MW01224760

INTERNATIONAL HANDBOOK OF DISTANCE EDUCATION

INTERNATIONAL HANDBOOK OF DISTANCE EDUCATION

Edited by

TERRY EVANS
Faculty of Education,
Deakin University,
Australia

MARGARET HAUGHEY
Athabasca University,
Canada

DAVID MURPHY
Centre for the Advancement of Learning and Teaching,
Monash University,
Australia

United Kingdom – North America – Japan
India – Malaysia – China

Emerald Group Publishing Limited
Howard House, Wagon Lane, Bingley BD16 1WA, UK

First edition 2008

British Library Cataloguing in Publication Data
A catalogue record for this book is available from the British Library

ISBN: 978-0-08-044717-9

Awarded in recognition of Emerald's production department's adherence to quality systems and processes when preparing scholarly journals for print

Contents

Contributors

Terry Anderson is Professor and Canada Research Chair in Distance Education, Athabasca University – Canada's Open University. He has published widely in the area of distance education and educational technology and has co-authored or edited five books and numerous papers. He teaches courses in educational technology in Athabasca University's Master of Distance Education programme. His current research interests involve the use of social software in providing support for students. Dr Anderson is also the director of CIDER, the Canadian Institute for Distance Education Research (cider.athabascau.ca) and the editor of the International Review of Research on Distance and Open Learning (IRRODL http://www.irrodl.org) (http://cider.athabascau.ca/Members/terrya/).

Jon Baggaley is Professor of Educational Technology at Athabasca University – Canada's Open University. He is author/editor of a dozen books/volumes including *Dynamics of Television* (with Steven Duck), *Psychology of the TV Image*, and *Evaluation of Educational Television*, and over 100 articles on media research and evaluation. He has consulted on the design of educational media campaigns for government and broadcasting organizations in Canada and the US, Bangladesh, Brazil, the Dominican Republic, Germany, Kenya, Mexico, Norway, Russia, Ukraine, South Africa, the United Kingdom, and thirteen other Asian countries. During 2006–2007, he was working throughout Asia, advising the PANAsia distance education projects of the International Research Development Centre.

Norman "Tut" Bailey is a senior marketing associate for Penn State Outreach Marketing and Communications. He has provided marketing strategy and overseen the implementation of marketing for more than twenty-five different distance education programmes ranging from homeland security and turfgrass management to special education and geographic information systems for Penn State World Campus, the university's online education arm. He has won UCEA's marketing strategy award twice, receiving gold in 2003 and silver in 2005. For the past 3 years, he has served as chairman of UCEA's marketing and publications community of practice.

Tony Bates is a private consultant specializing in e-learning in higher education. Between 1995 and 2003, he was Director of Distance Education and Technology at the University of British Columbia and Executive Director, Strategic Planning, at the Open Learning Agency, Vancouver, from 2000 to 2005. Before that he was Professor of Educational Media Research at the British Open University. He has written nine books on distance education and learning technologies and consulted for the World Bank, OECD, UNESCO, Ministries of Education in several countries, state higher education commissions in the United States, Volkswagen AutoUni, Open University of Catalonia, and Southern Alberta Institute of Technology. He has a PhD in educational administration from the University of London, and honorary degrees from Laurentian and Athabasca Universities and the Open Universities of Portugal, Hong Kong, and Catalonia (http://tonybates.ca).

Nigel Bennett is Professor of Leadership and Management in Education at The Open University, United Kingdom. He has been extensively involved in writing and teaching on courses in educational leadership and management for more than 20 years and was the coordinator of the leadership and management line in the university's Doctorate in Education programme. He is currently convenor of the Leadership, Lifelong Learning and Educational Governance Research Group in the Centre for Research in Education and Educational Technology.

Jane E. Brindley is a clinical psychologist with over 25 years' experience in open and distance learning. Currently, Jane is the Intake Coordinator at the University of Windsor Centre for Psychological Services, a training clinic for doctoral students in Clinical Psychology and is a course author and faculty member in the Masters of Distance Education Program jointly offered by University of Oldenburg and University of Maryland University College. She is author of *Researching Tutoring and Learner Support* (a research methods manual for practitioners), co-author of *Learning on the Information Highway: A Learner's Guide to the Technologies*, and lead editor and chapter author for *Learner Support in Open, Distance and Online Learning*.

Mark Bullen is the Associate Dean of the Learning and Teaching Centre at the British Columbia Institute of Technology (BCIT) where his main areas of responsibility are curriculum and instructor development and educational research and innovation. He has a PhD in Adult Education from the University of British Columbia and is an adjunct Professor in the UBC Master of Educational Technology programme and in the Athabasca University Master of Distance Education. Before joining BCIT in 2005, he was involved in managing, developing, and researching distance education at the University of British Columbia, where he held the positions of Director of the Centre for Managing & Planning E-Learning (MAPLE) and Associate and Acting Director of the Distance Education & Technology department. He has extensive international experience related to online course development and the planning and management of e-learning.

Elizabeth J. (Liz) Burge has worked through most of the post-1978 distance education years covered in this chapter. Her course design, librarianship, staff development, adopting new technology, teaching, book-making, researching, and national professional association activity for various distance education contexts around the world are all guided by a resolutely and critically reflective mindset. She is a Professor in adult education at the University of New Brunswick-Fredericton campus, in Atlantic Canada (http://www.unbf.ca/education/faculty/burge.html).

Katy Campbell is Dean in the Faculty of Extension (University of Alberta). She has been an Assistant Professor in the College of Education at the State University of New York College at Geneseo, a distance education developer at Keewatin Community College (Manitoba, Canada), and the Research Director of Academic Technologies at the University of Alberta. Her research interests include gender/technology interactions and resulting design issues, faculty transformative practice through collaborative instructional design, psychosocial issues of faculty teaching with technology, and the lives and practice of instructional designers. A recent study explores the role of the instructional designer as an agent of social change in higher education.

Chère Campbell Gibson is Professor Emerita in the School of Human Ecology and graduate programme in Continuing and Vocational Education at the University of Wisconsin-Madison. She brings over 30 years of experience in teaching and research on learners and learning at a distance, three national awards in distance education outreach programming, and international experience on the use of distance education for development. An author of numerous research articles on teaching and learning at a distance, she edited a book entitled *Distance Learners in Higher Education: Institutional Responses for Quality Outcomes*. She currently serves as a distance education evaluation consultant.

Ellie Chambers is Professor of Humanities Higher Education in the Institute of Educational Technology, the UK Open University. She is editor of the journal *Arts and Humanities in Higher Education: An International Journal of Theory, Research and Practice*. Recent publications include *Teaching and Learning English Literature* (2006), Sage, with Prof. Marshall Gregory, USA; *The Arts Good Study Guide* (forthcoming) (second revised edition), OU, with Prof. Andrew Northedge. She has worked as evaluator of projects funded by the European Union since 1997.

Dianne Conrad is Director, Centre for Learning Accreditation, Athabasca University, and a practising adult educator with extensive experience in distance, professional, continuing, and online education, particularly in the post-secondary sector. Her graduate research focused on interaction and support for distance learners. Dr Conrad is currently responsible for the management of the university-wide system of prior learning assessment and recognition. She is actively engaged in funded research projects involving both PLAR and e-learning. The latter studies focus on the development of community among online learners and the positioning of e-learning as a societal phenomenon.

Terry Evans is the Associate Dean (Research) in the Faculty of Education at Deakin University. His responsibilities include the management of staff and postgraduate research in the Faculty. Terry has conducted research in all educational settings from preschools through to universities. His recent research and scholarship is in the field of doctoral policy and practice. He has also researched and published widely in the fields of open, flexible, and distance education including work on professional and vocational education and training, and new educational technologies. He is a member of several editorial boards and has consultancy experience in various fields.

James Fong is an adjunct instructor of marketing and a management development associate for The Pennsylvania State University. He is currently the president for an international research consulting firm, Diagnostics Plus. Prior to joining the firm, he served as the director of marketing planning and research for Penn State Outreach where he was responsible for research and strategy for many distance education programmes and efforts. In 2004, he was the recipient of the University Continuing Education Association (UCEA) Adelle Robertson Continuing Professional Educator Award.

Suresh Garg is a former Acting Vice Chancellor and Pro-Vice Chancellor at the Indira Gandhi National Open University where he is also a Professor of Physics in the School of Science. He has held a wide variety of Directorships including the Schools of Computing Science, Engineering and Technology, Agriculture, and Law as well as being Director of the International Division. An established author and researcher in both physics and distance education, he has been founding editor of the Indian Journal of Open Learning and the Global E-Journal of Open and Distance Learning. He has served on national accreditation bodies and has also been Secretary of the SAARC Consortium for ODL and Head of the Secretariat of the Global Mega Universities Network.

Susan E. Gibson is a professor in the Faculty of Education at the University of Alberta, Canada. Her area of specialization is social studies education. Dr Gibson's ongoing research programme has been focused on the use of computerized tools to help pre-service teachers make critical theory to practice connections as they learn about teaching. Her latest project involved connecting her pre-service class to three elementary school classrooms using videoconferencing in order that her students could interact with the teachers and the children as they engaged in social studies activities.

Rosemary Green is Graduate Programs Librarian at Shenandoah University in Winchester, VA, USA, where she is responsible for coordinating library services and instruction for on-campus and off-campus graduate students. She holds a B.A. from Virginia Polytechnic Institute & State University and an M.L.S. from the University of North Carolina. Her areas of research interest and publication include graduate pedagogies, information literacy teaching and learning, and distance education. She is currently a PhD candidate at Deakin University in Geelong, Australia.

Charlotte Nirmalani (Lani) Gunawardena is Professor of Distance Education and Instructional Technology in the College of Education at the University of New Mexico. Her work concerns organizational learning and instructional technology in distance education. Her current research examines the social construction of knowledge and the socio-cultural context of online communities. Dr Gunawardena was a World Bank and Asian Development Bank consultant in Sri Lanka, and has also consulted in Brazil, Mexico, Norway, Turkey, and China. Her awards include the University of New Mexico's Regents' Lecturership, the General Library Faculty Recognition Award, and a Fulbright Regional Research Award for research in Morocco and Sri Lanka.

Sanjay Gupta is Senior Lecturer in Physics in the School of Science at Indira Gandhi National Open University. He holds a PhD from the University of Delhi and has worked as an Associate Director, Research with the Association of Indian Universities. His research interests involve specialized studies in physics and many aspects of distance education.

David Harris is a senior lecturer in social science at the College of St Mark and St John, Plymouth, UK. He has a long-standing interest in distance education with several publications in the field (including *Openness and Closure in Distance Education*). He is also interested in social theory and its possible e-applications to higher education. These include producing textbooks in various formats and maintaining a personal website (http://www.arasite.org/). He has a book offering critical reviews of both university teaching and study skills (written with H. Arksey) March 2007.

Margaret Haughey is the Vice-President, Academic at Athabasca University, Canada, a post she took up during the work on this Handbook. She has previously held administrative and academic appointments at a number of Canadian universities. A former editor of the *Journal of Distance Education*, she has served on a number of editorial boards for open and distance education and educational administration journals. She has been president of various educational professional organizations, consulted internationally on a wide range of topics related to distance education, and her publications involve administration and distance education in schooling and tertiary settings. Not surprisingly, her present academic work focuses on issues of distance education policy and practice in higher education.

S.R. Jha is a reader in physics in the School of Sciences at the Indira Gandhi National Open University.

Insung Jung is Professor of Educational Technology and Communications at the International Christian University in Tokyo. She has also worked at the Ewha Womans University in Seoul and the Korea National Open University, served as a consultant and technical advisor on distance learning to numerous national and international agencies, including UNESCO and the World Bank, and researched and written about e-learning designs and policies.

Olabisi Kuboni is Senior Lecturer and Campus Coordinator and Curriculum Development Specialist at the University of the West Indies Distance Education Centre. He has held senior coordinating positions with the University of the West Indies Distance Education Consortium (UWIDEC). Her responsibilities include the ongoing project to transform distance delivery in the University of the West Indies to a blended learning/asynchronous delivery mode; the specialized online course on local e-governance in the Caribbean, offered in collaboration with UNESCO; and the online capacity-building programme for drug demand reduction, implemented in partnership with OAS/CICAD. Her current research and development interests include learner participation in online teaching and learning, the design and development of staff training programmes for open and distance learning, and the design and development of student support systems for distance education.

Deborah LaPointe is Assistant Director for Education Development in the Health Sciences Library and Informatics Center and an Assistant Professor in the College of Education at the University of New Mexico. Her academic work ranges from educational development to organizational learning and technology. Her research interests include cultural considerations, the role of peer interaction in the facilitation of learning outcomes, online group development, and the appropriate use of synchronous and asynchronous technologies in the design of online learning environments.

Colin Latchem is a former head of an academic staff development, instructional design/educational technology and open and flexible learning centre at Curtin University of Technology in Western Australia, and President of the Open and Distance Learning Association of Australia. His publications include an award-winning book on leadership for twenty-first century learning and books on teacher education through distance education, staff development for open and flexible learning, telecentres, and multimedia. He now consults, researches and writes on leadership, strategic planning, management, and evaluation for educational development systems. In recent years, his work has taken him to the United States, Canada, Barbados, Netherlands, Turkey, Nigeria, South Africa, India, Indonesia, Brunei, Japan, Korea, Taiwan, China, Hong Kong, and the Philippines.

Fredric M. Litto has recently retired after 36 years as professor of communications at the University of São Paulo, where he founded and directed from 1989 to 2006 the "School of the Future" (http://www.futuro.usp.br), a self-sustaining research laboratory producing digital learning materials. He is currently in his third term as president of the Brazilian Association for Distance Education, a learned society which in September 2006 hosted the 22nd ICDE World Conference of Distance Education in Rio de Janeiro (http://www.abed.org.br). In the second semester of 2006, he was the "Rio Branco Scholar" in Education and Technology in the Institute for Education of the University of London, researching the issues involved in OER-Open Educational Resources in developing countries.

Fred Lockwood was previously a school teacher, College of Education, lecturer, and educational researcher before joining the Open University in 1975. He worked for 25 years within the OU Institute of Educational Technology before joining Manchester Metropolitan University as Professor of Learning and Teaching in 2001; he was appointed Emeritus Professor in 2006. Fred has an international reputation in the field of distance education, as evident in Visiting Professorships, Keynote addresses at conferences, and editorship of the Routledge Open and Flexible Learning Series. He has led consultancy teams associated with the design, production, presentation, and evaluation of self-instructional material in over twenty countries.

Peter Macauley is a senior lecturer in information and knowledge management at RMIT University, Melbourne, and prior to his commencement at RMIT, he had 30 years in public, special, and university libraries. Over the past decade, his research has focused on doctoral pedagogy, information literacy, and distance education. He is a chief investigator on two Australian Research Council funded projects: "Research capacity-building: The development of Australian PhD programmes in national and emerging global contexts" and "Working students: Reconceptualising the doctoral experience".

Mandla Makhanya is presently Professor and Executive Dean of the College of Human Sciences at the University of South Africa (UNISA). As executive Dean, he has played a significant role in transforming the college into a leaner, leading, efficient, and effective entity. Prof. Makahanya has served as Chairperson of the Culture Sector for the South African National Commission for UNESCO since 2001. Through his contribution to UNESCO, he has established a close relationship between the university, the South African Department of Arts and Culture, and the international community.

He also worked closely with South African Management Development Institute of the Department of Public Service and Administration. These affiliations highlight Professor Makhanya's social and academic interests which are also portrayed through his research and publications which deal with aspects such as culture and knowledge systems, education and learning, organizational development and transformative management.

Robin Mason is Professor of Educational Technology at the Open University in the United Kingdom, where she writes courses for a globally accessible Masters Programme in Online and Distance Education (http://iet.open.ac.uk/courses). She is co-author of two recent books: *E-Learning: The Key Concepts and The Educational Potential of e-Portfolios*, both published by Routledge. Her research interests relate to all aspects of online education.

Veronica McKay, a sociologist, is Professor and Director of the Institute Adult Basic Education and Training at the University of South Africa. She has a long history in ODL having been teaching at the University of South Africa (UNISA) for 24 years. She was the founding director of UNISA's Institute for adult basic education (ABET) established in 1994 with the view to "going to scale" to address the problem of adult illiteracy, as well as a wide range of critical developmental needs. Presently, Dr McKay is literacy and adult basic educational advisor to the South African Minister of Education. She has authored a number of journal articles and books and has conducted a wide range of research in areas such as curriculum, quality management, HIV/AIDS, health, gender, and development. In 2002, she was awarded the Commonwealth of Learning's award of excellence for materials distance education materials development.

Edith Mhehe is the Founding Dean of Education, Open University of Tanzania. Dr Mhehe completed her doctoral studies at the University of Alberta, Canada, in education administration and leadership focusing on the issues faced by women studying at her Open University. She has published several papers and book chapters as well as spoken at conferences on this topic. Currently, she is working to establish a number of community-based education support service centres for women in Dar-Es-Salaam. These were identified in her doctoral work as essential in providing women with the support of their peers and in learning how to achieve through their studies.

Jean Mitchell is an educational consultant with over 30 years' experience as a teacher/researcher at schools, teacher training colleges, and universities. Currently, she works at the University of South Africa (UNISA) where she is an education consultant. Her duties include instructional design and the development of learner-friendly distance education materials. Her research interests focus on learner support in open and distance learning and the development of academic literacy via contact tuition, distance education, and e-learning. She is the co-editor of the journal, *Progressio: South African Journal of Open and Distance Learning Practice*, published by Unisa Press.

John Mitchell is Managing Director of John Mitchell & Associates, an Australian company he founded in 1992. As a leading company in evaluation, research, and consulting, it specializes in the fields of education, health, and the public sector. A prolific author, John has recently produced evaluation and research reports on national programmes involving innovation, change agents, change management, strategic management, leadership, communities of practice, networking, e-learning, flexible learning, e-education, e-health, e-business, and professional development. View sample reports at http://www.jma.com.au.

Bill Muirhead is Associate Provost, Teaching and Learning in the Institute of Technology at the University of Ontario. His educational interests lie in the use of technologies in the design and provision of learning including its implementation in both schooling and higher education and has had extensive experience in the development of virtual schooling and the implementation of online education in the university sector as an administrator, practitioner, and researcher. Dr Muirhead has used his experience to be a strong proponent of the possibilities of distance education through serving on the boards of a number of professional associations. Currently, his research interests are in the areas of mobile computing, and the design of hybrid teaching-learning environments.

Stephen Murgatroyd is Chief Scout of The Innovation Expedition – a company dedicated to building networks that foster change, innovation, and development. Formerly with The Open University (UK), Athabasca University (Canada), and Middlesex University (UK), Stephen was the designer and creator of the world's first online MBA programme through Athabasca University. He also created a work-based learning masters degree in leadership for Middlesex. He worked for 5 years as Vice-President of Axia Netmedia and has consulted on human resource and strategic issues for many companies worldwide. Author of twenty books and over 200 papers, he holds a PhD from The Open University and an honorary doctorate from Athabasca.

David Murphy is Professor and Director of the Centre for the Advancement of Learning and Teaching at Monash University. Over the past couple of decades, he has also worked at the Open University of Hong Kong, Deakin University, and the Hong Kong Polytechnic University. His consultancies include work with the Commonwealth of Learning, Austrade, the United Nations High Commissioner for Refugees, and the World Health Organization. His research has most recently focused on ICTs in higher education. Recent publications include three edited books, titled *Online Learning and Teaching with Technology: Case Studies, Experience and Practice, Advancing Online Learning in Asia* and *Distance Education and Technology: Issues and Practice*.

Elizabeth Murphy is Associate Professor in Faculty of Education at Memorial University, Newfoundland, Canada. She is a scholar with a strong interest in online learning and schooling. She is presently conducting a 3-year, Social Sciences and Humanities Research Council of Canada (SSHRC)-funded study of the practice of the e-teacher in the high-school virtual classroom. In addition, she is a co-investigator on a SSHRC-funded Community University Research Alliance (CURA) on e-learning in which she is exploring learner-centred e-teaching. Dr Murphy disseminates her research widely to academic audiences using peer-reviewed journals and to non-academic audiences through workshops, media presentations, the web (http://www.ucs.mun.ca/~emurphy), and using YouTube.

Christopher Newell is an Associate Professor in the Medical Education Unit of the School of Medicine at the University of Tasmania. As a person with a disability, he has researched the social and ethical relations of disability with regard to a variety of technologies. He is a member of the National Health and Medical Research Council and the Australian Commission for Safety and Quality in Health Care. Recent books include *Digital Disability* (2003), *Disability in Australia* (2005), and *Disability in Education: Curriculum, Context and Culture* (2005). In 2001, he was appointed as a Member of the Order of Australia (AM) for his work.

Ted Nunan is an Adjunct Associate Professor with the Flexible Learning Centre of the University of South Australia. Prior to this, he worked in the centre with responsibilities in the areas of policy, scholarship, and research in teaching and learning. He is particularly involved with distance education and professional development of academics that teach at a distance and has published widely in journals such as *International Review of Research in Distance and Open Learning, International Journal of Inclusive Education, Journal of Higher Education Policy and Management* and provided conference presentations to the International Council for Educational Development Conference, Higher Education Research and Development Society of Australasia, Improving University Teaching and Learning International Conference, International Conference on New Concepts in Higher Education, and the Indonesian Distance Learning Network.

Jennifer O'Rourke is a consultant with over 20 years' experience as a distance educator, including instructional design, administration, tutoring, learner support, course writing, and research in academic, community, and professional development contexts. For the past 10 years, she has worked mainly with international organizations in planning and providing distance learning for staff in widely dispersed locations throughout the world. She is the author of *Tutoring in Open and Distance Learning: A Handbook for Tutors*, published by the Commonwealth of Learning in 2003.

Santosh Panda, a former Senior Fulbright Scholar, is a professor of distance education and currently Director, Staff Training & Research Institute of Distance Education, Indira Gandhi National Open University, India. Dr Panda has, in the past, been Director of Policy & Research at the Association of Indian Universities, and visiting professor at Manchester Metropolitan University and University of London, UK. Editor of two referred journals *Staff & Educational Development International and Indian Journal of Open Learning*, he has published internationally, and his forthcoming work includes *Economics of Distance and Online Learning* (Mahwah: Lawrence Erlbaum, 2007).

Ross H. Paul is President of the University of Windsor, Canada's southernmost university. He was previously President of Laurentian University in Sudbury, Ontario, and served 11 years at Athabasca University, 10 years as Vice-President Academic, and 1 year as acting president. A graduate of Bishop's, McGill and London universities, Dr Paul has particular interest in the sociology of organizations and the management of higher education. He is best known for his 1990 book, *Open Learning and Open Management: Leadership and Integrity in Distance Education*, and is a frequent contributor of book chapters and journal articles on the management of technology and higher learning.

Brian Pauling is a senior lecturer at the New Zealand Broadcasting School, Christchurch Polytechnic Institute of Technology, New Zealand. He founded the Broadcasting School in 1983 and was Head of School for 15 years. His employment background spans many years of working in radio, television, bookselling, publishing, community education, adult education, and tertiary education. He was also responsible for the establishment of the first independent community access radio station in New Zealand, PLAINSFM. He has a particular interest in the impact of digital technologies on broadcasting and education.

Otto Peters is Professor Emeritus of the FernUniversität (Distance Teaching University) in Germany. For nearly 10 years he had been its Founding Rector, and for 17 years he held a chair in a discipline called "Methodology of Distance Teaching" in the same institution. In this capacity, he conducted an extensive research project: "University Study for Persons who have to Work for a Living" ("Studium neben dem Beruf"). From 1969 to 1974, he was engaged in comparative distance teaching research at the German Institute for Distance Education at the University of Tübingen. His latest book is "Distance education in Transition" (University of Oldenburg, 2004).

Jody Polec is a graduate research student in Education at the University of New Brunswick-Fredericton Campus, in Atlantic Canada. Relevant to her studies are 17 years in the corporate world managing technology implementations and delivering accompanying training in North America and internationally. Her teaching and technology skills inform her research into how adults experience their learning via distance education. Of particular interest is the application of adult learning and teaching principles with the use of new technologies.

Adnan Qayyum is a PhD candidate in educational technology at Université Concordia (Montréal). He has worked as a researcher and instructional designer at Distance Education & Technology at the University of British Columbia. He has published on the economics of e-learning, the response of adult learners to using learning technologies, learning environments for non-formal adult education, cultural issues relating to using learning technologies, and, most recently, on how PowerPoint inhibits and can enhance e-learning. His other research interests include non-formal learning, evaluation issues, instructional design, and planning in education.

Greville Rumble obtained a PhD from the Open University in the costs and economics of open and distance learning. He was twice head of the Open University's corporate planning office and also director of a regional office and was later appointed to a personal chair as Professor of Distance Education Management. He left the Open University in 2001 and now freelances as a consultant. He has extensive international experience as a consultant in the planning, management, costs, and economics of distance education. In addition to many short-term consultancies, he was advisor in the Planning Vicerectorate of the Universidad Estatal a Distancia in Costa Rica in 1980–1981, a research fellow at Deakin University Australia in 1986, and in the mid-1990s Chief Technical Advisor at the Bangladesh Open University. He has written extensively on the planning and management of distance education.

Yoni Ryan is Director of the Centre for the Enhancement of Learning, Teaching and Scholarship at the University of Canberra. She has extensive experience in international education, staff development, and educational design and development with new technologies, at various universities in Australia and the Pacific. Recent publications include "Teaching and learning in the global era", in King, R. (ed.) (2004) *The University in the Global Era*, and, with Glen Farrell and Andrea Hope, "Globalisation", in Perraton, H. and Lentell, H. (eds) (2004) *Policy for Open and Distance Learning. World Review of Distance Education and Open Learning*. Vol. 4.

Sandi Shillington hails originally from South Africa, attending the University of Cape Town and the University of Port Elizabeth, where she was a senior lecturer in the Department of Psychology. Dr Shillington was part of the Phelophepa (which means good clean health) Project, a primary health care train that travelled to impoverished areas of South Africa helping communities to set up services and infrastructure. In New Zealand, she has worked in Community Mental Health in Hamilton and is now at Massey University. Here she first headed the Counselling Service and is now Regional Registrar: Student Life. Her responsibilities include on-campus Student Services at Palmerston North campus and the services for Massey's nearly 20,000 distance students.

Peter J. Smith is Associate Professor of Professional Education and Training at Deakin University in Australia. He has published a large number of journal articles and several books in distance education, workplace learning, and vocational education and training. Prior to joining the university sector, he was a senior manager in Australia's vocational education and training sector, and before that was the director of the division of off-campus studies in two of Australia's higher education institutions. His early career was in human resource development in the mining industry.

Christine Spratt has a PhD in Education from Deakin University in Australia and has taught at universities in Australia and Singapore. She is currently Senior Lecturer (Strategic Development Support) at Monash University in Australia, where she is responsible for coordinating a range of strategic institutional teaching and learning initiatives. She has a diverse professional background in open and distance learning, where she has worked as an educational designer, and in health professional education, where has worked in quality improvement and academic staff development. She has eclectic research interests including online learning, technology innovation and organizational change in universities, and the use of mixed methods in educational programme evaluation.

Barbara Spronk is Visiting Graduate Professor, Athabasca University, and a sessional lecturer at the University of Guelph. She has been working in distance education since 1974, primarily at Athabasca University (1974–1996), then as Executive Director of the International Extension College (1996–2002), and most recently as a freelance consultant and online course instructor. Dr Spronk has been privileged to work with colleagues on distance education initiatives in over twenty countries and is now enjoying staying close to her Canadian roots and providing academic and personal support to a wide range of online learners.

Alan Tait is based at the Open University UK, where he is Professor of Distance Education and Development in the Faculty of Education and Language Studies. He was appointed to the post of Pro-Vice Chancellor (Curriculum and Awards) in 2007 and was formerly Dean of Faculty. He is currently Vice-President of the European Distance and E-learning network (EDEN, http://www.eden.bme.hu), and is Editor-in-Chief of the European Journal of Open and Distance Learning (http://www.eurodl.org). His research and publication has been primarily in the field of learner support, institutional development, and policy in distance and e-learning.

Jennifer Thompson is the Deputy Regional Registrar, Student Life, at Massey University in Palmerston North, New Zealand. Formerly she was the Director of the Student Learning Centre at Massey. Her work includes the development of online and on-campus learning support services for distance and internal students. Jennifer is currently completing a PhD at Deakin University in Australia examining the provision of online learning support for tertiary students.

Mary Thorpe is Professor of Educational Technology at The Open University UK. At the University of Botswana, Lesotho and Swaziland (1972–1975), she led the materials and evaluation of a national radio learning campaign. Appointed to the UKOU in 1975, she has published in the fields of open and distance learning, student support, evaluation, and communities of practice and computer-mediated interaction. Her teaching has focused mainly on adult learning and courses for teacher development. She was Director of the Institute of Educational Technology from 1995 to 2003 and led a unit of over 100 staff with a thriving research and development culture.

Kevin Wilson is former UK Open University Arts Faculty staff tutor and is currently a visiting senior lecturer in the OU's Institute of Educational Technology. He has first-hand experience of transnational course design, development, and implementation and for many years chaired the Humanities Programme Committee of the European Association of Distance Teaching Universities. He has published extensively on open and distance learning course collaboration in international settings.

Alan Woodley is a Senior Research Fellow in the Centre for Institutional Research, which is part of the Institute of Educational Technology at the Open University of the United Kingdom. His work there concerns the evaluation of the OU in terms of meeting its aims to widen participation. He has published extensively, both on the findings and on the research methodology. In recent years, he has been exploring the possibilities of evaluation using ICT. He is currently working on comparative studies of graduate outcomes, both within the United Kingdom and across Europe.

Christopher Ziguras is Associate Professor of International Studies in RMIT University's Globalism Institute. He has published extensively on international education policy, transnational higher education, trade policy, skilled migration, and health behaviour. His books include The International Publishing Services Market co-edited with Bill Cope (Common Ground, 2002), Self-Care: Embodiment, Personal Autonomy and the Shaping of Health Consciousness (Routledge, 2004), and Transnational Education: Current Issues and Future Trends in Offshore Higher Education with Grant

McBurnie (RoutledgeFalmer, 2007). Previous appointments include Research Fellow at the Monash Centre for Research in International Education (1999–2001); Deputy Director of the Globalism Institute (2002–2004); and Head of RMIT's School of International and Community Studies (2004–2005).

Chapter 1

Introduction: from Correspondence to Virtual Learning Environments

Margaret Haughey, Terry Evans, and David Murphy

A handbook on a subject needs to encompass the substance of the field and its traditional practices, as well as its contemporary forms, concerns and contexts. In planning this handbook, we made these matters central to our task. We were keen, however, that we made room for critique and for some prospective thinking on the part of our authors. Each section of the book concludes with a critical chapter, where the authors have been asked to reflect on the topic of the section and to adopt a "critical edge" to their writing as they saw fit. Such an approach does have roots in distance education, in particular, to the publication in 1987 of *Openness and Closure in Distance Education* (Harris, 1987), and in 1989 of *Critical Reflections on Distance Education* (Evans and Nation, 1989). This handbook recognizes this "tradition" but also seeks to advocate the continuation of critique within the field, especially in these times when the "end-users" of distance education's "products" (graduates) appear to be exercising disportionate influence over the curriculum, assessment and "delivery" of distance education, at the expense of a tradition of distance education being for the intellectual and educational betterment of people who were effectively excluded from "traditional education" and needed some "access and equity" in their lives. Wedemeyer's (1981) work entitled *Learning at the Back Door: Reflections on Non-Traditional Learning in the Lifespan* used the folksy notion of peoples' education arriving "at the back door", which was very much about access. Faith's (1988) edited collection *Toward New Horizons for Women in Distance Education: International Perspectives* had a sharp focus on gender-equity. We argue that these are not just important features of the history of distance education. The contexts and circumstances may have changed to a degree, but social inequality remains as pervasive as ever and distance education has the means to address the educational bases of much of this inequality.

We wish to discuss the origins and transitions of distance education, as it has been formally known since 1982, when the International Council for Correspondence Education

(ICCE) became the International Council for Distance Education (ICDE). It is said that distance education includes "various forms of study which are not under the continuous immediate supervision of tutors present with their students in the same room but who benefit from the planning, guidance and tuition of a tutorial organization" (Holmberg, 1977, p. 9). This definition stresses that distance education is formal study supported by an educational organization as opposed to informal education; that it involves the separation of learners and teachers in real space; and that learners receive planned and guided tuition (by implication, in some mediated form) through non-contiguous communication. Subsequent definitions by various theorists have stressed the relationship between teacher and student rather than the separation, have ignored the formal organizational aspect, have been concerned with learner autonomy and prescribed materials, have defined it as an industrialized form of education, and have placed emphasis on the technology mediation rather than the guidance and tuition.

During the last 25 years, proponents and practitioners have tried to illustrate the underlying principles behind their understandings of distance education. Some have proposed theories with testable propositions while others have suggested models that are based on guiding principles. Their intent has been to grapple conceptually with a rapidly changing phenomenon that prior to 1982 had been categorized as independent or correspondence study and had depended on books, paper and the post. Even then, the development of large-scale correspondence institutions had raised pedagogical issues concerning the extent of student interaction and independence. Rapid changes not only in technology but also in our conceptions of society and learning have occurred during this time. It has resulted in the development of very large dedicated distance education institutions serving over 100,000 students and in the addition of distance learning options by conventional institutions.

Keegan (2000) identified four societal characteristics – immediacy, globalization, privatization (where the sense of community has been replaced with a focus on the home) and industrialization – as influencing the provision of distance education and training. We would add the imperative to lifelong learning as an aspect of training for the knowledge society and the impact of rapidly changing post-industrial systems. These, combined with demands for increased learner choice and flexibility and the technological possibilities of rapid feedback, mobility, multimedia and the Web, have resulted in the promotion of distance learning as a cost-effective alternative. As a number of authors (Hannafin and Kim, 2003) have commented, the adoption of some form of technology-based provision has more often focused on the attributes of the technology than on the underlying theoretical frameworks. We believe that with notable exceptions writers have ignored the socio-economic context that framed their analyses. However, despite this, these theories do help us see the concepts and questions that concerned distance educators over this period. In this chapter, therefore, we review and discuss the various distance education theories and models developed over the last 30 years and then place those models within contemporary discourses.

1.1 HOLMBERG'S GUIDED DIDACTIC CONVERSATION

One of the first major theorists of distance education was Holmberg (1976, 1983, 1995), who identified the presentation of learning matter, student–tutor communication, information technology and media, organization, and evaluation as components of any distance education system. Of these, Holmberg noted, "the communication element is rightly considered a corner stone of distance education" (1986, p. 54) He proposed a conversational theory as the pedagogical model for distance education.

> My theory implies that the character of good distance education resembles that of a guided conversation aiming at learning and that the presence of the typical traits of such a conversation facilitates learning. ...There is a constant interaction ("conversation") between the supporting organization (authors, tutors, counselors) and the student, simulated through the students' interaction with the pre-produced courses and real through the written and/or telephone interaction with their tutors and counsellors. Communication is thus seen as the core of distance education.
>
> (p. 55)

This model involved a number of assumptions about learning. First, interaction is at the core of teaching, facilitated in part by the materials that are designed to have students consider different opinions. This interaction which encourages a sense of belonging or rapport with the tutor and organization is provided by using a "friendly, personal tone" (1986, p. 122), making the study relevant to the individual learner's needs, and ensuring that the materials are designed to provide easy access to the study matter. Second, there is an interactive relationship among the student's sense of belonging, learning pleasure and motivation. Holmberg posits that learners who develop a positive relationship with their learning organization will find their learning more pleasurable, this feeling in turn supports their motivation, and both facilitate their learning.

Holmberg identified a number of strategies to help establish a cooperative conversational relationship between teacher and learner. His list of characteristics of good materials includes opportunities for learner choice. The course objectives should engage the student in the evaluation of their relevance and in the selection among them. The structure should build on earlier learning. He emphasized the use of the personal pronoun ("You" rather than "The student"), of highly readable and engaging prose, and of graphics and print design strategies, which aided reading, argument and retention. He described writing in a discursive conversational style, providing lots of examples and questions that were to engage the learner emotionally and encourage an exchange of views. Tutors and counsellors were to be constantly available to students for questions and exchanges of opinions. He proposed self-check exercises for learners as well as frequent submission of assignments, and quick handling of these with friendly, helpful, extensive feedback to promote the rapport necessary for student motivation and support. Holmberg called his theory, guided didactic conversation. He was concerned that students have the opportunity to make active choices throughout the course, and he focused on the individual learner rather than on learning as a social activity. His theory is reflected in the design adopted by the United Kingdom Open University (UKOU) that was based on the development of well-designed print materials to support student–tutor interaction.

As Thorpe (1979) from the BOU has noted, while the reading materials are designed for students in general, the tutorial system means that student and tutor work together as individuals.

At the time Holmberg proposed his model, the philosophical debates in education concerned two opposed views. One was the importance of supporting and encouraging the autonomous adult (Knowles, 1970) through greater choice and responsibility, and opportunities for unstructured interaction. The other was the more behaviourist position that educators should control the learning process and provide highly delineated materials that were designed to ensure that adult learners would be successful. Holmberg chose to include both well-designed materials and individual discussion and feedback as elements of his model. Moore also attempted to integrate these differing perspectives.

1.2 MOORE'S TRANSACTIONAL DISTANCE

Moore (1973, 1993) proposed a theory of transactional distance in which he sought to link notions of autonomy, interaction and structure. Moore based his definition of transaction on Dewey's notion of the "transactions" between teacher and learner and it was the distance that could be present in that relationship that Moore sought to capture in his term, transactional distance. For Moore, distance was not a geographical phenomenon but a pedagogical concept, involving "the universe of teacher-learner relationships that exist when learners and instructors are separated by space and/or by time" (1993, p. 22). He saw it as having three constructs: the extent of structure in the instructional design of the course, the extent of the teacher's interaction with the learner and the extent of self-directedness of the learner. These interact in the psychological and communications space resulting from the separation of teachers and learners. Moore termed these three inter-linking components structure, dialogue and autonomy. Structure referred to the level of openness or closure in the architecture of the course design. This included the course objectives, content and evaluation and hence involved the pedagogical philosophies of the instructor and designers. Dialogue referred to the opportunity for communication between learners and teacher and was influenced by the media choices and number of learners in the course, while autonomy meant the degree of freedom learners had to make course design choices. In delineating his model, Moore proposed that as student autonomy increased, i.e. when learners had more choice about what and how to study and about how they would be evaluated, then transactional distance, i.e. the extent of structure and dialogue should decrease. Such learners he contended are able to work successfully with less design structures and less frequent interaction with the instructor.

Subsequently, Moore and Kearsley (1996) noted that sometimes highly structured courses were necessary depending on the students' initial understandings and that the amount of autonomy may increase over the length of a course. One problem with Moore's model is that using very specific descriptors for common terms like "dialogue", "structure" and "autonomy" can be confusing. Autonomy for Moore is at one level about the choices presented to the learner but at another level, autonomous learners are those able to make and be comfortable with their choices so that autonomy moves from being a property of the course to being a property of the student. Similarly, while structure refers to how the course was designed, it also carries the connotation that highly structured courses are not open to learner choice, confusing structure and control.

While Moore was particularly concerned about student autonomy, Holmberg focused on the instructional materials and their capacity for interaction and motivation through interactive designs. Holmberg's work reflects his experiences in a large print-based institution with correspondence study while Moore's work reflects the importance of independent study to US institutions. However, Moore's work, like Holmberg's, speaks to three important elements in distance education theory: the design of the learning materials, the extent and kinds of communication and the choices available to the learner. The ways these three variables are configured in a distance education course or program are influenced not only by the pedagogical philosophies of the instructor and designers but also by the organizational and cultural contexts.

1.3 PETERS'S INDUSTRIALIZATION MODEL

The socio-economic context played a large part in the conceptualization of distance learning by Peters (1983). He had initially attempted to characterize distance education into its different forms of instruction such as by writing, by using printed material, by using teaching aides, communication of knowledge by radio, etc., but found that these 27 different forms did not identify the specific structure of distance education. Then he tried to formulate a definition based on the six aspects of a structural definition of instruction, i.e. aims, content, methods, media, etc., which proved equally unproductive. Ultimately, he looked at the separation of the preparation of materials from the instruction, the use of formalized and standardized procedures in the development of materials, the use of efficient, mechanized, mass production processes, and concluded that distance education was a more industrialized form of teaching and learning. Therefore, Peters defined distance education as

> a rationalized method – involving the division of labor – of providing knowledge which, as a result of applying the principles of industrial organization as well as the extensive use of technology, thus facilitating the reproduction of objective teaching activity in any numbers, allows a large number of students to participate in university study simultaneously, regardless of their place of residence or occupation.
>
> (cited in Keegan, 1994, p. 125)

While Peter's delineation which focused on the production of the materials and the infrastructure supporting their provision was helpful in explaining the development of distance education institutions as reflective of contemporary industrial society, it avoids the issue of the pedagogical assumptions underlying such a model, a point taken up by Harris (1987) in his critique of the processes at the United Kingdom Open University (UKOU). Harris argued that "Distance education and educational technology do have liberating sides but their current forms prevent them from emerging fully" and called for them "to be recolonized from below, subjected to the widest possible discussions instead of being isolated as anomalous to the mainstream of higher education, or treated as the latest enthusiasm of the rationalizers" (p. 150). This seeming misalignment between industrialized forms of production involving course teams of content specialists, instructional designers and educational technology specialists and the individualized interaction with the tutor, referred to by Thorpe, points to the difficulty of using exclusively either macro- or micro-based theories as reflective of distance education.

Unlike Holmberg and Moore whose models consider the learner, Peter's original two developments were entirely from the perspective of the teacher while his third reflected the larger contemporary context. Subsequently, he sees his interpretation as reflecting the developments in the 1970s to 1990s and notes that as we move into a post-modern era, new models need to be developed (2002, p. 23). New developments in technologies also posed difficulties for Holmberg and Moore's models. The 1980s saw the advent of various forms of audio and video conferencing, which introduced group processes into what had been conceptualized previously as essentially private study. Garrison based his model on the communicative advantages these new technologies could provide.

1.4 GARRISON'S TWO-WAY EDUCATIONAL TRANSACTION

While Holmberg and Moore stressed the separation of teacher and learner as integral to distance education, Garrison (1989) stressed the importance of two-way communication among students and with the teacher. He proposed that it was a mistake to define distance education through its differences from conventional education and hence, to focus on ways to overcome the separation or distance; instead, he defined distance education as "a species of education characterized by one structural characteristic – the noncontiguity of teacher and student" (p. 8). His two other defining criteria were two-way communication and technology mediation (Garrison and Baynton, 1987, p. 11). He did not include reference to a formal organizational presence, partly because he considered the presence of an institution to be irrelevant to the actual relationship between the teacher and the students and because increasingly, distance education courses were being offered by traditional institutions.

Garrison (1989) proposed a model based on the educational transaction between teacher and learner but focused on dialogue and debate as being essential for understanding and hence necessitating two-way communication between them. He rejected Holmberg's emphasis on the interactive quality of the print materials as being a simulation for interaction with the instructor and insisted that mediation through technology was an essential component of distance education. Garrison defines his model as a triangle linking teacher, student and content. The two-way linkages between teacher and student are termed dialogue, i.e. discussion and negotiation for meaning and personal understanding, and the link between teacher and content is labelled structure referring to the preparation and packaging of content. Garrison (1989) also proposed that the concept of learner autonomy be replaced with learner control as a more precise construct involving the learner in "influencing educational decisions" (Garrison, 1993). However, he argued that learner control was not one-way but involved, and had implications for, others so that it needed to be shared between teacher and learner and renegotiated throughout the learning process. Garrison and Baynton (1987) had proposed that the construct included three concepts: learner independence, proficiency and support. Independence referred to the learner being "free to choose and pursue educational goals" (p. 27). In a later discussion, Garrison redefined it as the learner "assuming responsibility for constructing meaning in a collaborative or interactive setting" (1993, p. 16). Proficiency referred to the learner's ability to be self-directed, and support meant the availability of the necessary human and non-human resources. He superimposed this conceptualization on his initial model so that support was provided through the dialogic relationship between teacher and student, while proficiency was linked to the student's work with the content, and the student's level of independence or self-directedness was evident in the level of structure the teacher had imposed on the content. He strongly supported sustained interaction as essential to the development of critical learning and saw the role of the teacher as essential to the process.

Garrison's concepts of dialogue, structure and control built on the concepts identified by Moore but while Moore used them to try to identify what was unique about distance education, Garrison used them as a means of dissolving any differences. His model could be applied successfully to an analysis of classroom instruction. Garrison's highlighting of the importance of two-way interaction reflected the new developments of group communication technologies. These were a way to bring the campus to the students and to provide a form of education that was similar to what was available in traditional classrooms. These practices have been called "classrooms at a distance" since in many instances, the use of technology is all that marks them out from other on-campus offerings.

1.5 LAURILLARD'S CONVERSATIONAL FRAMEWORK

A similar focus on aspects of the learning situation was delineated by Laurillard (1993, 2002), who saw "learning as a relationship between the learner and the world mediated by the teacher" (2002, p. 86). She set out a conversational framework which contained the requirements for any learning situation; it had to be "an iterative dialogue", "discursive, adaptive, interactive and reflective", "operate at the level of descriptions of the topic", and "at the level of actions within the related tasks" (p. 86). Her model is a rectangle. Like Garrison, she begins her model with two adjacent corners of the model linked with a series of two-way arrows designating the dialogue between teacher and student. She refers to them as "Teacher's conception" and "Student's conception". Linked to the teacher's corner is the "Teacher's constructed environment" (the context for the student's actions) and to the student's, "Student's actions". These four points form the rectangle. Laurillard used three concepts to activate her model: adaptation, interaction and reflection. Through interaction and reflection, there is ongoing adaptation for both teacher and learner.

Adaptation is the process of considering, reflecting, reiterating and changing actions based on what is received from the other person in the dialogue. This occurs simultaneously in both the teacher's and the student's conceptions as they interact and it is visible in their ongoing dialogue and in the student's actions. Interaction is part of adaptation and involves the teacher setting the task, the student doing something to achieve the goal, the student obtaining feedback on the action from the teacher and both student and teacher modifying subsequent actions. Reflection occurs internally as both the teacher and learner reflect on the experience, each adapting and changing their understanding of the task and the goal for future actions and revealing this in their dialogue. Laurillard used this model in identifying the learning experiences that were best supported by various media and concluded that no medium can provide all aspects equally well. Instead, a range of media should be used depending on the goals and tasks. Laurillard's model focuses only on the interactions (descriptions and tasks) between teacher and student that are integral to the learning process and like Garrison, the teacher is essential to the process.

Laurillard sought to delineate the actual learning process. She made interaction between teacher and learner integral to this process and included internal learning processes of adaptation and reflection as well as external discussion and action. Through these adaptive processes she captures the notion of control as discussed by Garrison. Garrison's model although also focused on the learning sequence is more general, separating content from dialogue and student choice, while Laurillard sees choice as embedded in the interactive process provided through the dialogue itself. Adaptation from Laurillard's perspective is less about control than about ongoing negotiation as a process of iterative communication. Also, unlike Garrison who argued for the "crucial and necessary role of the teacher" (1989, p. 35), Laurillard notes, "The dialogue may never take place explicitly between teacher and student. It could be a kind of internal dialogue, with the student playing both roles" (1993, p. 104) as it is when students reflect on lecture notes. Garrison's response would be that "it is the challenging of perspectives and the presentation of alternative viewpoints that the student is not likely to perform adequately [and] independently" (1989, p. 35). In his 1993 discussion, Garrison placed even greater emphasis on these, noting that they reflected "the cognitive/constructivist ideal of an interdependent teacher-learner" (p. 13) which was emerging. He outlined the challenge for distance educators as being between the tradition paradigm of prepared materials for independent learners and the emerging paradigm of sustained collaboration for meaning-making.

1.6 VARIOUS LEARNING THEORIES

The initial models of distance education were versions of traditional education, and were based on adaptations of the traditional lecture/discussion model to a distance education situation. Expertise was provided through print materials, or through audio or video-conferenced lectures and discussion and feedback came through written assignments. Essentially, students learned individually and they did so through the content provided by the instructor and through some form of iterative communication that allowed for adaptation. This is still the most common form of educational provision in post-secondary education.

It is based on what is now termed instructivism, i.e. teacher-directed teaching, where the teacher as expert decides what is to be known, how it is to be transmitted, and the criteria for evaluation. Student motivation and support are the responsibility of the teacher. The student's task is to learn and to reveal that knowledge for evaluation. As Thorpe (1995) notes,

> course designers have, for two decades and more, been using a cognitive approach to learning and searching for ways in which learners can mobilize their existing knowledge and create new frameworks which integrate old and new learning in new forms of understanding. Advance organizers, in-text activities, tutor-marked assignments and project-based assessment are some of the approaches which assume a cognitivist model of learning.
>
> (p. 175)

Cognitivism also stresses the importance of the teacher in the instructional process but unlike instructivist approaches considers the learner to be an active participant in the construction and manipulation of mental models in learning even if knowledge is a given.

These orientations to education have been challenged by constructivism, which believes that knowledge is not a given; it cannot be transmitted but must be (re)constructed by each learner. Constructivism places interaction at the centre of the learning process. First, the interaction is between the learner's present knowledge and what the person is hearing or observing in the surrounding context. The learner's prior meanings may be challenged in this situation and how the learner responds will influence others in the same context and their responses will also influence the learner. Hence, communication among learners is essential for meaning-making for the individual's learning is constantly shaped by what others say and how they react. Knowledge then is relative to the context and always open to question. There are two kinds of constructivism. Cognitive constructivism stresses the problem-solving aspects of individual knowledge-building while social constructivism focuses on the collaborative interaction among learners in their shared knowledge-building processes. In practice, these distinctions are less clear-cut. For one, the social context provides a supportive context of shared experiences while the other sees knowledge as constructed by and shared among the group rather than being concurrently constructed individually. However, the way people approach and solve problems is context-dependent, and more holistic and intuitive than logical (Winn, 1990) so that documenting these processes is difficult.

Both perspectives are oriented to problem-solving and critical inquiry. This means that instructors focus on the provision of a learning environment rather than on complete, previously designed, mass-produced course packages. Constructivist learning designs call for providing learners with realistic, meaningful, relevant, engaging, complex and information-rich resources to use in the process of meaning-making. Learners' interactions in aid of meaning-making are based on the higher-order thinking processes of analysis, synthesis and evaluation and should include creativity and experimentation. The learners should be given differing perspectives to consider rather than a single or dominant point of view. They also require incremental learning strategies such as scaffolding and sequencing of tasks to aid their knowledge-construction. Assessment should be authentic, using realistic tasks and providing feedback not only on content knowledge but also on the learner's learning processes. Social constructivism not only privileges interaction but more clearly shares the responsibility for learning between the teacher who should provide situations for dialogue and learners who must interact with their own knowledge base and that of their peers to try to achieve mutual understanding. While learner characteristics are important in deciding on appropriate situations and materials, the focus is on learning, and so constructivism is seen as both learning- and learner-centred. Over the last decade, it has become increasingly accepted as the most appropriate set of principles to direct educational endeavours.

1.7 VRASIDAS AND GLASS'S CONCEPTUAL FRAMEWORK

Vrasidas and Glass (2002) adapted Moore's theory and Garrison's model to reflect a constructivist orientation. They proposed a model with three concentric frames; in the centre frame is interaction, surrounded by the instructional design and content and embedded in the outer context frame which contains the technology, institutional politics and the teacher. Interaction is described as a set of concepts—dialogue, learner control, feedback and social presence—which they do not link these together conceptually but see them as parts of a system. They define social presence as the extent to which the medium allows the learner to feel socially present in the mediated situation. They extend the definition of dialogue beyond being a conversation between learner and teacher by including the four types of mediated interaction (Hillman et al., 1994; Moore, 1989) – between learners, with the teacher, with the content and with the machine interface – to highlight "the importance of technology in mediating and shaping interaction" (pp. 38–9). In the instructional frame, they point out that structure is dynamic, changing through negotiation as the course proceeds (p. 45). The outer frame is the context within which the rest occurs. It is both separate from and part of the process, ranging from institutional policies and teachers' philosophies to the attributes of the technology, all of which constrain and shape what is possible. They define technology broadly, listing the wide variety of technologies used in distance education.

Vrasidas and Glass are concerned to delineate a model that relates to the specific circumstances of distance education. Therefore they place interaction at the centre of their model and expand the traditional teacher – learner – content interactions to include student-interface interactions. They also point out that there is a difference between teacher–learner interactions and teacher-group interactions and suggest a distance learning model should address this option also. Their focus on technology is not meant to place technology ahead of learning but rather that research studies should focus on "how technology affords certain kinds of interactions and shapes content, context, interaction, and learner experience" (p. 50). They question whether the focus on social presence is part of the trend to replicate the "face-to-face ideal" (p. 42) and challenge the extent to which social presence is deemed necessary for individual learners, suggesting instead that while some learners seek a highly supportive and interactive environment, others may prefer one that is less so. They note their disagreement with Moore, contending that structure does not necessarily reduce dialogue. They give the example of required collaborative projects that increase interaction. Overall, their conceptual framework, as a series of concentric spaces, reinforces the interrelatedness of interaction within an instructional and organizational context.

1.8 GARRISON, ANDERSON AND ARCHER'S COMMUNITY OF INQUIRY MODEL

Garrison et al., (2000) designed a model for distance learning that returns to their core concept of two-way communications and whose goal is critical thinking. The model is premised on the notion of a community of inquiry and designed specifically for computer conferencing environments. The community of inquiry (or critical thinking) is formed through the interactions of teachers and learners and has three essential components: social presence, cognitive presence and teaching presence. Social presence refers to students' sense of their online identity as group members through their interactions with each other and the instructor. It is obtained through engaging, positively reciprocated interactions that recognize the contributions of others and include affective aspects such as humour and self-disclosure. These interactions, however, should be focused on the social construction of meaning, the focus of cognitive presence. Garrison et al., (2000) define cognitive presence as "the extent to which the participants in any particular configuration of a community of inquiry are able to construct meaning through sustained communication" (p. 89). They delineate a problem-oriented approach involving learner interest, engagement, exploration and resolution as four stages of cognitive presence. Teachers guide learners through these four stages through participation in the learning process. Teaching presence includes the design and organization of the learning sequences, the facilitation of interaction and active learning and the provision of subject matter expertise. It is labelled teaching rather than teacher presence, since learners can undertake some of these functions. Based on this model, they "hypothesize that high levels of social presence with accompanying high degrees of commitment and participation are necessary for the development of higher-order thinking skills and collaborative work" (p. 94). Also, "when social presence is combined with appropriate teaching presence, the result can be a high level of cognitive presence leading to fruitful critical inquiry" (p. 96).

Unlike other distance learning models that did not specify particular technologies although the technologies then available are evident in their formulation, this model addresses a specific rapidly growing technology, computer conferencing. However, as is evident from Garrison and Anderson's earlier work, the model predates its application to computer conferencing environments. Garrison et al., (2000) have argued that the concept of a community of learners focused on critical thinking is only viable via computer conferencing if the three elements are present. However, the elements are defined in such a way that it is not always clear whether they are an attribute of the participant, of the learning design or of the technology. For example, social presence is described as "the ability of the participants ... to project their personal characteristics into the community thereby presenting themselves to the other participants as 'real people' " (p. 89), while cognitive presence is "the extent to which participants are able to construct meaning through sustained communication" (p. 89). However, from the subsequent description of social and cognitive presence, it is evident that participants require not only the ability but more importantly the opportunity to project themselves socially and emotionally and to negotiate meaning with the other group members. High levels of ability alone would not help fulfil the hypotheses.

Garrison and his colleagues see the constraints on cognitive presence as partly dependent on the technology itself while the communicative norms established by the group rather than the technology is "the most salient factor in determining the degree of social presence" (p. 94). They further argue that there needs to be "a significant degree" of social presence for cognitive presence to be sustained. Garrison et al. see sharing as an essential aspect of critical inquiry since cognition can't be separated from its social context.

Their model is less clear in its comparative delineation of cognitive and teaching elements. Cognitive presence, seen as the core element, focuses on the learners' problem-solving activities while teaching presence refers to the design (subsequently referred to as instructional management), direct instruction and facilitation activities that support this process and that are usually attributed to the teacher. The overlap is labelled "supporting discourse" which Anderson et al., (2001) define as establishing and maintaining knowledge-based deliberations and supporting and encouraging participation through management of the learning space. The overlap is extensive since the teacher's instructional and facilitative activities are essential to the level of analysis sought in the cognitive activities and help sustain the socio-emotional context. For example, the learner's cognitive search for information for clarification and integration is integrally connected to the teaching presence role. In addition, the differentiation of cognitive presence to highlight the cognitive aspect of learning seems to suggest that the ongoing negotiation of meaning is an activity of the learners alone rather than of the teacher also. Similarly, separating the affective from the cognitive aspects of learning downplays the holistic, embodied characteristics of learning. Furthermore, little emphasis is given to the context in which this learning occurs. Vrasidas and Glass (2002) contend that interaction is not a variable one extracts from a context but rather that it is "an ongoing concept that resides in a context and also creates context" (p. 34). Both cognitive and teaching sectors seem to have similarities with Laurillard's more integrated adaptation process. Why these two sectors are called "presence" is also not obvious apart from the harmony of the sectors' names.

The importance of the learners' social context in learning and the concurrent rapid growth of computer conferencing have resulted in numerous programs and research studies that focus on interaction, collaboration and community (Duffy and Kirkley, 2004). The sustaining questions have been about the ways to use technology to achieve these three goals whether for classroom or distance learners. What are less evident are questions about how the learning style of the individual learner and learner control are accounted for, how different media influence learning models and what combination of content and context can best be accessed through learner-content rather than through learner–human interactions. These questions are taken up by Anderson.

1.9 ANDERSON'S EQUIVALENCY INTERACTION THEOREM

Anderson (2003) bases his model on the Anderson and Garrison (1998) version of Garrison's 1989 model. He begins by enumerating the three components added in the 1998 version to the triangular model of student, teacher and content, where learners interact not only with teacher and content but also with other learners. Similarly, teachers also interact with other resource people and content interacts with other content. However, in his latest model, Anderson (2003) does not separate interaction from content and instead places knowledge/content/interaction as an interface between the learner and the teacher. In this he is recognizing the mediated nature of the knowledge-based communications between the teacher and the learner. He includes links of students to other students and the teacher to colleagues and other resource people. He then provides two examples of the use of particular technologies and learning activities that illustrate his model. To the left, he outlines a learner–content–teacher linkage that privileges learner–learner interaction. He describes those web-based courses where synchronous and asynchronous conferencing is the basis for paced, collaborative learning involving the teacher and learners in a community of inquiry model. He notes that "the high level of student-student interaction capacity allows for reduced student teacher interaction ... and facilitates students sharing and discussing student-content learning resources gathered or created by students" (p. 7). Anderson notes that community of inquiry environments "encourage the development of social skills, collaborative learning and the development of personal relationships amongst participants as components of the learning process" (p. 8). To the right, the learner–content–teacher linkage privileges learner–content interaction. He describes the traditional distance education model that has migrated to electronic communication. It includes independent study and structured learning resources from e-books and tutorials to simulations, games and virtual labs. To these he added peer, professional and family support. Anderson explains that "although engaged in independent study, the student is not alone" and is likely to have an informal support group of friends, peers and family. In this version, students can but seldom do engage in academic discussions with their tutor. Also, "student–student interaction is minimized allowing for maximum flexibility, start and finish times for courses, and capacity for students to set their own pace through the learning content" (p. 6).

Using these two examples, and based on his model of student–student, student–teacher and student–content interaction, Anderson then proposes that "deep and meaningful learning is supported as long as one of the three forms of interaction is at a high level" (p. 3). He goes on to elaborate that an instructional designer can substitute one type of interaction for one of the others with little loss in educational effectiveness (p. 4).

Unlike Vrasidas and Glass's (2002) model or that of Garrison, Anderson and Archer (2000) which are based on constructivist learning principles, Anderson's model returns to the broader issue of mediated or distance learning and the various possibilities available. In placing the resources, materials and communications as the interface between the instructor and the student, he has broadened the notion of content to being inclusive of all three rather than separating out teacher–learner interactions from knowledge-based interactions or interactions with structured course materials. The two examples he gives use learning designs that are based in differing philosophies of learning. In the social constructivist design to the left, learning is believed to occur primarily through interaction with others facilitated by the teacher. The course materials, like students' experiences, are resources to encourage reflection, sustained discussion and meaning-making. In the cognitivist design to the right, learning occurs through interaction with the resources and with the teacher. As Heinecke et al., (2001) point out, basic beliefs about education influence how courses are designed and ultimately the roles of the teacher, students and content. Anderson's model is an attempt to reflect the diversity of actual and potential practices rather than a single orientation.

In this he is influenced by three concerns. First, he is interested in the migration to student–content interactions. He suggests that given the computer's increasing storage capacity and computing power and the comparative higher costs of learner–human interactions, some activities that are now student–teacher interactions will migrate to being student–content interactions. One example is that student–teacher queries, now in e-mail and computer conferencing formats, are moving to FAQs (web-based prepared responses to frequently asked questions), and to teacher demonstrations (online video clips or learning objects). This migration has the advantage of consistency, immediacy and flexibility. The responses are similar for all learners and learners can access them when they need them. They can also be individualized to better reflect a learner's competency level or specific learning needs or to provide personalization of interactions. Similarly, automated computing components can look after accounting and clerical tasks originally categorized as teacher–learner interactions.

Second, he believes that learners vary in their needs for flexibility and engagement in group-based learning. The community of inquiry model binds learners together within regular timeframes to interact in group-based activities. The issues of the centrality of interaction, and the extent to which communities develop in this context, have been the foci of multiple research studies. From the many case studies, context, task and purpose appear to be the most important variables (Hannafin and Kim, 2003) but like Vrasidas and Glass, Anderson questions the ubiquity of this particular design for all learners. Third, Anderson is concerned with the scalability of distance education models. He points out that since the number of students in an online conference using the community model is generally limited to fewer than 30, community-based models are inherently more expensive and "suffer from an inability to scale to large numbers of learners" (p. 8). He argues that we should "be focused on creating the most cost effective and accessible alternatives" that can scale to meet the burgeoning demand for distance learning and that this will mean reducing the amount of teacher–student interaction, and replacing it with increased student–student and student–content interactions. His contention is that these interactions can be as educationally effective as asynchronous communications although he also recommends that given the variety of learners in any situation, designers should incorporate and design activities to encourage "strategic amounts" of each of the three types of interaction (p. 5).

1.10 INTERACTIVE, SELF-PACED AUTONOMOUS LEARNING

The issue of learner choice is evident in Anderson's model, and in particular, in the example on the right. Learner choice or autonomy, an integral aspect of distance education for Moore, is seen by Peters (2001) as occurring when the learners take over the functions of the teacher and take control of their education. Peters argues that to do this the learners need to have metacognitive skills including critical contemplation, and to be motivationally and actively involved in their own learning. Constructivism argues that individuals "construct" their own knowledge networks rather than replicating an external reality and that they do this through a recursive process of internal and external dialogues seeking internal accord with their own experience and external agreement with others. This requires that the learning environment provide opportunities for learner autonomy and responsibility and that the teacher focus on developing the metacognitive skills the learner needs so as to be able to critique, analyse and synthesize from many differing sources and points of view. These are the skills of critical contemplation which provide the basis for emancipation and transformation.

Learners' engagement with the computer is unlike their involvement in other pedagogical forms. Already we take for granted that the virtual space we "call up" on the computer screen is an unlimited series of temporary, non-existent images usually in 2-D space, generated by computer software, in which the immediacy of tele-presence replaces our sense of distance. Furthermore, we, in part, control what we see. We use metaphorical terms for objects such as bulletin boards, desktop and recycle bin, and locations such as virtual classrooms, laboratories, libraries and coffee shops because we have a need to place these temporary spaces in some temporal location where the social norms for that object or place are an accepted part of our virtual activity. We have access to unlimited resources at our fingertips. We can scan, browse, skip, backspace and store what we find. We have a sense of immediacy and responsiveness, of control and choice, and of the opportunity to browse and search. The functions we employ can be divided roughly into four. First are the skills associated with the use of the computer's text-based programs involving composing, editing, storing and retrieval. Second are the communication functions involving messaging via e-mail, bulletin boards and in conferences and the posting and responding skills required. Third are the skills associated with obtaining resources through browsing, searching, following links and assessing information and integrating it with other knowledge. Fourth are the imaginative and creative skills associated with participating in simulations and virtual reality environments such as MUDs and MOOs. Essential are the metacognitive skills that we use to interpret these momentary happenings, to assess their worth and to integrate them into whatever topic we are coming to know. These learner-driven activities are changing our understanding of learning and of the combination of resources and activities we call virtual learning environments.

1.11 THE POSSIBILITIES OF VIRTUAL LEARNING ENVIRONMENTS

Virtual learning environments have been defined as "advanced, flexible, social systems, supported with ICT" (Koper, 2000, p. 2). As Peters (2001) and others have identified, virtual learning environments provide increasingly complex pedagogical structures and are powerful tools for independent as well as collaborative learning. Koper (2000) identified five characteristics of virtual learning environments: representation, personalization, integration, cooperation and process management, each of which has an influence on pedagogical design.

Personalization focuses on the needs of the individual learner. Since constructivist learning principles are based on meeting the differing learning needs of individuals, there has to be relevant individualization of various aspects of the process. Anderson (2003) referred to customized instructions, advice, methods and assignments as some examples of personalization. He noted, "student-content interaction is most accessible, and most readily adapted, via individualized "student portfolios" that can influence design, assessment, or delivery customizations" (p. 4). Students' learning styles and needs can be stored in a personal profile that is used by the computer software to customize responses to student queries. By reducing the amount of redundant materials, the learner is better able to focus on the task at hand. This is often referred to as adaptive instruction and may range from adapting goals and resources to providing opportunities for self-testing or for tutorial help.

Integration refers to the seamless way the course appears to the learner due to the properties of the computer, which can integrate files from people in different places and times. The learner can be time-independent and access the course at any time; time- and place- independent and communicate asynchronously; or place- independent and use video or audio computer communications. Connectivity, the sense of being connected to other learners has become a key term in research on computer-based communications. Integration also allows for the efficient handling and sharing of files stored in a central location among distributed personnel.

Cooperation refers to collective work on an object or report, usually through shareware. One variation is CSCL, computer supported collaborative learning which explores the ways socially constructed knowledge can be electronically distributed in solving common problems. The cooperation is usually self-managed by the group members. Koper identifies characteristics that can limit or derail cooperative activity including conflicts, counterproposals, uneven sharing of the workload and appropriation. Anderson (2003) also referred to the issues surrounding cooperative conferencing noting that some students did not find this a helpful pedagogical approach because of the time-bound dimension. It is evident from the literature that designing, facilitating and participating in appropriate learning activities involving collaboration or cooperation is part of a new skill repertoire for learners and teachers.

Representation is the capacity of the computer to provide a simulated environment that reflects actual situations but does not involve actual people. The video game industry is based on this capability. While large-scale simulations are often expensive, smaller segments of situations, called learning objects, which draw learners into the situation and encourage manipulation of the environment, are becoming increasingly common. One characteristic of learner participation in simulations is that the learner is a participant in the process and must make decisions with visible consequences. Again, Anderson (2003) mentioned the use of virtual labs, which would be one example of remote involvement in actual and virtual situations. However, he commented that "the value of the content is dependent on the extent to which it engages students or teachers in interaction, leading to relevant knowledge construction" (p. 5). He linked the capacity for interaction with resulting engagement, mindfulness and motivation, as do Duffy and Kirkley (2004).

Process management is an attribute of computer software that reduces complex forms of work and makes them manageable. Virtual learning environments that personalize learner activities or materials or that use alternative pedagogical features such as portfolio assessment generally require a complex administrative and management structure which can be computerized. Process management is meant to reduce the complexity for the learner and for the teacher. It can manage workflows, identify problems, collate information and provide information, resources or tasks appropriate to the particular situation. Anderson (2003) noted that computers could take over teacher's administrative tasks such as collating and sorting marks. For Peters (2002) it is the capacity of the virtual environment to provide different learning opportunities rather than the same pedagogical designs in a different media that is the attraction of virtual learning environments.

1.12 COMMENTARY

Anderson's call for more discussion within our community of practice is welcome and important. In a previous analysis of a number of these theories, Amundsen (1993) identified the general theme of communication and an emphasis on the adult learner. She noted the different conceptions of distance, from geographic to pedagogic, and the move to focus on the educational transaction, evident in Moore's (1973) and Garrison's (1989) work. Sauvé (1993), from a similar analysis, grouped the theoretical models into two main fields: those that focus on student autonomy and independence and those that focus on interaction and communication. She also noted the different views of separation, the constant comparison to classroom teaching, and the lack of an overarching model. She identified four constants in the various theories: communication, distance, technologies and planning and organization (p. 102). Since available technologies influenced the various models, Sauvé grouped them as those focused on individualized study with limited teacher–learner interaction (for example, Holmberg 1983; Moore, 1973) and those who saw technologies as closing the gap between teacher and learner (Garrison et al., 2000; Garrison, 1989; Vrasidas and Glass, 2002).

Theories reflect the philosophical beliefs of their authors and much of the theoretical work described above has reflected the modernist search for the overarching theory and its postulates. Gibson (1993) commented on the lack of recognition of context in these theories. She proposed more emphasis on the lifeworld of the learner, such as the influence of the family circumstances, the impact of gender, and the competing time demands of work and learning. Most of these analyses did not include Peters's work. One of the reasons that theorists may have had difficulty with Peters's model is that it was based entirely on the impact of the context on distance education, the penetration of industrial processes into the traditional provision of education and the workplace changes it brought about.

Even when the context has been ignored, distance education theories reflect their social context and values. By and large, the discussions of the last 30 years have been framed within the discourse of increasing access. Distance education has been promoted as a cost-effective means to overcome funding restraints to meet the demands of increasing numbers of students. At the same time that discourse of provision is being overlain by a discourse of lifelong learning, which proposes that people should have opportunities to learn throughout the life span. Distance educators have supported the discourse of access while being frustrated at some of its aspects. Within the mass production and large-scale provision of materials to students, distance educators have sought to recognize the multiple realities of students' lives and ensure alternative choices. And yet the model of large-scale provision limits those possibilities and reinforces the notion that the boundaries of education are controlled by the institution.

The discourse of lifelong learning reflects the post-industrial order discussed by Peters (2002). It is based on the increasing demands for flexibility and choice, the replacement of large-scale production with smaller, niche-based industries, and the globalization of trade. It gives precedence to individuals rather than to institutions, according individuals not only a sense of autonomy and choice but thereby greater responsibility for the outcome of these choices. This discourse prefigures learners as consumers and highlights the utility of learning. However, learners are not left to make these choices alone since employers' demands shape what learners may choose. The provision of education has become a marketplace, and there now is a wider range of providers. The concept of knowledge as being resident in stable bodies of knowledge has been challenged, as the boundaries of provision are reshaped to reflect these new demands. This uncertainty makes a place for situated knowledge and for greater diversity of information sources, but also challenges the identity of the learner.

The concept of the lifelong learner is one of choice and activity and hence identity formation is an ongoing process based on conscious reflection. We see these processes at work when we encourage learners to become increasingly aware of their learning processes, the better to shape them. Thorpe (1995) notes the use of Schön's (1983) work on reflective practice and suggests that we should encourage learners to develop internalized dialogues with themselves about their own learning processes. Overall, there is now much greater emphasis on the economic value of learning, and on learner choice. The state has taken a much greater interest in lifelong learning but has moved it from a social policy of emancipation to an economic model that it has then devolved to the market. This challenges the previous disciplinary boundaries of knowledge as new configurations are made available, and it also gives learners more opportunities to decide what constitutes practical knowledge. The concept of the lifelong learner supports individualized rather than communal learning and with information and communication technologies, learners have immediate access to information and can synthesize it for themselves, further challenging the foundations of institutional learning.

As distance educators, we place ourselves within these discourses, conscious that our actions can be interpreted as supporting either and yet recognizing that the process is complex and the meanings multiple and contested. We constantly renegotiate our positions, crossing by and forth across the borders of these options, as in Anderson's (2003) model, recognizing that each privileges some and marginalizes others. The lack of a single theoretical model could be taken as a positive reflection of our acceptance of the multiple narratives that make up distance education. One of the characteristics of competing, overlapping discourses is the permeability of boundaries. For us this is evident between the dedicated providers of distance education and conventional institutions that also provide distance education and between distance education and what are termed "blended" or "mixed mode" courses. One outcome is that distance education itself is questioned and its absorption and convergence into traditional education is promoted. Our defining concepts of communication, distance, autonomy and planning and management that demarcated our field are being challenged and are being re-interpreted in different ways. While Sauvé concluded her analysis commenting, "Distance is still at the heart of distance education" (p. 105), others would argue that given the immediacy of telecommunications distance is no longer a relevant concept. One alternative is to encourage a much richer discussion that uses concepts from a broader range of fields, as Peters did.

Another facet of our times is the discourse of flexibility. Edwards (1997) contends that flexibility as a discourse has been used to promote changes throughout our society. He sees it as central to the demands for change in educational provision as well as in the restructuring of established educational practices that has been prevalent in the last decade. Flexibility has been used to argue that learning should be reformed to support lifelong learning and be more responsive to the needs of students and employers. It is used to promote distance education and has become a positive value. Those who do not respond are accused of being self-interested professionals lacking adequate accountability, and subject to what Ball termed the "discourse of derision" (1990). It is a discursive strategy used to argue that the issue for educational institutions is not increased funding but more efficient institutional practices that are more responsive to learners. Its discourse promotes access and increased provision while cutting real costs. We see it used also in support of such diverse trends as individual learning portfolios, prior learning assessment and student-centred learning.

As distance educators, the discourse on technology has been of particular importance. While McLuhan (1987) and Franklin (1992) among others have warned of the integral value-positioning of communications technologies, these technologies are often promoted as a neutral tool, an inevitable part of the knowledge society. By promoting them as merely natural developments, the actual impact of the technological change can be removed from criticism. Communications technologies have provided us with significant and contested possibilities for distance education. They have been used to support the globalization of information often of a dominant culture but as well, they have drawn people from far-flung locations closer together in relationships that recognize and promote diversity. Digital communications technologies have transformed our notions of space and time.

Each technological change forces us to reexamine the practice and the theoretical foundations of distance education and the advent of the networked computer has brought new challenges. On one hand, it has provided not only a means to reach more people at times and places convenient to them, but also new possibilities for the ways we design and provide learning environments. However, at the same time as the provision of e-resources supports learners' autonomous behaviour, it shapes learners' beliefs about autonomy as a preferred freedom through its use. In addition, while its asynchronicity can foster isolation and privatization (home versus a public location), it also provides the choice of conferencing with dispersed others and forming social bonds to support collaborative learning.

In describing the large-scale provision of distance education between the 1970s and the 1990s, Peters considered that it was the technologies of post and transport, which came into being with the Industrial Revolution, that ushered in contemporary distance education. Before then, it was impossible on any large scale. More recently (2002), he has explored the possibilities and opportunities provided by digital learning environments. Peters contends that "there is no doubt that the digital learning environment can challenge students to more activity and intensified interactivity not only with regard to quantity but also to quality" (p. 63). Here Peters links aspects of virtual technology to parallel discourses on flexibility, activity and quality, or accountability. He is particularly interested in the challenges to the dominant pedagogical paradigm that these environments can provide. He sees a pedagogical process that has more of the attributes of personal research and proposes that "We are therefore confronted with a break with tradition never seen before. However we judge this process, the removal of the bonds above leads to a flexibility and variability of learning which was never before possible" (pp. 65–66).

Peters and Anderson find great possibilities in the virtual learning environment. Garrison et al., (2000) highlighted the possibilities associated with intense interactivity in their community of inquiry model. But there is still much that we can learn from earlier models. For example, two aspects of Holmberg's model continue to be important. One is his guidance concerning the ways to make print materials engaging and challenging to the learner which need to be reexamined as we develop digitized interactive resource materials. Second, the notion of empathic engagement which he proposed as the basis for his guided didactic conversation that was based on the work of Carl Rogers (1962), who identified three critical aspects of successful communication: open disclosure, warm affirmations and empathetic comprehension. This work could assist in the conceptualization and analysis of computer conferencing sessions that are meant to promote collaborative learning. As Burge (1995, p. 159) noted,

> Collaborative learning ... does not happen just because people have been collected together. This connection relates to the synergy of learning: "creating a shared experience of learning is qualitatively different from helping individuals share their prior experience"
>
> Johnson and Johnson, 1993, p. 146.

Similar links can be made with the other models to illustrate how they continue to help inform our multiple and diverse practices.

Finally, we argue that more attention is required to the discourse of knowledge/power. The permeability of traditional educational boundaries has already led to challenges to the profession as the source of knowledge. The possibilities of networked computers are also challenging our conceptions of the role of the teacher. Already we have had a change from the expository sage on the stage to the discussion-oriented guide on the side. But even with the emphasis on facilitation, the institution continues to control the boundary of knowledge. If we hesitate to adopt models of learning that encourage student autonomy more than student cooperation, or fear to include a teaching, rather than a teacher role, or are unwilling to differentiate the role of the teacher and share it with learning designers, educational technology specialists and tutors, then we need to ask ourselves why. We need to ask ourselves if it is that we fear the loss of professional control and whether new pedagogical models will provide for greater balance between the institution and the learner. How we weave our way among discourses of technology, flexibility, power, knowledge and lifelong learning will continue to influence the models of distance education that we create through our practices. As John Daniel noted recently, we hesitate to accept that distance education has become the flavour of the month because once it becomes part of the dominant discourse we don't know how it might be used. But at least, we should be on our guard for how we understand distance education as a reflection of our own positioning in the competing discourses of today's society.

This handbook canvasses a wide distance education policy and practice that we have positioned for our purposes as editors of the collection. The section topics help frame the reading of the chapters, indeed, as they helped frame the writing. The previous discussion of the origins and connections of theories and practices of distance education enables the work of the contributors to be understood in both historical and epistemological contexts. It is the case, however, that many of the chapters have implications and connections across sections. The distance education community has been an international one for many years (see, for example, Sewart et al., 1983). The contributors' contexts and experiences also reflect a diversity of national, social, political and economic perspectives that enable readers to appreciate the work and circumstances of distance educators in other nations. The practices of distance education have become infused into "mainstream" education over the past two decades (see, for example, Smith and Kelly, 1987; Evans and Nation, 2000; 2003); however, this handbook re-draws the boundary around distance education in order that its substance, theories and practices can be recognized and appreciated as distinct and important ways in which nations educate their citizens.

REFERENCES

Amundsen, C. (1993). The evolution of theory in distance education. In *Theoretical Principles of Distance Education* (D. Keegan, ed.) London, UK: Routledge, pp. 61–79.

Anderson, T. (2003). Getting the mixture right again: An updated and theoretical rationale for interaction. *International Review of Research in Open and Distance Learning*, 4, 2. Retrieved April 22, 2007, http://www.irrodl.org/index.php/irrodl/article/view/149/708

Anderson, T. and Garrison, R. (1998). Learning in a networked world: New roles and responsibilities. In *Distance learners in higher education* (C.Gibson, ed.) Madison, WI: Atwood Publishing, pp. 97–112.

Anderson, T., Rourke, L., Garrison, G., and Archer, W. (2001). Assessing teaching presence in a computer conferencing context. *Journal of Asynchronous Learning Networks* 5(2), Retrieved April 22, 2007 from http://www.sloan-c.org/publications/jaln/v5n2/v5n2_anderson.asp.

Ball, S. (1990). *Policy and politics in education*. London, UK: Routledge.

Burge, L. (1995). Electronic highway or weaving loom? Thinking about conferencing technologies for learning. In *Open and Distance Learning Today* (F. Lockwood, ed.)(pp. 151–163). London, UK: Routledge.

Duffy, T.M. and Kirkley, J.R. (2004). *Learner-Centred Theory and Practice in Distance Education: Cases from Higher Education*. Mahwah, NJ: Lawrence Erlbaum Associates.

Edwards, R. (1997). *Changing Places? Flexibility, Lifelong Learning and a Learning Society.* London, UK: Routledge.
Evans, T.D. and Nation, D.E. (eds) (1989). *Critical Reflections on Distance Education,* London, UK: Falmer Press.
Evans, T.D. and Nation, D.E. (eds) (2000). *Changing University Teaching: Reflections on Creating Educational Technologies.* London, UK: Kogan Page.
Evans, T.D. and Nation, D.E. (2003). "Globalisation and the reinvention of distance education." In *The Handbook of Distance Education,* (M.G. Moore and W. Anderson, eds) 2nd ed., Mahwah, NJ: Lawrence Erlbaum and Associates, pp. 767–782.
Faith, K. (ed.) (1988). *Toward New Horizons for Women in Distance Education: International Perspectives.* London, UK: Routledge.
Franklin, U. (1992). *The Real World of Technology.* Toronto, ON: Anansi.
Garrison, R. (1989). *Understanding distance education.* London, UK: Routledge.
Garrison, R. (1993). Quality and access in distance education: theoretical considerations. In *Theoretical Principles of Distance Education* (D. Keegan, ed.) London, UK: Routledge, pp. 9–21.
Garrison, R. and Baynton, M. (1987). Beyond independence in distance education: the concept of control. *The American Journal of Distance Education* **3**(1), 3–15.
Garrison, R., Anderson, T., and Archer, W. (2000). Critical thinking in a text-based environment: Computer conferencing in higher education. *The Internet and Higher Education,* **2**(2), 87–105. Retrieved April 22, 2007 from: http://communitiesofinquiry.com/
Gibson, C. (1993). Towards a broader conceptualization of distance education. In *Theoretical principles of distance education* (D. Keegan, ed.) London, UK: Routledge, pp. 80–92.
Hannafin, M. and Kim, M. (2003). In search of a future: A critical analysis of research on web-based teaching and learning. *Instructional Science* **31**(4), 347–351.
Harris, D. (1987). *Openness and Closure in Distance Education.* London, UK: Falmer Press.
Heinecke, W., Dawson, K. and Willis, J. (2001). Paradigms and frames for R and D in distance education: Towards collaborative electronic learning. *International Journal of Educational Telecommunications* 7(3), 293–322.
Hillman, D., Willis, D., and Gundawardena, C. (1994). Learner interface interaction in distance education. An extension of contemporary models and strategies for practitioners. *The American Journal of Distance Education* 8(2), 30–42.
Holmberg, B. (1976). Academic socialization and distance study. *Epistolodidaktika,* **1**, 17–25.
Holmberg, B. (1977). *Distance Education. A Survey and Bibliography.* London, UK: Kogan Page.
Holmberg, B. (1983). Guided didactic conversation in distance education. In *Distance Education: International Perspectives* (D. Stewart, D. Keegan, and B. Holmberg, eds) London, UK: Croom Helm, pp. 114–122.
Holmberg, B. (1986). *Growth and Structure of Distance Education.* Beckenham, Kent, UK: Croom Helm.
Holmberg, B. (1995). *Theory and Practice of Distance Education.* London, UK: Routledge.
Johnson, D. and Johnson, R. (1993). Cooperative learning and feedback in technology-based instruction. In *Interactive Instruction and Feedback* (J. Dempsey and G. Sales, eds) Englewood Cliffs, NJ: Educational Technology Publications, pp. 133–159.
Keegan, D. (ed)(1994). *Otto Peters on Distance Education.* London: Routledge/falmer.
Keegan, D. (1993). Reintegration of the teaching acts. In *Theoretical Principles of Distance Education* (D. Keegan, ed.). London, UK: Routledge, pp. 113–134.

Keegan, D. (2000). *Distance training. Taking Stock at a Time of Change*. London, UK: Routledge Falmer.

Knowles, A. (1970). *The Modern Practice of Adult Education: Andragogy Versus Pedagogy*. New York: Association Press.

Koper, R. (2000). *From Change to Renewal: Educational Technology Foundations of Electronic Environments*. Educational Technology Expertise centre, Open University of the Netherlands. Retrieved April 22, 2007 from: http://eml.ou.nl/introduction/docs/koper-inaugural-address.pdf.

Laurillard, D. (1993). *Rethinking University Teaching. A Framework for the Effective Use of Educational Technology*. London, UK: Routledge.

Laurillard, D. (2002). *Rethinking university teaching. A conversational framework for the effective use of learning technologies*, 2nd ed., London, UK: RoutledgeFalmer.

McLuhan, M. (1987) *Uniderstand Media: The Extensions of Man*. London, UK: Routledge. [Originally published 1964, same title, NewYork: Signet books.]

Moore, M. (1973). Towards a theory of independent learning and teaching. *Journal of Higher Education*, **44**, 661–179.

Moore, M. (1989). Three types of interaction. Editorial. *The American Journal of Distance Education*, **3**. Retrieved April 22, 2007 from http://cdl.panam.edu/Home/Files/MMOORE.doc.

Moore, M. (1993). Theory of transactional distance. In *Theoretical Principles of Distance Education* (D. Keegan, ed.) London, UK: Routledge, pp. 33–38.

Moore, M. and Kearsley, G. (1996). *Distance Education: A Systems View*. Belmont, CA: Wadsworth.

Peters, O. (1983). Distance teaching and industrial production: A comparative interpretation in outline. In *Distance education: International Perspectives* (D. Sewart, D. Keegan, and B. Holmberg, eds) London: Croom Helm.

Peters, O. (1993). Distance education in a postindustrial society. In *Theoretical Principles of Distance Education* (D. Keegan, ed.) London, UK: Routledge, pp. 39–60.

Peters, O. (2001). *Learning and Teaching in Distance Education: Analysis and Interpretations from an International Perspective*. London, UK: Kogan Page.

Peters, O. (2002). *Distance education in transition: New Trends and Challenges*. Oldenberg, FGR: Bibliotheks und Informationssystem der Carl von Ossietzky Universität Oldenberg.

Rogers, C. (1962). Toward Becoming a Fully Functioning Person. In *Perceiving, Behaving, Becoming, 1962 Yearbook* (A.W. Combs, ed). Washington, DC: Association for Supervision and Curriculum Development.

Sauvé, L. (1993). What's behind the development of a course on the concept of distance education? In *Theoretical Principles of Distance Education* (D. Keegan, ed.) London, UK: Routledge, pp. 93–112.

Schön, D (1983) *The Reflective Practitioner: How Professionals Think in Action*. London: Falmer Press

Sewart, D., Keegan, D. and Holmberg, B. (eds) (1983). *Distance Education: International Perspectives*. Beckenham: Croom Helm.

Smith, P. and Kelly, M. (eds) (1987). *Distance Education and the Mainstream*. London, UK: Croom Helm.

Thorpe, M. (1979). When is a course not a course? *Teaching at a Distance*, **16**, 13–18.

Thorpe, M. (1995). The challenge facing course design. In *Open and distance learning today* (F. Lockwood, ed.) London, UK: Routledge, pp. 175–184.

Vrasidas, C. and Glass, G. (2002). A conceptual framework for studying distance education. In *Distance Education and Distributed Learning* (C. Vrasidas and G. Glass, eds) Greenwich, CT: IAP, pp. 31–56.

Wedemeyer, C.A. (1981). *Learning at the Back Door: Reflections on Non-Traditional Learning in the Lifespan.* Madison: The University of Wisconsin Press.

Winn, W. (1990). Some implications for cognitive theory for instructional design. *Instructional Science* **19**(1), 53.69.

Section I

Diversity in Distance Education

Introduction

Margaret Haughey

Diversity in education speaks to inclusion in many forms, not only in terms of provision from schooling to vocational and post-secondary education and inclusiveness in the materials we develop and the learners we support, but also a recognition of inclusiveness in the services we provide. In this section, the writers have addressed diversity in some of these ways; others are detailed in chapters in other sections.

McKay and Makhanya begin the section with an examination of the role of open and distance learning (ODL) in the context of development. Based at the University of South Africa, they use their own experiences to raise questions about the ability of ODL to transform society by engaging in emancipatory politics and at the same time address the needs of those least advantaged in society. Their response "to think broadly, to partner wisely and to act courageously" is a challenge to all ODL institutions regardless of context.

Next, Gundawardena and LaPointe examine several aspects of the socio-cultural context that influence distance education. They explore in turn the diversity of expectations, learning styles, social presence, differences in communications styles, second-language issues and visual design interpretations and place these within a theoretical framework that acknowledges cultural variability. For them, the goals of distance education include "developing global citizens who can solve global problems without the diminution of indigenous culture" and they use examples from their own work in many different countries to help bring resonance to their ideas.

Gender has been recognized as an aspect of distance education for quite some time but how it manifests itself within a particular context is the focus of Mhehe's work.

She explores the lives of women students and their non-student friends in relation to the issues and barriers associated with participation in distance education at the Open University of Tanzania. In doing so, she identifies the many socio-cultural and institutional issues the women face in that society. Providing access is not enough she contends; as well, an exploration of the ways gender is embedded in distance education provision needs to be undertaken.

Learning styles, originally discussed by Gundawardena and LaPointe in terms of their socio-cultural aspects, are the focus of the chapter by Mitchell and O'Rourke. They critique the industrialized model of course development which subdues individual learner needs to the provision of "learner opportunities" rather than "opportunities for learning" with a "minimization of learner support." They base their chapter on a model in which learners' needs arising from learners' characteristics and experiences is at the centre. Responding to those needs through appropriate learning strategies and the relationship between those learning strategies and learning outcomes forms the discourse of the chapter. In the process, they provide a framework which visually integrates these aspects and then descriptions of various approaches which provide a narrative thread.

The question of structural impediments to inclusiveness is also taken up by Newell who examines disability and distance education from two perspectives: disability as a medical condition and disability as an aspect of the social group. In the former, the issues of accommodation and adaptation to the mainstream come to the fore while the construct of disability as an aspect of a social group requires that disability be included as one aspect which anyone may have. While movements like universal design go some way to reflect the second construct, Newell contends that the slide to the first position is still the norm and calls for a continuing critique of the "otherness" it enacts.

Diversity can also apply to distance learners' experiences, one aspect of which is informal learning. In this chapter, Conrad describes the use of prior learning assessment procedures in providing a platform for the recognition of these experiences. She uses her experience at Athabasca University to describe how various aspects of the recognition of prior learning are handled and elaborates on the underlying tensions entailed in the classification of experiential knowledge generally viewed by the learner as holistic and integrated. These tensions are highlighted when experiential learning recognition procedures are placed in a larger rhetoric of economic and political concerns.

The next two chapters explore the provision of first open schooling and then vocational education. Using a series of case studies, Haughey, Murphy and Muirhead provide an historical narrative of the provision of schooling through the various forms of distance education from the early provision of correspondence education to today's virtual schooling, first in Australia and Canada and then in India and Zambia. The various cases help illustrate the tensions between the replication and transformation agendas in schooling and the increasing use of blended learning in serving school learners.

Smith's chapter on vocational schooling also uses an historical narrative to document the changes in Australian vocational education and training through distance education from a centralized model to a decentralized provision. In particular, he documents the move from a career development educative approach to a skills upgrading economic imperative. Given government support, first the training itself and then its assessment were localized, providing a major challenge to centralized distance education providers. And yet these challenges of hand-on learning through direct experience, of learning specific to the local employment context, of assessment when the person has learned the skill rather than when the exam is set, all contributed to a reclamation of DE as flexible delivery which also includes learner control over "content, sequence and time to completion," an idea more often espoused that enacted in other DE environments.

The last two chapters explore technology. Anderson examines the possibilities of social software technologies for distance education. Beginning with a typology of technologies, he proposes a new space for social technology that is neither independent information nor collaborative communications centric, but overlaps both. He proposes that in addition to the freedoms documented by Paulsen (1993) of space, time, pace, media, access and content, a seventh should be freedom of relationship that lets "students to decide on the type of learning community and individual relationships" they desire for their learning. He then goes on to describe various tools which could be provided to assist students achieve this freedom.

In the final chapter in the section, Spronk provides a critical essay, but not in the sense that she engages with the topics identified by earlier authors. Instead, she focuses on what she terms as the essential issues. By this, she means the issues those beginning to engage in distance education provision in developing countries need to address cost, technology, level and culture. In addressing each of the four, she raises questions and provides practical advice that is critical to success. The chapter provides an important reminder of the diversity of issues which need to be addressed if distance education is to succeed in meeting learner needs.

Chapter 2

Making it Work for the South: Using Open and Distance Learning in the Context of Development

Veronica McKay and Mandla Makhanya

2.1 INTRODUCTION

> Why twenty years later am I forced to ask the question "Why is open learning at-a-distance failing the masses of Africa?"
>
> (Dodds, 2002).

Dodds (2002) asks this question despite the fact that open and distance learning (ODL) is increasingly becoming accepted in academic circles throughout the world as a legitimate, effective and even fashionable approach to educational provision. However, while it may be fashionable, to what extent is Dodds correct that ODL is failing the masses? To what extent can ODL be used for redress and social transformation, and how can it address the needs of the world's most disadvantaged people? These are questions that educators and policy makers need to bear in mind in their deliberations on educational delivery.

In responding to these questions, we will refer to certain endeavours by the University of South Africa (or, as it is generally known, Unisa) as examples, which may engender good practice in meeting the needs of the most disadvantaged. We start the chapter with some background information on Unisa, which after the demise of apartheid had *itself* to be transformed to take on these challenges.

We begin with a description of Unisa, and then focus on the challenges it has faced and the strategies it has employed in responding to the questions proposed by Tony Dodds.

In this way, we hope that the activities of Unisa will help illustrate the importance of distance education responses in the context of development.

2.2 TRANSFORMING UNISA TO MEET THE NEEDS OF SOCIAL TRANSFORMATION

Inspired by the philosophy outlined by the *New Partnership for Africa's Development* (NEPAD) of African ownership for the future development of the continent, and committed to translating NEPADs declaration into action, Unisa has responded by shaping its responsibility as an ODL institution of higher learning through partnerships with African governments and tertiary education institutions as part of its efforts in human capacity building, skills training, collaborative research and publications.

In his inauguration address as Principal and Vice-Chancellor of Unisa on 24 January 2002, Professor Pityana made the following statement:

> Finally, Unisa has an Africa-wide reach. Beginning with the SADC states and with the advances through the Constitutive Act of the African Union and the New Partnership for Africa's Development (NEPAD), Unisa can play a part in rapid integration, not just of the economies and trade of Africa, but also intellectual output, training, skills development, as well as research. In the prevailing economic climate, additional national universities may no longer be affordable, and, with co-operation agreements in place in education and other areas, Unisa is best placed to become the alternative provider of quality higher education to a growing number of African States.
>
> (Pityana, 2002, p. 1)

Professor Pityana highlights the need to position Unisa so that it can indeed confront African challenges. As he sees it, Unisa's experience in distance education can be readily harnessed to make education accessible to Africa, and its resources can be used as a basis for education throughout the continent. Unisa is a viable alternative to traditional delivery modes, since it is inexpensive and available to everyone in the continent. Unisa must play its role within South Africa, but must also understand that it should begin to design a broader understanding within the context of the African Union (AU) and NEPAD. All projects should be geared to what the continent wants to achieve. If Unisa is to fit in with this vision, it must have a clearly defined agenda, and it was for this reason that Unisa's Directorate for Africa was put in place, with the task of:

- forging links with the political leadership of the countries with whom the university is involved;
- mediating all Unisa's activities in Africa;
- reporting about Unisa to politicians in the countries with whom it collaborates.

The aims outlined above are envisaged to contribute to the mutual empowerment of the continent's scholars and reduce Africa's reliance on European and American scholars, who have for so long dominated African education. Unisa's partnerships with these institutions will also be in line with the South-to-South philosophy of NEPAD.

NEPAD bases its view of higher education on the philosophy that African institutions should contribute to the analysis and solution of the many problems that are plaguing the African continent. To make this an effective contribution, universities have to cooperate by building institutional linkages. Many African universities find themselves facing the sad reality that past and present political turmoil has resulted in a situation where they have limited resources at their disposal. Unisa sees its role as one of collaboration and partnership with other African universities, and it has taken on the role of spearheading this collaboration and partnership by signing various Memorandums of Understanding (MOUs) with other African institutions with regard to staff exchange programmes, exchange of academic information and other resources, and development of joint degree programmes.

For collaboration to work, it is essential to have the commitment of all concerned or directly affected. Leatt and Martin (2000, p. 2) identify a number of elements that are essential for effective collaboration:

- Each member is committed to incurring costs to pursue joint objectives that cannot be resolved by individual members acting alone.
- Agreements are in place that define what the collaboration does, how its activities are resourced and how collective decisions at all levels are taken.
- Collective decisions are taken and accepted by the members.
- Each member incurs costs that are not directly ascribable to benefits for itself. Likewise, each member receives benefits for which it does not directly bear the cost.

Makhanya and McKay (2004) add a further requirement, which is that the end beneficiaries of the collaboration should believe that the collaboration is working and is in their interest.

2.3 MEANWHILE BACK AT HOME: CHANGING STUDENT DEMOGRAPHICS

Since the 1990s, South Africa has experienced a demographic trend whereby blacks now constitute a larger share of the university population than whites. This is in stark contrast to the past when, as a result of apartheid legislation, the majority of blacks struggled to be admitted to a university because they were prevented from completing their secondary education. Those who succeeded were mainly from urban areas. Since the beginning of the 1990s, Unisa has seen an increasing number of university entrants drawn from educationally and socially disadvantaged communities, a majority of whom cannot afford full-time studies at residential universities. This means that the university is drawing in large numbers of young students and is no longer attracting only the traditional "mature aged" distance learner.

Also, in line with global trends for a learning society, students who are employed and who need to further their education (and who might be regarded as the "traditional" target group of distance education) have not stopped enrolling at Unisa. The rapid changes that are taking place within the world of work require a workforce that continuously sharpens its skills, and can thus never stop learning and furthering its knowledge. Hence, the report of the National Commission for Higher Education that today South Africa is following global trends towards the establishment of a learning society with institutions of higher learning having to make provision for ongoing learning so that learners can be competitive in their world of work (NCHE, 1996). For these learners, distance education is the answer to their quest to learn.

2.4 DISTANCE EDUCATION AND ODL DEFINED

Unisa was established in 1873 as the University of the Cape of Good Hope, serving exclusively as an examining body. In 1916, the university relocated from Cape Town to Pretoria, and took a new name – the University of South Africa. The institution became a federal structure incorporating almost all the university colleges that existed in South Africa at that time, and "parented" them until they were able to become autonomous. In 1946, Unisa transformed itself into an institution that provided postal tuition to nonresidential students.

A distance education institution is one that is dedicated to providing education to those who want distance education by choice and those who, through barriers to access, might not be able to study at a residential university. Today, such institutions use a set of multimedia channels to provide an education that is didactically appropriate to their students. Moore (1973, p. 664) defines distance education as:

> [t]he family of instructional methods in which the teaching behaviours are executed apart from the learning behaviours, including those that in a contiguous situation would be performed in the learner's presence, so that communication between the teacher and the learner must be facilitated by print, electronic, mechanical or other devices.

Keegan (1986, p. 49) adds to this, saying that distance education is a form of education characterised by the following:

- the quasi-permanent separation of teacher and learner throughout the length of the learning process; this distinguishes it from conventional face-to-face education;
- the influence of an educational organisation both in the planning and preparation of learning materials and in the provision of student support services; this distinguishes it from private study and teach-yourself programmes;
- the use of technical media - print, audio, video and computer - to unite teacher and learner and carry the content of the course;
- the provision of two-way communication so that the student may benefit from or even initiate dialogue; this distinguishes it from other uses of technology in education;

- the quasi-permanent absence of the learning group throughout the length of the learning process so that people are usually taught as individuals and not in groups, with the possibility of occasional meetings for both didactic and socialisation purposes.

Unisa's most recent Tuition Policy document extends this definition by stressing design and development of learning experiences, student support structures and the importance of interaction. It states that distance learning is

> a form of planned learning which provides learning opportunities aimed at limiting the constraints of time/place/pace. It involves the design and development of learning experiences using various technologies and student-support strategies to effect interaction among teachers and learners. It enables learners to become independent and critical thinkers, and to attain their educational goals. (http://www.unisa.ac.za/internal/cs98/pol.html:1)

The role of distance education in South Africa is further elucidated by the National Commission of Higher Education (NCHE), which notes the importance of openness of access.

> A key challenge for higher education is to enhance the quality of higher education programmes ... This challenge must be met in the context of greatly increased access to a wide diversity of students at varying entry levels, and within a higher education budget that increases significantly slower than enrolments rise. The Commission believes that distance education and resource-based learning are a fundamental part of meeting this challenge ... A further challenge is to move the higher education system in the direction of becoming an open learning system organised for use by learners at various stages of their lives and careers – a system that promotes lifelong learning, not merely at the margins for small groups of "mature" students, but in its basic shape and structure.
>
> (NCHE, 1996, pp. 118–119)

Distance education has evolved from a mode that was known as correspondence education as it started to use a wider and wider array of media. This is captured clearly by Rumble (1991, pp. 7–9), who says:

> Although the term "distance education" is now widely used in preference to "correspondence education", there is no inherent difference in the two methods. "Correspondence education" is the older term, reflecting the origins of distance education as a product of the development of a cheap, reliable postal service and the fact that the early means of communication was by letter. Nowadays correspondence education can be regarded as a particular form of distance education based on print and written assignments and letters, whereas distance education uses a wide range of media.

Unisa endeavours to provide quality ODL opportunities in higher education, conducts research and serves the community through the expertise of its personnel. It enrols learners in a flexible manner without the barriers that a traditional university would put in their way.

Having looked at the definitions of distance education, it is appropriate to define open learning so as to get a clearer picture of Unisa and how it functions. The Manpower Services Commission (1984, p. 7) offers the following succinct definition:

> Open Learning arrangements enable people to learn at the time, place and pace which satisfy their circumstances and requirements. The emphasis is on opening up opportunities by overcoming barriers that result from geographical isolation, personal or work commitments or conventional course structures which have often prevented people from gaining access to the training they need.

Wedemeyer's definition (1977, p. 217) of open learning reads as follows:

> All open schools have one principle in common: they are to a greater or lesser extent efforts to expand the freedoms of learners. Some are open only in a spatial sense ... while others provide freedoms in more significant dimensions – in admissions, selection of courses, individual adaptation of the curriculum and time, goal selection and evaluation.

Lewis (1988, p. 257) defines open learning as "essentially a means to enable [learners], of whatever age, to take responsibility for their own learning". This is how open learning is described in Unisa's Tuition Policy document:

> Open learning promotes open access to courses, flexibility in learning provision, and methods and criteria of assessing learning progress and achievement. Open learning denotes a shift of emphasis from the institutional lecturer or content-centred learning to a learner-centred and outcomes-based approach. (http://www.unisa.ac.za/internal/comserve/cs98/pol.html:1)

This presupposes a learner-centred approach in respect of curriculum development and the learning process itself.

2.5 UNISA AS A MEGA-UNIVERSITY

Unisa is the largest ODL institution in South Africa and on the African continent. It is also one of the mega universities in the world, that is, one with over 100,000 learners. Unisa achieves economies of scale in an environment of ever-increasing budgetary constraints on higher education. According to the South African National Student Organisation (SANSO) funding formula, the subsidies paid to institutions of higher learning have, at the time of writing, been reduced to half of what they should be. ODL institutions such as Unisa are a great deal more affordable for students than residential universities, and have the advantage of reaching multitudes of students. Unisa currently reaches around 240,000 degree students annually and about 50,000 diploma and certificate students.

2.6 STUDY MATERIAL: DESIGN AND DELIVERY

Unisa's success lies in its use of printed materials, consisting primarily of study guides and tutorial letters. Study guides are interactive materials with various activities aimed at keeping students actively involved in the learning process. Self-assessment exercises, for example, assist learners to practise what they have learnt in each unit or section of the guide, and a range of activities provoke students to think critically about what they are learning and to apply concepts and principles to practical situations. Additional reading lists complement the material, which addresses students in a direct, reader-friendly manner. Tutorial letters set out various assignments that students should complete. There are also a number of optional assignments aimed at giving learners a broader base of understanding of the course. They can choose whether or not to write these, although obviously doing so is to their own advantage. Recorded programmes are used in addition to printed materials. Among these are audiocassettes, videos and, CD ROMs. Radio, tele and video conferencing are also used, but the university has not, as yet, experimented with television as a medium for delivery. It does, however, provide face-to-face support in the form of group discussion lectures and tutorials presented at various provincial and other centres throughout South Africa.

ODL institutions require a support system infrastructure that must operate smoothly if they are to succeed. Unisa is no exception, and its infrastructure includes the following delivery departments or sections:

- Call Centre
- Examination Administration
- Finance
- Undergraduate Student Affairs
- Postgraduate Student Affairs
- Graduation Ceremonies
- Bureau of Student Counselling and Career Development
- Student Financial Aid Bureau
- Student Support
- Assignments (the section that handles the administration of assignments which includes implementing a policy of receipt and return of assignments to students in a workable timeframe)
- Dispatch (which distributes materials)
- Computer Services
- Library Services
- Telecommunication Services
- Corporate Communication and Marketing
- Editorial Services
- Bureau of Management Information
- Bureau of Learning Development
- Safety Services

These departments provide support to the academic and teaching departments spanning across three colleges. While this support is fundamental for the optimal running of the university, the general ethos of the university is to ensure a supportive and nurturing environment for students – especially first-year students who in South Africa tend to be drawn from disadvantaged backgrounds.

2.7 STUDENT SUPPORT

Student support takes on a number of dimensions from career counselling through to workplace support and student development.

In addition, accessible study material is also a means of providing support. This requires lecturers to move away from the kind of study material that students struggle to read and understand. Materials need to be student friendly. They need to make it clear to learners, from the very beginning, what they need to know or what they should be able to do once they have completed their course of study. Learner support materials need to give the learners a chance to see how well they are mastering the objectives of each unit or chapter by providing them with self-assessment exercises that they can do after each unit or chapter. In South Africa, with eleven official languages, the use of English as a medium of instruction means that the majority of students do not have English as their mother tongue. This makes it imperative to provide learners with support mechanisms, such as a glossary that explains difficult concepts, and to use a writing style which is consistently dialogical in order to stimulate students' interest in the material.

According to Moore (1973, pp. 664–665), a student support system may be defined as:

> a programme within the dominant institution aiming towards bridging the distance between teaching and learning whereby the distance learner can control the pace at which he[she] receives information and at which he[she] must make his[her] response through face-to-face dialogical intervention.

Rowntree (1990) perceives distance learners as students who will not be in regular contact with the teachers responsible for the course design, and with little or no face-to-face contact even with other learners. On the other hand, he points out that distance learners may include students who use the facilities of the institution sponsoring the course and who learn through self-instruction in a situation where they are able to meet one another, a tutor, and perhaps a more experienced colleague who can support their studies although he or she is not the actual course designer.

Moore's (1973) definition of student support corresponds with the approach adopted by Unisa when it decided to establish a network of learning centres from 1995 onwards, where tutors were contracted to render subject-related and study skills support to students. This was intended to address the needs of disadvantaged students by improving the level of communication between lecturers and students. Since 1995, Unisa has committed itself to offering student support in terms of tutorials, counselling and administrative services (including library services) to reinforce the study package.

Tutorials. A number of tutors were brought on board to do the following:

- Serve as facilitators of independent learning by students.
- Assist students to understand and relate to their materials rather than replace the study material.
- Provide explanations where required and diagnose problems students may be experiencing in grasping the material.
- Help students address such problems so that they can comprehend their work and ultimately pass their examinations at the end of each semester or year.

Unisa therefore started seeing tutors as an integral part of the university who could help take the distance out of its ODL endeavours to bring students and Unisa itself closer together.

To facilitate the effectiveness and efficiency of the tutorial programme, the university decided to appoint tutor representatives or coordinators to represent the different faculties, so that a relationship could be built between academic departments and tutors. Besides themselves offering tutorials, tutors are expected to oversee the tutorial support in terms of both content and process, and are also lecturers in their own departments.

Counselling. Student counsellors are required to guide and assist the students with study skills as well as to give them career guidance. Unisa has gone beyond counselling services provided by professionals only, the Bureau for Student Counselling and Career Development (BSCCD) having started a programme of assistance through peer helpers – a group of students who are specially trained to provide assistance to other students. The programme was developed for students who are nervous about sharing their problems with student counsellors and prefer to discuss them with peer helpers, who are their contemporaries.

Learning Centres. Learning centres have been established at the regional campuses and a number of other venues. These provide the following:

- adequate study areas;
- seminar rooms (where tutorials and group discussion lectures take place);
- discussion rooms for students;
- offices for staff and local Students' Representative Councils (SRCs);
- a post box for assignments;
- a recreation hall, micro-computer facilities;
- library services (the young students the university attracts need access to the library on a full-time basis);
- conference telephone, video and television facilities;
- small cafeterias serving light refreshments.

2.8 ACCREDITATION BY THE DISTANCE EDUCATION AND TRAINING COUNCIL

Unisa has now been accredited by the Accrediting Commission of the Distance Education and Training Council (DETC) of the United States. This means its quality multimedia instructional materials, tutorial support networks and highly qualified staff have passed the stringent DETC tests. The DETCs accreditation attests to the quality of Unisa's products, processes, delivery systems and general organisational philosophy (these are the four aspects of quality referred to by Normann in his 1984 work on quality in educational institutions). This accreditation gives Unisa the right to use the DETC seal on all its learning materials, and gives it continued access to quality assurance and peer review, which will guarantee the maintenance of its high standards.

2.8.1 Challenges that have been Met

In reformulating Unisa to better meet the needs of learners who are unable to access residential universities, as identified by Dodds (2002), Unisa has faced three broad challenges in the past 8 years or so. These challenges have been the impact of ICT on course design, delivery through local, multipurpose community centres (MPCCs) where students are able to access materials online, communicate with their lecturers, submit assignments online and request library materials.

2.9 INFORMATION AND COMMUNICATION TECHNOLOGY

With innovation and refinement, as well as with delivery, Unisa has accepted the reality of globalising world and has taken information and communications technologies (ICT) seriously. Work has already started on a project known by the acronym VMA (the Virtual Multimedia Academy). This is a UNESCO sponsored joint venture with Universidade de Eduardo Mondlane (UEM) of Mozambique and Sudan University of Science and Technology (SUST). The three institutions involved in the VMA project have decided to use the learning materials of an existing print-based Unisa course, a first-level Art History module, as the basis for the multimedia enhanced learning material. Unisa has set up its own team of people for the project: three members from the ICT Directorate, three members from the Faculty of Humanities and Social Sciences' Art History department (these members are multimedia specialists), three members who are isiZulu, tshiVenda and isiXhosa language specialists, and an administrator from the ICT Directorate. In addition to this team, the Unit for Video, Sound and Photography has recorded the voice-overs and provided the digital sound clips.

Unisa's dreams springs from a government initiative to build multipurpose community centres (MPCCs) in various disadvantaged communities to connect each and every South African to the Internet. The university has decided to collaborate with government in this initiative so that its students will, in the near future, enjoy all the benefits of the Internet and its related services.

Great strides have already been made in the area of ICT. The Department of Computer Services has, for example, already completed a number of major projects in the following areas: All the buildings on Unisa's main campus have been re-cabled with high-speed networks to give all staff an access speed to workstations of 100 MB/s. It has doubled the bandwidth of the institution's Internet access, and has done remote deployment of software as well as antivirus software. A new storage area of approximately 1.2 TB will assist staff in storing their academic and research data.

Students-On-Line communication has taken off in the past 3 years and its value is apparent in the significant increase in the number of students who use this communication tool each year. It is anticipated that in the years to come in South Africa, the majority of Unisa's students will come already equipped with intense media experience acquired in their homes and from recreational activities. These students will obviously learn more readily in the technologically rich environment that Unisa is preparing for them today.

2.9.1 Challenges of the Present with Regard to Mass Education

Our reflections on the use of ODL in the developing world need to be underpinned by questions about the role that education can and should play in development in general, and then about the role of ODL in the specific context of the developing world. Questions we might ask are:

- What kind of learning will prepare learners for participation in a global context without losing sight of the specifics of the local context?
- To what extent should curricula accommodate previously marginalized or indigenous knowledge as opposed to knowledge characterised as global or western?
- What lessons can be learned from the use of ODL in the provisioning of mass education in the context of the developing world?

2.10 THE NEED FOR BASIC EDUCATION WITHIN THE GLOBAL CONTEXT

The World Education Forum held in Dakar in 2000 committed itself to halving the adult illiteracy rate, which at that time stood at 860 million (UNESCO, 2002), by 2015. While some progress has been made, the Asian region has 614 million illiterate adults and the number of illiterate people in Africa stands at 182 million[1] people over the age of fifteen. The number of illiterate people in sub-Saharan Africa is said to be a staggering (and increasing) 137 million.

ODL within the context of the developing world must take cognisance of the need for mass education. Unisa is no exception. While addressing the need for market-oriented degrees and programmes, Unisa has had to locate itself within a developmental paradigm with programmes needed to address immediate development concerns. It has had to be aware of the important role that education *can* and *should* play in enabling the most disadvantaged to achieve self-actualisation and "true" emancipation, while simultaneously supporting the human resource development needs of a country.

Present inequalities in access to education seriously affect individuals and communities and, apart from reinforcing poverty and social inequalities, they determine whether people are part of – or excluded from – the learning society, and whether and to what extent they may participate in the creation and sharing of knowledge. At the same time, globalisation and the increasing "MacDonaldisation" of societies have impacted on indigenous value systems and placed indigenous populations at risk of losing their cultures.

Governments and education therefore have the obligation of ensuring the survival of cultures and languages – more especially those of minority groups – by developing educational as well as broader policies that authenticate local and traditional cultures. At the same time, they must open up opportunities for members of these cultures to access the economic and social benefits of globalisation. In this sense education is inextricably linked with what Giddens (1991) termed *emancipatory* and *life politics*, both of which, he argues, are pre-requirements for human emancipation and self-actualisation.

2.11 THE ROLE OF EDUCATION IN EMANCIPATION

Giddens's (1991) notion of emancipatory politics refers to the politics of societal divisions such as race and gender, or to divisions between ruling and subordinate groups, between the rich and poor, or between current and future generations.

Simply put, Giddens (1991) holds that for most social theorists (regardless of whether the theorist adheres to a structural or non-structural paradigm), discourses of *emancipatory politics* are concerned with ways of releasing under-privileged groups from their unhappy conditions. Emancipatory politics in this sense works with a hierarchical notion of power, which is understood as the capability of an individual or group to exert power or influence over another. In this sense, *emacipatory politics* is concerned with reducing or limiting exploitation, inequality and oppression, and considers as fundamental the imperatives of justice, equality and participation.[2]

Participation (in the full sense, which would involve cognitive participation) enables individuals or groups to influence decisions which affect them and which would otherwise be imposed on them. Freedom in this sense presumes responsible action in relation to others and the recognition that collective or intersubjective obligations are involved.

2.12 LIFE POLITICS AND ITS ROLE IN SELF-ACTUALISATION

For Giddens (1991), *emancipatory politics* supplies the foundation for the emergence of *life politics*. As he puts it, "it prepares the stage for life political concerns". Life politics is the politics of self-actualisation – it is concerned with questions of rights and obligations (Giddens, 1991, pp. 223–225) and how, in an arena which professes to be democratic and in which the *structures* are put in place for the exercise of democracy,[3] the individual can intersubjectively exercise her or his rights. This view suggests that social structures (and institutions) are in themselves unable to guarantee democracy in the absence of human participation, particularly in developing societies where vast numbers of people lack the skills that would enable them to participate. It is argued that the notion of true democracy can only be invoked by enabling people to acquire the skills and abilities (and the consciousness) with which to participate in the democratic processes. This view underlies the development of civil society and the progressive democratisation of social institutions.

It is therefore incumbent on education at whatever level and regardless of the mode of delivery, to instil the skills of creative citizenship – skills which are fundamental to ensuring human participation. According to this view, life politics or human citizenship is contingent on conscious or cognitive participation.

Life politics is therefore seen as any decision making that affects broader social communities. It is concerned with questions of rights and obligations, and it assumes greater and greater importance as globalisation impacts on countries in the South.

Clearly, equality and participation are goals with which educators at all levels, utilising all modes of delivery, are concerned.

2.13 THE NEED FOR LIFE POLITICS TO PERMEATE EDUCATION, ESPECIALLY BASIC EDUCATION

With the Jomtien policy shift towards basic education, ODL has come to serve as a central reference point for exploring a range of options with the potential to reach beyond the specific confines of conventional distance learning in higher education. This shift is underpinned by the Millennium Development Goals (United Nations, 2002), which highlight poverty reduction, economic development and the consolidation of efforts to overcome the HIV/AIDS pandemic in the developing world. It is in these arenas that the *politics of life* have a crucial role to play in enabling adults to acquire the knowledge, skills and confidence to creatively craft their own futures. Three aspects are important to highlight: the impact of HIV/AIDS, illiteracy and digital media, and lifelong learning (LLL) and the North/South divide.

2.14 THE IMPACT OF HIV/AIDS

In many developing countries, particularly in sub-Saharan Africa, the HIV/AIDS pandemic impacts almost every aspect of society and has grim implications for disadvantaged communities. This is especially so given the inadequacy of social protection systems within the developing context. The situation of the poor is exacerbated by this pandemic, which has decimated jobs and eroded household income. In the long term, the workforce of the future is also weakened as children are taken out of school early to help care for sick family members – a fact that suggests the long-term need for compensatory adult basic education.

In addition, the HIV/AIDS pandemic has meant that older women, who have already spent their lives looking after other people, are left with the responsibility of caring for their HIV-infected children and, then, their orphaned grandchildren. This means that older women are confronted with a greatly extended period of responsibility for family burdens – the ILO (2004, p. 32) terms this the "feminisation of poverty".

In developing countries, women bear the burden of poverty. If they are lucky enough to find employment, they usually end up with the double burden of working and at the same time carrying out their traditional functions at home. The double burden is, of course, not unique to women workers in the developing world. However, the fact that jobs in the formal economy, with the associated benefits and reasonable conditions of employment, are becoming increasingly scarce, means that women in developing countries are compelled to either face poverty or eke out a living from survivalist activities within the informal economy. That these women often have to care for those affected and/or infected by HIV/AIDS makes their hardships even more crippling.

The unemployed, the rural poor and people in informal work represent the largest concentration of "needs without a voice". They are excluded from or under-represented in social dialogue and from processes with and in institutions, including the institution of education. The HIV/AIDS pandemic threatens the livelihoods of these people, with women facing the most severe consequences. HIV/AIDS thus deepens poverty and intensifies economic inequalities.

2.15 MEDIA AND MARGINALISATION OF THE POOR

Coupled with poverty are the high levels of illiteracy across Africa – this further marginalising people and contributing to the "poverty trap". Although printing has a less important role today than it had in the early modern state, where it was one of the main information methods (followed by the telephone, radio and TV), the inability to access the written word remains a barrier in areas that lack the physical infrastructure necessary for communication. Thus while the virtual world exists and has the ability to establish a single or global world, there are many areas in the developing world where both the written word and other means of communication do not form part of people's everyday lives, and where people are doubly excluded. This begs the question of how the digital divide can be bridged in a developing context, leading to the next question: how can we use ICT to reach learners in communities that do not have access to electricity and telecommunication?

2.16 LIFELONG LEARNING AND THE NORTH/SOUTH DIVIDE

Confintea[4] V placed education within the paradigm of the *learning society*, with LLL as an overarching principle. ODL has a particular role to play in the discourse on LLL, which today may be regarded as a meta-discourse with a variety of underlying philosophies of human development. Torres (2001), however, unpacks the notion of LLL and succinctly analyses the debates on LLL in the context of developing countries. She states that the reality of a North/South[5] divide must be taken into account in these discourses. She provides an ideal type dichotomy, which underscores the wide gap between the "education for all" (EFA) policy in the South and the LLL agenda of the North.

Torres (2001) argues that the discourse of EFA refers to all levels of education ranging from basic learning to the provision of the minimum learning needs – especially of girls, children and women – where basic education shifts from being a *foundation* to being a *ceiling* in the developing world. This minimises the role of LLL and as long as basic education remains an unfulfilled right. LLL in the context of the developing world may be termed "just in time learning", which addresses mainly functional workplace learning needs. However, workplace learning is a privilege of the employed.

Lifelong learning, on the other hand, is generally the terrain of adults who have had the benefit of basic education and who may subsequently participate in the benefits offered by LLL. Torres (2001) points out, however, that where segments of the population have been excluded or marginalised (e.g. indigenous people, the poor, those living in remote areas or those, as in South Africa, disadvantaged by repressive regimes), LLL has limited application. Thus, Torres says, "EFA and issues of literacy and basic education are more prevalent in the South, and the philosophy of LLL is more prevalent among people living in the North."

LLL in developing countries, according to Torres (2001), is deemed useful and relevant to the extent that it addresses issues of poverty and exclusion. Basic education provides people with the basic foundation for LLL and equips them with the skills and critical capacity to participate fully in society. LLL debates therefore need to ensure that the following target groups are singled out as needing special attention and special motivation: women, especially those from the rural areas; out-of-school youth; the unemployed; prisoners and ex-prisoners; and adults with disabilities that prevent them from obtaining a basic education.

2.17 RESPONDING TO THE CHALLENGES: USING ODL AS A VEHICLE FOR DEVELOPMENT

In response to the kinds of problems referred to above, Unisa established the Institute for Adult Basic Education and Training (ABET). We will refer to an ODL programme presented by the Unisa ABET Institute, which attempts to address precisely those problems.

The delivery of adult education is contingent on, inter alia, the availability of well-trained adult practitioners[6] (see Singh and McKay, 2004), who should play a pivotal role in addressing critical economic, political and social problems specific to learners across a variety of contexts (such as health and HIV/AIDS, the environment and labour) and societal situations. They would be educators who might understand their roles as fitting in with the general principles of democracy, human rights, citizenship and development.

During the 1990s, in response to the democratic government's expressed desire for reconstruction and development in South Africa, the University of South Africa's ABET Institute undertook large-scale training of adult educators to develop a more professional cadre with relevant qualifications in South Africa. This required the Institute to be responsive to those areas where education could play a role in the development of communities.

The ABET Institute thus trains a cadre of practitioners who work in adult education programmes across various sectors and in different social contexts (such as health, environment, the workplace and water management) and in different types of settlements (urban, rural, formal and informal). This approach promotes key socio-economic benefits, especially for the most marginalised and disadvantaged communities, which are the Institute's primary target group. Training ABET practitioners in basic and generic skills allows them to work in a variety of specialised areas, including literacy, numeracy, primary healthcare and HIV/AIDS, English as another language, small business development and environmental education.

With development and the enhancement of livelihoods as the prime rationale for the courses presented by the ABET Institute, addressing the needs for literacy or numeracy could not occur without locating these needs within a broader development paradigm. This point of departure made the ABET Institute immediately different from programmes that focused primarily on literacy as a *method* or as a *technique*, and rarely on literacy as a component of a development strategy. The ABET Institute sees the practitioner as central to the enhancement of communities and directs its training at practitioners – in many instances nurses, community workers, literacy volunteers, trade unionists and so on – who will be able to teach skills like basic literacy, numeracy or health education, but with a *developmental bias*.

For this reason, the ABET practitioner's programme is useful to a variety of in-service and pre-service practitioners, including literacy practitioners; trainers for water and sanitation; trainers in health, nutrition, HIV/AIDS, family planning; environmental educators; job skills trainers; trade unionists; worker educators; adult educators who teach in state programmes; agricultural extension workers; youth workers; community organisers; and materials developers.[7]

How does the Institute implement a distance education programme that reaches thousands of pre- and in-service teachers who work across a range of developmental areas and across the country, in a way that can offer maximum benefit for the community while achieving maximum outreach? The programme trains up to 12,000 ABET practitioners per annum (and has, to date, trained more than 50,000 practitioners), who will work in a variety of fields in community development and community education. It is only through distance education that it has been possible for the training to go to scale.

After successfully completing the ABET practitioner course, students should demonstrate that they have or can do the following: undertake policy analysis; engage in policy debates; utilise a range of teaching/facilitation methods; utilise a range of assessment methods; counsel learners; identify and remedy learning difficulties; refer learners with complex learning difficulties to other professionals; develop teaching material; evaluate teaching material; profile learners; profile communities; identify target groupings; adapt teaching and learning situations to target groups' needs; improve knowledge in a selected teaching content/learning area; facilitate adult learning in selected areas of learning; plan a learning experience for group/individual learners; demonstrate teaching skills; demonstrate communicative skills; demonstrate assessment skills; relate teaching to social context; identify areas of research; design a research approach; compile research reports; utilise a variety of qualitative, quantitative and participatory research methods; contribute to the development of a common, shared vision for ABET across sectors; understand the situation within each district and its importance in terms of ABET; understand the usefulness of community profiles; know how to network and build partnerships with other stakeholders and institutions; form linkages between ABET and other developmental objectives and needs; have an understanding of terms like participation, development and people-centred development; know how to assess and prioritise needs and do a community profile; know how to collect information on relevant structures, organisations, institutions and other possible partners in an area; identify key roles that managerial staff may need to play; demonstrate skills such as collaborative management, teamwork facilitation, counselling, monitoring and strategising (Singh and McKay, 2004, p. 117).

In addition to the specific outcomes listed above, practitioners are expected to achieve certain *critical outcomes*, which are taught mainly indirectly. These should be achieved by all learners regardless of whether they are studying for a doctoral degree or a first-year certificate. Achievement of these critical outcomes should enable students to engage in problem solving; participate in group/syndicate task groups; encourage critical thinking; and organise group tasks.

The programme is delivered primarily by means of printed materials, and a central focus is that throughout the text, the student is given hints on how to study. These may be practical hints, for example to work in a quiet place, but often they involve important skills for learning. Students who study at a distance are often lonely, and many of those who enrol for this course are from educationally disadvantaged backgrounds. The text is written with this in mind.

As with the mainstream of the university, the ABET Institute also makes use of a national base of tutors, which enables it to reach its annual intake of students around the country. In 2005, the ABET institute had 12,000 enrolled students supported by its tutorial system, which entails placing students from the same areas into groups and ensuring that each group is assigned a local person who acts as its tutor/motivator.[8] Because the teaching is delivered in situ, practitioners conduct needs analyses and carry out mapping and other research in their areas. They are also able to conduct practice teaching in their areas, observe their peers and engage in group teaching initiatives. Since the final assessment requires that students engage with a local literacy/development project, the capacity on the ground is considerably enhanced. This has resulted in the emergence of a multitude of small income-generating, literacy/environmental projects in the local communities.

2.18 PARTICIPATING IN THE SA NATIONAL LITERACY CAMPAIGN

Having trained more than 50,000 educators since its inception, the ABET Institute was able to harness its graduates to serve as volunteer teachers in the South African National Literacy Initiative (SANLI) during the period 2003–2004 – a campaign which aimed to reach millions of illiterate adults. This partnership focused on delivering literacy training to the most needy learners across the country in some of its most isolated and impoverished communities. The ABET Institute enabled 350,000 to break through to literacy over the 2-year duration of the campaign.

The involvement of the university in the literacy campaign was instrumental in developing the necessary management support systems to effectively control, review and evaluate activities across the country and has been recognised by the South African Ministry of Education as having provided a replicable pilot of the proposed Ministerial Campaign for literacy to be started in 2008. The SANLI piloted many aspects to be drawn upon for the proposed campaign including creating a database to facilitate payment of expenses to the volunteer educators, and to monitor the learners' competencies by recording their scores on completing various tasks in their structured assessment portfolio.

The ABET Institute constructed the necessary frameworks to underpin what is seen as successful delivery of literacy and development opportunities throughout the country. By establishing learning centres located in the communities where the learners live, the partnership created considerable momentum[9] from the learners themselves. A characteristic of the literacy activities implemented by the Institute was the enthusiasm of the learners, gauged by their extremely regular attendance and the minimal drop-out rates of under 5 percent.[10] Another characteristic was learners' commitment to opening up new futures for themselves.

Classes were held where the learners live and where it was convenient for them to attend. Unlike other initiatives, which rely on volunteers who have received only short periods of training, the use of graduates from the Unisa ABET programme meant that educators were familiar with both the terrain in which the learners live and the methods of adult education.

The following quotations, taken from comments by adults who attended adult literacy classes in a variety of sites, including shelters for street children and prisons, reflect the difference that literacy made to their lives (Unisa SANLI, 2003). It is not uncommon for learners to identify benefits and achievements that are remote from the educators' aims.

> The world was painful because I used to use a cross when I signed a document and sometimes I would be doubtful of the implications.
>
> –Elderly learner in SANLI class; Soshanguvu, South Africa.
>
> My husband, who is blind, enjoys it when I read for him. Learning to read and write has made our lives happy. Even our children who stay far from us always ask me about this project.
>
> –SANLI learner and pensioner; Makenenge Ridge, Qwa Qwa, South Africa.
>
> I was always sad and depressed. Not any more. Now I wake up every day, pick up my books and stop complaining. My life feels good!
>
> –SANLI learner; Mabopane ABET Centre, South Africa.

During monitoring visits made by the DFID evaluation team (Bordia, 2002) to literacy learning sites, learners described what literacy meant to them. The benefits can be seen to have cut across sectors and needs. The following examples highlight the diversity of learners' responses.

> We now know our rights and I can now start a chicken business.
>
> –Elderly learner in SANLI class; East Rand, South Africa.
>
> Through the learning that I gained in the project, being a shoemaker, I can now count the number of stitches as I combine the sole and the top part of the shoe. This is very helpful because I can now make measurements.
>
> –65-year-old man; Makenenge rural centre, South Africa.
>
> I have opened a *spaza* [informal] shop – I can now count money and I have bought a fridge with the money I have made.
>
> –Female SANLI learner; Western Cape, South Africa.
>
> We have class in this primary school [a mud and dung structure]. Sometimes the children will visit us in class. They watch us learn, we hug them and then they leave. The children are very proud of us.
>
> –Mother of five; Makenenge Rural Centre, South Africa.
>
> I have started to teach my grandchildren numbers and letters of the alphabet and it is very exciting.
>
> –Elderly woman; Duduza Township, South Africa.
>
> I can now read my own letters. I used to hate it when the person reading my letters used to laugh at what the letter said before I knew what was in the letter.
>
> –Adult SANLI learner; Gauteng, South Africa.

2.19 CONCLUSION

To answer to the question posed by Dodds with which this chapter began: yes, it is possible that ODL can contribute significantly to the needs of development. What is needed for ODL institutions is to think broadly, to partner wisely and to advance courageously. This poses a challenge not only to Unisa to continue to reflect on its own role in the development of learners across the LLL continuum, but also for all universities to reflect on their roles in the life development of their learners.

NOTES

1. The World Education Forum (Dakar, 2000) has thus committed itself to halving these numbers by 2010.
2. It can therefore be likened to Habermas's (1972) definition of emancipation politics in terms of a theory of communication, which contributes towards an intersubjective understanding.

3. These may include constitutional rights, human rights, balloting and regular elections, the availability of social services and so on.
4. The International Conference for Adult Education.
5. This discussion acknowledges but does not take up the debate of the East/West divide – which in turn adds other dimensions to issues of education affected by globalisation.
6. A recently published book (2004) edited by Madhu Singh and Veronica McKay, entitled *Enhancing adult basic learning: training educators and unlocking the potential of distance and open learning*, provides many examples of how ODL can and has been used to train grassroots facilitators in development contexts across the continents of the world.
7. The programme has been continuously evaluated over the past 10 years by DFID teams including experts such as Professor Lalage Bown and Dr Anil Bordia, and the materials used for training educators received the Commonwealth of Learning award for the best distance materials in 2003.
8. Unisa ABET ameliorates the possible dilution of those at the lower levels of the cascade by training all tutors and closely monitoring all the levels of the cascade. In addition, the development of interactive material for students ensures a common curriculum which learners can apply to their own contexts. Learners' experiences are valued and there is much interplay between the various levels of the cascade. For example, learners' contributions towards materials are incorporated into texts.
9. The momentum is reflected by the over-subscription to the programme of 30,000 in its first two years.
10. Their completion of all their continuous assessment tasks is another signal of their enthusiasm. The fact that learners continued their own learning groups after the conclusion of the campaign highlights the significance of learning for them.

REFERENCES

Bordia, A. (2002). Evaluation of the Unisa ABET and SANLI programmes. Unpublished report for DFID.

Dodds, T. (2002). Non formal and adult basic education through open and distance learning in Africa. Paper presented at the Pan Commonwealth Conference.

Giddens, A. (1991). *Modernity and Self-Identity: Self and Society in the Late Modern Age.* Oxford: Polity.

Habermas, J. (1972). *Knowledge and Human Interests.* Boston: Beacon Press.

International Labour Organisation. (2004). *Working Out of Poverty.* Geneva: ILO.

Keegan, D. (1986). *The Foundations of Distance Education.* Beckenham: Croom Helm.

Leatt, J.V. and Martin, D.H. (2000). *Reflections of Collaboration Within South African Education by Two Bloodied but Unbowed Participants.* Paper No. 15, presented at CITTE and the Founding of the Tertiary Education Network (TENET), Cape Town.

Lewis, R. (1988). The open school? In *Open Learning in Transition: An Agenda for Action* (N. Paine, ed.). Cambridge: National Extension College.

Makhanya, M. and McKay, V. (2004). Challenges for UNISA as a distance education institution in Africa. In *Internationalisation and Human Resource Development in the African Union: Challenges for the Tertiary Education Sector* (J. Van Der Elft and C. Wolhuter, eds). Proceedings of the 7th International Conference of IEASA, North West University (Potchefstroom Campus), 3–6 September 2003.

Manpower Services Commission. (1984). *A New Training Initiative*. Pretoria: Department of Labour.

Moore, M. (1973). Towards a theory of independent learning and teaching. *Journal of Higher Education*, **44**, 661–679.

NCHE. (1996). *National Commission on Higher Education (South Africa). A Framework for Transformation*. Pretoria: Department of National Education.

Pityana, N.B. (2002). Inauguration Address as Principal and Vice-Chancellor of Unisa on 24 January 2002, Pretoria.

Rowntree, D. (1990). *Teaching Through Self Instruction: How to Develop Open Learning Materials*. London: Kogan Page.

Rumble, M. (1991). 'Open learning' 'Distance learning' and the misuse of language in course 2 – The development of distance education: A reader. Cambridge University, the University of London and the International Extension College.

Singh, M. and McKay, V. (2004). Improving the quality of adult basic learning and training adult educators, In *Enhancing Adult Basic Learning: Training Educators and Unlocking the Potential of Distance and Open Learning* (M. Singh and V. McKay, eds). Pretoria: Unisa Press & UNESCO.

Torres, R.M. (2001). Lifelong learning in the North and Education for all in the South? International Conference on Lifelong Learning: Global Perspectives in Education, Beijing.

Unisa. (2006). Tuition Policy. (http://www.unisa.ac.za/internal/cs98/pol.html:1)

Unisa SANLI. (2003). *Literacy Matters. A Commemorative Report*. Pretoria: Unisa.

United Nations. (2002). *Millennium Declaration*. New York: UN.

UNESCO. (2002). *EFA Global Monitoring Report. Is the World on Track?* Paris: UNESCO.

Wedemeyer, C.A. (1977). Independent study. In *The International Encyclopaedia of Higher Education* (A.S. Knowles, ed.). Boston: CINED.

Chapter 3

Social and Cultural Diversity in Distance Education

Charlotte N. Gunawardena and Deborah LaPointe

With the expansion of global telecommunication networks and the worldwide demand for higher education, distance education has the potential to reach out internationally to enhance learning for diverse learners and increase intercultural awareness and communication. By definition, distance education is borderless (Latchem, 2005), although differences in sociocultural contexts, values, and expectations of diverse educational systems and learners may prove to be its greatest challenge (Hanna, 2000). While distance education programs proclaim an international focus with international content and learners, instructional design and methods frequently carry Eurocentric Western bias. Distance educators need to be sensitive to social, cultural, and educational differences, cultural assumptions embedded in courses, and "the imposition of cultural values and practices" (Latchem, 2005, p. 189).

In Chapter 3, we examine several aspects of the sociocultural context that impact distance education. We begin by exploring reasons to study the sociocultural context along with issues in international distance education. Next, we look at theoretical dimensions that explain cultural variability and discuss the elements of the sociocultural context that impact distance education. These elements include (a) diverse educational expectations; (b) learning styles; (c) the sociocultural environment including social presence, help-seeking behaviors, and perception of time; (d) differences in communication styles including group process and development, perception of silence, and handling conflict; (e) language and issues related to second-language speakers; and (f) interpretation of icons, symbols, and colors used in Web design.

We address the above elements from our own research conducted in Mexico, Morocco, Sri Lanka, Taiwan, Mainland China, and the United States, the distance education course design and teaching experiences, and the supporting literature in distance education. As we discuss these elements, we provide design guidelines.

3.1 ISSUES IN INTERNATIONAL DISTANCE EDUCATION

Why is it necessary to understand the social and cultural factors that influence international distance education? Reasons that come to mind are (a) recognition that technology connects us but is not culture neutral; (b) demographics are ever changing; (c) globalization makes us interdependent; (d) education addresses global economic needs; (e) the growing peace imperative is a global initiative; (f) self-awareness of cultural perspectives and biases is key to designing learning for another; and (g) ethics influence behavior.

While new information and communication technology has its advantages and attractiveness, the problems of education are always more complex than the technology alone can solve. Solely focusing on the technology and the view of learning that it facilitates causes the designer and instructor to look at learning in only one way, ignoring other alternative cultural views (Visser, 2005). With technology, come the questions of who will use it and what meanings the users will assign to it (Heaton, 2001). Choice of one over another inadvertently encourages and discourages different individuals or groups from participating. The affordances of the technology are constrained by the traditional forms of expression that people use. While technology brings us together, the challenges and opportunities of networking far outshine the technology itself.

Demographics change as technology and transportation connect people. Cultural migration influences the formation of new communities as people cross borders, creating third cultures. We are becoming members of a planetary community as evidenced by transnational cultures that are not wholly based in any single place (Heaton, 2001, p. 221). International distance education can cater to those individuals who are unable to reside in one single location.

One of the main criticisms of globalization is the underlying tendency to colonize and import dominant paradigms into contexts that are either unfriendly to those paradigms or that can be harmed by those solutions (Carr-Chellman, 2005). Inherent within what is often perceived as a value neutral tool – the Internet-based technologies used for online learning – are culturally biased amplifications that have their roots in the American Industrial Revolution, which according to Bowers (cited in Carr-Chellman, 2005, p. 9) are: (1) context-free forms of knowledge; (2) conduit view of language; (3) Western view of autonomous individuals; (4) Western ways of experiencing time; (5) Western value of anthropocentrism; and (6) subjectively determined moral values. Traditional American measures of quality learning such as contact hours, physical attendance, proctored testing, and number of library holdings do not work globally. Carr-Chellman (2005) argues that making a single online course that is available worldwide is efficient, but culturally and contextually bankrupt. To make a product truly marketable globally, it is necessary to homogenize it. "Isn't learning necessarily contextualized in our own cultures and contexts?" (pp. 9–10). Globalization should not blind us to the need to help individuals and groups build on their own cultural traditions and unique strengths (Mintzberg, 2003).

From an economic perspective, educational systems in developing countries are judged by their ultimate contributions to the development of quality human resources and national development goals (Panda, 2005). The need for education extends beyond the individual's desire to learn to serving as an economic resource for national growth, competitiveness, poverty reduction, and quality of life (The World Bank, 2005). The developing nations look at the development of useful national skills (Badat, 2005; Day, 2005), courses that address the needs of those at the margins (Panda, 2005), address the whole person (Visser, 2005), and contribute to a peaceful globe. Since all nations can gain from incorporating the knowledge of other countries and cultures into their thinking and actions, international learning networks should be conceived as horizontal (localized), vertical (globalized), and bottom-up as well as hub periphery (Afele, 2003).

Intercultural awareness and competence are the foundation for peace imperatives. New threats to peace include civil wars, global disease, climate change, and desperation and hopelessness that accompany poverty. Peace imperatives become possible as people are connected, and the psychological and geographical distances between people narrow down. The world will benefit by the intersection of many minds and resources across the globe, as more teachers, doctors, and professionals are educated and involved in solving world problems. "Hence the need for distance education and partnerships to share knowledge and prosperity around the globe" (Latchem, 2005, p. 194).

One of the most important reasons for understanding cultural factors is the awareness it raises of our own cultural identity (Martin and Nakayama, 2004). "The reason man does not experience his true cultural self is that until he experiences another self as valid, he has little basis for validating his own self" (Hall, 1973, p. 213). A better understanding of one's own self as well as alternative approaches to learning lies in the capacity to provoke new ideas, techniques (Muirhead, 2005), strategies, and methodologies.

Developing international distance education also presents ethical challenges. Very often ethical principles are culture bound, and intercultural conflicts arise from different perspectives of ethical behavior. Understanding the sociocultural context helps us to distinguish ethical from unethical behavior given differences in cultural priorities and develop guidelines for ethical behavior within our courses.

3.2 THEORETICAL FRAMEWORKS FOR UNDERSTANDING CULTURAL DIMENSIONS

Culture is a difficult concept to define formally; many definitions define it as diverse, changing, concrete, and abstract. For this chapter, we adopt the definition of culture offered by Matsumoto (1996), who perceives culture as "the set of attitudes, values, beliefs, and behaviors shared by a group of people, but different for each individual, communicated from one generation to the next" (p. 16). As Matsumoto notes, this definition suggests that culture is an individual, psychological construct, and a social construct.

As we discuss cultural differences that impact distance education, we draw on the following theoretical frameworks that explain cultural variability in behavior and communication:

1. Dimensions of cultural variability proposed by Hofstede's (1980, 1986): individualism-collectivism (IC), power-distance, uncertainty avoidance, masculinity–femininity, and Hofstede and Bond's (1988) long-term versus short-term orientation or Confucian–Dynamism unique to some Asian cultures.
2. Dimensions of contextualization: high- versus low-context cultures and associated indirect and direct styles of communication proposed by Hall (1966, 1976).
3. Language: an important aspect of cultural identification (Rogers and Steinfatt, 1999).
4. Perception of time, categorized by Hall (1994) as polychronic and monochronic time, and by Brislin and Kim (2003) as ten concepts that affect intercultural interactions: (a) event and clock time; (b) punctuality; (c) task and social time; (d) one or many activities simultaneously; (e) sequential, efficient task performance or effectiveness; (f) fast or slow pace of life; (g) perception of silence; (h) past, present, and future orientation; (i) symbolic meaning of time; and (j) cultural differences in importance of work and leisure time.
5. Miike's (2000) three assumptions about communication based on an Asian paradigm of communication theory focusing on relationality, circularity, and harmony: (a) communication takes place in "contexts" of various relationships; (b) the communicator is both active and passive in multiple contexts; and (c) mutual adaptation is centrally important as adaptation is key to harmonious communication and relationships.
6. Martin and Nakayama's (2004) dialectical approach to understanding culture and communication, which emphasizes the processual, relational, and contradictory nature of intercultural communication, is evident in four components: culture, communication, context, and power.
7. Religion and its influence on shaping one's worldview.

Ross and Faulkner (1998) caution about over-reliance on dimensional information for understanding culture. While dimensional information serves as a excellent guide to approach understanding, the danger is in overgeneralizing or treating them as absolutes. For example, they advocate using Hofstede's dimensions with culture-specific approaches that provide contextual understanding. As we examine how cultural variability plays a role in international distance education, it is important to remember that "the variation within a culture in terms of situations, individuals, and socioeconomic status may account for as much or more of the variation in intercultural interpretations of messages as does the difference between the cultures of the individuals involved" (Rogers and Steinfatt, 1999, p. 96). With this understanding of the myriad ways in which cultural variability can be observed, we next explore how culture is manifested in distance education.

3.3 SOCIOCULTURAL CONTEXT OF DISTANCE EDUCATION

Learning is a social activity. Researchers have begun to examine how social interactions and the sociocultural environment affect motivation, expectations, attitudes, communication, teaching, and learning in the distance education context (Mason, 1998; McLoughlin, 1999; Pincas, 2001). Research on the link between cognitive and social processes in understanding learning (Vygotsky, 1978) has provided the impetus for examining the sociocultural context of learning environments. Our research, course design, and teaching experiences lead us to identify the following elements discussed in this section as essential areas for consideration as we design for distance education and facilitate learning communities through computer networks.

3.3.1 Diverse Educational Expectations

Different cultures bring different attitudes toward education and its purpose. Consider the philosophical differences reflected in the following two statements by learners we interviewed: "I don't know what I'll do with my education; I'm basically purposing my degree to meet a personal goal I set for myself" (Joan, an American student 2003). "The purpose of my education is to learn as much as I can and share that knowledge with others, so our nation can become great" (Luming, a Taiwanese student, 2005). The American student chose to pursue education for self-benefit while the Taiwanese student's purpose focused on economic well being and serving the nation.

"Learning like life in China is serious" (Chao, a Mainland China student, 2005) and has serious implications. Chinese and many other learners around the globe have no choice regarding the amount of invested mental effort devoted toward learning according to a personal cost/benefit analysis; for a student who does not perform excellently will be replaced by many learners waiting for acceptance in competitive higher educational systems (Jinghua, a Mainland China student, 2005). In contrast, the laughter, small talk, and self-disclosure found in American classrooms are considered inappropriate and offensive. For out of hardship and adversity, comes greatness.

Traditionally, teaching in Mainland China and many other countries involved the teacher standing on a raised platform lecturing and interrogating from the front of the room to large groups of fifty students. Choral responses in teacher-led recitations reflected the traditional value on the collective, the community consensus, and the uniform conduct in social interaction (Hu, 2004). Memorization is the most reliable and desirable attribute a student can have to ensure school success, for learning is attributed to "listening to the teacher" (Hu, 2004).

Today, Asia is using e-learning to explore innovative strategies to promote engagement through active and independent learning, self-assessment, digital libraries, and just-in-time learning. There is emphasis on (a) designing authentic learning tasks to facilitate learning engagement and (b) providing support and media-rich resources (Hedberg and Ping, 2005). Many online courses, being offered in Mainland China, Hong Kong,

Taiwan, and India, offer video lectures online and on demand, so learners can continue to "see and hear" their instructors giving lectures. Eye movement, gestures, gaze, and the human voice provide the contextual information, learners from high-context cultures rely upon to interpret meaning.

Turkey's culture and oral traditions have emphasized the sacredness of the text, honor the responsibility of the professor to interpret the text, and expect students to memorize the professor's words (Gursoy, 2005). In many developing countries, quality of education is not seen as a property of the system or the intelligibility of materials but as a property of the students measured by their performance on examinations. In such environments, assessment of student performance by group work presents a challenge. The paradigm of flexibility, openness, and the self-paced independent learner is not a value-free, neutral idea. Likewise, a teacher who functions primarily as facilitator, course designer, organizer, and friendly critic (Jin and Cortazzi, 1998) is not a global idea. The cultural values of individualism, secularism, and feminism are not recognized as desirable in other cultures that place higher values on religion, group efforts, and well-defined gender roles (McIsaac, 1993).

Most Western learners and instructors, especially American, believe that each learner (a) is a distinct individual, (b) controls his or her behavior, (c) is responsible for outcomes of behavior, (d) is oriented toward personal achievement, and (e) frequently believes group membership compromises goal achievement (Nisbett, 2003). Asian learners like Luming believe success is a group goal. Attaining group goals is tied to maintaining harmonious social relations. These differences in expectations have implications for designing the learning environment and learner support systems for distance education.

3.3.2 Learners and Learning Styles

How one learns and what one learns is culturally determined. People reared in different cultures learn to learn differently. Some do so by pattern drill, memory, and rote following behaviorist theory; some work in groups learning through interaction with others to cross the zone of proximal development (Vygotsky, 1978). In today's learning environments, whether face-to-face or distance, one will encounter diverse learners and learning styles. As Moore (2006) asks, "How do we design a course and manage it to induce the different forms of understanding that lie in the culture represented by each student to the greater benefit of the whole class?"

Facilitating learning for diverse learners requires putting learner needs first rather than institutional or national needs. Generally, the primary theory of knowledge construction underlying emerging online course designs emphasizes the exchange of ideas to construct meaning. Cultures have differing preferred ways – scripts – of transmitting culture, knowledge, and ideas. Ideas are expressed in symbols, and carry expressed meaning as well as emotional and cognitive perceptions (Chen and Starosta, 1998), deeply rooted history, and tradition reflecting cultural patterns of thinking. Learning often requires contextualizing complex, abstract concepts, using analogies as a learning aid (Day, 2005). Analogies are culturally dependent.

Students who are more holistic and visual may thrive in well-designed multimedia environments that present a global view, while those who have a concrete sequential orientation will prefer a linear organization of information. Chen (2000) notes that differences in thinking patterns and expression styles influence student reactions to teaching methods. In a global e-mail debate on intercultural communication, the debate format caused orientation problems for some participants as the "debate" is a product of low-context culture that requires a direct expression of one's argument by using logical reasoning. Students who come from high-context cultures in Asia and Latin America find an argumentative format uncomfortable, and this discomfort is exacerbated when the debate is facilitated through a medium devoid of non-verbal cues. Fahy and Ally (2005) in their study of online students at Athabasca University pointed out that when students are not permitted to participate in CMC in accordance with their individual styles and preferences, the requirement for online interaction ironically becomes a potential learning barrier.

Based on our study using nine instruments to analyze Hispanic learning styles (Sanchez and Gunawardena, 1998), we provide the following guidelines for accommodating learning styles. In general, it is best to design alternative activities to reach the same objective and give students the option of selecting activities, which best meet their preferred learning styles. We found that Hispanic adult learners show a preference for collaborative over competitive activities; reflectivity in task engagement; and a preference for an action-based, active approach to learning. For these learners, we recommend designing real world problem solving or case-based reasoning tasks in asynchronous learning environments that provide opportunities for reflection and active collaborative learning.

As we design, it is important to consider that within cultural groups, individuals differ significantly from each other, and therefore, it is equally important to identify and respond to an individual's learning style preference. While matching teaching and learning styles may yield higher achievement, providing learners with activities that require them to broaden their repertoire of learning styles more fully prepares them to function in our diverse society. There is a need to provide a delicate balance of activities that give opportunities to learn in preferred ways and activities that challenge the learner to learn in new or less preferred ways. Gibson (1998) made a plea for understanding the distance learner in context (e.g. in relation to classroom, peer group, workplace, family, culture, and society) and the impact of their learning on those who share their lives in the multiple interacting contexts that contain them. "Our challenge as educators is to consider how the context might be seen as a partner in teaching and learner support" (p. 121).

3.3.3 Social Environment

In defining sociocultural space, Rummel (1976) noted that a dyad of socially interacting individuals forms the smallest sociocultural field. This interaction comprises a cluster of values and meanings, a set of norms; is within a range of mutual expectations and roles; and has all the characteristics of the most comprehensive social systems, such as a nation. Bargaining, problems of credibility, threats and transactions, joint cooperation and conflict, status-quo testing, and undercurrents of power, status, and class occur. These social interactions become complex in international distance learning environments where there are many more individuals than dyads and individuals who represent diverse cultures.

In the following section, we explore factors that contribute to sociocultural space in distance education: social presence, help-seeking behaviors, and perception of time.

3.3.3.1 Social Presence

Social presence is the degree to which a person is perceived as a "real person" in mediated communication (Short et al., 1976). One of our studies (Gunawardena and Zittle, 1997) established that social presence is a strong predictor of learner satisfaction in a computer conference. Richardson and Swan (2003), adapting the survey we used, replicated and extended these findings. They determined that students' overall perception of social presence was a predictor of their perceived learning in seventeen different online courses. Tu and McIsaac (2002) observed that three dimensions of social presence – social context, online communication, and interactivity – emerged as important elements in establishing a sense of community among online learners.

Studies are beginning to examine cultural perceptions of social presence. Tu (2001) conducted a study of how Chinese perceive social presence in an online environment. In a cross-cultural study of group process and development in online conferences in the United States and Mexico, we (Gunawardena et al., 2001) found that social presence emerged as a theme addressed by both US and Mexican focus group participants. US participants felt that social presence is important to smooth group functioning to provide a sense that the group members are real people. Social presence builds trust and leads to self-disclosure. Building relationships enhances online civility. The Mexican focus group participants, however, felt that having personal information about the participants was unimportant. For these participants, how peers contribute to the conference is more important than knowing their personal information. The differences in the way that US and Mexican participants perceived social presence could be attributed to cultural differences related to power distance (Hofstede, 1980) in the two societies. The Mexican participants perceived computer-mediated communication as equalizing power and status differences in their society.

To further examine social presence from a cultural perspective, we undertook a study (Gunawardena et al., 2006) to generate a theoretical model of social presence from the perspective of two sociocultural contexts - Morocco and Sri Lanka - by examining the communication conventions and processes employed by Internet chat users who develop online relationships with people they do not know. Employing qualitative ethnographic analysis and grounded theory building, this study explored cultural perspectives on "social presence" and properties related to the construct "social presence" in online communication. Preliminary results indicate that social presence is emerging as a central phenomenon in the communication patterns of Internet chat users. Properties associated with social presence in both cultural contexts include: self-disclosure, building trust, expression of identity, conflict resolution, interpretation of silence, and the innovation of language forms to generate immediacy. Initial theoretical propositions that we developed from this research are as follows:

- Social presence is a key factor in building online relationships.
- There is a relationship between social presence and disclosure of private life. Participants tend to expect chatters to tell them about their problems, because that makes them "real." Self-disclosure enhances social presence.
- Anonymity increases the ability to self-disclose and generates a heightened sense of social presence.
- Social presence is closely linked to building trust. When trust is established, the sense of social presence increases.
- Attempts to resolve conflict depend on the strength of the relationship that has been built.
- Silence is often expressed as "no presence."
- Chatters have devised means to communicate in the native language, or short forms of the native language using a Latin keyboard, to increase social presence and the connection they feel to each other.

These findings provide insight into designing activities that generate social presence in online social spaces.

The instructor plays a critical role in facilitating social presence and the social environment. Social presence research has shown that teacher immediacy behaviors include using humor, personalizing examples, addressing students by name, questioning, praising, reinforcing, initiating discussion, sharing personal experiences, encouraging, and providing timely feedback. Other than the instructor's role in creating social presence, several of the following design techniques can be used to create social presence and build the social environment based on learner characteristics and the specific context.

- Virtual Pubs or Cafes – a specific virtual space assigned for social interaction where participants can demonstrate a sense of their own social presence and where participants feel fully represented as human beings.
- Introductions – usually done at the beginning of a course where participants introduce their professional and personal identities and interests. The amount of self-disclosure that participants are comfortable with will vary depending on cultural background, and introducing each other online may be more comfortable than self-introductions.
- Creating a sense of online community – moderators or facilitators play an important role in community building activities, facilitating discussions, summarizing, and by being present online frequently.
- Timely feedback, encouraging participation, and rewarding contributions.
- Developing formats for interaction – that would enhance the presence of others in the community, such as story telling and sharing experiences.
- Encouraging the use of online conventions such as emoticons.

3.3.3.2 Help-Seeking Behaviors

Cultures differ in help-seeking behaviors. Help seeking is a learning strategy that combines cognition and social interaction (Ryan et al., 1998) and involves the ability to use others as a resource to cope with difficulty encountered in the learning process. When learners do not seek help, performance and learning can suffer. In American classrooms that emphasize competition and normative evaluation, students are unwilling to seek help as they fear others would perceive that they lack ability (Ryan et al., 1998). Where the socio-emotional needs of students and learning for intrinsic reasons are emphasized over performance and competition, learners seek help.

The socio-emotional needs of students are recognized as part of the classroom design in other cultures. Chinese students communicate with their teachers outside the class for guidance with personal problems (Zhang, 2006). Teachers in China assume responsibility for educating the whole person instructionally, cognitively, affectively, and morally, and are expected to care about students' behaviors and problems inside and outside the classroom. The collaborative strength of home and school, parents and teachers work harmoniously toward the mutual goal of preparing learners (Hu, 2004) for rigorous national examinations and the country's economic development. In contrast, Western teachers are expected to perform academic duties, and generally are unconcerned about students' behaviors and problems outside of school. Westerns students are advised not to bring personal problems to the classroom. The warm interaction that Asian learners expect outside the classroom with their instructors is not expected by Western students.

Therefore, distance education designers must be cognizant of the expectations of diverse earners related to help seeking behaviors, and make teaching and learning philosophies, procedures and practices explicit in course design, and the syllabus or course outline.

3.3.3.3 Perception of Time

Use of time is a "silent language" that affects everyday behaviors (Hall, 1973). How people view time is a form of communication (Hall, 1973). Punctuality and sensitivity to deviations from appointed times have different levels of importance in a learning context. Where people's attitudes toward time are more approximate and lenient, such as in the Middle East, Latin American, and African countries (Polychronic time), handing in assignments "on time" will not be perceived as important as in North American clock time cultures (Monochronic time), which put a monetary value on time and treat it as a tangible commodity. Americans focus on tasks during the workday and become dismayed when others spend work time and classroom time socializing and chatting, unaware that socializing leads to supportive work relationships that can be called upon later when work needs to be accomplished quickly and well.

The analysis of past, present, and future orientations is another perspective to understand a culture's time use. Cultures do not exclusively have one orientation; however, Americans live in the present fully and want to move on toward the future. Present-oriented cultures consider the present to be the only precious moment. In contrast, past orientation honors tradition, history, and is influenced by the past. Chinese people attribute great importance to 2,000 years of history and their ancestors. People evaluate daily or business plans based on the degree to which their plans fit with customs and traditions; innovations and change are discouraged. When change is necessary, it is justified by the past experience.

Time orientation impacts communication. Cognition, knowledge, beliefs, and attitudes about time combine to (a) structure a model about how time itself operates and functions, and (b) set expectations for usage of time and tradition in the classroom. Time orientation lays the groundwork that learners use to understand and act on the world around them.

3.3.4 Communication and Interaction

Culture is communication (Hall, 1998); culture and communication act on each other (Chen and Starosta, 1998). In the online context, communication takes place through a computer-mediated environment, by which people create, exchange, and perceive information. Computer-mediated communication (CMC) can reduce patterns of discrimination by providing equality of social interaction among participants who may be anonymous in terms of gender, race, and physical features. However, there is evidence that the social equality factor may not extend to participants who are not good writers, but who must communicate primarily in a text-based format (Gunawardena, 1998).

In Western classrooms, autonomous learning involves understanding the complexities of an issue or concept and the learner's ability to address the complexities. Learner autonomy is promoted by feedback from instructors and other students that challenge the learner's own views and ideas by raising issues he or she might not have thought of otherwise. Critical discussions and philosophical arguments are a frequent component of many Western distance learning courses. However, critical discussions and debates may not be appropriate across cultures for face-saving reasons.

The learned conventions of turn-taking are universal, but differ in detail from culture to culture; for example, in the degree to which overlapping talk is tolerated. For the most part, the one-speaker-at-a-time structure predominates, and people adjust their turn-taking patterns as they negotiate role relationships, power relationships, or institutionalized procedures. Deviant users are called "disruptive," "irrational," "undisciplined" or even "unintelligent." Comparative studies of non-native and native English conversational discourse have become a rich territory for exploration of how culturally specific assumptions and strategies vary in cross-cultural encounters (Driven and Putts, 1993).

In written prose, Americans are direct and indirect. Chinese culture emphasizes beauty, tradition, poems, and the polite way in social interaction. The literate Chinese person memorizes the characters, idioms, wise sayings, classics, literary allusions, and the accepted patterns of expression. Words flow effortlessly, and ideas blossom into ideas in a human context that keeps social harmony and maintains hierarchy (Hu, 2004). The Chinese written language has no alphabet. Instead, it consists of thousands of different pictographic and ideographic characters. Each word consists of one to three characters. By the sixth grade, Chinese students must have mastered 3,000 characters, basically by memorization. Text-based communication between Americans and Chinese would mean understanding each other's writing style. Given the characteristics of the online environment, we as designers need to pay attention to cultural differences in communication conventions, which may be manifested differently in this unique space for communication devoid of non-verbal cues.

3.3.4.1 Group Process and Development

To study the impact of culture on group dynamics, Chan (2005) gave the Myers-Briggs type indicator (MBTI) and the Chinese personality assessment inventory (CPAI) to fifty-nine tutors at the Open University of Hong Kong and their 1,106 students. Only one dimension on the MBTI – extraversion – was connected with group effectiveness in the classroom. However, four dimensions from the CPAI – Renqing, Face, Harmony, and Leadership – promoted group effectiveness. Renqing refers to a "humanized obligation," carrying with it a continued expectation for mutual favor exchanges with a sentimental touch. Tutors who employed face saving strategies were considered more effective in creating harmony and balance in relationships. Tutors with a high concern for harmony subordinated personal needs and accepted group norms rather than their own norms. Tutors who were rated high on leadership were motivated, interacted well with their students, and made effective presentations. Chan's study reflects the social obligation to help others within the social group.

Employing survey and focus group data, we (Gunawardena et al., 2001) examined differences in perception of online group process and development between participants in Mexico and the United States. Survey data indicated significant differences in perception for the Norming and Performing stages of group development as described in Tuckman's (1965) model. The groups also differed in their perception of collectivism, low-power distance, femininity, and high-context communication. Country differences rather than age and gender differences accounted for the differences observed. Focus group participants identified several factors that influence online group process and development: (1) language, (2) power distance, (3) gender differences, (4) collectivist versus individualist tendencies, (5) conflict, (6) social presence, (7) time frame, and (8) technical skills.

With the increasing use of collaborative learning methods and community of practice models in online course design, we need to pay attention to how groups are formed and supported through the collaborative learning process.

3.3.4.2 Silence

Silence while frustrating for American and Western Europeans is quite comfortable for Asian and Pacific Island cultures (Brislin, 2000). For Americans, silence indicates rudeness, inattention, or uncertainty. However, in other cultures, silence indicates respect (Matthewson and Thaman, 1998). Silence allows people time to collect thoughts, think carefully, listen to others, and provide opportunity for reflection, integration and consensus of many diverse perspectives into a workable solution. In our experience, teaching English via Voice Over Internet Protocol, a synchronous technology to Chinese students (LaPointe and Barrett, 2005), initially, both American instructors and Chinese learners were uncomfortable in the classroom. The American instructors expected the Chinese learners to speak at will as students do in American classrooms. American teachers were initially uncomfortable with the long, reflective pauses in the synchronous voice communication. The Chinese respect for authority conditioned learners to wait for an explicit invitation rather than make the impolite gesture of raising a question or criticizing someone else's work.

3.3.4.3 Conflict

We conducted an exploratory qualitative study with six cultural groups (Native American, Hispanic American, Anglo American, East Asian, Middle Eastern, and Indian Subcontinent) to examine how participants negotiate face in an online learning environment (Gunawardena et al., 2002). Participants were asked to respond to three scenarios, one of which dealt with how they would handle conflict online. The hypothetical scenario asked participants how they would respond when a peer misunderstood what the participant said and posted a message demeaning the participant's contribution to the academic discussion. Results indicated both cultural and individual differences. Some would have apologized for being misunderstood; others would have been angry or offended and demanded an apology; some would react in a calm, non-confrontational manner; and others would have ignored the comment. Members of all six cultures would have posted a message in reply, saying that they had been misunderstood or their posting had been misinterpreted. Then they would have given further explanations to clarify the message.

Our study conducted in Morocco and Sri Lanka discussed earlier (Gunawardena, 2006) showed that the nature of the relationship determines reactions to insults and the resolution of conflict in chatrooms. Chatters will close the window if the relationship is weak and employ many techniques to resolve conflict if the relationship is stronger.

We can draw implications from these results for developing communication protocols for online environments. One protocol would be to encourage participants to clarify and explain their messages if they feel they have been misunderstood or misrepresented in the group discussion. Another protocol would be for online participants to direct conflicting points of view of a demeaning nature with names attached to the individual in a private e-mail, thus giving that individual an opportunity to explain his or her point of view. If the two participants then determine by this private e-mail that the discussion can be handled in a public forum, they can move it to the public forum. A third protocol would be to advise students to use high-context communication - providing the context so messages would not be misunderstood.

3.4 LANGUAGE AND SECOND LANGUAGE SPEAKERS

Language represents a different way of thinking and speaking, and cognition is mediated by language (Gudykunst and Asante, 1989; Pincas, 2001). Language also reinforces cultural values and worldviews. The grammar of each language voice and shapes ideas, serving as a guide for people's mental activity, for analysis of impressions, and for synthesis of their mental stock in trade (Whorf, 1998). Those from oral cultures may not embrace written communication (Burniske, 2003) and the abstract discussions that permeate Western discourse. Learners from oral traditions such as the Maori desire intimate connections with the instructor and a way to apply knowledge according to Maori customs (Anderson, 2005). Malaysia, strong in oral culture, uses storytelling while teaching history, culture, and moral values (Norhayati and Siew, 2004). Learners from visual and oral cultures expect that learning resources will be offered in media beyond mere text (Jiang, 2005) and prefer a great deal of detail and visual stimulation (Zhenhui, 2001). Chat may provide an outlet for interaction that more closely resembles spoken language (Sotillo, 2000). Learners from collectivist countries may refrain from contributing critical comments in text conferencing to avoid tension and disagreement to maintain interpersonal harmony (Hu, 2005). Limiting online learning to text-based expression restricts the voices and the richness that can be a part of the online class.

Using English to learn rather than one's native language puts learners at a disadvantage. Often English is a learner's third or fourth language with little opportunity to actually use English daily. Communicating in English requires Asian and Arabic speakers to enter individual letters, one stroke at a time, on a keyboard while frequently referring to online dictionaries. English-as-a-second language (ESL) learners need additional time for reading and need content provided in a variety of formats – written lectures, audio recordings, and concept maps.

Smith (2005) found that a lack of awareness to cultural differences and generalizations about others who use ESL may enable learners from dominant cultures to unknowingly deauthorize group members with group coping strategies that, although well intended, limit opportunities for discussion. Groups assign minimal responsibilities to their non-native English-speaking members because they felt these learners had faced unusual challenges of adapting to the United States and completing their studies. Non-native English speakers then feel uncomfortable and unproductive. This crystallized the recognition of difference among group members; non-native speakers were perceived as "others" and treated as a threat to the group in ways that mirror hierarchical structures within larger society, creating unsafe learning spaces (Smith, 2005).

To learn about the perceptions of Taiwanese and Mainland China ESL learners, bilingual teaching assistants, and staff regarding the *Speak2Me* program (Ladder Publishing Co., Ltd. of Taipei's web-based ESL program using an *iTalk* synchronous platform), those of us who taught English at a distance traveled to Taiwan and Mainland China to conduct face-to-face interviews over the past 3 years. In the preliminary results, we (LaPointe and Barrett, 2005) found that although students recognize the need to study English through materials from the target culture, when they have no prior experience with the content of the materials, they cannot participate. Students told us if neither they nor their families have prior knowledge about a topic, they find engaging in a conversation difficult. They cannot participate when the "topic is too far away." Such topics do not produce the intended level of critical thinking as much as topics that more directly affect students' lives.

Many individuals have a fear of speaking English with native speakers. Ping observed, "We Taiwanese – if we can't speak English very nice, very fluent – we want to learn English and speak, but we are afraid. We are afraid to talk with foreigners because we are afraid if I can't speak the proper words or listen to it." Students, particularly adults, seek a safe place to speak. The Internet provides that safe space through the removal of visual cues; informants have reported that they are more willing to try to speak English when they cannot see either other students who they perceive to be better English speakers or the teacher's dismay as they are speaking. They also feel safer participating from their homes.

Implications for design include creating an atmosphere that invites participation from ESL speakers. Some techniques include writing the instructor's welcome message in more than one language, translating the syllabus when possible, and developing clear communication protocols.

3.5 CULTURAL INTERPRETATION OF WEB ICONS AND IMAGES

When designing online learning, the interface designer must pay attention to how different cultures respond to the graphical interface, images, symbols, color, and sound. Simple issues of layout, format, and icons become increasingly complex as the diversity of learners increase. Since icons enhance the learner's ability to use and control the capabilities available within the environment, we conducted a study in the United States, Morocco, and Sri Lanka with participants in University computer labs and Internet Cafes, to examine differences in perceptions of the meaning of icons and images (Knight et al., 2006). Fifty-three participants from Morocco, sixty-eight from Sri Lanka, and fifty-eight from the United States completed a questionnaire containing eighteen icons and images drawn from twenty-six US academic websites. Participants were asked to assign meanings to each icon or image and to select a preferred image to represent; for example, group discussion online, chat, submitting an assignment, accessing a library, and so on. Results showed that icons and images that rely on literal interpretations may be the most reliable in developing Web materials for cross-cultural users. Images and icons, which were representational and contained little detail, were less likely to elicit unintended interpretations. Individual image preferences for online functions suggest most users preferred representations that were conceptually focused and visually simple. Icons that were photographic were least frequently selected. Differences in the interpretation of meanings and preferences for specific icons and images were related to the cultural context of the participants. For example, the calendar icon was interpreted with the highest accuracy in the United States, followed by Sri Lanka and Morocco. Morocco is an oral culture, and many people remember appointments rather than write them down on a calendar; therefore, there were varying interpretations of this icon in Morocco. In Sri Lanka, one participant identified the calendar as a temporary house. It is important to note that a large number of tents were put up in the coastal areas of Sri Lanka after the Tsunami incident in 2005, when this study was conducted. The aftermath of the Tsunami may have influenced the participant in identifying the slanting shape of the open calendar as a tent.

3.6 CONCLUSION

As we explore opportunities to provide international distance education, we should pay careful attention to developing global citizens who can solve global problems without diminution of indigenous culture (Latchem, 2005, p. 195) to meet national educational and economic goals. Mason (1998) recommends three approaches to globalizing education: beginning in areas of curriculum which have global content so that all participants have an equal status and an equal contribution to make; trans-border consortia, where each partner contributes courses to the pool to avoid the trap of the dominant provider and the dependent receiver; and focusing not on exporting courses at all, but on developing resources and international contacts to enable one's own students to become global citizens. In the hands of perceptive and creative designers, communication technologies have the potential to internationalize higher education and overcome challenges to honor the social–cultural diversity in distance education. Creativity is harnessing universality. Culture and awareness of differences among cultures are resources for the distance education instructor and designer.

REFERENCES

Afele, J.S.C. (2003). *Digital bridges: Developing Countries in the Knowledge Economy.* Hershey, PA: Idea Group Publishing.

Anderson, B. (2005). New Zealand: Is online education a highway to the future? In *Global Perspectives on E-Learning: Rhetoric and Realities* (A.A. Carr-Chellman, ed.). Thousand Oaks, CA: Sage Publications, Inc., pp. 163–178.

Badat, S. (2005). South Africa: Distance higher education policies for access, social equity, quality, and social and economic responsiveness in a context of the diversity of provision. *Distance Education*, **26**(2), 183–204.

Brislin, R. (2000). *Understanding Culture's Influence on Behavior*. 2nd edition. Fort Worth, TX: Harcourt.

Brislin, R. and Kim, E. (2003). Cultural diversity in people's understanding and uses of time. *International Association for Applied Psychology*, **52**(3), 363–382.

Burniske, R.W. (2003). East Africa meets West Africa: Fostering an online community of inquiry for educators in Ghana and Uganda. *Educational Technology Research and Development*, **51**(4), 105–113.

Carr-Chellman, A.A. (2005). Introduction. In *Global Perspectives on E-learning: Rhetoric and Reality* (A.A. Carr-Chellman, ed.). Thousand Oaks, CA: Sage Publications, pp. 1–16.

Chan, B. (2005). From West to East: The impact of culture on personality and group dynamics. *Cross Cultural Management*, **12**(1), 31–43.

Chen, G.M. (2000). Global communication via Internet: An educational application. In *Communication and Global Society* (G.M. Chen and W.J. Starosta, eds) New York: Peter Lang Publishing, pp. 143–157.

Chen, G.M. and Starosta, W.J. (1998). *Foundations of Intercultural Communication*. Boston, MA: Allyn and Bacon.

Day, B. (2005). Open and distance learning enhanced through ICTs: A toy for Africa's elite or an essential tool for sustainable development? In *Trends and Issues in Distance*

Education: International Perspectives (Y.L. Visser, L. Visser, M. Simonson, and R. Armirault, eds) Greenwich, CT: Information Age Publishing, pp. 183–204.

Driven, R. and Putz, M. (1993). Intercultural-communication. *Language Teaching*, **26**, 144–156.

Fahy, P. J. and Ally, M. (2005). Student learning style and asynchronous computer-mediated conferencing. *American Journal of Distance Education*, **19**(1), 5–22.

Gibson, C.C. (1998). The distance learner in context. In *Distance Learners in Higher Education: Institutional Responses for Quality Outcomes* (C. Campbell Gibson ed.). Madison, WI: Atwood Publishing, pp. 113–125.

Gudykunst, W. and Asante, M. (1989). *Handbook of International and Intercultural Communication*. Newbury Park, CA: Sage Publications.

Gunawardena, C.N. (1998). Designing collaborative learning environments mediated by computer conferencing: Issues and challenges in the Asian socio-cultural context. *Indian Journal of Open Learning*, **7**(1), 105–124.

Gunawardena, C.N., Bouachrine, F., Idrissi Alami, A., and Jayatilleke, G. (2006, April). *Cultural perspectives on social presence: A study of online chatting in Morocco and Sri Lanka*. A research paper presented at the Annual Meeting of the American Educational Research Association, San Francisco, CA.

Gunawardena, C.N., Nolla, A.C., Wilson, P.L. et al. (2001). A cross-cultural study of group process and development in online conferences, *Distance Education*, **22**(1), 85–121.

Gunawardena, C.N., Walsh, S.L., Reddinger, L. et al. (2002). Negotiating "face" in a non- face-to-face learning environment. In *Proceedings Cultural Attitudes Towards Communication and Technology* (F. Sudweeks and C. Ess, eds). Montreal, Canada: University of Montreal, pp. 89–106.

Gunawardena, C.N. and Zittle, F. (1997). Social presence as a predictor of satisfaction within a computer mediated conferencing environment. *The American Journal of Distance Education*, **11**(3), 8–25.

Gursoy, H. (2005). A critical look at distance education in Turkey. In *Global Perspectives on E-Learning: Rhetoric and Realities* (A.A. Carr-Chellman, ed.). Thousand Oaks, CA: Sage Publications, Inc., pp. 35–51.

Hall, E.T. (1966). *The Hidden Dimension*. Garden City, NY: Doubleday.

Hall, E.T. (1973). *The Silent Language*. New York, NY: Anchor Book Editions.

Hall, E.T. (1976). *Beyond Culture*. New York, NY: Anchor Books.

Hall, E.T. (1994). Monochronic and polychromic time. In *Intercultural Communication: A Reader* (L.A. Samovar and R.E. Porter, eds). Belmont, CA: Wadsworth, pp. 264–271.

Hall, E.T. (1998). The power of hidden differences. In *Basic Concepts of Intercultural Communication: Selected Readings* (M.J. Bennett, ed.) Yarmouth, ME: Intercultural Press, pp. 53–67.

Hanna, D.E. (2000). Higher education in an era of digital competition: Global consequences. In *Higher Education in an Era of Digital Competition: Choices and Challenges* (D.E. Hanna, ed.). Madison, WI: Atwood Publishing, pp. 19–44.

Heaton, L. (2001). Preserving communication context. In *Culture, Technology, Communication: Towards an Intercultural Global Village* (C. Ess, ed.). Albany, NY: State University of New York Press, pp. 213–240.

Hedberg, J.G. and Ping, L.C. (2005). Charting trends for e-learning in Asian schools. *Distance Education*, **26**(2), 199–213.

Hofstede, G. (1980). *Culture's Consequences: International Differences in Work-Related Values*. Beverly Hills, CA: Sage Publications.

Hofstede, G. (1986). Cultural differences in teaching and learning. *International Journal of Intercultural Relations*, **10**, 301–320.

Hofstede, G. and Bond, M.H. (1988). Confucius and economic growth: New trends in culture's consequences. *Organizational Dynamics*, **16**(4), 4–21.

Hu, Y. (2004). The cultural significance of reading instruction in China. *The Reading Teacher*, **5**(7), 632–639.

Hu, G. (2005). Using peer review with Chinese ESL student writers. *Language Teaching Research*, **9**(3), 321–342.

Jiang, J.Q. (2005). The gap between e-learning availability and e-learning industry development in Taiwan. In *Global Perspectives on E-Learning: Rhetoric and Reality* (A.A. Carr-Chellman, ed.). Thousand Oaks, CA: Sage Publications, pp. 35–51.

Jin, L. and Cortazzi, M. (1998). Dimensions of dialogue: Large classes in China. *International Journal of Educational Research*, **29**, 739–761.

Knight, E., Gunawardena, C., Bouachrine, F. et al. (2006). A cross-cultural study of icons and images used in North American web design. In *The Internet Society II: Advances in Education, Commerce, and Governance* (K. Morgan, C.A. Brebbia, and J.M. Spector, eds). Southampton, Great Britain: WIT Press, pp. 135–145.

LaPointe, D. and Barrett, K. (2005, May). *Language Learning in a Virtual Classroom: Synchronous Methods, Cultural Exchanges*. Paper presented at the meeting of Computer-Supported Collaborative Learning, Taipei, Taiwan.

Latchem, C. (2005). Towards borderless virtual learning in higher education. In *Global Perspectives on E-Learning: Rhetoric and Reality* (A.A. Carr-Chellman, ed.). Thousand Oaks, CA: Sage Publications, pp. 179–198.

Martin, J.N. and Nakayama, T.K. (2004). *Intercultural Communication in Contexts*, 3rd ed., New York, NY: McGraw-Hill.

Mason, R. (1998). *Globalising Education: Trends and Applications*. London, Great Britain: Routledge.

Matsumoto, D. (1996). *Culture and Psychology*. Pacific Grove, CA: Brooks/Cole Publishing Company.

Matthewson, C. and Thaman, K.H. (1998). Designing the *rebbelib*: Staff development in a Pacific multicultural environment. In *Staff Development in Open and Flexible Learning* (C. Latchem and F. Lockwood, eds). New York, NY: Routledge, pp. 115–126.

McIsaac, M.S. (1993). Economic, political, and social considerations in the use of global computer-based distance education. In *Computers in Education: Social, Political, and Historical Perspectives* (R. Muffoletto and N. Knupfer, eds). Cresskill, NJ: Hampton Press, Inc., pp. 219–232.

McLoughlin, C. (1999). Culturally responsive technology use: Developing an on-line community of learners. *British Journal of Educational Technology*, **30**, 231–243.

Miike, Y. (2000). *Toward an Asian Standpoint of Communication Theory: Some Initial Assumptions*. Paper presented at the Pacific and Asian Communication Association Convention, "Waves of Change: The Future of Scholarship in Communication and Culture," Honolulu, HI.

Mintzberg, H. (2003, October). Africa's Best Practices. Project Syndicate. Retrieved October 15, 2005, from http://www.project-syndicate.org/commentary/mintzberg1

Moore, M.G. (2006). Editorial: Questions of culture. *The American Journal of Distance Education*, **20**(1), 1–5.

Muirhead, B. (2005). A Canadian perspective on the uncertain future of distance education. *Distance Education*, **26**(2), 239–254.

Nisbett, R.E. (2003). *The Geography of Thoughts: How Asians and Westerners Think Differently ... and Why*. New York, NY: Free Press.

Norhayati, A.M., and Siew, P.H. (2004). Malaysian perspective: Designing interactive multimedia learning environment for moral values education. *Educational Technology and Society*, 7(4), 143–152.

Panda, S. (2005). Higher education at a distance and national development: Reflections on the Indian experience. *Distance Education*, **26**(2), 205–225.

Pincas, A. (2001). Culture, cognition, and communication in global education. *Distance Education*, **22**(1), 30.

Richardson, J. and Swan, K. (2003). Examining social presence in online courses in relation to students' perceived learning and satisfaction. *Journal of Asynchronous Learning Networks*, 7(1). Retrieved October 29, 2006, from www.aln.org/publications/jaln/v7n1/v7n1_richardson.asp

Rogers, E.M. and Steinfatt, T.M. (1999). *Intercultural Communication*. Prospect Heights, IL: Waveland Press.

Ross, R. and Faulkner, S. (1998). Hofstede's dimensions: An examination and critical analysis. In *Civic Discourse: Multiculturalism, Cultural Diversity, and Global Communication* (K.S. Sitaram and M. Prosser, eds). Stanford, Co: Ablex Publishing CT, pp. 31–40.

Rummel, R.J. (1976). *Understanding Conflict and War: Vol. 2: The Conflict Helix*. Beverly Hills, CA: Sage.

Ryan, A.M., Gheen, M.H., and Midgley, C. (1998). Why do some students avoid asking for help? An examination of the interplay among students' academic efficacy, teachers' social-emotional role, and the classroom goal structure. *Journal of Educational Psychology*, **90**(3), 528–535.

Sanchez, I. and Gunawardena, C.N. (1998). Understanding and supporting the culturally diverse distance learner. In *Distance Learners in Higher Education: Institutional Responses for Quality Outcomes* (C. Campbell Gibson, ed.). Madison, WI: Atwood Publishing, pp. 47–64.

Short, J., Williams, E., and Christie, B. (1976). *The Social Psychology of Telecommunications*. London, Great Britain: John Wiley & Sons.

Smith, R.O. (2005). Working with difference in online collaborative groups. *Adult Education Quarterly*, **55**(3), 182–199.

Sotillo, S. (2000). Discourse functions and syntactic complexity in synchronous and asynchronous communication. *Language Learning and Technology*, **4**(1), 82–119.

Tu, C.H. (2001). How Chinese perceive social presence: An examination of interaction in online learning environment. *Education Media International*, **38**(1), 45–60.

Tu, C.H. and McIsaac, M. (2002). The relationship of social presence and interaction in online classes, *American Journal of Distance Education*, **16**(3), 131–150.

Tuckman, B.W. (1965). Developmental sequence in small groups, *Psychological Bulletin*, **63**(6), 384–399.

Visser, J. (2005). The long and short of distance education: Trends and issues from a planetary human development perspective. In *Trends and Issues in Distance Education: International Perspectives* (Y.L. Visser, L. Visser, M. Simonson, and R. Armirault, eds). Greenwich, CT: Information Age Publishing, pp. 35–50.

Vygotsky, L.S. (1978). *Mind in Society: The Development of Higher Psychological Processes*. Cambridge, MA: Harvard University Press.

Whorf, B. (1998). Science and linguistics. In *Basic Concepts of Intercultural Communication: Selected Readings* (M.J. Bennett, ed.). Yarmouth, ME: Intercultural Press, pp. 85–95.

World Bank (2005). *Central America Education Strategy: An Agenda for Action*. Washington, DC: The World Bank.
Zhang, Q. (2006). Immediacy and out-of-class communication: A cross-cultural comparison. *International Journal of Intercultural Relations*, 30, 33–50.
Zhenhui, R. (2001). Matching teaching styles with learning styles in East Asian contexts. *The Internet TESL Journal*, 7(7). Retrieved December 1, 2005, from http://iteslj.org/

Chapter 4

Distance Education and Gender: Women's Experiences at the Open University of Tanzania

Edith Mbebe

In addressing the Fourth Pan-Commonwealth Forum on Open and Distance Education in Jamaica (2006), Dr Penina Mlama, the Executive Director of the Forum of African Women Educationalists (FAWE), pointed out that Open and Distance Learning (ODL)

> should move beyond simply advocating itself as a unique opportunity to provide education to large numbers, which of course it does. There is no denying the fact that ODL broadens opportunities for more women to access education, as a first or second chance. ODL should see itself as having the additional and bound duty to address the gender imbalances, inequities and inequalities which the overall education sector is struggling with or is even unable to handle.
>
> (p. 9)

She goes on to ask, "Has the ODL sector sufficiently interrogated, articulated and analyzed the gender construction in which ODL is delivered?" and concludes that "the challenge for ODL and the education sector as a whole is how to effect action on the ground and achieve genuine gender formation in our communities" (p. 12).

Such actions have to begin with the stories of the ODL women learners themselves so that we can indicate to policy makers and national governments the desires of women in Africa for ODL while at the same time taking into account the lives of these women. Women's groups form the poorest group of people of the world, the most marginalized and disadvantaged of groups in education; and yet women, in general, are the first teachers of *all* children for *all* generations of people of the world. Given their multiple responsibilities in the society and their low status in their cultures, providing ODL for women is difficult and complex. This chapter will focus on how women in Africa, particularly in Tanzania, have participated in open and distance education (DE), their educational barriers, their issues and their desire in the twenty-first century for opportunities to enhance their education.

4.1 DISTANCE EDUCATION IN TANZANIA

Tanzanians demanded and struggled for their right to greater access to formal education long before they had achieved independence (1961): first, before the First World War, when the country was under the German rule, and again after the First World War when the country was a British protectorate (Nyerere, 1964; Zindi and Aucoin, 1995). The private foreign-owned DE institutions that existed in Tanzania before independence and in Africa as a whole offered various forms of DE to both the local Tanzanians and expatriates mostly in correspondence form (Ntirukigwa, 1986). The programmes did not include face-to-face contacts with tutors or provide mentors to students. After independence in 1961, Tanzanians' need for formal education became more pressing and multi-purpose (Nyerere, 1964), for the new government found that the education it inherited was inappropriate and the majority of its people were uneducated and lacked skills needed to provide the leadership to carry out the development plans of the new government. The population was also growing fast, with a very low income of less than US$100 per capita. This situation necessitated the new government to immediately embark on expansion of education system at all levels, primary, secondary and tertiary, at the same time.

John (1991) explained that the Tanzanian government introduced DE programmes in order to provide mass education on a wider scale and to provide professional training for nationalists, who were already in such posts as teachers and cooperative or development workers. He said that like many other African countries, DE in Tanzania followed four different stages: correspondence institutes; radio programmes which were used to improve residential instruction; radio and visual campaigns to promote literacy, health and other issues of national importance; and formal DE and training institutions. In Tanzania, the development of the formal DE education followed such a path from the private correspondence schools of the 1960s to the proposal and establishment of the full-scale Open University of Tanzania (OUT) in March 1993.

4.2 THE OPEN UNIVERSITY OF TANZANIA

The University is the second single-mode distance teaching university established in Africa, south of the Sahara, after the South African Open University "SAOU" (UNISA), and the first post-secondary distance teaching institution in Tanzania. Since its inception, it has expanded rapidly, and to date, it serves the entire Tanzanian population of over 37 million people (2002 Census), and foreign students from several countries are registered in its various programmes. The University offers certificates, diplomas, degrees and post-graduate courses.

The University's main objective is in filling the gap left by conventional universities through opening up learning opportunities for the less advantaged in higher education, especially women (Tanzania Ministry of Education, 1990). Its teaching and learning system not only is based on print learning materials and two written assignments, but also includes an orientation, two face-to-face tutorial sessions, science laboratory sessions and teaching practice (for the teacher students), two timed tests and an annual and supplementary examination (if required) in each course. These activities occur in the twenty-five examination regional centres across the country, which also provide limited library services to reach them, often across long distances. Students need enough money to pay for transport, accommodation, food and any medical care. There are also over sixty-nine study centres, some in each region, where students meet subject peer groups and sometimes their tutors. The print course materials are delivered to students mainly by postal services, and also through public courier services, and personally by the OUT staff during their visits to the regional centres. Plans are underway to use the regional centres as the main venues for storing and distributing study materials. The OUT purchases study materials from other distance learning universities (Nairobi, Zimbabwe, South Africa, Abuja, Indira Gandhi), and ongoing are plans to get supplementary and reference materials from Open University UK. The OUT has to date more than 118 published materials of its own, written by its faculty members and those from other post-secondary institutions in the country.

At present, the University has five faculties (Arts and Social Sciences; Education; Science, Technology and Environmental Studies; Law; and Business Management) and two institutes (Continuing Education and Education Technology) with over 200 staff (OUT payroll list, November 2006). However, while the general mission of the OUT is to enhance adults' access to higher education, and despite efforts to attract female students, the extent of women's participation at the OUT is much limited, for less than 30 percent of the total students enrolled are women.

4.3 BARRIERS TO WOMEN'S PARTICIPATION AT THE OUT

The general mission of Tanzania in initiating DE, ODL and the OUT in general was to improve adults' access to higher education through distance teaching and learning methodologies. The third president of Tanzania, Benjamin Mkapa (1996), explained that for many Tanzanian women the OUT is their only hope of attaining higher education. However, despite the opportunities and efforts to attract female students to higher education, for example, establishment of Universal Primary Education (UPE), pre-university programmes in conventional universities, a foundation course at the OUT and university loans, women's participation in tertiary and university education in Tanzania is generally very low compared to men. On the whole, it is less than 30 percent of the total students registered in post-secondary education. This low participation is mainly attributed to the diversity of socio-cultural groups with their varied rules about succession, land holdings and responsibility for children, which have a strong influence on the expected social roles for women and men. They pose a limiting influence on women in being able to fully seize the opportunities brought by liberalization of education through DE and ODL programmes. This is due to many factors, some of which are related to the school, e.g. the curriculum, design and provision of the instructional materials. Some are gender related such as the gendered division of labour in production and reproduction in the society and parents' traditional beliefs that educating girls is transferring one's own wealth to other peoples' families and reducing her marriageability where the father gets paid a dowry. These limitations are based on the socio-cultural beliefs that women's participation in the society is naturally that of multiple roles of being a wife, mother, housewife and manager of the small economic projects in the families in addition (if they like and/or have their husband's or father's permission) to their paid jobs. As such, Tanzanians are torn between their traditions and modernization when it comes to developing their society through education, and the women are the most affected. Therefore, there is need to find ways and means to resolve the socio-cultural conflict so that women can be free to participate fully in their own educational development in order to fully participate in the development activities of the nation.

Muro (1988), who examined the provision of post-primary education through distance tutoring in Tanzania, noted that the proportion of women students at the National Curriculum Institute (NCI) was only 16 percent of the UPE students in Tanzania. She thought that one would expect more women to be studying with the NCI because their opportunities for getting selected to continue studying in the government regular secondary schools are less than those of men. She identified reasons that might be holding women back from registering as being that the courses offered do not meet women's expectations and needs since women are normally attracted to programmes which cater for their immediate problems and needs; and due to time constraints, because most women are so bogged down by farm work and routine household chores that they have no time and energy to study (pp. 60–61).

On the other hand, von Prummer (1988) noted that women in developing countries are affected by barriers such as problems related to distance, time, inadequate support, unsatisfactory tutorials, lack of childcare services and enabling study and learning space (p. 57). She attributed this to the economic and organizational conditions of the educational systems, and the traditional roles binding women to the roles of becoming wives, mothers, raising children and being homemakers.

As a faculty member of the OUT since its establishment, and as founding Dean of the Faculty of Education (1994–1996), I have been concerned about the low participation rates of women in higher education. I thought it important to help the OUT understand fully the underlying causes of women's low enrolment, inadequate participation and unacceptable completion rates. This understanding is expected to help guide OUT (and other higher learning institutions in Tanzania) adjust and improve its plans, management and administrative procedures to enable provision of appropriate learning opportunities for women.

For 2 years (1998–2000), I conducted a qualitative study on major barriers and issues concerning women's enrolment and participation at the OUT. I used interviews, discussions, observations and documentation in various OUT regional and study centres covering seventeen of the twenty-five geographical regions in Tanzania. I met over eighty OUT women students and a similar number of non-students who were close relatives and friends of the OUT women students and listened to and tape-recorded their stories carefully. What I heard enabled me to understand the women's participation issues in ODL, and the extent of the challenge for OUT in its goal to enhance and sustain Tanzanian women's access and academic success. Since then, I have continued to talk with women and research womens' educational issues which has further deepened and enlarged my original learning.

4.4 BARRIERS TO ENROLMENT

From the research findings, I identified two types of barriers: those associated with activities or non-activities of the OUT and those related to the socio-cultural context in which women students live. Each is discussed in turn.

4.4.1 Institutional Barriers

The information provided indicated that the low participation of women comes from various factors from the OUT not having enough funding, inadequate publicity and OUT programmes not being seen to be relevant to the women's lives to women's financial concerns, poor educational background, lack of confidence in studying by distance and lack of female role models.

4.4.1.1 Lack of OUT Operational Funding

The financial limitation was explained by the OUT chief executive officer as forcing the OUT to operate as business in order to survive. As such, the OUT is unable to waive the fees or provide loans to women. The OUT had to buy materials from other operating ODL universities, e.g. Nairobi, Abuja, Indira Gandhi and UNISA, to initiate programmes while struggling to be able to develop its own. The radio programmes could not be used due to the financial liberalization policy which resulted in exorbitant prices for everything in the country. For instance, Radio Tanzania, the national radio station, demanded Ts 150 million to run a half-hour air programme per week which the OUT could not afford, and the government was unable to provide extra funds. Since its inception, the OUT manages its programmes under financial crisis which has barred it from making use of the newer learning technologies. However, funds donated by the David Anderson Africa Trust enabled the OUT to initiate its own recording and dubbing facilities.

4.4.1.2 Inadequate OUT Publicity

The regional directors, some OUT personnel, students and non-students explained that the OUT lacks the publicity techniques to market its programmes. For instance, the student counsellor and regional directors said that the OUT had never provided them the opportunity to be able to conduct regional campaigns and counselling to students. They gave examples of Dar-Es-Salaam saying that although the OUT headquarters is in Dar-Es-Salaam, there are many men and women who have never heard of the OUT's existence and they live and work in the city. Other reasons explained for non-publicity of the OUT programme were the distances and costs involved. The regional directors also lacked manpower, transport and reliable communication facilities such as telephone and computers. On the other hand, the regional directors explained that, for DE, and in particular for women, very carefully planned publicity is needed as most women do not really get the time and/or the money to read publications in newspapers as they cannot afford to buy them, or to hear radio and see TV as most times the news is on and most women are busy with family chores while their husbands are watching the news, and the men may have had access to the newspaper in their offices. They explained that best contact for most women is in the religious places when they go to pray, in the hospitals when they are sick or have a sick child and in working places for those who are employed.

4.4.1.3 Financial Concerns

Many women explained that they had difficulties finding money to pay for the tuitions as well the overhead costs that a DE learner has to spend for travel costs to and from the regional and study centres, and for the library fees and stationery. Of OUT women students, the majority are primary school teachers with very low salaries (normally below Ts 100,000 equivalent to US$100 per month) compared to male students who are holding managerial positions and can afford fringe benefits and have better salaries than most female students. The women complained that many husbands were reluctant to support women's education, especially when it is a degree programme for fear that they will have hard time controlling a wife if she is well educated and financially stable. And that for men, in order to afford their tuition fees if they are studying, they can decide to abandon all family financial matters especially if their wives are employed, while for a woman it is not possible to leave her children suffering in order to do her university education, and this situation is worsened by the fact that for most women when they can find time and the energy to study is after the children grow up. However, this is complicated by the financial demands of paying school fees for their children who by then are attending secondary education; and if the child is a girl, most fathers are not very willing to provide daughters with much support for their education as they think it is transferring wealth to other families because when girls grow up they get married and live elsewhere.

4.4.1.4 No Role Modes for Women Students at the OUT to Market Its Programmes

Most regional directors, senior OUT personnel and the women students explained that the stresses on women students as they try to study with the OUT discourages other women from seeking admission to study with the OUT. They said that many people, including the non-studying women, actually have a low opinion of degrees obtained through the OUT as they perceive that it is not really possible, and it is not worth the troubles experienced for one to combine full-time employment, family care and studying for a degree without even having proper library facilities, or the ready availability of study materials which are necessary to perform well as a student in a conventional university.

4.4.1.5 Gender Bias

Most women students complained that they are not being understood by their tutors and administrators – particularly those who are males, and women without families – when sometimes they cannot cope with the timelines set by the university due to family and/or workplace demands. For instance, two women coming from remote rural area of their regional centres explained that it is not easy for them to be in time for examinations set first and second sessions in the morning because the place they live is too remote and has no reliable bus transport. At the same time, money to afford proper accommodation is not available because they have to pay very high private boarding secondary school fees for their children as there are no day secondary schools in their rural area where it could be cheaper for them to pay. Together with that, their husbands do not allow them sleep in guest houses which are cheaper since such guest houses have poor reputations and are not considered to provide safe accommodation for women.

When I interviewed a senior administrative official at the OUT about this complaint and requested his opinion on why many more women than men are not able to participate in programmes at the OUT he explained:

> My own view would be that DE program is designed to be for those who are ready to push themselves. There is lots of self-pushing rather than to be pushed by somebody. So, OUR [OUT] responsibility is to provide the enabling environment, and it is for the clientele to take the advantage of the environment that is provided. It's like lying pipes, water pipes in urban setting in a cosmopolitan centre – that is our [OUT] responsibility. But it's for the members of the cosmopolitan settings to make advantage of the water such an amenity thus provided. So, the responsibility rests on the general public, on the target group, on the clientele. The best that could be done within the system would be may be to raise consciousness, awareness of the existence of such programs, the levels of such programs, the potential of such programs, and may be the benefit of such programs.
>
> (Mhehe, 2002, p. 66)

A woman Senator when asked the same question explained that "many times since the OUT inception, women Senators and Councillors have brought up the issues of women participation in the OUT programmes at the Senate and Council meetings, but in her estimation, the OUT paid only 'lip-service' to the issue". She stated:

> Women Senators and Councillors have been raising this matter, over, and over, and over, and over, but usually what they do is just show their statistics – whatever statistics they give us they must tell us whether is female or male, every time – and now they've got used to it and they show us.
>
> We have proposed many ways of reaching women, and giving the idea of open learning as the way for women and girls to catch up with their education because it can be done along with their other family chores. It is of course another job on top, overburdening women with what they have already in their roles, but still it is an opening for them to go back into education. But, we have failed very much. I cannot say we have done much. We have paid "lip-service" more than really do something tangible.

I also think that the problem of such administrators in DE is that they lack the knowledge of principles of DE teaching as Kamau (1995, p. 262) while discussing DE programmes in Kenya explained that "it is important in course design to listen to the needs of potential and actual learners (before course design and implementation) in order to assess the support services required".

Some OUT personnel that I interviewed indicated that they accept as ideal a gender relationship where the husband has control over a wife because she is married to him. In this regard, the wife is bound to secure permission from her husband if she wants to do university studies because the husband is her head in marriage. Also, many women students complained of husbands refusing them permission to do university studies, especially when the children were still young. Some students also complained that some husbands allow wives to study but demand that the wives continue to do and manage all housework together with preparing all meals for the family. This, the students complained, is very difficult especially during the regional centre activities.

The above observations indicate that potential and actual students face cultural prohibitions through OUT staff who may not be aware of their own biases and their effects on women students. Similarly, from a societal perspective, some students and OUT personnel explained that the attitude of the society towards women denies the women the freedom to decide on their own to participate in higher studies. For instance, a senior OUT finance officer said:

> I think it is a kind of behaviour, or attitude that is in our society which makes a woman feel and accept that situation [that she is not supposed to go for higher education]. We have to accept a reality in the society that many people believe that women cannot do university studies unless they are asked/told/forced/ to do so by somebody usually a male.

This means that a woman's participation or non-participation in DE for higher studies really depends on her spouse's or father's income and encouragement. This societal yardstick sorts the ideal women from the deviant women in society, and as such make it difficult for women to seize the educational opportunities provided in the country by government, or any other sympathizer without the consent of the spouse/father.

4.4.1.6 Fear of the DE Systems

Unlike conventional education, DE involves much independent study. All regional directors and women students and non-students explained that both men and women fear studying by distance because they lack the confidence in their own abilities to study effectively. The regional directors noted that students, especially the women, persistently asked for tutor support lectures in order to be sure they can sit for their timed tests and annual examinations. This lack of confidence is an outcome of the long experience they have in learning through the conventional method. For women are the most affected because by their upbringing they have poorer exposure to academic studies than do their male counterparts.

4.4.1.7 Distance Education Not Relevant to the Women Lives

The DE and OUT programmes in Tanzania are organized in regional towns, leaving students to create their own study centres to their own convenience. Normally, very few urban women participate in these programmes, and the males who are the majority dominate the study centres. As such, women in rural areas feel the programmes are not really meant for them. Also, the programmes teach traditional subjects as in the conventional universities, ignoring the fact that rural women have long lived in the rural areas, and they have their own way of life such as doing agriculture, animal husbandry and horticulture which give them their daily bread. These women would appreciate the DE/OUT programmes more if they would teach them how to improve what they are already doing (Kamau, 1995, p. 262). This leaves only the few women in towns to participate. More to this, by culture, many rural women, especially married women, are not expected by their husbands and society in Tanzania to be sleeping in guest houses and hotels when doing examinations. A regional director told me that when he tries to encourage women in his region to enrol with the OUT, he often got responses such as

> Why trouble myself, how can I go there, what will I tell my husband I am looking for, after all, the education is located in town, while all I am looking for is just good life, nice family, nice children, good house, good environment to live in, which I already have in my village!

The kind of responses the regional directors get from women as they encourage them also indicate that most women are also "tamed" by their husbands' money power. It necessitates that Tanzanian women behave this way because they also observe from the society that for a woman, even with university education or more, the chances of securing good paying employment, as most men can get even with very minimal education, is a distant dream. And if one were to get such a position, most often she must have a man behind the deal. As such, for Tanzanian women, unless the government is to act deliberately, it is not easy to have many women as are men participating in the DE and OUT programmes.

4.4.2 Socio-cultural Barriers

Tanzania is a multi-cultural country based on about 120 tribal communities that are organized into three major distinct socio-cultural groups. While the culture in each case is patriarchal, the disbursement of land from one generation to the next follows the three distinct traditions. The dominant group is patrilineal, where the head of the family normally falls to the first-born son of each family unit. In the patrilineal groups, all property is owned by the male clan and is entrusted to the male members, and the first son in each family is usually in charge of all property in the family unit. The second group is matrilineal, where the wife's brother (the children's uncle) assumes responsibility for the care of his sister's children, and the third group is neutral sex bias, where the wife's uncle (known as the grandpa-uncle of the children) assumes the rite of succession.

In the matrilineal and neutral sex-bias groups, usually all members of the family unit share the family property. An extensive part of southern Tanzania is mainly matrilineal, but the dominant socio-cultural group for Tanzanians is patrilineal. However, although

Tanzanian people have no tribal conflicts, culturally they are strongly grounded in their tribal cultures, especially on the basis of sex roles, ownership of property and different aspects of life values including what counts as necessary to be accepted as normal human beings in their tribal group culture. As such, the socio-cultural context of women's lives in Tanzania places many constraints on women's involvement in education whether through the conventional or through the distance and open learning method. Within their descriptions, interviewees mentioned that the strong cultural expectations for women are around early marriage and childbearing, lack of societal support for girls' education, marginalization of women's concerns as "women only" issues and control of women's lives by men and society in general. Hence, my investigation of the gender issues in DE in Tanzania indicates that, to a great extent, the socio-cultural context of women's lives constrains many women's schooling. The issues they identified were poor education and social background, cultural expectations for girls and women, "women's only" issues, lack of support for girls' education, lack of role models for girls in society and control of women's lives.

4.4.2.1 Poor Education and Social Background

My research indicates that majority of girls and women applying for OUT degree studies are under-qualified. This results from poor socialization that hinders informed knowledge and life-coping skills. Traditions demand that girls and women be restrained from mixing with boys and men in public to protect their virginity and desired femininity characteristics (shy, tender, soft and not argumentative) that are highly respected for marriage to help men to easily control their wives in family and society matters. Furthermore, girls educated in girls' secondary schools usually experience poor teaching compared to boys in boys' secondary schools because most female teachers are under-qualified and the schools have poorer teaching facilities, especially for science subjects. Also, most girls are often engaged in helping their mothers with house chores. So, to equalize the academic competences of women and men, the women must be supported by additional re-socialization into the public sphere to update their academic competencies and aspirations.

4.4.2.2 Cultural Expectations for Girls and Women

Culturally, Tanzanians consider university education as fitting men more than women because it elevates people to public interaction and enables them to earn a bigger income for supporting a family, something women are not expected to do. Men are regarded as the main breadwinners of their families, and therefore, as an investment, families prefer educating sons more than daughters. What counts more for girls is to get married, bear and raise children. So, culturally, Tanzanians think that married women have enough tasks to do within the family and with childcare. They believe that adding employment and studying will create conflicts with her spouse because the woman will not have given all her time to care for her husband and children. From this perspective, women juggling family, employment and studies together are considered odd, and as such, they do not get the respect reserved for full-time wives and mothers.

The OUT male regional directors reported that many OUT women students lack conscientization, sensitization, encouragement and provision of their basic rights to education. They believe marriage, childbearing and rearing are the most respectable roles for them. The belief is a vicious circle inherited from the culture of past generations. It aims to prohibit women from getting more educated than their husbands. The women's focus group noted that culture and traditions make African communities feel educating girls is to destroy their marriageability because education destroys their traditional qualities while they get groomed for dowry. One OUT woman student explained that her father forced her to marriage at grade thirteen. She now struggles on her own as a married mature woman student to achieve the university education to which she aspired since her childhood. Five girls at the University of Dar-Es-Salaam pre-entry programme told me they had been pregnant at some stage in their secondary education, but their mothers' willingness to care for the babies enabled them to go back to school. They were grateful for the chance and were working hard not to disappoint their mothers. They said their mothers could decide to help because they were single parenting, but if they had their fathers in the family, the fathers would not have allowed them to help. Four of the five were among the top ten students in the course. This is encouraging; it indicates that, if girls are helped to access and remain in school, they are able to make full use of their intellectual abilities.

4.4.2.3 Women-only Issues

As an achieving woman artist explained, women have too many "women only" issues embedded in women's multiple roles, culture and traditions. The society encourages and subtly forces young girls into early marriage. This poses limitations to studying. Men are deliberately encouraged to get married to young women so that these women can have many children and care for them. Men believe that caring for offspring is the role of women alone. The women's focus group complained that women's many roles are repetitive, tedious, time-consuming and unpaid, and as such, they occupy minds, time and energy throughout the year limiting their academic aspirations, financial power and status in society. In contrast, men have specific employment or business interests earning them big money, social status and political and financial power in society. They have the time and energy to think, plan, socialize and relax which refresh motivation, studying and retention. The women's focus group also observed that relatively few wives of rich men seek education; the wives are not taking the trouble to educate themselves although money would not be their problem. These wives think they have good rich family which their husbands are providing for. The husbands like to see beautiful wives giving birth and caring for children and property. This way the roles in the family have become traditionally "a woman's responsibility only". Most men demand their wives assume the role upon marriage for this is what they married them for and most women accept this role. Tradition also reinforces this relationship as ideal for man and wife. This way women's education is limited by traditions that determine the ideal life for men and women in society, and anything different is not acceptable.

A female OUT administrator explained women's oppression as due to their lacking information and support on alternative choices. She said some NGOs, relatives, government and religious institutions are capable of helping women, but the culture and traditions are powerful enough to prevent it. One achieving woman presumed that the government controls men and leaves men to control women since the government does not impose laws to protect culture and traditions that oppress women, but instead favours men in the family and society. This observation is made by Thomson (1983) who commented that

> unless women think much more deeply about themselves, make sense of their experiences and expectations in reference to their own needs and interests, and consider strategies of redefining the relationship with men in ways which will change the distribution of power and oppression to one of equality and respect, learning new roles will continue to be a poor substitute for the practice of freedom and liberation.
>
> (p. 106)

4.4.2.4 Lack of Support for Girls' Education

An achieving women educationist from FAWE explained that from childhood there are many, multiple and complex constraints from different sources that limit girls' and women's education. Crucial ones are as follows: first, girls and women do not have high aspirations for education, employment and social status, because parents and society generally do not sensitize, motivate, encourage and support them as they do for boys. Many fathers do not invest in girls' education. Therefore, for many girls, schooling can stop at any level, because getting married and producing children is considered the ideal achievement.

Secondly, adolescent socialization done by illiterate elderly female relatives creates vicious circles of ignorant young females in society. Many girls believe that marriage is more important for them than a good education; men are more intelligent, and therefore, women should not compete with them; men should not be questioned; and women should not be heard in public or mix with men who are not their relatives. When young girls believe in such notions, naturally they lose their self-esteem and confidence and their personal capabilities do not really get developed. Hence, many families do not have ideal women role models for their daughters. As such, it is important that the society create centres to help re-socialize and update academic competence for girls and women.

Thirdly, many girls are stifled by early marriage and pregnancy. While boys repeat classes, re-seat examinations and attend extra private tuition, girls are expelled from school for pregnancy, are expected to get married and produce children instead of repeating classes to improve their education. Many girls become trapped in a vicious circle of acute poverty, prostitution and HIV when they produce children they are unable to care for.

Fourthly, multiple roles limit girls' and women's time and energy to study. Therefore, in doing examinations most girls fail to compete equally with boys. The government exacerbates the situation by opening more day secondary schools. So, Tanzania today has large numbers of girls who do not aim high in education.

4.4.2.5 Lack of Role Models for Girls in Society

Culturally, the status of women in the family and society is low. Most mothers therefore are unable to be good role models for daughters to emulate while their sons can emulate their fathers. As such, most girls grow up lacking the spirit and vision to compete for success and excellence in their development for anything. Many women, therefore, need guidance and counselling, to be told, pushed (empowered), encouraged and supported to achieve in education.

4.4.2.6 Control of Women's Lives

Girls are controlled by their mothers through requiring their help with house chores while their fathers make final decisions to send them to school or not, and to dictate the man to marry her and at what age. Girls are also controlled by society. When they attend school, they are expected to cope with male harassment in public. If they get pregnant outside wedlock, they become outcasts to their families, society and the government, which expels them from school. Expulsion from school normally leaves them prey to public prostitution to survive and today puts them at high risk of contracting HIV/AIDS. If they get married, they are considered as achieving regardless of their ability to sustain their marriage or children. They become the property of husbands whose demands they must obey including refusing them permission to work or study even after the children grow up.

4.5 CONCLUSIONS

Women experience institutional and societal barriers as they try to participate in the DE. While the institutional barriers relate to the OUT not having enough money to run the University and its inadequate publicity, the societal barriers are associated with the culture and its expectations regarding girls' and women's education and role in sustainable development in the society. In many African societies, marginalization of girls' and women's education is seen as a way to supplement the parents' income and ability to push forward the boy's development since girls can get married, and in raising a family get occupied and purposefully contribute to her society by raising future generations. To a poor country, educating boys is a family investment, for he can support other members of that family where the government does not function. But for women, the marriage, which is a necessary part of her growth and development, is dysfunctional in terms of helping members of her biological family since by marriage the women and girls are removed from their birth families to raise children in another family. Patriarchal control functions in political arenas where one must be superior to the other, and the married woman is a late entrant to her husband's family. Early marriage is focused on a woman's reproductive functions, which limits her opportunity for schooling, while men can become married and have families without losing time from their studies.

4.6 RECOMMENDATIONS

Although the barriers facing girls' education appear impossible to have quick or easy remedies, my personal recommendations to the DE practitioners, the governments of the developing nations of Africa, willing sympathizers and families are that since women are increasingly showing ability to participate in the public sector tasks as men are doing, and the threats from the HIV/AIDS continue to ravage marriages for many girls (at least for this century), women therefore need opportunities that can support their own initiatives of what they as women think and perceive they need in order to develop, and even more to leap forward their stunted development in order to catch up with their male counterparts.

I suggest that "women-to-women support services" be given optimal preference since, as one of the OUT students in my research told me, men and women are all human beings but are different and have different needs and ways of seeing, just as oranges and mangoes are all fruits, but the nutrients that the orange needs to thrive well are not the same as those needed by mangoes. She believed that the male-dominant plans for women are often lopsided due to their lack of knowing or being able to interpret well the issues of women's development. Also, during my research I asked one of the senior achieving OUT woman academic staff what technologies she thought would help women to better achieve their studies as men can do. She said that women in Tanzania need technologies such as refrigerators, electricity and cookers, running water in the house, vacuum cleaners, washing machines, transport, nearby effective clinics and day cares for the children so that these can help them finish quickly their home chores to give them time and energy to study. She added that women will study well using any of the learning technologies that men are using, but they need to be helped to get the time and energy. The women's focus groups agreed with the ideas of these individual interviewees and together concluded that the only thing that an African woman can own without it being taken away from her is good education, because this no one can take away from her and when she died it goes with her; no one can inherit another's good education.

I suggest that since most women have poor educations and social backgrounds, and lack role models, in particular the younger women and girls, the state has obligation to protect and advance these women, through organizing support such as through women-centred education support service circles, where other willing achieving women can help re-socialize and provide extra academic tuition support and recreational activities that are so much missing for most women in Africa.

As Dr Mlama pointed out, however, it is not sufficient to provide educational opportunities which provide for gender equity, we also need to keep track of enrolment figures and seek gender-disaggregated data to ensure that both groups not only enrol but also succeed in their studies. She concluded that this is one means of monitoring our success. What "ODL, therefore, needs is to be seen as a viable route to achieving what to us is a basic human right, the treatment of men and women as equal human beings in the provision of education" (pp. 12–13). Providing women-centred support centres is one means towards achieving this goal.

REFERENCES

John, M. (1991). A survey on distance education. *New Papers on Higher Education: STUDIES and Research 4*. Paris, France: UNESCO.

Kamau, J. (1995). Distance learners' perceptions of quality of course materials and student support in distance learning program in Kenya. In *On World Many Voices: Quality in Open Distance Learning*, Vol. 2, (D. Stewart, ed.), pp. 262–265.

Mhehe, E. (2002). Women's enrolment and participation issues at the Open University of Tanzania. Unpublished doctoral dissertation. University of Alberta, Canada.

Mkapa, B. (1996). Opening speech on the occasion for the inauguration of additional work space for the OUT at TIRDO premises. OUT, DarEsSalaam. In Mhehe, E. (2002). Women's enrolment and participation issues at the Open University of Tanzania. Thesis (Unpublished).

Mlama, P. (2006). The gender dimension of open and distance learning. Invited keynote address, *The Fourth Pan-Commonwealth Forum on Open and Distance learning (PCF4)*, Ocho Rios, Jamaica, November 2. Retrieved march 24, 2007 from: http://www.col.org/colweb/site/pid/4204

Muro, A. (1988). Providing postprimary education and training through distance tutoring in Tanzania. *ICDE Bulletin*, **17**, 5862.

Ntirukigwa, E.N. (1986). Distance education in Tanzania. In *Learning Strategies for Post Literacy, the Tanzanian Approach* (J. Muller, ed.) A Reader. Bonn, Germany: German Foundation for International Development.

Nyerere, J. (1964). Education for self reliance. In *Learning Strategies for Post Literacy, The Tanzanian Approach* (I.N. Resnik, ed.) A Reader. Bonn, Germany: German Foundation for International Development.

Open University of Tanzania. (2006). Payroll list, November 2006 (Unpublished).

Tanzania Ministry of Education. (1990). Report of the Committee on the Establishment of an Open University in Tanzania. Tanzania, DarEsSalaam, Ministry printer, 5859.

Thomson, J. (1983). *Learning Liberation: Women's Response to Men's Education*. London: Helm.

von Prummer, C. (1988, August). *Women in Distance Education*. Paper presented to the ICDE World Conference, Oslo.

Zindi, F. and Aucoin, R. (1995). Distance education in Tanzania and Zimbabwe. *Open Learning*, **10**(1), 32.

Chapter 5

Distance Education: Enabling and Disabling?

Christopher Newell

In this chapter, I argue that distance education (DE) may be seen as both enabling and disabling. The literature with regard to disability (including chronic illness) and DE displays some important examples of programmes around the world which have had a positive impact upon people who live with impairments. Yet, there are also cautionary voices that point to the problems associated with such technology, including that regarded as being inherently enabling. Indeed, drawing upon the critical literature with regard to disability and technology, it is argued that too often DE programmes incorporate into technological systems and approaches dominant ideologies and structures which may be seen to be disablist – that is, technologies which are often portrayed as enabling may be seen as disabling in impact.

Furthermore, a major challenge may be seen in terms of the tension between having *special* programmes aimed at people with disabilities,[1] including the use of adaptive technologies, and the *mainstream* incorporation of people with disabilities. In this way, even attempts at "inclusion" may be seen to leave unaddressed the structural dimensions of inequity. It is also suggested that in looking at the notions of openness and flexibility, we may see the development of technologies that are inherently controlling and indeed constitutive of the disabled body and mind.

Such a critical perspective may of course seem problematical given that the author has benefited enormously from DE to the extent that all of his studies have been undertaken using the distance mode. Yet, such experience combined with the critical disability studies literature helps us to encounter the structural dimensions of disability in the socio-political space which is DE, and to reflect upon the ways that a discourse of diversity often omits disability.

Finally, it is suggested that there are profoundly important challenges for the future in fostering DE programmes, which move from talking *about* the disabled student and academic to *listening to and learning from* the narratives of the students and scholars with disability. DE has the potential to be a liberating, indeed emancipatory, technology for students with disabilities. Yet, it also shows significant aspects of social control of those it is meant to liberate. The paradox of so-called flexible approaches may well be that in being enabling they are also disabling.

5.1 DE AS ENABLING?

This kind of thesis is of course a troubling start to a chapter. After all, the dominant myth of disability is that technology is always inherently good for people with disability and there is always a technological solution around the corner. Indeed, more than 20 years after I first started using DE as a mode of delivery as a young student with disability, I find myself reflecting on the variety of ways in which the technology which is supposed to liberate can also control. As I wrote in a piece with Judi Walker in the early 1990s as the globe was swept with the promises of so-called open education:

> The re-emergent concept of "openness", using distance education methods and communication technologies to expand learning opportunities to meet the needs of all learners whatever their vocations or circumstances, has the potential to increase rather than decrease social control, and to decrease rather than increase access.
>
> (Newell and Walker, 1992, p. 68)

In exploring the literature regarding disability and flexible in DE, this chapter suggests that rather than being inherently liberating, as is often supposed, Newell and Walker are correct to point to the way in which the technology, which is DE, has fostered control and even oppression of people with disabilities. Written in 1992, such a critical understanding needs to be complemented by contemporary disability studies, which helps us to understand more explicitly the structural nature of disability and to locate this within the notion of disablism, a concept which is explored later.

In arguing that DE may be seen as both enabling and disabling in its application to, and relationship with, people with disability, in this chapter I would seek to include those who live with chronic illness under the broad heading of disability. Amongst other things, in a variety of Western countries chronic conditions are accorded protections under relevant anti-discrimination legislation.

5.2 DE AND DISABILITY

A variety of recent work suggests that DE can provide a suitable route to support the studies of students with disabilities, including those who live with chronic conditions. As Newell and Debenham (2005) suggest, it is important that this should be regarded in terms of providing choice to students rather than requiring those who identify with, or who are identified as having, impairment/chronic illness to undertake studies at a distance. Despite the hype regarding fostering ability (such as removing the "dis" from disability as some Australian government programmes suggest) in many settings, choice is significantly wanting, and choice often revolves around specialised programmes which fail to problematise why such specialised solutions are necessary in the first place. A central concern of this essay, under-explored in much of the literature, is that unless well designed and evaluated, as with any technology, DE (including so-called flexible/open approaches) can also be significantly disabling in their impact (Newell and Walker, 1992; Goggin and Newell, 2003).

5.3 BRINGING THE PERSONAL TO THE LITERATURE

This critical account of the literature review emerges from my own particular struggles as a student with disability over many years. I have pursued all of my post-secondary education by DE, and have elsewhere documented the way in which flexibility of approach enables me when my body does not necessarily enable me to participate face to face not only on particular days but even particular weeks and months (Newell and Walker, 1991). While I have acquired further impairments since that early work, it does document the way in which flexibility of approach enables me (Newell, 1995). Yet, in returning to study recently in a Masters programme, where flexibility and openness are central discourses and supposedly of central concern, I was deeply disturbed to find that the cautionary work written by Judi Walker and myself has to a significant extent come true.

In researching the literature, it has emerged that since Walker and Newell's early work in the area of DE and disability, there has been comparatively little critical analysis of disability and DE. Yet, as the Australian Bureau of Statistics suggests, some 20 percent of the population lives with disability and in early contributions Walker and Newell had sought to document the way in which inflexible education environments actually disable rather than enable (see Goggin and Newell, 2005). For example, as I wrote with regard to my experience of failing at school, in a keynote address to a national conference regarding disability and open learning approaches:

> When I was at school, I learned a great deal, but not what I hope that you learned at school. I learned that I was a failure, that there were many things that I couldn't do, that I was lazy, and that I would never achieve in life... When I was at school, I was always struggling to catch up, and to seek to explain myself to teachers. I was struggling to get around the campus, and most importantly, I was struggling to meet other peoples' limited expectations of what it meant to learn, and what a proper education was all about... Anyway, I failed at school. Not because I was inferior, I now know, but because the system was inflexible and disabling.
>
> (Newell, 1995, p. 14)

After many years of other scholarly activity, especially in interrogating the technologies of disability (see, e.g. Goggin and Newell, 2003), in recent postgraduate study with its requirement for continuous online participation, I found myself struggling with an online delivery and broader systems which did not meet my needs, were not what I would call flexible and indeed were helping me to revisit ghosts as I re-learnt how much of a failure

I am. Yet, lecturers obviously influenced by their own on-campus experience as learners and dominant accounts of technology as the salvation for people with disabilities kept suggesting technology as inherently beneficial for people with disabilities. The situation became worse when I needed to be admitted to hospital where I did not have access to the Web, while the whole course required it. Despite claims by the course to being flexible, I found myself reflecting that old paper-based technologies enabled me far more than systems which did not anticipate me not being able to access the Web. Likewise, as someone with chronic pain in the hands, I found the requirement for online participation very painful. I write most of what I need to type using a Dictaphone, but the online environment my so-called flexible DE course required was always on and instantaneous. Frankly, it made me unwell.

I also came to realise that the inflexibility of the system (which had moved from paper to online in those years) was at the heart of my trouble, despite the fact that this is provided in the name of flexible options. "Flexible for whom?" I wonder. After all, I am someone who has utilised DE methodologies to enhance and enable, and to display significant levels of competence at undergraduate and postgraduate level. I have managed to do much of my education from very difficult circumstances, including institutions and when I have been totally in bed for months at a time.

5.4 STORIES AND PUBLIC ISSUES

Recognising my life and story as text itself, this essay has been deeply influenced by narrative theorists such as Hilde Lindemann Nelson (2001) who explore not just "damaged identities" but look at the way in which story can foster "narrative repair" amongst disadvantaged and oppressed social groups. Accordingly, I utilise this story to introduce DE, suggesting that this story is not just about deviant Christopher but flags issues that to a significant extent have not been adequately explored and discussed in the literature in terms of a disability critique of what it is to offer DE and an online learning experience. Wright Mills would suggest that this is not about a private trouble, but a public issue, and for Goggin and Newell (2005), the public issue is that people with disability are largely defined in ways which foster us as "other" outside of socially accepted norms and roles, a situation they suggest constitutes a form of "social apartheid". This approach moves us beyond the understanding of Newell and Walker (1992) in terms of "social control" to understanding the role of institutions and technologies in creating and replicating *otherness* such as disability via structures and ideology. Furthermore, it shows the under-examined role of normalcy in creating disability.

5.5 DISABILITY AND DISABLISM AS SOCIAL ISSUES

In short, my narrative as text moves us well beyond critiquing a course ethos and approach in one particular institution. I would go so far as to suggest that a review of the literature reveals much of the practice and theorisation conducted in the name of so-called DE actually revolves around dominant accounts of the world and the incorporation of these into technological systems as artefacts and ways of operating which are fundamentally disabling.

In this way, I wish to suggest that it revolves around a form of disablism. As Mike Oliver a leading disability studies theorist argues:

> If the category disability is to be produced in ways different from the individualised pathological way it is currently produced, then what should be researched is not the disabled people of the positivist and interpretive research paradigms but the disablism ingrained in the individualistic consciousness and institutionalised practices of what is, ultimately, a disablist society.
>
> (Oliver, 1996, p. 143)

Within the Western world some 20 percent of the population has some degree of disability (discussed further in Goggin and Newell, 2005). Yet, there are a wide variety of impairments and diverse ways of understanding disability. Taken together, these have significant implications for curriculum design and pedagogy, as well as research and development of educational programmes and technology. Considerable differences in life orientation may be found between those who are born with impairment (and for whom such a condition is "normal") and those who acquire impairment. Those who have visible disability and those whose conditions are hidden can have markedly different experiences, including whether or not their situation is seen as warranting disability support by institutions.

The UK, US, Australian and New Zealand Disability Studies literature highlights a marked shift in recent years from the so-called medical model of disability to a "social model" (Albrecht, 2001). As Fulcher (1989) observes, medical and charitable discourse still dominates everyday understanding of disability. The *medical model* constructs disability as a "personal tragedy" located within a deviant individual, to be overcome by providing assistance on an individual basis to a deviant individual. My everyday reality is that I am someone who still needs to prove my disability via medical certificates in order to gain access to services needed for daily participation in life. This is an unpalatable situation for many of us.

On the other hand, *social model* theorists argue that it is society that creates disability. This approach suggests barriers to participation need to be addressed systemically. One problem which leads some to suggest that this is somewhat ideological is that specificity is sometimes wanting. It is this social understanding which informs this chapter, and yet little of the DE literature reviewed draws upon such a social understanding of disability. This is to some extent hardly surprising, since many funding programmes rely upon dominant understandings of disability as medical deficit. Likewise, few writers in the area of DE seem to identify as having disability. In addition, the literature also highlights the importance attached by people with disabilities to the maintenance of personal control over decision-making regarding our lives (see, e.g. Finkelstein, 1990, 1991, 1996; Hunt, 1996).

One good example which serves to illustrate the marked differences that can occur within one broad category of disability is the experience of deaf and deafened (hearing impaired) people. A distinction may be drawn between deaf (or deafened) people (who are usually post-lingually deafened) and deaf people (who are part of the deaf community). Deaf cultures exist in most countries and consist of people who are born or become deaf, use a particular national sign language as their first language and identify themselves as being deaf (Padden and Humphries, 1988). A very real issue is whether education and training requires deaf people to conform to the dominant approaches to disability as deficit. Are they to be educated with English (or similar oral language) as the main language? Alternatively, there is a cultural understanding and pedagogical approach which regards deaf people as being a socio-linguistic minority, whose training should be provided using the appropriate sign language as the dominant form of language.

This is not just an issue of pedagogy, but also one of power and culture. For example, there is no doubt that deaf people prefer the delivery of material and conversation via video-conferencing with sign language more than written text. Sign language is their native language. Yet, this is not necessarily recognised in the literature regarding education and disability, where constructions of deafness as pathology dominate, reflecting the power relations inherent in conversations regarding pedagogy.

For example, Richardson (2001) provides a useful comparative study of deaf and non-disabled students undertaken in a distance learning environment, concluding that, in terms of both their persistence and performance, students with a hearing loss are similar to students with no reported disability. This is certainly useful for understanding regarding people with hearing loss. Yet, such a research approach starts with deafness as pathology. Berry (1999) also highlights the diversity of experience occurring amongst members of the blind and partially sighted population in relation to the issue of access to the World Wide Web.

Debenham (2001) is an example of a researcher who identifies as having a chronic condition which serves to disable her. Her research identifies differences between the needs of those with disabilities that are stable (or have stabilised) and those with long-term health problems. She explores the experience of distance learners with chronic illnesses in her tertiary education, what she terms "long-term health problems". As she notes, the impact of such conditions can be variable. She has a particularly important insight in observing that as they are often hidden, they may not be well understood in terms of "disability". It is notable that the stereotype of disability is the wheelchair. Yet, this is a small minority and most disabling conditions are hidden and not well understood in terms of impact of functioning. Good examples include mental illness and people with episodic presentation of symptoms which impact on functioning.

As someone who uses a wheelchair, I also find that the misunderstandings associated with this symbol are profound. Many of my limitations are hidden and yet because they cannot be seen are not well understood by many. The UK scholar Alan Roulstone (1994) provides another excellent example of the problems of the stereotypes of disability. He wryly describes his own experience of being regarded as "a fit person fallen from grace" describing a lack of understanding of his functional limitations. Of course, even physically obvious impairments differ in their impact in part because of cultural settings and norms. As someone who uses a significant amount of oxygen therapy, I find understandings associated with a sickness role rather than that of disability associated with my wheelchair!

5.6 TOWARDS A CRITICAL APPROACH

In reviewing the literature on technology and DE, we can find a significant amount of critical literature which lends support to a thesis whereby disability can be seen to be created via such technologies. This is despite the fact that disablism and, largely speaking, the situation of learners with disability are not examined. For example, Tony Bates explores the need for a comprehensive process in selecting technologies, even warning about the significant problem of "monomedia mania" where "a government, company or institution decides to invest heavily in a single technology for all teaching or training throughout its system" (Bates, 1995, p. 33).

Bates' well-expressed alternative framework makes it apparent that the needs of learners with disabilities are not well taken up in the online environment (not just by people such as myself who do not have unfettered access to the Web) but for a variety of people with vision impairments and intellectual disability, let alone for people for whom a Web-based browser may not necessarily be accessible by virtue of the slowness of their connection to the internet. Bates suggests a useful alternative framework in evaluating an approach with the following characteristics:

> It will work in a wide variety of contexts;
>
> It allows decisions to be taken both at a strategic or institution – wide, level, and at a tactical, or instructional, level;
>
> It gives equal attention to instructional and operational issues;
>
> It will identify crucial differences between different technologies, thus enabling an appropriate mix of technologies to be chosen for any given context;
>
> It will accommodate new developments in technology.
>
> (Bates, 1995, p. 35)

Likewise in a later essay, Bates (2000) stresses the importance of using technology to enhance the quality of learning and indeed to widen access. Yet, such writers as Bates fail to recognise the limitations associated with the increasing use of Web interfaces and a requirement for interactivity when this may not be a viable proposition.

Indeed, this is reflected in the way in which particular abilities are uncritically assumed by such writers as Collis, who cites authorities such as Norman suggesting that "the assessment of competence depends on listening, observing and responding to learners reflecting on their products" (as cited in Collis, 1998, p. 375). Not all of us have such abilities! For all that writers such as Collis suggest contact sessions and ways of participating via the digital world that are potentially exciting, there are some limitations. Such an uncritical quote shows the norms which operate in the literature in unchallenged ways. Functional norms are expressed which can be seen as an expression of disablism. Paradoxically, this is when they are writing of the importance of enabling learners. Yet, Collis et al. (2000) helpfully sum up the importance of particular characteristics of technologies utilised in terms of what they refer to as the 4-E Model: of perceived educational effectiveness, ease of use, engagement and environmental factors (Collis et al., 2000, p. 108).

In reflecting upon the characteristics of technology and the discourse we utilise with regard to disability, we find important learnings provided by Fairclough when he writes:

> People internalize what is socially produced and made available to them, and use this internalized MR [members resources] to engage in their social practice, including discourse. This gives the forces which shape societies a vitally important foothold in the individual psyche.
>
> (Fairclough, 1989, p. 24)

Indeed, in critically reflecting upon the work of such commentators as Fiske (1990) and Hartley (1994), it is immediately obvious that non-disabled norms, and ways of operating, can be found in what is manifested in the social dimensions of so-called flexible distance educational technologies.

Whilst writers such as Hawkridge (1995) have flagged some significant issues to do with a proper evaluation of DE, where "distance educators have many more media to choose between and very little good advice to depend upon" (p. 3), there would appear to be a particular dearth in the literature with regard to a critical examination of instructional technologies as building in disability. For example, Huang argues "… the internet provides distance learners more interactive activities and greater exchange of information. In addition, distance learners can easily receive the feedback to internet communications" (2000, p. 43). As a learner and educator with disability, it is difficult to say how devastating it is for my reality not to be recognised in such powerful statements.

Yet, the insights of Kelsey can be built into our critical understanding: for example, when he recognises that there can be advantages in "de-emphasizing discussion board activities where a minority of students participate" (Kelsey, 2000, p. 73). Likewise, for all that La Velle and Nichol recognise the way in which models mediate knowledge and relationships, this does not seem to be explicitly explored with regard to the characteristics of learners with impairments who may be disabled as a consequence of the particular model. As they argue:

> At the heart of such ICT applications is either an explicit or implicit model of how the student learns in relation to the educational training environment … Underpinning the design of virtual reality learning environments is a model or models of the users. A model serves as the basis for designing the software and related courseware.
>
> (La Velle and Nichol, 2000, p. 104)

The approach of a variety of people focused on online learning seems to be that of suggesting that online learning is inherently liberating, provided "best practice", to use Oliver's terminology, is entered into (Perraton, 2000; Robson, 2000; Oliver, 2001). Here we may note that Robson (2000), for example, in evaluating online teaching, tends to focus on reducing barriers without looking at the way in which technology can actually build those barriers in as an integral part of the technological systems which are supposedly flexible DE.

5.7 FOSTERING ACCESS

There are a variety of issues of access which emerge for students who need to study using DE, and/or to be connected via various technologies or educational services. One core issue, regardless of national variation, is the cost of disability – especially in terms of capital and running costs for those utilising information technology, where many people with disability are on low incomes, including pensions. In the UK, there is the example of the government-funded disabled student allowance (DSA) (Department of Education and Skills, 2003). However, such an initiative has sadly not been replicated in a variety of other nations. Furthermore, one of the issues which remain under-explored is the structural reasons why it is more difficult and expensive for learners with disability to participate in education and society.

This highlights the major differences in approach in terms of access as a construct. These may be summarised as the difference between *mainstream* and *adaptive/special solutions*. Mainstream approaches seek to move people with disabilities from specialist, often isolated, educational settings to the mainstream, seeking to integrate them into regular educational settings and contexts (Fulcher, 1989). Within the Western world, this has tended to raise important issues of ensuring equity, not just in terms of opportunity, but making sure that there is adequate support. It also requires an understanding of the needs and aspirations of learners with disabilities. In terms of distributive justice, equity can require further injections of funding in order to address structural inequality.

The incorporation of the needs of people with disability into the "mainstream" can include a variety of specific educational programmes. As the discussion of the "Universal Design" literature below suggests, programmes designed with disability access in mind will usually be more accessible for the general population. In the area of information technology, a variety of positive initiatives have made the initial inaccessible design of computers and the World Wide Web more accessible. In many respects, this has removed some need for special solutions (see, e.g. the WAI Web Content Accessibility Guidelines: http://www.w3.org/wai). As Foley and Regan (2002) suggest, "an essential part of web design today is designing for individuals with disabilities". Yet, even in this well-intentioned statement about mainstream access, we see the role of dominant approaches to disability, whereby it is individualised and privatised. Disability is not understood in terms of the way in which disability and/or ability is designed into technologies.

Accordingly, the emphasis in the literature is that no matter how effective mainstreaming is the other dominant approach, "adaptive" or "special" solutions will at times be needed. This is usually justified in terms of requirements of individuals, leaving unexamined the structural reasons why "special needs" emerge (Fulcher, 1989). An example of this is found in the Open University (OU, UK) offering to arrange home assessments (where necessary) where student needs are explored with students in their home environment. Adaptive equipment and running costs of students may be paid for from an individual's DSA, up to the limits of the yearly allowance (Open University, 2004). Such services are a double-edged sword, in that they certainly enable, and yet they help support a system which builds in disability, requiring such special solutions (Goggin and Newell, 2003).

Writers such as Linburger and Brown (2002) and Schenker and Scadden (2002) explicitly examine the way in which a proactive approach to creating accessibility is needed. While reports such as the Flexible Learning Advisory Group of the Australian National Training Authority (2000, 2002) explicitly explore the fact that there are significant issues in providing for online access, there is little evidence of systemic action following their important reports.

5.8 UNIVERSAL DESIGN

There is a significant and growing literature that looks at the way in which a Universal Design approach can enable learning, and a strong literature advocating the benefits of implementing this approach in policy and education (see, e.g. Anonymous, 1998; Burgstahler, 2000a,b; French, 2002). Foley and Regan (2002) explicitly suggest that "an essential part of web design today is designing for individuals with disabilities", referring to the Web accessibility guidelines created by the "World Wide Web Consortium" for accessibility (see http://www.w3.org/wai/wcag-curric).

Cutting-edge work with regard to DE has revolved around the concept of Universal Design, which may be defined as

> The design of products and environments to be usable by all people, to the greatest extent possible, without the need for adaptation or specialized design.
>
> (Connell et al., 1997)

One of the leaders has been the work of "The Trace Center", a US federally funded centre focused on developing more accessible products and services for people with disability, with a particular focus on technology. Their work includes the development of an online design tool aimed at assisting in the development of more usable products (Trace Center, 2004).

In 1997, a working group of architects, product designers, engineers and environmental design researchers collaborated to establish the following Principles of Universal Design:

1. *Equitable use*: The design is useful and marketable to people with diverse abilities.
2. *Flexibility in use*: The design accommodates a wide range of individual preferences and abilities.
3. *Simple and intuitive use*: Use of the design is easy to understand, regardless of the user's experience, knowledge, language skills or current concentration level.
4. *Perceptible information*: The design communicates necessary information effectively to the user, regardless of ambient conditions or the user's sensory abilities.
5. *Tolerance for error*: The design minimises hazards and the adverse consequences of accidental or unintended actions.
6. *Low physical effort*: The design can be used efficiently and comfortably and with a minimum of fatigue.
7. *Size and space for approach and use*: Appropriate size and space is provided for approach, reach, manipulation and use regardless of the user's body size, posture or mobility (Connell et al., 1997).

There is much to be said for such an approach. For all the rhetoric of the accessibility of the Web, it is increasingly apparent that claims to accessibility are not necessarily found in practice (Craven, 2003; Schenker and Scadden, 2002; Thompson et al., 2003). This is despite the development of BOBBY, a software tool established to ensure that text-based pages meet the criteria of accessibility (Bobby, 2002). The Web is a litmus test for the implementation of such Universal Design approaches.

Yet, for all the advantages of Universal Design as a practical approach and ethos, there is clearly an unremarked problem which underlies this work. That is, it has become necessary precisely because of the norms of what is nice, normal and natural which create disablist programmes and technology. Likewise, I find myself wondering at the majoritarian nature of such an approach. For all the talk of maximising participation, we find an old adversity of people with disability in the necessarily utilitarian calculus of the greatest good for the greatest number. Obviously, I ruefully reflect, yet again we find people excluded. Yet, paradoxically, this is in contrast to the promise found in the title of Universal Design. This reality is in sharp contrast to values statements such as the Universal Declaration of Human Rights, which is based upon the dignity (inherent worth) of all people.

5.9 ANTI-DISCRIMINATION LAW

While unremarked in much of the literature to do with DE, it is apparent that a sub-text and incentive on improving online accessibility and the accessibility of learning materials is found in anti-discrimination legislation. In most Western countries, there is specific legislation prohibiting discrimination on the grounds of disability. Such legislation provides exemptions for unreasonable hardship imposed by complying with such legislation, as well as specific exemptions.

In Australia, the national *Disability Discrimination Act 1992* provides a broad definition of disability and protection against "unreasonable" discrimination including in areas such as education. Countries such as the USA which has similar legislation in the *Americans with Disabilities Act* have also seen moves to revise the broad protections offered by such law, reclaiming narrow and stereotypical definitions of, and approaches to, disability (Johnson, 2003). Often, people with chronic health conditions are included under the provisions of such anti-discrimination legislation; however, they may not be aware of their rights or may well not initially identify as having disability. In the USA , it is also clear that recent legal action has sought to remove such a broad understanding of disability, showing a preference for reverting to disability stereotypes. Certainly, many people with functional impairment may well choose not to reveal their disabilities (if they conceptualise these as such) to institutions. This helps to make the case for the importance of a mainstream approach to provision of access for all.

One of the problems with such legislation and its impact on flexible and distance learning is that it reinforces stereotypes of disability. Even the important 1995 Human Rights and Equal Opportunity Commission decision in *Scott versus Telstra* required a deaf man (who identified himself as being part of a socio-linguistic minority not as having a disability) to adopt a definition of disability as deficit in order to gain access to justice (Goggin and Newell, 2003). In this way, we can also reflect that in a variety of approaches to disability support requiring students to access disability services, we can require identification as a student with disability, which may be contrary to their self-conception.

5.10 STUDYING AT A DISTANCE

There are certainly advantages associated with studying via DE. These include overcoming the inability to attend (or difficulty in attending) campuses and the flexibility of study hours. Often allowing students to work when it is optimal is crucial. Such flexibility addresses problems encountered with chronic fatigue and pain that can fluctuate from day to day.

As Newell and Debenham (2005) suggest, disadvantages can include (a) a lack of social engagement; (b) capital and running costs; and (c) the use of DE to avoid the issue of making campuses accessible.

A variety of scholars have suggested that access to a "Virtual Campus" environment of a distance learning institution can address some aspects of isolation for those studying at a distance (Jennison, 1997; Debenham, 2001). Capital and running costs are significant for those on a low income, as many with disability are (see also Paist, 1995; Ommerborn, 1998; Moisey and Moore, 2002).

Accordingly, a very real issue is whether DE (particularly using modern communications technology) promotes autonomy. On the one hand, there is a case to be made that it can re-enforce control of people with disability by defining them as having "special needs" requiring a professional response, learning from the medical model. The disabled body and mind is managed by the increasing number of dedicated professional responses to disability in the higher education and other environments. On the other hand, however, there is little doubt that, at its best, educational options for learners with disability are enhanced (Walker, 1989, 1994; Newell and Walker, 1991; Debenham, 2001).

5.11 METHODS OF COURSE DELIVERY: MULTIMEDIA

Distance education once utilised print media as its dominant form of presentation. In the Western world, particularly from the 1970s onward, this was variously supplemented, in particular with audiotapes, videotapes and TV in an effort to present material in as approachable a form as possible. After all, learners absorb, process and operate in different ways. In addition, "on-campus schools" geared to the needs of distance learners have been widely utilised. I still remember, however, as a person with disability whose reality barred me from travelling, how my "options" were curtailed to those courses that did not require such travel.

With the growth of the Internet in recent years, the emphasis shifted to e-mail, Web access, CMC (including the "Virtual Campus environment"), electronic resource material (e.g. on CD-ROM) and video and/or audio conferencing via the Internet. While the media may change, there are continuing issues for those with disability. This leads to a consideration of the need to ensure adequate and equitable access, particularly when mainstream technology has often historically served to disable people (Goggin and Newell, 2003). For all of this history, and the promise of the technology, why is it that we are still talking of issues of access and equity? Are the special cases of institutions which provide exemplary access the answer?

5.11.1 Exemplars in Access

There are many examples of institutions and projects that may be seen to have had an enabling impact. These are as follows:

5.11.1.1 The Open University, UK

The Open University, UK, (http://www.open.ac.uk) was inaugurated in 1971. The UK's largest university, with over 200,000 students, OU sources suggest that in 2005 the student population included almost 9,000 students who declared a disability, learning or mental health difficulty (Open University, 2006). A variety of special arrangements are available to support the needs of students with disability. There is no doubt that the University has an exemplary record in enabling students with disability to study at all levels of University education.

Since its earliest days, the University has employed a multimedia approach to support students. In the early days, this included specially written course units including material such as set books, TV and radio programmes and cassette tapes, plus face-to-face tutorials and residential schools. As with all learning institutions, the advent of CMC has led to dramatic developments in the use of e-learning. Debenham (2001) has pointed to the advantages of the way DE technologies have supported learners with disabilities in this institution. The work of Debenham, a former successful PhD student of the University, has illustrates the benefits of the University and its approach.

5.11.1.2 DO-IT Project (The University of Washington)

The award-winning DO-IT project (http://www.washington.edu/doit/) began in 1992, aiming to increase participation of disabled students in science, engineering and mathematics programmes and careers. The project supports scholars with a wide range of disabilities as they prepare for college. Significantly, advice is given on appropriate adaptive technology to meet individual needs. Equipment to enable participation in the programme is loaned, where necessary.

Participants communicate electronically throughout the year with mentors, DO-IT staff and other DO-IT scholars. Mentors are volunteers, often with a disability, who have been successful and can give advice based on their own life experience (see also Burgstahler, 2002c, 2003 and undated).

5.11.1.3 EASI

EASI is based at the Rochester Institute of Technology, arising from the work of Professor Norman Coombs, a blind professor (Coombs, 1989) (http://www.rit.edu/~easi/). It provides access to resource information and guidance on access-to-information technologies for those with disabilities. Online training courses are also offered on adaptive technology in the field of computer and information technology systems.

Yet for all that these case studies are excellent examples of providing access and solutions for students with disabilities, there is an under-explored dimension of these programmes. It is arguable that they do not address the structural reasons for why special solutions are needed in the first place. They do not address the political and power dimensions of technology and why in 2008 we still build in disability, even in the name of universal design and access.

5.12 CRITICAL DISABILITY PERSPECTIVES

Within the literature with regard to DE and flexible delivery, there has been work by people with disabilities which utilises narrative to identify structural issues. An early piece in the literature by Newell and Walker (1991) utilises my own narrative, identifying a variety of structural issues, and showing how educational attitudes can enable or disable someone who failed at school due to disabling (i.e. highly inappropriate) pedagogy. Later doctoral research by Margaret Debenham (2001), profoundly influenced by her experience of disabling chronic illness, extends this approach, utilising the narratives of a variety of people with chronicity and disability to identify needs and experiences.

Reflecting broader social power relations, very little of the material about disability is actually written by people with disabilities themselves. A rare exception is found in disabled American professor Art Blaser's work. Writing in the influential disability journal *Ragged Edge Online*, he suggests that "disabled people, more often than not, simply fall through the open "net". When it comes to the "digital divide," disability is a more significant variable than ethnicity, income or age' (Blaser, 2001).

Blaser suggests that while a variety of universities have been developing online access as part of their quality initiatives, what is really required is a tackling of the culture and norms found not only in the institutions but also in the technologies themselves. Goggin and Newell's (2003) critical study, *Digital Disability*, identifies the disablist nature of many online technologies, with the inherent characteristics reflecting broader social norms and power relations.

While the World Wide Web is utilised by many people with disabilities, Goggin and Newell (2003) suggest online usage is mediated and despite the rhetoric does not meet all of the needs of people with disabilities. People with intellectual disability and allergies to computer components have largely been forgotten. There can even be a significant ghetto effect for users who rely upon screen readers given the dominant use of graphical interfaces. Such a critique suggests that disablism operates in structures and taken-for-granted social norms.

5.13 STUDENTS WITH DISABILITY AS EXPERTS AND EDUCATORS

For all these criticisms a real advantage of DE is found when learners with disability become educators and professionals through their experience and use of DE technology. Examples include Margaret Debenham (ex Open University, UK) and Christopher Newell (University of Tasmania) (see also Evans and Newell, 1993). Tobin (2002) and Lance (2001) also document how people with disabilities as diverse as cerebral palsy and vision impairment can become instructors online.

Contrary to the experience of online learning I documented at the beginning of this chapter, Lance documents how her use of CMC has enabled her to take time to answer questions. She also notes that while she has impaired speech and mobility, her communication partners only become aware of this if she chooses to disclose it. As she notes, it is a complex issue as to whether or not to reveal a lecturer's disability to DE students. In my own case, I have always found it useful in building rapport at particular times and in explaining my research, or even why I did not manage to get things done within time frames.

5.14 CONCLUSION: TOWARDS ENABLING DE

In this chapter, it has been argued that the existing DE literature has significantly failed to engage critically with the way in which disability is built into education. I have drawn upon my own narrative and experience, suggesting that there are systemic issues including the impact of disablism, but that largely these issues are not recognised in the DE literature. The few critical studies that have been written have largely not been taken up in the significant move to online environments. Despite the hype and the way these meet the needs of some students with stereotypical disability, I would suggest that these DE environments inherently will continue to disable without remedial systemic action.

Yet, in drawing upon the insights of the critical DE literature, we can see that what is required is more than just an "access and equity" approach. Too many online courses fail to explore the characteristics of technology from the perspective of people with disabilities, largely reflecting the disadvantaged situation of people with disabilities and the way in which we are less likely to become administrators and designers. Even if they do use the perspectives of people with disability, too often this is within a dominant framing that fails to explore dominant norms and structures that impose disability upon people with impairments.

This is not a neo-luddite thesis. As a teacher who utilises such tools as the www and e-mail extensively in my teaching, I have come to realise the benefits. Yet, as a person with disability, I long for DE technology which will enable me totally and truly allow flexibility. I long to know that DE of the future will be undertaken in such a way that no matter what my situation (home, work or hospital) I can participate fully and learn of my value as a learner and teacher who just happens to live with disability. Sadly, the massive emphasis on the www as a medium seems to reflect a greater desire for control and containment of costs than a desire to foster access for all in a holistic approach to pedagogy which truly embraces flexibility.

It is only when we have effectively explored, tackled and purposely ameliorated the status quo, utilising the life experience of learners with disability, that the disablism unwittingly incorporated into DE, especially online learning environments, will be tackled. As Paulo Freire observes:

> The pedagogy of the oppressed, as a humanist and libertarian pedagogy, has two distinct stages. In the first, the oppressed unveil the world of oppression and through the praxis commit themselves to its transformation. In the second stage, in which the reality of oppression has already been transformed, this pedagogy ceases to belong to the oppressed and becomes a pedagogy of all men in the process of permanent liberation. In both stages, it is always through action in depth that the culture of domination is culturally confronted. In the first stage this confrontation occurs through the change in the way the oppressed perceive the world of oppression; in the second stage, through the expulsion of the myths created and developed in the old order, which like spectre haunt the new structure emerging from the revolutionary transformation.
>
> (Freire, 1972, p. 31)

The rise of critical work of scholars with disability suggests that there is hope we are closer to the second stage that Freire identifies. However, we need to attend to the broader social relations of disability and the ways these are incorporated into DE.

There is no doubt that DE can be useful and helpful for the studies of students with disabilities, provided it is well designed. It is, however, not a universal solution. Increasingly, learning environments utilise not only the discourse of customers, but also that of diversity. Yet, this is a discourse that has largely failed to connect with disability (Campbell, 2002) although other demographic variables such as race and sex have figured in fostering teaching and learning environments that embrace diversity. A very real challenge for society, educational institutions and educators is to ensure that disability is included in DE and flexible learning environments which explicitly embrace and evaluate their programmes against diversity guidelines. Accordingly, it emerges that the experience of disability and chronic illness becomes a crucial dimension for the evaluation and benchmarking of DE into the future. This needs to move beyond the account of technology being inherently good for people with disability and yet paradoxically value-neutral. It requires the use of critical work from disability studies scholars. The political question is whether we will dare to do so.

5.15 ACKNOWLEDGEMENTS

I am grateful for the opportunity to work with and develop ideas found in this chapter in relationship with many scholars. Thanks especially to Judi Walker, Gerard Goggin, Margaret Debenham and Terry Evans.

NOTE

1. In this paper, "people with…" terminology is utilised, reflecting the approach adopted in Australia (the writer's location) and countries such as the USA. This reflects a desire by people with impairments to be identified as people first. This contrasts with terminology adopted in the UK where the terminology "disabled people" is preferred. The logic behind this suggests people are disabled by society. Both approaches have merit.

REFERENCES

Albrecht, G. et al. (eds) (2001). *Handbook of Disability Studies.* Thousand Oaks: Sage Publications.

Anonymous (1998). *Universal Design for Individual Differences.* www.cast.org/udl/universaldesignforindividualdifferences1363.cfmaccessed/29/8/2003

Australian National Training Authority. (2000). *Strategy 2000: Access and Equity in Online Learning: Project Report RO117*, Australian National Training Authority.

Australian National Training Authority. (2002). *Strategy 2000: Access and Equity in Online Learning: Annotated with Biography RO13B*, Australian National Training Authority.

Bates, A.W. (1995). Selecting technologies: Sorting out the differences. *Technology, Open Learning and Distance Education*. London: Routledge, pp. 33–60, 250–255.

Bates, A.W. (2000). Confronting the Technology Challenge, *Managing Technological Change: Strategies for College and University Leaders*. San Francisco, USA: Jossey-Bass, pp. 16–29, 34–35, 217–220.

Berry, J. (1999). Apart or a part? Access to the Internet by visually impaired and blind people, with particular emphasis on assistive enabling technology and user perceptions. *Information Technology and Disabilities Journal*, **6**(3) http://www.rit.edu/~easi/itd/itdv06n3/article2.htm. Accessed 22 March 2004.

Blaser, A. (2001). Distance Learning – Boon or Bane? Ragged Edge on Line, (5), September. http://www.raggededgemagazine.com/0910/0901ft1.htm. Accessed 29 August 2003.

BOBBY (2002) BOBBY web page. http://bobby.watchfire.com/bobby/html/en/about.jsp. Accessed 29 March 2004.

Burgstahler, S. (2002a). Distance learning: Universal design, universal access. *Educational Technology Review*, **10**(1). www.aace.org./pubs/etr/issue2/burgstahler.cfm. Accessed 29 August 2003.

Burgstahler, S. (2002b). Universal design of distance learning. *Information Technology and Disabilities Journal*, 8(1). www.rit.edu/~easi/itd/itdvo8n1/burgstahler.html. Accessed 29 August 2003.

Burgstahler, S. (2002c). Working Together: People with Disabilities and Computer Technology. http://www.washington.edu/doit/Brochures/Technology/wtcomp.html. Accessed 22 March 2004.

Burgstahler, S. (2003) DO-IT: Helping students with disabilities transition to college and careers. In *Research Practice Brief: Improving Student Education and Transition Services Through Research*. Minnesota: National Center on Secondary Educational Transition, University of Minnesota. http://www.ncset.org/publications/viewdesc.asp?id=1168

Burgstahler, S. (Undated). Use of the Internet in DO-IT. http://www.washington.edu/doit/Brochures/Technology/internet.html. Accessed 22 March 2004.

Campbell, J. (2002). *Valuing Diversity: The disability agenda – we've only just begun, Disability and Society*, **17**(4), 471–478.

Collis, B. (1998). New didactics for university instruction: Why and how? *Computers & Education*, **31**, 373–93.

Collis, B., Peters, O., and Pals, N. (2000). Influences on the educational use of the web, email and videoconferencing. *Innovations and Education and Training International*, **37**(2), pp. 108–119.

Connell, B.R. et al. (1997). The Principles of Universal Design, Version 2.0 dated 4/1/97, NC State University, The Center for Universal Design http://www.design.ncsu.edu:8120/cud/univ_design/principles/udprinciples.htm. Accessed 25 March 2004.

Coombs, N. (1989). Using CMC to overcome physical disabilities. In *Mindweave: Communication, Computers and Distance Education* (R. Mason and A.R. Kaye, eds). Oxford: Pergamon Press. (http://www.icdl.open.ac.uk/lit2k/external.ihtml?loc=http://icdl.open.ac.uk/literaturestore/mindweave/mindweave.html. Accessed 25 March 2004.

Craven, J. (2003). Access to electronic resources by visually impaired people. *Information Research*, 8(4) Retrieved 07 April 2006, from http://informationr.net/ir/8-4/paper156.html

Debenham, M. (2001). *Computer Mediated Communication and Disability Support: Addressing Barriers to Study for Undergraduate Distance Learners with Long-term Health Problems*. Unpublished PhD Thesis. Milton Keynes: The Open University.

Department for Education and Skills (2003) Bridging the Gap: A guide to the Disabled Students Allowances (DSAs) in higher education in 2003/2004. http://216.239.59.104/search?q = cache:XdIqo5Bskr0J:www.dfes.gov.uk/studentsupport/uploads/Bridging-the-Gap-2003-webversion.doc + Disabled + Student + Allowances + UK and hl = en and ie = UTF-8 Accessed 28 March 2004.

Evans, T. and Newell, C. (1993). Computer mediated communication for postgraduate research: Future dialogue. In *Distance Education Futures* (T. Nunan, ed.). SA: University of South Australia, pp. 81–91.

Fairclough, N. (1989). *Language and Power*. Longman: London.

Finkelstein, V. (1990). Services for Clients or Clients for Services; Annual Course: 'Working Together'. Northern Regional Association for the Blind. Leeds: Centre for Disability Studies; University of Leeds. http://www.leeds.ac.uk/disability-studies/publish.htm Accessed 29 August 2003.

Finkelstein, V. (1991). Disability: An administrative challenge (The Health and Welfare Heritage). In *Social Work - Disabling People and Disabling Environments* (M. Oliver, ed.). London: Jessica Kingsley.

Finkelstein, V. (1996). Modelling disability. *Breaking the Moulds Conference*, Dunfermline, Scotland, May 1996. http://www/leeds.ac.uk/disability-studies/archive/archframe.htm Accessed 29 August 2003.

Fiske, J. (1990). *Introduction to Communication Studies*, 2nd edn, London: Routledge.

Foley, A. and Regan, B. (2002). Web design for accessibility: Policies and practice. *Educational Technology Review*, **10**(1). www.aace.org/pubs/etr/issue2/foley.cfma. Accessed 29 August 2003.

Freire, P. (1972). *Pedagogy of the Oppressed*. Harmondsworth: Penguin.

French, D. (2002). Editorial: Accessibility...an integral part of online learning. *Educational Technology Review*, **10**(1). www.aace.org./pubs/etr/issue2/french-ed. cfmaccess29/8/2003

Fulcher, G. (1989). *Disabling Policies?* London: Falmer Press.

Goggin, G. and Newell, C. (2003). *Digital Disability: The Social Construction of Disability in New Media*. Boulder, Colorado: Rowman and Littlefield.

Goggin, G. and Newell, C. (2005). *Disability in Australia – Exposing a Social Apartheid*. Sydney: UNSW Press.

Hartley, J. (1994.) *Designing Instructional Text*, 3rd edn, London: Kogan Page.

Hawkridge, D. (1995). An agenda for evaluation of distance education. In *One World Many Voices: Quality in Open and Distance Learning* (D. Stewart, ed.). Selected papers from the 17th World Conference of the International Council for Distance Education, Birmingham, UK, pp. 85–88.

Huang, H. (2000). Instructional technologies facilitating online courses. *Educational Technology*, July–August, pp. 41–46.

Hunt, P. (1996). A critical condition. *In Stigma: The Experience of Disability*, London: Geoffrey Chapman (Extract available at http://www.leeds.ac.uk/disability-studies/archiveuk/archframe.htm).

Jennison, K. (1997). Mutual support on the virtual campus. In *The New Learning Environment; A Global Perspective; ICDE '97* (CD ROM). Pennsylvania State University, USA.

Kelsey, K.D. (2000). Participant interaction in a course delivered by interactive compressed video technology. *American Journal of Distance Education*, **14**(1), 67–73.

Johnson, M. (2003). *Make them Go Away*. Louisville, KY: The Advacado Press.

Lance, G.D. (2001). Distance learning and disability: A view from the instructor's side of the virtual lectern. *Information Technology and Disabilities Journal*, **8**(1). http://www.rit.edu/~easi/itd/itdv08n1/lance.htm. Accessed 22 March 2004.

La Velle, L. and Nichol, J. (2000) Editorial. Intelligent information and communications technology for education and training in the 21st century. *British Journal of Educational Technology*, **31**, 99–107

Linburger, J. and Brown, C. (2002). Accessibility or flexible wording resources: a proactive approach to providing equitable access for students with disabilities. *Untangling the Web: Establishing Learning Links*, Proceedings of the ASET Conference, 2002, Melbourne, 7–10 July. Published at www.aset.org.au/comfs/2002/contents.htmlaccessed29/8/2003

Moisey, S.D. and Moore, B. (2002). *Students with Disabilities: Their Experience and Success at Athabasca University*. In ICDE/CADE Calgary 2002 Conference Papers. CADE, Canada http://www.cade-aced.ca/icdepapers/moiseymoore.htm.

Nelson, H.L. (2001). *Damaged Identities, Narrative Repair*. Ithaca: Cornell University Press.

Newell, C. (1995). *Towards High Quality Open Learning for People with Disability: Some Challenges and Opportunities*. Keynote Address presented to "Enabling Vision '95", A National Conference on Open Learning and People with a Disability, 20–21 February, 1995, the Carlton Radisson Hotel, Melbourne, Victoria. Published in Walker, J. ed. *Enabling Vision '95 Conference Proceedings*, Open Learning Technology Corporation Ltd., South Australia, pp. 14–25.

Newell, C. and Debenham, M. (2005) Disability, chronic illness and distance education. In *Encyclopedia of Distance Learning* (C. Howard et al. ed.) Vol. 1. Idea Group Inc, Hershey, PA, USA, pp. 591–598.

Newell, C. and Walker, J. (1991). Disability and distance education in Australia. In *Beyond the Text: Contemporary Writing on Distance Education* (T. Evans and B. King, eds) Geelong: Deakin University Press, pp. 27–55.

Newell, C. and Walker, J. (1992). 'Openness' in distance and higher education as the social control of people with disabilities: An Australian policy analysis. In *Research in Distance Education 2* (Evans, T. and Juler, P. eds) Victoria: Institute of Distance Education, Deakin University, pp. 68–80.

Oliver, M. (1996). *Understanding Disability from Theory to Practice*. Houndmills: MacMillan.

Oliver, R. (2001). Seeking best practice in online learning: flexible learning toolboxes in the Australian VET sector. *Australian Journal of Education Technology*, **17**(2), 204–222.

Ommerborn, R. (1998). *Distance Study for the Disabled: National and International Experience and Perspectives*. Hagen, Germany, FernUniversitat.

Open University (2004). *Learners Guide – Services for Disabled Students. What Services are Available? Disabled Students' Allowances*. http://www3.open.ac.uk/learners-guide/disability/services_available/factsheet_dsa.htm. Accessed 22 March 2004.

Open University (2006). *Learners Guide – Services for Disabled Students. What Services are Available? Disabled Students' Allowances*. Retrieved 07 April 2006, from http://www.open.ac.uk/disability/pages/funding/dsa-funding-answers.php#dsa

Padden, C. and Humphries, T. (1988). *Deaf in America: Voices from a Culture*. Cambridge, MA: Harvard University Press.

Paist, E.H. (1995). Serving students with disabilities in distance education programs. *The American Journal of Distance Education*, **9**(1), 61–70.

Perraton, H. (2000). Choosing technologies for education. *Journal of Educational Media*, **25**(1), 31–38.

Richardson, J.T.E. (2001). The representation and attainment of students with a hearing loss at the open university. *Studies in Higher Education*, **26**(3), Society for Research into Higher Education.

Robson, J. (2000). Evaluating online teaching. *Open Learning*, **15**(2), 151–172.

Roulstone, A. (1994). *New Technology and the Employment Experience of Disabled People: A Barriers Approach*. Unpublished PhD Thesis. Milton Keynes, UK: The Open University.

Schenker, K. and Scaddon, L.A. (2002). The design of accessible distance education environments that use collaborative learning. *Information Technology and Disabilities*, Vol. **VIII**(1) Retrieved 07 April 2006, from http://www.rit.edu/~easi/itd/itdv08n1/scadden.htm

Thompson, T., Burgstahler, S., and Comden, D. (2003). Research on Web accessibility in higher education. *Information Technology and Disabilities Vol. IX No. 2*. Retrieved 07 April 2006, from http://www.rit.edu/%7Eeasi/itd/itdv09n2/thompson.htm

Tobin, T.J. (2002). Issues in preparing visually disable instructions to Teach online: A case study. *Information Technology and Disabilities*, 8(1). www.rit.edu/_easi/itd/itdvo8n1/tobin.htm Accessed 29 August 2003.

Trace Center (2004). http://www.trace.wisc.edu/world/tool_nav.html). Accessed 28 March 2004.

Walker, J. (1989). *Mark's Story: A Disabled Student's Case Study in Distance Education*. Distance Education, **10**(2), 289–297.

Walker, J. (1994). Open learning: The answer to the government's equity problems? A report on a study of the potential impact of the Open Learning initiative on people with disabilities. *Distance Education*, **15**(1), 94–111.

Chapter 6

Meeting Diverse Learning Needs

Jean Mitchell and Jennifer O'Rourke

This chapter considers the reasons why open and distance learning (ODL) must consider and respond to learning needs that emerge from learners' diverse characteristics and contexts. We will explore strategies that have proven effective in meeting diverse learning needs, and examine the relationship between these strategies and learning outcomes.

Responding appropriately to diverse learning needs is especially important for ODL because some of its operating models assume large, relatively homogeneous learner cohorts. Distance education literature often refers to industrial terminologies and methodologies as models for providing education to learners at a distance. Terms such as "economies of scale", "delivery", "markets" and "mass production" appear frequently in distance education literature (Holmberg, 1982; Bates, 1995; Rumble, 2003). The terminology implies that an underlying principle of industrial production, using consistent processes to yield consistent products, is as applicable to the human dynamic of learning as it is to the process of turning out identical cars off the production line. As Franklin (1999) points out, models and structures can create the conditions they assume. Unfortunately, in the case of ODL, using a model that assumes large numbers of similar learners can lead to exclusion or disadvantage for learners who are different from the expected "norm". This chapter will argue that supporting a successful distance learning process involves identifying and addressing diverse learning needs.

6.1 BACKGROUND

For more than a century of provision, there have been two quite different paradigms for ODL that have affected the approach to meeting learning needs. One paradigm is that providing accessible education is a consumer service, operating on market principles that should generate a profit for the provider. The other is that providing accessible education for all is essential for sustaining a just society. These two potentially opposing threads continue to weave through the recent history of ODL: in some contexts balancing the two paradigms creates a major challenge.

In addition, distance education has served to bridge gaps in the provision of education brought about by social and geographical exclusion. In countries where populations are widely dispersed, such as Canada and Australia, distance education has been used to provide educational opportunities for those who were far from schools, colleges and universities.

Bridging geographical distance sometimes addresses social distance, by reaching learners who cannot afford the costs of conventional face-to-face studies, or who cannot be accommodated in conventional education institutions. Distance education has also bridged socio-political distances, as in apartheid South Africa where students from all racial groups could study at the same distance institution and meet together in tutorial sessions and study groups.

Throughout the world, ODL provision became a means of meeting the demand for mass education (Daniel, 1996) and access to a recognised qualification. Thus institutions with established reputations were in a good position to provide this service. For example, the University of London (UL) External Studies Programme began operating in the nineteenth century. In providing accreditation services to those in Great Britain and in British colonies, UL was theoretically addressing both social and geographical distance even though the programme was regarded as a financial enterprise (Pennells, 2003). Another example is the University of South Africa (Unisa) that began as an examining body in South Africa in the 1870s, evolved in 1916 into an accreditation body and changed in 1946 to a dedicated distance teaching institution (Dhanarajan, 1994; Glennie, 1995).

The British Open University (UKOU), begun in 1970, was one of the first large-scale efforts to use distance education to bridge social distance and give adult learners an opportunity for "second-chance" learning. The OU's underlying principles were intended to ensure that learners had a genuine opportunity for success. Courses developed by academic and design teams were comprehensive print, audio and video versions of university-level instruction. Learner support included group and individualised tutoring as well as advising and counselling services available at regional centres (Tait, 2003).

The OU's successful approach became a template for ODL provision worldwide, both for new providers and for some existing providers who revised their strategies in order to improve completion and success rates. Other examples of large-scale providers include Indira Gandhi National Open University in India, with over 1.5 million students, and the Botswana College of Open and Distance Learning (BOCADOL) that provides learning opportunities for primary and secondary education, teacher education and university education. Even though distance education started from similar models, it has expanded to meet increasingly diverse needs in different contexts.

Although the original UKOU model was based on the principle that good distance education requires both quality materials and effective learner support (Tait, 2000), providers tend to invest more in learning materials than learner support (Lentell, 1994).

This is probably because learning materials are visible evidence of quality and academic rigour, whereas learner support is distributed, less visible and more difficult to link to academic success (Tait, 2000; Gibbs and Simpson, 2002; Simpson, 2003, 2004).

Moreover, the cost-effectiveness of distance education is based mainly on reducing per-student costs by amortising course development expenses over large enrolments and an extended time frame (Rumble, 1986). Providing learner support represents a continuing per-student cost (Mills, 2003; Tait, 2003), and therefore, demonstrating its value in financial terms involves calculating its impact on learner success. Where ODL is part of an effort to create a more equitable society, there is usually more concern about providing effective learner support, despite the costs involved.

Open and distance learning was developed to serve learners who must overcome a range of challenges in order to obtain access to successful learning opportunities. It continues to evolve to meet multiple and more diverse learning needs Anderson and Spronk (2000). Even though distance education started from similar models, these models have changed to meet increasingly diverse needs in different contexts. Strategies for meeting diverse learning needs are situated in materials development, learner support and responsive administration, and this chapter will consider all the three areas.

6.1.1 Defining Distance and Diversity

Before examining in more depth why and how ODL providers should and can meet diverse learning needs, we should consider the implications of the terms distance and diversity.

As Haughey (1995b) pointed out, distance implies both a physical and psychological separation, "the notion of being different, apart, separate, also standing for, of confirming, of being from the place where I stand. These two notions of presence and apartness are contained in the concept of pedagogical distance."

Canadian social theorist Harold Innis (1951) developed the concept of "the centre" and "the margins" to explain how, in Canada, the original pattern of transportation routes leading to major centres rather than sustaining local networks of communities created a political, social and economic landscape in which decisions are made at the centre and imposed on the margins. This perception of a distant centre wielding more power than it should over the rest of the country or region also arises in European, Asian and African contexts. In distance education, there is often the sense of the provider being at the centre, and the students on the margins.

This perception can lead to assumptions that categorise learners as "typical" or "exceptional" in terms that are based on the provider's definitions, rather than on the learners' understanding of their situation. Providers then develop programmes that meet the needs of the pre-defined "typical" learner. However, learners may not share the providers' perspective, and may be so rooted in their own reality that they do not recognise that the providers' view of them is different from their own. The situation is comparable to that of the little boy who said calmly, after his frantic parents had searched for him in a busy store, "I wasn't lost, it's just that you didn't know where I was."

In addition to the psychological dimension of distance, there is also the metaphorical sense of distance as different. In many contexts, such as dual-mode institutions, distance learners are different simply because they are at a distance, and not on site, like "normal" students. For example, dual-mode institutions have not always recognised the implications of this difference or addressed the issue of distance in provision of services: they have often asserted that distance students can take advantage of all the services available to onsite students, simply by coming to the institution in person.

In many situations, distance learners are different because they represent a different age range, gender and life situation than do conventional learners. In addition, distance learners may have different prior educational experiences, skill levels and approaches to learning than those whose education has been continuous and classroom-based.

When ODL serves those who have experienced barriers to learning, distance learners are more likely to be different in other ways from mainstream learners. For example, learners may belong to a minority cultural or language group; or face poverty or a disability; or lack access to transportation, communications or information technologies.

However, it would be a mistake to equate difference with disadvantage. The concept of diversity is helpful because it can be interpreted more neutrally. In the context of ODL, diversity can encompass the range of learner characteristics, learning conditions and learning contexts within the milieu that the provider serves. In this chapter, we consider diversity from the learners' perspective, which can be much broader than a definition of diversity from the providers' perspective.

6.2 IDENTIFYING AND RESPONDING TO DIVERSE NEEDS

In the discussion of distance, difference and diversity, we take into account several dimensions: learners' individual characteristics; learning contexts and learning conditions; and barriers to learning that learners face. Each of these dimensions presents a range of learning needs. The challenge for distance education providers is in finding ways of responding to these learning needs that are consistent with their mandate, manageable within available resources and compatible with the goal of cost-effective provision. We will consider some underlying principles that can guide the process, such as equity for learners, a reasonable opportunity for learner success and consistency of practice.

Most distance education requires considerable advance planning to prepare learning materials, arrange learner support and coordinate administrative arrangements, such as enrolment, face-to-face meetings and examinations. The need for longer-term planning means that providers must anticipate learner needs as much as possible, and build in enough flexibility so that they can also respond to learner needs that emerge during provision. This flexibility should go beyond single programmes because the changing needs of learners can sometimes require providers to change focus and even reinvent themselves.

From an organisational perspective, distance education can respond to learner needs through any or all of its components: course materials, learner support and administrative systems.

However, in this chapter, we will start from the learners' perspective, taking learner characteristics, learning conditions and learner context, including barriers to learning, as the starting points for examining how providers can address learners' diverse needs.

6.2.1 Examples of Responding to Diverse Learning Needs

The following examples illustrate how distance learning providers identify and respond to diverse learning needs, and demonstrate that these strategies are feasible in practice as well as worthwhile in theory.

In order to illuminate how these strategies can work in real situations, we have included examples selected from different contexts, some with large enrolments and limited resources and some from contexts with small enrolments of learners with very specialised needs. Some examples show situations where there are many factors to address; some demonstrate the impact of just one strategy; and some illustrate the results of collaboration among several parts of an organisation, or several organisations. There are examples of formal, non-formal and workplace learning.

CASE STUDY 1

Academic Literacy Elements in Distance Courses at the University of South Africa (Unisa)

Learners: Learners who have not had the opportunity to develop academic skills required for tertiary-level education and who are enrolled in distance programmes offered by Unisa. A significant proportion of learners combine their studies with work and family responsibilities, and many have limited access to the Internet.

Learner needs: The academic literacy elements in Unisa courses address the needs of learners who:

- need stronger academic literacy skills to enable them to read the prescribed learning material and to write academically acceptable essays;
- need to develop learning skills for tertiary education;
- have a variety of prior knowledge, skills and education;
- have different learning styles and learning goals;
- belong to a range of cultures and nationalities;
- may use English (Unisa's language of instruction) as a second or third language;
- need to reinforce their ability to analyse questions and explore ideas in a spirit of academic inquiry;
- need to learn to develop and present logical arguments in academically sound English;
- need to develop thinking skills necessary for tertiary study;

- need to experiment with and develop the study skills that are most appropriate to their situation;
- need to build their confidence and self-esteem.

Provider: Unisa offers undergraduate and postgraduate programmes at a distance. Unisa offers formal modules that teach language and thinking skills, to enable learners to develop academic literacy skills, such as language skills appropriate to a specific discipline (*Language for Lawyers*; *English for Science Access*). As well, some programmes like the BA in Open and Distance Learning (BAODL) incorporate elements in each module that develop academic literacy skills: tutoring support for this programme addresses both academic literacy and subject matter issues. Unisa's learning support system for all learners includes counselling, tutoring and writing centres where learners can receive coaching in writing skills.

Learning goals: Learners have a range of specific, personal learning goals, but essentially they wish to

- develop the skills that will enable them to achieve their academic goals, such as completing a course, programme or degree;
- participate fully in learning programmes;
- acquire transferable skills that will increase their employability.

Programme goals: To enable learners to

- develop sufficient academic literacy skills to enable them to study successfully;
- develop the ability to adapt and apply their academic literacy skills to different learning situations and different courses;
- strengthen their ability to put ideas into writing through brainstorming, note-taking, preparing outlines, developing paragraphs and organising acceptable academic essays;
- apply their learning in practice in their own context.

Provider Strategies

Overview: Modules are either year-long or six-month semester courses offered at a distance with limited tutor support and contact sessions. Unisa hopes to develop more extensive learner support in the near future. Course materials are developed by teams and take into account learner profiles; modules are revised every three years and consider learner feedback.

Preparation: Unisa selects learners for admission who have passed the minimum grade 12 school level, and assesses their skills in numeracy and English language levels needed for specific courses (e.g. Mathematics).

Needs assessment: Learner profiles indicate that the learners are now in the age range of 18–80. More school leavers are studying through distance education because no other options are available to them. In general, these learners are the most at risk because they have not had an opportunity to develop academic literacy skills in their secondary education.

Learning materials design: Learning materials throughout the university are essentially print-based. Materials are designed to enable learners to reach specified learning outcomes. In courses that incorporate academic literacy skills, there are sections that guide learners as they apply specific academic literacy skills to a task related to the course content, for example, writing an academic essay.

Provision of learning: Although a relatively small proportion of Unisa courses include academic literacy, they demonstrate a range of approaches and have proven effective in practice (Mitchell, 2005).

Types of in-text support provided in study materials of different modules include

- general writing and reading programmes included as activities in study guides (e.g. BA in ODL);
- overt, developmental/graded guidance in the reading and writing required in the discourse of a particular subject (e.g. law, communication science and philosophy);
- incorporation of typical workplace-related reading and writing skills into study activities (e.g. public administration, information science);
- writing and editing skills embedded in learning materials (e.g. missiology, an application of theology and social sciences to mission work).

Application of learning: Learners apply their academic literacy skills to their course work, and tutor feedback responds to both the skills application and the content of the assignment. Tutors encourage learners to support their arguments and strengthen their case in response to feedback and to submit multiple versions of revised assignments.

Impact: Learner feedback, assignments and examination results show that the tuition in academic literacy across the curriculum is welcomed and helps learners to improve their academic reading and writing.

Lessons learned:

- Completing a guided process of researching, reflecting and writing in order to complete their assignments allows learners to gain transferable knowledge and skills.
- Most learners benefit from academic literacy elements in course materials, and in assignments. Even those learners whose background includes academic preparation benefit from the opportunity to hone their writing skills through practice and feedback.
- Clearly written course materials help to demonstrate the academic writing skills that learners should acquire and enable learners to strengthen their reading skills.
- In African states, learner access to advanced technology cannot be presumed. Because relatively few learners have easy access to the Internet and other electronic media, it is essential to include learner support and academic literacy elements in learning materials for all subjects at all levels (Nonyongo, 2003; Goodwyn-Darey, 2006; and Nothling, personnal communication, 2006).

CASE STUDY 2

Facilitation of Learning Programme (FOLP)

Learners: Staff who work with the UN Refugee Agency (United Nations High Commissioner for Refugees, UNHCR) who are responsible for coordinating, planning and providing learning programmes for colleagues and for staff in partner organisations and governments.

Learner needs: The programme responds to learners who

- need to strengthen their knowledge and skills about facilitating learning in UNHCR contexts;
- need to be able to apply their learning in their workplace;
- work in challenging environments, in widely dispersed offices and field locations, many in active conflict zones;
- face emergency situations and crises that may demand full-time attention for several weeks;
- may work in contexts with limited access to electricity, e-mail and the Web;
- need to balance learning with the demands of work and family commitments;
- have different levels of prior knowledge, skills and education;
- have a range of learning styles and learning goals;
- operate in many different cultures;
- use English as a second or third language.

Provider: UNHCR, whose mandate is to provide protection and support for refugees and internally displaced people, has about 6,000 staff in more than 116 countries, working with about 17 million refugees and persons of concern. Staff Development Section (SDS) implements a policy that supports widely accessible learning opportunities that are coordinated by local offices and by functional areas, such as protection.

Learning goals: The common learning goal for all participants is to develop skills in providing and coordinating staff development for their colleagues, whether in UNHCR or in partner organisations.

Participants in FOLP identify their own specific learning goals, depending on their needs and situation.

These goals may include acquiring the skills and knowledge they need to be able to

- prepare, implement and assess a coherent and cost-effective learning plan for all staff in one office, which enables each person to meet their learning needs;
- plan, provide and evaluate technical training (e.g. in computer use);
- develop, implement and evaluate strategies for facilitating learning in a specialised topic (e.g. refugee protection or programme planning) to government officials and NGO staff.

Programme goals: To enable participants

- to strengthen their skills and knowledge in needs assessment, planning and providing learning activities that meet identified needs, choosing appropriate

techniques and technologies, and planning, budgeting and coordinating a learning programme that meets the needs of a disparate group of learners;
- to apply their learning in practice in their own context;
- to build skills in collaborative learning, distance learning, communication and networking to create a corps of learning facilitators throughout the organisation.

Provider Strategies

Overview: The course, which lasts for 18 weeks, combines distance learning and a four-day face-to-face session that takes place in the 12th week.
Needs assessment/preparation: Course development and revision has been guided by consultation, needs assessment and evaluation. SDS initially assessed learning needs through surveys across the organisation.

The selection of participants is based on a detailed application form that enables careful consideration of applicants' readiness for the programme. Applicants must show that they are in a position to facilitate learning, are committed to the programme, have support from their supervisor and will be able to participate fully for the duration of course. Each offering of FOLP comprises two groups, of between 20 and 25 participants in each group, and each group has a facilitator who provides individual and group tutoring and ongoing support. The facilitators are external consultants rather than UNHCR staff members.

Learning materials design: The first version of the course was revised after some initial sessions. Course evaluations and indicators of unmet learning needs guided a subsequent major revision that integrated assessment as an essential element of the course (Oleniuk, 2006). The course is flexible enough to accommodate the needs of those with different levels of facilitation skills, experience and facilitation roles.

Course assignments are designed to enable learners to apply their learning directly to their workplace situations, to work collaboratively with colleagues and to design and facilitate a learning activity during the face-to-face seminar.

Provision of learning: SDS staff screen applications and handle administrative matters, such as preparing and distributing course materials and managing logistics for the face-to-face seminar. The course organiser at SDS helps to develop appropriate responses to difficult situations, follows up with logistical or financial problems and develops guidelines that clarify expectations of participants and facilitators (deVries, 2006).

The FOLP facilitators are primarily responsible for guiding and supporting the learning process. They do this by

- creating a supportive atmosphere for learning by encouraging online discussion, providing feedback, support and assessment of individual and group projects, and enabling groups to develop problem-solving strategies;
- promoting collaborative learning and development of collaboration skills;
- sustaining participants as they encounter difficulties, self-doubt or unfamiliar concepts;

- demonstrating adult learning principles in their practice, so that participants feel more confident in moving away from didactic to participatory approaches;
- providing individualised and group support during the distance learning phase and the face-to-face seminar;
- helping learners to participate at their level of competence and use it as the basis for further learning by making the best use of the resources in the course;
- assessing learning throughout the course and guiding participants as they apply their learning to their work situations;
- notifying SDS of technical problems affecting e-mail communications among learners;
- serving as a liaison between learners and SDS, and advising SDS of situations that require some flexibility or negotiation within the organisation.

Participants are encouraged to be supportive colleagues for each other, as part of the process of developing their skills as facilitators. For example, small groups working on a collaborative learning project often give each other permission to "check-in and check-out", to participate when they can, notify others they will be busy on assignment or out of e-mail contact, provide an informal handover to others in their small group so that they can carry on a task during the person's absence and then catch up after they return. In doing so, they are building on strategies they have developed for maintaining flexibility and continuity in a relatively unpredictable work environment.

Application of learning: Participants apply their learning throughout the course, and prepare a plan for implementing learning in their workplace after they have completed the course. After course completion, follow-up with learners and supervisors monitors transfer of learning to the workplace.

Impact: 92% of participants in the last eight cohorts completed the course successfully. The FOLP "graduates" frequently remain in touch with each other, and often recommend the course to other colleagues. Participants also apply for the course as a result of observing what a colleague has learned from it. By enabling participants from across the organisation to develop their facilitation skills, FOLP has helped UNHCR achieve its goals of making learning opportunities more widely available at every level, and providing accessible learning on issues important to UNHCR for staff, partner organisations and governments.

Lessons learned: The blended learning model that combines distance learning and a face-to-face session provides a more in-depth programme than is possible through using only one of these methods.

Offering a staff development programme that accommodates participants with a range of backgrounds can foster a richer collaborative learning situation in which participants share their specialised areas of expertise and support each other's learning. Continuing personalised facilitation of both group and individual learning is an important factor in ensuring that participants stay with the course despite a heavy workload and difficult circumstances (O'Rourke, 2003 and Wright and Camargo, 2005).

CASE STUDY 3

Women in the Fishing Industry Project (WIFIP)

Learners: Women from the many isolated fishing communities on the shores of Lake Victoria who struggle to make a living buying and selling small quantities of fish. As females in a male-dominated industry and culture, they are very vulnerable to fishermen's economic, social and sexual exploitation.

Learner needs: The programme responds to the needs of learners who

- have limited time;
- have limited literacy and numeracy skills;
- are involved in the same occupation;
- have practical prior knowledge;
- need skills and knowledge to enable them to have sustainable livelihoods;
- are oriented more towards group than individual learning.

Provider: The provider, the WIFIP Trust, evolved as a result of the initiative of Jennipher Kere, an MA student who research identified the needs of women in the fishing industry on Lake Victoria. Initially supported by International Extension College (IEC) and funded by The Big Lottery, the WIFIP Trust "exists to build a community in which anyone, and women in particular, is empowered and equipped with the necessary capacities to lead socially and economically prosperous lives" (Kere, 2003 quoted in Binns, 2004). The programme began on a project basis: WIFIP has since become an NGO focusing on education development that continues to provide non-formal, community-based distance learning.

Learners' goals: To acquire functional literacy status, entrepreneurship and life skills and ultimately to develop business management skills that they need to sustain themselves and their families in a self-sufficient way, and to lead healthy lives.

Programme goals:

- to use non-formal education to enable the women to develop a voice in their communities;
- to initiate socio-economic changes that enable participants to achieve self-sufficiency and improve community health;
- to build women's capacity in running small business enterprises in the fishing industry;
- to develop the capacity of women to have a voice in decision-making processes;
- to promote positive behaviour change in order to reduce and control water-borne and sexually transmitted infections and diseases.

Provider Strategies

Overview: WIFIP Trust provides a non-formal, community-based distance education programme delivered in Dholuo language using print, radio, audio and face-to-face support.

Preparation/needs assessment: WIFIP developed relationships with identified communities (including women fish traders, Beach Management Units and local government representatives) to explain the underlying principles and obtain support for the programme.

In the initial phase, there were eight learning groups of about 20 women each, based on existing social groups. WIFIP conducted a needs assessment that yielded data on awareness of and approach to the following:

- the use of elementary business practices;
- saving habits;
- hygiene and sanitation;
- diseases such as STIs, HIV and AIDS;
- women's rights including reproductive and children's rights.

Learning materials design: In consultation with participants, WIFIP developed a two-year informal learning programme that uses radio, audiotape and print to provide health, business and rights education.

The curriculum comprising five blocks of learning: two on Business Skills and Savings, two on Health Issues and one on Women's Rights, was developed into a story line based on the life experiences of people in fishing communities (Binns, 2006).

All materials are designed to accommodate varying levels of literacy. Broadcast radio dramas in the Dholuo language, created with participants' input, audiotapes and illustrated print materials are all resources for guided discussions and tutorials. Some of these materials have been translated into Kiswahili and English at the request of interested parties.

Provision of learning: Radio programmes in drama format are broadcast twice a week in Dholuo language. Participant groups receive audiocassettes of the programmes and illustrated booklets/flipcharts and discuss issues that arise from the programmes and materials. Discussions help to reiterate particular issues in the drama. These 15 minute programmes form the basis for group discussions that each last about two hours.

The women identify their own group leaders, who receive training in facilitation and leadership skills from WIFIP. These trained group leaders facilitate group learning using an easy-to-use facilitators' handbook. After each learning session, participants provide feedback that is then used in the production of feedback programmes broadcast on the radio and audiotapes for the groups.

Application of learning:

Participants are able to apply their learning in several ways. The learning groups and the wider community are invited to express opinions and share their stories in the project's newsletter "Samaki News", and to record music for the radio programmes.

Participants are involved in organising events for the wider community, such as Beach Days that combine socialising through sports, music and theatre performances and opportunities for free health services provided in collaboration with the Ministry of

Health and private pharmacies. This helps to build support and awareness of the programme, and to encourage others to participate.

Participants also benefit from mutual support:

> Within the groups, the more literate assist the less literate, and it seems that skill levels have improved, driven by the need to improve business and the desire to improve understanding of preventive health care.
>
> (Binns, 2004)

Once they have completed the business programmes, participants draw up simple business plans, and they can take part in the project's microcredit scheme to strengthen or expand their business, or engage in alternative income generating activities to support them when the fishery is not operating.

Impact: The programme has had a profound impact on the lives of the women as well as on their community. The radio programmes are successful because they tell the stories of people who live in fishing communities, and because they reach the wider community. The women are taking what they have learned and putting it into practice. They are working towards improving their businesses, resisting the fishermen's demands, increasing their savings, and they are now healthier and more confident.

> A wide audience has been primed, while a smaller group has been given the basic training that enables them to become valued members of their local community and the focus of change.
>
> (Binns, 2004)

A mid-point evaluation of the project confirmed that it had achieved its main goals (Fentiman et al., 2003). The programme for women in fisheries continues, and the WIFIP NGO has expanded programmes in topic areas, participant groups and geographical reach, to include Kitchen Gardening and Nutrition, a Poverty Alleviation Programme for Kisumu City, and an HIV/AIDS Positive Living Project. WIFIP also provides assistance for men who want to participate in learning programmes and support groups (Kere, personal communication, 2006).

Lessons learned: As the following quotes illustrate, the success of WIFIP is based on consultation and responsiveness to learning needs, ongoing participation by learners in the direction of the process, links to the wider community which in turn generate support, flexibility in design and implementation, and using radio, a medium that has a far-reaching impact.

The programme is "about finding a way to make things happen, rather than being restricted by a design that dictates how the programme should be" (Kere and McCulloch, 2003 and Binns, 2004).

The project's strength was that it operated on the principle that planners had to be "very flexible and recognise that they must look beyond the core of the programme to facilitate development, by enabling the participants to forge ahead according to their own needs and vision" (Kere and McCulloch, 2003 and Binns, 2005).

CASE STUDY 4

Equal Access to Open Learning (EATOL)

Learners: Adults with long-term illnesses and disabilities, and carers, whose situation prevents participation in onsite learning or in a tightly scheduled ODL.

Learner needs: The programme responds to the needs of learners who have

- a need for a learning programme that is adaptable to their specific situations;
- health or disability challenges, and/or substantial commitments as carers;
- limited time available for learning;
- a range of prior learning experiences and potential gaps in learning or qualifications;
- a range of learning styles and preferred approaches to learning;
- limited access to transportation or computer communication.

Provider: National Extension College (NEC) is a well-established distance learning provider in the United Kingdom whose brief includes course development and course provision for adult learners engaged in studies in academic, professional, occupational and interest areas. The EATOL project comprises two projects. Distance Learning for People with Disabilities provides access to open learning for people with long-term ill-health and disabilities. The Carer's Distance Learning Project provides access for people with carer responsibilities. Both programmes provide additional support customised to learner needs.

Learning goals: Participants have a range of goals, including

- to complete a short academic programme or courses;
- to test their ability to study a specific subject area;
- to take the first step towards a programme of study leading to a qualification or employment opportunities;
- to satisfy the need for an external interest beyond the home context.

Programme goals: These include

- to enable people who had not previously had access to learning to participate in distance learning courses;
- to provide increased support customised to learners' needs as a strategy for enhancing access to successful learning experiences;
- to develop and test models of providing access to learning for people with disabilities and people with caring responsibilities, and to demonstrate the viability of these models.

Provider Strategies

Overview: NEC worked in partnership with the Princess Royal Trust for Carers and nine Carers' Centres in the region to plan and implement the project. NEC has a very broad range of distance learning courses, and the course materials used were the same as those provided to conventional NEC learners. EATOL projects focus on providing the level of support and flexibility that learners need in order to succeed in an NEC course, given their particular circumstances. The Carers' Centres provide a local access point for information about the programmes and initial advising and support.

Preparation/needs assessment: The project needs assessment by NEC and the Princess Royal Trust for Carers identified learners' needs for flexible provision and support tailored to their specific needs. Flexible provision includes more time to complete assignments, help in strengthening basic skills and consistent encouragement in dealing with challenging situations.

Pre-enrolment advice and guidance provided through the Carers' Centres and NEC gives applicants a chance to discuss their situation and their interests in learning, to consider their learning goals, and to look at sample course materials. Pre-enrolment assessment of applicants to the 2006 programme entails completing a piece of work, such as some activities from the course materials, part of an assignment or some written work. This assessment helps to ensure that the learner enrols in a course that is within their capability.

Learning materials design: The learning materials are essentially the same course materials that are available for other NEC distance learners.[1]

In previous years, EATOL learners chose courses leading to a GCSE qualification (secondary school completion), courses related to their caring role, work-related courses and interest courses. Creative writing was the most popular course.

There were no special adaptations of the course materials, although NEC can provide courses in large print.

Provision of learning: Cohorts of learners in the EATOL projects are relatively small, about 100–150. They receive support from

- a mentor, who helps learners deal with challenges that impede learning, such as illness, and crisis situations;
- a tutor, who provides support tailored to individual learning needs, and who can provide some flexibility in scheduling when needed;
- local carers' centres, who publicise the project, provide some initial advising, help learners to enrol and host study days for learners.

Eligible learners also receive some funding support to help them obtain access to computers.

Application of learning: Many participants in the carers' project were able to apply their learning to their carer role. Some learners were able to build on an interest, for example, in creative writing, and publish their work.

Impact: Over half the participants in the 2003–2005 projects achieved significant goals, such as completing the course successfully, moving on to further study or moving into employment.

As well, many participants

- reported that the learning experience had improved their lives and enabled them to cope better with their situation;
- gained enough confidence to move on to a higher-level course;
- identified an interest or talent that they followed after the initial course;
- overcame isolation and low self-esteem as a result of the learning experience;
- developed longer-term goals that they planned to pursue.

As the project evaluator notes, "experience has shown that criteria such as completion of a course, qualification gained or length of time to complete do not adequately measure success for student carers. Many of the perceived benefits and successes reported ... would disappear or even appear as negative outcomes under an analysis that is not sensitive to the particular circumstances of carers." Provision of tutoring and mentoring at a distance is less costly, at least as effective, and more accessible for learners than the alternative: home visit support for house-bound learners who are studying course materials provided by a conventional institution (Edmunds, personal communication, 2005).

As a result of the demonstrated value of the EATOL projects, renewed funding will allow these initiatives to continue at least until 2009.

Lessons learned: Initial consultation and a prior assessment of learners enables learners to choose a course they can manage and provides valuable information to tutors about learners' needs. A requirement that learners develop learning plans should be treated with sensitivity and flexibility. A learning plan can provide a useful framework for learning but can create added pressure for learners already under stress. Learning plans should enable ongoing discussion between learner and tutor, and should be flexible, so that they can be changed in response to a learner's situation.

Making course materials fully accessible requires some adaptations, such as making print materials available on audio for those who are visually impaired.

A commitment to meeting a broader range of learning needs involves a reassessment of conventional definitions of success, such as completion rates or cost-effectiveness. It must take into account the broader social impact of enabling participation in learning for people in challenging situations. (For example, there are about 5 million carers in the United Kingdom who could potentially benefit from a programme like this. (Edmunds, 2003; Edmunds and west, 2003; Mares, 2005; Tarry, personal communication, 2005; and crowley, personal communication, 2006))

6.3 CONCLUSION

As the examples show, meeting diverse learning needs involves addressing those characteristics of learners that make their learning experience different in some way from an established norm. What is considered the established norm has changed in the recent history of distance education, and this in turn changes definitions of diversity. Thirty years ago, face-to-face education was an established norm, and distance education itself represented a different practice serving learners in a different way. Now that distance education has become part of mainstream provision in many places, diverse learning needs can be identified more specifically.

What is considered "difference" may be based on any of the many factors that prompt people to learn at a distance: distance from a conventional provider; social or economic exclusion that has limited a person's prior learning opportunities; work and/or family obligations that make conventional face-to-face learning impossible; and a physical condition that makes face-to-face learning or travel difficult. But in addition to the factors that affect whether or not people have the opportunity to learn, difference can also refer to the next layer of factors – those that affect how people learn. These can include

- learning approaches or learning skills that are not those anticipated by planners;
- a learner's cultural context that is different from the one that planners anticipated, or that planners assumed was compatible with the cultural assumptions of the course;
- language skills that are not the same as those assumed in the course design;
- background knowledge in the subject area that is not the same as assumed in the course design; and
- learners' life challenges (family, home conditions, medical conditions) that require more flexibility and support than planners may have anticipated as "the norm".

Addressing this layer of diversity involves a conscious effort to identify what specific learners need in order to be successful, and how to meet those needs through course design, administrative processes and learner support. But an underlying issue for any provider is to consider its own mandate, the characteristics of the learners it intends to serve and how to meet their learning needs in a way that is effective and feasible. The examples selected demonstrate the importance of considering these underlying questions first, and of deciding how meeting diverse learning needs matches the providers' mandate. This may be through special projects that provide opportunities to develop and test strategies for meeting specific learning needs, and for including improvements in subsequent projects. Another approach is one that is based on the providers' central mandate and is supported by core funding.

Distance education practice that meets diverse learning needs in a sustained way requires providers to

- examine the implications of its mandate and interpret what it means to meet learners' needs;
- be clear about their goals in meeting diverse learning needs;
- identify what is feasible and not feasible in its efforts to meet diverse learning needs and communicate this clearly and honestly to prospective learners;
- respect learners' indications of their own learning needs;

- carefully track the effect of strategies on meeting learning needs they were intended to address, as well as unintended outcomes;
- sustain an institutional memory about meeting diverse learning needs by documenting lessons learned about effective and ineffective practices, including information about the contexts in which they were applied and the learning needs they were intended to meet.

Learners also have an important role in helping distance education providers meet their learning needs by

- articulating their learning needs as clearly as they can;
- providing honest feedback to the provider about which strategies are most helpful in meeting their learning needs;
- remaining open to new approaches to learning, and identifying what help they need in order to try new approaches.

Advocates for learners (including advocates for learners with disabilities, social agencies, representatives of cultural or language groups) can help by

- working with learners to compile information about their learning needs, based on valid observation, tests and research information;
- supporting communication with providers that clarifies reasonable expectations about meeting learning needs;
- working in consultation with providers to provide any supplementary support that can help learners achieve their learning goals (e.g. the involvement of Carers' Centres in the NEC programme for caregivers, or local schools that serve as learning centres).

Tutors, as those with most direct contact with learners, can support the process by

- clarifying with learners their learning needs and goals;
- identifying any learning need that requires specific attention;
- communicating with the provider about patterns of learning needs among learner groups that the provider should consider addressing;
- recommending strategies for addressing specific learning needs, including tutoring and learning support strategies, administrative strategies and course design changes.

As Lentell (2003) has pointed out, tutors do not always have the ear of the organisation's decision makers, especially if the organisation is large and complex. Tutors and others in direct contact with learners can provide essential input to those who plan courses, support systems and special initiatives to serve diverse learning needs. As well, providers need to assess how well their practice matches their commitment to meet diverse learning needs and how well each strategy to meet learner needs is achieving its goals. If there is this kind of link between practitioners who work directly with learners and those who plan how best to serve learners, it is more likely that the organisation will choose strategies that are based on a clear understanding of learner needs. Meeting diverse learning needs is also consistent with sustainability. As both Gibbs (2003) and Simpson (2003, 2005) have pointed out, keeping learners is much more cost-effective than continually recruiting new learners, especially in funding models based on completion rates. Simpson (2005) cites examples showing the cost-effectiveness of proactive learner support, encouraging support for learners from their family and friends and providing resources that help learners make better course choices. As both project funding and core funding for education are increasingly linked to learning outcomes, meeting diverse learning needs would mean that providers, in enabling learners to achieve their goals, would also be able to sustain their programmes and their own organisation.

As ODL commits to serving an expanding range of diverse learners, there is an implied commitment to address their distinctive needs appropriately. This may require some rethinking of what is meant by appropriate provision, in the same way that dual-mode providers have had to rethink their strategy of offering services to distance learners only if they arrived in person at the institution's door.

NOTE

1. Each year, there are about 20,000 learners taking NEC courses directly through NEC, and an additional 200,000 learners who use NEC learning materials at schools and colleges.

REFERENCES

Anderson, L. and Spronk, B. (2000). Audiences for Basic education at a distance. In *Basic Education at a Distance* (C. Yates and J. Bradley, eds) London: Routledge.

Bates, A. W. (1995). *Technology, Open Learning and Distance Education.* Routledge: London.

Binns, F. (2004). *Learning Communities and Participation in Appropriate Education: The Women in Fishing Industry Project*, Paper presented at the Third Pan-Commonwealth Forum on Open Learning, Dunedin, New Zealand July 2004.

Binns, F. (n.d.) (2006). *Non Formal Education Radio Project in Kenya* http://www.harare.unesco.org/wgnfe_edf/bestpractices-pub.htm [accessed on October8, 2006]

Binns, F. (2005). Approaches to the challenges of literacy and livelihoods in Africa. In *Literacy and Livelihoods: Learning for Life in a Changing World Commonwealth of Learning*, Vancouver. http://www.col.org/colweb/webdev/site/myjahiasite/shared/docs/L&Lpublicationweb.pdf, accessed November 15, 2007.

Crowley, S. (2006). Personal Communication.

Daniel, J. (1996) *Mega-Universities and the Knowledge Media: Technology Strategies for Higher Education.* London: Kogan Page.

deVries, F. (2006). Personal Communication.

Dhanarajan, G. (1994). *Student Support Services: The First Challenge for Distance Education*, unpublished contribution to the International Commission on distance education in South Africa.

Edmunds, M. (2003). Distance learning for people with disabilities and caring responsibilities, www.nec.ac.uk [accessed on November 14, 2005].

Edmunds, M. *The Carer's Distance Learning Project*, www.nec.ac.uk [accessed on November 14, 2005, November 19, 2007].

Edmunds, M. (2005 and 2006). Personal Communication.

Edmunds, M and West, A. (2005). Involving part-time tutors in reflective practice. In *Reflective Practice in Open and Distance Learning: How do We Improve?* Proceedings of the 11th Cambridge International Conference on Open and Distance Learning.

Fentiman, A, Ochieng, M., and Othero, D. (2003). *WIFIP Evaluation.* Cambridge: IEC.

Franklin, U. (1999). *The Real World of Technology.* Totonto: Anansi..

Gibbs, G. (2003). The future of student retention in Open and Distance Learning. In *The Future of Open and Distance Learning*, Proceedings of the 10th Cambridge International Conference on Open and Distance Learning.

Gibbs, G. and Simpson, C. (2002). How assessment influences student learning, Student Support Research Group, http://www2.open.ac.uk/cehep/ssrg/reports/documents/42_02.pdf, accessed November 15, 2007.

Glennie, J. (1995). *Towards Learner-Centred Distance Education in the Changing South African Context*, Paper presented at Putting the Student First: Learner Centred Approaches in Open and distance Learning, Cambridge International Conference on Open and Distance Learning.

Goodwyn-Davey, A. (2006). Institute for Curriculum and Learning Development Unisa, Personal communication

Haughey, M. (1995b). Re-examining distance: losing distinctions, retaining difference, In *One World, Many Voices*, Proceedings of the International Council on Open and Distance Learning.

Holmberg, B. (1982). *Essentials of Distance Education.* Fernuniversitat: Hagen.

Innis, H. (1951). *The Bias of Communications.* Toronto: University of Toronto Press.

Kere, J. (2006). Personal Communication.

Kere, J. and McCulloch, V. (2003). *Radio and Audio Technology in Non-Formal Education: A Case Study of Women in the Fishing Industry Project*, Kisumu, Kenya. Paper presented at the 10th Cambridge Conference.

Lentell, H. (1994) Why is it so hard to hear the tutor in open and distance learning? *Open Learning*, **9**(3) 49–52.

Lentell, H. (2003). The importance of the tutor in open and distance learning. In *Rethinking Learner Support in Distance Education, Change and Continuity in an International Context* (A. Tait and R. Mills, eds) London: Routledge/Falmer.

McLoughlin, C. and Oliver, R. (2000). Designing learning environments for cultural inclusivity: A case study of indigenous online learning at tertiary level. *Australian Journal of Educational Technology*, **16**(1), 58–72, accessed Nov. 1, 2005 at http://www.ascilite.org.au/ajet/ajet16/mcloughlin.html

Mares, P. (2005). Making Learning Accessible to Unpaid Carers, Independent Evaluation of Carers' Distance Learning Project.

Mills, R. (2003). The centrality of learner support in open and distance learning: A paradigm shift in thinking. In *Rethinking Learner Support in Distance Education, Change and Continuity in an International Context* (A. Tait and R. Mills, eds) London: Routledge/Falmer.

Mitchell, J. (2005). Can writing skills be taught at a distance? In *Reflective Practice in Open and Distance Learning: How do We Improve?* Proceedings of the 11th Cambridge International Conference on Open and Distance Learning.

Nonyongo, E. (2003). Changing Entrenched Learner Support Systems: Vision and Reality. In *Rethinking Learner Support in Distance Education, Change and Continuity in an International Context* (A. Tait and R. Mills, eds) London: Routledge/Falmer.

Nothling, M. (2006). Institute for Curriculum and Learning Development Unisa, Personal Communication.

Oleniuk, C. (2006) Personal Communication.

O'Rourke, J. (2003). Lost and found, open learning outside the doors of academe. In *Rethinking Learner Support in Distance Education, Change and Continuity in an International Context* (A. Tait, and R. Mills, eds) London: Routledge/Falmer.

Pennells, J. (2003). Challenges in adjusting to new technology in supporting learners in developing countries. In *Rethinking Learner Support in Distance Education, Change and Continuity in an International Context* (A. Tait and R. Mills, eds) London: Routledge/Falmer.

Rumble, G. (1986). *The Planning and Management of Distance Education*, London: Croom Helm

Rumble, G. (2001). The costs and costing of networked learning. *Journal of Asynchronous Learning Networks*, 75–96, http://www.aln.org/publications/jaln/v5n2/v5n2_rumble.asp, accessed November 19, 2007.

Simpson, O. (2000). *Supporting Students in Open and Distance Education*, London: Kogan Page.

Simpson, O. (2003). *The Impact on Retention of Interventions to Support Distance Learning Students*, Paper prepared for symposium, Student retention in open and distance learning May 2003, OU Knowledge Network, www.open.ac.uk [accessed on November 23, 2005].

Simpson, O. (2004). The Impact on Retention of Interventions to Support Distance Learning Students, *Open Learning*, **19**(1), 79–95.

Simpson, O. (2005). Reflection or deflection: What's the evidence that we learn from evidence? In *Reflective Practice in Open and Distance Learning: How do We Improve?* Proceedings of the 11th Cambridge International Conference on Open and Distance Learning.

Staff Development Section. (2003). UNHCR Learning Policy and Guidelines, Parameters for the Enhancement of Staff Development in UNHCR.

Student Support Research Group, Student Vulnerability and Retention Project, http://www2.open.ac.uk/cehep/ssrg/reports/documents/40_02.pdf [accessed on March 31, 2003].

Tait, A. (2000). Planning student support for open and distance learning. *Open Learning*, **15**(3), 287–299.

Tait, A. (2003). Rethinking learner support in the open university UK. In *Rethinking Learner Support in Distance Education* (A. Tait and R. Mills, eds) London: Routledge/Falmer.

Tarry, R. (2005). Personal Communication.

Wong, A. (1998). *An Evaluation of the Internet-Based Math Readiness Course Trial*, Research report prepared for the Office of Learning Technologies, Human Resources Development Canada.

Wong, A. (1999). *Promoting the Effective Learning of Mathematics Among Aboriginal Adults: A Community-Based Adaptation of the MRC Package for the Internet*, Research report prepared for the Office of Learning Technologies, Human Resources Development Canada.

Wright, C. and Camargo, F. (2005). *Evaluation of Protection Learning Program*, EPAU2005/07, retrieved October 23, 2006 from www.unhcr.org.

FURTHER READING

Haughey, M. (1995a). Distinctions in Distance: Is distance education an obsolete term? In *Why the Information Highway: Lessons from Open and Distance Learning* (J. Roberts and M. Keough, eds) Toronto: Trifolium.

MacKeogh, K. (2005). Preparing students for online learning – The oscail experience in reflective practice, In *Open and Distance Learning: how do we Improve?* Proceedings of the 11th Cambridge International Conference on Open and Distance Learning.

Spronk, B. (1995). Appropriating Learning Technologies: Aboriginal Learners, Needs, Practices, In *Why the Information Highway, Lessons from Open and Distance Learning* (J. Roberts, and E. Keough, eds) Toronto: Trifolium.

Chapter 7

Recognizing Experiential Learning Through Prior Learning Assessment

Dianne Conrad

By definition and through practice, distance education has become synonymous with innovative models of program delivery that offer more generous open and flexible learning opportunities to a wider and more diverse audience than did the bricks-and-mortar classroom structures in which most of us were raised. The commonly accepted ways in which open and distance institutions serve a diverse student population center around issues of scheduling and geography, typically allowing easier access to post-secondary education for those who have not previously enjoyed that option. Such opportunities for learner access address the situational, attitudinal, and institutional conditions that have long been described in adult education literature as the types of barriers that prevent adults from realizing their educational dreams (Cross, 1981; Wiesenberg, 2001; Mackeracher, 2005).

The relationship between the concepts of diversity, access, and the issue of facilitating adults' learning through the recognition of their prior learning is both complex and dichotomous. Recognizing learners' prior learning (RPL) may appear to provide solutions to many aspects of traditional, situational, attitudinal, and institutional barriers. RPL, for example, can help gain access to post-secondary study for learners who have been blocked by institutionally erected barriers that deny admission to "unqualified" learners. Such learners, however, may themselves harbor deep-seated and self-undermining insecurities that arise from their not having strong academic backgrounds. In turn, these learners bring that level of attitudinal diversity forward into the RPL process. In short, an uneasy type of teeter-totter balancing exists between the fact of open and distance access and RPL processes, exacerbated by even deeper and more riveting philosophical and social power relationships.

Athabasca University (AU), Canada's open and distance university, celebrates the diversity of its learners' knowledge in many ways, not the least of which is its system of RPL. As a result, its use of RPL processes confronts, and opens the door to, a network of resulting tensions. In this chapter, using AU as a case study, I will outline AU's commitment to distance education, outline AU's prior learning policies and procedures, discuss the fit of prior learning into AU's spectrum of learning activities, and focus on the relationship of AU's prior learning systems to issues of diversity.

7.1 ATHABASCA UNIVERSITY: COMMITTED TO OPEN AND DISTANCE LEARNING

The commitment to serving learners at a distance involves a great deal more than what is quickly and easily visible. While it may appear that the only difference between open and distance institutions such as AU and traditional universities is that ODL institutions do not have learners sitting in campus classrooms, in fact the entire ODL infrastructure is pitched differently in order to accommodate all the facets of distance education. Far-flung faculty often function in isolation, apart from each other and from the ease of handy administrative support. Governance structures must accommodate the physical difficulties wrought by distance that manifest in communication systems and travel arrangements. A justifiably heavy infrastructure handles every business item at a distance, and a justifiably extraordinary student support service arm provides distance learners with the semblance of "being there" through all stages of their programs.

Athabasca University made this commitment in 1970 and, in doing so, established itself as the largest single-mode open and distance university in Canada. Over the years, some of AU's counterparts, such as the Open Learning Agency in British Columbia, have come and gone; conversely and more recently, other dedicated online institutions, such as New Brunswick's Yorkville University, have opened their doors. But 36 years after its incorporation by the Government of Alberta, AU continues to thrive and has doubled its student numbers in the last 6 years, currently serving 34,000 students annually.

Athabasca University's complex infrastructure is designed to oblige the many diverse needs of distance learners. It offers blended and flexible delivery models. Its individualized study courses permit self-paced learning and free learners from specified class schedules. Continuous entry offers year-round study opportunities. Anyone over the age of sixteen is eligible for admission to the University. Programs are designed to allow learners to maintain full-time careers while studying part-time. Study materials are sophisticated and carefully crafted. All student service transactions can be enacted electronically. All AU's library holdings can be downloaded onto mobile learning devices. Taken together, these innovations hallmark a progressive distance learning institution.

In meeting distance learners' needs through its extensive infrastructure and protocols, AU addresses the most obvious needs of its diverse student population. Inherent in its commitment to open learning, however, is another value system that is designed to address a largely unseen diversity – the very wide-ranging and unique educational backgrounds that its learners possess – or, more importantly, that they do *not* possess – as they attempt to move forward to pursue post-secondary university education.

In its mandate and vision statement, AU outlines its commitment to reducing the barriers to achieving a university education. Following on this, it adopts as one of the key pillars of its foundation a process of recognizing learners' prior experiential learning. To implement a coherent and integrated prior learning recognition policy, AU maintains a central office where personnel champion, direct, and manage the various processes that constitute the RPL enterprise. The existence of such an internal and integrated structure makes AU somewhat unique among Canadian universities; the size of its operation places it at the forefront of university prior learning practice in Canada.

7.2 PRIOR LEARNING ASSESSMENT AND RECOGNITION: THEORY AND PRACTICE

The recognition of prior learning is practiced globally as a means of honoring and building on mature learners' past experiential learning. UNESCO provides this short and effective definition of RPL: "The formal acknowledgement of skills, knowledge, and competencies that are gained through work experience, informal training, and life experience" (Vlăsceanu et al., 2004, p. 55). Grounded in ancient philosophies, Western educators can look back to a more recent history in the work of Pestalozzi and Dewey, who presented sound pedagogical rationales for recognizing adults' experiential learning: "The beginning of instruction shall be made with the experience learners already have ... this experience and the capacities that have been developed during its course provide the starting point for all further learning" (Dewey, 1938, p. 74).

Dewey's advocacy of a progressive philosophy that promoted real-world learning echoes through the work of many adult educators. In Canada, Moses Coady, Jimmy Tompkins, and Alfred Fitzpatrick were among those whose parallel views were instrumental in bringing educational opportunities to the oppressed and poverty-stricken. Farther abroad, Paolo Freire's work with farm workers in South America rested on the foundational premise of their experiential learning. More recently, in exploring transformational learning across the span of adults' lives, Welton (1995) cited Mezirow's understanding of the role of educators in helping learners mine their past for reflexive learning. The educator's role, Mezirow holds, involved these three inter-related activities: (1) helping self and others engage in reflection; (2) helping self and others redefine premises; and (3) helping self and others decide how to act on new insights and understandings (Welton, 1995). In this declaration, Mezirow worked toward giving experiential learning value as an active-learning occasion by implicating the teaching role in the re-creation of learners' pasts.

World-wide, educators' beliefs in the value of adults' prior learning are reflected in the practice of RPL, also understood as accreditation of experiential and prior learning (AEPL) or the accreditation of prior learning (APL). Within the broad parameters of RPL, there exist a number of more specific procedures that address various types of prior learning. Adults' prior learning opportunities are generally classified according to their origins, that is, according to whether the learning has been obtained formally, at recognized post-secondary institutions, or whether the learning has resulted from situations or environments outside formal institutions (Selman et al., 1998).

Credentials obtained from study at recognized post-secondary institutions are usually considered for transfer credit or qualification recognition at other post-secondary institutions. Transfer agreements among institutions exist to standardize the movement of credit from one institution to another, usually simplifying, for learners, accessibility to post-secondary credentials within established jurisdictions.

Non-formal and informal learning acquired by learners through training, workplace offerings, from non-accredited institutions, or simply from life's lessons, is generally not recognized for transfer by accredited post-secondary institutions. It is this type of learning that provides the material for the sub-area of RPL that is generally referred to as prior learning assessment and recognition (PLAR). In past years, PLAR was more commonly referred to as prior learning assessment (PLA). The addition of the "R" was designed to emphasize the final outcome of the assessment process through which learners' experiential learning is recognized – and, in that way, awarded credit toward post-secondary studies (Thomas, 1998).

The RPL and PLAR are large and complex concepts that currently do not enjoy much common understanding in Canada's post-secondary sector. The schema that is presented here, while fairly common, is not universally accepted. However, as this is the definitional structure on which AU bases its implementation of PLAR policy, this will be the understanding that frames the language of this chapter's discussion.

7.2.1 Prior Learning Assessment and Recognition at Athabasca University

Athabasca University's support of PLAR as a vehicle through which to recognize and accredit learners' prior and experiential learning is firmly rooted in the university's mission statement which captures its vision as an open and distance institution. As an open university, it is generous in its allocation of credit for formal transferred learning. AU also maintains a policy that guides applications from non-accredited institutions, largely private colleges and training institutions, through a rigorous process of evaluation.

The recognition of informal and non-formal learning, however, is addressed by AU's PLAR policy, with its focus on the assessment of learning. AU's implementation of PLAR through two channels, challenge-for-credit and portfolio assessment, reflect the field's general understanding of the two practices for PLAR implementation, challenge and equivalency (Ontario Ministry of Education, 2001). Although many Canadian universities have policies that clearly outline their PLAR processes, AU is one of very few universities in Canada that actively practice PLAR and perhaps one of only three Canadian universities that support a central office to manage university-wide PLAR implementation.

Athabasca University established its PLAR office as the Centre for Learning Accreditation (CLA) in 1997. Working collaboratively with programs across the university, CLA's first director created criteria for program-based learning outcomes for all of AU's programs.[1]

During this process, each program determined the maximum number of PLAR-awarded credits that was judged to be appropriate, given the configuration of the program, its purpose, and the nature of its studentship. Therefore, while some 120-credit degree programs offer a maximum of 30 potential PLAR credits, other 90-credit degree programs may offer only a maximum of six potential PLAR credits. A consistent variance also exists between degree program requirements and requirements for corresponding post-diploma degree programs, thus addressing the fact that learners entering a post-diploma degree program have already been awarded up to a maximum of 60 credits toward their degree requirements for the diploma credential that they hold.[2]

The implementation of PLAR, at AU and at other educational institutions that practice PLAR, encompasses both portfolio assessment and challenge-for-credit processes. Diverse understandings of the PLAR lexicon result in different types of applications of these practices among institutions. At AU, the CLA office is responsible for the university-wide implementation, management, and marketing of PLAR-by-portfolio assessment. Challenge-for-credit processes are currently handled collaboratively by personnel in the Office of the Registrar and faculty responsible for the course about to be challenged.[3]

7.2.2 Portfolio-based PLAR

Applicants wishing to receive credit for their prior experiential learning may choose to present their knowledge for assessment in the form of a portfolio. With the use of guidelines, templates, and examples, applicants assemble portfolios in which they document their learning histories and display the knowledge they claim to have in text form, supported by well-referenced documentation. The many parts of the portfolio – including a learning narrative, a resume, and a statement of educational goals – create a large collection of carefully chosen artifacts and reflexive pieces. Candidates pursue either a program-based or course-based approach, depending on which program they are enrolled in or how they feel their learning is best demonstrated. The CLA provides learners with both information and coaching by means of paper and electronic materials.

When portfolios are received by the CLA, they enter into a long process that includes pre-vetting and distribution to a team of assessors who have been selected according to the subject expertise demanded by the contents of the portfolio. Assessors follow explicit criteria in making their assessments and return their judgments to the CLA for review and compilation. As a final part of the process, CLA personnel determine the "fit" of assessors' suggested credit awards into the applicants' AU programs, ensure that all program requirements are accommodated, and notify both learners and appropriate university departments of the PLAR decision. The entire process can take as long as 6 months and is subject to the appropriate appeals process if PLAR recipients are dissatisfied with their results.

7.2.3 Challenge-for-credit

Athabasca University learners may choose, instead of preparing, a portfolio that demonstrates their knowledge through the selection, reflection, connection, and projection of learning artifacts, to target a specific course for which they feel they already possess the required knowledge or skills. Working with the course professor, they engage in a contractual relationship to meet the challenge conditions that have been pre-established for the course.

Both challenge-for-credit and PLAR-by-portfolio processes are well defined by AU policies and procedures. By university standards, both are generous in the opportunities they offer to learners as alternative avenues for achieving course credits. Each process is clearly designed to reduce barriers to educational accessibility and allow learners to progress toward their goals as quickly as they can. More than that, however, AU's prior learning options are testaments to its acceptance and recognition of the endless diversity manifested by its learners.

7.3 PLAR AND THE RECOGNITION OF DIVERSITY

As played out in classroom situations, diversities are most often recognized and acknowledged based on visual clues or other very tangible evidence. Racial, ethnic, and gender diversities are often not difficult to identify, although observing the fact of diversity is only the first step in comprehending how those diversities contribute to an individual's sense of self. Without prioritizing types of diversity, or their relative importance to each other, it can be said that some types of diversity are more difficult to identify. Social diversity may be outwardly identifiable by wardrobe or other items related to material acquisition. But evidence of cultural or political diversities may lurk, unseen or unheard, well hidden in the teaching-learning relationship among peers and instructors.

In distance learning situations, diversities are further obscured by the absence of visual and physical clues. In open learning institutions such as AU, the fact that there are no restrictions to entering the university community increases the potential for diversity even more. The PLAR option, constructed to provide maximum access to university credentials for eligible learners, implicitly invites applicants to bring forth experiential and cognitive diversities and pledges to accommodate those diversities to the degree that such recognition is possible within the university's policy framework.

Although AU maintains the two "arms" of prior learning assessment – PLAR-by-portfolio and challenge-for-credit – through which learners are able to demonstrate their prior knowledge for university credit, it is the portfolio option that accepts most fully the scope and latitude of learners' prior knowledge. The challenge-for-credit option that is also available asks learners to bring forth their knowledge in defined packages that closely resemble the shape of the university's courses. The university professor responsible for a particular course is able to determine what particular package of knowledge will satisfy his or her definition of what the learning outcomes for that course should be. In other words, learners applying to have their prior knowledge recognized in this fashion are obliged to tailor their learning histories to fit into predetermined knowledge clusters that look like AU courses. While this is just one model of PLAR – and an acceptable one – it is not a model that gives learners the opportunity to celebrate or explore their diverse learning histories.

On the other hand, the portfolio approach to PLAR offers learners the possibility of a richer, more self-directed learning experience. Two caveats must be stated here: first, not all learners avail themselves of the pedagogical possibilities offered by the portfolio method. Secondly, the portfolio approach is necessarily guided by sets of university-provided criteria and outcomes. That said, portfolio criteria and outcomes serve as guidelines, as structuring devices, rather than as hard-and-fast targets. They provide signposts around which learners can rally and organize their own learning, rather than stipulating for them what they *must* know in order to be successful in their petition.

7.3.1 Portfolio Assessment

In the portfolio process, learners undertake difficult and complex journeys as they mine the breadth and depth of their learning histories in bringing forward evidence of appropriate university-level learning. On the other end of the process, teams of content experts assume responsibility for assessing that knowledge and for determining its relevance to a learner's current program of study at the university. Assessors are also asked to respond narratively as fully as possible to the learner's portfolio presentation: What was missing? What strengths are displayed? How can the learner best complete his or her program in order to utilize past learning while at the same time remedying any perceived gaps in required knowledge?

As outlined by policy, assessors are looking for a minimum of a 60 percent overlay with either broad program outcomes or more specific course outcomes. The criteria that have been developed by each program contain levels of accomplishment for each listed criterion; roughly speaking, the levels of accomplishment mirror Bloom's Taxonomy. The benchmarks for meeting the stated outcomes reflect primarily the cognitive domain as most university-level learning that is put forward for assessment resides within the cognitive domain rather than in the affective or psycho-motor domains. However, at the program level, some programs have included more generic, or process outcomes, such as decision-making skills, critical thinking skills, or team communication skills.[4]

Assessors have a number of tools at their disposal to assist in the difficult assessment process. The relative ease or difficulty levels of their task hinges, of course, on how well learners have put forward their cases in their portfolios. Although a well-done portfolio can grow to become a formidable size, PLAR applicants are expected to have observed guidelines that caution again needless repetition, irrelevant documentation, or sloppy organization. It is incumbent upon the applicant to present a well-organized document that holds within it an appropriate structure and keys to finding one's way through that structure. To this end, portfolios end up often being three-inch binders with many colorful dividers and tabs to create direction and clarity.[5]

The central part of the portfolio comprises learners' collection of learning statements wherein, using Bloom's taxonomic verb structure, they arrange and display their knowledge in text form to satisfy the stated criteria. They meet the criteria using examples from their pasts that they have deemed relevant. Assessors triangulate learners' claims using a number of other documents within the portfolio: the resume, which outlines the learner's history chronologically; a statement of educational and career goals, contextualizing past learning, present endeavors, and future aspirations; and the largest piece, the autobiographical narrative, in which the writer makes sense of his or her past experiences and links them to occasions of learning, to insights, and to the creation of the current career path. A transcript of past formal learning and program progress is also included.

A large part of any portfolio is composed of documentation that learners use to validate their learning claims. Documentation can consist of copies of awards, certifications, commendations, and the like. The more telling documentation are the Letters of Attestation, which are templated letters written on behalf of the candidate by those in positions to speak to the learning or skills that the applicant claims to have. These are usually supervisors or mentors. The Letter of Attestation is critically important to assessment. Substantially different from a reference letter, it must speak clearly and with authority to the demonstrated ability of the applicant to perform or to have performed, using the knowledge in question. Using all these vehicles, assessors move back and forth through the portfolio, holding up the applicants' claims of learning against the body of evidence that supports those claims. They note areas of excellence and achievement as well as areas of "not quite" as they corroborate learning with learners' insights and reflections about their learning and how that learning has contributed to performance and to personal and professional growth.[6]

Ultimately, the assessors' feedback reaches the CLA office. In most cases, three assessors independently review a learner's portfolio. Their input will identify either specific courses for which they feel the applicant should be given credit or a course area for which they feel the applicant should be awarded credit; how much credit the applicant should receive; courses that the applicant should *not* take, considering his or her areas of demonstrated strength; or courses or areas of study that they feel the applicant should incorporate into his or her program. Assessors also provide narrative commentary on the portfolio.

7.4 RECOGNIZING LEARNING, ACKNOWLEDGING DICHOTOMY

The portfolio process at AU is rigorously designed and carefully executed. While the challenge-for-credit process has less "design" built into it, it too provides a much-used vehicle for honoring mature learners' prior learning. Still, underneath these attempts to give adequate voice to experiential learning sits an inherent contradiction that is well understood by PLAR devotees and critics alike. Validating learners' experience, Avis warrants (1995), could actually be a "conservative practice". Avis is not alone in asking the question, how are learners positioned within [institutional] notions of knowledge, experience and practice? As a corollary to the issue of "fit" within the institutional paradigm, both Harris and Avis also acknowledge that experience is not neutral. "An alternative is to see it as partial, socially constructed, highly contextualised and as already embodying knowledge" (Harris, 1999). Further exacerbating the unevenness resulting from learners' disparate experiential bases are the various discourses within which learners are situated. Harris (1999) explained the problems that her institution identified as a result of these conditions:

> In effect... we required candidates who could write with authority in distinct genres and who could hold to a reflective/academic discourse. Candidates with different holding discourses (for example, narrative, corporate, customary) or no particular holding discourse, were less successful. We expected that... we could "move the Diploma discourse into people's heads, experientially"... we also floundered because we did not have the tools, authority (or perhaps even the desire) to, in effect, re-engineer the Diploma curriculum.
>
> (p. 125)

Fenwick (2006) summed it up well with this analogy: "When learning is understood to be continuously co-emergent with persons and environment... it simply makes no sense to treat knowledge as a product that is carried around like a handbag, able to spill its contents upon request by RPL assessors" (p. 298). Similarly, Michelson (1996) reflected on the nature of the self in creating, from experience, appropriate demonstrations of learning for portfolio assessment: "Where, precisely, are we standing when we "reflect," and what kind of self is constructed in the process?" (p. 449).

In like fashion, at AU, where a PLAR process has been built to respect and accommodate diversities in applicants' educational backgrounds, it is likely the process itself invites the realization of more fundamental diversities among learners as they attempt to "spill" their learning into an institutionally acceptable discourse. The fact that the institution tries to make *explicit* the academic standard to which applicants are striving does not in any substantial way lessen the contradiction.

I have outlined, thus far, an ironic tension wherein a process that was set in place to accommodate diversity, in an institution that exists to celebrate and receive diversity, places learners in the middle of a philosophical debate around issues of social diversity, empowerment, and the nature of knowledge. What learner could possibly foresee stepping into this dilemma upon engaging in the PLAR process? More to the point, how does an institution such as AU that is committed to reducing barriers to access wrestle with an irony that potentially permits barriers to be erected on the shoulders of another type of less explicit diversity?

First of all, it should be made clear that there is neither surprise nor disgrace in the fact that a post-secondary system should exhibit some level of ambiguity. Shale (1987), when writing some years ago about innovation in open universities, observed rather presciently that "the very nature of the open learning enterprise has forced the universities associated with it to be innovative in ways and to an extent rarely realized in conventional universities". He concluded this line of thinking by outlining how actual innovations became juxtaposed with unintended innovations – a natural outcome of simply being innovative. Shale buttressed his argument by pointing out that pioneer distance educator Charles Wedemeyer held that "'openness' is not an absolute quality but rather a range of possibilities". Since, as an open university, AU encompasses a dramatic range of innovative features, it is not surprising that AU's move to diminish diversities among learners has in fact uncovered further layers of diversity. Still, the question remains, what is the university doing about it?

A foundational contribution to this discussion recognizes the argument around social diversity, empowerment, and voice as emanating from the critical pedagogies and radical practices of educators such as Freire (1972) and Illich (1970) who worked for social transformation through changed social structures. More recently, Michelson (2006) and Fenwick (2006) have written compellingly on the role of RPL practices and their relationships to power and the place of experience in knowledge. Without debating the relative merits of radical pedagogy and pointing out its own tendency to silence other voices (Harris, 1999), it can be simply stated that most publicly funded Canadian post-secondary institutions do not operate from – and most probably will never adopt – this philosophical stance. In fact, instead of moving *beyond* "an alliance between the market, individuals and providers [and] toward a broader alliance with group and social interests" (Harris, 1999, p. 135), Canada's post-secondary system has been recently moving the other way, away from the heightened social consciousness of the 1930s and toward market demand.

The political reality of an institution frames, to a large degree, the possibilities that are open to an innovative strategy such as PLAR. Against the backdrop of many types of diversity, the implementation of PLAR has the potential for a wide range of applications. As Usher et al. point out, "it offers a contestable and ambiguous terrain where different socio-economic and cultural assumptions and strategies can be differentially articulated. As a field of tension, it can be exploited by different groups, each emphasising certain dimensions over others" (1997, p. 105). At AU, PLAR administrators work to diminish the effects of potential exploitation, of imbalance, and of exclusion. We do this in the following ways:

Being informed. Understanding the nature of the dichotomy is critical to informed decision-making. Similarly, understanding the nature of the institution within which we work provides another important source of data.

Participating in collegial, informed debate. The university provides democratic, multi-layered fora for discussion and the provocative airing of issues. Through various fora, it is possible, and essential, to keep diversity issues at the forefront.

De-emphasizing the "diarist" element of the PLAR process. There is a tendency, among certain PLAR factions, to over-celebrate the self through extensive personal history activity. That said, Harris (1999) spoke of the relationships between personal biographies for self-therapy and of connecting personal experience to social history in meaningful ways. The challenge lies in finding a balance between the two approaches.

Focusing on critical reflection and meaning-making. At AU, we have found that one of the ways to de-emphasize the diarist approach to portfolios is to structure PLAR instruments that foster critical thinking and encourage the connecting of experiential critical incidents to life choices, especially educationally and professionally. AU's PLAR process has introduced a portfolio component called "framing the issue" wherein applicants are invited to focus critically on how they have come to be where they are – in their lives, in their work, and in their studies. This particular part of the portfolio encourages movement from what Crites (1971) has termed the "mundane" to the "sacred"; understanding experience beyond the isolated, secular level. Helping learners to settle at this level of interpreting their experiences is intended to elevate their stories beyond the confines of some types of diversity. For example, a single mother wrote recently about her demanding personal schedule that included shuttling her sons back and forth to hockey practice and assuming multiple parental roles. In her reflection, she used those experiences to thoughtfully consider the value of her organizational skills and the resultant value she brought to her workplace and to inter-collegial relationships in the workplace. The management-oriented assessors who reviewed her work were very pleased with the elevation of potentially socio-economic specifics to a more generic, and academically relevant, level.

Promoting the PLAR process as a critically reflective learning activity. As an open university, AU offers its students several alternate routes that include the range of RPL activities. Typically, not just at AU but at many post-secondary institutions that challenge traditional learning models, the differences between engaging learners in assessment processes and evaluating past learning for formal credit transfer are not well understood. Following on the establishment of the reflexive vehicle outlined above, by which learners are encouraged to find the "sacred" meaning in their experience, the CLA promotes this PLAR as a process that offers an alternate way of learning.

Developing target criteria that "speak" to a variety of experiential backgrounds. PLAR criteria, especially when expressed at program level, provide learners with a framework that should facilitate their move from Crites' "mundane" to the "sacred". The resultant expression of this deeply thoughtful and complex process is ultimately cognitive in nature. Using Bloom's Taxonomy, writers capture the essence of their learning according to stated criteria. In concert, then, the taxonomy offers the possibility of presenting a hierarchy of demonstrated knowledge while the breadth of well-chosen criteria makes possible the display of a wide range of diverse experiences and backgrounds.

Helping portfolio assessors identify and accept a variety of interpretations of learning. The last part of the portfolio process involves the assessment of learners' work by a team of content-knowledgeable assessors, working independently. Locating, training, and working with assessors is critically important, not only to the PLAR process in a logistical sense, but to PLAR's qualitative potential in addressing the existence of socially embedded diversity. By the very nature of their training, most academic assessors are poised to think about imparting knowledge through teaching. Traditionally, this university structure is framed by courses, course units, and topics; and benchmarked with assignments and examinations. Through exposure to PLAR literature and examples of well-prepared portfolios that have achieved the desired outcomes, faculty assessors can come to appreciate the "diversity and divergence of knowledges, experiences, and meaning . . . and inclusion, rather than alternative forms of exclusion" (Harris, 1999, p. 136).

Providing a mentoring process for PLAR applicants. The items outlined above include expressions of theoretical and ideal conditions as well as operational procedures. The need for a responsive mentoring process for PLAR applicants underpins many of the strategies and conditions mentioned above. While a combination of Bloom's Taxonomy and clearly defined criteria may provide appropriate guidelines to PLAR applicants, gaps may exist between applicants' grasp of their experiential learning and their ability to capture that learning thoughtfully and appropriately. It is critical to provide mentoring opportunities where learners can receive assistance in bridging those gaps (Arscott et al., 2007). Experience has shown us that the iterative nature of this process is time-consuming and arduous, but extremely valuable and highly appreciated by learners.

The measures described here have been put in place to make the best possible effort to make "the criteria of judgement visible, and therefore potentially negotiable: for whose knowledge gets to "count"; for who may judge whom, and on what basis; for the procedures whereby knowledge is rewarded; and whose interests those procedures serve" (Michelson, 2006, p. 157). In doing so, the processes of recognizing prior learning implemented at AU address issues of diversity as best they can, working within the confines of a structured and established power hierarchy.

7.5 DIVERSITY AND DICHOTOMY: A BIGGER PICTURE

Currently in Canada, national and government perspectives on recognizing prior learning are being driven by economic concerns surrounding issues of globalization, immigration, foreign credential recognition (FCR), and projected labor shortages due to the impending retirement of the first wave of baby boomers. These are international concerns that are shared by European and other Western and industrialized nations, and the linkage of PLAR – in its capacity as a training model – to the economy is not a new phenomenon. As Peters pointed out when looking historically at RPL in the UK:

> Prior learning assessment and recognition practices have, in many parts of the world, been loosely – or not so loosely – tied to economic tides. In the United Kingdom, in 1979 for example, APEL was first introduced [when], faced with a demographic downturn among 18-year-old school leavers, universities were looking for ways of attracting different people, particularly mature students.
>
> (2005, p. 273)

In Canada, government efforts are focused on the benefits that PLAR can bring to the workplace. PLAR literature emerging from government agencies highlights the engagement of various stakeholders from government, from the workplace, and from learning institutions and other agencies, including the Council of Ministers of Education Canada (CMEC), Forum of Labour Market Ministers (FLMM), HRSDC (cited as leading the way on PLAR), CIC, Industry Canada, sector councils, apprenticeship networks, regulatory bodies, employers, the Association of Universities and Colleges Canada (AUCC), the Association of Canadian Community Colleges (ACCC), Canadian Association for Prior Learning Assessment (CAPLA), and the Halifax PLA Centre (Lake, 2005).

In the current initiative to populate a potential new workforce, government-backed initiatives are moving toward credentialing large numbers of under-employed and unemployed recently arrived – and soon to arrive – immigrant workers. The learning potential of prior learning has been overlooked in light of economic and political concerns. If the current emphasis on these activities successfully reflects the funding resources that have been put in place to ensure results (Goldenberg, 2006), the subsequent influx to the middle class should solidify a measure of citizenship that results from reputable employment and increased social responsibility (Selman et al., 1998).

It is ironic that the government's emphasis on the "credit exchange" (Trowler, 1996) model of PLAR offers the potential to diminish some measures of diversity among Canada's citizenry. Conversely, AU's educationally oriented attempt to obviate some level of diversity through the application of the developmental model of PLAR serves to surface more pervasive applications of social, political, and cultural diversity while the tangible outcomes of such processes are credit exchanges.

7.6 CONCLUSION

While the recognition of prior learning at post-secondary institutions in Canada is not widely practiced, it constitutes a solid plank in AU's mission as an open and distance institution. Although both challenge-for-credit and portfolio assessment strategies are used at AU, learners are best able to control their destinies and celebrate their diversities by engaging in the reflexive portfolio processes. As is exemplified by the onion in the familiar metaphor, however, peeling back the layers of RPL "demonstrates that RPL, like most apparently bounded educational practices, is also a lens for examining the most fundamental questions about the purposes and practices of education" (Young, 2006, p. 321). As demonstrated through literature and practice, there is little consensus to be found around issues of prior learning. Philosophical musings could conclude that, given its ambiguities, prior learning is well suited to an enterprise as fluid, mercurial, and diverse as learning.

The practice of recognizing prior learning will continue to challenge, and hopefully inform, post-secondary educators' perceptions of learning. At AU, the implementation of RPL will continue to give voice to both diversity and dichotomy as it offers learners an alternate vehicle through which to celebrate their learning.

NOTES

1. The completion of a current initiative to develop and standardize learning outcomes for all undergraduate courses at AU will put in place a seamless matrix of learning outcome literature, against which assessments of learners' knowledge can be made. The learning outcomes project is currently in progress.
2. This is a generalization that describes the majority of degree regulations. There are some credentials that vary slightly from this formula. Each AU degree, post-diploma degree, or certificate has been individually evaluated for its capability for advanced standing.

3. Policy is being brought forward to relocate a redesigned challenge-for-credit policy in the CLA.
4. Learning outcomes can generally be broken into two broad categories: those outcomes that reflect course content and those more tacit outcomes that are connected with generic learning skills. The generic learning skills resemble Canada's list of nine essential skills which in turn are often reflected in an institution's high-level listing of the kinds of employability skills they wish their graduates to hold upon completion of their program of study. In some programs at AU, the nature of the program dictates that these generic outcomes should be explicitly stated as learning outcomes. A good example is the Bachelor of Professional Arts in Communication Studies, where the ability to display well-developed communication skills is critical.
5. The portfolio process at AU is currently mainly paper-based. Electronic portfolios are accepted if the applicant has utilized a functional design. Materials on CDs are also accepted, both as the portfolio itself and as documentation for learning claims. Tapes, videos, and other examples of multimedia are also accepted as documentation.
   The university is currently moving toward the establishment of an e-portfolio platform for use in portfolios. It is anticipated that AU will be dealing with both paper portfolios and e-portfolios in the coming years.
6. Giving learners the opportunity to engage in this type of mature and intense reflection is recognized as a critical strength of the portfolio method of assessment. For PLAR to be recognized as a learning activity within the university, the generation of this type of reflection is essential. Here is one learner's feedback on this process:

   > While I found the PLAR a very specific, detailed and time-consuming procedure, it was actually a piece of luck in disguise. Essentially it offered me, a part-time student, the following five advantages: an awareness of my previously acquired skills, improved self esteem, a better understanding of university programs and related coursework, possible future planning and most importantly, university credit.

   Using the PLAR procedure as an assessment tool allowed me to systematically order my formal and informal learning. Previous work experience, training, and education became *learning clusters* and, finally, *actual skills*. Numerous letters of attestation confirmed these skills.

REFERENCES

Arscott, J., Crowther, I., Young, M., and Ungarian, L. (2007). *Producing Results in Prior Learning: Final Report from the Gateways Project*. Athabasca University: Athabasca, Alberta.

Avis, J. (1995). The validation of learner experience: A conservative practice? *Studies in the Education of Adults*, **27**(2), 173–187.

Crites, S. (1971). The narrative quality of experience. *American Academy of Religion Journal*, **39**(3), 291–311.

Cross, K.P. (1981). *Adults as Learners*. San Francisco: Jossey-Bass.

Dewey, J. (1938). *Experience and Education*. New York, NY: Macmillan.

Fenwick, T. (2006). Reconfiguring RPL and its assumptions: A complexified view. In *Re-theorising the Recognition of Prior Learning* (P. Andersson and J. Harris, eds). Leicester, UK: NIACE, pp. 283–300.

Freire, P. (1972). *Pedagogy of the Oppressed*. Harmondsworth: Penguin.

Goldenberg, M. (2006). Employer Investment in Workplace Learning in Canada. Canadian Council on Learning. Available at: http://www.ccl-cca.ca/CCL/Home?Language=EN.

Harris, J. (1999). Ways of seeing the recognition of prior learning (RPL): What contribution can such practices make to social inclusion? *Studies in the Education of Adults*, **31**(2), 124–138.

Illich, I. (1970). *Deschooling Society*. New York: Harper and Row.

Lake, K.L. (2005). Prior learning assessment and recognition (PLAR) in Canada: The context. Presentation for the OECD Dissemination Conference, Dublin.

Mackeracher, D. (2005). Making sense of adult learning. 2nd ed. Toronto: University of Toronto Press.

Michelson, E. (1996). Usual suspects: Experience, reflection, and the (en)gendering of knowledge. *International Journal of Lifelong Education*, **15**(6), 438–454.

Michelson, E. (2006). Beyond Galileo's telescope: Situated knowledge and the recognition of prior learning. In *Re-theorising the Recognition of Prior Learning* (P. Andersson and J. Harris, eds) Leicester, UK: NIACE, pp. 141–162.

Ontario Ministry of Education. (2001). Policy/program memorandum No. 129. Available at: http://www.edu.gov.on.ca/extra/eng/ppm/129.html

Peruniak, G. and Welch, D. (2000). The twinning of potential: Toward an integration of prior learning assessment with career development. *Canadian Journal of Counselling*, **34**(3), 232–245.

Peters, H. (2005). Contested discourses: Assessing the outcomes of learning from experience for the award of credit in higher education. *Assessment & Evaluation in Higher Education*, **30**(3), 273–285.

Selman, G., Selman, M., Dampier, P., and Cooke, M. (1998). *The Foundations of Adult Education in Canada*. 2nd ed. Toronto: Thompson.

Shale, D. (1987). Innovation in international higher education: The open universities. *Journal of Distance Education*, **2**(1), 7–26.

Thomas, A. (1998). The tolerable contradiction of PLA. In *Learning for Life: Canadian Readings in Adult Education* (S. Scott, B. Spencer, and A. Thomas, eds) Toronto: Thompson, pp. 330–342.

Trowler, P. (1996). Angels in marble? Accrediting prior experiential learning in higher education. *Studies in Higher Education* , **21**(1), 17–30.

Usher, R., Bryant, I., and Johnston, R. (1997). *Adult Education and the Post-modern Challenge: Learning Beyond the Limits*. London: Routledge.

Vlăsceanu, L., Grünberg, L., and Pârlea, D. (2004). *Quality Assurance and Accreditation: A Glossary of Basic Terms and Definitions*. Papers on Higher Education. Bucharest: UNESCO-CEPES. Available at: http://www.cepes.ro/publications/Default.htm

Welton, M. ed. (1995) *Defense of the Lifeworld: Critical Perspectives on Adult Learning*. Albany, NY: State University of New York Press.

Wiesenberg, F. (2001). The roller coaster life of the online learner: How distance educators can help students cope. *Canadian Journal of University Continuing Education*, **27**(2), 33–59.

Young, M. (2006). Endword. In *Re-theorising the recognition of prior learning* (P. Andersson and J. Harris, eds) Leicester, UK: NIACE, pp. 321–326.

Chapter 8

Open Schooling

Margaret Haughey, Elizabeth Murphy, and Bill Muirhead

The provision of schooling to students at a distance has had a multitude of titles. Erdos (1967) defined correspondence education as a "method of teaching in which the teacher bears the responsibility of imparting knowledge and skill to a student who does not receive instruction orally, but who studies in a place and a time determined by his individual circumstances" (p. 10). This definition made sense when use of technologies such as audio tapes, radio broadcasts, or telephones in education was uncommon. Today, we would define distance education as involving mediated learning opportunities, whether available in synchronous or asynchronous time, individually or in groups, but involving a formal system of student support. Correspondence schooling depended on print and the postal service. Today, distance education is likely to involve a variety of technologies but the intent is the same: to provide through alternate means educational opportunities of similar or better quality than those proposed for a site-based programme. With the advent of the Internet, it is sometimes referred to as online schooling.

The term "open schooling" has a much shorter history. Open schooling refers to schooling which "concerns using alternative and, usually, less resource-based approaches which characterize distance education methods and open learning, to deliver basic education and training (Phillips, 1994, p. 149). Openness usually refers to the removal of barriers such as age, entry qualifications, ability to pay, and geography. Sometimes open schooling is provided through virtual schools where all students are studying online at a distance, while other providers are conventional schools which can provide some open schooling to selected students. The combinations and terms continue to proliferate and so while we have called the chapter "open schooling", the general intent is to encompass all the variations of open and distance learning".

While much of the original correspondence education literature focused on adult education, the focus in this chapter is on the provision of educational opportunities to school-aged children. There has been no single model of correspondence or distance education for children's schooling but, like adult education, the models which were developed had to fit within the parallel context of on-site provision and were judged in comparison to it.

Of all the open schooling initiatives occurring around the world, we have chosen to focus on the following cases: correspondence and distance schooling in Australia and Canada, the open school movement in India, developments in sub-Saharan Africa, and schooling in conflict situations. We believe that they provide a rich tapestry of the variety of contexts and ingenuity of distance educators in their search to solve the challenges of providing educational opportunities through open schooling. We begin with a historical overview of the development of open schooling.

8.1 THE DEVELOPMENT OF OPEN SCHOOLING

In general, while open schooling began as a way to provide education to children who were without access to schools, the rationale for its provision has depended on the times and the context. In both Australia and Canada, at the beginning of the last century, parental concerns of those living in isolated and remote rural areas who could not afford to hire a personal tutor or send their children to boarding schools led to the development of government correspondence programmes. In both countries, this model of school provision spread rapidly as new settlements in sparsely populated areas outpaced the capacity of the local governments to provide schools.

In some situations, the development of open schooling became a necessity when regular schooling was temporarily unavailable. This happened through widespread sickness – such as the polio outbreak in New Brunswick, Canada (1939), and the influenza epidemic in New Zealand (1922) – that closed down all schools in the province or country and provided the impetus for the provision of what was then termed "correspondence education".

The disruptions of war have also contributed to enrolments in what was then called "correspondence education". In Canada, all the provincial correspondence education institutions combined resources to provide a complete secondary education curriculum to Canadian soldiers serving in the Second World War. In Europe, as Daniel notes (2006, p. 2), "the largest open school outside the Commonwealth, France's Centre National d'Enseignement à Distance (CNED) was created to serve the thousands of French children who were evacuated from the cities at the outbreak of World War II". In various European countries, such schools continued in the post-war reconstruction era as countries sought to provide vocational education for civilians and schooling for children whose lives had been disrupted by war. Glatter, in his 1969 article on correspondence education in four European countries (The Netherlands, West and East Germany, and France), mentions the CNED (then called Centre National de Télé-Enseignement) as having 10,000 students in 1950–1951 and an enrolment of 124,701 in 1966–1967. Given the disruption of schooling, not only in France, but all over Europe, the high enrolment figures include adults as well as school children, some taking school-level education while others were registered in post-secondary education; for example, The Netherlands (723,000 in 1960), West Germany (Peters estimated it was approximately 300,000 in 1965), and East Germany (37% of all technical college and 25% of all university students).

The next major development of distance schooling coincided with the economic and social development movements of the late 1960s in Africa, Mexico, and India. In these initiatives, the emphasis was often on teacher-training schemes which used learning centres to help encourage the learners to study together without the aid of a teacher. During the 1980s, the emphasis was on secondary education and the need to provide greater access to selected secondary education subjects. Many of these projects used communications technologies, radio most often, but sometimes television, to reach students and a general audience simultaneously. In the 1990s, the focus moved to primary education provided through radio and print to students in their homes without any face-to-face interaction (Brophy, 2003). Now, the pendulum has swung again with a renewed emphasis on secondary education and on out-of-school youth, the latter often the result of HIV/AIDS, poverty, and conflict. Despite a general consensus that schooling is important, UNESCO noted that in 2003 over 104 million school-aged children were not in school. The reasons include "economic, social and cultural barriers, ill health, religion, accessibility, political conflict and gender discrimination" (Fentiman, 2004, p. 1). Distance education is seen as providing an option for these children, particularly those in conflict situations.

8.2 OPEN SCHOOLING IN AUSTRALIA

Stacey (2005) identified the first distance education school programme in Australia as occurring for secondary school students in 1909 and for elementary students in 1914, the latter in response to a parent's request from Beech Forest in the Otway mountains, west of Melbourne. The best-known correspondence schools are the Australian Schools of the Air. They had their roots in the first government correspondence schools developed in response to settlers' requests for lessons for their children. Prior to the correspondence schools, a number of states had appointed "travelling" teachers who were required to travel throughout their districts visiting children at least four times a year if possible. Only men were appointed and the transition from travelling teachers to a more centralized operation came about partly due to the shortage of males during and after the First World War (Longreach School, n.d.). Teachers in these schools developed lessons which were mailed to students on a weekly basis and returned for correction. For educational resources, students were dependent on any additional materials available in their homes. Teachers sought various ways to provide supplementary information to their students. In Western Australia, in 1940, the Correspondence School Head Clarence Eakins built on the provision of general school broadcasts and developed radio broadcasts which augmented the school curriculum, provided students with the sound of their teachers' voices, and content related directly to their written work.

Schools of the Air are synonymous with the use of radio broadcasts in education. They spearheaded the use of two-way radio educational broadcasts and the first one began broadcasting in 1951 from the Royal Flying Doctor Base in Alice Springs, Northern Territory (NT). The Western Australia School opened in 1959. By 1968, there were thirteen schools throughout Australia. Initially, the school broadcasts were provided by teachers in a local school near the Flying Doctors' air base. The lessons were broadcast to those students taking correspondence courses from the state's correspondence school. The role of the School of the Air teacher was to supplement the work of the Correspondence School teacher. As Margaret Hartley, the teacher at SOTA noted, "SOTA teachers tried to create a classroom atmosphere and provide standards by which individual students could compare their efforts with others. ...[and] to give prompt help with individual problems identified by the child and the home tutor" (Longreach School, n.d.). Attempts were made to link the broadcasts more closely to the correspondence lessons and eventually, in 1974, the Alice Spring School of the Air took over the correspondence programmes for all Central Australia children. Within the next two decades (1976–1996), in the various Australian states, state "radio" school services and correspondence schools were amalgamated and decentralized and multiple distance education centres or schools were established. This resulted partly from the concerns of parents who wanted a more integrated approach to their children's education and school sites closer to their homes since many children were unable to participate in extra-curricular activities due to long distances, inadequate road conditions, poor weather, and financial difficulties.

In Queensland, in 1987, two committees investigating the needs of correspondence students recommended the reorganization of distance education provision and the redevelopment of curriculum materials, some of which were over 30 years old. Parents could now register their children in the closest school of distance education which provided a wide range of services formerly provided by the Schools of the Air. These services included "marking of papers, individualizing papers to meet needs of students, conducting on-air lessons, home visits, mini-schools, home tutor sessions and seminars, camps, sports days and activity days" (Longreach School, n.d.). Teachers from the schools visit the homes on a yearly basis. Each of these schools provides educational services to approximately 250 students living in an area in excess of 300,000 sq. km. The distance education materials used by the students were developed by a Support Unit that was amalgamated with the Open Access unit and, in 2005, reorganized into the Distance Learning Unit "with responsibility for developing curriculum in a digital format" (Longreach School, nd).

In Western Australia, the Distance Education (DE) Centre was formed in 1983 from the amalgamation of the Correspondence School, the Early Childhood scheme, and the Isolated Students Matriculation scheme to provide distance education materials for K-12 students. Subsequently, in 1995, the DE Centre and the five Schools of the Air, which together catered for approximately 2,500 students, were combined to enhance the quality of services which could be provided. As conditions allowed, radio was replaced by satellite broadcasts, and video-conferencing and laptop computers were added to the technologies used in working with home-based students. These schools vary in programs using text-based materials where students work on weekly lessons with their home tutor (usually their mother) which are posted back to the school for marking by the teacher and those with the addition of a radio or satellite broadcast, audio-graphics system where regular lessons are broadcast to students at set time. Although the majority of children would have been living on isolated properties in the outback, groups from other areas were also added. These included children with physical handicaps and those convalescing, students whose parents moved frequently, children living overseas temporarily, children who wanted to pick up some subjects to complete their education,

Aboriginal children in pastoral areas and in Mission or small rural schools, and, more recently, those whose parents chose not to have them attend a school building.

In an insightful account of one Queensland family's distance education experience, Green (2006) identifies the importance of the home tutor's personal educational biography, the pressures of the daily chores required on a ranching property, and how the home tutor, in this case the mother, brought her past experiences and her daily routines to bear on her obligations as a home tutor. For this mother, the distance education lessons were "one more chore to be done" (p. 42). The materials "largely set the pace and tone of [her] home tutoring activities" and failed to "rescue school learning activities from becoming simply a chore" for both the mother and the children (p. 42). Nonetheless, the two children preferred to be tutored by their mother than by any of the visiting teachers they had met. Her interactions with the children in educating them about many of the natural happenings in their everyday lives on the property provided the basic meaningfulness for their tutorial time together.

8.3 OPEN SCHOOLING IN CANADA

In Canada, open schooling for school children began in 1919 in response to a British Columbia rancher's request for lessons for his children (Haughey, 1990). The development of the provincial correspondence schools fits a pattern very similar to that in Australia. Programmes were developed and lessons organized using print and mail. By 1946 almost all Canadian provinces had a provincial correspondence schooling system (McKinnon, 1986). Gradually, the focus of correspondence education shifted from primary to secondary education. The post-war years brought a demand for vocational trades and skills. The increase in the number of elementary and secondary schools meant that developments in correspondence education focused on post-secondary and adult learners. As a result, funding for primary and secondary school correspondence education declined in comparison to its classroom-based alternative.

The revitalization of K-12 correspondence education in the 1970s in the US and Canada resulted from economic and curricular concerns arising from the population decline in rural communities and the demographic shift to the cities (Williams et al., 1988). Stephens (1986) noted that over 77 percent of United States school districts enrolled fewer than 2,500 students. Barker (1986) listed the reasons for this migration as including the "farm crisis", the drop in the price of oil, fewer teachers entering the profession, higher graduation requirements, and more diverse curricula. In response, schools were "turning to technology to help broaden curricular offerings in light of low student enrolments and increasing per-pupil cost of programs, facilities, and certified personnel" (p. 5). A similar trend occurred in Canada in the 1980s. During the previous 20 years, social trends in Canada showed a declining birth rate, a move away from farming, increasing urbanization, modernization of farming practices, depression in the agriculture industry, and increased graduation requirements. These trends resulted in increased urbanization because cities were seen as providing better educational and employment opportunities. As the tax base shifted, the survival of rural communities became an increasingly important concern. Other concerns were the lack of specialist teachers in rural schools and the relatively high numbers of secondary students who did not complete high school.

Today, in many provinces across Canada the move to greater urbanization and the decline in rural populations continue. At the same time, the increasing availability of the Internet continues to change the provision of schooling for urban students. It has also meant that options especially for children in situations which are truly remote have received new emphasis. Schools in remote Aboriginal communities in Northern Ontario have used the Internet to develop and share materials and resources in the local language, thereby helping to sustain the cultural context of schooling. Teachers have cooperated in the provision of online courses thereby sharing their expertise among the many small schools in the region. Given Canada's climatic challenges and vast land mass it is likely that distance education will always be a part of its educational provision. The cases of Alberta and Newfoundland and Labrador illustrate the essential role of this form of education.

8.3.1 Open Schooling in Alberta

In Alberta, a new form of correspondence education emerged as a way to provide the desired high quality education to families who chose to remain in rural communities. Projects undertaken at this time include *Distance Learning in Small Schools*, which used local tutor-markers, fax, and audio-conferencing to provide better student support and faster feedback to the distance education students taking correspondence courses in the thirteen pilot schools. A subsequent project used competency-based tests from a computer-managed database system and audio-conferencing with audio-graphics to enhance the provision of mathematics in small schools. The success of these projects led to the development of a consortia of school districts that would be responsible for the provision of all aspects except course development associated with distance education provision to students in their own jurisdictions (Hough, 1989). Previously, in-school students had identified loss of interest and lack of frequent feedback as their reasons for abandoning correspondence courses (Balay, 1978). It is not surprising that the use of local tutors, a faster turnaround time, use of fax machines, active supervisors, and more support led to a dramatic decline in the number of student dropouts (Hough, 1989).

These programmes focused on students who could not access specialist teachers or appropriate courses. Less emphasis was placed on correspondence education for students who did not attend a school at all since the numbers of these students had declined. The numbers of those taking correspondence courses at the elementary level between 1987 and 1990 ranged from about 450 in Alberta, approximately 1,000 in British Columbia, to only about seventy students in Manitoba (Haughey, 1990). Two circumstances radically changed this scenario in Alberta. The first resulted from the impact of an economic downturn in the 1990s when 141 school jurisdictions were amalgamated into sixty-three, and each new jurisdiction had to rationalize costs by closing small schools. Concerns about the long distances elementary children had to travel daily by bus during the winter months led to a sharp rise in the number of parents who wanted to home-school their children. Changes in the provincial curriculum language arts programmes raised further concerns for some parents who subsequently demanded more control over their children's education.

> As a result, provincial legislation was changed to allow parents to undertake the education of their children under the general supervision of a willing school board.... In addition funding was restructured to reflect this change and parents could offset the costs of instructional materials and curriculum guides against a provincially designated amount for each student.
>
> (Haughey and Muirhead, 2004, p. 52)

However, many parents did not want to develop lessons and instead sought help from their local school district or the provincial Distance Learning Centre.

The second circumstance that changed in Alberta was the development of the Internet and the World Wide Web. The new technology gave students the opportunity to stay at home and yet participate in classes given by the local school teachers over the Internet. Approximately nineteen jurisdictions developed "virtual" school programmes, some designed to serve students in their own jurisdiction while others served students throughout Alberta and some registered international students. The programme enrolments varied from about 250 to over 2,000 students. Virtual schooling provided students with flexibility in attendance and with a more interactive environment than was initially available through home-schooling or correspondence lessons. Today, these schools use course management software such as WebCT or Moodle. The course materials are posted on the website and, depending on the school, students can work independently or in a group. Many schools use an interactive synchronous audio-conferencing groupware which provides a whiteboard and small group spaces for interaction. Teachers have developed their own lessons or work with materials developed by the Alberta Distance Learning Centre.

The former correspondence school, now called the Distance Learning Centre, has also changed. It began using e-mail in 1995, and by 1997 when it was placed under a school jurisdiction more than 100 students were registered in its virtual school programme. Today, the school works with students in isolated areas and those who choose to home-school through distance learning. In addition, it continues to develop courses which students can access independently and in print as well as online and to partner with school jurisdictions to make these materials available to their students and teachers. The government has, in cooperation with federal and provincial initiatives, implemented SuperNet, which provides a broadband network to most small communities around the province. Falling costs for hardware at home and within schools have made the Internet the vehicle for flexible learning and new combinations of learning environments.

8.3.2 Open Schooling in Newfoundland and Labrador

While the Alberta scenario shares many similarities with other jurisdictions across Canada, each province developed models of open schooling provision which fitted the provincial geography and educational policies. There is a range of pedagogical options from virtual schools with their own teachers and the work completed by students most often at home, to non-specialist teachers using distance education materials in a classroom setting or to in-school students working on materials at their own pace. The different models were all designed to extend the options available to secondary students in particular. The present provision of open schooling in Newfoundland provides one such example.

Distance education in Newfoundland and Labrador has evolved out of extreme demographic, socio-economic, and geographic conditions. The population of the province in 2005 was only 512,930 (Government of Newfoundland and Labrador, 2005a). However, this population is in decline as evidenced by a Statistics Canada (2001) survey, which revealed that between 1996 and 2001 about 47,100 people left the province as a result of a decrease in the importance of resource-based industries such as fishing, mining, and forestry. The remaining population is dispersed primarily in rural and coastal areas over a land mass of 405,720 sq. km or the equivalent of one and three quarter times the size of Great Britain.

Not surprisingly, of a total of 303 schools, 65 percent (198) are classified as rural and 35 percent (105) as urban (Government of Newfoundland and Labrador, 2005b). In 2003–2004, 14.1 percent of schools had enrolments of fewer than fifty students, and 30.5 percent had enrolments of 50–99 students (Government of Newfoundland and Labrador, 2004). Many of these schools have multi-grade, multi-age classrooms. Numerous schools exist with populations of under 100 students with some having enrolments as low as thirty-five students from grade K-12 (see Government of Newfoundland and Labrador, 2005c). These schools may have difficulty recruiting teachers in areas such as Maths, Science, and French (Dibbon and Sheppard, 2001), or may simply have enrolments too low to justify the hiring of a teacher in a specialty area. It is primarily as a result of these conditions and factors that distance education has developed in this province.

Distance education for rural high school students was first introduced by the provincial Department of Education in 1988 in response to the *Small Schools* report (see Government of Newfoundland and Labrador, 1987). The first course was Advanced Mathematics and other Mathematics and Physics courses followed. Courses were delivered through an audio-teleconferencing system developed by Memorial University's Telemedicine Centre (Telemedicine/TETRA, 2002), as well as a telewriter system and fax (Government of Newfoundland and Labrador, 1992). From one course with thirty-six enrolments in thirteen schools in 1988, delivery expanded to eleven courses in seventy schools with approximately 900 course enrolments in Advanced Mathematics, Physics, Chemistry, and French in 1999 (Brown et al., 2000).

In 2000, the Centre for Distance Learning and Innovation (CDLI) was created by the Department of Education upon the recommendations of the report of the Ministerial Panel on Educational Delivery in the Classroom (see Government of Newfoundland and Labrador, 2000). In the following year, CDLI implemented ten Web-based high school courses through digital intranets in partnership with the Centre for Telelearning and Rural Education (Coffin and Stevens, 2002). Whereas the traditional distance education model tended to target higher-ability learners in rural schools, CDLI's model of e-learning was designed for both rural and urban learners (Barbour and Mulcahy, 2004). The three main mandates of CDLI are online distance education, online teacher professional development, and the integration of e-learning in the learning environment (CDLI, 2005). CDLI e-learners attend conventional face-to-face schools but supplement their course offerings with virtual classes.

In 2005–2006, CDLI employed twenty-eight teachers and offered thirty-two Web-based courses with approximately 1,000 course enrolments in ninety-seven schools across the province (CDLI, 2005). Courses are designed according to provincial curriculum guidelines and rely on asynchronous modes of communication using WebCT™ with a percentage of synchronous communication conducted using Elluminate *Live*™. This audio-graphic learning environment includes various collaborative tools, including Class List Display, Direct Messaging, White Board, two-way audio, and Graphing Calculator. CDLI works with two categories of teachers: e-teachers are subject specialists who facilitate learning at a distance; m-teachers or m-teams are available for student consultation on site. They are not responsible for content delivery in the subject area and, instead, fulfill technical, coaching, and administrative roles.

Besides regular curricular offerings, CDLI provides additional support for e-learners. E-tutors are assigned to each e-learning site for troubleshooting equipment, tutoring, and presenting information about CDLI to junior high students. High school learners preparing to write public examinations can avail of free online tutoring from post-secondary students, and CDLI has created multimedia learning tools for supplementary study. Also available is a Guidance Room where CDLI students can contact an e-counsellor and access career planning and other resources. They can also attend online career presentations weekly during lunch hours. Other opportunities available to CDLI students include a variety of extracurricular opportunities. As an example, in 2003 and 2004, two Science students were selected in the Canadian Genetic Diseases Network national competition for placements during spring break working with scientists and their lab teams in molecular biology research labs. In 2004, twenty-four learners from eleven communities taking CDLI French courses travelled with two French teachers to Quebec. In 2005, forty-three learners (seven teams) from two districts participated online in the first CDLI Senior Math League. Later in the year, two teams of learners from different communities participated in Senior Math League Provincials competing against other school teams from across the province.

The CDLI also offers support to teachers and encourages parental involvement. Professional development includes Web-based opportunities for teacher professional development through online collaboration. M-team training sessions are also organized. Some teachers have had the opportunity to meet with parents and students face-to-face. Internships are available for university Education students. Parents can attend orientation meetings where they are introduced to the CDLI learning environment.

The successes of CDLI have been accompanied by a need to face a variety of challenges and issues. Technical issues include the spread of viruses and spam through e-mail; mail-box quota issues; system outages; Internet performance issues; bandwidth access; the need to constantly update software and equipment at learning sites; and the provision of adequate equipment and technological support to instructors, learners, and schools. Other issues relate to scheduling across four districts and ninety-seven schools in a province with two time zones. Learners at the various sites may have different timetables, calendars, and events. District schedules may change because of professional development dates, school events, or weather closures. Because teachers work across districts, the logistics of coordinating schedules, professional development meetings, and teacher-leaves sometimes presents challenges. Other issues include supervision and monitoring; exam security and confidentiality; and access to special materials and equipment for courses not offered at schools (e.g. books, headphones, and lab supplies). Another challenge relates to the development of course materials and learning objects (Barbour, 2006). In this regard, CDLI contracts out the development of some course materials through a bidding process. Other issues relate to recruiting professionals with the required expertise and technological knowledge; providing relevant training and professional development opportunities; and finding substitutes with the required technical expertise.

8.4 OPEN SCHOOLING IN INDIA

While open schooling in Australia and Canada began as a means to provide education for children who could not access conventional schools, it began in India in the mid-1960s as a means to help students from private schools perform better on the secondary-school examinations. As Sujatha (2002) notes, "it was a means to improve their academic performance" (p. 41). A number of states (i.e. Delhi, Rajasthan, Madhya Pradesh, Orissa, Uttar Pradesh) followed the advice of the Boards of Secondary Education and began correspondence courses. These materials followed the examination syllabus programmes of these states. Despite the rapid expansion in numbers and capacity of schools, the even greater numbers of students without access to education continued to lead to yet greater inequalities. This situation was exacerbated by the large number of communities without access to any schooling. The government-appointed working group, under the National Council for Educational Research and Training, examined the feasibility of an alternative system of schooling and proposed that an Open School be established catering to those over fourteen years of age. Over the next 4 years, the topic was debated and discussed in government and educational circles and, following the discussions generated at the International Conference for Correspondence Education (now ICDE) meeting in Delhi in 1978, the government gave approval for the Open School Project. It registered its first 1,672 students in May 1981 (Sujatha, 2002, p. 45). The Open School Project provided a parallel system to conventional education and targeted out-of-school learners, especially women, lower castes, the scheduled tribes, and those with little or no income. It used an open-entry system for anyone over the age of fourteen, and provided instruction in both Hindi and English. The courses were bridging courses designed to help student obtain the foundations acquired by a successful conventional schooling, and secondary education courses with a focus on vocational education which were equivalent to those in the conventional school.

A resource-centre model was developed where students came to register, obtain materials, and participate in classes on weekends and holidays, where assignments were evaluated and examination fees paid. Singh (1988) in his research on the Open School in Delhi found that these centres increased student attendance and student–tutor interaction and saved on costs associated with administration of materials and forms. By 1989, over 40,000 students were enrolled in the Open School Project (Sujatha, 2002) and a number of states who had initially developed correspondence education established their own Open Schools although some continued the examination syllabi while others adopted the Open School curriculum.

This move to form state Open Schools was accelerated following the 1986 National Policy on Education. This policy strongly supported distance education as a means to meet the enormous needs for education at both secondary and tertiary levels. As a result, the Open School project was amalgamated into a new National Open School (NOS) under the Ministry of Human Resource Development. The NOS was able to build on the foundational architecture for administration and curriculum development established by the Open School Project, and immediately began to expand the senior secondary course offerings. It continued the offering of bridging courses (equivalent to 8, 10, and 12 years of secondary education), vocational education, and life enrichment courses, and added an Open Basic Education component. Based on the objective of helping to achieve national literacy standards, the latter programme is for out-of-school 6–14-year-olds and adult learners. Like its tertiary distance education partners, the NOS uses a network of study centres in accredited institutions. NOS is responsible for providing the up-to-date curriculum materials and examinations. Its use of Information and Communication Technologies (ICTs) is increasing through the provision of on-demand examinations, published lists of examination results, and digitized access to library materials through its website. Students register at the network of regional centres throughout India, attend weekend classes, and obtain tutor assistance through a number of accredited institutions which provide premises, organize tutorial staff, and ensure student support. In 1999–2000, according to the NOS website (http://www.nos.org/enroltrend.htm), about 147,000 students were enrolled in the NOS. While these students come from almost all the Indian states, the small numbers in some areas may reflect the rise of state Open Schools and the importance of the state or local language which the state schools use. Raising awareness of the school and its possibilities continues to be an important concern for NOS.

By 2002, there were eleven Open Schools functioning under their respective state governments. As a result, NOS provided consultancy and quality assurance services to state Open Schools in addition to running schools of its own. In 1999, a National Consortium of Open Schooling was formed under the leadership of NOS to help support this network and encourage links with the public system. In 1998–1999, there were 318,000 students enrolled in these state Open Schools, which was still only a small fraction compared to the 11.9 million students in conventional secondary schools (Sujatha, 2002, p. 51). To reflect its work in assisting the provision and quality of open schooling in state Open Schools, NOS's title was changed to the National Institute of Open Schooling (NIOS) in July, 2002.

The state Open Schools have different operational structures: some are autonomous institutions while others operate as an arm of a government department or the State Board of Education. This has implications for their operation (Mishra, 2005). They have different priorities: some focus on Open Basic Schooling, while others have only secondary or vocational schooling. Some serve children while others serve only adult learners. Those linked to Boards of Education are more likely to have regulations that follow those in conventional schooling such as requiring students to take all five examinations in a single year, while NIOS, for example, provides examinations on demand and encourages students to study for only one to three examinations at a time.

The NIOS is an autonomous body operating under the government of India; in this regard, it is not unlike Indira Gandhi National Open University in having a monitoring and coordinating as well as a collaborative standard-setting role as Chair of the National Council of Open Schooling. NIOS also provides the headquarters for the Association of Open Schools of the Commonwealth, which receives support from the Commonwealth of Learning (COL). The National Institute's role is to coordinate services among the participating schools, particularly in personnel development and teacher training, provide coordination and consultation services, promote research and development, and help ensure quality standards. NIOS also coordinates the International Centre for Training in Open Schooling (ICTOS), which is supported by COL and UNESCO. The major function of NIOS is to aid other countries in capacity-building for developing open schools, and NIOS is beginning to offer a Certificate and Diploma in Open Schooling to aid in developing teachers' skills.

In a review of open schooling in India for UNESCO, Sujatha (2002) observed that research on the effectiveness of the processes and on student and tutor satisfaction was still spotty with most studies targeted at a small percentage of the entire enterprise. Sujatha noted that "the research on different aspects of NOS is not only limited, but also does not provide a wide cross-section of the country. Therefore, it is difficult to make generalizations" (p. 152). Recognizing this issue, the Association of Open Schools of the Commonwealth now funds the *Journal of Open Schooling*, devoted to research in this area. Mishra (2006) recently completed a study on gender and open schooling using data from NIOS. She noted that NIOS, the largest open school in the world, had a mandate to enhance opportunities for women and girls. However, while enrolments of girls in conventional schools have increased from 11 percent in 1950–1951 to 37 percent in 2003–2004, wide disparities still exist. Mishra reviewed NIOS's figures and found that while the proportion of female learners in NIOS was higher between 1990 and 1993, it has subsequently been falling even though the proportion of girls in conventional schools has been rising. She attributes this gap to barriers to schooling existing prior to 1993. Since then, the barriers in formal schooling situations have been reduced by government measures such as the recruitment of women teachers, the provision of appropriate facilities for girls, free elementary education and bicycles for travel to schools, and the assurance of spaces in schools. She found that in a number of state open schools the demand for secondary education through open schooling was higher for females. Mishra concluded that "access to education alone was not enough to create gender equality" (p. 7); female students certainly enrolled in open schooling but a minority registered in Mathematics although many chose Science. These trends indicate that the females may not have recognized the importance of mathematical skills as well as scientific knowledge in their future occupations.

While the NIOS in India has been the focus of this case, a similar project has been the Bangladesh Open School attached to the Bangladesh Open University. In a report on the project, Mattuber (2005) noted that some ongoing challenges were the maintenance of updated curriculum materials and recruiting sufficient numbers of students to ensure adequate revenue and to meet the university's mission to reduce educational equities. He quoted the 2005 enrolment as approximately 269,500 students, of which 40 percent were female. He added that the heavy reliance on print and "the lack of teachers trained in multimedia" (p. 26) resulted in difficulties in transforming the curriculum.

8.5 OPEN SCHOOLING IN SUB-SAHARAN AFRICA

The international development movement in the 1960s was the original impetus for distance education in various African countries. Most projects focused on providing teacher training and many of these endeavours did not persist beyond changes in government and termination of the initial funding. More recently, the United Nations' target of Education for All and the focus on early basic education, the realities of an inadequate secondary schooling infrastructure, the large numbers of out-of-school students, and the prevalence and ongoing impact of HIV/AIDS have brought renewed emphasis on the possibilities of open schooling. In particular, Botswana, Namibia, and Zambia have significant open schooling systems.

In several African countries the centres responsible for adult education have undertaken the provision of secondary schooling. The Institute of Adult Education in Tanzania, the Zambian College of Open and Distance Education, the Namibian College of Open Learning, Botswana's College of Distance and Open and Learning, the College of Distance Education in Malawi, and the Emalatine Development Centre in Swaziland all serve adult and or secondary learners through distance education. The numbers of students are still relatively small compared to their school populations, the largest being Namibia with over 30,000 learners.

8.5.1 Open Schooling: Botswana

The Botswana programme dates back to the establishment of learning centres for teacher candidates during the late 1960s, which, over time, as government policies changed became centres for learner services. The Botswana College of Distance and Open Learning (BOCODOL) has used the learning centre architecture in its provision of open schooling for secondary out-of-school students. The centres are located in the local village schools. Local teachers apply to become tutors and coordinator of the centre but the resources for the centre are supplied by the BOCODOL. At the local centre, potential students can obtain information and advice and enrol in courses. They can also receive their study materials, attend weekend tutorials, and have their assignments marked. Regional Offices coordinate, monitor, and evaluate the work of the centres, provide marketing and publicity, ensure organizational and tutorial support, and provide appropriate training programmes for part-time staff.

The quality of student services is an ongoing concern and BOCODOL uses a system of monitoring and evaluating not only learners, but also tutors and the learning centre. These supervisory functions are carried out mainly by Regional Office staff, who use data from random interviews with students, Learning Centre Supervisor reports of tutorial sessions, and their own assessment of the effectiveness of the Learning Centre Supervisor in monitoring the quality of the centre. Although they have study materials, students are expected to attend weekly tutorial sessions and do assignments regularly. Hence, there is a need for responsive, positive, and frequent feedback to learners. The students study materials include print and audio cassettes. In addition, radio programmes aired once each week contain a combination of course-specific and general study skills information.

According to Thuteotsile (2004), the challenges faced by BOCODOL vary from the digitization of records for automated record-keeping to ensuring the safety of tutors and students since most tutorials occur in the evening. Other challenges include tracking down learners who stop attending without notice, and the low examination pass rate due to infrequent assignment submissions. In addition, the problems of great distances and low population numbers, seasonal changes, competing family pressures, and work-shifts which influence attendance result in a number of very small centres with few students, which in turn impacts services, costs, and monitoring.

8.5.2 Open Schooling: Zambia

In general, those leading African open schooling initiatives have sought to adopt multimedia technologies despite the lack of a robust infrastructure in many instances, believing that the development of infrastructure will support growth and that multimedia approaches will enhance learning. Radio has proved to be an important medium in reaching children in a number of countries. The most famous is perhaps the Australian School of the Air. Others include the Radio Mathematics project in Nicaragua, the Brazilian radio, and television project or the Radio-Assisted Community Basic Education project in the Dominican Republic (Shrestha, 1997).

A recent project using radio as well as print resources is Zambia's Interactive Radio Instruction programme. The Zambian programme began as a result of a study initiated by the Ministry of Education in 1999 and undertaken by faculty from the University of Zambia. The study identified the numbers of out-of-school children, the reasons why they were not in school, the institutions that were providing some non-formal schooling, and the type of programmes provided. It also made recommendations for radio broadcast programmes which might assist these institutions (Lubinda, 2004). The result was a pilot programme, the Interactive Radio Instruction programme, undertaken by the Educational Broadcasting Services of the Ministry of Education and begun in 2000. It involved twenty-two centres in three different areas of the country including both urban and rural populations. One hundred radio programmes based on the national curriculum for literacy, numeracy, and life skills were developed and broadcast over a 6-month period to 900 registrants. Besides significant learning gains, the researchers found that older students also participated, and that, in general, the organizational partnership model worked very well with communities who identified volunteer mentors responsible for conducting the lessons and looking after the radios and some supplies associated with the project. Since 2000, "interactive radio centres have been established in all nine provinces" (p. 68) and "over 1,000 IRI programs for grades 1–5" have been produced (p. 70). By 2004, there were 642 centres with over 38,500 learners. The numbers of boys and girls have remained fairly even. However, there are "over 600,000 learners who cannot access formal education" (p. 73), which makes this project all the more important.

Lubinda (2004) described how children aged 9–15 years were put into learning groups and attended listening centres organized by the local communities and run by volunteer mentors chosen by the community. Each year, these mentors received a guidebook suggesting pre- and post-broadcast activities. Three days of formal training from the Ministry of Education focused on "how to organize learning in groups, how to play learning games and organize student-centred learning activities, how to ask and answer questions, how to teach reading, and how to talk about issues concerning HIV and AIDS" (p. 70). The volunteer mentor is paid (in cash or kind) by the local community, while the Ministry is responsible for the development of the scripts, the printing of the mentor guides, the payment of the radio actors, and the broadcast costs.

As the programme has grown, the Ministry has appointed outreach coordinators responsible for capacity-building in communities, linking closely with the Ministry officials, ensuring good communications, and developing partnerships. Partnerships with local radio stations that have publicized and often rebroadcast the programmes have not only ensured greater local involvement, but helped in areas where the signal has been poor. Non-governmental agencies such as churches have helped provide facilities and do local organizing. International partnerships have helped provide learning materials and resources.

The Ministry maintains the enrolment and accrediting database including demographic information on learners. The programme of continuous improvement calls for external evaluations by University of Zambia faculty and the Examination Council officials. These evaluations have been held annually since 2001 for grades 1–3. Nonetheless, the need for better programme design, distance education pedagogical training, and production techniques for the programme writers and developers remains a challenge. Recently, the new pedagogies for teaching literacy have been incorporated into the broadcast designs. In addition, while the Ministry has plans to expand the life skills programmes, to introduce the programmes into formal schools, and to develop programmes for adult literacy and in-service teacher training, several other challenges need addressing. These include the lack of material and financial support for the mentors and centres, which results in frequent turnover and poor learning conditions. Similarly, when these learning centres become community schools, the mentors sometimes abandon the radio programmes even though the Ministry prefers that the school continue to use them. Finally, the project depends on adequate numbers of quality broadcasts reflecting current curricula and contemporary pedagogy. As Lubinda (2004) concludes, the "poor and erratic funding to the department is a hindrance to the timely production of programs" (p. 73).

8.6 OPEN SCHOOLING IN CONFLICT SITUATIONS

Besides all the children who are not able to attend a school due to economic or social conditions (usually poverty and distance), there are over 60 million children who have been displaced by humanitarian emergencies and "at any one time over 6 million children worldwide are refugees from conflict" (Fentiman, 2004, p. 2). While there are many reasons for their displacement, HIV/AIDS and conflict are two major reasons for the disruption. According to UNAIDS (2003), it is estimated that by 2010 there will be 44 million children who will have lost at least one parent to HIV/AIDS. In these situations, the out-of-school strategies developed by programmes such as BOCODOL and NIOS and CNED created to serve French children during the Second World War are important in terms of providing an alternative to formal schooling. In conflict situations, the use of radio becomes particularly useful due to its ability to compensate for the mobility of the group. The Interactive Radio Instruction programme from Zambia is one model and is not unlike the radio programmes provided to children of the Fulani and other nomadic peoples in Northern Nigeria by the Nomadic Commission (Usman, 2001). Brophy (2003) listed a range of radio schooling programmes provided by the BBC World Service to children in refugee camps in various countries from Albania to Afghanistan.

8.7 COMMENTARY

From the isolation and distance which drove the initial impetus for open schooling in Australia and Canada to the social and economic issues facing the rapidly growing populations of India and sub-Saharan Africa, the opportunities provided by an alternative form of schooling were never in doubt. From among these opportunities, however, a number of commonalities seem evident.

In general, the form of open schooling has followed that of formal schooling. It has been seen less as an alternative form of schooling than as another way to provide formal schooling. It has seldom broken through the mirror of formal schooling. NIOS is one example where an alternative curriculum which allows students to study at their own pace has been constructed.

Most open schools follow a model which requires some face-to-face interaction. Whether it is the parent, the volunteer tutor, or the teacher, most schooling models require some combination of interaction as well as independent study.

Students who have support beyond the tutorial or school setting are more likely to succeed. A number of schools have encouraged study groups to help provide this ongoing support.

The impact of digital technologies has brought new challenges and opportunities. The reconfiguration of open schooling in Australia and the changes planned at NIOS and BOCODOL suggest that the rapid adoption of digital technologies from cell phones to CD ROMs, and for more immediate Internet access, is challenging open school personnel to decide how to integrate these technologies into their present systems.

The real challenge will be to decide how they can transform their systems to be more learner-centred and responsive to students' needs.

Governments and countries look to distance education to provide alternative ways to educate their young people. For many children and youth open schooling is the only avenue to education. In general, however, the open schooling initiatives as described in this chapter have been driven largely by economic, geographic, social, and political imperatives. They have evolved as a reactive solution to problems rather than as a viable proactive educational alternative adopted as a means to provide better or more effective forms of teaching and learning. Without a more pedagogical or educational imperative for open schooling, it will likely remain a poor cousin rather than a valued member in the tradition of education.

REFERENCES

Barbour, M. and Mulcahy, D. (2004). The role of mediating teachers in Newfoundland's new model of distance education. *The Morning Watch*, **32**(1). Retrieved September 7, 2005 from http://www.mun.ca/educ/faculty/mwatch/win05/barbourmulcahy.htm

Barker, B. (1986). *Interactive Satellite Instruction: How can Rural Schools Benefit?* Paper presented at the Rural Education Association Conference, Little Rock, AR. (ERIC Document reproduction service No. ED 274 499).

Brophy, M. (2003). Open learning and distance education for displaced populations, In *The Open Classroom* (J. Bradley, ed.) London: Kogan Page, pp. 85–98.

Brown, J., Sheppard, B., and Stevens, K. (2000). *Effective Schooling in a Tele-learning Environment*. St. John's, NL: Centre for TeleLearning and Rural Education, Faculty of Education, Memorial University of Newfoundland. Retrieved September 12, 2005 from http://www.tellearn.mun.ca/es_report/index.html

CDLI (2005). *The Centre-Overview*. Retrieved September 1, 2005 from http://www.cdli.ca/index.php?PID=AnnounceFull&NewsID=6352

Coffin, G. and Stevens, K. (2002). *Experiencing e-Learning: A Report of the First Experience with On-Line High School Courses in Newfoundland and Labrador Schools, 2001–2002*. Centre for Distance Learning and Innovation, Department of Education of Newfoundland and Labrador. Unpublished report.

Dibbon, D. and Sheppard, B. (2001). *Teacher Demand, Supply, and Retention in Newfoundland and Labrador*. St. John's, NL: Memorial University of Newfoundland. Retrieved September 26, 2005 from http://www.mun.ca/educ/faculty/ddibbon/report/report.pdf

Erdos, R.F. (1967). *Teaching by Correspondence*. London: Longsmans/UNESCO.

Fentiman, A. (2004). *Out of School Provision for Children and Adolescents*. An IRFOL report prepared for the EFA Monitoring team, UNESCO, Paris.

Glatter, R. (1969). Aspects of correspondence education in four European countries. *Comparative Education*, 5(1), 83–98.

Government of Newfoundland and Labrador. (1987). *Report of the Small Schools Study Project*. St. John's: Memorial University of Newfoundland.

Government of Newfoundland and Labrador. (2000). *Supporting Learning: Report of the Ministerial Panel on Educational Delivery in the Classroom*. Retrieved September 16, 2005, from http://www.edu.gov.nf.ca/panel/panel.pdf

Government of Newfoundland and Labrador. (2004). *Department of Education Annual Report 2003–04*. Retrieved September 26, 2005 from http://www.ed.gov.nl.ca/edu/pub.htm

Government of Newfoundland and Labrador (2005a). *About Newfoundland and Labrador*. Retrieved September 7, 2005 from http://www.gov.nf.ca/nfld&lab/

Government of Newfoundland and Labrador (2005b). *Education Statistics: Elementary – Secondary, 2004–2005*. Retrieved September 7, 2005 from http://www.ed.gov.nl.ca/edu/pub/stats04_05/stats04_05.htm

Government of Newfoundland and Labrador (2005c). *List of Schools 1996–97 to 2004–05 (sorted on school id and year)*. Retrieved November 9, 2005, from http://www.education.gov.nf.ca/sch_rep/history/histsch4.rpt

Green, N.C. (2006). Everyday life in distance education: One family's home schooling experience. *Distance Education*, **27**(1), 27–44.

Haughey, M. (1990). Distance Education in schools. *The Canadian Administrator*, **29**(8), 1–9.

Haughey, M. and Muirhead, B. (2004). Managing virtual schools: The Canadian experience. In *Development and Management of Virtual Schools: Issues and Trends* (C. Cavanaugh, ed.) Hershey, PA: Ideal Group, pp. 50–68.

Longreach School (n.d.). *School of the Air*. Retrieved from http://www.aasa.au/

Lubinda, F.M. (2004). The interactive radio instruction (IRI) program in Zambia. In *Proceedings of the Forum on Open Schooling in Secondary Education in Sub-Saharan Africa* (A. Fentiman, ed.) 5–8 October. Gabarone, Botswana. IRFOL: COL, pp. 67–73.

Mattuber, M.A.A. (2005). Contemporary issues in open schooling: A case of Bangladesh open university. In *Proceedings of Initiatives for Seamless Learning. International Conference on Promotion of Open Schooling* (pp. 25–26). 23–25 January, Goa, India. Delhi, IN: NIOS/COL. Also available at http://www.nios.ac.in/finalgoa3.pdf (Retrieved March 17, 2007).

McKinnon, N. (1986). Public elementary and secondary schools. In *Distance Education in Canada* (I. Mugridge and D. Kaufman, eds), Beckenham, Kent, UK: Croom Helm, (pp.194–203).

Mishra, S. (2005). Models of open schooling: State open schools in India. In *Proceedings of Initiatives for Seamless Learning. International Conference on Promotion of Open Schooling* (pp. 38–40). 23–25 January, Goa, India. Delhi, IN: NIOS/COL. Also available at http://www.nios.ac.in/finalgoa3.pdf (Retrieved March 17, 2007).

Mishra, S. (2006). Gender and open schooling in India. Presented at the Fourth Pan Commonwealth Forum on Open Learning, Oka Rios, Jamaica, Oct 30–Nov 3.

Mukhopadhyay, M. and Phillips, S. (eds). (1994). *Open Schooling: Selected Experiences*. Vancouver: The Commonwealth of Learning.

NIOS (2007). http://www.nios.ac.in/glance.pdf

Phillips, S. (1994). Conclusion: The Open Schooling Case Studies. In *Open Schooling Selected Experiences* (M. Mukhopadhyah and S. Phillips, eds), Vancouver: The Commonwealth of Learning.

Phillips, S. (2006). Vocational education and training through open schooling: challenges and future strategies. Opening speech delivered by J. Daniel. *International Conference on Open Schooling for Better Working*, (8–10 Feb), Kovalam, Kerala, India. Retrieved December 29, 2006, from: www.col.org/colweb/site/pid/3567

Shrestha, G. (1997). *A Review of Case Studies Related to Distance Education in Developing Countries*. A report for INFO21/ IT for Development Program. New York: United Nations Development Program.

Singh, J. (1988). The open school, Delhi. *Journal of Educational Planning and Administration*, **2**(3–4).

Stacey, E. (2005). The history of distance education in Australia. *Quarterly Review of Distance Education*, **6**(3), 253–259.

Statistics Canada. (2001). *Profile of the Canadian Population by Mobility Status: Canada, a Nation on the Move*. (Catalogue number 96F0030XIE2001006). Retrieved September 7, 2005 from http://www12.statcan.ca/english/census01/products/analytic/companion/mob/contents.cfm

Stephens, E.R. (1986). Resisting the obvious: State policy initiatives for rural school improvement should not mean just another round of massive school reorganization. *Research in Rural Education*, **4**(1), 29–34.

Sujatha, K. (2002). *Distance Education at Secondary Level in India: The National Open School*. Paris: International Institute for Educational Planning, UNESCO.

Telemedicine/TETRA (2002). *The History of Telemedicine/TETRA*. Faculty of Medicine, Memorial University of Newfoundland. Retrieved September 7, 2005 from http://www.med.mun.ca/telemed/telehist/telemulti.htm

Thuteotsile, T. (2004). Learning centres: The experience of Botswana College of Distance and Open Learning (BOCODL). In *Proceedings of the Forum on Open Schooling in Secondary Education in Sub-Saharan Africa* (A. Fentiman, ed.) (pp. 51–61). 5–8 October Gabarone, Botswana. IRFOL: COL.

Usman. L. (2001). "No one will listen to us"; Rural Fulbe women learning by radio in Nigeria. In *Using Learning Technologies. International Perspectives on Practice* (E.J. Burge and M. Haughey, eds) London: RoutledgeFalmer, pp. 92–101.

Williams, D., Eiserman, W., and Quinn, D. (1988). Distance education for elementary and secondary schools in the United States. *Journal of Distance Education*, 3(2), 71–96.

Chapter 9

Social Software Technologies in Distance Education: Maximizing Learning Freedoms

Terry Anderson

New technologies afford new ways to undertake existing tasks, alter cost–benefit models, and most importantly create new opportunities to resolve old problems. Distance education, more than other modes of formal education provision, is positioned, because of its closely linked relationship with communication and information technologies, to take maximum advantage of the affordances of new technologies. However, capabilities of technologies alone do not determine their actual use. Rather, social, political, personal economic, and other factors constrain and define the ways in which the technology is actually used in everyday life (Bijker, 1999). In this chapter, I overview the ways that developments in communications, information technology, and pedagogical theory are stimulating new ways to support and create formal learning opportunities available at a distance. In particular I examine educational social software and ways in which this new genre of net-based software promises to expand educational opportunity while increasing freedom for participants.

9.1 THE TECHNOLOGIES OF DISTANCE EDUCATION

Distance education is often defined both by its providers and by learners in terms of the technology used in its provision. This technological identification carries with it an underlying deterministic bias that has both positive and negative impact on distance education perceptions, attitudes, and practices. In this section, I examine the way in which distance education theorists have categorized the technologies used in distance education and highlight recent developments and applications using these technologies.

Building on the work of Rumble (1999), Hulsmann (2004) describes two major types of technologies that define and contextualize distance education delivery. The first of these is *Type I* for Information technologies that generally support delivery and engagement with content. This content is now increasingly available in a variety of media, packaged in units as large as full course and as small as discrete learning objects (McGreal, 2004) and capable of interacting with and engaging the learner in a wide variety of instructional activities. The *Type I* information technologies and applications are all migrating to the Web. Furthermore, simple Internet access is slowly being augmented by organization schema and meta-tag descriptions to allow access not only to humans but also to intelligent or autonomous agents. This capacity for machines or autonomous agents to search, analyze, and make inferences based upon networked data is the essence of Tim Berners-Lee second phase of the Web, which he termed "the Semantic Web" (Berners-Lee et al., 2001). In earlier works we focused this development on an educational context referring to the educational semantic web (Anderson and Whitelock, 2004).

The second type of technologies referred to by Hulsmann is *Type C* for communication or interactive technologies. Hulsmann and Rumble describe *Type C* technologies as those that support a wide variety of mediated human interaction. In distance education, these *Type C* technologies originally supported asynchronous text interaction such as postal correspondence and later e-mail and computer conferencing. Today, asynchronous tools have been supplemented by synchronous technologies such as text, audio- and video-conferencing, chats, and immersive educational worlds.

Although Hulsmann noted the capacity of both Type I and Type C technologies to exist on a common platform (such as a learning management system or LMS), we are seeing in the intersection of these two types of technologies the emergence of a new genre of distance education software – Type S for Social software technologies (Figure 9.1).

These technologies map closely to the well-known typology of generations of distance education (Nipper, 1989). The First-Generation, correspondence technologies and the mass Second-Generation technologies of radio and television telecourses are Type I technologies used in most part to support independent learning. The Third-Generation technologies of audio- and video-conferencing are based largely on Type C technologies. The so-called Fourth- and Fifth-Generation distance education (Taylor, 1995; Taylor, 2001) use the enhanced processing capacities of Type I information technologies with multimodal Type C interactive technologies. Type S technologies are therefore component tools of Fifth-Generation technologies. Because they support distance learning

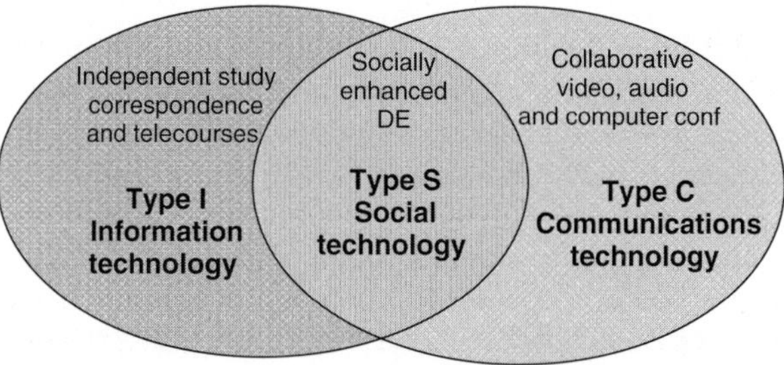

Figure 9.1: Distance Education Delivery Models and Technologies

applications that encourage collaboration even within self-paced and continuous enrollment courses, they can create opportunities for radically new conceptions of independence and collaboration in distance education (Anderson, 2005).

9.2 ISSUES OF ACCESS

Before discussing developments related to these three types of technologies in more detail, I should emphasize that almost all of the applications of the technologies discussed in this chapter assume ready, reliable, and affordable access to the Internet. Further, many of these applications are optimized for higher speed connections than supported by dial-up connectivity. Thus, these are technologies for a network-infused society. This precondition for access currently precludes many of those in developing countries and those in rural locations in nearly all countries.

Distance educators have traditionally chosen to use "lowest common denominator" type technologies in order to assure access by all. The distance education applications described in this chapter violate that tradition of prioritizing access over functionality.

While acknowledging the limitations of access, I believe that we are in the midst of an expansive era in which connectivity is rapidly increasing while associated costs are decreasing. The 2005 MIT announcement of the $100 computer (http://laptop.media.mit.edu/), plus expansion of wireless telephony to large areas of Africa and Asia, illustrates that connectivity and access to mobile-learning possibilities, while remaining an issue, is not problematic for a large and growing proportion of global lifelong learners. Finally, developments of solar-powered mesh routers give promise of network connectivity even in areas where electricity is not readily available (Islam, 2006).

Distance education must be broad enough to focus on access issues while at the same time exploiting new technologies to expand the breadth of opportunity to growing number of learners in Net-infused societies. New communities are being created that are native to these technologies. For example, LunarStorm, the Swedish language online community, has 1.2 million members and 90 percent of the country's high-school students are active members (Crampton, 2005). MySpace reported adding 260,000 users per day to the 65 million users in early 2006 (Gates, 2006). Access within these new communities necessitates a different form of distance education, one that challenges educators to create and sustain types of learning opportunities that exploit the specific learning affordances of the technologies upon which these communities are built.

9.3 DEVELOPMENTS IN TYPE I TECHNOLOGIES

The capacity of the Net to serve as a searchable (and findable!) repository of educational content and applications is perhaps the greatest innovation in Type I technologies. Although the promise of retrievable and reusable learning objects has not yet met the exuberant claims of early developers, there are a host of extraordinary

Type I resources available today. A few exemplar Net examples include Wikipedia, the world's largest and most popular encyclopedia, with its 2.5 million entries in ten languages, the search and retrieval capacity of free-to-use tools such as Google Scholar, the free publication and distribution of over 22,947 open-access scholarly journals (http://www.doaj.org, Nov. 2007), and the development of open-access texts and resource repositories such as the Internet Archive (http://www.archive.org/), the growing list of Open Access curriculum (see examples at http://www.oercommons.org), and the efforts by many to support and stimulate the open-source development and sharing of education resources (Keats, 2003). Many of these learning resources move beyond text to create animated, video, and audio enhancements with examples such as Google Earth (http://earth.google.com/) or educator-created, video-annotated learning objects such as the Conceptual Frameworks Learning Object (http://innovation.dc-uoit.ca/cloe/lo/cf/CF_LO_content.html). Net-based Type I technologies are being used extensively in distance education for a host of administrative functions including content management of course guides, student support and information portals, online registration systems, and online access to library collections. Downes (2005) argues that the Type I technologies of the very near future will be modeled on a "Read/Write Web" in which students are not only consumers, but also creators of learning content. My own work using student-created learning portals (Anderson and Wark, 2004) and recent use of educational Web blogs (see http://terrya.edublogs.org/) convince me that instructional design models are needed that allow students to actively participate in the cocreation of Type I learning resources. Finally, the development of individual e-portfolios (i.e. http://www.theospi.org) and institutional knowledge repositories (e.g. http://www.dspace.org) provide persistent storage and selective display of a large quantity of distance education artifacts. These artifacts range from scholarly works, to student-created content, to the course guides and texts used in course delivery. In sum, the decreasing cost of online storage, the ease of creation in multimedia formats, and the increasing capability for search and retrieval is affording a move from scarcity to abundance of distance education, Type I content.

9.4 DEVELOPMENTS IN TYPE C TECHNOLOGIES

The convergence of communication technologies on an Internet-based common platform, coupled with the rapid development of various forms of Net-based communication software, allows very low cost communications in multiple media for many distance education applications. Communication and subsequent interaction, via a mediating technology, has always been a critical component of distance education theory and practice (Holmberg, 1989; Moore, 1989; Anderson, 2003). However, the costs of these technologies coupled with access issues have always controlled and limited the amount of this interaction. The emergence of no-cost Net-based telephony tools such as Skype (http://skype.com) that support synchronous audio, text, and even video interaction amongst not only individuals but groups of distance education students, teachers, or administrators has fundamentally changed the costing factors related to the use of Type C technology.

A second notable development in Type C technologies is the move from access through expensive hardware located at learning centers to participation in distance education programming from individual home and offices. This enhanced distribution obviously increases accessibility and decreases transportation costs. However, it decreases opportunity for planned and spontaneous face-to-face interaction by groups of learners who would gather at learning centers to access distance education programming. This trade-off illustrates that every application of education technology both alleviates and creates access and pedagogical opportunities and concerns.

Although far from the mainstream of distance education practice, millions of users are now engaged in immersive virtual worlds and collaborative gaming environments (Castronova, 2002). These social and community environments use Type C technologies for entertainment and informal learning. It is easy to imagine distance educators creating institutions and learning spaces using these technologies. SecondLife, the largest of these immersive worlds, now hosts a wide variety of campus-augmented and virtual universities, and provides incentives and supports for educators wishing to offer programming in immersive contexts (see http://www.simteach.com/wiki/index.php?title=Second_Life_Education_Wiki). Finally, Type C interactions are moving from the ethereal to the persistent as they are captured in digital formats and replayed using a host of portable and desktop tools.

In summary, the examples above illustrate the convergence of distance education technologies on the Web, and the reduced cost and the increased functionality of these technologies. Before turning to a discussion of the pedagogy and learning activities afforded by the convergence of Type I and Type C technologies, I want to provide a context for the discussion by reviewing the types of freedom that distance educators seek to support in their distance education programming.

9.5 TECHNOLOGIES, DESIGNS, AND PARTICIPANT FREEDOM

Each model or form of distance education involves trade-offs and choices. Freedom to access learning through time and space has always defined distance education, but now the frontiers of access can be extended to new degrees of freedom, providing teachers and learners with new tools, techniques, and learning activities.

Paulsen (1993) identified six different dimensions of freedom relevant to distance educators in his "theory of cooperative freedom". These include the familiar *freedom of space* and *freedom of time*, which have defined much traditional distance education programming. But he also describes the *freedom to pace* one's learning in response to individual competencies, learning resources, or time availability. A fourth dimension concerns the *freedom of media*, which allows choice of learning medium to match a host of media access and usability constraints, and communication system qualities and preferences. The fifth is the *freedom of access*, which includes removal of barriers of prerequisites and high costs. Finally, Paulsen's sixth dimension is *freedom of content*, which allows the learner to have freedom to impact or control the subject and instructional style of their learning. To these six freedoms I have added a seventh, *freedom of relationship*, which allows students the capability to decide on the types of social relationships they will develop and maintain within their learning communities and individual relationships with other students, teachers, and local and online community members.

Program or course designers are afforded the options of curtailing, mixing and matching, or facilitating any and all of these freedoms by the instructional designs and tools they use to support the distance learning experience. Of prime importance is learning efficacy, but even this highest goal must be balanced with cost-effectiveness, and attention to access issues. As importantly, in an increasingly consumer-orientated education economy the learning experience must be compelling and motivating to learners.

9.6 FREEDOM OF SPACE AND RELATIONSHIP

Because freedom of pace and of relationship are arguably the most complex of the freedoms to provide in any formal education context, they are the focus of this section. Freedom to pace one's learning experience over a week, a month, or a year defined earliest forms of distance education such as postal correspondence. These forms also afforded freedom of time and place. Freedom of pace allows educational systems to support continuous enrollment, so that students can begin their program, not just once or twice a year at the convenience of the delivering institution, but whenever they have need or opportunity to engage in formal learning. Allowing for freedom of pace and continuous enrollment opens the door to access of formal learning in a "just-as-needed" format more closely aligning provision with need. This alignment is a critical feature of lifelong learning (Koper, 2005). However, past and current models of self-paced formal learning, based upon continuous enrollment programs, usually restrict freedom of relationship, in that not only are start times variable, but the length of time to complete a course also varies widely. Personal privacy concerns can also limit learners' capacity to work collaboratively or even to be made aware of other learners working on the same course. Creating learning groups or communities amongst students moving through a course of studies at varying times and pace created numerous obstacles and resulted in low registration levels in early pilots offering collaborative designs within this model of delivery (Anderson et al., 2005). We needed to make learners more aware that others have something of value to offer and would not hold them back. Despite these challenges we are seeing growing interest in more collaborative and community-based models of learning (Slavin, 1995) and in online learning communities (Palloff and Pratt, 1999).

To bridge this gap between promise and practice there is a need for new tools and instructional activities that allow students freedom of pace, time, and space, yet still support freedom of relationship, in which students are afforded an opportunity to collaborate with each other and share social space. In sum, we search for a way for learners to have their cake and eat it too!

9.6.1 Type S – Social Technologies

Type S technologies utilize the information processing, storage, and retrieval capacity of Type I technologies and couple them with the interactive communication capacity of

Type C technologies. Outside the formal world of distance education Type S technologies are synonymous with the set of Net-based applications often referred to as "social software". Social software has been heralded and hyped as the "next big thing" in Net-based tools for a variety of business, personal, and political applications (Kaplan-Leiserson, 2004). Social software technologies and applications are evolving very quickly and even the definition of social software is in flux.

The term "social software" is often attributed to Clay Shirky, who defined it as "software that supports group interaction" (Shirky, 2003). This definition is so broad that it includes everything from e-mail to SMS; thus it has been qualified by a number of authors. Allen (2004) notes the evolution of software tools as the Net gains in capacity to support human interaction, decision-making, planning, and other higher level activities across boundaries of time and space, and less adeptly those of culture and language. Similar to affordances of the semantic web outlined by Anderson (2004), Levin (2004) notes noted the ubiquity of the Net and especially the "findability" of content available to current generations of searching with brute force tools like Google. Second, she notes the pervasive and multiple formats of communication that are supported ranging from synchronous to asynchronous, from one-to-one to many-to-many, from text to full multimedia, and from communications in a dedicated home theatre to that supported on a mobile phone while in transit. Finally, Levin notes the affordance of the Web to support new patterns of interconnection that "facilitate new social patterns: multi-scale social spaces, conversation discovery and group forming, personal and social decoration and collaborative folk art".

A major function of social software is to facilitate the meeting (either online or face-to-face) of an individual with other individuals or groups who share common interests. Social software provides scaffolding that allows individuals and groups to share, extract, and organize new knowledge and build social relationships. This knowledge can be applied to a range of applications from stamp collecting to bicycle racing; from selling a product to finding a spouse. Meeting together in a shared space is likely not to happen by happenstance alone. Cervini (2003) notes that the capacity of social software to create links between individuals with particular interests or skills is done through a directed searching of individual profiles, writings, and other contributions to a shared Net space. This searching must be secure, effective, easy to use, and not violate the privacy of users. Applying this affordance to allow students to meet each other (online or off-line) has many positive and disruptive implications for systems built upon an independent study model.

To summarize, social software uses the information processing power of the distributed Net to contextualize and adapt Type I or information technologies. It uses this same power to enhance Type C communication technologies providing users powerful tools to locate, engage, and organize their communicative encounters with other learners and teachers. However, to be effective Type S or educational social software tools must offer the following list of qualities:

Ease of use: Very easy to use, allowing distributed individuals to communicate and participate in social activities with minimal technical skills.

Accessibility: The contributions of others are not hidden behind passwords or closed classroom door, or archived in inaccessible libraries. Rather, social software is an integral component of a globally networked and publicly accessible information and communication infrastructure.

Findability: Use of syndication, automatic and cooperative tagging, indexing and spider tools allows social software contributions and information about their authors to be searched, harvested, and extracted.

Ownership and identity: Social relationships are built on reputation and responsibility. Social software seeks to return ownership of comments to their creator. Thus persistence of contribution across formal and informal communities and the technical capacity for all participants to link, search, and archive contributions across these communities is critical.

Persistence: Being digital and thus searchable, social contributions (with permission of the participants) can be used, referenced, researched, extracted, reused, and recycled across time and space (Erickson, 1999).

Like other technologies used in distance education, social software tools were created for applications that are not directly related to formal education. Our task as distance educators is to identify the capacities and pull together the most useful features of these tools to apply them in the formal context of distance education. In the next section, I describe how these applications can be used, beginning with a definition of the term "educational social technology".

9.7 EDUCATIONAL SOCIAL TECHNOLOGY

A working definition of *educational social technologies* (EST), as applied to an open learning educational context, is "networked tools that support and encourage learning through face-to-face and online interactions while retaining individual control over the learners' time, space, presence, activity and identity" (Anderson, 2006).

Turning now to the application of Type S social technologies in an educational context (EST), I examine the component tools, pedagogies, and learning activities of the current generation of EST applications. By focusing on these critical components of education we see how these tools come to take their place in the constellation of technologies that afford quality distance education experiences.

9.8 THE COMPONENT TOOLS OF EDUCATIONAL SOCIAL SOFTWARE

The current generation of EST systems usually combine at least three kinds of generic affordances see Figure 9.2. These three major functions – profiling of participants, communicating tools, and collaborative tools – interact to create a more powerful social learning environment than any of the three applications alone.

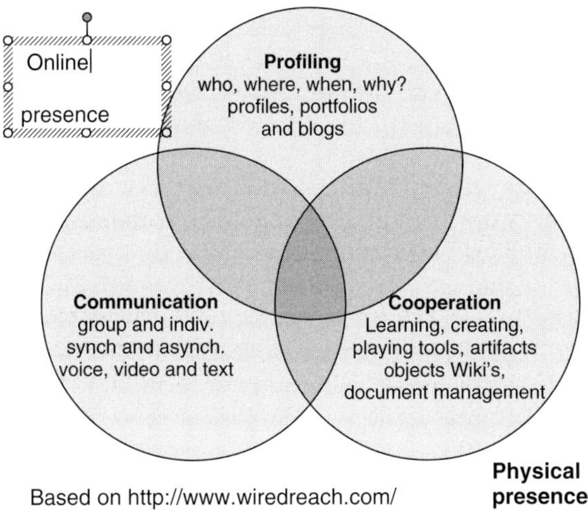

Figure 9.2: Typical Set of Tools Used in an EST Enhanced Distance Education Context

9.8.1 Profiling

In order to establish social connections among learners, tools must be used to allow users to create, edit, and search the profiles and postings of others to find similar interests, expectations, time frames, common locations, and other personal data. An educational profile typically contains fields including the learner's name, location, e-mail addresses, courses enrolled, willingness to collaborate on projects, and anticipated date of completion. Obviously, release of this data contains risk of privacy violation, and thus safeguards must be in place to allow selective release of this data (Nabeth, 2005). Figure 9.3 provides a screen shot of a social software tool set (elgg.net) being pilot

Figure 9.3: Example of Learner Profile Editing Illustrating Selective Control of Release of Personal Information (Me2u.athabascau.ca – powered by elgg.net)

tested at Athabasca University. Notice the capacity for the user to voluntarily release information and to control to which class of user the data in each individual each field is released. These control groups can be changed by the systems administrator but typically involve release to anyone, to only those logged into the institutional system, those enrolled in the student's program, those in a particular class, or those in a user defined subgroup or community of users. In Figure 9.3, a screen shot from the Elgg-powered social software system illustrates the profiling capability. Each of words entered in any of the fields at the left is instantly hyperlinked to others who share that interest. Thus, one can quickly and easily find other participants sharing interests, geographic location, or any other category of user information established by the institution in the profile. Secondly, it is important to notice the learner's control over the release of each filed in the profile (see right column). Access can be restricted in many ways ranging from public (including Goggle search spiders), logged-in users, or members of particular communities or groups.

Currently, most social software applications do not use emerging specifications such as the IMS Learning Information Package Specification, but one can easily imagine linking a student-owned profile to any number of institutional systems to allow students to efficiently control access to personal information. For the first time it becomes possible for online learners to find other learners in close physical proximity, those who share interests, courses, vocations, and other background characteristics upon which collaborative learning can be based. Additionally, the data in the profile may be used to customize the educational content, thus using the Type S technologies to individualize the Type I content.

Besides providing profiles, learners may make accessible their interests and ideas by creating essays and other documents, commenting on course content, or questioning, debating, and defending ideas. These productions are coming to be known as Webblogs or Blogs. Will Richardson's video on blogs at http://campus.belmont.edu/chenowit/dragonstale/WebLoggingSmall.mov provides an overview of the benefits of Blogging applications to campus education settings. Blogging has many characteristics in common with the familiar threaded discussion lists; however, they differ in the extent to which the BLOG is owned by the learner, persists beyond a single course, and is syndicated and thus shared beyond those enrolled in the course. The information shared in these BLOG components of an EST system allows the selective release of these learner-created artifacts so that others can find, retrieve, and comment upon these contributions. The technical linking of these contributions is sustained through tagging of content, selective release, and RSS syndication (see Richardson, 2005).

9.8.2 Communication Tools

Communication tools and techniques create the opportunities for interaction and for collaborative construction of knowledge. Net-based communications (Type S) tools are usually incorporated within or used in conjunction with educational social software suites.

I will not review all the text, audio, graphic, and video tools that support one-to-one, one-to-many, and many-to-many communications, but the overview of developments in Type S presented earlier underlines the increasing number of ways that communication among learners can be supported, recorded, archived, and reviewed.

9.8.3 Cooperation Tools

Effective cooperative creation of knowledge in distributed contexts often depends on tools to create and then manage these learning artifacts (Stahl, 2002). Very simple, first-generation networking tools such as threaded discussions can be used for these tasks, but their lack of support for group editing, version control, annotation, and graphics creates barriers to effective use. EST systems generally support Wikis for group editing (Thorne and Payne, 2005), dedicated tools such as concept mapping, ways to determine and assess the presence and contribution of co-learners, and finally ways to control the distribution of these artifacts.

The EST tools are currently being merged into next-generation LMS, and thus we can expect hybrid and customized combinations of social software to be used in conjunction with other forms of online learning and teaching support. Rather than huge monolithic tool sets, each unique to a particular educational institution, we image a day of disaggregated tools where individual learners, teachers, and institutions mix and match tools necessary for their own pedagogical and discipline-related use (Downes, 2005).

Figure 9.4 illustrates the function of four separate tools and overviews the component functions of each. The example is from a master's degree course at Athabasca University. The major learning activity of the course is the creation (by small groups of students) of

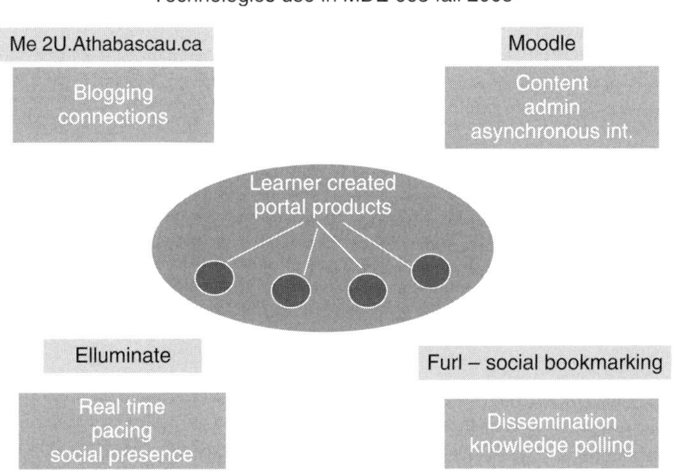

Figure 9.4: The Four Technologies Used in a Course at Athabasca University

extensive portals focusing on an emerging distance education technology. The Moodle LMS is used for posting of articles and other content, for its assignment drop box, calendar, and other administrative functions as well as asynchronous threaded interaction. The Me2U software is an instance of the open-source profile and blogging suite elgg.net that is used for blogging of personal reflections, commenting on others work, creating a blogging community, and finding common interests and building community through linkages of learner profiles. The Elluminate.com audiographic software is used for weekly synchronous sessions featuring presentations, group discussions, and other "virtual classroom" interactions. Finally, Furl.net is a social tagging system that allows learners to submit, evaluate, and share Net-based resources as found by the teacher and participating students.

Certainly, similar educational activities can be undertaken using more than one of the applications below, or others not used in the course. We can expect a period of experimentation, consolidation, and specialization in EST tool sets as new tools are created, and we learn to use effectively the tool appropriate for each unique context in which distance education is practiced.

I turn next from the tools to the pedagogical underpinnings of EST application in formal learning, and finally to a listing of appropriate learning activities.

9.9 PEDAGOGY OF EST

An educational tool is only as useful as its functionality in meeting teaching and learning goals and enabling positive learning outcomes within the learning context that it supports. EST resonates well with the social constructivist ideals of Dewey and Vygotsky and in the support of cooperative and collaborative learning activities developed and validated in educational contexts well before the Web. As importantly, EST fits with the learning perspective of the so-called "Net Generation" (Oblinger and Oblinger, 2005) and the "postmodern pedagogy" that acknowledges that "colleges do not exist to provide instruction; we exist to create learning" (Taylor, 2005).

Moreover, new EST tools also both beget and demand new pedagogies. Stewart and Kagan (2005) argue "that our educational discourse is largely stuck in a time warp, framed by issues and standards set decades before the widespread use of the personal computer, the Internet, and free trade agreements". Three relatively new insights into learning theory come directly from a deep understanding of the role of the Net in creating opportunities for new forms of teaching and learning.

The first relates to the capacity for learning to flow seamlessly between online and face-to-face educational contexts. Mejias (2005) has argued for a new "pedagogy of nearness" in which online interaction, collaboration, and learning are neither valued nor devalued as compared to interactions with those near at hand. Rather, in a network-infused environment we are "on our way to a more sustainable relationship with the world when we learn to inscribe our online experiences into larger systems of action meant to bring the epistemologically far near to us, and make the physically near relevant again". Increasingly, networked users are equally comfortable creating and sustaining productive social relationship in either online or face-to-face contexts and quite easily switch between the two. This obviously presents opportunities for distance education that must, by definition, operate in such distributed contexts.

The second pedagogical insight relevant to EST is George Siemen's (2005) "connectivism", which he describes as a way of knowing that is native to those immersed in networked knowledge construction and is particularly relevant to EST-based distance education systems. Connectivism is informed by chaos, network, complexity, and self-organizational theories and postulates that "the connections that enable us to learn are more important than our current state of knowing". Siemens notes that learning is a process of connecting nodes or knowledge and this knowledge resides in both humans and nonhuman appliances. To Siemens, learning is a process of encoding nodes (of information and knowledge) and connecting them to other internal and external nodes. These connections are fluid and expand and contract with the focus of the activity and the networked resources available to the learner. To optimize learning requires that learners be exposed to problems and challenges together with resources such that they can meaningfully encode new nodes and connect them as densely as possible with existing networked nodes. These connections create resiliency, force confrontation with contradiction, and through use are strengthened by exposure and repetition. EST serves to provide a means whereby distributed learners can in the first place become aware of each other and the strengths, insights, and contexts they bring to the learning context and then providing means by which communities of learning are both stimulated and nurtured.

A final insight comes from Stewart Hase and Chris Kenyon (2000), who updated pre-Net conceptions of pedagogy and andragogy to define "heutagogy" – the study of self-determined learning. Heutagogy functions as a guide for self-directed learners operating in a world in which

> information is readily and easily accessible; where change is so rapid that traditional methods of training and education are totally inadequate; discipline based knowledge is inappropriate to prepare for living in modern communities and workplaces; learning is increasingly aligned with what we do; modern organisational structures require flexible learning practices; and there is a need for immediacy of learning.
>
> (Hase and Kenyon, 2000)

Thus, learning content must be capable of being multifaceted such that it can speak to the many and changing contexts in which the learner constructs their own knowledge. These authors argue that teacher-directed learning packages often found in distance education require greater learner control, input, and flexibility that matches well with the technical affordances of EST.

The pedagogy of EST serves to integrate formal educational learning with real-life application. At primary and secondary levels, obvious participants in this open sharing of educational archives are parents and guardians. In professional and vocational education an increasing amount of the professional discourse is created and sustained on the Net (see, for example, the notions of community-centered learning of (Bransford et al., 1999) or the practical applications in teacher education as illustrated in Wiske et al. (2002)). By both allowing opportunity and creating challenging demands on learners to engage with the community of practice for which they are preparing, we accomplish a number of useful goals. First, learners acquire hidden curriculum goals allowing them to begin to think and act like members of their profession (Anderson, 2001). Second, higher education moves from an observer and trainer role to being a contributor to professional discourse that serves to integrate knowledge production in practice and in disciplinary inquiry (Gibbons, 1999). Finally, exposure to EST technologies and activities provides invaluable experience in the skill sets necessary to function in a Net-based economy and learning space and, as importantly, enhances learners' Net self-efficacy (Eastin and LaRose, 2000).

The EST pedagogy asserts the importance of learning with and through others and via adaptive content (Siemens, 2005). It stresses the need for and value of social connections both face-to-face and online (Mejías, 2005). It is most appropriate for self-directed learners who need to access and can contribute to views of others and the topic under study in a community of practice (Hase and Kenyon, 2000).

From the pedagogical theory I next turn to practical learning activities that have been developed for use in EST platforms.

9.10 LEARNING ACTIVITIES USING EST

I conclude this discussion with a brief overview of some of the learning activities that can be used in distance education programming that uses EST. The activities in Table 9.1 are generic, and of course must be customized and aligned with general and particular learning outcomes designed by developers, teachers, and the learners themselves.

Many designs developed for cooperative and collaborative learning in campus-based programs can be reconfigured for distance delivery in either cohort or self-paced distance models. However, we are just at the beginning stages of construction and testing of instructional designs that effectively exploit the affordances of all three types of distance education technologies as they become Net integrated.

The first applications of new technologies are usually instantiations of activities supported by earlier more familiar technologies creating the so-called horseless carriage effect (McLuhan, 1964). In such a fashion, Donna Cameron and I have mapped many of the collaborative and cooperative learning activities designed for classroom groups to online activity using educational social software.

In Table 9.1 we provide a listing of these activities as they have been modified to use the features of the Me2U instance of the elgg.net social software tool set currently being piloted at Athabasca University.

Table 9.1: Learning Activities Modified for Social Software

Use of Social Software	*Specific Activity*
Orientation activities using Me2U	• Registration • Lurking • Self-introduction • Who's who • Joining and creating communities • Online chats or calls
Collaboration using Me2U	• Jigsaws • Mentoring • Debates • Group response • Discussion groups • Posting a review • Surveys • Document sharing • Data/File collection • Information search
Advanced web activities using Me2U	• Creating Web sites • Developing E-portfolios • Reviews • Wiki-based projects • Collaborative FAQs • Course assignment library • Student advice pages or link lists • Collaborative glossary • Collaborative writing • Exam review • Additional collaborative tools

A description of each of these activities including suggested number of participants, assessments, support technologies, and suggested time to complete is available at http://cider.athabascau.ca/Members/terrya/socialsoftware/

9.11 CONCLUSION

In this chapter, I have attempted to document the impact that the Net has on the traditional methods and tools of distance education technologies. The most recent of these effects affords the development of a new genre of distance education technology referred to as Type S or educational social software. These technologies are being widely and enthusiastically used to enhance classroom and cohort models of distance education. But perhaps their most revolutionary impact will be to support adlib, short-term, and spontaneous communities among those learners enrolled in continuous intake programs. Adding a social element to these courses, while retaining freedom of relationship and pacing creates tools for the next generation of lifelong learning – available at any time, any place, any pace.

REFERENCES

Allen, C. (2004). Tracing the evolution of social software. *Life With Alacrity*, Retrieved February 2005 from http://www.lifewithalacrity.com/2004/10/tracing_the_evo.html

Anderson, T. (2001). The hidden curriculum of distance education. *Change Magazine*, **33**(6), 29–35.

Anderson, T. (2003). Modes of interaction in distance education: Recent developments and research questions. In *Handbook of Distance Education.*(M. Moore and W. Anderson, eds), Mahwah, NJ: Erlbaum, pp. 129–144.

Anderson, T. (2004). The educational semantic web: A vision for the next phase of educational computing. *Educational Technology*, **44**(5), 5–9.

Anderson, T. (2005). Distance learning – Social software's killer ap? In *Proceedings of the Open & Distance Learning Association of Australia*, Adelaide: ODLAA. Retrieved December 2007 from www.unisa.edu.au/odlaaconference/PPDF2s/13%20odlaa%20-%20Anderson.pdf.

Anderson, T. (2006). Higher education evolution: Individual freedom afforded by educational social software. In *Perspectives on the Future of Higher Education in the Digital Age* (M. Beaudoin, ed.), New York: Nova Science Publishers.

Anderson, T. and Wark, N. (2004). Why do teachers get to learn the most? A case study of a course based on student creation of learning objects. *e-Journal of Instructional Science and Technology*, **7**(2) Retrieved November 2007 from http://www.usq.edu.au/electpub/e-jist/docs/Vol7_no2/FullPapers/WhyDoTeachers.pdf.

Anderson, T. and Whitelock, D. (2004). The educational semantic web: Visioning and practicing the future of education. *Journal of Interactive Media in Education*, **1**. Retrieved December, 2007 from http://www-jime.open.ac.uk/2004/1

Anderson, T., Annand, D., and Wark, N. (2005). The search for learning community in learner-paced distance education programming or "Having Your Cake and Eating It, Too!". *Australian Journal of Educational Technology*, **21**(2), 222–241. Retrieved December 2007 from http://www.ascilite.org.au/ajet/ajet21/anderson.html

Berners-Lee, T., Hendler, J., and Lassila, O. (2001). The semantic web. *Scientific American*, **284**(5), 34–43.

Bijker, W. (1999). *Of Bicycles, Bakelites and Bulbs: Towards a Theory of Sociotechnical Change*. Cambridge: MIT Press.

Bransford, J., Brown, A., and Cocking, R. (1999). *How People Learn: Brain, Mind Experience and School.* Washington: National Research Council. Retrieved December 2007 from the http://www.nap.edu/html/howpeople1/.

Castronova, E. (2002). On virtual economies. *CESifo Working Paper Series No. 752*, Retrieved December 2007 from http://ssrn.com/abstract=338500

Cervini, A. (2003). Network Connections: An Analysis of Social Software that Turns Online Introductions into Offline Interactions. New York: New York University. Retrieved December 2007 from http://www.frimfram.com/thesis/thesis.html

Crampton, T. (2005, November 28). Online community takes Sweden by storm. *International Herald.*

Downes, S. (2005). E-Learning 2.0. *ELearn Magazine,* Retrieved December 2007 from http://elearnmag.org/subpage.cfm?section=articles&article=29-1

Eastin, M. and LaRose, R. (2000). Internet self-efficacy and the psychology of the digital divide. *Journal of Computer Mediated Communications*, **6**(1), Retrieved December, 2007 from http://jcmc.indiana.edu/vol6/issue1/eastin.html

Erickson, T. (1999). Persistent conversation: An introduction. *Journal of Computer Mediated Communications*, 4(4), Retrieved December 2007 from http://jcmc.indiana.edu/vol4/issue4/ericksonintro.html.

Gates, B. (2006). Keynote Speech at Mix06 Conference [Film]. Retrieved December 2007 from http://www.microsoft.com/billgates/speeches/2006/03-20MIX.asp

Gibbons, M. (1999). Changing research practices. In *What Kind of University? International Perspectives on Knowledge, Participation and Governance* (J. Brennan, J. Fedrowitz, M. Huber, and T. Shah, eds). Buckingham, UK: SRHE and Open University Press, pp. 23–35.

Hase, S. and Kenyon, C. (2000). From andragogy to heutagogy. *UltiBase*, Retrieved December, 2007 from ultibase.rmit.edu.au/Articles/ dec00/hase2.htm

Holmberg, B. (1989). *Theory and Practice of Distance Education.* London: Routledge.

Hulsmann, T. (2004). The two-pronged attack on learner support: costs and centrifugal forces of convergence. In *Supporting the Learner in Distance Education and E-Learning: Proceedings of the Third EDEN Research Workshop,* Oldenburg: Bibliotheks-und-Information system der Universitat Oldenburg, pp. 498–504. Retrieved December 2007 from www.uni-oldenburg.de/zef/literat/paper-huelsmann.pdf.

Islam, R. (2006, August 30). Solar power may soon bring the Web to remote areas. *The Christian Science Monitor.*

Kaplan-Leiserson, A. (2004). We learning: Social software and e-learning – Part 2. *Learning Circuits*, (January), Retrieved December 2007 from http://www.learningcircuits.org/2004/jan2004/kaplan2.htm

Keats, D. (2003). Collaborative development of open content: A process model to unlock the potential for African universities. *First Monday*, 8(2), Retrieved December 2007 from http://www.firstmonday.org/issues/issue8_2/keats/

Koper, R. (2005). Designing learning networks for lifelong learners. In *Learning Design.* (R. Koper and K. Tatterssall, eds), Berlin: Springer, pp. 239–252.

Levin, A. (2004). Social software: What's new. *Many 2 Many*, Retrieved December 2007 from http://www.alevin.com/weblog/archives/001492.html

McGreal, R. (2004). *Online Education Using Learning Objects.* London: Routledge/Falmer.

McLuhan, M. (1964). *Understanding Media: The Extensions of Man.* Toronto: McGraw-Hill.

Mejias, U. (2005). Re-approaching nearness: Online communication and its place in praxis. *First Monday*, 10(3). Retrieved December 2007 from http://firstmonday.org/issues/issue10_3/mejias/index.html

Moore, M. (1989). Three types of interaction. *American Journal of Distance Education*, 3(2), 1–6.

Nabeth, T. (2005). *Privacy in the Context of Digital Social Environments: A cyber-Sociological Perspective.* Retrieved December 2007 from http://www.calt.insead.edu/project/Fidis/documents/2005-PET-Privacy_in_the_Context_of_Digital_Social_Environments_A_Cyber-Sociological_Perspective.pdf

Nipper, S. (1989). Third generation distance learning and computer conferencing. In *Mindweave: Communication, Computers and Distance Education* (R. Mason and A.A. Kaye, eds), Oxford, UK: Permagon, pp. 63–73.

Oblinger, D. and Oblinger, J. (2005). *Educating the Net Generation.* Boulder, Co.: EduCause. Retrieved September 2007 from http://www.educause.edu/content.asp?PAGE_ID=5989&bhcp=1.

Palloff, R. and Pratt, K. (1999). *Building Learning Communities in Cyberspace.* San Francisco: Jossey-Bass.

Paulsen, M. (1993). The hexagon of cooperative freedom: A distance education theory attuned to computer conferencing. DEOS, 3(2). Retrieved December 2007 from http://www.nettskolen.com/forskning/21/hexagon.html

Richardson, W. (2005). *RSS: A Quick Start Guide for Educators.* (1.5 ed.). Retrieved December 2007 from http://static.hcrhs.k12.nj.us/gems/tech/RSSFAQ4.pdf.

Rumble, G. (1999). Cost analysis of distance learning. *Performance Improvement Quarterly*, **12**(2), 122–137.

Shirky, C. (2003). A group of its own worst enemy. Clay Shriky's writings about the Internet. Retrieved December 2007 from http://shirky.com/writings/group_enemy.html

Siemens, G. (2005). A learning theory for the digital age. *Instructional Technology and Distance Education*, **2**(1), 3–10. Retrieved December 2007 from http://www.elearnspace.org/Articles/connectivism.htm

Slavin, R. (1995). *Cooperative Learning Theory, Research, and Practice.* Boston: Allyn and Bacon.

Stahl, G. (2002). Groupware goes to school. In *Groupware: Design, Implementation and Use: Proceedings of the 8th International Workshop on Groupware. (CRIWG '02)*, La Serena, Chile: Springer. Retrieved December 2005 from http://www.cis.drexel.edu/faculty/gerry/cscl/papers/ch11.pdf.

Stewart, V. and Kagan, S. (2005). A new world view: Education in a global era. *Phi Delta Kappan*, **87**(3). Retrieved December 2007 from http://www.pdfintl.org/kappan/k_v87/k0511st2.htm.

Taylor, J. (2001). Automating e-Learning: The higher education revolution. In *International Conference on Emerging Telecommunications Applications (ICETA):* ICETA. Retrieved January 2005 from http://www.backingaustraliasfuture.gov.au/submissions/issues_sub/pdf/i43_3.pdf.

Taylor, J.C. (1995). Distance education technologies: The fourth generation. *Australian Journal of Educational Technology*, **11**(2), 1–7.

Taylor, M. (2005). Postmodern pedagogy: Teaching and learning with generation NeXt. *MCLI Forum*, **9**, 4–8. Retrieved December 2007 from http://www.mcli.dist.maricopa.edu/forum/spr05/mcliForumV9Sp05.pdf

Thorne, S.L. and Payne, J.S. (2005). Evolutionary trajectories, Internet-mediated expression, and language. *CALICO Journal*, **22**(3), 371–397. Retrieved October 2007 from http://language.la.psu.edu/˜thorne/thorne_payne_calico2005.pdf

Wiske, M., Sick, M., and Wirsig, S. (2002). New technologies to support teaching for understanding. *International Journal of Educational Research*, **35**(5), 483–501. Retrieved November 2007 from http://wideworld.pz.harvard.edu/_upload/wide_research/aera_ijer_042002.pdf.

Chapter 10

Vocational Education and Training at a Distance: Transformation to Flexible Delivery

Peter J. Smith

10.1 FOCUS OF THIS CHAPTER

This chapter will explore the position that distance education has held in the past in Australian vocational education and training (VET) and how that position has developed and transformed over the past couple of decades. It is argued here that after a period of VET provision through distance education that was largely based around an earlier centralised model, VET was early to recognise the potential that new technologies in distance education had for VET learners and learning. Concurrently there was recognition of the substantial limitations a centralised model of distance education posed for new demands on VET. Economic imperatives also contributed to what became a revolution in VET and its delivery to learners.

The chapter identifies these developments and the factors that have contributed to them, and tracks the transition of Australian VET distance education as it transformed away from centralised distance education provision towards its more recent forms of locally provided flexible delivery and blended learning.

10.2 HISTORICAL CONTEXT OF VET IN AUSTRALIA

Vocational education and training in Australia is provided at the levels of post-compulsory upper secondary school and post-school. The post-school sector forms the major focus of this chapter, and the majority of VET training provision in Australia occurs at that level. Although there are some complexities and qualifications in the complex national statistical reports on VET provision, it is reasonably accurate to state that in 2003, 1.72 million students participated in post-school VET studies and 0.20 million in the VET in Schools sector (NCVER, 2004).

After 1974 and until the end of the twentieth century, VET in Australia was nearly completely delivered through what is known as the Technical and Further Education (TAFE) system, which was set up as an outcome of the report of the Australian Committee on Technical and Further Education. That report established the TAFE system throughout the nation, and brought together under the one concept of TAFE what had previously been a fairly disparate set of arrangements. VET was largely delivered through a number of TAFE colleges set up in each of the Australian States, normally based around pre-existing technical institutes. TAFE has been the funding responsibility of State governments, and administered through State education bureaucracies, with some contributions being made by the Australian Commonwealth Government. As the result of a growing recognition that TAFE provision throughout the nation needed increased uniformity between States, the Australian National Training Authority (ANTA) was set up in 1992. Funded largely by the Commonwealth Government, ANTA had responsibilities to develop TAFE as a nationally coordinated response to industry and individual demand, with delivery assured through performance agreements with the States. In the middle of 2005, ANTA ceased to exist and its functions are now administered by the Australian Commonwealth Department of Education, Science and Training. That change is expected to signal a stronger Commonwealth Government interest in the provision of VET.

Readers so far may have detected some looseness between the terms TAFE and VET that requires some explanation. Prior to the 1990s, VET was delivered almost exclusively by TAFE colleges, such that the term VET was really taken to be synonymous with TAFE and, indeed, the latter was the term most commonly used. Since the early 1990s VET has been provided by a much broader set of training organisations than TAFE colleges, such that VET is now the term used to describe vocational education and training as a larger functional concept, and TAFE is now just one of the structures within the "VET system" that provides VET. Each State had set up its TAFE system, which comprised the publicly owned and funded TAFE colleges, including an organisation for the provision of VET studies at a distance.

Most States had developed separate organisations to provide distance education at TAFE level, such as the College of External Studies in New South Wales (NSW), or the Technical Extension Service in Western Australia. With some minor variations between States, these organisations were operated like any other publicly owned TAFE provider, and, along with their campus-based sister institutions, provided distance courses to TAFE students unable or unwilling to attend face-to-face classes at a TAFE college.

In 2007 none of those organisations dedicated to distance education continue to exist, and most have not existed since the early to mid-1990s. In the rest of this chapter, I intend to examine some of the reasons that have led to a major change in the conceptualisations and provision of distance education in Australian VET, and some insights into what is now provided instead.

10.3 ECONOMIC IMPERATIVES AND CHANGES IN VET

In the mid-1980s, Australia experienced some economic awakenings that changed the nation's view of itself. A history of world demand for traditional exports of primary production commodities such as wool, wheat, and metals, together with a history of adequate prices being received for these commodities, had meant that Australia had been a comparatively rich country with a high standard of living. The traditional reliance on its primary products to generate economic wealth had fostered a neglect of trading opportunities in other areas. The strong economic recovery following the recession of 1983–1984 showed a rapid increase in import growth resulting from the uncompetitive nature of Australian traded goods and services. The weaknesses in the economy that required high levels of imports were further exposed when the world prices for primary produce and metals fell sharply in 1985–1986.

The (then) Labor Government recognised that Australia had to change and that Australian industry had to develop a wider range of products and services, and do so in a context of increasing international competition. A highly trained and flexible workforce was seen by the Labor Government (Dawkins and Holding, 1987) as central to productivity improvement, which, in turn, was seen as essential to long-term economic well-being. It was clear that if Australia was to remain a country with a high living standard and play an active part in the global economy, attention would have to be paid to the nation's systems and processes for VET, and to the formation of productive skills. Mathews et al. (1988) observed widespread agreement that Australia was an underskilled and vulnerable society. Carter and Gribble (1991) observed that this underskilling represented

> ... a crisis in our human capital which has been created by a mismatch between rapid economic change and insufficient attention, particularly by the industry partners, to past workforce development.
>
> (Carter and Gribble, 1991, p. 4)

Calder and McCollum (1998), in the United Kingdom, and Carter and Gribble (1991), in Australia, have observed that in both nations a dynamic relationship between education and training systems and economic growth is accepted as a necessary, though not sufficient, condition for major economic reform. Nicoll (1998, p. 301) has suggested that post-secondary education has come to be viewed as an industry itself that "is required to contribute to the economic progress of the nation". Carter and Gribble (1991) cited the United Kingdom's National Economic Development Office (1990):

> The prevailing issue is no longer whether education and training is a factor in economic performance, but what needs to be done to improve its provision, by what means, and where responsibility for action lies.
>
> (Carter and Gribble, 1991, p. 66)

As a result of the need for greater productivity, and the analysis of Australia as a comparatively poor performer in training provision, the Federal Government in *Skills for*

Australia (Dawkins and Holding, 1987) set a number of policies and targets designed to increase participation in VET. These concerns and reforms were responsible for a wide range of changes within the Australian VET system, and largely formed the basis for what became known as the National Training Reform Agenda. Although these changes and reforms served Australia arguably well into the twenty-first century, more recently there have been new pressures on the Australian economy, and interest among State and Commonwealth governments for new training reforms has emerged (Department of Education, Science and Training, 2005). It is likely that further change and reform will impact on some of the argument within this chapter, but at this stage it is unclear what those changes might be.

The developments in VET in Australia as a response to economic concerns and aspirations most importantly represented a change in the way that governments conceptualised VET. Whereas VET had been largely viewed as a form of education and training that was to support individuals in their work and career aspirations, the new thinking saw it very much as an important part of government policy, of economic development and the development of the nation's stock of human capital. The relationships formed between VET authorities and employer and industry bodies were developed with some vigour to try and ensure that the content that was being taught was relevant to industry needs, and that the forms in which VET was to be delivered were amenable to participation by employees. Flexible delivery that was partially based in distance education mindsets and methods was seen as one of these important forms of training delivery.

10.4 DEVELOPMENT OF THE TRAINING MARKET

The economic and policy imperatives outlined above were accompanied by the deliberate creation of a "training market", where VET service providers were motivated through competition to more readily respond to enterprises and individuals in skill upgrading (Anderson, 1997). *Skills for Australia* (p. 30) reported that in 1974 there were 458,000 people enrolled in vocational and preparatory courses. In 2003 the National Centre for Vocational Education Research (NCVER) reported that 1,720,000 people were enrolled in the public VET system (NCVER, 2004). Clearly, VET has developed into a sizeable business between 1974 and 2003. State training authorities have been active in the development of a more open market, where the pre-existing publicly funded TAFE institutions have become subjected to winning much more of their business through open tender. Additionally, government has re-conceptualised itself as customer, rather than as provider (Osborne and Gaebler, 1992), and purchases a contracted number of places from VET providers, both public and private.

It is not easy to obtain good statistics on the contribution of private providers to Australia's VET effort. However, the Australian Council for Private Education and Training (2004) report for NSW (the most populous State in the Commonwealth) shows that there were 792 VET providers within NSW, of which 455 were private training providers. It is useful, though, to observe that the remaining 337 providers were composed of publicly funded VET organisations or providers operated by individual enterprises, by industry groups, or by professional associations. The same report also notes that 673 interstate providers operate in NSW, taking the total to 1,465 providers in that State alone. Prior to the creation and encouragement of the private training provider market, NSW would have been serviced for VET by a combination of the following:

- Publicly owned and operated TAFE colleges in the major metropolitan areas and larger regional towns;
- Some satellite centres of these TAFE colleges in medium-sized rural towns;
- A central College of External Studies providing distance education throughout the State; and
- A very small number of privately operated organisations that were not supported by government funding.

Other States were similarly serviced through their systems of TAFE colleges and publicly funded distance education provider.

The development of the training market and the growth in the number of training providers has, it is argued here, had a profound effect on the relevance of the older more centralised model of publicly funded distance education provision. Where a VET learner is not living in a town large enough to have a TAFE college or a satellite of one, the alternative is no longer only one of enrolling with a central distance education provider. The distribution of training providers throughout the nation has become much richer with the smallest of communities now most likely boasting a training provider of one sort or another. In small communities these providers are commensurately small as well, but they offer the VET programmes that are relevant to the industry and other economic activities of that community. Learners can respond to their local provider and gain access to group learning, to actual demonstrations, and to the physical contexts demanded by competency-based training (CBT) and assessment. These developments have not been friendly to centrally provided distance education models. The marketisation of VET in Australia, and the wider geographical distribution of training providers are not without problems, and Anderson (2004) has written cogently on some of the dysfunctions in user choice that are present.

Training providers and the communities they serve are supported in each of the States by new forms of organisations that have replaced the earlier distance education providers. Staying with NSW for a moment, the publicly owned Open Training and Education Network (OTEN) (http://www.oten.edu.au) provides distance education programmes to individuals throughout the State, as well as developing study materials and online learning programmes for local providers to use with their own enrolled students, and for business to purchase and use for employee training. In Victoria, the smallest and most densely populated mainland State, the TAFE Virtual Campus (http://www.tafevc.com.au) produces and provides online learning opportunities to students who are enrolled at a registered training organisation (RTO). Important here is that TAFE virtual campus does not directly enrol individual learners, but serves RTOs and the students who enrol with them. Western Australia, the largest and most sparsely populated State, has a similar organisation called WestOne (http://www.westone.wa.gov.au), which also does not enrol students directly, but produces learning resources (largely online) for use by students enrolled at RTOs throughout that State. The relationships here are similar to those between any wholesaler of goods and services and the retailers who sell those goods to the public. There are variations on that relationship, since local training providers and other organisations also develop curriculum and learning materials to suit local clienteles; and in some States (e.g. OTEN in NSW; the Open Learning Institute in Queensland) the "wholesaler" also retails its goods directly to the consumer.

In summary, the move to marketisation of the provision of VET has resulted in a wholesaler/retailer network providing for a rich geographical distribution of training providers throughout the nation, where each of these training providers is locally focussed and able to provide face-to-face training and demonstration, and assessment in situated contexts. These developments have overtaken the need for centralised distance education providers as they once existed.

10.5 COMPETENCY-BASED TRAINING AND ASSESSMENT

In pursuit of the development of a national training system through ANTA, the Commonwealth, State, and Territory Ministers of Employment, Education, and Training set up the Vocational Education, Employment and Training Advisory Council (VEETAC), which published its *Framework for the Implementation of a Competency-Based Vocational Education and Training System* in 1993. The framework comprised the following components:

- competency-based training;
- recognition of training;
- curriculum development;
- assessment; and
- administrative processes.

Competency-based training was seen as an approach to learning and a system for VET, as well as forming the basis for assessment. It emphasises outcomes and skills rather than the processes for learning and the time taken to reach a prescribed standard of competency. Not without its detractors (e.g. Marginson, 1992; Roffey-Mitchell, 1997), CBT is claimed to enable the training outcomes to be closely aligned to the level of skill required by the enterprise. Therefore, it is argued, the costs of training can be contained to support development of only those skills required by industries and enterprises. CBT can also be related to the quality assurance process (Hager, 1997). Additionally, since CBT instruction does not need to take place in a group or classroom setting, and learning programme length is not expressed in units of time, flexible delivery was viewed as part of the strategic responses to the need for increased training efforts and outputs (Kearns, 1997).

Assessment of VET outcomes were addressed through four key features – validity, reliability, fairness, and flexibility (Tovey, 1997). These features were to be implemented to provide equitability of assessment among all groups of learners, and to provide full information to learners on procedures and judging criteria. Also to be provided was a participatory approach to assessment that included the person to be assessed, and the requirement for a process to enable challenge to assessments and re-assessment. Some of these changes were not able to be implemented successfully within the previous distance education provision framework of VET organisations that specialised in distance education. First, as noted by Hyde et al. (2004), much of the assessment of competency needs to be carried out as demonstrations or execution of manual tasks and skills. Accordingly, assessment has to be quite localised. Adding further to the need for localisation, learning of competencies and their assessment can be achieved using the equipment and processes in use by the employer. As long as the competency is achieved, the actual vehicle of its acquisition and demonstration is largely immaterial, but what is important to employers is that the people they are paying to learn are learning directly applicable skills. Selection of the most appropriate training materials and delivery method has become a user-based decision. Again, the previous model of centralised distance education providers of VET was substantially challenged.

10.6 SITUATED LEARNING AND WORKPLACE LEARNING

Interest in situated and workplace learning has developed strongly since the publication of work by Resnick (1987) and Brown et al. (1989), each of whom questioned the hegemony of classroom-based instruction, and argued for learning that is undertaken in the same situation as the knowledge is used. Researchers were also recognising and exploring the value of workplace communities of practice as part of the legitimate learning experiences that take place in enterprises (Lave and Wenger, 1991). At the same time as this increased interest in situated learning was occurring, commercial and industrial enterprises were experiencing the rapid changes in production technology that occurred throughout the last two decades of the twentieth century, and continued into the twenty-first century.

The technological changes in the business world resulted in a stronger need for learners to learn skills on the equipment that was in-house. That was partly due to the difficulties confronting education and training providers in purchasing the highly expensive equipment for training purposes, and the decreasing amount of time elapsing before it became superseded or obsolete. A further consideration was the differentiation in the market for production equipment resulting in major differences between firms in the equipment that they purchased, and the way it may be configured, even among firms producing similar goods in the same industry sector. That differentiation among firms also made it less effective for training organisations to provide fairly standard learning experiences on the same piece of equipment to all their students, or to produce distance education learning materials that could be used by all students irrespective of where they worked.

Again, these changes in workplace circumstances represented a challenge to the more traditional model of distance education provision, where learning materials could be centrally developed, centrally distributed, and learning outcomes centrally assessed. What was more emergent in demand was training that could be more directly related to the processes and the equipment used in a particular firm where the learner was employed.

The VET authorities in Australia were quick to question the provision of pubic funds to purchase expensive equipment for training purposes in the context of limited currency for the equipment, and a larger variety of needs by the learners and their individual workplaces. Similarly, there was a reticence to provide funding to develop detailed materials for individual learners. The preference became one for developing materials to support trainers in workplaces and VET institutions. These trainer-support materials addressed the acquisition and assessment of prescribed competencies, but could fairly easily be supplemented by trainers to take account of enterprise-specific or otherwise localised processes and equipment.

In support of these changed circumstances, in which a great deal more training could be carried out and assessed in workplaces, courses were developed for trainers and assessors (e.g. Certificate IV in Training and Assessment) so that the people already working in enterprises could become proficient at training and assessing others within their workplace. Apart from enabling the training and assessment to be conducted in the workplace, using its own equipment and processes, this also enabled enterprises to train people whenever it suited them, and to have the requisite competencies assessed whenever the learner was ready. In that way the trainee could be deployed to the new task in a proficient way, and within quality assurance guidelines, at a time that suited the enterprise rather than at a time that suited the large and centrally organised distance education provider. Again, though, these developments were not kindly towards the traditionally organised form of distance education. Where an enterprise had access to a responsive local training provider there would be some interest in using that provider rather than being in the business of training themselves (Evans, 2001); but where they were not able to access a local provider the enterprise could now conduct the training and assess it in-house, rather than continue to depend on a distance education provider.

10.7 RECOGNITION OF STAKEHOLDERS

Distance education providers typically enrol individual students as their clients, and they develop their administrative and support processes to cater to individual learners. The recognition that training and skills development is an important contributor to the productivity and competitiveness of individual enterprises and of nations (Carter and Gribble, 1991; Nicoll, 1998) brought with it a further recognition that individual learners pursuing their own aspirations were not the only stakeholders in training, and possibly not even the most important ones in economic terms. Other stakeholders included the enterprises employing these learners, and paying for the time of their employees and the services of the training provider. Government also sees itself as a stakeholder (acting on behalf of the community), where all or part of the funding for training organisations is provided from the public purse. Government exercised its rights as a stakeholder in Australian VET by, typically, contracting with training providers (both public and private) for the purchase of an agreed number of training places (or training hours or training effort) in each field of vocational study. The training provider was then paid to deliver those outcomes. One result of that process was that no longer was the number of people enrolled in any course determined either by the provider or by individual learners. The actual number of individual subscriber enrolments was determined by what government had purchased on behalf of the community, based on manpower requirements data. Retention of students became something of an issue to governments in this context in that they were reluctant to be paying for a service that was not ultimately delivered, and an outcome that was not achieved. High levels of attrition in VET distance education were seen as a management and cost problem, and the amounts that government paid to the providers was discounted by attrition. Hence, providers became more urgent in their wish to reduce attrition. Whereas once they had been able to rather liberally and luxuriously view attrition as somewhat wasteful of human effort and aspiration, or argue it as the learners' achievement of something less than the entire course, but an achievement nonetheless, they now started to see it as a source of funding leakage. Accordingly, the attention of provider managements was more closely focussed on attrition than it had been, and a spotlight went on to distance education as characterised by high attrition (Misko, 2000).

The third stakeholder to be recognised by the public VET sector was the employer (King, 1996; Evans and Smith, 1999). Employers were free to purchase from training providers training effort and services above those funded by government. Providers were also free to make government-purchased places available to individual enterprises under certain conditions. Employers were the individual enterprises, big and small, that employed (or consumed) the products of VET, where these products might be student graduates, or other goods and services associated with training, such as training design, materials, advice, and consultancy. Employers were also represented by peak bodies, set up for each industry sector as Industry Training Advisory Boards (ITABs). Through these ITABs VET authorities and providers were provided with intelligence on the training needs of the industry sector, and the delivery modes that may best suit the sector.

These developments, it can be argued, changed the conceptualisation of distance education as it had been in the centrally operated more traditional organisations where the individual student had been the customer. In the context of enterprise training, this again raises the question of who is the learner and who is the customer. While the learner is likely to be an individual within the enterprise, that person may not be the customer who pays the bills and who makes the training decisions. The customer is most likely to be the enterprise and its management. King (1996) has examined the language used in ANTA reports and concludes that the principal client is seen as the enterprise, rather than the individual learner. It is the enterprise which largely determines content and sequence of training, along with the length of time provided to complete the learning programme. Again, this change in recognition of the customer did not sit well with centrally organised distance education. The flexibility and responsiveness required to negotiate content with the enterprise customer, and to also negotiate and deliver on timing and sequence at customer demand place enormous demands on large centrally driven systems. The attraction of moving towards flexibly and responsively provided local or workplace-based training is again apparent, at the expense of centrally provided distance education, with a purchase of training materials from the wholesale provider.

Evans and Smith (1999) explored the differences in conceptualisation of flexible delivery that are apparent between the higher education sector and the VET sector. They argued that in the higher education sector the notion of flexible delivery is very firmly rooted in distance education, and represents "the delivery of university-developed and controlled courses of study to students in such a way that they can study where and when they wish" (Evans and Smith, 1999, p. 120). On the other hand, the VET sector, according to Evans and Smith, saw flexible delivery as borrowing from distance education for some of its thinking and its methods, but central to the VET conceptualisation is the idea of customer control over content, form of delivery, timing, and sequencing.

The earlier central providers of VET distance education in fact saw their business in much the same way as Evans and Smith suggested that the university sector sees it – as providing supplier-designed courses at a distance (or at least remotely) to learners who largely studied to a provider-determined timetable. Although Evans and Smith did not make the argument in their 1999 paper, it is possible to suggest that it is the difference they identified between the two conceptualisations of flexible delivery that best represents the transformation that has occurred in VET distance education since the late 1980s.

10.8 FOCUS ON LEARNERS

The VET distance education had operated largely on a basis of what was feasible within the resources available. Accordingly, it meant that the majority of learning materials developed and provided to students were printed notes sent through the mail, and assignments were returned for assessment. In other words, it was a fairly typical correspondence education model (Foks, 1987).

The new technologies of the 1980s ushered in new opportunities for distance and other resource-based learning in VET. Household-owned video-cassette equipment provided opportunity for moving images to be cheaply distributed to learners; desktop personal computers provided opportunity for computer-based training materials and systems to be developed. Videodisc, although very expensive to produce and reproduce, was seen as a further opportunity because of its random accessing capability. Along with the new opportunities to provide VET in different formats came concerns for costs that would be greater than those incurred in the reproduction of printed notes. Together with increases in costs came an interest in whether higher-cost training materials produced through the newer electronic formats were indeed what learners would want and effectively use.

In the VET sector in Australia Thompson (1985) had explored the newly available individualised systems of instruction in each of the Australian States and concluded that catering to the characteristics of individual learners in VET is an important contributor to teaching and learning success. She also showed that selection of media and delivery methods to suit individual learner characteristics was an important factor in the effectiveness of individualised instruction. In 1986, Smith and Lindner published their report on learning styles among VET students and how well those student characteristics were served by teaching delivery methods. The report showed that the relationship between learner characteristics and teaching delivery was by no means strong, and that there was considerable room for development if VET was to become more client-focussed. Both the Thompson and the Smith and Lindner research projects were funded by government VET authorities, indicating an interest commencing at that level in the issues of client focus and service. At a national level the issues of learner characteristics and client focus were again revisited by Misko (1994a, 1994b) in her research conducted on behalf of the national VET research authority. Later research on student characteristics by Boote (1998), Smith (2000, 2001, 2003), and Warner et al. (1998) showed that VET learners were typically not self-directed learners and neither did they have a preference for learning from text. The most typical VET learner was characterised by a preference to learn through hands-on direct experience in an instructor-guided context. In other words, distance education through resource-based packaged learning materials and provided remotely from an instructor was almost diametrically opposed to learner preferences commonly observed among VET learners. Although showing there is diversity among VET learners, each of these studies indicated that large numbers, if not a majority, are typically hands-on learners who prefer an instructor-led learning context.

These same learner characteristics also represented a challenge for online learning. Australian State VET systems were enthusiastic to develop a sophisticated and comprehensive online learning platform and service (Mitchell, 2000). The motivations for these developments were partially associated with the State image and a sense of having to develop such a system to project currency (Zemsky and Massy, 2004), but also, as Mitchell (2000) has pointed out, with a genuine attempt to provide online programmes and services to learners and corporate clients. However, as Mitchell's research indicated, the business models underlying these developments seldom took account of desired educational outcomes nor the nature of the end users. Later, nationally funded research by Brennan (2003) confirmed that online courses frequently make unfounded assumptions about VET learners, such as that they are motivated, text-capable learners, well organised, and have well-developed higher-order cognitive skills. As Brennan points out, many VET students do not have those characteristics (Boote, 1998; Warner et al. 1998; Smith, 2000, 2001, 2003). Accordingly, as Brennan identified in her national study, the trend in VET has been to use online learning within a learning environment where online learning and face-to-face contact are blended.

In summary, a model of distance education where learners are typically remote from their teacher and access their learning materials from an education provider through electronic mediation has fallen from favour in VET. There is recognition that VET learners are not typically well suited to that independent and self-directed form of learning, and that good customer service in a competitive and marketised VET environment is not provided through that model. National research by Smith and Dalton (2005) has shown that VET providers claim that accommodating the learning styles of client learners is an important part of their business and customer service.

10.9 A TRANSFORMATION TO FLEXIBLE DELIVERY

Summarising to this point, by the early 1990s a number of threats to the success of the centrally organised distance education organisations available in each State could be identified; and a number of new opportunities had become similarly apparent.

The threats were related to the requirements of CBT and assessment; workplace learning relevant to the specific needs of the enterprise; and the need for VET learners to have hands-on learning through direct experience, and an instructor-guided context for learning. There were new opportunities related to the potential for new technologies to deliver resource-based VET in a wider set of forms than print-based learning materials; and the structures put in place to support the "wholesaler/retailer" model with its liberal distribution of competitive public and private training providers throughout the nation.

A move towards the flexible delivery of VET was a response to these threats and opportunities, where flexible delivery was conceptualised as a combination of resource-based learning, hands-on experience in workplaces, and a social context for learning with fellow workers or learners and with face-to-face instruction delivered through training providers or in workplaces. In the Australian VET sector, the Flexible Delivery Working Party (1992) proposed the following definition of flexible delivery:

> Flexible delivery is an approach to vocational education and training which allows for the adoption of a range of learning strategies in a variety of learning environments to cater for differences in learning styles, learning interests and needs, and variations in learning opportunities.
>
> (Flexible Delivery Working Party, 1992, p. 2)

The Working Party further suggested that flexible delivery provides students with greater flexibility in

- delivery modes;
- delivery venues; and
- assessment practices.

The Working Party suggested several features of flexible delivery, each of which was seen as providing considerable advantages for training. Flexible delivery has the potential to enable considerable customisation towards learner preferences. Through access to a wide range of learning resources, and a wide range of teaching options, it is possible for a learner to assemble the resources that best fit learning requirements, preferences, and the teaching methods that are most favoured, to yield a learning experience that is comfortable and effective.

Observing this identified capacity for flexible delivery to enable the learner (or other end-user) considerable flexibility in choice of place of learning, level of content to be learned, actual content to be learned, and the method through which the learning takes place, Misko (1994b) called it a "client focused" approach to the delivery of education and training. She listed the forms of learning available with flexible delivery as

- competency-based learning
- discovery learning
- self-paced learning
- resource-based learning

- group-paced learning
- mixed modes of learning
- integrated theory and practical learning
- integrated on-the-job and off-the-job learning
- problem-based learning.

(Misko, 1994b, p. 3)

Further development in the thinking is indicated in 1996 when the Australian National Training Authority's National Flexible Delivery Taskforce adopted the definition:

> Flexible delivery is an approach rather than a system or technique; it is based on the skill needs and delivery requirements of clients, not the interests of trainers or providers; it gives clients as much control as possible over what and when and where and how they learn; it commonly uses the delivery methods of distance education and the facilities of technology; it changes the role of trainer from a source of knowledge to a manager of learning and a facilitator.
>
> (ANTA, 1996, p. 11)

This description is precisely that proposed by Johnson (1990, p. 4) to define "open learning", and captures the two focuses most commonly associated with flexible delivery–extended access to learning through the removal of barriers, and a philosophy of learner-centred provision where learner choice is the key. Also evident in that definition is an understanding of the role that new technologies could play in converging resource-based or distance forms of training delivery with other face-to-face forms of teaching, demonstration, and practice (Smith and Kelly, 1987; Tait and Mills, 1999; *Distance Education* Special Issue, 2005).

As Rumble (1989) suggests, open learning is a very different idea from distance education. He also points out that there is no shortage of definitions of open learning. Rumble argues cogently that education practices fall on a continuum between contiguous and distance modes of teaching, but where on the continuum a practice lies has nothing to do with its openness. Rumble concludes by observing that

> The concept of open education is ill-defined but has to do with matters related to access, freedom from the constraints of time and place, means, structure, dialogue and the presence of support services.
>
> (Rumble, 1989, p. 41)

He points out that distance education systems may be quite closed, and not meet the criteria for openness that he has established. A different insight into the distinction between distance education and open learning was provided by Edwards (1995) as part of his analysis of these terms in a post-Fordist context. Edwards suggested that distance education, with its emphasis on provision of learning opportunities at a distance "... is consistent with a Fordist model of organisation in which mass produced products are available to a mass market" (Edwards, 1995, p. 242). In contrast, Edwards saw open learning, similarly to flexible delivery, as being more market sensitive with a greater emphasis on meeting the needs of the learner/consumer. He also saw the "privileged discourses of providers" (Edwards, 1995, p. 250) being replaced with discourses that place the learner as a consumer in the centre. In his suggestion that technologically mediated knowledge provides the vehicle for individualising learning, Edwards recognised that distance is subservient to the discourse of open learning, and becomes "reconstituted as relationships between producers and consumers in which knowledge is exchanged on the basis of the usefulness it has to the consumer" (Edwards, 1995, p. 251). It is through that notion of subservience that Rumble's and Edwards' analyses form congruence with, as Rumble (1989) has argued, the continuum of distance being independent from that of openness. This relationship between open learning and flexible delivery was further explored in the Report of the Australian Senate Employment, Education and Training References Committee, Part 2 (1995) when it suggested that

> If open learning is considered an expression of a certain educational philosophy, the notion of "flexible delivery" favoured by the VET sector may be considered as an education and training strategy which emerges from the philosophy.
>
> (The Australian Senate Employment, Education and Training References Committee, Part 2, 1995, p. 7)

The notions of learner control over content, sequence, and length of time to complete the programme are included in the conceptualisation of flexible learning as crucial components in the provision of learning programmes to enterprises (Evans and Smith, 1999). Behind the inclusion of those notions in flexible learning is the fundamental idea that flexible learning is learner (or customer) controlled rather than provider controlled. It is the learner or the enterprise that largely determines content and sequence, along with the length of time provided to complete the learning programme.

A definition of distance education and its key characteristics was comprehensively addressed by Keegan (1980) at a time before the newer terms of "flexible learning" and "flexible delivery" emerged in the language of educators. Keegan's work sought to examine the confusion between the then new term "distance education", and the older commonly used terms such as "home study", "external studies", and "correspondence study". Keegan reviewed a number of definitions of distance education and concluded that the main elements any definition needs to include are

- the separation of teacher and learner (to distinguish from face to face instruction)
- the influence of an educational organisation (to distinguish from private study)
- the use of technical media (including print) to unite the teacher and learner, and to carry the educational content
- the provision of two-way communication between teacher and learner
- the possibility of occasional meetings for both didactic and socialisation reasons
- the participation in an industrialised form of education where there is division of labour such as instructional design, graphics, word processing and typography, teaching etc.

(Keegan, 1980, p. 33)

The Keegan review provides an insight into the distinction that may be made between distance education and flexible learning in that he does not include any notions of flexible entry or exit, or learner control over content, sequence, and pace of progress, or the potential co-location of teacher and learner. The features of distance education proposed by Keegan are preserved in a provision of education or training that has a set syllabus which learners must cover, and determined periods of study such as semesters, and expected progression rates to meet provider requirements for assessment and receipt of accredited awards. The characteristics of flexible learning can be met, however, in a system of educational provision which provides for substantial learner control over content, sequence, and progression rate. Where controls are introduced, they are not initiated by the training provider but by another party such as the learner's employer. Support for this view, also expressed by Evans and Smith (1999), that the key characteristics of flexible learning lie within this notion of learner control is given by Ellington (1997) when he writes,

> ... I would suggest that we all try to promote the general adoption of this wider interpretation, and start using the term "flexible delivery" as a generic term that covers all those situations where the learners have some say in how, where or when learning takes place – whether within the context of traditional institution-centred courses or in non-traditional contexts such as open learning, distance learning, CAT schemes, wider access courses or continuing professional development.
>
> (Ellington, 1997, p. 4)

10.10 CONCLUSION

It has been argued in this chapter that in the VET sector, in Australia at least, what was provided as distance education at one time has developed into flexible delivery. It is also suggested here that this has not been a passive transformation, but rather one that has been deliberately planned and developed in response to change in economic circumstances and imperatives in the conceptualisations of relationships between providers and their customers. That transformation was largely forged by VET authorities at State and federal levels of government, and with industry and trade union support. Few, if any, of those people came from within the discipline of distance education, and the drivers of change were economic rather than educational. It is arguable that major changes such as those discussed in this chapter may have been easier to achieve in a politically stable, well-organised, and prosperous country such as Australia with its six States and Federal system of national government. A larger country with a more complex or fraught political structure may not have been able to complete the transformation quite as quickly.

Partially fuelling the transformation, but also stimulated as a result of it, has been the convergence that new technologies have forged between distance education and more traditional face-to-face delivery methods. However, in the context of VET, it is argued in this chapter that the transformation from distance education to flexible delivery has been even more strongly driven by other broader economic, organisational, and conceptual changes identified and discussed in this chapter.

REFERENCES

Anderson, D. (1997). *Competition and Market Reform in the Australian VET Sector.* Adelaide: National Centre for Vocational Education Research.

Anderson, D. (2004). Adult Learners and choice in further education and training markets: Constructing the jigsaw puzzle, *International Journal of Training Research*, **2**(2), 1–23.

ANTA (1996). *National Flexible Delivery Taskforce Final Report.* Brisbane, Australian National Training Authority.

Australian Committee on Technical and Further Education. (1974). *TAFE in Australia: Report on Needs in Technical and Further Education, April, 1974*, Canberra: Australian Government Publishing Service.

Australian Council for Private Education and Training, (2004). *The Importance of Private Providers of Post-Compulsory Education to the NSW Economy and to Meeting the State's Skills Training Needs.* Sydney NSW: ACPET.

Australian Senate Employment, Education and Training Reference Committee (1995). *Inquiry into the Development of Open Learning in Australia Part 2.* Canberra, Senate Printing Unit, Parliament House, March 1995.

Boote, J. (1998). Learning to learn in vocational education and training: are students and teachers ready for it? *Australian and New Zealand Journal of Vocational Education Research*, **6**, 59–86.

Brennan, R. (2003). *One Size Doesn't Fit All: Pedagogy in the Online Environment Volumes 1 & 2.* Adelaide: National Centre for Vocational Education Research.

Brown, J.S., Collins, A., and Duguid, P. (1989). Situated cognition and the culture of learning, *Educational Researcher*, **18**, 32–42.

Calder, J. and McCollum, A. (1998). *Open and Flexible Learning in Vocational Education and Training.* London: Kogan Page.

Carter, R. and Gribble, I. (1991). *Work Based Learning: A Discussion Paper.* Melbourne: Office of the State Training Board.

Dawkins, J. and Holding, A. (1987). *Skills for Australia.* Canberra: Australian Government Printing Service.

Department of Education, Science and Training. (2005). *Skilling Australia: New Directions for Vocational Education and Training*, Canberra: Commonwealth of Australia.

Edwards, R. (1995). Different disclosures, discourses of difference: Globalisation distance education and open learning. *Distance Education,* **16**, 241–255.

Ellington, H. (1997). Flexible learning-your flexible friend'. In C. Bell, M. Bowden, and A. Trott (eds) (pp. 3–13). *Implementing Flexible Learning.* London: Kogan Page.

Evans, T.D. and Smith, P.J. (1999). Flexible delivery in Australia: Origins and conceptualisations, *FID Review*, **1**(2/3),116–120.

Evans, T.D. (2001). Two approaches to workplace flexible delivery and assessment in a rural community. *Australian and New Zealand Journal of Vocational Education Research*, **9**(2), 1–22.

Flexible Delivery Working Party (1992). *Flexible Delivery: A National Framework for Implementation in TAFE,* Brisbane, Flexible Delivery Working Party.

Foks, J. (1987). Towards opening learning, In Smith, P.J., and Kolly, M. (Eds). *Distance Education and the Mainstream* (pp. 74–92), New York: Croom Helm.

Hager, P. (1997). *Quality Assurance in VET.* Adelaide: National Centre for Vocational Education Research.

Hyde, P., Clayton, B., and Booth, R. (2004) *Exploring Assessment in Flexible Delivery of Vocational Education and Training Programs*, Adelaide: National Centre for Vocational Education Research.

Johnson, R. (1990). *Open Learning.* Canberra National Board of Employement, Education and Training, Commissioned Report No. 4, June.

Kearns, P. (1997). *Flexible Delivery of Training.* Adelaide: National Centre for Vocational Education and Training.

Keegan, D. (1980). On defining distance education, *Distance Education,* **1**, 13–36.

King, B. (1996). Life, Learning, and Flexible Delivery. Sydney: South Sydney Institute of TAFE.

Lave, J. and Wenger, E. (1991). *Situated learning: Legitimate Peripheral Participation.* New York: Cambridge University Press.

Marginson, S. (1992). Competent for what? *Arena Magazine,* October–November, 35–37.

Mathews, J., Hall, G., and Smith, H. (1988). Towards flexible skill formation and technological literacy: Challenges facing the education system, *Economic and Industrial Democracy*, **9**, 497–522.

Misko, J. (1994a). *Review of Research 2: Learning Styles.* Adelaide: National Centre for Vocational Education Research.

Misko, J. (1994b). *Flexible Delivery: Will a Client Focused System Mean Better Learning?* Adelaide: National Centre for Vocational Education Research.

Misko, J. (2000). *The Effects of Different Modes of Delivery: Student Outcomes and Evaluations*, Adelaide: National Centre for Vocational Education Research.

Mitchell, J. (2000). 'The impact of e-commerce on online learning systems in the VET sector', paper delivered at the conference of the Australian Vocational Education Research Association, Canberra, 23–24 March.

National Economic Development Office (1990). Competence and Competition: Training and Education in the Federal Republic of Germany, the United States, and Japan. London: NEDO.

NCVER, (2004). *Australian Vocational Education and Training Statistics: Students and Courses 2003*, National Centre for Vocational Education and Training, Adelaide: Retrieved from www.ncver.edu.au June 19, 2005.

Nicoll, K. (1998). "Fixing" the "Facts": Flexible delivery as policy intervention, *Higher Education Research and Development,* **17**, 291–304.

Osborne, D. and Gaebler, T. (1992). *Reinventing Government: How the Entrepreneurial Spirit is Transforming the Public Sector.* Reading, MA: Addison-Wesley.

Resnick, L.B. (1987). Learning in school and out, *Educational Researcher,* **16**(9), 13–20.

Roffey-Mitchell, N. (1997). Cognitive skill development (CSD): The quality approach to training, *Training and Development in Australia,* **24**(6), 19–21.

Rumble, G. (1989). 'Opening learning', 'distance learning' and the misuse of language. In A. Tait (ed). *Key Issues in Opening Learning 1986–1992.* Harlow, Essex, Longman pp. 24–44.

Smith, P.J. (2000). Flexible delivery and apprentice training: Preferences, problems and challenges, *Journal of Vocational Education and Training,* **52**(3), 483–502.

Smith, P.J. (2001). Learners and their workplaces: Towards a strategic model of flexible delivery in the workplace, *Journal of Vocational Education and Training*, **53**(4), 609–628.

Smith, P.J. (2003). Learning strategies used by apprentices in flexible delivery, *Journal of Vocational Education and Training*, **55**, 369–382.

Smith, P.J. (Ed.) (2005). *Distance Education.* Special Issue **26**(2), 159–277.

Smith, P.J. and Dalton, J. (2005). *Accommodating Learning Styles: Relevance and Good Practice in VET*, Adelaide: National Centre for Vocational Education Research.

Smith, P.J. and Kelly, M. (eds) (1987). *Distance Education and the Mainstream*, New York: Croom Helm.

Smith, P.J. and Lindner, C. (1986). *Learning Style Preferences of Technical and Further Education Students, and Delivery Methods in Selected Teaching Programs*. Victoria: Office of the TAFE Board.

Tait, A. and Mills, R. (eds) (1999). *The Convergence of Distance Education and Conventional Education: Patterns of Flexibility for the Individual Learner*. New York: Routledge.

Thompson, J. (1985). *Individualised systems of instruction in TAFE Colleges*, TAFE National Centre for Research and Development, Adelaide: National Centre for Vocational Education Research.

Tovey, M.D. (1997). *Training in Australia*. Sydney: Prentice Hall.

Vocational Education, Employment and Training Advisory Committee. (1993) *Framework for the Implementation of a Competency-Based Vocational Education Training System*, Canberra: Commonwealth of Australia.

Warner, D., Christie, G. and Choy, S. (1998). *The Readiness of the VET Sector for Flexible Delivery Including On-Line Learning*. Brisbane: Australian National Training Authority.

Zemsky, R. and Massy, W.F. (2004). *Thwarted Innovation: What Happened to E-Learning and Why*, University of Pennsylvania: The Learning Alliance.

Chapter 11

Naming the Issues

Barbara Spronk

Suppose you are an education provider in one of the world's lower-income countries, one of those countries that appear in the lower half of the indexes published annually in the UNDP's Human Development Reports (e.g. UNDP, 2005). Perhaps you work for an existing educational institution, or a ministry of education, or a non-governmental agency that plays a significant educational role. Suppose in addition that your aim is to widen access to and opportunities for education and training for some particular population within your national boundaries. You are aware that distance education might have a role to play in this widening, and you find considerable appeal in this alternative to existing or conventional approaches. For example, your target learners may be widespread geographically or in locations remote from centres with education facilities. They may have educational needs that must be fitted in around demands of daily life: making a living, caring for families, maintaining communities. At the national level, resources for new schools or other institutions are likely scarce, in terms both of funds for erecting and maintaining buildings, and of qualified teachers, trainers and other staff. What are the particular challenges you will face if you include distance modes amongst your array of educational approaches?

This chapter is an attempt to present, in summary form, some major issues that arise for decision-makers such as you, grouped into four categories: technology, cost, level, and culture. The lists and discussion of these issues are not intended to be exhaustive or detailed. The aim is rather to provide an overview that will point the reader to more in-depth treatments in the literature of distance education.

11.1 TECHNOLOGY

Starting with technology goes against the best advice of expert and experienced distance educators; according to the distance education canon, one begins with the needs and context of the learner and the teaching/learning tasks to be accomplished, and builds one's distance education system accordingly. By beginning this overview with technology, however, we are being realistic rather than "right"; a preponderance of distance education projects now involve the newest information and communication technologies (ICTs), regardless of context and purpose. These technologies are seductive, offering access to enormous and growing assemblages of information about anything one can think of or even imagine. Even more exciting for those who have laboured in the fields of distance education for a number of decades, the new technologies make possible interaction between learners and teachers, among learners, and between learners and countless others who might have useful contributions to make to the learning process. No longer must distance learners study in isolation; they have a world at their fingertips via the Internet. Couple the communicative and informative capacities of these machines with their integrative capabilities, that is, their ability to make available for learning the entire range of media – text, visuals, video, and audio, when there is sufficient bandwidth available – and their appeal is almost overwhelming.

The siren call of these technologies is bolstered and amplified by the fact that they are developed, produced and promoted by some of the most influential corporations in existence. For the global giants in the software, hardware, media and networking industries, the educational market is appealing in terms not only of potential profit but also of social benefits and political support. The Millennium Declaration and its "Millennium Development Goals", adopted by the international community in the year 2000, provide "a set of time-bound and quantified targets for reducing extreme poverty and extending universal rights by 2015", amongst them universal primary education and gender parity in education and literacy (UNDP, 2005, p. 17). The newest technologies are bound to play a role in initiatives designed to meet these goals, given their central role in advancing the restructuring and unification of the global economy (cf. Burbules and Torres, 2000; Carnoy, 2000; Stromquist, 2002). The argument – and the hope – is that the accomplishments of the digital revolution in expediting international finance can be replicated in the educational arena in terms of both efficiency in deployment of resources and effectiveness of the outcomes. However, the ability of digital technologies, or of any technologies for that matter, to work such educational magic is tempered by the conditions or requirements that apply to all endeavours in distance education: development of appropriate learning materials; supporting learners on the system; administration of these learners; providing the necessary technical infrastructure and support; and planning and managing the system (cf. Rumble, 2001b).

- In terms of developing materials from which users can learn effectively, numerous books and journal articles have been devoted to the steps involved in this process. For example, materials development for web-based courses that run over the Internet requires some specialized skills, such as Web design and programming of appropriate learning platforms, but essentially the process is a subset of general distance education materials design and entails application of the same principles.
- Another principle applies here: regardless of the quality and thoroughness of the learning materials, in the implementation or delivery phase the users of those materials will need support as they work with them. This support at least includes the possibility of contact with the host or sponsoring agency or institution (e.g. who will answer the e-mails or take the telephone calls?), and at best enables and facilitates learner-to-learner contact and collaboration on a continuing basis.

- Regardless of the type and depth of support that is provided to learners, a crucial component of that support is administration, in the form of enrolling learners, collecting fees, getting materials to them, ensuring that assignments and examinations are marked and returned as quickly as possible and that mechanisms for contact among learners and between learners and their tutors operate smoothly.
- Then there is the matter of the infrastructure, both physical and human, that is needed to ensure that the foregoing conditions are in place. The physical infrastructure requires not only installation or means of access but also continuing maintenance and possibly upgrading. The human infrastructure comprises personnel who are qualified and trained for the jobs they must do. Students might also need training, depending on their level of familiarity with the technologies on which the course delivery depends. Both types of infrastructure are typically lacking in low-income countries, and require major investments of both one-time capital and continuing operational funding (more about this below).
- Finally, the entire system requires planning, management, evaluation and renewal, along with appropriate policy frameworks at the national level. This may seem self-evident. Nonetheless, it is worth emphasizing that planning in the case of distance education needs to be done as far in advance of implementation as possible. Project funding tends to focus on the production of visible outcomes, as quickly as possible, which leaves insufficient time for the complexities of audience analysis, course design, development and production, and design of learner support mechanisms, to say nothing of training of all the staff involved. Classroom courses can be mounted relatively quickly, once appropriate space, curriculum and staff have been assembled. Distance education courses and their supporting systems take far longer to get right; this is a major lesson from countless distance education projects around the world, but one that project planners continue to ignore.

11.2 COST

The costs of distance education are inextricably bound up with the technologies used in development and delivery. Despite the centrality of such costs to the decision-making process involved in planning for distance education, there are lamentably few actual costing studies. Nonetheless, the studies that do exist are instructive.

Rumble (1997, 2001a) has done the most complete job to date of detailing the costs of distance education provision. One of his major emphases has been the need to take all the costs of the system into account, including costs to the user. What are or will be the costs to the users or learners in the system? Fees and materials costs (e.g. textbooks), in all likelihood, but also access and usage costs. For example, in a relatively "low-tech" offering that relies on print as a medium and face-to-face tutorial sessions for support (still the typical delivery mode in low-income countries), students have to come up with money for transport to tutorial sessions; in many cases, both the transport and the money are hard to come by. In such situations, textbooks may also be an insupportable expense, especially if they have to be imported. Local and national publishers, especially in India, are providing a great service in the form of low-cost versions of standard textbooks, but the risks of copyright infringement can impose severe limits on local production. At the other end of the technology spectrum, users in Web-course environments typically have to bear the costs of hardware, software and connectivity, in addition to materials. Even in cases where all materials are provided online, many users will want to print them, perhaps to make them more portable or to share them with other users, an enterprise that can quickly become very expensive.

Passing costs on to the user lowers the costs of distance education provision. This strategy has severe limits in low-income countries, however, especially if one's aim is to extend access to low-income learners. Few of these learners, for example, can afford their own computers, printers and Internet connections. One of the most common responses to this problem is the provision of learning or access centres, as described in the studies of "telecentres" compiled by the Commonwealth of Learning (Latchem and Walker, 2001). One of the most significant lessons evident from these studies is the need for centres to have a business plan, so that their operation will continue once start-up funds are exhausted. In low-income countries, generation of sufficient operational funds from users alone is limited by users' ability to pay, and ongoing involvement of government and/or the private sector is critical to the continuing operation of the centres (cf. Oestmann and Dymond, 2001).[1] Rather than setting up their own networks of centres, institutions can ask students to use the Internet cafés that are becoming a feature of communities worldwide, locally owned and operated small enterprises that can stay in business only by making their services affordable.

Another approach to the access problem is to use existing technologies that are within reach of many if not most students, such as radio. A limiting condition of radio access has been power supply. Mains electricity is often unavailable, and batteries are expensive – hence the development of radio receivers powered by hand-cranking (cf. Freeplay Foundation website) and/or by solar batteries. In terms of programming, Worldspace™ Satellite Radio has launched two satellites, with footprints that cover all of Africa and much of Asia, with an accompanying foundation to help fund educational uses and make satellite receivers available to low-income groups (cf. Worldspace website).

A newer technology that is becoming increasingly common in even the lowest-income countries is the mobile telephone. Wireless technologies in general circumvent the need for costly land-line infrastructure, and agencies such as the International Telecommunications Union are working assiduously to widen access, lower costs and ensure cross-network compatibility. Educationalists are working on the programming side, developing creative ways of using mobile technologies for educational purposes (Traxler and Kukulska-Hulme, 2005).

Yet another approach to making technologies affordable is the development of low-cost yet powerful hardware and software. A current example is the "$100 laptop" that is under development by the One Laptop Per Child Foundation (cf. OLPC website), a machine powered by solar batteries and hand-cranking, equipped with wireless connectivity and loaded with free, open-source software. Another recent development is the "virtual laptop", which places onto a "flash drive" (portable storage device) the full range of programs available on the typical laptop, enabling users to carry their programming around with them in their pockets or handbags (Paul West, personal communication).

Exciting as these technological developments are, the challenge of keeping costs within range of low-resourced providers and students remains. In the developing world, distance education is commonly seen as a way of meeting public demand or need with a minimum of resources (cf. Perraton, 2000, Chapter 9). Distance modes can indeed be cheaper than conventional approaches, but only if economies of scale are realized by spreading the costs of course development and media use over a large enough population of learners, extending the life of course materials over a number of years, restricting the number of courses available and minimizing the cost of learner support (Rumble, 2001b; Hülsmann, 1999). All these measures, especially the last, although they decrease the cost per learner enrolled, may well result in low rates of learner retention, thereby increasing the cost per graduate. Appropriate use of sophisticated technologies can make the learning experience richer and more satisfying, but they seldom make it cheaper.

11.3 LEVEL

The way in which issues of technology use and costs play out varies with the level at which distance education is provided. Distance education approaches have been used at all levels of education, from literacy and livelihoods training to tertiary level and professional upgrading. In low-income countries in particular, distance methods have appealed because of their potential for reaching large numbers of people. For example, there are still 800 million people in the world lacking basic literacy skills, with women accounting disproportionately for two-thirds of the total. There are still over 100 million children not in school, mostly in Sub-Saharan Africa and South Asia. And access to higher education remains a privilege available mainly to citizens of high-income countries (UNDP, 2005, p. 24).

In terms of literacy and livelihoods training, radio has been probably the most successful medium, using the "read, listen, discuss, act" model, combining radio broadcasts with print material and community-based study circles. Funding and support for this level of the so-called non-formal education remains scarce, at both government and donor levels, but nonetheless initiatives continue, both on the programming side (e.g. the Developing Countries Farm Radio Network) and in terms of radio receivers with affordable power supplies, as discussed above.

At the level of primary school there are a variety of models operating, supported by both government and private sectors. In Asia, government-funded "open schools" offer a flexible timetable that appeals to disadvantaged or economically deprived children. For example, India offers self-instructional materials with no formal entry requirements for students; the Indonesian open school supports a teacher's aide who provides weekly supervised instruction from a base school attached to the regular junior-secondary school. The medium is generally printed material with some use of radio or audio cassettes (Perraton, 2000, Chapter 3). In Latin America, broadcast television is a medium of choice, particularly at secondary level. For example, Mexico's *Telesecundaria* has been a quiet success for over 30 years. The programme is large enough to have achieved economies of scale, and has become institutionalized as an alternative delivery system for children in scattered rural settlements. In Brazil, the Roberto Marinho Foundation, the world's ninth largest media organization, also uses television successfully, in this case for out-of-school youth and adults preparing for secondary-level equivalency examinations (Oliveira et al., 2001). In Sub-Saharan Africa, distance education at secondary level is provided primarily by the study centre model of print-based packages supported by face-to-face tutorial meetings and supplemented with other media where possible. Particularly successful examples include the "colleges" of open learning in Namibia and Botswana, which offer educational opportunities to adults in rural areas needing secondary-level credentials, at a modest cost per student (Perraton, 2000, Chapter 3).

Still at school level, technologies are also used in the classroom in low-income countries, enriching the learning experience for children and supporting teachers but unfortunately adding to rather than reducing costs of instruction. Interactive radio instruction (IRI), for example, brings broadcast radio "teachers" to the classroom, engaging teachers and pupils in lively learning activities that centre on subjects such as Maths and English in which teachers tend to lack skills. Once the initial funding for IRI disappears, however, governments have tended not to continue the programming. As for computers in the classroom, there are a growing number of experiments in low-income countries, and with the advent of the "$100 laptop" there are bound to be a great many more. Even with the costs of advanced technology coming down, however, studies to date indicate that the advent of computers in classrooms, although enriching, will add to the costs of primary and secondary education rather than reduce them (Orivel, 2000; Bakia, 2003). Amongst the costs associated with computers in the classroom is the cost of training teachers to make most effective use of these technologies. The training of teachers overall has been one of success stories of distance education provision in low-income countries (Robinson and Latchem, 2002; Perraton, 2000), using primarily paper-based courses with study centres in teachers' colleges and schools themselves. If computers are to be introduced into classrooms, teacher training programmes need to be amongst the first users to lay hands on them.

At the tertiary level in low-income countries, open universities feature very prominently in distance education provision (Perraton, 2000, Chapter 5). The Asian open and distance universities are the largest universities in the world, but the model is found also in Africa, Latin America and regionally in the island nations of the Caribbean and South Pacific. The delivery mode is largely print-based, but the China Radio and Television University (not technically an open university) uses the eponymous media extensively, and in the two regional universities satellite and conference technologies help link widely spread campuses and study centres. Many experiments with the latest technologies are underway, far too many to capture here; there have also been experiments with "virtual university" models, such as the African Virtual University (cf. Farrell, 2001). It is also in these large, single-mode institutions that most of the costing and other kinds of studies of distance education in low-income countries have been carried out, since this is where academics who have a vested interest in finance tend to be located.

11.4 CULTURE

Amongst the studies centred in these tertiary-level institutions are explorations of the issues that arise when one exports to a non-Western, low-income context educational models that arose in the affluent countries of Europe and North America, and Australia and New Zealand. These issues are fundamentally those of a difference in cultures, the term "culture" used in its anthropological sense. Culture involves beliefs and values, ways of seeing the world, and ways of knowing, thinking, doing and relating to the cosmos and to society. These beliefs, values and practices are learned from infancy onwards, and are shared with other members of a particular culture or subculture, even though they might take idiosyncratic forms in any given individual.

Our focus here, as it is in the literature, is the learner in an open university in a low-income country. There are a number of different cultures in play here, not only the learner's own culture but his or her academic culture; that is, the way in which he or she is accustomed to learning. Many features of the academic culture familiar to most learners whose first language is English or some other Western European language may strike learners from other linguistic and cultural traditions as alien. These features include the following:

- Linear logic, thinking in straight lines, rather than the more lateral or spiral logics of other traditions;
- An analytical approach that emphasizes dividing reality into its component parts, rather than more synthetic approaches that emphasize the whole over the parts;
- An expository, declarative and deductive rhetorical style that works from the "big picture" or thesis statement down through the supporting details or arguments, rather than an inductive style that requires learners to be more tentative, stating rationales and arguments before attempting a more generalized statement;
- Encouraging debate, discussion and original thinking, compared with academic traditions such as that which Robinson (1999) describes for Chinese learners, for whom three key rules are "memorize the lesson, practice the skill, and respect superiors";
- Privileging the written over the spoken word. Despite the continuing dominance of the lecture as teaching mode, learners in the West are assessed primarily on their ability to express themselves in written form. In contrast, most of the world's languages have only recently been written down, in the context of conquest and colonization; hence the cultures associated with these languages are based on the spoken word and oral traditions and histories that continue to inform daily existence. The impact of the written word on oral cultures has been powerfully described by Ong (2002), and in specifically academic contexts by Scollon and Scollon (1981).

To further complicate this disjunction of the so-called Western academic culture with other traditions of learning, there are also disciplinary subcultures. The essays required of a student in a course in English literature, for example, tend to take a form quite different from those required in psychology courses, and different again from the reports required from a physics lab. Distance education modes of presentation in many ways take on the characteristics of a sub-discipline of a broader academic culture; many of its characteristics represent a departure from the norm of academic culture, and an even greater departure from the norms of other learning traditions, in a number of ways:

- Learner autonomy as a desired goal – first- and second-generation distance education modes (Nipper, 1989) were founded on the concept of the autonomous learner working through prepared course materials with the support of a tutor.
- An emphasis of "learner-centredness" in development and presentation of learning materials and an effort to meet individual needs, especially through various forms of learner support.
- The teaching function of the learning materials and the consequent facilitating and mediating role of the tutor – tutors in first- and second-generation distance education are expected to support the learner in learning from the provided materials, a role that most academics find unfamiliar and even uncomfortable in their first encounters with distance students.
- Multiple sources for course content – following on the example set by the UKOU, most distance teaching providers do their best to provide a variety of perspectives and voices in their learning materials, in an effort to provoke the learner to challenge the authority of the materials rather than to take their authority for granted.
- Dialogue as a central feature of both the learning materials and the learner support system – materials encourage activity on the part of the learner in response to what she or he is reading, watching or listening to; two-way communication with tutors and, if possible, other learners is a fundamental requirement of learner support provision.
- Processes of learning as a central concern of designers and developers of distance education provision – because of this focus on promoting dialogue and activity/interactivity in distance teaching and learning, designers tend to pay a great deal of attention to the processes of learning at a distance, certainly more than is typical of the "stand-and-deliver" mode of face-to-face, classroom instruction.
- A focus on learning outcomes – this is a major feature of the emphasis on the processes of learning, typically in the form of aims and objectives, towards and around which instruction is designed and on the basis of which learner performance is assessed.
- The use of media for teaching and learning – most distance education continues to rely on text, but text that is presented in a variety of ways, including electronic. Other media, such as sound and moving images, can be used as the primary means of providing learning material, but typically these other media are used in support of text rather than in place of it.

This brings us to yet another set of cultures that intersect in the provision of distance education, those of the media. Each medium relies on a different set of symbols – the written word and static visual portrayals in the case of the print medium, moving images in video formats, and sound in audio. Each imposes on the users, both learners and teachers, a different set of rules, protocols and logics, not all of which are equally appropriate for all tasks; the presentation of a detailed argument, for example, is more effective in a print format than in video. Each medium also makes different requirements of the user; for example, in distance learning contexts, video or audio presentations are most effective when accompanied by text materials that provide a framework within which to watch or listen, especially since most learners are accustomed to using video and audio as entertainment rather than for formal learning.

The current preoccupation is with computer-mediated communication and its challenges to teachers and learners. Gayol and Schied (n.d., p. 1) describe its complexities: "CMC encompasses all the existing forms of narration: conversation, speech, written and visual... (and) is more powerful than other media not only because it allows for a fusion of technologies and texts, but because it allows people to have instantaneous, decentralized and always available interventions." The authors explore the cultural consequences of the global use of CMC, including its continuing reliance on English[2] and its cultural impositions, the possibilities for shaping and even creating identities in an electronic universe, and the potential for collaborative learning and communities of practice. Research on these issues is still at an early stage, and there is still much to know, especially about learners and teachers who use languages other than English (e.g. Aylward, 2002) or whose cultures are predominantly oral rather than written (e.g. Voyageur, 2001; Corry and Lelliott, 2002).

11.5 CONCLUSION

From even this brief review of the issues confronting an educational provider in considering the adoption of distance education as an alternative to existing provision, perhaps the most obvious conclusion is that distance education is far from a straightforward or unproblematic option. There are many trade-offs amongst the issues listed here: for example, heed the siren call of ICTs but be prepared to pay for them and their associated costs, and on an ongoing basis; shortchange planning or learner support and risk inefficient and ineffective deployment of resources and high dropout rates; ignore at your peril the lessons of other providers of distance learning at your level and in your region; question and query the cultural assumptions and demands that underlie the distance education "package" you are considering; and ensure that you are prepared for introducing what amounts to new cultures of learning. Experience to date in the developing world – over three decades of it – indicates not only that distance education is worth doing, but also that it is worth doing well.

NOTES

1. Even in affluent countries, financial support from communities, government and the private sector is important to the ongoing operations of access centres. For example, Contact North, a very successful network of access centres in Northern Ontario, Canada, relies on the continuing support of the provincial government, co-funding by communities, and inputs from the private sector (Maxim Jean-Louis, personal communication).
2. As of September 20, 2006, English was the language used by 30% of all Internet users. Chinese is gaining quickly, but still represents only 13% of Internet users (Internet World Stats, 2006).

REFERENCES

Aylward, L. (2002). Constructivism or Confucianism? We have the technology, now what shall we do with it? In *Rethinking Learner Support in Distance Education: Change and Continuity in an International Context* (A. Tait and R. Mills, eds). London: Routledge Falmer, pp. 3–13.

Bakia, M. (2003). The economics of open learning and distance education in primary and secondary schools. In *The Open Classroom. Distance Learning in Schools* (J. Bradley, ed.), London, UK: Routledge, pp. 39–52.

Burbules, N. and Torres, C. (2000). Globalization and education: An introduction. In *Globalization and Education: Critical Perspectives* (N. Burbules, and C. Torres, eds). London: Routledge, pp. 1–26.

Carnoy, M. (2000). Globalization and educational reform. In *Globalization and Education: Integration and Contestation Across Cultures* (N. Stromquist and K. Monkman, eds). New York: Rowman and Littlefield, pp. 43–61.

Corry, N. and Lelliott, T. (2003). Supporting the masses? Learner perceptions of a South African ODL programme. In *Rethinking Learner Support in Distance Education: Change and Continuity in an International Context* (A. Tait and R. Mills, eds). London: Routledge Falmer, pp. 28–40.

Farrell, G. (2001). Chapter 8. Issues and choices. In *The Changing Faces of Virtual Education* (G. Farrell, ed.). Vancouver: Commonwealth of Learning, pp. 141–152.

Gayol, Y. and Schied, F. (n.d.). Cultural imperialism in the virtual classroom: Critical pedagogy in transnational distance education. Retrieved September 16, 2006, from www.geocities.com/Athens/Olympus/9260/culture.html

Hülsmann, T. (1999). The costs of distance education. In *Higher Education Through Open and Distance Learning* (K. Harry, ed.). London: Routledge Falmer.

Latchem, C. and Walker, D. (2001). *Telecentres: Case Studies and Key Issues*. Vancouver: Commonwealth of Learning.

Nipper, S. (1989). Third generation distance learning and computer conferencing. In *Mindweave: Communication, Computers and Distance Education* (R. Mason and A. Kaye, eds). Oxford: Pergamon Press.

Oestmann, S. and Dymond, A. (2001). Chapter 1. Telecentres – Experiences, lessons and trends. In *Telecentres: Case Studies and Key Issues* (C. Latchem and D. Walker, eds). Vancouver: COL, pp. 1–16.

Oliveira, J., Castro, X., and Verdisco, A. (2001). Education by television: Telecurso 2000. In *The Open Classroom: Distance Learning in Schools* (J. Bradley, ed.). London: Routledge Falmer.

Ong, W. (2002). *Orality and Literacy: The Technologizing of the Word*. New York: Routledge.

Orivel, F. (2000). Finance, cost and economics of distance education at basic level. In *Basic Education at a Distance* (C. Yates and J. Bradley, eds). London: Routledge Falmer.

Perraton, H. (2000). *Distance Education in the Developing World*. London: Routledge Falmer.

Robinson, B. (1999). Asian learners, western models: Some discontinuities and issues for distance educators. In *The Asian Distance Learner* (R. Carr, O. Jegede, W. Tat-meg, and Y. Kin-sun, eds), Hong Kong: Open University of Hong Kong, pp. 33–48.

Robinson, B. and Latchem, C. (2002). *Teacher Education through Open and Distance Learning*. London: Routledge Falmer and Vancouver: Commonwealth of Learning.

Rumble, G. (1997). *The Costs and Economics of Open, Distance and Flexible Distance Education*. London: Routledge Falmer.
Rumble, G. (2001a). *Analysing Costs/Benefits for Distance Education Programmes*. Vancouver: Commonwealth of Learning.
Rumble, G. (2001b). E-education – Whose benefits? Whose costs? Open University Professorial Inaugural Lecture, February 2001. Available at www.iec.ac.uk/resources/e_education_costs.pdf.
Scollon, R. and Scollon, S. (1981). *Narrative, Literacy and Face in Interethnic Communication*. New Jersey: Ablex Publishing.
Stromquist, N. (2002). *Education in a Globalized World: The Connectivity of Economic Power, Technology, and Knowledge*. Oxford: Rowman and Littlefield Publishers, Inc.
Traxler, J. and Kukulska-Hulme, A. (2005). *Mobile Learning in Developing Countries*. Vancouver: Commonwealth of Learning.
UNDP. (2005). Human Development Report 2005. International cooperation at a crossroads: Aid, trade and security in an unequal world. Oxford: Oxford University Press.
Voyageur, C. (2001). Ready, willing, and able: prospects for distance learning in Canada's First Nations community. *Journal of Distance Education*, **16**(1), 102–112.

WEBSITES

Developing Countries Farm Radio Network: www.farmradio.org
Internet World Stats: www.intermetworldstats.com/stats7.htm
Freeplay Foundation: www.freeplayfoundation.org
One Laptop Per Child Foundation: laptop.org
Worldspace™ Satellite Radio: www.worldspace.com

Section II

The Transformation of Teaching and Learning at a Distance

Introduction

Terry Evans

Section 2 concerns the ways in which teaching and learning at a distance is being transformed in various international and practical contexts. Arguably, distance education has been characterised by transformation since its earliest correspondence days through to the integration of online media. Tony Bates pursues this latter theme in his opening chapter for the section where the range of new media and their implications and transformative features in distance education and from distance education to mainstream educational practices are discussed.

Distance education, however, is not merely educational which is particularly mediated by communications media; it is also an approach to education in which the educators, designers, support staff and students are engaged differently and often for purposes that have particular social and policy imperatives. As Liz Burge and Jody Polec argue, there are elements of change and consistency for the people involved which can be tracked through the evolution of distance education from its inception. Chère Campbell Gibson explores the ways in which non-formal education in the United States have been transformed by both new technologies and the changing circumstances and needs of the population for non-formal education, especially as lifelong learning.

At a large institutional level, arguably one of the major educational changes of the twentieth century was the conception, in the United Kingdom, of an "open university" and its subsequent development into a form which became one of the most important agents for educational change and educational provision in higher education. Otto Peters's chapter reviews the steps which led to these fundamental transformations in the provision of education at a distance to millions of people worldwide through that became 35 open universities. To a large extent, these 35 universities have focused on post-school courses, especially undergraduate diplomas and degrees, often followed by coursework masters degrees. Terry Evans considers doctoral education at a distance which has developed, either explicitly or in a de facto sense, both within distance education institutions and in "traditional" universities. This chapter deals with the courses that lead to the highest qualification offered by universities and which are substantially, or entirely, based on the students' own research.

Christine Spratt draws on her own doctoral research in a dual-mode university to explore the tensions that surround the technological change and structural changes as they are experienced by the teaching staff. This chapter shows that the critical intent of much intellectual and pedagogical work in universities sits uneasily with corporate approaches to the implementation and operations of computer-based learning systems that are created from corporatist ideological positions. Katy Campbell and Susan Gibson consider the ways in which assessment has evolved in both education and distance education to measure, sort, distribute and "gate-keep" individuals. They consider the constructive purposes to which assessment can be marshalled in distance education in order to enhance learning.

Peter Macauley and Rosemary Green present an overview and analysis of the development of library and information services in distance education. The impact of new media and technologies on the dissemination, storage, searching and access to knowledge is considered. The connections between these developments and the related technological changes in distance education enable different possibilities for the integration of knowledge management into distance education. Brian Pauling's chapter takes a complementary line through his exploration of the ways in which the new technologies have radically altered the mass media, and the nature of human engagement with the media is a globalising context. The consequences and potential for distance education and its mutations in education are considered.

David Harris closes the section with his critical essay on the transformation of teaching and learning in distance education. He explores the nature of the human and political interests involved in changes to distance education. Using various ideas from social theory, he focuses on specific examples, such as assessment and technology to analyse the transformations in distance education.

Chapter 12

TRANSFORMING DISTANCE EDUCATION THROUGH NEW TECHNOLOGIES

Tony Bates

12.1 INTRODUCTION

Technology has always been a defining feature of distance education. Each of the major developments in distance education has been strongly linked, if not driven, by advances in technology. This chapter examines the ongoing, dynamic relationship between technology and distance education.

12.2 THE IMPACT OF TECHNOLOGY ON THE ORGANIZATION OF DISTANCE EDUCATION

Distance education has gone through several stages of development.

Taylor (1999) has proposed five generations of distance education:

- correspondence education;
- integrated use of multiple, one-way media such as print and broadcasting or recorded media such as video-cassettes;
- two-way, synchronous tele-learning using audio- or video-conferencing;
- flexible learning based on asynchronous online learning combined with online interactive multimedia;
- intelligent flexible learning, which adds a high degree of automation and student control to asynchronous online learning and interactive multimedia.

The progression through these stages of development has been driven mainly by changes in technology and educational theory. At the end of the 1980s, Nipper (1989) and Kaufman (1989) identified three generations of distance education. The first generation is characterized by the predominant use of a single technology, and lack of direct student interaction with the teacher originating the instruction. Correspondence education is a typical form of first-generation distance education, although educational broadcasting is another version. Correspondence education makes heavy use of standard textbooks and the use of a contracted correspondence tutor, who is not the originator of the learning material and often works for a commercial company. Students, however, take examinations from accredited institutions.

Second-generation distance education is characterized by a deliberately integrated multiple-media approach, with learning materials specifically designed for study at a distance, but with two-way communication still mediated by a third person (a tutor, rather than the originator of the teaching material). Autonomous distance teaching universities, such as the British Open University, are examples of second-generation distance education. Second-generation distance education is based on specially designed correspondence texts, combined with standard textbooks and collections of readings from academic journals, and supported by television and/or radio programming. Open universities and distance education units in dual-mode institutions have been associated more with systems-based and behaviourist or cognitive-science approaches to learning. These may be considered more teacher-focused and "industrialized", in that all students get the same material, resulting in considerable economies of scale.

Taylor's third generation (two-way, synchronous tele-learning using audio- or video-conferencing) is based on replicating as far as possible the classroom model through the use of synchronous interactive technologies, such as video-conferencing, and relies heavily on lecturing and questions. This model of distance education is often used by multi-campus institutions, because it saves travel time between campuses for instructors. However, it provides relatively small economies of scale, and little flexibility for learners, because they still have to attend a campus at a set time, and the average cost per student tends to be high. Nevertheless synchronous teleconferencing is popular because instructors do not have to change or adapt their classroom teaching methods to any extent.

Taylor's fourth generation (Kaufman's and Nipper's third generation) is flexible learning based on asynchronous communication through the Internet and the World Wide Web (online learning). This model enables increased student–teacher and student–student interaction at a distance, collaborative group work, flexibility for learners to study anywhere at any time, and economies of scope, in that courses for relatively small numbers can be developed without high start-up costs. However, to exploit the educational advantages and to control costs, the design and delivery of asynchronous teaching must be different from both traditional approaches to classroom teaching and the large-scale design of open university programmes. Kaufman (1989) characterizes this as a progressive increase in learner control, opportunities for dialogue, and emphasis on thinking skills rather than mere comprehension.

Taylor's fifth stage is still experimental, and applied mainly in his own institution (University of Southern Queensland).

Although these are useful classifications of the technological and educational development of distance education, the situation on the ground at any one time is much more complex. Building on other studies by Cunningham (2000), Dirr (2001), Ryan and Steadman (2002), the Association of Commonwealth Universities (2002), and the OECD (2005), Bates (2005) provided an extensive analysis of the impact of technology on distance education organizations. He identified six main types of distance teaching organizations in operation in 2003:

- public autonomous distance education institutions;
- dual-mode institutions;
- for-profit distance education institutions;
- partnerships and consortia;
- workplace training organizations; and
- virtual schools.

Distance teaching organizations were using a wide combination of technologies, and there were many different variations on the basic six models. Bates concluded (p. 36) that "the most striking result from the analysis is the diversity and volatility of distance education in 2002–2003". Bates identified thirteen different types of distance education organization in 2003, nearly all resulting from experiments with Internet-based delivery.

Bates (2005) also noted that although private universities such as the University of Phoenix Online and Jones International were relatively successful and sustainable, focusing on niche markets and strong business models, nearly all the spin-offs from not-for-profit universities, such as New York University Online and e-Cornell, had "crashed and burned". His analysis also suggested that consortia "seem too cumbersome to work", although "smaller, simpler university to university partnerships, such as the one between UBC and Tec de Monterrey, where just two partners work together to provide a joint international degree" appeared to be more viable.

Bates also found (2005) that in 2002–2003, in the public sector, print and broadcast-based distance education still accounted for almost ten times more distance students than fully online programmes (5 million to 600,000). Bates pointed out though that

> Trends are more important than the actual figures. The overall trend is towards more online courses and fewer print-based courses in distance education. Private suppliers of online learning are increasing. Distance education continues to grow in the public sector, but more slowly than ... [the] rapid growth in the use of e-learning for company training and [for] support[ing] classroom teaching on university and college campuses.

Bates also commented that

> unlike the 1970s and 1980s when governments created large national autonomous open universities, governments have generally been reluctant to create new post-secondary institutions that are fully online (the Open University of Catalonia is an exception). Instead, governments have tended to encourage consortia of existing conventional universities and colleges moving into online learning for the first time. We have seen though that conventional institutions and consortia have not in general been successful in widening access, increasing quality, or becoming financially sustainable

through the use of online learning. There certainly seems to be an opportunity for political parties to make their mark by creating new virtual institutions designed from the beginning to exploit fully the potential of the Internet, possibly through a public private partnership.

Finally, Bates commented on the growing role of the private sector in distance education, again mainly as a result of moving into Internet-based delivery.

> The private sector now accounts for almost half of all distance learning globally, mainly through company training. In terms of formal post-secondary education, though, the private sector impact is still quite small, though growing. The large numbers still come from the national autonomous open universities, which account for approximately four million students. [Another million distance learners are in dual mode institutions].
>
> However, private sector university and college distance education will probably continue to grow rapidly, especially in Mexico, Brazil, Chile, China, Malaysia, Korea, India and other newly emerging economic powerhouses, where influential and impatient middle classes are increasing faster than the provision of good quality public sector education. Much of this private sector expansion of distance education in these countries will be online.
>
> In poorer countries, and for the poor in rapidly developing countries, the large public sector print- and broadcast-based autonomous open universities will continue to be important.

In summary then, the following conclusions can be drawn:

1. Technology has a major impact on the organization of distance education; as new technology develops, new organizational models develop to exploit better the new technology.
2. The large autonomous distance education universities have moved more slowly than conventional institutions and the private sector in adopting the Internet for teaching purposes. This is mainly because of structural rigidities in the large autonomous distance teaching universities due to heavy prior investment in print and broadcast technologies.
3. Although in 2003 in the public sector students in print- and broadcast-based distance education programmes far outnumbered students in online distance courses, nevertheless the trend is towards more online courses and fewer print-based courses, although for large enrolment courses and for students with poor access to the Internet, print- and broadcast-based programmes will remain important.
4. Although conventional universities have moved more rapidly into online learning or e-learning, quality, access, and sustainability remain problematic (see OECD, 2005). Many conventional universities have failed to adopt and adapt the strategies developed by distance teaching organizations to ensure quality, increased access, and sustainability from the use of technology for teaching.

12.3 DEFINING MEDIA AND TECHNOLOGY IN DISTANCE EDUCATION

"Media" and "technology" are everyday words that we use. Their meaning tends to be taken for granted, and the terms are often used interchangeably. However, their role in education is by no means obvious or without controversy. It is important then to define more closely what is meant by "technology" and "media". This distinction becomes particularly important when the issue of whether media actually influence learning is discussed.

Kozma (1994) defines "media" and "technology" as follows:

> *Media* can be analyzed in terms of their cognitively relevant capabilities or attributes (Salomon, 1978). These include a medium's technology, symbol systems, and processing capabilities. *Technology* is the physical, mechanical or electronic capabilities of a medium that determine its function and to some extent its shape and other features... *Symbol systems* are sets of symbolic expressions by which information is communicated about a field of reference. ... A particular medium can be described in terms of its capability to present certain representations and perform certain operations in interaction with learners who are similarly engaged in internally constructing representations and operating on these.
>
> (p. 7–8)

Media are means of communication. They require a source of information, a means of transmitting information (including technology and symbol systems), and a receiver, that is, someone who is interested in, has access to, and knows how to interpret the communication. Thus speech, writing, drama, radio, and television programming, computer programming, and Web-based courses are all communications media. In this definition, face-to-face teaching can be considered a medium of communication, even if it does not use electronic technology. Language is the predominant symbol system used in face-to-face teaching, and classrooms, schools, and campuses could be considered the technological components.

Technologies are physical things. Of themselves, they do not communicate. Thus classrooms, books, theatres, cinemas, radio sets and transmitters, cable, satellites, television monitors, computers, computer software, and computer networks are all technologies.

While there is usually an assumption that media will use technology of some kind for the means of transmission and communication, media, though, may not be related necessarily to any specific technology. For instance, although a television programme needs to be recorded and transmitted using technology, a television programme can use several different technologies, such as digital or analogue equipment, terrestrial broadcast, cable or satellite transmission, video cassettes, or digital video disc. Similarly, computer signals can be sent by telephone lines, wireless, co-axial or fiber optic cable, satellite, or any combination. Furthermore, everyday use of the term "media" usually includes the whole organization of a communications industry, such as television, newspapers, publishing, and the Internet, thus encompassing far more than just the technology.

12.4 COMPARING TECHNOLOGIES

Bates and Poole (2003) classified media and technology in terms of the communications functions that impact on teaching and learning. They grouped the media of face-to-face teaching, audio, video and digital, and their related technologies by three main dimensions: broadcast (one-way) versus interactive (two-way); synchronous (same time) versus asynchronous (available on demand); and transient versus permanent. In terms of teaching and learning, there are advantages when a technology can combine multiple media (allowing for richer representation of knowledge), when the technology allows for interaction between teachers and learners, and when the learning material and opportunity for communication are always available to the learner and teacher (asynchronous and permanent). Thus the Internet (including the Web) is the potentially most powerful educational technology because it is the only technology that integrates all these elements, thus providing more opportunities for teachers and learners when designing the learning experience.

Does this then automatically mean that Internet-based teaching is always the best? Not necessarily. There have been hundreds of comparative studies, comparing, for instance, the effectiveness of a broadcast lecture with a face-to-face lecture, or an online course with a face-to-face course. Generally, such studies have not proved very conclusive. From Schramm (1974) through Clark (1983) to Russell (1999), analysis of these studies have shown that there are *on average* no significant differences in learning between different technologies or media (including face-to-face teaching).

The reason for this is that the technology of teaching is only one of many different variables that influence the effectiveness of learning. In particular, the *way* a particular technology is used – more accurately, its quality – is very important. Thus a poorly prepared and delivered lecture will be less effective than a professionally produced television programme – and vice versa. Well-designed teaching using any technology is likely to be effective. However, this should not be interpreted to mean that the choice of technology does not matter. It is important to look at the conditions that lead to the successful or inappropriate use of different technologies. In particular, the appropriateness of a particular technology will depend on the context in which it is to be used. Consequently, much attention has been paid to the design of technology-based teaching.

12.5 THEORIES OF TEACHING AND LEARNING AND CHOICE OF TECHNOLOGY IN DISTANCE EDUCATION

Rational approaches to the design of teaching aim to demonstrate the links between desired learning outcomes, theories of learning, and teaching method (or pedagogy) (see, for instance, Edmonds et al., 1994). This section discusses the extent to which technology developments in distance education map to changes in educational theory, and the extent to which educational theory has influenced decisions about the use of technology in distance education.

Greeno et al., (1996) have identified three broad perspectives on theories of learning:

- the associationist/empiricist perspective (learning as activity);
- the cognitive perspective (learning as achieving understanding); and
- the situative perspective (learning as social practice).

To these three perspectives I would add two more:

- the constructivist perspective (learning as reflection and dialogue); and
- the didactic perspective (learning as comprehension and apprenticeship).

Each of these main streams of theory reflects somewhat different epistemological roots, but each theory stream provides a rationale that underpins the choice of learning outcomes, the design of learning environments, and teaching methods (pedagogy).

The *empiricist* perspective has strong routes in behaviourism. Mayes and de Freitas (2004, p. 7) state that in this perspective "learning is the process of connecting the elementary mental or behavioural units, through sequences of activity". Underlying this approach is the belief that learning is governed by invariant principles, and these principles are independent of conscious control on the part of the learner. Empiricists attempt to maintain a high degree of objectivity in the way they view human activity, and they generally reject reference to unobservable states, such as feelings, attitudes, and consciousness. Human behaviour is above all seen as predictable and controllable.

The *cognitive* perspective in contrast focuses on the mental processes – internal and conscious representations of the world – that are essential for human learning. Fontana (1981) summarizes this approach as follows:

> The cognitive approach ... holds that if we are to understand learning we cannot confine ourselves to observable behavior, but must also concern ourselves with the learner's ability mentally to re-organize his psychological field (i.e. his inner world of concepts, memories, etc.) in response to experience. This latter approach therefore lays stress not only on the environment, but upon the way in which the individual interprets and tries to make sense of the environment. It sees the individual not as the somewhat mechanical product of his environment, but as an active agent in the learning process, deliberately trying to process and categorize the stream of information fed into him by the external world.
>
> (p. 148)

The *situative* perspective puts more emphasis on the social aspects of learning by looking at the contexts in which learning takes place. For many educators, the social context of learning is critical. Ideas are tested not just on the teacher, but with fellow students, friends, and colleagues. Furthermore, knowledge is mainly acquired through processes or institutions that are socially constructed: schools, colleges, and universities. Thus what is taken to be "valued" knowledge is also socially constructed. In this perspective learning can take place through communities of practice, where learners with common needs and understandings can share experiences.

Crossing both cognitive and situative perspectives is the *constructivist* perspective. Individuals consciously strive for meaning to make sense of their environment in terms of past experience and their present state. It is an attempt to create order in their minds out of disorder, to resolve incongruities, and to reconcile external realities with prior experience. The means by which this is done are complex and multifaceted, from personal reflection, seeking new information, to testing ideas through social contact with others. Problems are resolved, and incongruities sorted out, through strategies such as seeking relationships between what was known and what is new, identifying similarities and differences, and testing hypotheses. Reality is always tentative and dynamic.

Lastly, the *didactic* perspective is based on the transmission of information by a subject expert through what Mayes and de Freitas (2004, p. 15) call "compelling explanations". This can be summed up by the professor who says to her student, "My job is to teach; your's is to learn." The learner's task is to understand and memorize the expert's knowledge and to learn by example.

It should be noted that although there is a surprising degree of agreement among educators about the existence of these five perspectives on learning, and some elaborate attempts to relate these perspectives to teaching practice and choice of technology, the position on the ground is once again much more complex. Teachers tend to mix and match these different approaches, again dependent on the context and the perceived needs of learners.

Despite this, there has been a close link between educational theory and choice of technology in distance education. Learning by association, and behaviourism have been the hallmarks of much of computer-based learning in the workplace. Second-generation print-based distance education has been heavily influenced by the empiricist, cognitive perspective. The first UK Open University courses were based on instructional systems design. The use of video-conferencing for multi-campus teaching was usually based on transferring the didactic approach to teaching in the classroom to the video-conferencing environment. Educators such as Harasim et al. (1995) and Peters (2002) have argued that online learning is a "paradigm shift" in teaching. Harasim emphasizes constructivist approaches based on knowledge construction, collaborative learning, and problem-solving, and Peters emphasizes the development of "self-autonomy" and "lateral thinking".

However, none of these features are unique to online learning; they can be found not only in face-to-face classroom teaching but also in cognitive approaches in second-generation print-based courses. The problem is that in practice, there is a wide variety of teaching approaches, irrespective of the technology being used. Thus one can find constructivist approaches to teaching by video-conference, didactic and behaviourist use of online learning, and cognitive approaches in classroom teaching. Technologies are generally flexible enough to accommodate a variety of approaches to teaching.

Nevertheless, in general, there is a strong argument to suggest that asynchronous online learning has considerable educational advantages over print-based distance education, provided that students have access to the technology. Certainly, the weakness of print-based or broadcast-based distance education is the difficulty of providing opportunities for student discussion. Expensive and optional arrangements have to be made through local study centres for face-to-face interaction, and in practice these are often used by local tutors for more lecturing, rather than group discussion of the printed material. Thus web-based learning offers a better opportunity to achieve academic goals such as creative and critical thinking, knowledge construction, problem-solving, and collaborative learning than print-based distance education (but not necessarily better than classroom teaching).

12.6 A GENERAL THEORY FOR MAKING DECISIONS ABOUT TECHNOLOGY IN DISTANCE EDUCATION

Is it then the educational theories that drive the choice and use of technology? While educational theories and preferred teaching methods have a role to play, they are not the main drivers of technology choice and use. In other words, they are necessary but not sufficient guides for decision-making about the use of technology in distance education.

In 2004, the Institute of Socio-technical Innovation and Research, University of Essex, produced several online reports on effective practice in relation to e-learning (available as PDF files at http://www.jisc.ac.uk/elp_learneroutcomes.html) for the UK's Joint Information Systems Committee. These reports provide a good overview of current thinking regarding the relationship between theories of learning, educational design, and e-learning. Building on the "core" learning theories outlined by Greeno et al., (1996), the University of Essex team designed a grid that identified for each learning theory the implied pedagogies, the power balance between teacher and learners ("desirable role combinations"), learning tasks, the type of interaction, and generic learning activities (Fowler and Mayes, 2004). Using this grid, they then identified "functionality requirements for [e-learning] tools" for each of the learning theories, with general descriptions and mini-scenarios for each row in the mapping table.

The final result is a good example of the difficulty in providing satisfactory guidelines for practitioners in choosing, in this case, technology tools. The further away the analysis moves from the general theories of learning, the more unwieldy it becomes. (The mapping table stretches over twenty pages with sixteen pedagogical perspectives each with nine columns of analysis, without identifying any specific existing tools as being appropriate or inappropriate.) This resembles many of the earlier attempts by instructional systems designers to match media to learning tasks (see, for instance, Reiser and Gagné, 1983). The approach becomes too reductionist to be of value.

Also, similar to the earlier approaches, the analysis focuses only on one set of variables, those associated with teaching and learning. In one of the papers for this study, Mayes and de Freitas (2004) recognize that "many of the decisions that are taken in the curriculum design process depend on pragmatic issues that will not be directly addressed in this document". These "pragmatic" decisions include costs, technical support, quality assurance.

Research by Bates and his associates (Bates, 1995) has shown that some of these "pragmatic" factors, such as access and cost, are better *discriminators* for choosing and using technology than teaching requirements, although the latter are still important. Access and cost are better discriminators because the differences between technologies in these factors are clearer and more easily defined. As a result, Bates developed a decision-making model called ACTIONS (Access, Cost, Teaching function, Interactivity, Organizational issues, Novelty, and Speed) to help choose the most appropriate combination of media and technologies for a particular context. These are listed roughly in order of importance for distance education.

Thus access is the most important criterion for distance education. If the aim is to increase access, and students cannot access the technology, either because it is not available or they cannot afford it, then it is a useless technology, no matter how great the pedagogic benefits. Cost is a more complex factor (see Rumble, 1997, for a good overview), but the core drivers of cost (planning, development, delivery, learner support, student numbers, fixed and variable costs) are now well understood, and in particular the different cost *structures* of different technologies allow for fairly accurate prediction and accounting of the costs of different distance education technologies in different contexts.

In the ACTIONS model, teaching functions include presentational features associated with a medium or technology, the way each technology structures knowledge, and the relative facility for the technology to develop different kinds of skills. Interactivity can be seen as a subset of teaching functions, but is considered significant in its own right, reflecting the different kinds of interaction supported by different technologies. Organizational issues too are important. If an institution cannot adequately support the application of a technology then it is likely to fail. Novelty and speed are of lesser importance. In the ACTIONS model, a set of questions is asked for each factor. When each question is answered within the specific decision-making context, decision-makers then would make a decision intuitively, taking all the factors into consideration, in contrast to using a grid or algorithmic approach to decision-making.

Of course, in practice such rational approaches to decision-making are rarely followed. Typical factors that have influenced decision-making about educational technologies are as follows:

- the availability of spare broadcasting capacity (an important factor initially influencing the BBC's partnership with the UK Open University – see Perry, 1976);
- an offer from technology suppliers of free or cheap equipment or services (for instance, IBM Thinkpads for laptop programs);
- the comfort level of academics with technologies that replicate traditional teaching formats (for instance, video-conferencing); and
- the enthusiasm of a key decision-maker for a particular technology (for instance, a college president influenced by a demonstration at a trade conference).

Nevertheless, the opportunity now exists to take advantage of a growing body of knowledge about the use of technology in distance education when making decisions. These decisions need to include other factors as well as educational theory if the right choices are to be made.

12.7 SOCIO-ECONOMIC FACTORS INFLUENCING THE USE OF TECHNOLOGY IN DISTANCE EDUCATION

Another way of looking at the synergy between technology and distance education is to step back from educational theory and rational decision-making processes, and to look at the complex relationship between technology, distance education, and socio-economic developments.

The development of second-generation distance education, and in particular open universities, was driven initially by the desire to fast-track access to post-secondary education. This in turn was linked to the desire to move from an elite to a mass higher education system (see, for instance, Perry, 1976). Government support for such initiatives stemmed from two sources, one idealistic and the other economic. The British Labour government under Harold Wilson in the 1960s was anxious to provide a second chance for many adults who had been unable to attend university because of the lack of places (only 8% of the 18-year-old cohort went on to higher education in the UK in 1969). The UK Open University survived a change of government (Mrs Thatcher became the new Conservative Minister for Education in 1971) because the Conservatives saw the economies of scale that distance education based on the mass media of print and broadcasting could achieve.

In other words, as Otto Peters (1965) so astutely predicted, technology would enable the industrialization of higher education. Distance education then can be seen as leading the charge towards the industrialization of higher education, but even more significantly is also now being affected by the move to a post-industrial or knowledge-based society. It is worth tracing these developments in more detail.

12.7.1 Agrarian Organizations

In an agrarian society, a skilled worker was responsible for all aspects of the production, manufacturing, and distribution of a product or service. The wheelwright would collect the wood and the materials required, manufacture the wheel, and transport and market it himself. He would teach his son or a neighbour's son the same skills and the same methods.

Similarly, the traditional university or college teacher is responsible for all aspects of teaching, from selection of content and the method of teaching, to the delivery of the teaching, to the assessment of students. Teaching in higher education generally remains based on an apprenticeship model of handing down knowledge and teaching methods from one generation to the next (which is one reason why the didactic approach to teaching remains so strong, to the dismay of educational theorists). A particular university subject discipline still resembles a closed community or guild, whose admission is controlled through doctoral study managed by peers. Thus, even modern universities still display many examples of pre-industrial or agrarian organizations. For instance, the semester system with the long summer break reflects the origin of the land grant universities, where students had to return home for harvesting and to tend the crops.

12.7.2 Industrial Organizations

Most manufacturing companies producing physical goods have until recently adopted a "Fordist" organizational model, named after Henry Ford, the car manufacturer. This is characterized by a number of features:

- the production of uniform products;
- economies of scale (initial set-up costs are high, but large volume results in each extra unit having increasingly lower marginal costs);
- a division of labor (work is broken down into different elements conducted by different classes of worker);
- hierarchical management (decisions are made at the top, and passed down the line of command);
- organization of people and processes into discrete, large units (divisions, for example, of manufacturing, sales/marketing, distribution, and administration) which themselves are hierarchically managed (each division with its own Vice-President, with departments such as accounting, payroll, personnel, each with its own level of hierarchy);
- standardized, bureaucratic policies and procedures operating across all divisions, with a high degree of central control, often characterized by company-wide collective agreements with highly organized unions, which reinforce and codify hierarchical structures and divisions within the organization.

The larger, national autonomous open universities in countries such as UK, Netherlands, Thailand, Indonesia, India, and so forth, many of which have over 100,000 students (what Daniel, 1998, calls "mega-universities"), are good examples of this kind of manufacturing organization and structure in education. Organizations such as these were designed from the start as industrial models of education (Peters, 1983).

However, there has also been a rapid increase in the size and scale of "conventional" universities in industrialized countries since the introduction in the 1960s of systems of mass higher education. This has forced even conventional universities and colleges to adopt many features of an industrialized or Fordist organizational model (see, for instance, Campion and Renner, 1992):

- large class sizes (economies of scale);
- a differentiation between tenured (research) professors and graduate teaching assistants, and between academic (professors), management (deans and vice-presidents), and administrative staff (division of labor);
- hierarchical management (Presidents, Vice-Presidents, Deans, Heads of Department), with managerial control increasingly replacing collegial decision-making;

- large, hierarchical, and distinctly separate core organizational structures (faculties, administrative departments, buildings and plant, and so forth);
- bureaucratic procedures, even – or especially – in academic areas, such as closely defined admission requirements, prerequisites, and credit banking, to ensure standardization across the organization.

Industrially organized post-secondary institutions tend to design teaching and learning in ways that suit an industrial economy. Students are organized into large classes and thus get the same material which may be of a high quality in terms of content but tends towards a didactic or cognitive approach to presentation.

12.7.3 Knowledge-based Organizations

In contrast to both the agrarian and the industrial forms of organization, information technology has led to the growth of many knowledge-based and service industries that have a very different structure from the industrial or agrarian models. These newer forms of organization have also been labelled as "post-Fordist" (or "post-industrial") in structure (see, for example, Farnes, 1993).

Knowledge-based organizations are characterized by the following:

- heavy dependence on information technologies (telecommunications, computers);
- customized products and services tailored and adapted to needs of individual clients;
- workers directly networked to clients: rapid and immediate feedback used to modify products and services;
- workers who are encouraged to create and develop new knowledge and new ways of doing things, or who transform and modify pre-existing information;
- decentralized, empowered, creative workers, often working in teams;
- "core" workers are well paid, well trained, and educated on contracts, often with ownership in the company through stock options, and are highly mobile; "non-core" workers and functions are often "outsourced", and lack secure conditions of employment;
- strong leadership characterized by clear but broad vision and objectives; senior management plays an integrating, co-ordinating, and facilitating role;
- often small-scale and specialist; dependent on partnerships and alliances with other organizations with related and complementary competencies;
- rapid development and change: post-Fordist organizations are dynamic and move very fast; and
- operate on a global basis.

Knowledge-based business sectors are often chaotic and characterized by new players, new amalgamations, and the unpredictable emergence of dominant technology-linked organizations. Examples of knowledge-based organizations are Apple Computers, started originally in a garage in California; Microsoft, which has the same revenues as Sony and Honda combined, but whose direct workforce is one hundred times smaller than each of those companies; and Google, whose stock is now valued as greater than General Motors.

12.7.4 The Post-industrial University?

We have not yet seen any advanced and sustainable form of such an organization in higher education. Nevertheless, despite some of its "agrarian" and "industrial" elements, there are certain features of a traditional university which are compatible with the new knowledge-based organizations. Despite its hierarchical organizational structures, a university is in practice an extremely decentralized organization. It has a large and highly creative "core" of staff, faculty, who are able and willing to operate relatively autonomously, are concerned with the creation and transmission of knowledge, and have the power to develop and implement new ways of doing things, if they wish. Furthermore, they have a research capability that enables them to generate new knowledge in a wide range of subject areas that can be assembled and disseminated through the use of technology. Lastly, the better-established research universities have the advantage of what marketers call "a strong brand image".

Since 1995, universities and colleges have been moving more and more into the use of information technology and computers for teaching, more commonly called "e-learning", driven mainly by the development of the World Wide Web. One rationale for e-learning is that it is not only a product of a knowledge-based economy, but also a means by which to develop appropriately skilled workers for a knowledge-based economy. E-learning develops appropriate IT skills and, in particular, trains or educates students to find, analyse, apply, and evaluate information appropriately within each field of study or discipline. As we have seen, there has been an emphasis on constructivist approaches to online learning, with a focus on knowledge construction, problem-solving, collaborative learning, critical thinking, and autonomous learning, all skills considered to be essential in a knowledge-based economy. It has been argued that e-learning lends itself to economies of scope, enabling teaching to be "tailored" to individual needs, with increasing responsibility and control placed on the learner/consumer, reflecting another feature of knowledge-based economies.

We also saw earlier that conventional universities have moved more aggressively into e-learning than distance education institutions or departments. This move by conventional institutions into e-learning is beginning to have a profound side effect on the organization and management of distance education. As King (2005) states,

> the impact of technologies on the delivery of face-to-face education enable any educator to replicate many of these dimensions of off-distance delivery that previously required a specialist infrastructure to provide. On-campus delivery has become more like distance education and – in so doing – undermined the distinctive contribution to overall provision of ODL practitioners.

Thus King is arguing that distance education is increasingly seen as just another way of doing e-learning, and since e-learning is becoming a central activity of academic departments, there is no need for a separate organization to manage distance education.

Thus we have seen in some jurisdictions the closure of dedicated distance education organizations (such as the Open Learning Agency in Canada) or attempts to close distance education departments in dual-mode institutions (such as at the University of British Columbia, also in Canada). This may also explain the reluctance of governments to create new institutions based on e-learning and to favour consortia and collaboration between existing institutions through structures such as the South Eastern Regional Board in the USA, the Open Learning Agency of Australia, BC Campus and e-learning Alberta in Canada, all of which enable students to pick and choose online courses from a variety of institutions.

Nevertheless, despite these moves, there are still some concerns about treating distance education as merely an extension of classroom-based teaching. First, students who take fully online courses tend to be older, want to study part-time and in short bursts of activity, and require specialist off-campus support (for example, "24 × 7" access) that regular academic departments find difficult to provide. Academic departments tend to underestimate the learner support issues, and are more focused on the needs of the full-time student on campus. It is interesting to note that at the University of British Columbia, after three years' planning to decentralize the distance education department's functions to the faculties, the decision was reversed at the last minute when the Dean of Arts at last realized the implications of having to manage another 4,500 distance course enrolments. There is clearly a strong argument for having a department or division that focuses on lifelong learners and their needs.

Secondly, many of the pedagogical approaches found in distance education departments – such as instructional design based on educational theory and advanced pedagogy, project management, team work, business cases, and quality assurance processes – have not yet been generally accepted or adopted in campus-based e-learning. On-campus e-learning still in many institutions resembles more of a cottage industry managed by individual academics than a re-structured knowledge-based operation. Quality remains an issue.

12.7.5 Implications of the Three Economies

The successful introduction of technology always requires changes in the organization of work, and both conventional and distance education institutions are no exception to this rule. New forms of work organization are needed to ensure that technology-based teaching is cost-effective. So far, few sustainable organizational forms reflecting the flexibility of knowledge-based organizations have yet emerged in post-secondary education. The main examples are the loose consortia that are being developed to share courses across institutions, and the two fully online universities of the Open University of Catalonia and the University of Phoenix.

Furthermore, in most economically advanced countries, access to conventional higher education has increased. For instance, in 2003 in Britain, approximately 37 percent of a cohort went on to higher education, with a target of 50 percent being set by the government over the next 10 years. In North America, access rates have always been high, with over 60 percent of the high-school cohort going on to higher education in 2003 in Canada. This has reduced (but not eliminated) the demand for open access.

Instead, one feature of a knowledge-based economy is the need for workers to continually learn and improve.

Thus the demand has subtly shifted from providing initial degrees through distance education to providing already well-qualified lifelong learners with additional opportunities for study. For instance, in 2005, 70 percent of the graduates from the Open University of Catalonia already had a first degree before applying for admission to the university (Cabrera et al., 2005). These are learners whose post-secondary education has already been state-subsidized, who are in reasonably well-paid jobs, and who are often able and willing to pay the full cost of lifelong learning programmes because of their immediate economic benefits.

In all countries, agrarian, industrial, and knowledge-based economies exist in parallel. Thus the large-scale industrial distance education institutions based on the mass media of print and broadcasting are still likely to be needed in countries where the industrial base is large, or where access to post-secondary education is restricted. (It is interesting to note that in Spain, both UNED and the Open University of Catalonia successfully exist side by side, but serving subtly different markets. However, enrolments are dropping at both UNED and the conventional universities, but increasing at the Open University of Catalonia). In countries though where the knowledge-based economy is significant, and where Internet access is high, online distance education – sometimes mixed with small chunks of campus-based teaching – delivered by small, flexible units using market research, business plans, and programmes tailored to the needs of individuals, is most likely to succeed.

12.8 WHEN WILL IT ALL END?

This is not so much a question about distance education but a desperate plea from a distance education manager about technological change. The answer of course is that it won't. The technology continues to evolve. At the time of writing, proprietary e-learning platforms such as WebCT and Blackboard were merging into one large global product. However, they will be challenged by the development of open source software that will allow institutions to build and customize their own platforms. New tools are being added, such as blogs, wikis, e-portfolios, and learning objects. M-learning, based on mobile technology such as wireless, cell phones, and PDAs, has already made its entrance in several projects (see, for instance, Alexander, 2004; Knight, 2005). Synchronous technologies allowing audio over the Internet through VoiP (Voice over the Internet Protocols) are resulting in tools such as Skype and Wimba being developed for online real-time discussions. Completely new online tools are now becoming available almost on a daily basis.

How will this rapid technological change impact on distance education? First of all, we will see not only a convergence of technologies, with synchronous and asynchronous tools being used together, but also a convergence of operations, with even more blurring between on-campus and distance activities, as a result. We will also see more student empowerment. Students will want to use the online tools themselves to create and manage their e-portfolios, to design Web-based assignments, and to manage their own blogs and online discussions. As a result, we will also see new course designs emerging, with more student choice and more tailoring of material. Thus we can predict constant development and change in distance education over the next few years.

The main challenge will be how to manage these rapid technological developments. Several things, though, are now becoming clear. First, institutions will need to choose software applications that operate to open standards. This will allow new tools to be plugged into existing platforms or learning environments. Second, portals that can offer a wide range of online tools will become more and more important, so that designers and students can plug and play as required, thus integrating, for instance, synchronous with asynchronous learning. Course design then will also need to be more flexible, allowing alternative routes and alternative approaches to learning, to suit the different needs of individual instructors and individual learners. Content management will become critical, so that digital materials can be easily created, stored, and retrieved. (This goes far beyond creating learning objects.)

In short, we will see a great deal more experimentation in teaching, and those distance education programmes that do not move with the new technologies will become increasingly obsolete, because the appropriate application of technology not only will be expected by learners, but will lead to learners who are skilled in operating in a knowledge-based society. However, appropriate use of such technology will depend on matching technology to appropriate teaching methods and learning outcomes – in other words, instructional design supported by pragmatic decision-making procedures for the choice of appropriate tools.

12.9 CONCLUSIONS

There has been a symbiotic relationship between distance education and technology. As the technology has changed, so has the structure and organization of distance education. Educators have found it difficult to control and master the impact of technology, because of factors to some extent outside their control, such as broader changes in society and economies. Distance education is now struggling to keep up with technological change, and as a result risks losing its unique identity and function. Nevertheless, distance education has developed procedures and practices which are valuable in ensuring the appropriate use of technology in teaching, and it would be a tragedy if this knowledge and experience is lost because of failure by distance and conventional educators to learn from one another.

REFERENCES

Alexander, B. (2004). Going nomadic: mobile learning in higher education. *Educause Review*, 39(5), 29–35.

Association of Commonwealth Universities. (2002). *Online Learning in Commonwealth Universities*. London: The Observatory on Borderless Higher Education (available as a pdf file at: http://www.obhe.ac.uk/products/sample.html#reports).

Bates, A. (1995). *Technology, Open Learning and Distance Education.* London: Routledge.

Bates, A. (2005). *Technology, e-Learning and Distance Education.* London/New York: Routledge.

Bates, A. and Poole, G. (2003). *Effective Teaching with Technology in Higher Education.* San Francisco: Jossey-Bass.

Cabrera, N. et al. (2005). *Estudi d'Impacte de les Titulacions UOC.* Barcelona: Open University of Catalonia.

Campion, M. and Renner, W. (1992). The supposed demise of fordism – Implications for distance education and open learning. *Distance Education*, **13**(1), 7–28.

Clark, R. (1983). Reconsidering research on learning from media. *Review of Educational Research*, **53**, 445–459.

Cunningham, S. (2000). *The Business of Borderless Education.* Canberra: Commonwealth of Australia, Department of Education, Training and Youth Affairs.

Daniel, J. (1998). *Mega-Universities and Knowledge Media: Technology Strategies for Higher Education.* London: Kogan Page.

Dirr, P. (2001). The development of new organizational arrangements in virtual learning. In *The Changing Faces of Virtual Education* (G. Farell, ed.) Vancouver, BC: The Commonwealth of Learning.

Edmonds, G.S., Branch, R.C. and Mukherjee, P. (1994). A conceptual framework for comparing instructional design models. *Educational Research and Technology*, **42**(2), 55–72.

Farnes, N. (1993). Modes of production: Fordism and distance education. *Open Learning*, **8**(1), 10–20.

Fontana, D. (1981). *Psychology for Teachers.* London: Macmillan/British Psychological Society.

Fowler, C. and Mayes, T. (2004). *JISC e-Learning Models Desk Study: Stage 2: Mapping Theory to Practice and Practice to Tool Functionality based on the Practioner's Perspective.* Colchester, UK: Institute of Socio-technical Innovation and Research, University of Essex (available at: http://www.jisc.ac.uk/uploaded_documents/Stage%202%20Learning%20Models%20(Version%201).pdf.)

Greeno, J., Collins, A., and Resnick, L. (1996). Cognition and Learning. In *Handbook of Educational Psychology* (D. Berliner and R. Calfee, eds) NY: Simon and Shuster Macmillan.

Harasim, L., Hiltz, S., Teles, L., and Turoff, M. (1995). *Learning Networks: A Field Guide to Teaching and Learning Online.* Cambridge, MA: MIT Press.

Kaufman, D. (1989). In *Post-Secondary Distance Education in Canada: Policies, Practices and Priorities* (R. Sweet ed.) Athabasca: Athabasca University/Canadian Society for Studies in Education.

King, B. (2005). Managing change for sustainability. In *Strategies for Sustainable Open and Distance Learning* (A. Hope and P. Guiton, eds) London: Routledge.

Knight, S. (2005). *Innovative Practice with e-Learning: A Good Practice Guide to Embedding Mobile and Wireless Technologies into Everyday Practice.* Bristol, UK: JISC Development Group (report available from http://www.jisc.ac.uk/eli_casestudies.html).

Kozma, R. (1994). *Will* Media Influence Learning? Reframing the Debate. *Educational Technology Research and Development*, **42**(2), 7–19.

Mayes, T. and de Freitas, S. (2004). *JISC e-Learning Models Desk Study: Stage 2: Review of e-learning Theories, Frameworks and Models.* Colchester, UK: Institute of Socio-technical Innovation and Research, University of Essex (available at: http://www.jisc.ac.uk/ uploaded_documents/Stage%202%20Learning%20Models %20(Version%201).pdf.).

Nipper, S. (1989). Third generation distance learning and computer conferencing. In *Mindweave: Communication, Computers and Distance Education* (R. Mason and A. Kaye, eds) Oxford: Pergamon.

OECD (2005). *E-Learning in Tertiary Education: Where Do We Stand?* Paris: OECD

Perry, W. (1976). *Open University*. Milton Keynes, UK: The Open University Press.

Peters, O. (1965). *Der Fernunterricht* ("Distance Education"). Weinheim: Beltz.

Peters, O. (1983). Distance Teaching and Industrial Production. In *Distance Education: International Perspectives* (D. Sewart., D. Keegan and B. Holmberg eds) London: Croom Helm.

Peters, O. (2002). *Distance Education in Transition*. Oldenburg. Germany: Biblioteks- und informationssystem der Universität Oldenburg.

Reiser, R. and Gagné, R. (1983). *Selecting Media for Instruction*. Englewood Cliffs, N.J.: Educational Technology Publications.

Rumble, G. (1997). *The Costs and Economics of Open and Distance Learning*. London: Kogan Page.

Russell, T.L. (1999). *The No Significant Difference Phenomenon*. Raleigh, NC: North Carolina State University, Office of Instructional Telecommunication.

Ryan, Y. and Stedman, L. (2002). *The Business of Borderless Education: 2001 Update*. Canberra: Commonwealth of Australia.

Salomon, G. (1978). *Interaction of Media, Cognition and Learning*. San Francisco: Jossey Bass.

Schramm, W. (1974). *Big Media, Little Media*. San Francisco, CA: Sage.

Taylor, J.C. (1999). Distance education: The fifth generation. *Proceedings of the 19th ICDE World Conference on Open Learning and Distance Education*, Vienna, Austria.

Chapter 13

Transforming Learning and Teaching in Practice: Where Change and Consistency Interact

Elizabeth J. Burge and Jody Polec

> Each branch of study [leader] gives such directions as she sees fit . . . , suggests books to be read in addition to the printed list, and advises or explains. This is done by . . . monthly correspondence which is made as regular as possible . . . All the students are requested to make notes, from memory, of what they read, in a book, this being the best method . . . by which private study may receive a test . . . and the notebook, after correction, a serviceable record for future reference.
>
> Agassiz, 1897, in MacKenzie and Christensen, 1971, pp. 29–30

> The nature of asynchronicity makes it harder for e-moderators to create positive group experiences and the excitement, rhythm, engagement and focus that we know as "flow" . . . compared with face-to-face groups. It is not impossible, though! Key issues are the ability to create clear goals and appropriate challenges, through a vision of the learning outcomes and very short focused steps, good timely feedback and appropriate motivation.
>
> Salmon, 2004, p. 61

In the last quarter of the nineteenth century, the famous Miss Ticknor of the Society to Encourage Studies at Home (in USA) was as much determined to send her interactive education "to the doors of families living far from libraries, museums, or colleges" (Agassiz, 1897; MacKenzie and Christensen, 1971, p. 29) as, 130 years later, equally determined distance educators apply Web technologies that help learners access learning resources. Between the 1870s and now, much has changed – at least technologically – and much is revisited – at least in terms of learning and teaching.

We outline here how experienced colleagues have reported the practicalities of distance learning and teaching and its technological mediation. We sought a broad geographic representation in sources relatively easy to access. We leave specifically theoretical discussions (e.g. Moore, 1993; Laurillard, 2001; Garrison, 2003; Gibson, 2003) to other literature and other chapters in this book. We exclude these areas of practice: distance education of children (e.g. Haughey, 2005), instructional designers *per se* (Campbell et al., 2005), student retention (*Open Learning* special issue, 19/1, 2004), issues specific to ethnicity (Gunawardena et al., 2003) and developing country mass education (Chapter 11), gender-related issues (von Prümmer, 2007; Faith, 1988), disability (Kinash et al., 2004), organizational/vocational education (Hawkridge, 2000; Moran and Rumble, 2004), language teaching (Holmberg et al., 2005), online teaching in traditional higher education contexts (McConnell, 2005), learner support – as in advising that excludes academic tutoring or teaching (Simpson, 2002), detailed evaluations of learning outcomes (Morgan and O'Reilly, 1999), distance technologies *per se* (Clark, 2001), and "no significant difference" studies (http://www.nosignificantdifference.org/).

This chapter has four sections: (i) teaching and learning pre-online communication (up to mid-1990s), (ii) the mediation effects of pre-online technologies, (iii) teaching and learning in online contexts (mid-1990s onward), and (iv) our perceptions of change and consistency.

13.1 TEACHING AND LEARNING UP TO MID-1990s

It was not until 1995 that the Web and online learning strategies were applied "in any systematic way" (Bates, 2005, p. 152). So what could possibly have happened between the early 1970s and mid-1990s, especially regarding communications to and from learners? Frankly, a lot!

During the 1970s and 1980s, distance educators developed various ways for learners to interact with learning resources, both material and human. What Peters originally named as "forms of industrialization", that is, "standardized, normalized and formalized procedures for design and delivery" (2001, p. 110), Campion and Renner (1992) and others as "Fordism", and Evans and Nation later named as "instructional industrialism" (2000, p. 172) was, for many larger-scale distance-mode operations, a combination of multi-skill, team-based, tightly scheduled, quality criteria–driven production processes that defined teaching in terms of "largely pre-planned, pre-recorded and pre-packaged" materials for large numbers of students (Rowntree, 1990, p. 11).

The overall quality of the planned materials had to be the highest possible because of three factors that differentiated this model of teaching from conventional on-campus teaching: "the need to 'teach in one's hand' [i.e. write down all that a face-to-face teacher would say] . . . the 'public' 'nature of the teaching' [anyone can see and assess the printed materials] . . . and 'the relative inflexibility of self-instruction' [course designs had to last several years because of the high costs of revision or correction]" (Rowntree, 1990, p. 35).

Detailed guidelines and criteria for quality distance teaching have been recommended since the late 1960s (e.g. Erdos, 1967; Jenkins, 1981; Bååth, 1983; Rowntree, 1990;

Lockwood, 1992, 1998; Holmberg, 1995). Generally, writers stressed helping each learner recognize and build upon her/his academic successes, feel respected academically and personally, get connected to learning resources (human and material) quickly, easily and regularly, and sustain motivation. Distance mode teaching via pre-designed, complete course packages showed often behaviourist and/or cognitivist approaches taken from educational technology literature, as in references to identifying and using the learner's own experiential knowledge and the provision of prescribed, pre-selected, chunked, and structured content, advance organizers, action- and outcome-oriented learning objectives, structured in-text activities, tutor-marked pre-designed assignments, and projects.

A key design goal was to stimulate the type of learning conversations to facilitate "Elaborative processing of text, i.e. the interaction of the text content with the prior knowledge of the reader" (Holmberg, 1995, p. 48). Some opportunities were also given for greater choice of topic to be researched, greater relevance to the learner's own context and needs, and greater reliance on an experiential and dialectical process of action, reflection in and on that action, evaluation, new actions, and so on. (Thorpe, 1995b). Where the content was not able to be clearly boundaried and where there were real-world ambiguities to be managed and used (not dismissed or ignored), "reflective action guides" (Lockwood, 1992) could prompt a learner into more independence of thought and action. "In short, teachers would expect the exercise of certain study skills by which the learner constructs his or her own picture of the subject and learns to integrate what has been taught with what had been learned before feedback was provided." (Lockwood, 1992, p. 25).

The term "self-instruction" was used for guiding course designers (Rowntree, 1990; Lockwood, 1992, 1998). Self-instruction referred to the concept of the almost solitary learner's reliance on well-planned and extremely detailed, content-carrying materials, with a secondary reliance on a tutor for feedback and grading. As Daniel and Marquis described this approach, "courses conceived in teams and studied in solitude" (1977).

Worth noting in more recent, generalist literature on designing teaching functions are the Moore and Kearsley course design principles (2005), the O'Rourke tutor handbook for the Commonwealth of Learning (COL) (2004), and COL's handbook for authors and instructional designers, promoting decision-making between behaviourist, cognitivist, and constructivist approaches as and when necessary (2005). Constructivist approaches have been more overtly discussed in relation to online learning (e.g. Jonassen et al., 1995; Duffy and Kirkley, 2004; Gunawardena, 2004), but we suspect that more constructivist learning and teaching occurred before 1995 than colleagues were able to name as such: they did design frameworks for multimedia-based learning activities calling for problem-solving inside real-world complexities that were relevant to learners.

While the provision of overall high quality and often costly material design standards was understandable from the institution's point of view, many learners, being time- and workload-stressed, used very pragmatic approaches to working through learning materials. They did not always decide to dutifully follow each activity as they privately assessed the intellectual and operational costs and benefits of each prescribed or suggested activity (Lockwood, 1992).

Overall, the principles of cognitive interaction and affective engagement guided the design of learning. Daniel and Marquis's discussion in 1977 about "getting the mixture right" between "interaction and independence" used four then-current problems – choice over content, institutional costs for sustaining interaction, matching of learning activities to learners' lives, and pacing – to propose more planned interaction in the forms of counselling, tutoring, and group meetings. Thus, they argued, the adult learner would gain "a variety of mixtures of instructional fuel" (p. 43) to pilot themselves effectively through their studies. Kaye later conceded that course designers had to assume that "the learner is likely to be much lonelier and to have access to only a limited range of reading materials" (1981, p. 64). Rekkedal's findings about the affective and cognitive importance of quick turnaround times for written assignments reminded his colleagues that dialogues on paper are more effective if the time delay is minimal (1983).

Dialogue and rapport were valued in these pre-online times. While arguing for more attention on individualized feedback to learners, especially to those who lacked confidence as "second chance" learners, Cole et al. (1986) listed seventeen student feedback needs that are still relevant today. They defined "dialogue" as a key operational concept: "Teaching/learning becomes a two-way process in which tutor and student are working *together* [sic] in a relationship of *mutual* [sic] respect. Establishing rapport through the written word is obviously not easy but it can be achieved" (p. 18). Twelve years later Evans and Nation (1989) wanted to see more dialogue designed into instructional materials; they saw it as essential for proactive meaning construction and critical thinking rather than as a limited reactive measure in a knowledge reproduction teaching model.

Holmberg's concept of guided didactic conversation (1995) was later merged inside his broader, less authoritarian concept of empathy (2003):

> Feelings of empathy and belonging ... are fostered by lucid, problem-oriented, conversation-like presentations of learning matter expounding and supplementing the course literature; by friendly mediated interaction between students, tutors, counselors, and other staff in the supporting organization; and by liberal organizational-administrative structures and processes.
>
> (p. 82)

In a variant on the functions and location of dialogue, Morgan and Thorpe (1993) reviewed the current benefits and issues associated with the 1-week residential schools run by the UK Open University (UKOU). By 1995, Thorpe was using Winn's critique of behaviourist teaching models to argue for a more sophisticated and reflective view of course design (Thorpe, 1995a). She wanted to see more decision-making *in situ* as the course progressed. She looked also for student learning that used the needs and benefits of reflective learning and the concomitant development of metacognitive skills:

> distance education may be a more promising site for the encouragement of deep approaches to learning ... explicit discussion of the learning process as well as the content of study, and activities oriented to meta-learning and awareness raising, may have the potential to affect learning strategy.
>
> (1995b, p. 157)

Her research led her to hope that "the course team or instructional designer creates space for students to reflect on their own learning in ways which encourage them to 'think out' to their own histories and current circumstances" (1995b, p. 165). She acknowledged the need to "work with the grain of the known pressures on students, of time and of the wish to succeed..." (p. 165). Her colleague, Morgan, also wanting more reflection in learning, asked, "How can interaction and dialogue be set up...?" (1995, p. 59). Berge (2002) included reflection in his recent review of forms of learning.

The emphasis on well-prepared materials to promote cognitive interaction and affective engagement was understandable, given that (i) the principles of equitable access, careful course design, academic support, and tangible educational success were driving many practitioners; (ii) student retention was a vexing issue; (iii) the broader, public credibility of distance education was at stake; and (iv) real-time conferencing technologies became adopted by some practitioners. So it is appropriate now that we outline developments in pre-online mediating technologies before moving to online contexts.

13.2 PRE-ONLINE TECHNOLOGIES

Hear the wisdom of extensive experience. Claire Matthewson observes of any technology that "Old is no more dead than new is uncritically better." (personal communication, December, 2004). Von Pittman uses his historian's eye: "...the development of distance education is not a simple linear progression, with each new medium topping the previous one...each medium or format can continue to have appropriate, legitimate, and beneficial uses" (2002, p. 118).

Any well-applied technology brings enabling and limiting (i.e. mediating) influences on information structuring and delivery, on learner-to-content interactions, and all forms of interpersonal communications (Clark, 2001; Bates, 2005). It is generally agreed that no substitute exists for also knowing the enabling and limiting factors in learners' and teachers' daily contexts, the principles of how adults learn, and how effective teaching intervenes in learning in dialogical and reflective processes (e.g. Kirkup, 2001; Laurillard, 2001; Kirkwood and Price, 2005). No single technology is ever inherently the best solution; rather that effectiveness and flexibility lie in a mix of information access/delivery and dialogue media (Burge and Haughey, 2001; Clark, 2001; Bates, 2005). Accessibility (cognitive, affective, and physical access to learning resources), portability, reliability, repeatability, and cost-effectiveness emerge as overall themes and principles for learner-centric use of any technology.

In the 1880s, Miss Ticknor used a variety of print media: "By a well organized system of distribution, she sent books, engravings, photographs, maps, all that makes the outfit of thorough instruction to the doors of families living far from libraries, museums, or colleges" (Agassiz, 1897, in Mackenzie and Christensen, 1971, p. 28–29). Later, in the early twentieth century, changes began as distance educators appropriated technologies designed for other purposes. Today we may look back 80 years ago to hear radio first being used for distance teaching, and 30 years ago to hear and see television programmes, audio and video-cassettes, and the beginnings of audio-conferenced classes across multiple locations.

Any print technology extends our reach for and storage of information but it requires its own principles for effectively operationalizing (Dekkers and Kemp, 1995; Hartley, 2003). Used appropriately inside a mix of media, it facilitates the transmission of text and visuals, the development of intrapersonal and interpersonal learning dialogues (spoken or silent), and the convenience of access. Print was used as a "deliberate attempt to structure explicitly a student's response to the material" (Bates, 2005, p. 71).

Print is alive and well in many learning contexts. Many distance-mode students still prefer to read from well-designed print-based learning resources, especially the required readings, rather than printing them out on a home printer.

Radio's long history reminds us of the relevance of the well-designed spoken word for auditory learning styles, the enabling of multitasking by listeners, the warmth and closeness of the human voice, and the reach of radio to thousands of listeners (Maskow, 2000; Thomas, 2001). Audio and video cassettes have been useful for alternative and highly portable supply of additional content on demand, private repetition of course content, expert discussions, and skill-building for language learning, counselling, engineering, and other topics that demand human interaction and/or motor skills.

The use of audio- and video-conferenced tutorials or classes moved at least some distance teaching into another phase or "generation". Learners and tutor now could hear each other in real-time dialogue, so "classroom" became an adapted concept (Burge and Roberts, 1998). A multi-skilled team was no longer necessary for the pre-production of detailed course content and instructions because real-time talk enabled anytime, any-reason changes to class process. Students could not see each other as they talked so they had to learn to listen carefully in order to cue their responses, assess peer opinions, ask questions, and share responsibility for class process (George, 1994; MacDonald, 1998). Effective teachers/tutors quickly surrendered any dark thoughts of using the microphone for lectures/monologues or conversational traffic policing; best use of the technology demanded cognitively high levels of multi-directional, unfettered talking-to-think, with the tutor doing a lot of respectful listening (Burge and Snow, 1990). "Effective audio-conferencing is just good small group work – with a few minor special features" (George, 1990, p. 248). As a person once said to Liz, "Oh, you have to connect the minds, not just the wires!"

With video-conferencing's additional capacity for spontaneous use of visuals – of learning materials and of each other – the cue load became richer. But such richness can come with a price, as practitioners quickly learned: inadequate lighting can render healthy people into pale shadows of themselves, the moving images may become distracting at worst and boring at best, and the medium used regressively for transmission teaching models.

As online technology improves to the point where we may securely use consistently high quality real-time audio and video for "classes" via laptops or mobile multimedia devices, it will be interesting to see how much use may be made of the earlier lessons learned about audio- and video-conferencing (Gaskell and Mills, 2004). And as Wisher and Curnow (2003) show about video-based instructional media, for example, the usefulness of each medium is directly dependent on the skill of its application, not on its inherent features *per se*.

13.3 TEACHING AND LEARNING IN ONLINE CONTEXTS

> Effectiveness, then, depends on an appropriate combination of factors related to student characteristics, course design and facilitation, and the attributes of computer conferencing.
>
> (Bullen, 1998, p. 26)

Since Chapters 12 and 18 of this book cover Web-based learning and teaching in detail, we confine ourselves to six key factors: increased learning resources, community, flexibility, teaching, learning objects, and mobile learning. In reviewing them here, we are not advocating that their sheer existence implies consistently successful application for bringing together teachers and learners. But applications so far do indicate that we might discard lingering ideas of an institutional centre and learners at the periphery, with the intervening psychological, financial, and geographical spaces named as forms of "distance".

As computer-mediated communication (Mason and Kaye, 1989) evolved into e-learning, learning resources for distance learners became time and place independent, more personally interactive, and greatly increased in volume. Online chats, user groups, task-focused discussion boards, e-mail, e-library databases, search services, digitized paper documents, and real-time conferencing each increased the potential for easy dialogue, not only between student and teacher but also freely among students (Bates, 2005). Linear, hierarchical, or even matrix styles of learning are possible inside multiple, divergent layers of presentation and multiple levels of cognitive engagement via hypertext (Peters, 2001). Even so, assigned course material competes for learners' attention with non-prescribed sources accessible via the Internet, each contributing to learners building their own individualized learning experiences (Collis and Moonen, 2002; Thorpe, 2002).

The terms "community" and "community of inquiry" (derived largely from Lave and Wenger's work on communities of practice) have gained understandable popularity, since the multi-directional messaging capacity of online software would be expected to create feelings of "groupness". However, in a serious learning environment evidenced by "critical discourse and reflection" (Garrison and Anderson, 2003, p. 27) and informed peer challenges to theoretical and experiential knowing (Wilson et al., 2004), effective learning communities should not be so easily assumed. Garrison and Anderson argue that three distinct forms of "presence" have to constitute a community of inquiry: social, cognitive, and teaching (2003, p. 28). But sustained evidence of learning community effectiveness is weak (Carabajal et al., 2003). Wilson et al. (2004) confront various community-inhibiting parameters – length of course, teacher-imposed course content, assignment requirements (inherently competitive), grading criteria, institutional regulations, and lack of free choice over membership of the class – to argue for using the more realistic and qualified concept of "bounded community" (as distinct from an organic community built up voluntarily over a long period of time). From that concept flow seven distinguishing features which resonate with much other literature about online learning: "shared goals ... safe and supportive conditions ... collective identity ... collaboration ... respectful inclusion ... progressive discourse ... and ... mutual appropriation" (p. 5).

The online learning environment carries great possibilities for flexibility. Learners have choices in when and where to access or create learning resources. Teachers may apply more collaborative teaching models when they feel comfortable with transferring some decision-making power to the learners, or if the learners appropriate some of that power themselves (Paulsen and Rekkedal, 2001; Collis and Moonen, 2002). The learner may exercise considerable autonomy regarding participation, even in the face of peer and/or tutor pressures to attend to group process requirements, and respond carefully and with academic rigour. Choices exist for articulating and sharing ideas and opinions, for anytime, self-convenient messaging, and for timely (or untimely) (Hannafin et al., 2003) withdrawals from the "community" to reflect alone or search out additional resources. Learners, however, need to attend to their meta-cognitive skills, including their reflective assessments of online strengths and weaknesses and the returns on their cognitive energy investments (Burge, 1994). Students have found that online asynchronous peer interaction is valuable in supporting each other in their learning (e.g. Fahy, 2003; Anderson and Simpson, 2004), with appropriate teaching skills and designs, of course.

Online technologies also give learners more self-directed control over other institution-related interactions such as access to their academic records, registrations in courses, transcript checking, fee payments, scholarship information, scheduling of advising consultations, and so on. As these academic services now operate constantly, institutions and teachers are denied excuses or responses based on the so-called delays or loss of "paperwork".

> The nature of asynchronicity makes it harder for e-moderators to create positive group experiences and the excitement, rhythm, engagement and focus that we know as "flow" ... compared with face-to-face groups. It is not impossible, though! Key issues are the ability to create clear goals and appropriate challenges, through a vision of the learning outcomes and very short focused steps, good timely feedback and appropriate motivation.
>
> (Salmon, 2004, p. 61)

As Gilly Salmon explains, online teaching is, unquestionably, demanding of the teacher's own time and contributive energies, of the separate creation and sustenance of "cognitive ergonomics" (our term), and of an affectively helpful "community" (Gibson, 2000; Stephenson, 2001; Hara and Kling, 2002; Garrison and Anderson, 2003; Lentell, 2003; O'Rourke, 2003; Commonwealth of Learning, 2004; Salmon, 2004; Wilson et al., 2004). As Cavanaugh et al. (2001, p. 67) remark, "every voice is authorized to speak" in online learning contexts and the teacher has to adapt to this dynamic as well as to a potentially increased workload, a changed model of teaching, and learners who do not hesitate to take full advantage of the flexibility – for them – offered in online environments.

Online teaching behaviours are generally discussed in terms of course "housekeeping", interventions in and management of academic discourse, maintaining interaction, and, as-needed, one-way transfer of content. Salmon's (2004) five-stage model for teaching and learning online focuses on scaffolding for guiding facilitation. Her stages of access and motivation, socialization, information exchange, knowledge construction, and development (self-responsible, constructivist approaches used with skill) are cumulative in process and effect, and bear some comparison to group development sequences used in other disciplines. Naidu (2003) argues that a learning scaffold supports online distance learners but expresses concern that distance educators are not designing learning in such a way, even though technology can be easily leveraged to do so. Hawkridge (2003) identifies key teaching skills as "acknowledging contributions, synthesizing and summarizing, drawing threads together, watching for and correcting conversational 'drift', spotting good ideas, opening up new avenues for development, identifying holes in arguments (and patching them), separating opinions from facts, clarifying areas of agreement and disagreement, encouraging further exploration, pointing to valuable sources, promoting selectivity and building patterns" (p. 23). Evidence of such active teacher presence online is easily identified; but presence may also be subtle and discrete. Such "absent presence" exists when the teacher remains silent yet present during online conversations, steering the learners only at strategic points to promote learning (Hult et al., 2005, p. 30). Such strategic and disciplined intervention requires restraint and extreme attention to the qualities of interaction and cognitive process and stages of group development. How sophisticatedly a definition of interaction is applied has drawn recent attention and arguments for going beyond the typical interpersonal communications to include a more holistic view that includes, for example, intrapersonal connections (Thorpe and Godwin, 2006).

Constructivist approaches to online learning facilitation have promoted more examples of course design that is learner-centred, collaborative, interactive, and reflective, thus helping learners construct their own mental frameworks under skilful guidance (Jonassen et al., 1995; Andrusyszyn and Davie, 1997; Duffy and Kirkley, 2004; Salmon, 2004). Berge (2002) presents a model for e-learning based on constructivism which echoes the design requirements above and includes active and critical thinking, multidimensional interaction with content, peers and instructor, and reflection. How far online teaching to "facilitate critical thinking and higher-order learning outcomes" (Garrison et al., 2003, p. 124) is actually achieved in the face of barriers to "bounded community" development remains to be seen. Wilson et al. (2004) used their seven features of bounded communities to categorize approximately fourty strategies for "leading, supporting and facilitating effective learning community membership" (p. 14). Anyone reaching all of them within the impacts of learners' behaviours and without undue workload pressures deserves a medal!

Developments in the use of learning objects for online learning may enhance features of constructive practice and flexible learning (Littlejohn, 2003; Thorpe et al., 2003; Ally, 2004; Cleveland-Innes et al., 2005). The introduction of learning objects in course design requires further role adjustment and cognitive flexibility from distance teachers: "creativity will revolve around unbundling and reassembly rather than original course content and development" (Abrioux, 2003, p. 30). Sharing reputable information, as a process in itself, will evolve as context-sensitive content expertise is built into learning objects using open standards and then shared worldwide. To encourage innovative design, Bates (2005) suggests having the learner build their own course using learning objects of their choice, starting with a framework provided by the teacher to gently guide the learner. The teacher facilitates towards required and clear learning objectives while acknowledging the need for non-linear learning activities.

The latest moves towards mobile learning enable high levels of personal portability, digitized, multimedia information, and personal convenience messaging via various devices. Mobile devices are rarely applied in isolation; they are combined with other technologies such as print to optimize the learning process (Taylor, 2004; Kukulska-Hulme and Traxler, 2005). M-learning practice also uses existing theories of learning in a blended approach to suit the learning objectives at hand. Although in the beginning stages of use, m-learning reflects the "just-in-time" learning phenomenon prevalent in our times. There are issues to be resolved, specifically around keeping learners engaged in the virtual classroom (Naismith et al., 2004) while they multi-task in their other life roles.

13.4 PERCEPTIONS OF CHANGE

We might categorize changes by referring to relatively bold, single-cause claims such as the change (for many distance-mode teachers) from mostly print directly to online technologies. Or we might refer to presumed paradigm changes promoted by the "early adopters" of each new technology (Rogers, 2003). We might even refer to opposing models of learning (from expository to experiential/constructivist; or, in our vernacular, from photocopying teachers' blueprints for their students' learning to being our own learning architects, albeit with some consultation and validation of our learning design).

But distinguishing dualistic, paradigmatic, or revolutionary change from adaptive, cumulative, evolutionary change depends on the experience and values of evaluators, not to mention what they know about the history of prior use of teaching and learning principles and technologies. We do not, for example, immediately, necessarily, or uncritically accept claims that the online environment is a new "paradigm" for distance education (e.g. Garrison et al., 2003) or that we consistently "are entering new territory and are experiencing an unequalled breach of tradition [and that learning] and teaching in the digital age have to be redefined" (Peters, 2003, p. 99). We do recognize that online learning and teaching is still in relatively early stages of research and agree with Garrison et al. that more attention is needed on using online teaching to "facilitate critical thinking and higher-order learning outcomes" (p. 124). Those outcomes are still needed in many face-to-face classrooms. Some educators, coming from transmission modes of teaching face-to-face in conventional higher education, realize after some online trials that they may need some new teaching models, but others may see online as a new vehicle for transmitting pre-digested information (Naidu, 2003): the "old wine in new bottles" syndrome. Many distance educators, however, who already can apply general facilitation and collaborative models via face-to-face or audio-conferenced contexts, will instead analyse how far the mediating effects of each new technology may influence their continuing use of those teaching models and extend possibilities for successful learning. Kenworthy (2003), for example, posits that "the principles of independent learning, self-direction and self-management of time and learning activities will basically remain unchanged" (p. 62) despite the move into online and virtual contexts. Olgren (1998) emphasizes the continuing relevance of established cognitive learning strategies. Salmon's principles for "e-moderating" (2004) reflect sound adult learning facilitation principles as well as shades of Lockwood's 1992 emphasis on "tutorial-in-print... reflective action guide... [and] dialogue". Moore and Kearsley's functions of and advice to the "instructor" (2005, pp. 135–160) knowingly echo decades-old distance course design discussions. George's lessons from audio-conferencing rest in established small group theory (1990). Pennells raises five questions that, if taken out of his online thinking context, would serve for any critical interrogation about learning technologies, old or new: "will our students have access?... will our students be able to afford it?... will our students and staff have the necessary skills?... can we guarantee the quality of the student experience?... will our students suffer loss of independence?" (2003, p. 160–162).

One historical parallel informs us too that change may not be as ecologically profound and paradigm shifting as early adopters would have us believe. The growth of distance learning and teaching in the second half of the nineteenth century was the result of new transportation technologies (train and paper mail for delivery and asynchronous interactions). It met the learning needs of the economically and socially mobile (upwards) and those needing even a second chance at access to education. The growth of distance learning and teaching in the final quarter of the twentieth century was due to the new information delivery and communication technologies that gained increasing sophistication and acceptance because they now also met the learning needs of physically mobile (literally) learners. Mobility – social, career, and physical – appears as much an ongoing theme as does cognitive interaction and affective engagement.

So we see key iterative and cumulative "changes"; or an evolution, not a revolution (Bates, 2005). Evans and Nation take a similarly incremental view, arguing that we have to build "a new phase of distance education... that incorporates the appropriate strengths and values of the past into a new form of multimedia education at a distance" (2003, p. 778). While Peters (2004) does use the stronger "paradigm" change to contrast a very traditional view of teaching with a postmodern view of learning, he at least argues that "paradigm" is not the most appropriate term but that it should represent a wide range of societal and educational changes.

We use three categories to organize the changes: (i) changes in learners' attitudes towards learning; (ii) increased access to learning resources; and (iii) changes in teaching and learning interactions. Then we revisit some technology matters to create a synthesis for your own assessment. We avoid the change issue of convergence *per se* (Tait and Mills, 1999), that is, the mainstreaming of distance education with conventional higher education, since it carries economic and administrative connotations broader than our remit.

13.4.1 Changes in Learners' Attitudes Towards Learning

Many of today's distance learners could not be described as deferential, patient, compliant, and grateful. Our own experience reveals learners who want overt signs of respect regardless of their academic capacities and who are time-stressed, credential-hungry, client service–oriented, and multi-tasking over long work days. They rationalize their increasingly high course fees by arguing that they are paying for an academic to select the world's best and most relevant literature as the basis for their course work. Our colleagues have noticed similar consumer-oriented and self-interest-oriented changes in students' behaviour and expectations (Powell et al., 1999; Rumble, 2000; Mills, 2003; Tait, 2003).

Mason's (2003) frank view refers to how pragmatic adult learners use the new technologies for greater self-control over their time and intellectual energies:

> I think we have to assume that the new breed of learner has neither the time nor the inclination for extended interactions and institutional affiliations – rather, ease of access, quality of information and tailorability of access are the key concerns (p. 95)... perhaps they will want much shorter learning opportunities which fit more closely with problems, gaps, or activities in their working or leisure concerns.
>
> (p. 98)

A contrast between earlier and current student attitudes noted by the UKOU refers to additional qualities of today's distance students; they are intolerant of institutional errors, impatient, IT literate, and expect high levels of personalized educational service (Mills, 2003, p. 109). In addition, Phillips reports that today's learners "do not want to be asked to choose between traditional methods and the new electronic media. They want whatever works best for them... they [want] a variety of media and will value a service that knows them and treats them as an individual" (p. 176, 180). Like Lockwood's earlier ultra-pragmatic, cognitive energy-saving learners (1992), today's learners look unabashedly for time, workload, and reward efficiencies (Kirkwood and Price, 2005).

If we factor in age-based societal generational differences – for example, as in baby boomers' versus millennials' lifestyles and needs or postmodern views of human needs and expectations (Peters, 2004, pp. 29–30) – the changing attitudes presented within learner cohorts may be analysed more effectively. Bates (2005) points to another implication regarding cohorts: "This diversity of the student body is growing fast" (p. 211), "... there is no longer a single mass market for adult continuing education, but an increasingly wider variety of needs, and increasingly smaller and unique target groups" (p. 224).

13.4.2 Increased Access to Learning Resources

E-library databases and librarian-designed e-services have extended the "reach" of learners and teachers into hugely expanded, reputable information sources, as explained in Chapter 19 of this book. The Internet is also a source of reputable information if the learner has the requisite search and evaluation skills. Such levels of accessibility, when consistently and easily available, also deny learners and teachers any excuse that they could not find enough information. Ironically, however, the continuing pragmatism and time-poverty of today's learners often work against their taking full advantage of such resources.

A stronger contrast between old and new learning resource capacities is seen with the development of learning objects. As Littlejohn (2003) says, we are moving from the aggregation of content in pre-designed omnibus course packages to the "disaggregation" of content into stand-alone, micro units that learners will be able to access and assemble into a whole as and when needed (see also Cleveland-Innes et al., 2005; http://www.merlot.org). We see echoes here of the earlier German "Baukasten-prinzip, the principle of the box of bricks" (Holmberg, 1995, p. 70).

The UKOU concept of "openness", that is, being open to people, places, methods, and ideas, will carry additional meaning as more learners access and modify "wiki"-mode materials and teachers modify open-source software.

13.4.3 Changes in Teaching and Learning Interactions

> the changes in teaching and learning at a distance really involve returning to the point from whence we came, so to speak – a recognition that teaching and learning are essentially human interactions that involve dialogue, respect and wisdom. After a brief Brave New World period in distance education that ran along the theme of "teacher-free" or "teacher-proof" materials, we've come back to an appreciation of what teachers, tutors, facilitators actually do in enabling people to make connections and to learn.
>
> (Jennifer O'Rourke; personal communication, April 13, 2006)

In a nutshell, we see the emphasis changing from course *Content* (high quality, pre-designed materials plus mostly written text correspondence) to *Connection* (real-time structured discussions and adaptive teaching responses) to *Community* (aiming for group synergies in a medium that enables both self-interest and group-interest behaviours). Morgan's 1995 question "How can interaction and dialogue be set up...?" (p. 59) indeed now has some answers.

We find it difficult, however, to claim a generally consistent shift, in actual practice, from fully transmission models of teaching to fully constructivist learning models as described by Duffy and Kirkley (2004), Hedberg and Harper (2002), Jonassen et al. (1995), and Vrasidas and Glass (2004). We may assume such a shift, at least in theory and from many reports of practice: for example, using the interactive features of online software, adopting new teaching skills, learners using opportunities to assume more responsibility for their learning activities and outcomes, teachers and learners designing activities relevant to real-world complexities, and teachers and peers guiding learners to challenge and critique problems, solutions, and their experiential knowledge. However, many solo course designers have to struggle their way into the new model (e.g. Gibson, 2000, 2005). It is not easy to reach raw data: online class records are guarded by various privacy regulations; not all students participate as anticipated; and no record is left after a three-hour audio-conferenced class. In arguing a proven move from a teaching model to a learning model, whose definitions of each model would most count – learners' or teachers'? How many credential-needy, time-stressed learners set their own limits for joining collegial discussions and use a pragmatic, assignment-driven focus? "Evolution" towards long-term, collaboratively structured discussion models, not revolution, is the safest general assessment (Bates, 2005, p. 16).

Compared with the earlier solitary learner's use of pre-designed, print-grounded learning media and written interactions with a tutor divorced from the course design processes, audio- and video-conferencing opened new opportunities for real-time, spoken dialogue and class-responsive, democratic decision-making. These conferencing technologies showed the need for high levels of interactive and constructivist teaching and learning skills, especially for generating additional learning resources from in-class dialogue. But relatively few writers, it seems, used or noticed these changes in distance-mode learning and teaching. With the advent of voice-over-Internet capability, the lessons learned in audio- and video-conferencing may regain currency.

The arrival of online learning literature increased opportunities for constructivist models of learning and text-based dialogues, this time amongst learners. Their written experience and textual dialogue became recorded learning resources and various forms and layers of interaction became part of the course design. The opportunities for easy communication between course peers have "the potential to overturn the emphasis on distance education as an individualized form of learning" (Thorpe, 2003, p. 206). A further factor here is leadership: how a teacher may enact her/his presence with each learner in the hypertext software environments. As Thorpe knows, "who or what is 'in authority' may be less clear..." (p. 205). Hult et al. (2005) argue for various forms of teaching presence but not all being vocalized or held by the person named as "teacher":

> Online pedagogues... may be present in person, participating in learning conversations. They may constitute an absent presence that, nonetheless, is embodied in the learning resources directed towards students... Or pedagogues may exist merely as inner voices, inherited from the language of others, that (invisibly) steer the desires, self-regulation, and self-direction of learners.

Pennells drew attention to two "downsides" of online learning, the now "new and unfamiliar pressure on the tutor... to manage the learning process and to ensure it works" and the "vagaries of peer participation" (2003, p. 162). It remains to be seen if Lentell's argument that distance education has failed to "grasp the centrality of the tutor..." in learning processes (2003, p. 66) will play out in online behaviours. Certainly, we believe that Rowntree's 1990 observation that to produce paper-based learning materials was to "teach in one's hand" (i.e. write down all that a face-to-face teacher would say) still applies in online contexts.

How a course develops from a teacher's original design and how learners develop as skilled learners *per se* are now relevant issues. If many teachers in online contexts operate as "lone rangers" – "designing" their own courses via whatever software templates their university supplies and without expert, on-site help from instructional design staff

(Bates, 2005, p. 164) – then Daniel and Marquis, 30 years on, might now refer to "courses designed in solitude and studied in teams". Or Gibson might continue to hope that change will focus more on learners expanding their learning-to-learn skills for real-world problems and less on learning content for its own sake (cited in Moore and Kearsley, 2005, p. 69).

13.5 CHANGES IN TECHNOLOGIES

Delineating "generations" of distance education argues a technology-oriented, easily understood, seemingly linear "progression", as, for example, in Moore and Kearsley's distinctions of "correspondence" (first), "broadcast radio and television" (second), "open universities" (third), "teleconferencing" (fourth), and "Internet/Web" (fifth) (2005). While the impact of online activities in the current generation still carries for some the "wow!" factor, it also may obscure the need to use earlier-generation technologies in certain resource-constrained or cultural contexts around the world. It also may lead to understating the levels of skill required to use effectively the earlier-generation technologies. Experienced designers of paper-based text, for example, follow certain principles when applying it for current contexts (Hartley, 2003). Facilitation skills learned two decades ago for audio-conferencing may return to broader relevance once voice-over-Internet protocols become more stable and widely accessible. Or they may not, if practitioner memories are short. Production values of earlier non-digitized audio and video (as in cassettes), long useful for pre-planned additional content, on-demand, private re-hearing or re-viewing of course content ought to be transferable to today's digitized contexts of ipodcasting, streaming Web video, and mobile "phone" technologies. One major difference is of course that much of that new material may be produced quickly, cheaply, and on demand by relative amateurs, that is, typical "lecturers" and professors.

To what extent e-learning as we know it becomes more broadly adopted depends on the answers to D'Antoni's four key questions: "Is it accessible? ... Is it appropriate? ... Is it accredited? ... Is it affordable?" (Daniel et al., 2006, pp. 3–4). For good measure, check the various forms of e-learning against Rogers' attributes for innovation adoption, especially those of compatibility with existing contexts, reliability, low level complexity, familiarity, and relative advantage (2003).

13.6 THE FUTURE EVOLVES – AS ALWAYS

Our review of change and consistency ends with a quotation designed, in the best tradition of interactive text, to help you interrogate your thinking. If you remove the m-word, how far might the remaining words apply to any technology for distance learning and teaching goals in any context?

> Mobile learning can take education back into the home, the workplace and the community. Mobile learning can be spontaneous, portable, personal, situated; it can be informal, unobtrusive, ubiquitous and disruptive. It takes us much nearer to "anytime,

> anywhere" learning but it is still too early to predict how our understandings of learning and teaching will evolve as a consequence.
>
> (Kukulska-Hulme and Traxler, 2005, p. 42)

But at least our predictions will be better with some knowledge about how informed evolutionary change depends on established principles of context-sensitive teaching and learning, not on each new technology's features. We suspect that Miss Ticknor would, today, use a judicious mix of learning strategies and media to meet her goals of access, care, and quality.

REFERENCES

Abrioux, D. (2003). Athabasca University: An evolution of an existing institution. In *The Virtual University: Models and Messages* (S.D' Antoni, ed.) Paris: UNESCO International Institute for Educational Planning. pp. 35 Retrieved March 12, 2006 http://www.unesco.org/iiep/virtualuniversity/home.php

Ally, M. (2004). Foundations for educational theory for online learning. In *Theory and Practice of Online Learning* (T. Anderson, ed.) (pp. 3–31). Retrieved March 29, 2006 http://cde.athabascau.ca/online_book/index.html

Anderson, B. and Simpson, M. (2004). Group and class contexts for learning and support online: learning and affective support online in small group and class contexts. *International Review of Research in Open and Distance Learning*, **5**(3). Retrieved March 22, 2005 from http://www.irrodl.org/index.php/irrodl/article/view/208/291

Andrusyszyn, M. and Davie, L. (1997). Facilitating reflection through interactive journal writing in an online graduate course: a qualitative study. *Journal of Distance Education*, **12**(1 and 2), 103–126.

Bååth, J.A. (1983). A list of ideas for the construction of distance education courses. In *Distance education: International perspectives,* (D. Sewart, D. Keegan and B. Holmberg, eds). London: Croom Helm, pp. 272–290.

Bates, A.W. (2005). *Technology, E-learning and Distance Education*, 2nd ed., London: Routledge.

Berge, Z.L. (2002). Active, interactive, and reflective e-learning. *The Quarterly Review of Distance Education*, **3**(2), 181–190.

Bullen, M. (1998). Participation and critical thinking in online university distance education. *Journal of Distance Education*, **13**(2), 1–32.

Burge, E.J. (1994). Learning in computer conferenced contexts: The learners' perspective. *Journal of Distance Education*, **9**(1), 19–43.

Burge, E.J. and Haughey, M. (eds) (2001). *Using Learning Technologies: International Perspectives on Practice*. London: RoutledgeFalmer.

Burge, E.J. and Roberts, J.M. (1998). *Classrooms with a Difference: Facilitating Learning on the Information Highway*, 2nd edn. Montreal: Chenelière/McGraw-Hill.

Burge, E.J. and Snow, J.E. (1990). Interactive audio classrooms: Key principles for effective practice. *Education for Information*, **8**, 299–312.

Campbell, K. Schwier, R.A., and Kenny, R.F. (2005). Agency of the instructional designer: Moral coherence and transformative social practice. *Australasian Journal of Educational Technology*, **21**(2), 242–262.

Campion, M. and Renner, W. (1992). The supposed demise of Fordism: Implications for distance education and higher education. *Distance Education*, **13**(1), 7–28.

Carabajal, K., LaPointe, D. and Gunawardena, C. (2003). Group development in online learning communities. In *Handbook of Distance Education* (W. Anderson and M.G. Moore, eds) Mahwah, NJ: Erlbaum, pp. 217–234.

Cavanaugh, C., Ellerman, E., Oddson, L., and Young, A. (2001). Lessons from our cyber-classroom. In *Using Learning Technologies: International Perspectives on Practice* (E.J. Burge and M. Haughey, eds) London: RoutledgeFalmer, pp. 61–71.

Clark, R.E. (2001). Evaluating distance education technologies. In *Learning from Media: Arguments, Analysis, and Evidence* (R.E. Clark, ed.) Greenwich, CT: Information Age Publishing.

Cleveland-Innes, M. et al. (2005). The Athabasca University eduSource project: Building an accessible learning object repository. [Electronic version]. *Australasian Journal of Educational Technology*, **21**(3), 367–381.

Cole, S., Coats, M., and Lentell, H. (1986). Towards good teaching by correspondence. *Open Learning*, **1**(1), 16–22.

Collis, B. and Moonen, J. (2002). *Flexible Learning in a Digital World: Experiences and Expectations*. London: RoutledgeFalmer.

Commonwealth of Learning. (2004). *Tutoring in Open and Distance Learning: A Handbook for Tutors*. J. O'Rourke. Retrieved March/06, 2006 from www.col.org/resources/startupguides/odlsystemsHB.htm

Commonwealth of Learning. (2005). *Creating Learning Materials for Open and Distance Learning: A Handbook for Authors & Instructional Designers*. Retrieved march 06, 2006 from www.col.org/resources/startupguides/odlsystemsHB.htm

Daniel, J., West, P., D'Antoni, S., and Uvalić-Trumbić, S. (2006). E-learning and free open source software: The key to global mass higher education? Retrieved April 10, 2006 from www.col.org/speeches/JD_0601eLearningKualaLumpur.htm

Daniel, J.S. and Marquis, C. (1977). Interaction and independence: Getting the mixture right. *Teaching at a Distance* , **14**, 29–44.

Dekkers, J. and Kemp, N.A. (1995). Contemporary developments in the typographical design of instructional text. In *Open and Distance Learning Today* (F. Lockwood, ed.) London: Routledge, pp. 311–322.

Duffy, T.M. and Kirkley, J.R. (2004). Learning theory and pedagogy applied in distance learning: The case of Cardean University. In *Learner-Centered Theory and Practice in Distance Education: Cases from Higher Education* (T.M. Duffy and J.R. Kirkley, eds) Mahwah, NJ: Erlbaum, pp. 107–141.

Erdos, R. (1967). *Teaching by Correspondence*. London: Longman.

Evans, T. and Nation, D. (2000). *Changing University Teaching: Reflections on Creating Educational Technologies*. London: Kogan Page.

Evans, T. and Nation, D. (2003). Globalization and the reinvention of distance education. In *Handbook of Distance Education* (M.G. Moore and W.G. Anderson, eds) Mahwah, NJ: Erlbaum, pp. 777–792.

Evans, T.D. and Nation, D. (1989). Dialogue in practice, research and theory in distance education. *Open Learning*, **4**, 37–43.

Fahy, P. (2003). Indicators of support in online interaction. *International Review of Research in Open and Distance Learning*, **4**(1). Retrieved March 22, 2006 from www.irrodl.org

Faith, K. (ed.) (1988). *Toward New Horizons for Women in Distance Education: International Perspectives*. London: Routledge.

Garrison, D.R. (2003). Self-Directed Learning and Distance Education. In *Handbook of Distance Education* (M.G. Moore and W.G. Anderson, eds) Mahwah, NJ: Erlbaum, pp. 161–168.

Garrison, D.R. and Anderson, T. (2003). *E-Learning in the 21st Century: A Framework for Research and Practice*. London: RoutledgeFalmer.

Garrison, D.R., Anderson, T., and Archer, W. (2003). A theory of critical inquiry in online distance education. In *Handbook of Distance Education* (M.G. Moore and W.G. Anderson, eds) Mahwah, NJ: Erlbaum, pp. 113–127.

Gaskell, A. and Mills, R. (2004). Supporting students by telephone: A technology for the future of student support? [Electronic version]. *European Journal of Open, Distance and E-Learning, 2004/I*.

George, J. (1994). Effective teaching and learning by telephone. In *Distance Learning in ELT* (K. Richards and P. Roe, eds). London: Modern English Publications/British Council/Macmillan, pp. 82–93.

George, J.W. (1990). Audioconferencing – just another small group activity. *Education and Training Technology International*, **27**(3), 244–248.

Gibson, C.C. (2000). The ultimate disorienting dilemma: The online learning community. In *Changing University Teaching: Reflections on Creating Educational Technologies* (T. Evans and D. Nation, eds) London: Kogan Page, pp. 133–146.

Gibson, C.C. (2003). Learners and learning: The need for theory. In *Handbook of Distance Education* (M.G. Moore and W.G. Anderson, eds) Mahwah, NJ: Erlbaum, pp. 147–160.

Gibson, C.C. (2005). Online learning: From high tech to high touch. In *Online Learning: Personal Reflections on the Transformation of Education* (G. Kearsley, ed.) Englewood Cliffs, NJ: Educational Technology Publications, pp. 101–112.

Gunawardena, C.N. (2004). The challenge of designing inquiry-based online learning. In *Learner-Centered Theory and Practice in Distance Education: Cases from Higher Education* (T.M. Duffy and J.R. Kirkley, eds) Mahwah, NJ: Erlbaum, pp. 143–158.

Gunawardena, C.N., Wilson, P.L., and Nolla, A.C. (2003). Culture and online education. In *Handbook of Distance Education* (M.G. Moore and W.G. Anderson, eds) Mahwah, NJ: Erlbaum, pp. 753–775.

Hannafin, M., Hill, J.R., Oliver, K. et al. (2003). Cognitive and learning factors in web-based distance learning environments. In *Handbook of Distance Education* (M.G. Moore and W.G. Anderson, eds) Mahwah, NJ: Erlbaum, pp. 245–260.

Hara, N. and Kling, R. (2002). Students' difficulties in a web-based distance education course: An ethnographic study. In *Digital Academe: The New Media and Institutions of Higher Education and Learning* (W.H. Dutton and B.D. Loader, eds) London: Routledge, pp. 62–84.

Hartley, J. (2003). Designing instructional and informational text. In *Handbook of Research on Educational Communications and Technology* (D.H. Jonassen, ed.) 2nd ed., Mahwah, NJ: Erlbaum, pp. 917–947.

Haughey, M. (2005). Growth of online schooling in Canada. In *Encyclopedia of Distance Learning* (C. Howard et al., eds) Hershey, PA: Information Science Publishing, pp. 984–989.

Hawkridge, D. (2000). Using media and technologies for flexible workplace learning. In *Flexible Learning, Human Resource and Organisational Development*, (V. Jakupec and J. Garrick, eds) London: Routledge, pp. 193–210.

Hawkridge, D. (2003). The human in the machine: Reflections on mentoring at the British Open University. *Mentoring and Tutoring*, **11**(1), 15–24.

Hedberg, J.G. and Harper, B.M. (2002). Constructivist approaches to authoring. *Australian Journal of Educational Technology*, **18**(1), 89–109.

Holmberg, B. (1995). *Theory and Practice of Distance Education* 2nd ed., London: Routledge.

Holmberg, B. (2003). A theory of distance education based on empathy. In *Handbook of Distance Education*, (M.G. Moore and W.G. Anderson, eds) Mahwah, MJ: Erlbaum, pp. 79–86.

Holmberg, B., Shelley, M., and White, C. (eds) (2005). *Distance Education and Languages: Evolution and Change*. Clevedon, UK: Multilingual Matters Ltd.

Hult, A., Dahlgren, E., Hamilton, D. and Söderström, T. (2005). Teachers' invisible presence in net-based distance education. *International Review of Research in Open and Distance Learning*, **6**(3). www.irrodl.org

Jenkins, J. (1981). *Materials for Learning: How to Teach Adults at a Distance*. London: Routledge.

Jonassen, D., Davidson, M., Collins, M. et al. (1995). Constructivism and computer-mediated communication in distance education. *The American Journal of Distance Education*, **9**(2), 7–26.

Kaye, A. (1981). Media, materials and learning methods. In *Distance Teaching for Higher and Adult Education* (A. Kaye and G. Rumble, eds) London: Croom Helm/The Open University Press, pp. 48–69.

Kenworthy, B. (2003). Supporting the student in new teaching and learning environments. In *Rethinking Learner Support in Distance Education: Change and Continuity in an International Context* (A. Tait, and R. Mills, eds) London: RoutledgeFalmer, pp. 55–63.

Kinash, S., Crichton, S., and Kim-Rupnow, W.S. (2004). A review of 2000–2003 literature at the intersection of online learning and disability. *The American Journal of Distance Education*, **18**(1), 5–19.

Kirkup, G. (2001). Teacher or avatar? Identity issues in computer-mediated contexts. In *Using Learning Technologies: International Perspectives on Practice* (E.J. Burge and M. Haughey, eds) London: Routledge, pp. 72–81.

Kirkwood, A. and Price, L. (2005). Learners and learning in the twenty-first century: what do we know about students' attitudes towards and experiences of information and communication technologies that will help us design courses? *Studies in Higher Education*, **30**(3), 257–274.

Kukulska-Hulme, A. and Traxler, J. (2005). Mobile teaching and learning. In *Mobile Learning: A Handbook for Educators and Trainers* (A.Kukulska-Hulme and J. Traxler, eds) London: Routledge, pp. 25–44.

Laurillard, D. (2001). *Rethinking University Teaching: A Conversational Framework for the Effective use of Learning Technologies* 2nd ed., London: RoutledgeFalmer.

Lentell, H. (2003). *The* importance of the tutor in open and distance learning. In *Rethinking Learner Support in Distance Education: Change and Continuity in an International Context* (A.Tait and R. Mills, eds) London: RoutledgeFalmer, pp. 64–76.

Littlejohn, A. (ed.) (2003). *Reusing Online Resources: A Sustainable Approach to e-Learning*. London: Kogan Page.

Lockwood, F. (1992). *Activities in Self-Instructional Texts*. London: Kogan Page.

Lockwood, F. (1998). *The Design and Production of Self-Instructional Materials*. London: RoutledgeFalmer.

MacDonald, D. (1998). *Audio and Audiographic Learning: The Cornerstone of the Information Highway*. Montreal, PQ: Chenelière/McGraw-Hill.

MacKenzie, O. and Christensen, E.L. (eds) (1971). *The Changing World of Correspondence Study: International Readings*. University Park, PA: Pennsylvania State University Press.

Maskow, M. (2000). Radio as a learning technology. In *The Strategic Use of Learning Technologies* (E.J. Burge, ed.) San Francisco, CA: Jossey-Bass, pp. 59–68.

Mason, R. (2003). On-line learning and supporting students: New possibilities. In *Rethinking Learner Support in Distance Education: Change and Continuity in an International Context* (A. Tait and R. Mills, eds) London: RoutledgeFalmer, pp. 90–101.

Mason, R. and Kaye, A. (eds) (1989). *Mindweave: Communication, Computers and Distance Education*. Oxford, UK: Pergamon.

McConnell, D. (2005). Examining the dynamics of networked e-learning groups and communities. *Studies in Higher Education*, **30**(1), 23–40.

Mills, R. (2003). The centrality of learner support in open and distance learning: a paradigm shift in thinking. In *Rethinking Learner Support in Distance Education: Change and Continuity in an International Context* (A. Tait and R. Mills, eds) London: RoutledgeFalmer, pp. 102–113.

Moore, M.G. (1993). *Theory of transactional distance*. In *Theoretical Principles of Distance Education* (D. Keegan ed.) London: Routledge, pp. 22–38.

Moore, M.G. and Kearsley, G. (2005). *Distance Education: A Systems View*. 2nd ed., Belmont, CA: Thomson Wadsworth.

Moran, L. and Rumble, G. (eds) (2004). *Vocational Education and Training through Open and Distance Learning*. London: Routledge.

Morgan, A. and Thorpe, M. (1993). Residential schools in open and distance learning: Quality time for quality learning? In *Reforming Open and Distance Education: Critical Reflections from Practice* (T. Evans and D. Nation, eds) London: Kogan Page, pp. 72–87.

Morgan, A.R. (1995). Student learning and students' experiences: Research, theory and practice. In *Open and Distance Learning Today* (F. Lockwood, ed.) London: Routledge, pp. 55–66.

Morgan, C. and O'Reilly, M. (1999). *Assessing Open and Distance Learners*. London: Kogan Page.

Naidu, S. (2003). Designing instruction for e-learning environments. In *Handbook of Distance Education* (M.G. Moore and W.G. Anderson, eds) Mahwah, NJ: Erlbaum, pp. 349–365.

Naismith, L., Lonsdale, P., Vavoula, G., and Sharples, M. (2004). *Literature Review in Mobile Technologies and Learning*. Retrieved march/07, 2006 from http://www.nestafuturelab.org/research/reviews/reviews_11_and12/11_01.htm

Olgren, C. (1998). Improving learning outcomes: The effects of learning. In *Distance Learners in Higher Education: Institutional Responses for Quality Outcomes* (C.C. Gibson, ed.) Madison, WI: Atwood Publishing, pp. 77–95.

O'Rourke, J. (2003). Lost and found: Open learning outside the doors of academe. In *Rethinking Learner Support in Distance Education: Change and Continuity in an International Context* (A. Tait and R. Mills, eds) pp. 142–154.

Paulsen, M.F. and Rekkedal, T. (2001). *The NKI Internet College: A review of 15 Years Delivery of 10,000 Online Courses*. Retrieved March/13, 2006 from www.irrodl.org

Pennells, J. (2003) Challenges in adjusting to new technology in supporting learners in developing countries. In *Rethinking Learner Support in Distance Education: Change and Continuity in an International Context* (A. Tait and R. Mills, eds) London: RoutledgeFalmer, pp. 155–167.

Peters, O. (2001). *Learning and Teaching in Distance Education*. London: Kogan Page.

Peters, O. (2003). Learning with new media in distance education. In *Handbook of Distance Education* (M.G. Moore and W.G. Anderson, eds) Mahwah, NJ: Erlbaum, pp. 87–112.

Peters, O. (2004). *Distance Education in Transition: New Trends and Challenges.* 4th ed.,) Oldenberg, Ger.: Bibliotheks-und Informationssystem der Carl von Ossietsky Universität.

Phillips, M. (2003). Delivering learner support online: does the medium affect the message? In *Rethinking Learner Support in Distance Education: Change and Continuity in an International Context* (A. Tait and R. Mills, eds) London: RoutledgeFalmer, pp. 168–184.

Pittman, V. (2002). Interview. *The American Journal of Distance Education*, **16**(2), 115–123.

Powell, R., McGuire, S., and Crawford, G. (1999). Convergence of student types: issues for distance education. In *The Convergence of Distance and Conventional Education: Patterns of Flexibility for the Individual Learner* (A. Tait and R. Mills, eds) London: Routledge, pp. 86–99.

Rekkedal, T. (1983). The written assignments in correspondence education: Effects of reducing turn-around time. *Distance Education*, **4**, 231–252.

Rogers, E.M. (2003). *Diffusion of Innovations* 5th ed., New York, NY: Free Press.

Rowntree, D. (1990). *Teaching through Self-Instruction: How to Develop Open Learning Materials.* London: Kogan Page.

Rumble, G. (2000). Student support in distance education in the 21st century: Learning from service management. *Distance Education*, **21**(2), 216–235.

Salmon, G. (2004). *E-moderating: The Key to Teaching and Learning Online.* 2nd ed., London: Routledge.

Simpson, O. (2002). *Supporting Students in Online, Open and Distance Learning.* 2nd ed., London: Kogan Page.

Stephenson, J. (ed.) (2001). *Teaching and Learning Online: Pedagogies for New Technologies.* London: Kogan Page.

Tait, A. (2003). Rethinking learner support in the Open University UK: A case study. In *Rethinking Learner Support in Distance Education: Change and Continuity in an International Context* (A. Tait and R. Mills, eds) London: RoutledgeFalmer, pp. 185–197.

Tait, A. and Mills, R. (eds) (1999). *The Convergence of Distance and Conventional Education: Patterns of Flexibility for the Individual Learner.* London: Routledge.

Taylor, J. (2004). A task-centred approach to evaluating a mobile learning environment for pedagogical soundness. In *Mobile Learning Anytime Everywhere.* (J. Attewell and C. Savill-Smith, eds) London, UK:Learning and Skills Development Agency. Retrieved March 29, 2006 from http://iet.open.ac.uk/pp/j.taylor/publish.cfm

Thomas, J.H. (2001). *Audio for Distance Education and Open Learning: A Practical Guide for Planners and Producers.* Retrieved March/12, 2006 from http://www.col.org/audiohandbook/

Thorpe, M. (1995a). The challenge facing course design. In *Open and Distance Learning Today* (F. Lockwood, ed.) London: Routledge, pp. 175–184.

Thorpe, M. (1995b). Reflective learning in distance education. *European Journal of Psychology of Education* **10**(2), 153–167.

Thorpe, M. (2002). Collaborative on-line learning: Transforming learner support and course design. In *Rethinking Learner Support in Distance Education: Change and Continuity in an International Context* (A. Tait and R. Mills, eds) London: Routledge, pp. 198–211.

Thorpe, M. and Godwin, S. (2006). Interaction and e-learning: The student experience. *Studies in Continuing Education*, **28**(3), special issue on 'Advances in Researching Adult e-Learning'.

Thorpe, M., Kubiac, C. and Thorpe, K. (2003). Designing for reuse and revisioning. In *Reusing Online Resources: A Sustainable Approach to e-Learning* (A. Littlejohn, ed.) London: Kogan Page, pp. 106–118.

von Prümmer, C. (2007). Distance education. In *Gender and Education: An Encyclopedia.* (B.J. Bank, ed.) Westport, CT: Praeger, pp. 163–170.

Vrasidas, C. and Glass, G.V. (eds) (2004). *Distance Education and Distributed Learning.* Greenwich, CT: Information Age Publishing.

Wilson, B., Ludwig-Hardman, S., Thornam, C.L., and Dunlap, J.C. (2004). Bounded community: Designing and facilitating learning communities on formal courses. *International Review of Research in Open and Distance Learning*, **5**(3), 23.

Wisher, R.A. and Curnow, C.K. (2003). *Video-Based Instruction in Distance Learning: From Motion Pictures to the Internet.* In *Handbook of Distance Education* (M.G. Moore and W.G. Anderson, eds) Mahwah, NJ: Erlbaum, pp. 315–330.

Chapter 14

From Chautauqua to Correspondence to Computers: Non-Formal Education in Transformation

Chère Campbell Gibson

> In our complex, interdependent, and increasingly overcrowded world, it is becoming evident that the human beings continual renewable capacity to learn has been the least appreciated and least exploited human resource.
>
> Wedemeyer, 1981, p. 3

14.1 INTRODUCTION

This chapter explores non-formal learning whose very existence is predicated on the assumption of the adult's ability and willingness, even desire, to learn across the lifespan. Following an exploration of the definition of non-formal education in North America, including its relationship to formal and informal learning; an array of non-formal learning opportunities over time will be presented as a foundation for a discussion of transformation both of and by non-formal learning. The transformation of non-formal learning as an enterprise as a result of the ubiquitous nature of technology will be highlighted as well as the transformative learning potential in technology-based non-formal education. The chapter concludes with a discussion of exploiting non-formal learning's potential to enhance perspective transformation and the challenges that face those who seek to foster such a change.

14.2 A MATTER OF DEFINITION

Merriam and Caffarella (1999), in their book *Learning in Adulthood: A Comprehensive Guide*, note that learning in adulthood has been categorized in a variety of ways over the life of the discipline, including as formal, non-formal and informal adult learning. They continue noting,

> Formal learning takes place in educational institutions and often leads to degrees or credit of some sort. Non-formal learning refers to organized activities outside educational institutions such as those found in learning networks, churches and voluntary organizations. Informal learning refers to the experiences of everyday living from which we learn something.
>
> (p. 21)

Coombs (cited in Merriam and Brockett, 1997) not only echoes the definitions above but helps us differentiate non-formal from informal learning by highlighting the **planful** nature of the learning with non-formal learning described as "any organized learning activity outside the formal system that is intended to serve identifiable learning clienteles and learning objectives" (p. 14). Informal learning in contrast is considered unplanned, serendipitous, experience based and incidental to living one's daily life.

But seldom are things seldom so cut and dry. Formal educational institutions are increasingly offering educational experiences that carry no credit, are offered in a short time frame and may be oriented to either professional, personal or community development. Additionally, non-formal and informal learning may result in formal credit as a result of credit for prior learning assessment and so on.

Furthermore, the National Forum on Partnerships Supporting Education about the Environment (1994) suggests using the term "lifelong learning . . . to encompass formal education as well as non-formal learning throughout one's lifetime. One reason for broadening the term is that education begins in the home, and this early learning does not find a comfortable resting place in the traditional definition of lifelong learning. But the main reason is that learning is a seamless process that occurs in myriad non-formal and informal ways during an individual's lifetime" (Chap. 1, para. 1).

For the purposes of this chapter, I have chosen to include those organized learning activities that are community based and emerge from a community-based agency or organization, a group of like-minded individuals working in a coordinated manner to address an educational need or an educational institution who have a community-based educational mission, for example, Cooperative and/or Continuing Education Extension. The key emphasis is therefore on community-based activities, with learning as part of the overall goal with no awarding of credit or technology specified.

14.3 NON-FORMAL EDUCATION OF THE PAST AND THE TECHNOLOGIES UTILIZED

In reflecting on the foundations of American distance education in a book by the same name, Watkins and Wright (1991) begin with a short discussion of the Lyceum movement begun by Josiah Holbrook, a movement begun in 1826. Described a powerful force in adult education, social reform and political discussion, many of the ablest leaders of the time lectured to Lyceum audiences. Public interest in general education was greatly stimulated by the movement. Following the Lyceum movement's demise after the Civil War, the Chautauqua, a more famous movement with similar purposes, emerged in 1873. The movement

> grew out of summer Sunday school institutes held by the Methodist Episcopal church during the 1870s....Thousands came to eight-week sessions to hear lectures by many of the period's most eminent politicians, authors, artists, and scientists, as well as to enjoy the entertainments and festive atmosphere of the gatherings. By the end of the nineteenth century the program had spread throughout the United States and Canada and had expanded to include a variety of educational and farm studies. Also sponsored were weekly lectures, forums, and concerts.
>
> [(http://www.answers.com/topic/chautauqua-movement), Chautauqua Movement, para. 1]

While neither of these movements would be considered distance education in any of the modern definitions of the term, they did meet one of the objectives of distance education – reaching out and making education accessible in local communities.

As the Chautauqua movement was developing, so was Anna Ticknor's "Society to Encourage Studies at Home" offering educational opportunities to women of all classes. As Watkins and Wright (1991) note, "This Boston-based, largely volunteer effort provided correspondence instruction to over 10,000 members over a 24-year period despite its resolutely low profile" (p. 3). Print became a vehicle for non-formal learning.

The Chautauqua experience, with its broad program, including educational and farm sciences, was not accessible to many unable to leave their homes for extended periods of time, especially farmers. What emerged to meet the educational need was creative uses of radio, with Farm Radio as an example. In Canada,

> CBC [Canadian Broadcast Corporation] created...the continuing story of a farm family to discuss, in an easy-to-absorb way, rural issues in different parts of the country. Given the nature of our country, it's perhaps not surprising that there were several different families, each facing different circumstances: the Carsons in BC, the Jacksons on the Prairies, the Craigs in Ontario, and the Gillans in the Maritimes. Broadcast live at noon each day from the 1940's through the 1960's, the series made an important contribution to the war effort, especially in food production, while post-war, they helped disseminate new methods of farming and household economy.
>
> (Redekopp, 2002)

As the telephone became more ubiquitous, it, too, became a tool for non-formal learning. Perhaps one of the best example was (and still is) a non-formal educational resource entitled infosource®. By simply dialing a toll-free number, the learner has access to over 600 audio messages on topics that range from agriculture, garden and landscaping and our environment to home and family, including parenting the first year and youth development http://infosource.uwex.edu/. These messages are also currently available in print form on a web server. The general concept of infosource® has been implemented in may cities, and listing can be found in many local phone books, linking citizens to resources that can answer their immediate questions at a time they occur and in anonymity. Topics often include those related to citizenship and the undocumented, sexually transmitted diseases and other sensitive topics.

But other media were becoming available for non-formal learning beyond print, radio and the telephone, including television. As an example, Wisconsin's Rural Family Development (RFD) program was designed to demonstrate and evaluate a new adult continuing education delivery system featuring communication, computation and life-coping skills. Directed at rural adults functioning below twelfth grade equivalency levels and in low socioeconomic strata, the program had three main goals: (1) to assist participants in upgrading living and coping skills, (2) to assist participants in improving basic skill proficiency toward the ultimate goal, and (3) to assist adults in participating in contemporary society. The program combined an array of components including a half-hour magazine format television program, radio programs and a monthly client-oriented newspaper. In addition, RFD provided a new print-based life-coping skill curriculum based on the introduction of living skills prior to the introduction of basic skills in a non-sequential, broad scope learning system that included a weekly home visit program by local community-based trained paraprofessionals. And, similar to many of the non-formal learning efforts of years gone by, nationally known show business stars were incorporated into the programs (Hiemstra, 2002). This program parallels in the British Open University's continuing education programs that also included television, plus audio and/or videotapes to supplement learning, however without the presence of a paraprofessional. And audio and videotapes continued to abound as delivery mechanisms for non-formal education ranging from audiotapes for language learners to videotapes for the home carpenter.

Bringing educational opportunity to many, through the movement of "learned" individuals to communities around the country in person or through the use of print, telephone, radio and television, as well as audio and videocassettes, continues to grow. For the most part, the pedagogies utilized in these programs mirror those employed in traditional formal education. Characteristics include the teacher/instructor as expert and the learners as passive recipients of information in what has been referred to as a banking concept of education (Freire, 1971). Interaction among and between individuals has diminished since the early Lyceum and Chautauqua movements with few exceptions. While potentially building capacity in individuals, the potential for building communities of practice and/or encouraging social action seems limited in most early forms of non-formal learning.

But while the efforts of the past, with the technologies of the past, focused on individual growth, the new interactive technologies have begun to transform non-formal learning and in doing so enhance the transformative potential of non-formal education.

14.4 NEW USES OF OLDER TECHNOLOGIES AND NEW TECHNOLOGIES IN NON-FORMAL LEARNING

One might argue that the use of radio, the telephone, and television had potential for interaction that might encourage new pedagogies, but that potential was rarely exploited. More recently, one-way video with two-way interaction provided through audioconferencing and/or email, two-way interactive video and computer-mediating conferencing have radically changed non-formal learning and associated pedagogies. Several examples provide illustration.

A universal truism, if such exists, might be that the teenage years are challenging and parents struggle to provide guidance to teens while trying not to stifle their growth. One might ask, "How do you raise a responsible teen?" One non-formal learning program tried to provide a learning environment to answer the question. "Raising Responsible Teens," an outreach program of the University of Wisconsin-Extension, combined one-way video satellite-based programs that enabled parents to hear from experts around the USA, with opportunities to chat with other parents face-to-face in community-based settings around the country and generate questions posed to the experts through the use of fax and audioconferencing encouraged both "real" and virtual interactions. In addition, agencies and individuals who interact with teens, from local law enforcement to educators, social workers and psychologists, joined the local discussion groups and Extension provided a facilitator. The weekly programs were supplemented with print-based materials and the opportunity to call a toll-free number to raise questions anonymously with experts.

But two-way interactive video has supplanted satellite-based educational delivery for many due to cost. Two-way interactive video is not inexpensive, at least at this writing; however, some agencies and organizations with community development as a mission find the tool extremely useful. What better way to solve community problems than to bring similar and dissimilar communities together virtually to discuss problems, both common and unique, explore solutions, assess interdependence and develop action plans with an "act locally, think globally" perspective.

But the technology that "puts power in the hands of individuals, completely reinventing our ability to reach people, acquire information and distribute knowledge" (Understanding the Internet and Society, 1995, Roots of the revolution, para. 4) is the computer and computer-mediated communications. Furthermore, they note that this technology,

> all forms of dynamic communications – one-on-one, small group, mass broadcasting and a wholly new form of many-to-many interactive mass communications. One of its most powerful characteristics is that it can enrich communication by combining all other forms of communication – text, audio, graphics and video – in a single message. It does so without regard to the distance or time differences between people, since it can store and hold messages until the receiver chooses to view and respond to them. It offers powerful and timely access to information and knowledge, which opens up a vast array of opportunities.
>
> (The new communications medium, para. 2)

An example of technology's power is its role in the e-Health movement, with its emphasis on the "development of a growing set of tools and resources designed to help stakeholders navigate the organizational, financial, legal and clinical aspects of health information exchange." (e-Health Initiative, 2005). In 2005, an estimated 212,930 new cases will be diagnosed, and 40,870 deaths from breast cancer will occur (American Cancer Society, 2005). Patients describe feeling lost and alone, helpless, out of control and so dependent on others. Enter the Comprehensive Health Enhancement Support System (CHESS, 2005), a computer-based health resource designed to educate and equip people facing a health crisis. CHESS:

- provides timely, easily accessible resources (information, social support, decision-making and problem-solving tools) when needed most;
- combines various services and resources into one system, meeting the needs of various coping and information-seeking styles, and making use more likely and rewarding;
- tailors and personalizes information and support to help users better manage their health and change behaviors that are harmful to their well-being;
- protects privacy, encouraging openness and honesty in dealing with health concerns;
- presents reliable, well-organized, detailed health information in language that is comprehensible to people at most educational levels.

(Gustafson, 2005)

The computer and the community associated with it become a lifeline – an online connection to those who suffered a similar fate: individuals who understand the hopes and fears of a breast cancer patient, who, even in the dead of night, were there to quell fears, empathize and strategize. Those who felt lost feel found in the company of others who share the struggle and armed knowledge to control their destiny. (It should be noted that the CHESS program model has been extended beyond breast cancer to other medical conditions.)

Examples abound of the use of these new interactive technologies, with specific emphasis on computer-mediated communications. As the Morino Institute (Understanding the Internet and Society, 2005) notes,

> The most important aspect of interactive communications [computer mediated communications] is that it inspires engaged participants rather than passive listeners or viewers. Its unique potential is that it empowers every participant to be a publisher or producer of information as well as a consumer.
>
> (The new communications medium, para. 3)

The potential for new pedagogies, communities of practice and individual, group and community growth potential emerges as well, thus transforming both distance education in general and non-formal learning in particular.

14.5 TRANSFORMATION OF DISTANCE EDUCATION AND NON-FORMAL LEARNING

Randy Garrison (2000), in his article entitled *Theoretical Challenges for Distance Education in the 21st Century: A Shift from Structural to Transactional Issues*, suggests "... the study of distance education in the 20th century was primarily focused on distance constraints and approaches that bridged geographic constraints by way of organizational strategies such as the mass production and delivery of learning packages" (p. 2). He continues noting that recently "... the focus in the study of distance education has shifted to educational issues associated with the teaching-learning transaction" (p. 2). In other words, the enterprise has moved from bridging the distance to enhancing teaching and learning.

Chris Dede (1995) in an article entitled *The Transformation of Distance Education to Distributed Learning* also reflects on the shift in focus within distance education noting,

> How a medium shapes its users, as well as its message, is a central issue in understanding the transformation of distance education into distributed learning. The telephone creates conversationalists; the book develops imaginers, who can conjure a rich mental image from sparse symbols on a printed page. Much of television programming induces passive observers; other shows, such as Sesame Street and public affairs programs, can spark users' enthusiasm and enrich their perspectives. As we move beyond naive "superhighway" concepts to see the true potential impact of information infrastructures, society will face powerful new interactive media capable of great good or ill.
>
> (Transforming distance education to distributed learning, para. 4)

Is non-formal learning also being transformed? Are the new technologies shaping the users and the message? Acknowledging Garrison's (2000) position that "conceptual confusion is created with the advent of new terminology (virtual, open, distributed and distance education) new technologies, new program demands, new audiences, and new commercially competitive providers" (p. 1), several of these concepts may be helpful in determining the extent to which the potential for a transformed non-formal learning has evolved and been exploited with the arrival of new technologies.

The concept of control, the variable placed at the center of the model of the educational transaction at a distance proposed by Garrison and Baynton (1987) and later revised by Garrison (1989), becomes a starting point. Defined as the opportunity and ability to influence the educational transaction (Garrison, 1989, p. 27), control exists within the larger relationship of teacher, learner and content. At the more micro-level, control includes a triad of elements, including (1) independence to select learning goals and objectives, activities to accomplish these and assessment strategies of their choosing; (2) proficiency, with its focus on the ability of the learner to learn independently; and lastly (3) support with its emphasis on the human and non-human resources that influence the teaching–learning transaction.

Have the newer technologies available for non-formal learning changed the dynamic of control? One might suggest the potential for wresting control from the teacher to the learner has certainly been made more possible. Print, radio, television, audiotapes and videotapes, even video satellite educational opportunities, result in static content over which the learner has little or no control in terms of the selection of goals, objectives, learning activities or even assessment beyond personal assessment of learning gains. Newer more interactive technologies such as audioconferencing, videoconferencing and computer-conferencing afford the learner the potential to assume some level of control over their learning IF the environment is designed to do so. That includes willingness and expertise on the part of the educator to share control over the learning goals and objectives and learning activities, including those that enable a learner to assess his/her own accomplishments within a personal definition of mastery of the content.

Furthermore, the learner must also be willing and have a sufficient level of proficiency and support as an independent learner to share in the control of the teaching–learning transaction. Teachers can help build that capability if they choose to do so. Without a willingness to engage in more collaborative and capacity building forms of teaching and learning, in contrast to the more "banking concept of education" noted earlier, we find ourselves as passive listeners as an expert drones on in an audioconference, as passive viewers of a videoconference and as passive readers of screen after screen of web-based content, the interactive potential of the technology all but ignored.

The newer technologies with their potential for high levels of interaction have the potential to transform non-formal education. The new media are indeed beginning to shape both the users and the message. New conceptions of learning and knowledge are emerging, with traditional definitions of teacher and learner being called into question. But as Dede (1995) notes, "... The most significant influence on the evolution of distance education will not be the technical development of more powerful devices, but the professional development of wise designers, educators, and learners" (Transforming distance education to distributed learning, para. 4). Being able to harness the potential of these new media to engage teachers and learners alike in the construct of knowledge that is contextually relevant and engages all parties in reflection and action toward the end of both individual and societal transformation is the ultimate challenge!

14.6 NON-FORMAL LEARNING AS TRANSFORMATION

Can non-formal learning meet this challenge? If learning is indeed being reconceptualized as discovery and development rather than as telling information to a passive audience (Pratt, 1998), and as transformational rather than informational, can non-formal learning play a role? To answer these questions, it seems important to quickly review the theoretical perspectives or conceptualizations of transformational learning. With a common understanding, we can then ask, what are the conditions necessary for transformation? In addition, to what extent is media-facilitated access to non-formal learning, the processes of non-formal education and resultant success (or failure) in non-formal education potentially transformational?

Baumgartner (2001) in her chapter entitled, "An Update on Transformational Learning," references Dirkx's four-lens approach to thinking about transformational learning philosophies. These transformational learning lenses include a cognitive rational approach, a social-justice approach, a developmental approach and a spiritual approach to transformational learning.

14.6.1 Perspective Transformation

The majority of the research in North America has focused on Mezirow and his perspective transformation, with its emphasis on rationale thought and reflection. Learning is understood as the process of using a prior interpretation to construe a new or revised interpretation of the meaning on one's experience as a guide to future action (Mezirow, 2000, p. 3). Mezirow (1985) points to the importance of the personal theories, assumptions, beliefs, propositions and prototypes that make up our higher order thinking schemata that undergirds our habits of expectation. Familiar role relationships, such as, employer–employee and teacher–student, are examples of habitual expectations familiar to everyone. He contends that our key role as educators is "to help learners make explicit, elaborate, and act upon assumptions, premises... upon which their performance, achievement and productivity are based" (Mezirow, 1985, p. 48). This perspective transformation begins with a disorienting dilemma that calls into question the effectiveness of previously held beliefs, values and assumptions and is theorized to progress through a ten-step process. This ten-step process includes the following steps: (1) a disorienting dilemma; (2) self examination with feelings of guilt or shame; (3) a critical assessment of epistemic, sociocultural or psychic assumptions; (4) recognition that one's discontent and the process of transformation are shared and that others have negotiated a similar change; (5) exploration of options to form new roles, relationships and actions; (6) planning a course of action; (7) acquisition of knowledge and skills for implementing one's plans; (8) provisional trying of new roles; (9) building of competence and self-confidence in new roles and relationships; and (10) a reintegration into one's life on the basis of conditions dictated by one's new perspective (Mezirow, 1991, pp. 168–169).

A critical component in the transformative learning process is critical reflection, more specifically critical reflection on assumptions, i.e. "reassessing of the presuppositions on which our beliefs are based and acting on insights derived from the transformed meaning perspective that results from such assessments" (Mezirow and Associates, 1990, p. 20). Additional and critical elements in the process of transformation that have emerged from recent research include the realization that the process is more fluid and recursive, less linear than earlier writings of Mezirow have suggested; that emotions and working through one's feelings are an essential element of change; and the most common finding across all research studies, the importance of relationships and relational knowing. Context and culture remain as possible predisposing factors and represent areas where additional research is needed.

14.6.2 Emancipatory Education

Paulo Freire from his early translated writings in "Pedagogy of the Oppressed" (Freire, 1971) to his later writings "Pedagogy of the Heart" (Freire, 1998) and "Pedagogy of Freedom: Ethics, Democracy, and Civic Courage" (Freire, 2001) has a recurring theme of social justice. He notes, "An education of answers does not help the curiosity that is indispensable in the cognitive process. On the contrary, this form of education emphasizes the mechanical memorization of facts. Only an education of questions can trigger, motivate and reinforce curiosity" (p. 31). And he suggests to what end that curiosity should be applied when he notes, "The world, in order to be, must be in the *process of being*" [emphasis in the original] (p. 32). And there have been countless efforts, both successful and less successful, to operationalize his teachings, to reinforce curiosity, to engage in liberating education and, in doing so, impact the world in positive ways. Many begin with circles of culture, discussion groups, reflecting on the situation they find themselves in, on their hopes and fears and the sociocultural and historical forces that impact their reality, often in response to a question generated within the group. Pictures often inform the later stages of the discussion. Additional reflection on the contradictions and limiting situations in the context leads to proposed action. The taking of action toward the end of social justice is but one end. Reflection on action and reflection in action are important aspects of praxis, i.e. reflection and action. Throughout, Freire advocates openness to dialogue, a caring for learners, recognition of our conditioning and unfinishedness and lastly, "the importance of decision making that is aware and conscientious" (p. 101).

Once again we see the importance of critical reflection to the process of transformation. In addition, dialogue with others and the creation of the knowledge in relationships emerge as essential elements, all within a specific context. Dale's (2004) recent research findings echo these themes and those of others when he concluded that

> (1) Educators should be aware that Freire is not a method. In other words, educators should create their own methods; (2) Critical reflection on practice has the potential to influence one's ontology; (3) Dialogue is a central element to critical reflection on practice; (4) Teaching and learning are enhanced by contextualization and politicizing of experiences and; (5) Problem-posing education engages students through dialogue and experiential learning.

14.6.3 Developmental Approach to Transformation

Daloz (1999), in his writings on learners in formal educational contexts, suggests that learners are often in developmental transition when they approach education. Mentoring that unique one on one supportive relationship can guide the learner on their transformational learning journey, a journey, Daloz notes, that is affected by the social environment that surrounds the learner.

Once again we see the importance of relationships, of dialogue and of the context in which the learner finds himself/herself as they continue to develop over time.

14.6.4 Spirituality, Learning and Transformation

Lastly John Dirxx (1997, 2001) directs our attention to the role spirituality can play in learning. "Soul-based learning that emphasizes feelings and images" (Baumgartner, 2001, p. 18) is advocated based on a position that the process of transformation goes beyond a cognitive-rational approach to transformation to a more all-inclusive integration of all aspects of the Self. Other analytical depth psychologists, advocate transformation to "expand consciousness itself or actually change personality through conscious awareness of the individuating process" (Scott, 1997, p. 43).

In sum, there are a variety of perspectives on transformation from a more individualistic orientation as represented by Mezirow to a more emancipatory view espoused by Freire. However, while Daloz's more developmental perspective is singled out in Baumgartner's four-lens classification system, Mezirow, Freire and Dirkx also recognize the potential for individual growth. In addition, the more spiritual and affective considerations reflected in the writings of Dirkx have been embraced by Mezirow in his more recent writings and are likewise represented in the recent writings of Freire. However, interestingly, there is no mention of transformative learning occurring in contexts other than face-to-face interaction.

14.7 THE CONDITIONS NECESSARY FOR TRANSFORMATIVE LEARNING

Kegan (2000), reflecting on transformative learning, noted "... learning aimed at changes not only in *what* we know but changes in *how* we know ... comes closer to the etymological meaning of *education* ('leading out')" in contrast to informational learning that represents "a kind of in-filling" (p. 49, emphasis in original). Later, he notes that "both kinds of learning are each honorable, valuable, meritable, dignifiable activities.... in given moments or contexts, a heavier weight of one or the other may be called for" (p. 51).

But if that moment or context calls for transformative learning, what conditions are necessary to facilitate this type of learning? Regardless of the lens brought to the discussion of transformative learning, several key conditions seem evident. There is a coming together (assumed face-to-face) of individuals in an open relationship of trust. This coming together enables an ongoing dialogue and "meaning forming" the activity by which we shape a coherent meaning out of the raw material of our outer and inner experiencing (Kegan, 2000, p. 52). Furthermore, Kegan would suggest we need to move to reforming our meaning-forming, i.e. "we change the very form by which we are making our meanings" (p. 53). As Belenky and Stanton (2000) have noted,

> This collaborative process of assessing and reformulating one's basic assumptions about the knowledge making process permits more inclusive, more discriminating, permeable and integrative ways of knowing the world. Reflective discourse and critical thinking thus provide the tools for continued intellectual and ethical development throughout adulthood.
>
> (p. 71)

But Brookfield reminds us that reflection or reflective discourse and critical reflection are not one and the same. To be truly critically reflective he suggests "that the persons concerned must engage in some sort of power analysis of the situation or context in which the learning is happening ... to identify assumptions they hold dear that are actually destroying their sense of well-being and serving the interests of others, that is hegemonic assumptions" (Brookfield, 2000, p. 126).

Furthermore, listening deeply, respectfully, in accepting ways, yet probing caringly for deeper meanings, unspoken assumptions and beliefs, is also critical. Through these connected conversations in a community of learners, members come to common understandings, co-creating shared knowledge.

Lastly, moving beyond reflection to action is also a critical condition. Freire (1971) speaks of praxis – the nexus of reflection and action. Action provides another opportunity for reflection – both reflection in action and reflection on action (Schon, 1983).

If non-formal learning is to go beyond informational learning and foster transformational learning, the technologies employed and the instructional designs must be able to support the development of trusting relationships, ongoing dialogue, critically reflective conversations and a movement from reflection to action within one or more contexts in which the constructed meaning has arisen.

14.8 EXPLOITING THE POTENTIAL FOR TRANSFORMATIONAL NON-FORMAL LEARNING

One might ask, can access to information be transformational unto itself? Are face-to-face group processes and group deliberations essential to foster transformation as suggested above? Are there conditions under which transformational learning leading to individual and social change is possible without the group and at a distance? To what extent is ongoing synchronous conversation important to the process? These and other questions are important to explore as we consider the multiple forms of non-formal education, from didactic delivery of information that typifies the use of early one-way media to the highly interactive synchronous and asynchronous educational environments made possible by two-way media.

14.8.1 Transformation as a Solitary Pursuit

Can the very access to non-formal learning be the start of individual transformation? Can an individual engage in transformative learning alone? Arseneault in her 1998 thesis (cited in Cranton, 2000) described the process of critical self-reflection in seven individuals. As Cranton notes, most participants described processes similar to many aspects of the transformation process – "disorientation, self-examination, critical assessment, exploration of options, engaging in discourse and planning a course of action" (p. 190). Thus, it seems from at least one small research study, individuals can engage in transformative learning individually although the study cited fails to detail the taking of action, only the planning of action.

Returning to the conditions deemed essential for transformative learning, problem-posing education, critical reflection, dialogue, contextualization and politicizing of experiences and the taking of action all seem integral to the process. In the absence of a group of learners, two conditions seem important to facilitate the process at a distance and in the absence of a face-to-face group – concept of the guided didactic conversation advocated by Holmberg (1983) and interaction with the learner's context (Gibson, 1993). Educational materials regardless of medium of delivery, be it print, radio, audiocassettes, videotapes or television, can embrace Holmberg's guided didactic conversation and through this "conversation" pose questions, guide critical reflection, in the true sense of the word. Furthermore, the learner can be also guided toward reflections on and in the context in which she/he lives and works – the context that may be oppressive, stifling individual and social growth. This context can be used as a forum for further face-to-face dialogue, a context in which to take social action and a context for further reflection in action and on action.

But do we as distance educators design to raise the difficult questions, help learners reflect on their very existence, on their habits of the mind, on their unexplored assumptions, values and beliefs and the resultant actions? Do we incorporate others into the conversation – others from the context in which the learner finds himself/herself? All in all, in spite of the Arseneault findings reported by Cranton (2000) and Cranton's own research on that suggesting "psychological preferences influence the way we engage in reconstructing frames of reference" (p. 195), the potential of transformative non-formal learning using the early technologies without the interactive capabilities of recent technological advances seems a challenge at best.

14.8.2 Transformation as a Group-Enabled Process

But in stark contrast, some would suggest the very presence,

> ...of interactive communications leads inescapably to one conclusion: the increasing importance and empowerment of individuals, regardless of location, economic status, political affiliation or any other criteria.
>
> (Understanding the Internet and Society, 1995, Individual empowerment, para. 1)

The report continues noting that

> By connecting people with others, to vast resources of information and by helping them bypass intermediaries who have monopolized access to knowledge and opportunity, interactive communications is helping people take greater responsibility and control over their lives and communities.
>
> (Understanding the Internet and Society, 1995, Individual empowerment, para. 1)

And most would hardily agree. Through the use of interactive communications media, especially computer-mediated communications, we can indeed meet the conditions, mentioned earlier, that are deemed essential for transformative learning – problem-posing education, critical reflection, dialogue, the sharing of multiple perspectives contextualization and politicizing of experiences and the taking of action within a safe, open, secure environment of caring and trust plus, with interactive communications media, we can have a virtual group.

Chris Dede (1995) reflecting on the potential of virtual communities to provide support from people who share common joys and trials, notes,

> We are accustomed to face-to-face interaction as a means of getting to know people, sharing ideas and experiences, enjoying others' humor and fellowship, and finding solace. In a different manner, distributed learning via information infrastructures can satisfy these needs at any time, any place. Some people (shy, reflective, comfortable with emotional distance) even find asynchronous, low bandwidth communication more "authentic" than face-to-face verbal exchange. They can take time before replying to compose a more elegant message, as well as to refine the emotional nuances they wish to convey. This alternative conception of authenticity may reflect a different dimension to learning styles than the visual, auditory, symbolic, and kinesthetic differentiations now used.
>
> (Virtual communities, para. 1)

Reflecting back on the CHESS Program and its impact on those who have made use of its resources, including the potential for conversation among and between those who face serious health conditions, individual transformation seems possible in virtual groups and a resource-rich environment. And certainly most would describe the CHESS breast cancer members as part of a community of practice, a group of people who share similar goals and interests, who, through CHESS, work with the same tools and express themselves in a common language. Through such common activity, they come to hold similar beliefs and value systems (Wenger, 1998). And as members of this community of practice, they take action outside of the group, but only as individuals.

An example of a community of practice through the use of interactive media that is often cited is Blacksburg, Virginia. A town of 36,000, over one-third of the population of Blacksburg is linked together on a computer network called the Blacksburg Electronic Village. This network links Blacksburg residents to each other as well as the city's businesses, government departments, schools, doctors, hospitals and entertainment. It enables them to communicate with their government, shop with local retailers, get medical advice and, most important, talk to each other. A collaborative effort among the city government, Virginia Polytechnic Institute, Bell Atlantic and local businesses and organizations, it provided an opportunity for research as well as social action. In addition to discovering that informed activist become more involved once going online and the less active and informed person becomes less engaged once online, they also noted "that in order to play a constructive role in creating a more civil society, community networks should explicitly pursue strategies that encourage community activism." Ensuring non-profit community groups have access to low-cost Internet applications (e.g. email for leadership, online discussion for members, web space) is important as well as providing and supporting innovative tools for non-experts, such as easy collaborative web-based tools for information production and collaboration. They conclude their research report noting, "Interactive services such as these might facilitate the formation, energizing, and maintenance of active subgroups in a community who shoulder the responsibility of raising, discussing, and resolving local issues." (Kavanaugh et al., 2005, p. 23.)

Smart mobs certainly represent the formation and energizing of active subgroups in a community! An online book summary of the new book entitled *Smart Mobs: The Next Social Revolution* (http://www.smartmobs.com/book/book_summ.html) notes that "Smart mobs emerge when communication and computing technologies amplify human talents for cooperation. The impacts of smart mob technology already appear to be both beneficial and destructive, used by some of its earliest adopters to support democracy and by others to coordinate terrorist attacks" (para. 1). Street demonstrators, using "dynamically updated websites, cell-phones, and 'swarming' tactics," as they protested in Seattle Washington, the site of the 1999 World Trade Organization, serves as a North American example of the use of technology for social action. The book summary ends with two questions. "Are the populations of tomorrow going to be users, like the PC owners and website creators who turned technology to widespread innovation? Or will they be consumers, constrained from innovation and locked into the technology and business models of the most powerful entrenched interests?" (para. 5)

14.9 A DEARTH OF EXAMPLES AND RESEARCH

What has become clear is that although a capacity to create the environment that is conducive to emancipatory education for social action is possible through the use of technology in non-formal learning, instances are few and far between. Optimism abounds for some as they view the new patterns of communications enabled by the new interactive communications.

- We can build new communities of communication, whether that means creating the "virtual communities" based on common interests that are so characteristic of the networks or facilitating contact and collaboration in our real local communities. This changes the patterns of how individuals communicate with other individuals;
- We can reach more people, more easily – singly or en masse – and we can develop new channels for interacting with – or bypassing – organizations and institutions. This changes the patterns of communication for organizations and their constituents;
- We can reach and treat information differently, getting it more quickly, in more forms, from more sources regardless of length or medium. This changes the patterns of access to information.

(Understanding the Internet and Society, 1995,
A new communications medium, para 1)

Others begin to devote more attention to capitalize on the potential described above. Examples of such attention include the Technology and Social Action Project. Their wiki describes their efforts as "a project to foster dialogue and collaboration between activists in social movements, voluntary and community organisations and technology designers [and] committed to supporting networks exploring effective ways of designing and using technology to support social action, and of ensuring that technological innovation responds to social priorities" (http://otho.cms.shu.ac.uk/pmwiki/pmwiki.php?n=Main.HomePage). Both face-to-face meetings and online dialogues are utilized to "identify key issues facing social actors using technology, and examine how designers can contribute."

Others also recognize the need to wrestle with design issues as they seek to maximize the potential of technology for social action as exemplified by a 2005 workshop in Sheffield England on "Technology and social action: Designing a future" (http://www.hrea.org/lists/huridocs-tech/markup/msg01256.html). The promotional website noted,

> The global diffusion of communication technologies in society has changed the speed with which situations of social need are noticed, and the ability of social actors to respond. Logistics and coordination within and between groups benefits from technologies, from mobile phones and email, from a simple spreadsheet, to complex project management software. How can technologies and organisations be designed to facilitate effective social action?
>
> (para. 2)

There is much work to be done if technology-based non-formal learning is to be transformational for both individuals and society. And it goes beyond researching the potential, designing to ensure transformative learning, and social change is one outcome of the use of technology for non-formal learning and assessing these outcomes.

14.10 ADDRESSING CHALLENGES AND DEVELOPING CAPACITY

Challenges abound, not the least of which is providing affordable and ubiquitous access to the technologies. A digital divide still exists within North America (Lenhart, 2003), a divide less evident with the use of print and analog technologies such as the telephone. Interactive technologies, especially the networked computer, are critical to non-formal learning and its transformative potential. Open source software that enables co-creation of knowledge, collaboration and social action is also vital and not currently available although projects, including the European FLOSS project (Free/Libre Open Source Software, http://www.infonomics.nl/FLOSS/report/index.htm), are exploring the availability, as well as political, economic and social implications of open source software.

In addition to readily accessible networked computers and open source software, it is also critical to ensure that education and training are available, without cost, to ensure that the necessary computer skills and computer literacy are universal – regardless of age, gender, geography, ability and so on. These skills that can be developed refined, shared and taught by community members include

> *Navigational skill:* the ability to move smoothly among arrays of autonomous and globally interconnected information, contacts, forums and discussion groups in order to locate and connect to information and expertise from relevant sources.

Information literacy: an understanding of which information is most useful, relevant, and reliable, as well as the ability to analyze, distill, integrate, compose and classify information to create knowledge.

Distribution skill: frameworks for rethinking methods of packaging, presenting, providing access and disseminating information and knowledge in this new medium.

Communications literacy: integrating new forms of information, knowledge and message development into evolving patterns of organizational and interpersonal communication.

(Understanding the Internet and Society, 1995, Providing education in the new skills and literacies, para. 1)

14.11 SUMMARY

We return to Wedemeyer's (1981) assertion that "In our complex, interdependent, and increasingly overcrowded world, it is becoming evident that the human beings continual renewable capacity to learn has been the least appreciated and least exploited human resource" (p. 3). Some might argue that lifelong learning has finally come into its own. Its importance in a rapidly changing world is well accepted and opportunities for learners to continue to grow abound. These opportunities include not only formal education, with close to 50 percent of its learners defined as adults, but also in the non-formal offerings as well as informal venues for learning.

Non-formal learning has gone beyond face-to-face offerings of non-profit agencies and organizations such as museums, horticultural and zoological societies and institutions of post-secondary education with their expanded non-credit offerings, to educationalopportunities offered via technologies. Older technologies such as print, radio and televisions promote primarily informational learning as a result of the one-way nature of the delivery, learners' limited control over learning and limited, if any, interaction with others. In contrast, the new interactive media have radically changed the potential for not only informational learning but also individual perspective transformation and/or social change. Bringing together, either synchronously or asynchronously, many individuals with their multiple perspectives, to engage in critical reflection, critical discourse, collaboration, co-creation of knowledge, coupled with action, in a resource-rich environment presents countless opportunities to "renew capacity" of both individuals and society. Our challenge is to ensure these powerful technological tools are harnessed toward these ends!

REFERENCES

American Cancer Society. *Cancer Facts and Figures 2005*. Atlanta, Ga: American Cancer Society, 2005. Retrieved November 25, 2005, from http://www.cancer.org/docroot/STT/stt_0.asp

Baumgartner, L. (2001). An update on transformational learning. In, *The New Update on Adult Learning Theory* (S. Merriam, ed.) New directions for adult and continuing education, no. 89. San Francisco, CA: Jossey-Bass, pp. 15–24.

Book summary of *Smart Mobs: The Next Social Revolution* (n.d.). Retrieved December 6, 2005 from http://www.smartmobs.com/book/book_summ.html

Brookfield, S. (2000). Transforming learning as an ideology critique. In, *Learning as Transformation: Critical Perspectives on a Theory in Progress* (J. Mezirow and associates, eds) San Francisco, CA: Jossey-Bass, pp. 125–150.

Comprehensive Health Enhancement Support System (CHESS). (2005). Retrieved November 28, 2005 from http://chess.chsra.wisc.edu/Chess/

Cranton, P. (2000). Individual differences and transformative learning. In, *Learning as Transformation: Critical Perspectives on a Theory in Progress* (J. Mezirow and associates, eds) San Francisco, CA: Jossey-Bass, pp. 181–204.

Dale, J. (2004). *A Critical Inquiry of Freirean Pedagogy: Implications for Contemporary Adult Education (Paulo Freire)*. Unpublished dissertation – Ball State University.

Daloz, L. (1999). *Mentor: Guiding the Journey of Adult Learners: Realizing the Transformational Power of adult Learning Experiences*. San Francisco, CA: Jossey-Bass.

Dede, C. (1995, July). *The Transformation of Distance Education to Distributed Learning*. Retrieved December 1, 2005 from http://www.hbg.psu.edu/bsed/intro/docs/distlearn/

Dirxx, J. (1997). Nurturing the soul in adult learning. In *Transformative Learning in Action: Insights from Practice* (P. Cranton, ed.) New directions of adult and continuing education, no. 74. San Francisco, CA: Jossey-Bass, pp. 79–88.

Dirxx, J. (2001). The power of feelings: Emotion, imagination and the construction of meaning in adult learning. In *The New Update on Adult Learning Theory* (S. Merriam, ed.), New directions for adult and continuing education, no. 89. San Francisco, CA: Jossey-Bass, pp. 63–72.

e-Health Initiative. Retrieved November 28, 2005 from http://www.ehealthinitiative.org/

FLOSS (Free/Libre Open Source Software) Retrieved December 7, 2005 from http://www.infonomics.nl/FLOSS/report/index.htm

Freire, P. (1971). *Pedagogy of the Oppressed*. New York: Herder and Herder.

Freire, P. (1998). *Pedagogy of the Heart*. New York: Continuum.

Freire, P. (2001). *Pedagogy of Freedom: Ethics, Democracy, and Civic Courage*. Lanhma, MD: Rowman and Littlefield Publishing Group.

Garrison, D.R. (1989). *Understanding Distance Education: A Framework for the Future*. London: Routledge.

Garrison, D.R. (2000). Theoretical challenges for distance education in the 21st century: A shift from structural to transactional issues. *International Review of Research in Open and Distance Learning*, **1**(1). Retrieved December 3 from http://www.irrodl.org/content/v1.1/randy.pdf

Garrison, D.R. and Baynton, M. (1987) Beyond independence in distance education: The concept of control. *The American Journal of Distance Education*, **1**(3), 3–15.

Gibson, C. (1993). Toward a broader conceptualization of distance education. In *Theoretical Principles of Distance Education* (D. Keegan, ed.) London: Routledge, pp. 80–92.

Gustafson, D. (2005). The Comprehensive Health Enhancement Support System (CHESS). Retrieved November 30, 2005 from http://www.psycho-oncology.net/forum/CHESS.html

Hiemstra, R. (2002). *The Adult Education History Project*. Retrieved November 25, 2005, from http://www-distance.syr.edu/cpae96.html

Holmberg, B. (1983). Guided didactic conversation in distance education. In *Distance Education: International Perspectives* (D. Sewart, D. Keegan and B. Holmberg, eds) London: Croom Helm.

Infosource® Retrieved November 25, 2005, from http://infosource.uwex.edu/

Kavanaugh, A., Carroll, J., Rosson, M. et al. (2005). Participating in civil society: The case of networked communities. *Interacting with Computers*, **17**(1), 9–33.

Kegan, R. (2000). What form transforms? A constructive-developmental approach to transformative learning. In *Learning as Transformation: Critical Perspectives on a Theory in Progress*. (J. Mezirow and associates, eds) San Francisco, CA: Jossey-Bass.

Lenhart, A. (2003). *The Ever-shifting Internet Population: A New Look at Internet Access and the Digital Divide*. Pew Internet and American Life Project. Washington, D.C.: The Pew Foundation.

Merriam, S. and Brockett, R. (1997). *The Profession and Practice of Adult Education: An Introduction*. San Francisco, CA: Jossey Bass Publishers Inc.

Merriam, S. and Caffarella, R. (1999). *Learning in Adulthood: A Comprehensive Guide*. San Francisco, CA: Jossey Bass Publishers Inc.

Mezirow, J. (1985). Concept and action in adult education. *Adult Education Quarterly*, 35(3), 142–151.

Mezirow, J. (1991). *Transformative Dimensions of Adult Learning*. San Francisco, CA: Jossey-Bass.

Mezirow, J. (2000). *Learning as Transformation: Critical Perspectives on a Theory in Progress*. San Francisco, CA: Jossey-Bass.

Mezirow, J. and Associates. (1990). *Fostering Critical Reflection in Adulthood*. San Francisco, CA: Jossey-Bass.

National Forum on Partnerships Supporting Education about the Environment. (1994).

Retrieved December 15, 2005 from http://clinton2.nara.gov/PCSD/Publications/TF_Reports/linkage-chap1.html

Pratt, D. (1998). *Five Perspectives of Teaching in Adult and Higher Education*. Malabar, FL: Krieger.

Redekopp, H. (2002). *The Role of Public Broadcasting in Fostering Civil Society*. Retrieved November 25, 2005, from http://www.cbc.radio-canada.ca/speeches/20021112.shtml

Schön, D. (1983). *The Reflective Practitioner*. New York: Basic Books.

Scott, S. (1997). The grieving soul in the transformative process. In *Transformative Learning in Action: Insights from Practice* (P. Cranton, ed.). New directions of adult and continuing education, no. 74. San Francisco, CA: Jossey-Bass, pp. 41–50.

Understanding the Internet and Society: The promise and challenge of a new communications age – Unlocking the doors to opportunity. (1995). Retrieved November 25, 2005, from http://www.morino.org/under_sp_pro.asp

Watkins, B. and Wright, S. (1991). *The foundations of American Distance Education: A Century of Collegiate Correspondence Study*. Dubuque, Iowa: Kendall/Hunt Publishing Co.

Wedemeyer, C. (1981). *Learning at the Back Door: Reflections on Non-traditional Learning in the Lifespan*. Madison, WI: The University of Wisconsin Press.

Wenger, E. (1998). Communities of Practice. Learning as a social system. *Systems Thinker*, http://www.co-i-l.com/coil/knowledge-garden/cop/lss.shtml.

Chapter 15

Transformation Through Open Universities

Otto Peters

15.1 INTRODUCTION

Open universities are autonomous single-mode distance teaching universities. Since the1970s the world has seen the establishment of more than 50 of these open universities (Table 15.1).

Table 15.1: List of 49 Open Universities in Many Countries All Over the World

Year of Foundation	*Name of Open University (in English)*	*Abbreviation*	*Country*
1969	The Open University	UKOU	United Kingdom
1970	Athabasca University	AU	Canada
1972	Universidad Nacional de Educacion a Distancia	UNED	Spain
1972	Korea National Open University	KNOU	Korea
1973	Open University of Israel	OUI	Israel
1974	Allama Iqbal Open University, Islamabad	AIOU	Pakistan
1974	FernUniversität in Hagen	FU	Germany
1977	Universidad Estatal a Distancia, CostaRica	UNED, CR	Costa Rica
1977	Universidad Nacional Abierta	UNA	Venezuela
1978	Sukhothai Thammatirat Open University	STOU	Thailand
1979	**China Central Radio and Television University** *and a network of 44 regional open universities. Eight of the more important ones are included in this list.*	**CCRTU**	**China**
1979	Henan Radio and Television University	Henan RTVU	China
1979	Tanjin TV and Radio University		China

(*Continued*)

Table 15.1: (Continued)

Year of Foundation	*Name of Open University (in English)*	*Abbreviation*	*Country*
1979	Sichuan Radio and Television University	SRTVU	China
1979	Tianjin TV and Radio University	TjTVRU	China
1979	Hangzhou Radio and Television University	HTTVU	China
1979	Jiangsu Radio and Television University	JRTVU	China
1979	Beijing Radio and Television University	BRTVU	China
1979	Shaanxis Radio and Television University	ShRTVU	China
1979	Qinghai Radio and Television University	QRTVU	China
1982	Dr. B.R. Ambedkar Open University	BRAOU	India
1982	Anadolu University	Anad U	Turkey
1983	The University of Air, Wakaba, Mihama-ku, Chiba City	UAir	Japan
1983	Shanghai Television University	STVU	China
1984	Open Universiteit Nederland	OUNL	Netherlands
1984	Universitas Terbuka	UT	Indonesia
1985	**Indira Gandhi National Open University** *and a network of nine regional open unversities, which are included in this list.*	IGNOU	India
1986	National Open University,	NOU	Taiwan
1986	Yunnan Radio and TV University	YNRTVU	China
1987	Kota Open University	KOU	India
1987	Nalanda Open University	NOU	India
1987	Payame Noor University	PNU	Iran
1988	Universidade Aberta	UA	Portugal
1989	The Open University of Hong Kong	OUHK	China
1989	Yashwantrao Chavan Maharashtra Open University	YCMOU	India
1990	Open University of Sri Lanka	OUSL	Sri Lanka
1991	Madhya Pradesh Bhoj (Open) University	MPBOU	India
1991	National Open University	NOP	Taiwan
1991	Al-Qud Open University	QOU	Jerusalem
1992	Bangladesh Open University	BOU	Bangladesh
1993	The Open University of Tanzania	OUT	Tanzania
1994	Dr Babasaheb Ambedkar Open University	BAOU	India
1996	Karnataka State Open University	KSOU	India
1996	University of the Philippines Open University	UPOU	The Philippines
1997	Netaji Subhas Open University	NSOU	India
1997	The Hellenic Open University	HOU	Greece
1997	The Open University of Kohsiung	OUK	Taiwan
1999	Uttar Pradesh Rajarshi Tandon Open University	UPROU	India
2002	National Open University of Nigeria	NOUN	Nigeria
Proposed	Wawasan Open University College	WOUC	Malaysia
Proposed	Cyprus Open University		Cyprus

The University of South Africa (UNISA) should be included in this list because it is the oldest single-mode distance teaching (mega) university. However, it was founded in 1873 as an examining body and started teaching at a distance in 1945. Its tradition is mainly that of correspondence education and it was not really part of the open university movement. The Universidad Oberta de Catalunya (UOC) in Spain should also be mentioned here, but this university, established in 1991, calls itself "La universidad virtual" and represents another type of open distance teaching university.

The emergence of so many entirely new institutions of higher education is remarkable in several ways.

- They are usually the product of governmental planning and fulfil a national mission.
- They provide educational opportunities to a larger segment of the population.
- They reach the previously unreachable: new groups of students who have up to now been barred from enrolment.
- They introduce and consolidate formal and informal studies for adults.
- They show an inherent tendency towards large-scale operations, even towards mega-universities, a previously unknown phenomenon. Quite a number of them cater for several hundred thousand students, and CCRTVU and IGNOU for over a million. These mega-universities "provide a powerful response to the crisis of access and costs" (Daniel, 1999, p. 8).
- They pave the way from elitist to mass higher education.
- They cross national boundaries easily and promote educational globalization.
- They have constructed a new model of higher education that is thoroughly industrialized. They apply management methods, organizational techniques, advanced technical communication media, and new appropriate methods of teaching and learning. This means that the pedagogical structure of higher education has been changed drastically as well.
- They have accumulated rich and detailed experience with the systematic use of multimedia and new information and communication technologies in higher education.
- They are beneficial in terms of cost-effectiveness.
- They mark a significant departure both from conventional higher education and from traditional correspondence education.
- They are "just emerging from non-traditional status" (Keegan, 2004, p. 98) and moving into the centre of mainstream of higher education.
- They are a milestone on the way towards the transformation of a university into an institution of independent learning.
- They are in line with universal postmodern trends of "delimiting" and "destructuring" traditional institutions and "individualization" (Kade, 1989; Arnold, 1996).

Educational specialists are aware of the powerful impact of these open universities on the innovation of higher education. They call the new institutions "the most dynamic and revolutionary component of education" (Yibing, 1998, p. 3), and their emergence "perhaps the most important" event "since the birth of the ancient universities in the

Middle Ages" (Garcia-Garrido, 1988, p. 200), "the most radical challenge yet to the traditional concept of a university" (Keegan and Rumble, 1982, p. 24), and "the most developed stage yet in the evolution of a concept of a university" (Keegan, 1993, p. 67), "a revolutionary change, a breakthrough in higher education" (Guri-Rosenblit, 1999a, p. XVII), and "a distinct phenomenon in the evolution of tertiary distance education over the last 150 years" (Curran, 1996, p. 21).

On the other hand, the international spread of open universities, although very significant because of its pedagogical, social, and educational innovations, has not yet become part of the collective consciousness, and even most educationists are scarcely aware of it, especially in countries in which open universities could not be founded.

15.2 ORIGINS

The appearance of these open universities in so many countries all over the world since the 1970s was not a coincidence. It was the product of the simultaneous occurrence of new pedagogical ideas, efforts to alleviate strong economical needs, the impact of new technical media and the growing awareness of distance education. In the 1960s and 1970s the movement towards "open learning" was widely discussed, governments explored new ways of producing more graduates for economic growth, the use of television and multimedia in education fascinated educationists, and the first academic publications spread the news of the peculiar advantages of distance education.

15.2.1 The Movement Towards Open Learning

During the 1960s and 1970s, educators and politicians were extraordinarily reform-minded. They believed that the welfare of society can be considerably improved by education. An intellectual, social, and political climate existed in which the "open learning movement" could develop.

After the Second World War higher education was "still the domain of upper and upper middle classes in Europe" (Ramanujam, 1995, p. 17). In many countries universities tended to work in seclusion, in Germany in "remoteness and freedom" (Schelsky, 1963), and in Great Britain in a "narrowly elitist educational system" (Bell and Tight, 1993, p. 133). As a reaction to this the ideas of "open learning" and "education for all" were taken seriously by progressive educationists. The opinion spread that gifted persons of all classes should be admitted to higher education. "Equality of educational opportunity" was the catchword. "Education for All" became the motto of the Open Universities of Hong Kong and Korea. Meanwhile it is considered "an imperative for world security" (Daniel, 1999, p. 5).

At the time, open learning experiments became "the most important innovation in post-secondary education" (MacKenzie et al. 1975, p. 502). They widened access to university study for persons who could not attend conventional full-time higher education, provided part-time higher education, succeeded in applying modern technical communication media, and developed new ideas about adequate curricula and individualized and autonomous learning.

In Great Britain the trend towards open learning impressed many educationists and politicians. Their ideas were collected and reviewed by Nigel Paine (1988). The first realizations of the concept were the Open Tec Programme, the Open College, and the National Extension College. The Open University was to follow.

In the USA the discussion of this new approach was lively as well and led to quite a number of experimental efforts. According to Charles A. Wedemeyer this movement was a reaction to "the general societal uncertainty respecting all conventional education, the effects of continued industrialization, the push for civil rights and full democratization, the unrest of youth in the sixties, political radicalism, changing needs and lifestyles, the yearning for some measure of control over personal destiny, disillusionment with institutional inflexibility, even a growing sense of the importance of education throughout life – all of these continued to the eruption of concepts and innovations that have marked a watershed in all levels of American education, not only in higher education" (Wedemeyer, 1981, p. 60).

In this situation reformers strove for the establishment of "non-traditional" and "alternative" forms and institutions of higher education for adults (Cross, 1981). High-ranking committees explored the possibility of such new approaches (Commission, 1973; NAEB 1974; Gould and Cross 1977).

The supporters of this movement not only envisaged the application of new technical (mass) media, the development of innovative teaching methods, and the creation of a new learning behaviour, but intended to achieve political, economic, and social goals as well.

- The message of this movement was that the acquisition of knowledge, skills, and attitudes should be open to all. Nobody should be excluded (*principle of egalitarianism*).
- Traditional educational barriers were to be removed; for example, the financial difficulties of those whose income is too low, gender-specific educational practices, unfavourable socio-cultural milieux, or membership of minority groups (*principle of equality of educational opportunity*).
- Learning is not bound to defined life cycles or to defined locations and times. It must be possible to learn at any time and anywhere (*principle of lifelong and ubiquitous learning*).
- Teaching programmes should not be completely developed and determined beforehand in an empirical-scientific manner, but should be "open" for unforeseen developments in the build-up of individual ability to act (*principle of flexible curricula*).
- The course of learning should not be stipulated rigidly and independently of the students, but start from and be shaped by their individual value perspectives, interests, and experiences (*principle of learner-orientation*).

- Students should not be the objects but the subjects of the teaching process. For this reason, learning and teaching institutions should be created in which students can organize their learning themselves (*principle of autonomous learning*).
- Learning itself is not initiated and steered by means of ritualized presentation and reception processes, but by discussion and active management of the student (*principle of learning through communication and interaction*).

15.2.2 Economic Forces

The movement towards open learning created a general atmosphere of educational optimism and raised hopes for innovation in higher education, but did not really lead to the establishment of open universities. The ulterior motive for a revolutionary change of this nature was the desire to overcome *economic* needs. It was the need to surmount economic stagnation in industrialized countries and economic backwardness in developing countries. The real factor that led to the establishment of open universities was the determination of politicians to improve their countries' economic situation. The examples of Great Britain, Germany, India, and China show this clearly.

15.2.3 Advances in Communication Technology

The advent of television gave a boost to the ideas of those who favoured the use of broadcasting for educational purposes. Enthusiastic instructional designers believed that radio and television could not only transport but also innovate and enhance education. A new academic discipline – educational technology – emerged in this period. It was to become especially important in open universities, which quite often established special units for the application of educational technology. The idea of mass higher education developed. Harold Wilson, the leader of the British Labour Party, announced the establishment of a "University of the Air", based mainly on radio and television, in 1963.

15.2.4 The Background of Distance Education

When government officials and educational planners explored possibilities of producing a more educated and trained workforce in order to solve acute economic problems they could not overlook previous experiences with teaching at a distance in higher education. This was facilitated as in those years this kind of learning was analysed for the first time by academics (Holmberg, 1960; Peters, 1965, 1967, 1968, 1971; Wedemeyer, 1971, 1977; Moore, 1976, 1977; Holmberg, 1977). The "legacy of distance education" (Daniel) attracted their interest not only because it was based on printed material – another mass medium – and communicated by post, but also because it represented a humanistic tradition by reaching the needy, underserved, and socially disadvantaged as well.

In Britain there is a long and varied tradition of correspondence education at the level of higher education which reaches back to the middle of the nineteenth century (Bell and Tight, 1993). Universities in the USA started correspondence study courses as part of their university extension programmes at the end of the nineteenth century. (Bittner, 1920; Bittner and Mallory, 1933; Houle, 1965). In the former Soviet Union, correspondence study ("study without interruption of employment") was one of the official three modes of study at most universities – besides on-campus and evening study (Anweiler, 1963). Their unconventional approach to educating workers in such an extensive way attracted the attention of Harold Wilson when he visited this country (Guri-Rosenblit, 1999a, p. 8). He was to become the most influential originator of the idea of a University of the Air which prepared the way towards the first Open University in Britain.

Only the merger of these four developments can explain the nearly simultaneous appearance of open universities in many countries of the world in the same period of time.

15.3 MANDATES

Universities are generally characterized by their performance of two main functions: the production of new knowledge, new understandings, through research; and the education of secondary school leavers in order to prepare them for professional careers. Open universities are to perform the same functions, but with different groups of students, by employing different methods and media and under entirely different circumstances.

In order to demonstrate how open universities differ from conventional universities we must examine the reasons why they were founded. What are their mandates? Most open universities are expected to carry out particular tasks in order to fulfil a national mission. This can be illustrated by the examples of some arbitrarily selected open universities shown in Table 15.2.

Table 15.2: Examples of "National Missions" of Open Universities in Nine Countries

Open University	*The Open University is to*
UNED, CR Costa Rica	widen "educational opportunities" and to alleviate "social demand at a lower unit cost than that which could be achieved by expanding conventional universities" (Rumble and Harry, 1982, p. 75).
UNED Spain	"provide a second chance to those who for various reasons had lost the first" (Rumble and Harry, 1982, p. 151)
AU Canada	provide "education for democratization, education for innovation, education for autonomous development" (Penalver, 1979, p. 15).
UKOU United Kingdom	"increase the numbers of graduate teachers and qualified scientists and technologists" (Rumble and Harry, 1982, p. 170).
FU Germany	create additional capacity for academic study and thus increase the capacity of the German university system, develop a system of academic continuing education, and be engaged in the reform of university teaching (Peters, 1979, p. 19, 1981, p. 14).
OUNL The Netherlands	exercise an innovative influence on traditional universities, and increase learning opportunities for adults, the disadvantaged, and women, and for lifelong learning (Leibbrandt, 1997, p. 102).

(*Continued*)

Table 15.2: (Continued)

Open University	*The Open University is to*
IGNOU India	establish a new flexible and cheap system that offers opportunities to those excluded from the formal system, equalize educational opportunity, and break the rigidities of the traditional university system with regard to curricula and modes of study (Perry, 1997, pp. 121–122), democratize higher education, promote education, training, research, and extension activities based on the rich heritage of the country, and promote education of the disadvantaged groups of the population (Ramanujam, 2002, p. 133).
BOU Bangladesh	provide formal and non-formal programmes in order to take the university to the doorsteps of the common man and woman. Emphasis is laid on non-formal programmes for enhancing their skills. (Ali, 1997, p. 158).
CCRTU China	"improve the general cultural and scientific standards of the whole nation", "educate more people at lower costs", "develop the Chinese economy" by educating millions of additional engineers and secondary-school teachers (Peters, 2001, p. 187). "To provide higher education opportunities for business, the army, other members of society; to set up modern distance education public service support systems for colleges, universities and other educational institutions through the use of RTVU education resources" (www.crtvu.edu.cn).

All in all these goals differ in several points from those of conventional universities. Open universities endeavour to expand the country's resources, produce more graduates at lower cost, provide for more equality of educational opportunity, cater for new groups of adult students, develop additional forms of professional qualification, innovate higher education, and assist in developing and democratizing the country.

15.4 ORGANIZATION

In order to carry out such mandates the new institutions have to be organized in an unusual, specific way. They are expected to perform tasks that are alien to all academic traditions. This was difficult before 1969 as there was no workable model for an organization of this type. Planners could not base their projects on experiences that had already stood the test of time. The first successful organizational model was created by the planners of the UKOU. The full and detailed first-hand account of its organization, written by its first vice chancellor, assisted many planners to take it as a model (Perry, 1976, p. 214).

A fundamental problem of open universities is coping with two main tasks: organizing teaching and research and constructing and running a reliably functioning technological-organizational system that enables faculty to use technical media in order to communicate with students who do not assemble on a campus, but live and learn elsewhere. The unusual task is to integrate the system of knowledge production, course creation, and dissemination, and support into this complex technical system, which is a significant precondition for teaching at a distance at open universities.

This task can only be fulfilled with the necessary number of staff, who must be balanced in the right way. In order to illustrate this by an example I will refer to the FU, which caters for 45,000 students. In 2006 it employed

76 full professors (tenure);
353 lecturers and academic staff;
397 mentors, students, and assistants; and
711 non-academic staff.

This composition of personnel differs from conventional universities as a relatively small number of full professors have to deal with a large number of persons who perform many specific functions.

The *organization of research and teaching* follows, as a rule, traditional patterns. This is naturally influenced by the prevailing national cultures of higher education. In this case the respective academic units are faculties, as, for instance, at the UKOU, UNED, FU, OUSL, AU, or departments (Guri-Rosenblit, 1999a, p. 174). KNOU has also established faculties, whereas the Open Universities of Hong Kong and Bangladesh use schools. The motive for establishing these units is to continue concentrated disciplinary research mainly in traditional ways in order to attain and preserve the academic respectability of the scientific community. At the FU the departments have established 14 institutes for special disciplinary research. Some open universities innovate university teaching by promoting interdisciplinary projects on an ad hoc basis, for example the OUI up to 1996 (Guri-Rosenblit, 1999a, p. 180).

The following functions must be enabled regarding the *organization of the operating technological system*: course creation, production, and distribution, student services, management of tutors and counsellors, and quality control (Rumble, 1992, pp. 48–79). These functions are often fulfilled in central service units: for example, in (1) Instructional Design and Educational Technology; (2) Computing; (3) Student Support; (4) Library; and (5) Distance Education (and Institutional) Research. In order to perform these functions open universities run units; for example, "Technical Production and Distribution", "Study Centres", "Support Services", "Cooperation with Broadcasting Corporations", and "Quality Control".

In most of these units pedagogical and technical functions merge in a unique way. This means that, ideally speaking, all persons are dedicated to the mission of distance education and consider themselves as part of the complex teaching and learning process. All are committed to making the system work by professional communication and cooperation and they all develop a special expertise that cannot be found in conventional universities.

The governance of an open university also differs, because the chief executives are involved in unusual tasks. The vice chancellors, rectors or presidents, and secretaries cannot restrict themselves to the administration and management of faculty members, their staff and students. They are also involved in problems of teaching at a distance, instructional design, educational technology, adult education, and educational policy, and must keep themselves informed about rapidly changing possibilities of information and communication technology.

The necessity of this kind of involvement can be illustrated by an example. A key problem of established open universities was to make it perfectly clear to all newly appointed faculty members that teaching at a distance is *not* traditional teaching transported by technical media. They had to gradually gain an accurate and deep understanding that teaching at an open university not only differs from teaching at conventional universities, but constitutes quite another pedagogical approach that must be fully understood and internalized. Finally, the traditional university must be transformed into an institution of independent learning. This means also that both the executive head and the administrative head and their staff have to perform new and unusual tasks: elicit a new attitude towards adult distance students; promote an understanding of the necessary role change of teachers, of the division of labour and cooperation with instructional designers and media experts in course teams; and provide insight into the necessity of applying management, evaluation, and control techniques. These processes take time, years even, but they develop by being involved in the complex teaching and learning processes. The chief executives of classical universities would never be expected to discuss pedagogical issues with their professors and staff.

15.5 TECHNOLOGICAL STRUCTURE

Open universities have a particularly close relationship with their technical media. Technical media and devices have constitutive significance, because these universities have to rely on quite a range of them. Without technical media and devices they could not exist. For this reason they are often called "media universities". They use technical devices for the production and delivery of teaching materials, and, even more importantly, to improve and enhance the pedagogical structure of teaching and learning. It is fair to say that open universities are pioneers in the application of technologies in both areas.

The most common technical media used for teaching purposes are print, radio, television, audio and video cassettes, computer, the Net, correspondence, e-mail, telephone, and fax. Two approaches in particular are typical and represent marked innovations: multimedia and networked computers.

15.5.1 Multimedia

When the UKOU was being planned and founded "multimedia" was the slogan chanted by many educators in many countries. The use of several combined technical media to make teaching more attractive and effective was recommended by instructional designers. However, classical universities remained sceptical and found it disconcerting that the UKOU decided to cooperate closely with BBC. The combination of print, radio, and television meant the absolute departure from important academic traditions and conventions. In fact, this was the boldest pedagogical innovation in the history of learning. To reach masses of students who cannot attend regular lectures and seminars at a university and to develop teaching broadcasts professionally was a formidable challenge. Radio and television were particularly attractive and the cheapest way of delivering teaching programmes to the homes of many students. Small wonder that in 1982 many open universities (for instance, AU, CCRTU, UNED CR, OUI, AIOU, and UNA) had followed the British example and used radio and television as transport and teaching media (Rumble and Harry, 1982, p. 214).

The adoption of this multimedia approach created new pedagogical problems. Should educational radio and television broadcasts be used as *delivering technology* or as *teaching media*? Should they offer regular obligatory or only supplementary optional learning programmes? Which is to be the major technology? In the beginning most people thought that television would be the dominant medium because of its appeal and glamour. However, when Tony Bates (1982, p. 9) analysed the use of radio and television in five open universities (AIOU, AU, OUI, UKOU, and UNED) he found that there was a "move from broadcasting". It had changed from the centre to the periphery of the learning environment. This process was partly influenced by the experience of students who found it more practical to work with audio and video tapes, but more so by a new awareness and reappraisal of the teaching power of print.

Printed course material, specially designed to meet the needs of distance students, now became the characteristic component of distance education. Rumble and Harry (1982, p. 212) observed that the situation was marked "by a curious mixture of public identification with and stress on the use of educational broadcasting and the playing down of their real basis in correspondence teaching and the use of print". It is no small wonder that the Open Universiteit of the Netherlands and the FU in Germany go without television. They use it for public relations purposes only.

In distance teaching universities in the Far East the role of broadcasting is quite a different one. At CCRTU television and radio broadcasts play an outstanding role (McCormick, 1982, p. 54). Here they represent the dominant media mainly used for delivering education. The system is reinforced by regular satellite transmissions that link the Central Radio and Television University in Beijing to "the network of 34 other open universities throughout the country" (Keegan, 1995, p. 116). The same can be said about the Japanese "University of the Air". KNOU also teaches mainly by TV and radio broadcasts (62 hours per week by TV and 7 hours daily by radio). Their pedagogical concept is to use these media for *presenting* lectures. The carefully designed and tested course material seems to be alien to these open universities. Printed material has complementary functions only.

Different academic learning cultures are the reason for this approach. In these countries students venerate their professors and wish to see their faces on the screen. In China and Japan the outstanding role of these broadcast media can also be explained by the necessity to transmit the pronunciation of the words, which cannot be presented in print because of the ideographic characters of the script (Peters, 2001, p. 196).

15.5.2 Networked Computers

The advent of computers and the Internet in the 1990s started to change the pedagogical structure of open universities again. The combination of these technologies provided a new distribution mode, an inconceivable potential for interactive information and communication, and a unique possibility of enabling students to become autonomous learners.

All open universities started exploring the new virtual learning spaces. Course units and later whole courses were distributed and taught on the Net, and virtual seminars and virtual examinations became standard components. Many units for developing new forms of learning and collaborating on the Net were established (Eisenstadt and Vincent, 1998). Quite a number of open universities assume and perform already functions of a future virtual university (Tiffin and Rajasingham, 1995, 2003; Hoyer, 1998; Ryan et al., 2000; Unger, 2003; Rajasingham, 2004).

It is true that "the development and utilization of interactive teleconferencing technologies and computer-mediated communication have accelerated both within distance teaching universities and classical universities" (Guri-Rosenblit, 1999a, p. 141). It might therefore be assumed that this new approach is not a real characteristic of open universities. However, open universities were prepared to adopt and integrate this innovation in a distinct way. Teachers and students already had the attitudes, strategies, and experience that support and facilitate the change that has become necessary. Advantageous institutional circumstances are added here, because at open universities not only the whole teaching body, but also the whole administration, a costly, complex organizational-technical operating system, and various support measures are all geared *exclusively* to the learning requirements of distance students. Learning in distance education is structurally strikingly close to learning in virtual spaces.

Distributed and asynchronous learning, so often referred to as innovations of online learning, are nothing new to open universities. They have already developed special strategies for bridging the distance between teachers and students in pedagogical ways (Moore, 1993), whereby this is not always a matter of geographical distances but also of mental, social, and cultural "distances". Teachers have already developed a positive attitude towards *technical media* based on 35 years of experience. An analysis of the development of the FU shows that long before the advent of personal computers and the Net there were 34 isolated technical and pedagogical approaches to online learning, a development that is without parallel in conventional universities (Peters, 2003a, pp. 91, 109).

15.6 PEDAGOGICAL STRUCTURE

Even the most sophisticated educational media are futile if they are not used in a pedagogical way. Teaching and learning at open universities grew out of the critique of traditional university teaching. They do not intend to reform traditional teaching and learning. They are in a continuous process of developing new systems of teaching and learning.

The pedagogical structure of teaching and learning can be characterized by the interplay of six components.

- The permanent, and not just occasional, use of the *technical media* already referred to.
- In many cases, the *self-teaching course material*. It is carefully planned, designed, developed, and produced by teams of professional experts: subject matter specialists, television and radio producers, educational technologists and instructional designers, print editors and course managers. High quality courses can be developed in this way, which also include video and audio cassettes or home experiment kits. Although the development of this type of course material may take a year or longer, developing high quality self-teaching courses in this way becomes cost-effective as soon as it is mass-produced and studied by a great number of students.
- Reading recommended *articles, reports, and set books* provided for by the system.
- The *study centre*. Typically, open universities establish nets of regional and local study centres where face-to-face counselling and tuition, classes, discussions, and group work take place and where tutors or mentors contribute to the teaching–learning system.
- *Mediated communication* between faculty and students by post, telephone, fax, or email.
- *Digitized learning*. Computers, the Internet, and the Web have grown during the last 10 years at an unbelievable speed. Increasingly, students are studying their courses online or off-line with the help of CD-ROMs or DVDs. Communication and interaction with faculty members, tutors, and fellow students develops in unforeseen dimensions. A significant asset of this digitalization of learning is the easy access to an inexhaustible supply of information.
- It is necessary to grasp that teaching and learning at open universities is based on a complex and integrated mix of approaches to learning. It requires new pedagogical approaches and new patterns of teaching and learning behaviours.

Working in such a distinctive learning environment, open universities strive to reach the following educational goals:

- New *attitudes towards students* are to be assumed. This means that curricula and teaching modes must be adapted to the life situation of adult students. Peter Jarvis (1981, p. 24) suggested referring to principles of andragogy rather than to those of pedagogy.
- The benefits of *curricular flexibility* are to be reaped. Because teaching and learning does not have to take place at fixed times and at fixed places, the study programmes can be flexible. Programmes for continuing studies, and up-date and refresher courses and programmes in cooperation with the labour market can be developed, which means a great amount of variety can be achieved. Developed and tested courses can be changed and improved as soon as this is necessary. Modular units can be combined according to individual preferences. Entirely new approaches could be developed (Peters, 2003b). Printed courses can be easily adapted to scientific advances and changes in the working world with the help of

other information and communication media. The most radical curricular flexibility can be achieved by enabling students to design and practise considerable parts of their learning themselves. Online learning in particular provides many new possibilities for the development of autonomous learners.
- Advantage must be taken of *methodical flexibility*. Open universities cannot replicate traditional expository teaching and receptive learning. They are able to explore and to exploit the wealth of new possibilities provided by distance and online education to create new approaches. This assumes the significance of a pedagogical paradigm shift. The goal to be pursued is that of "guided self-learning" and, ultimately, autonomous, self-regulated learning.

Critical objections to this system of teaching and learning are rare. Tunstall (1974, p. XVII) pointed to paradoxes, problems, and dilemmas (too many dropouts, abolition of lectures, inequality between one OU student and another). Doug Shale (1987, p. 9) referred to "Innovations that did not work out" (technology did not really revolutionize higher education, radio and television are more difficult to use than was originally expected, and so on). Simpson (2005, p. 1) argued that "distance education will fail unless it can increase its rate of student success".

15.7 ACADEMIC EXCELLENCE

Are open universities able to excel in teaching, given the technological and pedagogical structure described here? According to John Daniel (1998, p. 3), the key to such a success is "1) well-designed multiple media teaching materials, 2) personal academic support to each student, 3) efficient logistics, and 4) faculty who also conduct research". The UKOU, where this approach is practised, achieved excellence. In a government evaluation it ranked 10th out of 101 UK universities for the excellence of its teaching programme, just behind Cambridge and Oxford (Daniel, 1998, p. 3; Keegan, 2000, p. 78). Students like the way they learn at this university. In the 2005 and 2006 National Student Surveys the UKOU ranked even *first* with regard to students' satisfaction. This means that it is more popular with its students than any other publicly funded university in the UK. The students expressed their satisfaction with regard to the teaching, assessment and feedback, academic support, organization and management, learning resources, and personal development (National Student Satisfaction Survey, 2006).

15.8 STUDENTS

Students at open universities differ greatly from those at classical universities. Most of them are adults in full-time gainful employment, often in mid-career. Smaller groups are formed by housewives, retired persons, soldiers, sailors, the handicapped, or prisoners. Most of them live in densely populated districts, but in some countries this method is just used in order to reach students in rural and remote areas.

Students vary considerably in their *age*. At OUHK the youngest is 20 and the oldest 72 years old (Annual Report, 2004–2005, p. 69). This may be typical for all open universities. Sarah Guri-Rosenblit (1999a, pp. 67–69) compared the students of five open universities – UKOU, UNED, OUI, FU and AU – and presented the following findings.

The median age ranges from 30 to 34 years. This is to be expected because open universities are principally universities for adults. However, 10–30% of the student population of UNED, OUI, and FU are under 24 years. Some open universities wish to relieve overcrowded conventional universities and admit younger students as well. For instance, at the OUI the under-24 age group constituted 46% in 1996 (Guri-Rosenblit, 1999a, p. 69), and in **CCRTU**, which is to provide higher education for the great number of school leavers who remain unemployed, the median age was 24 years in 1994 (Runfang and Yuanhui, 1994, p. 70).

With regard to their *educational background* four groups of students can be distinguished: (1) second-chance students who are studying for the first time in their life with or without formal entry qualifications; (2) graduate students who wish to continue their studies after some years in gainful employment; (3) those in possession of several degrees who are eager to acquire another one; and (4) ambitious persons in senior positions in business and industry who wish to qualify themselves for their further professional development. It is telling that at OUHK 57.5% of the students are managers and professionals (Annual Report, 2004–2005, p. 69). All these data indicate that the educational level of open university students is on average markedly higher than at conventional universities. The composition of their students varies from country to country due to different economical and cultural differences.

As to *gender*, women are slightly in the majority at OUI and AU and in the minority at UKOU and FU (Guri-Rosenblit, 1999a, 67). They are in the majority at Shanghai CRTU (Information Brochure, 1997, p. 11) and OUHK, at 54.6% (Annual report, 2005). On the other hand women, at OUT are, at 13%, markedly in the minority (Bhalalusesa and Babyegeya, 2002, p. 584).

With regard to their status as students, open universities distinguish between graduate and postgraduate students, full-time and part-time students, single-course students, and continuing education students. Open universities that teach via radio and television broadcasts are also open to the public and often have millions of free listeners and free viewers – an unexpected realization of the slogan "Education for All".

Students in full employment usually enrol in degree *programmes* as *part-time students*. In Britain, the Open University dominates in the provision of part-time undergraduate places for adults. They have established twice as many of these places as all other institutions in the country (Runfang, 1997, p. 22). In Germany, a third group comprises students at *conventional* universities who are eager and permitted to use the pre-prepared course material of the FU and to acquire experience in studying at a distance.

Many students enrol in *non-degree education and training programmes*, for instance at UNED, UKOU, FU, PNU, UPOU, KNOU, and STVU. They usually constitute a considerable section of the student population, in particular in developing countries. In order to learn something about the nature of these programmes we can take a look at those at STVU: "In-service training", "Professional qualification", "Leadership Education", "Continuing Education", and "Programmes for the Aged" (Information Brochure, 1997, p. 15). BOU even has the explicit mandate to emphasize non-formal education. Here, half of the students are enrolled in non-formal studies in order "to make them more conversant with things that touch their lives: health, hygiene, nutrition, agriculture, environment and what not!" (Ali, 1997, p. 158). This open university performs the task of improving the living conditions of its students. In order to remind us of the humanitarian mission of distance education, Vice Chancellor Ali (1998, p. 158) reports that "a focus of the BOU is on the needs of the poor and underprivileged people of society".

15.9 FACULTY

It is not easy to describe the teaching academics at open universities. It is not possible to draw a clear picture of them, because teaching is organized in an industrialized way in the form of "systems approach" (Moore and Kearsley, 2005, p. 33). This means that the task of teaching is divided into several functions, which are performed by different persons: subject matter specialists, mass media experts, educational technologists, tutors, mentors, moderators, counsellors, markers of tests or essays, evaluators, external course-writers. All of them cooperate and convey a diverse picture of the teaching process.

The *academic faculty* is naturally of overriding importance. The professors and their staff are not only "subject matter specialists", but also and often mainly responsible for research in order to produce new knowledge. This is important for gaining recognition and prestige in professional associations and the scientific community. Both enhance the quality of teaching, motivate students, and improve the status of the institution. Usually a considerable core of fully-fledged and full-time professors with tenure is responsible for the academic development of their disciplines. If there is only a small nucleus of full-time professors who are compelled to cooperate with changing part-time academics from other universities, the university can neither develop its own scientific accomplishment and academic identity, nor establish its academic reputation.

Full professors conduct their research, train their academic staff, and take an active part in university committees very much in the same way as at conventional universities. But they differ entirely in their teaching behaviour. They do not lecture, but engage themselves in course writing together with experts of educational technology in "course teams", or together with members of their staff. They are challenged by quite another teaching–learning environment. They are ready and able to deal with adult students and to take into account their special living conditions, to work with technical media (of necessity and not as an option), to explore new virtual learning spaces, to develop a favourable attitude to professional upgrading and lifelong continuing education, and to be an active, adaptive part of a complex technical-organizational system. Above all, they are to develop a habit of cooperating with experts both inside the university, especially with educational technologists, instructional designers, and outside, in particular external course writers and leading representatives of their disciplines.

15.10 ECONOMICS

Open universities were founded in the belief that they will be able to cater for far more students than conventional universities at lower costs. This belief was based on the experiences of first-generation correspondence education, which distributed self-teaching printed material with minimal or no two-way communication. This led to the idea that mass production and mass distribution of objectified self-teaching material must have the benefit of economies of scale. Because open universities are able to enrol students from a wide catchment area, they are able to reach great numbers, often even extraordinarily great numbers, of students, and can reap the benefit of economies of scale.

This belief was partly confirmed by the experience that the industrialization of teaching and learning could bring the cost down. Ford managed to mass-produce first-rate cars in an industrialized way that were relatively cheap and could be sold to broad sections of society. In a similar way it was thought that education could be mass-produced and distributed and become available for broader sections of society at lower costs. This is exactly what takes place at large open universities. The assumption that this industrialized form of teaching is cost-efficient is furthermore substantiated by the argument that teaching great numbers of students without providing and maintaining the expensive infrastructure of campuses at many places must be particularly cost-efficient.

The idea of the cost-efficiency of mass instruction is convincingly supported by a Chinese experience: an eminent professor lectures in front of several TV cameras in a studio run by the Central Radio and Television University in Beijing knowing that more than several hundred thousand students everywhere in this huge country are listening to him attentively and taking notes at the same time.

All these notions were reaffirmed by Sir John Daniel (1999, p. 39), the second vice chancellor of the Open University in Britain, who speaks of the "superior cost effectiveness of the mega-universities, but not necessarily of the smaller distance teaching institutions". A government review of the UKOU compared the costs per graduate with three other institutions in 1991. "The UKOU costs were significantly lower, between 39% and 47% of the other universities' cost..." Daniel referred also to similar results at the Centre National d'Enseignement par Correspondence, Radio and Télévision in France and CCRTU.

However, it is extremely difficult to quantify the cost-efficiency of open universities (Hülsmann, 2000; Rumble, 2004). It is necessary to examine the development cost, unit cost production, distribution cost, and support cost, and relate these to the number of students. Much depends on the kinds of media that are used. If open universities base their teaching mainly on print, radio, and audio cassettes, they are likely to profit from scale economies (Rumble, 2004, p. 45). If they employ new and advanced media, develop intensive support systems and tutorial services, and integrate optional or obligatory labour-intensive face-to-face meetings in study centres, the advantage of scale economies will shrink. During the recent past the cost structure of *online learning* has also influenced the costs of distance education. Seemingly it will be "nearer to face-to face models than first- and second-generation models of distance education with their economies of scale" (Rumble, 2004, p. 48).

15.11 HISTORICAL CONTEXT

The significance of open universities can be demonstrated by interpreting their emergence as the beginning of a new era in the history of distance education. It is an era of profound innovation, which affects pedagogical, political, and social aspects of higher education.

It is possible to distinguish three generations of distance education. They are important in their special functions within the then prevailing systems of education.

The *first* generation is characterized by the establishment of *correspondence schools and colleges*. This began in the first half of the nineteenth century. After the University of London was established as a purely examining body (Bell and Tight, 1993, p. 29) a number of correspondence colleges were established that prepared its external students for taking their examinations there. This approach was an amazing innovation, a revolution even, as technical machines and equipment (printing office, postal services, and railways) were used in order to make higher education possible for them. Correspondence education was organized mainly in the same way as the industrialized production processes and was commercialized right from the beginning. It filled gaps and compensated for deficiencies in the educational system, which in many cases did not adapt to the transformation from artisan to industrialized work processes. Pedagogically it was based on two main media: printed courses and the exchange of letters. This kind of distance education prevailed from the middle of the nineteenth century until today. But the status of this kind of instruction, "both in correspondence schools and university departments, was fragile and often the subject of harsh criticism" (Keegan, 2004, p. 101).

The *second* generation of distance education, which started in the 1970s, is characterized by the establishment of *open universities* (See Reddy, 1988; Mugridge, 1997; Guri-Rosenblit, 1999a). They caused a second pedagogical revolution and "heralded a new era in the history of distance education" (Reddy, 2001, p. VII). They adapted teaching and learning systematically and consistently to the general technological advances of their time. They restructured and enhanced distance teaching. In order to demonstrate this structural change they dropped the designation "correspondence education" and adopted the term "distance education".

The very fact that nearly all of them are not commercial, but autonomous institutions established and funded by governments and that they cooperate with popular mass media added enormously to their prestige and freed them from the often-negative image of old-fashioned and outworn correspondence education. An important contribution of open universities is that they paved the way for the emergence of the next generation of distance education as they gathered and consolidated broad and first-hand experience with distributed, asynchronous, mediated teaching of part-time adult students.

This *third* generation is characterized by the swift rise of *digitized distance education,* which began in the 1990s. The exploration of virtual learning spaces led to new ways of information, communication, and collaboration. It represents major adaptations of higher education to the requirements of the knowledge society. Open universities are now at a premium because they promote the difficult process of breaking with tradition and designing something new with more relevance to the post-industrial knowledge society. They enabled the emergence of virtual universities and corporate universities.

As with generations of people, these three generations of distance education do not replace each other, but continue to remain important side by side, as well as in an integrated way, for quite some time. Each generation topped the previous one by its unforeseeable and unexpected new practicability and success.

15.12 PERSPECTIVES

The establishment of about 50 open universities since the 1970s is an outstanding phenomenon. It shows in a nutshell that higher education can be totally innovated with regard to its goals, groups of students, curricula, methods of acquiring knowledge, media, and advanced technologies. It is significant to see that these open universities represent a new type of university that is in accordance with marked political and educational trends: the democratization of university study, mass higher education, lifelong education, adult higher education, professional qualification, collaboration with the labour market, and globalization.

Strategies for future developments are of course discussed in the institutions themselves but also in their networks and associations. There are a number of influential organizations existing in the world on regional and global level (Observatory, 2004). I only want to name three of them explicitly: the European Association of Distance Teaching Universities (EADTU) and the Asian Association of Open Universities (AAOU) on regional level and the International Council for Open and Distance Education (ICDE) on global level, the latter having formal consultative relations with UNESCO. The proceedings of their conferences show strong experimental spirit, pioneering zeal, and pedagogical determination. They present research results achieved in open universities which indicate the growing importance of flexible and online learning in future open universities. A global survey of respective current open university research is published by the International Research Foundation for Open Learning in Cambridge (UK).

The very fact that the concept of the open university was adopted and realized by so many governments all over the world shows that the new model of a university corresponds with changes of post-industrial virtualized knowledge society. Another indication of success is their sustained growth, which has led to the emergence of a significant number of mega-universities (Daniel, 1998, 1999). Börje Holmberg (1996, p. 567) predicted that "most probably the future will see a further strengthened open university movement". Ten years later we can see that he was right. Even more, open universities are in the process of moving "from the margins to the centre stage of higher education" (Guri-Rosenblit (1999b, p. 281).

The specific experiences of open universities will have special relevance when the "University of the Future" comes to be designed and implemented. Conventional universities have also started to provide distance education courses and to explore the possibilities of virtual learning spaces. This means that they are entering the realm of distance teaching and enriching their arsenal of pedagogical media and methods. There will be a trend towards a new type of university. The University of the Future will probably be based on four fundamental pedagogical approaches: distance education, online learning, scientific discourses face-to-face, and many forms of intensified professional support, all of them have already been developed, tested, experienced, and consolidated at open universities. Open universities "can be viewed from many respects as forerunners in facing and dealing with challenges that confront higher education systems all around the globe" (Guri-Rosenblit 1999b, p. 281). So far, open universities have been trendsetters. According to Sir John Daniel (2001, p. 135), open universities and open learning will have a central role in the twenty-first century. The ultimate general goal will be the gradual transformation of the university into an institution of independent learning (Peters, 2004, p. 203).

REFERENCES

Ali, M.S. (1997). Bangladesh Open University. In *Founding the Open Universities* (I. Mugridge) New Delhi: Sterling Publishers, (pp. 152–165).

Annual Report. (2004–2005). *The Open University of Hong Kong.*

Anweiler, W. (1963). Fernstudium in der Sowjetunion. *International Review of Education,* 8(3–4), 224–226.

Arnold, R. (1996). Entgrenzung und Entstrukturierung der Hochschulen durch das Fernstudium. Paper presented to the Symposion Studium online, November 26/27 at the University of Kaiserslautern.

Bates, T. (1982). Trends in the use of audio-visual media in distance education systems. In *Learning at a Distance: A World Perspective* (J.S. Daniel, M.A. Stroud, J.R. Thompson, eds) Edmonton: Athabasca University.

Bell, R. and Tight, M. (1993). *Open Universities: A British Tradition?* Buckingham: The Society for Research into Higher Education and Open University Press.

Bhalalusesa, E. and Babyegeya, E. (2002). The Open University of Tanzania. In *Towards Virtualization: Open and Distance Learning* (V.V. Reddy and S. Manjulika, eds) New Delhi: Kogan Page, pp. 581–595.

Bittner, W.S. (1920). *The University Extension Movement.* Washington: Government Printing Office.

Bittner, W.S. and Mallory, H.F. (1933). *University Teaching by Mail.* New York: Macmillan.

Commission = Commission on Non-Traditional Study (1973). University by Design. San Francisco: Jossey-Bass.

Cross, K.P. (1981). *Adults as Learners.* San Francisco: Jossey Bass.

Curran, CH. (1996). Distance Teaching at University Level: Historical Perspective and Potential. In *University Level Distance Education in Europe Assessment and Perspectives.* (G. Fandel, R. Bartz, and F. Nickolmann eds). Weinheim: Deutscher Studienverlag, pp. 19–32.

Daniel, S.J. (1998). Knowledge Media for Mega-Universities: Scaling up New Technology at the UK University. Keynote speech at 1998 Shanghai International Open and Distance Education Symposion. Shanghai Television University: Symposion Abstracts, 3.

Daniel, S.J. (1999). *Mega Universities and Knowledge Media.* London: Kogan Page.

Daniel, S.J. (2001). At the Conference on ICDE Asia Regional Conference at Indira Gandhi National Open University, September 3, 2000.

Eisenstadt, M. and Vincent, T. (1998). *The Knowledge Web.* London: Kogan Page.

Garcia-Garrido, J.L. (1988). The Spanish UNRD: One way to a new future. In *Open Universities: The Ivory Towers Thrown Open* (G.R. Reddy, ed.). New Delhi: Sterling Publishers, pp. 200–214.

Gould, S.B. and Cross, K.P. (eds). (1977). *Explorations in Non-traditional Study.* San Francisco: Jossey-Bass.

Guri-Rosenblit, S. (1999a). *Distance and Campus Universities: Tensions and Interactions: A Comparative Study of Five Countries.* Oxford, UK: Pergamon.

Guri-Rosenblit, S. (1999b). The agenda of distance teaching universities: Moving from the margin to the center stage of higher learning. *Higher Education* **37**, 281–293.

Holmberg, B. (1960). On the method of teaching by correspondence. Lunds universitets aarsscrift, N.F. Avd. 1 Bd. 54. Nr. 2. Lund: Gleerup.

Holmberg, B. (1977). Distance education: A survey and bibliography. In: *International Encyclopedia of Educational Technology, 2nd ed.* (T. Plomp and D.F. Ely Eds). Oxford: Pergamon press.

Holmberg, B. (1996). Open Universities. In: *International Encyclopedia of Educational Technology*, pp. 562–567.

Houle, C.O. (1965). Correspondence instruction. In *Encyclopedia Britannica* (W.E. Preece Ed.), 14th ed. Vol. VI. Chicago: Encyclopedia Britannica, Inc., pp. 544–545.

Hoyer, H. (1998). A Virtual University. Challenge and Chance. In Universities in a Digital Era. European Distance Education Network, EDEN Conference Proceedings. University of Bologna, 24–26 June.

National Student Staisfication Survey (2006). In Education Guardian.co.uk. Guardian unlimited. http://education.guardian.co.uk/students/tables/0,1574395,00.html

Hülsmann, T.H. (2000). *The Costs of Open Learning: A Handbook.* Oldenburg: Bibliotheks- und Informationssystem der Universität Oldenburg.

Huan Quingyun (ed.) (1997). Shanghai Television University. Shanghai, 25 Fu-Xing Road, China: Shanghai Television University.

Jarvis, P. (1981). The Open University Unit: Andragogy or Pedagogy? *Teaching at a Distance*, **20**, 24–29.

Kade, J. (1989). Universalisierung and Individualisierung der Erwachsenenbildung. *Zeitschrift für Pädagogik*, **XXXV**(VI), 789–808.

Keegan, D. (1993). A typology of distance teaching systems In *Distance Education: New Perspectives* (K. Harry, M. John and D. Keegan) London: Routledge, pp. 62–76.

Keegan, D. (1995). Teaching and Learning by Satellite in a European Virtual Classroom. In *Open and Distance Learning Today* (F. Lockwood, ed.) London: Routledge, pp. 108–117.

Keegan, D. (2000). *Distance Training. Taking Stock at a Time of Change.* London: Routledge Palmer.

Keegan, D. (2004). The Competitive Advantages of Distance Teaching Universities. In *Papers and Debates on the Economics and Costs of Distance and Online Learning* (G. Rumble, ed.) Oldenburg: Bibliotheks- und Informationssystem der Universität Oldenburg.

Keegan, D. and Rumble, G. (1982). Distance Teaching at University Level. In *The Distance Teaching Universities* (G. Rumble and K. Harry eds). London: Croom Helm, pp. 15–31.

Leibbrandt, G. (1997). The Open Universiteit of the Netherlands. In *Founding the Open Universities. Essays in memory of G. Ram Reddy* (I. Mugridge, ed.) New Delhi: Sterling Publishers, pp. 101–108.

MacKenzie, N., Postgate, R. and Scupham, J. (1975). *Open Learning Systems and Problems in Post-secondary Education.* Paris: The UNESCO Press.

McCormick, R. (1982). The Central Broadcasting and Television University, People's Republic of China. In *The Distance Teaching Universities* (G. Rumble and K. Harry, eds). London: Croom Helm, pp. 54–71.

Moore, M.G. (1976). *The Cognitive Styles of Independent Learners.* Ph.D. Dissertation. University of Wisconsin-Madison.

Moore, M.G. (1977). On a Theory of Independent Study. *Papiere No. 16.* Hagen: Zentrales Institut für Fernstudienforschung der Fernuniversität.

Moore, M.G. (1993). Theory of transactional distance. In *Theoretical Principles of Distance Education* (D. Keegan, ed.) London: Routledge, pp. 22–38.

Moore, M.G. and Kearsley, G. (2005). *Distance Education. A Systems View.* Belmont, CA: Thomson Wadsworth.

Mugridge, I. (ed.) (1997). *Founding the Open Universities: Essays in Memory of G. Ram Reddy.* New Delhi: Sterling Publishers.

NAEB = National Association of Educational Broadcasting (1974) Report.

Observatory. (2004). Regional and International Distance Learning Associations. In The OBSERVATORY on borderless higher education, Key Issue, November 2004, http://www.obhe.ac.uk/cgi-bin/keyresource.pl?resid=26

Paine, N. (ed.) (1988). *Open Learning in Transition.* Cambridge: National Extension College Trust.

Penalver, L.M. (1979). Venezuela: Universidad Nacional Abierta. In *Report of the Conference of Executive Heads of Distance Education*, Walton Hall Milton Keynes: The Open University, pp. 46–50.

Perry, W. (1976). *Open University.* Walton Hall, Milton Keynes: The Open University Press.

Perry, W. (1997). The Open University. In *Founding the Open Universities. Essays in memory of G. Ram Reddy* (I. Mugridge, ed.) New Delhi: Sterling Publishers, pp. 121–126.

Peters, O. (1964+1965). *Der Fernunterricht.* Weinheim: Beltz.

Peters, O. (1967) *Das Fernstudium an Universitäten und Hochschulen.* Weinheim: Beltz.

Peters, O. (1968). *Das Hochschulfernstudium.* Weinheim: Beltz.

Peters, O. (ed.) (1971). *Texte zum Hochschulfernstudium.* Weinheim: Beltz.

Peters O. (1979). Federal Republic of Germany, Fernuniversität. In *Report of the Conference of Executive Heads of Distance Education* Walton Hall, Milton Keynes: The Open University, pp. 18–22.

Peters, O. (1981). *Die Fernuniversität im fünften Jahr.* Köln: Verlagsgesellschaft Schulfernsehen.

Peters, O. (2001). *Learning and Teaching in Distance Education.* London: Kogan Page.

Peters, O. (2003a). Learning with new media in distance education. In *Handbook of Distance Education* (M.G. Moore and W.G. Anderson, eds) Mahwah, New Jersey: Erlbaum, pp. 87–112.

Peters, O. (2003b). Models of open and flexible learning in distance education. In *Planning and Management in Distance Education* (S. Panda ed.). London: Kogan Page, pp. 15–30.

Peters, O. (2004). The Transformation of the University into an Institute of Independent Learning: In *Distance Education in Transition.* (O. Peters) Oldenburg: Bibliotheksund Informationssystem der Universität Oldenburg, pp. 203–214. First published in Evans T. and Nation D. (eds) (2000). *Changing University Teaching* London: Kogan Page, pp. 10–23.

Rajasingham, L. (2004). In *Search of a New University Paradigm in a Knowledge Society. ZIFF-Papier 124.* Hagen: Zentrales Institut für Fernstudienforschung der Fernuniversität.

Ramanujam, P.R. (1995) *Reflections on Distance Education for India.* New Delhi: Manak Publications.

Ramanujam, P.R. (2002). *Distance Open Learning. Challenges for Developing Countries.* Delhi: Shipra Publications.

Reddy, G.R. (ed.) (1988). *Open Universities: The Ivory Towers Thrown Open.* New Delhi: Sterling Publishers.

Reddy, M.V.L. (2001). *Towards Better Practices in Distance Education.* New Delhi: Kanishka Publishers.

Rumble, G. (1992). *The Management of Distance Learning Systems.* Paris: UNESCO International Institute for Educational Planning.

Rumble, G. (ed.) (2004). *Papers and Debates on the Economics of Distance and Online Learning.* Oldenburg: Bibliotheks- und Informationssystem der Universität Oldenburg.

Rumble, G. and Harry, K. (1982). *The Distance Teaching Universities.* London: Croom Helm.

Runfang, W. (1997). China's Radio and TV Universities and the British Open University. A Comparative Perspective. *ZIFF Papiere 104.* Hagen: Zentrales Institut fpr Fernstudienforschung der Fernuniversität.

Runfang, W. and Yuanhui, T. (1994). *Radio and TV Universities.* Nanjing, Jiangsu: Yilin Press.

Ryan, S.T., Scott, B., Freeman, H. and Patel, D. (2000). *The Virtual University.* London: Kogan Page.

Schelsky, H. (1963). Einsamkeit und Freiheit. Idee und Gestalt der deutschen Universität und ihrer Reformen. Reinbeck: Rowohlt.

Shale, D. (1987). *Innovation in International Higher Education: The Open Universities.* http://cade.athabascau.ca/vol2/Shale.html

Simpson, O. (2005). E-Learning and the Future of Distance Education in the Markets of the 21rst Century pp. 1–5. In EDEN 2005 Annual Conference Proceedings. Helsinki University of Technology.

Tiffin, J. and Rajasingham, L. (1995). In *Search of the Virtual Class. Education in an Infoormation Society.* London: Routledge.

Tiffin, J. and Rajasingham, L. (2003). *The Global Virtual University.* London: Routledge.

Tunstall, J. (ed.) (1974). *The Open University Opens.* London: Routledge and Kegan Paul.

Unger, Claus: E-Learning at the FernUniversität in Germany: The presence, the transition, the future. Paper delivered at the Conference of ODL Universities of the European Union organized by the Hellenic Open University. March 2003. Proceedings on CD-ROM.

Wedemeyer, Ch.A. (1971). Independent Study. In *The Encyclopedia of Education* (L.C. Deighton, ed.) New York: Free Press.

Wedemeyer, Ch.A. (1977). Independent Study. In *International Encyclopedia of Higher Education* (A. Knowles, ed.) San Francisco: Jossey-Bass, pp. 2114–2132.
Wedemeyer, Ch.A. (1981). *Learning at the Back Door. Reflections on Non-Traditional Learning in the Lifespan.* Madison, Wisconsin: The University of Wisconsin Press.
Yibing, W. (1998). Challenges Facing as well as Opportunities for Open Universities. In *Open Education Research.* A Special Selection for English Edition '99, pp. 1–8. Shanghai: Shanghai TV University.

Chapter 16

Transforming Doctoral Education Through Distance Education

Terry Evans

16.1 INTRODUCTION

This chapter draws on my two main areas of academic work over the past 30 years: distance education and doctoral education. I have been involved in distance education for all of this time as practitioner, scholar and researcher. I have been a doctoral supervisor (adviser) of distance students for about 20 years, and in the past decade, I have been a manager, scholar and researcher of doctoral education.[1] In bringing these two areas of work together for this chapter, I am intending to sensitise the distance education community to an area of educational practice that is special to university life (doctoral education) and which is fundamental to the future of contemporary societies: the development of people who can undertake research to produce new knowledge. The practical basis of my experience is based in Australia, so I shall draw particularly on Australian examples. However, my enquiries and research show that Australia has – mostly in a taken-for-granted way – blended distance education with doctoral education, that is, especially, off-campus, part-time doctoral studies. I shall make reference to various forms of earned doctorate, in particular PhDs and the professional doctorates. However, most emphasis will be given to the former because it is the PhD that dominates doctoral education: historically, numerically and culturally.

It is important to state that PhDs and many other doctorates have as their defining characteristic the production of a significant and original piece of scholarship. In PhD programmes in the UK and its ex-colonies – such as Australia, Hong Kong, New Zealand – PhDs are awarded solely on the basis of the (often external) examination of a thesis. The thesis is expected to report on a work of original scholarship and research that contributes, or has the potential to contribute, significantly to knowledge in the discipline or field of study. In other parts of the world, there is often preliminary coursework that is required before a candidate proceeds to their research and dissertation. However, the final examination of the dissertation (often by an internal committee) also conforms to requirements of originality and significance. Some candidates work on topics that have been provided by their supervisors, especially in the laboratory sciences; however, most PhD students pursue topics that are largely or solely of their own choosing. For distance educators, this is a major difference in the nature of the curriculum and the pedagogy. In effect, a candidate selects and structures their own "curriculum", and the pedagogy is based on "resource-limited" learning. This is somewhat exaggerated to make the point. Arguably, there is a curriculum centred around the knowledge, skills and values of research conducted in the candidate's field, through a topic being studied (researched) of the candidate's choosing. There is also pedagogy. This is typically based on individual "supervision" of the candidate's learning through research (Green and Lee, 1995, 1999). As is discussed later, this combination of a relatively open curriculum and a relatively individually tailored pedagogy may be seen as a high form of independent learning (Evans, 1998) which distance education can extend further still.

A review of the literature on distance education shows that doctorates have rarely been a topic of consideration. The field has been concerned with work in distance education involving the schooling, vocational and professional areas, and undergraduate and postgraduate coursework programmes. Doctoral programmes, especially PhDs, which constitute the vast majority of such degrees, have not been of much concern. This chapter shows that, in effect, there has been a considerable amount of distance education practice in doctoral education but that it is usually not named as such. It considers the work that has been done in distance education concerning PhDs and professional (or coursework) doctorates and argues that there is scope in the future for more consideration within distance education of the conceptualisation and development of doctoral pedagogies and practices "at a distance".

The particular focus of this chapter is on doctoral education and its relation to distance education. If a review of the literature on distance education shows that doctorates have rarely been a topic of consideration, then the literature on doctoral education shows that distance education has rarely been a topic within it. Although there is increasingly mention made of the use of the media that distance education has deployed so well: print, telephone, videoconferencing and online media, Sunderland (2002, p. 235) observed in the UK "... though they are not usually thus represented, PhD programmes are and have often been done through 'distance learning', i.e. by those doctoral students who are part-time and not resident on or near the campus of the university at which they are registered."

This chapter demonstrates the importance of distance education to doctoral education in Australia, and it argues that this is something that has been largely invisible or unrecognised for its importance within Australian educational provision. It is also significant that internationally, even amongst other nations with long histories of distance education, Australia is unusual, in that the main distance teaching universities [which are all dual mode, that is, they have both on-campus and off-campus (distance education) enrolments] have fostered "off-campus" doctoral education, in particular, within the professional disciplines. It will be argued that there are also examples of both real and de facto doctoral education at a distance internationally and that the signs are there that these forms are expanding and that distance education practitioners may have an important role to play in shaping the design, implementation and quality assurance of doctoral programmes offered at a distance.

16.2 OFF-CAMPUS DOCTORAL EDUCATION

In Australia – as is the case of other nations such as Canada, New Zealand, the USA – forms of distance education have been used for schooling, college and university education since the beginning of the twentieth century (Bolton, 1986). It has grown and developed over the past century as the needs, contexts and media have changed (Evans and Nation, 2003). Although there is relatively little literature from within the distance education field on doctoral education, the practice of doctoral education at a distance has occurred for some years, both formally and especially informally. Pearson and Ford show that, from outside of distance education, there has been a good deal of de facto distance education practised in doctoral education (Pearson and Ford, 1997; Pearson, 1999). This has occurred from the commencement of PhD programmes in Australia in the 1940s. For example, many candidates undertook their library work, fieldwork, writing and so on "off-campus" (even overseas), although they were not formally enrolled as "external students". Some candidates were formally undertaking their doctoral research in other institutions, such as the military, or in overseas universities, galleries etc. (Evans and Tregenza, 2004).

The first doctoral programme formally offered at a distance appears to be the Doctor of Education (EdD) programme at Nova University in the USA in the early 1970s. However, in contrast to the British-style thesis only PhDs, the Nova programme was based substantially on coursework together with a small research project. Therefore, the coursework components could be provided in the resource-based way of distance education at the time, together with face-to-face support. Such distance programmes were particularly criticised in the general education community (see White, 1980), although some distance educators would have (and still do) encountered similar criticisms of their other non-doctoral courses. Nova's EdD programmes have survived for three decades (see http://www.schoolofed.nova.edu/home.htm) and have developed with the times and the media available. However, as discussed below, doctorates at a distance (and other courses) are still viewed with suspicion in many contexts and nations, although much less so in Australia.

In Australia, Deakin University, the University of New England (UNE) and the University of Queensland were the first to offer masters degrees by coursework programmes at a distance in the early to mid-1980s (Bynner, 1986). As mentioned previously, some doctoral candidates may have been de facto distance education candidates for some or all of their candidature back to the 1940s when the first PhD programmes were offered in Australia. However, locating the first instance of the formal offer of external doctoral enrolment to PhD candidates is difficult to determine without some specific archival work in the likely universities. Deakin University offered off-campus doctoral study by the early 1980s, in effect, through the provision of part-time candidature married to its off-campus operations, in particular its library services – an essential aspect of doctoral studies (see McKnight, 2003, for a discussion of Deakin's "guiding philosophy" for enabling all students to use the library). It is also possible that at least UNE or the University of Queensland or the University of Western Australia did similarly to Deakin before this. In particular, the Universities of Queensland and Western Australia had established PhD programmes and were involved in off-campus enrolments for other courses soon after the Second World War (Bolton, 1986).

A related matter concerned with off-campus enrolment was whether a university permitted part-time enrolment or not. The University of Melbourne (the first Australian university to award a PhD, in 1948) did so from the outset (Evans and Tregenza, 2004); however, Monash University did not do so until the mid-1970s, a decade after its inception. Barnacle and Usher (2003) and Evans (2002) have explored the particularities and contexts of part-time doctoral study in Australia, and those in distance education would recognise the comparisons with research on distance education (part-time) students. One of the features of doctoral pedagogy is the interpretation of the supervisor as "looking over the shoulder" of the candidate (Green and Lee, 1995, 1999). This surveillance view contributes to peoples' concerns over both part-time and especially off-campus candidature. Full-time, on-campus candidature is favoured because it enables closer monitoring and surveillance. However, it is questionable how many supervisors actually do pay this level of attention to their candidates. Another concern raised over part-time and off-campus candidature is the "absence" of the candidate from the "research culture" of the department in which candidature is "located". In this view, research culture is reified and located physically in the lab, library or departmental tearoom. It is not understood as a social and intellectual entity that is shared principally through language, however, mediated. In much the same way that distance educators have fostered learning communities through language and media (print, radio, videoconference, online discussions, etc.), research cultures can be shared similarly. Indeed, arguably, scholarly communities have been "global" communities, principally by sharing texts (articles, books, etc.) and occasionally discussing them at international seminars and conferences. Therefore, the "absence" of the candidate from the supervisor's place of work does not mean that they are disconnected from the principal means through which research culture is represented and shared. This is especially the case in these days when email and other online facilities are ingrained in both on-campus and off-campus life for both teachers and students.

Turning to Australia as an example of a nation where doctoral education at a distance has gradually evolved and become widespread, if not widely recognised, Table 16.1 shows the distance education (called "external") doctoral enrolments in Australia for selected years. As Evans et al. (2006) show, the Australian (federal) Government is principally responsible for university education, although most individual universities are established under State acts of parliament and formally report to their particular State government. However, successive Australian governments have over recent decades increasingly monitored and influenced universities. The volume of data required by the government to be formally reported by universities on prescribed "census dates" has increased, apparently in line with computers' capacities to store, manipulate and transmit data. An advantage is that a year or so after the data are received, some of them become available via the appropriate government department's website, along with a steady stream of policy documents, statements, reports and so on (see http://www.dest.gov.au). It is this source that has enabled the data in Table 16.1 to be presented. The institutions

Table 16.1: External Doctoral Enrolments in Australia, Selected Institutions 1989, 1996, 2004 (source, DEST)

University	*1989*	*1996*	*2001*	*2004*
Adelaide	8	44	70	48
Charles Sturt	n/a	61	184	168
Curtin	0	0	261	425
Deakin	42	259	346	309
Monash	0	0	72	127
Murdoch	9	28	20	40
QUT	n/a	15	47	79
Tasmania	7	0	5	5
UNE	77	196	226	230
UniSA	n/a	27	243	115
USQ	n/a	18	69	62
UWA	10	0	0	0

selected are those with the major numbers of distance education doctoral candidates in one or more of the selected years (2004 is the latest year for which data were available). The first selected year, 1989, corresponds to the end of what is known in Australian education circles as the "pre-Dawkins" period. Dawkins was the Minister of Education in the late 1980s and he was responsible for major reforms to both higher education and distance education. His reforms led to the Colleges of Advanced Education (CAEs, these were established in the 1960s as "polytechnic" colleges where students typically undertook 3-year "sub-degree" diplomas; by the late 1980s, they were offering bachelors degrees and even some masters degrees) being transformed into new universities, or amalgamated into reformed universities. Therefore, these would have been well established by the next selected year: 1996. Charles Sturt University, Curtin University, Queensland University of Technology (QUT) and the University of South Australia (UniSA) were CAEs, not universities, in 1989 and, therefore, were not permitted to enrol doctoral students at that time. The following selected year, 2002, marked the commencement of the Research Training Scheme (RTS).

The RTS represented a reduction in the total number of government-funded domestic places and the application of a formula to allocate new research student places based significantly (50%) on the numbers of completions (graduations) of previous candidates. This led some universities to endeavour to predict and select "successful" candidates at the time of application for a place; often part-time students were seen as more risky because they had higher dropout rates (no surprise to distance educators here). However, those part-time students who complete do so on average with less candidature time than full-time students. Because external students are mostly part-time and more likely not to complete, some universities have shied away from enrolling them and given preference to on-campus, full-time students (although this is more expensive in terms of infrastructure costs, see Evans, 2002). Therefore, 2001 represents the last year before the RTS was introduced and 2004 is the latest year where its effect can be measured on the available data. (The full effect is expected to take until about 2007; for a discussion of the RTS and how it operates see, Evans et al., 2006)

Table 16.1 shows that the major universities in off-campus doctoral study in 1989 were Deakin and UNE: two of the most significant distance teaching universities in Australian history. These two universities sustained significant provision of doctoral education at a distance throughout the entire period. Deakin expanded its enrolments at a greater rate. This was probably due to it large increase in size as a consequence of its amalgamation with two CAEs in the early 1990s and UNE's less successful amalgamation experience. Over the past decade, a "Group of Eight (Go8)" universities in Australia prosecuted itself as the Go8 leading "research-intensive" universities. Of these, Adelaide University and Monash University are the only two Go8 universities currently involved in doctoral study at a distance (Monash University inherited a significant distance education capacity when it merged with a CAE, Gippsland Institute of Advanced Education, in the early 1990s). Two other Go8 members, University of Western Australia (UWA) and the University of Queensland, were noted for their external studies in earlier times, and UWA had a modest number of external doctoral enrolments in 1989. Three "new" (post-Dawkins) universities have developed significant profiles in doctoral education at a distance: Curtin University, QUT and UniSA. Each of these universities, as CAEs, had significant distance education capacity before they became universities. The Royal Melbourne Institute of Technology (RMIT) was an important distance education provider in Victoria as a CAE. It became a university but lagged behind Curtin, QUT and Unisa in its development of doctoral education at a distance. (It also gradually eroded its distance education capacity after Dawkins's reforms to distance education, which sought to concentrate provision in fewer universities.) RMIT had twenty-one external candidates in 2001 and fifty-one in 2004, too few to be tabulated here. The University of Tasmania had a consistent, but tiny, involvement in doctoral education at a distance in its State since 1989.

Table 16.1 also shows that there is some reduction in numbers in 2004 for five of the selected institutions. This may well be a consequence of the RTS which has led some universities to favour full-time, on-campus students. The national external doctoral enrolments totals for the above years are as follows: 173 (1989), 730 (1996), 2,270 (2001) and 2,454 (2004). These figures show that there was a rapid growth until 2001, and then a more modest increase to 2004. The aforementioned effects of the RTS toward reducing domestic doctoral places and part-time/external enrolments, in particular, are mediated by the increase in the number of international candidates. The RTS is for domestic students only: Australian and New Zealand citizens and Australian permanent residents. In recent years, there has been a marked increase in the numbers of international doctoral candidates studying at a distance; these mask what may well have been a reduction or stabilising of domestic enrolments by 2004. The increase in such international enrolments is partly a reflection of the limited or non-existent opportunities in some nations for doctoral study at a distance. If this changes, one might expect the growth and even the total numbers of international doctoral candidates studying at a distance to decline.

As mentioned in the introduction, the notion of supervision at a distance is seen as problematic in many nations. Some Asian governments, for example, have restrictions on the recognition of PhDs undertaken at a distance. Some, such as Taiwan, require mandatory periods or proportions of study on campus before recognition is given. However, there are problems with both the assumptions behind this approach and the practical aspects of administering it. The assumptions about the superiority or necessity of good study occurring in contiguous, face-to-face contexts are typical of those with which distance educators have had to deal for years. In the same way that for undergraduate study the uncritically accepted superiority of face-to-face tuition ignores the weaknesses of "instructing" didactically in the lecture theatre, the uncritically accepted superiority of on-campus doctoral study ignores its weaknesses, too. On-campus doctoral study may typically be a fairly solitary experience with the occasional meeting with a supervisor. However, all doctoral study these days is increasingly mediated by online media, with supervisors and candidates emailing each other and exchanging drafts of candidates' writing whether they are along the corridor or across the globe. A major concern is that the benefits (for the home nation, community, employer and/or the candidate) of candidates undertaking their doctoral research (that is, the fieldwork and data collection) in their own country are lost if it is mandatory that the candidates have to remain at the overseas institution. It may be argued that for many fields of study – perhaps less so for the laboratory-based sciences – there are many benefits to being flexible with doctoral enrolments (on-campus or distance education, full-time or part-time) during a candidature to enable the best circumstances for the needs of the research, the research context and the candidate. However, this sort of flexibility may be seen as too risky by some governments and universities.

16.3 RISKING DOCTORATES AT A DISTANCE

To some extent, every research project involves risks that need to be managed. Some risk has to be taken to invest time and resources into the planning and execution of a project in order to reap the potential (but not guaranteed) benefits. In the case of research on animals or with/on humans, there are also the associated ethical considerations (in most Western nations) of the harms and benefits of the research on the researched and to humanity in general. To the extent that doctoral education necessarily involves research that makes a significant and original contribution to knowledge, then it engages with these "risky" matters (Evans, et al., 2005, pp. 6–8). However, in the case of doctoral education at a distance, a significant part of the resistance to it comes from the concern over its "risk management" at a distance. The need for "supervision" to be conducted suggests, as noted above, that the supervisor needs to "look over the shoulder" or "keep an eye on" the candidate. In North American universities, amongst others, the term "supervisor" is not used, but "adviser" is used instead. This has a different connotation and appears to convey that less responsibility is taken for what the candidate does. However, the roles of each formally do not appear to be greatly different, although in North America a "committee" overseas the candidature, which may dilute the adviser's individual responsibility in comparison with a "British-model" supervisor.

Beck and Giddens are amongst several theorists who have characterised contemporary society as a "risk society" [Giddens, 1991a; Beck, 1992; Giddens and Pierson, 1998 or, with embedding of globalisation, a "world risk society" (Beck, 1999)]. This is not so much that life has become riskier but rather because the "rise of science" led people to assume that eventually societies would be able to manage (eliminate?) risks or at least ameliorate their consequences. A greater understanding of the complexities of global natural, social, economic and physical relationships has not entirely displaced this assumption, but it has led to organisations, such as universities, endeavouring to engage in forms of risk management, even become risk averse, for fear of reputational, financial or other damage (McWilliam et al., 2005; McWilliam et al., 2007). Doctoral studies is one of the areas that is exposed to such risk management (or aversion). Typically, the organisation reacts by individualising risk, in the case of doctoral education, especially by defining and entering into formal written agreements over candidates' and supervisors' responsibilities and obligations. Bauman (1998, 2001), Beck (1992, 1999) and Giddens (1991a,b) see the individualisation of risk and its bureaucratisation (the organisation defines and describes all the risks "you" must accept if you want to use in its service) as part of the ways societies or communities react when exposed to the forces of contemporary globalisation. There is a propensity for shifting the responsibilities for risks to individuals.

The "ethics process" in universities is a good example of both the bureaucratisation and the individualisation of risk: shifting the responsibilities for risks to individuals. In theory, the ethics committees of universities are expected to ensure that the research conducted by its staff and students is in the interests of society or humanity and that the "harm" (which may mean giving time to complete a questionnaire or an interview, and rarely means any real physical or mental harm) done to participants is worthy of the benefits. Such harm (involvement) is expected to be reasonable for the circumstances understood by the participants (with some exceptions) before they consent to participate and recorded and reported in a way that (normally) protects their identities. In practice, ethics committees (in several nations including Australia) have become risk management committees that exhibit varying degrees of risk aversion. Candidates who undertake their research "at a distance" from the university, and not under the gaze of their supervisor, may be seen as riskier prospects than those who are seemingly in full view.

The pertinence for distance education lies not just in the practical consequences but, perhaps ironically, because the media which have helped shape contemporary distance education are those, as Beck (2004) suggests, that "tele-mediate" social, cultural and economic flows between the local and the global, consequently challenging or dissolving the significance of nation-state boundaries. In this sense, the media and circumstances which create the potential of and for doctoral education at a distance are also those which create the circumstances in which universities are apprehensive of their risks for damage if a doctoral candidature "goes wrong". There is clearly much more control over a typical coursework student at a distance than there is over the "independent" learning of a doctoral student pursuing their research. However, to return to an early point, doctoral education, like research, always has risks associated with it. Doctoral education is partly about candidates learning how to design and manage a piece of research within the practical circumstances of a doctorate and within the intellectual circumstances of their field of study. The management of the risks at a distance may be viewed more appropriately as the management of a good-quality doctoral experience at a distance. A good quality doctoral experience is, presumably, much less "risky" than a poor one, in that the candidates are supported to undertake a good piece of research and produce a good thesis or dissertation. Arguably, the potential of such good research and theses undertaken at a distance is greater than for those undertaken on-campus. This is because research and its dissemination is already located in the wider, more diverse and "richer" world beyond the university's walls and is not constrained within them. It might well be a good research question to investigate the nature, quality and impact of doctoral research undertaken at a distance in comparison with doctoral research undertaken on-campus.

The author's involvement over many years in doctoral education at a distance provides an example of how matters of sustaining a good-quality doctoral experience at a distance may be achieved. The context in which this occurs will be discussed critically below to illustrate how the seemingly difficult and even questionable practice of doctoral education at a distance has been achieved over a long period and is now just seen as "normal practice" within the Faculty of Education at Deakin University.

16.4 DOCTORAL STUDIES IN EDUCATION AT DEAKIN UNIVERSITY

The Faculty of Education at Deakin University fosters off-campus doctoral education as an explicitly valued aspect of its practice (see Evans, Davis and Hickey, 2005). In the late 1970s, the Faculty (then School) of Education was at the vanguard of the provision of offering PhDs at a distance (in addition to on-campus) in the University: its first doctoral graduates were in 1984. There are currently about 145 candidates enrolled in its PhD programme which has two pathways: the "traditional" single project leading to a thesis and a "professional" workplace-based multi-project leading to a folio (with a dissertation and other forms of research dissemination). About 85 percent are off-campus and part-time, and many candidates live overseas, including North America, Europe, the Middle-East, Asia, Papua New Guinea and New Zealand. International students represent about 15 percent of the total enrolment, some of whom are studying in their own country, but most of whom are full-time, on-campus candidates. The domestic students (that is, Australian citizens or permanent residents and New Zealand citizens) are mainly off-campus and may be studying in Australia or overseas. Most of the doctoral candidates are mid-career professionals with ten or more years' experience and who work full-time in the education or training sectors. Many undertake research within and related to their own workplaces as part of their doctoral studies. In contrast to the non-professional disciplines in the University, none of the students are young graduates who have some straight from their undergraduate degrees. As noted previously, about 45 percent of doctoral students are part-time, yet they are largely ignored and undervalued in government and in institutional policies (Evans, 2002).

As is commonly the case in Australian universities, doctoral candidates are required to conduct their research and scholarship under the supervision of a principal supervisor and usually with an associate supervisor. The doctoral candidate–supervisor relationship is understood as an intensive, if somewhat solitary, experience whether on campus or at a distance. However, in the Faculty of Education, we have worked to bring typical distance education means together with what are more North American "coursework" approaches to doctoral pedagogy to build a doctoral community within the Faculty.

It draws substantially on collaborative work in order to moderate the isolation and solitariness of the candidate–supervisor relationship, especially for distance students. For experienced distance educators, the strategies deployed are far from innovative; indeed they reflect aspects of what has long been seen as good practice in distance education: intensive residential schools (see Morgan and Thorpe, 1993), telephone tutoring (see Thompson (now Challis), 1990) and online collaborative learning (Stacey, 1999). However, deploying these approaches in doctoral education, as we have been doing for about 15 years, was innovative at the outset and still remains "progressive" in this field.

Daniel and Marquis (1979) argued over a quarter of a century ago that good distance education is about "getting the mixture right" between interaction and independence. This is particularly the case in doctoral education, although the latter has a much stronger emphasis. The candidate has to pursue individual original scholarship (searching online library databases, solitary reading, thinking, analysis and writing) and communicate this to, and even become inducted into, a scholarly community, and also their profession and sometimes the general community. Therefore, from the outset the Faculty's distance education doctoral pedagogy necessarily involved a "mix" of interaction and independence: face to face and through communications media. However, again like all good distance education practices, matters of access and equity needed to be considered before deciding to require particular elements of participation by the candidates. A major consideration in this regard concerns the doctoral colloquium. For nearly 30 years, it has been a requirement that doctoral candidates attend their doctoral confirmation colloquium in person, usually on-campus at the University. At the colloquium, a candidate discusses their substantial (50–55 pages) doctoral proposal with a panel of five academics, including their supervisors, and occasionally other "critical friends". This occurs about one-third of the way through candidature (at about 18 months for part-time candidates) and represents a significant event and "rite of passage" for all doctoral students. The proposal is read carefully by the panel members prior to the event and they, especially the non-supervisors, come with questions, comments and advice that they wish to share and discuss on that day. Although attendance is compulsory for the candidate, occasionally a panel member may participate by teleconference or videoconference. The requirement to attend the colloquium – this is the only formal attendance requirement during candidature – does create an access barrier. However, the benefits of attending in person are seen to outweigh the difficulties involved. In particular, reading the body language of panel members and the intensive "de-briefing" with the supervisors afterwards are important qualitative components that cannot be experienced as well through communications media. There is also the matter of the occasional candidate who requires counselling about an unsuccessful outcome or a requirement for substantial revisions. It is recognised that these things are better handled responsibly face-to-face and in the knowledge that there is an array of support service available if required.

Obviously, arranging attendance at a doctoral colloquium for part-time students, especially those living interstate or overseas, requires co-ordination. The candidate's schedule is considered first and arrangements are made with the other panel members (one of whom is normally from outside the University) to suit this. International (that is, fee paying) part-time students, who are located overseas, have their return airfare paid by the Faculty. Other students meet their own costs of attendance. Although this is the only mandatory attendance at the University, commonly candidates make several visits during their candidature, sometimes studying on-campus for a few weeks or months.

Distance educators are often aware that a brief period of on-campus study, especially with other off-campus students, is highly valued by students. Although they are studying at a distance to be "liberated" from the classroom, a brief period of on-campus study is often an intensely rewarding educative experience and period of social contact with fellow students (Moodie and Nation, 1993; Morgan and Thorpe, 1993). Since 1994, the Faculty offers an annual residential summer school over 4 days in February for doctoral students on its Geelong campus. Since 2000, a residential winter school has been provided in New Zealand to cater for the significant number of students there (about 25) and any other students who wish to attend: in particular, northern hemisphere international students who find it useful to attend in their summer break. All candidates, on-campus and off-campus, are encouraged to attend these events, but they are not compulsory. Typically, about sixty candidates attend the summer school and about twenty attend the winter school. The programme for these schools involves staff presentations and discussions on matters to do with completing a doctorate (reviewing the literature, using SPSS, ethics, conducting interviews, writing a thesis, etc.), candidates' presentations and "roundtable" discussions on aspects of their doctoral work; staff presentations on aspects of their research or methodology; and social events, drinks and meals for conversation and "networking". The evaluations of the summer and winter schools are typically highly positive, and a real effort is made by staff to keep improving and revitalising the events so that distance students who come each year always have something useful and stimulating.

Over the past 15 years, the Internet has been used increasingly to provide support and resources for doctoral students. In the early years, due to concerns about some students lack of access, use of such facilities was optional. Since 2002, it has been mandatory for candidates to have access and make use of the Internet for their doctoral work. A range of listservs and webpages are used to promote communication between candidates and supervisors, in both social and academic forums. However, the most substantial development in these respects occurred in 2002 with the introduction of an online seminar programme called Doctoral Studies in Education (DSE) (http://education.deakin.edu.au/dse). This programme supports the candidate (and supervisor) around a sequence of core seminars that are required of all candidates. there are also optional research issues seminars (on methodology, research practices, etc.) and occasional seminars (research presentations by guests, staff and candidates). The seminars are "located" within the discussion or tutorial "spaces" of normal forms of online education software (The Faculty has used First Class, WebCT and, now, Moodle for this purpose). They are asynchronous discussions facilitated by a staff member over a 6-week period (occasional seminars are usually shorter). The core seminars focus on "generic skills and knowledge", such as, identifying and reviewing literature, doctoral proposal writing, research ethics. In addition, they also provide an induction into doctoral study and help to ensure that all doctoral graduates are familiar with online media for study, research and communication. An open discussion space and a blog space are elements of the DSE site and enable other forms of "free-flowing" discussion and contact between candidates. Although the compulsory elements are well "attended", and particular optional seminars likewise, the open spaces are less well subscribed. The nature of the busy professional, family and doctoral lives of the candidates probably makes it difficult to find time to "just chat", although, as noted above, this form of social contact is appreciated in the restricted time at a summer or winter school.

The Faculty is considering requiring all final year doctoral candidates to convene their own online seminar on an aspect of their PhD research. This will provide an opportunity to present online – a new skill for many and one we think all doctoral graduates should possess – and to share their ideas and findings with others. Doctoral candidates who convene their seminars will also benefit from having comments from the participants that may help them refine their thesis in some way. Additionally, they will provide role models to new doctoral candidates participating in the seminars, in terms of both the substance of and approach to their doctoral writing and the use of online media for research dissemination and discussion purposes.

The DSE site also provides candidates with access to information about other candidates, staff, research activities, research groups, publications, ethics, funding and conference opportunities and so on. These resources are essential for all candidates whether on-campus or at a distance. However, for the latter, it is essential to have a central "place" (online) to go to find resources required at specific points of time, without being dependent on another person being at work at a desk at the University (often in a different time zone to the candidate). In 2004, The Faculty extended its connections to include doctoral graduates through the Faculty of Education Doctoral Alumni Network (FEDAN). Here, an e-newsletter is circulated to all alumni members containing information about research and training-related activities, as well as profiles and information from previous and current candidates. There are also FEDAN events at summer and winter schools and at major research conferences locally and overseas. FEDAN can be seen as another subset of the Faculty's doctoral "distance" networking activities, which has both online and "real" presences.

Distance educators are likely to recognise that the DSE represents a particular blend of fairly conventional educational practices that have been deployed in distance education in recent years, although less so in developing nations where the infrastructure is less well developed. However, the use of residential schools has become less common in distance education as the pressure on costs and staff and students' time has increased. Doctoral educators are likely to recognise that this blend is innovative in doctoral education, especially before 2002, and that most doctoral students would still not be able to engage with such a range of educational practices because of the domination of traditional face-to-face practices in doctoral education.

16.5 CONCLUSION

It is perhaps not surprising that distance education is a matter that is rarely overtly considered in the doctoral education policy or scholarly literature or that doctoral education is rarely considered in the distance education literature. There is an important element of distance education practice buried in the enrolments of doctoral students in many Australian universities. Indeed, the DEST enrolment figures show that every Australian university has enrolled "external" (distance education) doctoral students at some time between 1989 and 2004. Some universities, especially Deakin and UNE, have enrolled significant numbers of external doctoral students each year since 1989. These data show that, at least at the formal level of enrolment, doctoral candidates have been enrolled at a distance in widespread and long-standing fashion in Australia. It is likely that Australia is somewhat unusual in these respects. However, the work of Pearson and Ford (1997) in Australia shows that there has been an enormous amount of de facto "open and flexible" doctoral study in Australia that is not captured in these enrolment figures. The regulations of even the oldest universities, such as Melbourne and Sydney, have allowed (full-time, on-campus) candidates to be flexible in their attendance and other requirements in order to complete their doctoral work, such as studying at other libraries, experimenting in outside laboratories or fieldwork in remote locations. It is arguable, therefore, that distance education is behind most, if not all, doctoral candidates' work irrespective of whichever university they are enrolled in or whatever country.

On this basis, it may be contended that doctoral education could benefit with more distance educators, especially those with research and doctoral education experience, moving into doctoral education with a view to enhancing and researching doctoral practices at a distance. To do so, it is necessary to understand the particular nature of doctoral scholarship and research and not merely attempt to transplant existing coursework undergraduate or postgraduate approaches. In particular, as has been illustrated through the Deakin University Faculty of Education experience, it is likely that effective practices will be those that develop communities of doctoral scholars through collaborative learning and through the presentation and critique of doctoral work (Evans, 1997, 1998; Barnacle, 2004). From this experience, although this may not suit all circumstances, which includes doctoral students scattered around the world, a mixture of distance education media and strategies together with face-to-face encounters seems to work well. However, it seems clear that there is scope for more creativity, and for more research, to explore new approaches to doctoral study at a distance.

NOTE

1. Some of the argument in this chapter arises from my research and scholarship with colleagues on both distance education and doctoral education. In particular, I acknowledge the various contributions to my ideas of Carey Denholm, Barbara Evans, Alan Lawson, Peter Macauley, Heléne Marsh, Erica McWilliam, Daryl Nation, Margot Pearson, Kevin Ryland, Peter Taylor and Karen Tregenza, Some of the research I have undertaken with these colleagues has been funded by the Australian Research Council and Deakin University.

REFERENCES

Barnacle, R. (2004). A critical ethic in a knowledge economy: Research degree candidates in the workplace. *Studies in Continuing Education*, **26**(3), 355–367.

Barnacle, R. and Usher, R. (2003). Assessing the quality of research training: The case of part-time candidates in full-time professional work. *Higher Education Research & Development*, 22, 345–358.

Bauman, Z. (1998). *Globalization: The Human Consequences*. Cambridge: Polity Press.
Bauman, Z. (2001). *Community: Seeking Safety in an Insecure World*. Cambridge: Polity Press.
Beck, U. (1992). *Risk Society: Towards a New Modernity*. London: Sage.
Beck, U. (1999). *World Risk Society*. Cambridge: Polity Press.
Beck, U. (2004). The cosmopolitan turn. In *Social Theory* (N. Gane, ed.), Vol. Continuum, London, pp. 143–166.
Bolton, G. (1986). The opportunity of distance. *Distance Education*, 7(1), 5–22.
Bynner, J. (1986). Masters teaching in Education by distance methods. *Distance Education*, 7(1), 23–37.
Daniel, J.S. and Marquis, C. (1979). Interaction and Independence: getting the mixture right. *Teaching at a Distance*, **14**, 29–44.
Evans, T.D. (1997). Flexible doctoral research: Emerging issues in professional doctorate programs. *Studies in Continuing Education*, **19**(2), 174–182.
Evans, T.D. (1998). Research as independent learning: Emerging issues in supervising postgraduate researchers in their professional contexts. In *Improving Student Learning: Improving Students as Learners* (C. Rust, ed.), Oxford Centre for Staff and Learning Development, Oxford Brookes University, University of Strathclyde, pp. 377–384.
Evans, T.D. (2002). Part-time research students: Are they producing knowledge where it counts? *Higher Education and Research and Development*, **21**(2), 155–165.
Evans, T.D. and Nation, D.E. (2003). Globalisation and the reinvention of distance education. In *The Handbook of Distance Education* (2nd Edition) (M.G. Moore and W. Anderson, eds), Mahway, NJ: Lawrence Erlbaum and associates, pp. 767–782.
Evans, T.D. and Tregenza, K. (2004). *Some Characteristics of Early Australian PhD Theses*. Paper presented at the Australian Association for Research in Education conference, The University of Melbourne, November 29–December 2.
Evans, T.D., Davis, H., and Hickey, C. (2005). Research issues arising from doctoral education at a distance. In *Research in Distance Education 6* (T.D. Evans, P.J. Smith and E.A. Stacey, eds), Deakin University, Geelong. http://www.deakin.edu.au/education/rads/conferences/publications/ride/2004/index.php
Evans, T.D., Evans. B., and Marsh, H. (2006). Australia. In *Forces & Forms of Change in Doctoral Education Internationally* (M. Nerad and M. Heggelund, eds), Seattle: University of Washington Press.
Evans, T.D., Lawson, A., McWilliam, E., and Taylor, P.G. (2005). Understanding the management of doctoral studies in Australia as risk management. *Studies in Research: Evaluation, Impact & Training*, **1**, pp. 1–11 http://www.newcastle.edu.au/group/sir/.
Giddens, A. (1991a). *The Consequences of Modernity*. Cambridge: Polity Press.
Giddens, A. (1991b). *Modernity and Self-Identity: Self and Society in the Late Modern Age*. Cambridge: Polity Press.
Giddens, A. and Pierson, C. (1998). *Conversations with Anthony Giddens: Making Sense of Modernity*. Cambridge: Polity Press.
Green, B. and Lee, A. (1995). Theorising postgraduate pedagogy. *The Australian Universities' Review*, **38**(2), 40–45.
Green, B. and Lee, A. (1999). Educational research, disciplinarity and postgraduate pedagogy: On the subject of supervision. In *Supervision of Postgraduate Research in Education* (A. Holbrook and S. Johnston, eds), Australian Association for Research in Education, Coldstream, Victoria.

McKnight, S. (2003). Distance education and the role of academic libraries. In *Handbook of Distance Education* (M.G. Moore and W.G. Anderson, eds), Mahwah, NJ: Lawrence Erlbaum, pp. 377–386.

McWilliam, E., Lawson, A., Evans, T.D., and Taylor, P.G. (2005). Silly, soft and otherwise suspect: doctoral education as risky business. *Australian Journal of Education*, **49**(2), 214–227.

McWilliam, E., Sanderson, D., Evans, T.D. et al. (2007). The risky business of doctoral management. *Asia Pacific Journal of Education*, **27**(2) (in press).

Moodie, G. and Nation, D.E. (1993). Reforming a system of distance education. In *Reforming Open and Distance Education* (T.D. Evans and D.E. Nation, eds) London: Kogan Page, pp. 130–149.

Morgan, A.R. and Thorpe, M. (1993). 'Residential schools in open and distance education: Quality time for quality learning?'. In *Reforming Open and Distance Education* (T.D. Evans and D.E. Nation, eds), London: Kogan Page, pp. 72–87.

Pearson, M. (1999). The changing environment for doctoral education in Australia: implications for quality management, improvement and innovation. *Higher Education Research and Development*, **18**(3), 269–288.

Pearson, M. and Ford, L. (1997). *Open and Flexible PhD Study and Research*, Department of Employment, Education, Training and Youth Affairs Evaluation and Investigations Program, Canberra. http://www.dest.gov.au/common_topics/publications_resources/All_Publications_AtoZ.htm.

Stacey, E.A. (1999). Collaborative learning in an online environment. *Journal of Distance Education*, **14**(2), 14–33.

Sunderland, J. (2002). New Communication practices, identity and the psychological gap: The affective function of e-mail on a distance doctoral programme. *Studies in Higher Education*, **27**(2), 233–246.

Thompson (now Challis), D. (1990). If it's good for your do you have to swallow it? Some reflections on interaction and independence from research into teletutorials. In *Research in Distance Education 1* (T.D. Evans, ed.), Geelong: Deakin University, pp. 219–229.

White, M.A. (1980). Graduate degrees by external studies: The Nova University programmes in Florida. *Distance Education*, **1**(2), 188–197.

Chapter 17

Innovating with Technology and Structures of Indifference in Distance Education

Christine Spratt

17.1 INTRODUCTION

In the global higher education sector, including distance education, the revolution in information technologies has created "flexibility" and "going online" as well entrenched policy discourses. Policy discourses are not typically "critical", and as such are silent regarding some areas of universities' business, for example the often deeply embedded pedagogical conservatism of academic groups. This chapter draws on case-study data from recent doctoral research to explore the way in which technology innovators engage as social agents within what I characterise as "structures of indifference" (after Sennett, 2001) in the contemporary academy. The doctoral research was framed within the epistemological paradigm of hermeneutic critical inquiry where life history interviewing within the framework of case-study research was the key method. The research undertook an investigation of the lived experience of critical pedagogues as technology innovators in distance higher education. This meant investigating ideas of "becoming" – becoming an academic, becoming a teacher, becoming critical, becoming interested in technology, becoming disengaged and how that was manifested – these concepts of "becoming" demanded an exploration of identity, structure and agency within the contemporary academy. In drawing on aspects of the doctoral research,[1] the intention of this chapter is to highlight several issues that seem relevant broadly across the sector in Australia and globally in distance education and higher education more broadly. Drawing on aspects of the case-based research provides "an evidential boundary within which to discuss key educational issues" (Walker, 2002, p. 120).

The chapter begins by explaining the research context; in doing so, it also offers a brief critique of information technologies in the corporate academy. The chapter introduces key areas of interest, what I call coming to teach with "critical intent" and related views of agency and identity before arguing that technology innovators in distance higher education face considerable personal and professional "costs" when they engage in innovative pedagogical practice given the prevailing ideologies of the contemporary academy. Indeed, the chapter argues that academic agencies of innovation are paradoxically reified and marginalised in ways that creates them as "absent presences" (Kemmis, 1989, p. 33). This has implications for academic agency and identity and the way in which pedagogical work in distance education and higher education may be conceived as the twenty-first century develops.

17.2 THE CONTEXT

17.2.1 Deakin University

The study which underpins this chapter was undertaken at Deakin University from 1998–2001. Deakin University, in Victoria, Australia, was then and is now a dual-mode multi-campus University which presents itself publicly as a corporate citizen committed to flexible learning. As such it teaches both on-campus and off-campus, using a range of online, print and multi-media technologies to support its distance education strategies, to undergraduate and postgraduate students, full time and part time. As a result of several amalgamations over the past 15 years, it includes campuses at Warrnambool and Geelong in regional Victoria (two campuses at Geelong: the Waterfront and Waurn Ponds). Recently, three campuses in metropolitan Melbourne have been rationalised; the major campus in suburban Burwood is the major campus. At the time this research was undertaken (1998–2001), Deakin's private company DeakinPrime [then Deakin Australia] was involved in offering commercial educational services to the private sector, and had its head office in the Melbourne central business district and offices in Geelong, Sydney and Canberra.

While not wishing to labour the process that Deakin University has undertaken to "corporatise" in the past 10–15 years,[2] it is important to contextualise the discussion particularly in relation to the policy discourses that are called upon to inform the University's practices and which create the structures of the "life-worlds" of academic agents engaged in Deakin University's flexible distance education and on-campus pedagogies. When the research that informs the chapter was undertaken, Deakin University had a longstanding international reputation in distance education and in some departments, unique approaches to curricula and curriculum development, for example in the Faculty of Education a tradition of and respected reputation in the area of socially critical curricula; such reputations remain and institutional policy makers have aggressively harnessed the now not so "new" technologies to further advance Deakin's expertise as a distance education provider and its international reputation for innovativeness.

The University's policy discourses remain quite unashamedly the discourses of the market: innovation, flexibility, entrepreneurship and building partnerships with industry. According to its strategic planning framework, Deakin University's vision in 2006 was to be recognised internationally as Australia's most progressive university for the quality, effectiveness and accessibility of its teaching and learning programmes, research in key areas, commercial and educational partnerships and international activities. It states that Deakin's goal is to

> provide excellent teaching in relation to undergraduate, postgraduate and professional development programs of contemporary relevance that are available to students wherever they are located and developed in consultation with potential employers, industry, government and professional bodies.
>
> (Deakin University Strategic Plan: Taking Deakin University Forward, 2006, p. 4)

In its contemporary policy discourses, Deakin University continues to enthusiastically, at an institutional level at least, promote its flexibility and characterises the use of information technologies, "going online", as a major strategic initiative to allow it to continue to "increase the number of units taught with extended use of online technology" and by

> ensuring that Deakin's distance education courses and services set world standards for excellence, are aligned to student needs and make innovative use of technology including, where appropriate, the delivery of the course online; [and] progressively introducing online resources and learning experiences to both distance education and campus based programs to enhance, and where appropriate, transform, teaching and learning.
>
> (Deakin University Strategic Plan: Taking Deakin University Forward, 2006, p. 4)

Deakin University as a dual-mode institution then is not uncharacteristic of its competitors in the current national and international market with flexibility and online learning as strategic discourses. For as Gallagher (2002, p. 1) summarised several years ago in Australia, the higher education sector has grown to reflect these now common key characteristics which also characterise the sector globally, including

> growth in the student body; diversification of student backgrounds and rising expectations of students (most of whom now pay a share of costs); more exacting public accountability requirements on universities, including for planning, performance reporting and quality assurance; increasing reliance of universities on non-government sources of income, especially through expanding involvement in the business of international education; accelerating application of Communications and Information Technology to teaching, learning, research, student services and administration. Associated with those big shifts we [see] several main effects: stronger corporate management of universities; greater instrumentalism in curricula for work-force skilling of graduates; closer research links between universities and industry; more aggressive competition and the beginning of increasing differentiation among universities; improved productivity (higher student throughput for lower unit costs without apparent diminution of quality); increasing threshold capability costs (for infrastructure and expertise); involved in world class research; changing nature of academic work, including a shift from "cottage industry" to "mass production"; specialization of curriculum design and assessment functions, and rising expectations of output and self-generated earnings.

In short, Deakin University presents itself to the world in the first years of the new millennium as a multi-campus geographically dispersed, dual-mode corporate university that has undergone a period of rapid change and innovation since its inception. It has an established reputation as a distance education provider, with an extensive infrastructure to support the mass production of print-based distance education materials and a comparatively robust information technology infrastructure to support a range of electronic and online strategies for pedagogy and administration.

It is important for the arguments of this chapter to appreciate that Deakin University at the time the research was conducted and in the ensuing 5 years has come to characterise the contemporary state of not just corporate "traditional" or predominately face-to-face higher education generally but distance education and open learning institutions specifically. To illustrate this, in an important study, *The Business of Borderless Education*, Cunningham et al. (2000) found that across the not-for-profit and the for-profit adult and higher education sectors in Australia and the United States of America, that "most education providers indicate an intention to employ combinations of delivery mechanisms in the future, for example mixing face-to-face contact with online availability of programs". In the United States, for example, Cunningham and his collaborators found that technology was driving the rapid growth of the distance education market rather than perhaps identified student need, among for-profit institutions (Cunningham et al., 2000, p. 124). Their update to that research (Ryan and Stedman, 2002) argued that

> What has become clearer since the 2000 Report is that quality online education programmes from "brand name" institutions have not delivered cost savings at the institutional level. Staffing costs have increased, reflecting both the longer time teaching staff must spend in interactive teaching, and the expense of technical and administrative support systems.

While traditional universities have corporatised and are "online" in various forms, distance and open universities continue to differentiate themselves through their expertise in teaching with technology and their understanding of the infrastructure needs and costs of large-scale off-campus learning that their distance education histories affords them. A decade ago, Daniel (1996) argued that the distance teaching universities, in particular those with over 100,000 enrolled students (the "mega-universities"), had the capability to "renew" forms of higher education through their interest and commitment to off-campus learning and technology-based teaching "at scale". Subsequently, he has argued that

> open universities and open learning will have a central role in higher education in the new century. Social, economic, political and technological forces are all pulling this form of education to the centre of the policy stage.
>
> (Daniel, 2000)

These ideas are important for those of us in distance higher education committed with Daniel (2000) to the

> democratic educational mission to reach and enthuse an enormously diverse student population; to insist that critical, informed, reflective engagement with the human condition is not a matter for elites or professional experts alone. By urging students always to be sceptical, always to ask questions and never to take things for granted we aspire to lead them beyond information and knowledge to understanding.

However, Daniel's enthusiasm for the mega distance teaching universities does not mean that they do not face complex challenges and that those challenges reflect those heralded by corporatisation in the sector broadly and which the chapter pursues – challenges that are pedagogical and related to the personal and professional challenges for innovative critical academics and which are influenced by the university as "corporation".

17.2.2 Corporatisation in Distance and Higher Education

Corporatising universities adopt the strategies of privatisation and corporatisation to build business acumen at any cost, to reconceptualise their students as consumers and customers and to find clients in the marketplace who can support their work beyond the retreat of State funding for teaching, learning and research. Such tactics are reflected throughout the scholarly discourses of the politics of change in higher education, and one is compelled to agree with Evans and Nation (2000, p. 165) that in accepting globalisation as a given in relation to contemporary social life, one must "... accept that capitalism has won the contest for economic domination, at least for the foreseeable future". New right political and economic agendas of economic rationalism therefore have created the "corporate university" where "utilitarian objectives are explicit and cultural objectives are implicit and democratic reflexivity is lost" (Marginson, 1999, p. 229). In a more recent paper exploring competition in the global higher education market, he has suggested that

> higher education is now situated in an open information environment in which national borders are routinely crossed and identities re continually made and self-made in encounters with diverse others.
>
> (Marginson, 2006, p. 2)

He paints a breathless picture of the sector reflecting Bourdieu's "fields of power" where the sector is "bounded, complex, hierarchical, fragmented contested, product making, subject-forming, [and] continually transforming [as a] world wide arrangement" (Marginson, 2006, p. 2).

One might argue then, that corporate universities like Deakin have succumbed to Habermas's (1987) "technical rationality" where knowledge is seen as an economic commodity, learning as "technique" and academic agency and identity homogenised to reflect the corporate ideal (Barnett, 2000, 2005; Marginson, 2000; Harris, 2005; Churchman, 2006). As universities continue to corporatise and globalise, then institutional change and change management strategies, those largely drawn from the "corporate" sector they wish to emulate, are inculcated into daily life.

Moreover, corporatisation expects the identity of individuals to merge with that of the organisation, a melding of cultures, to transform them as if this is an unproblematic ideal. There is an extensive literature in this field that is critical of the way in which the discourses of organisational structures and reorganisation operate. Casey (1999, p. 1) argues "reorganisation of the workplace, the production of new sets of attitudes, beliefs and behaviour among corporate employees to enable productivity and profitability for the organisation" are the key agendas of organisational change programmes. In many instances, metaphors of "team" and "family" precede discourses of discipline. Weil (1999) has discussed related issues in the context of change in tertiary settings. Such critiques serve to position the re-engineering processes that accompany corporatisation as "devices of control". Casey (1999, p. 13) argues that

> the new corporate culture provides, under the semblance of a caring team-family, and effective disciplinary and control apparatus that requires employees to sufficiently contain the disintegration or mobilisation of ambivalence by its displacement into obsessive compulsion to work and to belong.

Ball (2003, p. 215) has discussed these kinds of ideas in the context of "performativity" where he claims the reformations driven by globalisation which have characterised public bureaucracies including education, "does not simply change what people as educators, scholars, and researchers do, it changes who they are". He describes performativity as

> a technology, a culture, a mode of regulation, that employs judgements, comparisons, and displays as a means of incentive, control, attrition and change – based on rewards and sanctions (both material and symbolic). The performances (of individual subjects or organisations) serve as measures of productivity or output or delays of "quality" or "moments" of promotion or inspection.

Subsequently, he argues that the new performativity wants to "make us up" [our academic identity] differently from before by providing new modes of description for what we do and new possibilities for action' [or agency] (Ball, 2003, p. 217). I draw on Sennett's (1998, 2001) ideas, particularly, in this area in relation to the implications for academic agency and identity subsequently.

17.3 TEACHING WITH CRITICAL INTENT

Critical pedagogy claims to have the capacity to position learners and teachers as collaborators in the political and social life of their experience, to transform their thinking in the fundamental recognition, as Lusted argues (1986, p. 2), that

> knowledge is not just produced at the researcher's desk nor at the lectern but in the "consciousness": through the process of thought, discussion, writing, debate and exchange.

The theoretical and philosophical informants of critical pedagogy are generally accepted as the critical social science of The Frankfurt School especially, Habermas's (1970, 1987, 1988), as well as Freire's (1972, 1998) work. Critical pedagogy is contested by its proponents (Ellsworth, 1989, 1997; Lather, 1998) yet within these contestations, there lies a deep commitment to calls for "pedagogies of possibility" (Simon, 1992) which might be radical, robust, embedded in many forms of social critique and diverse enough to move beyond the contemporary challenges facing a globalised academy.

Academics practising within Lather's "big tent" (1998, p. 487) of critical pedagogy come to their praxis through their biographies and the evolution of their self-identities as academics. We can accept that the paths to critique are often circuitous, and when one arrives at the gate of critical pedagogy, the manner in which it is lived and enacted is embodied, situated and transformative. This is not to suggest that all agencies of critical pedagogy are the same agencies. For academic teachers, coming to ideology critique is a complex integration of intellectual risk taking, of living as a teacher authentically and of developing the capacity for reflexivity. Critical knowing arises in the lived experience of teaching over time, and for many academics, it is embedded in their engagement with the scholarship of practice that is with their engagement with their research and teaching in ways that are complex, creative, intellectual and critical.

Therefore, becoming critical and pursuing critique in higher education is enacted within the dialectic of agency and structure. Engaging with pedagogy as "critical intent" creates a *praxis* oriented form of critical pedagogy where praxis encapsulates the dialectical relationship between theory and practice in action. Critical academics as technology innovators are creative, risk-taking agents often compelled to "work against the grain" (Simon, 1992) within the market structures of the academy which from a pedagogical perspective, remain largely conservative. "Critical intent" in teaching is therefore concerned with building discursive, egalitarian relationships between learners and teachers to effect pedagogic experiences that might lay claim to reflective action and change.

17.4 CONCEPTIONS OF AGENCY AND STRUCTURE

Theories of agency, structure and various forms of an agency–structure dyad are an enduring theme in the social sciences. This includes the theoretical and empirical controversies about the nature of agency and structure respectively and their dualistic relationship. The *nature* of the agency–structure dyad is also one of the most contested concepts in sociology. Generally, in sociology, agency refers to human actors as individuals and structure refers to social systems. Ritzer and Gindoff (1994) provide a useful analysis of the competing views surrounding agency and structure; they make explicit the theoretical interest in the *relational nature* of the two concepts as it has come to dominate the literature on the one hand yet point out the "considerable dissimilarities" (Ritzer and Gindoff, 1994, p. 9) between the nature of the agent and the nature of structure on the other hand. For example, there are differences in the perceptions of agents as "perpetrators of action" in a reflexive manner (after Giddens' agents) and as seemingly more mechanical and dominated by "habitus [as a] source of strategies without being the product of a genuine strategic intent (after Bourdieu)" (Ritzer and Gindoff, 1994, pp. 9–10). The capacity for reflexivity is tightly integrated with Giddens' concepts of discursive and practical consciousness. Reflexive awareness is, according to Giddens (1991, p. 35), "characteristic of all human action" and in the monitoring of action, which is "practical consciousness", there are discursive features.

In conceptualising agency thus, Giddens conceives self-identity not simply as the result of "the continuities of the individual's action-system, but something that has to be routinely created and sustained in the reflexive activities of the individual" (1991, p. 52). It is in the context of self-identity as socially and culturally constructed biographical narratives that the "self as reflexively understood by the person in terms of his or her biography is presented to the world across time and space" (Giddens, 1991, p. 53).

Agency is a dialogical process embedded in time–space where agents

> are positioned within a widening range of zones in home, workplace, neighborhood, city, nation-state and a world-wide system, all displaying features of system integration which increasingly relates the minor details of daily life to social phenomena of massive time–space extension.
>
> (Giddens, 1984, p. 84)

Moreover, agency and structure are mutually constitutive creating a form of social life that is "... continually contingently reproduced by knowledgeable human agents – that's what gives it its fixity and that's what also produces change" (Giddens and Pierson, 1998, p. 90). Agency as knowledgability and the conception of agentic orientations are created in the lived experience of social agents "going on" in everyday life. "Going on" in everyday life acknowledges the ephemeral concept of time–space orientation and the way in which "... actors must continually reconstruct their view of the past in an attempt to understand the causal conditioning of the emergent present" (Emirbayer and Mische, 1998, p. 5).

Sennett (2001, p. 175) explores a form of identity in late modernity that is particularly concerned with "work and home, the street and the office". Here he speaks of the way in which "identity involves a life narrative rather than a fixed image of oneself"; he emphasises that the "ever shifting market reality disturbs fixed pictures of self" (Sennett, 2001, p. 176). Not only this but "agency" creating "voice" as the capacity for interpretive acts enables actors to "go on in everyday life".

In this sense, the university as a public corporation has, in "many instances sought to eliminate layers of bureaucracy, to operate via work teams and work cells ... [yet] ... the effort to create more flexible organisation centralises power at the top" (Sennett, 2001, p. 186). In the context of restructuring Australian universities, Lafferty and Fleming (2000, p. 26) conclude that the way in which management has appeared "as a universalising discourse" has created the "top-down implementation of structural change in universities signalling the simultaneous centralisation of power and devolution of blame". Marginson argues that there is (2000, p. 34).

> a serious deficiency in the norms and models of good governance which have emerged to assist universities in their struggle to stay relevant to contemporary conditions. At a time when universities might have helped to pioneer creative organisational structures and indigenous "learning cultures" capable of great flexibility, they often appear to have surrendered to highly derivative and dependent notions of themselves.

Further, he found in a recent major study of Australian universities that

> over and over again it became apparent that those in positions of greatest influence in the universities were often fixated on simplistic outside norms of good management.

> There was a loss of the sense of the distinctive character of universities, a forgetting of what it is that they do, and what makes them different to other institutions and an undue faith in generic organizational models. There is more here than just benchmarking for excellence. Being useful to business is interpreted as being like business.
>
> (Marginson, 2000, p. 35)

More recently, Barnett (2000, 2005) identifies what he calls the "supercomplexity" of social systems characterised by "contestibility, challengeability, uncertainty and unpredictability" (2005, p. 415), all reflective of the impacts of globalisation and marketisation which for the university threatens it role as the owner and arbiter of knowledge. However, in this supercomplexity, Barnett (2005) sees room for new epistemologies and the "rival discourses as to the meaning and purpose of the university abound". He goes on:

> "managerialism", "enterprise", "market", "collegiality", "access", "standards", "research" and, more recently, "engagement" and "the scholarship of teaching": all these are code words for rival discourses and ideologies. The contemporary university is a discursive swirl of contending ideas as to the proper character of each university itself.

Sennett's (2001, p. 186) interpretation of contemporary managerialist functions in the corporation of late modernity is also relevant where he argues the following:

> A split opens up between the command function and the response function. That means that an inner core will set production or profit targets, give orders for reorganization of particular activities then leave the isolated cells or teams in the network to meet these directives as best each group can. Those outside the elite group are told what to achieve not how to achieve it. The split between command and response often appears at the moments when an enterprise is trying to remake itself, feeling its way towards another structure. In reality, this equates to a *regime of indifference* (my italics).

In effect, the "split between command and execution means that power is retained while authority is surrendered" (Sennett, 2001, p. 189).

How are these kinds of structural and power agendas lived pragmatically and how do social agents engage with them? Sennett (2001, p. 188) argues, based on his research, that in the flexible corporation, workers on what he calls "the receiving end of the split between command and execution" appear to "lose what might be called a work-witness" (p. 188). By this, he means that the worker labours in a "vacuum" forced to make sense of his work in ways that become "internalised". One might then expect that this would allow the worker to contrive a meaning for work, as desired. However, he argues that

> without a witness who responds, who challenges, who defends and who is willing to take responsibility for the power he or she represents, the interpretative capacity of the worker becomes paralysed: [that the] lack of witness diminishes the power of agency.
>
> (Sennett, 2001, p. 188)

17.5 ACADEMIC AGENCIES OF DISENGAGEMENT

The stories that critical teachers as technology innovators in distance education tell about their engagement with technology as early adopters and their progressive disengagement over time resonates with Sennett's (2001) belief that the power of agency diminishes in the presence of institutional indifference. I do not mean, however, that they necessarily become disengaged with technology and the opportunities they perceive it offers their teaching nor that they become indifferent to their agency as teachers, rather they become disengaged from institutional structures and the associated discourses of flexibility and technology. As one participant claimed, "I guess I am disenchanted, the hype is just that and the investment in producing [good technology enabled teaching] too sparse" (P1). While Sennett's (2001) conception seems feasible, it may also be that the "lack of witness" creates a more *strategic* type of agency rather than a *diminishing power of agency*. Perhaps it means that agents, in taking a particular course of action, serve to redirect the power of agency in order to maintain ontological security and their identities as autonomous agents within structures of control. P2 for example, claimed that

> I felt part of and close to various groups of people, tasks and kinds of work (who and which were for me, the "university" i.e. that which was most worthwhile, of quality, congenial) but also increasingly alienated from the institutional facade and from those who took it upon themselves to "represent" the University to others (which I saw as unproductive, self-important). The gap was too much for me to bridge on a daily bases. I got caught between a probably outmoded and idealistic vision of the University and the new bureaucracy that is the contemporary Deakin.

To reiterate, despite the institutional rhetoric of flexibility as a "good" and online technology as a "saviour" that, so it is claimed will create institutional success by any measure, disengagement for critical academics is founded on a conception of themselves as "marginalised" in the settings of what they perceive as "institutional indifference" to the realities of practice. Forms of disengagement can also be seen as a response to the structural tensions that ideologies of technology create for critical teachers in that a "form of productive cognitive dissonance has gone missing: [that is], interaction with others in the environment so that difficulties, differences and dissonance can be renegotiated" as Sennett (2001, p. 188) argues.

As P3 explained

> I'm fed up with being seen as the person who's driving this [technology developments in his School] and being loathed for it, so I'm just going to shut up. One of the professors called my use of technology in my teaching as "cameo". He meant that he wanted a whole-school approach and he didn't want mavericks like me going off and doing my own thing. I happen to see this as a core part of the teaching that I do and if I want to do that, I'm going to do it, so sod you [the professor].

P4 reflected

> I wish sometimes I were not in the vanguard, because it's lonely, the opportunities for meaningful discussion limited, and the chances of technology-frustration over minor matters appallingly high.

P5 commented that

> if I think something is worth doing, I find a way to do it, regardless of the official line. I have to admit to finding it harder and harder to get motivated enough anymore to be subversive.

These comments reflect a sense of dissonance.[3] P5's reference to "being subversive" was in the context of trying to do what he believed was appropriate for his teaching practice rather than what the institution wanted him to do. It was P5's view that what the institution wanted him to do in relation to the evolution of online technologies in teaching[4] was not only impractical but clearly indicated that university executive had no real understanding of new technologies, nor how they might be applied in teaching enhancement or learning improvement. He is sceptical of the institution's capacity to be innovative and has little time for its rhetoric. He demonstrated this by explaining that while his School is "seen and often promoted as open and/or flexible", it runs its off-campus programmes as an extension of its on-campus activity:

> the semesters are the same, the materials are the same, the assessment is the same, and all the deadlines are virtually identical, apart from a two-day allowance for off-campus students to post their assignments. Students have limited choice. All major characteristics of the course are fixed. Flexibility resides in the mode of study and the variety of educational media employed. It is not about flexibility for the learner or their learning.

While the narratives here isolate frustrations with technology, with the "official line", and with being at the forefront, the added demands that being "obsessed with the possibilities of this kind of work" means to their daily lives as academics compounds their sense of frustration over technology matters.

Marginson (2000, p. 40) reporting on a major study of university management in Australia conceded that

> the academic profession needs radical strengthening in the material sense. It is stretched across more functions than before, and at the same time many academics are subject to a form of work intensification that has negative effects on the quality of research and scholarship.

In the context of this chapter, this is manifested in the way in which the self-identities of critical academics change to accommodate the often-overwhelming demands of having become Goffman's "blurs". As P2 describes it,

> The thing that I find most fracturing is the unpredictable nature of the multiplicity of demands. I can work for days on end and have nothing at all to show for it where

> I feel I've achieved very little really. Once there was never a reference that I wrote that I didn't know the kids inside out and I'd know them back to front. You knew your students really well. That's not possible any longer. I have them now for four weeks at a time. The standard load in my School is one hundred and twelve students a semester imagine learning a hundred and twelve students' names a semester! I'd have ten or twelve research students to look after; it's a big load, it's a huge load. I just don't feel that there are spaces in my brain where reflection can happen; it's just mush a lot of the time and you're just running from one demand to another.

The burdens of the "fracturing" of academic work for these critical teachers then are also compounded by their "innovativeness" as early adopters of technology:

P2 articulated this is terms that reflected considerable distress:

> I feel that I've got my nose against a brick wall a lot of the time. If there were someone here who was doing something similar it would be so much easier. I've been the kind of person who has been rapturous about what I do but I'm quickly coming to the point of just tiredness and of feeling that it's not worth the gamble.

P2's belief that her involvement in innovative pedagogy was a "gamble" creates the perception that creative pedagogical risk taking is marginal and unimportant. For P2, her pedagogical interests were creating difficulties for her in relation to the institutional demands for her to be "researching". It was implied institutionally (through a superior administrator) that much of her work was "too pedagogically focussed". She believed that this was an interesting comment in that the institutional rhetoric attempts to support the arguments that "teaching is enriched by research; but that teaching can contaminate research". This kind of institutional demeanour is common (Barnett, 2005; Churchman, 2006) in the contemporary academy. P3 too felt distressed and rather betrayed by the lack of collegiality among his peers in his School.

> I have spent an enormous amount of time and effort developing reasonably high skills in web technologies over the past two years. During that time I have had a fair amount of criticism from other staff and little or no support. Decisions are being made all over the University with little or no understanding of the technicalities involved or the processes in making them work. The demand now is for interactive dynamic websites that take account of the user's configuration, that connect to databases that work as applications rather than static pages. Sadly this is not realised by University decision makers.

P1 explained that

> The University frequently presents the innovation (especially to the outside world) as evidence to justify its image of itself as innovative within this field (a partial fiction in which we readily collude). For me it's interesting because distance education finds itself suddenly taken seriously by those who have previously dismissed it. In the push to flexible delivery, expediency and efficiency is to the fore and educational ideology pushed to the background.

Indeed, there is the perception among technology innovators that "executive is very uncritical of the pedagogies that they imagine are ideally delivered by technology. They seem to think that lectures available electronically are the end of the road and the high point of academic achievement" (P4). Moreover, that "executive doesn't understand the technology nor its potential so how can they make any decisions about it?" (P2).

How then did these critical teachers come to be disenchanted and how did they move to disengagement? What features of their lives as social agents in the academy and the structures within which they work have created the kind of dissatisfaction that the narratives reflect?

Sennett's (2001) ideas have appeal as a means of explaining the relationships that exist between agency and the structures of the contemporary academy. The fracturing of academic work creates uncertainty, and as Sennett (1998, p. 27) suggests, what is "...peculiar about uncertainty today is that it exists without any looming historical disaster; instead it is woven into the everyday practices of capitalism. Instability is meant to be normal". Moreover, he suggests that "detachment and superficial cooperativeness are better armour for dealing with current realities that behaviour based on values of loyalty and service" (Sennett, 2001, p. 28). Giddens (1991, p. 168) has discussed these kinds of issues as the "sequestration of experience" where the "frontiers" of sequestered experience are

> faultlines, full of tensions and poorly mastered forces; or, to shift the metaphor, they are battlegrounds, sometimes of a directly social character, but often within the psychological field of the self.

Giddens discusses the expansion of surveillance as the "main medium of the control of social activity by social means" (p. 149).

Further, he explains that the

> sequestration of experience is in some part the contrived outcome of a culture in which moral and aesthetic domains are held to be dissolved by the expansion of technical knowledge.

In essence, then the sequestration of experience for Giddens creates "fragility" in the framework of ontological security. For critical teachers as technology innovators, it may be that the dissonance they experience as social agents reflects developing "existential crises" as routines that they expect to maintain their day-to-day lives are "radically disrupted" (p. 167).

Their approach to and engagement with new technologies confirms innovative distance educators as pedagogical risk takers who see technology as another potential opportunity to improve and extend their practice, a powerful addition to their existing repertoires of pedagogical expertise. The previous excerpts reveal this and moreover situate the practice of innovators in the "social" and in the problematic complexities of teaching and the desire to innovate to improve practice.

Rogers (1995, p. 132) states that the identification of a problem usually generates the innovation-development process. Moreover, he demonstrates that the generation of problems that initiate innovation are not only political and social but also often serendipitous and that "*much innovation occurs when people talk*, when information is exchanged about needs and wants versus possible technological solutions" (my italics) (p. 137). Here we see this articulated clearly as these teachers recollect the settings of their initial interests. Their interests in technology are embedded in their histories and importantly, those interests remain essentially pedagogical. The practice orientation of engagements with technology occurs when pedagogical practice issues create opportunities for creative problem posing and problem solving.

In their wide-ranging study of problem finding in art, Getzels and Csikszentmihalyi (1976) explored the way in which artists become creative. They concluded that the evolution of creativity is bound up in the way in which artists come to formulate problems and the way in which they solve them. In the context of the arguments of this chapter, their concluding chapter is salutary.

In it they argue the following:

> The ability [to formulate problems] is not based on quantitative superiority in memory, reasoning or conventional cognitive capacities. The ability to formulate problems seems to be a faculty of a different order. It entails a process more in touch with the deeper layers of being than reason alone usually is: it is far more holistic in that it encompasses the person's *total experiential state*. The process is goal directed but it often pursues goals beneath the threshold of awareness. It seeks out similarities between external objects and internal states; it uses symbolic means to express formless feelings, thereby disclosing that which would otherwise go unperceived, articulating what would otherwise remain unarticulated. Problem finding may well be at the origin of creative vision (my italics).
>
> (Getzels and Csikszentmihalyi, 1976, p. 248)

If critical pedagogy can be conceived as a creative scholarship of praxis, it bears some resemblance to the way in which creative artists engage with the acts of problem finding and how they come to innovation. Creative scholars can be conceived as self-actualising persons, "aware of unformulated problems potentially present in the conflicts of their own experience, [and] unlike machines they devise their own programs and work on *discovered problems*" (Getzels and Csikszentmihalyi, 1976, p. 250). Rogers (1995) also highlights facets of the kind of "holistic experiential state" of creative problem posing described by Getzels and Csikszentmihalyi (1976) above as a characteristic of "early adopters" of innovations.

Technology innovators "look like" Getzels and Csikszentmihalyi's (1976, p. 183) creative problem-posing artists,

> who approach their work with personal commitment yet without stereotyped problems in mind, not only produce drawings that are rated more original and of greater aesthetic value, but persist in art longer. It would seem that problem finding is an

> integral part of a person's cognitive style: it is a reliable characteristic. A problem finding orientation seems necessary for creative work.

It is "the diversity and complexity of the intangible social, emotional, and intellectual experiences that produce existential tensions which artists translate into tangible creative problems" (p. 244). Getzels and Csikszentmihalyi (1976, p. 247) conclude that "a creative problem cannot be fully visualised in the 'mind's eye'; it must be discovered in the interaction with the elements that constitute it". Indeed, it can be claimed that "interaction with the elements that constitute it" in the context of critical teachers as technology innovators might equate to the intellectual, cognitive and emotional engagement with practice that so characterises the way in which they "become teachers".

Critical teachers engaged in technology innovations are prepared to take risks in their practice; they look for ways in which they might "shift the nature of academic work away from the sorts of things that Deakin had mostly done, and other people had done too, which is to oversimplify" facets of the curriculum. They look for ways to engage learners in authentic learning that reflects real worlds of work in ways that go beyond calls to active learning and which are more deeply concerned with transformative change, intellectually and socially (e.g. Ellsworth, 1989, 1997; Mezirow, 1991; Brookfield, 1992, 1995; Gore,1992; Lather, 1992; Sholle, 1994; Buckingham, 1998; Green, 1998). They recognise that such worlds are "complex and untidy" as Schön's (1995) "Swampy Lowlands of Practice". They ask critical and difficult questions of themselves in regard to their teaching with technology, for example, "what couldn't it be?" instead of "what is it?" as a necessary step in discovering problems that can be engaged with creatively to develop students' "intellectual autonomy". They see the challenges of new technologies not so much as a "curriculum challenge" but as heralding a need to "reconstruct ourselves as teachers" as P1 argued.

They want to give themselves opportunities within the structural constraints of the corporate institution, to think creatively about "preparing learning materials that engage students and allows them to interact with the material in more focussed ways". Increasingly though, it is becoming more and more difficult to do this as I have already discussed. Critical teachers as early adopters want to create innovative technologically mediated learning environments and opportunities for students that are not only intellectual and social but also, importantly "unbureaucratic". They want to create technologically mediated environments that "allows [them as teachers to do] more small group work" and which also creates complementary opportunities for students to be learning about and using online technology as an "informative and challenging experience". They are prepared to take risks, to make mistakes and to learn; to learn about "how long it takes to do these things, what works well and what doesn't" and importantly, "how much time, effort and other resources it takes to create something that looks trivial" as P2 argued.

In their creativity and innovativeness, they are ambitious about what they want to try and achieve, and they are often frustrated by institutional structures and their "huge workloads" that inhibit what they perceive to be a critical part of their teaching; the capacity to be innovative. They are distressed that they struggle to accommodate the myriad demands on their time where they "find it difficult to meet all [their] commitments and find [they are] constantly disappointed with the result".

Those who are breaking new ground, such as those who have participated in the research that informs this chapter, still feel "marginal", particularly where they do not have around them in the same physical and intellectual spaces, "a critical mass" of people interested in teaching and technology with whom they can interact and engage in intellectual debates that they believe contributes to the generation of ideas and the capacity to sustain themselves intellectually and emotionally. This is seen as part of the sociality of academic work where serendipitous conversations create the "exciting things that can happen with research: casual chats in the corridors" and for many of them while they may have this in their discipline-based research, they "don't have that with [their] teaching".

17.6 CONCLUDING COMMENTS

The chapter has argued that there are deep connections in contemporary discourses of distance and higher education between the marketisation and globalisation of higher education and the contributions information and communication technologies to ideological conceptions of flexibility and going online. I have suggested that the developing agency of critical teachers as technology innovators sees them as pedagogical risk takers committed to innovativeness and that such characteristics define the creative critical scholar. I have argued that the academy as a corporate entity presents itself to agency through structures of indifference where central executive power and authority in distancing itself from the pragmatics of practice serves to alienate and marginalise technology innovators.

The academy is engaged recursively in the risk society of late modernity. Giddens (1991, p. 191) claims that one of the major dilemmas that faces the "self" of late modernity and which nearly "all authors who have written on the self in society, discuss is the assertion that, individuals experiences feelings of powerlessness in relation to a diverse and large-scale social universe"; the corporatised academy as Sennett's (2001) "structures of indifference" reflects this. Policy discourses of flexibility" and going online within it operate ideologically as "the structural features of symbolic forms which facilitate the mobilization of meaning" and as a means of sustaining "relations of domination" (Thompson, 1990, p. 293). As agents of reflexive modernization, technology innovators take action to maintain ontological security in their often turbulent personal and professional lives within such a culture. The costs of the rhetoric of change in the academy therefore are complex and interrelated.

Beck (1992, p. 93) claims that

> The educated person becomes the producer of his or her own labor situation and in this way of his or her social biography ... the educated person incorporates reflexive knowledge of the conditions and prospects of modernity and in this way becomes an agent of reflexive modernization.

Theoretically, this can be explained by Giddens' (1991, pp. 192–193) analysis of the way in which

> powerlessness and reappropriation intertwine variously in different contexts and at various times; given the dynamism of modernity, there is little stability in the relations between them.

The pragmatic actions that social agents take within "structures of indifference" are complex, and they are dictated by their social biographies, the lived experience of practical consciousness, immersion in the culture and structures they reflexively inhabit, the stories they tell to frame their being-in-the world and the stories they tell themselves to understand it. Moreover, as Emirbayer and Mische (1998, p. 22) have suggested, "actors engaged in emergent events find themselves positioned between the old and the new and are thus forced to develop new ways of integrating past and future perspectives". Furthermore, they can "pioneer the exploration and reconstruction of contexts of action" (p. 23). The chapter has argued that as academics, technology innovators acknowledge their synergistic relationship with the structures and structural relationships they inhabit, they are capable of dissociating themselves from the often constraining environment – structures of an "unwieldy bureaucracy" and structures of indifference – to work in ways that are "subversive" so that they can "go on" in everyday life in ways that supports their conceptions of themselves as critical and authentic teachers. Either this or they leave the academy or retreat within it.

While they may be temporally and spatially situated as engaged actors within their schools and faculties, the pedagogical innovativeness and critical intent of academics as early adopters of technology marks them as "other" in sociological terms. Here lies the major paradox. They believe that the University's "off-campus print approaches teaches to the lowest common denominator [within] structures of *in*flexibility" (my italics). They are disinterested in "churning out capable young graduates" as the University's corporate model demands, rather than "educating them". They take action in their everyday lives to "subvert" what they see as educational and technological ideologies of the marketplace. Such beliefs and actions attest to changing ontologies of praxis. They are creative, innovative pedagogical risk takers. The challenge of seeking from their practice the intellectual and emotional capacity to "find a way to work within the system" can be confronting. The system, as they see it, is based on "rational planning models" which denies the "importance of a symbolic imagination" in personal and pedagogical relationships. Living within a regime of indifference, which abrogates responsibility while maintaining power centrally "makes it difficult for us to see ahead", and "persuades us uncritically to be led by the policies (even fantasies) of those with power" towards the ideological wastelands "flexibility" and "going online".

Perhaps it is not too great a leap to see links to the early critiques of distance education offered by Evans and Nation (1989a, 1989b) and Harris (1987); it may well be that the "instructional industrialism" of mass print-based distance learning systems is reconstituted by new media (enabling flexibility and going online) and a globalised economy; each demanding the business of education have a perpetual supply of its standardised products for lifelong learners seeking credentials and corporations that want work-ready graduates.

The discourses of flexibility and going online are lauded within and outside the university, yet the phenomenological lived experience of technology innovators within these discourses sees them and their interests unsupported and often marginalised; they perceive themselves "swimming through molasses" as they traverse the seas of pedagogical innovation within a more pedestrian pedagogical culture. In corporatised organisations, Sennett (2001, p. 187) contends that this amounts to agents working "without recognition", where he argues "efforts to create a more flexible organisation, centralises power at the top" and "shifts responsibility downwards". What this amounts to is all power at the centre that in effect exerts "diminished authority" creating structures which Sennett (2001, p. 187) argues are "regime[s] of indifference".

NOTES

1. Where participant research data is drawn on directly, it is identified P1, P2, P3, P4, P5.
2. The strategic initiatives it has taken to do this are reflected widely in the sector in Australia and abroad and have been discussed extensively in Australia for example by Marginson 1993, 1997, 2000; in Europe and the UK for example in Clark 1999 and Readings 1995 and Tierney 2000 in the US.
3. While the interviews were conducted over an 18-month period, aside from the conversations about their early lives, the discussions rarely took a linear path. It is worth noting that these comments were made towards the end of the interview series and after the protagonists had been engaged in using technology in their teaching at Deakin for at least 3 years. It was also a time at the University when several flexible online learning initiatives were occurring such as the *Online Teaching and Learning Enhancement Project.*
4. He is referring here to one of the executive's "ephemeral" and ill-defined dictates that "all units would be online" by the end of a particular academic year.

REFERENCES

Ball, S.J. (2003). The teacher's soul and the terrors of performativity. *Journal of Education Policy*, **18**(2), 215–228.

Barnett, R. (2000). University Knowledge in an Age of Supercomplexity. *Higher Education*, **40**(4), 409–422.

Barnett, R. (2005). Recapturing the Universal in University. *Educational Philosophy and Theory*, **37**(6), 785–797.

Beck, U. (1992). *Risk Society: Towards a New Modernity*, London: Sage.

Brookfield, S. (1992). The development of critical reflection in adulthood: Foundations of a critical theory of adult learning. *New Education,* **13**(1), 39–48.

Buckingham, D. (1998). Introduction, In *Teaching Popular Culture: Beyond Radical Pedagogy* (D. Buckingham, ed.) London: UCL Press, pp. 1–17.

Casey, C. (1999). Come join our family: Discipline and integration in corporate organizational culture. *Human Relations,* **52**(2), 155–173.

Churchman, D. (2006). Institutional commitments, individual compromises: Identity-related responses to compromises in Australian Universities. *Journal of Higher Education Policy and Management,* **28**(2), 3–15.

Clark, B. (1999). *Creating Entrepreneurial Universities: Organizational Pathways of Transformation.* Oxford: IAU Press and Elsevier Science Ltd.

Cunningham, S., Ryan, Y., Stedman, L. et al. (2000). *The Business of Borderless Education.* Canberra: Department of Employment, Training and Youth Affairs.

Daniel, J. (1996). *The Mega-Universities and the Knowledge Media.* London: Routledge.

Daniel, J. (2000). The University of the Future and the Future of Universities, Keynote Address, *Improving University Learning and Teaching: 25th International Conference*, July 18, 2000, Frankfurt.

Deakin University. (2006). *Taking Deakin University Forward*, Deakin University, Geelong. Retrieved February 17, 2007 from http://www.deakin.edu.au/vc/docs/TDUF06.pdf

Ellsworth, E. (1989). Why doesn't this feel empowering? Working through the repressive myths of critical pedagogy. *Harvard Educational Review*, **59**(3), 297–324.

Ellsworth, E. (1997). *Teaching Positions: Difference, Pedagogy and the Power of Address.* New York: Teacher's College Press.

Emirbayer, M. and Mische, A. (1998). What is agency? *The American Journal of Sociology*, **103**(4), 962–997.

Evans, T. and Nation, D. (eds) (1989a). *Critical Reflections in Distance Education.* London: The Falmer Press.

Evans, T. and Nation, D. (1989b). Dialogue in practice, research and theory in distance education. *Open Learning*, **4**(2), 37–42.

Evans, T. and Nation, D. (2000). Understanding changes to university teaching. In *Changing University Teaching: Reflections on Creating Educational Technologies* (T. Evans and D. Nation eds). London: Kogan Page, pp. 160–175.

Freire, P. (1972). *Pedagogy of the Oppressed.* Harmondsworth: Penguin.

Freire, P. (1998). *Pedagogy of Freedom: Ethics, Democracy and Civic Courage*, (trans. P. Clarke), Oxford: Rowan and Littlefield.

Gallagher, M. (2002). *Modern University Governance: A National Perspective*, Paper presented to the conference 'The Idea of a University: Enterprise or Academy?' Canberra, July 2001. Retrieved February 17, 2007 from http://www.dest.gov.au/highered/otherpub/mod_uni_gov/default.htm

Getzels, G. and Csikszentmihalyi, M. (1976). *The Creative Vision: A Longitudinal Study of Problem Finding in Art.* New York: John Wiley and Sons.

Giddens, A. (1984). *The Constitution of Society: Outline of the Theory of Structuration.* Cambridge: Polity Press.

Giddens, A. (1991). *Modernity and Self-Identity: Self and Society in the Late Modern Age.* Cambridge: Polity Press.

Giddens, A. and Pierson, C. (1998). *Conversations with Anthony Giddens: Making Sense of Modernity.* Cambridge: Polity Press.

Gore, J. (1992). What we can do for you! What can 'we' do for you? Struggling over empowerment in critical and feminist pedagogy. In *Feminisms and Critical Pedagogy* (C. Luke and J. Gore, eds) London: Routledge, pp. 54–73.

Green, B. (1998). Teaching for difference: Learning theory and post-critical pedagogy. In *Teaching Popular Culture: Beyond Radical Pedagogy* (D. Buckingham ed.) London: UCL Press, pp. 176–197.

Habermas, J. (1970). *Toward a Rational Society: Student Protest, Science and Politics* (trans. J.J. Shapiro), Boston: Beacon Press.

Habermas, J. (1987). *Knowledge and Human Interests* (trans. J.J. Shapiro), Cambridge: Polity Press.

Habermas, J. (1988). *On the Logic of the Social Sciences.* (trans. S. Weber Nicholsen and J.A. Stark), Oxford: Polity Press with Basil Blackwell.

Harris, D. (1987). *Openness and Closure in Distance Education.* London: The Falmer Press.

Harris, S. (2005). Rethinking Academic Identities in Neo-Liberal Times, *Teaching in Higher Education*, **10**(4), 421–433.

Kemmis, S. (1989). Absent presences in educational research, revised version of 'Action research revisited', Paper presented to the Annual Conference, American Educational Research Association, San Francisco, March/April.

Lafferty, G. and Fleming, J. (2000). The restructuring of academic work in Australia: Power, management and gender. *British Journal of Sociology of Education*, **21**(2), 257–268.

Lather, P. (1992). Critical frames in education research: Feminist and post-structural perspectives. *Theory into Practice*, **21**(2), 87–99.

Lather, P. (1998). Critical pedagogy and its complicities: A praxis of stuck places. *Educational Theory*, **48**(4), 487–498.

Lusted, D. (1986). Why pedagogy? *Screen*, **27**(5), 2–7.

Marginson, S. (1993). *Education and Public Policy in Australia.* Cambridge: Cambridge University Press.

Marginson, S. (1997). *Markets in Education.* St Leonards: Allen and Unwin.

Marginson, S. (1999). Introduction by Guest Editor: Education and the trend to market. *Australian Journal of Education*, **43**(3), 229–241.

Marginson, S. (2000). Rethinking academic work in the global era. *Journal of Higher Education Policy and Management*, **22**(1), 23–37.

Marginson, S. (2006). Dynamics of National and Global Competition in Higher Education. *Higher Education*, **52**, 1–39.

Mezirow, J. (1991). *Transformative Dimensions of Adult Learning*, San Francisco: Jossey-Bass.

Readings, B. (1995). The University without Culture? *New Literary History,* **26**(3), 465–492.

Ritzer, G. and Gindoff, P. (1994). Agency–structure, micro–macro, individualism–holism–relationism: A Metatheroretical explanation of theoretical convergence between the United States and Europe. In *Agency and Structure: Reorienting Social Theory, International Studies in Global Change* (P. Sztompa, ed.) Amsterdam: Gordon and Breach, pp. 3–24.

Rogers, E. (1995). *Diffusion of Innovations.* New York: The Free Press.

Ryan, Y. and Stedman, L. (2002). *The Business of Borderless Education, 2001 Update.* Canberra: Department of Employment, Training and Youth Affairs.

Schön, D. (1995). Knowing-in-action: The new scholarship requires a new epistemology. *Change* (November/December), 27–34.

Sennett, R. (1998). Why good workers make bad people. *New Statesman, September,* **127**(4406), 25–28.

Sennett, R. (2001). Street and office: Two sources of identity, In *On the Edge: Living with Global Capitalism,* (W. Hutton and A. Giddens, eds) London: Vintage, pp. 175–190.

Sholle, D. (1994). The theory of critical media pedagogy. *Journal of Communication Inquiry,* **18**(2), 8–29.

Simon, R. (1992). *Teaching against the Grain: Texts for a Pedagogy of Possibility.* New York: Bergin and Harvey.

Thompson, J. (1990). *Ideology and Modern Culture: Critical Social Theory in the Era of Mass Communication.* Cambridge: Polity Press.

Tierney, W. (2000). *Developing the High Performance Organisation: Impediments to Change and Innovation in Colleges and Universities*. Retrieved February 17, 2007 from http://www.usc.edu/dept/chepa/documents/papers/Tierney.doc.

Walker, R. (2002). Case study, case records and multimedia. *The Cambridge Journal of Education,* **32**(1), 109–127.

Weil, S. (1999). Recreating universities for beyond the stable state: From 'Dearingesque' systemic control to post-Dearing systemic learning and inquiry. *Systems Research and Behavioural Science*, **16**(2), 171–190.

Chapter 18

THE EVOLUTION OF ASSESSMENT IN DISTANCE EDUCATION

Katy Campbell and Susan E. Gibson

Dr Sandy Cobban is a member of a team developing a set of online courses for degree completion and the continuing professional education of dental hygienists. Her goal is to "give them [dental hygiene students] tools for professional practice and life long learning". She describes a blended course design in which senior students in the post-diploma program complete problem-solving activities, supported by computer conferencing. Students complete an individual activity to find a website that addresses an authentic problem of practice and, using the ethical and critical literacy guidelines that they developed, evaluate the site and post the evaluation in the conference. Since one of Sandy's goals for the learning is to acculturate dental hygienists to a community of learning and practice, she has integrated an authentic project of social activism in the course. She assigns leadership projects for which the participants identify a community health-related issue to which dental hygienists might contribute. During the activity the learners "identify a community agency that is currently addressing this issue, or could be addressing this issue, and work with that agency to develop or propose something that dental hygiene could do to contribute ... ". In this collaborative group activity, she "require(s) them to evaluate the process and the outcome", which includes self- and peer-assessments. During the course, students are also placed with a preceptor in a rural community. The students keep a reflective journal and communicate regularly with each other and Sandy. In this course, assessment is integrated with, and informs, student learning. Sandy's course is an example of assessment-as-culture, a case for which we hope to make in this chapter.

18.1 ASSESSMENT AS CULTURE: TRANSFORMING PRACTICE

According to Rogers (1989), "Despite our most valiant efforts, the taught curriculum and the experienced curriculum are not always the same.... Those things that a student chooses to emphasize, elaborate on, ignore or omit as he or she recounts learnings from a class – the learner's personal meanings – make up the experienced curriculum" (p. 714). As instructors we cannot assume that just because we taught a lesson "well", our learners understood it. Rather, we believe that the learner's experience, not our own, should be the focus of this chapter. How you understand assessment and what you think it is for, is dependent on your goals and your beliefs about how people learn, your personal experiences of being assessed, and your own values about learning.

No one reading this chapter is a stranger to assessment. Assessment is a constant in our lives. We have been assessed thousands of times, before we reach post-secondary education, and for many of us it has not always been a happy experience. Assessment may be formal, through a variety of paper and pencil tests, written essays, oral presentations, displays, skills demonstrations and performances; or non-formal, through observations of behavior, overheard conversations, sense of participation level–but, almost always, it is done *to* us, produces high anxiety, is summative, and only in the best circumstances measures what we've actually learned. We suggest that assessment has been a tool of evaluation, rather than a tool of learning, employed after teaching has taken place and not while learning is occurring. However, in designing e-learning environments, Sluijsmans and Martens (2004) suggest that a shift is occurring from a test culture to an assessment culture, one that emphasizes the integration of instruction, learning, and assessment. They align this shift with a theory of "constructive alignment" (Biggs, 1999; Pellegrino, 2004), where the conditions of learning "should match the learning outcomes that should match the assessment" (Jonassen, 2004, p. 146). In other words, the emerging view of assessment places it at the center of instructional practice rather than at the end. In fact, "situating assessment and evaluation as essentially social activities, influenced by unique affordances and constraints of a particular educational context, is a critical pedagogical component when designing and teaching online courses" (Matuga, 2006, p. 317). According to Morgan and O'Reilly (2006) online learning affords new opportunities for learning, which in turn influence assessment practices that reflect "the drama of multiple meaning, the contrary viewpoint, the search for credible sources, and the elusive nature of 'truth' in a postmodern world" (p. 87).

Distance education offers the higher education community an opportunity to rethink the role of education at many levels and to leverage this opportunity in positive social ways (Zemsky and Massy, 2004). Morgan and O'Reilly (2006) compellingly describe the potency of the online learning community as being "about the drama of the multiple meaning, the contrary viewpoint, the search for credible sources, and the elusive nature of 'truth' in a postmodern world" (p. 87). The transition from face-to-face teaching to e-learning has the potential to appeal to those learners, and their instructors, who are interested in the capacity of this community to contribute to social change. At its best, the virtual learning environment has the potential to be socially transformative in its power to be inclusive, that is to support diverse cultures, languages, work contexts, learning needs and styles, prior experiences, generations, economic circumstances, social contexts, and geographic location. Online learning has the capacity to span diverse online communities, organized communities, and exclusionary in-groups because it encourages an exploration of alternatives for example, breaking down the boundaries of the physical classroom where course participants meet at established dates and times.

This traditional space has had an important socialization function in shaping the nature of interactions that occur within it: members of the community know how to speak and act within these spaces, and understand power relationships by the way these spaces organize interactions, for example, locating the intellectual authority and control in the form of a fixed lectern at the front of the classroom. The learner in this emerging, inclusive context is a member of an international community of learners, and it is by addressing this potential that instructors and administrators can in part enable the transition from face-to-face learning to e-learning. "In other words, the formation of a learning community through which knowledge is imparted and meaning is co-created sets the stage for successful learning outcomes" (Palloff and Pratt, 1999, p. 5).

18.1.1 Purposes of Assessment

Assessments are often used to gatekeep rather than benchmark. But used as a tool for learning, assessment can assist both teachers and learners in diagnosing learning problems, and orient the learning environment to success rather than failure. In other words, we intend to make the case that assessment can and should be a "regular, inherent, and transparent" (Leskes 2002, 2/3, n.d.) process rather than a final product. By that token it involves teachers and learners in an equitable learning partnership based on connecting new learning with personal values and experience, interpretation of experiences in the social contexts in which it occurs, critical reflection that is both self-focused and collaborative, and social engagement and action. Consequently, assessment must "incorporate multiple approaches and a diverse array of assessment methods to accommodate various learning styles and provide continuous feedback . . . with opportunities for relearning and reassessment" (Bartley, 2006, p. 39).

Before making a passionate case for the transformative property of assessment, however, we want to clarify the terms we use throughout this chapter. In our view, "assessment" is not the same as "evaluation", although the terms are often used interchangeably. Assessment involves gathering information about the learner in order to make decisions about the instructional process. It is the process of observing, recording, discussing and documenting the work learners do, and how they do it. Evaluation concerns making a judgment about the learner based on interpretation of the assessment information collected. Reporting is sharing the assessment information and the evaluative judgment based on that information with learners and others who will make further decisions, including whether a learner may progress, on that report. Traditionally, learners have not participated in defining or designing the process.

According to Wiggins (1990) the instructor needs to distinguish between assessment *of* learning and assessment *for* learning. In the former, information in the form of numbers, scores, and marks are usually collected, used to check what has been learned (the learning process is finished), compared with the scores of other learners to make a final determination about standing, and does not involve the learners. Assessment for learning, however, is an ongoing conversation with learners that focuses on improvement, compares the learners to his or her own previous best, and informs the next steps in the learning process (learning is in progress).

18.1.1.1 Assessment of Learning

Instructors who advocate assessment of learning usually take a more traditional right-answer approach to assessment. Foundational to this approach is the belief that there is a body of knowledge to be accumulated. In this view the focus is on the knowledge that learners have acquired, the end product, from the sources of intellectual authority, that is the instructor and the text, and reflecting the authority of other experts. Objective-type questions and written examinations are often the instruments for determining what has been learned. The assessment tools used are instructor-focused and instructor-designed and reflect a one-way pattern of instruction from the instructor to the learner. The learner's role in the right-answer environment is to respond to the instructor's questions, to complete the required instructor controlled work and to "pass the test". The right-answer environment fosters a culture of competitiveness, rather than collaboration, in which the instructors assume the power to distribute success and failure.

We argue that this approach reflects a set of values about the sources of knowledge, who holds it, who shapes it, and who has the right to it. Proponents of this approach argue that the assessment of learning reflects fairness; however, others argue that "fairness does not exist when assessment is uniform, standardized, impersonal, and absolute; rather it exists when it is appropriate . . . " (Funderstanding website). Critical theorists, including those interested in the principles of the universal design of instruction, ask whether these forms of assessment uncritically reflect dominant culture values (c.f. Gordon and Musser, 1992; McLoughlin, 1999; Luppicini, 2002; Morse, 2003).

18.1.1.2 Assessment for Learning

Some theorists (c.f. Glaser, 1991; Jonassen et al., 1997; Tergan, 1997) believe that learning is most effective if it is embedded in social experience, and if it is situated in authentic problem-solving contexts entailing cognitive demands relevant for coping with real-life situations. This view entails a culture shift in education – a shift towards environments and approaches based on the ideas of social constructivism. In this worldview, learning is situated in rich contexts, and knowledge is constructed in communities of practice through social interactions in which participants seek common ground between the knower (the instructor) and the learner. This common ground must embrace interests and personal values, which requires a sharing at both the sociocultural and the cognitive levels (Ewing et al., 1998). Social constructivists are interested in prior experience that is shared through conversation and negotiation. In other words, a network of interactions is created through which the process of knowledge-making is collaborative. Palloff and Pratt (1999) describe this as the "web of learning" (p. 6). The assessment conversation occurring between and among learners and instructors in this web connects us to the real world and represents knowledge that is organic; evolving.

Advocates of open-ended assessment, in whose company we count ourselves, envision learning as interactive, purposeful, and process oriented. Through the use of problems and questions of importance, learners are required to actively engage in learning tasks in which they must work with their new knowledge by applying higher-order thinking skills. Here, the instructor is more interested in the ability to use knowledge to create personal solutions to problems than in "correct" answers. Because assessment is aimed at identifying and supporting growth in understanding, it fits the goals of instructors who want learners to grow in their ability to set goals for themselves and do inquiry.

Knowledge about individual learners and how they learn drives this approach. Through assessment, the instructor tries to reveal what learners know and understand and how those new understandings have developed. Instructors who advocate the open-ended approach assess student learning while they teach to gain insight into students' understanding as well as their level of cognitive development. Since the emphasis is on what the individual can do, everyone has an equal chance and opportunity to succeed. In this way, cooperative, collaborative learning is fostered. Learners play a more active role in the assessment of their own learning through the use of tools and activities such as reflective exercises, self-evaluations in tandem with peer assessments, collaborative projects, and ePortfolios. Through reflection they can identify gaps in their learning and strategize how to improve (Wiggins, 1990). This type of assessment is typically viewed by students as being more relevant, respectful, confidential, fair, timely, and helpful.

Most distance learners live and learn in the world of work. Relevant and productive assessment then is concerned with authenticity, or how closely the task or process being assessed replicates or illustrates the learning in daily practice. An instructor who assesses for authenticity would either create natural or real-life settings and activities or contextualize learning in the settings that already exist, in order to understand and document how learners think and behave over an extended period of time. In other words, the instructor uses multiple sources for gathering information that would reveal a more accurate picture of learning progress as well as emphasizing the process of learning, not just the final product.

In the remainder of this chapter, we present approaches to assessment that reflect our understanding of the transformative social nature of learning. These approaches are meaningful, process-oriented, democratic, and active. They reflect Newman's model of "authentic achievement", which includes assessment tasks that "embody construction of knowledge, discipline inquiry, and value beyond the classroom" (Peters and Kenney, 2006, p. 154).

18.1.2 Inclusive Assessment Practices

We believe that learning is contextualized. The notion that knowledge is a dialectic process shifts attention from the mastery of content to the sociocultural setting and the activities of the people in a learning environment. That is, if knowledge emerges from lived social practices, it can only be fully understood and assessed in relation to those activities (Luppicini, 2002). Luppicini (2002) cites the example of an online course involving participants in Mexico and the United States (Gunawardena et al., 2001) in which the two cultural groups differed significantly in "perceptions of language, power distance, gender differences, collectivist vs. individualist tendencies, conflict, social presence, time frame, and technical skills" (p. 90). As Morgan and O'Reilly (1999) point out, with increasing internationalization in higher education, we are likely to encounter an increasing diversity of learners from different experiential, educational, social, cultural, economic, and language backgrounds in online classrooms. As the boundaries between physical/geographical and sociocultural environments become more permeable, assessment needs to be responsive to diversity and reflect critical and inclusive practices. Gordon and Musser (1992) "recognize that various populations live their lives in multiple contexts, and that authenticity may vary not only with populations but also with contexts. Thus, in modern societies authenticity requires that competence be measured by multiple criteria met within the same person functioning in multiple contexts" (p. 2). Culture, age, gender, and life situation are four contextual factors that influence the design of assessment that respects learning needs, preferences, motivations, and readiness levels.

Cognitive research indicates that information learned and assessed as a linear set of objective facts, operating outside of the world in which they are applied, fails to yield the kinds of in-depth understanding needed to function in our modern, multicultural, multidisciplinary society. However, assessment that encompasses aspects of *connecting*, which involves the coherence of knowledge; *reflecting*, which allows individuals to recognize the gaps that exist in their understanding; and *feedback*, which provides information about performance and how improvement can be made, is an iterative and dynamic part of the learning process itself. Authentic assessment respects individual differences, is learning-oriented, measures learning in the form in which it will be used in the real world, is integrative, and reflects co-construction of knowledge for meaningful action. The following discussion of the forms authentic assessment can take in e-learning is framed by these principles; the principles of the social construction of knowledge.

18.2 ASSESSMENT-AS-CULTURE: CONSTRUCTIVIST APPROACHES AND TOOLS

Social constructivism challenges us to move away from decontextualized, fact-driven learning "in favor of approaches . . . that are active, collaborative, reflective, and that connect learning to . . . needs and life context" (Mathur and Murray, 2006, p. 239). At the institutional or macro-level, Angelo (1993, 1999) describes an "assessment–as-culture" model as one in which shared trust, shared vision and goals, shared language and concepts, and shared internal guidelines are necessary preconditions for designing assessments that meet the requirements for transformative learning. These aspects also frame the assessment culture at the micro-level of a course of program. Morgan and O'Reilly (1999, p. 35) discuss a list of assessment opportunities that support online learning, including peer and self-assessment; teamwork and collaborative tasks; online dialogue and debate; simulations and role plays; problem-solving; online testing, and digital scrapbooks and portfolios.

In this section we frame a discussion, by no means exhaustive, of many of these strategies and tools for assessment whose purpose reflects this goal of active change: e-Journals, self- and peer-assessment, ePortfolios, rubrics, and concept maps. Although in our descriptions of these tools we have linked them to four specific constructivist principles, naturally they are interconnected and serve many purposes in assessing learning. The four constructivist principles that contextualize assessment for learning are deep learning, new knowledge, collaborative learning, and critical reflection.

18.2.1 Assessing Deep Learning

Deep learning occurs through resolving complex problems and issues that are meaningful to learners in the contexts in which they live and work. Problem-solving is an activity that helps learners acquire an "integrated body of knowledge and skills in a domain that can be deployed in subsequent school and work settings in meaningful ways" (Dijkstra, 2004, p. 159). Problems are solved through questioning, making predictions, and testing hypotheses. The learning that occurs in these tasks may be assessed in a variety of ways, but we focus on online discussion. Online discussions, at their best, encourage the social construction of knowledge in contexts that require learners to use new concepts and defend their ideas. As a cognitive tool, online discussion requires thinking and writing in ways that are accessible to others and available permanently as a resource for both peers and instructor. The problem-solving process, rather than the product, is the focus of assessment: Peters and Kenney (2006) use online discussions as scaffolds to the acquisition of deeper understanding.

Meyer (2005) identifies five challenges for the instructor assessing learning through online discussions: (1) understanding how online discussions compare to face-to-face discussion; (2) deciding how to assess and what criteria and tools to use; (3) using technology; (4) metacognition, that is practice and reflection about the design of the online environment; and (5) keeping informed of the assessment research. We focus on the second challenge, deciding how to assess online discussions. Currently, there are three main tools to assess discussions: content analysis, rubrics, and frameworks (Meyer, 2005). For each, the learning goal is the heart of the process. For example, the goal of providing evidence for ideas may be assessed differently from that of using conceptual frameworks in argumentation. Models of assessing deep learning have been developed, for example the Community of Inquiry model (Garrison et al., 2001), in which developmental levels of thinking are determined.

Content analysis involves determining the words, phrasing, cues, and characteristics that illustrate learning of the skill, assigning codes, and analyzing transcripts for instances of appropriate language use, quality and frequency of response, proximity to others' responses, and so on.

As they are continuums of learning, rubrics are helpful for assessing complex skills and progress over time. Rubrics are ideal tools to be constructed collaboratively with learners, a process that supports metacognition ("What do *you* think is evidence for creative ideas?"). When rubrics are available and transparent to learners early in the assessment cycle they can also guide discussion. Meyer (2005, p. 122) provides an example of a rubric to assess the contribution of new ideas in a discussion. The rubric assigns values to conditions like "no new ideas offered", to "regularly contributes new ideas to discussion", evaluates the quality of the ideas, whether other learners built on them in their own postings, and whether learners provided evidence and evaluated their own ideas. Meyer goes on to identify rubrics that assess "teaching presence", "social presence", and "interactivity". The latter two reflect an individual's contributions to the social community.

Frameworks, like Bloom's Taxonomy, provide the instructor with a set of heuristics or a model against or within which to assess learning. For example, Bloom's Taxonomy of Cognitive Outcomes can be used to define stages of thinking from acquisition of lower-level knowledge to higher-order thinking that involves analysis, synthesis, and judgment. A sample of a rubric to assess contribution to the online discussion in Campbell's online graduate course "User-centred Design" is provided in Table 18.1.

Of late, online discussion as a cognitive tool that encourages critical thinking and discourse has come under closer scrutiny. In his doctoral work, Liam Rourke (2005) found that critical discourse is not a natural outcome of discussion; that it must be explicitly guided by a skilled facilitator. He offers a number of recommendations for designing computer conferencing that encourages critical thinking. For example, he describes a

Table 18.1: Assessment Rubric for Online Class Discussions

Level	*1*	*2*	*3*	*4*
Learning Goals	*Consistently does Most or All*	*Does Many*	*Does Most or Many*	*Consistently does Most or All*
Identifies and summarizes the **problem/ question** at issue (and/or the source's position), and identifies and assesses the key **assumptions.**	Offers biased interpretations of evidence, statements, graphics, questions, information, or the points of view of others.	Misinterprets evidence, statements, graphics, questions, etc.	Accurately interprets evidence, statements, graphics, questions, etc.	Accurately interprets evidence, statements, graphics, questions, etc.
	Does not surface the assumptions and ethical issues that underlie the issue.	Superficially discusses assumptions and ethical issues.	Identifies assumptions and addresses the underlying validity and ethics in most cases.	Identifies and questions the validity of the assumptions and addresses the ethical dimensions that underlie the issue.
Identifies salient **perspectives and positions** that are important to the analysis of the issue	Fails to identify or hastily dismisses strong, relevant counter-arguments.	Fails to identify strong, relevant counter-arguments.	Identifies relevant arguments (reasons and claims) pro and con.	Identifies the salient arguments (reasons and claims) pro and con.
	Regardless of the evidence or reasons, maintains or defends views based on self-interest or preconceptions.	Regardless of the evidence or reasons, maintains or defends views based on self-interest or preconceptions.	Offers analyses and evaluations of obvious alternative points of view.	Thoughtfully analyzes and evaluates major alternative points of view.

Table 18.1: (Continued)

Level	*1*	*2*	*3*	*4*
Learning Goals	*Consistently does Most or All*	*Does Many*	*Does Most or Many*	*Consistently does Most or All*
Identifies and assesses the quality of **supporting data/evidence** and provides additional data/evidence related to the issue	Argues using fallacious or irrelevant reasons, and unwarranted claims.	Draws unwarranted or fallacious conclusions.	Draws warranted, non-fallacious conclusions.	Draws warranted, judicious, non-fallacious conclusions.
	Does not justify results or procedures, nor explain reasons.	Justifies few results or procedures, seldom explains reasons.	Justifies some results or procedures, explains reasons.	Justifies key results and procedures, explains assumptions and reasons.
	Exhibits close-mindedness or hostility to reason.	Justifies few results or procedures, seldom explains reasons.	Fair-mindedly follows where evidence and reasons lead.	Fair-mindedly follows where evidence and reasons lead.
Shows evidence of **metacognition** and **conceptual growth.**	No evidence of critical reflection.	Reflects on own assertions; shows no critical change in thinking.	Objectively and critically reflects upon own assertions, some evidence of growth.	Objectively and critically reflects upon own assertions; demonstrates significant self-insight.
Identifies and considers the influence of the **context** on the issue.	Discusses the problem only in egocentric or sociocentric terms.	Does not present the problem as having connections to others.	Considers other pertinent contexts.	Analyzes the issue with a clear sense of scope and context, including an assessment of the audience of the analysis.

computer supported collaborative argumentation system (CSCA) designed to scaffold argumentation among learners (Jonassen and Cho, 2002). Based on a conversation analogy, this system offers options such as *rebut*, *add evidence*, and *challenge assumption*. Scardemalia and Bereiter's Knowledge Forum™ (1994) exemplifies this approach.

18.2.2 Assessing New Knowledge

Learning new knowledge is a process of building on and revising previous knowledge and experiences. Assessing new knowledge can and should occur at various stages in the learning process. Cognitive and diagnostic tools like concept maps and KWL charts have been used in educational settings for three decades to assess learning in domains as diverse as engineering and comparative literature. Concept maps are graphical representations of knowledge that are comprised of concepts and the relationships between them, often represented in a hierarchical fashion through "crosslinks" (Figure 18.1). Cañas et al., (2003)

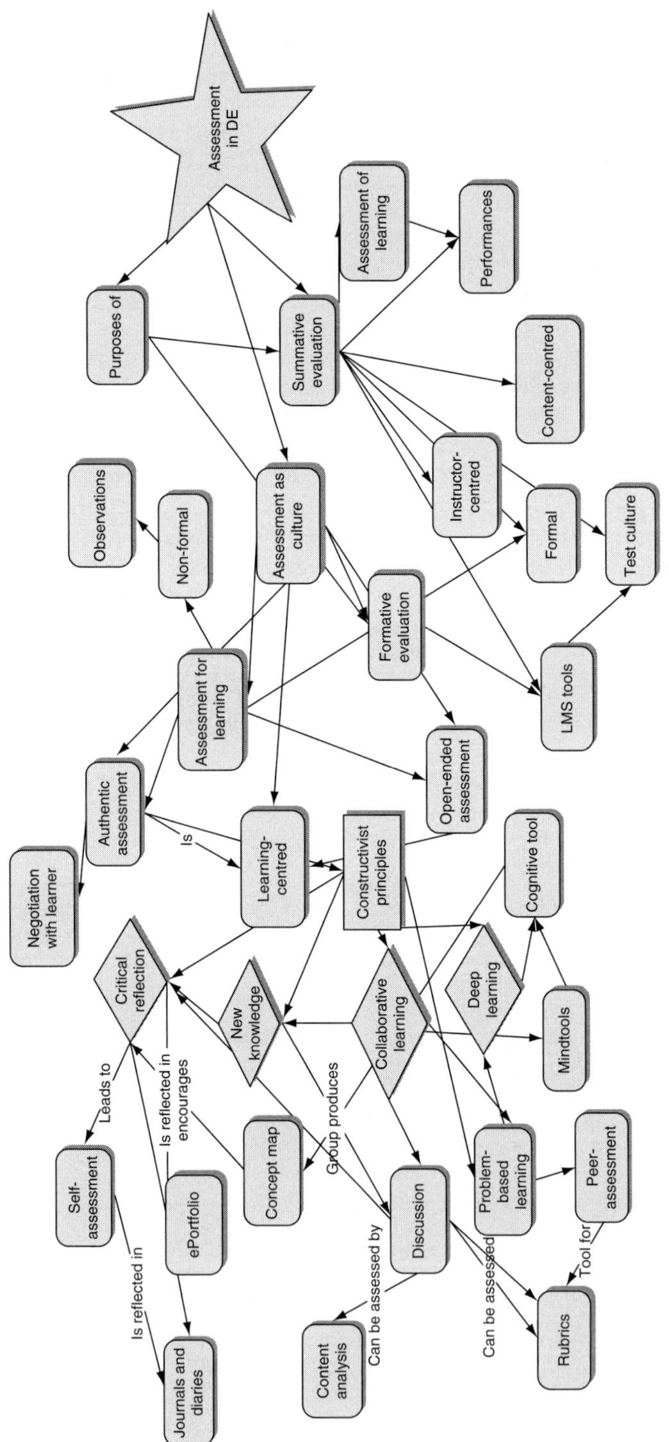

Figure 18.1: Concept Map

describe crosslinks as connectors that show how a concept in one domain of knowledge is related to a concept in another domain, noting, "in the creation of new knowledge, cross-links often represent creative leaps on the part of the knowledge producer" (p. 5).

18.2.2.1 Supporting Knowledge Representation: Concept Maps

As cognitive tools, or "mindtools" (Jonassen, 1996), concept maps encourage learners to demonstrate knowledge of a domain, reflect upon and elaborate new knowledge, link new knowledge to existing knowledge, support different learning styles and encourage the generation and organization of ideas in preparation for writing (Alpert and Gruenberg, 2000). As diagnostic/assessment tools, they provide a visual representation of learning and identify gaps in knowledge. Concept maps also support collaborative learning, as learners must discuss their ideas, support, or contradict arguments and perspectives and justify their own. According to Bromley (1995, in Alpert and Gruenberg, 2000) this sort of collaborative activity "helps the participants to co-construct evolving understanding of the subject matter, ultimately resulting in advancing individual learning and understanding" (p. 314). As a pedagogical tool, a concept map is effective at both formative (diagnostic) and summative (evaluation) stages. For example, if constructed as ongoing evaluation of knowledge within a course or across a program, concept maps may demonstrate conceptual change. For this reason, concept maps may be meaningfully included in learning portfolios (see below).

Ausubel and his colleagues (1978) identified three conditions for meaningful learning that relate to the conditions for meaningful or authentic assessment. First, material to be learned must be conceptually clear and presented with language and examples that relate to the learner's prior knowledge. Concept maps are effective for identifying the relevant knowledge a learner possesses before or after instruction (Edwards and Fraser, 1983, in Cañas et al., 2003). Second, the learner must possess relevant prior knowledge. Creating a concept map encourages learners to incorporate new meanings into prior knowledge. Third, the learner must choose to learn meaningfully. Concept maps may encourage students to use meaningful-mode learning patterns (Mintzes et al., 2000, in Cañas et al., 2003). Concept maps aid the instructor in identifying both valid and invalid ideas held by students.

A number of computer-based concept mapping tools currently exist, for example Inspiration™, SMART Ideas™, Mindmapper and Decision-Explorer™; newer tools include multimedia functionality. However, as straightforward as these tools are for learners to use, implementing concept maps as assessment tools can create a challenge in terms of instructor workload, reliability, and validity. In their comprehensive literature review, Cañas et al., (2003, pp. 25–29) briefly discuss two traditional methods of assessing learning through concept maps.

The traditional method of concept map scoring was proposed by Novak and Gowin (1984), and is based on the components and structure of the Concept Map. This method assigns points for valid propositions (1 point each), levels of hierarchy (5 points for each level), number of branchings (1 point for each branch), crosslinks (10 points for each valid cross-link), and specific examples (1 point for each example). This scoring technique has proven to be time-consuming, but it does give a great deal of information about the creator's knowledge structure. Others (cf. Pearsall et al., 1997) have adapted this method, scoring the same additional components to reflect more explicitly the knowledge domain; and some research is becoming available on the efficacy of computer-based scoring (see, in particular, the Concept Mapping Resource Guide).

A second method, proposed by Ruiz-Primo and Shavelson (1996) involves comparing a learner-generated concept map to that of an expert. Experts can be defined as domain experts, instructors, advanced learners, or a combination of the three. The comparison method has also been automated although, because human judgment is often involved, these tools have not had wide adoption. For a picture of a concept map, see the Utah State University Libraries Reference Services concept mapping tutorial (http://library.usu.edu/Tutorials/CMSamples.htm).

18.2.3 Assessing Collaborative Learning

Learning is collaborative and meaning is made through active engagement and negotiation with others with different experiences, values, and perspectives. The view of cognition as socially shared implies approaches that make thinking visible, generating and receiving feedback and revising (Pellegrino, 2004). Collaborative assessment involves negotiation between and among instructors and learners, observation of and participation in discussions, and contributions to group tasks and projects. At the same time, the development of the skills (e.g. conflict resolution skills, accountability; interdependence) implicated in effective collaborative can be assessed individually. Strategies such as e-journaling (individual) can be complemented by the use of social software, such as discussion boards, blogs, and wikis; and rubrics to assess collaborative group work.

The instructor who assigns collaborative problem-solving activities, for a portion of which the team is graded, will need to persuade learners of the benefits of this approach. Assessing group work is challenging, particularly when assigning grades – individual, group, negotiated, or a combination. Note that if learners have chosen distance delivery for convenience and/or because they prefer to work alone, any synchronous activity may defeat the purpose.

Negotiating roles and responsibilities at the beginning of an authentic problem-solving task and engaging team members in defining criteria for success serves both as a reflective activity for learners and as an opportunity to develop skills necessary for effective teamwork in the workplace. Nightingale et al. (1996; in Morgan and O'Reilly, 1999, p. 122) propose a set of assessment criteria to consider, including

- identifying indicators that the problem exists;
- identifying further information needed to understand the problem;
- demonstrating understanding of knowledge concepts underpinning the problem;
- using knowledge to generate ideas and propose alternative solutions to be evaluated;
- justifying a course of action that includes ethical and moral dimensions;

- carrying out the plan;
- evaluating the action plan and proposing revisions;
- reflecting on one's own and one's group learning.

As problem-solving and collaborative teamwork skills may improve along a continuum, these or similar criteria could easily be included in an assessment rubric.

18.2.4 Assessing Critical Reflection

Perhaps even more central to adult learning than elaborating established meaning schemes is the process of reflecting back on prior learning to determine whether what we have learned is justified under present circumstances. This is a crucial learning process egregiously ignored by learning theorists (Mezirow, 1990, p. 5). Thoughtful, personal reflection is necessary to ensure meaningful learning and growth, leading to personal and social action. Examples of strategies and tools to assess cognitive and affective change and growth include self- or group (peer) assessments, journal writing and ePortfolios.

In "How We Think", John Dewey (1933) writes, "reflective thinking is active, persistent and careful consideration of any belief or practice in the light of the grounds that support it and the further consequences to which it leads" (p. 9). John Barell (1991) adds that such reflectiveness is important because it "helps us gain more awareness and control of our thought processes and related feelings" (p. 7). Critical reflection is grounded in the understanding that all learners have personal preconceptions that act as powerful filters through which everything they experience is sifted. Taking frequent opportunities throughout the learning experience to uncover these preconceptions and critically examine their influence on the understanding of the new learning is an important step in ongoing assessment. Such reflection can lead to transformation in one's thinking.

Perspective transformation is the process of becoming critically aware of how and why our presuppositions have come to constrain the way we perceive, understand, and feel about our world; of reformulating these assumptions to permit a more inclusive, discriminating, permeable and integrative perspective; and of making decisions or otherwise acting on these new understandings (Mezirow, 1990, p. 14).

Critical reflection is an approach to assessment that places high priority on growth in the learner's independence, responsibility, ownership, and self-direction. By taking responsibility for their own learning, individuals are engaged at the outset in setting goals and planning to check back to see how and what they are learning relates to these goals. Such reflection helps learners to establish links between previous knowledge and new knowledge because as they monitor their own thinking, they notice connections between what they used to know and what they know now. Not only does making these connections help create meaning, but learners also come to better understand the processes involved in learning as they pay attention to these connections. Questions such as how is my thinking changing?, why is this important?, how does this fit with what I already know? help to reveal learning processes. Self-evaluation also helps them to discover what strategies best help them to learn. Additional questions could include what works best for me?, how do I feel about what I have accomplished?, and what would

I do differently the next time? Using such guided self-evaluation; individuals develop the capacity to assess their own learning.

Donald Murray states that "writing is the most disciplined form of thinking – a way of processing and remembering information and making meaning. It is thinking on paper" (Robb, 2003, p. 59). Journaling provides a place for this "thinking on paper" as well as an avenue for interaction through written conversation. Through threaded discussions and online journaling opportunities such as blogs instructors can foster metacognition by asking learners how to think about their own thinking using probing questions such as:

- What kind of thinking did you do?
- Why do you think this? Are there inconsistencies in your thinking?
- How did you come to understand . . . ?
- What influenced your thinking about . . . ?

However, individual reflection without peer interaction inhibits higher-order thinking. Collaborative reflection promotes learners' opportunities to articulate ways of thinking, develop divergent thinking styles, include multiple points of view, builds and modifies understanding through potential cognitive conflicts (Kim and Lee, 2002). Thus, a blend of self- and group evaluation, and/or peer-assessment, is an important part of successful collaborative group work. Learners can be encouraged to examine their own personal contribution to the group by responding to such questions as:

- Did I share my ideas effectively in the group?
- Was I accountable to my colleagues?
- Did I respect other's ideas in my group?
- Did my contributions to group discussions move the project forward?
- Was I a "force for good" in group interaction, or were others required to manage my behavior?

The group also needs to be encouraged to evaluate their group effort by reflecting on the strategies they used to cooperate with each other; their development of team-building skills; the challenges that they faced and resolved together; and constructive suggestions for improved collaborative processes. By using group and self-evaluation, instructors can also get at personal growth, social growth and attitudinal development including initiative, teamwork, leadership, problem-solving, decision-making skills, as well as respect for the perspectives and contributions of their peers.

As learning is at once an individual and a social experience and accomplishment, a blended assessment approach can provide the best picture of progress. For example, a course design in which participants complete an individual task, work with a partner to complete another task, and complete a collaborative project will provide opportunities for self-, peer-, and group assessment. However, the administrative (instructor) and individual (learners) workloads are substantial (Hanrahan and Isaac, 2001), and anonymity may be an issue to some participants. Li and Steckleberg (2005) describe a database-driven web-based peer assessment system, Peer Assessment Support System (PASS) that automates data collection and provides continual access to both learners and instructors. The model was designed to scaffold instructional design decision-making through a pre-service teacher education project to build a WebQuest, and was built according to "four critical attributes" of peer assessment (p. 82):

- the well-defined assessment criteria (i.e. a rubric) helped them understand the basic elements of good performance;
- scores and comments were immediately summarized and posted to the site to guide formative evaluation of the projects;
- a peer review editing function permitted reviewers to modify their comments and scores; and
- participants had instant access to feedback to their reviews and projects.
- Table 18.2 is an example of a peer or team assessment rubric Campbell uses in one of her online courses.[1]

Table 18.2: Peer Assessment Rubric

Evaluate your Team Development					
How do you feel about your team?	***Strongly Disagree***	***Disagree***	***Neutral***	***Agree***	***Strongly Agree***
1. I understand my team's purpose.	1	2	3	4	5
2. I feel like a member of the team.	1	2	3	4	5
3. My team has open communication.	1	2	3	4	5
4. My team has defined goals.	1	2	3	4	5
5. The team uses each member's skills appropriately.	1	2	3	4	5
6. There is adequate support for individuals.	1	2	3	4	5
7. The team discusses problems openly and directly.	1	2	3	4	5
8. All members influence decision-making.	1	2	3	4	5
9. Risk taking is encouraged and supported by all team members.	1	2	3	4	5
10. Team members make a satisfactory effort to work on their relationships.	1	2	3	4	5
11. Many members share the distribution of leadership.	1	2	3	4	5
12. I receive a considerable amount of useful feedback.	1	2	3	4	5

18.2.4.1 Supporting Critical Thinking: Portfolios

If integrated into the entire learning experience, portfolios may potentially help shape the entire approach to learning (Challis, 2005). As reflective tools that learners will accept as a holistic part of their growth, portfolios must be more than a loose collection of artifacts. Instead, a learning portfolio is a purposeful collection of individual work and collaborative work product that exhibits effort, progress, or achievement either in a specific domain (e.g. European history) or of learning in general (e.g. critical thinking skills). Portfolios help learners make connections between different contexts, such as academia, the workplace and the community (Tosh et al., 2005). Learning portfolios are celebratory because they focus on what an individual knows and can do while assisting instructors in monitoring and evaluating performance and in diagnosing learners' strengths and weaknesses. Portfolios also illustrate growth and learning over time, suggesting that integration over a curriculum or program better represents deep learning such as problem-solving and collaborative team skills, that is, learning outcomes that require a longer time to mature.

Portfolios have the potential to enhance one's learning through active involvement in the decision making about what to include in portfolios. According to Adams and Hamm (1992), the most powerful benefit from the use of portfolios is that learners participate in the selection of portfolio content. "Authentic (meaningful) assessment allows students to select, collect and reflect on their learning and gives them an opportunity to use critical-thinking skills as they select the academic efforts that might best represent them .... This process itself is a powerful educational experience" (Adams and Hamm, 1992, p. 103). Portfolios are also a form of personal development because they promote self-assessment and reflection. When deciding on pieces to include in their portfolios, learners need to be encouraged to ask themselves why they are making the choices they are; in this way they enhance their understandings of their thinking as they become accomplished at evaluating their own work, thus promoting intellectual autonomy and self-respect.

ePortfolios are defined as a "highly personalized, customizable, web-based information management system which allows students to demonstrate individual and collaborative growth, achievement and learning over time" (LDP, 2003–2004, in Challis, 2005, p. 19). They have the advantage of being readily and more broadly accessible, and allow users to store, search, retrieve, manipulate, refine, cross-reference and reorganize and repackage multimedia data that is "undeniably enhanced" by the functionality of computers, the Internet, and related software (Challis, 2005, p. 20; Mathur and Murray, 2006). Peters and Kenney (2006) characterize the use of ePortfolios in teacher education as encompassing deep understanding, reflection and metacognitive thinking, and scaffolding. ePortfolios in this course consist of lesson plans, assignments, analyses of student work, conversations with the mentor teachers, videoclips of practice teaching, classroom observation notes, interviews, and so on. In conjunction with a Literacy Journal the learners document the changes in their thinking and practice over 1 year. Integrating journal writing, online discussions, and the development of ePortfolios, Peters and Kenney (2006) are able to guide or scaffold the learners through the process of providing concrete evidence of their growth and transition from students to teachers. The ePortfolio conversation begins with reflective writing tasks (RWT) through which the preservice teachers write about their experiences from the beginning of the course, 10 months before the ePortfolio is due. The authors describe writing as the heart of the transformation. "Their examination of and reflection on their work that permits students to gain deeper and richer understandings of their own practice" (Peters and Kenny, 2006, p. 168).

While ePortfolios show great promise, the software tools are not yet mature; the danger noted by several researchers lies in the tool directing the process. Pilot projects in teacher education programs, and in other disciplines, have revealed several issues of concern for both institutions and learners, for example security, privacy, and safety; identity management; achieving buy-in from learners, instructors, and institutions; managing the volume of data collected over time; the ROI; and authenticity (Challis, 2005; Tosh et al., 2005).

18.2.5 Learning Management Systems and Assessment

Online assessment using the tools provided by portal-based learning management systems (LMS) is of particular concern to instructors who are institution-based. For example, at the University of Alberta WebCT Vista™ is the centrally supported LMS that delivers content, provides assessment tools, and manages student records in an integrated manner. As Williams points out, "the requirements for centralisation of the management and control of learning lead(s) to the implementation of large-scale web solutions, but this approach creates a conflict with the requirements for e-assessment". Williams' central concern is the security and reliability of the Internet. While we acknowledge the inherent problems of Internet-based assessment, our concern is that the assessment tools in LMS reflect a content- or instructor-centric approach. For example, WebCT™ provides a suite of assessment tools that includes multiple-choice and True/False tests and a short-answer facility (Figure 18.2).

The LMS have many features that facilitate testing through online item-banking, delivery, and reporting, three essential functions of these systems (Schnipke, Becker and

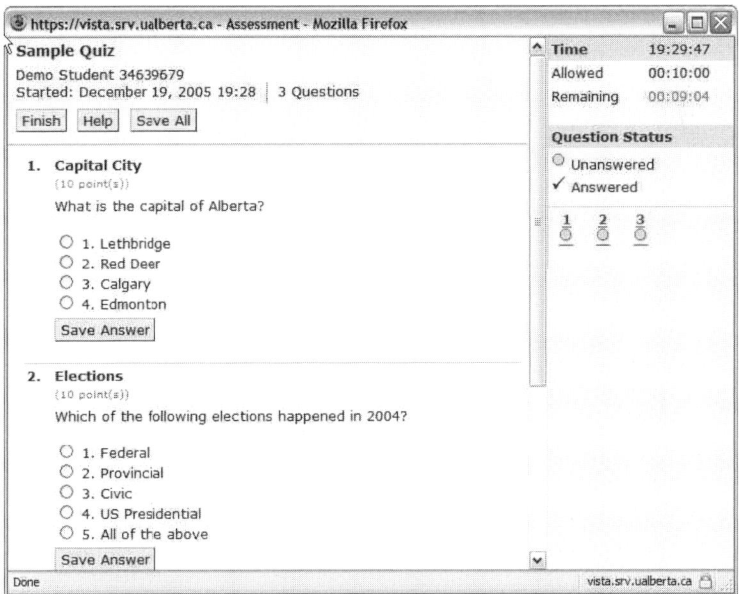

Figure 18.2: An Assessment Tool in WebCT™

Masters, 2006). For example, most of them include a test item repository, a grade book, and tools for designing and managing test items, including multimedia items. Students are able to manage their assessment activity only to the extent that they use "delivery" tools like the Drop Box™, or take a quiz multiple times if the instructor allows it in the system. For example, a psychology instructor might design the multiple-choice quiz so that students may complete it three times without being "recorded", but the fourth try is the one that counts. The tools in LMS may support assessment as a cognitive tool if users are permitted to manipulate them for self-assessment. In the previous example the course participants could test their knowledge and approach mastery. If the instructor uses the feedback feature to supply meaningful "knowledge of results" for each response, learners are able to self-diagnose. Going beyond text-based assessment, because an LMS supports the integration of multimedia materials, learners may submit assignments in formats that include digital objects such as a narrated slide show, video and audio. In general, however, LMS reflect an evaluation approach rather than an assessment approach. Nevertheless, for a good overview of features to evaluate when using an LMS, refer to Schnipke, Becker, and Masters' (2006) "Summary of sample prioritization features" (p. 302).

We submit that LMS can support a constructivist approach through triangulation. For example, a holistic picture of student learning could include multiple-choice tests for pre-assessment, and mastery of low-level skills and knowledge, and self-assessment. A tool such the Drop Box™ could manage ePortfolios. Implementing the synchronous tools (e.g. whiteboard, chat) for document sharing and revision, Voice-Over Internet Protocol (VOIP) tools like SKYPE™ for oral assessment, and an asynchronous discussion to encourage collaboration, while potentially difficult to manage, demonstrates a learner's range of knowledge. At the same time, using a synchronous tool assessment raises accessibility questions. For example, in certain areas of the world consistent and reliable access to the Internet may be a problem and time zones complicate scheduling and learner availability at various times in the day.

While by no means exhaustive, we have endeavored to provide the reader with a repertoire of assessment practices and tools to support constructivist learning environments. Peters and Kenney (2006) show us how to integrate several of these tools: they use concept mapping, journaling, online discussion, writing tasks, and ePortfolios through a 12-month teacher education program. Below, we offer an example of complementarity in the learning design of a course-in-progress for instructional designers. In this course, assessment is an integral component of the design for learning, that is, through asynchronous online discussion (writing), a simulated multidisciplinary team project, and the negotiated use of rubrics, the assessment strategy reflects learning that is deep, contextualized, collaborative and reflective.

18.2.6 Learning Design that Supports Transformative Assessment

"Theory and Practice in User-Centred Design" is an elective course in the course-based Master of Arts in Communications and Technology at the University of Alberta. User-centered design (UCD) is a client-centered philosophy in which the individual is at the center of an iterative design process. UCD considers cognitive, sociocultural, political, and technological factors involved in defining user tasks and goals that drive the design and development of software, websites, information systems and processes – anything with which people interact. UCD is concerned with the usefulness, usability, desirability, legibility, learnability, accessibility, and meaningfulness of an information product.

Offered online in one term, this course takes a case-based approach to the theory and practice of UCD. Because UCD is a multidisciplinary process, course participants are assigned project teams early in the course. The teams work together on three mini-cases that taken together comprise a client-proposal. In the second iteration of the course (the first was not case-based), Campbell designed the experience based on the Jigsaw method of the cooperative learning approach: within teams participants were asked to assign roles and responsibilities as "real" UCD teams do, based on UCD concepts like "universal design" or "user research". During the term, Campbell facilitated two parallel forums: the first, running for 13 weeks, was for the whole class and addressed theoretical ideas. In the second, each "role" was discussed. For example, each team identified a user-research expert. A special User Research forum was available for a deep discussion of this topic. At the same time, a Prototyping forum was running, and so on. The "experts" in each team returned regularly to their groups to share their learning. A third forum was available to each team for project management; Campbell did not moderate these forums.

Learning was assessed in two ways: 65 percent for the team proposal and client presentation (group grade); and 35 percent participation in the class discussion (individual grade). Two rubrics were presented, one for the class discussion (Table 18.1) and the other for the mini-cases (Table 18.3). As the course progressed, the criteria were adjusted and the

Table 18.3: Mini-Case Rubric

Criteria	*Poor 0–2*	*Good 3–4*	*Outstanding 5*
The problem identification and statement Up to 5 points	Neither implicit nor explicit reference is made to the problem that is to be examined. The problem is not valid. No indication of the importance of the problem to UCD.	Readers are aware of the overall problem or challenge, that is to be examined. The significance of the problem to UCD is not explicit.	The problem is introduced, and is relevant and significant. The groundwork is laid for the development of the argument and direction of the project. The problem has significance for UCD.
Development of argument Up to 8 points	Major sections of pertinent data have been omitted. The topic is of little significance to the UCD field.	Pertinent data is included, but not covered in as much depth or insight, or as explicitly as possible. Significance to UCD field is evident.	The appropriate data is covered in depth. Significance of topic to UCD field is unquestionable.

(*Continued*)

Table 18.3: (Continued)

Criteria	*Poor 0–2*	*Good 3–4*	*Outstanding 5*
Inclusion of evidence Up to 4 points	There is little evidence offered to support the authors' argument. Appropriate sources and references are not included.	Evidence for the argument is presented clearly but may not support the issue as well as expected. Sources are included but may not be relevant, current, or significant.	The evidence for the argument is clearly presented, supports the argument, and is valid. Sources are cited when specific statements are made. The author has included the most current, relevant and important UCD sources.
Clarity and quality of writing Up to 6 points	It is hard to know what the writer is trying to express. Writing is convoluted. Misspelled words, incorrect grammar, and improper punctuation are evident. Many errors citing references.	Writing is generally clear, but unnecessary words are occasionally used. Meaning is sometimes hidden. Paragraph or sentence structure is too repetitive. Some errors in citing references.	Writing is crisp, clear, succinct and compelling. The writer incorporates the active voice consistently. Excellent syntax, appropriate and use of inclusive language. No spelling errors. Citations are consistently and accurately referenced (preferably in APA).
Synthesis of ideas and evaluation of results. Up to 5 points	There is no indication the author tried to synthesize the information or make a conclusion based on the evidence under review.	The author provides concluding remarks that show an analysis and synthesis of ideas occurred. Some of the conclusions, however, were not supported in the body of the report. The hypothesis or research question is stated.	The author was able to make succinct, precise and insightful conclusions based on the evidence. Insights into the problem are appropriate. Conclusions are strongly supported in the report.
Communication of results Up to 3 points	Readers are not clear about the results or how they were arrived at. The form of communication was not appropriate to the problem. No connection to future action.	The problem and results are communicated appropriately. The author is able to address some questions related to the treatment of the problem, or the results.	The problem and results are communicated appropriately and innovatively. The author is able to satisfactorily address specific questions. Recommendations are made for future action.
Evidence of learning Up to 4 points	No evidence of critical reflection or new insight.	The author provides some evidence of critical reflection and personal insight.	The author critically reflects on the issue in a way that demonstrates personal insight and transformation of previous views.

workload was renegotiated. Each mini-case could be refined and resubmitted one time. Anonymous feedback midway through the course and again at the end was incorporated for the third iteration in which the weight given to online discussion is reduced, peer assessment is included, and an individual, personalized assignment is negotiated.

18.3 FINAL WORDS

In this chapter we have argued for an approach to assessment in distance education that places assessment for learning at the center of instructional practice. Such an approach not only acknowledges that assessment needs to be ongoing and frequent throughout the learning process but also that the learner must play a central role in the process, thereby empowering him or her to take a more responsible active role in the learning. Such assessment reflects learning that is deep, contextualized, reflective, and collaborative. While this view of assessment requires a radical change in thinking from more traditional views of assessment, we feel that the tools we have provided in this chapter can be implemented to begin to make the transition smoother for e-learning.

NOTE

1. Shared by Ms. Sandi Barber, Learning Innovation Consultant, Northern Alberta Institute of Technology.

REFERENCES

Adams, D.M. and Hamm, M.E. (1992). Portfolio assessment and social studies: Collecting, selecting, and reflecting on what is significant. *Social Education*, **56**, 103–105.

Alpert, S.R. and Gruenberg, K. (2000). Concept mapping with multimedia on the Web. *Journal of Educational Media and Hypermedia*, **9**(4), 313–331.

Angelo, T.A. (1999, May). Doing assessment as if learning matters most. *AAHE Bulletin*. Retrieved December 18, 2005 from http://aahebulletin.com/public/archive/angelomay99.asp

Angelo, T.A. and Cross, K.P. (1993). *Classroom Assessment Techniques: A Handbook for College Teachers*. San Francisco: Jossey-Bass.

Ausubel, D. (1978). In defense of advance organizers: A reply to the critics. *Review of Educational Research*, **48**, 251–257.

Ausubel, D., Novak, J., and Hanesian, H. (1978). *Educational Psychology: A Cognitive View* 2nd ed., New York: Holt, Rinehart and Winston.

Barell, J. (1991). *Teaching for Thoughtfulness. Classroom Strategies to Enhance Intellectual Development*. NY: Longman.

Bartley, J.M. (2006). Assessment is as assessment does: A conceptual framework for understanding online assessment and measurement. In *Online Assessment and Measurement: Foundations and Challenges* (M. Hricko and S.L. Howell eds). Hershey, PA: Idea Group, pp. 46–66.

Biggs, J. (1999). *Teaching for Quality Learning at University: What the Student does.* Buckingham: Open University Press.

Bromley, K. (1995). *Graphic Organizers: Visual Strategies for Active Learning.* Markham, ON: Scholastic Canada Ltd.

Cañas, A.J., Coffey, J.W., Carnot, M. et al. (2003, July). *A Summary of Literature Pertaining to the use of Concept Mapping Techniques and Technologies for Education and Performance Support.* The Institute for Human and Machine Cognition. Retrieved December 5, 2005 from www.ihmc.us.

Challis, D. (2005). Towards the mature ePortfolio: Some implications for higher education. *Canadian Journal for Learning and Technology*, **31**(3), 17–32.

Concept Mapping Resource Guide. Retrieved December 20, 2005 from http://www.socialresearchmethods.net/mapping/mapping.htm.

Dewey, J. (1933). *How We Think.* Boston: D.C. Health & Co.

Dijkstra, S. (2004). The integration of curriculum design, instructional design, and media choice. In *Curriculum, Plans, and Processes in Instructional Design: International Perspectives,* (N.M. Seel and S. Dijkstra, eds) Mahwah, NJ: Erlbaum, pp. 145–170.

Edwards, J. and Fraser, K. (1983). Concept maps as reflectors of conceptual understanding. *Research in Science Education,* **13**, 19–26.

Ewing, J.M., Dowling, J.D. and Coutts, N. (1998). Learning using the World Wide Web: A collaborative learning event. *Journal of Educational Multimedia and Hypermedia,* **8**(1), 3–22.

On Purpose Associates. (2001). *Authentic assessment.* Retrieved December 19, 2005 from http://www.funderstanding.com/authentic_assessment.cfm

Garrison, D.R., Anderson, T., and Archer, W. (2001). Critical thinking, cognitive presence, and computer conferencing in distance education. *American Journal of Distance Education*, **15**(1), 7–23.

Glaser, R. (1991). The maturing of the relationship between the science of learning and cognition and educational practice. *Learning and Instruction*, **1**(2), 129–144.

Gordon, E.W. and Musser J.M. (1992). *Implications of Diversity in Human Characteristics for Authentic Assessment.* National Center for Research on Evaluation, Standards, and Student Testing (CRESST): UCLA Graduate School of Education. pp. 1–7.

Gunawardena, C.N., Nolla, A.C., Wilson, P.L. et al. (2001). A cross-cultural study of group process and development in online conferences. *Distance Education*, **22**(1), 85–121.

Hanrahan, S.J. and Isaacs, G. (2001). Assessing self and peer assessments: The students' views. *Higher Education Research and Development*, **20**(1), 53–70.

Jonassen, D. (1996). *Computers in the Classroom: Mindtools for Critical Thinking.* Englewood Cliffs, NJ: Prentice Hall.

Jonassen, D. (2004). *Learning to Solve Problems: An Instructional Design Guide.* San Francisco, CA: Pfeiffer.

Jonassen, D. and Cho, K. (2002). The effects of argumentation scaffolds on argumentation and problem solving. *Educational Technology Research and Development*, **50**(3), 5–23.

Jonassen, D., Dyer, D., Peters, K. et al. (1997). Cognitive flexibility hypertexts on the Web: Engaging learners in making meaning. In *Web-based Instruction* (B.H. Khan, ed.) Englewood Cliffs, NJ: Educational Technology Publications, pp. 119–133.

Kim, D. and Lee, S. (2002). Designing collaborative reflection supporting tools in e-project-based learning environments. *Journal of Interactive Learning Research,* **13**(4), 375–392.

LDP: Leadership Development Program 2003–2004. (2003–2004). LDP ePortfolio Report. Regents of the University of California. Retrieved December 16, 2005 from http://bearlink.berkeley.edu/ePortfolio.html.

Leskes, A. (2002). Beyond confusion: An assessment glossary, *Association of American Colleges and Universities Peer Review*, **4**(2/3). Retrieved December 19, 2005 from http://www.aacu.org/peerreview/pr-sp02/pr-sp02reality.cfm

Li, L. and Steckleberg, A.L. (2005). Peer assessment support system (PASS). *TechTrends*, **49**(4), 80–84.

Luppicini R.J. (2002). Toward a conversation system modeling research methodology for studying computer-mediated learning communities. *Journal of Distance Education*, **17**(2), 87–101.

Mathur, S. and Murray, T. (2006). Authentic assessment online: A practical and theoretical challenge in higher education. In *Online Assessment, Measurement and Evaluation: Emerging Practices* (D.D. Williams, S.L. Howell, and M. Hricko, eds) Hershey, PA: Idea Group Publishing, pp. 238–258.

Matuga, J.M. (2006). The role of assessment and evaluation in context: Pedagogical alignment, constraints, and affordances in online courses. In *Online Assessment, Measurement and Evaluation: Emerging Practices* (D.D. Williams, S.L. Howell, and M. Hricko, eds) Hershey, PA: Idea Group Publishing, pp. 316–330.

McLoughlin, C. (1999, June). *Culture on-line: Development of a Culturally Supportive Web Environment for Indigenous Australian Students.* Paper presented at EdMedia99, Seattle, WA.

Meyer, K. (2005). Best practices in the assessment of online discussion. In *Online Assessment and Measurement: Foundations and Challenges* (M. Hricko and S. Howell, eds) Hershey, PA: Idea Group, pp. 118–130.

Mezirow, J. and Associates. (1990). *Fostering Critical Reflection in Adulthood.* San Francisco: Jossey-Bass.

Mintzes, J.J., Wandersee, J.H., and Novak, J.D. (2000). *Assessing Science Understanding: A Human Constructivist View.* San Diego: Academic Press.

Morgan, C. and O'Reilly, M. (2006). Ten key qualities of assessment online. In *Online Assessment and Measurement: Foundations and Challenges* (M. Hricko and S.L. Howell, eds) Hershey, PA: Idea Group, pp. 86–101.

Morgan, C. and O'Reilly, M. (1999). *Assessing Open and Distance Learners.* London: Kogan Page.

Morse, K. (2003). Does one size fit all? *Journal of Asynchronous Learning Networks*, 7(1), 37–55.

Nightingale, P., Tewiata, I., Toohey, S. et al. (1996). *Assessing Learning in Universities.* Professional Development Centre, University New South Wales, Sydney, Australia.

Novak, J.D. and Gowin, D.B. (1984). *Learning How to Learn.* New York: Cambridge University Press.

Palloff, R.M. and Pratt, K. (1999). *Building Learning Communities in Cyberspace: Effective Strategies for the Online Classroom.* San Francisco: Jossey-Bass Publishers.

Pearsall, N.R., Skipper, J. and Mintzes, J. (1997). Knowledge restructuring in the life sciences: A longitudinal study of conceptual change in biology. *Science Education*, **81**(2), 193–215.

Pellegrino, J.W. (2004). Complex learning environments: Connecting learning theory, instructional design and technology. In *Curriculum, Plans and Processes in Instructional Design: International Perspectives* (N.M. Seel and S. Dijkstra, eds) Mahwah, NJ: Erlbaum, pp. 25–48.

Peters, C.W. and Kenney, P.A. (2006). Online assessment in a teacher education program. In *Online Assessment, Measurement and Evaluation: Emerging Practices* (D.D. Williams, S.L. Howell, and M. Hricko, eds) Hershey, PA: Idea Group Publishing, pp. 153–178.

Robb, L. (2003). *Teaching Reading in Social Studies, Science and Math. Practical Ways to Weave Comprehension Strategies into Your Content Area.* Toronto, ON: Scholastic.

Rogers, V. (1989). Assessing the curriculum experienced by children. *Phi Delta Kappan*, May, 714–717.

Rourke, L. (2005). *Learning Through Online Discussion.* Unpublished doctoral dissertation. Edmonton, AB: University of Alberta.

Ruiz-Primo, M.A. and Shavelson, R.J. (1996). Problems and issues in the use of concept maps in science assessment. *Journal of Research in Science Teaching*, **33**(6), 569–600.

Scardamalia, M. and Bereiter, C. (1994). Computer support for knowledge-building communities. *Journal of the Learning Sciences*, 3(3), 265–283.

Schnipke, D.L., Becker, K., and Masters, J.M. (2006). Evaluating content-management systems for online learning programs. In *Online Assessment, Measurement and Evaluation: Emerging Practices* (D.D. Williams, S.L. Howell, and M. Hricko, eds) Hershey, PA: Idea Group Publishing, pp. 153–178.

Sluijsmans, D. and Martens, R. (2004). Performance assessment in integrated e-learning, In *Integrated e-Learning: Implications for Technology, Integration and Organization* (W. Jochems, J. van Merrienboer, and R. Koper, eds) London: Routledge/Falmer, pp. 39–50.

Tergan, S.O. (1997). Misleading theoretical assumptions in hypertext/hypermedia research. *Journal of Educational Multimedia and Hypermedia*, **6**(3/4), 257–283.

Tosh, D., Light, T.P., Fleming, K., and Haywood, J. (2005). Engagement with electronic portfolios: Challenges from the student perspective. *Canadian Journal for Learning and Technology*, **31**(3), 89–110.

Wiggins, G. (1990). The case for authentic assessment. *Practical Assessment, Research and Evaluation*, 2(2). Retrieved December 19, 2005 from http://PAREonline.net/getvn.asp?v=2 and n=2

Williams, N. (2004). *Internet Based E-Assessment: Design Principles.* Retrieved December 19, 2005 from http://www.ecdl.nhs.uk/resources/technicalinformation/e-assessment_paper_1g.pdf.

Zemsky, R. and Massy, W. (2004). *Thwarted Innovation: What Happened to E-Learning and Why.* A Final Report for The Weatherstation Project of The Learning Alliance at the University of Pennsylvania in cooperation with the Thomson Corporation. University of Pennsylvania.

TOOLS

Conception: Found online December 19, 2005 from *http://www.parlog.com/en/conception.html*

Concept Mapping Bibliography. Retrieved December 20, 2005 from http://users.edte.utwente.nl/lanzing/cm_bibli.htm.

Decision Explorer: Banaxia Software Found online December 5, 2005 from http://www.banxia.com/

Inspiration Software, Inc. Found online December 5, 2005 from http://www.inspiration.com/

Knowledge Forum: Found online December 16, 2005 from http://www.knowledgeforum.com/

Learning Innovations Forum d'Innovation d'appentissage Found online December 16, 2005 from LIflA:http://www.liifia.ca

Mindmapper. Found online December 5, 2005 from http://www.mindmapper.com/

SMART Ideas Concept Mapping Software. Found online December 5, 2005 from http://www.smarttech.com/products/smartideas/

SKYPE: Found online December 19, 2005 from http://www.skype.com/helloagain.html

WebCT: Found online December 19, 2005 from *http://www.webct.com/*

Chapter 19

The Transformation of Information and Library Services

Peter Macauley and Rosemary Green

19.1 INTRODUCTION

Of all the elements of library and information services, none has changed more dramatically than the support of distance education. Technology is driving the development and expansion of distance education in general, demonstrating a critical effect on the delivery of library services to students in distance learning programs. As a result, the expectations of students for personalized content, services, and instruction have increased. Students, educators, and librarians are now engaged in the processes of locating, critiquing, using, and managing information in ways that are significantly different from just a decade ago. Innovative technology has also transformed pedagogical practices, and the methods by which knowledge transfer occurs in turn accelerate technological change. Librarians have shifted their traditional service, collection, acquisition, and instructional models from the proactive to the reactive and now to the personalized approach. The just-in-case model was replaced by the just-in-time approach, and now students expect services and resources to be tailored just-for-me. Such adaptations provide filtered packages that are geared to students' individual needs. Consistent with these adaptations is disintermediation, the self-service paradigm whereby students and other members in the teaching and learning community undertake their own information seeking without intervention by information professionals. While technological advances and the freedom of disintermediation are attractive and advantageous for students, particularly those at a distance, these changes have essential implications for the provision of library resources and for the teaching and learning of information literacy.

In the context of this revolution in the information environment, the subject of discussion in this chapter is the convergence of library collections, services, and instruction provided to students situated both on- and off-campus. The differences in the delivery of library services have diminished significantly over the past decade; now electronic access to information resources is available whether a student is sitting in a library or working in an airport lounge waiting for a flight. The transition from providing the traditional, exclusively print format to electronic access of information and bibliographic resources has been swift and dramatic in the new millennium. Electronic full-text journals, comprehensive multidisciplinary bibliographic databases, electronic reference and inquiry services, online tutorials, and electronic document delivery services are heavily used by those studying at a geographical distance and on-campus. Institutionalized practices such as face-to-face instruction using print-only materials have given way to modalities of teaching and learning that can occur at temporal and geographical distances, using a broad range of technologies and pedagogies.

Different sectors and institutions use a variety of means to provide information services to those studying at a distance. Initially, academic libraries developed segregated services and collections that were designated specifically to support students enrolled in distance learning programs. In the recent past, shared collections of items implanted in the libraries of other institutions, satellite libraries, large compilations of readings, and reliance on slow postal services commonly provided the necessary access to resources; these methods are still used in some locations. Librarians and students have also typically communicated via telephone, facsimile, courier services and by walk-in access, although e-mail and web-based methods are used predominantly. Wider broadband availability enhances and amplifies transmission speeds. The growth of new technologies, especially the Internet, has enormously affected libraries' capacities to provide informational services to both on- and off-campus constituents. The print-based resources of the 1960s and 1970s have given way to the electronic full text, on demand information retrieval of the new millennium. The advent of consistent computer protocols enables a seamless interface between suites of software, thus offering access to an array of services previously unimaginable, especially for those studying at a distance. Access to information has become much more equitable, transparent, and homogenous to larger numbers of researchers and information seekers.

This chapter considers these issues by first exploring the changes in library services relative to the growth of distance education, discussing the convergence of off-campus and on-campus library services, and relating the effects of changes in information-seeking patterns to the ways in which librarians respond through information literacy instruction. The chapter concludes with a look ahead to the future of library services, collections, and instruction to all learners.

19.2 CONTEXTUALIZING LIBRARY SERVICES FOR DISTANCE EDUCATION

Historically, libraries have played a key role in ensuring both the success of students and the success of colleges and universities. Academic libraries are expected to provide simultaneously accessible collections of books, electronic resources, and other information materials for use by students, faculty members, and the wider community. The 1960s proved to be the final decade wherein the central mission of the academic library was to provide traditional, print-based reading materials. In the 1970s, computers began to revolutionize technical and management activities such as cataloguing and acquisitions, and in the 1980s, the introduction of online catalogs, automation of interlibrary loans, and the provision of electronic databases supplying bibliographic citations dramatically affected user services (Miez, 1995, p. 28). At the same time, mediated reference services allowed researchers a new window into bibliographic content. The 1990s brought the World Wide Web, a medium easily navigated by end users, so full-text articles and other documents arrived at researchers' desktops through unmediated searching. Paralleling the expectations pervasive in the retail marketplace, libraries began to respond to researchers and scholars as consumers by offering self-service and full access to bibliographic databases, library catalogs, and other library tools.

In 1984, Rosenberg proclaimed that "a current debate of the major importance in the library and information providing fields is how rapidly technological changes will affect libraries. Some think that by the year 2000 library materials will be replaced by electronic document files and terminals" (p. 387). Her statement, perhaps controversial for the time, foretold the massive changes in the informational environment seen at the commencement of the new millennium. The proliferation of scholarly information over recent decades, combined with advances in information technologies, has changed the environment in which students function, whether they study on- or off-campus. Access to information appears to have become easier than ever before, particularly for those at a distance, yet this proliferation of information has made the evaluation and organization of information more difficult. The influences of more modern technology on scholarly communication effectively commenced with the invention of the computer, although, to an important extent, early technologies such as the telephone, photocopier, and facsimile also greatly influenced the way that educators, learners, and researchers communicate. At one time, physical distance was a consideration in the sharing of scholarly communication; it was once necessary to attend in person to converse with colleagues. Now electronic mail and the Internet have revolutionized scholarly communication. Today, those at a distance, whether they are across the corridor or across the globe, can easily communicate from any location that affords an information and telecommunications infrastructure. In the latter decades of the twentieth century, many countries made the transition from postindustrial societies to greater reliance on information and knowledge as technology rapidly changed information forms and systems of delivery. While this electronic transition has taken place rapidly in developed countries, regions of some countries or even entire nations still have not established an adequate or reliable information and communication technologies (ICT) infrastructure. The high cost of access to a telecommunications and information infrastructure in some areas discriminates against learners' abilities to take advantage of modern forms of distance education and the services that sustain it. For those cases, digital video disc (DVD) and compact disc (CD) technology can be used to provide library and other instructional tutorials to distance learners who are located in areas lacking a sufficient ICT infrastructure. Instruction placed on DVD or CD enables learners to bypass problems of large audio and video files and instead take advantage of the tutorials with a faster response rate absent the Internet access or affordable telecommunication systems. Flexible technologies allow timely delivery of instruction based on student needs rather than instructor's convenience.

Students studying via distance education have the right to expect the same level of service, instruction, and access to print and online resources as their on-campus counterparts. These equivalencies have been codified and clearly articulated in the Association of College and Research Libraries' (ACRL) *Guidelines for Distance Learning Library Services* (2004). The ACRL standards established a benchmark by articulating measures of accountability and defining assessable library responsibilities for distant learners, such as

1. reference assistance;
2. computer-based bibliographic and informational services;
3. reliable, rapid, secure access to institutional and other networks, including the Internet;
4. consultation services;
5. a program of library user instruction designed to instill independent and effective information literacy skills while specifically meeting the learner-support needs of the distance learning community;
6. assistance with and instruction in the use of nonprint media and equipment;
7. reciprocal or contractual borrowing, or interlibrary loan services using broadest application of fair use of copyrighted materials;
8. prompt document delivery, such as a courier system and/or electronic transmission;
9. access to reserve materials in accordance with copyright fair use policies;
10. adequate service hours for optimum access by users; and
11. promotion of library services to the distance learning community, including documented and updated policies, regulations and procedures for systematic development, and management of information resources (n.p.).

In the past, publications external to library and information science have remained nearly silent on library provision or the role of libraries in the distance education field. The inference here was that library services were not considered in the process of initiating and implementing distance learning programs, or that librarians functioned as silent partners. In the decade preceding the adoption of the ACRL standards, Cavanagh (1994) surveyed 250 papers presented at the 14th World Conference of the International Council for Distance Education, and he examined 109 articles reviewed in the 10th anniversary issue of the journal *Distance Education*. Across the board, he found a "complete absence of discussion by distance educators on the role of the library as a support system for external students" (p. 91).

Over time, the literature has reported a growing trend toward collaborations, joint efforts, and shared planning, and the library now has an acknowledged role in supporting and augmenting distance learning initiatives. McKnight (2003) clearly outlined and projected forward in her essay "Distance education and the role of academic librarians" in the *Handbook of Distance Education*. Publishing by librarians on the provision of library services for distance education in library related forums continues apace and demonstrates the influence and transformation of the field. This convergence is articulated in the four comprehensive bibliographies produced by Slade and colleagues. The first three (Latham et al., 1991; Slade and Kascus, 1996, 2000) were published in traditional print format, while the fourth bibliography (Slade, 2005) migrated to a dynamic web-based resource that enables frequent updating. The bibliographies have served as an historical overview to the progression of library services, collections, and instruction dominated by print-based formats to technologically shaped models of access and instruction. Early on, the face-to-face approach to resource provision and information skills training was most commonly cited; over time, focus has shifted to electronic and virtual means for resource delivery. Increasingly too, the literature describes the integration of teaching and learning information skills into course management software. The transformation and emphasis of library services for distance education can be judged in part by the changes of the titles of Slade's bibliographies over the years. The first and second editions were titled *Library Services for Off-Campus and Distance Education*, while the third and fourth editions were titled *Library Services for Off-Campus and Distance Education* and *Library Services for Distance Learning*. The inclusion of the term "learning" by 2000 demonstrates a major change in focus for librarians, reflecting a role shift from primarily service providers to that of educators, both directly and indirectly involved with teaching and learning processes.

While libraries provide an enormous range of services to students studying via distance education, significant variations in the depth and quality of offerings can be found. Cooper (2000) described differing interpretations of library support for distance learners, ranging from minimal to optimal support. She found that organizations offering minimal support directed their distance education students first to their public libraries for books and other resources, or perhaps they offered distance learners the opportunity to purchase a library card in order to use library services. She also found that some online universities did not directly provide instructional materials but instead referred their students to online book vendors for textbooks and supporting materials. Others provided support by establishing reciprocal borrowing arrangements and contracting with another university's library for its services and collections. The optimal service is provided by those who employ specialist librarians to support the specific needs of distance education students and who state clearly defined standards and strategies for meeting informational and instructional needs. This chapter focuses upon the optimal service model that accommodates complete and transparent access and delivery, as this level of expectation should be met for all distance students who enroll in a distance education program.

Universities of the late twentieth and early twenty-first centuries have realized the opportunities afforded by incorporating distance education programs into existing academic structures, and the imperative to start new programs and react to marketing opportunities is considerable. In some cases, the silo model is followed, in that several academic units and administrative units respond simultaneously yet independently to distance learning initiatives; later these units may discover that they have been traveling on the same tracks but not communicating with each other. Library staff may not realize that a new distance learning program has come on board until students begin to contact the library for access to e-collections and instructions for using them. Libraries often make the rapid transition from zero to nearly full service because librarians, library staff, and administration tend to respond to institutional needs with relative agility and flexibility. As one way of responding quickly to distance learners' needs, librarians' responsibilities are reallocated well in advance of more expensive changes, such as layering on more online tools and collections.

As lines of communication evolve and collaborations begin to take shape, coordinated and institution-wide adjustments are made in response to a university's entrepreneurial initiatives. Institutional decisions relative to financial pressures, accreditation and quality assurances, and globalization imperatives affect change. Consequentially, universities often find that relationship building among academic units strengthens its capacity for responding and accountability. The demand for accountability in higher education, related to accreditation and the assessment of student learning outcomes, is a critical element affecting information services and distance education. In the United States especially, regional accreditation standards have been reformulated to recognize technological changes at play in higher education. Institutions that choose to offer distance education programs must ensure that off-campus courses are integrated with the more traditional delivery modes. For libraries, the need to establish equivalent information services in support of distance education has been quick to follow. The ACRL (2004) *Guidelines* articulate minimal differentiation in services provided to students in all modes of study, as do accreditation standards established by the Society of College, National and University Libraries (SCONUL, 2001). In a growing number of instances, academic units and university administration welcome the integration of library programs and librarians into planning for distance learning initiatives because, as educators and information specialists, librarians contribute a unique package of training, education, and experience to the effort. Together, faculty members, librarians, and others in the education community have essential and increasingly visible roles in teaching and learning in an Internet-influenced society (Olson, 2001), in articulating responses to the informational and educational needs of distance learners, and in measuring the efficacy of distance learning programs.

19.3 THE CONVERGENCE OF ON-CAMPUS AND OFF-CAMPUS LIBRARY SERVICES

Convergence may finally put to an end the definitional and interpretive issue of distance learners. Terms such as "off-campus" and "distance education" in the library literature have often been based on geographical criteria, although temporal circumstances can be equally influential. This connotation of the term "distant" may be understandable because the circumstance of being at a distance has been equated with residing an hour's drive from a physical campus (Gandhi, 2003). While this interpretation of student status and information needs may have been relevant to a certain extent some years ago, such a definition is overly simple and outdated. Given the burgeoning collections, resources, and instructional modes that students can access conveniently from multiple locations and at all hours, growing numbers of students indicate that they do not want to come on campus for their courses or to visit the library. Technological and pedagogical changes have greatly altered assumptions about students based on geographic location. By initially providing web-based library catalogs, bibliographic databases, full-text journal and monograph collections, and electronic tutorials for their distance learners, libraries have also opened more opportunities for all students wishing to access the virtual library. Library services and collections are becoming seamless and cojoined; a student reading an online journal in the physical library experiences the same interaction and engagement with the information as a colleague who accesses the same journal at a site away from campus. Residential students who seek the campus-based experience choose to enroll in online courses for many of the same reasons as their off-campus counterparts; they too value the flexibility and convenience of distance learning modes (Olson, 2001; Moyo, 2004). Boundaries are blurred as the information-seeking behaviors and means of conducting library research by virtually all students are the same, regardless of physical location. As Burich (2004) observes, "this once discernable group of distance learners is no longer distinctly different from their on campus counterparts" (p. 101). For the sake of meeting students' informational and instructional needs, our discussions of on- and off-campus services and collections and instruction are no longer dichotomous; we are quickly reaching the point of discarding the distinction between off-campus and on-campus learning and learners.

Writing in the inaugural issue of *The Journal of Library Services for Distance Education*, Marie Kascus (1997) addressed the "Converging vision of library service for off campus/distance education." She stated that in the future, technology would change library service provision to distance education students and

- may help to alleviate the problem of duplicating resources at multiple satellite sites as electronic access can be provided to many more resources than libraries are able to purchase with diminishing budgets;
- can help to reduce the isolation of distance education students by providing many options for human interaction through electronic communication;
- will help to bridge the gap between the distant learner and the library;
- will enhance delivery of education and access to libraries making it important to reexamine accreditation standards to insure their relevance to an evolving academic setting;
- will enable libraries to serve distant learners better through networked access and web connectivity.

Kascus' observations from a decade earlier have proven to be prophetic. Now, multisite licenses for bibliographic databases enable full-text access to resources simultaneously to numerous concurrent users, regardless of their location. Self-directed learning, enhanced by technology, enables students to undertake their own library and information seeking. In response, libraries have shifted emphasis on collection building from a model based on acquisition of materials to one based on access to informational resources. The collection management strategies of the past that were defined by libraries acquiring and maintaining substantial, permanent collections have been overtaken by reciprocal and consortial lending agreements, document delivery, and electronic access to full-text documents. Added to these adjustments are timely, on-demand, just-for-me access geared to the requirements of the learners and student consumers. At the same time, the distance learner's sense of isolation has been reduced by e-mail, Internet chat, course management software, virtual reference capabilities, and other synchronous and asynchronous forms of communication.

The changing demographics of students have also contributed to the trend toward convergence of on- and off-campus resources, instruction, and methods of access. The typical description of the distance learner, either undergraduate or postgraduate, has in the past tended to profile an adult student, one who is older than other on campus fellows and faced with balancing the complex requirements of work, family, and study. These generalized characteristics have changed; however, as many younger students now enroll in off-campus courses while studying full time and working part time to help fund their studies. Mixed mode study has become more common, a trend further expedited by online learning (McKnight, 2003). This preference for a blend of on-site and distance learning modes reflects the worldwide trend of reduced visitation rates for university libraries as not only library resources are available online but also as students are spending less time on-campus. The distinctions between campus-based and off-campus students are diminishing and, as a consequence, library services have become less differentiated.

19.4 THE TRANSFORMATION OF INFORMATION SEEKING

The decade of the 1990s brought an increase in self-serve conveniences, as consumers in the marketplace made purchases and learners in higher education performed library research functions without an intermediary. End user searching, the direct access to bibliographic databases by researchers, replaced the mediated searching previously carried out by a librarian or information specialist. In the early days of electronic information access, databases required complex searching protocols and were packaged with fee structures based on numbers of citations retrieved and high telecommunication charges. By mid-decade, bibliographic databases on compact disc, such as ERIC and PsycInfo, were commonly found in college and university libraries, and Internet access to databases was rapidly advancing. Disintermediation was welcomed as database users gained "access to information without assistance or intervention of an information professional" (Edwards et al., 1996, p. 357). End user searching became more feasible as user-friendly software was developed, as natural language searching was introduced, and as database publishers offered flat-rate subscriptions with unlimited printing. Distance learners in particular benefited from the shift to online access of bibliographic resources; no longer did researchers face temporal and geographical limitations to information seeking. Distance learners as well as onsite users consistently demonstrate that disintermediation complements both their preference for self-directed learning as well as their inclination toward convenience and flexibility in information seeking and delivery.

Rapid deployment and acceptance of networked full-text databases made available not only bibliographic content but also entire journal articles, conference papers, and other professional documents, delivered to the desktops of library users. Importantly, many databases are now multidisciplinary in nature, such that researchers at any location can avail themselves of massive amounts of information using a single search interface and easily locate material otherwise difficult to acquire through single, discrete bibliographic sources. Access to copies of papers shortly after their electronic publication has considerably enhanced the usefulness of end user searching. Consequently, bibliographic searching has changed dramatically, and now librarians rarely undertake extended database searching for researchers. Simultaneous use of databases by multiple users and multisite licenses for electronic databases afford much more liberal and timely access, regardless of users' locations. During the early advent of computerized library resources, library catalogs available on compact disc appeared at the forefront of electronic bibliographic tools, followed quickly by Internet-based OPACs or online public library access catalogs. From the convenience of their desks, laboratories or homes, researchers were afforded unmediated searching, allowing them to investigate their own library's holdings and, in some cases, to order materials electronically. Individual libraries rapidly committed their collections to electronic indexing and management, and now most library gateways also provide an interface to online library catalogs worldwide. Historically, academic libraries have been among the first to respond to an institution's need for implementation of educational and information technologies; oftentimes the academic library was the first department on campus to make computers publicly available (Stoffle and Williams, 1995). Libraries are not necessarily tied to the tradition-bound model of developing and housing only physical collections or providing services and instruction only on site. As a result of libraries' early involvement with technology, librarians have been among the first to realize that rapid change is inevitable and to respond accordingly.

Electronic browsing enables serendipitous discoveries and affords online learners a sense of intellectual empowerment. Learners continue to respond to this unprecedented growth in electronic collections and searching capabilities by increasing their reliance on e-resources. While altering the ways that learners use libraries, rapid and convenient bibliographic access has also increased users' knowledge of information technology in general, enhancing methods of conducting online research and learning as a result (Lyman, 1993). Inevitably, users have changed their information-seeking behaviors. With increasing regularity, college and university constituents, regardless of their status as on campus or distance learners, demonstrate a reliance on online resources to seek information. Researchers also indicate a clear preference for convenience and are more inclined to conduct research in an online environment, regardless of their proximity to campus (Kelley and Orr, 2003; Moyo, 2004). In this way, the library as a physical presence is less apparent to researchers, both on- and off-campus.

The current literature consistently illustrates a fundamental alteration in the ways that students seek information, now choosing the Internet rather than the library as the central research source. A recent report by the Online Computer Library Center (OCLC) titled *Perceptions of Libraries and Information Resources* (2005) confirmed that students overwhelmingly prefer online resources as the first and often the only point of reference for research. Typically, students do not distinguish between open source, Internet-based search engines such as Google and library online sources, such as proprietary databases, e-journals and books, and online catalogs. All these tools are available via the Internet, many with similar interfaces, and often conveniently linked from the library gateway. Distance learners who seldom, if ever, come to campus are likely to confine their information seeking to the virtual library environment where seamless availability of resources is possible and preferred. Distance users now find that neither their own physical locations nor location and ownership of information are issues of concern. And because much of the information found online is unmediated, standards such as authority, quality, and reliability that typically apply in selection of traditional library materials do not necessarily hold true in the online environment. Given their predilection for conducting research on the Internet, users can benefit from help in filtering and selecting their results. The functions of unmediated and on-demand searching do not necessarily equip students or even academics to undertake in-depth and complex database searching. Electronic tools and particularly the proprietary database search engines accommodate sophisticated library searches; however, users seem to prefer the simpler, quick, and dirty searches that yield immediate and plentiful results. An assumption often made of students in general including distance learners, is that, as members of a technologically facilitated setting, they have the sufficient skills to choose and evaluate the information they retrieve from all sources including those coming from the Internet. Students do not necessarily acquire information literacy skills as an automatic process, despite the assumption by faculty that they can become proficient on their own. Stephens and Unwin called for caution regarding the available technologies when they said, "Visions of the autonomy of the electronic library may obscure what should be seen as the real issue for new information technology which is to reconsider the interface between new and traditional technologies" (1996, p. 86).

19.5 INFORMATION LITERACY INSTRUCTION FOR ALL LEARNERS

This climate of change requires new understandings, definitions, and standards for teaching and learning. No longer is an introduction to basic bibliographic tools sufficient; students must demonstrate information literacy, an ability to locate and understand information available from any number of points of origin. Drawing on the term first proposed by Zurkowski (1974), educators characterize an information literate individual by the ability to harness information wisely. From the final report of the American Library Association Presidential Committee on Information Literacy (1989), this widely adopted description of information literacy reads

> Information literate people have learned how to learn. They know how to learn because they know how information is organized, how to find information and how to use information in such a way that others can learn from them.
>
> (p. 1)

In an altered, technology-rich environment, a new generation of students is entering academic programs relatively sophisticated in the use of electronic resources. Students readily accept "technology as the cornerstone of an ideal information environment" (Brown, 1999, p. 436). For many, the perception is that an entire world of information is at their fingertips, and they need to look no further than the Internet. "Many users believe that if they have searched an electronic index they have searched the entire world of information. If it's not in the computer, they assume that it must not exist" (Manoff, 1996, p. 221). On balance, however, many students are actually quite skeptical of the resources they find on the Web and do not appear to be as easily seduced as others presume (Moyo, 2004). The critical challenge then for all educators is to harness this healthy skepticism, adding to learners' abilities to filter, contextualize, and use proliferating amounts of information. Further to this, institutional commitments to supporting students' acquisition of information literacy not only sustain academic success but also ensure attributes for lifelong learning.

As more distance students gain access to the Internet, the need for further information literacy skills increases, as do the possibilities for developing information literacy (Catts et al., 1997). As a result, librarians must also reflect on their own informational role and accept the challenge "to understand precisely what kinds of information handling skills people will need, and how they might acquire them, in a fundamentally different learning environment" (Heseltine, 1995, p. 432–433). Both on- and off-campus students and their teachers now engage with an increasingly complex informational environment. Information professionals and librarians join with information users in making the transition. As Todd (2000) reflects

> The information literacy movement has emerged in the last fifteen years as a field of academic inquiry and a focus of professional practice in the wake of notions of an information society, and an information environment rapidly moving from print to digital; from local to international; from secure to uncertain; from poverty to overload; and from service to self service. In addition, it has been stimulated by concerns about the impact of the explosion of information and advances in information technology on individuals, societies and nations.
>
> (p. 25)

Advances in distance education have made part-time study in quality programs both feasible and attractive to students seeking degree completion while continuing to balance other responsibilities. Information, filtered and reviewed, continues to migrate to the Internet; whether the need for information literacy that results from this new environment is increased or diminished is uncertain (Campbell, 2006). As new generations of technologically supported methods in distance instruction evolve, strategies for teaching information literacy continue to advance as well. Information literacy instruction to distance learners arises from the need to provide equivalent services to all students regardless of instructional mode, an essential responsibility of educational institutions. Attention to the equivalence of services is demonstrated by an increased emphasis on the importance of information literacy skills. Technology shapes the focus of the curriculum, methods of delivery, and the ability to do so. Information literacy standards that support of academic success and, ultimately, lifelong learning are open to issues of accountability as would be any instructional component.

Following the 1989 release of the American Library Association standards for information literacy, the concept of information literacy received international acceptance, and interest in information literacy and codification of standards can be traced through publications in America, Australia, Asia, Europe, and Africa (Bundy, 2001). Consistently threaded throughout these statements is the association of information literacy with lifelong learning. For example, the Australian and New Zealand Institute for Information Literacy (ANZIIL) promotes lifelong and transferable application of good information skills in this way: "Sheer abundance of information and technology will not in itself create more informed citizens without a complementary understanding and capacity to use information effectively" (ANZIIL, 2004, p. 3). Predictably, statements on information literacy incorporate the role of technology as a means to gather information, but ultimately the contribution of information literacy to lifelong learning must be independent of the delivery modes. Bundy (2002) has called for an adoption of standards of information literacy at local, national, and global levels in support of better education and allocation of resources and to the benefit of all information seekers.

Information literacy instruction now reflects the learner at the center, a shift in educational practice at large that emerged in the latter decades of the twentieth century. With the prevalence of CD and DVD technology, then the mainstreaming of the Internet, computer-assisted information skills training and tutorials were introduced primarily for distance learners as a form of instructional equivalence, comparable to the face-to-face training available to students who came to campus. These formats allow conventionally provided training to be transformed into online methods, making information literacy instruction available to all categories of students. In the past, librarians have often traveled some distances to undertake information literacy classes for students who are geographically remote; however, this practice is diminishing, particularly with the expansion of online tutorials and, importantly, with the embedding of information literacy into the curriculum. Course management software such as Blackboard, WebCT, and Moodle enhance the collaborative ventures between librarians and educator colleagues, allowing seamless integration of library resources and services into the academic curriculum. The introduction of this software has escalated the equitable provision of online instruction even more, further diminishing the practice of differentiating the delivery of information literacy instruction based on learners' locations.

Worldwide, the literature offers examples of information literacy instruction being delivered electronically and often collaboratively, primarily via the Internet, by e-mail, virtual reference, or using electronic tutorials (Campbell, 2004). The most prevalent delivery modes for distance-based information literacy instruction at present are stand-alone, web-based library tutorials and guides, online credit-bearing courses and short sessions, and information literacy instruction that is integrated into online academic courses. One-shot, informational literacy instructional sessions that are typically taught in an on-campus mode do not readily translate into distance formats; additional staffing and travel time are required if equivalent instruction is delivered in person. Course management software accommodates single-course instruction as well as blended library tutorials and communication across courses. When information literacy instruction is offered through a learning management system, the instruction may be more closely integrated into the academic disciplines. Embedded courses incorporate elements of seeking and academically exploiting information into the curriculum and ultimately into a more complete educational experience. In this way, information as an entity becomes integral to the learning process (Orr et al., 2001). Additionally, students may have the opportunity to join in a community of online students, further enhancing their learning. Regardless of the pedagogical design, instruction must be customized, designed, and delivered appropriate to the information needs and seeking behaviors of the learners. The curricular goals and learning outcomes must also be integral to the instructional design of online information literacy teaching if this instruction is to have an established place in the curriculum.

Contemporary strategies in information literacy instruction routinely emphasize the phenomenon of information, the resources that hold the information, and the search strategies needed to access information. As Webber and Johnston (2000) observe, the processes for information seeking have changed, but the way that those processes are taught has not. Although the media have changed, the agenda of teaching types of sources and search concepts has remained much the same. Furthermore, information literacy instruction may tend to concentrate on print and electronic information sources and address only a checklist of information literacy attributes (Macauley, 2002). The variability of search interfaces across e-sources requires that learners be trained in the basic skills necessary to negotiate using them. However, as more common standards for database structure and public interfaces are adopted, instruction can focus on the message rather than the messenger. Instruction should also address multiple media familiar to the current generation of students and endemic to the environment of all learners, especially distance learners. The basic focus of information literacy learning should and in many instances does mirror that of distance education, emphasizing learning rather than teaching and placing the learner at the center. Burich (2004) reminds us to anticipate the diverse learning styles and range of experiences that all students, regardless of their mode of learning, bring with them to the educational setting. Sound principles of instruction must apply, with learners engaged as active participants at the center of their own learning. The focus of informed information literacy instruction acknowledges information seekers' impetus to make sense of the information that they retrieve and to construct individualized meanings from information.

Reflecting most articulated standards for information literacy, instruction has typically focused on a set of generic attributes and transferable skills that progress from an individual knowing when information is needed to continuing as a lifelong learner. Information literate students understand how to gather, evaluate, and use information, regardless of their specific need and the sources of information encountered. In recent years, information literacy has come to be framed as a discipline-specific attribute, more closely associated with particular academic fields required of learners. Information literacy constructs embedded in course instruction represent a new development of the ways that information literacy is taught and learned, placing it more holistically into an institutionalized, academic perspective. In this way, instruction becomes more learner-focused and tailored to students' individual skills and knowledge base. Even though each student is considered as an individual, learners are also assumed to be situated in a community constructed of other learners and instructors. These pedagogical features then must compel changes to both content and instructional design. Increasingly, librarian collaborations with faculty instructors as well as other academic units demonstrate a convergence of participants as multiple teachers and learners come together in shared learning communities. As distance education pedagogies continue to emerge, information literacy becomes established not only as a set of identifiable attributes but also as a process that is valued in a collectivity of online teachers and learners (Bruce, 2000). Increasingly, students approach educational settings acclimated to learning collectively with others in shared activities and to participate with other learners in making sense of information (Green, 2006); technological capabilities allow collaborative online learning to occur. When information literacy is viewed not only as a process but also as a means of engaging in a learning community, participative learning that occurs in both physical and virtual communities can be understood and accommodated.

19.6 CONCLUSION

The advent of new communication and educational technologies has dramatically changed information and library services for distance education in recent times, particularly as the Internet has influenced the ways that these services are developed, formatted, and delivered. Growing bodies of professional, academic, and scholarly publications are now offered exclusively in electronic format; consequently, the widespread tendency to discount the e-format is fading in many sectors of the scholarly community. Transformation of educational technologies, offering innovation, opportunity, and challenges for distance teachers and learners will continue into the foreseeable future. Patterns of Internet use will continue to affect the development of library collections and the provision of library services. Libraries and librarians will maintain an essential role in facilitating the identification, acquisition, organization, and dissemination of information in both customary and novel ways. Central needs of learners of all profiles and in all locations will persist; learners must be taught how to learn, how to seek and critique information, and most important, how to turn information into knowledge. The emphasis in information literacy instruction will continue to shift from skills-focused training to more contemporary, appropriate pedagogical practices that dovetail effective methods of teaching distance learners. Information and library services for those studying via distance education will remain at the cutting edge and, in turn, influence the services provided to on-campus counterparts. Institutionalized distinctions between on-campus and off-campus students will continue to fade; planning for academic and support programs will emphasize pedagogical and technological advances that are transparent for all learners, without considering geographical locations or student demographics. In time, the terms "distant" and "off-campus" may have little relevance, as all learners will engage in some way with virtual instruction and resources.

Until now, libraries have performed as reactive agents to changes in academic programs and institutional directives. Now it is incumbent of all members of university learning communities to respond in more unified ways to distance education initiatives. Strategic planning that is founded on the broader view of current circumstances blended with future projections should engage the talent and expertise located in all university sectors. Any institution that anticipates or maintains programs in distance learning should, in dialogue across all constituents and participants, discuss realignments of curriculum, library services, programs, and instruction, and information technology so that all areas coordinate and operate effectively for all students, not differentiated groups of students. The focus of such coordination is to the benefit of students in all categories, undergraduate and graduate, on-campus and distance-based, part time and full time. Distance learning initiatives will continue to present challenges in the assessment and evaluation of university curricula and pedagogies, services, and infrastructures as the effectiveness of distance education demands examination.

REFERENCES

American Library Association Presidential Committee on Information Literacy. (1989). *Final Report.* Chicago: American Library Association.

Association of College and Research Libraries. (2004). *Guidelines for Distance Learning Library Services.* Retrieved February 4, 2006 from http://www.ala.org/ala/acrl/acrl standards/guidelinesdistancelearning.htm

Australian and New Zealand Institute for Information Literacy. (2004). *Australian and New Zealand Information Literacy Framework; Principles, Standards and Practice,* 2nd ed., Adelaide: Australian and New Zealand Institute for Information Literacy.

Brown, C.M. (1999). Information literacy of physical science graduate students in the information age. *College and Research Libraries,* **60**, 426–438.

Bruce, C. (2000). Information literacy research: Dimensions of the emerging collective consciousness. *Australian Academic and Research Libraries,* **31**, 91–109.

Bundy, A. (2001, February). *For a Clever Country: Information Literacy Diffusion in the 21st Century.* Background and issues paper for the First National Roundtable on Information Literacy conducted by the Australian Library and Information Society, State Library of Victoria, Melbourne. Retrieved February 6, 2006 from http://www.library.unisa.edu.au/about/papers/clever.htm

Bundy, A. (2002, April). *Growing the Community of the Informed: Information Literacy – A Global Issue.* Paper presented at the Standing Conference of East, Central and South Africa Library Association Conference, Johannesburg, South Africa. Retrieved February 6, 2006, from http://www.library.unisa.edu.au/about/papers/growing-community.htm

Burich, N.J. (2004). The changing face of distance learning: Implications for distance learning librarians. *Journal of Library and Information Services in Distance Services,* **1**(1), 99–104.

Campbell, J.D. (2006). Changing a cultural icon: The academic library as a virtual destination. *Educause,* **41**(1), 16–31.

Campbell, S. (2004, August). *Defining Information Literacy in the 21st Century.* Paper presented at the World Library and Information Conference: 70th IFLA General Conference and Council, Buenos Aires, Argentina. Retrieved February 4, 2006 from www.ifla.org/IV/ifla70/papers/059e-Campbell.pdf

Catts, R., Appleton, M., and Orr, D. (1997). Information literacy and lifelong learning. In *Lifelong Learning: Reality, Rhetoric and Public Policy* (J. Holford, C. Griffin, and P. Jarvis, eds) Guildford, England: Department of Educational Studies, University of Surrey, pp. 70–75.

Cavanagh, A. (1994). The role of libraries in off campus study. In *Research in Distance Education 3: Revised Papers from the Third Research in Distance Education Conference, Deakin University 1993* (T. Evans and D. Murphy, eds). Geelong, Australia: Deakin University Press, (pp. 91–102).

Cooper, J.L. (2000). A model for library support of distance education in the USA. *Interlending and Document Supply,* **28**, 123–131.

Edwards, C., Day, J., and Walton, G. (1996, December). *Disintermediation in the Year 2010: Using Scenarios to Identify Key Issues and Relevance of IMPEL2 eLib Project.* Paper presented at the Online Information 96: Proceedings of the International Online Information Meeting, London.

Gandhi, S. (2003). Academic librarians and distance education: Challenges and opportunities. *Reference and User Services Quarterly,* **43**, 138–154.

Green, R. (2006). Fostering a community of doctoral learners. *Journal of Library Administration,* **45**, 169–183.

Heseltine, R. (1995). The challenge of learning in cyberspace. *Library Association Record*, **97**, 432–333.

Kascus, M. (1997). Converging vision of library service for off campus/distance education. *The Journal of Library Services for Distance Education,* **1**(1), http://www.westga.edu/library/jlsde/jlsde1.1.html.

Kelley, K.B. and Orr, G.J. (2003). Trends in student use of electronic resources: A survey. *College and Research Libraries,* **64**, 176–191.

Latham, S., Slade, A.L., and Budnick, C. (1991). *Library Services for Off Campus and Distance Education: An Annotated Bibliography.* Ottawa, Ontario: Canadian Library Association.

Lyman, P. (1993). Libraries, publishing, and higher education: An overview. In *Changes in Scholarly Communication Patterns: Australia and the Electronic Library* (J. Mulvaney and C. Steele, eds) Canberra: Australian Academy of the Humanities, pp. 15–28.

Macauley, P. (2002). Menace, missionary zeal or welcome partner? Librarian involvement in the information literacy of doctoral researchers. *New Review of Libraries and Lifelong Learning*, **2**, 47–65.

Manoff, M. (1996). Revolutionary or regressive? The politics of electronic collection development. In *Scholarly Publishing: The Electronic Frontier* (R.P. Peek and G.B. Newby, eds). Cambridge MA: MIT Press, pp. 215–229.

McKnight, S. (2003). Distance education and the role of academic libraries. In *Handbook of Distance Education* (M.G. Moore and W.G. Anderson, eds) Mahwah, NJ: Lawrence Erlbaum, pp. 377–386.

Miez, P. (1995). The view from a university library: Revolutionary change in scholarly and scientific communications. *Change*, **27**(1), 28–33.

Moyo, L.M. (2004). The virtual patron. *Science and Technology Libraries*, **25**, 185–209.

Olson, J.E. (2001). Distance learning and the transformation of higher education. *The Reference Librarian*, **74**, 221–232.

Online Computer Library Center (2005). *Perceptions of Libraries and Information Resources. A Report to the OCLC Membership.* Retrieved February 13, 2006 from http://www.oclc.org/reports/2005perceptions.htm.

Orr, D., Appleton, N., and Wallin, M. (2001). Information literacy and flexible delivery: a conceptual framework and model. *Journal of Academic Librarianship*, **27**, 457–463.

Rosenberg, J.A. (1984). New ways to find book: Searching, locating, and information delivery. *History Teacher*, **17**, 387–391.

Slade, A.L. (2005). *Library Services for Distance Learning: The Fourth Bibliography.* Retrieved February 5, 2006, from http://uviclib.uvic.ca/dls/bibliography4.html.

Slade, A.L. and Kascus, M. (1996). *Library Services for Off Campus and Distance Education: The Second Annotated Bibliography*. Englewood, CO: Libraries Unlimited.

Slade, A.L. and Kascus, M. (2000). *Library Services for Open and Distance Learning: The Third Annotated Bibliography*. Englewood, CO: Libraries Unlimited.

Society of College, National and University Libraries. (2001). *Access for Distance Learners: Report of the SCONUL Task Force.* Retrieved February 19, 2006 from http://www.sconul.ac.uk/pubs_stats/pubs/distancelearners_report.doc.

Stephens, K. and Unwin, L. (1996). *Revisiting "Openness and Closure in Distance": A Critical Look at the Access Image of Distance Learning in the United Kingdom.* Paper presented at the Research in Distance Education 4. Revised papers from the Research in Distance Education Conference, Deakin University, Geelong, Australia.

Stoffle, C.J. and Williams, K. (1995). The instructional program and responsibilities of the teaching library. *New Directions for Higher Education*, **90**, 63–75.

Todd, R. (2000). *Information Literacy: Concept, Conundrum, and Challenge.* Paper presented at Concept, Challenge, Conundrum: From Library Skills to Information Literacy. Proceedings of the Fourth National Information Literacy Conference, Adelaide, Australia.

Webber, S. and Johnston, B. (2000). Conceptions of information literacy: New perspectives and implications. *Journal of Information Science*, **26**, 381–397.

Zurkowski, P.G. (1974). *The Information Service Environment: Relationships and Priorities.* Washington, DC: National Commission on Libraries and Information Science.

Chapter 20

Engaging the Digital Natives

Brian Pauling

> Anyone who tries to make a distinction between education and entertainment doesn't know the first thing about either.
>
> T-Shirt message attributed to Marshall McLuhan

This chapter is based on 40 years of personal experience as a broadcaster, a broadcast educator and, in recent years, some involvement in distance learning. The key elements of that experience used to inform this discussion are the following:

- The nature of the student entering higher education has changed and will continue to change;
- We are in the midst of a technological revolution and like all revolutions there will be a period of instability as the outcomes impact on the very nature of human behaviour and modes of existence;
- We need to understand this more;
- Higher education has been slow to adapt to technology changes but cannot avoid the challenges and changes that will impact on the sector;
- Large media conglomerates faced with increasingly fragmenting markets and challenges from start-up Internet-based services will respond by taking more than a marginal interest in distance learning.

This chapter examines in a somewhat discursive manner some of the current media behaviours of young people, reviews the technologies that digital natives engage with and comments on the engagement or non-engagement of learning providers with those same technologies. Finally, it makes some suggestions as to how the developing but sometimes fractious relationship between digital media and digitally mediated learning might reach a satisfying consummation.

20.1 MEDIA CONSUMPTION BY YOUNG PEOPLE

When the New Zealand Broadcasting School[1] was first established 25 years ago, the student intake was noted for the high level of language, literacy and comprehension skills.[2] The School's curriculum needed to introduce the students to the visual and audio "languages" of broadcasting at a very basic level. They were unfamiliar with the grammar of the screen, uncomfortable in writing for the ear and had virtually no knowledge of the technologies of broadcasting. They were however well read, had inquiring minds, a willingness to learn and high attention levels.

The contrast with today's students is marked. The curriculum no longer assumes lack of visual and aural skills. Many of the students have run a school radio station, created videos that have been entered into competitions and composed their own music which they have recorded, edited and post-produced themselves. They know what a storyboard is, can "set white balance" on a camera, have sometimes more than a basic understanding of visual grammar, can compose quite sophisticated screen shots and quite early on are producing sophisticated products that students of an earlier generation could only attempt at the end of the 3-year program. They watch much more television and listen to more radio, probably because there is now much more to watch and listen to! They are less well read but very knowledgeable about Google, Yahoo and the World Wide Web. Their years of soaking up multiple media messages and getting to "know what they like" lead them to have more definite opinions. They engage with each other in the "Internet 2" social networking sites of You Tube and My Space creating "virtual" relationships all over the physical world.[3] They are not less inquiring but perhaps more cynical and in need of more persuading. Their attention spans are indeed shorter but they are much more able to multi-task, work quickly and take risks.

Whilst these are very subjective observations informed by many years of teaching media and involvement with young people seeking a broadcasting career, there is evidence of major changes in the way young people behave as a result of their engagement with digital space. Just take three short examples from New Zealand:

> Emma[4] is a member of a team that has produced an award winning interactive Web site. The site provides a simulated exercise in setting up and running a small business. Embedded within the site are MP3 audio tracts, streaming video and Flash animations. The objective of the Web site is to provide fellow students with the opportunity to learn basic business and entrepreneurial skills by designing their own business and making it successful. Emma's primary school supports the project and encourages students to participate in the online simulation. Emma is 10 years old.[5]
>
> Hohepa attends a small school in the central North Island of New Zealand. He has become a skilled digital video editor because the school has established a fully functioning television studio complex. The facility includes a three-camera studio with lighting grid and cyc-screen, a control room with a production consul and a digital post-production edit suit. The school produces a weekly current affairs and news program focusing on events in the town and surrounding rural community. The students have produced material with sufficiently high production values to gain exposure on national network television. Hohepa is 12 years old.[6]

> Joanna spends a lot of time in a real-time online game. She has created an alto ego character (avatar) and role plays that character in the game. The character is a 25 year old male warrior who engages with a range of other avatars in a complex online community that is struggling to protect its safety and security. Joanna is also twelve.[7]

These three short examples have been chosen randomly from a plethora of sophisticated technologically engaging activities currently seen in hundreds of New Zealand primary schools around the country that range from the stylish middle-class suburbs of large cities to remote rural communities and reflect an equally broad range of ethnic, social and economic diversity. With strong support from the government and a national broadband network, thousands of New Zealand children are being introduced to ICT and the resources of the Internet and the Web.

These young people are "screenagers", Douglas Rushkoff's (1996) term for "digital natives", the first generation of students brought up in an entirely digitally mediated world. Cell phones, portable media players, personal digital assistants and laptop computers are part of their standard "dress code". They have been exposed to digital media from a very young age and embraced without question the ever increasing babel of media messages aimed directly and explicitly at them. They distress their parents with their constant daily engagement with ubiquitous digital tools out of which emerge vast amounts of digital data free from the traditional constraints of the mediated analogue traditions. It is media full of richness, complexity and diversity on the one hand, on the other it contains much risk – a "dark side" which both excites the screenager and frightens the parent!

They are comfortable and confident in handling a complex mix of sound, vision, graphics and text in their screen-based multimedia world. Many of them move effortlessly between the "real world" and the "virtual world" of cyberspace assuming, like Joanna above, complex personas as avatars in online real-time multiple-user interactive games. They share files in peer-to-peer chat rooms, engage in complex multi-tasking, have their own pages on You Tube, My Space and Bebo and create their own blogshperes, podcasts and online productions. By the time they reach university, they will have been exposed to thousands of hours of television, a medium that in their lifetime has moved from being a few regulated and relatively conservative channels to an unregulated aggressively commercial multi-channel environment that bombards society with countless images calculatingly designed to seduce the viewer and "hold" an audience, a far cry from the Reithian tradition of educate, inform and entertain!

Meanwhile the "digital immigrants", those who have had to change and adapt from the old linear analogue world to the new asynchronous digital one and who bring with them much of the "baggage" of that old world and a reluctance to fully hold onto the new, are the teachers! How ironic that one of the significant online projects supported by the New Zealand Ministry of Education, aptly called "Tech Angels", is where roles are reversed and the teachers in the schools become students as their students tutor them in the intricacies of the digital world![8] The "digital divide" is just not a geographical and economic concept, it is also an intergenerational one.

The "digital natives" are using media technology in ways that are perplexing, worrying and threatening to many older people. Perplexing in the sense that they do not understand how the technology functions, they fail to see the "logic" in spending long periods of time text messaging on the cell phone, and their own attempts to grapple with the technologies themselves often fail because they lack the patience to learn about the subtleties and intricacies of computing. Worrying because they witness the increasing amount of media consumption by young people and the perceived shortened attention span many young people bring to the traditional learning tasks of reading and writing. They feel that sense of ubiquitous "moral panic", which has been an intergenerational presence for generations, as they observe the content of much of the media aimed at youth. And threatening because in not understanding it, not participating in it and feeling that moral panic they begin to fear both the technology itself and the generation that consume it.

Young people are engaging with digital media in unprecedented amounts.[9] Eighty-seven percent of teenagers in the United States use the Internet, 81 percent play games online and 76 percent get news online. Half of US teenagers use cell phones daily, but in Europe, 88 percent of early teenagers (12–14) own a mobile phone! Surveys suggest that many hours a day (6–7) are spent using various forms of media. It has become the most significant time-consuming activity outside of sleeping. It's more than the average working week of 40 hours. Further, they are rejecting traditional analogue electronic media (radio and television) in favour of new forms. Over the last 5 years, the television viewing of British 16- to 19-year olds has reduced from 22 hours to less than 16 hours. According to the survey, that age group engages with messaging (SMS or IMS) for 6 hours a week, 15 hours a week on digital gaming and 9 hours a week on the Internet. It must be noted that this particular outcome shows that while television watching reduced by over 6 hours, the new activities exceeded those 6 hours by a factor of four. This has been explained by the practice of "multi-tasking", doing things simultaneously. Young people are increasingly adept at using more that one form of media at once. Half of the young people responding to the Pew survey use IMS to carry out several conversations at the same time on a regular basis, and less than 4 percent of IMS users say they have never carried out multiple simultaneous conversations. One European media executive has said that the "average child in 1 hour consumes 1 $\frac{1}{2}$ hours worth of media. The way it works is that every device is on and they are just pick-and-mixing" (Woods, 2005). Many have a range of online personas that have characteristics and practices different to their owners. Being online is second nature:

> I use it (the Internet) more on a daily basis than I did when I was younger. I would get online maybe in the evenings or something, if I had nothing else to do. But now, it's kind of like you get home, sign-on, turn your music on.
>
> (Pew, 2005)

The average young person's life is surrounded by technology.

> New homes come complete with special nooks for oversized TV screens and home entertainment centres, while new cars come with personal TV screens in the back of each seat. The amount of media a person used to consume in a month can be downloaded in minutes and carried in a device the size of a lipstick tube. Today

> we get movies on cell phones, TVs in cars and radio through the Internet. Media technologies themselves are morphing and merging, forming an ever-expanding presence throughout our daily environment. Cell phones alone have grown to include video game platforms, e-mail devices, digital cameras and Internet connections.
>
> (Kaiser, 2005)

There is a sense in which young people are permanently "plugged in" staying connected, either to their digital devices or to each other via the devices. The "MTV generation", a phrase coined by the music channel MTV to describe the teenagers that dominate their ratings, is totally at home in a world that is in many senses a virtual one. Talking on online chat rooms, short-text messaging frequently and to a wide range of friends and acquaintances, downloading digital music (legally and illegally) using software like Bit Torrent to download television and movies (most often illegally) and playing an increasing range of multimedia digital games either online and in real time or interacting via personal gaming machines with structured gaming has turned the teenager's bedroom into a "connected cocoon". According to Active Research (Woods, 2005), more than a third of all kids' bedrooms in Europe contain all of the following:

Television set (72%)
CD Player (64%)
Games consul (62%)
DVD player (55%)
Radio (49%)
Video cassette recorder (43%)
Personal computer (35%)

But it is not just in the home that children are being exposed to the media tsunami. More and more primary schools are introducing students to the Web at an early age. In schools, the Internet is used to encourage global communications across cultures and national boundaries. It is used as a major, sometime primary, source of information reducing the significance of the library.[10] Keyboard skills are considered as of equal importance in the curriculum as handwriting skills. Digital cameras, video recorders and associated software programs are used to create a classroom online presence. Students are encouraged to create narrative using sound and vision as well as text. There are increasing opportunities for children to enter into sponsored competitions for short videos, Web site design and audio podcasts. Many are growing up with an innate understanding of what looks and sound "good". By the time they get to secondary school, they have a grasp of productions values that used to be the sole purview of the film and television producer!

Perhaps the most significant change in young people's behaviour as a result of digital technologies is gaming. A vast new industry has been created to cater for the demands of the gaming market. Research indicates that revenue from online gaming subscriptions will exceed one-and-a-half billion US dollars by 2006 when it will generate $773.8 million in online PC games advertising (Greenspan, 2003). Even more significant is the role that will be played in the gaming market by emerging wireless technologies, such as third-generation (3G) cell phones. Sophisticated handsets, colour screens and dynamic sound allow for the development of a portable gaming environment. Games on mobile phones and PDAs are already proving popular in Asia. And games are becoming an increasing part of cultural experience in the West. The online gaming population is continuing to grow, and the demographic is getting broader. Once the major preoccupation of young males, more and more women are now engaging with gaming, and in 2005, there is almost a balance, 49 percent women vs. 51 percent men (Nielsen, 2005). The Nielson report suggests that playing video games of all kinds is increasing. What was once "considered the domain of teen boys, has evolved into a medium that is now capable of reaching expanding demographics of gamers, including females . . . and older players, ... It's quite possible playing video games will assume a significant role as a common cultural experience, in the way that movies and television do today." According to another Myers (2005), among teens, 71.5 percent of all males and 47.7 percent of all females played video games either on consoles or online in 1 week, with males spending an average of 1 hour and 54 minutes daily and females an average of 36 minutes daily.

Finally and perhaps most importantly, the social pressures to join the world of digital devices are also strong. To feel connected socially requires being connected digitally. Being "switched on" is essential to belonging. It also changes the content of personal communication. Surveys (Pew, 2005) show that many young people are less inhibited when in digital contact, and comments suggest that a large number have made remarks in the digital environment that they would not make face to face. More than anytime in our history, technology is dominant in creating cultural phenomena surely fulfilling Marshall McLuhan's prophetic statement, the "medium is the message" (McLuhan, 1964).

> Many students are entering their school or college with multiple literacies that go beyond text, and this trend will strengthen over the coming years. Educators will need to acknowledge and recognise these new literacies, and build upon and extend them.
>
> (Education.au.Ltd, 2005)

In terms of distance education, what sort of learning situations will "neomillennial" university students expect? How will educators react to students with shortened attention spans in linear communications but highly skilled attributes in multi-tasking and strong abilities in asynchronistic interaction? Will such students embrace distance education more willingly than their predecessors?

Or to paraphrase Steve Simpson:

> Now picture the average lecture theatre, say 60 students, some books, perhaps an overhead projector, and a teacher. How does a mere mortal communicate with a generation of human beings raised 40 plus hours a week in a media-saturated environment?
>
> (Simpson, 2005)

However, before leaving this part of the discussion, some global perspective and a small dose of reality would not go astray. Only 15 percent of the world's population is connected to the Internet.[11] Sixty percent of the world's population lack access to a telephone service. Rich countries have per capita GDPs of much greater magnitude than those of the poorest countries. Much more is therefore spend on ICT. And within countries, the rich tend to appropriate more of the benefits of the Information Revolution than do the poor. It is not just the technologies but the human knowledge and understanding that needs to benefit from them. This is no better illustrated than in the United States. That country can afford the most sophisticated and computerised weather prediction technology. The coasts are studded with a network of sensors; satellite mapping monitors every weather pattern, and specially equipped aircraft can fly into the very centre of storms and hurricanes. Yet Hurricane Katrina in 2005 demonstrated that even with such technology, only those with the resources (i.e. wealth) could take advantage of the knowledge and escape, and poorly trained and understaffed agencies could not use the knowledge to effectively minimise impact. In contrast, similar levels of technology coupled with the depth and breadth of military training saw the swift defeat of Iraq's large, and very experienced military in the first Iraq war, by an ICT intensive US force that could accurately predict the outcome of such conflicts knowing with some certainty that the initial war would be quick and US casualties would be quite low. In both cases, it was those on the wrong side of the digital divide that suffered: on the one hand the local poor and on the other a poor nation.

20.2 THE TECHNOLOGY

Jorma Ollila, former chief executive of Nokia is cited by Rossiter (2003) as arguing that there are three technology pillars that have shaped the development of society: digital convergence, the Internet protocol and mobility. He believes that these three together provide us with the long-predicted (McLuhan and Fiore, 1967) networked information society. These are the technologies so heavily embraced by the "digital natives".

20.2.1 Digital Convergence

This can be discussed in two modes. The first focuses on the technologies and the second on content. Whilst the former is the "driver" of digital convergence, the latter is the significant outcome. "Convergence" refers to the profound changes in the structure of media caused by the emergence of digital technologies as the dominant method for representing, storing and communicating information. In the past, information and communication technologies were segmented into discrete economic and technical systems with minimal capabilities for interoperability. For example, cable television used a discrete coaxial cable while telephony used the PSTN copper wire and computers used the Ethernet LAN[12] (Scales, 1999). These "vertical" models of applications developed as separate services throughout the twentieth century. Towards the end of the century the development of digitalisation began the "horizontal" integration of such technologies that enables a complex "diversity of implementations and approaches to coexist and evolve" creating "bitways" which can simultaneously transport sound, video, text and other data (Messerschmitt, 1996). Over the last 30 years four previously discrete technologies, text-based print media (books, newspapers, magazines, etc.), broadcasting (radio and television), telecommunications (telephones) and computers have, as a result of digitalisation, "merged" to provide a seamless "single" platform for storage and distribution. Two further consequences are that there is a growing amount of overlap in the functions that can be performed by different physical communication networks, and there is a growth in the interactivity, interoperability and connectedness of different networks and information appliances used in the home, in business and industry.[13] The development and application of these new convergent technologies have impacted, to a greater or lesser extent, on virtually every human activity.

In terms of content, the history of information storage and retrieval has for thousands of years been of a "single order" in nature and that order was first-written codex and then print (Luke, 1996). Except for illustration and the development in the nineteenth century of photography, it was text based. However, a "second-order" distribution system was developed just over 100 years ago with the invention of electronic media, such as radio, television, telephony and mechanical moving pictures. This created a "dual-order" media and information environment, electronic and mechanical analogue based non-text media on the one hand and print-based traditions on the other.[14] The second-order media developed rapidly reaching the "maturity" of social saturation in very quick time (Bittner, 1985). They remained discrete and functioned independently of each other relying on different technology platforms. Large industries developed around each medium and people had increasingly sophisticated content choices delivered over each platform. However, content creation was restricted because of two factors. The first was that content was confined to the capabilities of the platform (radio waves, celluloid, copper wire) and the second was that content was limited by the capacities of the platform (spectrum, camera and film speeds, cable reticulation and signal capacity).

Digital convergence enabled the data from the previously discrete technologies, no matter the form – text, pictures, moving images, audio and graphics – to be converted into a series of binary numbers. It enabled those numbers to be transmitted at high speed via cable, wireless or satellite to virtually any destination. At the destination, the data is able to be stored for later use in its binary form or converted back to the original source – text, pictures, moving images, audio and graphics – for immediate use. The data can be used and reused countless times without any diminution of quality. It enables the creation of mixed media and multimedia formats in ways not previously possible.[15] Furthermore, digital compression technologies enable vast quantities, some would argue infinite quantities, of data to be stored. Lyman and Varian (2000) see us as "drowning in a sea of information". They argue that "it's taken 300,000 years for humans to accumulate 12 exabytes of information.[16] It will take just 2.5 more years to create the next 12 exabytes".[17] Figure 20.1 attempts to model Luke's single/dual/single order concept.

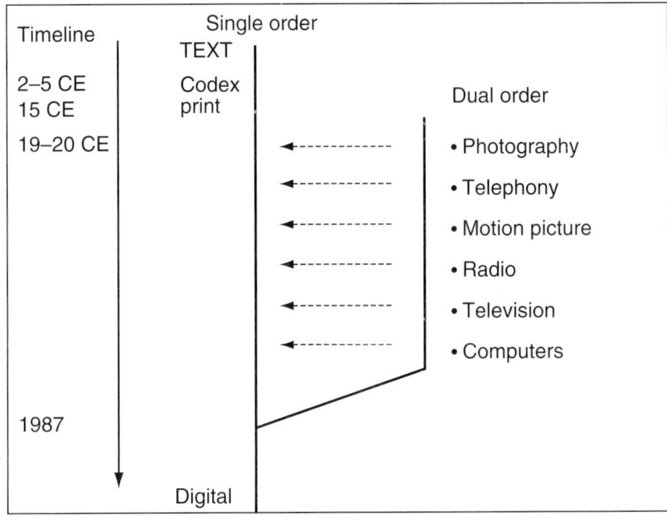

Figure 20.1: Graphic Schema of Luke's Model

20.3 THE INTERNET PROTOCOL

The development of the Internet from a small military experiment in the late 1960s to the technological force it is today was unexpected as it was rapid. Two elements were significant in the rapid uptake of the Internet. The first was the development of the personal computer and the second the changed role of the telecommunications industry. The development of the personal computer in the early 1980s put computing power into the hands of individuals, and a new economy was created around the creation and development of PCs. It is indicative of its significance that a product that didn't exist 20 years ago is so ubiquitous today. Current statistics indicate that PCs exist in 95 percent of businesses in the Western economies and in 50 percent of homes (CIA, 2005). No product in the history of technology has experienced such a rapid uptake.[18] Secondly, the rapid deregulation of telecommunications companies occurred during this same period. Released from state management or strict regulation, the telcos were looking for new and innovative business opportunities. To develop their voice networks to carry the new digital data was a way of generating fresh revenue to fund new products, such as the roll out of the new carriage technologies of fibre optic and satellite. The involvement of the telcos who have a history of legislated for international cooperation (spectrum allocation, interconnection protocols, international call pricing, etc.) enabled the development of universal standard communications protocols. With the common Internet Transmission Control Protocol/Internet Protocol (TCP/IP) universally accepted, service providers could use the worldwide networks to develop product, such as data services, electronic mail, file transfer, remote login, bulletin boards and the World Wide Web (Huurdeman, 2003).

The Internet has provided opportunities for and challenges to a range of businesses and organisations with its enabling of both synchronous and asynchronous interactive communication, instant and delayed, over vast physical distance. Moreover, the unprecedented technological developments associated with computers and the Internet are still occurring. The two areas of greatest development and continual change are the speed with which data can be transferred and the capacity for increasing amounts of data to be stored in decreasing physical space.[19]

The development of broadband is perhaps the most significant technological feature after the digitalisation process itself. It challenges the very nature of electronic communication and provides opportunities for new delivery platforms for video and audio. It also provides the capacity for emerging platforms, such as satellite and fibre optic cable to provide multiple channels of data and a high-speed return path to permit complex interactivity.

Broadband is a transmission and switching system that has very high bandwidth, i.e. it can carry large amounts of data extremely rapidly. Bandwidth and compression are two key elements of the new broadband delivery system. Bandwidth is the amount of the frequency available or needed to transmit data (pictures, sound, digital packets, etc.) over a medium, such as a cable, the airwaves or through an electronic device; the higher the bandwidth available, the greater the amount of data that can be transferred per second. Bandwidth within the spectrum is always a limited usable resource, thus there has been a tradition and a need for either regulation or a market to ration its use. Bandwidth on cable is only limited by the cable's size and capacity. In terms of today's fibre optic technology, this is almost limitless. Compression is the ability to reduce data to minimal size by not resending redundant data. For example, if only the face changes between two frames of a moving picture showing a human body, only the data related to the facial changes is sent (Norris and Pauling, 2005).

Today, broadband is more than bandwidth and compression, more than simple, static content. It is a combination of interactivity, access speed, delivery mode and demanding content. It means faster access and better performance of electronic data sent from a source to a recipient. Broadband therefore challenges the accepted model of the Internet being mainly a data stream and television being mainly an entertainment stream. Successful broadband applications blur the line between television and PCs and suggest that previously separate uses of these may blend with the development of hybrid platforms. Indeed, broadcasters are now beginning to "bring their whole content portfolio to the PC" (Kerschbaumer, 2005).

20.3.1 Mobility

Wherever one looks, the evidence of mobile penetration and adoption is irrefutable. The number of worldwide cellular subscribers is predicted to be close to three billion by 2009, up from 1.6 billion in 2004 (David, 2005). With increased saturation comes increased functionality and services. The mobile phone has quickly become ubiquitous in the West. In less than 15 years, it has moved from a single service device to multiple services with the launching of 3G networks opening up new opportunities for the delivery of content to mobile devices. Third-generation technology enables video to be streamed or downloaded to mobile devices in close to broadcast quality. Today's mobile phone can incorporate PDAs (personal digital assistants), cameras, Web browsers, e-mail clients, music players, portable games, radio services, television and global positioning systems. Specific services for individuals and groups are being developed that permit a vast range of activities.[20]

Full-service mobile devices are being installed in buses, taxis, trains and motor vehicles.[21] Radio Frequency Identification Devices (RFID) installed in vehicles enable the payment of tolls and other transport charges. They are also revolutionising the inventory and supply services in industry. RFID tags are attached to domestic animals and, in the United States increasingly to children as a security protection. New-generation wireless systems provide broadband always-on connectivity and the capability to track individual devices wherever they may be (Wolleben, 2005).

Thus as "mobile connectedness continues to sweep across the landscape" (Wagner, 2005), the modality changes produced by the three Ollila pillars are no better demonstrated than by the rapid adoption by business of new 3G mobile services. Research company Gartner claims that the abilities of executives to send and receive all forms of data to a portable mobile device that can fit in a pocket has caused the worldwide sale of PDAs to jump 34 percent in the first quarter of 2005 (Jenkins, 2005). As further evidence of the modality changes there are calls for universities to recognise the ubiquitous nature of the mobile phone in the hands of students on campuses and utilise them as both "m-learning" (mobile learning) and e-commerce (administration) tools (Alexander, 2004; Wagner, 2005, p. 16). It is the establishment of the Ollila pillars that enable world leaders to optimistically state that the world is

> entering a new era of enormous potential, that of the information society and expanded human communication. In this emerging society, information and knowledge can be produced, exchanged, shared and communicated through all the networks (mobile or fixed) of the world.... We trust that these measures will open the way to the future development of a true knowledge society.
>
> (WSIS, 2003)

20.4 THE SEARCH FOR NEW PRODUCT

Throughout the media world, Ollila's pillars significantly reduce the geographical and social barriers that previously inhibited the rapid exchange of information. They also make possible a high degree of interaction between information providers and consumers, enable the linking of specific groups with similar interests to each other and facilitate a higher degree of control by individuals over the time, place and pace of their information consumption. Organisations with previously clearly defined roles (broadcasting, telecommunications, publishing) are now faced with challenges that threaten their previously secure and defined territories. For example, Negroponte (1995) argued 25 years ago that there would be a dramatic switch in technology platforms as broadcasting, particularly television, moved from wireless mode to wired mode, while telephones would move in the exact opposite direction from wired to wireless. This is now increasingly the case as coaxial cable, fibre optic cable and enhanced compression technologies on copper wire (ADSLx) permit the transmission of high-definition television signals to the home and 3G wireless mobile phone technologies make mobile phones the personal communications application of choice. Publishers are now seeing an increasing number of books and journals made available in digital form. New services and new technologies are on the cusp of creating a new communications, information and entertainment environment.

These new services and new technologies are not exclusive to one platform or medium. Traditional players are responding to them by changing their behaviours as new core functionalities are discovered. The traditional broadcaster, telecommunications provider and publisher who had exclusive control over the creation, aggregation and distribution of their own product are reshaping to play multiple roles as content providers creating content for multiple platforms, content aggregators supplying content for distribution over multiple platforms and content distributors providing access to content on discrete or multiple platforms.

For example, telecommunications companies are taking multimedia content from a range of content providers, broadcasters, newspapers, libraries and behaving as aggregators (SBC). Broadcasters are using telco networks to distribute content on Web pages that contain print material from newspaper sources as well as audio and video (BBC Online). Publishers are using the Internet to provide digital copies of their print-based product that includes audio and video product as accompaniments to their books (Taylor and Francis, Prentice Hall, etc.). Newspapers are producing online versions of their papers that contain not just print, photographs and graphs but embedded video and audio enhancements taken from broadcast sources (www.stuff.co.nz). All services are developing digital archives for the storage and retrieval of their material and providing access to subscribers and on occasion the general public (BBC Archives, The Guardian Archive).

This is creating what some see as a revolution and just as the previous agrarian and industrial revolutions created instability this one is too. The most immediate impact on the once stable and discrete media industries is a struggle for identity and perhaps even survival. Telecommunications traditionally controlled the voice and analogue data networks that linked society; broadcasters traditionally controlled the visual and aural networks that entertained society. The arrival of the Internet coupled with the aforementioned convergence enables the existing traditions to encroach on each other's territories. Lower barriers to entry are also attracting new players and entrepreneurs into markets over which, previously, network broadcasters and telecommunications organisations could claim exclusivity.

Thus as the homes in Western nations acquire greater information technology power by the day people have the chance to explore global networks and utilise increasingly sophisticated multimedia technologies to a level never before experienced. As this happens, the pressure grows for information providers (publishers, broadcasters, libraries, educational institutions, etc.) to redesign their operations, take advantage of the technologies and create new product.[22] A new term "datacasting" has been coined to encompass all of this.[23] It's an obvious enough blend of *data* and *broadcasting*, and it's a cover-all term for the transmission of various kinds of data as a service on digital networks. Initially, the phrase was used to describe enhancements to traditional broadcasting but now it covers the total spectrum of converged communications services providing capability for e-commerce and a host of applications for business, personal use, education and entertainment, some of which, it has to be said, have yet to be created.

Digital is an enabling technology. How far and fast the digital revolution proceeds depends on factors, such as consumer behaviour, business models, the roles of the broadcasters, telcos and government regulation. But predicated on existing behaviour changes and new services already in existence, a model of datacasting services can be predicated.

In this model, the personal computer and the television set are merged and the screen becomes the focus of information and entertainment services to the home. First, there are the video centric elements common to any subscriber to a multi-channel pay service, news weather, sports, music, comedy, drama, games shows and specialty channels. Closely linked are a range of enhanced video programs usually interactive in nature and focused more on the individual consumer's needs, including gambling, online gaming, in-depth information services (sporting statistics, news archives, financial, market statistics). Finally, there are the datacasting services where the computer role of the screen enables a range of Internet-based, interactive data totally customised to meet interest and need and include health and education services, government services (including polling), banking, insurance and other financial services, travel and online shopping.

Mobile phone companies are not going to be left out of the revolution. They are already offering, trialling or talking about providing all of the following services via the cell phone screen (Table 20.1).[24]

New players are emerging; many of them are organisations not previously engaged in media distribution. They include government agencies, Internet service providers, satellite distribution companies, multimedia production houses, universities and corporations from the large transnational conglomerates to small businesses offering multimedia presentations of their products on the Internet. Existing organisations previously outside of electronic media are becoming players. Examples of these include newspaper, magazine and book publishers, and film studios.

Table 20.1: A Range of Mobile Digital Services

E-commerce	*Marketing and Advertising*	*Financial Information*
Tele-surveillance	Remote diagnosis	Voice activation
Mobile conferencing	Video telephony	Global IP telephony
Remote training	Virtual universities	Multimedia kiosks
Home entertainment	News and information	Home banking
Sports coverage	Gaming	Email
Web access	Home multimedia	Travel
Navigation	Distance learning	T-commerce

Consumers will decide the right mix for them at any given time. Predictions as to the nature of the industry as it absorbs these developing technologies are necessarily tentative. However, it could be argued that the development of such all pervading technologies coupled with the aforementioned wide continuum of services will dramatically change the behaviour of the consumer. The passive mass audience attributes of the traditional media will be overtaken by the targeted, interactive, multi-dimensional attributes of the "Me Channel"[25] (Norris and Pauling, 2005).

But there are risks and uncertainties as there are with every paradigm shift. If the technological changes are producing social upheavals similar to the previous agrarian and industrial revolutions, then there will be disruptions because of the inability of existing social, economic and political structures to provide support and guidance. A clear indicator that this is the case can be seen in current commercial behaviour. For example, new and untested business models have arisen but the markets, not sure how to respond to them, have become unstable. In both previous revolutions, boom and bust cycles occurred. The so called dot.com period (1995–2000) was one that produced a remarkable range of successes and failures as entrepreneurs sought new products and services. The behaviour of economies, governments and societies (and also many institutions of higher education) through the dot.com period demonstrated confused responses to the challenges of the revolution. Indeed, the uncertainty surrounding the behaviours of national governments and their regulatory agencies as they wrestle with appropriate policies and procedures to support new markets to develop and to mitigate market failures is overt (Bonnett, 1999; Jalil, 2000) and this also impacts on institutions of higher education (HE) (see later).

Whatever the outcome, we are in the digital age, these are the technologies that young people are engaging with, and demonstrably, young people are the target audience for most of the new product that the unstable media industries are developing in their rush for a place in the digital millennium. Whither education?

20.5 HIGHER EDUCATION'S ENGAGEMENT WITH NEW MEDIA

One of the criticisms of education in general and HE in particular is that it has failed to change with the times, and this was no better illustrated than in the university's use, or to be precise, non-use of technology. Someone once said that if a person from the nineteenth century were to return today, the only thing they would recognise would be the classroom. For over 500 years text formed the basis of every learning experience in the West.

20.5.1 Disengagement

Universities were never keen on electronic technologies and failed to embrace non-print mass communications technologies in the first 100 years of their existence. They played little role in the classroom at any level despite the "promises" that proponents of the technologies touted. For example, radio was going to "liberate" learning for the masses and reduce the "tyranny of distance" with educational broadcasts (Waniewicz, p. 58). Film and television were going to revolutionise instruction by adding pictures to voice and replace text as the dominant means of distance learning. "Educational Television is the most powerful tool of all and it won't be so long before it is universally available. We should be planning and experimenting in anticipation of that day," said Potts (1979, p. 22). Computers were going to make teachers redundant with computer-aided learning (Stonier and Conlin, 1985) and Skinner (1954, p. 97) pushed for the development of a "teaching machine" that would "free" the teacher. While none of this happened, the newer media existed side by side with traditional print, and during that time, they played an increasingly important role in just about every other communications activity. To use an analogy, education's engagement with mass communications covers a gamut of experiences that epitomise an "on-again-off-again" relationship – attraction, excitement, fear, and loathing. But on the whole, it has been an unconsummated relationship (Rushkoff, 1994). During much of their development, the technologies of radio, cinema and film, telecommunications, television, computers, videotext and multimedia, were located outside of mainstream academe to the extent that concepts, such as "technoculture" and "cyberspace" recognisable in the discourses of other disciplines were not been identified in discourses on formal education until very late in the twentieth century (Luke, 1996). Meanwhile, the rest of society became saturated with electronic media and operated comfortably in the dual print and electronic modes. To continue with the preceding analogy therefore, whilst education has "flirted" with each medium as it developed, there was never a commitment to any substantial long-term relationship.

20.5.2 Re-engagement

However, with the arrival of digital technologies and the ability to store and transmit every previously discrete medium in a series of one's and two's, educational agencies have engaged with technology in a manner not seen in the preceding 100 years (Watts, 1999). Maybe it is too harsh to suggest that newer analogue technologies were ignored because their impact would have been felt mainly in the classroom, the least valued role within the university. But it is clear that when computers were first developed, their value in research became immediately apparent. The ability to sort and analyse large volumes of data had particular appeal to the quantitative research model that dominated academic research at the time. Mainframe computers sprung up everywhere, and as the cost of computing came down, the use of computers spread from, initially, scientists and mathematicians to the wider university community.

Just a few years after the arrival of the PC, Abraham Peled (1987) was able to say, "The way computing has permeated the fabric of purposeful intellectual and economic activity has no parallel". The PC was transforming human behaviour and interaction in just about every field of endeavour, business, science, entertainment, the military, government, law, banking, travel, medicine, agriculture and, of course, the world of education.

Today computers are prominent in all facets of HE ranging across administration, data storage and distribution, library technologies, electronic mail, as alternative tools for teaching and research and, of course, distance learning. The large number of courses available on the Web is testimony to this. Yet the elusive "virtual university", the holy grail of distance learning where time, distance and space become irrelevant as the student interactively accesses the best university minds irrespective of location while still a distinct possibility is far from being a reality.

> The proliferation of VLEs running on desktop, networked computers, has allowed a number of institutions to offer subjects online to some extent. But, on the whole there is not a well articulated, homogenous, online learning strategy rather, "the majority... are patchy initiatives using piecemeal methods to deliver uncoordinated services via the Web."
>
> (McKey, 2003)

This criticism has some currency. Currently, there is little coordination so that different institutions and even different faculties within the same institution are using different software systems based on a range of ad hoc decisions which include cost and using what staff skills are available. Often it's a question of taking existing course material and "digitising" them making no changes to meet the unique opportunities offered by the new medium. Often the support and administration services offered by these programs are based on the 9 a.m.–6 p.m. mindset of the campus institution and do not accommodate the 24/7 needs of the online student.

And while students are taught using an increasing variety of teaching methods, print is still by far the most common mode. For distance students, it usually includes a subject outline, study guide, readings or laboratory manuals and student purchased textbooks. In some subjects, audio cassette tapes or video tapes are used as supplements to text. Increasingly, faculty are using e-mail to communicate with students and provide one-on-one feedback.

And despite the costly failures and overenthusiastic visions, distance learning continues to increase its share of the higher education "marketplace". However, it is far from the vision that has been idealised in the literature where the ideals of digitally produced and delivered material technology dominate.

That vision sees technology permitting for the first time the full replication of the classroom. The previously mentioned analogue electronic technologies could not do that. They formed at best only a part of the three essential elements of the classroom – teacher–student interaction, student–student interaction and an accessible source of stored information. Those three elements and knowledge have enabled the teacher a controlled classroom to dominate educational practice for centuries. Current digitally enabled asynchronous communications comes close to replicating these. Furthermore, the technologies of interactivity entice the institution into a belief that effectiveness and efficiency (in economic and time terms at least) will increase as a result of much larger numbers of students engaging via the Internet thus increasing the number of students able to be accessed by one tutor and without the costs of building and maintaining more lecture theatres. The temptation has been to see more off-campus students as leading to more fees and greater revenue at less cost. Students would be off-campus thereby reducing the stress on such facilities as libraries, facilities and computer suites.

Governments also see value in providing digital technologies to education. The state has the contrary goals of wanting to reduce the costs of education, whilst at the same time wanting to achieve a better informed, educated and trained workforce. Distance learning technologies are seen as a way of creating the so-called knowledge society so dear to the hearts of politicians seeking security in the increasingly competitive globalised economy.

There is also appeal in the value of flexibility that distance learning technologies appear to bring. More teachers would be needed for shorter periods and for easily defined tasks. Higher education could become increasingly casualised enabling a business model for managing staff to develop with easier hiring and firing, avoiding the "difficulties" of tenure (Brabazon, 2003).

However, "success has yet to come" (Williams, 2003). While convergence of the technologies can enable the vision, other events are impacting at the same time, and they may be as significant as the technology. Barriers to the successful implementation of the virtual university include economic issues, issues of the political economy that HE is engaged with, the nature of teaching and learning and the very essence of the university itself as it struggles to maintain relevance in an increasingly "hostile" world. The reality is that students are not engaging with online learning in the numbers expected; institutions are finding the costs of creating and delivering online learning greater than expected; and other forces, such as economic, political and social, are putting pressures on educational institutions at unexpected levels.

Strong elements of cultural history and political economy also inform a technology's development (Williams, 1974). It must be remembered that while the engagement with online learning that has been so noticeable over the last decade is enabled by the technology, technology itself has never been the sole factor of any change. Technology is an enabler and other factors need to exist before a technology will be developed. Many dot.com crashes were examples of technologies desperately seeking a reason to exist! If there is no demand, no "business model", then the technology remains sidelined. Further, technology can be developed that people just don't see as useful at the time. The fax machine prototype was developed in the 1930s but it was not until the mid-1980s that they became prominent.

Again, failure in the use of digital technology and the fear of failure has become a strong factor in HE thinking. Most countries have their share of IT projects that have gone horribly wrong, and universities have had high profile failures in technology driven distance learning projects. Brabazon (2003) points out that both the Columbia University and the New York University spent large sums of money ($25 million each) on ventures that either folded or where greatly reduced. The University of Maryland, Virtual Temple (the online offering from Temple University) and the University of California closed their first attempts at online services and the London School of Economics stopped charging for its online courses and put them up for free, using them as a taster for conventionally delivered programs. The author, who notes these failures, suggests that e-learning has failed because of a desire to make money – and quickly and cites that the spending by companies supplying online material for the education market in the United States dropped to US$17 million from US$483 million just 2 years earlier

(Brabazon, 2003, p. 35). More recently, in 2004, the highly promoted and state of the art e-university in the United Kingdom (UKeU) folded. With UK£32 million of a budgeted £62 million spent, it was said to have less than 1,000 students enrolled worldwide for its courses (Williams, 2003). The United Kingdom's Open University lost $US9 million in an attempt to enter the US HE market which prompted one commentator to write

> E-learning was seen as an opportunity to cut costs by automating a recognised process (learning), cutting out the middlemen (teachers and admin staff), reducing inventory (books) and minimising real estate (classrooms).
>
> (MacLeod, 2004, p. 4)

Critics suggest a number of reasons for these problems. There was some resistance from faculty both in terms of technophobia and perceived increased workload. Lack of training and at times poor technical support meant that much of the online menu was far from appetising. Course notes and lecture notes were thrown up on the Web; there was little genuine interactivity either between students and lecturers or between students, and standards of design both of the content and the screen varied. The Internet promised much but delivered less especially when it came to bandwidth and was often frustratingly slow. And, most importantly, it turned out to be far more expensive to establish and maintain than the early adopters believed. These high-profile first generation online mistakes have led to caution if not scepticism when faced with making heavy financial commitments to online delivery.

Further, the costs of establishing and maintaining a technology infrastructure are significant. The major costs of installing, maintaining and keeping up with the rapid changes in information technology have been a strain on institutions and an inhibiting factor in the growth of distance learning and the electronic classroom. Certainly, HE expenditure on information technology has increased dramatically over the last 30 years but it still remains low in the overall comparison with commercial institutions (Leach, 2003).[26]

Technology has also aided the development of a more competitive and market-driven HE environment and played a key role as the language of the marketplace has infiltrated HE. Students are now seen as "customers" and learning has become a "product". Major changes to the administrative structure of universities have occurred as an outcome of the market approach to HE. The business model of fiscal responsibility and accountability has quite quickly replaced the public service model of funding based on need. Universities now promote and market themselves. Universities are competing for students and, as the technology allows, seeking custom from outside of their traditional geographic boundaries.

The technology is also aiding competitive threats external to the HE sector, some of which are a direct challenge to the hegemony of the university. Scott (1997) identifies new forms of "knowledge" institutions adapting to or created to benefit from, digitalisation that are not based on the same structural ideas as the university which he sees as direct rivals to the university. The university as the local repository of knowledge no longer has a monopoly when other repositories can be accessed online from around the globe. Moreover, as Kumar points out, there are two key roles that appear to be changing as technology intervenes. The roles of the teacher and the library seem to be most under challenge. It appears that the personal quality of teaching is losing value and is slipping in status in this age of mass education and large classes.

> It is not at all clear that the instruction provided through the new media technologies, especially those involving interactivity, is markedly inferior to that provided by teachers. As for libraries, for anyone who has a personal computer the best libraries in the world will soon be available to be screen-read at home. Universities need libraries but libraries do not necessarily need universities.
>
> (Kumar, 1997)

Nor does the university have dominance in the distribution of knowledge. New institutions, often lacking both the traditions and value of the university are evolving that play an increasingly important role in distributing ideas and information.

Technologies have enabled the rise of the "corporate university", developed for the advanced training needs of knowledge-based companies and large R&D units in both industry and government departments. They are a direct challenge to university exclusivity. There are new, alternative and open sources of knowledge that also claim some authority, Learning Channels owned by media companies, commercially owned and operated Web portals, and the Web itself are current examples of a rapidly increasing field.

Digitalisation has enabled a "re-branding" of many organisations. Examples include BBC Television, Thomson Publishing, a host of private research bodies (e.g. Gartner) and many Internet sites, all of whom are claiming authenticity and authority equal to HE institutions and openly challenging the university's position as the sole and "rightful" place for the discovery and dissemination of knowledge. Some argue that fragmentation is inevitable when difference is such a strong factor (Smith and Webster, 1997). In future, HE institutions may form only a part and maybe a small part of the knowledge-producing centre. Few, if any, universities have the technological resources to match the large transnational media conglomerates that are staking a claim to knowledge creation.

Then there are the pedagogical issues. Universities are facing challenges to the traditional mode of educational delivery. The industrial societies of the nineteenth and early twentieth centuries wanted workers who were skilled in replicating knowledge and actions and not thinkers who challenged them. Over time, the litany changed and the belief was that HE required students not only to understand and do but also to think, to challenge and debate. But the teaching was still classroom based, the teacher dominated and the curriculum was prescribed. The nature of the student has now changed. They are more consumers of learning who want what they want. They know, sometimes more than the teacher, that the new "knowledge economy" needs original thinkers (Florida, 2002), that the new "product" is not material or stable in nature, rather it is intangible, unstable and forever in need of reversioning or, to use the language of the media, repurposing. They know that gaining access to knowledge is no longer limited to the classroom. Time and place constraints have ceased to be issues for information and entertainment sources, and they ask why they should remain issue for learning sources.

Just-in-time learning, at the student's pace and in the student's place, delivered as original and compelling content, should be possible. Learning that is sui generis in thought and able to compete within and sustain a return from the post-modern marketplace of ideas is being sought. New theories of teaching place more power and control with the student and challenge the traditional classroom and suggest changes to the political and social thinking around the role of HE.[27] Faculty have been slow to investigate them and even slower to accept them and much online delivery is heavily constrained from reaching its potential because of this theoretical hiatus. But universities are being warned that

> As the nation's homes acquire greater information technology power by the day and provide [students] with the chance to explore global networks and utilise increasingly sophisticated multimedia technology, so the pressure will grow for [teaching institutions] to redesign their operations.
>
> (Lee, 1995)

Others have written extensively on the many other issues facing twenty-first century HE and the role and status of HE in modern society. Such issues include massification, globalisation, corporatisation, intellectual property rights, the urge to privatise and/or make HE institutions into businesses, the reduced influence of governments and the rise of the knowledge industry. Each and every one is a major challenge to the sector (Kumar, 1997; Scott, 1997, 1998; Smith and Webster, 1997; Kelsey, 1998, 2003).

So despite the initiatives and best efforts to foster the development of learning technologies, institutions of higher education in the West are heavily affected by so many factors many of which are hindering the abilities of institutions to embrace technology and grow distance learning. Indeed, they are so substantial that it is hard not to observe that currently HE is challenged in every sense – epistemologically, sociologically, economically, politically and technologically, so much so that the future of the traditional university is not assured (Readings, 1996). Schilling (2005) puts the student challenge in sharp perspective:

> Today's students have formed their habits of mind by interacting with information that is digital and networked. They are, in a way, older than their teachers, whose relationships with information are governed by earlier generations of technology. There is more. Not only do our students possess skills and experiences that previous generations do not, but the very neurological structures and pathways they have developed as part of their learning are based on the technologies they use to create, store, and disseminate information. Importantly, these pathways and the categories, taxonomies, and other tools they use for thinking are different than those used by their teachers.

So, the combination of technologically libidinous young people, a rampant media landscape and a technologically challenged higher education system under siege from many directions is, to say the very least, problematical. But clearly there has to be a way through because young people continue to need educating and society continues to need skilled and well-educated citizens.

20.6 DIGITALLY MEDIATED LEARNING IS HERE TO STAY

The purpose of this chapter is not to resolve the many complex problems posed by the current crisis in higher education (Barnett and Griffin, 1997; Preston, 2002). Its concern is with suggesting how higher education may better engage with its upcoming catchment by utilizing digital media to create satisfactory digitally mediated learning that enhances the classroom and provides for attractive distance learning opportunities that will engage with "screenagers" on their terms and within their territories. There will be many that see this as capitulation. Knowledge should be created and shared on terms dictated by teachers and the institutions of learning. Using the Internet and other forms of digitally mediated learning is "poisoning" teaching (Brabazon, 2003). This position may hold in an educational environment that is privileged, stable, based mainly on the canon and funded by grants and the state. But as Western society moves from the industrial base of advanced modern capitalism to a form of society where information and knowledge are the primary product, the "goods" on offer from the institutions of HE may no longer be as relevant.

Indeed Strathdee (2005) argues that universities may be "missing the boat" in the sense that they are doing things that no longer matter. He argues that "credential inflation and the expansion of higher education has reduced the value of university degrees" with too many qualified people competing for too few good "middle-class jobs". Thus a good deal of "over-education" exists. He also argues that the growth in jobs in the post-fordist economies has not been in areas where qualifications are a good measure of performance. He sees the so-called soft skills of interpersonal relationships, "aesthetic labour" and the ability to sound and look "right" as more important. It is the individual's abilities with creative skills, innovative ideas and adaptive talents that matter. Such skills are not easily translated into "codified knowledge" that can be transmitted in the abstract form of a text book, manual or lecture. This is readily demonstrated by students at the Broadcasting School. They are given all of the basic skills of media creation, the rules and the processes, but this is not what creates the award-winning program, attracts the audience or generates the revenue. It is what eventuates when all of this is taken by the student and then moulded by their unique creativity, vision and ideas into the outcome that only they can see – their own sui generis production.

It is unfortunate for institutions of higher education that in a knowledge economy, it is not the knowledge that is written down which has value, rather it is the pool of tacit knowledge that gives the competitive advantage because it can be harnessed by those "in the know" to give the product its unique selling point advantages. Artists and broadcasting students alike are aware of this. Strathdee goes so far to suggest that

> It is clear that innovation is poorly related to qualifications. Qualifications do not measure the qualities, knowledge or dispositions associated with innovation.
>
> (2005, p. 453)

The "knowledge society" is one where creativity gives value to ideas, information and knowledge (Florida, 2002). In such an environment, learning is lifelong, constant and forever "on tap". To continue the analogy, the learner needs to be able to control the tap by being able to turn the flow up or down according to need. Sometimes the need for learning will be intense and time specific, on other occasions just a steady "drip". For many, such learning needs will be required just-in-time. Creative industries like the arts, cinema and the Web do not offer much traditional "steady" employment. Many people will require opportunities to retrain, to learn new skills to tackle the new jobs, some of which have yet to be even thought about, and to stay employed in the knowledge economy.

If this is the scenario, the message seems to be clear. Digitally mediated learning will play a primary role in satisfying twenty-first century learner needs, will be a key variable in providing the enormous range and diversity of learning objects that will be demanded and will be the technology of choice for the delivery of much of the learning. What is also clear is that if universities and other higher education institutions are not prepared to provide this, there are others who will – the aforementioned rampant media for example. Some of them are taking seriously the reported statement of Alan Gilbert, Chair of Universatis 21 that "education will become the biggest industry in the world" (D. MacLeod, 2000). Further, they recognise that the digital native needs to be "caught" early and so, on the assumption that you get them while they're young, they are providing the type of compelling content that will appeal to young people. The BBC has provided over 250,000 digital items for use in the United Kingdom K-12 curriculum. ABC Kids is one of the most visited Web site in Australia. The Learning Channel in the United States has the vast resources of media giant AT&T with Kids Discovery, Animal Planet, etc. PBS in the United States has a range of sophisticated programming for kids, parents and teachers. Further up the chain, Thomson Learning aims for post-secondary and graduate-level students, teachers and learning institutions in both traditional and distance learning environments.[28] The BellSouth Foundation, the charitable arm of US telco giant BellSouth, announced in late 2005 the spending of US$20 million over 5 years to improve online education and technology access in nine states. The aim of placing this money is to ensure that "all kids, not just the privileged, could be part of the virtual learning movement" (AP, 2005). It is not without some irony that three of these examples are actually public broadcasters funded by the state but as broadcasters not educators.

The crux of the matter lies with the profile of the MTV generation, the digital native young person portrayed earlier. They are increasingly cyberspace aware, with daily access to a complex range of technologies used for both leisure and work. Their use of technologies will sometimes, maybe often, mean that they will know more than their teachers, meaning that all of us teacher or student will be "sometimes teacher sometimes learner" and they will want to refer to the Web probably more that they will want to refer to texts.[29] Thus understanding the nature of informal learning will be the challenge for HE as more and more students take advantage of ways to learn that fall outside the formal educations structures. There will be much more demand from students for learning opportunities that don't necessarily lead to qualifications or formal recognition.

Let's return to the traditional media for a moment. They played a significant role in creating audiences. These audiences became communities that shared together the experiences of watching and listening. Before digital, the behaviours of the analogue non-print based communication industries were stable, profitable and culturally normative. Radio, television, cinema, telecommunications and cable systems did what they did best – produced content, aggregated that content for their discrete platform and distributed it. The arrival of digital technology changed all of this. Suddenly, a new instability emerged as the previously benign media environment turned upon itself, television vs. cable vs. satellite vs. telecommunications. Each platform no longer had its own monopoly. Entry into the field was made easier by deregulation and economies of scale. A new model is emerging where breaking away from platform dependency produces new opportunities. Producers of content are now able to reversion their product for multiple platforms[30] and distributors are now able to provide multiple platform services.[31] A new media "food chain" is emerging with industry specialisation in the areas of content production, content aggregation and content distribution. The emphasis in the value chain is moving from the platform itself to the program itself. People no longer watch channels they watch programs, programs that they themselves will schedule on a device and at a time that is suitable for them. In other words, "content will be king" and the content that has value will be the content that consumers find best excites them, informs them and is the most compelling.

Perhaps it's this that distance educators should pay most attention to. Rather than getting "bogged down" in worrying about systems (learning management systems, student management systems, digital student report card systems, plagiarism detection systems, online collaborative workspaces, virtual classroom software, systems, e-portfolios, content syndication, etc.) or about platforms (broadband, digital TV, podcasting, vodcasting, blogs, wikis, VOIP, etc.) attention should be given to content. And the content needs to be appropriate to the platform.

And in this respect, distance learning providers at present are perhaps a little hard on themselves. As new media technologies developed, they initially reflected the values of the technologies they emerged from. For example, early radio was "read" text, early movies were films of a theatre's stage and early television was "radio with pictures". But each medium quickly found the exclusive elements that made the technology "different" and began to create content that was in part made compelling by the uniqueness of the medium itself thus confirming McLuhan's tenet that the "medium is the message" (McLuhan, 1964). Early attempts at distance learning were indeed replications of the classroom; lecture notes were posted, texts for reading were put up as PDFs and a minimal amount of interaction was permitted, usually just with the teacher. And it has not been without success. Higher education has been engaged with digitally based learning for some years and the number of students taking online courses, and the number of courses continues to grow. At the turn of the century, it was estimated that over 6 million students were studying online worldwide (Walsh, 1999). Teachers are doing it and there is nothing to be ashamed of. However, if the field of distance learning is to move on, then the virtual classroom must take on its own uniqueness and create its own compelling material. The challenge is to find that uniqueness and "capture" the digital native's attention in a more convincing way.

20.7 CAPTURING THE AUDIENCE

This chapter concludes by suggesting that the way into the mind of the MTV generation needs a three-pronged approach. The first can be adapted from broadcasters, the second from gaming and the third can be found in the material that is being generated by distance educators themselves, a seamless open source conduit for creating, storing, retrieving and reversioning learning objects.

Broadcasters have a long history of knowing how to "capture" an audience and it is through creating compelling content. Today, there is no doubt in the broadcaster's mind that survival is based on the premise that content is king. Traditionalists may not like it but to engage the young audience, course material needs to have high production values with a strong emphasis on good design, engagement with sound, vision and graphics (animation, drawings, graphs) and less emphasis on print. Such material cannot be produced by a single teacher. Good broadcasting engages creative teams to conceive, develop, pre-test, produce and post-produce. Educators will need to do likewise. The time has come perhaps for broadcasters and educators to work collaboratively, like the early days of the Open University, UK and the BBC, to combine the talents of the screen producer and the content creator to produce to the level required. There is a synergy particularly between universities and public broadcasters around the world that should be exploited for mutual benefit.

Secondly, those content values will need to be combined with high levels of interactivity, and the model that best illustrates this is gaming. Online games and simulations will need to be recognised by HE as they become pervasive in students' lives and increasingly include educational goals and outcomes. Primary school teachers know how quickly children learn when playing games. The airline industry and the military know how well and quickly adults learn when involved in simulators and complex games. Why are they missing from the secondary school and university classroom? Could it be that those that play the games are young, whereas those that teach are older and have had little contact with games since primary school? Is it because learning styles based on sound, vision and touch are considered of less cognitive value than text-based learning? Is it because of cost? The simple games of the primary school classroom cost little, whereas the complex games designed for high-risk jobs in industries (airlines) and fields (military) where the costs of failure could be catastrophic cost a great deal. Interactivity allows for so much. It can measure progress towards a goal, enable "discovery" learning, permit mistakes (this is well recognised in the medical profession when training surgeons), facilitate problem solving and provide for individual and group participation. The three dimensionality of the gaming screen provides a "virtual" experience no traditional classroom can match. Add interactivity to compelling content and the digital natives will be tempted![32]

Finally, educators must embrace open platforms and open source software and middleware to enable a seamless exchange of digitally versioned objects and the development of repositories that enable the reuse and repurposing of created data. Open systems are necessary for this to be possible. For it is essential that material is accessible, interoperable, reusable, durable and affordable. Accessible, in the sense that access to distance learning components at one location can permit delivery of them to many other locations.

Metadata sets also need to be standard and "granulated" to the level appropriate for each user. Interoperable, in the sense that digital objects developed at one location can be used with a different platform in another location. It must be possible to reuse digital objects in multiple applications over both time and location. Open source ensures that components are able to operate when the base technology changes, without redesign or recoding. And, most importantly, it needs to be affordable and affordability is gained when data can be used and reused over time by a large number of people effectively and efficiently, thereby reducing time and cost factors.

Interestingly, just as the Internet had its beginning in the US military, it may be that the way forward is again being led from that source. Advanced Distributed Learning (ADL)[33] is a US government initiative which initially focused on the education and training needs of the US military. The traditional training methods of "right time, right place" learning which required face-to-face interactions at set times and in set places were considered increasingly ineffective for a mobile, geographically dispersed rapid response force. In its short history, ADL has been widely adopted within the US forces to deliver thousands of courses to military personnel in their homes, in classrooms and on personal digital assistants around the globe.

ADL initiatives were at first limited to US Department of Defence needs but a collaborative model was quickly developed which saw ADL activities spread to other government agencies, industry, higher education and US local government agencies. This resulted in the establishment of what are termed "co-laboratories" where the initial ADL organisation works collaboratively with other interest groups in a sense "gifting" the ADL initiative to the wider e-learning community. As well as the central coordinating laboratory located within the Department of Defence, there are currently three co-laboratories – the Academic ADL Co-Lab which focuses on promoting ADL technologies to assist distributed learning in education, the Workforce ADL Co-Lab which provides the focus for workforce education and training and the Joint ADL Co-Lab which implements ADL instruction and technology within the US military.

ADL operates on the twin principles of platform neutrality and software reusability. Its commitment to open source is based on the belief that this is the best way to "create new markets for training materials, reduce the cost of development and increase potential return on investment" (ADL, 2005).

As it stands at present, three key technologies inform the ADL initiative: SCORM (Sharable Content Object Reference Model),[34] CORDRA (Content Object Repository Discovery and Registration/Resolution Architecture)[35] and S1000D (Specification 1000 Defence). SCORM is a set of standards designed for Web-based learning that enable the finding, sharing, reusing and exporting of learning content in a standardised way. While it is principally designed to assist with the construction of learning management systems (LMS), SCORM, in association with other standards, has implications for repositories, simulations, intelligent tutoring systems and educational and instructional gaming. CORDRA is an open, standards-based model for how to design and implement software systems for the purposes of discovery, sharing and reuse of learning content through the establishment of interoperable federations of learning content repositories.

Like SCORM, CORDRA is not a specification per se rather it is a reference model that combines a number of existing standards and specifications. It is designed to be an enabling model to bridge the worlds of learning content management and delivery, and content repositories and digital libraries. S1000D[36] is an emerging international specification for technical publications utilizing a Common Source Data Base (CSDB) and is used for the procurement and production of technical publications within the digital environment. Importantly, the principles of the specification can easily be applied to non-technical documentation and as it is compliant with the Web and ISO standards the specification should be useful to organisations that use extended documentation within their digital environment. Whilst not a direct development from ADL (S1000D is a product developed by the aerospace industries of Europe and the United States), this standard is considered to be integral to the full development of the ADL strategy. A memorandum of understanding has been signed that integrates S1000D into the ADL suite of services.

The Advanced Distributed Learning (ADL) Initiative began in 1997 with the laudable goal of enabling high-quality education and training to be delivered anytime and anywhere. ADL models are being adopted in many different contexts and sectors for implementing technology-based learning across the world. It is hard to argue with the principle tenets of ADL which seeks a scalable and sustainable infrastructure for teaching, learning, education and training based on global interoperability and open standards. However, to do so requires a collaborative approach on an international scale. Unlike the TCP/IP, mentioned earlier and developed by state-owned or regulated telecos familiar with cooperation, ADL has arisen in an educational environment that is competitive, infiltrated by the closed standards of proprietary systems and lacking the financial resources of large communications entities. There needs to be a massive collaborative effort to optimise the advancement, development and maintenance of a global system of this nature. The recent formation of a global stewardship for ADL in Melbourne in late 2005 may go some way to effecting that collaboration.[37]

20.8 CONCLUSION

This chapter has attempted to address some of the challenges to educators in meeting the needs of the next generation of students and in particular those who will choose to learn from a distance. It argues that the three key elements are compelling content with high production values, sophisticated interactivity involving attributes of simulation and gaming and open source storage, retrieval and distribution platforms. It suggests that universities may face challenges from a more aggressive and well-funded media industry looking for new products and new markets to compensate for the loss of the exclusivity they had in the pre-digital environment. It further argues that academe needs to recognise the changing relationship between teacher and learner and acknowledge that in the digitally mediated knowledge society, sometimes the student knows best what the student most needs. There is a synergy between digital media and digitally mediated learning that could be harvested for the benefit of both sectors and the student.

However, like all revolutions, there may be more cycles to come. Is it too provoking to suggest that whatever happens now is just the beginning of the digital revolution? Tiffin and Terashima (2001) would argue that, really, we're engaged with an interim technology. We should be preparing for the next stage, the stage he calls hyper-reality, where the real and the virtual become seamless and we move between both without being aware of the transition. Sophisticated blends of digital technology, bio-technology and nano-technology will produce environments for informing, entertaining and learning that are still in the realms of science fiction. Imagine a child opening a book out of which jumps fully active three-dimensional characters that act out the story as the child reads and who interact with the child's questions and comments. The eye-magic book being developed by HitLab New Zealand is working towards this outcome.[38] Imagine donning a helmet and gloves and entering a virtual world which allows you to walk down the streets of Pompeii before the eruption (Drexler, 1990). That's truly distance learning!

NOTES

1. The author founded the School and was head for the first 15 years.
2. The School has been fortunate, in that demand for places has always required a selection process.
3. Over 50 percent of US youth with access to the Internet use online social networking sites (Pew Internet Project (retrieved 10/01/07 from http:www.pewinternet.org.).
4. Real names are not used.
5. See http://www.etime.co.nz/entrepreneurs.htm.
6. Makirikiwi School in the Rangitaki near Marton. The students built the studio were the swimming pool used to be. Reported TVNZ Close Up, October 26, 2005.
7. The game is "The World of War Craft".
8. See http://www.digiops.org.nz/projects/currentprojects/techangels/
9. Statistical data taken from Highfield (2005), Pew (2005) and Woods (2005).
10. The free online interactive encyclopaedia "Wikipedia" is popular.
11. Source: www.InternetWorldStats.com.
12. PSTN (Public Switched Telephone Network) LAN (Local Area Network).
13. As an example of the first, both telephony and broadcasting can be delivered wirelessly and over wire whilst previously they were discrete. As an example of the second, the interoperability of the Web connects to broadcasting networks, newspaper distributors and public libraries through the one computer.
14. The concepts of "single order" and "dual order" in this context are used to describe the methods of distribution of stored information.
15. Video games, for example, will include on the same platform video, text, graphics and full-spectrum surround sound.
16. An exabyte is a billion gigabytes.
17. Quotes taken from AFP Report "World Drowning in Data: Researchers", October 20, 2000, http://www.afp.com/english/home.
18. Although mobile phones may overtake PCs in the next few years (Dataquest 2005).
19. The phenomenon called Moore's Law suggests a doubling of storage capacity (transistors) and a halving of size every year.

20. The Economist reports that Catholics can sign up for a daily inspirational text message from the Pope and Muslims by using the F7100 handset from LG Electronics can be reminded via the phone's alarm system of prayer times and the device includes a compass pointing in the direction of Mecca ("Mobile Touches All Facets of Life" (excerpt from The Economist) reported in the San Francisco Chronicle, March 15, 2005, B7).
21. In Taiwan, the public broadcaster has a digital channel that broadcasts direct to more than a hundred buses in Taipei providing a mix of news, information, weather and entertainment. Taxi TV became a reality in London in 2005, with passengers offered a choice of seven channels of news, sport, music and comedy (Norris and Pauling, 2005).
22. This pressure is particularly strong from the "digital natives", the new generation of technologically savvy young people and is demonstrated in the way media companies have embraced digital and online gaming.
23. The term first appeared in popular literature in a New York Times article on Silicon Valley on November 02, 1995. The headline was "Silicon Valley Says Datacasting Is Hot".
24. As indicated by a presentation by Verizon, a US mobile operator, at the NAB convention (Las Vegas, April 2005).
25. The "Me Channel" refers to the ability of the consumer to program their own information and entertainment services so they totally determine what they engage with, where they engage and when they engage.
26. One observation argues that in the US education, overall spends less than $1,000 per employee compared to media companies that spend over $5,000 per employee and top spending telecommunications and banking organisations that spend in excess of $10,000.
27. A number of theories and methods are being developed to provide sound pedagogical grounds for the new learning environments. These theories include the UK Royal Society of Arts' "learning for capability", immersion learning, cooperative education and contract-based learning (Stephenson, J. and Yorke, M., 1998).
28. BBC: http://www.bbc.co.uk/schools/; http://www.bbc.co.uk/learning/
    ABC: http://www.abc.net.au/broadband/categories/kids.htm
    PBS: http://www.pbs.org/teachersource/; http://pbskids.org/go/; http://www.pbs.org/parents/
    Thomson Learning: http://www.thomson.com/learning/learning.jsp
    The Learning Channel: http://corporate.discovery.com/brands/discoverykids.html.
29. This may lead to a new core curriculum for search and evaluation skills!
30. For example, producers of television programs can reversion them for delivery over the traditional terrestrial network, through the Internet, via mobile devices, such as cell phones and PDAs or on DVD.
31. Many cable providers are now offering television, radio, telephone and Internet services via the one conduit.
32. The popularity of virtual reality environments, such as Second Life will assist in driving interest.
33. www.adlnet.org.
34. www.adlnet.org/scorm/index.cfm.
35. http://cordra.lsal.cmu.edu/cordra/.
36. www.s1000d.org/.
37. http://adlaustralia.org/aatgc/melbourne-declaration.html.
38. See: http://www.hitlabnz.org/route.php?r=prj-view&prj_id=18.

REFERENCES

ADL. (2005). *Learn, Distribute, Advance: Advanced Distributed Learning*. Washington DC: ADL Initiative.

Alexander, B. (2004). M-learning: Emerging pedagogical and campus issues in the mobile learning environment. *Educause Centre for Applied Research Bulletin, 2004,* **16**. Retrieved December 12, 2005 from http://www.educause.edu/MobilityandMobileLearning/5527

AP. (2005, November 20). Bellsouth Foundation Donates Money for Online Education. *Associated Press*.

Barnett, R. and Griffin, A. (1997). *The End of Knowledge in Higher Education*. London: Cassell.

Bittner, J. (1985). *Broadcasting and Communications*, 2nd ed., Englewood Cliffs: Prentice Hall.

Bonnett, T.W. (1999). *Governance in the Digital Age: The Impact of the Global Economy, Information Technology and Economic Deregulation on State and Local Government*. Washington D.C.: National League of Cities.

Brabazon, T. (2003). *Digital Hemlock: Internet Education and the Poisoning of Teaching*. Sydney: University of New South Wales Press.

CIA. (2005). Press release. *Computer Industry Almanac*. Retrieved August 13, 2005, from http://www.c-i-a.com/pr0305.htm

Dataquest (2005). Determine the Appropriate Level of ITAM Controls for Mobile Assets. Retrieved December 01, 2005 from http://www.gartner.com/it/products/research/dataquest.jsp

David, C. (2005). 3 billion mobile subscribers by 2010. *Wireless World Forum* Retrieved August 14, 2005, from http://www.w2forum.com/item/26_bn_mobile_subscribers_2009

Drexler, E.K. (1990). *Engines of Creation*. London: Fouth Estate.

Education.au.Ltd. (2005). *Emerging Technologies, a Framework for Thinking, Final Report*. Canberra: ACT Department of Education and Training.

Florida, R. (2002). *The Rise of the Creative Class*. New York: Basic Books.

Greenspan, R. (2003, January 21). *Online Wireless Gaming Gaining*. Retrieved December 01, 2005, from http://www.clickz.com/stats/sectors/entertainment/article.php/1572231

Highfield, A. (2005). Bbc online, *Digital and the BBC*. Wellington: Ministry of Culture and Heritage.

Huurdeman, A.A. (2003). *The Worldwide History of Telecommunications*. New York: Wiley-IEEE Press.

Jalil, T. (Writer) (2000). *Dot.Com [Film]*. In (T. Dillmann and T. Jalil (Producer). USA: IFILM Worldwide Video.

Jenkins, C. (2005, Tuesday, August 16). Email to go. *The Australian*, p. 4. Retrieved December 12, 2005 from http://w3.nexis.com/new/search/homesubmitForm.du

Kaiser. (2005). *Generation M: Media in the Lives of 8–18 Year-Olds*. Retrieved December 06, 2005, from http://www.kff.org/entmedia/upload/Ececutive -Summary-Generation-M-Media-in-the-lives-of-8–18-Year-olds

Kelsey, J. (1998). *Policy Directions for Tertiary Education: A Submission on the Government Green Paper a Future Tertiary Education Policy for New Zealand*. Auckland: Tertiary Education Review.

Kelsey, J. (2003). *Serving Whose Interest?* Christchurch: Action Research and Education Network of Aotearoa.

Kerschbaumer, K. (2005, August 08). TV on the pc gets real Time Warner launches trial in San Diego. *Broadcasting and Cable.*

Kumar, K. (1997). The need for place. In *The postmodern university* (A.W.F. Smith, ed.) Buckingham: Open University Press.

Leach, K. (2003). *Benchmarks for it Investments, Trends and Insights.* Paper presented at the National Association of College and University Business Officers' Annual conference, Sydney.

Lee, M. (1995, June 13). Illiterate teachers block superhighway. *The Australian.*

Luke, C. (1996). Ekstasis@cyberia. *Discourse Studies in the Cultural Politics of Education,* **17**(2), 96–116.

Lyman, P. and Varian, H.R. (2000). *How Much Information 2000.* Berkeley: School of Information Management and Systems.

MacLeod, D. (2000). Clever business. *Guardian.*

MacLeod, D. (2004). The online revolution, mark ii, 2004. Retrieved from. *The Guardian.*

McKey, P.T.T.S.E. (2003). *The Total Student Experience.* Retrieved June 06, 2004, from http://www.nexted.com/nexted/white-papers/2/default.asp

McLuhan, M. (1964). *Understanding Media: The Extensions of Man.* New York: Mentor.

McLuhan, M. and Fiore, Q. (1967). *The Medium is the Massage.* New York: Bantam.

Messerschmitt, D.G. (1996). The future of computer and telecommunications integration. *IEEE Communications Magazine, April 1996*, pp. 66–69.

Myers, J. (2005, November 15, 2005). *Gaming Medium Growing in Pervasiveness, Not Fully Tapped.* Retrieved from <http://www.adrants.com/2005/11/gaming-medium-growing-in-pervasiveness.php>

Negroponte, N. (1995). *Being digital.* New York: Knopf.

Nielsen. (2005, Monday, November 21). *Benchmarking the Active Gamer.* Retrieved December 01, 2005, from <http://biz.gamedaily.com/features.asp?article_id=11161§ion=feature&email>=

Norris, P. and Pauling, B. (2005). *Public Broadcasting in the Digital Age: Issues for New Zealand.* Wellington: New Zealand On Air.

Peled, A. (1987). The next computer revolution. *Scientific American,* **257**(4), 56–68.

Pew. (2005). *Teens and Technology, Youth are Leading the Transition to a Fully Wired and Mobile Nation.* Washington DC: Pew Institute.

Potts, J. (1979). ETV and the less developed countries, In *Visual Education*, Magazine of the National Committee for Audio-Visual Aids in Education, London, pp. 21–23.

Preston, D. (2002). *The University of Crisis.* Amsterdam: Rodopi.

Readings, B. (1996). *The University in Ruins.* Cambridge MA: Harvard Univeristy Press.

Rossiter, K. (2003). The future of broadcasting, presentation at the New Zealand Broadcasting School, July 14, 2003 by the Director of Satellite Services of Television, New Zealand.

Rushkoff, D. (1994). *Media Virus.* New York: Random House.

Rushkoff, D. (1996). *Children of Chaos: Surviving the End of the World as we Know it.* London: Harper Collins.

Scales, S.D. (1999). *Planning for Convergence: Who's Doing it, who's Not, and Why?* Retrieved August 15, 2005.

Schilling, P. (2005, May 31). *Technology as Epistemology.* Retrieved December 01, 2005, from http://www.academiccommons.org/commons/essay/technology-as-epistemology

Scott, P. (1997). Crisis: What crisis? The crisis of knowledge and the massification of higher education. In *The End of Knowledge in Higher Education* (R. Barnett and A. Griffin eds.) London: Cassell.

Scott, P. (1998). Massification, internationalisation and globalisation. In *The Globalisation of Higher Education* (P. Scott, ed.) Buckingham UK: Open University Press, pp. 108–129.
Simpson, S.W. (2005, November 20). *The Media Generation: A Million Attention Shifts Later*. Retrieved November 21, 2005, from edbriefs@mailman.olympus.net
Skinner, B.F. (1954). The science of learning and the art of teaching. *Harvard Educational Review*, **24**, 86–97.
Smith, A. and Webster, F. (1997). *The Postmodern University? Contested Visions of Higher Education in Society*. Philadelphia: Open University Press.
Stephenson, J. and Yorke, M. (1998). *Capability and Quality in Higher Education*. London: Kogan Page.
Stonier, T. and Conlin, C. (1985). *The Three c's: Children, Computers and Communication*. Chichester: Wiley and Sons.
Strathdee, R. (2005, July). Globalization, innovation, and the declining significance of qualifications led social and economic change. *Journal of Education Policy*, **20**(4), 437–456.
Tiffin, J. and Terashima, N. (2001). *Hyper Reality: Paradigm for the Third Millennium*. London: Routledge.
Wagner, E.D. (2005). Enabling mobile learning. *Educause Review*, **40**(3), 40–53.
Walsh, M. (1999, October 28). *Online Education in Australia Full of Potential*. Retrieved December 12, 2005, from http://www.clickz.com/stats/sectors/ geographics/article.php/228181
Watts, R. (1996). Cyber war for students: Competition on campus. *Campus Review*, **6**(35). Retrieved December 10, 2005 from http://www.opennet.netau/news/campus_review_article.htm
Williams, D. (2003, March 22). Success Still in the Distance. *The Guardian*. Retrieved November 16, 2005 from http://education.guardian.co.uk/elearning/story/0,10577,919318,00.html
Williams, R. (1974). *Television, Technology and Cultural Form*. London: Fontana.
Wolleben, M. (2005). *Wimax Telecom – Ready for Wimax Deployment*. Retrieved August 14, 2005, from http://wimax.com/commentary/spotlight/wimaxtelecom-spotlight
Woods, A. (2005). *Kids Supplement – Total Engagement*. Retrieved December 06, 2005, from <http://www.mediaweek.co.uk/features/index.cfm?fuseaction=detail>
WSIS. (2003, December 12). *Declaration of Principles*. Paper presented at the World Summit on the Information Society, Geneva.

Chapter 21

Transforming Distance Education: In Whose Interests?

David Harris

21.1 INTRODUCTION

There is some dispute about what is meant by the term "interest". I am using it in what follows to refer to the calculation of some kind of tangible benefit, as in "vested interest", but without the connotations of dogmatism and exploitation. I want to argue that educational ideas and policies are developed not just from philosophical reflection, the pursuit of research or the adoption of an ethical commitment but from calculations of benefit. I am not arguing that all action can be seen as the outcome of rational calculation, as in notions of Economic Man or some variants of game theory, since interests stretch beyond the narrow and calculable. The role of interests is clear when moving to the stage of trying to implement ideas and policies, but they have a role in the construction of ideas and policies too.

There are many colleagues who have devoted their professional lives to pursuing the goal of open access and mass higher education at macro- and micro levels, driven by a strong moral and political commitment to ideals of universal entitlement and universal benefit. However, we can introduce controversy by suggesting that an equally powerful impulse towards open access has its origins in more mundane interests – the pursuit of a favourable market position. This is not to condemn this interest as morally inferior, but simply to insist that it has had an effect on actual policies. Market interest might be seen as perfectly compatible with political commitments since efficient markets enable widespread distribution, energized by tangible benefits not just personal commitments. However, market interests might be seen as a threat for those who think that making educational materials assume a commodity form might devalue them as politically empowering – but compromises might still be possible, or struggles around the precise weight to be given to interest and commitment.

Specifically, distance education has become accepted and indeed valued by conventional universities because it does empower non-traditional students who would have been excluded otherwise. But it also offers to open up a worldwide market for educational materials, and it would be short-sighted to ignore this interest as an important explanation for the development of policy. Similar calculations of the possible market were influential if not decisive in winning consent for the establishment of the United Kingdom Open University (UKOU) too (Harris, 1987).

For various reasons, it is sometimes slightly controversial to argue this case, however. This is partly because of the tendency for professional scholars and academics to drift to philosophical idealism (roughly, an overestimate of the role and importance of abstract ideas). Ironically, it is also in the interests of universities to claim to be disinterested, to appear to lack mundane interests in education, to be pursuing loftier and more prestigious goals. All institutions claiming universal appeal (implicit still in the "uni" prefix to "university"?) have to conceal specific interests in order to retain legitimation, not simply for sinister reasons (to preserve the privileges of an elite), but also to gain a basis for converting traditionally alienated groups. If all goes well, expanding university provision becomes one of those policies that seems "above politics".

21.2 HOW INTERESTS WORK

Identifying the interests embedded in particular policies or descriptions of institutions used to be the hallmark of a proper critical social science. The activity turned on a notion that surface appearances concealed deeper underlying structural political forces. This surface/depth metaphor enabled social sciences to claim a particular cognitive status: whereas other flawed approaches operated exclusively on the surface, proper social sciences could penetrate to the real explanatory factors beneath.

There was an important claim about practical benefits too. Proper analysis was crucial to guide effective politics (of all kinds, including reformist versions). Superficial analysis would not uncover a number of traps for the unwary, such as failing to realize how deeply embedded social practices were. The classic cases in educational policy turn on the attempts to reduce social inequality by pursuing measures such as opening access or abolishing pupil selection based on "merit". We know that social class divisions are much more resilient than these measures imply and that they can easily re-assert themselves – elite groups avoid State systems altogether, middle-class groups soon manage to organize to take more than their fair share of advantage (by operating effectively in housing markets, for example, to access "good" schools and universities), new barriers and constraints emerge to replace any of the old ones that are weakened (cultural aspects of social class increase in importance as economic ones diminish). Gender divisions also persist as women and sexual minorities continue to be devalued culturally even though they are granted equality formally and legally. Unintended consequences chronically haunt the best-designed policies, as Weberian sociologists could have predicted: policies designed to empower ethnic minorities can contradict with those designed to empower sexual minorities; individualization can lead to alienation; affluence to dissatisfaction; expansion in higher education to "grade inflation" and credentialism.

Marxism offers one of the best examples of this kind of analysis. Marx identified suppressed interests beneath bourgeois economics and idealist philosophy alike. The former claimed to be describing the workings of a natural, evolved, efficient and fair system with its own market forces and equilibrium-achieving mechanisms, such as the price mechanism that magically brought together and resolved the interests of supply and demand. The most insidious version of bourgeois economics identified the wage labour relation like this, and one of Marx's major projects was to investigate this relation, pursuing its misleading surface appearance into the mechanisms below, to reveal the underlying exploitation involved in treating labour as a mere commodity. The same analysis was also to expose the apparent neutrality and ubiquity of "private property" and the legal system that supported it, or to reveal the misleading abstractions in describing the operations of the state as democracy: the state did indeed have one democratic moment – polling day – when all voters were equal, but for every day thereafter until the next election, substantial inequalities of political power were reproduced.

Idealist philosophy, and Marx's targets ran from the British Utilitarians to Hegel, pursued the same kind of false method of abstraction. Apparently universal concepts were really based on the much narrower experiences of dominant classes. In one of his most spiteful sections, Marx (1977 [1887], p. 570) refers to Bentham as "that insipid, pedantic, leather-tongued oracle of the ordinary bourgeois intelligence of the nineteenth century", taking the common-sense perceptions of English shopkeepers and turning them into a universal account of the pursuit of human happiness. More thoughtful philosophers were more self-critical, but they still failed to give an account of where ideas came from, and nor did they analyse sufficiently the social realities around them. Thus Hegel was able to systematically confuse abstract notions of the state with the rather specific characteristics of the Prussia in which he lived, so that the former lent a philosophical depth to the latter (see Colletti, 1975). Critiques of these more thoughtful and "scientific" thinkers point to the fact that the surface reality in capitalism is extremely misleading, and that it is easy to take aspects of it for granted. A special consistently critical methodology is required to really get to grips with what appears to be so self-evident. There has been much debate since about what this methodology might be, and, for that matter, how radically critical the project should become.

The most radical development of Marxist thought, it could be argued, is displayed in Critical Theory, which pursued a thoroughgoing attempt to avoid all premature limits and compromises threatening critique. Although, for many commentators, this project would lead only to philosophical dead ends and a politics of despair and sterility (Habermas, in Bernstein, 1985), the project certainly offers penetrating investigatory techniques. I borrowed heavily from them to guide my own critique of the UKOU (Harris, 1987). In a subsequent volume (Harris, 1992), I also used critical theory to expose the limitations of a rival critical approach based on Gramsci, and usually known as British Cultural Studies (I called it "gramscianism"), which featured strongly in a very well-known UKOU course (Open University, 1982).

This approach is popular and well developed in Cultural Studies, Media Studies and Youth Studies, and it has contributed to critical analysis of education (for example CCCS, 1981; Education Group II, 1991), but it has had much less to say about distance education specifically. Despite powerful analyses of ideologies of the mass media, Parliamentary politics and managerialism, prominent advocates of the approach remained completely silent about the conditions they were encountering at the UKOU in their own practice. The consequences of this limited form of radicalism have recently been noted by Cohen (2004), in what is partly a self-critique – radical gramscianism helped overthrow traditional conceptions of education but failed to replace them. Modern managerialism colonized the empty ground. In terms of the theme of this chapter, gramscianism's unfortunate incorporation indicates what can await critics who offer only partial critiques of interests, with a limited battery of privileged concepts.

Habermas is one of the more prominent modern thinkers who have thoroughly evaluated the marxist tradition and tried to open it to modern social science. His early attempts to critique the limits of conventional social sciences have an immediate relevance for this chapter because they turned on the argument that all forms of knowledge were inevitably grounded in human interests (Habermas, 1972). Failing to recognize the effects of these interests led to the usual limits identified with positivism. These limits provided "blocks" to thinking, unanalysed constraints, because practices and structures were taken as being incapable of being affected by action based on different human interests, as being somehow fixed, "natural" or inevitable. There happened to be three sorts of general human interests – an interest in "work" (producing science and technology), in interaction (the humanities and social sciences) and in emancipation. The latter was just as much an important interest as the other two, and must be reawakened and developed, in political practice and in a new kind of political philosophy and critical social science. These arguments are familiar to any reader of the influential work of Carr and Kemmis (1986 for example), who applied the ideas directly to educational politics and curriculum design.

One immediate problem is apparent, however, which led Habermas himself to abandon this framework of interests. The status, source and origin of these interests are very debatable. Were they "transcendental" in the classic philosophical sense of being grounded in "human nature" or implicit in human consciousness? If so, the whole project seemed based on dubious philosophical foundations. Did they have a more mundane status as sociological or anthropological generalizations? If so, they could be challenged on the grounds of typicality – human history seemed to show an equally dominant interest in oppression as well as emancipation, for example. Habermas himself tried a middle way by suggesting that these interests were "quasi-transcendental", but the problems were not really solved. Indeed, all arguments based on identifying fundamental interests "behind" social realities and practices face versions of the same problems, it could be argued.

Feminist analysis, for example, seems to offer a familiar range of alternatives to account for the underlying interests in patriarchy, which limit and constrain what can appear to be natural or neutral. It might be the specific interests of specific men that are responsible, for example, like those who control the media, or a more methodological flaw, revealed when even the most critical of thinkers such as Habermas or Foucault failed to break with concepts that reflect the binary logic of patriarchy: Fraser (1989) makes a strong case for insisting that a discussion of concrete interests would also help avoid this idealization. There is an obvious contradiction involved in feminists wanting to substitute other equally foundational concepts, however, as the contributors to Humm (1992) argue.

In many ways the crisis for critical social science emerged when these classic traditions were exposed to thorough critique by various "post" positions. Post-structuralism in particular raised substantial questions about the status of the underlying mechanisms that had been identified, and, eventually, came to question their privileged "foundational" status. The famous "skepticism towards [all] metanarratives' (Lyotard, 1984) was to follow, and to dethrone marxist and structuralist approaches in particular.

Apart from the rather scholarly criticisms of foundationalism based on acute deconstructionist readings of the key texts, some more familiar and immediate points have also led to problems with the stories of grand underlying interests. One concerns the observation that the cultural sphere (including education) has indeed become more autonomous, less likely to be influenced by interests based in other areas such as the economic. The extent and nature of this autonomy is still debated, woven into more general discussions about whether the current era is best described as "late modernity", "late capitalism" or "postmodernism" (Crook et al., 1992). However, certain trends seem to be evident to all commentators. Cultural matters do not change because of some underlying shift in the balance of power between contending parties, rooted in economic or political structures, but because those working in the cultural sphere itself reflect on current practices and modify them according to various kinds of theories of their own.

The case can be seen in a number of areas, principally the "creative industries", as in Eco (1987, pp. 148–149):

> A firm produces polo shirts... and it advertises them. A generation begins to wear the polo shirts... A TV broadcast, to be faithful to reality shows some young people wearing the... polo shirt. The young (and the old) see the TV broadcast and buy more [brandname] polo shirts because they have the "young look"... at this point, who is sending the message? The manufacturer of the polo shirt? its wearer? the person who talks about it on the TV screen? Who is the producer of ideology?...

The education system is another classic example. There clearly is an attempt to influence it from "outside", seen most clearly in the activities of various politicians representing particular ideological views of the economy and society. However, there is also an internal dynamic, easily recognized by anyone who has actually been involved in educational innovation. Educationalists reflect on existing practices and research them, and use a self-conscious turn to theory to introduce change. So do consumers. There is also a necessary instability peculiar to education, noticed by reflective marxists such as Gintis and Bowles (1980). Educational ideas and skills cannot easily be harnessed to dominant interests but have a constant tendency to yield critical reflection and innovation.

Many of these points have found theoretical expression in the work of Anthony Giddens. After a considerable and highly fruitful theoretical encounter with the classical accounts of interests that we began with, including marxism and structuralism (Giddens, 1979), and some of their leading advocates (Giddens, 1982), Giddens was in a position to insist on the crucial role played by human agents themselves. This was not a simple voluntarism, however. The activity of these agents was first of all constrained by "rules" and "resources" emanating from a social level, and, secondly, activities had unintended consequences which led to unanticipated constraints on further action. Some of the complex interactions between agents, social rules and resources and "structuration factors" that produce actual institutions are well developed in Giddens' discussion of class formation, but the whole approach has had a number of important applications, not least in the work of Evans and Nation, of course. The work has also been widely discussed and criticized (for example, in Stones, 2005).

Giddens' account certainly seems to permit a much more concrete analysis of the role of interests, say in the development of distance education at the UKOU. To simulate his approach, it would be quite possible to see the particular definition of openness which emerged as the result of both unreflected "resources", such as ideas about the universal applicability of academic knowledge and the social reasons for uneven uptake, and the specific tactical activities of individuals and parties like the "modernizers" in the Labour government of the time. A key role was played by a number of educational theorists, specifically educational technologists, in responding to tactical initiatives, but also in adding their own understandings of openness and how these understandings might be operationalized. As a result, the peculiar compromise emerged that saw a public commitment to "openness" which also embodied an advanced selection system for candidates (not actually used) and a largely unchallenged conception of scholarly knowledge that had been traditionally favoured. In my view, it would be impossible to understand the actual policy without considering interests at both the general social level and the specific professional level and how they were able to be harmonized. The policy also had the usual unintended consequences – probably causing substantial drop-out rates among the educationally inexperienced, and reifying the system so that it looked like an immovable constraint for subsequent academics, even those professionally interested in critique and radical change (see the Introduction to Bennett, 1998). The advantage of pursuing Giddens' framework systematically would be to provide a coherent account of what might seem like unconnected developments.

Giddens' approach seems to offer a workable model to enable sociology to continue despite the "post" critiques. His "applied" work on modernity also attempts to argue that suitably tweaked sociological concepts can explain the apparently "new" phenomena heralded by postmodernists trying to break with modernity (for example, Giddens, 1991). However, that still leaves one aspect of "post" critique turning on the notion of the "centred" reading. Briefly, it is still clearly possible to offer sociological readings and interpretations, but why should they be privileged above other readings – Christian ones, perhaps, those of evolutionary psychology, or those practised by devotees of Nostradamus? This point has led to some insightful work on how sociologists (and historians and philosophers of course) actually "write" in such a way as to maintain some privileged perspective, how they quietly defend their concepts deploying processes such as "différance".

To take a small but relevant aspect of this critique, it is clear that we can identify interests of various kinds in policies and analyses of them, but is it essential to do so? All was well in the high modernist period, when sociologists and other academics imagined they were acting as "public intellectuals", speaking for and on behalf of humanity as a whole, or, at least, the populations of their countries. Again, marxism offers the clearest example, perhaps, with the view that proletarian political action, and marxist theories that underpinned it, would install a genuinely universal regime instead of yet another class dictatorship. Disillusion with that project and other universalist claims (in Freud, for example) is said to have brought the whole issue into doubt, so Foucault (1980) argues, academics were recognized as representing only themselves or their social fraction, later identified by Bourdieu (1986) specifically as the new petit bourgeoisie, awash with educational and cultural capital but lacking economic capital. Ironically, the universal analysis of interests turned out to be based on specific interests itself.

A more empirical point can be added. Educationalists were sometimes reminded (and self-critique is warranted here) that "progressive" techniques merely reproduced the obedient self-monitoring citizen of advanced capitalism, or that university expansion would lead only to a deeper consumerism. Not surprisingly, some of those actually engaged in the field felt patronized or badly misunderstood: what external critics took to be ideological blockage requiring acute critique was really a knowing and perceptive strategy for the powerless. They were fully aware of the constraints facing them and were not fooled or naively convinced politically or ideologically, but were still trying to exploit any minor cracks or fleeting opportunities to challenge the system. The denunciations of a specialist quoting Gramsci, and often digressing to a scholarly discussion of which of Gramsci's works were the most relevant, were not likely to be much help.

These points lead to a new and more modest role for the academic critic. Instead of claiming to speak on behalf of the oppressed when we diagnose deep interests at work behind the scenes, we must offer our analyses as only one of a possible set of readings. If we want to persist in the claim that critique leads to better-informed action, and not just another profitable research programme, we must be prepared to let the activists be the judge of that. There is no dishonour in pursuing "purely" academic analyses, of course, but we must be clear that we are doing it for ourselves and not "humanity".

21.3 SOME ILLUSTRATIONS

The advantages and limits of an analysis of underlying interests can be illustrated by pursuing some of their specific debates and arguments about what might be taken as the central activities involved in education – teaching, learning and assessment. As a number of commentators in the past and in this current collection have noted, the emergence of distance education has done much to question practices in these areas that had remained unanalysed for decades. The literature on distance education has now affected discussions of teaching, learning and assessment in conventional institutions in the United Kingdom, as they have also attempted to change from elite to mass organizations, and as they have turned to the characteristic technologies of distance learning for solutions. Much of the specific advice on offer on government-sponsored websites – the "learning and teaching subject networks" organized under the aegis of the Higher Education Academy, and much of the material featured in training courses for new lecturers – will be instantly familiar to any distance educator. An insistence on planning by objectives, or rational curriculum planning models, is universal. Encouragement to experiment with "new" forms of assessment such as multi-choice testing or peer assessment is widespread. The purchase of a commercial Virtual Learning Environment (VLE) even produces earnest speculation about design of the kind that was pressing and urgent at the UKOU in the 1970s – given that we can stream video as well as provide text, which content is best expressed in which medium?

In conventional education as well as in distance education, there seems to be a tendency to represent the issues in an idealist form: that is as a series of ideas (sometimes approaches or perspectives). Developing ideas seems to be the main activity, ideas are seen as the main source of institutional change, and differences of policy are seen as reflecting different ideas. Can anything be gained by introducing the notion of conflicting interests?

21.4 TEACHING AND COURSE DESIGN

To take teaching first, how might we explain the widespread adoption of objectives or learning outcomes as a crucial guide to teaching activities? It can be difficult to persuade colleagues to try to discuss the issue at all, in the 2000s as much as in the 1970s, since they can see these approaches as self-evidently superior or as natural. This kind of rational approach simply seems the only alternative to complete chaos. It is easy to point out problems and contradictions to advocates of the approach. There are very interesting philosophical objections to underlying behaviourism or positivism in the approach that were well developed in 1970s curriculum design literature (Golby et al., 1975). There is careful work by Melton (in Henderson and Nathenson, 1984) showing that the presence of specific learning outcomes, objectives or other "advanced organizers" actually makes little difference to learning. It is still possible to provoke some kind of puzzlement by insisting that advocates actually approach seriously the challenging problem of operationalizing aims as objectives, instead of cheerfully thinking up some rewritten phrases using the key words in Bloom's taxonomy. It is always possible to demand to know what else is left as a remainder beyond that which can be specified. Those who believe that human thought is impossible without clear objectives can often be teased by insisting that they outline their objectives before making that point.

However, current audiences are probably more impressed by pointing out that objectives or outcomes are simply not used in the intended way in practice. Advocates of the approach will openly admit that they tend to write their own learning outcomes at the last minute, after having decided much of the contents of their courses, and in order to meet bureaucratic requirements for standard templates. Learning outcomes are often never referred to again, either by designers or by students, unless a formal evaluation exercise reminds everybody. Pushed a little, most people can see that the use of objectives or outcomes does not simply offer the best, most common or most obvious way to design teaching sequences, and does not persist as a result of the sheer power of the ideas. So why are they so widespread? My answer would be that they clearly reflect the interests of powerful groups in management. Rendering course design in terms of a logical means to achieve a tightly specified and simply defined end permits management interests to play a crucial role in what is widely agreed to be one of the more tedious but politically important tasks endured by working academics – the course validation process.

Managers have an interest in imposing a simple model because it justifies their existence and assists them in the micro-political struggle with specialists and subject experts, it could be argued. This struggle was necessary in one aspect of the "industrialization" of education – the emergence of a specialist management stratum to replace the older collegiate model. One implication, incidentally, is that planning by objectives is only one way to manage an educational system, and it may be best seen as a halfway house of limited appeal, as other kinds of cost–benefit analysis familiar to accountants take hold. Already there is a suspicion that evaluating courses in terms of how well they achieve learning outcomes is being replaced by simpler criteria such as the UK Quality Assurance Agency's "iron triangle": recruitment, quality rating and financial viability.

The term "industrialization" could point to another level of analysis as well. Rational curriculum planning is the manifestation in education of a much broader trend towards the deployment of a particular means-ends rationality – bureaucratic or scientific rationality as it is sometimes called. The origins and effects of this broader trend have been much discussed by social theorists. Weber sees the growth of such rationality as an essential but dangerous component of modernization, and warns of the threat to liberty that it carries. Adorno (1976) might see the trend as resulting from the logic of commodity production, and point to the connections in positivism between cognitive and political domination (and the need to stabilize occupational identity). Braverman (1974) has written an influential analysis of "deskilling" as an essential stage in capitalist development: the advanced level of division of labour and consequent casualization in the UKOU is one possible outcome.

Similar points might be made in order to critique current support for "study skills". This issue has been put firmly on the agenda by the growth of "mass" education, and, in the United Kingdom at least, much of the foundational work has been developed in distance education systems, principally the UKOU. Study skills are usually seen as an obviously good thing and as an effective solution to the problems faced by first-generation students, although there are the usual contradictions and problems with solid evidence. It is common, for example, for advocates of study skills to note ruefully that students do not actually seem to use them, even after they have made their best efforts. Advocates also disagree among themselves about the effectiveness of particular techniques. Disputes are usually rendered in the familiar format of different "approaches" or ideas, and students are usually advised to choose the most effective techniques for themselves. What interests might be concealed here, however?

One obvious point is that it is students who are being urged to adjust and not teachers. To adopt a critical question developed in the sociology of education of the 1970s (Young, 1971), how is it that publicly funded universities seem to be so unsuccessful at teaching the majority of citizens? This question appeared much earlier of course, in distance education systems, and changing both curriculum and pedagogy (in the direction of the rationality we have discussed) was part of the overall package of reform. However, it is the conventions of academic work that still remain largely uncriticized. Bourdieu (1988) offers an example of how this might occur. Academic judgments underpin actual formal assessments and grading, and are displayed best in discussions about grades or in the additional comments offered to students. In those discussions, "style" seems to be important, for example. This leads to a discussion of what the preferred style might look like, what its social origins are, and whose interests it serves. To cut a very long and powerful analysis short, Bourdieu refers to an unconsciously held and acquired "high aesthetic", which stresses the value of matters such as abstractness and emotional detachment. These values, and a system that uses them to make concrete judgments, are supposed to be universal, to represent "value" itself (see also the Postscript in Bourdieu, 1986), but Bourdieu suggests that their energy arises from social class divisions. The high aesthetic requires considerable cultural and economic capital if it is to develop, and it also enables not only judgment, but social distanciation. It is no accident that the high aesthetic is the polar opposite of the popular aesthetic that characterizes the tastes of those with less cultural and economic capital. Deploying the high aesthetic is one way to reproduce class boundaries.

It seems perfectly possible to offer the same kind of critique of the very popular work on "deep" and "surface" learning, and its more recent manifestations. This work is apparently the most popularly cited material in the extensive discussions on teaching and learning in both distance and conventional (higher) education. Ostensibly, these divisions appear to be psychological ones. One reason for the popularity of the work is its technical soundness, and it is one of only two approaches to learning styles to have survived a recent critical survey (Coffield et al., 2004).

However, what if these dispositions are not psychological but social and cultural after all? The characteristics of the "deep" learner bear a striking resemblance to those of the "high aesthetic" that we discussed above – the same ability to become detached, ignore detail, go for underlying generative principles and so on. Is it possible that the undoubted success of the deep learner in the current university system is due not to some cognitive superiority but because there is a congruence between the values of the deep learner and the values of the university academic? A clue might be found in some of the descriptions of the surface learner, which certainly seem far from value free. Many examples of value judgements can be found in the actual coding procedures used in the empirical research (turning on matters such as "inappropriate relations between concepts", or "vacuous analogies" for example, see Entwistle and Ramsden, 1983, p. 80), and surface learners are described having the disappointing tendency to treat tasks "as an external imposition" (Morgan, 1993, pp. 72–73).

21.5 ASSESSMENT

The discussion of the strategic learner also shows that something is often missing in discussions of assessment techniques and regimes. It is common to begin by noting that assessment practices can express different ideas and represent different purposes – assessment diagnoses student difficulties, but also serves to evaluate teaching, for example, although it is hard to see how the same instrument can possibly do both. Similarly, the empowering and transformative potential of suitably designed assessment is noted and welcomed, but there is often at the same time a strange silence about another function of assessment regimes. Grading is also used to differentiate among students, and it commonly does so very effectively, dividing students and putting a strain on those wishing to develop collective forms of education. Practising academics are only too aware of how important the grading and differentiation function can become: managers and external examiners seem obsessed by it, and much discussion at various boards is devoted to notions of acceptable distributions of grades. It seems obvious to suspect that this particular function of assessment has a considerable degree of institutional support. It represents powerful interests, revealed in comments made by university spokesman and national politicians about national standards, grade inflation, the need to introduce more discrimination by splitting the UK first class degree and so on. Although on paper, the discrimination function is simply another option, approach or characteristic, usually gladly passed over in favour of more interesting functions, in practice the discrimination function dominates in the last instance.

It might be painful to do so, but the discrimination function of assessment must be addressed and acknowledged. The worst possible outcome arises when assessment designed to reward student success, to empower them or to strengthen their self-esteem has to be reconsidered at the level of exam boards. A recent scandal in school assessment in the United Kingdom revealed the difficulties, as A/S level examinations had to be regraded by examination boards, acting at the national level, away from actual schools, to introduce what was seen as a necessary discrimination (Bright and McVeigh, 2002). Actual grades were awarded using marks gained on assessment devices that had not been designed with discrimination in mind. As a result, students with broadly similar clusters of marks ended up with very different grades, to their dismay.

A similar problem arose in the early days of the UKOU, which had tried to operate with a "criterion-based" assessment system that did not focus on discrimination. Problems arose when it was clear that on the basis of coursework alone, 40 percent of students in one Faculty were on course to receive a First or 2:1 grade. Managers and politicians felt that such a bunched distribution would lead to questions about the quality of UKOU courses, and steps had to be taken at the final examination board to make the distribution more politically acceptable (Harris, 1987).

These examples should not be seen as offering simple moral condemnations of managers and politicians, of course. Much of the shock and disappointment felt by academics and students arises from not realizing that a legitimate interest in acceptable distributions is going to be a major factor in the practice of student assessment. We may not support, admire or welcome such an interest, but it is quite a reasonable one – few would welcome an assessment scheme that did not effectively discriminate between talented and hard-working students at one end, and the idle at the other. It seems crucial that this legitimate interest is given full recognition in discussing assessment design, especially with students. Attempts to diminish the overall importance of the discrimination function in determining the final grade should be seen as necessarily political, even if this threatens the preferred idealism of the discussion.

It is also the case that assessment plays a key part in course design, although this is often glossed. Systems thinkers have long insisted that course designers consider assessment as an integral part of the cycle instead of leaving it to be "bolted on" right at the end, but there is another connection as well. The notion of "good design" or "quality" itself implies that materials must be capable of being assessed, it could be argued. "Proper" university knowledge is assessable, one of the characteristics that make it different from "common sense" or journalism. On a more immediate level, when study skills writers urge students to choose a suitable or "do-able" topic for their coursework or dissertations (O'Leary, 2004), what they mean is that it must be assessable, although this implication is often left implicit. I am sure students are well aware that their choice will be affected by what is likely to gain a good grade, despite the usual exhortations to pursue "a project of your own".

Students have contradictory interests of their own, as the considerable work on plagiarism, cheating and "playing the game" indicates (for example Norton et al., 2001). A strange evasiveness can affect academics discussing this matter: quite understandably, they find such practices distasteful and wish they would go away. However, student cheating should perhaps be understood first. It is not surprising that many students take a predominantly "instrumental" approach to assessment, especially if we see this as another manifestation of broader trends towards the narrowly-conceived bureaucratic rationality we were discussing above. Higher education itself is often promoted most prominently in terms of the qualifications that can be gained. The organization of higher education follows a calculating and instrumental path. The expectation that students pay more for their education can be implicated in a growing consumerism directed at educational commodities. A rational consumer decides how to acquire the goods with the least possible effort and expenditure, and the market is indifferent to appeals to traditional values. It is unlikely that simply adopting draconian punishments for those who are unlucky enough to be caught (naive plagiarists?) will diminish the activity if it has these broad cultural and social roots. The mass university is encountering genuinely different interests as it admits members of different social groups, yet it is often assumed that merely formal equivalences will overcome these social differences. A socially mobile single mother paying her own way might share the same broad policy commitments as the elderly male professor who is grading her work, but they will have very different interests in the outcome.

If, as seems likely, student cheating is likely to persist, or even increase, it seems evasive and contradictory not to discuss it openly when designing assessment. Of course, it may be in no one's interest to actually do so. There is more than a hint of staff collusion in "playing the game" in some of the studies, and some equally interesting material on "teaching to the test", largely confined to secondary schools at the moment (Hammersley, 1990). Again, it is necessary to insist that this is not to condemn the participants from some moral high-ground: turning a blind eye, or operating some kind of truce, can be seen as a sophisticated way to reconcile public ideology with private practice, pursued by all organizations that claim to be socially responsible. Nevertheless, this sort of activity, known to all but acknowledged by none, serves to make official advice on study skills or curriculum design look even more idealistic.

21.6 (EDUCATIONAL) TECHNOLOGY

The discussion of technology is a scarlet thread running throughout most of the contributions here, and through most of the classic literature on distance education. It is obvious that technology only ever gets developed in a social and political context in which interests have a major role. It is also true that phrases like "knowledge economy" clearly imply a connection with economic interests and whether they are likely to shift in particular directions. At the same time, both technology and knowledge have unpredictable effects and offer possibilities for action based on new and emergent interests.

The new requirements of distance education made the old technology of face-to-face teaching redundant and inefficient, while the new technologies of print and electronic media raised entirely new possibilities. It is the complicated interactions between the interests of designers and users and the unintended and emergent qualities of the technology itself that are of interest here. There are some historical examples of the unintended consequences of combining the technology of cheap printing and early literacy programmes – the lower orders in Britain were supposed to develop sufficient skills to be able to read simple instructions, but rapidly developed a taste for much less suitable political and critical literature (Rose, 2002).

More familiar and recent threads in the overall argument include discussion of some of the origins of Internet and Web (in military interests and in the interests of elite natural scientists) and its current financial organization, compared to the uses to which the technology is actually put, which are dominated by the diverse interests and intentions of millions of users. Whether this popular use of Computer-Mediated Communication (CMC) was ever actually intended is debatable, but it has certainly emerged as a central element of practice. As any educational user knows, for example, students using electronic educational materials are chronically likely to stray off-task and browse far more popular materials, or to use the enormous amount of educational material on the Web to pursue the sort of interests in plagiarism we were discussing above.

Nor is it just students who follow their own rather less respectable interests using the new technology. Kibby and Costello (2001) point out that the low-cost video conferencing software CU-SeeMe is now used to generate an intriguing kind of participatory pornography. One effect of this usage, incidentally, is to undermine the commercial pornography industry, an example of how the Web is undermining genres and collapsing cultural boundaries. Another study (Marshall, 2003) followed some respectable UK, Australian and American academics into the private chat area provided by an online conference (on postmodernism!) and discovered that they were engaging in some rather explicit flirtation. Following the argument in another direction, the Web is also used extensively to pursue that interesting area of convergence between education and leisure – educationists tend to call it "informal education" and leisure theorists "serious leisure". This area is occupied by people learning languages, discussing philosophical ideas about reality, reading about everyday life in foreign countries, discussing military strategy, uncovering family histories, or swapping spare parts for steam engines – for fun. For some zealots, this kind of activity signifies the end of privilege for academic discourses, the "death of the University", with both good and bad consequences, of course.

Enthusiasts have also noticed a number of social changes which appear to be emerging from the central importance of electronic communication to everyday life. Feminists like Haraway (1991) suggested that the electronic world offered far more possibilities for communication than did the old world of face-to-face. This would permit radical experimentation with our identities, which would not only allow women to ignore their bodies and gender, but would push at the very boundaries between humans, machines and even animals.

On another tack, there are a number of writers who suggest that mechanical and electronic forms of communication have now become central and indispensable to our lives. One implication might comfort those in Distance Education who are still faced with a legitimation problem – face-to-face communication has long been privileged as some essential human activity, but this claim is now much in doubt. Not only does electronic communication replace face-to-face as the dominant form, it transforms human communication as a result. For some writers, advocating variants such as Actor Network Theory (Ryder, 2006), this centrality and transforming power means that we should start to think of electronic machines as agents in their own right, playing an equally important role as humans in the networks which we all inhabit and which provide us with our sense of subjectivity and sociality.

This might come as no surprise to devotees of the latest electronic games, who can easily experience the sense of interacting with an equal if not superior partner, in a kind of populist Turing test. There has been much discussion about virtual reality and especially virtual communities, and whether it is possible any longer to sensibly differentiate between them and the older versions based on face-to-face and physical contact (compare Chesher, 1998; and Miah, 2000). In some more mundane examples, Silva (2000) has argued that domestic technology has played a substantial transforming role – the widespread use of microwave ovens, for example, has altered gender relations. I have recently explored myself the impact of accessing full-text electronic databases in transforming the notions of authorship of the textbook I was writing (Harris, 2005). Discussions like this add a new dimension to the old anxieties about limited access to electronic communication: the range of social identities available is being restricted as much as the specific content as such.

It is not known if participants in educational discussion forums have been known to log on with an avatar, possibly one with a different gender. It is not clear what the effects might be of permitting or even encouraging registered students to choose to read a range of materials from the entire Web, or to construct an online Web page from freely chosen materials and from freely chosen joint authors. There are discussions of the effects of using mobile technologies to access educational materials, but these seem largely turn on simple matters of access and popularity with students – what would be the social effects of being able to download educational materials immediately in order to support a trade union spokesperson in an industrial dispute (an old leftwing fantasy from the early days of the UKOU)?

It seems that universities are being extremely cautious and conservative with the possibilities raised by CMC. It seems common to try to regulate access to educational materials: in my own college, the VLE organizes us into tiny learning cubicles, according to which modules we are registered with. There is no chance for either staff or students to use the VLE to communicate across the strangely artificial module boundaries imposed by management. Less formally, there are latter-day Canutes who are desperately trying to enforce restrictions on the use of unauthorized websites in essays, or on communications in discussion forums. This sort of activity is perfectly explicable once we consider interests, of course. The university may have a theoretical, philosophical or cultural commitment to widespread discussion and learner involvement, but it also has a strong interest in legitimating and certifying the knowledge that it claims to monopolize.

REFERENCES

Adorno, T., Dahrendorf, R., Pilot, H. et al. (1976). *The Positivist Dispute in German Sociology*, London: Heinemann.

Bennett, T. (1998). *Culture: A Reformer's Science*. London: Sage Publications.

Bernstein, R. (ed.) (1985). *Habermas and Modernity*. Oxford: Polity Press.

Bourdieu, P. (1986). *Distinction: A Social Critique of the Judgement of Taste* (trans. R. Nice) London: Routledge and Kegan Paul.

Bourdieu, P. (1988). *Homo Academicus* (trans. P. Collier) Oxford: Polity Press.

Braverman, H. (1974). *Labour and Monopoly Capital: The Degradation of Work in the 20th Century*. New York: Monthly Review Press.

Bright, M. and McVeigh, T. (2002). How the A-level scandal caught fire. *The Observer*, Sunday September 22, 2002.

Carr, W. and Kemmis, S. (1986). *Becoming Critical*. Lewes: Falmer Press.

CCCS. (1981). *Unpopular Education Schooling and Social Democracy in England since 1944*. London: Hutchinson.

Chesher, C. (1998). Colonising Virtual Reality. Construction of the Discourse of Virtual Reality, 1984 – 1992. *cultronix*, **1**(1) [online]. http://eserver.org/cultronix/chesher/

Coffield, F., Mosely, D., Hall, E., and Ecclestone, L. (2004). *Should We be using Learning Styles? What Research has to say to Practice*. Published by the Learning and Skills Research Centre, and online. http://www.lsda.org.uk/files/pdf/1540.pdf.

Cohen P. (2004). A Place to Think? Some Reflections on the Idea of the University in the Age of the 'Knowledge Economy'. *New Formations*, **53**(12), 12–27.

Colletti, L. (ed.) (1975). Introduction. In *New Left Review, Marx: Early Writings*. London: Penguin Books.

Crook, S., Pakulski, J., and Waters, M. (1992). *Postmodernization: Change in Advanced Society*. London: Sage Publications.

Eco, U. (1987). *Travels in Hyperreality*. London: Picador.

Education Group II. (1991). *Education Limited Schooling and Training and the New Right Since 1979*. London: Unwin Hyman.

Entwistle, N. and Ramsden, P. (1983). *Understanding Student Learning*. London: Croom Helm.

Foucault, M. (1980). *Power/Knowledge Selected Interviews and Other Writings 1972–1977*. Brighton: The Harvester Press.

Fraser, N. (1989). *Unruly Practices: Power Discourse and Gender in Contemporary Social Theory*. Cambridge: Polity Press.

Giddens, A. (1979). *Central Problems in Social Theory: Action, Structure and Contradiction in Social Analysis*. London: Macmillan.

Giddens, A. (1982). *Profiles and Critiques in Social Theory*. London: Macmillan.

Giddens, A. (1991). *Modernity and Self-Identity: Self and Society in the Late Modern Age*. Cambridge: Polity Press.

Gintis, H. and Bowles, S. (1980). Contradiction and Reproduction in Educational Theory. In *Schooling Ideology and the Curriculum* (L. Barton et al. eds) Barcombe: Falmer Press.

Golby, M., Greenwald, J., and West, R. (eds). (1975). *Curriculum Design*. London: Croom Helm.

Habermas, J. (1972). *Knowledge and Human Interests*. London: Heinemann Educational Books Ltd.

Hammersley, M. (1990). *Classroom Ethnography Empirical and Methodological Essays*. Buckingham: Open University Press.

Haraway, D. (2003) [1991]. *A Cyborg Manifesto: Science, Technology, and Socialist-Feminism in the Late Twentieth Century* [online]. http://www.stanford.edu/dept/HPS/Haraway/CyborgManifesto.html.

Harris, D. (1987). *Openness and Closure in Distance Education*. Brighton: Falmer Press.

Harris, D. (1992). *From Class Struggle to the Politics of Pleasure*. London: Routledge.

Harris, D. (2005). Leisure studies as a teaching object. *Journal of Hospitality, Leisure Sport and Tourism Education*, **4**(1) [online]. http://www.hlst.ltsn.ac.uk/johlste/vol4no1/academic/0080.pdf.

Henderson, E. and Nathenson, M. (eds) (1984). *Independent Learning in Higher Education*. Englewood Cliffs, New Jersey: Educational Technology Publications Inc.

Humm M. (ed.) (1992). *Feminisms: A Reader*. Hemel Hempstead: Harvester Wheatsheaf.

Kibby, M. and Costello, B. (2001). Between the Image and the Act: Interactive Sex Entertainment on the Internet. *Sexualities*, **4**(3), 353–369.

Lyotard, J.F. (1984). *The Postmodern Condition: A Report on Knowledge*. Manchester: Manchester University Press.

Marshall, J. (2003). The Sexual Life of Cyber-Savants. *The Australian Journal of Anthropology*, **15**(2), 229–248.

Marx, K. (1977) [1887]. *Capital*, Vol. 1. London: Lawrence and Wishart.

Miah, A. (2000). Virtually nothing: re evaluating the significance of cyberspace. *Leisure Studies*, **19**(3), 211–224.

Morgan, A. (1993). *Improving Your Students' Learning: Reflections on the Experience of Study*. London: Kogan Page.

Norton, L., Tilley, A., Newstead, S., and Franklyn-Stoakes, A. (2001). The Pressures of Assessment in Undergraduate Courses and their Effects on Student Behaviours. *Assessment and Evaluation in Higher Education*, **26**(3), 269–284.

O'Leary, Z. (2004). *The Essential Guide to Doing Research*. London: Sage.

Open University. (1982). *Popular Culture (U203)*. Milton Keynes: Open University Press.

Rose, J. (2002). *The Intellectual Life of the British Working Classes*. New Haven and London: Yale University Press.

Ryder, M. (2006). Actor-Network Theory [online]. http://carbon.cudenver.edu/mryder/itc_data/act_net.html.

Silva, E. (2000). The cook, the cooker and the gendering of the kitchen., *Sociological Review*, **48**(4), 612–629.

Stones, R. (2005). *Structuration Theory*. London: Palgrave.

Young, M. (ed.) (1971). *Knowledge and Control New Directions for the Sociology of Education*. London: Colllier-Macmillan.

Section III

Leadership in Distance Education

Introduction

David Murphy

This section turns the focus to leadership, not just in terms of the individual who heads a distance education institution but more broadly with respect to how the concept of leadership is applied throughout an organization, and how increasingly significant leadership has become in the distance education sector.

In the first of this section's chapters, Paul and Brindley alert us to the changing context of higher education and the consequent pressures on leadership in distance education. Technological change is of course identified as a major driver of change, along with the "new breed of student", the emergence of whom has been partially responsible for the blurring of distinctions between distance and traditional universities. The authors visit the role of the university in this challenging environment and offer a range of strategies that institutions may choose to take in order to respond appropriately. This is not simply through adjustment of delivery models, but also involves rethinking curricula and the organization of knowledge, the training of staff and paying increasing attention to accountability.

Latchem, Lockwood and Baggaley pick up on the theme of technological change, outlining the leadership challenges and management requirements for those involved in development projects in low-income nations. What is initially surprising when perusing their chapter is the number of technology-based development projects they present (most with associated websites), illustrating both the scope and the extent of worldwide efforts to support educational advancement. The authors are not unfamiliar with ongoing inequity in the provision of education and starkly outline the enormous challenges facing agencies, NGOs and the private sector. They also discuss the reasons that some projects fail and, in doing so, present eight scenarios that illustrate the role of effective leadership in achieving successful outcomes.

In his examination of strategic planning in distance education, Panda emphasizes the leadership roles that must underpin such activity at a variety of levels in the organization. Links are also drawn with governance and policy issues, as Panda argues for a holistic approach to strategic planning, using examples from a variety of distance education institutions in a number of countries to illustrate the required underpinnings and models. He concludes by noting that appropriate contextually based strategic planning cannot be ignored – it is a basic requirement for a successful distance education system or organization.

In her chapter, Mason takes us to the practical topic of assessment, offering leaders in distance education institutions a viewpoint that appeals to both administrative imperatives (the effective use of resources) and academic concerns (practices that lead to effective learning). She argues for the need to rethink assessment, offering a theoretical model that empowers learners and overcomes the deficiencies of traditional assessment methods. Issues of cheating and plagiarism are also addressed, and a range of proven assessment methods are presented. The need for preparing both staff and students for innovative assessment methods is emphasized, along with the positive implications of adopting such strategies.

Using Massey University as a case study, the chapter by Thompson and Shillington tackles the issue of student support services, presenting a model that has been successfully applied at a major distance education institution. In presenting the services excellence model, they outline the challenges facing similar institutions, in terms of responding to new cohorts of learners, costing implications and the role of technology. The overall aim is to provide appropriate services in a timely and flexible manner, all developed within a strategic framework based on institutional policy and practice.

Leadership development, a rarely considered topic in the distance education literature, is the focus of the chapter by Tait, who presents an argument on how it can be promoted and supported in distance education contexts. Interestingly, he spends time presenting a case (significantly, including values) for believing that distance and e-learning requires separate consideration in terms of leadership from other institutional settings. The kinds of leadership that are important in this context are discussed, and he presents a case study from the UKOU of a leadership development program.

To round out this section, Bennett presents an essay that both critiques the other chapters and examines the concepts of leading and leadership. In doing so, he takes a disarmingly simple question such as "Where are leaders and what do they do?" and dissects the chapters in terms of their responses. He posits the view that the concept of leadership is slippery, in terms of both definition and practice, using arguments from both the cases and the literature to support his arguments. He also concludes that there is an overemphasis on rational models in the cases and the literature, at the expense of consideration of concepts such as power, trust and morality, at the same time calling attention to the notion of distributed leadership.

Chapter 22

New Technology, New Learners and New Challenges: Leading our Universities in Times of Change

Ross H. Paul and Jane E. Brindley

22.1 INTRODUCTION

The impact of technological change on society and its educational institutions over the past decade has been profound. In North America, especially, technological advancements that were supposed to give us more leisure time have dramatically increased the pace and the hours given to the workplace. Educational leaders are feeling intense pressure not only to keep up with the pace of change but to be at the forefront in creating learning communities that are models for the knowledge society.

In universities, access to digital resources and communication technologies is reshaping teaching, learning and scholarly research in ways that reach far beyond institutional walls. Students, familiar with the cyber world of instant messaging, gaming and information access, are bringing a whole new set of orientations, skills and demands to their educational institutions.

In this chapter, it is argued that the convergence of these forces is resulting in huge challenges to our post-secondary institutions and that the pressures for change are as great on our open universities and distance learning institutions as they are on traditional university campuses.

It is our perception that the evolution of distance education in European and Commonwealth countries, led by the open universities, has been significantly different from that of the USA. In the former, higher education was less accessible and more elitist so that the great success of the distance education universities over the past three decades was directly associated with providing opportunities to adult learners that they otherwise never would have had. In Australia, the development of dual-mode institutions resulted in better integration of the two systems and the two groups of learners. In America, given the broad range of diverse post-secondary institutions, accessibility was always much greater, and so there was less need for open universities dedicated to extending it. Instead, economists and educators embraced technology as the primary response to pressures to improve the quality and cost-effectiveness of post-secondary education.

In the twenty-first century, the differences between countries and institutions are disappearing quickly. Post-secondary education is much more accessible in relative terms in all countries, and technology is having a huge impact on educational delivery in all but the poorest jurisdictions. With greater accessibility, not only to higher education but also to increasingly sophisticated and rapid communication technologies, has come a new breed of students. Our particular interest here is the impact of this technological evolution on our students, the skills and aspirations that they bring to their studies and the implications of all of this for the organization and management of our universities. Our central thesis is that the new values and expectations that students bring are a huge challenge to the ethos of universities, both traditional and modern.

Thirty years ago, in most countries, there was a very clear distinction between the emerging open universities and their traditional counterparts. The respective clienteles were very different. Open universities were dominated by adult learners, usually part-time and often employed, who were highly motivated by the new opportunities offered to them by distance learning and open admissions. They studied at home or in the workplace, by correspondence and telephone tutoring, and had relatively little interaction with peers except in summer schools or in periodic weekend retreats or field trips. The traditional baccalaureate student, on the other hand, was young, full-time and carried out his or her studies almost exclusively in a campus and classroom setting.

In many countries, these distinctions are rapidly disappearing. The explosive development of online learning and changes in the way students learn have transformed both types of institution – the traditional campus-based university and our distance teaching institutions.

Today's campus-based student may still be full-time, but he or she brings a much more complex set of expectations and skills to university than was previously the case. Evening classes and distance education courses once designed for adult learners have been seized by younger on-campus students seeking more personalized timetables and the flexibility, course choice and convenience of online learning. Even a full-time undergraduate who takes no courses at a distance is often more comfortable working in a busy hallway or cafeteria than in a classroom or library, taking advantage of the wireless environment offered by more and more institutions. Such students do not take notes at lectures anymore but download the professor's lessons beforehand or afterwards. This changes the whole approach that many take to formal classes – they do not expect the professor to lecture or write notes on a board unless these illuminate or extend content to which they already have access. They seek to benefit from his or her application of the learning to real-life situations through facilitated discussion, pertinent stories and case studies or hands-on activities through collaborative projects, cooperative education and internships.

Although students are entering university programmes with greater and more sophisticated expectations for their educational experience and are often much more comfortable and adept with technology than their instructors, they may lack the requisite self-directed learning skills that flexible learning and use of extensive digital resources require. They will need learning activities that not only engage their imaginations but also help them to acquire these skills.

All of this puts huge strains on the organization of today's universities, campus-based or non-traditional. Higher education is increasingly accessible, and as students view it more as a right than a privilege, there are strong pressures for universities to respond to a much broader range of learners and learning styles and preferences. Students want quality, "just-in-time" services, access to faculty and preparation for jobs, but they also want convenience, independence and more control over their own learning environment. They are much more concerned about "value for money", especially where higher tuition and living costs increase their subsequent debt loads. Their assumption of higher education as a right brings a concomitant sense of entitlement that seldom existed among previous generations.

These trends have tremendously blurred the distinction between open and campus-based institutions and the clientele they serve. Both types of institutions have to take account of significant changes in their students – their profiles, their aspirations and the skill sets they possess or lack.

This is particularly a challenge for the traditional, campus-based university today. Even where the profundity of these changes is recognized, it is quite another challenge to adjust to the new learners. There is a very strong need to adjust the culture of the institution in support, taking into consideration such key factors as faculty and staff expertise and orientations, existing and needed infrastructure and reward systems.

At the same time, open universities are seeing new groups of learners. Campus-based students are looking to open universities for courses to complement or supplement their classroom timetables, and young working professionals who have already attained at least one degree are turning to them for professional and graduate degrees. These learners often bring a different set of expectations and much more sophisticated skills in communication technology to their studies than did adult distance learners of an earlier era. They may not have the same motivations as more traditional adult learners and they bring much higher expectations for the quality and variety of support, including a full range of online services.

In many ways, serving new types of learners has challenged the prevailing ethos of the open universities as much as it has the much longer traditions of campus-based universities. Even if they are only 30 or 40 years old, open universities have developed a very strong culture around the industrial model so well described by Peters (1983) and changing it has been a major challenge for institutional leaders in recent years. Following Hall (1996), while distance education sought to broaden the base of the "convocation" role of traditional universities (elite academics in secluded settings), technologies today are changing "all of learning" so that both kinds of institutions become universities of "convergence". With the advantage of 30 years' hindsight, the distance education movement seems far less radical or as different from the traditional university as it may have seemed at the outset, and the demands of today's learners are as profoundly challenging to the values and practices of open universities as they are to campus-based ones.

In somewhat different ways, both types of institutions face these challenges and the answers are increasingly similar at each. The first two sections of this chapter consider some of the challenges, first by looking at trends related to technology and its impact on current learners and then by reflecting on the role of the university. The final section of the chapter proposes responsive institutional strategies that strive for a balance between anticipating and adapting effectively to change, and valuing and nurturing the important role of universities in a democratic society.

22.2 ACCOMMODATING A NEW GENERATION OF STUDENTS

Much is made of the technological changes in the lives of our younger students and how these are having a major impact on the ways in which students learn and think (cf. Dede, 2005). There are those who downplay these assertions, noting that universities have survived for centuries with very little change in the basic model, but there are societal shifts associated with rapidly evolving communication technology that have major implications for the type of student seeking higher education and persuasively make the case that our traditional institutions must change fairly dramatically if they are to respond successfully. Issues and trends discussed here include demand for accessibility and the resulting student diversity, change in student expectations and experience, change in conceptualization of work and leisure time, importance of social networking, the impact of faster and easily accessible search engines and the virtual library and changes in the students' sense of entitlement.

22.2.1 Student Diversity and the Demand for Accessibility

Our universities are taking an increasing proportion of the age cohort, and lifelong learning is bringing a much more diverse set of learners to our institutions. There is no turning back from these trends, and an institution that is providing mass higher education has to be much more responsive to its wider and more diverse student clientele than was the case in more selective times. The challenges include catering to a much wider range of ability, previous achievement, motivation and aspiration. This requires a greater range of services and the capacity to respond to broader and more extensive expectations and demands.

22.2.2 Changes in Students' Expectations and the Way they Learn

In his useful notion of "digital immigrants" (faculty and staff) struggling to cope with "digital natives" (today's students), Mark Prensky (2001) notes that "today's students are no longer the people our educational system was designed to teach" (p. 1). Duderstadt et al. (2005) suggest that responding to new learners is forcing significant changes that will transform the modern university.

> Adept at multitasking and context switching, they approach learning in a highly nonlinear manner, which is a poor fit with the sequential structure of the university curriculum.
>
> (p. 2)

Responding to these new types of learners obviously requires significant change from faculty and staff. As Bates (2000) notes,

> Any strategies for implementing the use of technology for teaching need to take into account the prevailing culture of the university, and, above all, that of the faculty members.
>
> (p. 96)

In a very useful anecdotal approach to the challenges these changes in incoming learners pose for our educational institutions, four current American university students address their expectations for today's universities (Aviles et al., 2005). Representing three supposed generations of students (baby boomer, Generation X and two from the Millennium generation), the students agree on most of the shortcomings of the institutions they attend and are very clear on what they expect from them. In each case, the pressure for change emanates from the new communication technologies and their ease with them, which, in most cases, transcends the capacity of the institution to cope.

What is striking about these students is how articulate they are in defining their expectations for the educational institutions they attend. Previous generations, attending more selective universities in times when higher education was seen more as a privilege than a right, were much more apt to accept whatever the prevailing mode of educational delivery and service was at the given institution. In fact, very few support services were provided as it was up to the individual to cope in his or her own way. Dropouts were signals not of failure but of high academic standards. Poor teachers were mocked and satirized by students, but it was almost never the case that the students would get angry and demand better teaching or better professors as they are much more apt to do today.

22.2.3 The Impact of Technology on Notions of Work and Leisure Time

> Leisure-time pursuits will become an increasingly important basis for differences between people, as the society shifts from a work orientation toward greater involvement in leisure.
>
> (Toffler, 1970, p. 289)

Few recent predictions have been more off the mark than the very frequent assertion in the 1970s that emerging communication technologies would greatly increase our leisure time. While perhaps the best known proponent of this notion, Alvin Toffler (1970) was by no means inaccurate in his predictions of the "shock" of adjusting to a new age of high technology. Ironically, however, the shock has come not from trying to cope with increased leisure time, but with the stresses and strains of a dramatically extended and faster work life.

Indeed, technological advances have blurred the distinction between work and leisure time and, especially in North America, the pace and stress of working life have multiplied exponentially as advances in communication technology have enabled us to work at any time and from any place. In post-secondary education, this has not only affected the work habits of academics but also profoundly affected the expectations and behaviours of our students. It is the argument of this chapter that the changing culture within which today's student operates has profound implications for the organization and delivery of post-secondary education and, hence, for educational leadership.

If we accept the notion that technological advances have increased both the pace and the volume of work, it follows that time management becomes a vital challenge, especially for faculty. For example, e-mail opens the possibility of providing instant access for students to their professors, but the sheer volume of demand for quick response can be a challenge for already busy faculty members. This pressure is exacerbated by a culture that expects almost instant responses to electronic queries, where even a day's delay in responding is seen as far too long. This underlines the importance of faculty members, tutors and others establishing very clear protocols around the use of electronic communications, including expectations for response times. Each technological advance almost inevitably increases the gap between the students' ("natives") and professors' ("immigrants") familiarity with it, putting pressure on faculty to learn new systems and to cope effectively with them.

The pressures of time are constant and they often conflict with a faculty member's own concept of how to spend that valuable commodity. If technological innovations require more time dedicated to "teaching" (as opposed to research, grantsmanship or community service), they will induce new tensions and resistance to them among already beleaguered staff.

22.2.4 Importance of Technology in the Social Networking of Today's Student

The implication of technological change for today's institutions goes beyond its impact on teaching and learning. More fundamentally, students not only bring new ways of learning and seeing the world but have significantly different social orientations and skills. Previous notions of "nerds and geeks", isolated in their obsession with computers, are disappearing as electronic communication (cell phones, instant messaging, file sharing, portals) become the norm. There are less clear distinctions between "study" and "play" as multi-tasking and rapid shifting in activities take place at astonishingly quick rates. These trends have profound implications for education, both positive (collaborative learning, multi-tasking, ease at surfing the net) and negative (blurring distinctions between education and entertainment, shorter interest spans).

The rapid pace of today's digital world also challenges the traditional university role of reflection and taking a critical perspective of social trends. Students with busy lives and an instrumental view of the purpose of their education may be resistant to a professor's deliberate attempt to slow things down, to wonder about meaning and interpretation and to challenge students to do likewise.

In many ways, communication technologies are a force in the opposite direction, facilitating and creating a culture of speed and excitement. Peters (2002), in describing the transition from modern to post-modern curricula, notes that "Prefabricated courses for very large numbers of students will, however, lose their present significance as will the expository method of teaching which is linked to a receptive way of learning" (p. 29). Whether in a face-to-face or an online classroom, the challenge is to encourage critical reflection without losing the attention of the student. Interacting with students who have grown up in an environment of multimedia (IPods, MP3 players, cell phones, personal digital assistants) or whose workplace is characterized by sophisticated technology (learning management systems, e-mail, videoconferencing) requires a host of new skills on the part of the faculty member.

22.2.5 Impact of Google and the Emergence of Virtual Library Services

The explosion in the accessibility of knowledge is astounding, not only because of the development of the Internet and the World Wide Web but it is directly proportional to the incredibly rapid improvement of search engines for libraries and general interest. The Google phenomenon has dramatically increased access to knowledge, but it also makes great new demands on the student's ability to distinguish between academically sound knowledge and trivia, to know the difference between breadth and depth and to discern the veracity and validity of the source.

Just as the media blur the distinction between information and entertainment in today's news broadcasts, there are concerns about the impact of the digital culture on a faculty member's ability to induce "deep learning" among students used to multi-tasking, finding information quickly and moving rapidly from one issue to another.

The ease of access to information also makes new demands on the learner's knowledge of copyright and plagiarism and the sheer volume of information can be debilitating to rather than supportive of clear thinking and analysis. This places a much greater premium on the need to develop research and inquiry skills in our students. Notwithstanding the development of electronic vehicles to discover plagiarism on the Web, it also challenges a faculty member's ability to discern to what extent the work is that of the student and not something copied from someone else's work.

Nowhere are the impacts of new technologies more visible than in the rapid evolution of today's university library. For centuries, the library was a repository of books, journals and other written materials which were catalogued and borrowed on site. Quiet study carrels were provided and students were encouraged to treat them reverentially.

Today's "learning commons" is a far different place. Card catalogues have been replaced by sophisticated electronic search engines that can be used from any location with an Internet connection; librarians are readily available to assist students in their research in person or at a distance; and the physical facilities are as apt to include busy common rooms and coffee shops as quiet work spaces where silence is golden. The virtual library is fast becoming a reality, and in the process, one of the long-standing disadvantages of isolated learners in distance education has been overcome. Not only can they access materials, but they can learn the necessary research skills to do so, closing another gap between the on-campus and virtual learning experience. At the same time, campus-based students who are used to using the Internet as their main source of information are now just as apt as distance learners to use off-site online services as a library visit for their catalogue searches.

22.2.6 Student Sense of Entitlement

With the democratization and even commodification (cf. Peters, 2002, p. 28) of higher education has come a greater sense of entitlement among students, not only for how they are taught but even for how well they do. Competition for second-entry professional schools and for graduate programmes has bred a much more mark-conscious generation, as merely obtaining a good degree is no longer a guarantee of admission to an academic programme of choice. As well, the combination of higher accessibility and increased tuition fees in many jurisdictions may be breeding more of a "consumer" approach to post-secondary education whereby students expect certain results for their investment, sometimes seemingly independent of their own efforts!

Winzer (2002), in a report based on an extensive literature review on grade inflation for a university task force on this issue, concluded that factors affecting the trend of awarding higher grades included the extensive use of student evaluations of faculty in promotion and tenure (and the documented correlation between high grades and positive faculty ratings), "student expectations" and "student entitlement mindset". Citing Levine and Cureton (1998) and Trout (1997), she notes the following:

> The business model that preaches that the customer is always right has permeated academe, and resulted in a marked consumer orientation on the part of students and their families. Lead by this, students work to get what they paid for.
>
> (p. 10)

Levine and Cureton (1998) describe current post-secondary students as approaching their studies as they do any other service in a marketplace. They are looking for convenience, availability at all hours, helpful and efficient staff and return on investment. While this increased sense of entitlement can be viewed negatively by faculty and staff, it also has its positive manifestations. Students are far less apt to accept poor teaching or badly designed materials and they put legitimate pressure on an institution to be responsive and accountable for its programmes and services.

The central point is that earlier versions of the university, both campus and distance based, were not really overly responsive to learners while, today, very few institutions of higher education can afford not to do everything possible to accommodate their students in order that the core activities of research, teaching and learning remain relevant and accessible.

22.3 ROLE OF THE UNIVERSITY

In considering the most appropriate institutional responses to the challenges posed above, it is quickly evident that the answers are more complex than they at first seem. Once embarked on the road of accommodation, an institution can never look back and the challenges and changes will come quickly and furiously.

There are obvious practical responses to the new generations of students which have led universities to be much more complex organizations than they once were. Indeed, a whole range of support services (academic advising, career placement, study skills assistance, special needs and counselling offices, centres for women, international, and First Nations students, ombudspersons, human rights offices) are offered that were not even dreamed of a few short decades ago.

Of course, new technologies have also rendered some services much more effective and responsive. Online registration systems have eliminated the beginning of term line-ups, and libraries have been transformed by increasingly sophisticated search engines with access to ever-expanding digital resources. Portals create personalized environments where students can access services such as academic advising and registration as well as their individual courses (e.g. syllabus, lecture notes and assignments), review their academic records, do library searches and communicate with peers and professors. At the same time, as new technologies transform teaching and other core services, institutions are compelled to offer corresponding support such as extended hours help desks and online and classroom seminars on the effective use of various systems and tools.

These are natural and predictable responses to the rapid changes we have documented. However, real institutional change goes well beyond such adjustments to confront the prevailing campus culture and to require a fundamental rethinking of the institution's approach to carrying out its mission and mandate.

In this context, it is vital to develop a conception of the attributes that a graduate should have. More and more students are thinking instrumentally about their higher education – whether or not it will provide ready access to a good and well-paying job. Institutions can respond directly to this interest by promoting job placement statistics and providing good career counselling.

Surely, however, the university in today's society has much more responsibility than simply producing tomorrow's workers. It must go beyond knowledge and skill enhancement to developing graduates who are thoughtful and reflective about that world and their place in it. They must be at one and the same time comfortable with and critical of new technology. They must have the capacity to perform many tasks simultaneously and quickly but always with the self-awareness and critical perspective that is central to the management of an effective democratic society (cf. Duderstadt et al., 2005).

Of course, every institution cannot be expected to address all of these issues. There will always be room for more narrowly defined training programmes that use technology effectively to produce skilled workers for a given industry or set of tasks. However, any institution calling itself a university, whether campus or distance based, has responsibilities that go far beyond the utilitarian. Sophistication in the use of technology is not necessarily accompanied by sophistication *about* its meaning and impact and yet the latter is crucial if we are to produce more than technocrats for future societies.

The particular challenge is to adjust to the new realities of mass higher education without sacrificing the traditional academic roles of social criticism and critical reflection. While the fact that governments increasingly view the modern university as a key economic engine has led to more political and financial support, it has also emphasized its instrumental side. It is vitally important that the intrinsic value of higher learning is not lost in the process and that among the graduate outcomes most highly valued are the ability to think critically and deeply about society and one's role in it.

In short, institutions of higher education have a responsibility to change much more fundamentally than is required to deal with immediate economic and technological challenges. We turn, now, to some of the strategies that follow from this perspective.

22.4 RESPONSIVE INSTITUTIONAL STRATEGIES

All of the above forces have conspired to make much stronger and more complex demands on our formal educational institutions. In this context, universities can no longer merely carry on doing what they have been doing for hundreds of years. Instead, they have to provide for a much more diverse set of learners and in contexts that are quite foreign to the traditional campus-based university. The implications are significant and the responses must both be practical and philosophical.

22.4.1 Engaging in Strategic Planning

The primary path through the maze of burgeoning and often conflicting demands on our institutions of higher learning is effective strategic planning. This includes defining clearly the mission and mandate of the organization, its primary clientele, the sorts of outcomes it expects to produce and how it expects to go about achieving these.

Effective strategic planning is based on thorough environmental scans which locate the institution in the context of its strengths and weaknesses, opportunities and threats and the competition it faces in advancing its mandate. While it requires strong central leadership, it also must be widely consultative so that there is significant ownership among those most directly involved in the implementation of the institution's strategic directions.

The balance between leadership and grassroots consultation is a delicate one, and many such plans have failed because it has not been attained (Paul, 1990, pp. 178–182). An overly "top down" process may produce the illusion of change, but no strategic plan can be effective if it is not "owned" by those whose responsibility it is to carry it out (notably faculty members and front-line staff). On the other hand, an overly democratic a process may yield "planning by committee", the all-too-familiar strategic plans that read as the sum total of everyone's wish list and which provide very little guide to priorities or action.

One very effective strategic planning process is for the leader to solicit widespread community feedback as to the institution's perceived strengths, weaknesses, opportunities and threats and, on the basis of the findings, to forge a preliminary version of a strategic plan. This, in turn, sets off another consultation period, the purpose of which is to sharpen the proposals and to forge a plan which will have broad support but also be precise and incisive enough to be a clear guide to subsequent action.

A prerequisite to all that follows, an effective strategic plan must be not only broad and long term enough to provide vision, confidence and even excitement, but also specific and realistic enough to be a clear guide to action and results. The ultimate test of the effectiveness of a strategic plan is how useful it is in helping to determine the subsequent allocation of scarce resources so that the annual budget process directly reflects its priorities.

22.4.2 Choosing Which Delivery Models will be Supported and Integrating them Thoroughly into the Culture and Technology

To respond effectively to much more demanding students, as suggested above, both open and traditional universities must provide more clearly specified "flexible learning" opportunities that cater to a much more diverse clientele.

However, this provision can be anything but glib, for, as Thomas (1995) emphasizes,

> Flexible learning is not about producing variously deliverable learning packages or pick-'n-mix courses to an otherwise undifferentiated mass market. It is about being prepared to configure all available resources, expertise and learning opportunities in the way that fits the learning purpose best.
>
> (p. 2)

The degree of competition in the system means that it is no longer good enough for an institution to ignore student differences and their demands for maximum flexibility in timetabling and delivery mode. Instead, each institution must decide exactly what delivery strategies it will employ and plan these very carefully, giving full support to each.

"Full support" is an all-encompassing term that must take account of the needs, skills and aspirations of the learners, the systems that support them and the orientations, expertise and skills of faculty and staff. It must emanate from very thorough strategic planning processes that involve faculty, staff and students from the outset.

If new delivery systems are not carefully planned and implemented, an old lesson is learned the hard way, over and over again. If new technologies are introduced in superficial or incomplete ways, they have a profound long-term impact on the institutional culture and the consequences are frequently unintended. Educational television was going to transform schools, and yet almost no attention was given to designing how it would be integrated into the curriculum and teaching. As a result, so much of it was wasted with boring "talking head" productions, and soon school principals were wondering what to do with all the unused television sets. Disappointment with the initial promise of educational television has been replicated with just about every technological innovation since, including text messaging (such as Telidon), interactive video and many manifestations of computer-based learning.

No amount of planning will anticipate all possible outcomes, but a concerted effort to introduce new ways of teaching and learning that takes full account of the existing institutional culture and their impact on it will have a much better chance of succeeding.

22.4.3 Rethinking Curricula and the Organization of Knowledge

Following Duderstadt et al. (2005), the combination of new learners and new technologies may have profound implications for curricula and the organization of knowledge.

> The university may need to reorganize itself quite differently, stressing forms of pedagogy and extracurricular experiences to nurture and teach the art and skill of creativity and innovation. This would probably imply a shift away from highly specialized disciplines and degree programmes to programmes placing more emphasis on integrating knowledge.
>
> (n.p.)

While it may be unrealistic to expect universities to change approaches to the organization of knowledge that have prevailed for centuries, there are very strong trends to inter-disciplinarity, problem-based research and scholarship and a much more concerted effort to encourage students to engage in activities which test the theoretical constructs they have learned through practice and application. These include increasing emphases on group projects, cooperative programmes and internships and collaborative partnerships. Sophisticated technologies also can provide fascinating opportunities for simulations and gaming and foster international collaborations that could only have been dreamed of a few short years ago.

22.4.4 Training of Faculty and Staff

It follows closely on the section about delivery models above that once the delivery strategies have been determined, it is critical that faculty and staff are well prepared for each. An ill-supported distance-learning course, for example, can undermine the whole value of distance delivery if students feel confused and lost with no easy recourse to help. Even where there are sophisticated technological support systems (portals, chat rooms, bulletin boards, e-mail contact with faculty), they are far less effective if faculty and staff have not been well trained to use them and if they are not integrated into the overall design of an academic programme.

It is widely acknowledged in the literature that faculty and staff development is the key component in transformation of universities with regard to effective use of information and communication technologies (cf. Bates, 2000; Roberts et al., 2002). However, the shift that must take place goes far beyond faculty development. One does not just "train" professors for changes that are not supported by the prevailing culture. As Bates (2000) has noted, faculty development in itself may be insufficient if professors are not "totally immersed" in a culture that combines teaching and learning with technology (p. 100). The challenge is not only to consider prevailing institutional norms but also to take full account of the extent of the cultural changes between generations of faculty. Failure to take this into account too often leads to disappointment or unintended consequences and is often the basis for the gap between vision and reality in effective adaptation of universities to technology (Roberts et al., 2002).

This challenge cannot be understated or underestimated. Faculty tend to teach the way they were taught, not for the least reason that the vast majority have been very successful in their own university studies, and most have grown up in the culture of a university with little external experience. There are huge demands on their time as they try to juggle teaching loads with higher and higher expectations for their research productivity. Teaching effectively in the current environment requires not only new skills and knowledge with regard to technology but also a shift from an expository style of teaching to a focus on facilitation of learning activities that engage students and help them become better learners as well as addressing content knowledge. It is asking a lot of an academic who quite likely has never been trained in teaching and learning to experiment with new approaches dependent on complex technology and with significant implications for how they teach and how students learn.

While many faculty members put an inordinate amount of time into experimenting with new approaches to teaching and learning, the traditional reward systems do not always recognize these efforts. A great deal more could be achieved with greater support for and recognition of innovation in teaching. Otherwise, overburdened younger faculty, on whom the future of the institution is most dependent, will quickly learn that their best guarantee of career success is not innovative approaches to teaching and learning but high productivity in research. Both are critical to the success of the modern university.

This is not to suggest that faculty will only respond to formal reward systems or that change is not already taking place, at least in terms of research. Duderstadt et al. (2005) point to the emergence of global research communities supported by sophisticated communication technologies, common electronic data bases and the shared use of sophisticated research equipment such as particle accelerators through the Internet as important signs of transformation in scholarly and investigative activities in universities. In terms of transforming pedagogical approaches, the greatest driver for most faculty is still their love for their field of study and the impact that they can have on bright young minds. Ultimately, faculty will respond most positively when they are persuaded of the true value of new approaches to teaching and learning – that is, when they see the impact of their efforts on their students' ability to think critically and creatively. Any such innovation requires strong leadership, resource support (both financial and human) and recognition and reward. A new approach will not be achieved easily, but once it has been proven effective, it can be very powerful in an institution that is ultimately driven by ideas.

22.4.5 Accountability

The increasingly direct association of higher education with economic development has undoubtedly led to greater investment in universities but, with that investment, have come much higher demands for accountability and demonstrable outcomes. While these should normally be welcomed by educational institutions, undue emphasis on top-ten tables and other manifestations of these pressures can sometimes distort whole systems and lead to unintended consequences that actually undermine accessibility by valuing certain factors over others that are equally important (for instance, by denigrating excellent regional institutions that cannot always compete with the best known research-intensive universities on mandates well suited to the latter but less appropriate to the former).

A core problem in any institution is the difficulty of measuring the effect of processes that are not easily quantifiable and where the impact may not be seen in the short term. For example, the outcome of teaching effectiveness is difficult to measure, and a student may not even appreciate the impact of a particular instructor or course until long after graduation. We can measure research productivity through publications or citations much more readily than we can assess the impact of a particular approach to teaching. One unfortunate manifestation of this challenge is a tendency to measure inputs (which are quantifiable and immediately available – entering averages of students, class sizes, amount of money spent per enrolment) rather than outputs (which tend to be longer term and possibly more complex to correlate with educational experience – graduation and job placement rates and alumni success stories).

One positive response to pressures for accountability is for institutions to develop and publicize prescribed and specific graduate outcomes and strategies for their achievement for each academic programme. These can include specified areas of knowledge, demonstrable skills and core values and persuasive ways of demonstrating them through examinations, competitions, cooperative programmes, simulations and measures of performance in subsequent graduate school or in the work force. Some institutions are now using e-portfolios as a method for students to document and communicate their skills and achievements to potential employers or graduate school selection committees (cf. Walti, 2004).

This is one area where distance educators with their history of an emphasis on mastery learning may have much to teach their more traditional counterparts. Given the critical importance of curriculum to any degree programme, it is often astounding how little attention is paid to its regular review in many universities. In this context, an institution's ability to demonstrate the values, knowledge and skills of its graduates has much to recommend it and it is a worldwide trend on university campuses.

One effort of interest that goes some way to attempting to measure the impact of approaches to teaching and learning is an American-based instrument, the National Survey of Student Engagement (NSSE) (Ewell, 1999). This comprehensive survey is designed to collect data from students each year as to the level of their self-perceived engagement and interaction on campus – in and out of the classroom, with each other and with faculty and staff. According to the NSSE website, the data collected focuses on "how students spend their time and what they gain from attending college", and can be used "to identify aspects of the undergraduate experience inside and outside the classroom that can be improved through changes in policies and practices more consistent with good practices in undergraduate education" (See Quick Facts on the NSSE Website, http://nsse.iub.edu/html/quick_facts.cfm). While not completely an output measure, it is a useful instrument to determine the extent to which today's students are actively involved in their own learning and gives valuable information back to institutional leaders as to which of their strategies and services have been the most effective.

As an indication of the perceived value of this instrument, all eighteen universities in the Province of Ontario, Canada, are participating in this survey in 2006–2007 as they strive to improve the impact of what they do on students' learning (Eisenkraft, 2006). It would be fascinating to conduct a similar survey among the students of open universities around the world.

22.5 CONCLUSION

With the growth of mass higher education and the rapid evolution of communication technologies, a new breed of students is placing unprecedented pressure on our post-secondary institutions. Whether campus based or catering to distance learners, today's university can no longer be operated in the traditional manner of either type of institution. Indeed, the decades' old traditions of open universities are no less resistant to change than those that have prevailed for centuries in our most traditional institutions and the challenges faced by each are remarkably similar.

The emphasis now and for the future is so much less on the institution and so much more on the learner – his or her aspirations, skills, needs and expectations. New technologies have given students much more choice and independence, and they are increasingly forcing institutions of higher learning to respond to them. It is no longer a question of "look right, look left, only one of you three will be here next year", which was the mantra of so many highly selective universities in an earlier age. Students are much less apt to strive to fit into the learning culture of the institution they attend – instead, they expect it to adjust to their own needs!

In the face of such challenges, leaders of both types of universities can learn a lot from each other. However, the central response from both must be to be very clear as to the modes of educational delivery their institution will provide and to ensure that each mode is well supported and integrated into the entire institutional culture.

In this context, distinctions between campus based and distance learning are rapidly disappearing and increasingly irrelevant. As students gradually achieve the ability to study in their own time and in their own space, regardless of the institution(s) they attend, the ideals that once drove the establishment of open universities are being attained and the need for specialized institutions dedicated to them is increasingly unnecessary.

REFERENCES

Aviles, K., Phillips, B., Rosenblatt, T., and Vargas, J. (2005). If higher education listened to me. *EDUCAUSE Review*, **40**(5), 17–28.

Bates, A.W. (2000). *Managing Technological Change: Strategies for College and University Leaders*. San Francisco: Jossey-Bass.

Dede, C. (2005). Planning for neomillennial learning styles. *EDUCAUSE Quarterly*, **1**, 7–12.

Duderstadt, J.J., Wulf, Wm.A., and Zemsky, R. (2005). Envisioning a transformed university. *Issues in Science and Technology Online, Fall Issue*. Retrieved March 13, 2006 from http://www.issues.org/22.1/duderstadt.html.

Eisenkraft, H. (2006). Students get their say. *University Affairs*, **47**(3), 28–32.

Ewell, P. (1999). (Chair, Design Team). *National Survey of Student Engagement*. Boulder, CO: National Center for Higher Education Management Systems. Retrieved March 13, 2006 from http://nsse.iub.edu/index.cfm.

Hall, J. (1996). The revolution in electronic technology and the modern university: The convergence of means. In *Opening Education: Policies and Practices from Open and Distance Education* (T. Evans and D. Nation, eds) London: Routledge, pp. 7–20.

Levine, A. and Cureton, J.S. (1998). *When Hope and Fear Collide: A Portrait of Today's College Student*. San Francisco: Jossey-Bass.

Paul, R.H. (1990). *Open Learning and Open Management: Leadership and Integrity in Distance Education*. London: Kogan Page.

Peters, O. (1983). Distance teaching and industrial production. In *Distance Education: International Perspectives* (D. Sewart, D. Keegan, and B. Holmberg, eds), London: Croom Helm, pp. 95–113.

Peters, O. (2002). *Distance Education in Transition: New Trends and Challenges*. Oldenburg, Germany: Biblioteks- und Informationssystem der Universität Oldenburg.

Prensky, M. (2001). Digital natives, digital immigrants. *On the Horizon*, **9**(5). NCB University Press. Retrieved March 13, 2006 from http://www.marcprensky.com/writing/default.asp

Roberts, J., Brindley, J.E., Mugridge, I., and Howard, J. (2002). Faculty and staff development in higher education: The key to using ICT appropriately. Commissioned Report for *The Observatory*, London, UK: Association of Commonwealth Universities.

Thomas, D. (1995). Learning to be flexible. In *Flexible Learning Strategies in Higher and Further Education* (D. Thomas, ed.) London: Cassell, pp. 1–11.

Toffler, A. (1970). *Future Shock*. New York: Bantam.

Trout, P.A. (24 July 1998). Incivility in the classroom breeds 'education lite.' *Chronicle of Higher Education*, p. A46.

Walti, C. (2004). Implementing Web-based portfolios and learning journals as learner support tools: An illustration. In *Learner Support in Open, Distance and Online Learning Environments* (J.E. Brindley, C. Walti, and O. Zawacki-Richter, eds), Oldenburg: Bibliotheks- und Informationssystem der Universität Oldenburg, pp. 157–168.

Winzer, M. (2002). *Grade Inflation: An Appraisal of the Research*. Retrieved March 13, 2006 from http://people.uleth.ca/~runte/inflation/index.html.

Chapter 23

Leading Open and Distance Learning and ICT-Based Development Projects in Low-Income Nations

Colin Latchem, Fred Lockwood, and Jon Baggaley

23.1 INTRODUCTION

> Asked what she needed most in life, a mother of five in one the refugee camps in the conflict-torn Darfur region in southern Sudan replied, "First, an education for my children, then food, then peace so I can go back to my village". At the time, there were 1.3 million children in these refugee camps.
>
> (Chan, 2005)

While the developed world enjoys the benefits of the twenty-first century, in terms of education, information, technology transfer and living standards, many people in low-income nations are trapped in earlier eras. Millions have their lives disrupted by natural disasters, wars and civil upheavals, and even children are not safe from sexual slavery, being sent into combat and other crimes against humanity.

Worldwide, about 113 million children, mainly female, are denied schooling, and there are 861 million illiterate adults, two-thirds of whom are women (UNICEF, n.d.). Almost half of the world's 2.8 billion people must survive on less than US$2 a day (World Bank, 2005). The social tensions, environmental pressures and political instabilities bred by such ignorance, inequity and poverty are everyone's responsibility and put everyone at risk.

World Bank Infrastructure Economist Charles Kenny (2001) argues that combined with other development initiatives, open and distance learning (ODL) and information and communications technology (ICT) can help to bring education to the world's poorer communities and alleviate poverty. This chapter examines how ODL/ICT initiatives for socio-economic development and empowerment are being supported by international and national agencies, NGOs and the private sector and outlines the required leadership and management for such initiatives to succeed.

23.2 FORMAL EDUCATIONAL DEVELOPMENT

The world is still far from achieving the 1990 Jomtien target of Education for All (EFA). However, inequities are being addressed and enrolments are increasing (UNESCO, 2000), partly through ODL/ICT development projects supported by such agencies as UNESCO, World Bank, Commonwealth of Learning and Centre International Francophone de Formation à Distance, national agencies such as Australia's AusAID, UK's Department for International Development (DfID) and Canada's International Development Research Centre (IDRC) and private sector players such as Microsoft and WorldSpace.

EFA Goal 3 is concerned with gender equality and the empowerment of women. The World Economic Forum (Lopez-Claros and Zahidi, 2005) still rates gender inequality as one of the world' s greatest injustices, although Perraton and Creed (2000) note that female enrolment is growing faster than male enrolment. ODL/ICT are contributing to this. Girls and women are among the top priority groups of India's National Institute of Open Schooling (formerly National Open School) (http://www.nos.org). Also in India, the Indira Gandhi National Open University's Women Empowerment Project provides a nationwide certificate program via satellite and study centers for trainers of women's self-help groups (http://www.ignou.ac.in/aboutus percent5Cprojemwomen.htm). Such ICT-based initiatives as Malaysia's Mothers4Mothers and the Women of Uganda Network (Green, 2004) also help women build coalitions, educate themselves and collaboratively resolve their problems.

The capacity of ODL/ICT to meet the unsatisfied demand for junior-secondary schooling is shown in, for example, Mexico's Telesecundaria (Estrada, 2003) and India's National Institute of Open Schooling. New open schools are being established in a number of developing countries to provide mixed-mode primary, post-primary and secondary schooling for children, youths and adults previously unable to access conventional schools or catch up on their earlier schooling. ODL/ICT are also being used by technical and vocational education (TVET) colleges to increase their outreach and offer more flexible means of study, by mega-universities and open universities (Daniel, 1996), by traditional institutions moving into dual-mode to meet the high demand for tertiary study, by new institutions such as the Virtual University of Pakistan (http://www.vu.edu.pk), and by new networks, alliances and consortia.

The World Bank and Australian Government initiated African Virtual University (http://www.avu.org/) is managed by a Nairobi-based inter-governmental organization which collaborates with African universities in identifying program and development needs, with Australian, Canadian and US universities in developing courses, and with a network of institutions and learning centers to deliver these programs. Commonwealth Ministers of Education have recently endorsed Commonwealth of Learning proposals for a Virtual University for Small States of the Commonwealth

(VUSSC), a consortium of tertiary institutions concerned with improving classroom and distance education, increasing access, reusing or repurposing courseware, enhancing quality, reducing costs, accreditation, credit transfer, and research and development (http://www.col.org/Consultancies/02virtualu.htm).

Networks are replacing traditional hierarchies, and developments are no longer simply initiated and supported on a North–South basis. South–South collaboration is seen in Indonesia's open university, Universitas Terbuka, helping distance educators in Afghanistan, India's Indira Gandhi National Open University (IGNOU) and the New Delhi-based Commonwealth Educational Media Centre for Asia (CEMCA) playing an important regional role in ODL/ICT collaboration and networking, and the New Partnership for Africa's Development (NEPAD) helping to improve ODL/ICT provision across Africa (http://www.nepad.org/).

The low-income nations need many more knowledgeable teachers and teacher trainers. ODL/ICT pre- and in-service teacher training have proved effective in increasing the numbers and improving the capacities of teachers (Robinson and Latchem, 2003), and Perraton and Creed (2000) estimate the cost of such training to be one- to two-thirds of face-to-face provision. Today's teachers also need training in ICT. To date, this has mostly been attempted through crash programs in computer literacy rather then helping teachers integrate the technology and pedagogy (Kobayashi et al., 2005). Now governments, donors, NGOs and the corporate sector are collaborating in providing better ICT teacher training. Washington-based NGO World Links (http://www.world-links.org) is providing in-service training for Indian secondary school teachers in partnership with Intel Corporation and Schoolnet India with funding from the Dutch government. The World Bank, through its Intel®Teach to the Future initiative (http://www.intel.com/education/teach), is collaborating with ministries of education in developing countries. And Intel and UNESCO have co-developed a model syllabus to improve classroom applications of ICT worldwide.

Teachers are also able to share ideas, experiences and resources across schools, regions and national borders through Internet-based Schoolnets such as those in

- India (http://www.schoolnetindia.com);
- Africa (http://www.schoolnetafrica.net);
- Malaysia (myschoolnet.ppk.kpm.my);
- Thailand (http://www.school.net.th); and
- the Asia-Pacific(http://www.unescobkk.org/education/ict/v2/info.asp?id=10966).

ODL/ICT is also being used to provide accredited professional development for health professionals. Two examples of this are IGNOU's distance education postgraduate diploma in maternity and child healthcare and certificate program in surgery for doctors in rural clinics and village primary health centers in India. In the case of the latter, not only have these innovative programs proved that the diagnostic and treatment procedures of rural doctors can be improved through a combination of ODL/ICT and doctors in district hospitals acting as mentors at the local level, but they have overcome the Medical Council of India's longstanding prejudice against ODL and the idea of medical education being provided outside the medical colleges (Panda and Jena, 2001).

23.3 NON-FORMAL EDUCATIONAL DEVELOPMENT

23.3.1 Agricultural Extension

In most low-income nations, farmers comprise the majority of the workforce. Numbering about 2 billion, these smallholders are among the world's poorest people. They lack land tenure and farm with impoverished land and limited resources and technologies. In some sub-Saharan regions, death through HIV/AIDS in farming communities has reduced food production by 40 percent and over the next 20 years it is predicted that over 25 percent of these farmers will die from this pandemic. This is increasingly leaving farming in the hands of women who often lack knowledge and means to farm efficiently. The Food and Agriculture Organization (FAO) emphasizes the massive need for more agricultural extension to help these poor farming communities adopt new practices, increase cropping intensities and diversify into higher value commodities (Swanson et al., 2003). Improving knowledge and skills in the food-market chain on such a scale can be achieved through ODL/ICT-based extension programs that engage with the farmers' concerns and empower the farmers themselves to identify problems, find solutions and disseminate findings to others (Lightfoot, 2001; Latchem et al., 2004).

The Commonwealth of Learning's Poverty Reduction Outcomes through Education Innovations and Networks (COL-PROTEIN) (http://www.col.org/programmes/capacity/protein.htm) program is helping to improve food security, environmental protection and rural development. COL, the State Bank of India, n-logue Private Limited and a consortium of universities are partners in The Lifelong Learning for Farmers project in Tamil Nadu, a project that enables farmers to access to ICT-based education, information and communications through local kiosks. An International Development Research Centre (IDRC) Pan Asia Network (PAN) project in Vietnam enables the Bac Ninh Fisheries College to use ODL/ICT for aquaculture training for around 4,000 farmers, 60 percent of whom are female (Baggaley, 2004). In Bangladesh, an extension program in double cropping employs vernacular language audiotapes to teach peasant farmers how to grow Nile Tilapia in their irrigated spring paddies and thereby almost double their incomes by selling both the rice and the fish (Barman and Little, 2006). In Africa, Asia and Latin America, dryland development extension workers are providing web-based text, sound and images to rural communities lacking telephone access via WorldSpace digital satellite broadcasting technology (http://www.alin.or.ke/activities/initiative.htm; http://www.worldspace.org). Internet-based agricultural extension and information exchange services are also being provided by, for example:

- Rice Knowledge Bank (http://www.knowledgebank.irri.org);
- World Agroforestry Centre (http://www.worldagroforestrycentre.org);
- Virtual Academy of the Semi-Arid Tropics (http://www.vusat.org);

- Access to Global Online Research in Agriculture (http://www.agineretwork.org/en); and
- Virtual Extension and Research Communication Network (http://www.fao.org/sd/SDR/SDRE/Vercon.ING.pdf).

Satellite communications and wireless technology are bringing ubiquitous mobility to agricultural extension. In Thailand, FAO-trained extension workers use hand-held computers to guide farmers in fertilizer usage, planting dates, yield expectations, etc. In Honduras, Fintrac Agribusiness Support uses GPS, portable weather stations, digital cameras, laptops, portable printers and cell phones to enable its extension officers to spend 95 percent of their time in the field, immediately access vital agricultural information and make on-the-spot recommendations to farmers (http://www.fintrac.com/default.htm).

23.3.2 Healthcare and Welfare

In the developed world, infant mortality rates are 15:1,000 live births. In Africa, they are 175:1,000 and in India 100:1,000 (*The Róbinson Rojas Archive*, 2005). In sub-Saharan Africa, people rarely survive beyond the age of 50. Worldwide, 6 million people die annually from HIV/AIDS, malaria and tuberculosis. Women are twice as likely to become infected with HIV/AIDS as men (United Nations, 2005). The hardest hit regions are sub-Saharan Africa and the Caribbean but HIV/AIDS infection rates are increasing throughout all of the low-income nations, devastating communities and damaging their economies.

There is clearly a great potential, as yet far from fully realized, for distance education, media and health organizations to use print, radio, television/video and the Internet to raise awareness of the causes and prevention of HIV/AIDS and to overcome the cultural taboos, stigma, myths and cover-ups associated with this pandemic. Brazil has used such methods to train teachers in HIV/AIDS education in Botswana (http://ww5.aegis.org/news/afrol/2002/AO020101.html), the African Medical and Research Foundation (AMREF) includes material on HIV/AIDS in its continuing education correspondence programs for health workers in Eastern Africa (www.amref.org) and UNESCO Bangkok's Culture Unit and its research and broadcasting partners have developed research-based radio soap operas in local languages for broadcast and audio cassette distribution in Thailand, Lao PDR and China (UNESCO Bangkok, 2005). BBC World, in collaboration with Viacom and the Kaiser Family Foundation, has exploited radio's high penetration in Africa and the Caribbean to broadcast AIDS awareness programs in vernacular languages (http://www.bbc.co.uk/worldservice/trust/pressreleases/story/2003/11/031118_hivaidshealthlaunch.shtml). As Pridmore and Yates (2006) point out, there is a real opportunity to radically rethink ways of delivering HIV/AIDS education and ODL/ICT could play a much greater role in such reforms.

ODL/ICT are also used for in-service training for health workers. In Makati City in the Philippines, an IDRC Pan Asia Network (PAN) project is helping the Molave Development Foundation's Water, Sanitation and Hygiene Education (WASH) program progress from using magazines, comic books and posters to online delivery (Baggaley, 2004).

Health professionals in the Cook Islands, Fiji, Kiribati, Marshals, Federated States of Micronesia, Palau, Samoa, Solomons, Tonga and Vanuatu can bring themselves up to in advances in medicine and healthcare through the WHO Pacific Open Learning Health Net (http://www.polhn.com/index.php?id=1).

ODL/ICT can also be used for telemedicine, online research, consultation, reporting and collaboration between doctors and health personnel in rural areas (Edworthy, 2001). In Mongolia, the Health Science University uses online methodologies and a diagnostic database for distant consultation (Baggaley, 2004). In the Peruvian Amazon, the Biomedical Engineering and Telemedicine Group of the Technical University of Madrid and NGO Engineering Without Frontiers are developing low-cost telecommunications and information services for rural healthcare personnel (Martínez et al., 2004).

23.4 BRIDGING THE DIGITAL DIVIDE

Modern economies depend heavily on the global technology for their functioning and so it is important that all nations and all people should be able to access and use these powerful tools for change and communicate freely. Much is made of the digital divide but World Bank economists Fink and Kenny (2003) observe that the truly remarkable thing about this divide is not its size but how rapidly it is closing. Computers, Internet hosts and servers may be predominately in the developed world but mobile phones and Internet access are actually increasing more rapidly in the low- and middle-income countries and while the per capita access gap may be larger, more users access every computer than in developed countries.

The developing world is also becoming more computer savvy. When drought and famine struck remote northeastern Niger, the Fulani leader and chairman of the local herders' association traveled into the regional center Maradi, searched out potential international donors through his free, web-based email account, approached them and persuaded them to provide 100 tonnes of food aid (CNN, 2005).

The UN's Digital Solidarity Fund (http://www.dsf-fsn.org/) aims for "digital leapfrogging" but the costs of this are daunting. UNDP (1999) estimated that adding one billion telephone lines, subsidizing 600 million households' telephone charges and providing computers and Internet access in schools in the poorer countries would require an annual outlay of US$80–100 billion over 10 years. However, UNDP also noted that this was no more than Europe's annual expenditure on alcohol and only amounted to 11 percent of the world's annual military expenditure. And even in 1996, when Internet use was far less, UNDP estimated that a one cent a day "bit tax" on every hundred 10-kilobyte e-mailed documents per user would yield US$70 billion, a sum far exceeding that year's total aid monies.

There is undoubtedly an *access* issue. Barely 6 percent of the world's people have logged onto the Internet and only 10 percent of these are in the developing countries (ILO, 2001). But lack of access is not the only barrier. There is a *capability* barrier – providers and users need the mindsets, knowledge and skills to exploit the technology. There is a *technical support* barrier – maintenance and repair skills are needed. There is a *cost* barrier – few people can afford the connections charges, few institutions can find the US$78 per student per year estimated to be needed to provide one computer for every twenty students, and few providers can afford the license and staffing costs incurred with proprietary platforms such as WebCT. There is also a *regulatory* barrier – the deregulation and privatization of telecommunications are tending to eliminate the free access previously enjoyed by distance educators and trainers (Perraton and Creed, 2000). Digital inclusion also requires *appropriate applications*. Learners need information, education and training that are relevant to their cultures, needs and understandings. They also need to be enabled to use their own indigenous knowledge and empowered to use their own social means of learning. People in low-income nations are less likely to find web-based content generated in their own countries which means they are paying to access Western culture and polarized into those who have access *and* English language skills and those who lack these (Baggaley, 2004). There can also be a *political barrier*. ICT-based initiatives require political and technical openness. Authoritarian regimes are fearful of access to knowledge and information they cannot monitor or prevent and are battling for control of the Internet, most recently at the 2005 World Summit on the Information Society in Tunisia where some nations demanded more say in its running (Twist, 2005).

The Internet is lowering communications costs, opening up new markets and transforming the ways in which the world informs, educates and works. However, in the kinds of development contexts discussed in this chapter, the answers do not always lie with the latest gizmos. Technologies should never be ignored because they seem old-fashioned.

Radio is the most ubiquitous, inexpensive and cost-effective technology. The average radio costs less than US$10 (compared to over US$800 for a telephone line) and radio can deliver in local languages and to large audiences. In Tajikistan-Uzbekistan, the Silk Road Radio Project uses story-telling and dramas in Uzbec and Tajik to educate communities in family and reproductive health, farming and the need for ethnic harmony (http://www.unescobkk.org/index.php?id=1226). In Bolivia, farmers raise queries with community leaders which they pass on to a local radio station which then directs them to UNDP which in turn posts the answers on the Internet and e-mails them to the radio station for broadcast. Considerable ingenuity is being shown in developing new technologies for low-income nations. In Commonwealth of Learning Media Empowerment initiatives in Africa, Latin America and the Caribbean, broadcasts are made from a radio station that fits into a suitcase, hooks up to commercial FM networks and satellite feeds, has a 50 km radius, runs on car batteries or solar power, and costs about US$3,500 (http://www.col.org/colme/about percent20COLME.htm).

Seeking a solution to providing radio programs on HIV/AIDS for people lacking electricity and unable to buy batteries, inventor Trevor Baylis (1999) adapted the principles of the early wind-up phonograph to create the "Freeplay" radio. A solar battery/clockwork hybrid version of this is now assembled by disabled workers in South Africa and sells at a rate of 120,000 a month.

WorldSpace Foundation (http://www.worldspace.com), an NGO devoted to improving information access for disadvantaged rural communities via satellite-linked radios, is collaborating with the South Asia Foundation, a secular, non-profit/non-political regional youth movement, to serve 500 communities in Bangladesh, Bhutan, India, Maldives, Nepal, Pakistan and Sri Lanka using WSF-provided satellite receivers and multimedia adapters in solar-powered community information centers (http://www.unescobkk.org/index.php?id=1549).

Some rural Indian communities lacking online connection to the Internet can now do this through VSAT (Very Small Aperture Terminal) technology, a communication network set up through a series of receiver/transceiver terminals connected by a central hub through a satellite (San Miguel, 2001). It is also possible to connect to the Internet via bi-directional microwave satellite links and power the network and laptops through solar energy and even pedal generators. As a consequence of the Khmer Rouge regime, some 3,000 Cambodian villages have no schools. American Assistance for Cambodia is soliciting online adopt-a-school donations to reconstruct these schools and provide access to Internet-connected computers powered by solar panels (CambodiaSchools.com).

Low cost alternatives to PCs are promised by India's Simputer (http://www.simputer.org/simputer/), the Massachusetts Institute of Technology (MIT) Media Lab and Canada's Mercurial Innovations International Inc. The Amida Simputer is projected to cost about US$207, making this pocket computer affordable for communities if not individuals in low-income nations. Its simple user interfaces are based on sight, touch and audio, so illiteracy is no longer a barrier, and using a browser for the Information Markup Language (IML) solutions are provided on any platform. The MIT Media Lab US$100 Internet-enabled, wind-up laptop is designed for the non-profit One Laptop per Child (OLPC) project. Its backers include Rupert Murdoch, Google and computer chip maker AMD. Working in partnership with industry, it is aimed to launch 1 million of these laptops in 2007 (AFP, 2005). Mercurial Innovations is already manufacturing a US$180 Read Only Memory-based computer, the Ink-PC. Like the Media Lab computer, this runs on Linux and is fully Internet capable.

Every year many millions of usable and serviceable computers are discarded worldwide. These can be refurbished for use in low-income nations. Obsolescence, incompatibility, inappropriate software, language, fonts and maintenance can be avoided by working through the well-established channels for recycling and shipping computers (see, for example, http://www.schoolnetafrica.net/index.php?id=677; http://www.digitalequalizer.org/practices.htm).

Licence- and royalty-free Internet-provided open source software can also reduce costs and increase access and interoperability. This issue is being explored by, for example, Free and Open Source Software for Africa (http://www.fossfa.net/tiki-index.php) and UNESCO (http://portal.unesco.org/ci/en/ev.php-URL_ID=12034&URL_DO=DO_TOPIC&URL_SECTION=201.html).

There is also rapidly emerging low-cost net telephony. Meanwhile, mobile phones have a great potential in developing countries. The Economist (2005) estimates that by reducing transaction costs, broadening trade networks and reducing jobseekers' travel, every additional ten mobile phones per 100 people increases a developing economy's GDP growth by 0.6 percentage points.

While the number of mobiles per population in the poorer nations is much lower than in developing countries, 77 percent of the world's population is already within range of a network and people in developing countries actually spend more of their income on telephony than people in developed nations. They have been quick to recognize the social and economic benefits of voice calls and text messaging. Handsets can be shared or rented by the call, they don't need permanent power supply and Short Message Systems (SMS) and Wireless Application Protocol (WAP) enabled mobile phones with cameras can be employed in a wide range of development activities. Handset-makers are busily developing cheaper models for this vast market, and billionaire inventor of Priceline.com Jay Walker aims to provide mobile phones to 20 million people earning less than $3 a day to help them improve their lives (Cadwalladar, 2005).

Iqbal Quadir's non-profit GrameenPhone program in Bangladesh has provided 95,000 women in 50,000 Bangladeshi villages previously lacking in telecommunications services with mobile phones. These women are able to earn US$700 a year by on-selling phone services. This model is now being replicated in joint ventures with MTN Uganda and with MTN RwandaCell in Rwanda (http://www.gfusa.org/technology_center/village_phone/).

Educators are also exploring the potential of small, portable devices such as PDAs, palmtops, smartphones, and Tablet PCs in classroom situations or "on the move" (Kukulska-Hulme and Traxler, 2005). One example is Bridgeit, a collaborative program involving Nokia, the International Youth Foundation, Pearson and UNDP that has piloted the delivery of digital educational material into schools in the Philippines using mobile technology (http://www.nokia.com/nokia/0,60303,00.html).

Given the developments in telecommunications and the convergence of technologies, it is questionable whether the best strategy is to build low-cost computers or develop mobile phones that compute, based on Linux or other open-source software.

ICT, education and information can also be provided in rural and other disadvantaged communities through telecenters (Hunt, 2001; International Telecommunications Union, 2001; Latchem and Walker, 2001; PICTA, 2001; APC, n.d.; Etta and Parvyn-Wamahui, 2004; Márquez, 2004). Some question whether telecenters really achieve access and equity and wonder whether the high equipment and annual running costs can be justified where the majority of the people lack literacy and other material benefits. Such arguments hold true if telecenters are merely conceived as providing technology training and delivering digital products from one economy to another. But they work well where they provide opportunities for education, training, information access, telework and local enterprise, where they are in accord with local needs and strongly supported by local communities, and where the managers and staff are well trained for the work offer user-friendly and well-maintained technology and run the centers in accordance with sound business planning and quality control (Whyte, 2000; Hudson, 2001).

Telecenters fulfill a variety of functions. In Lao PDR, they focus on helping rural youth. In Sri Lanka, the Sarvodaya Shramadana Movement telecenters and Mobile Multimedia Units serve as community centers and village banks. In Thailand, the focus is on inter-village connectivity, learning and community development and in Indonesia, on information flow between local communities and government (UNESCO Bangkok, 1999). In Shakhooh in Iran, the telecenter is in a mosque and enables villagers to access education and job-related websites (http://www.shahkooh.com/). In rural Sri Lanka, a wireless telecenter operates in a Bhuddist temple with the Internet receiver tower on its roof re-broadcasting to computers in the village school and library (http://www.sarvodaya.org/). In India, telecenters have proved their worth in both rural and urban settings (see, for example, http://www.sustainableicts.org; http://www1.worldbank.org/publicsector/egov/gyandootcs.htm; http://www.is.cityu.edu.hk/research/ejisdc/vol4/v4r3.pdf).

Telecenter development in low-income nations is being supported by the following:

- the International Development Research Centre (IDRC);
- Microsoft;
- the Swiss Agency for Development and Cooperation (SDC) (http://www.telecentre.org);
- the International Telecommunications Union (ITU);
- Open Knowledge Network (http://www.openknowledge.net/);
- One World South Asia (http://southasia.oneworld.net);
- Hewlett-Packard;
- Open Society/Soros Foundation;
- Ford Foundation; and
- MS Swaminathan Research Foundation (http://www.mssrf.org/special_programmes/ivrp/ivrpmain.htm).

The Indian National Alliance for Mission 2007, a joint initiative involving MSSRF and various public, private and social/community development organizations plans to establish 100,000 rural knowledge centers and information kiosks in every village by the year 2007 and train over a million people to run these centers (http://www.mission2007.org). In India's Education for All project, an educational train (Vigyan Prasar) is being used to bring scientific information, small business training and farming extension programs to remote communities (Padmanabhan, 2004; Baggaley and Ng, 2005). In the Japanese Funds-in-Trust (JICA)/UNESCO E-learning Bus project in Cambodia (http://www2.unescobkk.org/education/ict/v2_2/info.asp?id=17156) and a similar UNDP scheme in Malaysia (http://www.undp.org/dpa/choices/2000/june/p15-17.htm l), ICT services are brought into rural communities by specially equipped buses. And in the COL-PROTEIN/Shidhulai Sanirvar Sangstha Mobile Internet-Educational Unit on Boats project in Bangladesh, boats equipped with solar-powered computers and projectors travel the extensive river network, providing children, women and others in remote villages with free access to education, library resources, small business training and farming extension programs (http://www.undp.org/dpa/choices/2000/june/p15-17.htm).

23.5 WHY SOME PROJECTS FAIL

The preceding sections of this chapter provide ample evidence that the world possesses the knowledge, skills and means to support low-income nation development through ODL/ICT. However, success can never be guaranteed. The political will and organizational vision and commitment may be lacking. There may be a lack of awareness of the needs and possibilities. Research, reports and recommendations may be ignored. Enthusiasts attempting change may be impeded by governmental bureaucracies, organizational politics and individuals' intransigence. Developments may founder once donor funding ceases. Political priorities may change. Providers' knowledge and skills in developing and delivering courses and support services may be inadequate.

Sheldon Schaeffer (2004), Director of UNESCO Bangkok, suggests that there have been numerous examples of countries wasting scarce resources on hardware, training and production without achieving their targets. Former President of the Commonwealth of Learning, Gajaraj Dhanarajan (2002) claims that providers may fail because they lack the necessary funds, time, staff development, technical support, technology, infrastructure or learner support systems.

So there are important leadership and management issues to consider if the world is to succeed in achieving the kinds of initiatives and interventions described above. These are discussed in the following section.

23.5.1 Leading and Managing ODL/ICT Development Projects

There is no single simple formula for success in applying ODL/ICT in development. However, it is possible to identify some key issues in leadership and management. These are discussed below. The anonymous scenarios accompanying the outlining of these issues derive from the authors' experiences and reports on ODL/ICT projects. Readers may wish to consider the following questions: What more could the applicants have done before these projects? What more could the providers have done before and during these projects? What more could the consultants have done before and during these projects?

SCENARIO 23.1: INCORRECT DIAGNOSIS OF NEEDS AND CIRCUMSTANCES

A Ministry of Education in a low-income nation was concerned about the high drop out/failure rates in its distance teaching universities. It successfully applied for international donor funding for consultants to develop remedial programs to help the students in their studies. Discovering that there had been no research into the possible causes of these drop out/failure rates, the consultants reported to the Ministry that they might be due to the students' shortcomings, the quality of the courses and/or courseware, slow or inadequate feedback on assignments, a lack of face-to-face or online support, conflicting family or work commitments or the costs of study. They requested a change of mandate to conduct research into these possible causes but the Ministry insisted that the funding was tied to the development of the remedial programs and that this should continue as planned. Left with no alternative, the consultants developed these programs but when they were applied, they were shown to have little effect on the success and completion rates. Three years later, a second consultant reviewing the universities' performance came across the earlier consultants' report and recommended the implementation of their earlier research proposal. However, the Ministry refused to fund this, fearing that it would expose the failure of the previous project.

SCENARIO 23.2: INADEQUATE NEEDS ANALYSIS

A traditional university decided that it needed to move into e-learning. It successfully applied for funding from an international donor for a consultant to train its staff and involve these staff in developing some pilot e-learning programs. On arriving at the college, the consultant found that there had been no prior needs analysis, environmental scanning or consultation with the stakeholders to justify such a development, that the university's managers and staff had no experience or understanding of what was entailed in distance education, let alone e-learning, that the syllabuses, teaching, staff commitment and morale were poor, and that the university's senior managers had provided no time release for the staff participating in the training and pilot programs. The consultant advised the college to "walk before it could run", suggesting that before it moved into e-learning, it should first train its staff in course and instructional design and learner support and utilize more traditional forms of distance education. After the consultant departed, totally disregarding this advice, the college signed up with an overseas commercial provider offering online advice and support for Internet-based delivery – without even questioning the cost per enrollee or who was going to develop the necessary materials and support services.

Project planning needs to be based on careful situational analysis conducted in collaboration with all of the stakeholders, including the learners, and in accordance with local needs and circumstances. The nature, scale and outcomes of the projects need to be commensurate with the available resources and human capacities, and the educational development and ICT aspects need to be part of the same research and development agenda. There also need to be clearly enunciated policies and procedures regarding educational outcomes, resourcing and quality assurance of projects. Dhanarajan (2002) attributes the fast growing contribution of ODL in India and South Africa to the far-sighted policies and unequivocal commitment of the authorities in these countries.

Tools to help policy-makers and planners integrate ODL/ICT into educational and training systems may be found in, for example, the UNESCO Bangkok ICT in Education Policies (http://www.uneswcobkk.org/education/ict/policy) and Commonwealth of Learning's policy-making for literacy skills acquisition and livelihoods development (http://www.col.org/literacyandlivelihoods).

SCENARIO 23.3: LACK OF INFORMED CHAMPIONS

A government's aim of applying e-learning to the Education for All agenda was impeded by a lack of informed champions in high places and an absence of enlightened government policies to support the kinds of system-wide changes needed. The politicians and bureaucrats declared a preference for funding and showcasing a few short-term high-profile distance education and government information programs rather than encouraging and resourcing those teachers and trainers who were already struggling to apply ODL/ICT in helping disadvantaged and marginalized adults and children. The high-profile government-funded educational and information programs had little impact and the absence of positive outcomes came to the attention of the national media which condemned the government's funding as wasteful and branded the innovative approaches in ODL/ICT as inappropriate to community needs. The government then reduced funding for ODL/ICT projects and avoided taking any new initiatives to advance the Education for All agenda.

SCENARIO 23.4: LACK OF FOLLOW-THROUGH TO THE STRATEGIC PLANNING

The principal of a technical and vocational college developed a strategic plan for her institution, stressing the need to improve the quality of the distance learning and move into blended learning. There was a disconnect between the plan's rhetoric and the subsequent actions taken by the principal and between her views and those of the other members of the senior management team and the staff. There was also no follow-through to her plan. As a consequence, there was widespread confusion and misunderstanding amongst the managers and staff. The principal charged the departmental heads with seeing through the changes but a yawning credibility gulf developed between these managers and the teaching and support staff. The college succeeded in gaining donor funding for a consultancy in support of the strategic plan but the consultant's report and recommendations gained no support because of disagreements over the institutional priorities, the managers' unwillingness and/or inability to make the necessary changes in organizational structures, roles, policies, procedures and practices, and suspicion, intransigence and low morale amongst the majority of the staff. As a consequence, the strategic plan was consigned to the shelves and things proceeded as before.

High-level champions can be invaluable. However, it is not enough that they "talk the talk". They also need to "walk the talk" of their policies and plans, ensuring that their and others' actions accord with these and empowering those responsible for implementation. To be sustainable, projects also need strong internal support, to be energized by bottom-up as well as top-down initiatives. And all of the stakeholders must be fully conversant with and committed to collaborating in the projects.

SCENARIO 23.5: LACK OF EVALUATION AND ACCOUNTABILITY

A number of low-income nations and an international donor collaborated in a number of projects aimed at providing ICT-based non-formal adult and community education. After 3 years, a team of evaluators visited the countries involved with the aim of conducting a meta-survey to monitor progress and guide future planning, funding and activities. They found that there were wide gaps between the ideals and the realities of these projects. While the donors had set explicit objectives for the projects, no key performance indicators (KPIs) had been set by the donors or the host countries by which to judge the processes and outcomes, and only a few, poorly conducted qualitative and quantitative evaluations had been carried out into what had occurred and been achieved. The local coordinators were vague about how funds had been expended and were unable or unwilling to state the true costs or resource requirements of the projects and whether or not the projects would be sustainable in the longer term. In some cases, it was suspected that there were misuses of funding. The evaluators therefore found it impossible to provide robust findings that would persuade the international donor or the governments concerned to commit further resources to these initiatives.

Evaluation, accountability and transparency in reporting what works and what doesn't and why are critically important. Without admitting to failure, it is impossible to reliably inform future planning and action. Failure in projects should be a stepping stone to success, not a stumbling block. Rerup (2003) and Denrell (2003) point to the dangers of focusing on success alone, warning that a failure to investigate, analyze and report on the causes of failure leads to self-delusion about the effectiveness of policies, plans, actions and outcomes. Researching failure requires imagination, diligence, courage and a willingness to ask awkward questions. These may be difficult to achieve in some cultures but they are essential in order to avoid repeating errors.

Project planning should be based on a results-based management and accountability framework that clearly articulates the roles and responsibilities of those responsible for the policy-making, implementation and evaluation, the key performance indicators (KPIs) regarding the inputs, activities, outputs and outcomes (see for example, http://www.unescobkk.org/index.php?id=894), and how the work is to be evaluated and reported on and by whom (see for example, http://www.tbs-sct.gc.ca/eval/pubs/RMAF-CGRR/rmafcgrr_e.asp).

Budgets are invariably constrained, so realistic and detailed costing is also essential. There should be transparency in who provides what funding for what purposes, especially where partnerships are involved. Budgets should focus on the core project elements with as much of the funding as possible granted to those working in the field and the end users. Project managers must be held accountable for expenditures. Progressively releasing funds as each stage of a project is completed and reported on ensures accountability and means that where necessary, funds can be redirected to where they may be more usefully employed.

Projects dependent on short-term external funding that excludes recurrent costs are likely to be non-sustainable in the longer term. So business plans are needed to cost the ongoing infrastructure, technology, staffing and operations and identify how these costs are to be paid for.

Project timelines need to allow for plans to be disseminated, understood and acted upon by bureaucracies, funds to be released, staff to be recruited and trained, infrastructure, technology and support to be put in place and other nettlesome issues to be resolved.

It may be useful to conceive ODL/ICT projects as "applied research" rather than "development" projects. All bids for support could then be required to specify how the work is to be researched, evaluated and disseminated and this aspect of the work could also be budgeted for.

Developing countries are usually weak in research capacity but managers and practitioners can now be trained online through the Commonwealth of Learning's Practitioner Research and Evaluation Skills Training Programme (PREST) (http://www.col.org/resources/startupguides/prest.htm).

Meta-analyses of ODL/ICT projects (Farrell and Wachholtz, 2004) are important in providing reform-minded governments, donors, and providers with hard evidence of system-wide gains in access, economy, efficiency, effectiveness and impact. They can show where particular policies, systems, methods and technologies work or fail and what is needed to ensure success.

SCENARIO 23.6: INADEQUATE COSTING, POOR PROVISION AND LACK OF COLLABORATION WITH OTHER PROVIDERS

An international agricultural research-extension agency aimed to become an online provider of information and training to improve farming methods in low-income nations. After 2 years of operation, it conducted a survey which revealed that relatively few farmers had actually accessed and used the agency's services. Large-scale farmers regarded the agency as too remote and unfamiliar with local conditions and the smallholders could not easily access the programs and lacked competence in using the technology. It was also found that the farmers did not understand the learner-centered, problem-based training methods and were incapable of self-managed, independent study. Trainers were needed in the field to help the farmers with their learning, adapt the new knowledge to local needs and apply the new practices – which meant that costs were much higher than estimated. It was also found that the services had not been sufficiently promoted, that more attention should have been given to the instructional design and training team members and that more frequent and meaningful interaction was needed between the farmers and online trainers – none of which had been adequately budgeted for, so the cost benefit was far less than envisaged.

It was further found that several other organizations, some international, some national, some private and some NGOs, were providing similar programs and services and that there were overlaps and gaps in provision. The experience, capacities and resources of these providers varied and some had withdrawn due to donor fatigue and perceived lack of progress. There was clearly an opportunity for formal organizational linkages, informal networks and joint planning and implementation. But then it was asked, who would co-ordinate such partnerships, how would the political, technical, organizational and funding issues be resolved, and how could such a system be made to achieve a maximum impact in the farming communities?

Projects supported by various organizations may run in parallel and even ignorance of each other. Some may address problems that others have already answered and some may spend money and time developing programs, materials and services that already exist elsewhere. Given the scale and extent of the needs, there is need for maximum synergy between international and national agencies, NGOs, the private sector, regulatory bodies, educational/training organizations and community groups interested in applying ODL/ICT to development. An initiative by the International Development Research Network addresses this problem by funding and coordinating parallel ODL projects in nine Asian countries that complement rather than replicate each other, monitoring their progress and analyzing the outcomes and providing practical advice for similar educational and training systems derived from evidence-based research (Baggaley and Ng, 2005). In adopting such an approach, considerable attention needs to be paid to ensuring that the projects' aims, methods and outcomes and partners' roles, responsibilities and resource and expertise inputs are clearly understood by all of the participants and that government, donors and other stakeholders fully appreciate who is in charge and what will help or hinder implementation and outcomes in the local contexts.

In providing e-learning, it is not enough to provide access to the content and assume that users will click onto sites and learn automatically. Much web-based material is presented from the providers' perspectives, not the users', is informational rather than educational, is in English, and is Western-oriented. The instructional design needs to be appropriate to the culture, gender, language and circumstances of the users and should enable situation-based learning to occur through dialogue and collaborative problem-solving. It is also important to ensure that the websites are easy to locate and use, accurate and up to date.

Courses and materials can be shared through knowledge repositories such as

- the Commonwealth of Learning Knowledge Resources (http://www.col.org/resources/) and Knowledge Finder (http://www.colfinder.org/);
- International Foundation for Research in Open Learning (http://www.col.org/irfol/);
- UNDP Info21 (http://www.undp.org/info21/index5.htm);
- Global Development Learning Network (http://www.gdln.org/); and
- World Bank Global Distance EducationNet (http://www1.worldbank.org/disted/).

Searches can be made, inventories created and generic ODL/ICT materials of proven quality adopted and/or translated into local languages, forms and contexts.

Portals and learning objects have a great potential but need to entail far more than converting print material or lecture notes into hypertext. This only replicates the worst features of traditional teaching and training and represents a "transmission" model that denies "construction of meaning" and "testing against other experiences and judgments" (Postle, 2002; Rushby, 2005). In sharing courseware, copyright and intellectual property also need to be taken into account (Swales, 2003).

SCENARIO 23.7: SHORTCOMINGS IN INTRODUCING NEW TECHNOLOGY

A team of international computer experts was invited by the senior managers of a distance teaching consortium to develop a cutting-edge learning management system through which learners could access study material, share information with their tutors and peers, and submit assignments. The consultants found that the teaching staff and instructional designers in the partner institutions were overworked and firmly wedded to the print/correspondence modes. Moreover, they found no provision for sustaining the system after the consultancy concluded. The consultants reported to senior management that the introduction of the system was premature but were instructed to proceed with developing a prototype. After the consultants had completed their work and departed, there was no further development work and no one used the system. A subsequent consultancy team stressed the need to add new online methods to the consortium's distance education offerings and demonstrated how this could be achieved using the learning management system. But their recommendations were undermined by the teaching staff in the institutions who were reluctant to adopt the new online learning approaches and so the learning management system and systemic introduction of e-learning proceeded no further.

It is important to integrate ODL and ICT development and to ensure that the providers possess or can develop the necessary knowledge and skills in teaching, training and learning methods as well as using the technology.

Projects that are wholly reliant on leading edge technology may be at risk or inappropriate. It is important to select the most suitable technology – which may not always be the latest – or the best mix of technologies. In some contexts, computers and the Internet may only play an adjunct role. Connectivity, electricity supply, usage, maintenance and repair costs incurred by providers need to be taken into account and the users' capacity to pay for the hardware, software, consumables and connectivity. Users should never be expected to pay beyond their means or contribute a greater proportion of the costs than those in more privileged settings.

SCENARIO 23.8: SHORTCOMINGS IN STAFF DEVELOPMENT

An international agency expended considerable funding on staff development in low-income nation educational and training institutions. An evaluation of these locally provided programs found that while they were appreciated, there were a number of failings.

Providing programs in response to organizational requests resulted in piecemeal rather than consistent or comprehensive provision. Where staff development programs were provided in the institutions where the participants worked, there were often interruptions with staff being called away to perform other duties. Whether due to nepotism or a lack of understanding, it was shown that some of the participants lacked the necessary experience or qualifications, that some showed little real interest in the sessions and that some failed to attend, arguing that they were too busy.

Some of the local trainers' reports provided useful insights into the workshops, participants and institutions. But most of them simply summarized what took place. Few of the trainers used formative evaluation to shape the training events and none had evaluated the longer term outcomes or impact of the programs. A lack of follow-through and support often prevented participants from implementing the ideas and methods considered in the programs. And the participants complained of a lack of awareness and commitment among their line managers and recommended that there should be more training for these personnel.

While considerable sums may be expended on ODL/ICT projects, it is often the case that staff development is underfunded and one of the first areas to be cut when funding is in short supply. It is essential that there should be adequate budget provision for training, mentoring and supporting all of the managers, administrators, teachers, trainers and technicians involved in ODL/ICT projects. This is particularly important in low-income nations where staff need to become developers and collaborators rather than for over dependent on knowledge and skills in the developed world.

Older teachers and training are often entrenched in their attitudes and younger staff may be more familiar with the latest developments in ICT rather than pedagogy. Both sets need help in learning how to develop and deliver high-quality teaching, learning and support services at a distance. Such capacity building cannot be achieved by means of short workshops alone. Trainees need to be collaboratively and continually involved in defining problems, learning through their actions and reflecting upon processes and outcomes. Trainees are often more willing to learn from their peers than external advisers and so a "training the trainers" approach can be extremely useful, selecting and skilling personnel who already have some of the aptitude for this work and giving them the tools and resources to train and support their colleagues in the local contexts.

Online resources such as the Commonwealth of Learning Start-up Guides and Training Resources (http://www.col.org/resources/startupguides/) can help to share, provide professional development at the time, place or pace of the trainees' choice.

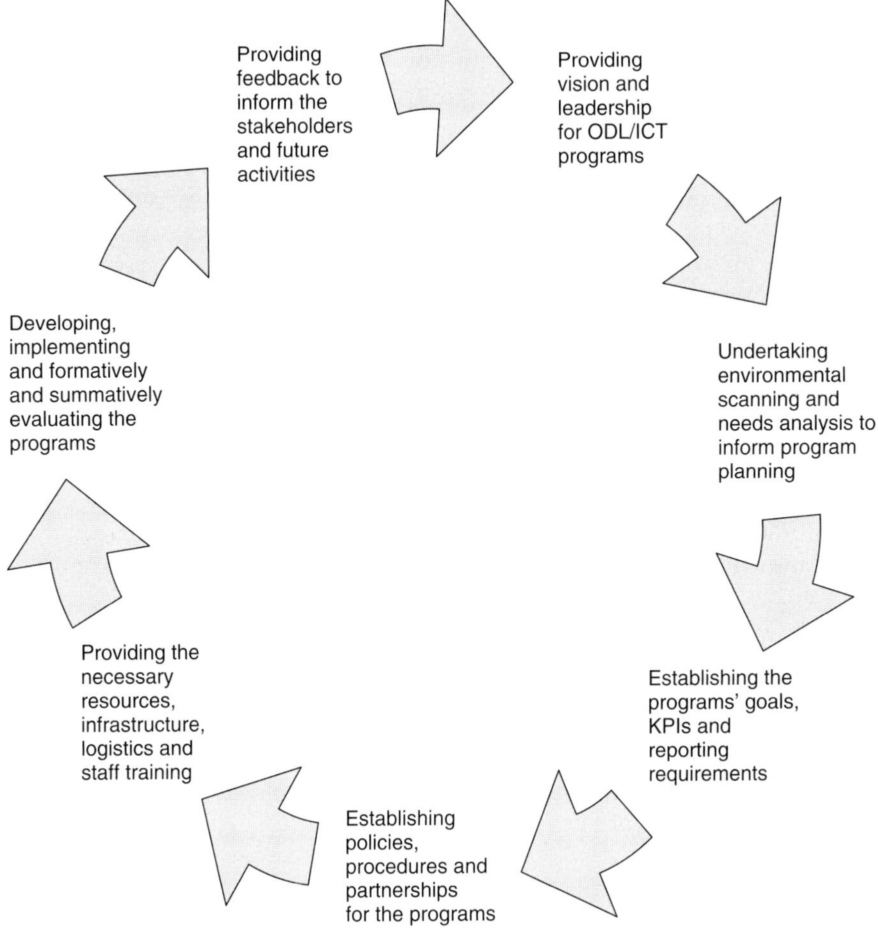

Figure 23.1: The Development Process

Wherever possible, meetings, training and communications should be provided via ICT. This will both economize and demonstrate the potential of the technology.

Staff development will not result in change where there is low energy, distrust and inadequate time release, where resources are limited resources and where there is no a recognition and reward. So these issues must be addressed in parallel.

In summary, as Figure 23.1 shows, ODL/ICT projects for development in low-income nations require careful analysis of the needs, contexts, circumstances and intended outcomes, and their quality and accountability to the stakeholders needs to be assured by formative and summative evaluation in accordance with key performance indicators and failure needs to be acknowledged and enquired into wherever this occurs.

23.6 CONCLUSION

Significant applications of ODL/ICT to the realization of the UN's Millennium Development Goals are increasing access to formal and non-formal education, bridging the digital divide and helping to overcome ignorance, poverty and discrimination in low-income nations. The Commonwealth Heads of Government Meeting (CHOGM), UNESCO, the Commonwealth of Learning and other international bodies have pledged to strengthen their networks of co-operation and use ODL/ICT to support and assist such initiatives. While others address the ideological, political, military and economic causes of poverty, hunger, disease, conflict and destruction, this chapter has shown that there is a rich seam of opportunity to be mined by ODL/ICT providers who are willing to turn their vision, leadership, professionalism, inventiveness and stamina to educational development in the developing world.

REFERENCES

AFP. (2005). Free wind-up laptops for the world's poor. *The Australian*, Friday, November 18, 9.

APC. (n.d.) *Telecentres – Training Materials*, The Association for Progressive Communications. Retrieved February 12, 2006 from http://www.apc.org/english/capacity/training/telecentres.shtml.

Baggaley, J. (2004). *Distance Learning Technologies: Deploying Canadian and Southern Technology Engines to Build an Asian Research Network*. Consultant's Report, IDRC-CDRI. Retrieved February 12, 2006 from http://www.idrc.ca/uploads/user-S/11280236271JPB-PAN_Asia_edit.pdf.

Baggaley, J.P. and Ng, M. (2005). PANdora's Box: Distance learning technologies in Asia. *Learning Media & Technology*, **30**(1), 7–16.

Barman, B.K. and Little, D.C. (2006). Nile tilapia (Oreochromis niloticus) seed production in irrigated spring rice-fields in Northwest Bangladesh – an approach appropriate for poor farmer? *Aquaculture*, **261**(1), 72–79.

Baylis, T. (1999). *Clock This: My Life as an Inventor*. London: Headline Book Publishing.

Cadwalladar, C. (2005). What's the big idea? *The Observer Review*. Sunday, July 24. Retrieved March 15, 2006 from http://observer.guardian.co.uk/review/story,0,6903,1534821,00.html.

Chan, A. (2005). Hunted, hungry victims in Darfur: UNICEF team member reports. *The Japan Times*, May 10, 13.

CNN (2005). Niger's nomads e-mail appeals for aid. CNN, July 29. Retrieved February 12, 2006 from http://www.cnn.com/2005/WORLD/ africa/07/28/niger.nomads.email.ap/.

Daniel, J.S. (1996). *Mega-Universities and Knowledge Media: Technology Strategies for Higher Education*. London: Kogan Page.

Denrell, J. (2003). Vicarious learning, undersampling of failure, and the myths of management. *Organizational Science*, **14**(3), 227–243.

Dhanarajan, G. (2002). *Open and Distance Learning in Developing Economies*. Paper presented at the UNESCO Conference of Ministers of Education of African Member States (MINEDAF VIII), Dar es Salaam, Tanzania, 6 December.

Economist. (2005). Technology and development: The real digital divide. *The Economist*, March 10. Retrieved March 15, 2006 from http://www.economist.com/printedition/displaystory.cfm?Story_ID=3742817.

Edworthy, S.M. (2001). Editorial: Telemedicine in developing countries may have more impact than in developed countries, *BMJ*, **323**, 524–525 (8 September). Retrieved February 12, 2006 from http://bmj.bmjjournals.com/cgi/content/full/323/7312/524.

Estrada, R.Q. (2003). (transl. Brown, T.) Telesecundaria: Students and the meaning they attribute to the elements of the pedagogical model. *Mexican Journal of Educational Research*, 8(17), January–April, 221–243. Retrieved March 15, 2006 from http://www.comie.org.mx/revista/PdfsEnglish/Carpeta17/17invest3Engl.pdf.

Etta, F.B. and Parvyn-Wamahiu, S. (eds) (2004). The experience with community telecentres. *Volume 2: Information and Communication Technologies for Development in Africa*. Retrieved March 15, 2006 fromwebdrc.ca/uploads/user-S/105552662601._PAN_AFRICAN_STUDIES_VOL_2-_TELECENTRES_Prelim_Pages.doc

Farrell, G. and Wachholtz, C. (2004). *Metasurvey on the Use of Technologies in Asia and the Pacific* (2nd ed.). Bangkok: UNESCO Asia & Pacific Regional Bureau for Education.

Fink, C. and Kenny, C.J. (2003). W(h)ither the digital divide? *Info: The Journal of Policy, Regulation and Strategy for Telecommunications*, 5(6). Retrieved March 15, 2006 from http://www.developmentgateway.org/download/181562/w_h_ither_DD_Jan_.pdf.

Green, L. (2004). Gender-based issues and trends in ICT applications in education in Asia and the Pacific. In *Metasurvey on the Use of Technologies in Asia and the Pacific* (G. Farrell and C. Wachholtz, C., eds) (2nd ed.) Bangkok: UNESCO Asia & Pacific Regional Bureau for Education, pp. 30–39. Retrieved March 15, 2006 from http://www.unescobkk.org/fileadmin/user_upload/ict/Metasurvey/2Regional29.pdf.

Hudson, H. (2001). Telecentre evaluation: Issues and strategies. In *Telecentres: Case Studies and Key Issues – Management |Operations|Applications|Evaluation* (C. Latchem and D. Walker, eds) Vancouver: Commonwealth of Learning. Retrieved February 12, 2006 from http://www.col.org/telecentres.

Hunt, P. (2001). True stories: Telecentres in Latin America and the Caribbean. *EJISDC*, 4(5), 1–17. Retrieved March 15, 2006 from http://www.is.cityu.edu.hk/research/ejisdc/vol4/v4r5.pdf.

ILO (2001). *World Employment Report for 2001*. International Labour Organization. Retrieved March 15, 2006 from http://www.ilo.org/public/english/support/publ/wer/overview.htm.

International Telecommunications Union (2001). *Papers on Multipurpose Community Telecentres*. Retrieved March 15, 2006 from http://www.itu.int/ITU-D/univ_access/telecentres/.

Kenny C. (2001). Information and communications technologies and poverty. *TechKnowLogia*, July/August, @Knowledge Enterprise, Inc. Retrieved March 15, 2006 from http://www.digitaldividend.org/pdf/kenny.pdf.

Kobayashi, T., Ueno, M., Hirasawa, T., and Kuroda, K. (2005). *Report on the Evaluation Mission on the Japanese Funds-in Trust (JFIT) for the Promotion of the Effective Use of ICT in Education*. Bangkok: UNESCO Asia & Pacific Regional Bureau for Education, mimeograph.

Kukulska-Hulme, A. andTraxler, J. (eds) (2005). *Mobile Learning: A Handbook for Educators and Trainers*. London: RoutledgeFalmer, Taylor & Francis Group.

Latchem, C. and Walker, D. (eds) (2001). *Telecentres: Case Studies and Key Issues – Management |Operations|Applications|Evaluation*, Vancouver: Commonwealth of Learning. Retrieved March 15, 2006 from http://www.col.org/telecentres.

Latchem, C. Maru, A., and Alluri, K. (2004). *Lifelong Learning for Farmers (L3Farmers)*. Vancouver: The Commonwealth of Learning. Retrieved February 6, 2006 from http://www.col.org/Consultancies/04L3Farmers.htm.

Lightfoot, C. (2001). *Transforming Conventional Extension to Farmer Driven Extension: Actions and Operational Guidelines for Extension Reform Managers*. Retrieved March 15, 2006 from http://www.isglink.org/LIGHTFOOT_PRACTICAL_GUIDE.pdf; http://www.eldis.org/static/DOC12963.htm.

Lopez-Claros, A. and Zahidi, S. (2005). *Women's Empowerment: Measuring the Global Gap*. Geneva: World Economic Forum. Retrieved February 13, 2006 from http://www.weforum.org/gendergap.

Martínez, A., Villarroel, V., Seoane, J., and Del Pozo, F. (2004). Rural telemedicine for primary healthcare in developing countries. *IEEE Technology and Society Magazine*, Summer 2004, 13–22. Retrieved March 15, 2006 from http://www.ece.osu.edu/~passino/Telemedicine.pdf.

Márquez, H. (2004). *Communications-LATAM: Telecentres to Narrow Digital Divide, IPS-Inter Press Service*. Retrieved March 15, 2006 from http://www.ipsnews.net/interna.asp?idnews=20182.

Padmanabhan, B.S. (2004). Science for social progress. *Frontline*, **21**(9), April 24–May 7. Retrieved March 15, 2006 from http://www.frontlineonnet.com/fl2109/stories/20040507003409900.htm.

Panda, S. and Jena, T. (2001). Changing the pattern: Towards flexible learning, learner support and mentoring. In *Innovation in open and distance learning* (F. Lockwood and A. Gooley eds) London: Kogan Page, pp. 172–178.

Perraton, H. and Creed, C. (2000). Applying new technologies and cost-effective delivery systems in basic education. *INFOSHARE: Sources and Resources Bulletin*, **2**(1), Bangkok: UNESCO Asia & Pacific Regional Bureau for Education, 30–33.

PICTA (2001). *PICTA Work Programs: Telecentres*. Partnership for Information and Communication Technologies in Africa. Retrieved March 15, 2006 from http://www.bellanet.org/partners/picta/tele.html.

Postle, G. (2002). *Emergence of Fourth Generation Technologies*. Australia: IDP Education Australia. Retrieved May 18, 2006 from http://www.usq.edu.au/electpub/e-jist/docs/html2002/pdf/g_pos.pdf.

Pridmore, P. and Yates, C. (2006). From a distance: HIV interventions for out-of-school youth, *id21 Health: Communicating Development Research*. Retrieved March 15, 2006 from www.id21.org/zinter/id21zinter.exe?a=l&w=b5.

Rerup, C. (2003). In the grey zone. *Impact: Management Research in Action*, **11**(1), The Ivey Business School, The University of Western Ontario, Retrieved March 15, 2006 from http://www.ivey.uwo.ca/publications/impact/Vol11No1-Rerup.htm.

Robinson, B. and Latchem, C. (2003). Open and distance teacher education: Uses and models. In *Teacher Education through Open and Distance Learning: World Review for Distance Education and Open Learning* (B. Robinson and C. Latchem eds) London and New York: Commonwealth of Learning/RoutledgeFalmer, pp. 28–47.

Rushby, N. (2005). Editorial. *British Journal of Educational Technology*, **36**(3), 359–360.

San Miguel, S. (2001). *Connecting Rural India to the Internet: The Challenges of using VSAT Technology*. Sustainable Development Communications Network. Retrieved March 15, 2006 from http://www.sdcn.org/webworks/cases/vsat_da1.htm.

Schaeffer, S. (2004). Are we getting any closer to bringing quality education for all people in Asia and the Pacific? In (UNESCO) *Harnessing Technologies Towards Quality*

Education for all in Asia and the Pacific. Bangkok, UNESCO Principal Regional Office for Asia and the Pacific, 01.

Swales, C. (2003). *Establishing Copyright Procedure in Distance Education*. Vancouver: Commonwealth of Learning. Retrieved March 15, 2006 from http://www.col.org/knowledge/pdf/ks_library.pdf.pdf.

Swanson, B., Bentz, R., and Sofranko, A. (eds) (2003). *The Special Programme for Food Security: Responding to New Challenges*. Rome: Food and Agricultural Organization (FAO).

The Róbinson Rojas Archive (2005). Retrieved February 6, 2006 from http://www.rrojasdatbank.org/pvfaces.htm.

Twist, J. (2005). Essential test for UN net summit. *BBC News*, Saturday, 19 November. Retrieved March 15, 2006 from http://news.bbc.co.uk/1/hi/technology/4451950.stm.

United Nations (2005). *Progress made in the Implementation of the Declaration of Commitment in HIV/AIDS: Report of the Secretary-General*, 4 April. Retrieved March 15, 2006 from http://www.unaids.org/.../un + special + session + on + hiv_aids/ 2005 + general + assembly + high + level + meeting + on + hiv_aids.asp.

UNDP (1999). *Human Development Report*. Retrieved June 6, 2005 from http://hdr.undp.org/reports/global/1999/en/.

UNESCO (2000). *UNESCO Education for All – EFA 2000 Assessment*. Retrieved June 6, 2005 from http://www.unesco.org/education/efa/efa_2000_assess/index.shtml.

UNESCO Bangkok (1999). *Evaluation of the Asia Pacific Information Network in Social Sciences (APINESS) 1986–99*. Bangkok: UNESCO Principal Regional Office for Asia and the Pacific.

UNESCO Bangkok (2005). *Trafficking and HIV/AIDS Project*. Retrieved June 6, 2005 from www.unescobkk.org/index.php?id =475.

UNICEF (n.d.). *Literacy as Freedom: United Nations Literacy Decade 2003–2012*. Retrieved June 6, 2005 from http://portal.unesco.org/education/en/ev.php-URL_ID=12920&URL_DO=DO_TOPIC&URL_SECTION=201.html.

Whyte, A. (2000). *Assessing Community Telecentres: Guidelines for Researchers*. Ottawa: IDRC. Retrieved March 15, 2006 from web.idrc.ca/en/ev-10572-201-1-DO_TOPIC.html.

World Bank (2005). *PovertyNet*. Retrieved June 6, 2005 from http://web.worldbank.org/WBSITE/EXTERNAL/TOPICS/EXTPOVERTY/0,,menuPK:336998~pagePK:149018~piPK:149093~theSitePK:336992,00.html.

Chapter 24

Strategic Planning and Distance Education

Santosh Panda

24.1 INTRODUCTION

As is widely reported and argued, educational institutions are inherently different from business organisations. Traditionally, they have preserved their academic identity through graduate teaching, disciplinary research, and collegial decision-making. For some time, educational institutions have been facing pressures to reform. These pressures are mainly from, but are not confined to, two quarters:

1. As a consequence of policies to widen access and promote lifelong learning, flexible and blended modes of learning are coming to occupy a sizeable chunk of educational space. This is also transforming policy and management.
2. Technological developments coupled with globalisation and continuing professional development needs (of especially the niche markets) necessitate adoption of new educational technologies. These developments demand new strategies of planning and management.

Haughey (2003) submits that the recent developments affecting postsecondary institutions require "a redefinition of academic work life" (p. 56), which includes re-engineering, restructuring, and transforming (though she underlines the need for holistic planning, to which we shall return towards the end of this chapter). Distance/open/flexible/online/blended learning are part of this redefinition and have been at the forefront of this transformation. In the first instance, though, such new teaching-learning systems require the dynamics of strategic planning.

24.2 STRATEGIC PLANNING

The definition of "planning" is somewhat difficult, in terms of confining its description to one framework. The interpretation of planning includes

- future thinking, to plan action in advance;
- controlling the future, to act on the plan; and
- decision-making, to determine in advance actions, resources, alternatives and the best alternative.

(Mintzberg, 1994b, pp. 7–8)

Mintzberg further emphasises that " 'Planning' may be so elusive because its proponents have been more concerned with promoting vague ideals than achieving viable positions, more concerned with what planning might be than what it actually became . . ." (pp. 6–7).

The concept of "strategy", associated with scientific planning, originated from military applications, where operations involved coherent actions designed by the strategist and not known to the enemy (Whipp, 1998). The arrival of "strategic planning" for business dates back to the 1960s, when corporate houses adopted strategies to further empower their competitiveness (Mintzberg, 1994a). At this time, higher education institutions globally started experiencing dwindling public subsidy and increasing institutional costs, and therefore planning a long the lines of strategic planning within the business community became important, to expand the student base, contain unit cost, and enhance the institutional competitive niche. Strategic planning "as a structured management discipline and practice" (Dorris et al., 2002, p. 6) was considered a rational tool for systematic institutional advancement by institutional leaders. The academies started to be viewed as academic enterprises. The seminal work of Keller (1983) on academic strategy had the most significant influence on higher education institutions to move towards mission and vision, environmental scanning, situational analysis, goal setting, strategy formulation, strategy implementation, feedback loop, and other features of strategic planning.

The meaning of strategy is very clear: "the pattern or plan that integrates an organisation's major goals, policies and action sequences into a cohesive whole" (Quinn, 1980, p. 7). This cohesive whole puts the organisation in a competitive advantage against its competitors or similar providers.

Strategic planning is a systematic, disciplined, and data-based decision-making process in which internal and external contexts are analysed, based on which resource commitment is exercised to conform to pre-stipulated mission and vision, so that the organisation's strengths and opportunities are optimised, and it surpasses its weaknesses and threats. If the mission is what one is and what one stands for, the vision refers to what one wants to achieve in the coming years, and strategic planning underlines how to achieve it (Kilfoil, 2003, p. 14). Strategic planning may be cyclic, take place only for the initiatives of transformation and innovation, be used to solve specific problems, and augment the particular area of institutional strengths and take advantage of its opportunities. Such planning has many benefits, all of which may not necessarily be achievable:

- promotion of strategic thinking and action;
- enhancement of institutional preparedness and responsiveness;
- improvement of decision making;
- enhancement of institutional performance; and
- facilitation of working together with clear roles to achieve organisational goals.

(Bryson, 1995, p. 7)

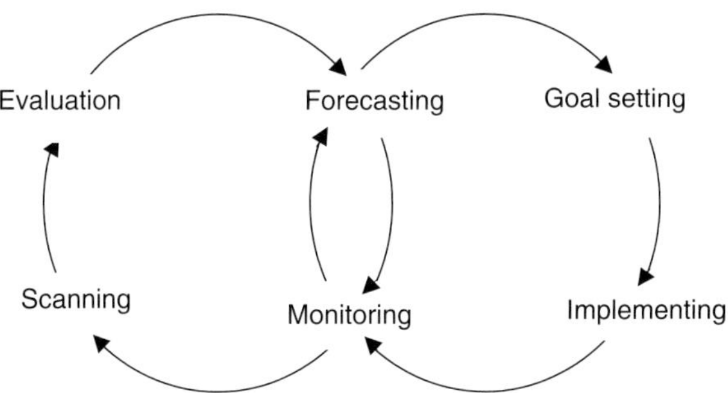

Figure 24.1: The Process of Strategic Planning

The process of strategic planning (Figure 24.1) proceeds with environmental scanning, through evaluation of issues, forecasting, goal setting, implementation, and to the end process of monitoring as a cycle (Renfro and Morrison, 1984, quoted in Morrison et al., 1984).

Strategic planning is described as the process of determining the alignment of the institution with the external environment. It is the response to environmental changes. It is a decision-making process based on analysis of internal and external environments, with accurate resource deployment based on maximising strengths and opportunities, and minimising weaknesses and threats. These must be compatible with the institutional vision and mission. As compared with long-range planning which strengthens internal strengths over a period of time to optimise preparedness for the future, strategic planning strategises the present, based on the prediction of future developments and opportunities.

Within education, strategic planning has emerged in response to market-driven programme development and delivery, and concerns of cost-efficiency. SWOT analysis (for internal strengths and weaknesses, and external opportunities and threats) (Figure 24.2) is an important component of strategic planning, and environmental scanning and focus on the strategic niche are core to this exercise.

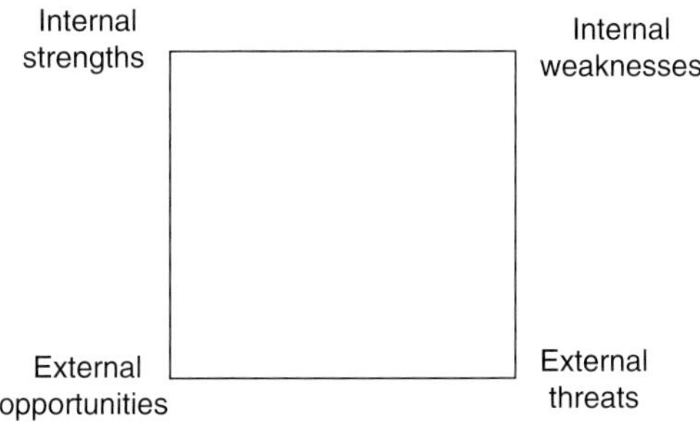

Figure 24.2: SWOT Analysis

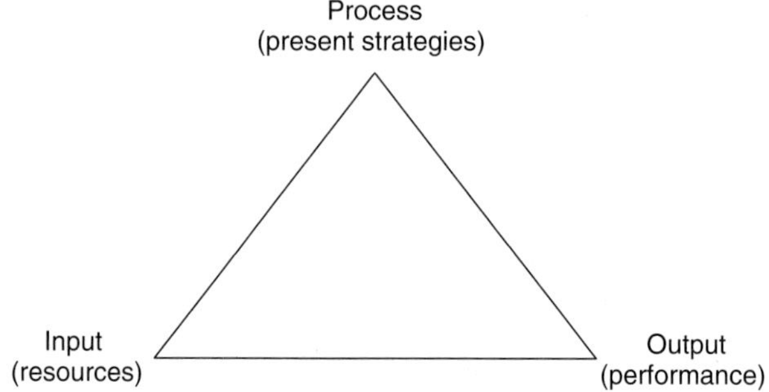

Figure 24.3: Input-Process–Output Linkage

An input (resources)–process (present strategies)–output (performance) analysis (internal to the environment) (Figure 24.3) is also conducted on the external environment forces and trends, competitors and collaborators; and key resources are determined. The mission, vision, and strategies are then interlinked.

The strategic positioning of the institution to best predict the future needs to be combined with looking into the institutional history to create the future – therefore, such planning would emphasise the process over the product (Lorenzo, 1993).

The process of strategic planning has matured in recent years, especially during the 1990s. Organisations are gradually introducing flexibility, dynamism, imagination, and inventiveness into their strategic planning and implementation. "Strategic thinking" has come to greater focus – a synthesis involving intuition and creativity (Mintzberg, 1994b). The distinction by Loewen (1999) is worth consideration (Table 24.1).

Given this distinction, it is not surprising that organisations are gradually replacing strategic planning with "strategic management" – that is the gelling of strategic thought and action with strategic planning.

Table 24.1: Strategic Planning and Strategic Thinking

Strategic Planning	*Strategic Thinking*
• Top management	• Entire personnel
• Structured planning	• Continuous planning
• Structured agenda-based sessions	• Theme-based, unstructured
• Correct answers (conforming top management)	• No immediate answer
	• Creative
• Definite steps	• Innovative measuring based on client satisfaction
• Normative measuring through control	
• Formal	• Informal

24.3 STRATEGIC PLANNING IN DISTANCE EDUCATION

In the past two and half decades, there has been tremendous worldwide growth in distance education. A variety of models of institutional delivery have emerged across the regions. These include

- Single-mode open universities;
- Dual-mode university distance education centres;
- Consortia and networked learning;
- Corporate/private for-profit institutions; and
- Single-mode virtual universities.

While all these models or institutional delivery mechanisms devise their own institutional policy and planning, their operation (including the mechanisms of accreditation) heavily depends on their national education policy and the planning initiatives to effect such a policy. In most national contexts, though there is a synergy between national policy intents and institutional mission and vision, this synergy is rarely visible for definite national policies for distance and online learning within the national educational policy. This is depicted in Figure 24.4.

The above situation can be exemplified by considering the case of the Indira Gandhi National Open University (IGNOU), the second largest mega-university in the world (Panda et al., 2006). For instance,

- While there is lack of a full-fledged national policy for distance and online learning, the detailed national Five Year Plan documents for education attach significant importance to distance education, with substantial state funding.
- The models of institutional delivery in the open and dual-mode universities are, therefore, guided by concerns of access and equity. Such models for consortia and private providers (including online learning institutions) are out of this purview.

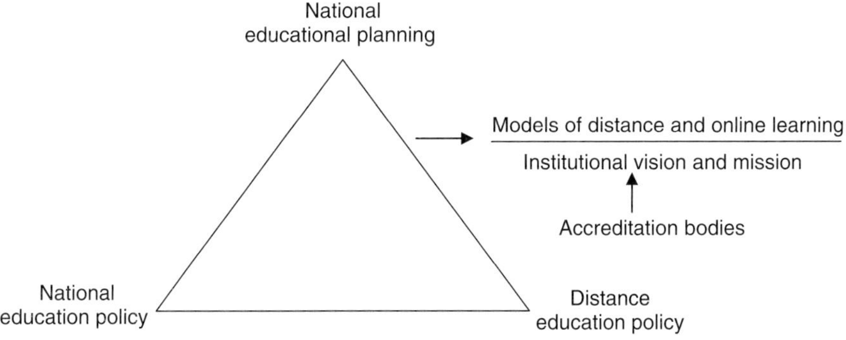

Figure 24.4: Distance Education Policy, Models of Delivery and Accreditation

- The existing national mechanisms of institutional evaluation and accreditation for conventional higher education heavily influence the accreditation process for distance teaching institutions. The private providers of distance education have managed to stay out of this jurisdiction.
- The national open university has the dual responsibility of being an open university as also a national nodal agency to promote, fund, evaluate, and assure quality for the distance education system in the country. Therefore, the institutional vision and mission of provincial open universities and dual-mode distance education universities are heavily guided by the *vision* of the national open university:

> Indira Gandhi National Open University, the National Resource Centre for Open and Distance Learning with international recognition and presence, shall provide seamless access to sustainable and learner-centric quality education, skill upgrading and training to all by using innovative technologies and methodologies and ensuring coverage of existing systems for massive human resource required for promoting integrated national development and global understanding.
>
> (IGNOU, 2002, p. 7)

In today's world of competition and need for collaboration and consortia (as in the case of India through the Distance Education Council of IGNOU), the teacher is no longer the sole arbiter of knowledge with full control over teaching and learning (as was in the past). Gumport and Pusser's (1997) description of institutions as loose networks of connected and interdependent work processes holds good in today's context in which a teacher depends on a host of teaching–learning support centres, without much control over any of them. Today's teacher therefore, by compulsion and by necessity, is part of a strategic planning process.

Institutional strategic planning exercises vary, depending upon institutional vision and policy. Outlined below are brief descriptions of institutional cases of dual-mode and single-mode distance teaching institutions, exemplifying strategic planning in a particular thematic area for each:

1. Texas Tech University, USA, for *technology*.
2. Open Learning Institute (now OUHK), Hong Kong, for *focus*.
3. Athabasca University, Canada, for *mission* and *research*.
4. University of South Africa, South Africa, for *quality distance education*.
5. Indira Gandhi National Open University, India, for *SWOT analysis*.

For a sophisticated technological institute like the Texas Tech University, USA, the strategic process in planning for outreach/distance education programmes had to be meticulous and clear. The University's strategic plan of 2006 presents the mission, followed by the vision statements, which are broken down to goals, with each goal having critical success factors, and objectives which included strategies and assessments. Consider the goal on *technology*:

Goal 4. Technology: Maximise the use of technology in instruction, operations, and community engagement.

Critical Success Factors (measures of the degree of success over the next 5 years):

- Offer 15% of all programs on-line.
- Effectively employ advanced technology in 50% of the Divisions' operations.
- Perform 40% of communications with students electronically.

Objective 4.1: Integrate the use of technology in distance learning and community engagement offerings, while ensuring electronic privacy.

Strategies:

- Systematically research new technologies and software applications that support our strategic endeavors.
- Develop additional electronic courses and expand the number of non-credit electronic programs.
- Establish electronic student bulletin boards.
- Establish programming for IVC delivery based on market demand.
- Hire additional technical staff and provide technical training needed to integrate technology into our operations.

Assessments:

- Implementation of appropriate technologies and software applications.
- Number of courses and programs offered electronically.

Objective 4.2: Offer programs electronically consistent with appropriate pedagogies.

Strategies:

- Include instructional design specialists in design teams.
- Keep up to date on research on pedagogy and technology.
- Work with the Teaching, Learning, and Technology Centre and Information Technology Division to investigate pedagogical and technological issues.

Assessments:

- Courses meet Principles of Good Practice and other indicators of quality.

(Texas Tech University, 2006, pp. 5–6)

Goal 4 had in total five objectives, with the last three objectives being to:

- assure appropriate maintenance of technology resources;
- integrate the use of technology to disseminate information to students, employees and the general public; and
- implement e-business applications to streamline operations.

The nine goals (i.e. access and diversity, academic excellence, engagement, technology, partnerships, human resources and management, tradition and pride, fiscal stability, and accountability) have twenty-seven objectives to comprehensively articulate the vision statements. Such detailed articulation is obviously reflected in the detailed planning document of the university, which includes strategies for implementation.

The Open Learning Institute (OLI) (now the Open University Hong Kong: OUHK) case stands out as significantly different, since it represents a not-for-profit business model of Open and Distance Learning (ODL). The OLI's strategic planning was therefore very clear:

> Our strategic planning therefore was not meant to be a paper exercise full of platitudes, it was an exercise that clearly and unambiguously stated the nature, types and names of courses we intended to offer during the plan period, the number of enrolments we hoped to achieve, the level of fees we wished to impose, the number of hours of tuition we planned to provide and the income we had to generate in order to support the level of anticipated expenditure.
>
> (Dhanarajan, 1993, p. 20)

The planning exercise involved all the stakeholders – it exemplified collective leadership. Any unit's or department's planning activity is reflected university-wide thereby giving the unit full confidence of its importance and the university full responsibility for its achievement.

A case to closely observe is that of the Athabasca University (AU), which has significantly transformed itself over the past years. Its strategic case for *research* deserves attention. AU received self-governing status under the Alberta's Universities Act in 1978, and the 1985 Mission Statement read as follows:

> Athabasca University is dedicated to the removal of barriers that traditionally restrict access to and success in university-level studies and to increasing equality of educational opportunity for all adult Canadians regardless of their geographical location and prior academic credentials.
>
> In common with all Universities, Athabasca University is committed to excellence in teaching, research and scholarship, and to being of service to the general public.
>
> (AU, 1996)

The Vision of the 2006–2011 strategic plan for the open university stated

> Athabasca University will continue to be an open and distance university, a research university and, above all, a university focused on excellence. The university continues to provide open university-level distance and e-learning education (to anyone over the age of 16). In 2015, Athabasca University will be acknowledged as one of the top three universities of its kind in the world – not the largest, but one of the very best
>
> (AU, 2006, p. 2)

with "barriers that traditionally restrict access" replaced by "barriers that restrict access"; "educational opportunity for adult Canadians" replaced by "educational opportunity for all adult learners worldwide"; and "In common with all universities, Athabasca University is committed to" replaced by "We are committed to". The changes were obvious and strategic.

The emphasis in both its Vision and Mission was reflected in its latest strategic plan including values, requirements, goals (strategic objectives and achievements within each goal). Its values statement read as:

> We value *excellence*. The search for excellence is the hallmark of all our endeavours. We value *learning*. Student learning and satisfaction are measures of our success. We value *scholarly research*. We engage in reflective practice through the scholarship of discovery and the scholarship of teaching. We value the *free exchange of ideas*. A respectful climate for open discourse promotes innovation, discovery and social responsibility. We value *openness and flexibility*. Reducing barriers to education enhances access and social equity. We value *diversity and inclusiveness*. Diversity and inclusiveness enhance the quality both of learning and of the workplace. We value *our employees*. The commitment, innovation, creativity and continuous learning of every employee contribute to our success. We value *accountability*. We are accountable to our students, to each other and to the public.
>
> (AU, 2006, p. 4)

Till 2011, the university has committed itself to six strategic areas: ensuring quality in learning; enhancing open access; focusing on quality research; building communities; recruiting and retaining excellent people; and allocating resources.

Commensurate with the mission statement, AU had developed a strategic research plan to align with its mission. The "mission-oriented" research themes included distance and online learning applied to particular disciplines; electronic publishing; space science and astronomy; globalisation and technology; changing workplace/workplace and community education; indigenous education; interdisciplinary research in environment and sustainability; health research; and those identified for/by the Canada Research Chairs (CRCs) (AU, 2003). The research activities are guided broadly by the philosophy of removing barriers to educational opportunities in order for graduates to participate fully in society. The research agenda was also designed to match the high teaching profile, under a new trademark *Canada's Open University*^{TM}. The alignment of research, teaching, and strategy was in keeping with views of the teaching and research profiles of OU academics, as well as identifying niche areas to which scholars are invited through the CRCs.

Examples of serious strategic planning initiatives for distance education in developing countries are rare. One of the best examples is that of the University of South Africa (UNISA), which has emerged strategically stronger after its merger with Technikon Southern Africa and the distance education centre of Vista University in 2004. The new UNISA, which promises education to every African (with the slogan "African University in service of humanity"), had developed a comprehensive *2015 Strategic Plan* (UNISA, n.d.) with detailed consideration of context, mission, situation analysis, strategic objectives with key strategies and targets. The university had ten strategic objectives. An example of the second strategic objective on "quality distance education" is outlined below to highlight strategic initiatives in this area and to illustrate the rigour that had gone into this exercise.

6.2 Position Unisa as a leading provider of quality distance education programmes through an academic product range that expands on its comprehensive character.

Unisa is recognised world-wide as a major provider of distance education. The University's programmes provide a flexible option for students who choose to study at their own place and pace using appropriate technologies and having access to a range of learning support. Our product range incorporates general academic, professional and vocationally-oriented programmes that are aligned to legislative and socio-economic imperatives and are nationally and internationally accredited. Although Unisa's objective is clearly to be an Open and Distance Learning institution we must strive to ensure that access is translated into success. The University's open access policy provides opportunities while its materials, quality assurance and student support based on best practice in open and distance learning ensure success for the reasonably diligent student.

Strategies

Establish a common understanding of the nature and role of Unisa as a comprehensive open and distance education university: internally, among all staff; and externally, among our students, market and stakeholders. This will be accomplished through communication and assertive and targeted marketing, placing an emphasis on what it means to be a comprehensive university.

Strive to make distance education a method of choice for South African and African students in particular and position Unisa as a university of first choice and not last resort, by instituting a tuition model appropriate to the purposes of the programmes, and the context and needs of students.

Develop an appropriate and relevant programme and qualifications mix (PQM) aligned with the comprehensive nature of the institution, its vision to become "the African University in the service of humanity", its need to maximize economies of scale wherever possible, as well as legislative and socio-economic imperatives.

Ensure the relevance of Unisa's PQM and research by regularly conducting needs analyses of our markets, our students and our stakeholders, both at an institutional level and within Colleges and organisational units, while at the same time benchmarking these with the highest international standards.

Manage access by providing students with the necessary competencies through RPL, access and foundation programmes and a more deliberate engagement with the Further Education and Training (FET) sector.

Maintain and improve on Unisa's position as a quality provider of distance education through committing to continuous quality improvement in internal systems, liaison with professional bodies, liaison and partnerships with business, industry and the public service, peer institutions. Actively seek out national and international benchmarks, accreditation and financial support.

Ensure that the curriculum for each module is up-to-date and well-researched, with aims and learning outcomes appropriate for the level of study; and with teaching, learning and assessment methods that are consonant with those aims and outcomes.

Increase headcount enrolments in line with national parameters to a plateau of 250,000 students by 2015. Growth will be encouraged particularly in the fields of Science, Engineering and Technology, as well as Agricultural and Natural Sciences. Appropriate enrolment caps and targets within the programme profile of Unisa will be used as an instrument.

Targets

- To maintain Unisa's position among the top ten mega-universities of the world (currently number 6) – using critical benchmarks of comprehensive learner support, use of ICTs, research output, ODL methods, and output (UG and PG) rates.
- To position Unisa as one of the Top 5 Universities in South Africa by 2015, based upon criteria such as outputs (UG and PG), research units published, number of NRF rated researchers, number of full professors, size, etc.
- To position Unisa as the top comprehensive university in the country by 2010 based upon appropriate and relevant evaluation criteria.
- A review of all curricula and the PQM in a phased approach to make transparent the teaching, learning and assessment assumptions; and to demonstrate consonance with the values, objectives and character of Unisa, as well as its Africa orientation, by July 2007.
- In line with the new programme and qualification mix, and with the intended paradigm shift, 100 priority modules revised or developed each year according to Unisa's new tuition and ICLD models.
- All quality assurance systems related to teaching and learning in place and operational by January 2007.
- General Unisa Satisfaction Index (GUSI) aspiration of 100% in 2015 (Currently 76.86%) with a minimum threshold of 90%.
- Full-time student headcount enrolment of 235,000 by 2010 and 250,000 by 2015 (Currently 215,825 students) in the light of enrolment-capping. Growth will be pursued after vigorous advocacy of Unisa's strategic positioning to cater for a larger proportion of the target pool.
- As a general rule no non-strategic undergraduate courses with less than 20 students enrolled per year by 2008. A threshold for viability of a programme will be set at 300 enrolments. The targets will be less in the Sciences and considerably more in the high volume programmes.
- Academic and academic professional staff-to-student ratio of 1:140 by 2015.

(UNISA, n.d., pp. 15–16)

UNISA strives hard and invests considerable time and energy (and publicly displays so) to implement its strategies in a manner almost commensurate with any business enterprise. In contrast, the second largest university in the world (i.e. IGNOU) that had contributed a considerable amount of scholarship, dialogue and articulation to develop its Vision and Mission (IGNOU, 2002) has never publicly presented, within and outside the institution, reference to the implementation of its 2002 document. In examining its positioning nationally and globally, it is worth quoting its realistic SWOT analysis, which further guides its strategic mission and twelve thrust areas, with the corresponding strategies to enable their achievement.

Threats and Challenges to the System

- Attracting best talent and retaining them.
- Sustain quality education under resource constraints and pressure of large numbers.
- Continued efforts required to upgrade standards in the context of global competition.
- Increased focus on learner-centric learning, particularly for those from remote and rural areas.
- Developing mechanisms and capabilities to compete internationally to advance frontiers of knowledge to emerge as the leader of ODL system.
- Continuing professional development of faculty and staff, especially for technology-enabled education and training.

Strengths of the System

It is now well accepted that the ODL system has reached a stage where highly professional inputs are required for the design, development and delivery of education. The very effective intervention of Information and Communication Technologies (ICT) has made it even more effective, technical and dynamic. Such a system can be handled only by experts. As a premier open and distance learning institution, IGNOU has developed in-house expertise to design, develop and deliver multi-media self-instructional materials. The other major strengths include

- Centre of Excellence for disseminating knowledge through the distance mode.
- Leadership in technology-enabled education.
- Internationally acclaimed quality instructional materials in diverse need-based areas.
- Extensive, efficient and functionally effective network for diversified student support and collaborative learning.
- National capability for delivery through educational TV channel – *Gyan Darshan* and *Gyan Vani* – the network of FM radio stations.
- Increased acceptance by national and international agencies.
- Phenomenal growth of students due to credibility and cost-effectiveness of the system.
- Internationally recognised training capabilities in diversified areas of education, HRD and extension.

Weaknesses of the System

- Reliance on conventional communication links.
- Weak Wide Area Network with Regional Centres and Study Centres.
- Scope for better database management.
- Access not beyond district level.
- Insufficient component of interactive multiple-media in courseware.
- Lack of tracer studies on learners and quality research studies on the system.
- Inadequate mechanism for continuous professional development of faculty and staff due to phenomenal growth of the system.
- Lack of initiative to promote collaborative inter-university alliances/ consortium.

Opportunities

In the emerging scenario, the ODL is probably the only sustainable system for enhancing seamless access to education in the country. The University has continuously strived for improving the credibility and quality of the system. The opportunities stem from:

- Ever increasing demand for higher education and upgradation of life-coping skills.
- Need for continuous training of a huge workforce in the developing countries with large populations, projects and plans.
- Enhancing access to education to the employed (with low qualifications), drop-outs, adults learners.
- Global alliances of ODL systems to provide and share rich learning experiences through collaborative educational programmes.
- Convergence between the open and conventional university systems (and other educational and training organisations) to enhance sustainable access.
- Scope for imparting education using emerging technologies.
- Focussing on disadvantaged groups and less developed regions.

(IGNOU, 2002, pp. 4–6)

Accurate matching of its SWOT analysis with its ambitious and all embracing *vision* (noted earlier) reveals significant challenges with respect to implementation. Some scholars and leaders have expressed surprise as to how such a huge university, with about 1.5 million cumulative student enrolments from 32 countries, can manage its operation to the satisfaction of all (Panda, 2005).

A detailed discussion of strategic planning in distance education, including SWOT, input–process–output analysis, strategy design and implementation, and monitoring and evaluation with examples from three types of institutions – home network, office college, and public university – could provide a useful guide for this system (Kilfoil, 2003). Consideration of the approach to planning (such as top-down or bottom-up) is also crucial. In case of the Australian Universities, the Hoare report had noted that "Some universities favour a "top-down" approach in planning, where the broad directions are set by the vice-chancellor and advisers, while others favour "bottom-up" where the corporate plan is the amalgamation of the faculty and other subsidiary plans" (Anderson et al., 1999, p. 6). Both the approaches are equally applicable to distance education. While, for instance, the provision of learner support services across all the learning or study centres may be the responsibility of the top management, departments and faculties (and even individuals) must be encouraged to devise innovations, for instance, in course development models and the nature of self-learning materials. These decisions will of course vary across institutions.

The application of strategic planning in distance education aligns with Watson's (2000) summation of higher education in the United Kingdom – that is, there is a gap between the promise of strategic planning (as theory) and the existing management strategies of higher education institutions (as practice). The reasons are varied and complex:

- The paradox of competition versus collaboration.
- Marrying "volatile and unpredictable external environment with the internal dynamics and trajectory of their own institution" (p. 1) which leads to "blandness and inclusiveness" where there should be differentiation. It is therefore not surprising that mission statements result in "list of imprioritised promises" (broad, universal, and all-embracing statements that are difficult to focus and follow).
- Existence of cynicism, including the mission and the university itself: "At the core of such cynicism is the issue of loyalty. Traditional academics do not regard themselves so much as working *for* a university as working *in* it" (p. 3)

In such a context a very important aspect of success in institutional management has been the "management of morale", to take action concerning low morale in organisations. In higher education, there "… is the lack of power of managers (individually and in teams) to act upon their instincts without considering (some would say calculating) how to carry along with them the other individuals and groups with whom they share direct responsibility for the quality and success of the enterprise" (Watson, 2000, p. 5). Consideration of alternatives is therefore inevitable.

Strategic planning in distance education tries not only to respond to the changing environment by repositioning the institution and by ensuring flexibility in the operational tasks and units of the institute, but also to capture and own the environment as its niche/specialism, and to continue to command the area for a long period of time. In the strategic planning process, various sub-units and tasks like curriculum design and development, media and technology choice and mix, instructional delivery, learner support, assessment and evaluation, certification, and so on are inter-linked to conform to the broad mission and vision. It is, however, argued that strategic planning models have limited applicability in distance education in so far as wider and effective involvement of its people (Panda, 2004) is concerned. "Leadership" holds the key for effective institutional planning and management in distance education.

24.4 LEADERSHIP AND GOVERNANCE

It is therefore important to consider what leadership roles and what patterns of governance exist and/or are intended to be achieved. Institutional strategies must be linked to detailed curriculum development and staff development (Cowan, 1978), and have clear implications for instructional transaction and learner support. The role of the leader both at the institutional and at the departmental/project level is crucial. Contributions in this area (Perry, 1976; Paul, 1990; Daniel, 1999; Bates, 2000; Evans and Nation, 2000; Latchem and Hanna, 2001; and Panda, 2003) are useful to both experienced and inexperienced practitioners. Of particular use and application for policy makers and planners are the strategic questions underlined by Robinson (2004, pp. 183–186), including

- What forms of governance are in place?
- Is the policy for ODL adequate for its governance?
- Does the policy for ODL accommodate different forms of ODL and their governance?
- Are responsibilities of stakeholders and implementing agencies well defined?
- Are there mechanisms for reviewing and monitoring governance, and for accreditation?
- How is quality assurance mechanism used for governance?
- What relationships exist among self-regulation, external control, and globalisation?
- Is there transparency in governance, and is it oriented to protect the students?

Crucial to institutional development is also the existing models of governance. For the OLI Dhanarajan wrote, "Rather than compile each unit's individual plan into an institutional one we plan for the institution as a whole when departments have or are ascribed a role. It is neither a "top-down" nor "bottom-up" process" (1993, p. 20). Effectiveness of any organizational productivity depends on effective leadership and good governance. Policy studies and R&D in this area for distance learning are the most neglected of all. In a recent study by Tsui and others (Tsui et al., 2000) on fifteen ODL institutions in the Asian region, it was pointed out that, except for a few institutions, the leadership style was "commanding", and the administrative style was "bureaucratic", "managerial", and "directive". Correspondingly, the institutional culture was perceived to be bureaucratic and of corporate culture. The authors suggest that institutions in the region need to shift to a new paradigm:

- Flexible and dynamic structure within the organization and its networks.
- Power shared by and empowerment of all.
- Valuing creative contribution of faculty and staff.
- Dynamic, intuitive, and expanding process of management.
- Inspiring and caring people to develop institutional ethics and commitment.

It has also been suggested that leadership in the four areas of budgeting, infrastructure, staffing, and policy revisions are essential in linking strategic planning to implementation of specific programmes (Berge and Schrum, 1998). This is certainly difficult to strategise and put in place the process of strategic planning. Paul's (1990) description of the adoption of a democratic process of consensus building resulting in disaster, and the subsequent corrective action concerning shifting decision from "what" to "how", speaks a lot about the difficulties the top management encounter in institutional planning and implementation. Therefore, leadership is critical to both strategic and other planning approaches. Writes Paul (2003):

> It is a serious mistake to castigate opponents of major change in our universities as dinosaurs or Luddites. Instead, the effective leader must encourage real debate on issues of change and capitalize on the positive energy that can be generated by an open and thorough consideration of alternatives. University faculty members are highly articulate and forceful in the presentation of their opinions and, while that doesn't make change any easier, at its best, it can ensure that every major step has been well thought through and really does have significant support in the institution.
>
> (p. 79)

It is also argued that "Successful, forward-looking and democratic institutional heads have involved researchers and critics of the system in an advisory role so as to enhance institutional performance reflected through transparent research data, critical reflection and public opinion" (Panda, 2004, p. 95).

While a Fordist approach to "quality control" is neither possible nor desirable, a process-oriented quality assurance mechanism can better facilitate individual and group reflection and reform. Given academic freedom and professional autonomy, especially with respect to the faculty/teachers, quality can be ensured through self-regulation, though external control/monitoring/audit/accreditation will reconfirm the self-regulation. Alternatively, a sense of institutional professional ethics can be imbued and will constantly evolve if we follow a holistic planning approach towards dialogue, discourse, and innovation and change.

24.5 CHANGING NATURE OF PLANNING

It seems we are obsessed with "planning", and also use it to achieve a number of "hidden" aims other than to plan for the future. This is where strategies may fail – planning is used to achieve something which is neither articulated nor intended clearly in the planning exercise and its documentary output. This relates to what Quinn (1980, quoted by Mintzberg, 1994b) remarked about corporate planning as a rain dance – the people involved in it think that it will have an effect on the weather, whereas the planning results in improving dancing than affecting the weather.

It has been contended that strategic planning succeeds in only ten percent of cases (Rosenberg and Schewe, 1985), and therefore it is not surprising that it is at times considered a management fad (Birnbaum, 2000). Since doing is better than saying, one needs to implement to make management difference and facilitate change. Leaders therefore prefer using the term "strategic management", which combines both – effectively implementing a well-articulated strategic plan. In reality, strategic planning has often been critiqued on the basis of cases of its poor implementation. Mintzberg (1994b) emphatically notes the malady of "lead boots" and "paperwork mills" that generally guide an organisation's strategic process – papers and words alone do not lead to effective action. Further, in any organisation or system, things must change over time, which is not usually the case. Pacey (1992), in considering strategic planning for open learning, notes, "It is natural not to question why the turkey tail is removed before roasting when generation after generation has followed that procedure. But the turkey tail was removed because of the limits set by the size of the oven. When ovens became larger there was no need to continue following past practice. When does an organisation begin to question its practices or recognise that the limitations that were once there have disappeared or could be removed? With the removal of these limitations, new opportunities become possible" (p. 9).

Has strategic planning in higher education failed? Dorris et al. (2002) write, "After reviewing the literature and consulting with knowledgeable colleagues, we have concluded that a convincing, generalizable empirical study on the efficacy of strategic planning in higher education has yet to be published. There is, of course, no shortage of anecdotes from both sides of the aisle – that is, from the proponents and the critics of strategic planning in academe" (p. 9).

Strategic planning often results in long-term planning and is designed as a linear process by the top management to be implemented mostly by the majority in the organisation. Bell (1998) appropriately remarks

> It can be seen, therefore, that strategy is deployed in most contemporary organisations . . . is based on power and social relationships derived from modes of activity which are rooted in conflict and competition as the prime determinants of social order. It is also based on inaccurate assumptions about organisational dynamics, the predictability of the environment and the capacity to know about that environment. The world is required to be an orderly, predictable place where the whole is equal to, but no greater than, the sum of its parts. Change comes through planning, usually by those at or near the top of the organisational hierarchy. This involves deploying strategy through the construction of a neat and linear alignment between ends and means for others in the organisation to implement. Thus, the paradigm from which those organisations are derived which was appropriate in its time, have now outgrown its usefulness, as has the concept of strategy which is associated with Newtonian organisations.
>
> (pp. 456–457)

Wilkinson (2006), in a recent work, analyses the Virginia Tech's evolution of its *holistic* approach to distance education from a three-dimensional model (academic, administrative, and support sub-systems), through a five-dimensional model (education, access, communication, technology, and satisfaction sub-systems) to the current six-dimensional model (learning effectiveness, student satisfaction, faculty satisfaction, access, cost effectiveness, and system effectiveness). Many universities, especially in the dual-mode and consortia sectors, do vie for such holistic models to increase satisfaction in their clients or stakeholders (a term which Wilkinson has used to represent students, faculty, instructional designers, service personnel, and institutional leaders). Most appropriately, strategic planning could address such a holistic approach to DE quality. What requires special attention is the way such quality parameters are defined. Wilkinson (2006) encapsulates the six dimensions in to two aspects of quality – access, and system effectiveness. Consider the key quality indicators for "access":

> 1. By 2012 at least 95% of academic departments are engaged in developing and/or delivering distance and distributed eLearning courses.
> 2. Distance and distributed eLearning enrolments increase by 10% annually.
> 3. Programs and courses provide for timely and appropriate interaction between students and faculty and among students.
> 4. Students have access to and can effectively use appropriate library resources, and have access to laboratories, facilities and equipment appropriate to the course or programs.
> 5. Students have adequate access to the range of services appropriate to support the programs, including admissions, financial aid, academic advising, delivery of course materials, and placement and counselling.
>
> (p. 3)

A close examination of the key quality indicators would suggest a very important learner requirement, that is access to the content and presentation of the learning resources and facilitation of learning, which is missing from the representation of quality in "access". It is therefore not surprising that in many strategic planning initiatives such crucial essentials miss out to the mundane but strategically important elements based on environmental scanning and institutional niche.

There has been an established trend in the higher education institutions in the strategic planning era to place greater stress on cost saving, institutional restructuring, and adoption of best practices (Kezar, 2000, quoted in Haughey, 2003). However, the practice of strategic planning towards a culture of "best practices" in lieu of "research" or R&D is a potentially dangerous trend, more suited to commercialisation than innovation.

In the strategic planning exercise, there is considerable ICT reengineering, restructuring of work practices (e.g. outsourcing, privatization, partnership, and alliances), and transformation of the instructional system (e.g. knowledge management, best practices, and the like). It is contended that the approaches of outsourcing and best practice (in place of context-specific R&D and system-wide reflective work structure, including technology applications) are not going to help much in the long run because of their inadequacy and inefficiency to create and sustain a system-wide/systemic knowledge base and sustained capacity building. Further, for example,

- simple convergence of units, tasks, technologies, and systems is not working any more (nor even any incrementalism);
- project-based implementation is not getting into the whole institution; and
- it is not able to address the traditional faculty culture.

Therefore, it is not enough to just have a strongly planned strategic niche – setting objectives and gearing the institution to achieve them. It requires a holistic transformation of the institution.

Distance education, and for that matter any educational system or learning environment, is constructivist in nature and is grounded in the context of one's own institutional and social culture. Therefore, adoption of best practices and outsourcing to partner or collaborator institutions is not going to produce desired institutional transformation. Planning and management of the DE system and its sub-systems in an institutional context need to be holistic (i.e. system-wide and comprehensive), and to be grounded in the R&D context of the institution and/or the system itself. Technology adoption and media deployment is a case at hand. Even if the latest full-scale digital technology is in place, the faculty and staff may not necessarily be predisposed towards it; and, therefore, may not integrate this into their work environment, work culture, and work ethics. What is therefore suggested is

- adoption of blended learning (and therefore blended media) strategies for institutional course design and media mix, and for addressing diversified learners' learning styles; and

- an institution-wide holistic planning perspective and mechanism to which all the stakeholders, especially the faculty and staff, contribute through internal strength, diversity, debate, discussion, dialogue, and personal development.

It is worth noting what Bell (1998) has argued in the case of holistic planning in the school system, in which there should be wider distribution of power to ensure multi-functional (rather than hierarchical) and holistic work relationships. Bell quotes two works by Handy and Aitken (1986) on right brain and left brain functioning, and by Tarule (1998) on problem-solving by women in management. The left–right brain perspective tells us that while the left brain activities are sequential, rational, logical, analytical, and time-oriented (and therefore strategic), the right brain activities are intuitive, creative, imaginative, and timeless (and may be holistic). The dominance of the left over the right needs to be reversed. One feminist perspective that can facilitate this is the discourse on problem-solving by women managers, accepting Tarule's (1998) distinction between "separate knowing" (which is objective, exclusive, critical, away from personal relationships, and therefore Newtonian and strategic) and "connected knowing" (which is collaborative in which meanings are constructed through narratives within inclusive relationships and commonality of experiences, and therefore holistic). Such a holistic process brings in flexibility in inclusive policy formulation, and sharing in differentiated values and perspectives. Bell (1998) quotes Zohar (1997) to compare the two perspectives to symphony and jazz – in a symphony orchestra, the players play individual scores to the script of the conductor and the whole is the sum of the individual scores; in jazz, individuals may be experts in many instruments and perform without any conductor or set score. "There is an evolving background theme that organises the parts, but the composite sound is always a surprise" (Zohar, 1997, p. 126). In the context and organisational set up of distance education, with multispecialism and teamwork, it is not easy to hold the flexible and diversified parts to the evolving (if at all) background theme and the unpredictable composite sound.

24.6 CONCLUDING REMARKS

Contextualising the process of planning and implementation by providing flexibility and opportunity to experiment with institutional work, including curriculum and course design, and even media mix and media integration, is presumed to work better than simply setting strategic objectives and efficiently mobilising resources to achieve them. Technology deployment is an issue in which every leader wants to engage and which every faculty is required to become involved. Writes Haughey, "If academics view the move to transformation of the instructional system as the imposition of technology they are unlikely to support the venture" (2003, p. 60). While such technology-enabled mass experimentations imposed from the top (unfortunately) continue to dominate institutional decision-making, it is extremely important for any leader to locate traditional established (may be best) practices which had been contexualised over a period of time, and encourage faculty and staff to initiate best alternatives and even supplementaries to address, for instance, student heterogeneity, massification, and quality processes, including student learning experiences. Instead of (or even besides) undertaking an accountability perspective (with quantitative performance indicators – how many came in and how many went out with what cost), it is essential to devise a managerial perspective (Panda, 1991) to seriously examine the quality of processes and build research and scholarship into its very foundation.

What is therefore emerging is that institutions cannot escape strategic planning and thinking (even if it is inadequate) – it is a basic requirement. They need to account for student registration, progression, graduation, attrition, and for cost efficiency. However, they must simultaneously go beyond to contextualise their planning for greater flexibility, quality, and long-term sustainability.

This chapter does not intend to end with a passive note (especially for strategic enthusiasts) about transformation of universities as seats of scholarship. However, it is worth noting the recent excellent study on tracking strategies at McGill University by Mintzberg and Rose (2003, p. 289): "... universities exhibit a sensible kind of stability in a world of often senseless change. And so they may well be beacons for a more reasonable future for our organisations. Perhaps the proper response to all the hype about change and turnaround and turbulence is not more dramatic intervention but more respect for institution".

REFERENCES

Anderson, D., Johnson, R., and Milligan, B. (1999). *Strategic Planning in Australian Universities*. Canberra: DETYA, Commonwealth of Australia.

Athabasca University (1996). *Strategic University Plan 1996–1999*. Athabasca: Athabasca University. Retrieved March 3, 2007 from http://www.athabascau.ca/html/info/sup/sup.htm.

Athabasca University (2003). *Athabasca University Strategic Research Plan*. Athabasca: Athabasca University.

Athabasca University (2006). *Strategic University Plan 2006–2011: Highlights*. Athabasca: Athabasca University.

Bates, A.W. (2000). *Managing Technological Change: Strategies for College and University Leaders*. San Francisco: Jossey-Bass.

Bell, L. (1998). From symphony to jazz: The concept of strategy in education. *School Leadership and Management*, **18**(4), 449–460.

Berge, Z.L. and Schrum, L. (1998). Linking strategic planning with programme implementation in distance education. *Cause/Effect*, **21**(3), 31–38.

Birnbaum, R. (2000). *Management Fads in Higher Education*. San Francisco: Jossey-Bass.

Bryson, J. (1995). *Strategic Planning for Public and Non-profit Organisations: A Guide to Strengthening and Sustaining Organisational Achievement*. San Francisco: Jossey-Bass.

Cowan, J. (1978). *Patterns of Institutional Development*. Paper presented at the Staff and Educational Strategies Development Conference, Manchester.

Daniel, J. (1999). *Mega Universities and Knowledge Media: Technology Strategies for Higher Education*. London: Kogan Page.

Dhanarajan, G. (1993). Strategic planning: The experience of the Open Learning Institute of Hong Kong. *Open Praxis*, **2**, 19–21.

Dorris, M.J., Kelly, J.M., and Trainer, J.F. (2002). Strategic planning in higher education. *New Directions for Higher Education*, **116**, 5–11.

Evans, T. and Nation, D. (eds) (2000). *Changing University Teaching: Reflections on Creating Educational Technologies*. London: Kogan Page.

Gumport, P. and Pusser, B. (1997). Restructuring the academic environment. In *Planning and Management for a Changing Environment* (M. Peterson, D. Dill, L. Mets and associates eds) San Francisco: Jossey-Bass, pp. 453–478.

Handy, C. and Aitken, R. (1986). *Understanding Schools as Organisations*. London: Pelican.

Haughey, M. (2003). Planning for open and flexible learning. In *Planning and Management in Distance Education* (S. Panda ed.) London: Routledge, pp. 53–62.

IGNOU (2002). *Vision and Mission of IGNOU*. New Delhi: Indira Gandhi National Open University.

Keller, G. (1983). *Academic Strategy: The Management Revolution in American Higher Education*. Baltimore: John Hopkins University Press.

Kezar, A.J. (2000). *Higher Education Trends (1997–1999)*. ERIC Clearinghouse on Higher Education.

Kilfoil, W.R. (2003). *Strategic Planning in Distance Education*. Washington, D.C: Distance Education and Training Council.

Latchem, C. and Hanna, D. (eds) (2001). *Leadership for 21st Century Learning: Global Perspectives from Educational Innovators*. London: Routledge.

Loewen, J. (1999). *The Power of Strategy*. Johannesburg: Zebra.

Lorenzo, A.L. (1993). Managing uncertainty: Thinking and planning strategically. *New Directions for Community Colleges*, **84**, 47–60.

Mintzberg, H. (1994a). The fall and rise of strategic planning. *Harvard Business Review*, **72**(1), 107–114.

Mintzberg, H. (1994b). *The Rise and Fall of Strategic Planning: Reconceiving Roles for Planning, Plans, Planners*. New York: Free Press.

Mintzberg, H. and Rose, J. (2003). Strategic management upside down: Tracking strategies at McGill University from 1829 to 1980. *Canadian Journal of Administrative Sciences*, **20**(4), 270–290.

Morrison, J.L., Renfro, W.L., and Boucher, W.I. (1984). *Futures Research and the Strategic Planning Process: Implications for Higher Education*. ASHE-ERIC Higher Education Research Reports – Report 9.

Pacey, L. (1992). *Strategic Planning and Open Learning: Turkey Tails and Frogs*. Paper presented at the World Conference of the International Council for Distance Education, Bangkok.

Panda, S. (1991). Programme evaluation in distance education: a perspective and proposed agenda of actions. In *Educational Technology: Third Yearbook Vol. 1* (M. Mukhopadhyay et al. eds) New Delhi: All India Association for Educational Technology, pp.168–181.

Panda, S. (ed.) (2003). *Planning and Management in Distance Education*. London: Routledge.

Panda, S. (2004). People: Staffing, development and management. In *Policy for Open and Distance Learning* (H. Perraton and H. Lentell eds) London: Routledge, pp. 76–99.

Panda, S. (2005). Distance education and national development: Reflections on the Indian experience. *Distance Education*, **26**(2), 205–225.

Panda, S., Venkaiah, V., Garg, S., and Puranik, C. (2006). Tracing the historical developments in open and distance education. In *Four Decades of Distance Education in India: reflections on policy and practice* (S. Garg et al. eds) New Delhi: Viva Books.

Paul, R. (1990). *Open Learning and Open Management: Leadership and Integrity in Distance Education*. London: Kogan Page.

Paul, R. (2003). Institutional leadership and management of change. In *Planning and Management of Distance Education* (S. Panda ed.) London: Routledge, pp. 75–85.

Perry, W. (1976). *Open University: A Personal Account of the First Vice Chancellor*. Milton Keynes: Open University Press.

Quinn, J. (1980). *Strategies for Change: Logical Incrementalism*. Homewood, IL.: Irwin.

Renfro, W.L. and Morrison, J.L. (1984). Detecting signals of change: the environmental scanning process. *The Futurist*, **18**(4), 49–56.

Robinson, B. (2004). Governance, accreditation and quality assurance in open and distance education. In *Policy for Open and Distance Learning* (H. Perraton and H. Lentell eds) London: Routledge, pp. 181–206.

Rosenberg, L.J. and Schewe, C.D. (1985). Strategic planning: fulfilling the promise. *Business Horizons*, **28**(4), 54–62.

Tarule, J. (1998). *The Characteristics of Connected and Separate Modes of Knowing*. Paper presented to the Joint UCET/AATCDE Seminar, London.

Texas Tech University, (2006). *Division of Outreach and Distance Education Strategic Plan*. Lubbock, TX.: Texas Tech University.

Tsui, C., Jegede, O., Zhang, W. et al. (2000). *Leadership Styles and Institutional Cultures in a Changing World: A Survey of Open and Distance Learning Institutions in Asia*. Paper presented at 14th Annual Conference of AAOU, Manila, October 25–27.

UNISA (n.d.) *2015 Strategic Plan: An Agenda for Transformation*. Pretoria: University of South Africa.

Watson, D. (2000). *Managing Strategy*. Buckingham: Open University Press.

Whipp, R. (1998). *Creative Deconstruction: Strategy and Organisations*. Paper presented to the ESRC Seminar Series "Redefining Educational Management", Cardiff.

Wilkinson, T. (2006). *The Holistic Quality Thread in Distance Education*. Paper presented at the Annual Conference on Distance Teaching and Learning. University of Wisconsin, Wisconsin.

Zohar, D. (1997). *Rewriting the Corporate Brain*. San Francisco: Berrett-Kochler.

Chapter 25

LEADERSHIP DEVELOPMENT FOR DISTANCE AND E-LEARNING

Alan Tait

25.1 INTRODUCTION

This chapter seeks to identify how leadership development can be promoted and supported specifically in distance and e-learning contexts, and primarily in post-secondary and higher education not-for-profit institutions. While there has been a small stream of significant works in the field of management of distance education (Paul, 1990; Rumble, 1992; Panda, 2003), there has been little about leadership, as Beaudoin (2004, p. 91) has pointed out, and very little indeed said about leadership development (for a brief mention, see Latchem and Hanna, 2001, pp. 61–62).[1] This chapter draws on what is available but has substantially to build from the ground up, on a topic that is now more than timely and indeed can be regarded as urgent. Firstly, we will seek to identify what it is in distance and e-learning contexts that leadership development needs to address for that broad set of activities and purposes, including consideration of whether the distinction that marks the domain of distance and e-learning remains helpful. Secondly, we will examine what sorts of leadership are needed. Lastly, we will examine an example from the Open University UK of how leadership development was provided and review what might be generalised from that experience.

25.2 DISTANCE AND E-LEARNING: A VALID DOMAIN?

The extent to which management skills are generic or context specific is a familiar topic: can a senior manager in education move easily and usefully to health or retailing, and of course vice versa? This is a relevant issue at this early stage of development of the argument here because if educational leadership can be drawn from a range of sectors, or effectively move around the sector, say between distance and e-learning institutions, dual and multi-mode institutions, research-led institutions, campus-based teaching-focused institutions or even from outside the education sector altogether, the approaches to leadership development might be very different.

What can then be said about the distance and e-learning domain that deserves attention at this stage? There are significantly different streams in terms of the history of distance and e-learning (a history that has yet to be written) that permit some broad categorisations of the sort of institutions and organisations that need leadership. These include the following:

- The "for-profit model" that has been represented from the beginning in the UK with Isaac Pitman's course in shorthand in the nineteenth century, and all the other programmes of study and training that offer immediate reward in terms of career and pay. These programmes work primarily in the vocational curriculum areas.
- The "development" model, which seeks to change the social relationships for individuals and groups in terms of individual opportunity, social justice and/or national economic and social development. This tradition is primarily value driven and is represented by both the open universities and the dual or multi-mode universities and colleges, which now form such a significant part of the post-secondary sector.

The reality is of course much more complex than this simple schematisation suggests. The for-profit sector can of course be value driven, although it can too simply be income driven, closing down a business if greater income can be developed elsewhere. Students who succeed there can change social developments around them. The "development" model has at the same time to be sustainable, that is to say it has to be able to create enough surplus income to be able to invest in the business as it changes and develops. It is also true that where institutional mission finds it difficult to sustain survival, institutions can and do seek any way to make a living in order to avoid closure. Such survival tactics can bring success in those limited terms; although when institutional fit to a contemporary landscape is so bad, institutional closure may follow anyway (and there have been some notable cases of this sort in both the for-profit and the not-for-profit sectors in distance and e-learning in the recent period).

However, this chapter concerns itself primarily with the "development" model and regards this as a significant discriminator in terms of the kinds of leadership that are needed, although what it has to say will be relevant to those parts of the "for-profit" sector that are value driven.

The next question to be examined is the extent to which distance and e-learning remains a valid domain in the sense of a distinct sector that has specific leadership development needs. There are three dimensions proposed that demand attention in this context in defining distance and e-learning as a domain, namely

- technologies for learning and teaching;
- the political, social and educational environments; and
- the values base.

25.3 TECHNOLOGY-SUPPORTED LEARNING

It is clear that distance and e-learning has developed through the application of technologies. This applies from the use of the postal system to carry correspondence education by rail in the nineteenth century, through to the use of radio and television, and now to the use of digital media, especially the web and mobile learning. Does this remain a discriminator for distance and e-learning? The arguments against would derive from the "convergence" school of thought: that distance and e-learning and what used to be called "conventional" educational systems are in fact converging (Tait and Mills, 1999). Many students now use the web to search for resources, communicate at least in part with their teachers by email and do not need to spend so much time on campus (and indeed as many have to work so substantially to keep themselves during full-time study they cannot actually spend so much time on campus). It is of course also true that many institutions have adopted distance and e-learning programmes as part of their provision, and in some cases so much of their provision that they can truly be termed dual or multi-mode institutions.

There are also significant differences between the instructor-led or boutique model of distance and e-learning, which is predominant in North America, and the "at scale" model of the open universities dependent on learning materials that are taught by a range of tutors with institutional populations of two million or more (Daniel, 1996). The first model provides extension off the campus through the use of technologies such as telephone conferencing and/or or web-supported learning but retains important continuities with the classic artisan model of teaching in a group led by the one professor. The model cannot be scaled up significantly. The second model, pioneered by the open universities, demands a commitment to the breaking of that mould and to an understanding of the industrial scale of this model of distance and e-learning. This is in fact no small thing and makes significant demands in terms of culture change. This is partly an issue of technical competence that can be learned, but equally importantly a capacity of imagination that allows a senior manager or would-be senior manager coming in from outside to leave behind the concept of classic teaching in favour of large-scale systems that put the students at the centre of the organisation's concerns (Tait, 2003, p. 156). For some university academics in "classic" universities or at least aspiring to the mindset of classic universities, it is not now so much the notion of distance and e-learning that is a barrier. However, such people may find very challenging the rupture with the approach to teaching where the teacher has a group of students, who see themselves affectively as well as intellectually as "her" or "his" students' now and in the future. They are asked in the second model to accept a new division of labour where the academic creates the learning materials but may not as an individual substantially or at all engage with the learner (that task being undertaken by tutors). This has the great advantage of specialisation – highly developed expertise; the economics of mass production; strength from scale – but the realities of industrialisation risks creating a sort of alienation. Just as Adam Smith's pin maker might have felt she or he became a cog in the machine of industrialised production rather than an artisan who was mistress or master of the craft, so an academic in a distance teaching university can feel that her or his status is transmogrified in the same way. Thus, while distance and e-learning is no longer necessarily distinct in its commitment to the support of learning by technology, its leaders may have to extend, dependent on the model of distance and e-learning that is used, to a commitment to an industrial model of education which is not only technically based but also culturally challenging.

25.4 THE POLITICAL, SOCIAL AND EDUCATIONAL ENVIRONMENT

Distance and e-learning has grown and continues to grow in relation to its educational environment, and this environment of course develops and changes within broader social and political contexts. The development of distance and e-learning has seen a very considerable change over the last 25 years. While the pioneers of distance education from the 1960s onwards had to believe in an approach to education that was substantially at odds with the rest of the system, this has changed to its widespread adoption by institutions and in terms of policy. The origins of this development can be seen in the creation of the External Studies Programme at the University of London in 1861, when the fundamental break of study with place was made (Bell and Tight, 1993). This allowed study all over the world, predominantly within the UK outside the very few number of university towns, but also widely throughout the then British Empire, free of constraint from Church (as was the secular mission of the University of London), race or residence. This left a very significant burden of freedom on the students concerned who had to manage their learning independently, not to say in many instances without support, and it was in that space that the tutorial college movement grew up, which was so influential on the student support activity that now is integral to model distance and e-learning (Tait, 2004, pp. 283–284).

Major distance teaching activity in this field was established in the UK and internationally because existing systems were seen as inadequate, in terms of access and scale. This derives from two streams of thought, both of which need to be located in current political debate. The first of these is that of social justice: the conviction that opportunity has not hitherto been equitably distributed. This is a transparent attack on the status quo and may be opposed by those with the conviction that there is no more capacity within the population to benefit from education (a point of view that owes its origins to the nineteenth century opposition to universal schooling); that society cannot afford more opportunity; or the usually implicit view that current privilege should be protected. The second stream of thought relates to human capital theory and derives from the view that in order to be competitive within current economic development, education and training needs to be more widely taken up. This was conventionally expressed in the nineteenth century in the UK in terms of competition with Germany, while today it is the rise of China and India that provides the context. A senior manager in a distance and e-learning institution or one that has significant distance and e-learning activity will find herself or himself today, even after the substantial move of professional opinion about the capacity of distance and e-learning to deliver education effectively, at times substantially in opposition to established interests, and to the status quo. It is important to note that the issue of marginalisation and social exclusion is not one that is ever finally "solved". Leadership in this context has to have the capacity to assess and reassess where society is going and who is being excluded. The mission that a university may, for example, manage for 25 years will need renewal as social trends change and new issues emerge. Failure to live beyond the founding mission is a problem that has beset a number of the major distance teaching universities in Europe, and leadership in this context is needed to avoid the complacency and inherent tendency of all organisations in greater or lesser part to serve their staff rather than their purposes. It is not only in distance and e-learning contexts of course that this organisational entropy has to be challenged.

In one of the few contributions to the study of leadership and management in distance and e-learning, Beaudoin (2004) comes to the view that distance education represents a special context for leadership. He writes,

> Leadership in distance education, as distinct from managerial functions in a variety of settings, is defined by a set of attitudes and behaviors that create conditions for innovative change, that enable individuals and organizations to share a vision and move its direction and that can contribute to the management and operationalization of ideas.
>
> (p. 73)

While there has been enormous progress over the last 25 years, leaders in this field have to have the conviction that social change is both necessary and possible. Whether it is leadership within a dual or multi-mode institution or within a distance teaching institution, leadership is not going to be comfortable. This context for leadership is significantly different from the classic universities, teaching the intellectual and social elites or seeking to do so (and so often they seem to be elided). Despite convergence, distance education contexts remain an uncomfortable place to be, and leadership development has to identify and support those committed to such work.

25.5 VALUES

This leads us to the area of values that has been emphasised on a number of occasions in this chapter. The importance of the definition and support of organisational purpose through strategic planning is well established. The surfacing and identification of values in that process in the context of distance and e-learning was effectively addressed by Paul (1990) in the context of distance learning:

> A value-driven leadership approach defines and articulates a clear set of guiding values and principles which form the basis for decision-making.
>
> (p. 71)

I have suggested that the major value clusters that are specific to this context relate to social justice and social development, which include but are not identical with human capital approaches to education and training. What the issues are for social justice and how society might or should develop remain of course highly contested; the position to be developed here is that leadership in distance and e-learning contexts needs to address these within and outside the institution explicitly. There could be nowhere further from the proverbial ivory tower. The "guiding values and principles" that Paul highlights do not of course come only from those in leadership positions or seeking them: they derive from a negotiation with values that are salient in contemporary society, those that are being driven by government and by other leading forces in a society such as employers, trades unions, faith-based organisations, major NGOS and Foundations. They are also legitimately driven by the range of values that can be identified within the institution, which may derive from supra-institutional research agendas, professional associations and those more loosely of the academy. In seeking leadership in the academic or educational sectors, a commitment to and indeed an enjoyment of negotiation across such a range of stakeholders, and a recognition that this is legitimate and necessary for distance and e-learning, represents a prerequisite.

While I have identified social justice and social development as the prime nexuses of values, there needs to be more definition of how these are played out. The values of social justice will be played out primarily across the dimensions of gender, race and social class, and the ways in which they constrain and support equity of opportunity. There remains a fundamental debate as to the adequacy of meritocracy as the sole vehicle for social justice, or the need in addition for redistribution and redress. Those who are at base uninterested in such issues or whose understanding of their society is that there is little to challenge are unlikely to find a distance and e-learning institution a satisfying or worthwhile place to work for long: its characteristics imply if they do not say explicitly that the value-based questions as to who, why and how we teach are explicitly and dynamically related to what we teach (see Figure 25.1).

The same will be true of research priorities and their relationship to teaching: the social mission of the institution will need to frame the research agenda. These big questions are in active relationship with each other, surfaced with unusual profile in post-secondary

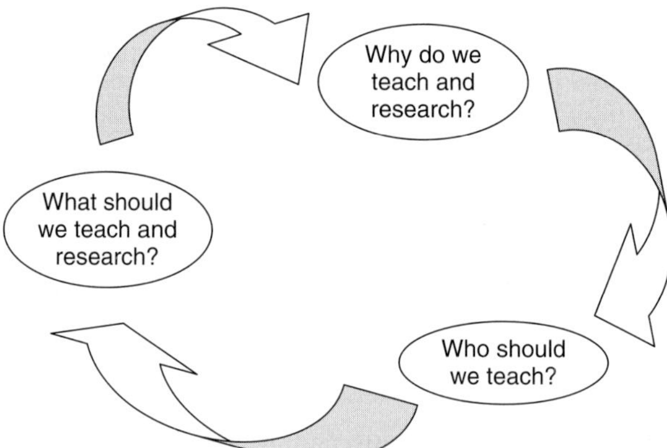

Figure 25.1: Organisational Purpose in a Distance and e-Learning University: Unpacking the Big Questions

and higher education contexts by the singular characteristics of the institutions that have a major or sole commitment to distance and e-learning. Colleagues who lack that critical attitude to their society will also not be able to contribute to one of the core purposes of the institution and that is doubly so for those in leadership positions.

The same is true of social development and of human capital development that is tasked with its support. While this is significantly dominated by discourse that takes the development of and competition between international economies at face value, there is in fact much that can and should be challenged here by those in leadership positions in institutions that contribute at major scale to the education and skills development of significant numbers in the population. The view that straightforward economic growth is the core goal of all societies is increasingly challenged by those who foreground the issues of environment and sustainability of both human networks and ecosystems. The nature of relationships between economies, in particular those of North and South, also provides a range of perspectives on how human capital could be developed to change those relationships from what are seen by a less and less marginalised view as unbalanced and unjust, and ultimately damaging to all.

25.6 WHAT CAPACITIES IN LEADERSHIP ARE IMPORTANT FOR THE DISTANCE AND E-LEARNING CONTEXT?

We now proceed to examine what kinds of leadership are important primarily for the development model of distance and e-learning. The development of the argument has sought to demonstrate that the following capacities are essential:

- an openness to the contested values of both society and the contribution that post-secondary and higher education makes to it domestically and globally;
- the imagination of educational opportunity as being other than it is now, in the face of established political, social and professional interests;
- the invention and management of learning and teaching systems that are radically different in the ways in which they use academic labour to provide programmes of study at scale and quality;
- the competence to integrate complex systems developed with a division of labour that can be industrial in nature.

It is clear then that the overall style for leadership in this context is that denoted as "transformational", concerning itself above all with meanings, as opposed to "transactional" that concerns itself primarily with operations (Bass, 1985). These meanings are associated above all with values; with the appraisal of, response to and intervention with the environment; and the deployment of technologies to support learning.

Turning now to a more functional analysis, we are therefore looking to identify what capacities are needed by those aspiring to leadership. These are more generic than the specific contexts that have been focused up until this point, as they relate to the capacity to manage in organisations with social purposes and in situations of contested values (this applies to many not-for-profit organisations both in the formal and in the non-formal sectors).

My own summary of these capacities can be succinctly defined as being able to

- tell the truth with energy;
- develop alliances around the truths that emerge from that process; and
- put into action the plans that are made as a result of agreement.

I have elided "telling the truth" and the issue of energy, as they seem to me to have a critical relationship. However, to clarify, first of all I do not mean that someone in leadership has a monopoly position of knowing the truth. If we are to be convincing in rescuing the term "leadership" from its historic vulnerability to the promotion of top-down hierarchy, we have to be clear that it refers to responsibility and service rather than privilege and power. There have been too many leaders with the insistent moral vision that is oppressive rather than liberating for their co-workers, which thereby diminishes the gathering of intelligence and understanding that support development. However, there is no doubt that someone in a leadership position has the right and the obligation to develop and deliver their perceptions about issues and questions that an organisation faces, and that obligation is perhaps the most central. Many writers about leadership have talked about courage and this is undoubtedly needed. Equally important is the capacity to manifest and sustain energy, which forms a crucial element in the charisma that is needed, at least as an element within an overall leadership style. The link with energy identifies the leadership role over and above the option of sharing insight as a private intellectual recreation with a few close colleagues; sustained energy is a crucial element that underpins all leadership activity, and it is the decline of energy that suggests when a particular role is coming to an end.

The inevitable limitations to the telling of truth by one individual are mitigated by the need to build alliances, and in that exercise of course, the vision is changed and indeed usually improved on. However, the nature of the leadership role demands that questions and insights lead to action rather than only to reflection or publication, and the capacity to build alliances to achieve that within an organisation identifies the political skills which those in leadership positions need to develop and sustain.

Finally, of course, as has already been stated, all this needs to lead to change. This means that those in leadership positions, while they may be able to call on managers to implement, cannot walk away from the outcomes of an exercise in examination of change without retaining a responsibility to ensure that implementation will happen.

I want to turn now to the notions of leadership that are broadly covered by the term "distributed leadership". While this term has a set of meanings (Bennett et al., 2003), core amongst them is the notion that leadership arises in a range of places within an organisation, and that expertise is not concentrated in one place. This chapter then is attempting to analyse leadership development issues not only for the most senior colleagues in an organisation but for all those who may wish or who may be called on to tell the truth with energy. Nonetheless, it remains true that leadership elements within a role are more and more concentrated at the higher the position in an organisation, and that for the senior tier of staff, leadership will be most of what they do, while for more junior posts leadership will be selective and less frequent. While distributed leadership has associated values of collegiality and of open and more democratic approaches, which I share and aspire to, I do not in fact think it has to be so associated (for example, in a hierarchical organisation such as found in the armed forces, expertise and responsibility are also widely distributed). This leads me to identify the need for a leadership development strategy that addresses both the need for those moving towards more senior posts and for a more widespread strategy in support of the distributed concept.

25.7 THE OPEN UNIVERSITY UK LEADERSHIP DEVELOPMENT PROGRAMME

The Open University UK conceived a Leadership Development Programme (LDP) in 1998, which ran for some 5 years. It was the brainchild primarily of Alan Bassindale, then a pro vice chancellor, from whom I was able to gather information (Bassindale, 2006). There were number of objectives set for the scheme:

- to develop individual leaders, and to include in particular those who would be post holders at senior level in the future;
- to set an agenda that would support leadership throughout the organisation;
- to enhance work in teams through the use of learning sets; and
- to break down silos across organisational boundaries and staff categories.

There was the desire by the University's senior management to change the culture by identifying "rising stars" who would be supported into career development at more senior levels. While there was broad support, it was not universal, with some heads of department believing this would be a distraction from day-to-day tasks. However, the LDP was established and over three presentations supported some seventy-five people. The programme was built around both external inputs from a range of contributors on leadership from various contexts, but put even more weight on team-based work in learning sets. This was a considerable investment by the University in both time and money, and it was clear to participants that the institution was taking a significant interest in them as individuals. Informal evaluation suggests that a significant number of participants, though by no means all, were promoted to new posts within 2 years or so of finishing the LDP, and that this was evidenced by an unusual bulge in the number of promotions, secondments and new posts. Units who received seconded staff were reported as having highly valued them. It was also felt by the University that new talent had been uncovered through this scheme. Some heads of department made the criticism that the LDP did not provide benefits directly to the unit, but this was perhaps a misunderstanding of where the benefits were primarily intended to accrue (i.e. at the institutional level).

It is also questionable whether it has yet adequately changed the nature of management as a whole in the university, where there has tended to be a dependency culture on senior management, as distributed leadership was not adequately in place. The situation was understood to be increasingly dangerous for an institution that had to rethink its role for a higher education system and a society that was markedly different from that in which it had flourished with relatively little change through the 1970s and 1980s.

Clearly the culture of leadership in the institution is in transition, and there is some way to go. The LDP has been replaced more recently by a Senior Leadership Programme (SLP) which is more explicit in selecting people already in senior roles rather than from those aspiring to them from a middle tier in the organisation.

We see in these interventions attempts by a major distance and e-learning institution to invent avenues for leadership development, which have had some success in changing the culture and practice. The programmes have worked both to address the future leadership needs of the university, and within that wider approach with a clear commitment to the notions of distributed leadership, and in the more recent programme to current leadership. It is worth noting that activity of this sort creates turbulence for the institution as a whole, where hierarchies are challenged by those who have had their horizons raised through leadership development. Interventions on such a scale are of course the privilege of a large and well-resourced institution. They also raise the question as to the need to balance leadership development from inside the organisation with recruitment of colleagues from outside who can challenge the culture and practice. External recruitment also of course contributes substantially to leadership development for distance and e-learning. There can be preciousness in institutions of a special type that have distance and e-learning as their sole or dominant modes of activity about the secret garden that they represent. Such protectionism represents a kind of immature or naïve professionalism in seeking to erect barriers to those who seek to enter from outside.

The OU UK has therefore in the recent period made a substantial investment both in the development of leadership in a distributed sense and in the more selective sense of those already in senior management positions. As the University moves out of the first phase of its history after some 35 years, this investment will surely be seen to have been critical in assuring that the second phase can be identified and achieved as one of the significant further contribution to social justice and educational innovation rather than decline.

25.8 LEADERSHIP DEVELOPMENT FOR DISTANCE AND E-LEARNING

I now want to review what might be the content and process for leadership development activity for distance and e-learning. This will be built on the three pillars of the specific distance and e-learning domain as it has been set out here, namely technology-supported learning; the political, social and educational environments; and values. It will be assumed that access to management education can be provided in order to ensure that core competences can be secured where they do not already exist.

From this basis, it is clear that leadership development needs to ensure

- knowledge of the current state of play in terms of technologies that support learning, and the capacity to stay updated;
- knowledge of main competitor activities and how to say abreast of them;
- understanding of the ways in which technologies can provide market leadership in a range of fields, e.g. Internet sales and other activities where the customer is distanced from the product;
- understanding of the ways in which service provides market leadership and of where and how this is developing;
- knowledge of the post-secondary and higher education policy arenas domestically and internationally, of main competitors and trends and of how to analyse such developments;
- knowledge of demographies nationally and internationally and trends of educational aspiration and qualification;
- knowledge of the contested value base for education and capacity to negotiate, develop and steer a value base that offers leadership within the institution;
- understanding of the courage needed for leadership and the capacity to support others as well as oneself;
- capacity to assess, manage and contribute to alliance building within an organisation; and
- knowledge and competence to work in and build teams in a variety of roles.

It is clear that an LDP that attempts to provide the basis for such knowledge, understanding and competences needs to develop by

- exposure to external speakers on environments and trends in technologies for learning, social and educational policy and major organisational change processes in a range of industries, especially those serving customers "at a distance";
- team-based case study and problem-solving projects;
- development and rehearsal of performance through role plays;
- engagement with key texts in leadership studies; and
- mentoring and personal support.

It is clear that leadership development organised within such parameters will demand sophisticated support from a training and development function, and support from senior management for the commitment of resources.

25.9 INTER-INSTITUTIONAL AND INTERNATIONAL LEADERSHIP DEVELOPMENT

Irlbeck, in an article on leadership in distance education in the USA, comments that there is "little education for the management of this field" (Irlbeck, 2002, p. 3). Her judgement is true not just for the USA. The reasons for this may be manifold, but a plausible hypothesis for part of the explanation is that institutions do not have the resources to manage this on their own. One approach that has not been adequately prioritised by the field, in my view, has been the need for leadership development on an inter-institutional and international basis. There have been some interventions in this field on an international basis, both by UNESCO for leadership in education more widely and by the Commonwealth of Learning in the field of distance and e-learning more specifically. The International Council for Distance Education (ICDE) also through its Standing Conference of Presidents (SCOP), bringing together institutional heads, makes an informal contribution to this sphere of activity. The Masters Programme in Distance Education offered by University College University of Maryland and the University of Oldenburg has offered a course in this field.

However, the field of senior management in distance and e-learning is now of a critical mass and is increasing in its sphere of operation across all continents to such an extent that this issue becomes urgent. The range of organisational development activities that are represented at an international level in conferences and workshops does not offer much in the ways of opportunity for discussion and development of leadership. The aspiration to change this is now at least timely and perhaps urgent. There is enough evidence of success in leadership to demonstrate that the ability to mount such professional development programmes exists and enough evidence of institutional decline or failure to recognise that this task is important. For all institutions, the challenges that competition poses are accelerating. Even more crucially, offering educational opportunity at scale and at quality in order to meet the challenges of social justice and national and economic development are no less pressing. The field has therefore everything to gain from developing current and future leaders together, and indeed to support their movement from one institution and organisation to another. If this chapter were to stimulate the institutions and professional organisations to examine how this could be done, supporting co-operation within a competitive environment, it will have served a valuable purpose.

25.10 CONCLUSIONS

To return to Beaudoin, I support his view that what is needed in leadership in distance and e-learning above all is an understanding of and commitment to change (Beaudoin, 2004, p. 91). This does not mean to say that there is an entirely separate field of practice in distance and e-learning, at least to the extent that only those who come from the field can be expected to provide leadership to it. To identify the need for leadership development in distance and e-learning should not act as a pretext to move back to some naïve and emergent professionalism for distance education that has been evident at some times and in some places, with its insistence that everything in this field was qualitatively different from the so-called conventional education. Such caution does not, however, take away from the specificities of the distance and e-learning field as they have been set out here: the understanding that technologies have a core role in rethinking learning and teaching; that the political and social environments represent a context of challenge rather an assured place; and that the values base has to steer activity and is contested. Nonetheless, we can identify what we seek in those occupying leadership positions, and the field is of a scale and of a character that we have the need to develop leadership skills and qualities for staff from within distance and e-learning institutions, as well as for those who move into them. We should work together across institutions, organisations and continents to make this happen.

NOTES

1. For the best available bibliography of management and leadership in distance education, see Beaudoin (2004, pp. 88–89). It can be cross-referenced with the bibliography of this chapter for an overall account of the literature.

REFERENCES

Bass, B.M. (1985). *Leadership and Performance Beyond Expectations*. New York: The Free Press.

Bassindale, A. (2006). Personal communication.

Beaudoin, M. (2004). *Reflections on Research, Faculty and Leadership in Distance Education*. Band 8, Studien und Berichte der Arbeitstelle Fernstudienforschung der Carl von Ossietsky Universität, Bibliotheks-und Informationssystems der Universität Oldenburg, Germany.

Bell, R. and Tight, M. (1993). *Open Universities: A British Tradition?* Society for Research into Higher Education, Buckingham: Open University Press.

Bennett, N., Wise, C., Woods, P., and Harvey, J. (2003). *Distributed Leadership*. Report for the National College for School Leadership. Retrieved October 1, 2006 from http://www.ncsl.org.uk/media/3C4/A2/distributed-leadership-literature-review.pdf.

Daniel, J. (1996). *Mega-Universities and Knowledge Media: Technology Strategies for Higher Education*. London: Kogan Page.

Irlbeck, S. (2002). Leadership and distance education in higher education: A US perspective. *International Review of Research in Open and Distance Learning*, 3(2). Retrieved October 7, 2006 from http://www.irrodl.org/index.php/irrodl/article/view/91/571.

Latchem, C. and Hann, D. (2001). *Leadership for 21st Century Learning: Global Perspectives from Educational Innovators*. London: Kogan Page.

Panda, S. (Ed.) (2003). *Planning and Management in Distance Education*, London: Kogan Page.

Paul, R. (1990). *Open Learning and Open Management: Leadership and Integrity in Distance Education*. London: Kogan Page.

Rumble, G. (1992). The Management of Distance Learning Systems, International Institute for Educational Planning, Fundamentals of Educational Planning 43, UNESCO, Paris.

Tait, A. (2003). The management of services to students. In *Planning and Management in Distance Education* (S. Panda ed.) London: Kogan Page, pp. 155–169

Tait, A. (2004). On institutional models and concepts of student support services: the case of the Open University UK. In *Learner Support in Open, Distance and Online Learning Environments* (J. Brindley, C. Walti and O. Zawacki-Richter eds) Band 9, Studien und Berichte der Arbeitstelle Fernstudienforschung der Carl von Ossietsky Universität, Bibliotheks-und Informationssystems der Universität Oldenburg, Germany, pp. 283–293.

Tait, A. and Mills, R. (1999). *The Convergence of Distance and Conventional Education: Patterns of Flexibility for the Individual Learner*. London: Routledge.

Chapter 26

Preparing Teachers and Learners for New Forms of Assessment

Robin Mason

26.1 THE ASSESSMENT CRISIS

Assessment processes are known to be one of the most powerful influences on learning (Ramsden, 1992), yet most instructors treat assessment as a necessary evil, or at best, an add-on at the end of the course. This "head in the sand" approach is not only ineffective and a waste of resources, but is actually damaging to learners. Research on assessment practices and experience of teachers and learners confirm the fact that the negative side effects of much assessment have long lasting, counter-productive outcomes (Rust et al., 2005). If learners perceive assessment as primarily to examine content knowledge, they will tend to do little more than rote learning. If course materials are over-burdened with factual content, the result is commonly a poor level of overall understanding. Where learners feel anxious or threatened, they are more likely to adopt mechanical, surface approaches to tasks (Gibbs, 1992; Tang, 1994).

In this chapter I examine current assessment practices and consider a wide range of alternative methods and approaches for integrating assessment with learning.

26.2 THE NEED TO RETHINK ASSESSMENT

Most current assessment practices fall into the following trap – we know they don't assess the real learning we think is taking place, but they are the only methods we have that promise high validity, reliability and ease of marking. Traditional multiple-choice exams are limited in their ability to evaluate complex thinking, deep understanding or skill in applying theoretical knowledge to real problems. Their strength typically lies in their ability to evaluate knowledge of facts and understanding of concepts. In order to assess learners' ability to use what they know to solve complex problems, to communicate their understanding or to work together cooperatively, different types of assessment must be used. A true test should engage the learner – in making judgements, interacting with others, in short, in doing something worth doing so that others can observe and evaluate it. "A true test provides [the learner] with opportunities to apply their knowledge and skills to enduring and emerging issues and problems – ill-defined problems – and it requires the integration of discipline-based knowledge and general skills." (Huba and Freed, 2000, p. 221). Too often discussions of assessment are reduced to a discourse on measurement.

It has been argued (Boud, 2000) that traditional assessment fails to provide opportunities for learners to learn the very thing they most need to know: how to assess their own learning. One of the aims of education must surely be to prepare learners for an increasingly unknowable future. There is a need for universities to offer opportunities for learners to reach not just immediate course-related goals but much wider learning and self-development goals.

Existing assessment practices frequently dis-empower learners and put the control and the judgement of learning in the hands of the assessors and tutors. For a learning society, it is the individual learners who need to develop the skills to assess their own and others' materials, to make judgements about quality and value, to give and receive feedback. One of the most significant tasks of the tutor is to help students develop these lifelong learning skills.

26.3 THEORETICAL FRAMEWORK

Many authors have defined the basic attributes of good assessment (e.g. Ramsden, 1992; Brown et al., 1996; Rust et al., 2005):

- Assessment should be a vehicle for educational improvement
- It should be explicit in values, aims, criteria and standards
- It should be relevant, authentic and holistic
- It should be reliable, valid and consistent whilst also being flexible enough to cater for diverse learning styles and needs.

However, Biggs (1999) has developed a theoretical framework for the integration of assessment with the whole course design process, which he calls Constructive Alignment. The basic premise of his framework is that the curriculum is designed so that the learning activities and assessment tasks are aligned with the learning outcomes that are intended in the course. (See Figure 26.1).

In short, the learning outcomes, the learning activities and the assessment must all be aligned. The teacher should make clear to the students what they are meant to achieve and then assess them against these criteria. This is a straightforward matter of establishing trust between assessors and assessed which encourages students to take responsibility for their learning.

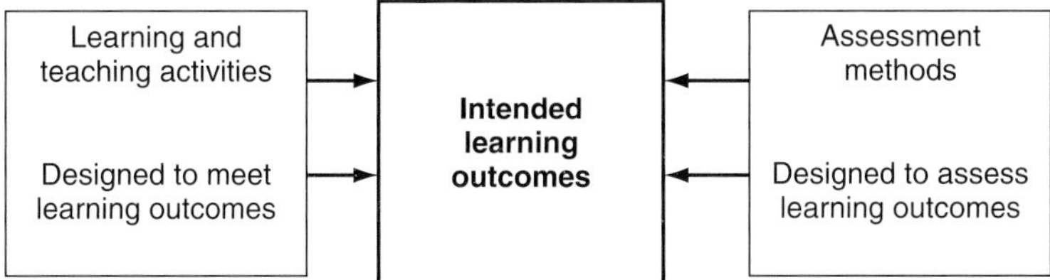

Figure 26.1: Aligning Learning Outcomes, Learning and Teaching Activities and the Assessment (Adapted from Biggs 1999, p. 27).

26.4 ASSESSMENT IN DISTANCE EDUCATION

Traditionally the construction of assignments and examinations are the last tasks undertaken in delivering a subject. This approach may be justified in small classes that meet face-to-face, and where the lecturer knows the class well. Students and the lecturer are able to discuss assessment requirements in class and the lecturer has the opportunity to adapt assessment requirements and/or lectures to better meet the needs of each group. These options are not so readily available when students are not, or not regularly, on campus. Therefore, in distance education, where there are limited opportunities for dialogue between students and teachers, assessment needs to be carefully planned right from the beginning so that it can be integrated within the course as a whole. In fact, experienced designers of distance education courses recommend that after the aims and objectives of a proposed new course have been identified, the assessment methods for each main objective should be the next design element (Rowntree, 1987). This process fits well with the theory of Constructive Alignment, as distance education requires course designers to plan the learning outcomes, the course content and the assessment before the students begin studying.

A well-designed assessment should help develop learners' independent study skills and allow students to assess their own progress. For instructors, assessments should help identify any student misconceptions and provide feedback about the strengths and weaknesses of the study materials. Finally, the assessment process should lead to fair, valid and reliable marking.

Typically the Course Guide, sometimes called a Subject Profile, is one of the first documents that students read because it contains the main details about assessment and assignments. It usually gives assignment topics, resources required, assignment preparation advice, layout, assessment criteria and weightings.

It should also indicate to students any opportunities provided for assignment guidance and feedback like tutorials, either online or face-to-face, and should show students how and when to prepare for these events. The following information should be provided to students about each assignment:

- size (number of words)
- recommended preparation time (hours)

- assignment expectations
- due dates
- suggested workplans and strategies
- assessment criteria (marking scheme)
- how the assignment relates to the subject
- citation and referencing style
- presentation standards (typewritten, cover sheets)
- procedures/penalties for late submission, plagiarism.

The purpose of the assignment should be clear to students. Most distance learners are mature-aged and want to know why they should do an assignment and how it will benefit them in their occupation or further studies. Not only should the purpose of the assignment be explicit, student guidance also should be explicit. Accurate and meaningful assessment of distance education assignments is fundamental to the assignment design process. When providing details about assignments the criteria for successful assignments and the weightings for individual components should be included for both students and tutors. For example, weightings for individual components of an assignment may be specified thus for students:

10 percent	Relevance to topic/question
10 percent	Style
30 percent	Content
30 percent	Problem analysis
10 percent	Structure of Essay
10 percent	Use of Resources/Referencing

26.5 THE ROLE OF FEEDBACK

Providing meaningful feedback to students about their assignments is an effective teaching strategy. Ideally, the role of feedback is to promote educational dialogue between the instructor and the student. Feedback can be presented in a number of ways.

- Model answers may be presented on paper, audio or video tape (depending upon the type of assignment set). Preparation of model answers may also help the teacher by clarifying assignment tasks and ensuring that they are workable, and reducing the amount of marking time or time required to guide tutors.
- Audio conferences or personal telephone calls can be used to provide students with feedback on their assignments and deal with common errors.
- Computer conferences can be used to provide a general overview of the student assignments: what was answered well, what was not, what the range of marks was etc.
- Email and email lists can be used to provide quick feedback and dialogue opportunities to students with online access.
- Exchanging assignments between students for critical comment and/or peer assessment can be useful especially if students can choose projects from a range of topics. Students may be given an opportunity to revise their work before submission for assessment.

26.6 CHEATING IN THE ONLINE ENVIRONMENT

While plagiarism is hardly a new problem in higher education, it has taken on new dimensions with the billions of pages of information "freely" available to students on the Internet. There is considerable evidence that plagiarism is a growing problem (e.g. Hickman, 1998; Walker, 1998; Cavalier, 2005). It takes a number of forms:

- Phrases and passages used verbatim without quotation marks or reference to the author
- Paraphrasing an author's work without a reference
- Taking material found on the web – text, images, graphics – and inserting it into an assignment without acknowledgement or permission
- Submitting an assignment written by someone else as one's own work.

It goes without saying that all of these forms of plagiarism are very much easier with the web, and it is common knowledge that sites exist where students can buy assignments – either "off the shelf" or "tailor made" (Groak et al., 1998). A number of studies have investigated the practice from the student perspective. The first problem they identify is student ignorance of:

- how and when to paraphrase
- how to reference correctly
- the basic rules of copyright, and particularly that web material is not copyright free
- what constitutes plagiarism.

An example of such research is the detailed analysis of both deliberate and unintentional reasons for plagiarizing produced by the University of Alberta, available at http://www.library.ualberta.ca/guides/plagiarism/index.cfm. The article notes that: The idea that an author has "ownership" of language may be a ludicrous concept to students from different cultures. In some cultures, copying someone else's words or ideas is a high form of flattery. The notion that words can be "owned" is a facet of Western culture.

The second problem lies in the nature of assignments set by the instructor. Tasks that require regurgitation rather than application and interpretation and poor instructions or guidelines as to what is required are both highlighted as leading students to take an instrumental approach to assessment. Where assignments are perceived as a hurdle to get over, rather than an integral part of the learning experience of the course, students will respond accordingly, using whatever means are at their disposal. The web provides an almost tailor-made solution.

This raises the most telling aspect of plagiarism as we struggle with information overload: surely we should be actively encouraging students to demonstrate an ability to use and re-use the material on the web, rather than forcing them "to go underground". If we rethink assessment, surely we can devise assignments that value the skill of synthesizing existing material, of applying it to individual contexts, of selecting, transforming and critiquing it. As the curriculum evolves with the impact of the web, these "process" skills are more important for the digital age than content knowledge.

In fact, rethinking the nature of assignments is the approach favoured by most academic researchers on plagiarism. Best practice advice includes assignments which require students to:

- use their own experiences
- apply ideas to their own or at least to real world contexts
- work collaboratively with their peers
- negotiate the assessment process with the instructor.

Nevertheless, many institutions are also pursuing technology-based approaches to the growth of plagiarism. Software has been devised to check for verbatim use of web materials, but this is costly and slows down the marking procedures and in time would lead clever cheaters to change the appropriate number of words to defeat the program. In fact, the threat of random use of such software might be as effective as the actual use of it.

A more problematic form of cheating in online courses centres on the identity of the student receiving the final accreditation. Distance education institutions have operated a system of remote examination sites with various procedures for ensuring that the student who sits the exam is the student who originally registered and eventually graduates. With the advent of online courses, offering access to higher education to a whole range of potential students needing flexible learning, there is a great demand for completely location-free study options. Furthermore, online courses attract a global student body, which makes place-based examinations difficult and expensive to operate. The problem is, "how can totally online procedures ensure that students are not cheating?" Of course a wide variety of cheating is practised on campuses which have the benefit of student identity cards, invigilated exams and security procedures to handle question papers. So we cannot demand 100 percent certainty, but we must look for "reasonable assurance". Even so, the greatest activity in this direction seems to be talk and speculation; no one claims to have solutions, despite there being great interest and demand for procedures which allow individual students to take examinations from home (or indeed any other location) without any certified person on site.

Regarding web-based examinations, the problem is who or how many are answering the multiple choice questions? Some technological approaches look to webcams which someone from a central site can use to "identify" the student at the other end. Iris identification is another hoped-for solution. Neither are foolproof – because someone could be seated nearby and passing answers to the identified student.

Regarding timed essay-type final examinations the problem of international time zones is also problematic. One solution is to have two different papers and two different exam times, so that no student will have to write the exam during the night-time.

With untimed, project-type final "examinations", the problem is being reasonably sure that it is the registered student who does the background work and writes the essay. Some approaches to this include

- requiring a person of local standing to sign a document stating it is the student's own work
- setting a task so rooted in the course work or the student's context and experience that no one else could write it
- insisting that the student submit photocopies of all documented or referenced material along with their own work.

In fact, it could be argued that on courses where there is extensive online interaction amongst students and with the tutor, there is much more active involvement with the student, and hence it is more readily apparent if a student's final assessed work is radically different from their written interactions during the course.

26.7 ASSESSMENT METHODS

The following methods all have their pitfalls, but they attempt to counteract some of the shortcomings of traditional assignments and examinations. Most of them offer opportunities for self-assessment and are easily adaptable to the Constructive Alignment Framework.

26.7.1 Learning Contracts

Learning contracts are usually individually negotiated processes between the learner and the instructor, in which an individual programme of study is mutually agreed in order to achieve specified outcomes. The following elements are usual in the contract:

- The learner's personal objectives
- The specification of a coherent body of knowledge to be mastered
- An agreed timetable
- Resources that can be accessed
- Support from the organization (sponsor, mentor or line manager).

Learning contracts are ideal for negotiating non-standard programmes of learning that reflect personal and, in the case of workplace learning contracts, employer needs.

Brown and Knight (1994) describe four stages in learning contract development:

1. Constructing a profile of the skills, knowledge and understanding of the learner
2. Specifying the learning outcomes to be achieved
3. Devising an action plan either individually or in small groups or with a tutor, to identify timescales, resources and actions
4. Evaluation of how successfully the learning outcomes have been met.

26.7.2 E-portfolios

An e-portfolio is personal digital record containing information such as a personal profile and collection of achievements. E-portfolios represent a move towards learner-centred, self-directed, autonomous learning. Primarily they help users define and reflect on their learning; in addition, their use increases students' IT skills and develops their digital literacy.

The process of collecting and selecting items for the e-portfolio is made easier because users can hold, organize and reorder contents easily and quickly. Being able to go back and re-work various components of the portfolio is a significant advantage of electronic portfolios. As a method of end-of-course assessment, e-portfolios provide many opportunities to integrate all of the student's work on the course and to connect new ideas with the student's existing knowledge and context. Collections can be the work of an individual, or assembled and shared by a group.

The value of using an e-portfolio is that reflection over time increases a learner's ability to make sense of concrete experience. Realization of competencies comes through reflection on activities and products that the student experiences and generates in a social context (Cambridge and Cambridge, 2003).

26.7.3 Projects

As a form of assessment, projects have to involve set goals. Participants should demonstrate a project plan, use of resources, anticipated and actual outcomes. It might involve the development of a product, in which case both the process and the quality of reasoning that led to it are evaluated. Projects can be carried out individually or through group work; they can be assessed by the instructor, the group or the individual. Applying criteria and making judgements are high-level learning activities, and the learning value of self-assessing and/or peer-assessing is often much higher than that of undertaking the assessed task on its own. Even more, when learners are involved in formulating and prioritising assessment criteria to use in peer-assessment, this activity in its own right has considerable learning benefit relating to the learning outcomes being addressed by the assessment (Race, 2001, p. 21).

26.7.4 Online Assessment

While many forms of online assessment are simple copies of practices common in traditional, face-to-face teaching environments, others build on the unique properties of the web. Examples copied from traditional environments include

- assessment in the form of portfolios of work
- research and critical review of resources
- computer marked quizzes
- reflective journals
- negotiated learning contracts.

All these have direct online equivalents, though they can be enhanced and improved through web delivery. Examples which have arisen because of the unique properties of the web include

- online debates
- group discussions which form the basis of either individual or group assignments
- individual and collaboratively produced web sites
- peers in remote locations commenting on assignments
- repositories of student assignments for consulting and re-use.

The increased interactivity afforded by the web provides the most exciting area for innovative assessment, especially for distributed learners. The access to a wider range of resources as well as to fellow learners leads to a new set of skills and understandings that online courses are providing. These should be included in the course aims and objectives and also in the assessment of the course. Networking presents new challenges for designers of assessment where accreditation is involved, because of the need to establish student identity and to ensure that students are aware of guidelines on plagiarism.

Electronic submission and marking of scripts lends itself to the use of a variety of formats in assignments, notably html. This opens up new opportunities for innovative assignments, which encourage research beyond conventional course materials and caters for a variety of interests and levels of experience.

26.7.5 Web-based assessment

Web-based assessment offers much more scope for comprehensive testing of course objectives and student understanding than the old multiple-choice systems (Brown et al., 1999). Examples include fill-in-the-blanks, matching questions, multiple right answers, graphical hotspots, ranking, sequencing, assertion-reason and so on. They are demanding and expensive to develop but are cost effective with large numbers of learners and are particularly appropriate for multi-national training. They are easy to quality assure, to "deliver" and to mark and record. They require very little input from tutors.

The literature on web-based assessment, the software and support tools and the availability of case studies from which to discover the pitfalls are more extensive than the equivalent in the much broader category of online assessment. Software vendors maintain sites full of useful tips, case studies and practice sessions, for example,

- http://www.questionmark.com/us/home.htm
- http://www.i-assess.co.uk

Portals on the practice of web-based assessment are also a rich source of resources, tools, papers and FAQs, for example,

- http://www.caacentre.ac.uk/

From these and other sources it is possible to draw a number of conclusions. First of all, learners are generally positive about this type of assessment because of:

- the immediate feedback and grading (if applicable)
- the convenience and flexibility for part-time and remote learners
- the clarity and objectivity of the procedures
- the fact that they are less demanding than other forms of assessment.

However, there is growing evidence that the most useful application of web-based assessment is for formative and self-assessment strategies rather than as summative and graded assessment. Innovative practitioners are beginning to regard web-based assessment as part of the learning process, by building in extensive feedback, opportunities to go back and re-do the tests, especially as a revision exercise, and as an integrated activity with simulations and other interactive teaching materials.

A further benefit was noted by these adult distance teaching researchers:

> Our discussions with some of the non-native English speakers in the class and our observations of the performance of these students indicated that this group might have especially benefited from the web-based assessment regime employed in this module. Informal survey of these students indicated that most found it easier to express their knowledge within this assessment strategy than by writing essay responses to exam questions, the norm in many of our courses. In addition, we noticed that a number of these students showed substantial improvements in their assessment scores through the module.
>
> (Baggott and Rayne, 2001, p. 7)

Where instructors are using web-based assessment as a means of reducing their marking workload, the results are somewhat less positive. Many novices to the process have discovered that writing good multiple choice questions is challenging and time-consuming. The use of multimedia – graphics, photos, audio clips and simulations – broadens considerably the types of question that can be set, but usually means the process of assessment design becomes a team production requiring IT support and even developmental testing.

26.8 PREPARING TEACHERS AND STUDENTS

Students who have developed effective techniques for obtaining high marks on traditional exams and assessments, who have successful exam strategies and who, consciously or unconsciously, have learned to adapt their study approach to the nature of the examination process, may not welcome the move to innovatory assessment processes. Helping them, as well as weaker students, has to be part of the change process.

An obvious way of preparing students for the move away from traditional assignments and examinations is the process of scaffolding. Essentially this involves moving gradually from the traditional to the more innovative, whilst providing explanatory material, tutor support and explicit instructions and marking guidelines. Formative assessments, which do not count towards the final grade, but which provide extensive feedback, are another useful form of scaffolding. Iterative assignments help students learn from feedback, by submitting a revised version of the same assignment, having considered the remarks of the tutor. This process can be combined with peer feedback, whereby the revised assignment is accompanied by comments made by the student on the work of two other students. By completing the feedback loop in this way, students are encouraged to see assessment in a wider context and to develop their ability to assess written work themselves.

Teachers are, on the whole, well aware of the shortcomings of traditional assessment practices. However, articles underlining the destructive effects of assessment on students' learning should be made available to them as part of staff development (see, e.g. AUTC, 2002). At the same time, case studies of new approaches such as portfolios, online assessment, contracts and so on should be offered with a view to generating ideas and broadening awareness. There are, of course, drawbacks or at least challenges to all of these innovative assessment processes, and these should not be minimized.

Many of these innovatory forms of assessment rely on a mature, self-directed and highly motivated learner to be most effective. It may be, therefore, that introducing new forms of assessment at post-graduate and Masters level is advisable until teachers have built up their expertise and confidence in the new methods.

In terms of computer-marked assignments, a more concerted form of staff development is required involving desk research, trials, pilot testing and real teamwork.

26.9 IMPLICATIONS OF INNOVATIVE ASSESSMENT STRATEGIES

While the problems of cheating and the need for improved learning outcomes from assessment indicate that a rethinking of assessment strategies is required, it is important to look at the impact this will have on students and online tutors. Feedback from the early adopters of innovative assessment strategies reveals some of the implications.

The first point to note is that innovative programme design has vastly outstripped innovative assessment design in online courses. A number of studies document the mismatch students have experienced between the philosophy of student-centred learning espoused by the course (e.g. a participative, less hierarchical approach to teaching and learning, tutor as guide etc.) and the teacher-centred approach to assessment, where the assessor is still all-powerful, objective and controlling (see Trehan and Reynolds, 2001). On one resource-based learning course, students were encouraged to develop the skill of browsing and selecting material to study in depth, but were then confronted by a traditional examination where they were unsure that they had covered the right materials (Macdonald et al., 1999). Best practice always underlines the need for the assessment strategy to reflect the underlying pedagogy of the course. However, there are tensions becoming increasingly apparent between traditional curricular imperatives, grading policies and institutionally devised evaluative criteria, and the online environment that inhibits such teacher-centred approaches and has defined a new role for the online tutor. McConnell (1997) highlights the contradiction between the intensively supportive and encouraging role of the online tutor and the need to grade assignments and uphold the institutions quality standards. Lauzon (1999) argues that many online tutors are somewhat unnerved by the multiple forms of authority which the web and online interactions produce. While some educators have avoided online courses because of a perceived undermining of their authority, others have welcomed this levelling effect as a sign of students' new empowerment. Nevertheless, the multiple subjectivities of the online environment, the expectation of being available at all times to students, the relatively louder voice given to student criticism of all aspects of the course, plus the ambiguity of being both guide and assessor, have led to the role of online tutor being challenging and relatively uncharted.

The implications for the assessment of courses with an online component can be summarized as follows:

- Web-assisted assessment has a powerful role to play in a formative and self-testing mode and a contributory role as a diagnostic and summative tool.
- The increased interactivity afforded by the web provides the most exciting area for innovative assessment, especially for distance education. The access to a wider range of resources as well as to fellow students leads to a new set of skills and understandings that online courses are facilitating. These should be included in the course aims and objectives and also in the assessment of the course.
- Networking presents new challenges for designers of assessment, in establishing student identity and in ensuring that students are aware of guidelines on plagiarism.
- Electronic submission and marking of scripts lends itself to the use of a variety of formats in assignments, notably html. This opens up new opportunities for innovative assignments which encourage research beyond conventional course materials and caters for a variety of interests and levels of experience.
- Students and tutors of online courses need considerable support in adapting to the new demands of the online environment. As assessment is the most critical point of the process, this is where support is most needed: clarity in the requirements of assessment, openness regarding the marking procedures and flexibility in the demands of the assignments are some of the ways in which this support can be demonstrated.

26.10 SELF ASSESSMENT

Black and Wiliam (1998) argue that students should be trained in self-assessment so that they can understand the main purposes of their learning and thereby grasp what they need to do to achieve. Teachers will need to help students develop their self-assessment capabilities, by providing them with appropriate models of this way of working. For example, many teachers now require students to indicate the strengths and weaknesses of their work as part of the assignment.

Nicol and Macfarlane-Dick (2004) argue that:

> The student or learner is always engaged in monitoring gaps between internally set task and personal goals and the outcomes that are being progressively produced. This monitoring is a by-product of purposeful engagement in a task. However, in order to build on this process, and the student's capacity for self-regulation, teachers should create more formal and structured opportunities for self-monitoring and the judging of progression to goals. Self-assessment tasks are a good way of doing this, as are activities that encourage reflection on both the processes and the products of learning.
>
> (p. 3).

These authors conclude that increasing students' motivation and self-esteem can be enhanced by designing into courses multiple opportunities for formative feedback rather than one or two summative assignments.

26.11 CONCLUSION

From the description of alternative approaches, a tension is apparent between assessment processes that are too focused on skills development and hence miss the wider value of learning, and those that are too process oriented and hence miss the point of the original learning objective. Finding the appropriate balance between these two extremes is always the aim.

A second tension lies in the balance between pedagogical effectiveness on the one hand and the practicalities of marking, providing reliability and assuring validity.

Implicit in this whole analysis is that the role of the instructor is even more vital than before:

- with web-based assessment, there is considerable skill needed to devise appropriate, challenging and workable questions
- with most other assessment methods, the instructor needs to understand the relationship between course content, outcomes and assessment methods, and to identify real criteria for assessment.

Given the impact and importance of assessment on student learning, it follows that instructors should give the design of assessment processes no less attention than they accord to the content of the course. In distance education especially, assessment can play a vital part in overall student learning in addition to being an opportunity for judging student performance and assigning a grade.

REFERENCES

AUTC. (2002). Online assessment. Retrieved 25 February, 2006 from http://www.cshe.unimelb.edu.au/assessinglearning/03/online.html.

Baggott, G.K. and Rayne, R.C. (2001). Learning support for mature, part-time, evening students: providing feedback via frequent computer-based assessment. Loughborough: Fifth International CAA Conference.

Biggs, J. (1999). *Teaching for Quality Learning at University*. Buckingham: SRHE and Open University Press.

Black, P. and Wiliam, D. (1998). Assessment and classroom learning. *Assessment in Education*, **5**(1), 7–74.

Boud, D. (2000). Sustainable assessment: Rethinking assessment for the learning society. *Studies in Continuing Education*, **22**(2), 151–167.

Brown, S. and Knight, P. (1994). *Assessing Learners in Higher Education*. London: Kogan Page.

Brown, S., Race, P., and Smith B. (1996). "An Assessment Manifesto" from 500 Tips on Assessment. London: Kogan Page. Retrieved 25 February, 2006 from http://www.lgu.ac.uk/deliberations/assessment/manifest.html.

Brown, S., Race, P., and Bull, J. (1999). *Computer Assisted Assessment in Higher Education*. London: Kogan Page.

Cambridge, B. and Cambridge, D. (2003). The future of electronic portfolio technology: Supporting what we know about learning. *ePortfolio 2003*. Poitiers, France.

Cavalier, R. (2005). *The Impact of the Internet on our Moral Lives*. New York: SUNY Press.

Gibbs, G. (1992). *Improving the Quality of Student Learning*. Bristol: Technical and Educational Services.

Groak, M., Oblinger, D., and Choa, M. (1998). Term paper mills, anti-plagiarism tools, and academic integrity. *Educause Review*, **36**(5), 40–48.

Hickman, J. (1998). Cybercheats. *The New Republic*, 218, 23 March, 14–15.

Huba, M. and Freed, J. (2000). *Learner-Centered Assessment on College Campuses*. Boston: Allyn and Bacon.

Lauzon, A.C. (1999). Situating cognition and crossing borders: Resisting the hegemony of mediated education. *British Journal of Educational Technology*, **30**(3), 261–276.

Macdonald, J., Mason, R., and Heap, N. (1999). Refining assessment for resource based learning. *Assessment and Evaluation in Higher Education*, **24**(3), 345–354.

McConnell, D. (1997). Computer support for management learning. In *Management Learning: Integrating Perspectives in Theory and Practice* (J. Burgoyne and M. Reynolds, eds) London: Sage, pp. 57–75.

Nicol, D. and Macfarlane-Dick, D. (2004). Rethinking formative assessment in HE: A theoretical model and seven principles of good feedback practice. HEA Briefing Document. Retrieved 25 February, 2006 from www.heacademy.ac.uk/assessment/ASS051D_SENLEF_model.doc.

Race, P. (2001). *A Briefing on Self, Peer & Group Assessment. LTSN Generic Centre Series No 9*.York, UK: Learning and Teaching Support Network.

Ramsden, P. (1992). *Learning to Teach in Higher Education*. London: Routledge.

Rowntree, D. (1987). *Assessing Students: How Shall we Know Them?* London: Kogan Page

Rust, C., O'Donovan, B., and Price, M. (2005). *Assessment and Evaluation in Higher Education*, **30**(3), 231–240.

Tang, C. (1994). Effects of modes of assessment on students' preparation strategies. In *Improving Student Learning – Theory and Practice* (G. Gibbs, ed.) Oxford: Oxford Centre for Staff Development.

Trehan, K. and Reynolds, M. (2001). Online collaborative assessment: Power relations and "critical learning". In *Networked Learning: Perspectives and Issues* (C. Steeples and C. Jones, eds) London: Springer, pp. 279–292.

Walker, J. (1998). Student plagiarism in universities, What are we doing about it? *Higher Education Research and Development*, **17**(1), 89–107.

Chapter 27

Leading Student Support Services for New Times

Jennifer Thompson and Sandi Shillington

27.1 INTRODUCTION

This chapter examines the challenges facing universities in supporting and retaining students in a changing educational market place. It also suggests institutional strategies for meeting such challenges.

Massey University is used as a case study to explore pertinent issues facing a long-term dual-mode provider of university education.

The incorporation of the service excellence model is described and the purpose, design, development and implementation of an extensive range of new student support services are outlined. The services developed include a range of on-line services as well as face-to-face and telephonic services.

The support services model is based on a vision to provide "Timely professional support for busy people", which means providing access to success and being able to substantiate the success of these measures.

Having examined best practice across a range of institutions, there was a conscious decision made, not simply to supplement more traditional forms of support, but instead to develop a model of distance support services which would enable the university to meet not only present requirements, but also the demands of emerging contexts.

27.2 THE CHALLENGES

Tait (2003) in looking back over the last 30 years of student support at the Open University in the United Kingdom (UKOU) reflects on the changing world in which students and universities now find themselves. In many ways new technologies have made life easier, but at the same time they have brought their own challenges in terms of providing access to economically disadvantaged students within both developed and developing countries. The nature of work and study are also changing with the growth in the notion of "lifelong learning" and its co-existence with a need for students to be at least in part time employment, living in increasingly crowded conditions which, for them, are not conducive to study.

Modern fiscal arrangements are also dictating a move from seeing students primarily as learners at the metaphorical feet of experts, to a customer/ consumer model where the student seeks both bargains and good service from institutions.

Tait (2003) concludes by pointing out that the new order demands a greater complexity in the provision of programmes and support for students, and that there is "no way back to a simpler world" (p. 196).

Key trends and influences shaping modern Student Support Services:

- *Widening participation and the growing diversity of the student body, including an increasing number of non-traditional students.*

Distance education has become a real option for thousands of students in developing nations across the globe. Many of these students would not have considered tertiary education before, but with governments now increasingly seeing education of their populations as being a way of achieving wealth and prosperity, more non-traditional students are entering the distance education pathway than ever before.

In developed nations, the average age of students has increased and students are more likely to be working at least part-time. Students see distance education as a way of juggling other commitments with study and so are undertaking distance study as a lifestyle option.

Students living with disabilities are able to utilize the distance mode to overcome sometimes very significant disabilities, and thus join the world of learners. For some, the ability to be "online" without disclosing their disability allows them to participate in ways never possible before (Bowker and Tuffin, 2002).

- *Developing nations may not have immediate access to the more modern technologies, nor may they have students who are able to utilize them. Finding bridges to meet needs and overcome skill deficiencies is essential.*

Although the uptake of new technologies is perhaps even more rapid in developing nations than elsewhere, there is still a significant number of learners for whom new technologies remain inaccessible. This is as true for students living in the far north of Canada as it is for students living in Southern Africa or remote Pacific Islands.

- *Changing learner expectations about the provision and delivery of student services in an increasingly customer-focused and learner-centred culture.*

The concept of lifelong education does not include the concept of staying with one provider for life. In an increasingly commercial view of education the focus has changed irrevocably from that of dutiful student to a consumer/customer model where students will be keenly aware of cost and quality and will demand high levels of service from their educational provider, or else seek another provider.

- *Growing demand from staff and students for an increasingly flexible approach to the delivery of student services, especially the use of online delivery.*

Modern technology has the potential to allow for study at any time and at any place. However, the reality is that a totally flexible approach to study comes with caveats in the form of difficulties in establishing an interactive community of learners, and difficulties for institutions in knowing whether students have dropped out or are simply taking a "breather" before continuing. Human nature is such that many people will fail to complete courses of study, unless there are explicit deadlines. The increased need to use personal time for study at the expense of sleep or family life further exacerbates the problem. Likewise, staff may not see the need to have formal office hours or even to offer regular "online times". The obverse is that staff may find having to communicate constantly by e-mail with an ever-changing student body simply too demanding of their time and often their personal space. Mason (2001) reports that student demands for instant feedback results in staff having to devote excessive time to this activity which often leads to "interaction fatigue".

- *Increasing costs at a time of decreasing government funding.*

The proportion of funding supplied to universities by governments appears to be on the decline in many parts of the world. Universities must find new income streams or else suffer financial difficulties. The temptation to withdraw from the provision of apparently "add on" support is obvious. This can only be countered by the demonstration of improvements in retention of students, and the rise in "retention strategies" and student-focused units amongst universities has been an outcome of this trend.

- *The increased emphasis on transnational distance education, where institutions are having to move swiftly to retain their position in the market place or risk losing out to competitors, means the focus may not be on providing the support needed.*

The rush by institutions to provide tertiary education for the emerging superpower – China – has a significant impact on the ability or willingness of institutions to focus on the provision of quality support for students. In a climate where time is of the essence in order to gain market share, it is difficult to see how this can be achieved in conjunction with the development of quality services.

- *High levels of enthusiasm for new technologies may override an understanding of what students want or require.*

The digital divide has been much discussed elsewhere (White, 2003). However, there is another divide that is perhaps just as pertinent for universities and that is the divide between the proponents of "e-learning" and those who ascribe to a more traditional form of distance education. Clearly there is a need for both, and, along with this, a real understanding of the pedagogical advantages or disadvantages of any particular delivery system ahead of a "bells and whistles", or alternatively a fiscal, approach.

- *An understanding of who students are, through careful market research and involvement of students in the development of services, will ameliorate misunderstandings and prevent unnecessary expenditure.*

With the increased focus on the customer–consumer approach comes an increased need to understand the demographics of the particular student body attached to a particular university. Without this, there will be little understanding of the requirements or wants of such students. This may result in unnecessary expenditure on services that are no longer required or relevant, or, alternatively, a deficiency in the level of support supplied.

27.3 PLANNING A RESPONSE TO THE CHALLENGES

Relatively little has been written about the planning and management of distance learning support, although there is an extensive body of research literature on distance education that can inform our response to the challenges.

Researchers have outlined the limitations of past attempts to provide support services. Initially services were conceived of in terms of counselling and health issues (Quintrell, 1985). Evidence of this early association can be seen in the medical connotations surrounding learning support particularly in the implication that support services staff were there to "cure" some "deficiency" (Chanock, 1995, p. 32). Failure (or success) was regarded solely as the responsibility of the individual student. It enabled the blame for failure to be placed on the student rather than on institutional practices. Assistance was transmitted to the student by experts rather than being based on the belief that the student was an individual who would actively participate as an equal in their own emotional and intellectual development. Tinto (1987) notes that the work of support services staff was often viewed as remedial, something outside the "real" academic work of the institution and divorced from the discipline-specific teaching role of academics. In the past many support services were based on an assimilationist process: fitting the student to the institution. Little concern was given to the necessity of paying more attention to considering the needs of individual students.

A report by The Commonwealth of Learning (1993) records a change in perceptions regarding support services and some evolution in support theory and practice. It refers to the awareness of a need to move beyond providing only generic, remedial and supplemental services that were directed exclusively to helping distressed students. Instead the modern model involves a more holistic and expanded role for support services that also provides resources, which are directed towards "the intellectual and personal development of students as well as their problems" (p. iii). The report also outlines "the progression towards a higher priority for students services in the policies and activities of distance education institutions" (p. 2).

More recent research outlines the need for more flexibility and willingness for the institution to adapt to the needs of the student. Noting the need for this more learner-centred approach, White (2003) emphasises the necessity to respond to individual distance learners and their response to distance learning contexts. The need to be aware of the diverse cultural and social backgrounds of individual learners and the impact that this has on their way of learning, and their interaction with others in a learning environment, is essential.

Understanding the dynamics of the impact of the social dimension of online environments on students" learning experiences is another challenge for support services staff. Gunawardena and Zittle's (1998) research examines knowledge construction in online learning communities. They draw attention to the need to understand how learners actively influence each other's learning experiences, knowledge and understanding through the social networks created online. Anderson (2005) also draws our attention to the challenges of supporting the building of communities of learners online.

The challenge of providing for different cultures must also be taken into consideration. The learner support practices associated with distance learning have for the most part been designed and implemented in developed nations. As online learning is increasingly used as the vehicle for the delivery of support services to diverse populations in global settings, there is an urgent need to understand how different cultural influences affect the experience of learners in online learning environments. Jegede (2000) argues that consideration should be given also to the various borders learners need to cross in undertaking distance and online learning, and that relatively little attention is given to their socio-cultural environments which may mediate or inhibit Learning Support Services which need to provide for global markets.

27.3.1 The Challenge of Costs

There are of course significant challenges that arise around the costs in terms of human and financial resources, including what institutions can afford and are able or willing to provide. Simpson (2000, 2002, 2003) asks how we can best support the ever-growing numbers of non-traditional students and also improve their retention rates. He notes the necessity for a more extensive and flexible range of support services (Simpson, 2003) if the experience of these students is not to be akin to what he describes as "educational passchendalism" – that is, allowing a mass of ill-prepared students into courses in the hope that some will pass (Simpson, 2000). Although providing support services may appear to be expensive:

> the costs of not providing such services are even greater in terms of student frustration and failure, wastage of institutional resources and the immeasurable loss to any society of a citizenry lacking the education it desires.
>
> (p. 8)

27.3.2 The Challenge of Technology

Evans and Nation (2000) observe that the technology itself can be a major hurdle for non-traditional learners with limited experience in using computers, and that insufficient consideration has been given to the impact of this additional obstacle for learners.

The ways in which technology is used can also create additional obstacles for learners. Murphy (2000) notes that technology has often been used inappropriately as educators have applied traditional teaching models and methods to the online environment with "screen after screen of content notes which students end up printing out to read later" (p. 2). This inappropriate use also has been applied in the area of student support services.

The challenge for support services providers is to work out how best to use technology and incorporate the principles of constructivism into the delivery of services. Laurillard (1993), emphasising the need for a constructivist approach rather than an instructivist model, provides an outline for the use of technology. She mentions that teaching materials, audio, audiovisual multimedia and print must be used as integral parts of the teaching process rather than as supplements to it. Laurillard argues that "there is no room for mere telling, nor practice without description, nor experimentation without reflection, nor student action without feedback" (p. 85). Oliver (2001) has also emphasised the need for a constructivist approach rather than an instructivist model of learning.

Perraton (2000) cautions against a wholesale introduction of these technologies in distance education services for students in the developing world. Students may be excluded from services because they are unable to afford equipment or gain access to online technologies. They may also face the added obstacle of the shift in costs from producer to user that online support can create. Developing nations may lack the stable government structures, available capital, efficient power supplies, telecommunication links and the service industry necessary to develop and maintain a reliable telecommunications system. In such nations, more conventional delivery systems are likely to be more accessible and affordable for students.

27.3.3 The Importance of Learner Support

Support is becoming a greater component than before. There is an increasing realisation that without support, the number of students who drop out or who go elsewhere for their educational experience will grow. The human face of the university has never been more important than it is now.

The Open University has long provided support for students as might be expected from an institution that is able to offer tertiary level education to a very diverse student body, many of whom will have very different levels of university preparation than universities with limited access. The work of Simpson (2000, 2002, 2003) indicates that the motivation of the student is the most deciding factor in retention. In addition, the support system that a student has outside of the university is primary to the ongoing involvement of the student at university. The student has invested a great deal of time, money and self-esteem in the successful outcome of the proposed course of study. The services put in place by a university are decidedly lower on the ranking of importance to the student, but nonetheless need to support each student's unique support system. Simpson (2000, 2002, 2003) is clear that proactive intervention is vital and is also sure that the "human face" is what makes the difference. In order to achieve an appropriate level of support, largely on line, it is important to develop "self help" strategies for students such as a range of "teasers" that either allow students to get a taste of what the course might contain or, alternatively, give the student and idea of what prior knowledge or skill base is likely to support success in the course. Alternatives can also be suggested if the material appears to be either at too high or too low a level for the student.

Anderson (2005) is perhaps one of the most advanced thinkers in the field of computer-based learning communities and is based at Athabasca University, "*the*" distance University of Canada. It is hardly surprising, therefore, that Athabasca is another distance provider with a very "human face". The system of tutors employed at Athebasca has been in place for a number of years and is well established and highly regarded. In addition, Athabasca provides in-depth interviews with students who need learning support, counselling and careers advice through its free phone system and its website is becoming increasingly user friendly. Further evidence of the importance placed on the development of engaged and immediate computer-based communities is provided by Perry and Edwards (2005).

27.3.4 The Advance of New Technologies

Most universities that have traditionally provided distance education (with some notable exceptions) are moving from paper-based to computer-based delivery formats (at least in part). Those new providers who have not developed a significant paper-based infrastructure are moving even more swiftly into the new technologies to support their deliveries. Indeed there are examples where "defunct universities" are being bought up and turned into distance education providers (Hilsberg, 2005).

However, to be successful, considerable thought and innovation is needed on behalf of the initiator. This thought and innovation cannot be a "once off", instead an ongoing relationship has to be built with the student and an ongoing electronic presence is needed. Williams and Wache (2005) demonstrated the pitfalls of not doing so at the recent ODLAA conference in Adelaide, Australia.

Lockwood (2005) from Manchester Metropolitan University is passionate about the uptake of online components of learning and is excited about the shift over the last 5 years from paper-based to online. However, he is concerned about the "add on" risk whereby new technologies are simply added to existing curricula. The student workload is increased proportionately, and unfairly (Lockwood, 2005).

27.3.5 Flexibility and Timeliness of Services

The development of student portals is in progress at many universities with substantial differences in the level of sophistication and usefulness. Portals, when well developed, can provide a real level of customisation that can deliver a sense of belonging for the student who can access personal information at any suitable time. The University of Delaware provides an excellent example of such a portal. Other portals are still in their infancy and may not display any real level of customisation other than simply a line welcoming the user.

27.3.6 A Case for Paper-Based Delivery

Corry and Lelliot (2003) caution against the blind adoption of technology as a means of reaching students, since many students in developing areas do not have ready access to these technologies. Instead, interactive paper-based materials with responsive and personalised feedback appear to be effective. The University of South Africa serves approximately 250,000 students from Southern Africa and beyond. There are several regional centres where students can drop in for help. The services are supported by peer helpers and assistant counsellors. The distance courses also appear to be paper-based rather than computer-driven. This is not likely to change because of the lack of ready access to computers in the communities forming the student body (van Schoor, personal communication, 20 October 2005).

It is clear that different models of support are being successfully utilised by different institutions, and, to a large part, the nature of services provided depends on the size of the distance component in comparison to the on campus component for that particular university, and also on student demographics appertaining to each university.

27.3.7 Evaluating Possible Model Strategies and Translating these Strategies into Institutional Policy and Practice

Tait (2003) sets out three primary functions of learner support – cognitive, affective and systemic. Support providers need to be aware that support should be given in all three areas and coordinated to result in an improved learning experience for students.

Hicks et al. (1999) have outlined a range of online approaches to the provision of support for students studying in online learning environments at the University of South Australia. Essentially they have developed three forms of online support for students:

- generic, stand-alone resources;
- parallel and adjunct resources closely aligned with the subject/course requirements; and
- integrated support developed as a result of close collaboration between academic and support staff.

These three forms of support can take the form of downloadable text-based documents or interactive online workshops. Generic resources apply across a range of subject areas. However, some skills are more deeply embedded in a field or discipline, and such skills can only be developed in conjunction with the discipline of the field.

Thorpe (2003) reminds us that in traditional approaches to the provision of learning support, the support is something that happens after course content has been created.

However, in an online environment with online interaction and collaboration, much of the content cannot be specified in advance. She notes that "the old model of course design first, learner support second, should be questioned and possibly reversed" (p. 199).

Oliver (2001) provides a very useful framework for the design and development of online resources. Clerehan et al. (2003) also supply a useful description of the development of the Online Student Resource Centre site at Monash University. Tait (2003) offers a framework for the development of a planning tool for student support services.

All too often support services provided online have been little more than printed resources. Oliver (2001) notes that many of the learning support sites put up on the web by universities have too many text-based resources and very few interactive resources. One exception is Monash University's Language and Learning Online site, which provides not only downloadable resources, but also interactive resources including online tutorials and interactive exercises. The site also provides access to resources by faculty and degree type, thereby meeting the need for support embedded in the context of a student's personal study discipline.

Some distance teaching institutions such as the UKOU offer alternative approaches and models for the support of students. One example is the closer co-operation between academic and tutorial staff, and another is the services provided through a network of regional centres and localised study centres. Amongst other services, the study centres provide for some individual and group tutoring. The work of the support staff is not simply to provide remedial services. Many students find face-to-face meetings with staff at the centres to be a valuable and enjoyable part of their studies. (Tait and Entwistle, 1996).

27.4 THE RESPONSE – PLAN AND IMPLEMENTATION

At Massey University, the community of extramural learners is made up of a large number of mature students, a few, more than 80 years of age. Increasingly, New Zealanders can be expected to study extramurally as they age and either have increased leisure time or need to retrain in order to keep on earning an income in the light of the removal of compulsory retirement at 65 and the probable retreat of the age at which government superannuation becomes available. New populations of extramural students may include more Maori and Pacific Island students, as well as foreign full fee paying (FFP) students, as Massey University expands its International Distance portfolio. Clearly support has to be tailored to meet their diverse needs.

Massey University is similar to the UKOU in that it has been providing distance education for approximately 40 years. However, it is unique among New Zealand universities in its tradition of provision of quality, accessible distance or "extramural" education. This tradition makes possible admission to higher education for many students who might otherwise be excluded from the opportunity to participate in university study. This is in contrast to other models (such as the case for most American Universities) where only students who achieve high grade point averages at secondary school are admitted to university.

Notwithstanding the tradition of providing accessible tertiary education to New Zealanders, the student body accessing tertiary education is becoming increasingly diverse in terms of educational preparedness for tertiary education, and in terms of student expectations of what university study comprises. There has also been an increased uptake of tertiary education by students living with disabilities and students for whom English is not a home language. Given the trend to increasing diversity within the student body, the provision of responsive support services becomes an evermore important feature of this commitment. These services constitute an essential element in the university experience of the extramural student population. They are in place to assist Massey University to lower barriers to student achievement, retention and completion, particularly for groups still under-represented at university.

27.4.1 Principles Guiding the Implementation of a Student Services Policy

The strategic importance of extramural education to Massey University has been emphasised by the Vice Chancellor, Professor Judith Kinnear, in her reference to the extramural programme as "the jewel in Massey's crown" (Off Campus, 2003, p. 5).

The University's commitment to the provision of student services (in *the Charter*, *Ten Year Plan* and *Statement of Objectives for 2003–2005*) is based on a combination of broad aims and quite specific objectives.

Of particular relevance:

> Massey University is, and will remain, the pre-eminent provider of university distance education (Charter)
>
> To provide student support services and a physical environment that will attract students and support greater academic success and retention

Massey University had been at the cutting edge for the delivery of extramural support services in the early days of development. However, more recent reports on extramural provision noted possible shortcomings in services and emphasised the need for more information on the levels and models of service provided. They also outlined the necessity for the development of a comprehensive support policy for extramural students. (Prebble, 2000; Prebble and Pullar, 2002).

27.4.2 The Challenges had Clearly been Identified, but How to Meet Them?

Having decided that a new model was needed at Massey University for the delivery of services to Distance students, the search was on for one that could provide flexibility and an overarching framework for the future. This is particularly important in the rapidly developing field of distance education, at a time when resources are tight and personnel changes are frequent. There was also a reluctance to introduce anything that would have to be completely revamped in the short-to-medium term, and where considerable investment in terms of human, technological and fiscal resource would be needed. The most appropriate model to achieve the above appeared to be the Service Excellence

Model, since this model can be applied to a range of different business situations, and has built-in flexibility and ongoing improvement components.

27.4.2.1 The Service Excellence Model

The usefulness of the Service Excellence Model becomes apparent when one tries to extrapolate "best practice" from the multitude of systems and structures employed at other universities. It is very difficult to compare single-mode institutions with dual-mode institutions because of the inevitable split in focus for "core business" and the competing need for infrastructure, human resource and differing ways of relating to students. It is even difficult to make comparisons between dual-mode institutions. For instance, how does one compare an institutional mode with a dedicated Distance Unit (such as Simon Fraser University), with the devolved model that exists at Massey University? It is clear that a "one size fits all" model is not going to be achievable or even desirable. In a rapidly changing educational world any model is also likely to become obsolete in a very short length of time.

As mentioned previously, the need to review the range of services offered at Massey University had become urgent in the light of the range of new developments, particularly changing student demographics and expectations, together with the advent of new technologies. In a climate of rearrangement and restructuring of units within universities, and the rapid turnover of staff at all levels, a model that would be flexible and that would allow for regular updating and review of itself and services provided is needed.

The Service Excellence model allows for some of these difficulties to be overcome because comparisons can be made on how the particular institution, utilizing a particular approach, succeeds or fails in its intent to deliver quality services to Distance Students.

The Service Excellence Framework is based on recent New Zealand-based research (Innes, 2005) and the internationally recognised Baldrige Criteria for Performance Excellence (NIST, 2005). It provides a business management framework, including best practice findings from a range of successful organisations throughout the world. The Services Excellence Framework represents the BE journey as five integrated elements as presented in Figure 27.1.

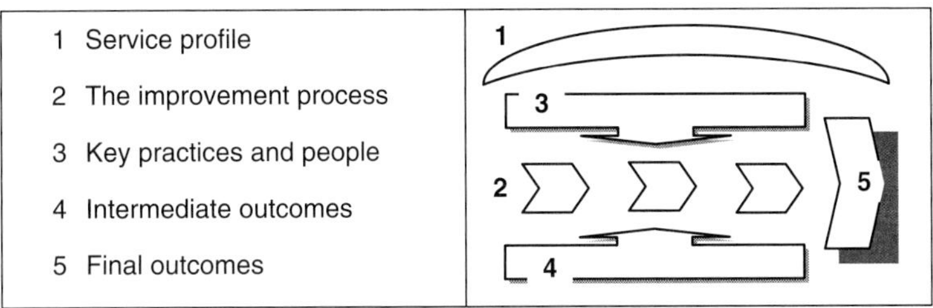

Figure 27.1: The Services Excellence Framework (Adapted from Innes, Services Excellence Framework, 2005, p. 1).

(1) *Service profile*
A clear picture of the service to be provided needs to be articulated in order to move forward. In Massey's case, student services had historically been offered on each of its three campuses. One of these campuses, that of Palmerston North, has been charged with the provision of services specifically for distance students. However, many administrative services, and also the Library, have been provided by other units with no direct reporting lines. The initial step involved the establishment of a small working group to establish a profile of services for all students. Most of these would be delivered from the Palmerston North campus. However, assistance from other units and other campuses would be imperative to the overall success of the services. Thus the profile reflects this multiplicity.

(2) *The improvement process*
The improvement process, as the phrase suggests, is more of an ongoing journey, rather than a destination. First, the decision is made to embark on the process, followed by the actual implementation of services, and, thirdly, the maintenance of these services is as critical as the preceding stages of the process. The small working group set up to manage the process consistently monitors progress along this continuum.

(3) *Key practices and people*
Key to the development and long-term improvement of services is the determination to communicate and collaborate with other units within the university, and with students. This is a challenging task, particularly in a complex organisation such as Massey University with its dual mode delivery and three Campus and five College matrix structure. People involved in the roll out of services are required to be good communicators and collaborators.

(4) *Intermediate outcomes*
The initiation of services is perhaps the most important intermediate outcome and this is detailed below. Increasingly, intermediate outcomes include additional information about what students want and need. This information is utilised as part of the improvement process to update and enhance the services as they are developed.

(5) *Final outcomes*
These will (hopefully) be more advanced, student useful and cost-effective services. Services at this stage will be firmly based on research and best practice through the continual update provided through the improvement process.

27.4.3 Risk Reduction

The number one risk is lack of "buy-in" from the top management and from the wider university – we are facing exactly this issue at Massey – how to build in a cost-effective manner, enduring systems that will survive? In any enterprise, there is the possibility of failure and so too with the implementation of a new model. The greatest risk to this – or any other model – is lack of sufficient "buy-in" either from the top or from the people tasked with the implementation of the new system. To some extent the Service Excellence model overcomes this by having as a necessary starting point the "buy-in" from top management. However, as "top management" at many universities ages and approaches retirement, the level of "buy-in" can, and frequently does, undergo change.

A second protective factor is the built-in reassessment of the system. This includes close monitoring of the process by the team involved in the implementation and a shaping of the services to meet the needs of the evolving student population. Such management allows for a testing of principles and a solid foundation to be established.

Other risks are of a political nature, and no large organisation is free of such influences. It may be politically expedient for a particular group to work against the new system and what is being achieved, but, again, the provision of measurable outcomes in a transparent system will do much to alleviate this risk.

The development of an international interest group alongside the implementation of the programme and the sharing of outcomes between groups would also assist with future proofing the system.

27.4.4 Implementation

A more detailed exposition of the implementation process can be found elsewhere (Shillington and Thompson, 2005). However, briefly, these services include the following.

27.4.4.1 Welcome and Orientation

The first personal contact students have with the university sets the tone of future interactions between Massey University and its distance students. A welcome pack, sent out by "snail mail", has proved to be an effective way to establish initial contact with students.

27.4.4.2 Early Contact with all "new to distance study" Students

The first 6 weeks are crucial to the successful experience of being at university, not only for campus-based students, but also for distance students. However, very little is known about how extramural students are finding their first few weeks studying at Massey University, or how they felt they were doing. For this reason, all students "new to distance study" are contacted to determine how they are coping with their new studies and to refer them to services, if needed, before they get into difficulties. Most students report that they are happy with their studies, but feel supported by the contact, and know how to access assistance, if needed.

27.4.4.3 Extraconnect

This is a dedicated e-mail address that provides students with a point of contact to ask questions, provide comments, make suggestions or make complaints. Topics raised by students include administrative questions, personal issues and academic difficulties.

27.4.4.4 Regional Workshops

Three campus-based Student Learning Centres provided introductory study skills and exam preparation. Students are delighted to meet Massey University staff members face-to-face, and find the workshops very useful and reassuring.

27.4.4.5 Career and Course Advice

After feelings of isolation and the need for contact with the university, students identify the need for course and career advice as being of greatest importance. Students often struggle to identify appropriate courses and career paths, or battle to juggle family, work and study commitments. A suite of online, phone and face-to-face services have been developed including the Careers "short job search" web page; specialist career counselling; effective course advice from academic specialists in the Colleges; and a virtual Careers fair.

27.4.4.6 OWLL

A recent survey by Meyer (2003) indicates that the majority (98%) of extramural students now have computer access, e-mail and Internet capability. OWLL – the Online Writing and Learning Link – is a specialised suite of increasingly interactive online learning support which includes features for all students as well as some specifically targeted to extramural students.

27.4.4.7 CROW

Counselling Resources on Web (CROW) are provided in virtual pamphlet form on a variety of topics from "difficulties with sleep" to "bereavement". These pamphlets have been used by students and others from beyond the university community.

27.4.4.8 Online Pre-Reading Service

This service provides students with the opportunity to receive feedback on assignment issues such as structure, focus, presentation or referencing. The turnaround is three working days. It is proving popular with both under-graduate and post-graduate students. Usage continues to grow significantly.

27.4.4.9 On Campus Support

This provides access to Health, Counselling and Recreation services. Extramural students are increasingly accessing services on campus and attending lectures (Meyer, 2003).

27.4.5 Additional Resources

27.4.5.1 CD Rom

Academic Writing Skills are provided in an accessible format (for students with print disabilities) on CD Rom. These are proving to be very popular with a range of extramural students.

27.4.5.2 Students with Disabilities

Many students with disabilities study extramurally as it is easier to do so. The Disability Service provides support for them in their homes and also when they come onto campus for "Contact Courses".

27.4.5.3 Māori

Additional Māori-centred services are provided. Many of these services had been provided prior to the provision of the new services and have, in fact, been used to inform the development of the generic new series.

27.4.5.4 Pacific Island Students

As part of the new series, services to this community have been extended, particularly in terms of additional regional workshops.

27.5 CONCLUSION

Whilst acknowledging that there is no universal blueprint for student services, this chapter offers background, a potential structure, and an example of the development and continuous enhancement of services for distance students. The Service Excellence model is presented as an option for achieving a measurable way forward into the foreseeable future. It allows for consistent re-evaluation and correction or enhancement as needed. This allows services to keep up-to-date with emerging technologies, but also to ensure that investments are appropriate.

Where to from here, for Massey and other distance student support providers? Managers of support services for new times must themselves be engaged in a constant learning process to research, understand, monitor and evaluate the services provided.

Tait (2003) maintains that this ongoing monitoring and evaluation of new services is essential and that we should not allow ourselves to make the mistake of believing that more provision automatically equates with more or improved service. New provision, especially that delivered through new technologies, needs to be carefully researched so that it can be effectively and appropriately resourced.

There is also a need for research findings that will inform those working in distance education on which support services are most effective in reducing student drop-out. As White (2003) reports, there are no consistent and thoroughly researched findings that "indicate that investment in a particular type of support will reduce drop-out by a certain amount" (p. 175).

From 2004 to 2005 we used the Service Excellence model to evaluate existing services and to guide the development and implementation of new services. In 2006 we moved to the next stage of monitoring and evaluating the impact of the new services on student satisfaction and retention rates.

Our response to the challenge to provide services for distance students is diverse, varied and still evolving. There is, of course, no single solution or final objective as we continue to develop and evaluate new provisions in response to ever-changing needs and demands for support. We are aware that there is no single model or set of experiences at any particular institution that will be totally effective. As Tait (2003) observes, there is no universal blueprint for the establishment of student support systems. Each distance education provider will need to consider the context of their institution and the particular characteristics and requirements of their student population. Given the complexities of challenges that face student support services, as effective practitioners, we must share our practices with others and constantly seek to find examples of best practice elsewhere.

REFERENCES

Anderson, T. (2005). *Distance learning – Social software's killer ap?* Adelaide, South Australia: 17th Biennial Conference of the Open and Distance Learning Association of Australia, 9–11 November.

Bowker, N.I. and Tuffin, K. (2002). Disability discourses for online identities. *Disability & Society*, **17**(3), 327–344.

Chanock, K. (1995). Counselling and academic skills teaching: What person-centred counselling can tell us about person-centred skills teaching. In *Academic Skills Advising: Towards a Discipline* (M. Garner. et al., eds) Melbourne: Victorian Language and Learning Network, pp. 28–37.

Clerehan R., Turnbull J., Moore T. et al. (2003). Transforming learning support: An online resource centre for a diverse student population. *Education Media International*, **40** (1–2), 15–32.

Corry, N. and Lelliot, T. (2003). Learner Perceptions of a South African ODL programme. In *Rethinking Learner Support in Distance Education* (A. Tait and R. Mills, eds) London: Routledge, pp. 28–40.

Evans, T.D. and Nation, D.E. (eds). (2000). *Changing University Teaching: Reflections on Creating Educational Technologies*. London: Kogan Page.

Gunawardena, C.N. and Zittle R.H. (1998). Faculty development programmes in distance education in American higher education. In *Staff Development in Open and flexible Learning* (C. Latchem and F. Lockwood, eds) London: Routledge, pp. 105–114.

Hicks, M., Reid, I., and George, R. (1999). *Enhancing Online Teaching: Designing Responsive Learning Environments*. Paper presented at HERDSA Conference, Cornerstones, What do we value in higher education? Melbourne, 12–15 July.

Hilsberg, T. (2005). *The Peaceful Rise of China as a Major International Higher Education Competitor*. Keynote paper presented at Adelaide, South Australia: 17th Biennial Conference of the Open and Distance Learning Association of Australia, 9–11 November.

Innes, J. (2005). *Service Excellence Framework*. Unpublished manuscript. Palmerston North: Massey University.

Jegede, O. (2000). The wedlock between technology and open and distance education. In *Changing University Teaching: Reflections on Creating Educational Technologies* (T.D. Evans and D.E. Nation, eds), London: Kogan Page.

Laurillard, D. (1993).*Rethinking University Teaching: A Framework for the Effective Use of Educational Technology*. London: Routledge.

Lockwood, F. (2005). *Estimating Student Workload, Readability and Implications for Student Learning and Progression*. Paper presented at Adelaide, South Australia: 17th Biennial Conference of the Open and Distance Learning Association of Australia, 9–11 November.

Mason, R. (2001). *IET's Masters in Open and Distance Education: What have we Learned?* Retrieved May 6, 2006, from http://iet.open.ac.uk/pp/r.d.mason/downloads/maeval.pdf.

Meyer, L. (2003). *Review of Codes and Modes Discussion Document*. Palmerston North: Massey University.

Murphy, D. (2000). *Instructional Design for Self-Learning for Distance Education*. The Knowledge Series, Commonwealth of Learning.

NIST. (2005). *Baldrige Criteria for Performance Excellence*. National Institute of Standards and Technology. Retrieved July 10, 2006, from http://www.quality.nist.gov/.

Off Campus. (2003). *Massey University Extramural Students' Society*, **8**(1), 8.

Oliver, R. (2001). Seeking best practice in online learning: Flexible Learning Toolboxes in the Australian VET sector. *Australian Journal of Educational Technology*, **17**(2), 204–222.

Perraton, H. (2000). *Open and Distance Learning in the Developing World*, London: Routledge.

Perry, B. and Edwards, M. (2005). *Exemplary Educators: Creating a Community of Enquiry Online*. Adelaide, South Australia: 17th Biennial Conference of the Open and Distance Learning Association of Australia, 9–11 November.

Prebble, T. (2000). *Support Services for Extramural students*. Report to Vice Chancellor's Executive Committee (VCEC 00/79 revised).

Prebble, T. and Pullar, K. (2002). *Extramural Student Support: Report on a Planning Workshop*, Tuesday 12 March 2002. Report to participants, VCEC and board of extramural studies.

Quintrell, N. (1985). A summary of the provision of language and learning skills support in Australian universities: 1985. In *Learning to Learn: Language and Study Skills in Context: Proceedings of the Sixth Annual Australasian Study Skills conference* (2nd ed.) (N. Quintrell, ed.) Adelaide: Flinders University of South Australia, pp. 159–165.

Rudzski, A. (2002). *Retention Statistics for Extramural Students*. Presentation at extramural student support planning day. Massey University, Palmerston North.

Shillington, S. and Thompson, J. (2005). *Breaking the Boundaries: Improving the Accessibility, Extent and Responsiveness of Support Services for Distance Education Students*. Paper presented at the 17th Biennial Conference of the Open and Distance Learning Association of Australia, Adelaide, 9–11 November.

Simpson, O. (2000). *Supporting Students in Open and Distance Learning*. London: Kogan Page.

Simpson, O. (2002). *Supporting Students in Online, Open and Distance Learning* (2nd ed.) London: Kogan Page.

Simpson, O. (2003). *Student Retention in Online, Open and Distance Learning*. London: Kogan Page.

Tait, A. (2003). Rethinking learner support in the Open University UK. In *Rethinking Learner Support in Distance Education* (A. Tait and R. Mills, eds) London: Routledge, pp. 185–197.

Tait, H. and Entwistle, N. (1996). Identifying students at risk through ineffective strategies. *Higher Education*, **31**, 97–116.

The Commonwealth of Learning. (1993). *Perspectives on Distance Education: Student Support Services: Towards more Responsive Systems*. Report of a Symposium on Student Support Services in Distance Education, Vancouver: Author.

Thorpe, M. (2003). Collaborative on-line learning: Transforming learner support and course design. In *Rethinking Learner Support in Distance Education* (A. Tait and R. Mills, eds) London: Routledge, pp. 198–211.

Tinto, V. (1987). *Leaving College: Rethinking the Causes and Cures of Student Attrition*. Chicago: University of Chicago Press.

White, C. (2003). *Language Learning in Distance Education*, Cambridge, UK: Cambridge University Press.

Williams, M.T. and Wache, D. (2005). "*Just Link and Leave*": A *Recipe for Disaster for Online Discussions*. 17th Biennial Conference of the Open and Distance Learning Association of Australia, Adelaide, 9–11 November.

Chapter 28

LEADERS AND LEADING IN OPEN AND DISTANCE LEARNING

Nigel Bennett

28.1 INTRODUCTION

The six chapters that explore issues associated with leadership present us with two distinct arenas for discussion. Five of them – those by Paul and Brindley, Mason, Thompson and Shillington, Panda and Tait – examine the issue from the point of view of organisational practice within universities that are concerned wholly or partly with open and distance learning (ODL). The sixth, by Latchem, Lockwood and Baggaley, addresses the wider question of how distance learning strategies might be explored and exploited in pursuit of wider economic development activities through international projects that are not institutionally located. Further, they represent different kinds of discussion. Three of the chapters – those of Paul and Brindley, Tait and Mason – are concerned with developing scenarios and exploring the demands that they see as being presented to academics and others in ODL organisations; a fourth, by Panda, explores these issues by reference to specific examples of university strategic planning; one – Thompson and Shillington – presents a case study of innovation in practice, making reference to the leadership activities and roles involved; and one – Latchem, Lockwood and Baggaley – combines the two by exploring ways in which large-scale international development projects can be implemented on the ground, and then examining the demands placed on project leaders through a range of scenarios that they have drawn from their experience as consultants. This variety of both context and focus enables us to analyse the nature of leadership in quite different ways; what is striking, however, is the extent to which they share a common perception of how leaders should address the concerns that they face. All of them present, to a greater or lesser extent, a profoundly rational approach to the tasks of leadership.

In this discussion, we will look first at some basic assumptions that are made about the location of leaders relative to those they lead, and how this defines the core task of their work. We will go on to examine the particular interpretations of the task/location relationship that the writers bring to their analyses, and the extent to which they share particular elements but interpret them differently. Finally, we consider some aspects of the leadership literature that relate to the explorations of leadership provided in the chapters we have discussed.

28.2 WHERE ARE LEADERS AND WHAT DO THEY DO?

We will focus our attention first on the five chapters that examine ODL universities. Three of them analyse the work of university senior staff who have a policy-making remit in the context of an environment that is presented in terms of dynamic change, whilst the other two explore work being undertaken by less senior staff. All five demonstrate that leaders are located at the boundary of the organisation or activity with which they are associated. They are faced with the responsibility of dealing with the immediate and wider environment within which they work and the area of work for which they are responsible. Thus Paul and Brindley and Tait are both concerned with how university policies are aligned with external pressures and demands, what has to be done to understand them and how to bring about practice within the university that reflects the policies that are framed to deal with environmental demands. Panda addresses a similar set of issues by discussing the basic principles of strategic planning, and considering the leadership issues involved in moving strategic *planning* – a process undertaken by senior management – to strategic *thinking*, which he sees as a holistic and all-embracing process. Thompson and Shillington and Mason are looking at the work of leadership from the other end of the telescope, being concerned with developing practice within the university and persuading the policy makers that new practice needs to be supported. Mason's primary concern is with diagnosing issues in the development of more sensitive assessment techniques that can exploit the opportunities presented by new technologies and aim at promoting learning rather than assessing it, and her attention to leadership within this area is relatively limited. Leadership as addressed in her chapter is more to be understood as innovative practice rather than leadership in the sense of an organisational activity. However, both perspectives can be seen to be addressing issues of alignment in the sense that they rest on identifying a need or requirement and looking for ways in which this might be met. Thus two key leadership tasks emerge: environmental scanning in order to carry out a needs analysis and promoting changes in practice that will meet the perceived needs not currently being addressed, or at least not being addressed satisfactorily. Leadership, in all these chapters, is seen as necessarily promoting change.

Within this basic analysis, we can differentiate between the kinds of change that leaders have to promote. In the scenarios discussed by Panda, Paul and Brindley and Tait, the leaders whose role they explore are concerned with promoting change within the organisation. As Tait clearly recognises, it is leadership and change from above. All three chapters see senior leaders needing to impose new practices in some way, exercising the powers that are inherent in their roles within essentially hierarchical and bureaucratic organisations. Because of this hierarchical structure – which stands strongly at odds with the traditional perception of academe as essentially a collegial world – the analysis of the environment is clearly defined as a task of senior staff, despite the possibility that others in the organisation might also have a finger on the environmental pulse.

Within the approach presented in these two chapters, "middle leaders" are concerned with ensuring that the changes mandated at senior level are implemented properly. We shall look shortly at the ways in which these authors see this work as being achieved.

It is interesting that although Panda's emphasis on strategic planning, strategic management and strategic thinking is also concerned with policy development, target setting and performance review, he sees this as less top-down than the other authors whose focus is on the policy and implementation process. By moving his thinking from strategic planning to strategic thinking, he attempts to incorporate other academic staff into the strategic decision making. A major reason for this is that he acknowledges, as the others tend not to, that academic institutions are loosely coupled arrangements (Weick, 1976) in which individual loyalty can be as much to their academic discipline as it is to the institution they work in. This is the case even though strategic plans will typically begin with a statement of organisational mission and vision which assumes, as does Tait, that organisational members subscribe to the values that underpin the plan.

Whereas the chapters by Paul and Brindley and Tait are concerned with implementing changes in the practice of their junior colleagues in order to align practice with revised policy demands, the chapters by Mason and by Thompson and Shillington present different perspectives. Mason examines the demands of assessment in the light of the changing technology of ODL and what she sees as the continuing acceptance by academics that we do not necessarily assess what she calls "the real learning we think is taking place" (p. 513) and presents a range of possible strategies for meeting both pressures. She is concerned with identifying new potential practices and promoting their use, as it were, on the ground, which may require facilitating activity from senior staff but are not necessarily dependent on it.

Unlike the other HEI-focused chapters, Thompson and Shillington report in some detail on an actual case study that studies the implementation of a new model of organisation and practice. Like the scenarios presented by Paul and Brindley and Tait, this case study rests practice on a careful and detailed situational analysis; however, the difference between this chapter and the others is that the analysis appears to come from within the organisation, examining the perceived needs of current students rather than the expectations attributed to current and potential students, and then looking to gain support – "buy-in" from the university senior staff, something they state to be a continuing concern.

These chapters make it clear that leaders are located on the boundaries of their area of responsibility. This creates a duality: on the one hand, they need to be aware of the environment within which they are working, and on the other, they must attend to the demands of the field of work for which they are responsible. The environment may be external to the organisation, as with Panda, Paul and Brindley and Tait, who see organisational leadership as concerned with dealing with the demands of the wider society in which the ODL institution is located, or it can be within the organisation, as in the chapter by Thompson and Shillington. All of them address specifically issues of technological change, which is the central environmental pressure underpinning Mason's exploration of assessment issues.

We can summarise the task of leaders as presented in these chapters as being concerned with carrying out systematic and continual situational analysis, developing alternative forms of policy and practice and getting them implemented by their colleagues, and where necessary for reasons of political support and resource acquisition, obtaining their acceptance by others. An important aspect of the chapters by Paul and Brindley, Thompson and Shillington and Tait is the implication they present that leadership is about the creation of systems, structures and policies that constrain colleagues and command adherence to them. Mason's chapter is rather different, suggesting that academics should recognise the weaknesses of current assessment practices but presenting options and a range of alternatives that might be employed instead. In this, she is closer to the discussion of leadership position and practice that underpins the first part of the chapter by Latchem and his colleagues.

The discussion of leadership we find in their chapter on the possibilities of ODL in developing countries reveals considerable similarities with the chapters we have discussed already, but important differences. Much of their discussion focuses on the roles and actions of project leaders in relation to the senior members of the state or organisation where the project is located, and in this they follow to some extent the chapters that are located within ODL organisations, locating leadership specifically within individuals who have organisational roles that place them on the border between their responsibility areas and their environment. However, they appear to position the idea rather differently. We can summarise the difference by suggesting that instead of locating the position of a leader or leaders at the boundaries between their responsibility areas and their environment, they place it at the interface between the project and its host. The difference may be significant. The concept of "boundary" implies a strong division between the two sides that it separates, which has to be policed and managed. A more permeable division between different elements is that suggested by the term "interface", and this seems to describe better the points at which leadership is exercised in the examples that Latchem and his colleagues present. It may be that it provides a better description of the kinds of relationship that exist between project leaders and the project users. One example of this is the way in which they describe a computer-based project being turned to their advantage by the Fulani of northern Niger, whose local leader exploited his free web-based email account to find potential donors and obtain 100 tonnes of food aid during a period of drought and starvation. This isolated specific example of an international project in action, rather than our having the purposes and methods of operation described, suggests that a key potential leadership role is the creative adaptation of opportunities in the interests of others – in this case, the local community of which this individual was a leading figure.

This raises the question, within project-based activities such as those they outline in the first part of their chapter, of who are the leaders and who provides leadership. In their outlines, they appear to make a clear distinction between those who generate and establish the project and those who develop and use the materials and equipment that is generated. There is a tension between the authors or creators of the project, the "on-the-ground" supporters and employees who are charged with putting the project into practice and those who actually use it. Each has a key role to play in defining the purposes to be served, assisting the target population to exploit the materials for those purpose, and turning these to their own advantage, which may not be what was intended nor within the project's original scope. This suggests strongly a view of leadership location as shifting and both situation- and task-specific, providing opportunities for extensively creative leadership that is responsive to immediate situations as well as to the overall plans of the project itself. Unfortunately, although we are given a lot of information about what was planned and what the practical outcomes have been, we are given rather less about the ways in which the projects turn from intention to practice, and about the implications of these developments for the communities they are targeted at. The nature of such projects appears to be creative rather than directive, although as their later scenarios indicate there can be formidable obstacles if this is to be achieved, and there is, as they state, a danger that they can be culturally insensitive.

This discussion suggests, then, that leaders stand on the edge of their formal area of responsibility, fielding and interpreting environmental pressures and opportunities and responding to them in ways that derive from that interpretation and promote new practices. Their response may be proactive in its view of their environment, viewing it as open to influence, or reactive in that the pressures it generates are not susceptible to resistance or influence but must be accommodated; however, both responses can be creative and radical. It can also be developmental, in that individuals may exploit opportunities created within the environment to their own, or, hopefully, their community's advantage, changing or extending the purpose of initiatives away from those originally intended. Leadership, then, can be located at a variety of points within a system, be it an organisation or a project. We will return to this in our concluding discussion, when we explore the idea of leadership as an "organizational quality" (Ogawa and Bossert, 1995) and the concept of distributed leadership (Bennett et al., 2003; Woods et al., 2004).

28.3 HOW THE AUTHORS INTERPRET THE LEADERSHIP TASK

In this section we will examine the similarities and dissimilarities between the ways in which the authors interpret the relationship between the organisation/project and its environment, and how these influence the ways in which they present the work of leaders. Two elements stand out. The first is presentation of the environment as fluid and potentially hostile; and the second is the rational approach to responding to that environment that all the authors take, although Thomson and Shillington and Latchem, Lockwood and Baggaley, drawing more directly on case studies, also acknowledge the importance of political issues. However, within these broad elements we can find considerable differences.

All of the writers in ODL institutions see the environment as a challenge to existing organisational practice. Panda sees this as creating the need for strategic planning that can link organisational mission (overall purpose), vision (medium-term goals) and achievement or performance targets. For Paul and Brindley, the challenge is the changing expectations that students bring to their contacts with the ODL organisation, which they see as deriving from two pressures: technological and values-driven. The second drives the use that is expected of the first. This view also underpins the discussion of student services presented by Thomson and Shillington and Tait's examination of the demands of leadership development; Mason also addresses the environment of changing technology, but her position is a more pragmatic and less values-driven one. Latchem and his colleagues, writing from the ODL development project perspective, see the relationship from the other end of the telescope: the environmental challenge is one of disadvantage and deprivation which requires change, so that change is the purpose of the project that its leaders must promote, rather than something that they must respond to. Interestingly, Tait develops a similar argument as the basis for his programme of leadership development.

The differences summarised in the previous paragraph, and the impact that these have on the authors' interpretation of leadership and the leaders' role, need to be explored separately. Paul and Brindley see the environment as not merely hostile but confrontational, prompting a student perspective on what ODL institutions should provide that demands radical change. This perspective is driven, in the first instance, by a culture of consumerism that leads to their seeing success in their studies as an entitlement and demanding the forms of support and assistance that will ensure this. The result of this is that, as they put it,

> The emphasis now and for the future is so much less on the institution and so much more on the learner [...] students are much less apt to strive to fit into the learning culture of the institution they attend – instead, they expect it to adjust to their own needs.
>
> (p. 449)

This is in itself an interesting conceptualisation of the ODL institution, in that the students are seen as an externally generated challenge rather than as a part of the institution itself, and this extends the confrontation from the environment – something outside the organisation – to a part of the organisation itself. The senior leaders of the institution, whose work is the focus of their chapter, are therefore concerned with the impact of the environment on members of the organisation itself, who become part of "the problem" that has to be addressed.

The second part of the environmental problem that Paul and Brindley identify is technology related. As part of the changing pattern of student expectations noted above, they point out that changing technology creates different expectations of how learning opportunities can be presented and accessed. Perhaps in part because they are working from a perspective in which ODL is frequently an extension of the work of traditional face-to-face universities rather than the fundamental basis on which all its teaching is designed, they see this as demanding profound changes in the expectations that university teachers have to fulfil. This, they suggest, needs to be addressed through the generation of protocols on matters such as response times to queries and student contacts, and the use of particular forms and levels of technology, that staff should adhere to in preparing and presenting their teaching programmes.

The organisation-wide approach through protocols and requirements for teaching practice that is suggested in this chapter necessitates a response to environmental pressures that is essentially based on a rationally based analysis of those pressures and predicting how they will develop. Although the protocols they suggest as a strategy can be framed in general terms, they will need to be adaptable to continuing technological development. They recognise the importance of having staff "buy in" to the changes, suggesting a consultative process that will gain broad support for a strategic plan, and acknowledge that major change can challenge the prevailing culture of the organisation, but although they emphasise the importance of staff training and development, their approach is essentially a top-down one across the institution as a whole, in which new delivery systems will be "determined" and "implemented". This appears to understate the extent to which staff in what Graetz (2000, p. 556) calls "the middle and lower levels of management" can act as blockages to change.

This strategy may face two problems. The first is the different ways individuals respond to change, such as Rogers' (1995) distinction between innovators, early adopters, early majority, late majority and laggards, which could make developing and policing such protocols problematic and divisive. By focusing on the relationship between the leader or the leadership team and their colleagues as a collectivity, rather than as individuals, they may be reducing the degree of creativity and innovation that is available to the organisation in responding to the twin pressures of consumerism and technological change they are seeking to address, and which they are facing on a daily basis. There is a danger that creating a rationally based, whole-organisation response will make the ODL institution less well placed to address the hostile environment they outline.

The second issue is concerned with the technological change they accurately identify. Although we may reasonably assume that a consumerist attitude will continue to inform students' attitudes to their teaching, predicting the development of technology is far more difficult. Rational planning such as they propose can surely be only at the most general level, and must be made open to significant and potentially radical adaptation in response to changing needs. Certainly this will be the case in relation to the kinds of protocols they appear to envisage. Paradoxically, their approach to addressing the challenges of rapid and culturally and technologically driven changes to the organisational environment may be too close to the period of environmental stability that they see us having left behind as we move from a convocational view of higher education to a convergence model.

We have dwelt a little on Paul's and Brindley chapter because their discussion raises many of the issues that run through the other chapters. They clearly view the changing cultural and technological environment of ODL organisations as presenting significant demands for the academics who teach there. They also acknowledge the tension between the development of organisation-wide policies and their implementation. Theirs is a responsive rather than a proactive approach to leadership in the field.

A slightly different response to a similar analysis of the environment is presented by Thompson and Shillington. They also argue that the demands and expectations of the student body have changed significantly towards a more consumerist and technologically driven position in which access to higher education is deemed to be access to success, and they comment that student decisions are driven increasingly by issues of cost and quality, with loyalty to the institution becoming much less important. In such a market-driven situation, ODL institutions must move quickly to identify potential markets and then to acquire sufficient market share, and this, they argue, changes what is seen as the nature of student services from the traditional view of remediation towards one of support and ultimately collaboration between academics and students in the learning process. This collaborative approach, it is suggested, will weaken the confrontational stance between the student/consumer and the ODL organisation/provider, and help to promote the institutional loyalty which will sustain student-led funding for the university, and which has traditionally been a hallmark of university/student relationships. However, their analysis of student needs suggests that taking too strong a technology-driven approach to providing course materials and student services may not always be helpful: there is, they say, a case for paper-based delivery being at least an option for the students, and refer to the value of opportunities for students to have face-to-face contact with their tutors.

The outcome of Thompson and Shillington's work on analysing the needs of the ODL students at Massey University was the development of a new student support service that rested on a model that would both provide a clearly defined set of academic and pastoral support services for students and have within it a built-in procedure for ongoing evaluation and review. This constant review process was an important route for obtaining the support of senior staff for the innovation, for it involves monitoring both the degree of use of the service and the levels of satisfaction communicated by the students. What they call management "by fact" (p. 539) is, they argue, a powerful tool in persuading senior staff to provide the resources for the innovation to continue.

Thompson and Shillington, then, start from the same premise as Paul and Brindley, that the relationship between the organisation and its students (both current and potential) is more confrontational and consumerist than collaborative and loyal, but argue that the proper response is to present a range of services that can support their needs and promote a culture of collaboration rather than going directly to meet the technological imperatives that leads students to articulate almost infinite flexibility in terms of course format and delivery. In both chapters, the environment is seen as a hostile force for change that must be met by changed institutional practice. Tait, on the other hand, sees the environment as hostile in a different way, in that it resists the challenge that the ODL institution presents to traditional values.

Tait shares with Paul and Brindley the view that a convergence perception of higher education is replacing the convocational view, but he argues that the role of ODL institutions has always been to promote the convergence view and challenge traditional cultural views of HE. Further, whereas Paul and Brindley appear to view rapid technological change as a part of the environmental threat that ODL institutions face, Tait argues that e-learning and technological change can further the work of cultural challenge and change that he argues should be central to their mission, both by strengthening individual ODL universities and through their potential for promoting inter-institutional collaboration. In his view, ODL and e-learning are potentially subversive forces, both in their impact on social justice and human capital development, through the articulation of the convergence model of HE that he sees as industrial higher education (though he might question whether this could be equated with mass production) as opposed to the convocation model which he equates with the artisan view of society, privileging some at the expense of others. It is essential, then, for leaders within ODL organisations to engage in "negotiating with values that are salient in contemporary society" (p. 504), such as are expressed through the actions and policies of governments, employers associations, trade unions and other quasi-public and representative bodies. From his point of view, leadership in ODL organisations is concerned with responsibility and service rather than privilege and power. Hence, a key task of the ODL leader is to identify and keep under constant review the direction of society and who may be excluded, and to seek to provide for the excluded. It may be relevant to his analysis of the relationship between the organisation and its environment that he is writing from within a university whose *raison d'etre* was to provide higher education for those who had been unable to obtain it when they were younger, and whose entire curriculum has been provided through forms of open and distance learning since its creation in 1969, whereas Paul and Brindley and, to a much lesser extent, Thompson and Shillington, appear to write from the viewpoint of traditional face-to-face universities that see ODL strategies as a means of promoting wider participation and greater market penetration.

However, Tait's view of the role of the senior leader within the institution remains more directive than his perception of the role towards the outside world. Alongside the importance of engaging with salient values in the wider society, he also argues that leaders must engage with the internal values of the organisation. In this he is in agreement with the arguments of Paul and Brindley. He acknowledges the potential significance of distributed leadership models (Gronn, 2002; Bennett et al., 2003; Spillane, 2006) for widening leadership activity within the organisation away from the senior staff who are formally charged with leadership roles, but goes on to argue for charismatically driven transformational leadership that challenges traditional practice and demands radical change. This is because he sees the key tasks of leadership in the context of challenges to social values as being so fundamental that they must be undertaken at the highest levels of the organisation.

What is interesting about Tait's chapter is that although his interpretation of the relationship between the ODL organisation and its environment is radically different from that of Paul and Brindley, he comes ultimately to the same perception of what is appropriate leadership. He also sees it as a purely rational process: emotion has no place in leadership, except perhaps in his injunction to "tell the truth with energy" (p. 506), and ten of the eleven capabilities of effective leadership that he argues development programmes should strengthen are presented in terms of knowledge and understanding. In both these analyses, leadership is basically a matter of situational analysis and policy formulation, followed up by strong action through junior colleagues to put the policy into effect.

It can be argued that this view of leadership presents a potential problem for both the leader and the led. There is a tendency in both Tait's chapter and that of Paul and Brindley to underplay the extent to which the boundaries of organisations are permeable rather than secure. External values, whether supportive of the key features of the environment or supportive of the practices being enjoined by senior leaders, are transacted into the organisation by those who work in it (Archer, 1981). Promoting a sense of shared values and collective commitment to organisational values, especially when this is being attempted in a large organisation, where the nature of practice is necessarily individualistic, as teaching is, and where traditional values are sometimes strongly held, creates pressure on the leaders who aspire to this kind of organisational transformation to become directive and autocratic, a danger that is to some extent acknowledged by Paul and Brindley. When this occurs, questions of perceived legitimacy can arise, with consequences for the actions of less senior staff (Hales, 1997). It may be that this rationalist approach to whole-organisational leadership has embedded in it the seeds of significant resistance. It may also be that the pressure for change is so intense that this simply has to be overridden, although this argument may be more appropriate to the analysis offered by Paul and Brindley, which sees the environment as aggressively hostile, than it is to that offered by Tait, who locates the challenge in the relationship between the organisation and its environment within the ODL organisation itself, and sees the current situation as a stronger opportunity for ODL to assert its long-standing role than it has ever had since its inception.

So far, we have shown that the writers who discuss leadership in ODL institutions have adopted a broadly rationalist perspective in response to the environmental pressures that leaders face. Panda's view of the leadership role, though still fundamentally rationalist and resting on the principles of strategic planning, takes more account of the loose coupling (Weick, 1976) that characterises academic institutions. He focuses his early discussion on the principles of strategic planning, that emphasise the formal search for organisational strengths and opportunities as well as opportunities and threats, but emphasises that there must be a sense of holism in the planning process: top-down is not enough.

Mason's chapter is rather different from the other ODL writers in that her primary concern is with discussing the nature of assessment in higher education and how online tuition and assessment provides opportunities for much more wide-ranging and sophisticated assessment of both skills and processes, and for students to take greater control of their own learning. Thus the environment, as represented by the development of online tuition and technological change, demands significant changes to how students' work is assessed simply by virtue of the technological developments that are occurring. She pays little attention to leadership practice *per se*, but unlike the other writers in this section she does indicate that technological change can create as much uncertainty and as many problems for students as it does for tutors.

As we said in the previous section, Latchem, Lockwood and Baggaley indicate how individuals who are recipients or targets of project activity have been able to adapt the technology to their own advantage. The discussion of projects that makes up the first half of their chapter suggests strongly that a key aspect of leadership in ODL projects is the process of empowerment so that the target population of a project can take control of the activities and develop their new opportunities to their own advantage, rather than remaining dependent on the assistance of project members. This point, that projects need both top-down and bottom-up support if they are to be successful, is made again when they discuss through eight scenarios of failed ODL/ICT projects what they define as key issues for successful project leadership and management. However, this point is rather lost in their summary of these issues that they present at the end of the chapter, when they state (p. 471) that

> ODL/ICT projects for development in low-income countries require careful analysis of the needs, contexts, circumstances and intended outcomes, and their quality and accountability to the stakeholders needs to be assured by formative and summative evaluation in accordance with key performance indicators and failure needs to be acknowledged and enquired into wherever this occurs.

One of the points that emerges strongly from the scenarios that Latchem and his colleagues describe and discuss is that much of the behaviour of both consultants and clients is non-rational. Strategic plans are not created with any degree of consensus or commitment, activities are not funded because they would demonstrate that a previous, related activity was a failure, advice is rejected and alternative action taken without any attempt at considering the cost implications, and technological innovations are introduced for which the recipients are not prepared or trained. It is clear that a rational planning model is seen as the way to avoid such failures. Interestingly, however, one scenario stands out by its acknowledgement of a political rather than a planning/implementation failing: the importance of "informed high level champions" who will support a project when it runs into difficulties and see it through to implementation. In this, they reflect the point made by Thompson and Shillington about the need to gain the commitment and support of senior staff if a successful innovation is to be achieved.

These six chapters, then, present us with a view of leadership as promoting change, largely through a rational process of situational analysis, policy or project planning and implementation. Evaluation is seen as essential, usually against performance targets. There is some variation between the writers whose positioning of the leader is best described as being at the boundary between the organisation and its environment and those who appear to locate it at the interface between parties to a relationship. The two positions produce different understandings of the how leadership might be analysed, and in the last part of this chapter we offer some points that might be considered in relation to the chapters we have discussed.

28.4 LEADERS AND LEADERSHIP

The initial focus of this chapter was on the location of leaders within the organisation or activity being examined, and how this affected the interpretation of their role. It is worth pointing out at this stage that in the chapters reviewed here the discussion is all about leaders even when the term leadership is used. Tait's focus on leadership development offers the most explicit association of leadership tasks with a leadership role, but the idea of leaders who are "in charge" is clearly visible in the chapters by Latchem, Lockwood and Baggaley and Paul and Brindley.

This short paragraph indicates that the concept of leadership is a slippery one, both in terms of what how the task of leadership is defined and in terms of how it is (and should be) done. It shows how we might be talking about individuals who act in particular ways or about some sort of procedure or process that may (or may not) be provided by specific individuals. Conventionally, leadership is seen as exercised from the apex of a hierarchical pyramid or the centre of a web or network by a single leader, who may be supported and advised by a team of senior colleagues, but who is ultimately responsible for decisions and policies. This view differentiates between "leadership" – exercised by leaders who set directions and create policies – and "management" – carried out by those who are charged with putting policies into practice. This view of leadership is visible in all of the papers to some extent, although it is perhaps most explicitly stated in the two chapters by Paul and Brindley and Tait, who articulate a view of the proper relationship between the ODL university and its environment. However, this is not by any means a universal view. Mintzberg (1990), for example, argued that leadership was just one of a range of activities that made up the management role, recognising in an analysis that reflects the policy implementation perspective of policy analysts such as Pressman and Wildavsky (1973) that leadership is necessary at every point in a system in order to bring action about and "keep the ship afloat". Panda acknowledges this in his later discussion. This view admits of the possibility that individuals might have their own agendas in implementing formal policies, so creating variations of practice between different parts of an organisational system. Paul and Brindley recognise this when they examine the need to address cultural concerns in implementing the large-scale changes in practice that they see as necessary. Latchem and colleagues state explicitly that projects need both top-down and bottom-up support, and for a clear connection between plan and action if success is to be achieved, and provide scenarios of projects that have not resulted in any changes in practice despite their having led to major plans for strategic change.

Closely associated with this perspective is the leadership activity that results from the creation of what Handy (1991) calls a task culture within organisations. In this, leadership is exercised in what is essentially a project-by-project basis, as people and other resources are brought together for a specific purpose, which is directed by a specific individual, and which is then disbanded when the task is completed. This is, of course, the underpinning view of leadership in the chapter by Latchem, Lockwood and Baggaley, whose focus is on leadership in ODL projects. In this, as in the Mintzberg-derived analysis just indicated, we find a sense that individuals have more influence over what is done, and importantly, we see that the task of leadership is to some extent disconnected from specific roles within the organisation, although it is likely that one individual will have some sort of generic formal role such as "project manager". Indeed, although the clear message in the early part of their chapter, when they demonstrate the range of possible ODL projects in the undeveloped world, is the importance of leadership at all levels of a project, their later discussion focuses on project leaders, and the questions they pose for us to use when considering their scenarios are all focused on what more the project directors or managers might have done.

More closely associated with leadership within organisations is the concept of distributed leadership that Tait refers to in passing. In some ways this reflects Mintzberg's view of leadership as part of the management role, but it differs from Mintzberg by decoupling the exercise of leadership from any particular role within the organisation. Distributed leadership theorists argue that leadership can be exercised by anyone within the organisation, regardless of whether they have formal management or leadership roles. Graetz (2000) argues that organisations with simultaneous loose–tight properties (Peters and Waterman, 1982) will cope best with change that results from external pressures through a process of distributed leadership in which a strong personalised leadership at the top of the organisation is supported by a group of trusted and experienced staff. Among writers on schools (Harris, 2003; Muijs and Harris, 2007), it is frequently equated with "teacher leadership", a view of school culture and structure that largely removes hierarchies, although it then has to address issues of accountability.

Although Tait acknowledges the concept of distributed leadership, he argues that it has limited value since it can only ever form a small part of a person's role, and that therefore it is necessary to address leadership development by focusing on senior staff, for whom leadership is a more substantial aspect of their work. This returns him to a more traditional hierarchical view of leadership within organisations, and to connect it with specific individual roles. "Leadership" remains connected to "leaders" as something they do, concerned with setting visions, establishing values and "telling the truth with energy" so that colleagues acknowledge it and sign up to the values it expresses.

However, another analysis suggests that we can disconnect "leadership" altogether from individual roles when studying organisations. For example, Ogawa and Bossert (1995) suggest that leadership can be understood as a "force" that "flows through the organization" as part of the everyday activity that keeps things happening. In this view of leadership, it is not positioned in any one permanent place or office within the organisation but arises from wherever it is most appropriate in relation to the task involved. This analysis decentralises leadership away from specific individuals to recognise that it is being exercised in a multitude of ways and in a multitude of locations throughout an organisation at any moment in time. This view of leadership can allow for the exercise of informal leadership by individuals within an organisation who can influence action and practice as opinion-formers, often creating resistance to change and reinforcing traditional practice and the cultural status quo. It also recognises the potential decoupling of elements of organisational practice from one another. Such informal leadership is acknowledged implicitly by Paul and Brindley when they point out that leaders need to do more than merely train professors in new techniques of teaching and assessment, but must also pay attention to wider cultural expectations if they are to avoid the possibility that all sorts of unintended consequences and forms of resistance to the planned changes will occur.

Ogawa and Bossert's concept of leadership as a force flowing through the organisation allows us to distinguish between perceiving leadership as a role and perceiving it as a construct. Seeing it as a role connects it to individuals, whereas seeing it as a construct enables us to identify it as a set of activities or events which will be undertaken by individuals, and which may be undertaken by virtue of their formal role or position within the organisation, or through more informal roles within their personal or professional role set. It emphasises the relational nature of leadership: we lead other people, and, as is made clear by Paul and Brindley in writing about ODL universities and Latchem, Lockwood and Baggaley writing about projects, we are dependent on them for agreeing to follow and supporting what we want them to do. Further, relationships are two-way affairs which require both parties to agree to sustain them, and they are rarely between equal partners. Grint (1999) points out that where action depends on the willingness of one party to agree with the wishes of another, it is actually the follower rather than the leader who has more power in the relationship, because their decision to refuse forces the leader to back down or find alternative means of getting their way – which may, of course, involve ending the relationship. This is why agreement and an element of consensus are essential in any setting where compulsion is problematic.

By raising the question of power, we introduce an issue that is often avoided by writers on leadership, particularly in the field of education. Yet it is clear that power is a key concept that runs through all the chapters. All of them are concerned with ways in which organisations or activities analyse and engage with their environments, and explore the extent to which they can influence the pressures upon them. The scenarios that Latchem and his colleagues analyse all demonstrate failures on the part of key players to position themselves so that they can achieve what they have set out to do: failure to secure a strong follow-through to ensure the implementation of a strategic plan, for example, or to persuade a university to prepare for the introduction of ODL rather than going ahead without analysing what it involved, indicate that the project leaders or their clients did not have the power they needed to carry out the task. Thompson and Shillington recognise the power of senior staff to block their initiative and to affect it by allocating insufficient resources: their argument for management "by fact" is a recognition of how one form of power – in their case, knowledge – can be set against another – in the case of senior staff, resources. The key difference between the environmental analyses of Paul and Brindley and Tait is that Tait sees the environment as an opportunity for the ODL university to challenge established values, whereas Paul and Brindley see it as a challenge to be taken as a given and responded to. Tait's argument claims power for the university leader to address key opinion formers and value-creators in the wider society and subvert traditional elitist values; Paul and Brindley accept the power of a consumerist student body and see the leadership role as one of responding to its wishes. But both also acknowledge the power of members of their organisations to resist policy and procedural decisions that they take in their leadership roles, although their responses are rather differently expressed. Again, we find different kinds of power being available to the parties to the relationship: resources on the part of senior leaders, and knowledge of practice on the part of the academic teaching and research staff.

Much of the literature on leadership and change presumes that our response to the exercise of power is primarily rational and calculative, and this stance is clear in all the chapters we have discussed. Central to this is the extent to which the power being exercised is deemed to be legitimate. The use of non-legitimate power results in what Hales (1997) calls alienative compliance, with serious consequences for the motivation of those involved. However, Hales goes on to argue that individuals respond to what they deem to be legitimate power by a calculative process of bargaining and exchange that deepens into commitment over time: the more they find that what is asked for and given in return is to their benefit, and results in continuing delivery of their obligations over time by the person who exercises that power, the more this calculative relationship develops into a commitment and ultimately into a relationship of trust that accepts the values of the other party as valid and appropriate. Whilst we may dispute the details of his analysis, his basic proposition that followership moves from a level of calculation towards one of trust is one that is widely argued (see Bottery, 2004). Surprisingly, relatively little attention is paid specifically to issues of trust in these chapters, although it is clearly a major issue in some of them: Latchem, Lockwood and Baggaley are concerned with building trust between donors, project members and clients in their ODL projects if they are to succeed, and a number of their scenarios indicate that lack of trust between project members and clients, and within the client organisation, are key features in the project's failure. Thompson and Shillington are concerned to ensure that students can trust the support service being provided, and their use of the term loyalty as a counterweight to consumerism indicates that they are looking for trust from the consumer-student.

The introduction of power into the discussion of leadership does not only lead to the issue of trust. It also introduces issues of morality – what makes leadership "proper". The moral dimension of leadership has been emphasised repeatedly in the educational leadership literature, regardless of whether it is seen from a broadly constructivist standpoint (for example, Sergiovanni, 2001; Lambert et al., 2002) or from more managerialist positions (e.g. Harris, 2002; Fullan, 2003; Leithwood et al., 2006). Harris describes the headteacher of one school where she identified a high degree of distributed leadership as "morally ruthless"; Fullan (2003) entitled his most recent book *The Moral Imperative of School Leadership*. Values therefore have a major part to play in defining "good" leadership and "good" leaders, which is the sub-text of all the chapters in this section. However, picking them out is not as straightforward as one might hope. Tait is quite clear about his stance in relation to both the role of the ODL institution in relation to society – subversive – and the obligations of the academics (and presumably others) who work there – acceptance of the values-stance. Latchem, Lockwood and Baggaley are clear about the purpose of the ODL projects they report, and also about the demands that success makes on project planners and consultants. Mason is clear that "good" assessment, both in terms of its robustness, reliability and validity and in terms of its effectiveness, must be integrated into the pedagogy and function as a tool for learning in its own right. It is less clear whether the authors of the other two chapters, who write from a student consumerist perspective, accept the values that they identify, or whether they simply view it as a given that the university must respond to. Thompson and Shillington do have a clear value position about the service obligation that an ODL institution has to its students, but that is overlaid by the same market-driven response that drives Paul and Brindley to offer services in a form and of a quality that promotes loyalty to the institution. In their chapter, Paul and Brindley accept the situation, analyse its implications clearly and incisively and advocate clear strategic responses, but it isn't clear whether their propositions are driven by the demands of survival or a belief in the "rightness" of the actions they suggest.

Earlier in this part, we indicated that conventional current views of leadership equate it with the promotion of change, and pointed out that all the leadership chapters we have discussed are actually discussions of how to bring about and ensure change. It was clear from all of them that the long-orthodox ideas of incremental change without any clear sense of vision and direction (Lindblom's (1959) "science of muddling through") and of change and policy making on an ad hoc and uncertain, almost anarchic basis

(Cohen et al.'s (1972) "garbage can" theory of organisational choice) have given way to rational, focused, vision-driven change. However, our discussion of issues of power and morality raise the question of the kinds of change that might be attempted, and what kinds of leadership can promote them. Tait refers in his chapter to "transformational" leadership (Burns, 1978; Bass and Avolio, 1994), which is conventionally defined in the literature as a form of leadership that brings about radical, vision-driven change. It is set against "transactional" leadership, which is a process of more incremental change that doesn't necessarily challenge the underpinning values of the status quo. Much of the current literature is by implication if not explicitly dismissive of transactional leadership on the grounds that it cannot cope with the constant environmental pressure for radical changes in practice, and it is clear that these chapters sign up to the argument that current circumstances require if they do not encourage radical change.

Transformational leadership is radical and challenging, and is synonymous with strong leadership. Fineman (2003) points out that transformational leadership frequently rests on particular charismatic individuals, for the promotion of radical change can provoke strong emotional responses that are not easily overcome through rational argument. Most advocates of distributed leadership argue that it is a vehicle for promoting radical change because it undermines traditional hierarchical models of organisation, which would appear to deny Fineman's argument. However, most of them acknowledge that distributed leadership can be – some would argue, can only be – developed within a strong framework that is policed by powerful individuals, often working through motivated teams whose members have "signed up" to the vision that has been articulated by the strong leader. Harris's (2002) "morally ruthless" headteacher set clear standards and boundaries for action which were not to be crossed, but within which high levels of distributed leadership were encouraged. Transformational leadership may depend for its achievement on widespread leadership activity throughout the organisation – indeed, this may be a part of the change that is being brought about – but it requires a very strong sense of direction if it is to be effective and avoid organisational fragmentation. Tait's argument about the importance of ODL academics sharing the subversive goals of their organisation's leaders recognises this point. Transformational leadership rests on a presumption of very significant power disparity between the leader and the led. Where this does not exist through the structure and culture of the organisation, it has to be created, and the result can be high levels of demoralisation, leading to exit. Fullan (2003) sees this as a necessary part of what he calls the "moral imperative" of leadership. Paul and Brindley and Panda are more inclined to acknowledge the need to bring potentially recalcitrant staff along with them.

28.5 CONCLUSION

The six chapters reviewed here have a number of elements in common. They all see leadership as an activity undertaken by individuals to align an organisation or unit with the demands of its environment. This process can be proactive or reactive. There are issues of implementation that need to be addressed as analyses of the environmental demands are converted into policies and then into practice. How these are faced and dealt with depends to some extent on the nature of the policy response, but they are strongly affected by the nature of power relationships between leader(s) and led, the extent to which the power they seek to exercise is deemed legitimate and the moral acceptability of the policies and practices that are proposed. None of the chapters pay particular attention to issues of what might be called distributed leadership, although Tait mentions the term explicitly and Latchem, Lockwood and Baggaley stress (but do not develop) the importance of bottom-up as well as top-down support for a project. All of the chapters adopt a rational model of leadership, and it could be argued that the issue of emotion, which is in any case underplayed in the leadership literature, receives less attention than is appropriate. However, what is clear from all of the chapters is the ODL faces major challenges and opportunities in the early twenty-first century, and that it is up to those who have leadership roles and capacities within ODL to promote effective and creative responses and to bring colleagues with them along the journey.

REFERENCES

Archer, M.W. (1981). Educational politics: A model for their analysis. In *Politics and Educational Change*, (P. Broadfoot, C. Brooke, and W. Tulasiewicz, eds) Croom Helm, pp. 29–55.

Bass, B.M. and Avolio, B.J. (1994). *Improving Organisational Effectiveness Through Transformational Leadership*. Thousand Oaks, CA: Sage.

Bennett, N., Harvey, J.A., Wise, C., and Woods, P.A. (2003). *Desk Study of Distributed Leadership*. Nottingham: National College for School Leadership. Available at http://ncsl.org.uk/literaturereviews.

Bottery, M. (2004). *The Challenges of Educational Leadership*. London: Paul Chapman Publishing.

Burns, J.M. (1978). *Leadership*. New York: Harper and Row.

Cohen, M.D., March, J.G., and Olsen, J.P. (1972). A garbage can model of organizational choice. *Administrative Science Quarterly*, **17**(1), 1–25.

Fineman, S. (2003). *Understanding Emotion at Work*. London: Sage.

Fullan, M. (2003) *The Moral Imperative of School Leadership*. Thousand Oaks, CA: Corwin Press.

Graetz, F. (2000). Strategic change leadership. *Management Decision*, **38**(8), 550–562.

Grint, K. (1999). *The Arts of Leadership*. Oxford: Oxford University Press.

Gronn, P. (2002). Distributed leadership as a unit of analysis. *Leadership Quarterly*, **13**(4), 423–451.

Hales, C. (1997). *Managing Through Organization*. London: Routledge.

Handy, C. (1991). *Gods of Management*, 3rd ed. London: Century Business.

Harris, A. (2002). Effective leadership in schools facing challenging contexts. *School Leadership and Management*, **22**(1), 15–26.

Harris, A. (2003). Teacher Leadership as Distributed Leadership: heresy, fantasy or possibility? *School Leadership and Management*, **23**(3), 313–324.

Lambert, L., Walker, D., Zimmerman, D.P. et al. (2002). *The Constructivist Leader*. New York: Teachers College Press.

Leithwood, K., Day, C., Sammons, P. et al. (2006). *Seven Strong Claims about Successful School Leadership*. Nottingham: National College for School Leadership.

Lindblom, C. (1959). The science of muddling through. *Public Administration Review*, **19**(2), 79–88.

Mintzberg, H. (1990). The management myth – folklore or fact? *Harvard Business Review*, March/April, 163–176.
Muijs, D. and Harris, A. (2007). Teacher leadership in (in)action: Three case studies of contrasting schools. *Educational Management Administration and Leadership*, **35**(1), 111–134.
Ogawa, R.T. and Bossert, S.T. (1995). Leadership as an Organizational Quality. *Educational Administration Quarterly*, **31**(2), 224–243.
Peters, T.J. and Waterman, R.H. (1982). *In Search of Excellence*. New York: Harper and Row.
Pressman, J. and Wildavsky, A. (1973). *Implementation*. Berkeley: University of California Press.
Rogers, E.M. (1995). *Diffusion of Innovation*. New York: Free Press.
Sergiovanni, T. (2001). *Leadership: What's in it for Schools?* London: RoutledgeFalmer.
Spillane, J.P. (2006). *Distributed Leadership*. San Francisco: Jossey-Bass.
Weick, K.E. (1976). Educational organizations as loosely-coupled systems. *Administrative Science Quarterly*, **21**(1), 1–19.
Woods, P.A., Bennett, N., Harvey, J.A., and Wise, C. (2004). Variabilities and dualities in distributed leadership: Findings from a systematic literature review. *Educational Management Administration and Leadership*, **32**(4), 439–457.

Section IV

Accountability and Evaluation in Distance Education

Introduction

David Murphy

This section focuses on the combination of a long-established and well-researched practice in distance education (that of evaluation) with an emerging and increasingly significant concern to all distance educators, accountability. Intertwined with these two are a number of associated topics, particularly quality assurance, assessment and accreditation.

Murgatroyd provides the first chapter in this section, wherein he examines the concept of quality and its multiple uses and frameworks, which leads nicely into accreditation and its manifestations in the distance education community. In particular, he takes us through the process by which Athabasca University was accredited by the Middle States Higher Education Commission in the United States. Moving to a different level, approaches to program review are outlined, with special emphasis on student services and other features peculiar to the distance education context. Stepping out into the wider context, examples of accountability frameworks are presented, emphasizing the growing interest in the public accountability of our institutions.

Woodley turns the focus firmly to evaluation, a topic with which he has enjoyed decades of experience at the UKOU. Further, while most of the examples he presents are from that institution, the models and approaches, coupled with his historical perspective, make for an engaging and relevant review of the field. His "geological model" of open and distance learning evaluation provides a vehicle for an examination of evaluation in terms of public and institutional research. The chapter also looks to the future, and ends with a return to the thorny issue of evaluating the cost-effectiveness of distance education.

Jung, like Murgatroyd, looks at quality in distance education, first taking us on a brief history of the quality movement and associated issues and challenges, such as the rise in use of information and communication technology and the globalization of higher education. She takes us on a journey across a number of countries and contexts (from Anadolu to Athabasca), illustrating the ways in which models of quality assurance are applied and an associated quality culture has emerged. Finally, Jung offers a number of strategies to enable institutions and nations to achieve their quality assurance objectives.

Murphy takes up the issue of accountability, introduced by both Murgatroyd and Jung, and discusses its rising role in higher education in general and distance education in particular. Using the Accountability Triangle (the balance among government, academic and market forces) as a conceptual lens, he briefly examines global trends before offering a couple of case studies from Australia and Hong Kong. Overly, he argues that accountability is here to stay and that distance education institutions need to demonstrate their responses and results to its manifestations.

The issue of transnational distance education provides Ziguras with the opportunity to discuss the failure of the recent wave of global distance education providers, citing their lack of understanding of students as fundamental to their overall failure. The transnational providers who have succeeded, he contends, are those who have offered students local support. This discussion provides him with the opportunity to discuss the associated issues of partner support, curriculum, cultural diversity, and teaching and learning styles in an effort to unravel the complexity of transnational education and explain the factors that make for success.

Thorpe provides the critical essay for this section, within which she analyses the contributions of the chapters from a number of standpoints, including the challenges of the expansion of distance education and its role in development in particular. Drawing on aspects of the discussions and examples from a variety of contexts, she examines the relationships between the key issues under consideration (evaluation, quality assurance, accreditation and accountability) and urges practitioners to avoid developing a compliance culture through commitment to internal evaluation and quality improvement.

Chapter 29

Managing for Performance: Quality, Accreditation and Assessment in Distance Education

Stephen Murgatroyd

29.1 INTRODUCTION

The term "quality" is in widespread use in education. It means different things to different people. For some, it relates to an "absolute standard", such as "the ideal staff:student ratio". For others, it refers to a process of peer review which permits assessment against a set of criteria, rather like a jury of peers sitting in judgment of others with a set of regulations as their guide. Others take the view that quality is determined by the market – if the outcomes of an educational process are valued by students, employers and others, then quality exists: quality is "fitness for use". Quality needs to be defined and this chapter will look at three frameworks for the definition of quality, focusing on the implications of each definition for distance education.

Quality, especially at the level of an institution, is variously assessed in different countries. Canada, for example, has no formal national accreditation or quality standards for post-secondary institutions, but has different standards in different provinces. Accreditation of universities or colleges or of professional programs in the United States is undertaken largely through a combination of self-regulating regional peer review against a set of agreed criteria, some objective data (e.g. student satisfaction, diversity measures, access to resources) and a set of judgments about the appropriateness of an institution's governance and decision making. There are several different accreditation bodies, each with their own standards and processes. Some, including the US Congress, are suspicious of the ways in which quality is assessed. A discussion paper issued in 2006 for the US Secretary for Education's Commission on the Future of Higher Education states (Miller, 2006),

> A major objective for the Commission on the Future of Higher Education is to insure that consumer-friendly information about colleges and universities be easily available

> to the public with little or no cost. The following issue paper/proposal is designed to produce that outcome through a recommendation to implement a free, comprehensive information system about higher education available from the U.S. Department of Education, in consumer-friendly form.... This comprehensive data system will allow all consumers or other analysts to create rankings of colleges and universities in an individual or customized format and allow the unlimited development of college rankings as needed and demanded by the public.
>
> [underlining in original] (p. 1)

This reveals that quality is an issue of public concern as well as one of academic integrity. This chapter will review the range of public concern issues and ways that are emerging of assuaging these concerns. It will also examine accreditation as a process.

In addition to reviewing quality, accreditation and competency-based outcome assessment, this chapter will also explore the practice of accountability for the management of performance outcomes in a distance education organization or program and review some recent developments.

29.2 THREE FRAMEWORKS FOR QUALITY

In an earlier contribution to this literature (Murgatroyd and Morgan, 1992), it was suggested that there are three distinctive uses of the term "quality". These are (a) quality assurance, (b) contract conformance and (c) customer-driven quality.

29.2.1 Quality Assurance

Quality assurance in education refers to the determination of standards, appropriate methods and quality requirements by a self-regulating expert body, accompanied by a process of review or inspection that examines the extent to which a particular institution's practices meet these standards. Critical to the process of quality assurance are the publication of standards and their interpretation, the transparency of the process of review and clear indications of whether or not an organization or program meets these standards.

Institutional accreditation is based on a set of published standards which an institution has to meet, a set of guidelines about how to interpret these standards, a clear description of the process of review and published reports which result from that review aimed at ensuring transparency.

For example, 125 medical schools in the United States and the seventeen in Canada each have to meet standards established by the Association of American Medical Colleges (AAMC) as outlined in their publication *The Functions and Structure of a Medical School* (LMCE, 2006). Following the submission of an extensive self-study and a visit by a peer review body of up to twenty persons, a specific medical school will receive a systematic written review of its performance against the standards. Once it has responded to this review, accreditation will be granted, be made conditional on some specific change or be denied. The process is repeated periodically and institutions are required to offer an annual review of their activities and notify the accrediting body of any substantive changes.

Within such guidelines, distance education is usually seen as an optional activity rather than mainstream. The expectation is that students pursuing some aspect of their studies by this means will normally be expected to be treated "not significantly differently" from others who are not, and that such students will be seen to have at least no significantly different outcomes from their learning (Russell, 2002) or even better outcomes (Shachar and Neumann, 2003). The Association to Advance Collegiate Schools of Business (AACSB) – the international program accrediting body in business education with 515 accredited programs, eighty of them outside the United States – says this in its guidelines about students pursuing some or their entire program at a distance:

> Distance education programs have particular support issues related to technology support and assistance for students and faculty, security and confidentiality safeguards, accountability for learning, and technology to provide sufficient interactive components for quality education.
>
> (AACSB, 2006, p. 27)

In the United States, however, there is an accrediting body for distance education and training – the Distance Education and Training Council (DETC) – which has accredited degree granting institutions in Australia (Deakin, Monash, Southern Queensland), the United Kingdom (University of Leicester, Rhodec International Inc.), South Africa (UNISA) and over one hundred post-secondary institutions in the United States. While having the same status in law as the regional accrediting bodies, most seeking accreditation would do so through a regional body. The University of Phoenix, for example, is accredited by the Higher Learning Commission of the North Central accrediting body. Athabasca University (Canada) and The Open University (UK) are both accredited by the Middle States Commission on Higher Education.

29.2.2 Contract Conformance

Under this conception of quality, a contract is negotiated between the party receiving a good or service and those delivering it. Quality is a measurement of the extent to which the promise of the contract is matched by the delivery of an outcome. An e-learning program offering, such as that from W3 Schools (http://www.w3schools.com/cert/default.asp), which commits to providing the learner with the knowledge to achieve certification in a range of specific skills (HTML, XML, ASP programming skills, for example) either does or does not deliver these skills. In this case, assessment is web-based to a set of industry standards agreed for each of these skills. Some courses, such as those in real estate, can be reviewed by a third party such as The International Distance Education Certification Centre in Montgomery, Alabama, who will certify that the courses and those providing them are legitimate and meet certain standards.

A great deal of the work on competency-based assessment (CBA) can be seen to be a form of contract conformance. The Australian training system for trades and technical skills is based on the concept of competency. Using both the National Training Framework (NTF) and Australian Recognition Framework (ARF), required knowledge for a trade or skill is defined in competency units. Each unit of competency describes a specific work activity, the conditions under which it is conducted and the evidence that may be gathered in order to determine whether the activity is being performed in a competent manner. The components of a unit of competency – the elements, performance criteria, range of variables and evidence guide – provide the basis for assessing the unit of competency. A learner completes the required learning through distance education, classroom activities or work-based learning or some combination of these methods. On completion of their preparatory activities, a learner submits themselves for assessment using a learning portfolio and a formal assessment. Britain has a similar process with the National Vocational Qualifications (NVQ).

Key to the contract conformance conception of quality is the ability of the provider of a learning opportunity to specify both exactly what skills and competency a person will have because of their learning and how this will be assessed. It is a design principle of most distance education courses that such specificity will be made clear at the beginning of a learning module and that students will be clear as to how they will be assessed against the objectives of the course: there is a transparency about the learning process "designed in" to distance education (Institute for Higher Education Policy, 2000; Council for Higher Education Accreditation, 2002).

29.2.3 Customer-Driven Quality

A third form of quality is where the end user – the learner or, more likely, their subsequent employer – determines the quality of the learning a person or group has received in terms of its value to them. For example, a student who has completed a university entrance qualification (e.g. High School Diploma, appropriate "A" levels in the UK, International Baccalaureate) who arrives at a college, university or employment with poor skills in analysis, mathematics or languages will not be seen as a "quality" product of their school system, especially when compared to others who possess these skills. The customer – in this case a college, university or employer – will judge the quality of the feeder school appropriately and may choose not to accept their students in future. This has been a particular concern for colleges and universities assessing overseas students' abilities in English as a Foreign Language.

Customers are concerned about quality outcomes from education. The Confederation of British Industry (CBI), for example, has suggested that one third of UK employers have to provide basic literacy and numeracy training for employees who leave the compulsory school system without these skills and are unable to make effective use of the web or related resources in their work (BBC, 2004). A UK House of Commons report from the Public Accounts Committee (see summary at http://www.management-issues.com/display_page.asp?section=research&id=2957) shows that some 16 million adults in the United Kingdom hold down regular employment despite having numeracy skills of level one or below – the equivalent of someone aged 11 years old or younger. In terms of literacy, around 12 million people in employment are struggling at the same level.

In the United States, concerns are even stronger. Here is a summary of the public concern issues which have been presented before the US Commission on the Future of Higher Education at some time in 2005/2006:

- The percentage of students entering higher education in the last 20 years has increased by 20 percent but the number graduating has increased by just 3 percent in this same time.
- Less than one third of college graduates could read instructions for a complex task and make complicated inferences, according to a study by the National Assessment of Adult Literacy (NAAL).
- Rates of adult literacy have declined since 1990 – only 25 percent of college graduates are deemed to have adult literacy levels appropriate to their qualifications.
- A similar study by the National Survey of America's College Students of numeracy shows that 20 percent of 4-year degree graduates and 30 percent of 2-year degree holders have only very basic numeracy skills. They find calculating the total on a grocery bill difficult. Worse, 50 percent of 4-year degree holders and 75 percent of 2-year degree holders had only basic literacy – not dissimilar to the position in the United Kingdom.

Customers have a right to be concerned about educational outputs, especially when these outputs flow from "accredited" institutions.

29.3 THE DOMINANT QUALITY FRAMEWORK: ACCREDITATION AND PEER REVIEW

The quality assurance model dominates educational assessment and review processes. It is used at the K-12 school level through such processes as that used by the Office for Standards in Education (OFSTED) in the United Kingdom, by the eight regional accrediting bodies in the United States as well as the sixty-six specialist accrediting bodies (e.g. Society of American Foresters, Accreditation Council for Occupational Therapy Education); by the quality assurance bodies for post-secondary education in British Columbia, Alberta, Ontario and Quebec; and by almost all of the accrediting bodies worldwide. The International Standards Organizations (through ISO 9000–04) have also created an approach to quality in distance education. In the ISO system, external controllers examine and interpret the quality of a distance education system (an institute) by means of documentation and guidelines within the framework of globally agreed standards.

It is the dominant model because it is

- general enough to permit accreditation for most applicants, but not all – it is therefore inclusive;
- while time consuming, relatively straightforward – the process is clear, the work required is clear, and there should be no surprises as a result of the process;

- both periodic and continuous – there are major assessment points and continuous reporting; and
- relatively low cost, both in terms of time and money, especially once initial accreditation has been achieved.

It is a disputed process for several reasons, including

- it is overly general – the standard criteria are not absolute and are open to varied interpretations, and are general rather than specific;
- while some systems have reviewers who are not employed in "sister" institutions, most accreditation systems use peer review and this in itself is problematic; and
- accreditation is generally at the institutional or program level, not necessarily in terms of student outcomes.

At the heart of these concerns is the process of peer review. Peer review is often a problematic and ineffective process. In academic publishing, for example, peer review is increasingly under suspicion. The Cochrane Collaboration undertook a systematic review of some 135 papers in biomedicine and found that in only twenty-one studies was the data presented credible (Petit-Zeman, 2003). Each year in the United States, there are several instances of significant peer review failures. One of the most startling was revealed in October 2002 when the work of Bell Laboratories' Jan Hendrick Schon came under scrutiny. Schon published twenty-five papers over the period 1999–2003. Of those, sixteen have been declared false (Piller, 2002). This finding caused the prestigious journal *Science* to repudiate eight of his papers. All of these repudiated papers had been peer reviewed. These examples raise more general doubts about peer review for all academic matters – a scientific paper's peer review can be problematic when this uses the core competence of the reviewers, what is the likelihood of institutional and program review also being problematic when most academic administrators have not been trained as managers, administrators or leaders? Dr Tom Jefferson, from the Cochrane Collaboration Methods Group claimed "If peer review were a new medicine, it would never get a license. Peer-review is generally assumed to be an important part of the scientific process and is used to assess and improve the quality of submissions to journals as well as being an important part of the process of deciding what research is funded. But we have found little empirical evidence to support the use of peer review as a mechanism to ensure the quality of research reporting" (Petit-Zeman, 2003, n.p.). Similar issues can therefore be assumed to exist with all forms of peer review.

There is another issue relating to the peer review process and distance education: the inhibiting effect of peer review on the development of distance education and technology-supported learning. Peer review is meant to be about standards for teaching and learning but is de facto also about the theories of peers concerning appropriate models of institutions, teaching, learning and assessment. Peers use their experientially developed rules to determine the appropriateness of that which they are reviewing (Mills and Murgatroyd, 1991). In 1996 when Athabasca University first approached AACSB to discuss accreditation of the new, online MBA program, the prospect of accreditation was dismissed out of hand since distance education was "unacceptable" as a teaching method at that time and online distance education even more problematic. Accrediting bodies can be gatekeepers, closing the gate on innovation, at least at the early stages of innovation adoption.

29.4 HOW ACCREDITATION WORKS

To illustrate the process of accreditation, the following is a short case study of the process. Athabasca University used to achieve US accreditation through the Middle States Higher Education Commission – an accreditation it secured in 2005.

An institutional decision was made as part of the strategic plan for the University to seek accreditation, and Middle States was recognized as the appropriate regional body for this process, since it was inviting international institutions to engage in such a process. A steering group was established to "manage" this relationship and work began in 2001 to achieve accreditation. They began by studying the Commission's comprehensive publications on accreditation and discussing their prospective application with the staff of the Commission.

Once an application had been made, a preliminary review is undertaken to ensure that there is a "fit" between the institution and the Commission. This preliminary documentation and a "readiness" visit is mutually informative: the commission begins to look at the institution critically and examines its operations, drawing attention to activities or concerns which will need to be addressed in the full submission and the University better understands the criteria and process required by the Commission. The resulting readiness review documentation from the Commission guides, the preparation of a substantive self-study.

Athabasca University's self-study, which was not unlike that conducted by any institution undertaking accreditation, involved over a third of all academic staff and all of the administration. It is substantial – a document of over one hundred pages – and supported by evidence ranging from systematic data analysis, survey material and quotations from students and staff. It paints a realistic picture of the University, raising issues as well as presenting the University in a systematic way, using the standards of the Commission as the framework for the study. Once submitted, it is reviewed for completeness and is then passed to the team which will be responsible for determining if accreditation should be granted.

The institution seeking accreditation can normally suggest specific individuals whom the Commission may appoint to the review panel, but the decision on who will undertake the peer review is a matter for the Commission. The chair of the peer review team makes an initial visit to familiarize him or herself with the institution and to meet with staff and students to ensure that they understand the process and that they can raise issues with the chair before the visit takes place.

A site visit from the peer review team – 15–20 persons – takes place over a number of days. The team works in small groups to meet with different staff, students and reviews the self-study, related materials and discusses these in depth. They then present an interim review which is followed by a full-written review, normally within a few working days. The institution can then respond to this review, correcting errors of fact or clarifying issues raised. The review team then makes its recommendation to the Commission and an accreditation decision is made at the next normal meeting of the Commission.

Once accreditation is granted, the institution is required to report on its activities annually and to inform the Commission of substantive changes. For example, Athabasca University is accredited to offer undergraduate and master's degrees. Once it begins to offer doctoral programs, it will need to undertake a similar process to that just described to have its accreditation status changed to permit it to be accredited as a doctoral institution. Periodically, the University will be required to repeat the process.

It is important to note that what is being accredited here is the University. Its programs are not reviewed in this process. What is reviewed is the process by which the institution undertakes quality assurance at the level of programs and courses. Rather than asking "is the Bachelors of Professional Arts (Communications) a quality program?" the question the commission asks is "does Athabasca University have a good process for determining whether such a program is a quality program?"

The accreditation process is thorough, informative, challenging, demanding (especially in terms of time and labour) and also revealing – some key issues associated with the University's online learning platforms were raised as were issues about governance, all of which were dealt with. It was a process useful to the administration of the institution in that it provided feedback and systematic, thoroughgoing peer review for the first time in the University's history. It led to Athabasca University being the only Canadian University to be fully accredited to operate in the United States.

Some of the accrediting bodies have reformed their criteria for evaluation, embracing the framework for institutional excellence developed by the Malcolm Baldridge Quality Awards or the European Foundation for Quality Management (EFQM). They have also embraced institutional capability analysis (Gibson, 1998), capacity analysis and reviews of evidence-based decision making, including work in New Zealand to improve the e-learning capability of its institutions (see Neal et al., 2005). Others have also offered benchmark review processes by which institutions can compare themselves against others in key measures of outcome and performance – AACSB has done this for over a decade, permitting institutions to learn from best practice and understand their position in the "league" of practitioners.

Distance education is generally treated as a teaching option within this process. That is, using the assumption of "no significant difference" in learning experience and outcomes between students taught through distance learning and those taught in classrooms, accrediting teams look at such issues as scalability and student satisfaction.

29.5 PROGRAM REVIEW

Program review, for example for programs in nursing or programs that are required to meet "industry" or professional standards, generally follows the same process as that for accreditation. The focus is on the program, its students and the strengths and weaknesses of the approach to learning and student performance. Increasingly in such reviews, the focus has moved from just reviewing the program to a critical examination of outcomes – what are the competencies which students possess because of completing the program.

Typical elements of a program review within an institution are these:

- Scheduled on a 5- to 8-year cycle, or the year prior to an outside accreditation review.
- The academic centre or department prepares a self-study that describes the unit's contributions to the institution, curricula, student profile and performance, faculty, facilities and resources, comparison to peers and other programs, and the unit's plan for the future.
- The future plan includes a discussion of ways to build on strengths and remediate weaknesses, expected reallocations or ways to obtain new funds to support any planned changes, and planning for the expected needs of students, the community and the state. In particular, distance education programs are expected to review their technology strategy and their strategy for student support.
- A review committee that includes a broad range of representatives from the institutions academic administration approves the self-study and collaborates with the unit in the selection of a team of reviewers.
- The review team usually includes three or more experienced faculty from other institutions and one "home" institution member.
- The review team provides a systematic report that is reviewed at all levels of the institution and is the basis for an action plan.
- An action plan is developed and then monitored for completion of action items. A more comprehensive review of the action plan occurs 3 years following the APR.

To better take into account learning outcomes in this process, many distance education organizations have developed a more focused process for outcome-based program review, such as this from the State University of Florida system:

1. Articulate the mission(s) and purpose(s) of the program(s) within the context of the institutional mission.
2. Identify program goals/objectives, including expected outputs and outcomes. Specifically, identify and publicize expected measurable student learning outcomes.
3. Develop assessment systems to determine how well students are achieving those learning outcomes.
4. Implement and/or modify the program(s) to achieve the articulated goals/objectives.

5. Collect data and information on actual outputs and outcomes.
6. Analyze – and have external expert(s) in the discipline analyze – the data and information to determine how well-articulated goals/objectives have been accomplished within the context of the mission.
7. Specifically, analyze – and have external expert(s) in the discipline analyze – how well students are meeting expected learning outcomes, both as articulated by program personnel and as deemed appropriate in the discipline within the context of the individual institution's mission.
8. Assess – and have external expert(s) in the discipline assess – the sufficiency of resources and support services to achieve the goals/objectives.
9. Identify – and have external expert(s) in the discipline identify – strengths, opportunities, and barriers that support or impede achievement of goals.
10. Review – and have external expert(s) in the discipline review – responses to recommendations from previous reviews.
11. Generate – and have external expert(s) in the discipline generate – recommendations based on review findings.
12. Plan for continuous program improvement based on the results of the review.

In such systems, students' work (assignments, projects) and engagement (involvement in discussions, project team work online) and contribution (formal assessment of the value of a student's participation) are reviewed and assessed. Typically, reviewers wish to see samples of the top 10 percent, average students and those near failing.

29.6 ONLINE STUDENT SERVICES

Education is about more than courses and programs. It also involves enabling a student to explore career choices, improve their learning skills and competencies, deal with financial concerns and overcome anxieties, distress or feelings of isolation. A key quality question for an institution developing a distance education program is "what kind of student support services shall we offer?" and "how shall we ensure the quality of these services?"

Organizations offering distance education offer a range of student services online, ranging from library services, financial advising and support for financial aid, career guidance, academic advising, counselling, skills training for learning and examinations, anxiety management and other services. Guidelines exist as to best practices for these services and the Western Co-operative for Educational Technology (WCET) has established a systematic review and evaluation practices which looks critically at all aspects of online support for student services through the Centre for Transforming Student Services (CETSS), based in Colorado, which also offers audit and benchmarking services.

Enhanced web services are rapidly emerging to support students, including

- Career Connections at Colorado State University;
- Disability Supports and Services at the University of Illinois; and
- Psychological services at the Help Your Self site used by a number of institutions.

There is also a growing number of online counselling sites (psycho-social problems), some of which are now making extensive use of artificial intelligence engines to support meaningful dialogue with individuals (see, e.g. Ask The Internet Therapist athttp://www.asktheinternettherapist.com/). Peer review of the functioning of these sites and the algorithms which drive them is also taking place.

29.7 SPECIAL CONCERNS WITH DISTANCE EDUCATION

Quality assurance, accreditation reviews and the assessment of programs and student services are all conducted within distance educational institutions or institutions whose offerings include distance education on the assumption of no significant difference. Students pursuing distance education will have meaningful learning experiences, be treated equitably with students studying through other means and will achieve the same or better results.

There are, however, some specific issues which many evaluations now attend to which are unique to distance education. These include the following:

- the assessment and management of quality, reliability and accessibility of technological systems to support distance learning;
- the availability of academic support services and peer support services for learning and problem solving;
- the coherence, completeness of distance education programs and ensuring that appropriate courses are offered in a sequence or configuration that allows timely completion of requirements;
- application of the same faculty qualifications to distance education programs as all other academic programs. Faculty design, deploy and deliver distance learning or supervise delivery where the learning is "franchised" in some way;
- provision of clear statements of learner responsibilities and expectations of student participation and learning;
- provision for appropriate and flexible interaction between faculty and students and among students;
- the selection of appropriate technologies for a specific distance learning opportunity for the intended learning outcomes, content, relevant characteristics of the learning and the learner, and student cost;
- adequate verification of learners' work; and
- faculty and program administrators' determination of the appropriate enrolment that can be supported in the distance learning program and in individual courses, based upon the content and learning activities, the nature of the learners, the technologies used and the support available to faculty.

Of these, the most frequent concerns are expressed over the verification of a learner's work – how does the organization ensure that the enrolled student is the one whose work is evaluated through both formative and summative assessment as well as examinations. Some have developed proctoring systems so as to undertake verification (Ahern, 2001). Others are now beginning to use biometric security systems – fingerprint, iris matching, palm identification – so as to ensure that the student sitting an examination online is in fact the student who registered for the course (Lin et al., 2004; Chaudhari et al., 2005; Sickler and Elliot, 2005).

29.8 STRATEGIC REVIEWS OF INSTITUTIONAL PERFORMANCE – INSTITUTIONAL CAPABILITY REVIEWS[1]

Self-study, peer and program review provide some indication of whether the institution or program is meeting expectations and living up to its commitments. But these are relatively "soft" measures. Increasingly, distance education organizations and others are turning to what might be termed "commitment performance reviews" – evaluating whether the institution or program is "on target" to achieve the measurable goals to which they are committed. Such reviews also examine the extent to which the institution is capable of achieving the plans it has established for itself. Many see this as very important, since many new kinds of organizations have emerged which offer distance education and online educational programs.

There are several approaches to such capability reviews (Ewell, 2002), but they all have in common:

- a focus on understanding the goals and objectives for which capacities are being developed;
- a review of the organizational will, resources and managerial capacity for change;
- a systematic analysis of the priorities and performance of the institution against these priorities; and
- an examination of what remedial action is taken when the data shows that a specific performance measure or group of measures is not being met.

This process begins with a review of the institution's strategic and business plans and the identification of planned measurable outcomes. These may be such things as budget outcomes, growth in student numbers, performance of students in terms of time to completion, completion rates, drop-out rates and so on. Attention is then placed on the systems the institution uses to track its performance on key measures and understand its capabilities to impact key variables. Particular attention is then paid to situations in which key targets are "missed" and what remedial action is taken and how the impact of such action is analyzed.

For example, Athabasca University had a measurable goal of increasing the number of students taking more than two courses – most of its students take just one or two courses. Between 1972 and 2003, a total of 490,516 students had taken undergraduate courses with Athabasca University. Of these, 55 percent had taken one (37.6%) or two (17%) undergraduate courses. A key retention strategy was to increase the number taking three of more courses (45%). Part of the motivation for this is to move the University to becoming more program focused than course focused, and part of the motivation is financial – costs of securing a student in an additional course are less than securing a new student for their first course, and there are different rates of government subsidy for students in some programs. Systematic analysis of the differences between the student profiles of the two groups (one or two courses takers versus 3+ course takers) and a systematic analysis of the impact of different intervention campaigns (proactive calling, mail campaigns, targeted campaigns for specific programs, etc.) then became part of the work of the University – always looking at continuously improving its capacity to retain students.

This is a very focused example. A more typical example may be to look at the planned expansion of an institution, say from undergraduate to graduate level or from master's to PhD and to assess its capabilities to make this transition. One methodology increasingly used in such capability reviews is simulation – the use of computer models to forecast and analyze capability requirements and capacity. For example, if an institution plans to grow its student volumes at 10 percent per year, at what point do what systems in the institution become problematic and at what point do investment need to be made (capital, people, infrastructure, technology) so as to meet the demands a growing student body makes on the organization? In distance education, such work is usually done in relation to the scalability of technological systems to support growth in learner demand, but simulation technologies are now being used to model institutions as a whole.

Capacity and capability evaluations are generally a continuous process undertaken within the institution, made available to external reviewers. Some make use of balanced scorecards (Elloumi and Annand, 2002), qualify function deployment tools (Murgatroyd, 1993) or other systematic tools, but the general principle is that there should be a thorough review of the capacity of the organization to sustain and improve the delivery of a course, program or service and that such reviews should be multivariate and include a systematic study of all variables that affect capability. Specific approaches to this work for distance education have recently been developed by New York State's Office of College and University Evaluation (see http://web.nysed.gov/ocue/distance/icrdescription.htm).

29.9 UNDERSTANDING ACCOUNTABILITY FRAMEWORKS

We began by seeking to understand accountability and assessment in terms of three different frameworks for quality. So as to understand the system of accountability and assessment, we need to understand how course, program, general learning objectives and institutional capability assessment and accreditation connect. Figure 29.1[2] shows the interrelationship between each level of accountability and assessment. The idea is that we can look at a slice of the institution at any time from a variety of perspectives – student as an individual, a group of learners at the level of a course or program or student service, the institution at a variety of levels and across a variety of issues or capabilities. Using evidenced-based analysis, we can begin to understand what works and what doesn't and what impact change efforts have (Fullan, 2005). By understanding the dynamics of change, we can continuously improve educational activities.

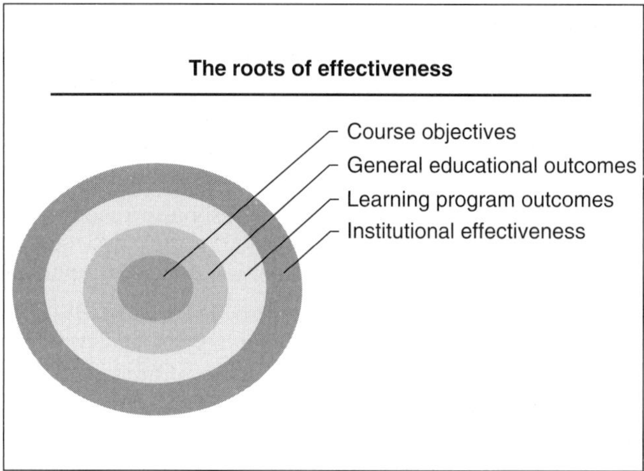

Figure 29.1: Four Layers of Accountability for Institutional Effectiveness

29.10 PUBLIC ACCOUNTABILITY

Most of the activities described to this point in this chapter refer to assessment or accreditation processes which are within an institution, undertaken through peer review or make use of models, benchmarks or best practices against which an institution can compare themselves.

Governments and funding agencies, however, are often not satisfied with such processes and have introduced ways of standard "testing" programs or "institutions". The development of standardized testing of students as a way of evaluating institutional performance is a rapidly growing phenomenon, especially at the K-12 level (Tucker and Codding, 1998; Sacks, 2000; Sahlberg, 2006), and there are efforts to spread this to post-secondary institutions.

For example, The Teaching Quality Information (TQI) initiative of the British Government is intended to provide information to prospective students and employers on the quality of post-secondary programs at each of the 329 institutions across the United Kingdom. Using data collected in the National Student Survey (NSS) and the Teaching Quality Assessment (TQA), statistics on admission, progress and completion as well as information provided by each institution about the quality of a specific program, the Government seeks to provide "best value" information on which decisions can be made (see http://www2.tqi.ac.uk/sites/tqi/home/index.cfm?tab=hei). Britain also publishes performance "league tables" for schools and for post-secondary education, as do a number of other jurisdictions.

In a different approach to institutional and systems accountability, the Government of Alberta periodically reviews the outcomes of post-secondary education at a more general level 2 years after graduation using telephone interviews and other methodologies. It looks systematically at "customer" satisfaction with the experience of learning, at employment outcomes and other aspects of the post-secondary system. Performance against a range of criteria has been used to shape funding decisions on discretionary funding to institutions. Alberta is not unlike many other government systems around the world.

Australia also has a national quality assessment framework (see http://www.aqf.edu.au/quality.htm). This sets out the different roles for different actors in the play for quality:

- National Government – assessing research plans and capabilities, agreeing the framework for quality assurance and undertaking "value for money" audits of the system.
- State Government – accreditation based on agreed, national protocols.
- Australian University Quality Agency – audits and peer reviews with best practice as the aim.
- Universities/Colleges – responsible for academic standards and capabilities.
- Australian Qualifications Framework – national registers and qualifications guidelines.

Distance education is treated as a delivery option in these frameworks at each level, again the assumption being that there are "no significant differences" between distance learners and others pursuing the same program.

The fundamental questions Governments are asking are the following:

- can we assure our students that they are receiving a quality education at all of the organizations authorized to offer such education in our jurisdiction – the quality question?
- are we assured that we are securing a good social return on our investment in our educational services and systems – the value for money question? and
- what are the long-term implications of decisions we make as a government for the performance of the education system – the consequences question?

The quality question is usually answered by the kind of framework developed in Australia or the public listing services offered in the United Kingdom – both briefly described here. The value for money question is explored in studies such as that described in Alberta or by systematic studies. For example, Brady et al. (2005) have looked at the social outcomes of investments in post-secondary education in California. Using scenario planning and forecasting models, the authors look at the impact investment in post-secondary education will have on health, crime, the economy and other factors. The authors suggest that for every dollar invested in post-secondary education, the State secures a three dollar return. The consequence question also used studies like Brady et al. (2005) to help shape policy and action choices, especially in terms of accessibility, fees and cost and quality.

29.11 CONCLUSION

This chapter has provided a framework for understanding how quality, accreditation and assessment is practised and how these practices relate to distance education. It has used examples from several countries and brief accounts of key processes to establish how quality is assured in distance education.

There are challenges, the most notable of which is the emergence of new kinds of institutions which offer distance education – virtual networks and franchises which, while they may take courses from a range of accredited institutions, are offering them in "packages" different from those originally intended. A second set of developments relate to the emergence of artificial intelligence and other technologies which may transform the nature of online learning – especially when linked to three-dimensional simulation technologies and the semantic web (Contact North, 2006). Such developments will pose challenges for the providers of quality assurance services, such as accrediting bodies or professional associations. Such bodies have demonstrated over the last 100 years that they are adaptable. They will need to be.

NOTES

1. I acknowledge the work of Dr Nancy Parker, Director, Institutional Studies and Acting Executive Director, External Relations at Athabasca University in shaping this section.
2. With thanks to Dr Nancy Parker for this diagram.

REFERENCES

AACSB. (2006). *Eligibility Procedures and Accreditation Standards for Business Accreditation*, Tampa, FL: Association to Advance Collegiate Schools of Business. Retrieved May 6, 2006, from http://www.aacsb.edu/accreditation/business/STANDARDS.pdf.

Ahern, T. (2001). *Online Testing in Distance Education.* Paper presented at the 17th Annual Conference on Distance Teaching and Learning, Madison, Wisconsin (mimeo).

BBC. (2004). *Basic Skills "Employer's Guarantee"*. BBC News, 18 October. Retrieved May 6, 2006 from http://news.bbc.co.uk/1/hi/education/3753220.stm.

Brady, H., Hout, M., Stiles, J., Gleeson, S. and Hui, I. (2005). *Return on Investment: Educational Choices and Demographic Change in California's Future.* Berkeley, CA: Survey Research Centre (mimeo).

Chaudhari, S., Sudarsan, S.D., and Kavitha, A. (2005). *Architecture for Secure Distance Education Through Virtual Learning*. Bangalore, India: ELELTECH (mimeo).

Contact North. (2006). *Technology and the FUTURE OF LEARNING*. Sudbury, ON: Contact North Thought Leadership Paper (mimeo).

Council for Higher Education Accreditation. (2002). *Accreditation and Assuring Quality in Distance Education.* Washington, DC: Council for Higher Education Accreditation Monograph.

Elloumi, F. and Annand, D. (2002). *Integrating Faculty Research Performance Evaluation and the Balanced Scorecard in AU Strategic Planning: A Collaborative Model.* Athabasca, AB (mimeo).

Ewell, P.T. (2002). A delicate balance: The role of evaluation in management. *Quality in Higher Education*, **8**(2), 159–171.

Fullan, M. (2005). *Leadership and Sustainability – Systems Thinkers in Action*. Thousand Oaks, CA: Corwin Press.

Gibson, C. (1998). *Distance Learners in Higher Education – Institutional Responses for Quality Outcomes*. Madison, WI: Atwood Publishing.

Institute for Higher Education Policy. (2000). *Quality on the Line – Benchmarks for Success in Internet Based Learning*. Washington, DC: Institute for Higher Education Policy (mimeo).

Lin, N.H., Korba, L., Yee, G. et al. (2004). *Security and Privacy Technologies for Distance Education Applications*. 18th International Conference on Advanced Information Networking and Applications (AINA '04), Vol. 1, 580.

LMCE. (2006). *Functions and Structure of a Medical School*. Liaison Committee on Medical Education. Retrieved October 27, 2006 from http://www.lcme.org/pubs.htm#fands.

Miller, C. (2006). Accountability/Consumer Information. Issue paper for the Secretary of Education's Commission on the future of Higher Education. US Department of Education. Retrieved March 5, 2006, from http://www.ed.gov/about/bdscomm/list/hiedfuture/reports/miller.pdf.

Mills, A. and Murgatroyd, S. (1991). *Organizational Rules – A Framework for Understanding Organizational Action*. Milton Keynes: Open University Press.

Murgatroyd, S. (1993). The house of quality: Using qfd for instructional design in distance education. *American Journal of Distance Education*, 7(2), 34–48.

Murgatroyd, S. and Morgan, C. (1992). *Total Quality Management and the School*. Milton Keynes: Open University Press.

Neal, T., Frielick, S., and Wilson, A. (2005). Developing e-Learning Leaders & Institutional Capability Through Collaboration. eCDF Project 3 brief update. Retrieved March 28, 2005 from http://www.e-learnz.org.nz/news/project3.htm.

Petit-Zeman, S. (2003). *Trial by Peers Comes up Short*. EducationGuardian, January 16. Retrieved May 11, 2006 from http://education.guardian.co.uk/higher/research/story/0,9865,875363,00.html.

Piller, C. (2002) Prominent physicist fired for faking data research. *The Los Angeles Times*, 26 September. Retrieved April 10, 2006 from http://www.drproctor.com/os/latimesschon.htm.

Russell, T.L. (2002). *The No Significant Difference Phenomenon*. Montgomery, AL: The International Distance Education Certification Centre.

Sacks, P. (2000). *Standardized Minds – The High Price of America's Testing Culture and What we can do to Change it*. Cambridge, MA: Persues Books.

Sahlberg, P. (2006). Educational reform for raising economic competitiveness. *Journal of Educational Change*, **1**(1), 1–29.

Shachar, M. and Neumann, Y. (2003). Differences between traditional and distance education academic performances: A meta-analytic approach. *International Review of Research in Open and Distance Learning*, **4**(2), 1–20.

Sickler, N. and Elliott, S. (2005). *VNC's, Web Portals, Biometrics and the Verification of Distance Education Students*. Purdue, ID: Symposium on "Security in Motion" (mimeo).

Tucker, M. and Codding, J. (1998). *Standards for our School – How to Set them, Measure them and Reach them*. San Francisco, CA: Jossey-Bass.

Chapter 30

But Does it Work? Evaluation Theories and Approaches in Distance Education

Alan Woodley

30.1 INTRODUCTION

Evaluation can be defined as a type of applied research aimed at improved decision-making within open and distance learning (ODL). Here "research" is considered an activity which covers all forms of systematic investigation. "Applied research" is a subset of "research" – one that is directly aimed at changing things. In turn, "evaluation" is a subset of "applied research". Evaluation differs from other forms of applied research, in that it attributes "worth or merit" to things. For example, it concludes that teaching method A is "better" than teaching method B, or that institution X has "improved" over time in offering educational opportunities to women. It is noted that in some cultures "evaluation" is the term used for the process of grading students. Here this process is referred to as "student assessment".

Evaluation as a form of research occurs in all disciplines and professions and is frequently referred to as "evidence-based decision-making". As applied to education, this process came into its own in the 1950s and 1960s when governments invested large amounts of money in innovatory educational campaigns. These took place both in developed countries, where they attempted to eradicate poverty through literacy and supplementary school programmes such as HeadStart, and in developing countries as an attempt to boost national economic development. The research questions were plain: "Do the campaigns work?"; "How much learning takes place?"; "Are they cost-effective?"; and "What is the relative cost of the learning gains that were achieved?" Evaluation was carried out by the government or its agents acting as "neutral", objective outsiders.

Such types of evaluation are still carried out today. However, "evaluation" has taken on much broader meaning where it has been carried out *within* institutions of ODL by members of that institution.

30.2 MAPPING ODL EVALUATION

The "tip of the iceberg" is a frequently used metaphor, implying that you only see a fraction of the whole thing. Similarly, with ODL evaluation, you only see a small fraction of the results, namely the ones that appear in books, journals, government reports, etc.

However, in the case of the iceberg, the invisible part is just more ice. While this metaphor might work for a discipline such as chemistry, with ODL evaluation, I would argue that the unseen part is generally very different. A better metaphor might be a Hawaiian island – as an extinct volcano it is mainly underwater, it is cone-shaped with a very large base, and it has different geological layers. I have attempted to illustrate this in Figure 30.1.

- The large "bedrock" (Layer 4) is labelled "Reflection". As Calder (1995) pointed out, this is the normal human practice of evaluating our own actions, thinking about them, and then choosing future actions. This is rarely written down and may barely qualify as research if it is not done systematically.
- Next comes Layer 3, "Communities of practice". This is where groups of workers, usually within a profession, evaluate their own practices but usually informally.
- I have called the next layer "Institutional Research". This is research commissioned by and for the institution itself to improve its performance. Its outcomes in the form of memos; internal or semi-published reports are commonly referred to as "Grey literature".
- The final public or "visible" layer of evaluation is the world of books, journal articles, conference papers, government reports, etc.

In this chapter, I am going to concentrate on the top two layers, discussing how they differ and how they shade into one another. It is important to note that this will be done from a particular perspective. While anybody can tackle the "visible" layer, the

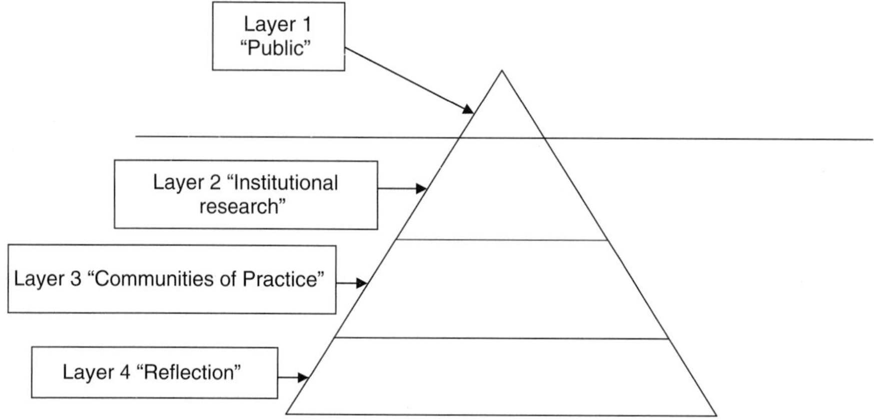

Figure 30.1: A Geological Model of ODL Evaluation

next layer down is only available to an insider. I can offer a description of institutional research as it is carried out at the Open University of the United Kingdom (UKOU), but the insights that I have derived from working there may have limited relevance elsewhere. I do not see the UKOU as a "distance teaching 'cathedral' " (Rumble, 2004, p. 5), but its sheer longevity has allowed certain patterns to emerge.

30.3 A REVIEW OF EVALUATION AT THE UKOU

When the UKOU was created (it received its Royal Charter in 1969 and the first students began their courses in 1971), it was always intended that its activities should be closely monitored and evaluated. One can adduce several reasons for this:

- The University had to be accountable to the Government which was the main source of funding.
- The University was to be funded directly by the Department of Education and Science rather than through the Universities Grants Committee and therefore would be scrutinised as a unique institution rather than as just another university.
- The University represented a major innovation in terms of teaching methods.
- The teaching material would be available for public examination and would therefore need to be of a consistently high standard.
- Most of the teaching and learning would be "invisible" because it would be carried out at a distance.
- The students were to be admitted on a "first-come, first-served" basis, regardless of prior educational qualifications. It would be necessary to know just who the students were and what progress they made.

Whatever the reasons, formative evaluation activities were already underway in 1970. Some of this took the form of developmental testing, with volunteers being recruited to try out the brand new foundation courses. Other researchers were studying those people who had enrolled on preparatory courses designed by the National Extension College, their purpose being to get an idea of who the first OU students were likely to be. The staff involved in this work were soon brought together in the new and rapidly expanding Institute of Educational Technology (IET). A large part of current evaluative research in the top two geological layers is carried out by members of IET, which now has over fifty academic staff. However, not all of its members are involved in evaluation, and much research that could be categorised as evaluation is in fact carried out by staff in other areas such as the Planning Division, the Business Development and Marketing Office (BDMO), and the Faculties and the Regions.

The UKOU now has over 200,000 students each year. Over 400 courses are on offer leading to more than 100 different qualifications. From 2007, students will be expected to have access to a computer.

In the next section, I attempt to map out the types of evaluation that have or are being carried out anywhere in the University. In later sections, I return to the questions of how and why the research agendas and styles have changed over time. A basic distinction is made between "programme" and "course" evaluation. The former refers to aspects of the whole institution and the latter to actual teaching.

30.3.1 System Evaluation

30.3.1.1 Basic Measures of Activity

Any system evaluation must begin with certain basic measures. How many courses have been produced? How many students are there? How many applicants had to be turned away? This data is drawn from administrative records and is presented regularly, often in the form of annual reports or "Statistical Digests".

30.3.1.2 Measures of Efficiency

Allied to measures of activity come those of efficiency. How many students successfully complete the courses? What workload do they attempt? What is the throughput of students? Again, this data comes from administrative records and is produced as part of regular monitoring procedures (McIntosh, Woodley and Morrison, 1980).

An obvious efficiency measure concerns cost-effectiveness. On the face of it, distance education is a cheap teaching method, but just how cheap or whether it is cheap at all has never been settled in relation to the OU. An early published paper claiming the cost-effectiveness of the UKOU (Wagner, 1977) was immediately challenged by Mace (1978). Disagreements among the economists centred upon difficulties in making comparisons with conventional institutions. How does one allow for the fact that distance students generally remain economically active while studying? Is it important that mature students have less years of economic activity in which to employ their new knowledge?

The UKOU was reviewed by the Department of Education and Science in 1991 (DES, 1991). They were looking to expand part-time higher education in the United Kingdom and insisted on a study by a major accounting company into the costs of producing graduates at the UKOU and several other major part-time providers. The results were never published, but the UKOU must have come out reasonably well because the DES continued to support its expansion.

I have not come across any further evidence in the grey literature that this line of evaluation is being developed per se. However, it is clear that the Finance and Planning departments continue to monitor costs and funding.

30.3.1.3 Outcomes

In the Open University, the measurement of whether adequate learning has taken place has usually been left to the formal exams and assessment system. This in turn relies upon the intricate, interlocking External Examiner system practised throughout the UK higher education system.

Some evaluation of teaching effectiveness has taken the form of research into the understandings developed by students as a result of their studies. Qualitative changes in the understanding of key concepts and relationships formed the focus of a study of Open University social science students (Taylor et al., 1981a and 1981b), based on a method for evaluating the content of students' learning developed in Sweden by Dahlgren (1978).

The study was concerned with finding out not *how much* students know but *what* they understand about particular concepts and principles. A group of university students taking an introductory social science course were individually asked a set of questions about key concepts and principles taught in the course. They were interviewed before commencing their studies and again after completion of the course. The findings of this study informed the writers of the replacement course, not only by identifying problem areas in the teaching but also by illustrating the different levels of pre-course understandings that students were likely to have.

There have been very few attempts to directly compare the learning achieved by UKOU students with that of full-time university students. In one isolated case, Open University economics students were compared with conventional students by administering a standardised test of economic knowledge (Lumsden and Scott, 1980).

On some OU courses, there are no formal exams, and follow-up surveys have to be carried out to see whether there have been appropriate changes in behaviour or attitudes. For example, in one study, people who had bought a "Study Pack" on energy efficiency in the home were contacted several months later to see whether they had carried out the energy-saving measures that had been specifically recommended. In another study, young mothers from deprived inner-city areas in Glasgow who had taken short "Community" courses were followed up to see what impact the courses had on their lives (Farnes, 1988).

Mail surveys of Open University graduates have been carried out to measure the long-term outcomes for individuals following an extended period of OU study (Swift, 1982; Woodley, 1988). These studies have looked at personal, occupational, and educational outcomes. It has allowed the University to say to what extent its qualifications have been accepted by other educational institutions for admission to postgraduate programmes and by professional bodies for membership. It has also recorded career changes and determined which, in the opinion of the graduates, occurred as a result of their studies. On a personal level, individuals have been asked about other changes such as growth in self-confidence and ability to communicate.

In recent years, more attention has been paid to the increasing proportion of students who gain a number of credits from the OU but leave before graduating. It is important to know whether these "dormant" students are leaving because the OU system is failing them or because they have already gained the benefits that they wanted. It is already known that many of these students have used their credits to transfer into full-time courses in conventional institutions of higher education.

The recognition of OU qualifications has also been approached from the other direction. A survey of employers was carried out to establish the standing of the Open University degree and the acceptability of its graduates (McIntosh and Rigg, 1979; Kirkwood et al., 1992).

Distance teaching can have other outputs besides the more obvious ones and several of these have been looked at. These include the use, acknowledged or otherwise, of OU teaching materials on courses in other institutions (Moss, 1979; Glaister and Carr, 1986); the passing on of OU materials to other learners (Stainton-Rogers, 1984); and effects on the educational motivation of the children of distance learners (Fenster, 1982).

30.3.1.4 Programme Aims

The Open University is committed to greater "open-ness" and to an increase in social equity. Consequently, much of the system evaluation work has been devoted to investigating how far these goals have been achieved. Particular attention has been focussed on formerly disadvantaged groups such as women, ethnic minorities, working class people, and those with low educational qualifications. As well as measuring their representation among the student body and looking at the progress they make on the courses, barriers to greater participation have also been examined. This has taken the form of surveys of the general public to determine the levels of awareness and knowledge of the institution (Swift, 1980), surveys of people who sent for details but decide not to apply (Woodley and McIntosh, 1977), and surveys of applicants who decline the offer of a place (Woodley, 1983).

30.3.1.5 Policy Evaluation

Formative evaluation in the policy area has sometimes taken the form of market research. Surveys of prospective students and employers have been carried out to measure the likely demand for possible new courses. Surveys of current students have also been used to sound out opinion on various policy options facing the University. For example, one study tested the reactions of Open University students to the possibility of reduced tutorial provision on higher level courses (Thorpe et al., 1986).

Policy evaluation has also taken the form of monitoring. The Open University carries out regular surveys to monitor the financial impact of study on its students, thus gauging the effects of fee increases, changes in local authority assistance, the effects of its own financial assistance schemes, etc. (Blacklock, 1982). Other survey data on the ownership of televisions, cassette recorders, home computers, etc. can assist course planning (Grundin, 1983; Kirkwood, 1997).

Research has also been used to evaluate the impact of policy changes. In one study, researchers looked at the effects of an OU policy to "de-register" undergraduates who had made no progress with their studies over a number of years (Heron et al., 1986). The results showed that one unforeseen consequence of this policy was that the University had de-registered many of its own graduates.

Finally, policy evaluation studies have also taken the form of experiments or pilot schemes. Perhaps the best-known example involved the admission of school-leavers to the Open University. The University and the Government of the day disagreed about the suitability of the OU for school-leavers, and so limited numbers were admitted on a trial basis and the outcome was evaluated over several years before making a final decision (Woodley and McIntosh, 1980). More recently, there have been evaluations of "access" pilot schemes devised to prepare people for OU studies (Fung and Woodley, 1997).

30.3.1.6 Organisational Evaluation

The Open University, just like any other large and complex organisation, can and has been evaluated in terms of its internal arrangements and procedures. In general terms, this has involved scrutinising the financial management and general "organisation and methods" of the University. More specifically, it has involved tasks such as the monitoring of tutors' marking patterns and the turnaround time for assignments. Evaluations have also been conducted into the course team approach to distance course writing (Nicodemus, 1992).

30.3.2 Course Evaluation

The second major strand of institutional research at the OU is "course evaluation", the aim of which is to improve the quality and effectiveness of the teaching and learning that take place. The evaluation of distance education teaching materials may seek to provide information that can be used during the process of developing or preparing materials or learning experiences – *formative* evaluation procedures, or information about how well the "finished" instruction has worked in normal use – *summative* evaluation procedures (Scriven, 1967). In practice, it is often impossible to draw such a clear distinction, but it provides a useful way of considering methods of evaluation.

30.3.2.1 Formative Evaluation

Critical Commenting The great majority of OU teaching materials are prepared by course teams, and consequently, peer review of draft materials is commonplace. At an informal level, this may simply involve one or more colleagues reading, listening to, or looking at draft materials and providing comments in terms of the suitability of content and the style of presentation. On the other hand, arrangements may be made for systematic critical commenting, with teachers or writers reviewing the materials prepared by all the others working on the same course or programme. Here there is the potential to improve not only individual teaching materials but also the overall course of instruction. The reactions of colleagues can also be augmented by adopting the more formal procedure of inviting one or more experts in the field to act as Assessors to comment on the draft materials.

Developmental Testing Developmental testing takes place during the preparation phase and involves trying out draft teaching materials with students. The feedback obtained is used to guide and inform writers' revisions to the materials before they are committed to print or tape (Nathenson and Henderson, 1980). Such testing may range from a fairly informal student try-out of a single piece of teaching to an elaborate procedure for testing draft materials for a whole course of instruction.

Students study the draft materials in the usual manner and may be asked to undertake any other requirements, for example, submitting assignments, attending tutorial sessions, and possibly sitting an examination upon completion of the course. Their comments on and reactions to the teaching can be collected by means of questionnaires and/or interviews and observations and are fed into the process of revising the course materials for "final" presentation.

Experience of developmental testing at the Open University (Henderson et al., 1983) indicates the strength of the procedure for the revision of materials within the overall structure of the course and that these can be of benefit to both course writers and students. It is, however, not particularly suitable for enabling major structural changes to be made to the course. In an attempt to allow for greater flexibility, a number of other procedures have been tried that are part formative and part summative (Henderson et al., 1983). These involve collecting feedback from students and tutors on a short-term "published" version of course materials, to inform revisions to be made for subsequent presentations.

30.3.2.2 Summative Evaluation

The "product" of course development in distance education is not just the materials that are delivered to students by one means or another. Rather it is the interaction of learners with those materials and other resources, possibly including tutors and fellow students (Thorpe, 1979). Summative evaluation procedures are intended to provide information about a course or materials in use.

Feedback from Tutors At the OU, most of the part-time tutors are not involved in the development of teaching materials for the courses they tutor. Their role is to support courses by running tutorial sessions (face-to-face or by means of telecommunications and information technology), marking assignments, teaching at summer schools, etc. They clearly have more direct contact with students, and mechanisms can be implemented to collect, on a systematic basis, evaluative comments from them on a range of issues. For example, they can give their own reactions to the teaching materials, and also accounts of problems their students have encountered in their studies and assignments (Ryan, 1982). The experience of tutors in making the course work can provide particularly useful information for subsequent modifications to or adaptations of the teaching materials and instructional arrangements.

Feedback from Students Feedback is gathered frequently from OU students while they are taking a course or shortly after its completion. In some cases, it may be possible to implement some revisions during the presentation of a course as a result of students' comments, for example, by providing a supplement to update information or to clarify a problem area. More frequently, the student feedback from one presentation of a course helps to determine revisions for subsequent presentations. After a course or programme of instruction has been presented in substantially the same form to many cohorts of students, feedback may be collected to inform decisions about remaking or replacing the course. Information gained by course writers about the success (or otherwise) of approaches and strategies employed in their distance teaching may prove to be of great value when they prepare further courses.

Mail questionnaires are the most widely used method for collecting feedback from students, and the types of information sought tend to fall into the following areas:

Extent of utilisation. Students may be asked to indicate which parts of the course or programme they have studied, which components they have used, how much time they have spent on their studies, etc. They may also be asked to report on any problems they have encountered in obtaining the course materials or in gaining access to resources.

Overall view of the teaching. Students may be asked to rate the teaching of a particular unit of instruction in terms of its interest, perceived relevance or usefulness, level of difficulty, etc. They may also be asked to rate individual components of a course (e.g. teaching text, audio tape) in terms of their relative usefulness.

General style of presentation. Course writers may be keen to receive students' comments on the style of presentation, in terms of both layout, design, etc. and the coherence and clarity of the teaching. Perhaps more importantly, students could be asked to comment on the extent to which the teaching style or strategy had enabled them to become actively engaged in learning from the materials.

Specific content issues. It is important to know how well the teaching has achieved its aims and objectives. To this end, information about students' problems with key concepts, ideas and relationships, etc. can be of great value to course writers when it is time for revisions to be made.

30.3.3 Cross-Sectional Evaluation

Some evaluation work has involved study of a particular innovation or component used in a number of courses. The aim of such studies has been to draw out generalisations from the use of a particular aspect of the teaching or to establish the effectiveness of a particular strategy or teaching medium.

The role of particular course components has been of concern to the Open University and has been the focus of much research into the use of, for example, audio-visual media (Grundin, 1985), tutorials (Kelly, 1981; Kelly and Swift, 1983), and computer-assisted learning (Scanlon et al., 1982). The research has involved collecting information from students on their access to and use of particular components and resources, as well as eliciting their views on the contribution made to the teaching and the overall effectiveness of courses.

The introduction of an innovatory teaching strategy has also given rise to evaluative research across a range of courses, for example, the use of project work to encourage greater independence in distance education (Henry, 1994).

30.4 TRENDS IN EVALUATION AT THE UKOU

The scope and nature of evaluation at the UKOU has changed a great deal over the 35 years of the institution's existence. In what follows I attempt to find what appear to be patterns among these changes.

30.4.1 The "Greying" of Evaluation

It seems that more evaluation now falls within Layer 2, "Institutional research" (see Figure 30.1). Furthermore, the "grey literature" that emerges there is becoming less accessible to outsiders. There seem to be several, interlocking, reasons for this:

a. All evaluation at the "pre-student" stage has been devolved to the marketing department. They in turn commission outside market research agencies to do studies of the potential student population.
b. Evaluation staff in IET are now principally on non-academic grades. This means that it is not in their job contracts to seek publications.
c. A lot of the data that is produced is now seen as being "market-sensitive". This means that internal reports and working papers are less likely to be distributed widely in case competing institutions use the information to capture the UKOU's share of the market.
d. Much of this evaluation is "standard" and repeated on a regular basis. Hence, it is less likely to result in journal articles that document theoretical thinking and methodological innovations.

30.4.2 The Demand for Management Information

There has been a growth in the number of senior managers with budgets and policy-making powers. In turn, they have requested more and better management information systems in order to make better decisions. This has led to complex, interactive databases that can be interrogated. However, they are inaccessible to outsiders.

30.4.3 The Obligation to Evaluate

Since the UKOU has become accepted as a full-blown university and is funded by the same procedures, it is now subject to the same evaluation procedures placed on all HE institutions. These include The National Survey of Students and The Destination of Leavers Survey.

In the former, all students about to graduate are asked to rate their courses in terms of teaching quality, support, skills acquisition, etc. These results are then subject to national comparisons with league tables appearing in the media.

Similarly, with the Destination of Leavers, graduates are surveyed to find out whether they are in paid employment, taking further courses, etc. Again the results are eagerly pored over by the institutions and the media.

With both surveys, the results are also made available to potential students so that they can pick a course with the best ratings.

So in our geological model, this is growth in evaluation in the top public layer, but it is growth that has been caused by "top-down" government pressure.

30.4.4 The Growth in Course Feedback

Course feedback was popular in the early years of the UKOU. In 1971, large numbers of students completed detailed questionnaires on each unit of each foundation course throughout the year. By 1990, the main source of feedback came from the Annual Survey of New Courses. This was a single questionnaire completed by samples of students after the courses had finished and, as the title implies, only affects courses in their first year of presentation. I have suggested that the lack of attention paid to this area had several causes:

- The great increase in the number of courses being offered;
- The decrease in staff numbers in IET;
- The routine nature of this work means many researchers found it boring and there were no junior research staff to delegate it;
- The type of information collected did not often lead to simple messages for course improvement, and the nature of OU course production means that very little actually could be changed in any case; and
- Academics who had been in the OU for a long time felt that they knew how to produce good courses.

However, the situation is now dramatically different. Every course is surveyed in its first year, in mid-term, and in the year before it is due to be remade. This means that large samples of students are surveyed on some 120 courses each year – a massive increase in survey activity. Again the driving force has been from outside, in the form of external subject reviews being carried out on a systematic basis throughout British Higher Education. Universities are meant to able to show evidence of regular collection of student feedback leading to improvements in teaching and support.

30.4.5 Changes in Policy Issues

The evaluation agenda has changed over the years in response to changes in the issues facing policy-makers. I note four major areas as examples.

1. **Student retention** While this has always been a much-researched area, considerably more attention has been paid to it now that funding is more closely tied to course completion rates and the achievement of student targets each year.

2. **Student costs** National changes in how much and when full-time students pay for their higher education (the "top-up fees" debate) have produced knock-on effects for part-time students. This has led to further studies of Open University students' incomes and the extent to which they pay their own fees (Woodley, 2005).
3. **Younger students** In the 1970s, an evaluation of a pilot scheme to admit school-leavers to the UKOU indicated low demand and a high dropout rate (Woodley and McIntosh, 1977). Today, the University sees a growth in younger student numbers, and faced with a need to meet student number targets in a very competitive market, it is carrying out research to identify which types of young persons are attracted, how to make the University more accessible to young people, and how to support them with their studies.
4. **Open content** The UKOU is about to launch an "Open Content Initiative" in which a large amount of its teaching material will become freely available on the Web. A major strand of the initiative will be an evaluation – who uses the material, how do they use it, do they go on to formally register as UKOU students, etc.? This would have occurred automatically with any major policy initiative, but in this case, it is also required by the outside funding body, the Hewlett Foundation.

30.4.6 The Effects of New Technology

This has always formed an important evaluation strand. Back in the 1960s and 1970s, it revolved around TV, radio, and audio cassettes, but now it concerns Information and Communication Technology. It also involves many parts of the University apart from IET. These include the Knowledge Media Institute, Learning and Teaching Solutions, the Telematics Department and the Computer-Assisted Research Group.

1. Although all students will soon be required to have access to a computer, it will continue to be necessary to carry out surveys to find out the capabilities of these computers and the type of access that students have to them.
2. Evaluation of the new technologies is very focussed on new developments – e.g. online student discussion groups, electronic assessment – and the effects on student learning.
3. The technology also means that "old" forms of evaluation can now be performed more quickly and more cheaply. Three examples are
   - PRESTO, a system whereby a panel of student volunteers can be electronically surveyed very quickly to measure student opinions on various policy issues;
   - DALS, recently introduced so that students can rate the performance of their tutor. The e-survey contains certain core questions plus others selected by the tutor. The aim is to incorporate the results in staff development activities; and
   - Staff surveys, which are now carried out electronically on issues such as workload and the rewards system.

30.4.7 The Growth of Specialist Journals

Although I have argued that more evaluation is becoming "grey", some of it is becoming less visible for other reasons. Rather than papers being published in the "general"

ODL journals, many are now being published in the increasing array of more specialist journals. Rather than submitting papers to *Open Learning*, say, I might send it to a journal concerned with learning *and* computers, or disability, or human resources, or economics, etc.

30.5 THEORIES AND APPROACHES

Attentive readers will have noticed that I have not yet referred to "theories", despite the word appearing in the title of this chapter. The main reason for this is, while there is general agreement about the need for evaluation, there remain many disagreements within the evaluation discipline about how best to practice it. In particular, the role of theory in evaluation is still the subject of much debate. Donaldson (2006) puts it this way:

> Reference to theory is widespread in the contemporary evaluation literature, but what is meant by theory encompasses a confusing mix of concepts related to evaluators' notions about how evaluation should be practiced, explanatory frameworks for social phenomena drawn from social science, and assumptions about how programs function, or are supposed to function.
>
> (n.p.)

He goes on to bemoan the fact that it is almost impossible to distinguish between terms such as theories of practice, theory-based evaluation, theory-driven evaluation, programme theory, evaluation theory, and theory of change that are scattered, often interchangeably, throughout the literature. He also notes that while the great majority of evaluators seem to argue that theory does, and should, play important roles in modern programme evaluation, distinguished evaluators such as Scriven (2004) and Stufflebeam (2001) continue to assert that there is little need for theory in evaluation.

While there is no agreement on what constitutes an evaluation theory, nor on whether such a thing is needed, there have certainly been evaluation "models". These include the Objectives Approach (Tyler), Goal-Free (Scriven), CIPP (Stufflebeam), Hierarchy of Evaluation (Kirkpatrick), Naturalistic (Guba), and Illuminative (Parlett). Each model has its own philosophy and recommended research methods. Stufflebeam (2001) himself has listed 22 such models. However, after rating them in terms of utility, feasibility, propriety, and accuracy, he concludes that only nine merit continued use and development. The point here is that most evaluation professionals think that some models are better than others, but it is up to the individual evaluator to select which is the most appropriate in a given situation.

Within IET, there have been debates on qualitative versus quantitative methodologies. Some researchers allied themselves to the so-called Gothenburg School and its use of phenomenography (Marton, 1988), and there were attempts to carry out Illuminative Evaluation when Parlett joined the staff. However, in my experience, the debates on evaluation theory and models have largely passed the Institute by. Most evaluators have settled for empirical, statistical, and survey-based methods, with some "mixed methods" solutions where possible. This may be explained in part by the a-theoretical pragmatism that is often attributed to British academics. However, it is also the case that ODL evaluators have all of the difficulties faced by those researching conventional education plus others caused by ODL. In the words of Philip Larkin,

> "They fill you with the faults they had
> And add some extra, just for you."
> *Philip Larkin, This be the Verse*
>
> (Larkin, n.d.)

In particular, the fact that students are scattered throughout the United Kingdom means that it is very difficult to carry out face-to-face interviews, run psychometric tests, or carry out the learning "experiments" used by Marton and others. Also, the very act of learning at a distance is a solitary, private experience that is not amenable to observation. Thus, one's selection of research methods is constrained by the learning context.

While it is difficult to identify the theoretical underpinnings of evaluation at the UKOU, one can typologise the approaches in various ways that locate the research in terms of how it is shaped by other external constraints and pressures, apart from the practical constraints already mentioned. These arise from who the researcher is, their values, their position in the workforce, etc. and from the social and political situation in their society. In particular, there are issues of power and control and how these shape knowledge.

MacDonald (1977) outlined three forms of evaluation that were distinguished by the different power relations that can exist in evaluation work. He called them "bureaucratic", "autocratic", and "democratic".

- Bureaucratic evaluation
  With this type of evaluation, researchers offer unconditional service to the funding agency. They accept the values of those who hold office and offer information that will help the policy-makers to achieve their policy objectives. The techniques used in the research must be credible to the policy-makers and not lay them open to public criticism. The researchers have no control over the use that is made of the information, and their research report is owned by the bureaucracy.
- Autocratic evaluation
  Here research is a conditional service to the funding agencies, offering external validation of policy, provided the recommendations emerging from the research are acted on. Researchers act as expert advisers, deriving the values from their perceptions of the constitutional and moral obligations of the bureaucracy. The researchers strive for neutrality and objectivity. Their contractual arrangements guarantee non-interference by the client, and while the bureaucracy gets its report, they the researchers are free to publish the results in academic journals.
- Democratic evaluation
  In this type of evaluation, the researchers try to represent the interests of all groups affected by the educational programme, rather than just the funding agency or the academic community. The aim is "an informed citizenry" and the evaluators act as information brokers between the different groups. Their techniques of

data-gathering and presentation must be accessible to non-specialist audiences. Informants are given control over the researchers' use of the information. The main activity is to collect definitions of, and reactions to, the educational programme. The final report does not contain recommendations.

Elsewhere I have sketched out a similar typology that was also based on power relations but was grounded in my own evaluation work and experience, and described various approaches adopted by internal evaluators (Woodley, 1991). I identified market, liberal, and radical evaluations.

- Market evaluation
  Here evaluation corresponds to the sort of research done by a market research department within a profit-making manufacturing company. Students are seen as customers and research is devoted to maximising their number and their throughput. Research reports will be confidential to the institution.
- Liberal evaluation
  With this type of evaluation, the researcher is the student's friend. Information is gathered on why people drop out, what they think is wrong with the course, what extra support they need, etc. so that the system can be made better for them. The research is likely to be shared with organisations such as student unions.
- Radical evaluation
  This can take several forms but essentially it involves the evaluator taking a critical stance concerning what sorts of people become or do not become students, what they are taught, which students make better and worse progress, and the effects on their lives. The evaluator will want to publish the results in theoretical journals and in newspapers in order to maximise their impact.

MacDonald's typology arose from his work as a university academic where he was hired by external agencies to study a variety of innovative programmes in schools. Mine came from my work as an academic institutional researcher. Nevertheless, there are great similarities between the two schema. Both revolve around the nature of the "contract" between the researcher and the person paying for the research. My contention is that within the OU there has been an increase in "Market evaluation" carried out within a "Bureaucratic" model.

"Market evaluation" was of key importance in the early years when the OU's viability was in question. Was it attracting sufficient students and was it producing graduates in a cost-effective fashion? This has been a continuing concern but takes on greater importance in years when the flow of new applicants slows down or when, as in 1990, the Department of Education and Science mounts a review to see how well the OU is performing. This is when evaluation clearly takes the form of self-defence rather than self-improvement (Woodley, 1993). Here the role of the institutional researcher is to provide the information that the University can use to convince its paymasters that the high level of state-funding is justified. In the last year, this has included attempting to demonstrate to the National Committee of Inquiry into Higher Education (the Dearing Report) that, among other things, the OU produces large numbers of graduates in maths, science and technology, that its graduates perform well in the labour market, and that it attracts large numbers of students from educationally disadvantaged groups.

Market evaluation has grown in importance in terms of potential student demand. Increased attention is being paid to identifying possible courses that will attract large numbers of students, that will be sponsored by employers, and that can command high fees. Members of IET have been involved in such work but it has increasingly come under the remit of the Marketing Department. This office has grown greatly in size and in turn has frequently used outside market research companies to carry out surveys whose aim is to find ways of maximising sales.

Institutional researchers within IET who are not on academic contracts could be said to fit the bureaucratic model with "unconditional service to the funding agency", in that their contractual obligation is towards their employer. However, their allegiance could be said to stretch beyond their employer. Many feel they have a duty to be the voice of the student and thus shade into "liberal evaluation". Sometimes, they have to become "super-bureaucratic" and accede to the demands of the university's funding agency – their employers' employer!

Academic evaluators at the UKOU have more independence, and it is up to them to negotiate with the University or with external funders whether their role is to be bureaucratic, autocratic, or democratic. Personally, I have argued for the important role of "the partisan guerrilla" which, using the present terms, constitutes a democratic, radical approach (Woodley, 1991).

30.6 THE FUTURE OF EVALUATION AT THE UKOU

Predicting the future from present trends, it is difficult to see anything other than a continuing increase in "bureaucratic/market" evaluation, plus evaluations of developments in new technology. However, there are one or two countersigns that might indicate changes in direction and methods.

- Developments in new technology in general, and in electronic surveys in particular, mean that evaluation has the potential to make the institution more democratic. Staff and students can be surveyed rapidly and cheaply on a wide variety of policy-related issues. Similarly, the findings and reports can be distributed to all participants.
- With the arrival of Virtual Learning Environments (VLEs) comes the possibility of digitally recording in minute detail how a learner behaves when in the VLE. This will generate enormous amounts of data that can be used for certain types of evaluation purposes. However, with the concomitant increase in surveillance and reduction in privacy, it is not clear that this will improve learning (Joinson, 2006).
- Qualitative research methods have been underused at the UKOU. This is due to a number of factors, but cost and practicality are among them. However, with all students being online, it is now possible to gather digital data from interviews,

conferences, chatrooms, etc., and there is increasingly sophisticated software with which to analyse this data.
- Universities will shortly have to publish annual data on Equal Opportunities issues concerning staff and students. This will cover gender, disability, ethnicity, and age. Where discrimination appears to be taking place, the University will have to provide a commentary suggesting explanations and solutions. Research exists in this area and it is likely to grow.

30.7 ODL EVALUATION ELSEWHERE

Earlier, I justified my decision to concentrate on evaluation at the UKOU. It is time now to return to the broader picture and to attempt the difficult task of considering what is happening elsewhere. Now, while somebody like Hilary Perraton has the experience and courage to attempt a book like *Open and Distance Learning in the Developing World* (Perraton, 2000), I have neither. Therefore, my thoughts in this area will be partial and based on limited information.

a. **Large single mode distance teaching organisations**
   Visits to other "Open University-like" institutions, collaborations with colleagues there, and observations of their research output suggest that the trends I have observed at the UKOU are present in all of them to varying degrees.
   - Departments dedicated to evaluation have become much smaller or have totally disappeared, absorbed into other departments, such as planning, marketing, or the vice chancellor's office.
   - The remaining evaluators have been encouraged to draw in external resources, either by producing distance learning courses of their own or by competing for external research and evaluation contracts.
   - Institutional research findings are increasingly internalised. There is less sharing of findings between institutions in the same country and between similar institutions in different countries. (The exceptions are where evaluative data is collected centrally by government departments and then made publicly available.)
   - Research publications are increasingly authored by academic staff whose main job is to produce learning material within their own discipline.

   For a more formal attempt to identify similarities and dissimilarities, see Rathore and Schuemer (1998).
b. **Dual mode institutions**
   Here, in my limited experience, distance learning has generally been "bolted on" to a full-time teaching institution. One consequence has been that the evaluation component has also tended to be marginal. People whose main job has been to transform full-time courses into distance learning material and to deliver it have tried to add on the function of evaluation. They tend to do it with few resources, little training, and little encouragement. Again it is academic staff who teach both full-time and distance students who have started to publish in this area.

c. **Private institutions**
When attempting to review research findings for UK correspondence colleges in the 1970s, I was unable to unearth any reliable published data. It was not even possible to establish the number of student enrolments. It seemed that they were being run purely on market-economy terms, with popular courses continuing and undersubscribed courses being cancelled if they could not be run cheaply. If anything else was being done in the way of "market research", it was not being shared with a wider audience.

Today, there are huge private institutions such as the University of Phoenix operating globally via the Web. In terms of evaluation, apart from their claims of large student numbers, I have no evidence to suggest that they are operating any differently to the early correspondence colleges.

d. **Major experiments and innovations**
Major ODL initiatives that are funded by public money are invariably subject to evaluation. The initiatives might take the form of a brand new institution such as the UK e-University, or a major expansion of an institution such as the UKOU's attempt to launch a version in the United States, or a major change within an institution such as the UKOU's Open Content Initiative. The evaluation might be carried out internally by the institution or externally by academics from other institutions or by external evaluation consultants. Whatever form it takes, and however sophisticated the evaluation methodology proposed, the bottom line is inevitably cost and cost-effectiveness.

In February 2000, the United Kingdom e-University (UKeU) was set up with £62 million government funding as a commercial, global e-university. In February 2004, the government withdrew its funding and, to all intents and purposes, the institution ceased to exist. The exact causes of its demise have been debated (Garrett, 2004), using what could be described as the "autopsy" model of evaluation, but failure to meet targets was the key factor. By November 2003, only 900 students had been recruited (against a target of 5,600), and many people rushed in to calculate the extremely high per student cost.

In spring 1999, the UKOU created the United States Open University (USOU). It was closed three years later in June 2002. According to Meyer (2006), the problems afflicting USOU arose from five sources:

- Loss of an important advocate and diminishing support from the parent institution;
- Conflicts with the OU's established curriculum;
- Challenges in entering a new market;
- Lack of accreditation; and
- Problems with business planning.

However, as she acknowledges, the main problem was a new vice chancellor faced with domestic financial problems and an overseas investment that was not generating any revenue. The latter's "evaluation" was that the project should end.

There have been other high-profile failures, or at least high-profile "lack of successes". Garret (2004) notes, "Along with NYU Online, Scottish Knowledge, and Fathom, UKeU has now failed. Others such as Universitas 21 Global and Global University Alliance, stumble on with no evidence of particular success" (p. 6). The UKOU's Open Content Initiative is different, in that no revenue is expected, and learning material will be free to all. However, it will be a failure if, despite considerable investment, it doe not generate huge numbers of learners who are seen to benefit from participation.

I am going to conclude by returning to the question of evaluating costs and cost-effectiveness in ODL. This situation can be likened to the "elephant in the room". It is large, it is a problem, everybody knows is there, but nobody knows how to deal with it, so everybody ignores it. Well, almost everybody. Hülsmann (2000) has approached the problem by attempting to calculate the comparative costs of various educational technologies. Using case studies from several countries and institutions, he used the costs involved in providing for "one student learning hour" using different media. His general conclusion for what he called "resource media" was that

> Taking the costs of a text, and reproducing it in print, as a basis, or default option, the evidence shows that that using any more sophisticated medium is likely to increase the development costs for resource media.
>
> (p. 20)

He also considered "communication media". These involve dialogue with a student and may involve tutor-marked assignments, face-to-face tutorials, video-conferencing, and computer-mediated communication. These will produce variable costs depending on the number of students and the costs of equipment and of online charges. He concludes, unsurprisingly, that

> If the costs per student for communication media rise as high as the costs that would be required for face-to-face teaching, then open and distance learning can never have an economic edge over conventional teaching.
>
> (p. 18)

Hülsmann's approach has its problems:

- The "student learning hour" is a questionable concept. Is there equivalency across media?
- The question of relative effectiveness is dismissed rather too easily by a reference to the research literature that shows that choice of medium does not effect learning outcomes (Clark, 1983).
- Choice of teaching medium is rarely made solely on the basis of cost.

Hülsmann is trying to help managers choose between teaching media. However, a full cost-effectiveness approach involves calculating input costs (course production and maintenance costs) and outputs (the number of successful learners). Rumble (2004) is the main writer in the area of what he has termed "the economics of mass distance education" and he addresses the major issues involved such as the different modes of course production, the number of registrations, progression rates, and life expectancies of courses. However, there is little in the way of actual data, and when asked to summarise his findings on whether ODL is cost-effective, he wisely replies, "It depends" (Rumble, 2002, n.p.).

The simplest approach to the problem is to divide input by output and to calculate something like "cost per graduate". Perraton (2000) is one of the few people to attempt this on an international basis, and it is difficult to know how trustworthy the results are, given the variations in how institutions are funded and in how they measure student progress. Data is also scarce for the UKOU but there are some interesting developments. The publication of figures for all universities on teaching costs, the number of students, and progress rates will mean that comparisons will be possible. Initial results suggest that UKOU is relatively cost-effective, but not extremely so. However, it can and will be argued that we are not comparing like with like because the UKOU caters for people that conventional universities do not serve, such as the geographically remote, those with low previous educational qualifications, and the geographically mobile.

I end with a quotation from Sir John Daniel, currently the President of the Commonwealth of Learning. After a speech in which he outlined a possible research agenda for ODL, I asked him whether the shortage of published research on the economics of ODL was because it is too difficult or because people do not like the answers. His one word answer was "Both!" (Daniel, 2002). I urge you to be aware that gaps in the ODL evaluation literature, be they about costs, student numbers, teaching effectiveness, or whatever, can be just as important as what is there.

REFERENCES

Blacklock, S. (1982). *What the OU Cost the Undergraduate Student in 1981 (Mimeo). Survey Research Department Paper No. 229*, The Open University.

Calder, J. (1995). *Programme Evaluation and Quality*. London: Kogan Page.

Clark, R. (1983). Reconsidering research on learning from media. *Review of Educational Research*, 53(4), 445–459.

Dahlgren, L.O. (1978). Qualitative differences in conceptions of basic principles in economics: A contribution to the discussion of the validity of examination results. *4th International Conference on Higher Education*, University of Lancaster.

Daniel, J. (2002). *Why Research Distance Learning?* Keynote address at CRIDALA Conference, Hong Kong, June 5–7. Retrieved August 4, 2006 from http://www.unesco.org/education/html/speeches/CRIDALA_Conference.shtml.

DES. (1991). *Review of the Open University*. UK: The department of Education and Science (internal document).

Donaldson, S. (2006). *Using Theory to Improve Evaluation Practice: Resources to Enhance your Knowledge and Skills*. Retrieved August 4, 2006 from http://mechanisms.org/modules.php?name=Content&pa=showpage&pid=9.

Farnes, N. (1988). Open University community education: Emancipation or domestication? *Open Learning*, 3(1), 35–40.

Fenster, E. (1982). *College Attendance by Working Adults and its Effects on the Educational Motivations of their Children*. Detroit: To Educate the People Consortium.

Fung, P. and Woodley, A. (1997). Evaluation of an access pilot. *Student Research Centre Report No 125*, Institute of Educational Technology, The Open University.

Garrett, R. (2004). The Real story behind the failure of UK eUniversity. *Educause Quarterly*, **4**. Retrieved August 4, 2006 from http://www.educause.edu/ir/library/pdf/eqm0440.pdf.

Glaister, B. and Carr, R. (1986). Education open to all. *Open Learning*, **1**(3), 50–52.

Grundin, H. (1983). *Audio-Visual Media in the Open University (Mimeo). IET Papers on Broadcasting No. 224*, The Open University.

Grundin, H. (1985). *Report on the 1984 Audio Visual Media Survey (Mimeo)*. Institute of Educational Technology, The Open University.

Henderson, E., Kirkwood, K., Mayor, B., Chambers, E., and Lefrere, P. (1983). Developmental testing for credit: A symposium. *Teaching at a Distance Institutional Research Review*, **2**, 39–59.

Henry, J. (1994). *Teaching through Projects*. London: Kogan Page.

Heron, M., Kelly, P., and Marshall, J. (1986). *Student Progress and Non-Progress (Mimeo). Regional Research and Development Papers, No. 15*, The Open University.

Hülsmann, T. (2000). *The Costs of Open Learning: A Handbook*. Oldenburg, Germany: Bibliotheks-und Informationssystem der Carl von Ossietzky Universität Oldenburg.

Joinson, A.N. (2006). Does your VLE virtually undress its users? *Times Higher Education Supplement*, September 15th. Retrieved August 4, 2006 from http://elsa.open.ac.uk/presto/prisd/Files/THES_article.pdf.

Kelly, P. (1981). *An Overview of Student Use and Appreciation of Tuition (Mimeo)*. RTS Research Group, The Open University.

Kelly, P. and Swift, B. (1983). *Tuition at Post Foundation Level in the Open University – Student Attitudes Towards Tuition (Mimeo)*. RAS/IET, The Open University.

Kirkwood, A. (1997). Computing access survey 1996. *PLUM Paper*, 80–83 Institute of Educational Technology, The Open University.

Kirkwood, A., Farnes, F., Hales, G., and Hughes, A. (1992). Employers study 1992: Report on the qualitative phase. *Student Research Centre Report No 72*, Institute of Educational Technology, The Open University.

Larkin, P. (n.d.). *This be the Verse*. Retrieved August 4, 2006 from http://www.artofeurope.com/larkin/lar2.htm.

Lumsden, K. and Scott, A. (1980). *An Output Comparison of Open University and Conventional University Students (Mimeo)*. Edinburgh: Esmee Fairbairn Research Centre, Heriot-Watt University.

MacDonald, B. (1977). A political classification of evaluation studies. In *Beyond the Numbers Game* (D. Hamilton, D. Jenkins, C. King, B. MacDonald, and M. Parlett, eds) London: Macmillan.

Mace, J. (1978). Mythology in the making: Is the Open University really cost-effective? *Higher Education*, **7**(3), 295–309.

Marton, F. (1988). Phenomenography: Exploring different conceptions of reality. In *Qualitative Approaches to Evaluation in Education. The Silent Scientific Revolution* (D. Fetterman, ed.) New York: Praeger.

McIntosh, N. and Rigg, M. (1979). *Employers and the Open University (Mimeo)*. Survey Research Department Paper No 162, The Open University.

McIntosh, N., Woodley, A. and Morrison, V. (1980). Student demand and progress at the Open University – The first eight years. *Distance Education*, **1**(1), 37–60.

Meyer, K. (2006). The closing of the US Open University. *Educause Quarterly*, **29**(2). Retrieved 20, October, 2006 from http://www.educause.edu/apps/eq/eqn06/eqn0620.asp.bhcp=1.

Moss, C.D. (1979). The influence of Open University distance teaching in Higher Education. *Teaching at a Distance*, **14**, 14–18.

Nathenson, M. and Henderson, E. (1980) *Using Student Feedback to Improve Learning Materials.* London: Croom Helm.

Nicodemus, R. (1992). Understanding course teams: organization and dynamics. *Teaching and Consultancy Centre Report No 62*, Institute of Educational Technology, The Open University.

Perraton, H. (2000). *Open and Distance Learning in the Developing World.* London: Routledge.

Rathore, H. and Schuemer, R. (1998). *Evaluation Concepts and Practice in Selected Distance Education Institutions.* Ziff Papiere 108. Hagen: Fernuniversitat.

Rumble, G. (2002). Personal Communication.

Rumble, G. (ed.) (2004). *Papers and Debates on the Economics and Costs of Distance and Online Learning.* Oldenburg, Germany: Bibliotheks-und Informationssystem der Carl von Ossietzky University.

Ryan, S. (1982). Developing tutor feedback. *Teaching at a Distance*, **22**, 9–14.

Scanlon, E., Jones, A., O'Shea, T. et al. (1982). Computer assisted learning. *Teaching at a Distance Institutional Research Review* **1**, 59–79.

Scriven, M. (1967). The methodology of evaluation. In *Perspectives of Curriculum Evaluation* (R.W. Tyler, R.M. Gagné, and M. Scriven, eds) Chicago, IL: Rand McNally, pp.39–83.

Scriven, M. (2004). *April 26, EvalTalk Posting.* Retrieved May 4, 2006 from http://www.aime.ua.edu/archives/evaltalk.html.

Stainton-Rogers, W. (1984). Alternative uses of materials: Research findings. *Teaching at a Distance* **25**, 58–68.

Stufflebeam, D.L. (ed.) (2001). *Evaluation Models (New Directions for Evaluation, No.89).* San Francisco, CA: Jossey-Bass.

Swift, B. (1980). *Trends in Awareness and Beliefs About the Open University Among the General Public (Mimeo). Survey Research Department Paper No.185*, The Open University.

Swift, B. (1982). *What Open University Graduates Have Done (Mimeo). Survey Research Department Paper No. 230*, The Open University.

Taylor, E., Gibbs, G., and Morgan, A. (1981a). *The Outcomes of Learning from the Social Science Foundation Course: Students' Understandings of Price Control, Power and Oligopoly (Mimeo). Study Methods Group Report No. 9*, The Open University.

Taylor, E., Gibbs, G., and Morgan, A. (1981b). *Students' Understandings of the Concept of Social Class (Mimeo). Study Methods Group Report No. 10*, The Open University.

Thorpe, M. (1979) When is a course not a course? *Teaching at a Distance* **16**, 13–18.

Thorpe, M., Woodley, A., Morgan, A. et al. (1986) *Effective Study in the Open University: The Human Dimension (Mimeo). Student Research Centre Report No. 1*, IET, The Open University.

Wagner, L. (1977). The economics of the Open University revisited. *Higher Education* **6**(3), 359–381.

Woodley, A. (1983). Why they declined the offer. *Teaching at a Distance* **23**, 2–7.

Woodley, A. (1988). Graduation and beyond. *Open Learning*, **3**(1), 13–17.

Woodley, A. (1991). Evaluation at the British Open University. In *Evaluation Concepts and Practice in Selected Distance Education Institutions* (R. Schuemer, ed.), Hagen: Zentrales Institut fur Fernstudienforschung, Fernuniversitat.

Woodley, A. (1993). Improving distance education universities through institutional research: A consideration of the roles and functions of the institutional researcher. *Student Research Centre Report No 79*, Institute of Educational Technology, The Open University.

Woodley, A. (2005). *Earning, Learning and Paying: The Results from a National Survey of the Costs and Financing of Part-time Students in Higher Education. DfES Research Report RR600.* Retrieved August 4, 2006 from http://www.dfes.gov.uk/research/programmeofresearch/projectinformation.cfm?projectid=14277&resultspage=1.

Woodley, A. and McIntosh, N. (1977). People who decide not to apply to the Open University. *Teaching at a Distance* 9, 18–26.

Woodley, A. and McIntosh, N. (1980). *The Door Stood Open: An Evaluation of the Open University Younger Students Pilot Scheme.* Lewes: The Falmer Press.

Chapter 31

Quality Assurance and Continuous Quality Improvement in Distance Education

Insung Jung

This chapter discusses challenges of a changing distance education (DE) environment at the higher education level to existing quality concepts and policies, and analyzes how DE institutions in different countries and regions are dealing with these challenges to promote quality assurance (QA) and continuous quality monitoring in DE. Finally it suggests future policy objectives and some possible areas for initiatives that might be taken by DE institutions, QA agencies, governments, and international organizations.

31.1 CHANGES AND CHALLENGES

The 1970s and 1980s were decades when DE was driven towards widening access. During these two decades, many countries and territories around the world established DE institutions at the higher education level to meet the growing educational needs of society. The concentrated efforts of governments with respect to improvement in higher education saw the establishment of dedicated single-mode ODL institutions during this time. With limited resources and the need to expand education rapidly, countries saw DE as an alternative mode of delivery to widen access to education, to satisfy the continuing educational needs of adults, to expand the trained workforce, and/or to train teachers to improve the quality of schooling.

The 1990s was a decade of concentration on effectiveness and efficiency. DE institutions utilized an instructional design team approach in developing and delivering DE programs and provided extensive capacity-building opportunities for their staff to improve the quality of DE courses and support services. Quite a few DE institutions began to experiment with the possibilities of information and communication technology (ICT) in improving effectiveness and efficiency in instruction, services and administration.

Computer-assisted testing, video-conferencing, online registration, and the use of email were examples of the application of ICT for DE in the 1990s.

The first half of our current decade (the 2000s) has witnessed a period of greater challenges than ever in DE. The most distinctive feature of this period is the increased student population in DE institutions (Jung, 2005b). For example, in the Asia and Pacific region, at least seven DE institutions have become mega-universities (universities with over 100,000 active students in degree-level courses). The Allama Iqbal Open University (Pakistan), Anadolu University (Anadolu, Turkey), China Central Radio and TV University (China), Indira Gandhi National Open University (IGNOU, India), Korea National Open University (KNOU, Korea), Sukhothai Thammathirat Open University (Thailand), Universitas Terbuka (UT, Indonesia), and Payame Noor University (Iran) had more than 5.6 million active students in total in 2004. Besides these well-known mega-universities, quite a few DE units within conventional universities in the region have been established more recently and provide tertiary level education to those seeking continuing education opportunities. With two-thirds of the global population, the Asia and Pacific region is estimated to have over 500 million potential students for DE institutions (Shive and Jegede, 2001).

Another recent change in DE is the rapid growth of ICT use. The growth of ICT in general has stimulated DE institutions to increasingly introduce ICT into the teaching and learning process. Most institutions have adopted ICT as a supplementary mode of instruction and also as a way of improving student services. E-tutoring, e-testing, one stop online services, online discussions, and digital libraries are representative examples of using ICT for DE. Some DE institutions have created totally online courses or programs. Examples include the e-MBA of Athabasca University (Canada) and Anadolu, and the online Lifelong Education Graduate School at the Korea National Open University.

The recent globalization of higher education has also had significant effects on DE. Over the last few years, there has been a noticeable surge in the export and the import of educational services. DE, including e-learning, is one of the many manifestations of the current trend, and it has been steadily gaining ground. For example, universities in Australia, United Kingdom, United States, and Canada have actively exported their DE programs to other parts of the world. China, Hong Kong (China), India, Malaysia, and Singapore are the major importers of those programs. However, among the importers, Hong Kong (China), India, and Malaysia have also exported their programs to some other countries such as Bangladesh, China, Indonesia, and Sri Lanka (Jung, 2004a). Global e-learning providers such as Thomson Learning, Apollo International, and UNext have been recruiting students especially from Asian countries such as Hong Kong (China), India, Korea, Malaysia, and Singapore.

All these trends challenge the existing definitions and assurance mechanisms of quality in DE. Especially with the increasing number of student enrollment in DE institutions, the issue of QA has become more pressing than ever before. Several recent studies have attempted to review current changes in DE and to evaluate QA systems of DE for higher education both at the national and at the institutional level. Some studies discussed issues related to QA and the emergence of virtual universities or e-learning programs and cross-border higher education (for example, Farrell, 2001; Lockwood and Gooley, 2001; UNESCO, 2003; Jung, 2004a; 2004b; 2004c; OECD, 2004). The findings show that DE institutions are in the midst of instructional and technological changes and that QA frameworks of DE in the globalized context are still at the early stages of development. In fact, the existing QA systems within DE have more focus on widening access than on assuring quality, and often do not address e-learning, for-profit, and/or transnational activities.

31.2 QUALITY IN DISTANCE EDUCATION

Quality in education in general is difficult to define since it depends on many factors. As we can imagine, a wide variety of definitions of quality in education are currently in use. Green (1994) says that "quality, like 'freedom' or 'justice', is an elusive concept. We all have an instinctive understanding of what it means but is difficult to articulate" (p. 12) and suggests five different approaches to defining quality in higher education:

- quality as excellence;
- quality as conformance to specification or standards;
- quality as fitness for purpose;
- quality as effectiveness in achieving institutional goals; and
- quality as meeting customers' stated or implied needs.

Some of these approaches have been identified in the DE context. The following section discusses four differing definitions of quality in DE, based on previous research, and looks at their relation to QA.

31.2.1 Quality as Conformance to Standards of Conventional Education

The traditional concept of quality in DE is related to the notion of quality as conformance to standards that have been set for conventional education. The standards are the basis of assessing the quality of educational programs and services. The QA of DE in this context is seen as the effort to ascertain whether a DE program or service meets these standards or not. This approach to quality has been and still is popular in DE. For example, in many countries, the QA policies and regulations for distance teaching universities are in general in conformity with the national QA frameworks for conventional higher education (Jung, 2004c). The QA or accreditation agencies in those cases have expanded their already existing standards to evaluate DE based on the belief that the existing standards assess resources, processes, and outcomes for effective teaching in any educational mode.

Based on the notion of quality of DE as conformance to specifications of conventional education, many distance educators have tried to demonstrate that DE is at least as good as that offered in a face-to-face mode. A review of early studies (Capper and Fletcher, 1996; Moore and Thompson, 1997; Jung and Rha, 2000) comparing effectiveness of DE with face-to-face instruction led to the conclusion that in many instances, DE was as effective as conventional classroom teaching and showed no difference in learning outcomes.

However, this notion of quality has a disadvantage in measuring and assuring the quality of DE. It does not address the particular features of DE such as technological aspects, the borderless and open nature of educational services, and collaborative processes in course development and delivery.

31.2.2 Quality as Fitness for Purpose

In this notion of quality, quality of DE is measured in terms of the extent to which a DE program or service meets its unique purpose. If the purpose of a DE institution is to provide educational opportunities to adult learners worldwide to meet the educational needs of the workplace, quality in the DE institution should be measured in terms of its achievement of that purpose. At the institutional level, QA of a DE institution focuses on developing clearly stated goals and adopting effective and efficient strategies in meeting the goals it has set itself.

A problem with this model of quality is that the purposes may change over time, different stakeholders of DE may have different views on the purposes, and DE may have multiple, often conflicting purposes. As Perraton (2000) discussed, conflicting ideological, economic, and political aims of different stakeholders in DE exist. For example, some governments have invested in DE to empower the disadvantaged or realize equity, whereas other governments aim to equip the workforce. To some non-government organizations, the main goal of DE is to empower rural people and women. It is clear that in defining quality of DE, it is impossible to have one gold purpose or standard.

Even though this type of approach does not seek one general standard for all the DE institutions, it provides a basis for developing what the standards for a high quality DE program or service should be. Since the late 1990s, several QA or accreditation agencies have developed the standards set or specific guidelines for measuring quality of DE which incorporate some distinctive natures of DE (Lezberg, 2003; Sherry, 2003). Examples include Guidelines for Distance Education (1997; 2005), Best Practices for Electronically Offered Degree and Certificate Programs (2000), and DE Accreditation Handbook (2005) in the United States; and Guidelines on the Quality Assurance of Distance Learning (1999) in the United Kingdom.

This model of quality as fitness for purpose has important implications for QA of DE, since it recognizes the distinctive features of DE and individual DE institutions, and emphasizes goal-oriented performance and efficient management of DE institutions.

31.2.3 Quality as Meeting Customers' Needs

This concept of quality has been popular in industry. As DE programs continued to increase and the market became competitive, DE institutions began to pay more attention to customers and placed high priority on customers' needs in providing DE programs and services.

However, there is a question about the customer of DE. And related to the question, there is a problem with conflicting needs of different customer groups. Two main student groups for DE at higher education level are those young people who have missed the opportunity to attend regular schools and are now seeking higher education, and those adults or working people who seek job-related knowledge and skills (Perraton, 2000). The needs of these two customer groups may conflict with, for example, one asking for more academic fields of study and more frequent interaction, while the other may demand practical courses and more flexible and independent study arrangements. In quite a few cases, customer groups do not know their needs!

This model of quality has been applied to the QA of support services in DE, as seen in the case of some DE institutions obtaining ISO9001 certification for their quality services. However, unlike for industry where the producer and the customer are clearly distinguishable, the students (the customer of DE) are also participating in the process of service production. This feature makes it difficult for an educational institution to specify and maintain quality standards for its services (Green, 1994).

While this approach to quality has helped some DE institutions to pay more attention to customer groups and their needs, and improve support services, there still remains the question about who should define the quality in DE and how it should be assured and measured.

31.2.4 Continuous Quality Improvement

The concept of continuous quality improvement also came out of industry, shifting the QA focus from product (e.g. DE programs) or services to process. It emphasizes the process of input, implementation, output, and back-to-input as a key element in assuring the quality of DE practices, and promotes capacity building or staff development as an enabling factor to establish such a quality process.

Continuous quality improvement focuses on dynamics in work processes rather than the product itself, whereas the primary focus of quality assurance activities in many DE institutions appears to be more on meeting standards, often external requirements in developing and implementing their programs and services. As we consider the fast-growing transnational education market and the diversification of DE learners' needs, this continuous improvement approach seems to provide a more flexible and systematic way of meeting these challenges in a borderless context than other approaches.

The continuous improvement approach to quality requires organizational and cultural changes and thus takes longer time and requires more systematic planning to implement. To continuously improve the performance of a DE system, one necessary condition is to develop its human resources and accumulate a body of knowledge which will help its members learn how to better support and facilitate distance learning. Where the system of continuous staff development has been integrated in DE institutions, the culture of research has not always been developed. We should remember that as in conventional higher education, research is the heart of professional practice and continuous quality improvement in distance education.

31.2.5 The Practical Approach to Quality in Distance Education

The definition of quality in DE is broadening as the range of customers and purposes of DE widens and the modes of teaching and funding vary. As explained above, quality is a relative concept and a number of different approaches to quality and QA are possible. One DE institution may be of high quality in relation to one aspect but low quality in relation to another. And one DE institution may be of high quality from the perspective of students but low quality from that of other interest groups. The most appropriate approach to quality in DE may be to recognize the difficulties in defining quality in DE and try to specify as clearly as possible the criteria for measuring quality of various aspects of DE and the procedures for assuring quality that reflect different perspectives of each stakeholder and society. In addition, continuous quality improvement needs to be embedded in the accreditation or QA process for DE institutions and quality review agencies.

Figure 31.1 shows a conceptual framework for QA and continuous quality improvement in DE. Recognizing different views on quality of DE, it is intended to present various levels and aspects of QA efforts at the institutional, national, and international level.

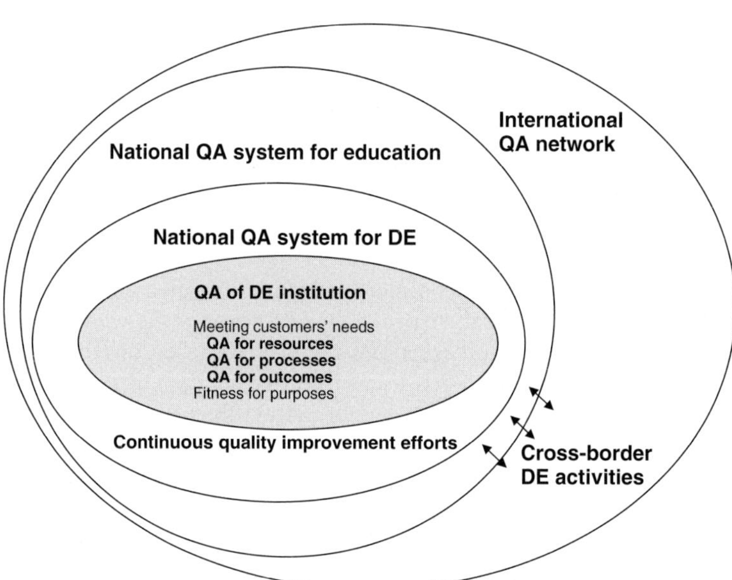

Figure 31.1: A Conceptual Framework for QA and Continuous Quality Improvement in DE

31.3 RECENT TRENDS OF QUALITY ASSURANCE IN DISTANCE EDUCATION

In the context of growing globalization in DE, there has been an urgent need to review existing QA mechanisms of DE at the national and institutional level, discuss new challenges of a changing DE environment, and enhance the quality provision of DE. Over the past years, developing and implementing policies to assure quality has become a priority of DE institutions. This section discusses general trends of QA efforts in DE institutions, based on the results of a survey conducted in 2004 (Jung, 2004c).

31.3.1 Convergence of Quality Culture

The survey showed that a quality culture has been emerging, if not yet fully integrated, in the nine mega-universities and the other six DE institutions investigated. In the survey, QA was defined as "planned activities carried out with the intent and purpose of maintaining and improving the quality of learning rather than simply evaluating activities". A majority of the institutions surveyed have developed and implemented QA standards and procedures in key areas of DE activities such as planning, program/course design and development, learner supports and tutoring, media and technology, and assessment. Most of the universities tend to have more detailed criteria especially for program/course design and development and learner supports. Half of the DE institutions surveyed have institutionalized a central QA unit and thus sought the development of a more systematic and coherent quality culture. Another indicator of the emergence of a quality culture is capacity building efforts made by the institutions. At least half of the institutions surveyed have provided continuous staff development opportunities to their academic and administrative staff in pursuit of continuous quality improvement. Inviting external experts at various stages of DE provision in a majority of the DE institutions surveyed is also an identified capacity-building effort. Moreover, most DE institutions have shown an aspiration of obtaining national recognition as a high quality DE provider. Some have gone beyond the national level accreditation and recognition and pursued international recognition such as ISO certification for their services.

31.3.2 Diversity of Quality Systems

The survey also revealed the existence of a variety of QA systems of DE, even though the globalization and competitiveness of higher education and the development of technology have brought distance teaching universities closer together in terms of developing a common quality culture. First, the level of QA policy integration in an overall university policy framework varies across the institutions. In some institutions, where the internal QA system is closely linked to the national QA framework, internal QA policies comply with the national QA standards and procedures, and are well integrated into the general university policy and performance framework. However, in some other cases, QA policies are established only at the unit level, and are thus not firmly integrated into the larger university policy and performance framework. Second, some DE institutions apply a set of standards and criteria pre-determined by the institution or by the national QA agency to the assessment of key areas of DE, whereas other institutions provide only general guidelines or areas for QA and leave room for the internal and external review teams or individual units to make QA judgments. Third, some mechanisms for assuring quality of DE adopt rigorous internal QA measures, whereas in systems where the accountability concerns do not dominate, the QA system is less centralized and the primary objective is self-improvement of the institution. Fourth, even though core areas – such as course and program development and delivery – for QA are similar in most institutions, some QA areas draw more attention than others. In some institutions, assessment of staff performance and tutoring services is emphasized, whereas in other institutions, learner assessment or monitoring of e-learning courses receive more attention.

31.4 INNOVATIVE APPROACHES TO QUALITY ASSURANCE IN DISTANCE EDUCATION

As indicated above, in the context of DE, striving for high quality is a relatively new strategy. Further, more focus has been given to widening access. But with the changes in the educational environment, new and innovative approaches to quality have been experimented with and adopted by several DE institutions. This section analyzes some of the recent and innovative approaches to QA and continuous quality improvement in DE, based on a series of surveys conducted by the author (Jung, 2004a, 2004c, 2005a, 2005b). Each case presented does not address QA issues across all the aspects shown in – Figure 31.1. Instead, each highlights QA efforts of selected DE institutions to meet specific challenges they have been facing.

31.4.1 Introducing the Concept of Learner-Centered QA

Of particular interest to students in any DE institution is whether they can receive enough support services from the institution and successfully complete their study. To improve the quality of its DE practices in general and student support services in particular, some DE institutions have developed a Total Quality direction. One example can be found in Anadolu University. Anadolu has implemented Total Quality Management (TQM) as the main management strategy since 1998. The Anadolu University Improvement Project was initiated by the Quality Commission of the university to create QA strategies within the TQM framework. Representatives of all the University faculties were invited to participate in the project. As a result, a widely shared quality consciousness in individuals and organizational units was developed and QA measures were tried out in various service processes. Each faculty (school) has developed its own Faculty Quality Management (FQM) model, leading to the clarification of the University Overall Quality Assurance Policy.

In this FQM model, the Faculty perceives itself as a service provider and students as a service receiver, to be satisfied individually concerning their unique educational needs and expectations. Changes in perception, from teacher-centered to learner-centered, have led to major revisions in mission statements, organizational policies, and implementation strategies. Priorities have been given to the students rather than the university members or organizational units. Specific changes include

- initiating highly interactive e-learning projects and virtual class models to meet the needs of Anadolu students to study in a more flexible environment,
- introducing an online academic advising system to increase two-way-communication opportunities,
- implementing the policy which requires all the faculties to respond to students' inquiries within 24 hours,
- adopting the strategy of blending physical and virtual contacts to introduce need-based student services, and
- including output variables such as students' satisfaction and graduation rate as QA factors.

Anadolu's learner-centered QA system, defining quality as meeting students' needs, is still at its developmental stage and thus more detailed QA standards and procedures are yet to be developed. However, the learner-centered QA approach still provides insight for other DE institutions that wish to implement QA measures in ways that assist in the progress of students in their studies and go beyond QA for the production and the delivery of course materials.

31.4.2 Linking QA to Staff Performance Evaluation

As mentioned, while DE institutions share a quality culture in general, the level of QA policy integration in an overall university policy framework varies across the institutions. In the case of Universitas Terbuka (UT) in Indonesia, the internal QA policies are well integrated into the general university policy and staff performance framework, and QA results are often used for staff evaluation and promotion.

The UT developed a new "Quality Assurance System for UT" based on modifications and contextualization of the "AAOU (Asian Association of Open Universities) Quality Assurance Framework" and further developed manuals to put QA into practice. This new QA system encompasses nine components and 107 quality criteria or statements of best practices (Zuhairi, Pribadi, and Muzammil, 2003). Each criterion is further delineated into indicators and methods of achievement.

Once the new QA system was developed, UT undertook unit-by-unit and university-wide self-assessment and priority setting. Managers from all units were invited to conduct self-assessment using the criteria of the QA system and set priorities for quality improvement over the next 4 years. All operational units were involved in producing these job manuals. Under the supervision of the Quality Assurance Centre at UT, 197 job manuals have been developed. These job manuals include

- systems and procedures in performing particular jobs and activities,
- standards relating to time, output, workflow, resources and competencies needed to perform the task, and
- the relationship of tasks among different units.

To ensure that the manuals are used consistently by all the members of UT in carrying out their daily responsibilities, assessment forms have been developed to monitor and assess tasks performed by individual staff, to support self-assessment of each unit, to record processes and outputs of the tasks, to identify problems, and to offer solutions. Each manager is responsible for implementing QA and assessment in his or her unit. All the assessment forms are analyzed and the result summary is reported to the Rector. UT's QA is linked to staff performance evaluation in such a way that units and individuals performing high quality works are fairly rewarded.

More than anything else, human resources play a significant role in QA implementation. Their performance is what makes a difference in DE quality. In this regard, UT's performance appraisal system, based on clear performance indicators, provides other DE institutions with a benchmark for monitoring organizational performance against objectives and key principles, and thus improving DE quality.

31.4.3 Developing National Level QA Mechanisms for DE

Whereas other countries adopt the QA system for higher education to oversee and monitor the quality of DE institutions, India is one of few countries which have a separate agency for assuring and managing the quality of DE. Being the separate QA body for DE in India, the Distance Education Council (DEC) has provided a comprehensive and consistent guidelines for QA in DE.

The DEC was established in 1992 within IGNOU with the mandate to promote an open and distance education network, and to plan and implement schemes for ensuring quality in DE in close collaboration with the National Assessment and Accreditation Council. The DEC can be seen as a QA and accreditation system that has been developed independently of the constraints of the organization, management, and funding that govern the conventional universities.

The DEC has developed a Handbook for the recognition of DE institutions and programs. The Handbook includes criteria set for the approval of a new conventional distance education institution or program. A DE institution or an open university that considers application for approval or recognition is requested to fill out three forms, Form I for institutional details, Form II for assessment details, and Form III for impact of grants/audits (Details can be found at http://www.dec.ac.in). Major evaluation criteria for Form II include

1. curricular aspects,
2. teaching, learning and evaluation,
3. research, consultancy, and extension,
4. infrastructure and learning resources,
5. student support services,
6. organization and management, and
7. healthy practices.

It appears that over the years, the DEC's efforts to establish a system of sharing DE courses and facilities among open universities and to build a formal assessment and accreditation system have contributed to collaboration among open universities and refinement of a QA and accreditation mechanism for DE in India. To countries where a centralized mechanism of QA for DE needs to be developed, the case of India provides a useful benchmark.

31.4.4 Obtaining Foreign Accreditation

Most of the DE institutions were initially accredited by their own government or a higher education accreditation body recognized by the central or local government. There are some exceptions. A recent trend is for a DE institution to obtain accreditation outside of its own country. This implies that DE institutions want to gain the confidence of current and prospective students around the globe in their DE programs and services by meeting rigorous international QA standards. For example, Monash University (Australia) has obtained ISO9001 certification for its DE services. UT and the Open University Malaysia (OUM) have been also awarded ISO9001:2000 certification. UT is also in the process of seeking international accreditation and quality certification from the International Council for Open and Distance Education (ICDE). Athabasca University and the University of Southern Queensland (USQ, Australia) both recently obtained accreditation from agencies in the United States.

- In June 2005, Athabasca University was accredited by the Middle States Commission on Higher Education, one of the six regional higher education accreditation boards in the United States. This accreditation is seen as "an indication of quality assurance and recognition of institutional excellence". During the lengthy evaluation process, Athabasca was able to reflect itself and identified both opportunities for improvement and areas of strengths.
- USQ was recently accredited by the Distance Education Training Council, one of the accreditation agencies recognized by the Council for Higher Education Accreditation in the United States, dedicated to identifying quality distance learning institutions. The accreditation is seen as "an endorsement that will allow the University to better sell its distance education programs overseas". By achieving the US accreditation, USQ's US-based students may be able to claim student financial assistance from their government.

In both cases, the US accreditation is seen as an opportunity to increase access to the DE market in the United States and around the world. In the rapidly changing and evolving field of DE and e-learning, foreign accreditation will certainly contribute to supporting capacity-building efforts of a DE institution and build international confidence in the quality of its courses and services.

31.4.5 Developing QA Guidelines for Transnational DE

In most cases, QA and accreditation criteria for transnational DE have not been developed. However, there is a tendency for the mandate of national or institutional policies to include evaluation criteria for transnational education with the growth of the export trade in borderless education products during the last several years. The following cases discuss QA for transnational DE in two institutions.

Monash University has developed specific QA guidelines for offshore courses including DE courses. Consistent with the Australian Vice-Chancellors' Committee's "Provision of Education for International Students: Code of Practice and Guidelines for Australian Universities", Monash's Off-Shore QA Committee approves all new and existing courses including those offered offshore. QA criteria for offshore courses include

1. details of Monash provider and partner(s), structure,
2. content and delivery of the course,
3. admissions requirements for students,
4. human resources to support the course,
5. teaching approaches and assessment,
6. facilities,
7. course management and evaluation,
8. marketing the course, and
9. financial resources and contract arrangements.

IGNOU, being an exporter of its DE programs, has also set QA guidelines for exporting programs. First, the credibility of partner institutions will be reviewed in collaboration with Indian High commissions and Embassies abroad. Second, IGNOU approves local tutors and counselors appointed by the partner institutions, based on their curriculum vita. Those approved tutors and counselors receive training sessions on student support services from IGNOU faculty. Finally, the examination scripts are marked centrally by IGNOU to provide reliability of student assessment.

The issue of QA for transnational DE – exports and imports – is still in the initial stages of development. Serious attention has to be given to the development of QA guidelines for transnational DE both at the national and at the institutional level. The above-mentioned cases should help in devising QA mechanisms for transnational DE operations.

31.4.6 Addressing Quality Issues in for-Profit e-Learning

More recently, for-profit e-learning providers have expanded locally and internationally. At the national level, for-profit e-learning companies in most of the countries have not been authorized to award degree programs independently. A few exceptions include the United States, Japan, and Singapore. An increased for-profit involvement has challenged the existing QA frameworks of DE, which often do not address for-profit education. The following cases show how two for-profit e-learning institutions have emerged and how some of QA issues have been addressed.

In Japan, a new government initiative to promote structural reform and revitalize the economy in some selected special zones has been implemented since 2003. This initiative enables a selected zone (town or district) to promote its structural reforms and boost the economy in an approved field, with some regulatory exceptions. In selected zones, a for-profit online university can be established in principle as long as the following conditions are met.

- A for-profit university must have one professor per 15 students. However, online universities can hire professors on a non-tenure track, part-time basis while keeping 1:15 faculty–student ratio.
- A for-profit university must execute faculty development programs for its members.
- A for-profit university must show the evidence of enough assets to run the organization.
- A for-profit university must have accumulated enough knowledge about school management.
- Top management of a for-profit university must have obtained social reputation in Japan.
- A company running a for-profit university must disclose its business affairs and financial statements.
- In addition to the evaluation by one of the university accreditation agencies authorized by the central government, a for-profit university in a special structural reform zone must be evaluated for its quality by the local government of that zone.

This case stresses that national policies should provide QA guidelines for for-profit involvement in DE. At the same time, for-profit DE institutions should be allowed to develop an organizational structure where they can purchase, lease, or modify facilities quickly, develop, devise, or distribute materials efficiently, focus on a specific niche of the education market, respond to market changes quickly (Rumble and Latchem, 2004), and utilize human resources in a flexible way.

U21G was established as a joint venture between Universitas 21, an international network of 16 prominent research universities, and Thomson Learning, a for-profit company that provides learning solutions, and now offers online programs including an MBA. U21G's MBA Program is registered by the Singapore Ministry of Education under the Distance Learning Program. Its programs are accredited by U21Pedagogica, the wholly owned QA subsidiary of Universitas 21. Degrees awarded by U21G will bear the names of the universities that are shareholders in this venture. U21G also offers opportunities for member universities to exchange students and faculty and conduct joint research.

The case of U21G highlights its efforts to gain public-confidence in the quality of its e-learning programs and services. It seems that one of those efforts is to collaborate with prestigious conventional universities around the globe in creating and delivering e-learning courses and administering the institution. Even though the president and CEO of U21G is from Thomson Learning, most member universities are shareholders and own 50 percent of U21G, and many of faculty members and deans in 16-member universities serve as academic consultants or part-time faculty member. Another way of gaining public-confidence is to apply its own QA framework through U21Pedagogica, with particular emphasis on the process governing the recruitment of adjunct faculty, training, supervision and mentoring, and teaching performance evaluation. Without hard evidence, we cannot conclude that these efforts of U21G have or have not contributed to the improvement of its e-learning practices. However, it is evident that U21G has addressed issues of QA in collaborative ways.

31.5 FUTURE DIRECTIONS

Based on discussions above, the following policy objectives can be suggested for the further development of quality in DE.

- The mission or purposes of DE need to be continuously reviewed, based on changing needs of society and learners.
- Learners should be protected from low-quality provision of DE. In this regard, for-profit, e-learning, and transnational DE activities require special attention.
- QA policies of DE institutions should cover major input, process, and output factors of distance teaching and learning, and be integrated into the general university policy and staff performance framework.
- The national QA system for education should include QA policies and procedures for DE.
- DE institutions need to review foreign or international accreditation considering the cross-border nature of DE.

To achieve such policy objectives for QA, individual DE institutions and nations need to further investigate context-sensitive QA strategies. The following areas are suggested for further investigation that DE institutions, QA agencies, governments, and international organizations can undertake (Jung, 2005c).

- There is a strong need to address the challenges of expanded cross-border and for-profit e-learning provisions in reviewing the existing QA policies or establishing new QA policies in any DE institutions. In a cross-border DE or an e-learning context, learners can be distributed anywhere and education can be delivered to them wherever they are. In the near future, people will be able to take some part of their courses from one university, another part from an alternative university, and a further part from a different university within their own nation or beyond the nation. To protect students from the risks of low-quality programs and education of limited national and international validity, further efforts to link the QA policies of a DE institution to the national and international QA frameworks need to be made.
- Each government and DE institution needs to develop a comprehensive QA structure, in collaboration with QA agencies, at the national and institutional level. There is little doubt that, in the future, DE will certainly dominate the post-secondary arena and continuing education market for professional development. There will be more and more requests to validate the credentials of DE institutions and the quality of programs and services in those institutions. To meet the demand for QA by its own students, a DE institution needs to develop

a more coherent and comprehensive QA organizational structure to coordinate and oversee the institution's various QA activities.

- The definition of quality and QA in DE should be widened as the range of stakeholders and purposes widens. For example, over the past years, internal QA efforts in DE institutions have been focusing mostly on course and material development from the perspective of DE providers. There is a need to extend the internal quality audit to other areas such as learning outcomes, experience of learners, cost-benefits, and improvement of staff performance from the perspectives of learners and sponsors.
- Finally, collaborative international efforts need to be made to promote QA activities in cross-border DE. QA in DE is not an institutional or a national issue anymore because DE reaches beyond local and regional boundaries and new forms of DE provision are increasing. The key to successful QA activities in the future may lie in DE institutions' commitment to international debates and international decision-making processes related to QA issues. International and regional organizations such as UNESCO, OECD, the Commonwealth of Learning, the European Association for Quality Assurance in Higher Education (ENQA), the Asia Pacific Quality Network (APQN), and the International Network of Quality Assurance Agencies in Higher Education (INQAAHE) can play an important role in promoting such international efforts and collaboration.

REFERENCES

Capper, J. and Fletcher, D. (1996). *Effectiveness and Cost-Effectiveness of Print-Based Correspondence Study*. Alexandria, VA: Institute for Defense Analyses.

Farrell, G. (2001). *The Changing Faces of Virtual Education*. Vancouver: Commonwealth of Learning.

Green, D. (1994). What is quality in higher education?: Concepts, policy and practice. In *What is Quality in Higher Education?* (D. Green, ed.) Buckingham: Open University press and Society for Research into Higher Education, pp. 3–20.

Jung, I.S. (2004a). *Quality Assurance and Accreditation Mechanisms of Distance Education for Higher Education in the Asia-Pacific Region: Five Selected Cases*. UNESCO Workshop on Exporters and Importers of Cross-Border Higher Education. 20–22 March 2004. Beijing, China.

Jung, I.S. (2004b). Review of policy and practice in virtual education: in the context of higher education in S. Korea. *Educational Studies,* **48**, 111–123.

Jung, I.S. (2004c). Convergence and diversity of quality assurance systems in distance education. *The SNU Journal of Educational Research,* **13**, 75–106.

Jung, I.S. (2005a). Implications of WTO/GATS on quality assurance of distance education (including e-learning) for higher education. Paper presented at the UNESCO Regional Seminar on Implications of WTO/GATS on Higher Education in Asia and the Pacific, 27–29 April, Seoul, Korea.

Jung, I.S. (2005b). *Innovative and Good Practices of Open and Distance Learning in Asia and the Pacific*. Report commissioned by the UNESCO, Bangkok Office.

Jung, I.S. (2005c). Quality assurance survey of mega universities. In *Perspectives on Distance Education: Lifelong Learning and Distance Higher Education* (C. McIntosh, and V. Zeynep, eds) Vancouver: Commonwealth of Learning and Paris: UNESCO, pp. 79–98.

Jung, I.S. and Rha, I. (2000). Effectiveness and cost-effectiveness of online education: a review of literature. *Educational Technology*, 40(4), 57–60.

Lezberg, A.K. (2003). Accreditation: quality control in higher distance education. In *Handbook of Distance Education* (M.G. Moore and W.G. Anderson, eds) New Jersey: Lawrence Erlbaum Associates, pp. 425–434.

Lockwood, F. and Gooley, A. (eds) (2001). *Innovation in Open and Distance Learning*. London: RoutledgeFalmer.

Moore, M.G. and Thompson, M.M. (1997). The effects of distance learning: revised edition. *ACSDE Research Monograph, 15*. Penn State University.

OECD. (2004). *Quality and Recognition in Higher Education: The Cross-Border Challenge*. Paris: Center for Educational Research and Innovation.

Perraton, H. (2000). *Open and Distance Learning in the Developing World*. London: Routledge Studies in Distance Education.

Rumble, G. and Latchem, C (2004). Organizational models for open and distance learning. In *Policy for Open and Distance Learning* (H. Perraton and H. Lentell, eds) London: RoutledgeFalmer, pp. 117–140.

Sherry, A.C. (2003). Quality and its measurement in distance education. In *Handbook of Distance Education* (M.G. Moore and W.G. Anderson, eds) New Jersey: Lawrence Erlbaum Associates, pp. 435–460.

Shive, G. and Jegede, O.J. (2001). Introduction. In *Open and Distance Education in the Asia Pacific Region* (O.J. Jegede and G. Shive eds) Hong Kong (China): Open University of Hong Kong Press, pp. 1–26.

UNESCO. (2003). *The Virtual Universities: Models and Messages*. Retrieved November 11, 2005, from http://www.unesco.org/iiep/virtualuniversity/home.php

Zuhairi, A. Pribadi, B., and Muzammil, M. (2003). Quality assurance as continuous improvement in distance higher education: we write what we do, and we do what we write! Paper presented at the seminar of the Association of the Southeast Asia Institutions of Higher Learning, 9–11 December, Jakarta, Indonesia.

Chapter 32

ACCOUNTABILITY AND DISTANCE EDUCATION

David Murphy

32.1 INTRODUCTION

"Distance education to be made accountable" boldly announced a headline in the *Times of India* (2004), heralding moves "to regularise open learning courses offered by various universities across the country." India is, of course, not alone in such actions, with governments around the globe jumping onto the accountability bandwagon. How well are distance educators responding to the accountability call, and what evidence is emerging of effective approaches to responding to emerging demands in this area?

Despite its emergence as a key issue and force, it is rare to find "accountability" in the contents list or index of any standard text on distance education. Nevertheless, accountability has become increasingly important in education in general over the past few decades, and more recently in higher education. It is gradually creeping into the distance education literature and is likely to remain a topic of discussion and debate for at least the near future.

In terms of basic meaning, accountability is related to taking responsibility for one's actions and has similarities with the notions of answerability, liability and blameworthiness. Where accountability becomes difficult and complex is not in providing a definition but in finding answers to questions associated with "*Who* is accountable to *whom*, for *what* purposes, for *whose* benefits, by *which* means, and with *what* consequences?" (Burke, 2005, p. 2). It is the struggle with questions such as these that has seen the issue of accountability remain elusive over the past few decades, as those both inside and outside higher education seek ways to make it more transparent and responsive (Evans, 1999).

32.2 HIGHER EDUCATION AND ACCOUNTABILITY

In evidence of its relatively recent emergence, Ravitch (2002) traces the interest in accountability to the 1966 Coleman Report (*Equality of Educational Opportunity*) from the USA, which studied the distribution of resources and opportunities among children of different races, and included an examination of differences in outcomes. As the author notes, the "study was significant for many reasons, one of which was its shift in focus from inputs to results, which followed the authors' decision to examine how school resources affected achievement" (n.p.). The fallout from this shift continues to this day, often in a non-harmonious environment, as "professional educators and their allies in higher education continue to focus on inputs (resources for reducing class size, increasing teachers' salaries, and expanding teacher training, for example), whereas policymakers representing the public seek accountability for results" (n.p.). Despite the tension, educators are nevertheless reminded that "Better accountability in higher education is required, not to fix blame, but to help improve performance, and build public confidence in and support for higher education" (Lingenfelter, 2005, p. 1).

Other governments have followed suit. More than a decade ago, it was noted that "the British government has adopted a series of principles for organising [higher education]... These principles include the need for increased access, greater integration of private/commercial interests, and allocation of public funds to fund such expansion. All this activity is hoped to pave the way to higher standards and greater accountability" (Prebble, 1995, p. 2).

So, accountability is increasingly significant, but, as Burke (2005, p. 1) wryly notes, "*Accountability* is the most advocated and least analyzed word in higher education." Essentially, though, accountability means that institutions of higher education must be answerable for their actions, in terms of the following:

- Demonstrating the proper use of power;
- Showing that they are working to achieve their mission;
- Reporting on their performance;
- Demonstrating efficiency and effectiveness;
- Ensuring the quality of their programs and services; and
- Demonstrating that they are serving public needs.

(Burke, 2005, p. 2)

The variety of ways in which institutions have responded to the accountability call is reflected in the array of models of accountability, with Burke able to list at least six: bureaucratic, professional, political, managerial, market and managed market (Burke, 2005, p. 10). The passage of time has seen a shift in emphasis, at least in the USA, from the early days of efficiency to quality, on to productivity and most recently to the goal of responsiveness to public priorities and market demands. The common deficiency of historical accountability models is that they fail to address the need to reconcile collegiate, civic and commercial cultures.

In demonstrating accountability, higher education institutions must at the same time achieve a delicate balance with their carefully nurtured and guarded autonomy, as it is fundamental to their purpose that universities "must simultaneously serve and scrutinize the society that supports them" (Burke, 2005, p. 5).

Based on Clark's governance triangle for analysing higher education systems (Clark, 1983), which used *state control*, *academic oligarchy* and *market models* as the dominant forces, Burke offers the Accountability Triangle (Burke, 2005, pp. 21–24) as a simple model to assist in unlocking the complexities of accountability in higher education. In this model, the three interests and pressures that allow assessment of accountability are *state priorities*, *academic concerns* and *market forces*. Although having primary application to the USA, the model can easily be modified for international contexts by substituting *government priorities* for *state priorities*. Fundamentally, Burke's model posits that higher education institutions and systems are accountable to *government priorities*, *academic concerns* and *market forces*. In achieving accountability, a balance should be attained and maintained in responding to the three "corners" of the triangle, ensuring high levels of service that at the same time avoid subservience (see Figure 32.1).

Government priorities (representing political accountability) "reflect the public needs for and desires for higher education programs and services, often expressed by state officials but also by civic leaders outside government" (Burke, 2005, p. 22). *Academic concerns* (professional accountability) focus on the issues identified by members of the academic community, both faculty and administrators, while *market forces* (market accountability) involve the needs and demands of the customers, primarily students, but also including others such as parents and the commercial world.

Evidence of attention to the Accountability Triangle can be gleaned in the recently released (26 September 2006) Report of the Commission on the Future of Higher Education (http://www.ed.gov/about/bdscomm/list/hiedfuture/index.html) in the US. Accountability was one of the four key areas that the Commission was charged to examine, the

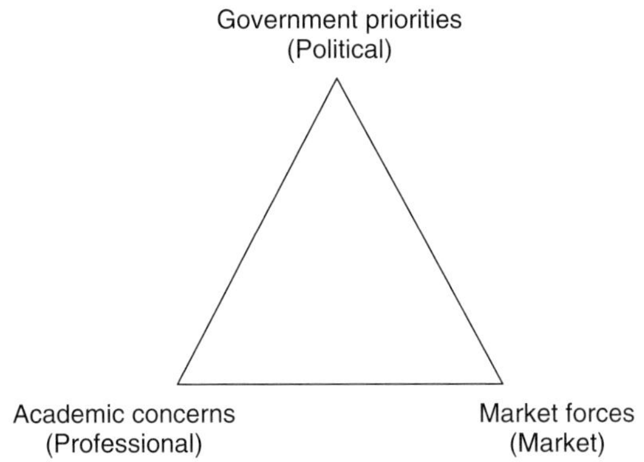

Figure 32.1: The Accountability Triangle

other three being access, affordability and quality. Under "Transparency and Accountability", the following strong statement is made:

> We believe that improved accountability is vital to ensuring the success of all the other reforms we propose. Colleges and universities must become more transparent about cost, price, and student success outcomes, and must willingly share this information with students and families. Student achievement, which is inextricably connected to institutional success, must be measured by institutions on a "value-added" basis that takes into account students' academic baseline when assessing their results. This information should be made available to students, and reported publicly in aggregate form to provide consumers and policymakers an accessible, understandable way to measure the relative effectiveness of different colleges and universities.
>
> (US Department of Education, 2006a, p. 4)

One of the recommendations specifically addresses this concern, calling for the creation of a publicly accessible database on higher education that will contain baseline data on providers. Information that allows easy comparisons with respect to costs, admissions, completions and, eventually, learning outcomes is specifically targeted. This move clearly lends particular focus to market and political accountability. Furthermore, with respect to market forces, a press release from the office of the US Secretary of Education states that

> In an effort to increase transparency and accountability, Secretary Spellings plans to provide matching funds to colleges, universities and states that collect and publicly report student learning outcomes. She will also convene members of the accrediting community this November to move toward measures that place more emphasis on learning and less on inputs. These proposals will improve higher education's performance and the ability to measure that performance.
>
> (US Department of Education, 2006b, n.p.)

It is noted that other countries have already introduced data and associated information sources that reflect the sentiments expressed in the USA. The Australian government publishes comparative data on student progression and retention, graduation statistics and the results of the nationwide Course Experience Questionnaire (CEQ) on its website (http://www.dest.gov.au), and universities in Australia make the results of student evaluation of individual subjects publicly available.

Thus, whether higher education institutions and systems like it or not, accountability is here to stay, and thus sustained efforts are needed to build and maintain systems of accountability that balance public, academic and market concerns.

32.3 DISTANCE EDUCATION AND ACCOUNTABILITY

It can be argued that accountability has been a cornerstone of distance education since its inception, at least with respect to academic concerns. While classroom teaching is, paradoxically, a somewhat private act, distance education makes the teaching function explicit through the publication of learning materials. The quality of the teaching is at least partly judged on the quality of the materials, and institutions have always striven to ensure that such materials are as exemplary as possible. The use of course teams, reviewers and evaluation and survey methods illustrates that distance education institutions consider themselves accountable to their students and the academic community.

The notion of accountability in a formal sense has become increasingly significant in distance education around the globe, as nations and institutions strive to make best use of their educational dollar. Accountability is one of the three requirements (the other two being good governance and transparency) of society in order for education to flourish, becoming "elements of freedom on which other freedoms can be built" (Daniel, 2002, n.p.).

The emphasis is not just on financial accountability, as Dhanarajan noted when speaking on "Open Learning: The Distance Ahead", reflecting the "market forces" (that is, students or student demand) corner of the Accountability Triangle:

> Good practice in distance education calls for... effective internal decision-making procedures for the setting up of standards, goals and priorities as well as a periodic self-evaluation of the system of accountability to learners.
>
> (Dhanarajan, 1966, n.p.)

This increasing attention is well recognised by Howell et al. (2003), who cite the growing emphasis on academic accountability as one of their thirty-two trends affecting distance education. Related to the adult distance education population, it is claimed that "accountability has become the driving force behind most of the laws, funding decisions and goals established for progress in adult education. Various stakeholders want evidence that adult learners are making the kinds of gains that will enable them to become more productive contributors to society." (Young et al., 2002, p. 3)

Do distance education institutions recognise and emphasise accountability in their mission statements and values? Athabasca University is clear in its view and matches precisely into the Accountability Triangle by including in its Business Plan (2006–2010) the statement that "We are accountable to our students, to each other, and to the public" (Athabasca University, 2004).

However, the pathway for accountability within distance education has not necessarily been a smooth one thus far. Shale and Gomes (1998) discussed some of the issues clouding the application of standard higher education accountability measures to distance education. As they explain,

> Higher education systems in many countries have come under increasing public and governmental scrutiny with respect to what they do, how well they do it, and at what cost. In some instances, a formalized accountability exercise has been implemented, usually based on the notion of "performance indicators".... In general, though, performance indicators are developed for application to conventional campus-based institutions.

> In the case of university distance education providers, these indicators have not generally been appropriate. For example, counts of students in conventional universities are based on an assumption that the norm is a full-time student carrying a full course load. By their nature, distance education providers typically cater to a group of students who necessarily must study part-time. Moreover, the mandates of distance education providers may often be antithetical to the mandates presumed by performance indicators formulated for conventional universities. For example, many distance education institutions have a stated commitment to lifelong, continuous learning. Numbers of degrees awarded, graduation rates and time to degree completion might (arguably) be indicative of how effective or efficient a conventional university may be. However, these kinds of indicators are less meaningful for most distance education providers because many of their students will not have a start-to-end degree program as an objective.
>
> (Shale and Gomes, 1998, n.p.)

Similar concerns have been raised in the USA, where accountability with respect to distance education has thus far been primarily linked to issues of accreditation. This has led to the question of whether existing accreditation practices are adequate and effective for this mode of education. The regional accreditation agencies have been required to demonstrate their ability to effectively review distance education, and all have done so. An emerging issue is whether this is adequate for distance education programmes, and thus whether there should be "separate and specific standards and procedures to ensure their quality" (Wolff, 2005, p. 97). The agencies argue that it is simply a matter of mode of education, so that existing procedures are adequate, nevertheless still adopting a specific policy on distance education, along with best practice guidelines (Wolff, 2005).

To be more specific, though, how does this issue of accountability in distance education play out in practice? This can be illustrated with reference to two different distance education contexts, those found in Australia and Hong Kong.

32.4 ACCOUNTABILITY IN AUSTRALIA

Australia does not have any open universities. Rather, distance education is offered by many conventional universities, via what has become known as a dual mode operation. The issue of accountability has, not surprisingly, thus been inextricably linked with its application in conventional tertiary education. Furthermore, the Australian government has shown keen interest in the issue of public accountability with respect to education:

> Accountability is a fundamental aspect of public administration. As large amounts of taxpayers' funds support the higher education sector, the Australian Government has an obligation to ensure it gets value for the money it spends and to hold the recipients of those funds accountable for their use.
>
> (Department of Education, Science and Training, 2005, p. 5)

The clear message being annunciated is increasingly acknowledged by Australian universities, as exemplified by the following statement from the University of Southern Queensland:

> Governments, funding agencies, professional bodies, employers, students' sponsors and students are demanding a greater say in setting priorities and more accountability for outcomes. Students are increasingly being seen as consumers. Educational organisations are having to take increasing account of customer demand. The demands of industry and commerce, as employers of graduates and consumers of university services and products, are changing.
>
> (University of Southern Queensland, 2002, n.p.)

The primary accountability mechanism for Australian universities is the Institution Assessment Framework (IAF), an information collection exercise undertaken annually by the government's Department of Education, Science and Training (DEST). The performance of higher education providers is assessed with respect to four key areas, organisational sustainability, achievements in higher education provision, quality and meeting legislative requirements (DEST, 2006, p. 94). The 2005 assessment portfolios added research performance to the list, the overall conclusion being that the "assessments continued to indicate a financially sustainable, high achieving, high quality and accountable higher education sector in Australia" (DEST, 2006, p. 95).

A significant recent government initiative with respect to quality and accountability has been the establishment in 2000 of the Australian Universities Quality Agency (AUQA), which is charged with promoting, auditing and reporting on quality assurance in Australian higher education. The particular application of the notion of quality adopted by AUQA is fitness for purpose. Its audit reports are publicly available and can thus be analysed to reveal emerging issues with respect to distance education, especially those related to offshore activities. Many Australian distance education providers are exporters of education (principally in Asia) through distance learning, and the feedback provided by AUQA audits has been timely.

An investigation of twenty-five of the AUQA reports (2002–2005) that provides specific useful quotes is Stevens (2005). An overall comment from AUQA related to distance education and relationships with third-party providers is as follows:

> Offshore activities with third party partnerships require more stringent quality assurance systems than "home" campus-based education, just as does the provision of distance education. However, assuring the quality for offshore activities, including through third parties, involves identifying further layers of differences in culture, politics, learning styles and business practices.
>
> (Stevens, 2005, p. iii)

Noting that institutions are particularly interested in the number of commendations they receive in AUQA reports, the following specific instances of positive feedback are reported:

> USQ's [University of Southern Queensland] strategic objective is to be a leader in flexible learning and the use of communication and information technologies in a tertiary education context. AUQA noted the international recognition of USQ and its robust processing distance education systems. AUQA commended its achievements and successes in the area of flexible learning.
>
> (Stevens, 2005, p. 13)

> USQ's online or distance education materials are produced to be stand alone in terms of not requiring extra tuition. However, certain offshore agencies add tuition support from local tutors or from visits by USQ staff. USQ research shows that this is beneficial with a positive impact on course progression rates and retention rates, particularly for undergraduate students.
>
> (Stevens, 2005, p. 59)

It is worth noting that the AUQA audit panels treat offshore provision seriously and typically visit at least some of the offshore agencies as part of the overall audit process. In the case of USQ, this involved three overseas countries.

> Another core commitment of DU [Deakin University] is to improve equity and access for individuals to higher education. AUQA commended DU's manifest commitment to equity and access, continuing education and lifelong learning, and rural and regional engagement through distance education.
>
> (Stevens, 2005, p. 15)

> UniSA's [University of South Australia] aim is to be "an innovator in blending online and campus-based learning" and AUQA commended UniSA for its successful flexible delivery models. UniSA draws on its distance education experience to provide flexible program delivery and a wide range of learning environments. Students blend full-time and part-time, face-to-face and online study, cutting across multiple campuses and accessing different staff and different types of support.
>
> (Stevens, 2005, p. 57)

The benefits of well-run, technology-supported distance education within some of Australia's dual mode universities is thus well acknowledged. However, while celebrating their commendations, institutions wish to minimise any negative feedback, in particular the number of recommendations they receive. The perennial problem of turnaround time for assignments is noted in the following list of quotes:

> AUQA found UNE's [University of New England] performance not strong enough against its goal to have the highest reputation for supporting the aspirations of its metropolitan distance education students.
>
> (Stevens, 2005, p. 14)

> USQ students informed AUQA that turnaround times for returning assessments are often longer than specified. With the success of distance education learning highly dependent on tutor feedback AUQA considers this requires attention.
>
> (Stevens, 2005, p. 37)

Issues associated with evaluation are naturally high on the AUQA agenda, illustrated by the following recommendations made for two distance education providers.

> Current students at ECU [Edith Cowan University] studying by distance are not evaluated. AUQA recommended that ECU urgently develop and implement a system for evaluating the quality of its distance education activities.
>
> (Stevens, 2005, p. 60)

> AMC [Australian Maritime College] distance education provision is increasing but the approach needs to be more team based. Outcomes need to be systematically evaluated to avoid overlooking stakeholder needs whilst the example of providing a compulsory online course decreases flexibility. The progress report states that better coordination is anticipated as a result of the amalgamation of services.
>
> (Stevens, 2005, p. 61)

Even more recently than the creation of AUQA, Australia has begun a move towards performance-based funding of teaching through the introduction of the Learning and Teaching Performance Fund (LTPF), the first two rounds of which took place in 2005 and 2006. As mentioned earlier, Australian universities are beginning to be held accountable for the quality of the education that takes place within them, based on a number of criteria chosen by the federal government's DEST, http://www.dest.gov.au. At the end of 2005, $54.4 million was distributed to fourteen universities, leaving twenty-four eligible institutions with none of the available pool. The 2006 allocation of $83 million has been made to twenty-one universities, the increased number largely a result of the introduction of four discipline streams. The criteria upon which the funding decisions were made are comprised of

- the outcomes of the CEQ;
- the Graduate Destination Survey (GDS); and
- progression and attrition data.

The third set of criteria may be of concern to distance education providers, as such data for distance education students typically do not match those of their face-to-face counterparts. Informal feedback in the first round suggested that thus far the inclusion of distance education students has not skewed the data negatively for distance education providers, though it was surmised that for the first round, only full-time undergraduate local students were included. For the second round, part-time students were included in the calculations. An adjustment process was introduced, based on the feedback from universities after the first round, and the factors of both mode (external/internal) and type of study (full-time/part-time) were included. It is noted, though, that distance education providers made up around half of the universities who failed to attract any LTPF allocation.

32.5 ACCOUNTABILITY IN HONG KONG

At first glance, the issue of accountability with respect to distance education in Hong Kong may seem unproblematic and straightforward. Hong Kong has its own Open University (http://www.ouhk.edu.hk), which undergoes regular review by (and is thus accountable to) the government via the Hong Kong Council for Academic Accreditation (HKCAA). The institution began its life in 1989 as the Open Learning Institute and following successful validation in 1995 gained university status and became the Open University of Hong Kong in 1997 (Murphy and Fung, 1999). Since its establishment it has produced more than 45,000 graduates, and in 2006/2007, its distance education students numbered just over 15,000.

Accountability in Hong Kong becomes a much more fascinating topic when the focus shifts to the offering of distance education courses by overseas institutions. The numbers of such courses grew rapidly during the 1980s and into the 1990s, so that by 1994 it was estimated that there were at least 319 tertiary institutions from seventeen countries offering their courses to potential students (Lee and Lam, 1994). This in itself is not necessarily problematic, except that the quality of such courses was highly variable, leading to increased concern within the community, especially when examples of Hong Kong students suffering the negative outcomes of dubious local agents linked to unscrupulous overseas operators appeared regularly in the local press. Concerns had been raised as early as 1987, when Pagliari and Frost (1987, p. 434) declared that "the public needs to be protected from the incompetent and the substandard".

It took a while, but finally the "Non-local Higher and Professional Education (Regulation) Ordinance was enacted in 1997. The objective of the legislation is to protect local consumers of higher educational services against the marketing of substandard non-local courses conducted in Hong Kong. It is also there to enhance the reputation of Hong Kong as a community which values standards of academic and professional education provisions in an open and free market" (HKCAA, 2005, p. 33). Under the Ordinance, all non-local distance education programmes and their agents/operators have to be registered. Under the regulation, all institutions offering non-local university distance education courses conducted in Hong Kong must apply for registration. The major criteria for registration are that the institution must be recognised in its home country and that the course offered to Hong Kong students must be at the same level as the equivalent offered in the country of origin. It is significant, though, that courses offered in collaboration with local institutions of higher education are exempted, the local institution being required to provide the registrar with certification of the collaborative arrangement (Murphy and Fung, 1999). There is thus, as also noted by Ziguras, a seeming loophole in the provisions, as exemption also applies to "pure" distance education courses with no local support.

The costs of registration are significant, and potential penalties for offences or non-compliance with certain provisions are severe (including forcible police entry to premises, personal detention, seizure of documents and possible fines and imprisonment). In addition, the regulation requires the use of safe premises for conducting tutorial and other student support activities. This provision was apparent recognition that at least in the past many commercial buildings used by overseas institutions and their local agents did not comply with the fire, building safety, approved planning and land use provisions for educational purposes.

The body overseeing the process is the HKCAA. As explained on their website (http://www.hkcaa.edu.hk):

> As the sole advisor on academic standards to the Registrar of Nonlocal Higher and Professional Education Courses under the Nonlocal Higher and Professional Education (Regulation) Ordinance since 1997, the HKCAA offered professional advice on the registrability of the non-local courses against stipulated criteria in the relevant legislation.... Apart from assessing new applications, the HKCAA also monitors that the registered courses continue to comply with registration criteria through the assessment of their annual returns.... So far, the total number of cases assessed is over 750 new applications and over 1,600 annual returns.
>
> (n.p.)

For 2004/2005, the HKCAA reported the assessment of fifty-seven new applications covering courses from Australia, UK, the USA, Macau and the Mainland (HKCAA, 2005, p. 33). Interestingly, and perhaps not surprisingly, 43 of the 57 courses were from the UK (27) and Australia (16).

Evans and Tregenza (2003) have reported on the experiences of students enrolled in Australian courses in Hong Kong, focusing in particular on course selection, experiences with teaching staff and experiences of Australian curricula, pedagogies and assessment. With respect to course selection, financial considerations were found to be significant, as were the status and prestige of the host institution. The authors noted that the latter two considerations were at times based more on the length of time that a particular Australian university had operated in Hong Kong than on more traditional notions of prestige in the host country. Also noted was the lack of prominence in the use of the phrase "distance education", as it was not always viewed positively. The value of flexibility, in terms of courses which blended elements of distance education, independent learning and face-to-face tutorials, was viewed favourably (Evans and Tregenza, 2003, p. 331).

With respect to teaching staff, while students in general liked meeting local tutors, they particularly appreciated the presence of visiting teaching staff from the host institution, as they "valued the international culture and perspectives they were obtaining. This includes understanding Australian contextual matters, the difference in people's understanding of knowledge and its ownership, and also of teaching and learning processes, especially notions of learning at a distance" (Evans and Tregenza, 2003, p. 332). Australian curricula, pedagogies and assessment presented particular problems to significant numbers of students, especially concerning language (studying in English, for example, presentation of argument), plagiarism (differing perceptions evident between students and staff) and lack of local content. This last point has special relevance to accountability, as the courses being offered in Hong Kong have to be the same as those offered in the home country. This clearly mitigates against any significant localisation.

32.6 CONCLUSION

So, for distance education, accountability is here and it is here to stay. Distance educators have long appreciated that they are accountable to their students, so have built their course development procedures and processes, along with their support systems, in ways that reflect their academic concerns. It is only more recently, though, that distance education has, along with other educational sectors, come under more formal accountability scrutiny and systems.

Returning to the Accountability Triangle, Burke (2005, p. 296) stresses that "responding to state priorities, academic concerns, and market forces offers a challenge, not a choice, for higher education." Institutions must serve all three, but submit to none. That is, the "three corners of accountability... balance each other, ensuring service to all but submission to none of the civic, collegiate, and commercial interests." Furthermore, despite the common calls for more accountability, what is needed is better coordination and implementation of the accountability programmes already in place, working towards "360-degree accountability" rather than "360-degree harassment" (Burke, 2005, p. 323).

The evidence gleaned from the cases of Australia and Hong Kong reveals that these two exemplars have made some progress towards these aims, including the accountability processes for distance education providers. The case studies also reveal strong contextual factors, including the significance of overseas providers of distance education courses in Hong Kong and the beginnings of a move towards performance-based funding in Australia. The case studies also provide indications, though not completely definitively, of where each jurisdiction might be placed in the Accountability Triangle. Both are certainly influenced by all three concerns, but each probably tends to be most strongly influenced by political forces, with Australia being next influenced by academic concerns and Hong Kong more attuned to market forces.

More significantly, the Accountability Triangle provides a useful tool for individual distance education institutions or systems to assess their approach to accountability. It encourages them to pay proper attention to the three forces of accountability, reminding them that their response should be balanced, in order that accountability concerns do not overtake their need for autonomy.

Finally, in drawing a final conclusion about accountability and distance education, it is tempting (and the temptation will not be resisted) to quote Burke's (2005) final reflection and replace the phrase "higher education" with "distance education". This leads to the statement that although there may be differences in "attitudes and approaches to accountability, all agree that [distance] education has become too important to the success of society and its citizens to leave the academy unaccountable for its responses and results.... accountability for [distance] education is much too important to be left to a single segment of society, whether drawn from government, education or business" (Burke, 2005, pp. xvii–xviii).

REFERENCES

Athabasca University. (2004). *Business Plan 2004–2008*. Retrieved October 6, 2006 from www.athabascau.ca/main/bizplans/04_2008_Plan.pdf.

Burke, J.C. (ed.) (2005). *Achieving Accountability in higher Education: balancing Public, Academic and Market Demands*. San Francisco: Jossey-Bass.

Clark, B.R. (1983). *The Higher Education System: Academic Organization in Cross-National Perspective*. Berkeley; University of California Press.

Daniel, J. (2002). *Development as Freedom: The Contribution of the Open Universities*. Keynote speech at the Pan-Commonwealth Forum on Open Learning Durban, South Africa, 29 July–2 August.

Department of Education, Science and Training (DEST). (2005). *Our Universities: Backing Australia's future*. Commonwealth of Australia. Retrieved October 6, 2006 from http://www.backingaustraliasfuture.gov.au/implementation/iaf.htm.

Department of Education, Science and Training (DEST). (2006). *Higher Education Report 2005*. Canberra, Australia: Department of Education, Science and Training. Retrieved October 6, 2006 from http://www.dest.gov.au/sectors/higher_education/publications_resources/profiles/highered_annual_report_2005.htm.

Dhanarajan, G. (1966). *Open Learning: The Distance Ahead*. Cambridge, UK: Anniversary Symposium, International Extension College, October 14.

Evans, G.R. (1999). *Calling Academia to Account: Rights and Responsibilities*. Buckingham, UK: Society for Research in Higher Education.

Evans, T.D. and Tregenza, K. (2003). Students' experiences of studying Australain courses in Hong Kong. In *Global Perspectives: Philosophy and Practice in Distance Education* (W.Y. Zhang, ed.) Vol. 1, Beijing: China Central Radio & Televsision University Press, pp. 322–336.

HKCAA. (2005). *Annual Report 2004–2005*. Hong Kong: Hong Kong Council for Academic Accreditation. Retrieved October 6, 2006 from http://www.hkcaa.edu.hk/Forms/Publications/Annual%20Report%2004_05.pdf.

Howell, S.L., Williams, P.B., and Lindsay, N.K. (2003). Thirty-two trends affecting distance education: An informed foundation for strategic planning. *Online Journal of Distance Learning Administration*, 6(3). Retrieved October 6, 2006 from http://www.westga.edu/%7Edistance/ojdla/search_results_id.php?id=208.

Lee, N. and Lam, A. (1994). *Professional and Continuing Education in Hong Kong: Issues and perspectives*. Hong Kong: Hong Kong University Press.

Lingenfelter, P.E. (2005). *The National Commission on Accountability in Higher Education*. American Council on Education, February 15.

Murphy, D. and Fung, Y. (1999). The Open University of Hong Kong. In *Higher Education Through Open and Distance Education* (K. Harry, ed.) London: Routledge, pp. 190–198.

Pagliari, M. and Frost, J.A. (1987) Distance education in Hong Kong. *Distance Education in Asia and the Pacific*, Volume II. Proceedings of the Regional Seminar on Distance Education, Bangkok, Thailand, November 26–December 3, 1986, 432–438.

Prebble, T. (1995). Holding the decision makers accountable: Relocating the locus of financial accountability within a dual-mode institution. In Indira Gandhi National Open University, *Structure and Management of Open Learning Systems*. Proceedings of the Eighth Annual Conference of the Asian Association of Open Universities, New Delhi, February 20–22, 1995. Vol. 1, 1–7.

Ravitch, D. (2002). A brief history of testing and accountability. *Hoover Digest*, **4**. Retrieved January 15, 2007 from http://www.hoover.org/publications/digest/4495866.html.

Shale, D. and Gomes, J. (1998). Performance indicators and university distance education providers. *Journal of Distance Education*, **13**(1). Retrieved January 15, 2007 from http://cade.athabascau.ca/vol13.1/shale.html.

Stevens, K. (2005). *Promoting and Advancing Learning and Teaching in Higher Education: The Messages from the AUQA Reports*. Sydney, Australia: Carrick Institute for Learning and Teaching in Higher Education.

Times of India. (2004). Distance education to be made accountable. Retrieved October 12, 2006 from http://timesofindia.indiatimes.com/articleshow/408551.cms.

University of Southern Queensland. (2002). *University Strategic Plan, 2003–2005*. Retrieved October 6, 2006 from http://www.usq.edu.au/planstats/Planning/Docs/StrategicPlan 2002–06.doc.

US Department of Education. (2006a). *A Test of Leadership: Charting the Future of U.S. Higher Education*. Washington, D.C.

US Department of Education. (2006b) *Press Release: Secretary Spellings Announces Plans for More Affordable, Accessible, Accountable and Consumer-Friendly U.S. Higher Education System*. Retrieved October 6, 2006 from http://www.ed.gov/news/pressreleases/2006/09/09262006.html.

Wolff, R.A. (2005). Accountability and accreditation: Can reforms match increasing demands? In *Achieving Accountability in Higher Education: Balancing Public, Academic and Market Demands* (J.C. Burke, ed.) San Francisco: Jossey-Bass, pp. 78–103.

Young, S.J., Johnston, J., and Hapgood, S.E. (2002). *Assessment and Accountability Issues in Distance Education for Adult Learners*. Institute for Social Research, University of Michigan.

Chapter 33

Cultural and Contextual Issues in the Evaluation of Transnational Distance Education

Christopher Ziguras

The term "transnational education" refers to programmes "in which the learners are located in a country different from the one where the awarding institution is based" (UNESCO and Council of Europe, 2001, n.p.). There are essentially three ways of delivering transnational programmes – through distance education, partner-supported delivery, or a branch campus. While each of these approaches involves a different level of local support to students, they all involve the production and dissemination of curriculum to remote students using information and communication technologies. In this chapter, I will use the term "distance education" to refer to online or print-based distance education without face-to-face teaching. Curriculum materials are designed for independent study and usually transmitted across national borders by a combination of posted print materials and Internet-based resources. Students and their teachers communicate to varying degrees using email, web-based discussion forums and increasingly Internet telephony. As will be discussed in detail below, most transnational education involves distance education materials combined with a wide range of forms of local support to students.

Cross-border distance education enrolments are spread very widely, if thinly, across the globe. For example, in 2004, Australian universities enrolled students from 159 countries in their offshore programmes, even though partnered programmes are only offered in forty-three. In 100 countries there are less than 20 students enrolled in Australian programmes in 2004 (DEST, 2005). As well as foreign students, many distance education programmes enrol domestic students who are located overseas. Some programmes, such as those designed for professionals working in international development, international education or the armed forces, may have very few foreign students enrolled but have a high proportion of their domestic students working overseas. One of the objectives of Turkey's Anadolu University, the country's only distance higher education provider, is to educate the Turkish diaspora in an effort to "re-acculture expatriate Turks to their language and culture" (Gursoy, 2005, p. 123). For the most part, the experience of expatriate students in distance education provided from their country of origin is very similar to that of domestic students located in the institution's home country, except perhaps for time-zone differences and variations in access to communications systems. This chapter, therefore, will focus on distance education programmes that seek to recruit students from other countries, which pose very different cultural and contextual issues. The first half of the chapter explains the recent history of transnational distance education, and the ways in which students' preferences have shaped the commercial environment in which these programmes compete with a range of local and foreign programmes. The second half of the chapter looks at how educators can most appropriately teach to the very diverse student populations that one finds in many transnational distance education programmes.

33.1 EVALUATION AND VALUATION

In the past, transnational programmes could often be overlooked by accreditation and quality assurance systems in both the institution's home country and the country in which the programme is being offered, effectively slipping between the cracks of national systems. Within the last decade, however, these agencies in most of the major education importing and exporting countries have developed extensive regulatory frameworks for transnational programmes, some relating to educational issues and some relating to commercial features in order to mitigate their impact on local providers. Quality assurance and accreditation processes in the major education exporting countries (the UK, Australia and the USA) now routinely scrutinise programmes offered overseas, whether these are offered through branch campuses, in conjunction with local partners, or through distance education without a local presence.

In the importing countries, however, the processes of evaluation, accreditation and regulation of transnational distance education vary widely, as do the meanings of these terms themselves. In many countries, foreign distance education programmes cannot obtain formal approval unless they have a local presence. Purely distance learning programmes are in most countries able to enrol students and award qualifications, but usually need to seek approval in order to advertise their programmes or to engage in any teaching or assessment in country. Unless there is some local presence, fully online distance education programmes are effectively invisible to the host government and are very difficult to track (Middlehurst and Woodfield, 2004). For example, in Hong Kong, "purely distance" transnational programmes are exempted from registration requirements if they are "conducted solely through the delivery of mail, transmission of information by means of telecommunication (e.g. TV, radio or computer network), or sale of materials in commercial outlets, and so on., but without the institutions, professional bodies or their agents being physically present in Hong Kong to deliver any lectures, tutorials or examinations" (Ip, 2006, p. 23). While this lack of regulation simplifies matters for a university offering online programmes to students in many countries, the downside is that because these programmes have no legal status in the students' country, these qualifications are often not recognised for the purposes of public-sector employment or professional accreditation.

Where there is some form of local presence, transnational distance education programmes are often evaluated in the same way as other foreign programmes using different delivery models, such as branch campuses and partnerships with local educational institutions. First, they are subject to laws that apply to all enterprises, such as those governing employment conditions of their locally employed staff, their payment of taxes, occupational health and safety and related matters. Second, they are subject to regulations that apply particularly to educational institutions and programmes, such as rules dictating the types of facilities that must be provided, the requirement to provide enrolment figures and other data to educational authorities. Third, they are also subject to regulatory frameworks that apply more particularly to private, non-government, institutions, which in many countries are different from those applying to government institutions, such as regulation of tuition fees, accreditation and quality assurance requirements, and qualifications of teaching staff. Fourth, they are usually subject to regulations that apply only to foreign institutions or programmes, such as the requirement to be accredited in the institution's home country, and to demonstrate equivalence of qualifications.

It is widely assumed that transnational education is regulated only in the sense that it is foreign, but these other forms of regulation are often much more burdensome than the restrictions on foreign companies, especially in the case of branch campuses which must navigate a wide range of regulatory requirements that can differ substantially from those applying to the institution's campuses in other countries. Transnational programmes that do not involve a commercial presence tend to be much more affected by the third and fourth types of regulation listed above, while branch campuses are more affected by the first and second. In addition, these regulations may be applied across a number of levels of government (local, state and national), further complicating the task of establishing an overseas operation.

The governmental evaluation processes described above establish hurdle requirements for transnational distance education programmes, restricting market entry to those institutions and programmes that are able to meet the required minimum standards. While formal *evaluation* of programmes through quality assurance and accreditation mechanisms is a vital precondition for success, the ongoing viability of a transnational programme is determined much more by the *valuation* of the programme's worth by consumers (students and their families). This chapter will consider the ways in which consumer valuation of various forms of distance learning has had a profound impact on its development over the past decade.

33.2 WHATEVER HAPPENED TO THE GLOBAL ONLINE UNIVERSITY?

At the height of the dot-com bubble in the late 1990s, the potential to create a global online mega-university or a global consortium comprising of several universities' online programmes excited and terrified educational planners and commentators.

Online courses, it was widely prophesied, would mean the formation of a global distance education market, in which geographical access limitations would be overcome, allowing prospective students to choose between courses offered by providers based in many different nations. Despite the best laid plans, fully online global delivery failed to capture the imagination of students and teachers in the same way it excited senior administrators. Millions of dollars invested by universities the world over was lost in a succession of failed online endeavours with global pretensions; the Universitas 21 international consortium, Western Governors University, the Global Universities Alliance, the UK e-University and the UK Open University's efforts to establish the United States Open University all collapsed due the their inability to attract students.

The desire to establish a global distance education provider was not new. A decade earlier, the Commonwealth Heads of Government in 1987 proposed to create a University of the Commonwealth for Cooperation in Distance Learning, so that "any learner anywhere in the Commonwealth shall be able to study any distance teaching programme available from any bona fide college or university in the Commonwealth' (Briggs et al., 1989). In the following years, a tension emerged among the individuals and agencies charged with implementing the proposal. On one side, education exporting countries advocated a high-tech global distance education provider (a university of the Commonwealth), and on the other, aid agencies and developing countries pushed instead for cooperation between distance education providers operating on a local or national scale. They argued that a global distance education provider which aimed at equalising access to distance education by using the educational and technological capacity of the rich countries of the Commonwealth to provide distance education to students in developing countries would invariably result in cultural imperialism. For this reason, instead of a new global provider, an agency – the Commonwealth of Learning – was established with a mandate to assist national distance education initiatives in each country, thereby seeking to equalise access to the technology, skills and information required to develop distance and online education. Former President of the Commonwealth of Learning, John Daniel, looks back upon the discussions that led to the formation of the organisation as a choice between cultural imperialism and intellectual national independence (Farrell, 2001; Daniel, 2004).

Since that time, most discussion of transnational education has become more pragmatic and less ideological, with most governments seeing it as a way of building the capacity of the domestic higher education sector by drawing on existing foreign expertise. The fears of cultural invasion of nationalist educators in developing countries has evaporated in relation to distance education largely because national open and distance education providers that have been established in many developing countries since the late 1980s have been much more successful in attracting large numbers of students than have foreign universities (Murphy et al., 2003). This is partly because the cost of production of distance education is lower in developing countries than they are for universities in rich countries. Also, national distance education programmes are often heavily subsidised by governments to keep tuition fees low, whereas governments rarely subsidise foreign students in transnational programmes. Another major advantage for national distance education providers is that they normally teach in the national language, while transnational programmes are most often taught in English. Critiques of cultural imperialism in the Asian region have subsided also because greater economic openness has generally led to increased prosperity and national self-confidence, while fears of re-colonisation are subsiding.

Like many failures during the dot-com bubble, the collapse of the aspiring global online universities was caused by an overemphasis on how technological changes would affect supply but without understanding the nature of demand for these services. This supply-driven focus in education meant that much energy and resources went into developing standardised curricula, web-based courseware, video-conferencing, and email discussion forums for global providers but very little thought went into understanding students' preferences. The bulk of students who consider studying in transnational education programmes are concentrated in cities which are experiencing rapid economic growth, most notably Singapore, Hong Kong, Kuala Lumpur, Shanghai. These cities' internationalised economies pay a premium for Western business skills and English language proficiency, and local institutions are often not able to develop new programmes to respond to labour market demand as quickly as foreign universities with established programmes. Students in most of these emerging global cities are able to choose from a wide range of foreign programmes with varying levels of local facilities, face-to-face teaching, and support services. These programmes are priced according to both the status of the awarding foreign university and the level of service provided by the local partner. The most expensive programmes are a small number of "full-service" branch campuses of foreign universities, which try to replicate the learning environment of their home campuses. The bulk of foreign programmes compete with one another on price, the status and reputation of the awarding university and the quality of the learning environment provided by the local partner. The cheapest programmes are those distance education programmes that have no local partner and offer very little face-to-face teaching or support to students. Failing to understand the nature of students' preference for local teaching, peer-contact, and support, the new global online university start-ups invested considerable sums of money into expensive programmes that students were not prepared to pay for. Consequently, in a succession of startling failures of market research, online programmes launched by the Global Universities Alliance, Western Governors' university and others with expectations of hundreds or thousands of online students were forced to sheepishly announce enrolments in the single digits.

Those transnational distance education operations that remain are generally those with longstanding domestic distance operations, where the infrastructure is already in place and international students can be taught alongside domestic students at little marginal cost. The main cost involved for such programmes is in marketing to international students, given the competition posed by competitors with a local presence who are able to market the programme locally and offer students more extensive teaching and administrative support. Distance education programmes that remain viable are those in niche fields in which there is insufficient demand in any one place to support a local presence (a graduate programme in international education for example). These operate with a relatively small student population dispersed across a large number of sites and are commercially viable precisely because of the low level of demand for such specialised courses they do not face competition from local providers or partner-supported programmes.

As well as these commercial impediments to cross-border distance education, they face difficulties with accreditation and recognition by the state and local educational institutions in many countries. Some governments are wary of transnational distance education programmes that do not have a local presence, especially in Asia, where their credibility is widely questioned and formal recognition is rare (WTO, 2002). One reason for this is the perception that cheating by students is much more likely in distance education programmes. In China, for example, students in domestic online courses must in most cases sit examinations at assigned locations so that photo identification can be inspected. Foreign distance education programmes that do not have such measure to prevent cheating in assessment are viewed with scepticism (Zhang, 2005).

33.3 PARTNER-SUPPORTED TRANSNATIONAL DISTANCE EDUCATION

Partner-supported delivery involves a local partner who provides a range of services to students, usually including face-to-face teaching, a library, computers, and administrative support. Partners vary enormously, and include *inter alia* public or private universities or colleges, the commercial arms of public institutions, for-profit or not-for-profit companies, professional associations, government departments, or agencies. There is a range of models of partner-supported delivery, which vary widely in terms of the division of responsibility for the components of the programme between the awarding institution and the local partner. This includes academic matters (such as the provision of curriculum, tuition, assessment, credentialing, and academic quality assurance) and operational matters (such as marketing, administration, provision of physical and financial resources, non-academic services to students, and operational quality assurance). In some contracts these may be broken down into dozens of sub-components. A common variation on this is "twinning", whereby students complete the first component of the qualification in the host country and – if successful – complete their studies at the home campus of the awarding institution. The curriculum materials are either those of the provider country or a local course adapted to or validated by the foreign provider. The student is normally enrolled throughout with the foreign provider. In cases where the student is enrolled initially with the local partner and subsequently enrols with the foreign provider, this is more often referred to as an "articulation" arrangement. Another variation is a "franchise", whereby the local provider is licensed to provide the foreign course under conditions set out by contract. Those conditions – that may include stipulations about class size, contact hours, teacher qualifications, and the role of the home country institution in conducting quality assurance – will determine the shape and quality of the programme. Nearly all Australian public universities deliver programmes overseas through local partners or branch campuses, and in 2003 they offered 1,569 such programmes in 43 countries, the vast majority through local partners (Table 32.1). Seventy percent of these programmes are in Singapore, Malaysia, and China (including Hong Kong) (AVCC, 2003).

Nevertheless, we can see that these two leading exporting countries between them enrol nearly 200,000 foreign students in their transnational programmes, and that the students

Table 33.1: Foreign Students Enrolled in UK and Australian Transnational Programmes

	UK (2002/03)	*Australia (2004)*	*Total UK and Australia*
Singapore	10,838	18,960	29,798
Hong Kong	13,928	15,594	29,522
Malaysia	10,506	14,579	25,085
China	1,491	9,654	11,145
Russian Federation	6,919	46	6,965
Israel	5,377	10	5,387
Ireland	5,325	32	5,357
Greece	4,397	3	4,400
United Arab Emirates	961	2,174	3,135
Trinidad and Tobago	3,079	4	3,083
Canada	1,896	1,168	3,064
United States of America	2,258	556	2,814
Germany	2,339	163	2,502
South Africa	1,408	995	2,403
Romania	2,277	4	2,281
Japan	715	1,358	2,073
India	1,203	621	1,824
Sri Lanka	956	791	1,747
Oman	1,506	41	1,547
Pakistan	1,156	373	1,529
Slovak Republic	1,359	1	1,360
Switzerland	1,085	118	1,203
Mauritius	1,031	152	1,183
Others	19,635	9,178	28,813
Total	101,645	76,575	178,220

Source: McBurnie and Ziguras (2007), drawing on data from Garrett and Jokivirta (2004) and DEST (2005).

are concentrated in Asia. In fact, the majority of students (54%) in the published data are in just three countries – Singapore, Malaysia, and China (including Hong Kong). A widely cited study by marketing company IDP Education Australia (2002) forecasts that global demand for international education will increase fourfold to 7.2 million in the year 2025. The predictably upbeat report proposes that Australian higher education institutions alone will enrol between 300,000 and 700,000 transnational students by 2025.

33.4 PACKAGED CURRICULUM AND LOCAL TEACHERS

While most large-scale transnational education involves a local partner, the diverse teaching models employed in these programmes in many ways resemble locally supported distance education. Most transnational programmes use teaching and learning resources that are able to be produced on the home campus and ensure consistency wherever the programme is offered. These curriculum resources include paper or electronic collections of assigned readings, lecture slides and notes, discussion questions and assessable tasks arranged into weekly modules. These have often grown out of the resources prepared for students in distance education programmes. For example, some of Monash University's business programmes, which are taught on their seven local and international campuses, have been standardised to the extent that 80% of the content of each course is common across the all delivery sites. One degree that has been developed primarily for offshore delivery, the Bachelor of Business and Commerce, has 100% commonality, so that each student, irrespective of the campus, studies the same curriculum, undertakes the same assessment and is assessed by the same criteria. Detailed weekly learning objectives guide teachers through the material, ensuring consistency while limiting the flexibility and autonomy of academic staff across the university (Schapper and Mayson, 2004). Monash has also developed an online English language and academic skills support site, with resources designed for a globally dispersed and diverse student population (Clerehan et al., 2003).

Applying distance education techniques to transnational programmes has some distinct advantages. The materials can be developed and refined over time with different academic staff having input into those sections where they have expertise. Material is able to be structured and sequenced to best suit students at a particular level. Students can study at their own pace, read ahead if they want to, and spend more time on the material they find difficult. The readings are readily available to students, who need to spend less time in libraries sourcing texts. Rather than stifling teaching, these resources can provide extensive supports for lecturers to cover the core curriculum, allowing them to focus their energies on questions and problems, providing illustrations and facilitating discussions. Pre-packaged material is a useful tool, providing a solid base for the course, which then allows the input of the teacher to range from a minimalist role of answering student questions and clarifying concepts in the readings, to using the package as a starting point and presenting lectures or seminars based upon the teacher's own work. Many lecturers see these materials as an extension of the course-specific textbook. Rather than stifling creativity, such materials can free up more of the lecturers time to engage in research. Various aspects of this reorganisation of academic work to emphasise efficiencies, predictability, and control have been referred to widely as the "McDonaldization" of higher education argument following the popularisation of the term by Ritzer (1993; see also Mok, 1999; Hayes and Wynyard, 2002). Schapper and Mayson (2004) have extended these analyses to show how transnational provision is intensifying of these trends.

The availability and relative costs of academic in the offshore setting is one of the most significant of the locational advantages that make transnational provision viable (Edwards and Edwards, 2001, p. 80). This is especially the case where the strategy is to deliver the bulk of the curriculum using locally employed staff. Teaching is often contracted out to a partner organisation in transnational programmes, primarily due to the lower costs and practicality of employing local staff rather than flying in teaching staff from the home campus. There has been surprisingly little written on outsourcing of tuition in education, and what has been published refers to the employment of casual or part-time teaching staff rather than to contracting out service provision to other organisations (e.g. Schibik and Harrington, 2004). Within the literature and on campuses there is much discussion of the merits of local staff versus expatriate teachers from country of origin of the programme. On the one hand, many students and parents expect that if they enroll in a foreign programme, they will be taught by teachers from that country, and preferably from that institution's home campus. After all, this is one of the features that would distinguish a transnational programme from its domestic competitors. On the other hand, the linguistic and cultural familiarity possessed by local teaching staff may help to facilitate a process of staged acculturation (Coleman, 2003, p. 365).

The profile of an average locally employed teacher in a transnational programme is quite different from that of a traditional academic in a conventional university. He or she may not be expected (or allowed the opportunity) to conduct research, will be more likely to need a teaching qualification and/or practical experience in their field, will probably be engaged on a casual or part-time basis, and may have little interaction with academic colleagues (Cunningham et al., 2000, pp. 117–122). As well as the separation of teaching from research, there is often a separation of other tasks into specific components. In terms of education functions, curriculum development, production of learning materials, delivery, support and assessment can each be handled by separate individuals. The staff member may concentrate on only one of these and this "unbundling" of academic work raises questions about the role of the educator. So far, offshoring tuition has been done primarily to serve local students, and even then only the lower level tasks have tended to be outsourced while assessment and curriculum development remains in the hands of the awarding institution. In time, some institutions will surely attempt to offshore other aspects of their teaching for offshore students and teaching for students on the home campus also.

33.5 DEALING WITH CULTURAL DIVERSITY IN TRANSNATIONAL DISTANCE EDUCATION

One of the most difficult issues facing teachers in transnational distance education is to develop a curriculum that is relevant to students with different educational and cultural backgrounds and which prepares them for living and working in widely varying social and economic contexts. Clearly the challenge is not so great for a programme that is delivered to students in a small number of overseas locations, as teachers are able to get to know these students and learn about their situation. For a more global programme whose students may be more widely dispersed, teachers can do very little to tailor the curriculum to the particular experience of students.

A common approach to developing international programmes that are attractive to students from different countries is to "globalise" the curriculum so that it is largely independent of the local context of the student (Ziguras and Rizvi, 2001). The success of global online education, in particular, relies on being able to develop curriculum that, in the words of Bates and de los Santos (1997), "is relevant to learners wherever they happen to reside" (p. 49). Globalised curricula are generic, universalised programmes produced in one location for global consumption. This relies on removing specific references to local experiences and examples that may confuse or distract remote students, and focusing on universal approaches that can be applied in any context. Transnational higher education has commonly involved Western educators exporting a locally developed curriculum, albeit with local references removed (Wells, 1993; McLaughlin, 1994; Kelly and Tak, 1998). Removing location-specific content is often necessary to confusing offshore students, but by trying to universalise a course, lecturers run the risk of abstracting the curriculum from real-world contexts. Such curricula invariably reflect the worldview of those who are constructing it, and so these programmes are often criticised as being eurocentric (Latchem, 2005) or culturally imperialist (Chambers, 2003).

The interrelationship between the universalistic forms of knowledge being taught and the particularistic experiences of students is a major issue for curriculum development. Students never read and use texts exactly as intended by their authors, and will invariably read selectively, and with a concern to create meanings that are relevant to their particular experiences. Some exceptional students are able to do this along, but most need help from interactive sessions with teaching staff who understand the student's intellectual and social context and can act as an interpreter of abstract texts. Most current transnational programmes combine such globalised curricula with face-to-face teaching for this very reason. Local teaching staff in offshore programmes play a more important part in localising generic international courses and can help their students participate in an international online environment. However, they commonly have little control over the content and form of generic study materials, which are often produced in the central campus by teachers with little familiarity with offshore students.

The Internet does make it possible to develop and share information across a network of teachers and students, and so many teaching staff can be involved in developing online courses and in teaching online. Such interaction with a suitably diverse teaching team can in turn help educators to better understand and cater to the diversity of the student population. Within all classes, there are differences based on prior life, educational and work experience, age, gender, ethnicity, motivation for study, and so on. Lecturers and tutors who are engaged with their students are able to respond to these particularities by tailoring their teaching to the needs of their students, and by providing a range of ways to approach study in any course so that students can engage with teachers, each other and materials in the most effective way for them and for the task. The aim should be to develop an international curriculum that is broad and inclusive enough to be relevant to the range of students in the course.

33.6 TEACHING AND LEARNING STYLES

One way of responding to cultural diversity in transnational distance education is to create more flexible and student-centred learning environments, so that students can choose to engage with the teaching materials and their teachers in the way that is most comfortable and familiar to them. In Anglophone countries there has been a tendency to believe that e-learning invariably has this effect, to the extent that "flexible learning" is often used as a euphemism for technologically mediated learning, so great are the perceived links between technology and flexibility. "Flexible learning", an approach that attempts to provide students with greater choice about how, where, when they learn

(Wade, 1994), offers a way of engaging with diverse student groups without imposing one particular set of expectations upon diverse student groups. It is worth remembering at the outset that the introduction of educational technologies does not necessarily transform learning, and may simply replicate pre-existing learning practices in a new medium. E-learning can be used in ways that rigidly circumscribe students' options, or in ways that lead to greater flexibility for students and encourage self-directed learning and student autonomy (Laurillard, 1993).

In practice, the adoption of e-learning in the West has been imbued with expectations of greater independence and autonomy on the part of students. For example, The British Council's advice to students contemplating distance education courses highlights these new demands:

> The new electronic technologies used in distance learning can provide students with far greater involvement in the process of learning. These interactive technologies also allow students the exercise of far greater control over that process than is possible in many traditional learning environments. This means that students must take more responsibility for, and be more active in, their learning...
>
> (The British Council, 1999, n.p.).

Such uses of interactive technologies can increase the autonomy of the learner, requiring them to choose the time, place, and pace of study. More study is conducted in isolation and the extent of face-to-face contact with lecturers and classmates is often diminished in the shift from traditional forms of university teaching to technologically mediated learning. At the same time Asian international students, for example, are often characterised by Western lecturers as being less self-directed learners who defer more to the authority of the teacher and prefer more structured learning environments (Ballard and Clanchy; 1997; Biggs, 1997; Kelly and Tak, 1998; Smith and Smith, 1999). While educational technologies, and the flexibility they bring, may be welcomed by Western students, these observations would suggest that students from Asian countries may not be so comfortable with such innovations (Jensen et al., 1997, Gunawardena, 1998). Joo (1999), for example, argues that:

> Because the Internet promotes pro-active teaching and learning, it may affect the balance of power in countries where the educational system is centralised and authoritarian.... In societies in where discipline and submission to authority is praised rather than individualism and freedom, teachers might feel too uncomfortable to take initiatives, to accept the scrutiny of peers, or to hand greater control to their students. Likewise, students accustomed to traditional methods may find it hard to adapt to active and innovating learning techniques.
>
> (p. 247)

There is a compelling argument, then, that flexible learning using educational technologies is not as appropriate in Asian countries as it is in more individualistic educational exporting countries. By expecting offshore learners to conform to Western expectations of student behaviour, multinational educators are engaging in a form of cultural imperialism, seeking to assimilate a diverse student body into an ethnocentrically defined norm. Many have argued that teaching in transnational education should be tailored to the specific cultural context in which the students are located (Kelly and Tak, 1998). Smith and Smith (1999), for example, conclude that:

> ...in those cases where a significant difference has been shown, it is prudent to consider adjusting teaching and support strategies to reflect those differences. Failure to take account at all of those differences runs the danger of being new colonialists who assume that the organisational, knowledge and belief structures that we develop in the English speaking West will transfer without adaptation to another culture.
>
> (p. 77)

As has been discussed earlier, adaptation is feasible if a programme is being taught in a small number of distinct locations but if the student body is more geographically and culturally diffuse, such adaptation would seem impossible.

Another option, and the most common in practice, is to accept that the forms of teaching being used are culturally and geographically specific and to expect students to adapt. Biggs (1997), for example, has argued (rather ethnocentrically) that cultural differences can be overcome by applying the same universal principles of good teaching wherever a course is taught and in many ways this reflects the views of most transnational educators. Invariably educators from different cultures will disagree about what the "universal principles" are, most would accept, but all we can do is to teach the best way we know how and let the students choose what type of education they want to undertake. It needs to be remembered that the main reason that students seek out a foreign education is that they are highly valued in their home country. That is, students are seeking out a new and different learning experience from foreign programmes and we should assist them to thrive in new learning environments rather than thinking that we should try to replicate the learning environments that students would find in their local institutions.

33.7 CONCLUSION

A whole wave of new global distance education providers failed due to lack of understanding of students, who voted with their feet and ignored fully online programmes and instead flocked to transnational programmes that offer local support for their studies. This is a key lesson for distance education, and not just for the choice of delivery models. Such a focus on students' preferences has also been noticeably lacking in much of the scholarly discussion of curriculum development and learning styles in transnational distance education programmes. Here, the commercial nature of most transnational distance education programmes makes life easier, for these are students who are choosing between a wide range of foreign programmes. If these programmes were being imposed on students who had no choice it would be another matter. In such an environment, the best an institution can do is to be very transparent about the type of curriculum and teaching that is involved and let students decide if this is what they want. It is unrealistic to expect that a programme offered to a diverse international student group should be tailored to the specific needs of all students, but it is also probably unnecessary. Education is always transformative, and we need to understand that students seek new and different forms of knowledge and learning, and they expect to be changed by the experience. We should not be afraid to celebrate and promote what is distinctive about the type of education we are offering, but we need to be open and honest about the distinctiveness and relevance of our approaches so that students can make informed decisions. Distance educators of course need to be aware and supportive of the diversity of their student groups and learn from and adapt to their students just as they expect students to learn from and adapt to them.

REFERENCES

AVCC. (2003). *Offshore Programs of Australian Universities*. Canberra: Australian Vice-Chancellors' Committee.

Ballard, B. and Clanchy, J. (1997). *Teaching International Students: A Brief Guide for Lecturers and Supervisors*. Canberra: IDP Education Australia.

Bates, A.W. and de los Santos, J.G.E. (1997). Crossing boundaries: Making global distance education a reality. *Journal of Distance Education*, **12**(1/2), 49–66.

Biggs, J.B. (1997). *Teaching Across and Within Cultures: The Issue of International Students*. HERDSA 1997 – Learning and Teaching in Higher Education: Advancing International Perspectives, Adelaide: Higher Education Research and Development Society of Australia.

Briggs, A., Adesola, A., Christodoulou, A. et al. (1989). *Towards a Commonwealth of Learning: A Proposal to Create the University of the Commonwealth for Co-operation in Distance Education: Report of the Expert Group on Commonwealth Co-operation in Distance Education and Open Learning*. London: Commonwealth Secretariat.

Chambers, E. (2003). Cultural imperialism or pluralism? Cross-cultural electronic teaching in the humanities. *Arts and Humanities in Higher Education*, **2**(3), 249–264.

Clerehan, R., Turnbull, J., Moore, T. et al. (2003). Transforming learning support: an online resource centre for a diverse student population. *Education Media International* **40**(1/2), 16–31.

Coleman, D. (2003). Quality assurance in transnational education. *Journal of Studies in International Education*, 7(4), 354–378.

Cunningham, S., Ryan, Y., Stedman, L. et al. (2000). *The Business of Borderless Education*. Canberra: Department of Education, Training and Youth Affairs.

Daniel, J. (2004). Distance learning across borders: Cultural imperialism or intellectual independence? Paper presented at the 18th IDP Australia International Education Conference: *International Education: The Path to Cultural Understanding and Development*. Commonwealth of Learning. Retrieved October 6, 2006, from http://www.col.org/speeches/JD_IDPAustralia_Oct04.htm.

DEST. (2005). *Higher Education Statistics Collection*. Canberra: Department of Education, Science and Training.

Edwards, R. and Edwards, J. (2001). Internationalisation of education: A business perspective. *Australian Journal of Education*, **45**(1), 76–89.

Farrell, G. (2001). Issues and Choices. In *The Changing Faces of Virtual Education*. (G. Farrell, ed.) Vancouver: Commonwealth of Learning.

Garrett, R. and Jokivirta, L. (2004). *Online learning in Commonwealth universities: Selected data from the 2004 Observatory Survey, Part 1*. London: Observatory on Borderless Higher Education.

Gunawardena, C. (1998). Designing collaborative learning environments mediated by computer conferencing: Issues and challenges in the Asian socio-cultural context. *Indian Journal of Open Learning*, 7(1), 101–119.

Gursoy, H. (2005). A critical look at distance education in Turkey. In *Global Perspectives on E-Learning: Rhetoric and Reality* (A.A. Carr-Chellman, ed.) Thousand Oaks: Sage.

Hayes, D. and Wynyard, R. (eds.) (2002). *The McDonaldization of Higher Education*. Oxford, Greenwood.

IDP Education Australia. (2002). *Global Student Mobility 2025: Forecasts of the Global Demand for International Higher Education*. Sydney: IDP Education Australia.

Ip, C. (2006). Quality assurance for transnational education: A host perspective. In *Quality Audit and Assurance for Transnational Higher Education*. (J. Baird, ed.). Melbourne: Australian Universities Quality Agency.

Jensen, S., Christie, A., and Baron, J. (1997). Online' teaching in an 'offshore' program: a recent pilot of a business management subject in Singapore. ASCILITE 97 – *What Works and Why: Reflections on Learning with Technology*, Curtin University of Technology, Perth: Australian Society for Computers in Learning in Tertiary Education.

Joo, J.-E. (1999). Cultural issues of the Internet in classrooms. *British Journal of Educational Technology*, **30**(3), 245–250.

Kelly, M.E. and Tak, S.H. (1998). Borderless education and teaching and learning cultures: the case of Hong Kong. *Australian Universities' Review*, **41**(1), 26–33.

Latchem, C. (2005). Towards borderless virtual learning in higher education. In (A.A. Carr-Chellman, ed.). *Global Perspectives on E-Learning: Rhetoric and Reality*. Thousand Oaks: Sage.

Laurillard, D. (1993). *Rethinking University Teaching: A Framework for the Effective Use of Educational Technology*. London: Routledge.

McBurnie, G. and Ziguras, C. (2007). *Transnational Education: Current Issues and Future Trends in Offshore Higher Education*. London: RoutledgeFalmer.

McLaughlin, D. (1994). Contrasts in learning in Asia and the Pacific. *Pacific-Asian Education*, **6**(2), 41–50.

Middlehurst, R. and Woodfield, S. (2004). *International Quality Review and Distance Learning: Lessons from Five Countries*. Washington DC: Council for Higher Education Accreditation.

Mok, K.-h. (1999). The cost of managerialism: The implications for the 'McDonaldisation' of higher education in Hong Kong. *Journal of Higher Education Policy and Management*, **21**(1), 117.

Murphy, D., Zhang, W.-y., and Perris, K. (2003). *Online Learning in Asian Open Universities: Resisting 'Content Imperialism'?* London: The Observatory on Borderless Higher Education.

Ritzer, G. (1993). *The McDonaldization of Society*. Thousand Oaks, CA: Pine Forge Press.

Schapper, J.M. and Mayson, S.E. (2004). Internationalisation of curricula: An alternative to the Taylorisation of academic work. *Journal of Higher Education Policy and Management*, **26**(2), 189–205.

Schibik, T.J. and Harrington, C.F. (2004). The outsourcing of classroom instruction in higher education. *Journal of Higher Education Policy and Management*, **26**(3), 393–400.

Smith, P.J. and Smith, S.N. (1999). Differences between Chinese and Australian students: some implications for distance educators. *Distance Education*, **20**(1), 64–80.

The British Council. (1999). *Study for a UK Higher Education Qualification by Distance Learning*. The British Council. Retrieved October 6, 2006, from http://www.britishcouncil.org.uk/distancelearning/index.htm.

UNESCO and Council of Europe. (2001). *Code of Good Practice in the Provision of Transnational Education.* UNESCO-CEPES. Retrieved October 6, 2006, from http://www.cepes.ro/hed/recogn/groups/transnat/code.htm.

Wade, W. (1994). Introduction. In *Flexible Learning in Higher Education* (W. Wade, K. Hodgkinson, A. Smith and J. Arfield, eds.) London: Kogan Page.

Wells, M. (1993). *The Export of Education: Exploitation or Technology Transfer.* Sydney: Research Institute for Asia and the Pacific, University of Sydney.

WTO. (2002). *Communication from Japan: Negotiating Proposal on Education Services.* Geneva: World Trade Organization, Council for Trade in Services.

Zhang, K. (2005). China's online education. In *Global Perspectives on E-Learning: Rhetoric and Reality.* (A.A. Carr-Chellman, ed.) Thousand Oaks, CA: Sage.

Ziguras, C. and Rizvi, F. (2001). Future directions in international online education. In *Transnational Education: Australia Online.* (D. Davis and D. Meares, eds.) Sydney: IDP Education Australia.

Chapter 34

Accountability and Evaluation in Distance Education: A Critical Overview

Mary Thorpe

34.1 THE CHALLENGES OF EXPANSION

The chapters in this section focus on quality issues arising from the expansion of courses and qualifications delivered by distance methods. This growth in provision of distance education has often been targeted at tertiary education, and all the chapters focus on accountability or evaluation in higher education institutions. It is in this sector specifically that the predicted convergence of distance and campus-based education has continued to grow (Smith and Kelly, 1987; King, 2001). As King asserted in 2001, "As the last century ended, the production and delivery services that represented the defining characteristic of distance education were confronted by technological changes that made them potentially available for educators everywhere to replicate" (p. 48).

These technological changes are transforming both distance- and campus-based forms of provision and the differences between the two are less marked than they used to be. Not only are both using similar information and communication technologies, but economic pressures in some countries are forcing campus-based students to work part-time while they study. In a study commissioned by Universities UK, just over half the students in a representative sample of UK universities were found to be working between 12 and 14 hours a week in term time (CHERI and London South Bank University, 2005). These students reported difficulty in accessing the resources of the institution and participating fully in campus activities. They experienced time pressures similar to those of the distance student with all the responsibilities of adulthood. It could be argued that they would have been better to study within a distance system that was designed for the needs of the off-campus and time-pressured adult. Some campus-based institutions assert that they are already offering flexible modes of provision that take these pressures on "full-time students" into account. As King comments on the dual-mode institutions in Australia (combining both campus and distance modes for the same course), "the infrastructure of distance education in dual mode universities – expertise in planning and scheduling, facilities for production of learning resources, experience in non-traditional delivery, appreciation of the administrative and support needs of students not on campus and the provision of systemic response to these, and professional development programmes for academic staff – can be deployed to better support all students" (King, 2001, p. 51).

However, many universities have not made such thorough-going accommodation to provide flexible study options for students who are officially studying full-time. Part-time routes have also increased but they may still not be designed to fully meet the needs of the student studying off campus. These considerations also illustrate one of the themes running through the chapters in this section. This theme is that while distance- and campus-based methods should be, and in many countries are being given parity, there are significant differences between the two that impact on the staff and the students in important ways. The question is how these differences should be treated in terms of the assessment and development of quality, specifically within distance education.

If, as Murphy says, accountability is not a term that features in the distance education literature, the fact that it now directly impacts on so many distance providers is evidence of the expansion of distance education forms of provision, rather than advocacy by distance education theorists. Distance education has been expanded in order to enable individuals to gain the skills and qualifications that are needed by the modern sector in economies all over the world. This has been the case in India for example, where distance education accounts for about 27 percent of the total enrolment in higher education and is set to rise to 40 percent (Sharma, 2005). Concerns about quality in that country in 2005 led the governor of the State of Uttar Pradesh to close down all distance education programmes offered by state universities as part of attempts to address shortfalls in quality (p. 239). However, here as elsewhere, the growth in distance methods and institutions is part of growth in the demand for and provision of higher education generally, and it is the massification of higher education that has fuelled the demand that it become accountable, whether delivered on a campus or at a distance. "As higher education has expanded and its aggregate budget has increased, the pressure has grown for greater productivity and efficiency... increasing financial dependence on the state... has fuelled demands for greater accountability" (Scott, 1998, pp. 110–113).

As the chapters by Murgatroyd and Jung show, it is by participating in quality assurance processes, often managed by public sector bodies, that distance providers now demonstrate their accountability within territories where they wish to operate. However, when the first distance education universities were being established, evaluation was the route through which providers could demonstrate their accountability. As with other forms of innovation in education, there were strong pressures to provide evidence of the impact on learners of a new mode of learning, and to demonstrate that the claims made for it could be substantiated. Evaluation does appear in the distance education literature and has been positioned as an essential component in the development of institutions, courses and programmes that meet high standards of quality (Thorpe, 1993; Calder, 1994).

34.2 THE ROLE OF EVALUATION AND ITS RELATIONSHIP TO QUALITY

Evaluation of distance education provision and its impact is intended to feed into decision-making and action. It involves data collection and analysis as part of a systematic process of judging effectiveness. This requires robust systems of capturing data from ongoing monitoring of effectiveness and performance, which should feed into both formative and summative evaluation. An external element in evaluation may be necessary, as a counter weight to the tendency for staff to react defensively when evidence shows weaknesses as well as strengths. However, external evaluators will also require the kind of evidence that can only be provided by effective and ongoing systems of monitoring and data collection by the distance education provider itself. The demands of setting up such systems require specialist expertise and the contribution of professional evaluators. Reliable and objective data delivered by such systems is essential for evaluative studies of retention, drop out, student performance and outcomes.

Studies of these issues have been essential in making the case for distance education and in some cases for continued state funding (Woodley et al., 2001). Woodley's account in this volume of the importance of evaluation in the early years of the UKOU shows accountability to the government as a key element within evaluation which was seen by the institution itself as both a practical and a moral imperative. The university had been established with high expectations around access and openness, and evaluation was a key means of checking out on its delivery. It was accepted within the institution as a way of keeping faith with its aspirations and being open to the needs of its students. Institutional evaluation is still being undertaken for similar reasons of checking on performance and impact. For example, in a study of the Universal College of Learning (UCOL) in New Zealand, evaluators undertook a 360-degree study of the views and reactions of staff and students for the introduction of more flexible forms of provision. Evidence of practices that were not in the best interests of student learning were revealed by the evaluation, as well as those that were. This enabled the institution to recalibrate its trajectory of change and to better orientate course providers to its preferred approach to flexible provision. "The institutional evaluation has enabled correction to some course practices, and has helped to make the target of flexible delivery better defined for staff... UCOL management has approved the evaluation report for general dissemination among UCOL staff. This communicates UCOL's dedication as a learning organisation... Further evaluations will take place on a regular basis, and will identify further opportunities for targeted staff development" (Nichols and Gardner, 2002, pp. 20–21).

However, evaluation is a very diverse set of practices that can stretch from methods close to journalism at one end of the spectrum to the standards of theoretically sophisticated applied research at the other (Oliver et al., 2007). Thorpe has identified three main approaches, for example – ideology critique and conceptual review, institutional research and practitioner self-evaluation (Thorpe, 1996). The first two tend to be carried out by either external academic researchers or internal specialist evaluators, while the third involves practitioners using evaluation for the development of their own practice (see also Thorpe, 1993). However, the differences between these and between research and evaluation generally are not primarily to do with methods. They are to do with the context and relationships within which each is carried out. The evaluator is generally required to work with issues already framed by a particular practice or policy, whereas the researcher usually has freedom to develop these in relation to previous research and theory. The evaluator also has to work within the time constraints relevant to the policy or practice being evaluated, since findings are usually expected to influence or to be applied to what has been evaluated. However, the practices of research and of evaluation overlap. Rather than trying to seek out categorical differences between the two, it is more important to note the importance of evaluation within distance education, and its core role in quality assurance (Freeman, 1991; Fage and Mayes, 1996; O'Shea et al., 1996; Rowntree, 1998). Indeed Calder has gone further and comments, "evaluation is used . . . to enable institutions to operate as learning organisations" (Calder, 1994, p. 19).

34.3 EVALUATION OF KEY ISSUES

Distance educators have typically had to justify their methods, and to find out about their impact using a range of data collection approaches to explore the behaviour and responses of learners studying in their local context. One of the key areas here is the quality of the relationship between students and tutor. Timely and detailed feedback to students on the quality of their assessed work has had high importance within distance education. Rekkedal's early study of the impact of turn-around time in marking students' work established the importance of monitoring this area of practice (Rekkedal, 1973). This contrasts with campus-based higher education where students have criticised institutions for inadequate feedback on their work (Barefoot, 2004). The importance in distance education of continuous assessment with good tutor feedback reflects the lack of other opportunities that students have to check out their understanding and to interact with a tutor.

Very large-scale distance education providers are still working out how best to provide this kind of continuous assessment. Jian and Hamp-Lyons (2006) report an evaluation of student reactions to its introduction by the China Radio and TV University (RTVU), under the title of progress assessment. In the context of the China RTVUs, this was a small-scale study of twenty students, but it confirms earlier research in finding that students value continuous assessment as a mechanism for pacing their studies and helping them learn more effectively. It also reports strong student feeling that contact with tutors should be increased, particularly between the face-to-face sessions provided. Students also request that progress assessment should be given a value higher than the 20 percent set by the China RTVU, with consequent reduction in the weighting of the final examination.

Studies such as this cannot claim to be representative of all students in a very large-scale institution, but they provide indicative insights into the student experience through direct reporting of student views. They illuminate (Parlett and Dearden, 1977) a particular issue and help ensure that the institution listens to the voice of its students. This is particularly important in an area where campus-based provision is less strong than the best of what distance education provides. Thus tutors who mark students' work, but have no experience in distance education, need help to learn how to teach through commenting on students' work, rather than merely grading. Monitoring of tutor marking should therefore be a regular feature of the evaluation and development of quality within distance education. The results of such monitoring can be used as part of staff development, so that standards of support to students are being continually reviewed and improved.

As the technologies used within distance education have changed, this has influenced the topics being evaluated. Thus the digital divide has been a key area for surveys of access to computers in the United Kingdom (Kirkwood and Price, 2005), and is a current concern in many countries still lacking universal Internet access. Enoch and Soker (2006) report a study on the issue at the Open University of Israel, which has added web-based components to all its courses, offering instructional materials, discussion groups, links to libraries and relevant sites. They relate their work to one of the issues that has dominated evaluation in distance education, which is whether the methods used serve to meet the needs of under-represented groups or not. They argue that access to technology is not a measure of use of technology, where evidence suggests that, for the OU of Israel, structural factors of age, gender and ethnicity are associated with lower usage of web-based instruction by these groups.

34.4 PEER REVIEW

The quality of distance education can also be maintained by adopting practices that *are* used by campus-based institutions. Well before the introduction of accountability in higher education, for example, the UKOU adopted the practice of external examining and peer review that is the bedrock of maintenance of standards in UK higher education generally. All courses produced by the UKOU have an external assessor appointed by the faculty who is a leading academic in the area. Their role is to review all the course resources as they are being developed and to advise the course team on their quality academically and in terms of their teaching effectiveness. Once the course is being studied by students, an external examiner is appointed who is also a leading academic in the area and whose appointment is ratified by the Faculty and the University. The role they play is the same as for any course delivered within the UK higher education system, which is to comment on the quality of teaching and to oversee the process of marking, standard setting and agreement of course credit for all students examined. As a result of these procedures of external peer review, a large body of leading academics has vouched for the standards of teaching and assessment at the UKOU and continues to contribute to ongoing processes of quality assurance within the university.

34.5 ACCOUNTABILITY, ACCREDITATION AND QUALITY ASSURANCE

The use of external examiners in the UKOU is an example of peer review that demonstrates a principle Murgatroyd makes in his chapter in this book, which is that accreditation of distance education providers now operates on the principle of no significant difference in expected outcomes. Distance education must meet the same standards as other providers, albeit using different processes and methods. In the context of the developed education systems of the United States, Canada and the United Kingdom, Murgatroyd outlines the impact of the quality frameworks that have brought accountability processes to a dominant position for all providers of accredited provision at higher education level. These frameworks typically require distance education providers to become accredited through procedures involving a mix of peer review, objective measures and oversight of management processes. Each element in this process is, as Murgatroyd shows, vulnerable to weaknesses that can undermine any quality system.

Peer review, for example, requires that reviewers behave as objectively as possible and undertake their role conscientiously. Some may not always do this, as Murgatroyd reminds us, but that is why their input needs to be balanced by evidence of performance and impact that relies on robust data. Such data can only be produced by institutions that have effective systems of monitoring and evaluation, which thus become an essential component in complying effectively with systems of accountability. This is also true in the case of programme review, which Murgatroyd introduces and relates to industry and professional standards. However, a similar review process has been the bedrock of quality assurance in higher education for at least a decade in the United Kingdom. All universities have had the quality of their programmes evaluated against the learning outcomes and aims that they set for themselves.

Jung's chapter also documents attempts by national and regional authorities to ensure that the expansion of distance education, particularly when provided by external organisations expanding their operations outside their country of origin, meets acceptable standards of quality. She outlines the impact of globalisation in education provision, where many countries have become both exporters and importers of distance education provision. The expansion has been fuelled by the availability of technologies that make communication and provision of materials internationally both easier and cheaper. Providers include private sector institutions and organisations that may not see themselves as distance educators, though what they offer uses the methods of distance education. She argues that more emphasis has been placed on widening access than on assuring quality, in this period of expansion.

Ziguras picks up on this issue in his examination of transnational education, noting that while there is generally a high standard of evaluation with respect to most exporting countries, standards vary widely in importing countries. Even when the evaluation and accountability procedures of an importing authority are robust, such as in Hong Kong, the particular context (e.g. degree of local presence) and measures of protection for consumers can leave some suppliers of distance education programmes unregulated. He also argues that consumer valuation of a programme can be a stronger force for its viability than formal evaluation.

Jung further reminds us that quality is a contested concept and that it can be judged using different criteria. Conformance to the standards of conventional provision can be used as the basis, and evaluation studies have shown that effectiveness of learning outcomes can be as good for distance education as classroom-based teaching. However, as she notes, such studies tend to ignore the features that distinguish distance education, and these may be more adequately represented using "fitness for purpose" approaches. The specific aims of a distance education system can be more easily accommodated and appropriately judged, if quality is judged against the purposes of the provision. Various countries have documented standards for quality that reflect the fitness for purpose approach.

However, Jung rightly emphasises that the degree of integration of systems of accountability within the core processes of an institution will determine whether quality is developed as well as assured. She reports the results of a survey of a number of large-scale providers that demonstrates a growing quality culture. Some have set up specialist quality assurance units, while others have left matters more to individual units. In some areas there are national guidelines and these are used to drive standards across the institution. The Universitas Terbuka, Indonesia, has a highly structured system of documenting and assessing performance, based on the Asian Association of Open Universities Quality Assurance Framework. Elsewhere there is less control with local staff more responsible to set their own standards and quality assurance methods.

Exporters of their systems to other territories have set up specific procedures to ensure that there is no loss of quality. Australia has a code of practice for provision to international students, and this is used by Monash University. Indira Gandhi National Open University has also set up specific guidelines for its transnational operations. However, it is the impact of for-profit providers that creates a new challenge for governments who need to protect citizens from poor quality provision. Jung outlines the need for the development of structures ensuring quality, by both international and national organisations, and a widening of areas for review. She argues that insufficient attention has been paid to the quality of learner experience and learning outcomes.

Murgatroyd and Jung both present quality and accountability from the perspective of the practices of distance educators. Murphy reflects on the origins of the accountability pressures originating in government concerns that increased spending on higher education should be both effective and efficient. Three key stakeholders are involved here: academic authorities, the intended beneficiaries of the system (both students and employers) and the government. One aspect of accountability systems that has brought a new emphasis is the pressure to communicate evidence of performance and quality, so that users can decide for themselves whether provision is appropriate for their needs.

The United Kingdom, for example, has recently initiated a national student satisfaction survey of graduates of all universities and the results are documented on a national site providing performance indicators and rankings for all universities (http://www.tqi.ac.uk). This has been a positive experience for the Open University, in that its graduates gave it the highest ranking for overall satisfaction with their studies. A total of 8,800 OU students took part in the survey in 2005, completed by a total of 157,000 from 129 institutions. Their responses also placed the OU first of all institutions in relation to the quality of assessment and feedback and third for academic support. However, performance indicators, as Murphy stresses, should not be taken at face value and need to be interpreted against the purposes of different providers. Distance education, for example, is often unable to match the retention rates of campus-based institutions, but this reflects the nature of the students for whom the system is intended and the contexts and purposes of their study. While it is always appropriate to know what the retention, course credit and degree achievement rates of a distance education provider are, it is not appropriate usually to expect that these ought to be the same as those of a campus university for school leavers. The two institutions may differ crucially in their intake and in the conditions and purposes of study by their students.

34.6 ACCOUNTABILITY AND EVALUATION

Evaluation, quality assurance and accountability could be said to be mutually constituted, in that versions of all three are involved in the many different approaches outlined in the chapters in this section. However, accountability and the setting up of processes for accrediting providers and their courses as meeting specified quality standards has eclipsed the earlier emphasis on evaluation within distance education. Is this a good thing? I fear that the answer has to be both yes and no.

As Woodley has outlined in this book, external review of quality by agencies and accreditation bodies has led to an increase in bureaucratic evaluation, where the data and evaluative procedures are directed primarily by the need to comply with the accrediting or quality assurance system. This is a game played for high stakes. Failure to achieve accreditation or high-quality assurance standards would impact negatively on the institution and might lead to its demise, given negative publicity and inability to attract students. There is obviously pressure to comply with the requirements and paperwork of the accrediting body – including the requirement with some agencies to demonstrate appropriate self-criticism and improvement of less good quality. However, it is much easier for a large established institution of distance education to take a self-critical and open-minded stance to the process than it is for one not so well established or so well-staffed. There are risks of a compliance culture developing rather than a genuinely self-critical quality improvement culture.

However, if the accountability culture has strengthened bureaucratic forms of evaluation rather than more democratic or critical approaches, it has also had a positive impact in that it tends to make practitioners pay attention to evaluation evidence and to demonstrate responsiveness to the results of evaluation. This has certainly been the case at the UKOU, whose teaching quality is assessed by the Quality Assurance Agency acting on behalf of the Higher Education Funding Council. The need to attain high grades in these reviews of teaching quality makes every faculty review the statistical evidence of student performance and the evaluations of their courses carried out by the Institute of Educational Technology (IET). The process of external scrutiny brings external teams of academics from the disciplines under review, who question their OU colleagues about the impact of their teaching (O'Shea et al., 1996). Evidence from the evaluation of teaching is an important resource in judging this, and persuasive because this is carried out using rigorous methods of data collection and analysis by professional evaluators in IET. While this is not the only source of data, it takes on high importance in this process of external accountability and quality review, a process which ensures that the results of evaluation are taken more notice of, and are more applied to practice, than was the case before it was implemented.

34.7 OPEN AND DISTANCE EDUCATION AND DEVELOPMENT

It is important to draw attention to a large area in the implementation and evaluation of distance education that is not emphasised in the chapters included here. This is the use of distance education methods as part of projects or development programmes that target some of the extremely challenging goals faced by developing countries. Correspondence and distance education, for example, have been used in training school teachers. Bertram (2006) notes that the South African Institute for Distance Education reported in 1995 that more than a third of existing teachers in South Africa were involved in some form of distance education. She reports on a current programme provided by the University of KwaZulu-Natal that uses tutorials plus self-instructional learning guides to make a postgraduate programme available to serving teachers on a part-time basis.

However, in a thorough analysis of the situation in Africa generally, Unwin identifies a lack of initiatives on a scale that will make significant improvements in the problem of untrained and unsupported teachers in service (Unwin, 2005). Trained teachers are essential if the Millennium Development Goals are to be achieved by 2015 (UN, 2004) and the urgency of the issue is clear. Ghana has 30,000 untrained teachers for example, and HIV/AIDS is creating a new crisis of supply. Estimates for Zambia are that more teachers are dying than are being trained (Unwin, 2005). The experience of supporting student learning within distance education can demonstrably be applied to using ICT to support appropriate forms of teacher training. The UKOU, for example, is in a partnership with the University of Fort Hare's Unit for Rural Schooling and development and the Nelson Mandela Foundation, to provide resources, activities, videos and websites supporting the teaching of literacy, science, numeracy and citizenship using ICT. The Digital Education Enhancement Project is building in evaluation of its activities (Leach et al., 2005) and this helps inform other activities, such as the provision of distance education resources for teacher training in universities in Sub-Saharan Africa, versioned to suit different cultures and five languages – Arabic, French, isiZhosa, Kiswahili and English.

Moving out from formal education into lifelong learning, Singh and McKay (2004), for example, record the huge scale of need for training of adult educators and trainers as part of mass provision of adult basic learning and literacy. They report the World Education Forum in Dakar in 2000 that set the goal of halving adult illiteracy levels by 2015, from their total of 860 million in 2000. They report no significant reduction as yet in these high rates of illiteracy, across Asia, the Pacific, Africa and Arabic countries. While all countries in these regions strive to provide universal primary education, there are still millions of illiterates within the age cohort of 15–24 years (UNESCO, 2002). The scale of the need, and the impossibility of funding classroom-based provision, leads policy makers to turn to the application of distance methods, particularly where these have been evaluated and can be shown to be adaptable to local conditions (Robinson and Latchem, 2002). Singh and McKay (2004) bring together key authors who argue that, with priority on opening up learning rather than mere delivery, distance education methods offer the best opportunity for meeting the needs for adult educator training, as well as for the provision of programmes of lifelong learning. We have decades of experience, for example, in using radio campaigns and correspondence plus study group approaches to distance learning for adult basic education (Siacewena, 2000; Perraton, 2000; Dodds, 2004). However, Yates (2004) documents the way in which these efforts have not continued to have such high government funding and support since the 1990s. "...the persistent low rate of investment in adult education is hardly surprising, given the continued dominance of the modernisation paradigm and human capital model of development" (p. 202).

Although radio farm forums have not had a transformational impact on society, evaluations have documented individual impact in terms of participation and learning (Siacewena, 2000). The International Extension College continues to use radio in its work with women in the fishing industry in Kenya. In collaboration with the Tropical Institute for Community Health and Development, a radio programme is part of a programme to deliver health and small business education. There remains a role for radio, as part of a combination of support and delivery methods (Perraton and Creed, 2000). Evaluation of projects using the methods of distance education rather than setting up distance education institutions is crucial for monitoring the impact and justifying funding for continuation of the approach.

Dodds, who has long campaigned for increasing use of open distance education (ODE), argues that this should not be seen as a panacea, rather as a key element in a strategy for provision and support of adult basic education. He provides an example of its use for training of adult educators on the job, in Namibia. Here the University of Namibia has offered since 2001 a diploma in Adult Education and Community Development through distance methods, providing an off-campus version of courses previously only available on campus. He advocates such use should be expanded – particularly to support adult educators who are expected to support a wide range of development-related activities and achievement of relevant and functional literacy skills. The key point in relation to evaluation is that, while authors may differ in the role they advocate for ODL, they draw on evaluations of previous programmes (Perraton, 2000; Siacewena, 2000) as the only source of evidence that may help make well-founded strategies for both which technologies to use, and in what ways.

While the key stakeholders in this context must continue to be national governments, a number of international organisations and non-government organisations play key roles in advocating, sponsoring and even funding what are felt to be beneficial applications of open distance education for development purposes. Yates reports that there is even a squeezing effect on national governments, consequent upon the "increasingly diversified nexus of state/private educational provision" (Yates, 2004, p. 201). UNESCO, as one of the supra-state bodies involved, has convened international conferences such as the 5th International Conference on Adult Education, which stressed the key role of adult and lifelong learning, and the importance of using information and communication technologies to provide open and flexible forms of provision (UNESCO, 1997).

UNESCO has also developed its role of supporting policy makers develop their understanding of ODL. It promotes publications of evaluation and research in the field of ODE and has also funded recently The Higher Education Open and Distance Learning

Knowledge Base, working collaboratively with the Commonwealth of Learning (COL) and other specialist bodies such as the South African Institute for Distance Education (SAIDE) and the Malaysian Open University in Kuala Lumpur. The project makes regional databases on open and distance higher education in Africa, Asia, the Pacific, the Community of Independent States and the Baltic States available on the Web (Varoglu, 2005). A search tool provided by COL enables the user to locate material relevant to regional needs via the site at www.unesco.odl/unesco. It aims to provide support for the planning and management of high-quality ODL, through access to regional information and also to a decision support tool. The tool has been developed in collaboration with regional authorities and has been informed by a study of the quality assurance mechanisms in cross-border higher education (Jung, 2005). The decision support tool is available on the website and provides a proforma of key questions through which to evaluate provision of ODE.

34.8 CONCLUSION

The establishment of large-scale institutions specialised for distance education led to a need for evaluation in order to demonstrate accountability to national governments that had provided funding and to justify the effectiveness of distance education methods. Formal methods of evaluation have worked best when built on widespread commitment to monitoring practice and building in quality-oriented development of practice. Thus evaluation and quality assurance and enhancement have been closely linked.

Alongside the successful expansion of distance education methods has come pressure from governments to make educational providers accountable. Distance education has been increasingly accepted in well-regulated systems of higher education provision, where it is expected to conform to the same high standards as the rest of the sector, if delivered in different ways. However, forces of globalisation have brought the import and export of distance education courses into prominence, particularly in the fast developing economies of India and South East Asia and the Pacific. Ensuring the quality of this provision has become a major concern of the state sector. Standards particular to distance education have been developed and in some areas these are being enforced. However, commitment to internal evaluation and quality improvement is required in order to avoid a compliance culture developing in these circumstances.

While the state is a crucial stakeholder in the accountability process, international organisations and NGOs are also playing constructive roles. Their role includes providing information about distance education methods, and reviewing the evidence of their impact. Distance education projects have played and arguably should play an even greater role in meeting the needs of adult and lifelong learning. Evaluation of such projects is always necessary if decision-making is to proceed on a sound basis. Thus we see accountability and evaluation as two approaches to quality that have played different roles, more or less important, at different times and in relation to different forms of provision. They are mutually constituted in that evaluation is often undertaken as a way of being accountable, and accountability processes require robust evaluation procedures to be in place for the process to be most effective. Their use reflects differences in the scale and nature of funding for distance education and while accountability has attained dominance in higher education, its effectiveness is inextricably linked with good internal evaluation, and its remit has been limited to particular institutional forms. For the use of distance education within projects and informal and non-formal learning opportunities, where the needs for provision in developing countries are huge, evaluation has a vital role to play. Whatever the limitations of "evidence-based practice", evidence of what has been implemented and its impact on the intended beneficiaries is surely the primary starting point for deciding whether, where and how to use distance education approaches. Evaluation is also key to the embedding of good practice and the achievement of quality enhancement by practitioners of distance education, whatever its purposes, forms and methods.

REFERENCES

Barefoot, B. (2004). Higher education's revolving door: Confronting the problem of student dropout in US colleges and universities. *Open Learning*, **19**(1), 9–18.

Bertram, C. (2006). Exploring teachers' reading competences: A South African case study. *Open Learning*, **21**(1), 5–18.

Calder, J. (1994) *Programme Evaluation and Quality: A Comprehensive Guide to Setting up an Evaluation System*, London: Kogan Page Open and Distance Learning Series.

Centre for Higher Education Research and Information and London South Bank University. (2005). *Survey of Higher Education Students' Attitudes to Dept and Term-Time Working and their Impact on Attainment: A Report to Universities* UK and HEFCE. London: Universities UK.

Dodds, T. (2004). Open and distance learning: Training and support for adult educators in the field. In *Enhancing Adult Basic Learning: Training Educators and Unlocking the Potential of Distance and Open Learning* (M. Singh and V. McKay, eds) Hamburg: UNESCO Institute for Education and Pretoria: University of South Africa, pp. 261–272.

Enoch, Y. and Soker, Z. (2006). Age, gender, ethnicity and the digital divide: university students' use of web-based instruction. *Open Learning*, **21**(2), 99–110.

Fage, J. and Mayes, R. (1996). Monitoring learners' progress. In *Supporting the Learner in Open and Distance Learning* (R. Mills and A. Tait, eds) London: Pitman Publishing, pp. 206–221.

Freeman, R. (1991). Quality assurance in learning materials production. *Open Learning*, **6**(3) 24–31.

Jian, N. and Hamp-Lyons, L. (2006). Progress assessment in Chinese distance education: the voices of learners, *Open Learning*, **21**(2), 111–123.

Jung, I. (2005). Quality assurance survey of mega-universities. In *Perspectives on Distance Education: Lifelong Learning and Distance Higher Education* (C. McIntosh and Z. Varoglu, eds) Vancouver: Commonwealth of Learning and UNESCO.

King, B. (2001). Managing the changing nature of distance and open education at institutional level. *Open Learning*, **16**(1), 47–60.

Kirkwood, A. and Price, L. (2005). Learners and learning in the twenty-first century: what do we know about students' attitudes towards and experiences of information and communication technologies that will help us design courses? *Studies in Higher Education*, **30**(3), 257–274.

Leach, J., Ahmed, A., Makalima, S., and Power, T. (2005). *DEEP Impact: An Investigation of the Use of Information and Communication Technologies for Teacher Education in the Global South*. Sevenoaks, Department for International Development, UK.

McIntosh, C. and Varoglu, Z. (eds) (2005). *Perspectives on Distance Education: Lifelong Learning and Distance Higher Education*, Paris: UNESCO & Commonwealth of Learning.

Nichols, M. and Gardner, N. (2002). Evaluating flexible delivery across a tertiary institution. *Open Learning*, **17**(1), 11–22.

Oliver, M., Harvey, J., Conole, G., and Jones, A. (2007). Evaluation. In *Contemporary Perspectives in E-Learning Research: Themes, Methods and Impact on Practice* (G. Conole and M. Oliver, eds) London: Routledge, pp. 203–216.

O'Shea, T., Bearman, S., and Downes, A. (1996). Quality assurance and assessment in distance learning. In *Supporting the Learner in Open and Distance Learning* (R. Mills and A. Tait, eds) London: Pitman Publishing, pp. 193–205.

Parlett, M. and Dearden, G. (1977). (eds.) *Introduction to Illuminative Evaluation: Studies in Higher Education*. Cardiff, CA: Pacific Soundings Press.

Perraton, H. (2000). *Open and Distance Learning in the Developing World*. London: Routledge.

Perraton H. and Creed, C. (2000). *Applying New Technologies and Cost-Effective Delivery Systems in Basic Education*. Paris: UNESCO.

Rekkedal, T. (1973). The written assignments in correspondence education: Effects of reducing turn-around time: An experimental study. Oslo: NKI-skolen, also (1984) *Distance Education*, **4**(2), 231–252.

Robinson, B. and Latchem, C. (2002). (eds) *Teacher Education Through Open and Distance Learning*. Vancouver: Commonwealth of Learning and London: RoutledgeFalmer.

Rowntree, D. (1998). Assessing the quality of materials based teaching and learning. *Open Learning*, **13**(2) 12–22.

Scott, P. (1998). Massification, internationalization and globalization. In *The Globalization of Higher Education* (P. Scott, ed.) Buckingham: The Open University Press, with The Society for Research into Higher Education.

Sharma, R.C. (2005). Open learning in India: Evolution, diversification and reaching out. *Open Learning*, **20**(3), 227–242.

Siacewena, R. (ed.) (2000). *Case Studies of Non-Formal Education by Distance and Open Learning*. Vancouver, Commonwealth of Learning. Retrieved January 4, 2007 from http://www.col.org/Consultancies/00nonformal.htm.

Singh, M. and McKay, V. (2004). (eds) *Enhancing Adult Basic Learning: Training Educators and Unlocking the Potential of Distance and Open Learning*. Hamburg: UNESCO Institute for Education and Pretoria: University of South Africa.

Smith, P. and Kelly, M. (1987). (eds) *Distance Education and the Mainstream*. North Ride: Croom Helm, Australia.

Thorpe, M. (1993). *Evaluating Open and Distance Learning* (2nd edn). Harlow, UK: Longman.

Thorpe, M. (1996). Issues of evaluation. In *Supporting the Learner in Open and Distance Learning* (R. Mills and A. Tait, eds) London: Pitman Publishing.

UNESCO. (1997). *Agenda for the Future*. Hamburg: UNESCO Institute for Education.

UNESCO. (2002). *EFA Global Monitoring Report. Education for All. Is the World on Track?* Paris: UNESCO.

UN. (2004). *UN millennium Development Goals*. Retrieved January 4, 2007 from www.un.org/millenniumgoals/.

Unwin, T. (2005). The use of ICT in teacher training in Africa. *Open Learning*, **20**(2), 113–129.

Woodley, A., De Lange, P., and Tanewski, G. (2001). Student progress in distance education: Kember's model re-visited. *Open Learning*, **16**(1), 113–131.

Yates, C. (2004). Can open, distance and flexible learning assist with adult basic education? Pursuing the concept of quality in the context of education for all. In *Enhancing Adult Basic Learning: Training Educators and Unlocking the Potential of Distance and Open Learning* (M. Singh and V. McKay, eds) Hamburg: UNESCO Institute for Education and Pretoria: University of South Africa, pp. 191–221.

Section V
Policy

Introduction

Margaret Haughey

Recognizing how difficult it was to obtain accounts of policy in relation to open and distance education, I had high hopes that this section would provide a variety of chapters that could address the issue. Unfortunately, for a variety of reasons, a number of authors had to withdraw. One of the difficulties with policy work is that those who are in the midst of it are often too busy to write about it and those who are on the edge don't know the whole story. Academics involved in policy work have noted the dangers of this work since it can be intensely political, and yet we need to obtain these narratives to inform our own understanding of how complexities are interwoven in the policy process. I am especially grateful therefore for the three authors whose chapters form this section. They are focused on policy making and its implications.

Litto describes how Brazil's colonial and cultural legacies continue to be represented in its present decisions and the difficulties of surfacing these beliefs so they can be put in juxtaposition to today's realities and possibilities for change created. The issues while embedded in Brazil's context are not unique; the purpose of distance education, its credibility, assumptions about education for all and its relationship to the economy and the general uplifting of civil society, centralization and cooperation – all are issues we recognize and can fruitfully examine in our own situations.

While Litto explores the ideas behind the implementation of distance education, Kaboni focuses her chapter on the implications of such a policy on the organization that is required to lead its implementation. The issues are ones of autonomy and control, centralization and decentralization, consistency and flexibility in the provision of distance education and they are also about the value of distance education to residential campuses and the impact of information communication technologies on jurisdiction. In Kaboni's case the organization is the University of the West Indies and the context involves the sixteen nation states that make up CARICOM, a Caribbean common market, committed to providing further education to enhance the economy of the region. The additional issues of national identity and competing agendas add a further layer to the complexity.

India has had an enviable record of embracing distance education in its national planning documents and encouraging its implementation at all levels from schooling to tertiary education. Garg, Jha and Gupta reexamine this period and look at the role of IGNOU in leading the implementation for the national government. The issues that Kaboni details in the relationships among the nation states is not unlike the complementary and yet competing developments among the Indian states and the issues facing the Distance Education Council are similar: how to enforce quality assurance among the participating institutions whose autonomy and expertise in the field is continuing to increase and in a context where there is a constant stream of new developments especially through digital education technologies.

Together these chapters provide a rich terrain for the exploration of policy in distance education.

Chapter 35

PUBLIC POLICY AND DISTANCE EDUCATION IN BRAZIL

Fredric M. Litto

35.1 THE HISTORICAL–CULTURAL CONTEXT

At the risk of appearing to oversimplify, but feeling the need to establish the premises necessary to understanding why one country's view of conducting its affairs might differ from that of others, I take the liberty of extracting, from a recent reference work, *The Encyclopedia of Distributed Learning*, a very reasonable definition of the term "policy":

> Policies are written guiding principles designed to ensure decision-making that is consistent with an entity's mission and philosophy . . . and tend to be *broad statements* [italics mine] that have the effect of a law in that violation of established policies generally carries a penalty or prescribed consequences.[1]

The present study addresses the situation of governmental (as opposed to institutional) policy-making with regard to distance learning in Brazil, a nation of continental proportions in both size and population, with an uneven history of growth and development in the use of learning at a distance. If it is possible to grossly distinguish European policy-making in the educational sector, with its high degree of centralization, from North American policy-making, highly decentralized, normally delegating responsibility for questions of accreditation and quality to mechanisms of self-regulation and confirmation by regional associations of institutions, then Brazil certainly belongs to the European school of administering educational efforts. But as I hope to demonstrate in this chapter, it is entirely possible that the highly centralized and "fine-grained" regulatory context in which distance learning finds itself in Brazil may turn out to be a phenomenon contrary to the public interest. Most likely, it will be unsustainable over time, since the constantly augmenting number of learners, courses and institutions, and the ever-more-scarce financial resources available will surely create, if the present regulatory context is maintained, an unmanageably complex environment.

"Each policy has its own politics" is the underlying motif of the interesting study recently released by the Inter-American Development Bank, *The Politics of Policies: Economic and Social Progress in Latin America*.[2] Though concentrating principally on areas like pension reform and export subsidies, the study offers fascinating observations of characteristic policy-making processes in the region:

> In Latin America ... government tends to have a very short time horizon ... there is not a sizable corps of public servants with the ability to steer or to preserve long-term policies .... Hence, this produces educational systems with an extreme reliance on rigid rules and institutional definitions that become untouchable and non-negotiable.

The authors affirm that, independent of its being meritocratic or clientelistic in nature, the bureaucracy in power generally reveals the degree of institutional strength or weakness in any given country. There may or may not be "veto players" on the scene, whose final word determines whether a policy is put into operation or not. Frequently, bureaucrats decide what they believe to be best and then bring in "yes-men" to confirm the measure. The longer the same bureaucrats are in power, the more likely there is a "continuation of rigidity instead of adaptability."

> Educational change is very difficult to achieve in practice ... some fundamental things have hardly changed at all. Why? In-depth analysis reveals that there is not one but rather two kinds of education politics. The first involves a group of core policies, dealing with quality and efficiency improvements, that is very rigid and resists fundamental change. The other involves a group of peripheral policies, dealing with expansion and growing enrollments, that is highly adaptable and even volatile: subject to regular – perhaps too frequent – modification .... Education policy brings in a more idiosyncratic set of actors ... not every change in the area of education is politically feasible.

Only in recent decades has education become a serious priority in Brazil. Though the Portuguese, brilliant and courageous navigators, first set foot on the land in 1,500, unlike the Spanish in their colonies, the Portuguese stifled every effort at the development of a literate, informed society. Formal education, dispensed by private tutors and ecclestiastics randomly and sparsely distributed throughout the rural, slave-based economy, reached only a pitiful minority. For the first 300 years in the life of the colony, the Portuguese crown prohibited the publishing of books and periodicals. Practically alone among the Catholic countries of Europe, Portugal did not experience the Reformation, which provoked many countries to initiate public schooling (really only literacy programs) as a form of combating Protestantism. When the Monarch of Portugal and his entire court, fleeing from Napoleon at the beginning of the nineteenth century, relocated to Rio de Janeiro, conditions began to change: schools of medicine, law and mining were created and publications were permitted (but note that these were institutions to prepare professionals for specific tasks, and not universities in which critical thought could take place). At the end of the century, with the arrival of waves of immigrants from Central and Eastern Europe and Japan, the composition of society was altered with new values, among them the desire for learning; and the first teacher-training institutions were begun in the province of São Paulo, then the richest area of the country because of the cultivation of coffee and its exportation throughout the world. Nevertheless, during the period called Brazil's "First Republic" (1890–1930), only 25 percent of the population was literate.[3]

A substantial part of the relations of power, policy and control in Brazilian society today are vestigial elements of this Portuguese legacy, a conceptual model dating from the absolutist monarchies of Europe in the seventeenth and eighteenth centuries: to guarantee the continuation of power and control, it is necessary to "maintain unaltered the domination from the center, annihilating any and all attempts at organized activity or spontaneous solidarity."[4] It was exactly this holdover from the centralizing and paternalistic figure of the monarch over the nation that Alexis de Tocqueville criticized in his celebrated works *The Ancient Regime and the Revolution* and *Democracy in America*: tutorship by an absolute power; minute controls, applied mildly and with foresight; regulating, disciplining, obstructing, ordering and restraining. "Apparently the characteristics of a father's authority, wishing only to desire to prepare men for adulthood, but, in reality, doing just the contrary – keeping them in perpetual infancy."[5]

In Brazil, and other nations that may still have the legacy of older monarchies, "the apparatus of the State functions as an extension of the sovereign's power; its coadjutants, public servants, possess the status of royalty; their functions are considered sinecures; the *res pública* is no different from the *res principis*... consequently, corruption and nepotism are inherent to this kind of administration."[6] The confusion between the public and private spheres, in which private individuals appropriate as theirs that which in reality is public, is rampant in Brazilian society. *Coronelismo* (power of the political chief in rural areas), *clientelismo* (favoring one's clients), *compadrio* (excessive favoritism or protection), *empreguismo* (arranging jobs for favored subordinates or friends), all of these behavior patterns are part of the culture of *patrimonialismo* (increasing or preserving one's patrimony, just as the monarchs did). The person of the governor is confused with that of the government itself.

> The emergence of the bureaucracy in Brazil [in the colonial period] occurred in a cultural context strongly influenced by the patrimonialist tradition of the country. Among the diverse concepts characterizing the Brazilian patrimonialism is loyalty related to other people. This fact, in itself, demonstrates an important cultural "tension" affecting university organizations: the bureaucratic pressure in the direction of the impersonal versus the patrimonialist pressure in the direction of personal favoritism. It is not by accident that in Brazil one sees a clear differentiation between individuals and persons. The individual must follow the rules, the norms and the bureaucratic procedures in effect; the person receives special treatment, on the basis of exceptionality. This favoritism permeates all bureaucratic organizations and could not be expected to be absent from the university.[7]

Regulating, disciplining and obstructing – the creation of hurdles to be overcome by those without protection, so that one could lower these hurdles to help those one favors. The construction of formalistic barriers to getting things done continues until today. In Brazil, there have always existed *cartórios*, or registry offices, where everyone must register deeds, contracts, birth and death certificates and the like in order for them to be considered "legal." The general operating principal, which carries over into general society, is that "every citizen, until he or she proves the contrary, is considered a liar and a cheat"; hence, it is necessary to have an elaborate series of laws, decrees, norms, resolutions and regulations, with great detailing and centralized decision-making, so as to guarantee that any and every action is honest and efficient. Heteronomous laws, those to which all citizens and institutions must submit themselves, regulate educational policy in Brazil – at the municipal level for primary education, the state for secondary education and the federal for post-secondary learning.

> [In Brazil, there is a] tendency of Ministries to legislate by means of "decrees" that are not required to go through a parliamentary process to be voted into law, but are drafted by committees appointed by the Minister and then become binding as soon as they are signed and published.[8]

The general society accepts, unchallenged, the "right" of the authorities to "make uniform in the entire country the rule of prescriptive conduct... [and that] of an education that is 'watched-over.' "[9] Consequently, curricula at all levels of learning have the same general structures and content, and one finds little innovation, experimentation, or creativity due to the risk of "stepping out of line," and not having one's courses approved. But as Noel Samways has related, this all-powerful authority derives from the acceptance, on the part of those subordinated to it, of the authority's power to command and decide: "the administrator only maintains his authority while it is conferred by those subordinated to him... even when [the results of such] imposition arise from caprice or even of not-very-clear motives on the part of the educational authority."

Surely, the most curious example in Brazil of societal acceptance of a legal incongruity is the question of university autonomy. The country's most recent Federal Constitution dates from 1988, and has 250 Articles (not exactly the document of "broad statements" defined at the beginning of this study), in which Article 207 declares that "Universities enjoy autonomy in didactic-scientific, administrative, financial and endowment areas, and will adhere to the principle of the necessary interrelation of teaching, research and extension." The term "Autonomy" is normally considered an absolute, like the terms "always" and "never." Even so, the approximately 200 public and private institutions (out of a total of over 2,000 offering programs of higher education) which are authorized by the Ministry of Education to use the term "university" in their names regularly submit requests for the approval of new courses and programs to the Ministry and are advised to not initiate such planned activities until approval is granted. Even the highly respected and publicly funded universities of the State of São Paulo, legally subordinated only to the local state government, follow this inexplicable practice.

If we consider Bernadette Robinson's observation that in recent decades, there has been a shift from emphasis on 'government' ("the state ruling and controlling through institutions and regulation over a given territory") to "governance" ("the control of an activity by some means such that a range of desired outcomes is attained... a function that can be performed by a wide variety of public and private, state and non-state national and international, institutions and practices"), then we must admit that in the educational sector, Brazil has not yet begun this shift.

> [Governance] relates to funding, regulation and provision or delivery of educational services... instead of carrying out most of the work of education itself, [authorities] determine where the work will be done and by whom... [it moves] from a state-controlled to a state-supervised [activity]. It brings more actors and voices into the policy process and transfers control to bodies other than government or state.[10]

Legacies die very slowly, however. The *PNE-Plano National de Educação, 2001–2011* (National Plan for Education, 2001–2011) prepared by the Federal Government in power in 2001, and still officially valid, sets forth 294 "goals" for education in Brazil. But critics have noted that those responsible for its preparation did not in any way guarantee the financial resources necessary to achieving those goals, and, more seriously, if *everything* is to be considered priority, then *nothing* is priority. In a clear example of the commentary with regard to governmental decision-making in Latin America by the authors of *The Politics of Policy*, there is a constant *discontinuity* of policies with regard to goals, whereas in countries which have earned international respect for their educational policies (such as Canada, Cuba, Finland and South Korea), policy is a question of the state and not of government. "While some countries can adapt their policies rapidly to changes in external circumstances or innovate when policies are failing, other countries react slowly or with great difficulty, retaining inappropriate policies for long periods of time."[11]

Alexander Romiszowski in 2005 studied how six developing countries were able to increase their capacity for extending delivery of higher education through the use of distance learning. India, Pakistan, Sri Lanka, Malaysia and Indonesia were able to increase capacity by 20 percent or more, and only Brazil made no progress in this approach. Romiszowski remarks that in the aforementioned Asiatic countries, 10–30 percent of all higher education is currently based on distance learning, and in India, Pakistan and Indonesia, with dual-mode learning, 50 percent of *all* post-secondary students in the very near future will be involved in distance learning at least part of the time. He notes that Brazil's tardiness in the employment of distance learning in higher education is the result of lack of experience. At the governmental level, he comments, policies reflect a paucity of experiences, good and bad, in the use of distance learning on a large scale in higher education; at the technical level, there is a much smaller number of experienced professionals to draw upon to create and run major distance learning programs than is to be found in the other developing countries, most of which received funds from the World Bank, UNDP and first-world nations to initiate their programs.

Brazil invests only 4.3 percent of its Gross National Product in education in general, and there is currently no specific provision for the financing through public funds of distance learning for higher education, and even highly successful state-inspired projects such as the CEDERJ (Centro de Educação Superior a Distância do Estado do Rio de Janeiro) in the State of Rio de Janeiro, and the imminent Universidade Aberta do Brasil (Brazilian Open University) are or will be paid for mostly from non-governmental monies. Figures show that Brazil has only 3 percent of its 4 million students in higher education enrolled in officially approved distance learning programs. Since the Federal Constitution prohibits public institutions from charging students tuition, and since there is no provision in the announced budgets for regular financing of public distance learning, only two scenarios seem possible: the private sector will dominate in this area of learning (as it already does in conventional higher education), or, as Romiszowski surmises, there will continue to be "discretionary financial incentives and disincentives," with short-term financing for distance learning given by the Ministry of Education only to favored public institutions.

The *Lei de Diretrizes e Bases* (Law of Policies and Standards), a Federal law of 1996 which governs all of education in Brazil, is highly favorable to the employment of distance learning at the secondary and tertiary educational levels, but its terms have never been adequately applied. The accreditation process it suggests is too complex and too slow and requires new approval for proposed distance learning courses on the part of institutions *already accredited* for conventional learning in the same academic areas; the "special treatment" it proposes for educational programs carried over commercial media has never taken effect; and, as Romiszowlski notes, most of the evaluators used by the Ministry to verify the quality of courses proposed for approval come only from Federal universities, and lack extensive practical experience in distance learning, thereby "reflecting vested interests against distance learning." Perhaps most detrimental of all was the series of decrees and regulations issued by the Ministry of Education in the period 1998–2001, which I have treated in depth elsewhere,[12] and which happily are no longer in force, but which included measures such as the *prohibition* of granting recognition to diplomas from foreign universities if they were earned in distance learning programs and the requirement that *every* distance education course at the post-secondary level includes 80 percent of face-to-face presence of the total time, as well as a face-to-face final examination.

Distance education in Brazil still suffers from what Bernadette Robinson has identified in the larger international community: "... an ongoing struggle to establish its credibility and legitimacy, even when its quality is good ... much doubt has been cast on its quality, especially in contexts where it is new or it faces a history of poor-quality provision."[13] A good example of this was the opinion written by one of the leading educational authorities of Brazil in 1984, in relation to a proposal to create an "open distance learning university." In the activities of the Federal Council for Education, Brazil's maximum body for policy in education, Opinion PL 32/84, related by a Council Member, and approved by the Council on 9 April 1984, concerned a proposal for the creation of an Open University. After "recognizing the success of the Open Universities of England, Spain and Venezuela ... and recognizing that Brazil's laws in force permit distance education in institutions having the necessary conditions appropriate to distance learning", he concluded *against* an Open University under the proposed terms and recommended returning the proposal to the Office of the Minister for further study. His reasons are as follows:

> [There exists an] understandable hesitation, considering the existence of deficiencies in the monitoring mechanism of the school system and of certain negative traits of social behavior, notably those related to this "philosophy" of *jeitinhos* [ability to employ "astute" solutions], *facilidades* [ability to employ "easy" or "indulgent" solutions], *levar vantagens* [ability to always "come out on top"], *e cousas pela rama* [and things of this ilk], which favor a certain climate of enticement in the following of duties on the ethical plane and of obligations on the legal plane. The occurrence of irregularities

> in the functioning of certain educational institutions, some of which were serious, such as the "weekend courses" and the periodical waves of diploma falsification, require that the idea of an Open University be considered with restrictions and trepidations.[14]

Although over 20 years have passed since that opinion was approved by the Federal Council of Education, there are still many persons, within and without the educational power establishment, who continue to harbor these attitudes. Some fear the imagined dishonesty of average learners, others fear that web-based learning is merely a rebirth of computer-based training, with its "drill-and-kill" pedagogic structure and hence an inability to educate more profoundly. Instead of seeking out the new approaches to education currently in use in web-based learning, many of which make use of the latest discoveries of the cognitive sciences, these critics prefer to appeal to nostalgic ideas of the teaching and learning process, using distance learning as a scapegoat. Romiszowski points out that there needs to be more attention drawn to the difference between policies treating distance learning (1) as a "separate professional category" and (2) as a "tool, available among other tools, for a professional to use."

Certainly, Brazil is still a long way from having a fruitful environment for the full development of distance learning as part of the total scheme of capacity building. Nevertheless, at the present time, some 3 million learners are involved with distance education in the country: one and a half million in the corporate world, half a million studying through the "Telecurso2000" (primary and secondary school education delivered to adults through open-circuit television and printed material) and the rest made up of university programs, both authorized and extension courses, vocational education, radio-based courses for owners of small- and medium-sized business and other segments. It is probably safe to affirm that the growing credibility of distance learning in the general population is the result of the increasing use of this modality, especially the "Telecurso2000". And the growing acceptance of distance learning in the academic community most probably stems from the international conferences, national seminars and scientific publications of the Brazilian Association for Distance Education – ABED, which for the last 10 years has attempted to develop a community of serious professionals in the area so as to increase awareness about questions of quality and effectiveness in distance learning. Even so, public policy is sure to keep a close watch on this approach to learning. As Samways has observed, "The proliferation of courses in the country feeds the normative voraciousness of the public power, which considers all education a 'public concession,' much like the concessionaries of public services in general"; and Romiszowski remarks that since it has taken on characteristics of "big business," distance learning will continue to draw ever greater attention to itself.

35.2 THE CURRENT POLICY SCENE[15]

On 19 December 2005, the president of the Republic of Brazil signed into law an extensive instrument establishing the policies and norms of distance education in the country. Decree No. 5,622 provides the detailed regulations which are covered only summarily in Law No. 9,394 of 20 December 1996, the all-important legal document governing all aspects of formal education and informally called the "LDB-Lei de Diretrizes e Bases"

(Law of Policies and Standards). That is, the more general law of 1996 devoted fifteen lines to distance learning, and the specific law, which took 9 years to elaborate and gain approval, offers thirty-seven Articles spread over twenty-four pages. Our focus in this study, however, is not the development over time of policy-making regarding distance learning in Brazil, which would be of interest principally to the legal or political science scholar. It is, rather, the thinking at the present moment, situated within the historical–cultural context just described, and pressured most recently by the increasing importance of the new communications technologies in the agitated climate of a learning society. Suffice it to say that the first examples in the country of legislation dealing with distance learning appeared in 1967 and 1971, encouraging the use of radio, television and correspondence courses for remedial primary and secondary education, with highly successful results. In subsequent years, some sixteen legal instruments held sway over the development of distance learning, and on the whole, they created so many hurdles for interested practioners that Brazil lost the lead it shared with the United Kingdom, Canada, Spain and India early in the decade of the 1970s. For those interested in a historical perspective, these instruments can be found in the literature.[16]

In some countries, the general policy regarding distance learning is that it is a part of education as a whole and does not require specific legislation. The evaluation of the quality of its implementation in individual institutions is considered part of the overall evaluation made of any institution's instructional objectives and performance. As we will see below, this view does not prevail in Brazil at the present time. Four versions were necessary, from early 2004 to the end of 2005, to obtain the new law, which had the contributions of learned societies and ad hoc committees of specialists advising the technical staff of the Ministry of Education responsible for preparing the document. Although not revealing a firm acceptance, on the part of the Ministerial staff, of *all* of the recommendations made by the academic community, the new law has met with a generally favorable reaction. There is a belief that the suggestions offered by the specialists received consideration and reflection on the part of the staff, in a spirit of openness for dialogue, even when the new ideas were not included in the resulting text. The consensus of opinion is that it is favorable to the growth of distance learning in Brazil, and deserves praise, even though it will have to be reviewed very shortly in order to excise some measures which are in conflict. There is also the question of the need for still further legislation, detailing even more some of the regulations, such as those treating pre-university and post-baccaulaureate studies (the law stipulates a maximum of 180 days for the completion of these additional regulations).

Almost 70 percent of the new law deals with higher education, a natural consequence of the Federal Constitution attributing the responsibility for primary and secondary education the cities and states respectively, and that for tertiary education to the Federal Government.

- Brought forward from the past is the procedure of accreditation by the Ministry of Education: all proposed programs and courses must be authorized by the Ministry before students are recruited and matriculated; programs are evaluated at the mid-point in time of their authorizations, and then renewed once every 5 years thereafter.

- The document promotes and offers incentives for inter-institutional collaboration, partnerships and agreements, especially within the same geographic region, as long as all of the institutions involved are educational in nature. It also permits the creation of programs or courses, "to be offered for a limited time only," of an "experimental" nature. But it does not make clear if *all* of the partners must be authorized to proceed, or only that one involved with the teaching/learning process.
- Institutions, both public and private, not necessarily educational in nature, but recognized for their excellence, may request authorization to offer courses at the following post-baccalaureate levels: specialization (programs of 360 hours of study), masters, doctorate and professional technology education.
- The new law revokes the earlier prohibition of legally "recognizing as equivalent to Brazilian degrees" university diplomas awarded in foreign universities if they were earned through distance learning (a just measure considering that (1) foreign universities frequently do not indicate in the student's transcript the mode of study used and (2) the LDB of 1996 stipulated that degrees earned in Brazil through distance learning have the same academic value as those earned conventionally).
- The new law, however, reserves to *public universities* the exclusive right to "recognize as equivalent to Brazilian diplomas" those degrees earned abroad at a distance. This restriction may be considered unconstitutional since "all are equal before the law," and it ignores the question of the presence of excellent private institutions on the national scene.
- Perhaps the greatest advance the new law brings is the possibility of offering, through distance learning methods, the sacrosanct degrees of masters and doctorate, although it remains to be seen just what will be the nature of the controls, qualitative, quantitative and procedural that will be required by the Ministry for this new category of studies.
- The different sectors of the Ministry of Education and the State Secretariats of Education have 180 days to issue regulations standardizing norms and procedures for accrediting distance learning programs in their spheres of concern.
- It is generally believed that the law is in error in limiting the use of distance learning in primary and secondary education only to "exceptional cases," meaning that of adults who left school early and must now resume their studies. It is expected that many organizations, public and private, which have decades of good experience in this line of work, will take this issue, excessively restrictive, into the courts to preserve their rights.
- Although it establishes the principle that diplomas awarded by authorized institutions have validity throughout the entire country, the law in not clear in its treatment of geographical jurisdiction on the part of different states, which supposedly have autonomy in matters of primary and secondary education. For example, if an institution operating at the secondary school level is recognized in one state and wishes to serve students residing in other states where its courses are not recognized, the new law says that it should request authorization from the Ministry. But what are the legal responsibilities and duties of the state governments where the students reside if they were not involved in the original authorization? What of state laws which are incompatible with one another? Or states which choose *not* to approve specific legislation regarding distance learning? Must institutions wishing to operate programs of pre-university education negotiate separate agreements

with each of Brazil's twenty-six states and the Federal District? Should not the same freedom over the entire national territory, given to institutions of higher education, be extended to those of primary and secondary education?

- Though advised by specialists to avoid attempting to define (even generically) in the new law the phenomenon called "distance learning," since rapid advances in pedagogy and technology are making it almost impossible to "pin down" anything that involves the human mind and communicational processes, the new law makes this attempt. The result, subject to divergent philosophies and inevitable obsolescence, is the following: "an educational modality in which the didactic–pedagogic mediation in the processes of teaching and learning occur with the utilization of the media and the information and communication technologies, with students and teachers developing educational activities in diverse places and times." Some of the elements of this definition are already obsolete when we consider (1) the totally automated web-based learning at the University of Southern Queensland in Australia and (2) that a great number of North American university students do distance learning in the *same* cities and in the *same* institutions where they are already enrolled in conventional mode learning.
- Many of the further criticisms of the new law arise from the fact that the thinking behind the regulations continues to reflect a by-gone paradigm, perhaps appropriate for conventional studies, but certainly inflexible and even inappropriate in the context of a complex, new urban reality.
  - The number of places for students in each course is regulated, essentially the same as in conventional learning (although distance learning requires "scaling up" course enrollments, while maintaining cohort groups small).
  - The calendar of the periods when courses are held must follow an annual or semesterly schedule (which places greater emphasis on administrative convenience, and ignores the convenience of learners, for whom courses could begin at any time, say, when the cohort group is filled).
  - The new law requires that courses for distance learning have the *same duration* as conventional courses (a measure which hinders mature, highly motivated learners from accelerating their studies; as one critic noted, this means that "repeating" a course is permitted – but "accelerating" learning is not. Who is to say what is a "normal rhythm" for learning?).
  - The new law requires that *all* distance learning courses have components of face-to-face contact between students and instructors, and that the principal element in the evaluation of the student's performance be examinations held in a face-to-face situation (this obligation negates the virtue of eliminating barriers of time and distance, so characteristic of distance learning, and in a country as vast as Brazil, the fifth largest in area in the world, it essentially eliminates the possibility of students acquiring knowledge and qualification in regions other than their own, not to speak of those incapacitated and restricted to their homes; it also ignores the advances made to date of evaluating student work at a distance).
  - The law requires that all new courses through distance learning be approved also by the respective professional societies which govern their practice (medicine, law, engineering, psychology), although the Ministry reserves the right not to accept a negative decision in certain cases.

  - Institutions receiving authorization to begin a distance education course have 12 months to initiate the course or lose the privilege (this measure ignores the fact that while conventional courses are relatively easy to prepare, those for distance learning require a significant and complex team effort, the possible elaboration of innovative technological supports and the production of new study materials, the establishment of partnerships, and so forth, with the recovery of the investment extending perhaps to 5 years).
  - The decree cites the possibility of appeal on the part of institutions which feel wronged by the legislation; but it does not clarify under what circumstances an appeal may be made, nor does it clarify to whom it should be directed.
- A key omission in the new law is any mention of what has been accomplished, by either or both the Ministry of Communication and the Ministry of Education, as stipulated in the LDB of 1996, that measures be taken to permit the use of commercial channels of radio and television, under favored conditions, for the transmission of educational content. No mention is made of this important possibility, while at the same time, the seventy-odd university-owned non-commercial television stations do nothing in the way of formal instruction, confining their programming merely to journalistic and cultural matters.

35.3 BY WAY OF A CONCLUSION

The considered opinion of many leaders of distance education in Brazil is that the new law treats distance learning "as a shadow of conventional learning," not really coming to grips with the full potential of this mode of extending access to knowledge and qualification to new segments of the population. No mention is made, for example, of "self-directed learning," or "just-in-time" learning or other forms of capacity building, which surely will take on greater importance in the coming years. Specialists believe that the law is excessively restrictive on some accounts, and seriously omissive on others. It places the Ministry of Education squarely in its old role of "policing" civil society, a function that will become ever more complex, slow-moving and occasionally subject to the customs of favoritism and privileges which have always been present in this culture. At the end of 2005, local newspapers decried the fact that hundreds of young people had received scholarships from the Ministry of Education so as to matriculate in 2006 in institutions whose accreditation had been revoked 2 years earlier by the same Ministry. And only 20 km from the offices of the same Ministry in Brasília, there are institutions which temporarily "rent" entire libraries or the professional biographies of university professors to unprepared and unqualified new institutions seeking accreditation. The complexity of the modern world makes difficult the effective monitoring of processes involving questions of quantity and quality in human affairs.

Nonetheless, no one in Brazil is talking today about the possibility of initiating a new system of self-regulation in education, one in which each institution does a profound self-evaluation and then periodically presents its findings before a panel of representatives of similar institutions. Instead of a policing action, instead of living under "supervised autonomy," institutions could come to know themselves deeply through serious self-evaluation; and, if they are honest with themselves, they can correct their educational "flight-plans" and move steadily in the direction of qualitative improvement. The recent decree regulating distance learning in Brazil represents an advance over prior conditions. It will still require a revised version, suppressing certain excesses, rectifying certain omissions and correcting some minor formal errors. But Brazil must break free of its cultural legacy of centralized control and command, of suspecting that a goodly number of people and institutions in society seek to come out on top at any cost. Distance learning may not be the cure for most of society's problems, but it has a significant role to play in many of them. "Over-legislating" stifles initiative and creativity. It creates a playing field that is not level and that discourages serious players from attempting to enter the game. The time has come for those who set public policy regarding education in Brazil to make a fresh start, transferring the question of setting policy into the hands of civil society. Minor problems may occur during the transitional phase, but in the long run, there is bound to be a more just and workable system than is presently the case.

NOTES

1. *Encyclopedia of Distributed Learning.* Anna Di Stefano, Kjell Erik Rudestam and Robert J. Silverman, eds, Thousand Oaks, California: Sage, 2004.
2. Inter-American Development Bank. *The Politics of Policy: Economic and Social Progress in Latin America 2006 Report.* Accessed on 18 November 2005. [www.iadb.org/res/ipes/2006/index.cfm?language=En&parid=1]
3. Simõn Schwartman, "Os Desafios da Educação no Brasil," in Colin Brock and Simon Schwartzman, orgs. *Os Desafios da Educação no Brasil.* Rio de Janeiro: Nova Fronteira, 2005.
4. Ricardo Vélez Rodriguez, "José Osvaldo de Meira Penna – O Homem e s sua Obra". Accessed 15 December 2005. [www.ensayistas.org/filosofos/brasil/meira/introd.htm]
5. Ibid, p. 2.
6. "Plano Diretor da Reforma do Aparelho do Estado," Câmara da Reforma do Estado, República Federativa do Brasil. Accessed 16 December 2005. [www.planalto.gov.br/publi_04/COLECAO/PLAND12.HTM]
7. Clovis L. Machado da Silva, "Modelos Burocrático e Político e Estrutura Organizacional de Universidades," in *Temas de Administração Universitária*, Florianópolis, S.C.: Universidade Federal de Santa Catarina, 1991. Cited in Noel Edmar Samways, "Problemas da Cultura Formalista na Administração Educacional Brasileira," Masters Thesis, Universidade Católica do Paraná, 1997, p. 62. Favoritism continues unabated in Brazil, as seen in a recent investigative story in a leading São Paulo newspaper relating that over half a million public employees in the country enjoy the status of holding "cargos de confiança," positions for which they were "indicated," instead of following the normal procedure of passing in competitive public examinations, as required by law. Gabriel Manzano Filho, "País tem 524 mil cargos de confiança, que emperram luta contra nepotism," *O Estado de S, Paulo*, 26 February 2006, p. A4.
8. Alexander Romiszowski, "A Study of Distance Education Public Policy and Practice in the Higher Education Sectors of Selected Countries: Synthesis of Key Findings." Accessed 17 December 2005. (www.che.ac.za/documents/d000070/Background_Paper1_Romiszowski.pdf) It is also worthy of note that there presently exist 177,875 valid laws at the national level in Brazil, "a good part of them not in use; others which are repetitive or even in conflict" (Veja, 21 February 2007, p. 32).

9. Samways, pp. 15, 23 and 29.
10. Bernadette Robinson, "Governance, Accreditation and Quality Assurance in Open and Distance Education," in Hilary Perraton and Helen Lentell, eds, *Policy for Open and Distance Learning*. London: Routledge Falmer and Vancouver: The Commonwealth of Learning, 2004.
11. *The Politics of Policy*, Chapter 1, p. 2.
12. Fredric M. Litto, "The Hybridization of Distance Learning in Brazil – An Approach Imposed by Culture." *International Review of Research in Open and Distance Learning:* 2, 2 (January, 2002). [iuicode: http://www.icaap.org/iuicode?149.2.2.6]
13. Robinson, p. 181.
14. Quoted in João Roberto Moreira Alves, *A Educação a Distância no Brasil: Síntese Histórica e Perspectivas*. Rio de Janeiro: Instituto de Pesquisas Avançadas em Educação, 1994, p. 91.
15. I wish to thank here, for their help in analyzing the implications of the new legislation governing distance learning, Professors Candido L. Gomes of the Universidade Católica de Brasília, João Roberto Moreira Alves of the Instituto de Pesquisa Avançadas of Rio de Janeiro, Manuel Marcos Maciel Formiga of the Universidade de Brasília, Roberto Palhares of the Instituto Monitor and Waldomiro Loyolla of the Faculdades Integradas de São Paulo.
16. An especially good source, bringing together the full texts of Federal and State legislation, as well as statistical data covering the field, is the *Anuário Brasileiro Estatístico de Educação Aberta e a Distância – ABRAEAD 2005*. São Paulo: Associação Brasileira de Educação a Distância – ABED e Instituto Monitor, 2005.

Further details on recent developments in distance learning in Brazil can be found in Fredric M. Litto, "Perspectivas da Educação a Distância no Brasil: Três Cenários a Ponderar [1997–2002]," *Revista Brasileira de Aprendizagem Aberta e a Distância/Brazilian Review of Open and Distance Learning*, Vol. 2, No. 3 (November, 2003). (http://www.abed.org.br/publique/cgi/cgilua.exe/sys/start.htm?UserActiveTemplate=1 por&infoid=888&sid=69).

Readers interested in the tendencies seen in 847 research studies on distance learning in recent years in Brazil may consult Fredric M. Litto, Andrea Filatro and Claúdio André, "Brazilian Research on Distance Learning, 1999–2003: A State-of-the-Art Study." *Open Praxis – the Electronic Journal of the International Council for Open & Distance Education (2005)*. (http://www.openpraxis.com/index.php?option=com_ content&task=view&id=40&Itemid=41).

Chapter 36

Transnational Policies and Local Implementation: The University of the West Indies Distance Education Centre*

Olabisi Kuboni

The University of the West Indies (UWI) is a regional institution that serves and is supported by fifteen countries of the English-speaking Caribbean.[1] It has three campuses, namely the Mona campus in Jamaica, the Cave Hill campus in Barbados and the St. Augustine campus in Trinidad and Tobago. In light of increasing concerns that the non-campus countries were not adequately served, the University took the decision to increase access for these countries using the distance education modality. To this end, in 1996, it set up the University of the West Indies Distance Education Centre (UWIDEC) with the mandate to work with the faculties to develop and deliver their offerings in the distance mode, targeting all contributing countries but in particular potential students in the non-campus countries (NCCs). Thus, when UWIDEC started operations in 1997, it did so with the clear mandate of increasing the university's enrolment, in particular from among potential applicants in the non-campus countries of the region.

In addition to satisfying its outreach responsibility, the UWI was following in the tradition of other institutions in two ways. Firstly, it had entrusted the management of its distance offerings to a separate department, and secondly, it was transforming itself into a dual-mode institution offering its programmes in both the face-to-face and distance modes. UWIDEC would be the mechanism through which the parent institution would realize these important goals.

* The UWI is currently in the process of setting up the UWI Open Campus (UWIOC) and UWIDEC is being incorporated into that structure. A brief statement will be made about this development at the end of the chapter. The above notwithstanding, the author is of the view that an examination of UWIDEC's role is still very pertinent at this time.

UWIDEC plays a major role in course development and manages the delivery of the University's distance offerings to students attached to thirty-two sites in the sixteen countries listed earlier.

Over the period 1997–2002, enrolment in distance programmes grew from 1,510 to 2,328, an increase of 54.2 percent (UWI, 2001, *Strategic Plan 2002–2007*, pp. 8–9). In the academic year 2005–2006, enrolment stood at approximately 3,000 students, some 28 percent higher than the figure for 2001–2002. The reduction in the growth rate is primarily because of the termination of three sub-degree certificate programmes, given a policy decision by the parent institution to discontinue offerings at that level.

As stated above, the UWI serves sixteen countries and is supported by fifteen. However, while this situation renders it a public institution, it is, however, not a state-run institution. Rather it is described as an "autonomous regional institution supported by and serving" the countries named. Its three campuses are described as being "quasi-autonomous but... integrated by a set of centrally administered functions and operations" (UWI website, http://www.uwi.edu). The implications of these organizational and governance arrangements for the implementation of distance education in the University will be discussed in greater detail later in this chapter.

Most of the countries referred above are themselves members of the regional body, the Caribbean Community (CARICOM). CARICOM was established in 1973 to continue efforts to reinstate a mechanism for regional integration subsequent to the demise of the West Indies Federation in 1962. The discussions that followed the collapse of the Federation eventually led to the formation of the Caribbean Free Trade Area (CARIFTA) in 1968, which, by 1971, numbered twelve members. By 1973, CARIFTA had evolved into the Caribbean Community and Common Market (CARICOM) with the signing of the Treaty of Chaguaramas. Over the ensuing years, new members joined, the latest being Haiti which, in 2002, became the first French-speaking Caribbean state to become a full CARICOM member (http://www.caricom.org).[2] Two things are to be noted about the two country lists. First, even though the number of countries supporting the University is the same as the number that are members of CARICOM, and while many belong to both lists, the two lists are not identical. Further, while all the countries supporting the University are former (or current) British colonies, CARICOM now comprises one former Dutch colony and, as stated above, Haiti.

While not directly governed by any of the regional governments, the UWI has the status of being an important regional institution. In fact, Article 22 of the revised Treaty of Chaguaramas, names the UWI as one of five associate institutions "with which the Community enjoys important functional relationships which contribute to the achievement of the objectives of the Community" (CARICOM Secretariat, 2001, p. 15). Consequently, even though it is an autonomous institution as stated above, the UWI must take on board the goals and expectations of the Community, in particular those that relate to higher education.

This chapter will therefore seek to examine the impact of policies from the University on the implementation of distance education within the UWI. Given the fact that the

University is a regional institution, the paper will also refer to relevant policies and practices at the level of CARICOM as a whole or its individual members.

36.1 CARICOM AND REGIONAL HIGHER EDUCATION

Earlier mention was made of a revised Treaty of Chaguaramas. The primary purpose of the revision was to transform the Common Market into a single market and economy, with the overall goal being to benefit the people of the region by providing more and better opportunities to produce and sell goods and services. To this end, the CARICOM Single Market and Economy (CSME) would seek, inter alia, to realize

- free movement of goods and services
- a common external tariff
- free movement of capital
- free movement of labour.

The CSME can therefore be regarded as the vehicle through which the Community would achieve its own objectives.

The objectives that inform the operations of CARICOM today are contained in Article 6 of the revised Treaty of Chaguaramas. Two of the objectives of the Community as listed in that article are improved standards of living and work and enhanced functional cooperation. The specific activities that the latter subsumes are

- more efficient operation of common services and activities for the benefit of its peoples;
- accelerated promotion of greater understanding among its peoples and the advancement of their social, cultural and technological development; and
- intensified activities in areas such as health, education, transportation and telecommunications.

It is against this background that the role of the UWI as an associate institution of the Community has to be considered. That role carries with it the responsibility of assisting the Community to achieve its objectives. In this regard, the 18th meeting of the Heads of Government Conference, held in Montego Bay, 30 June–4 July 1997, is of particular significance. In the communiqué issued at the end of that meeting, the Heads reported on agreement reached in relation to key strategic objectives regarding education and human resource development. Among the measures listed for priority implementation by member countries was the attainment of 15 percent enrolment of the post-secondary group in tertiary level education by the year, 2005.

This proposed measure was no doubt borne out of concerns that the Caribbean rate of enrolment in higher education was far lower than that attained by other regions of the world. In a 2001 address to the Council for Human and Social Development (COHSOD), one of the organs of the Community, the Community's Secretary General noted that while tertiary level enrolment in the English-speaking Caribbean stood at

6 percent, it was 12 percent in Latin America, 15 percent in South East Asia and over 20 percent in Europe and North America (Carrington, 2001).

It should be emphasized though that increasing the participation rate was not the only objective to be achieved. The 1997 Communique also highlighted the Heads' perspective on the role of education in regional development. It stated,

> Heads of Government recognised that knowledge had become the central factor of competitiveness. They emphasized the importance of life-long learning and continuing education.... Heads of Government re-emphasized that education and training must be relevant and should lead to the development of a creative and adaptive individual.
>
> (p. 5)

Some may suggest that the 1997 Communique was an attempt by the Community to bring some measure of cohesion to initiatives that were already being implemented by the Heads in their own states. The 1990s saw a proliferation of initiatives on the part of regional governments to reform the education systems of their respective countries. Howe and Cassell (2003) make the point that in spite of differing approaches, there were a core set of themes and issues at the centre of the reform process across all states. Citing Miller (1999), the writers identified one such theme as

> Expanding tertiary education, including the use of the distance education modality and linking this level of education more closely to the labour force demands, especially in the priority economic sectors such as tourism and hospitality.

It can be argued therefore that the decision of the UWI to increase access to its programmes of study through the distance mode may have been influenced by prevailing thinking among regional governments, and in particular the governments of the contributing countries.

The remarks of the St. Kitts–Nevis Minister of Education, in his feature address at the opening of the University Centre/UWIDEC site in that country, are instructive in this regard. He stated,

Let me mention my vision of having UWI at the cutting edge of technology to assist... St. Kitts and Nevis in our educational thrust into the New Millenium. By this prescription I hope to remedy the triumvirate evil, which has long been associated with UWI:

- Limited accessibility
- Exorbitant costs, economic cost, and residential cost;
- Discrimination based on unrealistic criteria of students who have the ability to pursue courses at UWI, but are unable to uproot themselves [and relocate to] one of the campus territories.

(Harris, 2000, p. 26)

It is evident that remarks such as the one above would not escape the attention of the University administration. Responding to regional needs would feature prominently in successive Strategic Plans of the University. Thus, one of the four core objectives of the 1997–2002 Plan states in part that UWI would "contribute to the expansion of access to Caribbean people to tertiary level education and training... ". The 2002–2007 Plan makes an even greater commitment. The mission statement of this latter Plan states, in part that the University would "provide the population of the region with access to high quality academic programmes that are effectively delivered and that help to build strong individual, national and regional capacities in response to changing human resource needs" (p. 22).

Given such a mission, it was evident that distance education would be given a high priority in the Plan, as the University set about to realize the intentions of its mission statement.

36.2 DISTANCE EDUCATION AND THE 2002–2007 STRATEGIC PLAN

The heightened emphasis on distance education is very evident in the 2002–2007 Strategic Plan. In addition to the strong demands of regional governments, another reason for this emphasis was the general dissatisfaction with the performance of the UWIDEC in the first 5 years of its existence. In the current Plan, distance education is identified as one of the "several discernible weaknesses that, if left unheeded, would seriously impair competitiveness and effectiveness". Specifically, the Plan notes that the University's distance education programmes "are not efficient and competitive" (p. 20). The University was keen to take steps to remedy this situation. Consequently, two of the nine strategic objectives of the Plan target distance education either wholly or in part. These objectives are

- expansion of access
- restructuring of distance education and deepening the impact of outreach programmes in the NCCs (non-campus countries).

In terms of expansion of access, the Plan calls for enrolment in distance education programmes to be expanded by 5,000 students "after radically reforming the system, to facilitate wider regional access to higher education" (p. 27). The Plan goes on to state clearly that the major distance education initiative must be to "make the restructuring of distance education a major undertaking of the highest priority during the plan period". Following are some of the objectives identified in relation to that initiative:

- Make higher education and training opportunities accessible to more people in the NCCs.
- Ensure that the University's distance education programmes are responsive, learner-centred and cost-effective.
- Implement a shift to asynchronous delivery of distance education programmes.
- Budget adequate resources for the delivery and management of the distance education programme, on a centralized basis that gives UWIDEC effective control of the required resources and facilitates accurate costing of services and accountability.

(pp. 30–31)

36.2.1 The Shift to Blended Learning

In light of the mandate outlined in the Strategic Plan and based on a paper presented and adopted by UWIDEC's own Academic Programmes Committee (UWIDEC APC P.4), the decision was taken to shift the delivery mode of the University's distance education programmes to a blended learning approach, one that placed greater emphasis on the use of web-based asynchronous technologies.[3] In furtherance of that decision, the blended learning project team was set up at the beginning of the academic year 2004/2005 to begin preparation to deliver twelve pilot courses in 2005/2006 in this new mode. These courses were selected from programmes already offered at a distance.

In embarking on this project, UWIDEC was attempting to satisfy the twin objectives of expanding access and attaining a higher quality in its offerings. In specific terms, the project was intended to minimize the prevailing heavy reliance on synchronous modes of interaction which both restricts the institution's ability to expand access as well as encourages the persistence of the didactic top-down modes of teaching and learning. It should be noted that in terms of the amount of time allocated to the respective components of the current mixed delivery mode, the allocation was clearly biased towards the core print-based self-study instructional materials. Of the estimated 100 study hours recommended for the study of a distance course, it was recommended that 80 hours should be spent on individual study of the course materials, with 12–16 hours allocated for face-to-face tutorials, and 8–10 hours for audio-conferencing. However, notwithstanding the intended bias towards the single asynchronous aspect of the delivery mix, the practice had evolved whereby students were making heavy demand on tutors and course coordinators in the two synchronous interactive aspects, thus heightening the emphasis on these two components of the delivery mix in ways not intended.

Consequently, the project sought to reduce the importance of the face-to-face tutorial and the course coordinator-led audio-conference. By extension, it is designed to shift focus to a web-based learning management system (LMS) that would allow flexibility in time and place for study, provide an environment capable of supporting less hierarchical relationships in the teaching–learning transaction, thereby encouraging greater responsibility on the part of learners. It would also make it possible for UWIDEC to attain greater scalability, offering its courses to groups ranging in size from 100 and less, to several hundreds.

The new mode therefore blends different technologies to attain these goals. The print-based self-study instructional materials remain at the core, with the active, interactive components now taking place largely online through the vehicle of various asynchronous technologies that together constitute UWIDEC's selected LMS.

At the time of writing, one semester of the year-long project had been completed. In spite of the short period, the potential of the new approach to attain the objectives set were already discernible. The challenges that were still to be overcome were also very real. However, when one examines the possibilities and the challenges, what was also evident is that, overall, the primary factor impacting UWIDEC's capacity to deliver an efficient distance education service lies in the organization and governance structure of the parent institution. The capacity of blended learning to deliver on its promise would be significantly compromised if this matter was not addressed.

I therefore wish to propose that the University should re-examine its governance structure if the expectations it holds for distance education are to be realized. In this regard, this chapter will address two issues, namely distance education and the "quasi-autonomous" campus and arrangements for quality assurance and accreditation. In doing so, it will also make reference to wider regional issues as these are deemed pertinent.

36.3 DISTANCE EDUCATION AND THE "QUASI-AUTONOMOUS" CAMPUS

The governance structure that is currently in effect in the University formally came into being in 1994, as a result of the recommendations made by the Commission set up by the then Chancellor for that purpose. These recommendations are contained in the 1994 *Report of the Chancellor's Commission on Governance of the University of the West Indies*. This document provides the basis for much of the discussion to follow.

The aspect of that structure that is of most relevance in this context is the relationship between the University Centre and the campuses. As indicated earlier, the campuses are currently described as "quasi-autonomous". Emmanuel (1993), while making a strong case against the centralized approach taken in introducing the semester system, as well as the system itself, nonetheless observes that, in the emerging structure, "the devolution of functions to the campuses has introduced elements of federalism and presented challenges to the authority of the office of the Vice Chancellor" (p. 6).

Based on its own evaluation of prevailing arrangements, the Commission makes the following recommendations about the balance of power between the Centre and the campuses:

> Part of the present problem lies in the University Centre being required by the current distribution of functions to take on too many responsibilities, so that the business of the University is clogged with decisions which would be better taken closer to the scene of the activity involved. For the governance of the University to be effective, the balance of responsibilities between the campuses and the Centre needs to be readjusted.... The Commission strongly supports the University's long-term plans for an expansion of student numbers.... But the Commission does not believe that these targets can be met unless the current governance and managerial structures are reformed and modernized ... For this policy to succeed, the excessive burden of central University control, that is, of involving all the campuses in central decision-making needs to be loosened so that individual campuses can take their own decisions about first degree matters and can experiment with new arrangements without the constraints which are imposed by central committees.... The Commission therefore recommends that all questions relating to first degrees: new degree programmes, syllabus amendments, matriculation and examinations be devolved to the individual campuses.

It is very likely that the Commissioners did not fully grasp the potential conflict within the very policy framework that they were proposing. In concrete terms, increased devolution of power for matters related to first-degree programmes was being proposed within the same context that the Commission was recommending the setting up of a single distance education centre to implement the development and delivery of the University's distance programmes.

36.3.1 Effect of the Devolution of Power

The "quasi-autonomous" nature of the campuses has brought with it several developments which, at best, can be regarded as hindering the work of UWIDEC. The mandate handed down in the 1994 Report encourages campuses to experiment with new arrangements with regard to first-degree matters. One important example of this is the articulation and franchising arrangements that each campus has worked out between itself and individual tertiary level institutions (TLIs) in the contributing countries. Typically, the TLI offers Level 1, and in some instances Level 2 of a UWI degree programme, under the direction and guidance of the relevant faculty; students pursue part of the degree at the TLI, then transfer to the campus to complete it.

There is the perception that campus principals favour these arrangements since they provide a ready pool of new enrolments. With each campus aggressively seeking to increase its own cohort, any commitment to building a distance programme that would undermine the campus' own goals would hardly be entertained. What makes the situation even more challenging for UWIDEC is that these franchising arrangements mainly involve programmes in the Faculty of Social Sciences, which is also the faculty from which UWIDEC draws its main distance offering. The University is therefore competing against itself in a fairly limited market.

Of interest though is the fact that, within recent times, the thrust to increase access to higher education at the level of the individual country seems to be moving in directions that do not necessarily involve a relationship with the UWI. Chevanne (2003) brings an interesting perspective on the ever-changing status of the UWI in light of developments within individual countries to address their higher education concerns. He contends,

> On the local level, the pressure of accountability to a local constituency plus the inability of the regional University to meet the rapidly expanding demands in a timely manner, have fueled the development of local institutions of higher learning. Thus, within recent times the arena of higher education has been widening rapidly within each island with the rise of public and private associate degree and degree-granting institutions.

Interestingly, Chevanne does not view these developments as adversely affecting UWI's position in the region. On the contrary, he asserts,

> While this appears contradictory, insofar as local higher institutions have the potential to be competitors of the regionally funded University of the West Indies, wise

> leadership has seized on this development as an opportunity to deepen coordination and cooperation.
>
> (p. 2)

It is likely that the "wise leadership" that Chevanne is referring to has to do with the articulation and franchising arrangements discussed above. However, contrary to his view, some may argue that the ability of the UWI to enter into these arrangements has not kept pace with the rapid increase of these country-specific institutions within the last few years, with many of these institutions forging ties with other institutions outside of the region.

It is important to emphasize at this juncture that the intention is not that the distance programme should displace the relationship that the University now has or which it will continue to build with other tertiary level institutions in the region. Any such move would be completely counter productive, since one cannot underestimate the value of partnerships in the current higher education market place. What probably needs to be re-examined is the campus-specific approach to building these relationships. There is obvious need for a holistic and less fragmented approach to these developments, one that does not serve the interest of some sectors at the expense of other sectors, and ultimately, at the expense of the whole.

The "quasi-autonomous" operation of the campuses adversely affects UWIDEC in other ways. One has also seen situations where resources are put into the strengthening of a part time face-to-face evening programme targeting candidates who would otherwise fit the profile of a typical distance student. In another situation, efforts at building a single unified professional degree programme to be offered at a distance for the entire region have been thwarted as the relevant faculties on each campus focus their attention on their respective country-specific markets, drawn by the pull of national government initiatives.

The irony of the above situation is that simultaneous with the drive to meet country-specific needs, national governments and other agencies with developmental agendas are themselves making demands of the respective campuses for programmes to be offered at a distance. Thus, in order to maintain their viability within their respective constituencies, the campus-based administrations are becoming more and more concerned that they should make the shift to a more open-learning mode, one that also involves the use of online technologies. Against that background, ad hoc, uncoordinated approaches have been made to UWIDEC units on the respective campuses for assistance in developing and delivering distance/online programmes. In spite of efforts to bring some order into these initiatives, there has not been any marked success in realizing intended goals.

36.3.2 Impact of Devolution on UWIDEC Core Operations

UWIDEC itself has not remained unaffected by this situation. For all of its existence, in terms of its core operations, it has been obliged to develop strategies that, while being consistent with its overall status as a single unit within the regional institution, must also be responsive to campus-specific processes and procedures. While the department has made reasonably satisfactory progress in establishing and maintaining systems for managing its operations, one cannot ignore the fact that at any given time, the reliability of these systems can be weakened by the need to shift gears to accommodate the way things are done on a particular campus.

This situation has also limited progress in terms of defining a clear set of rules for interacting with the various arms of the parent institution with which UWIDEC must do business. One critical area is the appointment/contracting of course developers, course coordinators and tutors. While much of the faculty-driven model as originally conceptualized (Renwick, Shale & Rao (1992)) no longer applies, the policy of the Faculty having the major responsibility for selecting these functionaries remains an ideal to which all subscribe. However, the rules governing this activity are still not clearly defined. Also not clearly defined are the conditions under which these persons are to be retained to perform their functions. As a result, campus-based UWIDEC offices adopt varying approaches for undertaking this very important activity.

Another important area that has been affected by the absence of a single set of rules to guide the UWIDEC–UWI interaction is the admissions and registration process. Up to the academic year 2007–2008, distance students were admitted to and registered in all three campuses, depending on their location in any of the sixteen countries that UWIDEC serves. As a result, all registry-related operations from admissions through to graduation were campus-specific.

It should also be noted that all three campuses are currently have transitioned away from a paper-based to an online system for student registry matters. Unfortunately, the online processes themselves are campus specific. Thus solutions that have been rolled out do not cater to the needs of the distance students spread across the region. UWIDEC's response to this development will be addressed later in this section.

36.3.3 Governance in Multi-campus Settings: Two Examples

As the demand for higher education continues to grow, university governance structures are coming under very close scrutiny as these institutions seek to determine the extent to which their prevailing structures are allowing them to evolve and be responsive to the complex demands of their environments. Such concerns become even more highlighted in situations where there are multi-campuses and, as in the case of the UWI, issues about the centralization and decentralization of authority become critical areas of debate. The experiences of the Cape Higher Education Consortium (CHEC) of South Africa, and Deakin University of Australia can provide some useful insight. Even though neither arrangement is exactly the same as the UWI, they both speak to the issue of governance in a multi-campus situation.

According to Leatt and Pretorius (2004), since the dismantling of the apartheid system in South Africa in the early 1990s, the government's higher education policy has been to encourage regional inter-institutional cooperation, while not necessarily mandating it. It is this policy that gave rise to the Cape Higher Education Consortium, which brought together three universities and two technikons to facilitate cooperation in strategic areas of their operations. The writers acknowledged the failure of the first projects that the Consortium had undertaken and assessed the lessons learnt this way:

> We have had to learn by trial and error to balance competing interests, resolve conflict and find diplomatic solutions to difficult problems. In fact, the literature of international affairs, conflict resolution and diplomacy has assisted us more than the management literature.
>
> (p. 3)

The Strategic Vision that was subsequently formulated, therefore established that the Consortium should aim to

> establish Western Cape as a strong higher education region...which, through systemic inter-institutional cooperation and academic programme collaboration, will be distinctively responsive to regional, national and international developments.
>
> (p. 3)

It was against that background that the libraries of the respective institutions embarked on the project to build the Cape Library Consortium (CALICO), described alternatively as "a library without walls", and as a "shared library and information system", that would be accessible to some 70,000 users (Leatt and Pretorius, 2004, p. 3).

As a result of mergers in the early 1990s, Deakin University was established as a single university with six campuses spread widely across the state of Victoria. Calvert (2001), in analysing the capability of the institution to embark on online learning, describes its existing operations this way:

> In spite of these distances, Deakin is not a federated university. Its five faculties...operate on multiple campuses, offering the same programs in different locations and off-campus (by distance). Similarly, the administrative and academic support divisions of the university are integrated and provide their services in multiple locations...Deakin has always served off-campus and on-campus students through the same administrative and support infrastructure; there has never been a separate unit responsible for the broad range of off-campus services.
>
> (p. 2)

The difference between the approach to governance of these two institutions and that of the UWI is clear. Whereas the first two place a high value on collaboration and integration, the UWI views its situation as requiring greater control at the individual campus level.

It would be very simplistic to assume that the CHEC and Deakin experiences are without their challenges. At the same time, it is likely that the fact that each is contained within a single political context may be a factor favouring their unified approach. In the case of the UWI, one wonders whether the fact that the three campuses are each located within a separate and distinct sovereign state is not an important factor that consciously or unconsciously may be influencing the strong pull towards autonomy. As indicated earlier, the administration of each campus will no doubt be very aware that even as the respective governments continue to acknowledge the UWI as the regional university, and as an important associate institution of CARICOM, they are also aggressively pursuing their own individual agendas to increase access to higher education within their respective countries. Moreover, the experience with CARICOM has shown that its integration agenda does not appear to be strong enough to override the separatist pull, whenever this appears to be necessary. The question that the University as a whole must therefore ask itself is, whether it has the capacity to maintain its oneness in a political environment that does not appear to have much success doing so. The fortunes of its distance education programme rest to a considerable extent on the answer that it gives to that question.

36.4 QUALITY ASSURANCE AND ACCREDITATION

Another critical area in which the governance structure has impacted the implementation of distance education in the UWI is its virtual exclusion from the processes of quality assurance that are currently in place in the institution. In the academic year 2001–2002, the Quality Assurance Unit (QAU) was set up within the Office of the Board of Undergraduate Studies (OBUS). This initiative came, in part, as a result of the proposal of the Commission on Governance, which states as follows:

> An essential element of the recommendation that first degree matters be devolved to the campus level is that the University establishes a quality control function under the auspices of the new Board of Undergraduate Studies chaired by a Pro-Vice Chancellor.... Even if the Commission were not recommending a transfer of responsibility for first degree work to the campus level, the Commission does not believe that UWI could stand aside from the international concern about monitoring quality in higher education.

36.4.1 The Two Boards

Before proceeding, it is important to examine the roles of two of the three new Boards whose establishment the Commission had recommended. These are the Board of Undergraduate Studies (BUS) and the Board for Non-campus countries and Distance Education (BNCCs&DE).[4]

BUS describes itself as having responsibility for general policy, quality assurance and quality audit and the preservation of the regionality of the University. In terms of general policy, the Board sets guidelines for matters within which the campuses may act and against which they must measure their proposals. Overall, the Board has the ultimate responsibility to set policy guidelines for such matters as matriculation, programmes and examinations.

With regard to the preservation of regionality, the Board draws attention to the 1989 Grande Anse Declaration of the CARICOM Heads of Governments in which the Heads recognized the pivotal role of the UWI in the region. Consequently, BUS views its role of setting policy on the structure of programmes as a way of preserving and strengthening the regional content and orientation of the degree programmes of the University.

Finally, with regard to quality assurance and audit, BUS has the power to monitor, audit and review teaching/learning activities of the campuses that impinge on the undergraduate programmes (UWI website, http://www.uwi.edu/vicechancellery/offices/undergraduatestudies/aboutobus.aspx).

In keeping with its overall mandate to promote, develop and administer the work of the University in the non-campus countries, the BNCCs&DE sets policies for and coordinates the work of three agencies namely the Distance Education Centre, the School of Continuing Studies (SCS) and the Tertiary Level Institutions Unit (TLIU). The SCS is responsible for the University's outreach activity through programmes of continuing education, public education and adult education in all contributing countries. The TLIU has the main responsibility of linking the University's programmes and services to those national tertiary level institutions throughout the region in the interest of the development of an integrated and collaborative tertiary education sector. In summary, the Board facilitates the work of these agencies and executes programmes that underpin their common interests and needs (BNCCs&DE, *Draft Strategic Plan 2002–2007*, October, 2001).

36.4.2 Quality Assurance and UWIDEC

As stated earlier, quality assurance is one of the responsibilities of BUS. Expanding on its stated role of monitoring, auditing and reviewing the teaching/learning activities of the campuses, the Board asserts that the main aims of its Quality Assurance Unit (QAU) are to

- maintain and enhance the quality of the learning experience of the UWI students and to ensure the maintenance of appropriate output standards;
- provide assurance to all of our stakeholders of the continuing high quality and standards of the work of the UWI (http://www.uwi.edu/vicechancellery/offices/undergraduatestudies/aboutobus.aspx).

Though performing a critical teaching/learning function, UWIDEC is virtually excluded from the quality assurance processes of the University. Two possible factors may be cited for this situation.

The first has to do with the initial conception of distance education in the University as being faculty-driven. The understanding was that all the core activities related to teaching and learning at a distance would fall under the purview of the faculty. Thus, these activities would be monitored and audited as part of the quality assurance exercise within the faculty. The faculty-driven model was based on practices being applied in other dual mode institutions. The Deakin model, referred to above, does not even have a separate unit for distance education functions. As indicated then, Deakin has always served both its off-campus and on-campus students through the same administrative and support infrastructure, without having a separate unit responsible for off-campus services (Calvert, 2001). As Calvert noted elsewhere in her work, Deakin was always a dual-mode institution and thus did not face the challenges of transitioning from a single-mode institution.

It is beyond the scope of this chapter to examine this matter further, but the UWI will do well to do a thorough investigation into the challenges it has been experiencing in making this transition. The point to be made here is that over the years, as the faculty-driven model has continued to be ineffective, UWIDEC has taken over the central role of managing the development and delivery of the University's distance programmes, drawing on the relevant faculty and other university services as required. The systems that it has put in place for this purpose certainly need to be subject to quality audit and review.

The second factor has to do with the role and function of the two Boards described above. UWIDEC falls completely under the aegis of the BNCCs&DE. As an agency of the BNCCs&DE, UWIDEC is required to serve three purposes. It can be argued that the activities to be implemented to realize these purposes are all interrelated and probably even integrated. Nonetheless, I would like to suggest that the purposes themselves are distinct and should be disaggregated, given the influence each can have on policy formulation and implementation. One purpose is to satisfy the University's outreach responsibility to the non-campus countries to increase enrolment in the University's programmes from among potential applicants in these countries. The second is to implement the distance education services of the University, and the third is to serve as the mechanism through which the University transforms itself into a dual-mode institution.

It would seem to me that the decision of the Commission on Governance, to subsume the distance education function entirely under the BNCCs&DE was influenced almost exclusively by the first purpose. I would suggest further that essentially, a core responsibility of UWIDEC is to support teaching and learning at a distance. As such, UWIDEC brings an important set of complementary strategies to the overall teaching–learning enterprise of the university that the conventional structures will ignore at their peril. Further, at a time when online technologies are assuming greater importance in providing the environment for teaching and learning, the very notion of the dual-mode institution, with its assumed separation between distance and face-to-face delivery, is itself receding. The emergent paradigm of online teaching and learning is breaking down the barriers and bringing greater convergence in the higher education setting. It is also for this reason that there needs to be a reappraisal of UWIDEC's position as far as Board responsibility is concerned.

36.4.3 Overview of UWIDEC's Operations

Because of the configuration of the Boards, UWIDEC's operations are not subject to the review processes of the University's Quality Assurance Unit. Nonetheless, the following should be acknowledged, as over the years, it has moved to assume the dominant role for managing the development and delivery of the University's distance programmes:

- A well-defined set of procedures underpins the approach to course development. Included in this approach is a mechanism for peer review of materials, as well as measures, albeit informal, for obtaining feedback from tutors and students.
- After a prolonged period of inefficiency, there is now in place a satisfactory system for the distribution of materials across the thirty-two sites in the sixteen countries. That notwithstanding, there is still the problem of customs regulations in a few places that continue to hamper the best intentions to distribute in a timely fashion.
- Every semester, some twenty course coordinators are contracted, based on the recommendation of the faculty, and supported in their role of monitoring the delivery of their respective courses.
- Every semester, UWIDEC organizes for the selection and appointment of approximately 200 tutors, who are provided with a relatively standardized set of procedures for providing learner support. Tutor-training workshops are conducted periodically.
- There is in place a robust wide area network that also allows for Internet connectivity. This network facilitates both web-based and audio-conference communication and provides the infrastructure on which UWIDEC has built aspects of its multi-dimensional delivery system.
- Alongside, the technological network is the administrative network of thirty-two sites, all staffed to manage the student support and delivery functions at the remote locations.

With the shift to blended learning described earlier, the following should also be noted:

- A more clearly articulated set of tutoring tasks have been developed to better equip tutors to support the online learner. These are detailed in the *Guidelines for the UWIDEC tutor*.
- Strategies have been devised to assist students to build the necessary self-confidence and capability to engage in online learning. Many of these strategies are implemented through online orientation courses for incoming students, specifically *Improving Your Study Skills* and *Improving Your Reading Skills*.
- A more detailed set of course coordinator responsibilities and duties have been developed to facilitate more efficient management of online teaching-learning.
- Periodic teleconference sessions are conducted with site-based staff with a view to enhancing capacity at that level to support tutor and student participation in online learning.
- The eLearning environment is subject to continuous review to ensure that its design allows for optimum meaningful participation by tutors and students alike.

While blending learning has brought with it new systems and new processes and procedures, it has also re-focused attention on existing ones that must be strengthened to support the additional demands of the enhanced delivery mode. One important system

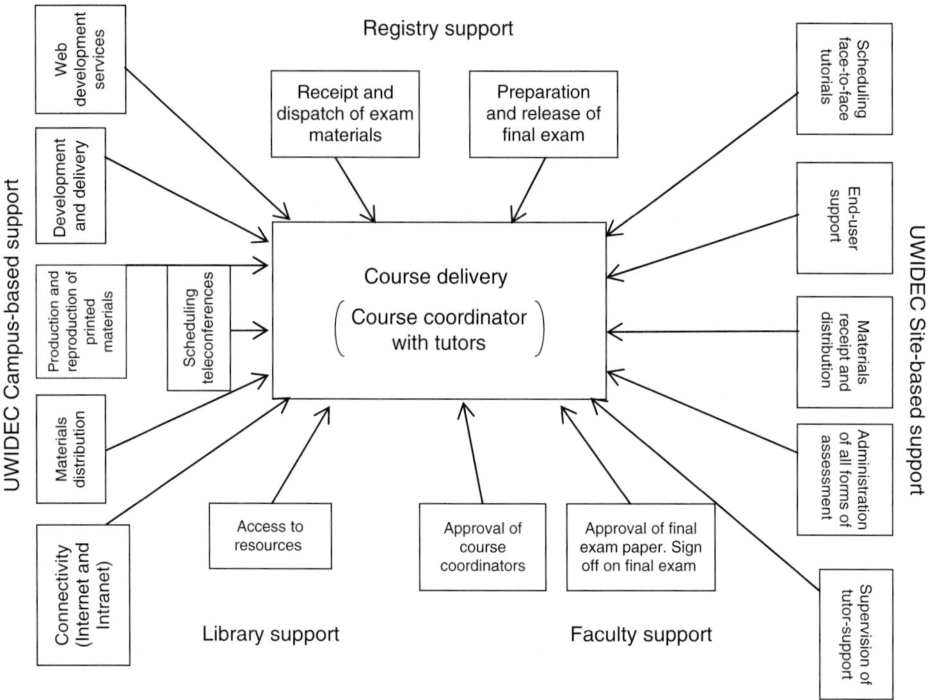

Figure 36.1: System Of Course Delivery

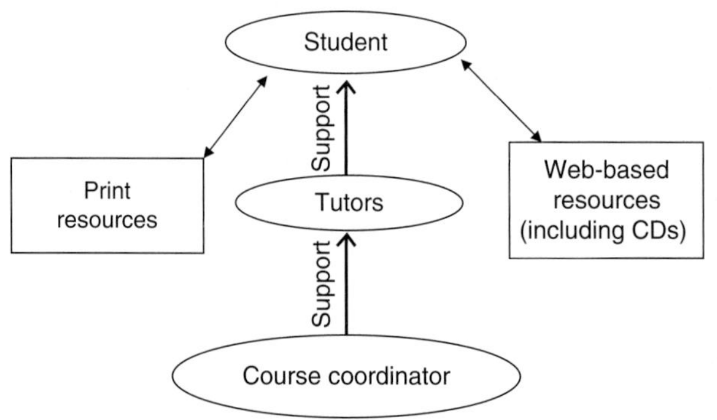

Figure 36.2: Relationship Among Core Elements in Teaching/Learning Process

that is receiving attention is the overall system of course delivery (see Figure 36.1). At the core of that system is the course coordinator–tutor interface, with the course coordinator providing guidance and monitoring tutors as they perform their role of providing learner support (Figure 36.2).

As a complement to the web-based learning management system, UWIDEC has introduced a web-based management information system with a view to bringing greater efficiency to the function of information dissemination among its various stakeholders. This facility may be accessed at http://www.dec.uwi.edu.

Steps are currently being taken to further enhance the capability of this system, expanding its scope to include application, admissions and registration functions for all distance students spread across the thirty-two sites. After much deliberation, UWIDEC considered it necessary to undertake this exercise to bring greater efficiency to this aspect of its student support services in order to eliminate the unevenness and fragmentation that are a constant by-product of its continued efforts to fit itself into the separate campus arrangements. However, even as we are taking this path, we recognize that there are risks involved in developing and using such important systems that are independent of those of the parent institution. So the debate continues, so too the search for the best possible solution for UWIDEC within the framework of a truly integrated University-wide system.

All of the above represent UWIDEC's attempts to define itself and streamline its operations in order to offer the best possible service to its students. However, one cannot ignore the challenges that are ever present as UWIDEC seeks to carry out its functions and to achieve compliance with a common set of agreed procedures and practices. That is not to say that operations have not improved. However, it is also the case that processes and procedures are not always uniformly applied or sometimes not even recognized in all sectors of the organization. The issue of quality is an important one that needs to be addressed.

The underlying reason for this situation may very well be the unit's inability thus far to fashion an appropriate organizational structure that would allow it to govern itself in an efficient manner, but which is also sensitive to the need to maintain a balance between centralization and decentralization. Like the parent institution (and some may say, like CARICOM itself), UWIDEC, with a presence on each of the three campuses, and with thirty-two sites in sixteen countries, has its own Centre-periphery issues to address.

36.4.4 Accreditation

Beyond internal quality assurance, there is the issue of accreditation. At this level, the matter is not primarily a UWIDEC one; rather it is a matter that is being deliberated by the University itself. The dilemma that the UWI faces is how to validate its worth in the public domain. There are two hurdles that the University has to surmount in this regard. First, it needs to move beyond what some may regard as an elitist conception of its worth and embrace a new set of validating conventions that are shared by higher education institutions of various types. The second is to identify the accreditation body. To date, there is no regional accreditation mechanism for Caribbean higher education institutions.

This does not mean that there have not been attempts to move in that direction. Over a decade ago, in 1990, the then vice chancellor of the UWI, Sir Alister McIntyre, led discussions that culminated in the formation of the Association of Caribbean Tertiary Institutions (ACTI). ACTI's objectives are to

- facilitate cooperation, collaboration and articulation among regional TLIs;
- facilitate more effective use of resources in seeking to enhance access, mobility and quality in tertiary education;
- assist in identifying and meeting the ongoing tertiary education needs of the region.

There is also the agreement that ACTI will be the implementation agency for equivalency, articulation and accreditation. To this end, ACTI, in collaboration with the Caribbean Examinations Council (CXC) and the CARICOM Secretariat has already prepared a manual outlining, inter alia, procedures for the conduct of accreditation, equivalency, articulation and quality assurance exercises.

To date however, the proposed regional accreditation mechanism has not yet materialized. At the same time, steps are being taken at national levels to introduce and/or strengthen local efforts. For example, in Trinidad and Tobago, the law to set up the Accreditation Council of Trinidad and Tobago was passed and the Council has since been established. In Jamaica, the University Council of Jamaica has been in existence since 1987. Its vision is "to establish and maintain a quality assurance system which is responsive to national and global changes while enhancing the development of a coherent Jamaican tertiary education system" (London et al., 2004).

In the absence of a clearly defined regional mechanism, with what entity will the UWI negotiate?

The administration on one campus had previously expressed an intention to seek accreditation for the campus from a body outside of the region. It is probably in light of this view that Gayle (2004) raised the question of the University as a whole seeking accreditation through a US agency. He contends,

> Universities everywhere are now functioning in a global market where students have more options than ever before, and where international recognition increasingly helps to create a competitive edge. The UWI should respond to the evolving environment for tertiary education institutions, as well as best practices in internal and external quality review...including an initiative directed at securing university accreditation from an appropriate US commission as a transitional measure.
>
> (p. 47)

It is evident that the matter of accreditation has to be settled sooner rather than later in the interest of both the UWI and its distance education sector.

36.5 CONCLUSION

The 2007–2012 Strategic Plan has recently been finalized and is currently operational. Based on that Plan, the decision was taken to establish the University of the West Indies Open Campus (UWIOC). Thus the objective of a re-structured UWIDEC in the previous Plan has evolved into a decision to set up the UWIOC based on the current Plan. This new campus will be established on a merger of the three units now subsumed under the BNCCs&DE, namely the UWIDEC itself, the School of Continuing Studies and the Tertiary Level Institutions Unit. The BNCCs&DE will cease to exist. The UWI will now comprise four campuses. The University's governance structure is also being reviewed. It is still to be seen if and how this review will impact on the 'quasi-autonomous' operations of the existing campuses and the relationship between these campuses and the UWIOC. In the context of the continuing discussion and debate, I would like to suggest that the University.

- adopts a policy that there will be a core set of common services for the University. In the immediate short term, this will mean establishing a single technological platform for student services for *all* students of the University, to be supported by a single set of related processes and procedures across all campuses. A closer examination of the CALICO experience of the Cape Higher Education Consortium, mentioned earlier, may be helpful in this regard.
- makes whatever adjustments are necessary to ensure that the operations of UWIOC are included in the Quality Assurance exercises of the University, using measures appropriate for a distance/online delivery mode.
- takes the lead (as it did with the formation of ACTI) to bring into being a regional accreditation body. As the University continues to take steps to strengthen its relationships with other regional TLIs, this is probably the most important activity that it should engage in at this time.

NOTES

1. The countries are Anguilla, Antigua and Barbuda, Bahamas, Barbados, Belize, British Virgin Islands, Cayman Islands, Dominica, Grenada, Jamaica, Montserrat, St. Kitts and Nevis, St. Lucia, St. Vincent and the Grenadines, Trinidad and Tobago. For the purpose of distance delivery, the Turks and Caicos Islands has been added. UWIDEC therefore serves sixteen countries.
2. Currently, CARICOM comprises fifteen members, namely Antigua and Barbuda, Bahamas, Barbados, Belize, Dominica, Grenada, Guyana, Haiti, Jamaica, Montserrat, St. Lucia, St. Kitts and Nevis, St. Vincent and the Grenadines, Suriname, Trinidad and Tobago.
3. It should be noted that prior to this project, there were efforts to introduce web-based technologies into the delivery mix (see Kuboni et al., 2002a,b; Kuboni and Martin, 2004). Nonetheless, the scope of the current project, the clear intention to transform the delivery mode, as well as the fact that the project itself was officially mandated, all combine to make this initiative a new beginning in its own right.
4. The third is the Board for Graduate Studies and Research, which is not relevant to this discussion.

REFERENCES

Calvert, J. (2001). Going online at a dual mode university. *International Review of Research in Open and Distance Learning*, **1**(2). (http://www.irrodl.org/index.php/ irrodl/article/view/20/52), accessed December 15, (2005).

CARICOM. (1997). *Communique*. The eighteenth meeting of the Conference of Heads of Government of the Caribbean Community, Montego Bay, Jamaica, 30 June–4 July. Retrieved November 30, 2005 from: (http://www.caricom.org/jsp/pressreleases/pres 56.html)

CARICOM Secretariat. (2001). Revised treaty of Chaguaramas establishing the Caribbean community including the CARICOM single market and economy. Retrieved November 30, 2005 from: http://www.caricom.org/jsp/community/revised_treaty-text. pdf

Carrington, E. (2001). Remarks at opening of the fifth meeting of COHSOD, 3 October 2001. In *A Rationale for Reconfiguring Tertiary Education in Montserrat and the OECS to Meet the Life-Long Learning Challenges of the Twenty-First Century* (G. Howe and D. Cassell, eds) (http://www.uwichill.edu.bb/bnccde/montserrat/conference/papers/howe&cassell.html, accessed November 30, 2005).

Chevanne, B. (2003). Legislation of tertiary education in the Caribbean. IESALC, May, 2003. (http://www.iesalc.unesco.org.ve/programas/legislacion/nacionales/caribe/leg_cb.pdf, accessed November 30, 2005).

Emmanuel, P.A.M. (1993). *Academic Relations of Power: The Case of UWI*. Paper presented for the XVIIIth Annual Conference of the Caribbean Studies Association, May 1993, Jamaica.

Gayle, D.J. (2004). University accreditation in the United States: Implications for the University of the West Indies. *YouWe, Quality Education Forum*. Kingston, Jamaica: Office of the Board of Undergraduate Studies, UWI. No. 10, pp. 33–49.

Harris, T. (2000). Perspectives of the role of the UWI in St. Kitts-Nevis. *YouWe, Quality Assurance Forum*. Kingston, Jamaica: Office of the Board of Undergraduate Studies, UWI, No. 5, pp. 23–27.

Howe, G.D. & Cassell, D. (2003). A rationale for reconfiguring tertiary education in Montserrat and the OECS to meet the life-long learning challenges of the twenty-first century. http://www.cavehill.uwi.edu/bnccde/montserrat/conference/papers/howe&cassell.html, accessed 30 November, 2005.

Kuboni, O., Thurab-Nkhosi, D., and Chen, T. (2002a). *The Expanded Use of IVTs in UWIDEC: An Analysis of Readiness for Online Course Delivery*. Paper presented at the conference on Problems and Prospects of Education in Developing Countries, University of the West Indies, Bridgetown, Barbados.

Kuboni, O., Thurab-Nkhosi, D., and Chen, T. (2002b). *Incorporating Web-Based Learning into a Mixed-Mode Distance Education Delivery Format: Challenges and Possibilities*. Paper presented at the second Pan-Commonwealth Forum on Open learning: open learning: transforming education for development, Durban, South Africa.

Kuboni, O. and Martin, A. (2004). An assessment of support strategies used to facilitate distance students' participation in a web-based learning environment in the University of the West Indies. *Distance Education*, **25**(1), 7–29.

Leatt, J. and Pretorius, T. (2004). *Regional Collaboration and the Transformation of Higher Education in South Africa*. Paper prepared for European Higher Education Society (EAIR) Conference on Knowledge Society Crossroads, Barcelona,

5–8 September 2004. (http://www/chec.ac.za/introduction/Barcelona.pdf, accessed December 15, 2004).

London, E., Commissiong, M., and Gordon, G. (2004). Accreditation of tertiary level programmes in Jamaica: The role of the University Council of Jamaica. *YouWe, Quality Education Forum*, Kingston Jamaica: Office of the Board of Undergraduate Studies, UWI, No. 10, pp. 5–18.

Miller, E. (1999). Educational reform in the Commonwealth Caribbean: An assessment. In *Educational Reform in the Commonwealth Caribbean* (Errol Miller, ed.) Washington DC: INTERAMER/Organisation of American States, p. 8.

Renwick, W., Shale, D. & Rao, C. (1992). *Distance Education at the University of the West Indies*. Vancouver: Commonwealth of Learning.

University of the West Indies. http://www.uwi.edu, accessed December 20, 2005.

University of the West Indies Distance Education Centre. http://www.dec.uwi.edu, accessed December 20, 2005.

University of the West Indies. (1994). *A New Structure: The Regional University in the 1990s and Beyond – Report of the Chancellor's Commission on the Governance of UWI*, July, 1994.

University of the West Indies, Board for Non-Campus Countries and Distance Education. (2001). *Draft Strategic Plan, 2002–2007*, October 2001.

University of the West Indies, *Strategic Plan II 2002–2007, Updated March*, 2003.

University of the West Indies, Academic Programme Committee of UWIDEC (2004). *Blended Learning/Asynchronous Delivery: A UWIDEC Project 2004/5*. UWIDEC APC P.4 2004/2005. Presented by Professor Stewart Marshall, Director, UWIDEC, October, 2004.

Chapter 37

Distance Education in India: Policies and Practices

Suresh Garg, S.R. Jha, and Sanjay Gupta

37.1 INTRODUCTION

India has one of the largest educational systems – from school to university level – in the world as it has to cater to one out of every six human beings on this planet. The enormity of the dimensions can be gauged by the fact that we are home to 50 percent of the illiterates/neo-literates of the world and there are very high drop out rates at the school level. It is estimated that out of every 100 student enrolling in standard one, only eighteen reach standard twelve. Though in absolute terms, even 18 percent is large enough, the backlog of out of school children and requirements of lifelong learning are exerting unprecedented pressure on the education system. To cater to these requirements, India has advocated and practised open and distance learning (ODL) at the school as well as tertiary level, but here we will confine our discussion to the latter. (Open schooling began in 1974 with the establishment of the M.P. Open School in Bhopal, Madhya Pradesh.) As of 2005, our tertiary education system comprised 329 universities, 16,885 colleges, more than ten million students and about 0.45 million teachers (GoI, 2005). By late 2007, the number of universities had increased to 364, colleges to approximately 18,000, and the number of students in higher education to 12 million, which according to the University Grants Commission is about 10 percent of the total number in the eligible age group. While more than 88 percent of students are enrolled in undergraduate programmes, only about 5 and 3.5 percent respectively study engineering and technology, and medicine. About 1.5 percent of students are enrolled in agriculture. Of the total learners in higher education, about 40 percent are women and 12 percent are from disadvantaged and excluded communities. In terms of the number of universities, colleges and enrolments, the system has grown 14-fold, 33-fold and 50-fold, respectively, if we take the year of independence as base. This development is indicative of the transition from an elitist and monopolist system to a democratic and mass system of higher education, where the youth has rising aspirations to contribute to the development of a knowledge society.

In spite of this, we are able to cater to only 7.5 percent of the eligible age group of 17–23 years. This percentage is an order of magnitude less than that of developed countries. The deficit is because of unmet demand; the annual requirement for education grew at 10 percent whereas the provisions for it increased at 5 percent. Even now, 70 percent of our post-matriculation students do not have access to any higher education institution within a reasonable distance from their neighbourhood (Dikshit, 2003a). A simple perusal of the 9th Five Year Plan reveals that in some states, literacy increased by 25–30 percent. The goal of universalisation of elementary education for the 6–14 years age group by 2010 in terms of access, retention, equity and quality through *Sarva Siksha Abhiyan* – Education for All – has generated pressure on the primary education sector and is likely to create further pressure on secondary and higher education in the coming years. By a rough estimate, India would need an additional 3 million primary schools by 2008 and 15 million secondary schools by 2010 (Dikshit, 2003b). We may need to establish a university every week, which puts severe constraints on already limited resources. This obviously is an inadequate response to societal needs in a fast growing economy where aspirations for higher education are set to rise further as an outcome of the escalation in the proportion of the young and educated population keen to be part of the success of an India in transition. The gap between demand and supply threatens to be further compounded by the requirements of continuous professional development, lifelong learning (L-3), and the fast rate of obsolescence of knowledge.

The open learning system has its genesis in the concerns for access and equity, relevance and quality, and affordability and sustainability. Open learning has now been accepted as a philosophy of education and accorded national credibility and acceptability, but its journey of about four decades in India from print-based correspondence education to web-based intelligent-flexible learning has been exciting, though arduous: from being just acceptable, to some parity of esteem, to showing promise, to being seen as a possible solution to universal education. It has evolved in a very complex socio-politico-economic environment as a vast, organised, vibrant and dynamic system endowed with capabilities to bring high-quality education to millions at low costs but with very enriching, even superior, learning experiences using satellite-supported ICT-networks. In India, we have witnessed a silent paradigm shift in the ways and means of imparting education at different levels through distance mode but we are yet to reach the last mile.

37.1.1 The Beginning

In India, the first reference to increasing opportunities for higher education outside the formal system through private study facilitated by radio talks and correspondence courses was made in the 1st Five Year Plan (1951). However, not much was done until 1961, when the issue of large numbers was considered seriously. Distance education, in its initial incarnation as correspondence education, for expanding educational opportunities at the tertiary level, has its origin in the farsighted recommendations of Kothari Committee (1961) appointed by the Central Advisory Board of Education and its implementation by the University of Delhi in 1962 as

> a step designed to expand and equalise educational opportunity, as it aimed at providing additional opportunity for several thousand students who wished to continue their

> education and the persons who had been denied these facilities and were in full-time employment or were for other reasons prevented from availing themselves of facilities at college.
>
> (Government of India, 1963)

However, the offerings were initially restricted to the Bachelor of Arts on a pilot basis. Enthused by the success of the experiment, the Education Commission (1964–1966) headed by Prof. D.S. Kothari recommended that

> the opportunities for part-time education through programmes like evening colleges, and for own-time education through programmes like correspondence courses, should be extended as widely as possible and should also include courses in science and technology. There need be no fear that they will lead to a deterioration of standards, especially if care is taken to maintain personal contact with the students receiving correspondence education by organising academic programmes during vacations and holidays. We suggest that by 1986 at least a third of the total enrolment in higher education could with advantage be provided education through a system of correspondence courses and evening colleges.

The Commission suggested that gifted teachers should be engaged to develop study materials. These recommendations found their way into the Government of India's National Policy on Education (1968) and created a highly conducive climate for the growth of correspondence education (Table 37.1).

The 1968 National Policy on Education also highlighted the concept of continuing education, continuous professional development and lifelong learning for the employed and parity between the correspondence education and face-to-face (F2F) classroom-based educational transactions. Ball (1994) echoed these sentiments about 25 years later in redrawing the maps for learning, noting that

> learning can no longer be the monopoly of the 18–25 age group nor can it be limited to full-time study. An increasing number of students can be expected to be part-time, employed, above 25 and making a late entry into higher education. In addition to these, many who are today's non-participants in education will need to be brought into the fold if we are at all serious about offering all people equal opportunity. Such a diversity of learners will require courses to be organised so that they are flexible, can be studied off-campus and credits received to be portable.

Table 37.1: Institutional Growth of Distance Education

Year	*Open University*	*Correspondence Colleges/Institutes*	*Remarks*
1962–1981	0	34	Correspondence era
1982–1985	2	04	Transition to open era
1986–2000	7	32	Consolidation of open era
2001–2006	4	38	Expansion of ODL system
Total	**13**	**108**	

To make this happen, it was important to liberate learning from the constraints of rigidities or the arbitrariness of mechanisms in vogue and the preferences of a teacher.

The correspondence system of education was well appreciated initially as it opened a new channel but the student support in the system was based mainly on providing print materials, which were devoid of instructional design inputs and principles of educational technology. Moreover, the system inherited rigidities of the conventional system; run of the mill courses, same entry requirements, same duration of programmes and examination. Also, no study whatsoever was made of the learning habits and needs of self-learners who were isolated, with the result that serious concerns began to emerge to improve the quality. As a result, correspondence courses began to lose parity of esteem and by the 1980s were regarded as the "poor cousin" of the conventional system; it came to be considered as the mode for those rejected by the system though about 8 percent of students in higher education were enrolled in it by then. In 1982, the Shah Committee emphasised the need to utilise and coordinate the intellectual and physical infrastructure to create an effective system of distance learning using communication technologies and other mass media options.

The first open university – Andhra Pradesh Open University, now known as Dr B.R. Ambedkar Open University – was established at Hyderabad in 1982. It marked a watershed in the history of development of distance higher education in India; the Ivory towers were thrown open. Its success played a crucial role in the establishment of Indira Gandhi National Open University (IGNOU) in 1985 by an Act of Parliament as a resilient, responsive, innovative and flexible institution with dual responsibilities to democratise higher education and work towards promotion, coordination and regulation of an open system of education in the country. Notwithstanding the belated start, IGNOU has progressed fast and emerged as the leader in the world of ODL; it is the second largest mega university in the world offering 125 programmes with an annual intake of more than 400,000 students in thirty-five countries.

Major developments since the Education Commission (1964–1966) were the New Education Policy (1986) and Programme of Action (1992). The ODL system found considerable space in these documents because of its inherent capabilities to cater to heterogeneous and widely spread learners with multilingual and multicultural backgrounds. The 1986 National Policy on Education recorded that IGNOU, established to democratise education, would support State Open Universities (SOUs).

The expansion of the open-distance learning system throughout the country, after the establishment of IGNOU, has been tremendous. However, the distribution of enrolled students has been markedly uneven; the system is most popular in southern states while eastern states have been slow to accept it. The reach and extent of DE in India continues to experience imbalance on account of gender (30% female), location (25% rural) and people with special needs (<1%), among others. In December 2005, India had thirteen Open Universities and 108 Distance Education Institutes enrolling about 2.8 million students (Table 37.2) and offering 576 academic programmes through 3,962 courses. These institutions have established a network of 122 regional centres, 4,662 study centres and 71,186 tutors/counsellors (Table 37.3). Since the system is learner-centric, it is geared to be more efficient, innovative and futuristic and endowed with immense

Table 37.2: Growth of Enrolment in DE System and Share of DE as Percent of the Total

Year	*Enrolment*	*% share*
1967–1968	8,577	0.62
1970–1971	40,753	2.05
1975–1976	64,210	2.58
1980–1991	166,428	5.70
1985–1986	355,090	9.04
1990–1991	562,814	11.28
1994–1995	803,176	13.14
1999–2000	1.58 million	17.00
2004–2005	2.8 million	25.00

Source: Based on UGC Annual Reports and DEC Database (2005).

capacity and capability to respond to issues and challenges emerging from lifelong learning (L-3) including to accommodate prior learning at different levels. In the initial years of the Tenth Plan (2002–2007), the DE system grew by 27 percent and is expected to enrol 30–40 percent of post-secondary students; IGNOU alone will have a cumulative enrolment of about 2 million by the end of the 10th Plan. Today, India stands out for its farsightedness in having clearly enunciated a policy framework on ODL at the national level. The issues such as recognition of qualifications obtained by the learners, provision for funding, expression of the quality of the learning environment, accreditation of prior learning on the job or by age for those without prior learning were settled long back. In fact, the University Grants Commission (UGC) issued circulars to all universities in 1991 recognising degrees offered by IGNOU and reiterated it for all open universities in 2004.

It may be noted however that the recommendation of the Education Commission concerning enrolling one-third of all students in a non-formal alternative system of higher education by 1986 remains unrealised even after 20 years and despite the CABE recommendation that every state must have an open university, and conventional universities should offer programmes in all areas.

37.1.2 Practices

As such, India's ODL system has emerged from the mainstream conventional system. Moreover, the structures and practices of the ODL system use conventional resources. Therefore, it is only natural to expect that there would be some similarities in the educational provisions and practices – course curriculum, examination, evaluation and certification, etc. (This, however, is in spite of the fact that the requirements of a distance learner are much different from those of a day scholar.) Pragmatic considerations of parity for acceptability of our product also limit the scope of deviations. For instance, the content to be transacted is invariably not much different from that in the conventional system, at least in general education courses, though the mode of transaction of the curriculum in ODL is sought to be different, at least in principle. We seek to substitute for the teacher a multiple-media learning package. Development of such packages and delivery of education have introduced significant changes and we now intend to discuss some of these here with particular reference to the ODL system in India.

Table 37.3: Status of Open Universities (2004–2005)

Indicators	*IGNOU**	*BRAOU*	*VMOU*	*NOU*	*YCMOU*	*MPBOU*	*BAOU*	*KSOU*	*NSOU*	*UPRTOU**	*TNOU**	*PSSOU*	*UOU*	*KKHAOU*	*Total*
Programmes	115*	25	26	22	78	77	43	19	26	50	60	35 proposed	Recently established and yet	Recently established and yet	576
Courses	900	332	255	148	355	611	140	n.a.	n.a.	603	618		To be functional	To be functional	3,962
Students ('000)	366.1	190.2	13	1.8	102	192.2	23.46	19.5	64.0	8.7	17.2				998.16
On Rolls('000)	1,311	190.2	–	8.4	800	199.2	68.8	33.1	225.2	30.9	40.9				290.77
RCs and SRCs	54	23	6	8	10	12	7	1	1	–	–				122
SCs	1,298	149	64	7	1,425	1,070	142	186	142	81	98				4,662
ACs	33,366	5,344	3,015	452	8,949	8,000	979	1,050	2,473	58	7,500				71,186
Audio	1,293	127	–	–	345	19	9	77	207	240	–				2,317
Video	1,792	121	–	–	333	6	16	7	13	–	–				2,288
Staff	1,369	565	303	46	277	240	84	419	16	71	94	12			3,496

*Data for 2005.

IGNOU = Indira Gandhi National Open University; BRAOU = Dr. B. R. Ambedkar Open University; VMOU = Vardhman Mahavir Open University; NOU = Nalanda Open University; YCMOU = Yashwantrao Chavan Maharastra Open University; MPBOU = MP Bhoj Open University; BAOU = Babasaheb Ambedkar Open University; KSOU = Karnataka State Open University; NSOU = Netaji Subhash Open University; UPRTOU = UP Rajarshi Tandon Open University; TNOU = Tamil Nadu Open University; PSSOU = Pt. Sunderlal Sharma Open University; UOU = Uttaranchal Open University; KKHAOU = Dr. K.K. Handique Assam Open University.

When correspondence courses were introduced into India in the early sixties, it was considered enough to get the study material put together. The print constituted the mainstay and unfortunately it had little input of instructional design and curriculum development. Moreover, no capacity building mechanism as envisaged in Education Commission (1964–1966) was put in place and the distance educators tended to land up in an academic wilderness. Also, the lack of an adequate learner support infrastructure meant that there was little concern for the academic requirements of distance learners due to insufficient research data on learner motivation, study skills, learning habits, etc., and inherent rigidities of the conventional system. As a result, serious concerns began to emerge about the quality of education imparted as well as the products. The system was considered a weaker option and this led to the crisis of identity, parity and esteem. However, the emergence of the open era and the reformulation of strategies – synergy with the conventional system in the development of self-instructional materials strongly grounded in principles of instructional design and development, use of multimedia (A/V), and provision of effective learner support – helped remove some of the deficiencies and apprehensions; the system began to take on a national character and receive credibility.

Open universities began to use technology for instruction gradually. However, the system laid greater emphasis on quality by blending technologies for systemic improvement. The methodology initially developed by UKOU for course design, development and delivery was adopted by OUs in India. It appeared simple but was very challenging and time consuming. Even gifted teachers and recognised experts, invited from the length and breadth of the country to pool best practices, had to be trained on the instructional design methodologies. The use of multimedia in curriculum delivery was a completely new experience for almost everyone who shifted from the conventional system. It posed an immense challenge in the initial years and had to be supported by staff development initiatives for capacity building. In IGNOU, all distance teachers were initially given exhaustive training in principles of A/V production – writing academic notes, developing working media scripts, presentation recording, programme preview, etc. Structured training is now imparted through orientation programmes at different levels as required by IGNOU for its own faculty as well as those of other universities for developing print as well as electronic ware (A/V, CD-ROM, online). In the initial years, a few teachers and professionals were sent on secondments with the UKOU and JICA for instructional design and multimedia, respectively. That is, the teacher who was initiated into the system as a trainee, later was recognised as a master trainer who oriented academic counsellors, highlighting finer requirements of the programme/system. Moreover, working with instructional designers and media experts, teachers perfected skills in multitasking and as a presenter, course writer, editor, proofreader, designer and innovator.

The media options used in Indian Open Universities range from print to videoconferencing (Table 37.4). However, the launch of an exclusive educational satellite, EduSat, in 2004 with footprints all over the country, has created a lot of enthusiasm for use of technology in education; five national and twenty-eight state level networks based on VSAT technology are being created. These utilise extended C-band and Ku-band connectivity. An effort is now being made to network these and share their utilisation (Dikshit, 2005).

Table 37.4: Media adoption in Open Universities in India

Open University	*Instructional Support*	*Audio Cassettes*	*Video Cassettes*	*Interactive Radio-Counselling*	*CD-ROM*	*Web-Based*	*Tele Conferencing*	*Video-Conferencing*
IGNOU	Print, multimedia mix online	√	√	√	√	√	√	√
BRAOU	Print, multimedia mix	√	√	√	√		√	√
YCMOU	Print, multimedia mix online	√	√	√		√	√	√
MPBOU	Print, multimedia mix online	√	√	√	√	√	√	√
KSOU	Print, A/V radio	√	√	√			√	√
VMOU	Print, A/V	√	√				√	
BAOU	Print, A/V CD, radio	√	√	√	√			
NSOU	Print, Audio radio	√		√				
UPRTOU	Print, A/V radio	√	√	√				
TNOU	Print, Audio radio	√	√	√				
SLSOU	Print							
UOU	Print							
HSOU	Yet to offer programmes							

We are on the threshold of an ICT-based knowledge revolution because of our enhanced capability to take quality education to the remotest and the most deprived nationwide. It is now possible to decrease the digital divide since EduSat networks have capabilities to support virtual classrooms, video-on-demand, database access, national and state level digital repositories, and on-line operations linking FM radio stations for simultaneous broadcast of programmes. (IGNOU is mandated to create forty FM radio stations all over the country. As of now, twenty-three are in operation and others are at different stages of commissioning. These are being operated in collaboration with SOUs and conventional universities. We also operate six TV channels, which beam curriculum-based general education as well as technical programmes, apart from general empowerment programmes. These efforts are being supported by the Indian Institutes of Technology (IIT), the University Grants Commission (UGC), the National Institute of Open Schooling (NIOS) and the National Council for Educational Research and Training (NCERT), among others.)

IGNOU has created 131 Satellite Interactive Terminals (SITs) across the country for video-conferencing. MPBOU, KSOU, YCMOU, BRAOU and other SOUs are in the process of establishing such centres in collaboration with ISRO. ICT solutions provide opportunities for synchronous as well as asynchronous interactions. In a new and innovative pilot project, 900 primary schools are being connected in the four most backward districts of the country. More than 500 teachers have been trained to prepare software. Once successful, it will be extended to all parts of the country and made available in different languages. It is believed that in this way we would be able to overcome the disadvantages accruing from a lack of availability of trained teachers, the resource crunch and geographical remoteness.

37.2 COURSE DESIGN AND DEVELOPMENT

Development of self-learning packages is the main curricular task of an institution offering education at a distance. The open university system in India has evolved a variety of course development models based on a course-team approach ranging from the coordinator-writer-editor model, the workshop model, the wrap around text model, the text transformation and contract author-editor models (Panda and Garg, 2005). The *course team model* essentially comprises subject experts from within and outside the institution. Media experts (radio and TV producers), educational technologists, graphic designers and the course editor actively participate at different stages with varying levels of responsibilities. The material is essentially written by outside experts, transformed/vetted by internal faculty and edited by an eminent expert. Because of the active involvement of different categories of experts, the quality of materials so produced has been usually very high, and very widely acclaimed. But it takes a long time and is cost-intensive. Many times, interpersonal incompatibilities sour the process and in many cases now, a single teacher is contracted to take up the entire responsibility of course development (*contract author-editor model*).

In the *workshop model*, authors and designers come together to design the course and identify content, format and assignments. Hence, the time taken to produce materials is relatively shorter. This model has been used to develop materials for the Certificate in

Guidance Programme, B.Sc. (Physics) Laboratory Courses and partly edit the M.A. (Education) and M.Ed. programmes (Panda and Garg, 2003).

Since development of high-quality self-instructional materials (SIM) is time consuming and cost-intensive, a few universities, including IGNOU, adopted existing text books with a *wrap around text*. This is particularly useful for low enrolment programmes or those in a fast changing area such as IT. When published literature in a subject is limited and/or the subject is in the nascent stage of development, this *seminar model* turns out to be a better option.

A variety of individuals/agencies/institutions are involved in the use of these models for course development and each model has its own complexities and constraints. In India, these are 108 dual-mode universities and institutions of higher learning, offering programmes ranging from undergraduate programmes to professional programmes in IT, management, electronics, agriculture, etc. As a typical example, we have considered the case of ICE, Madras, as it was one of the first few institutions that offered education through correspondence. It is also one of the largest enrolling institutes.

37.3 ICE, UNIVERSITY OF MADRAS

The Institute of Correspondence Education (ICE), University of Madras was established in 1981; and till the University of Madras Act was amended in 1984, the ICE depended on university faculty for course design and development. In 1984, the state government deputed faculty against substantive posts to ICE. The planning of a programme/course starts with the Advisory Committee, which acts as the Planning Board for the ICE and comprises the VC, Director of ICE, one expert from IGNOU, two members from the university Syndicate, and the senior-most Professor from the ICE. The recommendations are placed in AC for policy decision on the desirability of a programme. The proposal is then put up to the Syndicate, Senate and the Academic Council in that order for final approval. Any proposal for a new programme passes through the Board of Studies (BOS) to go to the Syndicate. Recently, a decision had been taken to constitute a BOS (the fiftieth one) exclusively for ICE by amending the university Act with the approval of the Chancellor. The ICE-BOS shall act for those courses which do not exist in the university. Such approved programmes can simply be adopted by the main university Subject-BOSs for their offer in the mainstream departments.

One lesson, on average, consists of twenty pages, and 20–25 lessons comprise a paper. Only a few lessons are in SIM format, and, except for some selected programs, (MCA, BCA, M.Com. and MA (Eco)), all the papers are offered in both English and Tamil. After approval by the AC, the DE staff or a committee recommended by the DE Staff Committee identifies course lessons/units: sometimes, it is just a one-person committee. Lessons are written by ICE or outside faculty, who edit, proofread and prepare the final course materials, vis-à-vis the DE Staff Committee (Figure 37.1).

The course development processes at the open universities are more rigorous and sophisticated. For the Yashwantrao Chavan Maharashra Open University (YCMOU) and IGNOU, the programme development processes are depicted in Figures 37.2 and 37.3.

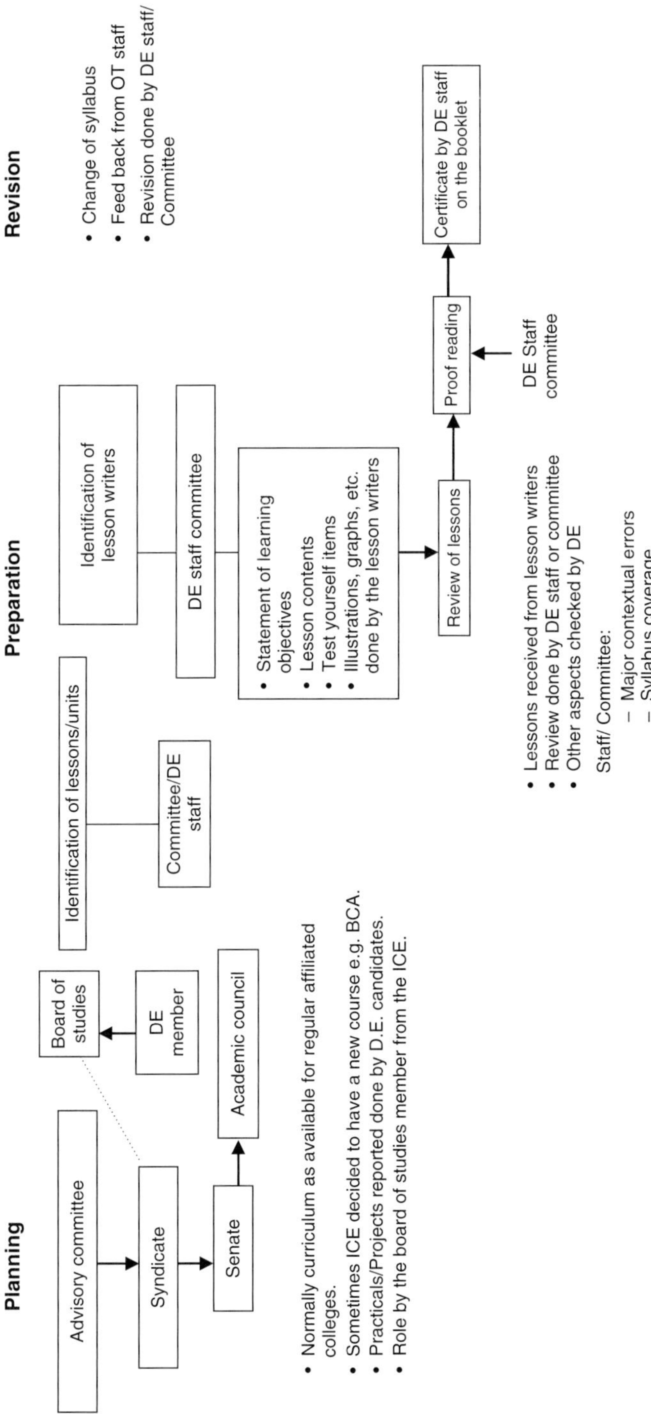

Figure 37.1: Process of Development of Materials: ICE, Chennai (Courtesy: Prof. R. Narasimham)

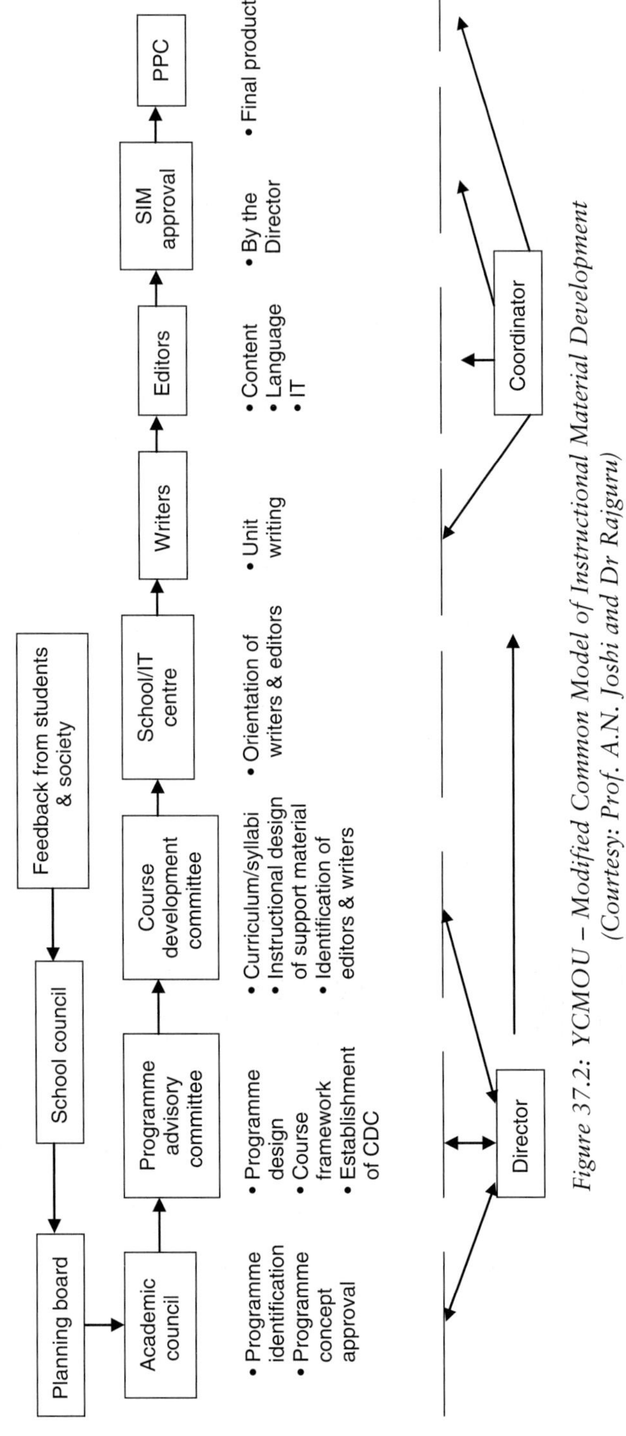

Figure 37.2: YCMOU – *Modified Common Model of Instructional Material Development*
(Courtesy: Prof. A.N. Joshi and Dr Rajguru)

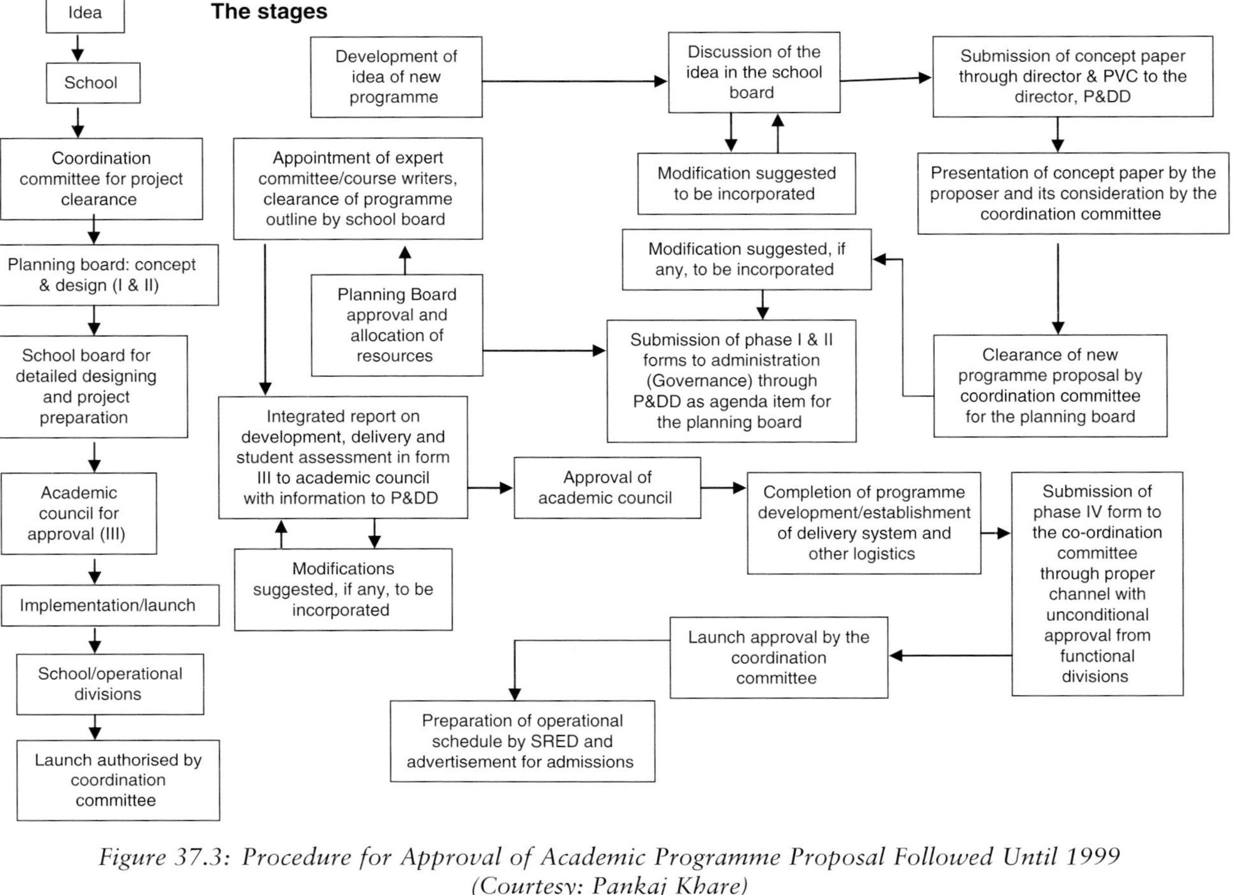

Figure 37.3: Procedure for Approval of Academic Programme Proposal Followed Until 1999 (Courtesy: Pankaj Khare)

At IGNOU, the entire process of programme development and launch has been divided into four stages:

Phase I: Programme Proposal is developed by the faculty and put up for approval by the respective School Board.
Phase II: Programme Concept is approved by the Academic Programme Committee or Planning Board.
Phase III: Programme Design and detailed curriculum is approved by the Academic Council or its Standing Committee after it has been cleared by the School Board.
Phase IV: Programme Launch is approved by the Academic Programme Committee after Services Divisions (Regional Services, Student Registration and Evaluation, Material Production and Distribution and Electronic Media Production Centre) have been alerted for their preparedness. It is mandatory that at this stage, at least 50 percent materials should have been printed and put on the shelf.

The course development process followed at IGNOU is depicted in Figures 37.4.

Following a variety of reformative models, a national pool of high-quality learning materials developed by various institutions has been created in DEC. This enables us to harness a diversity of experience and encourage innovation. Special emphasis has been laid on socially relevant and emerging areas. For example, IGNOU has developed programmes in human rights, women's empowerment, intellectual property rights, community cardiology, nautical sciences, environment and sustainable development, HIV/AIDS, teacher-training, medical waste management, empowering the physically challenged, food management and dietetics, rural artisans, disaster management and public policy. Online programmes are offered in IT, food-safety, library automation, management,

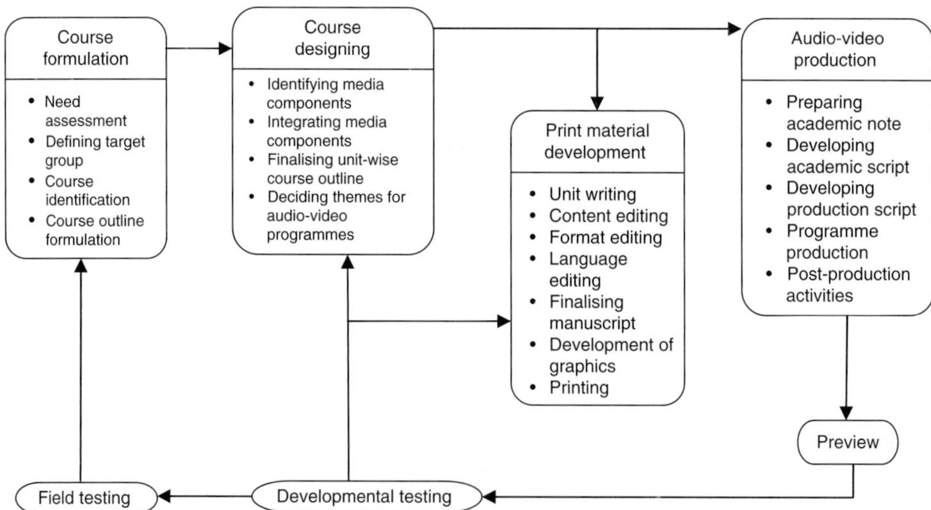

Figure 37.4: Course Development Process at IGNOU

and training of mid-career diplomats, among others. MPBOU has developed expertise in special education programmes, whereas YCMOU has excelled in agriculture and extension. TNOU and BAOU have focused on life coping skills for the excluded. These programmes are now being put in a national repository for tele-education.

37.4 COLLABORATION AND PARTNERSHIP

The open system practices an ethos of sharing and collaboration by pooling intellectual and physical resources. This helps to avoid reinventing the wheel, keeps costs low, replicates best practices and facilitates learner mobility. Other practices include

- forging alliances for seamless convergence with conventional universities/organisations, both national and international; developing/offering joint programmes based on market trends and empirical evidence as well as social relevance to cater to the unreached and special groups;
- nurturing talent and encouraging in-house capacity building with a focus on multi-skilling for multi-tasking;
- working towards self-sustainability by generating funds through sponsored projects, grants-in-aid, fee and consultancy and refraining from developing cost-intensive programmes;
- collaborating with central and state governments in catering to the emerging needs of education and training, such as teacher training in the North-Eastern states and newly created states of Chhattisgarh, Jharkhand and J&K, among others to meet the goal of universalisation of elementary education, and develop a critical mass of experts in various areas.
- exporting education, which has now become a marketable commodity.
- providing forums such as inter-university consortia and national centres of excellence for learning from the experiences of each other; and
- promoting research and innovation in Distance Education.

Acknowledging its strengths, the Government of India identified IGNOU as the nodal agency for the Government of India tele-education programme for fifty-three African Union Countries launched in November 2006, starting from Ethopia.

37.5 QUALITY ASSURANCE

Quality is a defining element of a knowledge society. It is also one of the most important vectors of the Daniel triangle (1996); the other two being access and cost-effectiveness. For us, it is a crucial issue as it is closely related to the credibility of the ODL system, because even now some functionaries and institutions, probably due to their ignorance, continue to believe that it is not possible to provide good learning experiences through open education. However, it is important to observe quality in all processes and operations so that our graduates can relate well to the world of work and compete with their conventional peers on equal terms and without any disadvantage whatsoever. In India, the responsibility of regulation and determination of standard of education delivered through ODL system (open universities, CCIs, IITs, IIMs/Deemed to be Universities) is vested with the Distance Education Council (DEC), an apex authority created by IGNOU under sections 4 and 5(2) of its Act and Statutes. As such, DEC visualises quality as an ongoing process; a search for excellence in design, development and delivery as well as the evaluation and certification processes used. Some of the practices which are leveraged in India to achieve these have been discussed by Garg and Kaushik (2005) in detail.

37.5.1 Design

Since study materials seek to be a substitute for the teacher in content as well as motivation, the curriculum must be strongly grounded in principles of instruction design. Some of the more important aspects are

- Standardisation of a well understood and clearly defined system of credits to be assigned to different components of course work and consequently the credit worth of each course, module and programme in terms of learner workload. This enables establishing equivalence and credit transfer across institutions.
- Constituting fairly broad-based programme expert committees, and pooling the best available expertise in the country.
- Involving stakeholders in the expert committees to incorporate a realistic picture of employer needs in terms of required competencies.
- Conducting a need survey to ensure that the programme is reflective of learner and societal needs in that domain.
- Identifying possible areas of technological intervention, accessing expertise across institutions, and building collaborative dynamic networks.
- Collaborating with educational institutions both national and transnational, and/or industry and professional organisations where a knowledge or experience pool exists, to conceptualise and design innovative, contemporary programmes.
- Institutionalising open and transparent mechanisms to review and approve the programme design by academic bodies to ensure that a less than excellent programme is not put on offer.
- Reviewing the programme through an internal and/ or external system of peer review and learner feedback every 3–5 years to ensure continued relevance.

37.5.2 Development

Developing learning materials by integrating print, A/V and other media solutions is now an advanced science and requires extensive effort and expertise. Development of quality materials involves the following:

- Identification of learning outcomes for each module, programme, course and unit for clarity of vision about what should form part of the content and how it should be presented, ensuring that learning habits, attitudes and contexts of distance learners are not obscured.

- Building the teacher into the text by ensuring interactive content with possibilities of formative self-evaluation and testing; bringing live examples from the immediate environment and context to make the materials more comprehensible and lively. Ensuring that the material is comparable with the best in the world in terms of level of academic excellence, by pooling the best subject experts from across the institutions.
- Participation of stakeholders in the development of content generation to ensure relevance and "fitness for purpose" aspects of quality in ODL materials.
- Orientation of course developers and experts, available in the conventional institutions as well as in professional spheres, in the principles and best practices in self-instructional material development for uniform and acceptable standards.
- Institutional mechanisms for language and content editing by acknowledged experts to bring authenticity, clarity and comprehensibility.
- Developmental testing among intended target segments to give feedback on relevance on content, difficulty levels, achievement of learning outcomes and effectiveness of self-evaluation components.

India is a multi-lingual, multi-cultural nation in a diverse and complex socio-economic milieu. To exploit the lack of availability of opportunities and generate funds, a few institutions were more interested in offering professional programmes such as the B.Ed., MBA and MCA. When it was observed that many of them were not well prepared in terms of intellectual capital, resource materials and/or delivery infrastructure/mechanisms, the DEC encouraged in-house capacity building for material development and supported the initiative financially. It facilitated organisation of regional/institutional workshops with resource persons from institutions with identified strengths. Even the high-quality study materials are being pooled to enhance access, save resources and time, help strengthen the ethos of sharing, promote excellence through collective wisdom and innovation in diversity, and forge strategies and alliances. This has shown positive results and a growing number of institutions are coming forward. It is expected that by the end of 2006, all public institutions offering educational through distance mode would be assessed and as the numbers grow, more ODL institutions shall contribute to the common pool.

37.5.3 Delivery

Quality assurance in the delivery of education includes the relationship between the institution and its students, reliability of schedules and effective student support services. For these, the ODL system utilises a variety of options and media, the key objective being to create as responsive and effective a network of learner support systems as possible. An entire spectrum of possibilities – from a brick and mortar network of study centres, which facilitate face-to-face interaction and serve as the focal point of all academic services, to web and wire-based learner support services – is available to choose from, depending on the requirements of the programmes and the respective learner segments. Similarly, a variety of media options, blended into the optimum media-mix can add value to the teaching–learning transaction. Academic services like counselling, mentoring and assignment evaluation are performed by counsellors or mentors available at the centres or at the serving ends of the web-based service networks. Maintaining parity in standards of quality across nationwide learner support networks is often an issue that defines the differentiation between an excellent ODL service provider and an average one.

Measures to assure quality in the delivery of ODL programmes include but are not limited to:

- Ensuring easy access to routine information on counselling schedules, the conduct of examinations and assignment evaluation.
- Developing benchmarks for all key aspects of service delivery, such as material despatch, counselling sessions, examination schedules, assignment delivery and evaluation, declaration of results, responsiveness to learner queries and complaints, timing and conduct of interactive teleconferencing and radio counselling sessions, and broadcast of A/V programmes and ensuring implementation of these desirable performance standards across the board for all programmes.
- Maintaining a responsive relationship between an institution and its learners by institutionalising systems of receiving formal and informal feedback about all aspects of programme content and delivery.
- Aiming at zero error student support services and complete reliability of all schedules.
- Taking complete responsibility for investing in the quality of part-time academic resources, like counsellors and mentors, through sustained programmes of counsellor orientation, training and re-training so that they can develop an empathy with their learners and pace their study through didactic interaction in the form of tutor comments within stipulated turn around times.
- Institutionalising mechanisms of monitoring the quality and adequacy of learner support services regularly.
- Putting in place an efficient complaint redress mechanism to minimise the possibility of grievances.
- Investing in research to constantly look for higher levels of effectiveness and efficiency in service delivery.

37.5.4 Evaluation

In the world of ODL, evaluation methodology comprises two components: Continuous Assessment (CA) and Term End Examination (TEE). These components essentially emphasise processes and outcomes, respectively. Continuous assessment encourages a learner to engage himself/herself with the learning materials throughout the period of study, understand his/her strengths and weaknesses and work accordingly. The tutor monitors and paces his/her progress through tutor comments and personal contact programmes. The CA can be in the form of tutor-marked and computer-marked assignments, workbooks, projects, class-tests and self-evaluation in answering in-text questions. In India, ODL institutions have adopted a judicious mix of these options depending on the requirements of the subject. Quality assurance in evaluation and certification, requires

- providing feedback on CA through positive tutor comments in the identified turnaround time of six weeks;
- ensuring uniformity in evaluation through model answers and marking schemes so as to minimise subjectivity;
- moving towards CMAs and on-demand examination on the pattern of GRE and GMAT;
- covering the entire course content to encourage deep learning;
- setting thought provoking questions which encourage problem-solving skills, develop ability and self-confidence for tackling unknown situations and discourage plagiarism/copying;
- ensuring proper maintenance of records preferably digitised, timely transmission of performance data, and timely uploading on a website; and
- putting in place a monitoring mechanism for CA as well as TEE components.

In India, there are two schools of thought on the desirability of CA in open education; arguments for and against are based on pedagogical requirements and operational logistics, respectively. In IGNOU, nearly 2.5 million assignment grades and 1 million TEE grades were transmitted, retrieved and uploaded in the year 2005. We are of the considered view that though it is a huge task, it is extremely crucial for the credibility of ODL system; efforts should be made to improve the management systems and new strategies need to be evolved. Based on such pragmatic considerations, IGNOU decided to drop assignments and projects for 6-month certificate programmes. The faculty has been advised to reflect and reconsider the issue for each subject/programme and make appropriate recommendations.

The poor and sub-standard programmes offered by correspondence course institutes in initial years and franchising to non-educational organisations by some of our universities, in recent years, have been some of the soft spots of our ODL system. This necessitated corrective measures to meet the challenges of credibility arising from such practices. Following extensive consultations with the National Assessment and Accreditation Council (NAAC) and highly reputed academics in Distance Education, both past and present, quality indicators and basic norms and guidelines specifying minimum infrastructure (physical as well as human capital) and with a focus on self-evaluation have been issued for new and existing centres of open learning as well as for the delivery mechanism. The Chairpersons of the UGC, AICTE and DEC issued a joint letter to all the Institutions of Higher Education in the country highlighting the Gazette Notification No. 44, F. No. 18–15/93-TD, V/TS.IV dated April 8, 1995 issued by MHRD, Govt. of India, which made it mandatory for every ODL institution, created by an Act of the Indian Parliament or a State Legislature, to seek recognition of their distance education programmes through validation of their certificates. The process of assessment of learner support capabilities through on the spot visits has now been established and accepted. On the basis of such reports, the Distance Education Council has advised State Open Universities to avoid "controlled franchising" in the offering of professional programmes in collaboration with private providers. Instructions have also been issued that failures in compliance will attract penalties, including withdrawal of financial support and de-recognition of programmes. In fact, recognition of the programmes offered by a few Deemed to be Universities and State Universities has been withdrawn.

37.6 PROMOTION OF AN ODL SYSTEM

Since correspondence courses were initially established in conventional universities, the responsibility for its promotion and support was vested in the UGC. However, it contented itself with laying down norms for an academic framework and funding; UGC did not evolve any mechanism to determine and maintain the standards of Distance Education programmes until IGNOU was established. In 1985, the mandate for promotion, coordination and regulation of an ODL system was transferred to IGNOU but UGC continued funding till 1996.

Since 1997, State Open Universities and Directorates of Distance Education/CCIs in the conventional universities are being funded by DEC. The size of the grant sanctioned to the State Open Universities has risen from about IRs 29 million in 1997 to IRs 156 million in this financial year, 2005–2006. Likewise, the amount sanctioned to the CCIs increased from IRs 10 million to IRs 49 million over the same period. This has enabled the ODL institutions to strengthen their infrastructure, augment student support services, and conduct staff development and training programmes. The grants have also helped in the networking of institutions leading to overall improvement in the quality of distance education. Special on the spot committees closely monitor the utilisation of the annual grant released to the ODL institutions.

One important aspect of the mandate of the Distance Education Council is to identify, from time to time, priority areas in which distance education programmes need to be developed and supported. It has recently identified professional programmes in areas such as management, computer science and information technology, teacher education, and library science and has come out with norms and standards for the development and launch of these programmes through distance mode in a way that would ensure quality of education. The development of norms and standards in other areas is also being contemplated. These norms include guidance on aspects such as curriculum design, eligibility criteria, selection procedures, duration, student intake, learning resources, delivery mechanisms, student evaluation and library services. In addition, the guidelines give concrete suggestions on monitoring and performance review, stressing the importance of evolving mechanisms of quality assurance in various phases of a given programme.

For foreign universities interested in running a Distance Education programme in India (independently or collaboratively with Indian higher education institutions), the regulations remain to be finalised in the light of the policy of the Government of India. It is "mandatory for all institutions to seek prior approval of the Distance Education Council for existing and new programmes and accreditation by the Board of ongoing programmes offered through Distance Education mode" (DEC, 2005).

In 2006, the Prime Minister set up National Knowledge Commission with the mandate to recommend ways to prepare the Indian nation to face the challenges of emerging knowledge society.

In January 2007, the Commission recommended five-fold increase in the number of universities (to 1,500) to attain a gross enrolment ratio of 15–20 percent by 2015. It is estimated that by the end of the 11th Five Year Plan (2007–2012), India will have to cater to a three-fold increase in learner population in higher education and the ODL system is being mandated to increase its share to about 40 percent. This additional load has put the system in a state of flux and it is looking for newer strategies. The Task Group on Distance Education constituted by the National Knowledge Commission has recommended a developmental modal of education, which is learner-centric with sufficient learner autonomy, trans-modal which facilitates convergence of all systems and integration of all methodologies, dynamic and distributed based on ICTs and value oriented, where the teacher–learner interface creates a new paradigm for generation of new knowledge. To help achieve these targets, the Government of India has raised the allocation to education by 50 percent for the 11th Plan Period.

37.7 CONCLUSION

India has over 40 years of experience in correspondence education and 20 years in ODL. It has witnessed a rapid rate of growth but there is a growing and disturbing trend on the part of the conventional and deemed to be universities to start Distance Education programmes to augment their finances and help support the conventional system. However, the Distance Education Council has now started acting firmly; encouraging performers and discouraging sub-standard systems. The decision of the Government of India to create the Distance Education Council as an independent authority by an Act of Parliament to monitor all forms of distance education, with due regard to the authority of other apex authorities, should empower it further to enable the system to emerge as more vibrant, innovative, learner-centric and dynamic and improve access to high-quality education at affordable costs.

Recently, Distance Education Council has decided to relax the condition of jurisdiction and changed the policy of recognition from programme to institution. The onus of ensuring quality is now on the academic bodies of the institution concerned rather than DEC. This shift is based on the argument that only those institutions shall survive which offer quality education. These initiatives are bound to have far-reaching implications and decide the future of Open and Distance Learning in the country.

REFERENCES

Ball, C. (1994). Lifelong learning in a learning society. In *Economics of Distance Education* (G. Dhanarajan et al. eds) OLIHK Press.

Central Advisory Board of Education (1961). 28th Meeting (January 1961), *New Delhi: Ministry of Education and Social Welfare*, Govt. of India.

Daniel, J. (1996). *Mega-Universities and Knowledge Media*. London, UK: Kogan Page.

DEC (2005). Database of Distance Education Council.

Dikshit, H.P. (2003a). Growth of open and flexible learning in India: Emerging challenges and prospects. *Indian Journal of Open Learning*, **12**, 7–15.

Dikshit, H.P. (2003b). Developing open and distance education into a science, Muktaye. *Journal of Netaji Subhash Open University*, **1**, 1–6.

Dikshit, H.P. (2005). Knowledge revolution through satellite based education In *Four Decades of Distance Education in India: Reflections on Policy and Practice* (Suresh Garg et al., eds) Viva Books: New Delhi, p. 244–262.

Garg, S. and Kaushik, M. (2005). Quality assurance in distance education: DEC initiatives In *Four Decades of Distance Education in India: Reflections on Policy and Practice* (Suresh Garg et al., eds) New Delhi: Viva Books, pp. 370–379.

Govt. of India (1963). Report of the Committee on Correspondence Courses, New Delhi: Ministry of Education and Social Welfare, Govt. of India.

Govt. of India (2005). Annual Report 2004–2005, New Delhi: Ministry of Human Resource Development, Govt. of India.

Panda, S. and Garg, S. (2003). Revisiting distance education course development: workshop method for development of science lab courses. *Staff and Educational Development International*, 7(2), 153–163.

Panda, S. and Garg, S. (2005). Models of Course Design and Development. In *Four Decades of Distance Education in India: Reflections on Policy and Practice* (S. Garg et al. eds) Viva Books: New Delhi, pp. 107–126.

Chapter 38

FRAMING AND TAMING POLICY

Margaret Haughey

Lentell in her concluding chapter in *Policy for Open and Distance Learning* (Lentell, 2004) highlights the overall lack of policy development in open and distance learning (ODL). The chapters in this section then provide an important contribution to help overcome this absence in the literature of ODL.

Lentell suggests several reasons for our lack of policies on ODL, such as a lack of clarity around the concepts that make up ODL or a lack of contextual or operational information such as on its costs and effectiveness. These, she proposes, may lead governments to hesitate in developing a national policy. What do we mean by policy? Edwards et al. (2002) see policy as statements being "put in place to address certain issues and achieve certain goals" (p. 2). Lentell has a similar definition, seeing it as an implicit or explicit course of action that is to be followed in support of some specific goal or outcome. However, these definitions, while trying to bring clarity to the difficult area of policy itself, may give it a concreteness and purpose that is ultimately unreal. In an overcrowded policy arena, the purpose of providing a structure for the provision of education can be waylaid by the more seductive siren of economic strategies and it is the issue of the provision of education that lies at the heart of ODL. Policy reflects the "relationship between the state, employers, civil society, families and individuals" (Edwards et al., 2002, p. 5). How that relationship is understood, influenced and enacted in relation to education, its purpose and its stated and unstated outcomes, gives rise to the different national forms of ODL policy.

Policy can be examined from a number of perspectives: the focus can be on policy development, how the actual policy is created and what policy discourses inform it; on policy purpose, what is intended by the policy; on policy assumptions, the ideals and theories on which the policy is based; on policy implementation and all the issues that have to be addressed in trying to align multiple policy desires with realities; or on policy evaluation, an exploration of the actual outcomes and effects of the policy. Not only are there multiple aspects of policy analysis, but there are multiple approaches used in addressing these questions. As Edwards et al. (2002) conclude, "policy work is multiple, contested and complex. There is no linearity in its assumptions, intentions or effects" (p. 5).

Policy creation occurs at the nation or state and at the level of institutions. Often national policies are more concerned with direction while institutions are more focused on implementation. Whether the focus is direction or implementation, policy makers require knowledge of the immediate context and a solid understanding of all the issues to be addressed. How they approach these questions and their response to the issues inform a policy response that will shape the eventual public policy. Many times however policy makers have some sense of the issue or policy problem but inadequate information to shape the proposed process. Mitroff and Emshoff (1979) believed that the major reason why policy so seldom works as intended is that there is inadequate attention to this early stage of policy development. They proposed that the problem with "ill-structured" messy policy issues was that their parts were so interdependent as to affect all aspects of an organization. In response, they stressed the importance of assumption surfacing and assumption challenging as critical methodologies in coming to a policy. The development of a national ODL policy may well fit into the category of an "ill-structured" policy issue since many of the factors on which good planning depends are not under the purview of the educational policy makers, for example, the adequacy and control of national telecommunications or postal services, the quality and quantity of housing for students who have to travel to examination centers, the aspects of the culture which accord decisions about education to the male head of the family and the gap between likely fees and average salaries.

In the field of ODL, Dodds and Youngman (1994) have already identified the factors that national policy makers have to consider. They are as follows:

- The rationale for the development of distance education and its priority in relation to other options.
- The perceived needs for distance education and the appropriate level of provision, namely secondary, tertiary and adult basic education.
- The direct costs and opportunity costs of investing in distance education provision and the potential cost–benefits.
- The appropriate institutional arrangements and the capacity for developing and maintaining an effective distance education system in terms of the recurrent resources, management capability, trained staff, materials production, student support and (information) communications infrastructure.
- The status of distance education and the acceptability of its qualifications within the national system of educational credentials.
- The possibilities for international cooperation in developing and sustaining a distance education system (p. 63).

While acknowledging the difficult questions in ODL policy development, it may be that not only lack of knowledge but also the influence of the present neo-liberal orientation which attempts to minimize overt government involvement work together to reduce the likelihood that governments would consider developing a structural rather than a strategic response to ODL. While a structural response would commit governments to a vision of ODL provision in a systematic way as an aspect of social policy, a strategic response would seem to be the more likely response today. With the impact of globalization, free markets, digitization and the integration of our economies, governments now focus more on strategic initiatives that are targeted and specific in shaping and supporting the realization of certain economic conditions. Griffin (2002) points out that, at least in post-welfare states, governments continue to develop policies for schooling because it is compulsory and every aspect can be regulated. They are less likely to formulate policies for adult learning because learning is not a topic for public policy and cannot be regulated in the way education is and partly because

> the political choice is *not to do so*. The strategy of governments is to create the conditions in which people, families, communities and organizations are most *likely* to learn for themselves, thus obviating the need for educational policy in the traditional sense.
>
> (p. 133)

Another interesting development related to ODL policy is the increasingly important role of international organizations. UNESCO, the World Bank, the Commonwealth of Learning and various European organizations have all played a role in attempting to keep ODL firmly on the policy agenda by developing policies themselves. Their models of learning provision suggest that these organizations see the provision of educational opportunity as their core value. They also, as Lentell (2004) points out, are able to not only share experiences but also address those issues best dealt with internationally: "Perhaps most important, the issues of credit recognition and transfer and the concerns for consumer protection ... demand a global response" (p. 257).

While the literature on national policies for distance education is somewhat lacking, this is less the case at the institutional level. Here several authors have provided lists of policy issues which an organization needs to address. Most often, the issues are raised by conventional colleges or universities that want or need to adopt distance education provision or who have adopted a technology infrastructure and now find that there are many other policy issues which need resolution. As Gellman-Danley and Fetzner (1998) conclude, while the technology often arrives ahead of the policy and planning phases, "advanced policy deliberation and development is essential to the success of distance learning programs and their students" (p. 1). They proposed a set of seven policy development issues (p. 2) which arose from their work on distance education policy with the State Education of New York (SUNY) (Table 38.1).

It is interesting to compare this list with that developed by Jegede and Okebukola (2002) and expanded on by Freeman (2002), both discussed by Lentell (2004). Jedgede

Table 38.1: Seven Policy Development Issues

Policy Development Area	***Key Issues***
Academic	Academic calendar, course integrity, transferability, transcripts, evaluation process, admission standards, curriculum approval process, accreditation
Fiscal	Tuition rate, technology fee, FTE's, consortia contracts, state fiscal regulations
Geographic	Service area regional limitations, local vs out-of-state tuition, consortia agreements
Governance	Single vs multiple board oversight, staffing, existing structure vs shadow colleges or enclaves
Labor management	Compensation and workload, development incentives, intellectual property, faculty training, congruence with existing union contracts
Legal	Fair use, copyright, faculty, student and institutional liability
Student support services	Advisement, counseling, library access, materials delivery, student training, test proctoring

Adapted from Gellman-Danley and Fetzner (1998, p. 2).

and Okebukola developed their list based on their experience in developing the Open University of Nigeria and it contains the following ten critical issues:

- Identifying the target population and needs
- Choosing the type of system
- Choosing the appropriate technology of delivery
- Business planning and costing ODL systems
- Materials – developing or acquiring
- Tutoring and supporting students
- Recruiting and enrolling students
- Assessing students
- Managing and administering the ODL system
- Monitoring, evaluating and quality assurance.

On analyzing this list, some issues relate to a general direction for ODL, while others focus on implementation. Some are more likely to engage policy makers who are examining the general issue of ODL provision, while others are more focused at the institutional level. Neither list is complete but together they give a sense of the wide range of issues that need to be addressed in a coherent and comprehensive way if the ODL system is to function as a whole. What is missing from both lists is context and in particular the specific political and ideological contexts in which the policies are being formed. Lentell (2004) mentioned lack of information about costs and effectiveness. Providing a financial base for an ODL policy is crucial to its sustained success. The formation of an ODL policy without reliable and sustainable strategies for continued investment means that the policy implementers have to rely on irregular funding from donor agencies and similar bodies. While the initial achievement of the policy proves to be a major political coup for the government, the lack of a strong financial base suggests that the policy makers did not think beyond the short-term advantages to ensure its longer-term provision.

A policy on ODL may be embedded in larger international exchanges. This is the case with the University of the West Indies' commitment to distance education. As Kuboni notes, CARICOM is essentially a free trade agreement among sixteen independent states that make up the Caribbean community. The document that confirms this relationship, the Treaty of Chaguaramas, includes reference not only to education but also to the University of the West Indies, which is itself a regional institution with campuses in three countries. This, Kaboni explains, requires the institution to help CARICOM meet its stated goals, a point reiterated in a Communiqué signed in 1997 which set the target of a 15 percent increase in post-secondary enrolment by 2005. Throughout the discussions for the original community common market and in the discussions surrounding the Communiqué, it is clear that economic advantage was a major priority for the various state leaders and their ministers. Lifelong learning was important but so was the development of individual adaptiveness, suggesting that some of the negotiators saw the strategic value of further education as a personal value while others saw it as contributing to a better educated workforce.

In planning for greater access to post-secondary education, especially for people who could not attend one of the three campuses, the possibilities of distance education came to the fore. The university had been offering ODL for some time mainly by audio-conferencing but was not satisfied with the low level of student success. The combination of the advent of web-based technologies, the needs of its own academic community and its responsibilities to CARICOM coincided in a proposal which could enhance its own DE programs and give clearer budgetary control and accountability to UWIDEC, the university's distance education center. The proposal was to develop a combination of asynchronous independent study and synchronous audio-conferencing or face-to-face classroom activities for each course and to gradually shift the synchronous activities to a web-based environment which provided for greater flexibility in place and time. On analyzing the effectiveness of this plan, Kaboni points out that it is not the ODL design itself which is the issue, but the governance and organizational structure of the institution.

The "quasi-autonomous" nature of the campuses, situated as they are in different countries, and each anxious to provide full-service facilities for its citizens, is reflected in the decision-making structure with regard to first degrees. Functionally, distance education organizations have major costs in their course development and student support infrastructures. To be effective and cost-efficient, they need to be able to scale up and amortize costs over a large number of students. This is what gives the impression of distance education as being a cheaper alternative, but cost efficiencies are only possible when the organization is able to sufficiently increase numbers since so much of the service cost is at the front end. This scalability was in direct conflict with the aspirations of the individual campuses. Part of the confusion rests on the conflation of the UWI's own aspirations and its commitment to provide access to tertiary education for the sixteen partner states.

Another aspect of this case is the impact of web-based technologies on the face-to-face activities at the various campuses. As the individual campuses began to develop the capacity to include web materials within classrooms, they were also beginning to develop blended and possibly distance education option outside those organized and coordinated by UWIDEC. This is a challenge faced by many distance education units which are part of residential organizations. It raises questions about the centralization of these program decisions, especially when the semi-autonomous campuses see themselves as national institutions, and it calls for a redistribution of control without necessarily the redistribution of accountability. There is much to be learned from the development and organization of consortia and the governance changes that have to be made when the original impetus for cooperation shifts and dissipates as expertise is increasingly shared among the members. Kaboni's paper is rich in policy issues and I have only highlighted some of them here.

The other two chapters in this subset focus on specific countries, Brazil and India, and again each provides excellent examples of how context shapes practice in ODL. Litto begins his chapter with a description of the historical and cultural background which provides both context and orientation for his subsequent description of Brazil's latest policy on ODL. He describes how the original colonization of Brazil has left a legacy of centralization and privilege that is still present. Fundamentally, it is one which is still suspicious of education and where the government views its role as "governing" by directly approving, regulating and essentially doing the work of education rather than through governance, or putting in place the mechanisms which decide who will do what and under what circumstances. Governance results in a much greater emphasis on accountability without the same sense of apparent, direct control. This is part of what I referred to earlier as the move from implementing structure to proposing strategic initiatives. However, this is not the case in Brazil, which still retains its emphasis on the development of large numbers of laws and regulations which seek to control every aspect of public life. For Litto, another complication retained from Brazil's previous colonial period is the use of the exceptional circumstance so that even though the lacework of rules might seem to provide a system that its citizens could trust, the alternative network of favors raises questions about the system's dependability. In addition, the process of policy making is focused on the bureaucracy where career administrators can ensure the retention of particular perspectives over the lives of many different political perspectives from governing parties. In such a context, it is not surprising that political dialogues and policy discussions around the meaning and interpretation of particular laws are of immense importance.

For ODL at the tertiary level, how it is understood is also in relation to government politicians' and bureaucrats' beliefs about traditional university education. Where the curriculum is highly regulated, the set books approved and examinations established for every course, acceptance of alternative forms of learning that give more autonomy to the individual to choose when and where and how to study is a major challenge. Within such a context, the meanings of ODL take on particular hues. Despite the success of an alternative, secondary school, distance education program that engages over half a million learners, it is still acceptable to suggest that ODL is not really as good as traditional learning and these beliefs can find their way into national policies. Part of this, Romiszowski (n.d.) contends, is due to a lack of experience with distance learning among both the bureaucrats and the professionals. The issue then is still one concerning the credibility of distance education. It is also, he suggests, an issue about how distance education is conceptualized. Is it a separate alternative system for those outside the traditional system, or is it an aspect of the system that needs to be included as an alternative in response to a changing population? If it is seen as the former, then one expects that the established system will seek to marginalize it and restrain its resource allocation. If it is viewed as the latter, then it is likely that a government would adopt a governance model of regulation and accountability and that ODL institutions would have to cope with the issues of dual model provision.

Examining a national policy then has included not only reviewing aspects of its historical past and its cultural present in relation to the way it governs but also how these are evident in the present system of education. For Brazil, Litto suggests that the recent law may be a harbinger of change although he is concerned that the rhetoric is not matched by any sustained fiscal support. There are many issues which still remain to be clarified and resolved, particularly difficult when there are likely to be many competing agendas from various educational sectors. While he sees hope in the platform of ideas for ODL that has been visualized, his own extensive experience reminds him that this step is still more like "a shadow of conventional learning" and that the Ministry is still controlling the system. It will take time for institutions and learners themselves to be able to propose policies that reflect contemporary thinking in ODL and demonstrate that the system is not only rigorous and demanding but equally creative in responding to the needs of Brazil's learners.

Litto's chapter reminds us to spend time examining how policy making and governance in a state reflect in its cultural practices and assumptions about its citizens and its view of the role of education in civil society. In contrast, Garg and his colleagues, Jha and Gupta, have provided an overview of how the Indian state has moved to develop a comprehensive system of distance education at primary, secondary and tertiary levels in less than 40 years. Like Brazil, India is made up of a series of individual states that have autonomy over certain aspects but are also expected to follow the national government's decrees. The national government has overall control over educational funding and directs the focus of educational development through its national 5-year plans.

In 1964, the Indian government set up the Kothari Commission to provide a comprehensive review of India's educational system. It recommended significant changes to the entire educational system. It also published the first 20-year National Educational Scheme. Its recommendations included changes in the methods of education, training needs and standards for teachers, equity and access in education for all, providing suitable environments for higher education, giving autonomy to universities, the introduction of agricultural education and adult education and the need for professional, technical and engineering colleges. These recommendations for change in the educational system got an excellent response.

The first attempt to introduce distance education in India had been in 1962 when the University of Delhi established a Directorate of Correspondence Courses on an experimental basis. The 1970s saw the expansion of correspondence education to over thirty universities. The government set up a National Open School in Delhi in 1979 to offer bridging courses for out-of-school learners to enable them to complete their secondary education. Gradually, the first two open universities, Dr B.R. Ambedkar Open University (BRAOU) in Andhra Pradesh state in 1982 and Indira Gandhi National Open University (IGNOU) in 1985, were established. In 1986, the government announced its National Policy of Education that promoted "Education for All" and suggested implementing distance education throughout the nation. As the national university, IGNOU's mandate was to democratize education through provision of ODL and to promote, coordinate and regulate a national system. Two decades later, India has at least thirteen state-based open universities, each offering its own courses, many developed independently but some based on IGNOU or another open university's materials, some in English and Hindi and many in their own state languages. Together with the distance education institutes, the ODL units associated with conventional universities, the open universities serve at least 2.8 million students.

It is useful to review the policy processes through which India has been able to achieve this remarkable success. Initially, the Ministry of Education worked through the University Grants Commission, which had been set up in 1954 essentially to monitor the universities. This included responsibility for the quality of the correspondence programs offered by the conventional universities. Then, in 1985, the coordination and regulation of ODL became the responsibility of the newly formed IGNOU. The body that provides for oversight of ODL is the Distance Education Council (DEC), which IGNOU coordinates. Over the years, DEC has not only become the funding body for all distance education institutions (1997) but also became the accrediting body for the quality of ODL programs (1995). As such, DEC and IGNOU have become the guardians of quality assurance for the national government. The DEC has three other tasks. First is the identification of new program areas, second the development of norms, standards and guidelines for a wide variety of aspects of distance education and third the adjudication of applications from foreign universities who want to offer ODL programs in India.

As Litto noted, "each policy has its politics" and that is equally the case in India. Culturally, India has both class and caste issues. It has over eighteen official languages and despite the growth in ODL, a high percentage of its people are barely literate resulting in wide disparities between the rich and the poor. The combination of state governments, which provide some, but never sufficient amounts of the national funding for their open universities, with their own political parties and competing agendas, and the national government with its parties and national 5-year plans, mean that policies may or may not be more than rhetoric and open university officials have to tread a delicate path in seeking for sustaining support for their programs. At the same time, the rise of IGNOU as the flagship university has been embedded in its control of the DEC. There would seem to be an increasing likelihood of a challenge, not unlike what occurred among the "quasi-autonomous" campuses of UWI. Garg and his colleagues note that not only is the DEC doing spot checks to ensure that funding is being properly allocated and learner support capabilities are actually present, and increasingly setting out standards for new programs which will have to be followed, but also that DEC has closed the door on state universities working with private providers. Contravention of this latter mandate can result in withdrawal of financial support, and de-accreditation of programs. This would seem to suggest that the balance between central control and state autonomy may prove to be a delicate one. On one hand, IGNOU has a strong national mandate and yet the requirement that it nurture the development and support of its competitors, the state-based universities, would seem to require careful steering to avoid a collision course. However, the numbers of people seeking further education who are as yet unserved may enable this structure to survive for quite some time to come.

Policies arise within political contexts that are complex and disputed. These contexts include both the goals that policy is supposed to address and the reactions of those influential stakeholders who are trying to shape the formation of the policy. These stakeholders may be individual bureaucrats or networks of people who hold similar perspectives in relation to the policy goal and processes. Likely they include government officials, party influentials and informed experts among others. Yet they are not alone. There may well be several competing groups involved in the policy debate, and in the end, the likelihood of the policy's acceptance by the electorate may torque the final version quite severely or even result in its termination. It may be a timing issue, dependent on what else is happening in government or where in the mandate of the government it occurs. Much can influence policy making besides the beliefs of the participants. The authors of the three chapters have provided ample evidence of the messy and contested nature of policies whether in their creation or their implementation. However, what is equally evident is that ODL policy making not only requires the research that provides information on aspects such as costs and effectiveness but also requires that those who know and understand the possibilities of ODL have to take a part in influencing the outcome. From Kaboni who asks that UWI reexamine its governance and organizational structures that she believes limit the potential of ODL for CARICOM, to Litto who worked to help shape opinions about the 2005 Law, to Garg and his associates who are monitoring the role of IGNOU among its sister institutions, involvement is key. Only by participating in the policy process can our beliefs and vision for ODL be heard.

REFERENCES

Dodds, T. and Youngman, F. (1994). Distance education in Botswana: Progress and prospects. *Journal of Distance Education*, **9**(1), 61–80.

Edwards, R., Miller, N., Small, N., and Tait, A. (2002). Introduction: making policy work in lifelong learning. In *Supporting Lifelong Learning, Vol. 3: Making Policy Work* (R. Edwards, N. Miller, N. Small and A. Tait, eds.) London: Routledge Falmer & Open University Press, pp. 1–15.

Freeman, R. (2002), *Planning and Implementing Open and Distance Learning System: A Handbook for Decision Makers*. Vancouver, BC: Commonwealth of Learning.

Gellman-Danley, B. and Fetzner, M.J. (1998). Asking the really tough questions: Policy issues for distance learning. *Online Journal of Distance Education Administration*, **1**(1), Spring. Retrieved march 30, 2007, from: http://www.westga.edu/%7Edistance/ojdla/spring11/danley11.html

Griffin, C. (2002). Lifelong learning and welfare reform. In *Supporting Lifelong Learning. Vol. 3. Making Policy Work* (R. Edwards, N. Miller, N. Small, and A. Tait, eds.) London: Routledge Falmer & Open University Press, pp. 123–149.

Jegede, O. and Okebukola, P. (2002). The re-emergence of ODL in Nigeria and its use for transforming education for national development. Paper presented at the *Pan Commonwealth Forum on Open Learning, Open Learning: Transforming Education for Development*," Durban, SA, July 29 to August 2.

Lentell, H. (2004). Framing policy for open and distance learning. In *Policy for Open and Distance Learning* (H. Perraton and H. Lentell, eds.) London: Routledge Falmer & COL, pp. 249–259.

Mitroff, I. and Emshoff, J. (1979). On strategic assumption-making: A dialectical approach to policy and planning. *The Academy of Management Review*, **4**(1), 1–12.

Romiszowski, A. (n.d.) A study of distance education public policy and practice in the higher education sectors of selected countries: Synthesis of key findings. Retrieved March 30, 2007, from: http://www.che.ac.za/documents/d000070/Background_Paper1_Romiszowski.pdf

Section VI
The Business of Distance Education

Introduction

Terry Evans

The relationship between education and business grows stronger with each passing year. Notwithstanding the mutuality in this relationship, it is not without its tensions, inconsistencies and contradictions. Indeed, there are strong critics of each sector from within the other. Many in education lament and resist the rise of corporatism in educational sectors and institutions, and many in business criticise the absence of "job ready" knowledge and skills being taught in schools, colleges and universities.

Distance education has been deployed both within business and universities for training and professional development, and some businesses are in the business of distance education as trainers or management educators. The potential flexibility of distance education – in time and pace – and its potential for supporting workplace-based provision or on-the-job training has proved attractive to many organizations. In this section, the business of distance education is considered from the perspectives of distance education being both a business and for business.

Yoni Ryan has been involved with colleagues on major transnational projects concerned with the ways in which new technologies are enabling transnational educational business to be conducted from within both the public and the private sectors. She shows that there are various elements and problems in the ways in which the commercial provision of e-learning is planned, developed and operated, whether it is crossing borders or not. Greville Rumble provides another important perspective on this matter in his economic analysis and modelling of distance education in particular contexts and circumstances. His work draws on analyses and formulae developed for the cost of distance education in its various pre-online forms of mediation, especially print. He then deals with the emergence and establishment of online media in distance education and the implications for economic models when online course development, delivery and management alter the economic variables.

John Mitchell considers the business skills, which include financial planning skills, required by vocational education and training managers of organizations which need to deal with e-learning, flexible learning, workplace learning, distance education, etc. He argues that these skills may be usefully categorised as strategic and operational, and that they are similar to those that any manager of medium-sized business requires, especially one which is operating in a knowledge industry and with new technology.

Having established the business case, this section then moves into considering specific elements and examples of the business of distance education. Jim Fong and Tut Bailey discuss the matter of understanding markets and marketing in distance education. They make the case for a careful and rational approach to this aspect of the business of distance education, whether this being the public or private sectors. Mark Bullen and Adnan Qayyam pursue the matter of the costs and effectiveness of distance education. The matter of the effectiveness of the investment made in distance education by all the parties is of considerable importance if a distance educational business is to prosper. Ellie Chambers and Kevin Wilson provide a detailed exploration of global and European policy that affect the conduct of international business and relate this specifically to the business of distance education. They explore the case for collaboration for the mutual cost and quality benefits in distance education.

Ted Nunan provides the critical essay for this section. He considers the new businesses of distance education and asks, who profits and who loses? His critical perspective shows that the rational and logical analyses to business models are useful for operating a distance education business, but that a consideration of the political and ideological forces at work, and how these may operate to weaken distance education, or more particularly the mutating and converging forms of education of which distance education is a fundamental part – for the public good to enhance the conditions for those who wish to use distance education for private or corporate profit.

Chapter 39

Borderless Education and Business Prospects

Yoni Ryan

39.1 INTRODUCTION

So much has the worldscape of higher education altered since the first of the Borderless Education reports was commissioned from Queensland University of Technology (QUT) (Cunningham et al., 1998) that it is useful to review the varied pressures and trends which have become clearer, and more potent, since that time. After all, few then predicted that a commercial search engine, Google, would become a *verb*: to "google one's way to a degree", and a portable *library*.

These pressures and trends include distinctions of terminology – borderless and transnational education, internationalisation and globalisation, marketisation of education, distance education, online/e-learning – and the clear dominance of neo-liberal theory and practices, including the notion of education as a "private good" denoting "user pays", at national and supranational levels. The commitment of development banks to macroeconomic policies is exemplified in such documents as the World Bank's 2002 assessment of directions for tertiary education, which emphasises required reform of national policy on free or low-cost education as a condition of loans in the developing world.

I start from the position that distance education has as its core philosophy the provision of educational opportunity to those disadvantaged by distance, socio-economic position, or disability, although increasingly in the Western world, the convenience factor is a major driver. In the developing world, the disadvantaged remain primary users.

It is the contention of this chapter that digital technology will ultimately drive the convergence of online and class-based education, that existing business models for distance and online education are fragile because of this convergence, and that therefore the prospects for distance education as a successful and sustainable mechanism for development are not promising within the dominant neo-liberal paradigm.

39.2 BORDERLESS EDUCATION

The term "borderless education" first seeped into the lexicon of higher education in the late 1990s in the context of concerns in the Australian federal education department about the apparent threat posed by rapidly emerging "corporate universities" (Meister, 1998), the presumed enthusiasm of media companies to enter the education market via their investments in new technologies, and the seemingly insatiable appetite among international students for higher education in information technology and business and for English-language programmes, as the recognition grew that English had become the global language (Crystal, 1997). The Department already held fears that international students, by 1997 a vital funding source for many universities, would be lost to US media-education consortia, crossing borders via the Web or satellite broadcast to "deliver" education directly to students in their home countries, thus eroding onshore Australian markets.

The term "borderless higher education" refers to a range of interlocking activities – including e-learning, other forms of transnational provision, and new providers (e.g. for-profit universities) – that cross a variety of "borders", whether "geographic, sectoral or conceptual" (Observatory, 2006). As Knight (2005) observes, borderless education connotes the erosion of national borders in education policy and practice. Clearly, while these borders have been breached via technology and physical delivery, national educational policies still exert a strong if diminishing influence on higher education, as a result of globalising trends.

While geographical borders have been the main focus of most studies, it should not be forgotten that conceptual and sectoral borders are being eroded in like measure: it is no longer possible, for instance, to divorce education policy from national policies in respect of immigration. In Australia, for example, the potential to gain Permanent Residency (PR) visas through degree studies in Australia has become a major platform for migration, with graduates constituting 40 percent of PR applicants and PR visa "success" [*Times Higher Education Supplement* (*THES*), 2006, p. 12]. Student mobility directly correlates with global migration flows, and increasingly via *trade* qualifications, not merely *university* qualifications. Education policy has also become a major element of trade policy: while the University of New South Wales Asia was certainly in planning before the Singapore Australia Free Trade Agreement, the signing of that agreement did not harm the venture (*The Australian Higher Education*, 2005). As yet, there has been no reverse entry by Singapore to Australia in higher education, although a number of Singapore companies are heavily invested at the Vocational Education and Training (VET) level.

From the first, "borderless education" connoted commercial exploitation via new information and communication technologies, as vendors sought mainstream applications for their products. From the perspective of a media provider such as News Corporation, the business case required a decision to buy "content" (education), provide "carriage" (technical infrastructure such as satellite transmission), or, more alarmingly for the higher education institutions, both.

For public, private non-profit, and for-profit education institutions, the business case demanded a decision to develop "content" alone (since content or knowledge is considered core business for a university), to onsell to an infrastructure provider, or to collaborate with other universities to develop, sell, and "transmit" programmes. Some of the projects that emerged from the university sector were well intentioned, even altruistic: Fathom and Cardean come to mind. However, few were without hope of profit, market expansion, or brand recognition.

Since the complementary Australian and UK Business of Borderless Education reports were published in 2000, the dot.com crash and the downturn in world economies have caused a re-assessment of the *business* cases of most borderless ventures – not least, the assumed lucrative returns from e-learning, and market expansion offshore.

39.3 TRANSNATIONAL EDUCATION

According to the 2001 *UNESCO-CEPES/Council of Europe Code of Good Practice for the Provision of Transnational Education*, transnational education *subsumes* distance education and refers simply to programmes delivered in a State different from that in which the awarding institution is located. However, this does not adequately account for the increasing trend to establish offshore campuses of a university, where the offshore institution must be registered and incorporated in the "host" country. The "main" campus may be located elsewhere, but the entity is an awarding institution in its own right, being subject to local legal, financial, and educational regulatory regimes, which pose challenging "partnerships", as King (2004) observes in his analysis of the University of South Australia's entrepreneurial activities. Knight (2005) observes that the term "transnational" was devised in the Australian context to differentiate offshore from onshore international programmes, whether by distance or twinning or franchise arrangements. The focus is on *where* the student is studying, not on the mode of delivery.

Many in the sector are convinced that offshore enrolments are the "growth area" of higher education, and there is good evidence of this trend, with 56,000 international students enrolled offshore in Australian university programmes in 2004 (*Campus Review*, 2005a), compared with 150,000 onshore. By way of comparison, Garrett and Verbik (2004) estimated over 100,000 international students were enrolled in UK offshore programmes in 2004, constituting 41 percent of all international enrolments. IDP (*Campus Review*, 2005b) as well as the British Council (*THES*, 2005) has now predicted that offshore enrolments will outpace onshore enrolments within 5–10 years. Clearly, this is a significant market at present, whatever its future prospects.

The emerging model of transnational education combines distance and class delivery and is gaining strength because of the patent failure of many of the early models of e-education. For example, Monash University, one of Australia's largest providers to international students at 30 percent of its student population, educates 35.6 percent of these students using distance materials supplemented with local tutoring. Its over 2,700 international distance students offshore constitute 14.75 percent of Australia's total offshore distance enrolments, and as such it dominated provision in this segment of the market (IDP, 2004). Nearly 3,000 offshore students in Monash campuses in South Africa and Malaysia also utilise distance materials in their class-based tuition.

Such provision raises many issues in relation to standardisation of programmes and facilities between onshore and offshore campuses. National higher education quality agencies, such as Australian Universities Quality Agency (AUQA) and the Quality Assurance Agency (QAA) in the UK, have issued warnings about the damage done to a nation's educational reputation by questionable programmes "exported" to a host country in the stampede expansion of markets. Government response to Australia's third largest industry was to extend AUQA's charter to include inspection of overseas campuses (at the cost of the auditee) and greater attention to overseas-delivered programmes. The latter typically involve the use of distance education materials, supplemented by "fly-in/fly-out" teachers from Australia, and often by local tutoring in face-to-face classes. Thirty-eight of Australia's thirty-nine universities now offer some form of transnational education; many of these are "niche programmes", small, single discipline, and often serendipitous; others are the result of strategic commercial decisions to offer a suite of courses to a high-demand market, such as Hong Kong or Singapore, where a local partner provides the administrative and infrastructure support. Woodhouse (*Campus Review*, 2006) reports AUQA's concerns on some Australian providers' "weakness of contract monitoring . . . quality is fragmented and variable because quality control was left to departments, without central control". Moderation, and coordination of student evaluations were other causes of concern. AUQA is not alone in its attention to failings in transnational education, as we shall see.

National jurisdictions which have not signed free trade agreements on education may exercise various controls over the entry of foreign providers. The Indian government's treatment of foreign private providers (*Times of India*, 2006), in barring profit and enforcing quotas for under-represented classes, is one example, but recent examinations of US "exports" to China reveal that there are other methods of distorting the effect of the purpose of "free trade in services", which is profit, or, at the very least, no loss. Mooney (2006) quotes the International Finance Corporation of the World Bank as listing over 700 programmes operating in China, 150 of them from the United States. Thirty-six percent of all programmes are MBAs, a fickle market, as recent Australian enrolments reveal. "China is clearly the Klondike of higher education", according to the President of the State University of New York at Albany, which is developing a campus near Nanjing with other North American institutions. Typically, providers such as the University of Maryland at College Park (UMCP) use "fly-in/fly-out" staff to deliver intensive teaching once or twice a semester, utilising videoconferencing, web-based resources, and online delivery for most of the programmes. The logistics are challenging, and the commercial benefits have been limited by Chinese government fiat, that the institution should be run like a non-profit. The economics of such distance programmes appear tenuous when one considers the costs of travel for US teachers, inducement allowances for US staff, and the fact that tuition fees must be competitive with the fees charged by local providers. Only where the programme is recognised as conferring benefits that local providers cannot can higher comparative fees be charged. One UMCP staff member pointed out that the government's regulations on jointly provided programmes are "a flagrant violation" of China's WTO commitments (Mooney, 2006). Yet individual providers relying on international agreements to conduct their borderless operations have little recourse to the WTO. Curricula must align with (non-defined) Chinese public morals and ethics, and course outlines and teaching materials must be approved by higher education authorities.

Such restrictions have shaped what Mooney calls "a British-style curriculum" at the University of Nottingham's Ningbo campus, with 930 students in 2005, and aspirations to 4,000 by 2009. One of the students quoted by Mooney says she chose Nottingham because of its Western approach to teaching via discussions between staff and students, a contrast to "the Chinese way", where "the teacher stands in front of the class talking and the students just take notes". One might question how closely Nottingham Ningbo can replicate UK teaching approaches, when China blocks Sky TV, CNN, a number of websites, and routinely monitors chat rooms for signs of political subversion. Such oversight is particularly restrictive, one might imagine, in the Nottingham courses of international studies and business management, although Moody notes with approval that the BBC World News is broadcast on campus, despite restrictions elsewhere in the country.

39.4 INTERNATIONALISATION OF HIGHER EDUCATION

The term "internationalisation of higher education" has highly divergent applications. In almost all operational documents of Australian universities, it connotes increasing enrolment of international students, with or without rhetorical gestures towards the importance of expanding both local and international students' mental and cultural horizons through exposure to other cultures. Knight (2005) notes the same trend. It is the market orientation embedded in this conception of internationalisation that fosters the sardonic observations of Ninnes and Hellsten (2005, p. 1):

> For the academic with a taste for adventure, an insatiable desire to know and experience a wide range of exotic "others", a willingness to board the entrepreneurial bandwagon, a hankering after airport departure lounges, and an immunity to the effects of long term exposure to radiation at 10,000 metres above sea level, the internationalization of higher education is an enticing and intoxicating cocktail of possibilities. From teaching intensive residential schools off-shore in the "glitz and glamour" of Hong Kong, to educational consultancies in remote Kingdoms "lost in time",...internationalization...appears to provide increasing opportunities for academics to become global travellers, makers of difference, effectors of personal change, and facilitators of social progress.

However, when the term first emerged around 20 years ago, it referred specifically to the study abroad programmes common in US private universities, and then evolved to include all higher education processes and policies (Knight, 2005). Knight's 1994 use of the term envisaged a less commercial orientation: it was to describe curriculum perspectives and content that acknowledged the increasingly "connected" world and to teach tolerance and respect for non-Western epistemologies. Knight (2005, p. 4) differentiates the terms internationalisation and globalisation thus:

> ...internationalisation stressed the notion of relations between nations, people, culture and globalisation stressed the idea of a world wide flow of people, technology, economy, ideas, knowledge, culture but did not focus on (but nor did it exclude) the relationships between countries.

Pedagogical issues concerning Western and non-Western styles of teaching and students' learning are a dimension of borderless education briefly canvassed in Cunningham et al. (1998) as requiring close attention to curriculum and delivery mode. With the high numbers of international students onshore in the United Kingdom, Australia, Canada, and New Zealand and declining but still high numbers in the United States, as well as the export of provision offshore, increasing numbers of teachers are exploring the complex issues of cross-cultural teaching, previously a matter of little concern to distance educators, who simply assumed that foreign students wanted a purely "Western" qualification, with all that implied of an inward-looking national curriculum and a Western epistemology. Doherty (2004) outlines how a transnational online programme affords both positive and negative learning experiences. Doherty is one of an increasing number of commentators (see also Kelly, 2000) who recognise the importance of educating for global citizenry and intercultural competence.

Now, "internationalisation" is a keyword for most education agencies and providers: Department of Education, Science and Training's (DEST) Australian Education International database features "International Education" as a dedicated term, and monthly updates to the database canvass not only marketing and "market updates" but also socio-cultural issues, descriptive reports of staff teaching internationally and in online international programmes, student mobility, and regulatory control, as well as learning style differences and policy matters (AEI, 2006).

39.5 GLOBALISATION AND HIGHER EDUCATION

As enrolment figures in transnational education ventures indicate, globalisation of education markets is a significant dimension of many universities' operations. Yet there are many who have questioned the impact on the institution of "the university", including Castells (2000). Neave (2002) warned of the potential for further commodification of knowledge "as a purchasable and saleable good" (a process now sealed by the inclusion of education in the General Agreement on Trade in Services (GATS)), and the rise of for-profit providers, with the consequent likelihood of an increasing exclusion of less developed countries and their citizens from the benefits of globalisation.

National education and micro-economic polices have struggled with the implications of globalisation for education. South Africa has wrestled with the dual problems of reforming its apartheid era higher education sector, while expelling some of its foreign providers to secure its domestic education agenda of equal opportunity. Several countries have protested the inclusion of higher education in the GATS agreement: the

South African Council of Higher Education, for example, has argued that as a public good, higher education should not be included and that "free trade will undermine national values" (*THES*, 2005). However, the trend seems inevitable. India, which had initially welcomed foreign investment in education, maintained its policy of refusing to recognise the degrees of foreign onshore providers, causing Sylvan (now Laureate: http://www.Laureate-Inc.com) to abandon its planned campus there in 2004.

Nevertheless, not all non-Western nations have succumbed to beggardom at the bowl of globalising trends in education, as Currie et al. (2003) appear to suggest. Malaysia, Hong Kong, and Singapore, once the largest "exporters" of students to Australia and other Western nations, and the target of many offshore operations, have escalated investment in their own education systems, aspiring to become hubs for higher education in the Asia-Pacific region. Since many Australian universities have nursing programmes in Singapore, the establishment of a Bachelor of Science (Nursing) by the National University of Singapore (NUS) in 2006 may significantly dent those programmes' enrolments. Harman (2006) reports that Singapore intends to expand its international student numbers from 60,000 to 150,000 within a decade, via its own institutions, or by direct investment in "foreign" providers, as with the UNSW Asia campus.

One response to globalisation of education has been positive: greater attention to quality, albeit often in the name of "consumer protection", and protecting the reputation of "exporting" countries' educational systems. AUQA's David Woodhouse, for example, has said that "globalisation... is one of the causes of the increased attention to quality assurance" (*Campus Review*, 2006).

Many national education bodies now include some form of quality or accreditation agency, and these are increasingly concerned to root out substandard or non-registered institutions, including many distance providers. The Sri Lankan University Grants Commission, through its QAA, for example, has recently moved to screen a number of UK, Australian, and Indian universities offering distance programmes through local private providers without the required local accreditation. Leicester University's MBA, offered through the Business Management School, managed only thirty-two passes from 153 enrolments in 2004, raising concerns about local tutors, how the Leicester curriculum was delivered, and the facilities available to students (*THES*, 2005). Such concerns intersect with AUQA's new powers, and should ultimately lead to international accreditation and quality regimes, but in the meantime, students are often the victims of poorly administered "distance" programmes.

Kaplan's proposed entry into Australia via its purchase of Sydney-based Tribeca Learning is a local example of how globalisation of higher education occurs through the private sector. Kaplan does not appear to be "re-branding" Tribeca, but buying an established brand and listed Australian company (*Financial Review Education*, 2006). This may avoid the legal impediments to setting up a "foreign" university in Australia, although the issue of whether Kaplan will use the title "university" is moot. It is unlikely to want to seek university status, since it is best known in the United States as the "test-prep" subsidiary of *The Washington Post*. A second business "line" is professional education in the financial services sector (http://www.kaplan.com/AboutKaplan/), which is also Tribeca's focus. In the United Kingdom, Hong Kong, Singapore, and Shanghai, Kaplan operates under an established name, Financial Training Company.

39.6 MARKETISATION OF EDUCATION

Throughout the 1990s, we saw national governments across the world reduce their historical commitments to free higher education and encourage the growth of private providers. In the absence of the wealthy philanthropists who established the non-profit elite US private institutions, new private providers have been almost entirely for-profit organisations. By its inclusion of trade in educational services as a component of free trade agreements, GATS itself has contributed to the increasing marketisation of education (Knight, 2005). Furthermore, as numerous commentators (Marginson and Considine, 2000; Koelman and de Vries, 1999) have observed, governments, with the encouragement of supranational agencies such as the World Bank and the Asian Development Bank, have progressively shifted financing of higher education to the demand side, introducing or extending tuition fees. At the same time, governments have strengthened contestable funding programmes for specific university "services", such as research. As Koelman and de Vries (1999, p. 173) point out, this has resulted in "hybrid" institutions, combining "public duties and...commercial market activities".

The outcome is remarkable: Central Queensland University, for example, now earns most of its income from its satellite metropolitan campuses and international students, and only 20 percent of its 2005 income was derived from federal funding (*The Australian Higher Education*, 2006).

However, marketisation of education in a borderless society is not without economic and financial challenges. No one seems to have foreseen the inevitable problem of debt collection of student fees in Europe once "top-up" fees are introduced in the United Kingdom in September 2006. Tuition will be "free at point of entry" to UK institutions, and EU students will not have to re-pay until their income on graduation reaches £15,000 in their home countries (*THES*, 2006). What mechanisms are in place to trace graduates and collect the fees?

39.7 DISTANCE EDUCATION

Supranational bodies, finance agencies, and established distance providers such as the United Kingdom Open University (UKOU) continue to espouse the urgent need for distance education as a mechanism for development, particularly in Africa, Central Asia, and Latin America (UNESCO, 2002; Gourley, 2004). Yet the lack of government support for distance education (in World Bank terms "weak mandates for distance education", Murphy et al., 2002, p. 28) within those countries inhibits take-up, as do the high financial and social costs of most distance programmes (Darkwa and Mazibuko, 2000; Mhehe, 2001).

However, in Western countries, the notion of distance education as complete separation of teacher/institution from student is altering, as delivery modes converge. The National Centre for Education Statistics (NCES) (2002) study on US student participation in distance education notes that 44 percent of 2 and 4 year institutions were offering distance programmes by 1997, up from 33 percent in 1995. This figure does not include those institutions which were not eligible for Title IV funding at that time, and hence the participation rate is almost certainly much higher. The study included those who took one or several subjects by distance, not only those completing an entire distance programme.

What has occurred, among entrepreneurs (including many in public institutions) and policy makers, is an unfortunate conflation of "distance education" with "e-learning", and of "distance education" with "borderless education": unfortunate, because it belied the many worthy programmes and institutions using "old" technologies such as print, radio, even audio cassettes. Historically and currently, print and to a much lesser extent radio remain the primary media for delivery of distance education, whether in small-scale operations or the "mega-universities" identified by Daniel (1996). It should be remembered that in 1998, the year the first "borderless education" report commissioned by the then Department of Education, Employment, Training and Youth Affairs (DEETYA) (Cunningham et al., 1998) was released, the first issue of *Distance Education* for that year carried articles based on the then standard mode of distance education, print, and examining historical distance education concerns – persistence in open universities (Belawati, 1998), evaluation, quality, understanding learners, and embedding learning strategies. Only one article (Dymock and Hobson, 1998) concerned the then "new" technologies of audioconferencing and voicemail. Yet by Issue 2 of that year, seven out of nine articles explored the potential of new communications technologies for distance education, and that trend has persisted in the journal since. Replicated in numerous journals of distance education, this focus on new technologies has reinforced the linkage of "distance" with "online" learning.

The high failure rates of distance (and open) students, as much as 95 percent in some Asian institutions (Daniel, 1996; Belawati, 1998), as well as the potential of digital technologies to overcome the recognised disadvantages of traditional distance study, have prompted many practitioners and researchers in developing countries to urge radical change to the historical conception of distance education. For instance, the Higher Education Quality Committee (HEQC) of South Africa (2003), in investigating reform of that country's distance institutions, issued a comprehensive list of criteria to improve student success, most of which involved establishing study centres across the country, staffed with administrative, technical, and academic staff, running supplementary face-to-face classes, and supplying the digital technologies needed in contemporary educational settings. The HEQC acknowledged the power of computer-based group communication to overcome lack of motivation induced by isolation, but stressed the importance of *social* learning, and the need for *in-person* teaching and feedback. The World Bank's Africa Region Report of 2002, a more measured and thoughtful assessment of the possibilities for distance education in Sub-Saharan Africa than those it produced in the 1990s, argued for the same support measures.

Clearly, these approaches represent a significant shift in conceptualising "distance" education, and introducing them will add enormous costs to distance systems, reducing the conventional argument (UNESCO, 2002; Moore and Kearsley, 1996) that distance education is more cost-efficient than class-based education. Once high recurrent costs in staffing, equipment maintenance, and connection costs are added to high initial capital costs, economies of scale diminish, as Bates (2004) argues. Not unexpectedly, Murphy et al. (2002) in the World Bank Africa Region Report argue that student fees should meet the additional costs. The technology affords speedy communication and retrieval of information, but who will afford the technology?

As will be discussed further below in examining some specific models, distance modes which are heavily reliant on online interaction are expensive to develop and maintain, most particularly in regions where telecommunications costs are prohibitive and infrastructure is limited and unreliable.

39.8 ONLINE EDUCATION

As the dot.com bubble expanded, entrepreneurs like Glenn Jones (International University) and Bill Gates (Microsoft), prophesised a future where "star professors" would educate the world's masses through virtual or cyber universities. Rupert Murdoch (News Corporation) briefly shared the vision with Universitas21 (U21), brainchild of the former vice chancellor of the University of Melbourne, until it became apparent that News could not use education as a Trojan Horse for Sky TV's entry to China. Famously, John Chambers, CEO of Cisco Systems, declared that use of the Internet in education would make email take-up "look like a rounding error", and investment companies such as Morgan Keegan (2000) trumpeted the returns to be made with online education providers.

"Irrational exuberance" was certainly a feature of supranational agencies' embrace of e-learning in the early 1990s. Ryan (2002b) reported that thirty-five US states had established "virtual universities" by that date. Few remain; even the most ambitious Michigan Virtual University, has reverted to providing resources to the K-12 sector (http://www.mivu.org/content.cfm?ID=1). Even such enthusiastic proponents of online training for business as Corporate University Xchange (http://www.corpu.com/) note that classroom-only training was still preferred by 36 percent of such organisations, with another 36 percent blending online and class delivery (*Sixth Annual Benchmarking Report*, 2004). Thus with some notable exceptions, outlined below, online provision is dominated by short-run training programmes. As Aldrich Clark, of Gartner Group, noted in our interviews for the Business of Borderless Education report, the vast majority of e-learning activities fall "at the low end of the pyramid" in government mandated programmes such as occupational health and safety, and sexual harassment courses, the intent being "simply to put a big check mark there and say 'done' ".

Some of the early e-education models and the reasons for their failure are canvassed in Ryan (2002b). Since then, many pressures have emerged to alter the environment for distance and e-learning endeavours. Among these are the effects of the GATS agreement as it relates to trade in educational "services" via the codification of transnational trade (Knight, 2002), the entry of China to the WTO, and the resurgence of bilateral FTA agreements. Where GATS encouraged distance education as a mode of service delivery, limiting the extent to which signatory countries could legislate against "foreign" providers, bilateral agreements have encouraged national government support of "foreign" institutions from a bilateral trade partner keen to establish branch campuses. The US/Australia FTA has improved the climate for US branch campuses. Carnegie Adelaide campus is one example, as well as a pointer to the use of "public" monies to subsidise private institutions. The commercial environment for transnational education via *physical* facilities has therefore improved, while the challenges of purely online education in terms of scale and learning preferences have remained.

Online learning as a *purely* technologically mediated institution–student delivery modality has had limited appeal. CNN.com (cnn.worldnews, January 13, 2006) reports a Sloan Foundation finding that 1.6 million students in its collaborating colleges and universities using the Sloan Asynchronous Learning Network were enrolled in an online subject in 2002–2003, though most were also studying the majority of their subjects face-to-face. South Dakota University reports in the same article that 42 percent of its online students were actually on-campus for most of their subjects.

As a means of promoting global education, it has had even more limited success, as the case of U21 Global will demonstrate. Staff and students alike have found combining international student groups challenging and fraught with cultural difficulties (Vermeer, 2004). The initial tendency to use digital technologies for "shovelware", basically print "lectures" or PowerPoint presentations uploaded to a website, did little to exploit the potential of those technologies, or to retain student motivation.

In summary, "the business of borderless education" grew in the interstices of macroeconomic policy shifts to globalisation of trade and services, the obvious potential of digital technologies to network the world's population, the needs of media companies in the late 1990s to recoup the exorbitant prices they had paid for 3G spectrum, and the growth of a middle class in developing countries hungry for education. Added to these factors, institutions in the Western world noted the changing demographic as the school-leaver population, the traditional higher education source, declined. While few public universities were initially prepared to adapt their modes of delivery to a growing adult market, for-profit institutions such as The University of Phoenix (UoP) and DeVry saw a niche market for the time-pressed worker seeking convenience and "speed to degree".

The years since the dot.com crash have seen the demise of many online and distance ventures, public and for-profit, and a high level of merger and acquisition activities amongst for-profit providers. Blackboard and WebCT, then the two dominant LMS, have "merged", leaving many higher education providers uncertain about their mission critical platforms. Sylvan has focused on expansion of its international campuses, mainly in Europe and South America. Its foundering National Technological University, an online provider, has been absorbed into the online Walden University, which it also owns. Fathom, the ambitious consortium of several US prestige institutions including

Columbia, finally folded in 2003; Cardean University appears to be struggling, with its MBA enrolling only 905 students in 2003–2004 (*Business Week*, 2006).

Among the failures are NYUOnline, Caliber, Harcourt Higher Education, Scottish Knowledge (SK) (which was part-owned by News Corporation), Temple University, SmartForce, the UKOU's US subsidiary USOU, and, of course, the UK e-University, which finally closed in 2004, having squandered £50 million to attract 900 students against the advice of many consultants appointed by Higher Education Funding Council for England (HEFCE).

39.9 MODELS OF BORDERLESS EDUCATION

Examination of the operations of a number of providers exemplifying a typology of borderless institutions will provide evidence of the argument regarding convergence of on- and off-campus modes, and the fragility of distance education in non-commercial operations. The models and institutions examined have been chosen because they represent a spectrum of provision:

- the niche market elite single-brand model – Duke's Global Executive MBA;
- University of Phoenix Online (UoP Online) – US mass market for-profit online provider;
- the World Bank development model – the African Virtual University (AVU);
- the media giant–elite university partnership – U21Global; and
- the print-dependent late twentieth century "mega-university" transitioning to new media – Indira Gandhi National Open University (IGNOU).

39.9.1 Duke's Global Executive MBA

This was one of the earliest MBA programmes to enter the "e-learning space". Launched in 1996, it blends residential sessions in Asia, South America, Europe, and the United States with online learning. The programme is based on an 18-month five-term programme, with three subjects completed per term: each term includes "a three-week reading period, a two-week residential classroom session, a one-week break, 10–12 weeks of Internet-enabled course work and a one-week break. As the class travels across the globe, students take the curriculum together in the same sequence" (Duke FUQUA School of Business, 2006a). Despite its global rubric, its students are predominantly North American citizens aspiring to or in careers with multinational companies (46%). Europeans account for 19 percent of enrolments, with executives from Africa and the Middle East 5 percent (Duke FUQUA School of Business, 2006b). Women comprise only 12 percent of enrolments the most common background is in sales/marketing. Workload is intensive: students are expected to be online a minimum of 5 hours a week, and to study for 20 hours per week. (A National Survey of Student Engagement, incidentally, found that 44 percent of US undergraduates spend fewer than 10 hours per week studying (Chronicle of Higher Education (CHE) online, November 15, 2004). Overall, 40 percent of MBA instruction is face-to-face.

Students are attracted by its exclusivity: enrolment averages 80–90 for each cohort, divided into two classes of 40–45; tuition fees are US $115,700, which does not include a mandated IBM ThinkPad, or travel expenses to each residency. The high quality of faculty in terms of experience and research is another attraction, as is the attention devoted to educational design of its material. It has eschewed partners since its technical platform, Pensare, collapsed not long after it had launched the Global Executive programme. Its success can therefore be attributed to a number of factors – high-cost tuition allows high-quality teaching and resources, the cohort is highly motivated and ambitious, the Fuqua School of Business has full control of the programme, unencumbered by partner compromise, and it combines online and significant face-to-face elements and syndicate learning in proportions appropriate and familiar to its students.

39.9.2 The University of Phoenix Online

By contrast, the UoP Online targets the convenience-motivated mass market of middle-class North America, a market UoP had already captured in its "bricks and mortar" operations in twenty-nine US states, and 244 centres (The University of Phoenix, 2006a), in rented rooms near major car parks, operating nights and weekends, for the convenience of working adults. Only when UoP had perfected its mass market model did it expand into the distance market. UoP, like other for-profits, exploited the growing vocationalist trend in post-secondary education.

UoP, the parent University, is now 30 years old, and has developed a sound reputation among the mass market for-profit providers, though like other high-profile for-profits such as Integrated Business Technologies Education (IBT) and Education Services, it has not been immune to legal challenges over its aggressive marketing practices and misrepresentation of employment rates for its graduates. UoP cautiously translated its face-to-face model of small classes, taught by practising professionals in its areas of specialisation (business management, IT, and more recently health care, nursing, education, and human services), into the online environment (The University of Phoenix, 2006b). It floated UoP Online from the parent Apollo Group in 2001, presumably to quarantine possible failure of the online business as dot.com industries floundered.

Curricula are centrally developed by full-time staff in close consultation with the main employer bodies for each profession and are taught by 10,000 part-time teachers. Unlike the situation in online subjects in many public universities in Australia, students are assigned to a class with a *maximum* size of twenty for each tutor (up from 8 to 10 when UoP Online first started), they are required to log on for online activities and discussion at least four times per week, and assignments are constant over the abbreviated 6-week "term". Such a staff:student ratio guarantees the attention few distance students receive in either traditional print or public university online programmes. Exercises are geared to syndicated learning activities, replicating the professional learning environment of many students in business and IT: 41 percent of enrolments are in business. Students undertake one subject a term, and can graduate in two years, especially if they are granted credit, which UoP encourages. "Time-to-degree" is a strong motivation, as is the group work required in each class. There are few or no electives, making the economics of development and delivery comparatively inexpensive compared with most non-profit, and public distance programmes, which attempt to gain efficiencies through large student:staff ratios.

Nevertheless, there are signs that the astounding growth in online enrolments may be moderating. UoP Online paid no dividends over the 2001–2004 period, before the listed company was reabsorbed into the parent company via the issue of shares in Apollo Group (2005). Comparative graduation rates are difficult to locate in the company reports. The Annual Report for 2005 notes that online enrolments now outnumber class enrolments (125,000:100,000), but graduate numbers are given as 69 percent from class-based programmes, compared with 25 percent from online programmes. The contribution of private for-profit providers to the marketisation of higher education is also evidenced in the fact that sales and promotion costs at UoP for FY 2005 were a full half of teaching costs: what public university could afford such marketing expenditure? Perhaps a further innovation in UoP's delivery method signals a recognition that blended or hybrid approaches to combining online and face-to-face methods may prove more beneficial for student retention and graduation: the fastest growing "segment" of UoP's business is FlexNet, in which online materials, resources, and communication are combined with regular face-to-face classes. FlexNet thus accommodates convenience, social contact, and an e-learning environment.

39.9.3 U21Global

Universitas21 attracts little attention in education media today, a very different situation from its inception, when the public/private partnership between a group of elite international and Australian universities and News Corporation was first announced (somewhat prematurely) in a Memorandum of Understanding in 1997. It was possibly this which prompted the disquiet in the Australian federal education department of the potential threat of media companies entering the higher education market.

The vision for U21 had two distinct elements: one the consortium relationship between the institutions as a network of physical institutions, the other the commercial arm U21Global. There are less "virtual" aspects of the consortium which have proceeded as planned, and with little attention, such as staff and student exchanges, sharing of learning objects, benchmarking of courses and administrative and internet infrastructure, and joint research activities. Some 1,200 students, according to Dr Chris Robinson, Managing Director of the Executive, had participated in such exchanges by 2001 (Ryan and King, 2004). In late 2001, U21 signed the U21Global arrangement with Thomson Corporation, to exploit U21 developments through commercial online education services.

"U21pedagogica" is a wholly owned subsidiary of U21 in perpetuity; "U21Global" can offer nothing that has not been certified by U21pedagogica, which ensures the quality of programmes. According to Thomson's press release (September 7, 2001):

> The unique structure of Universitas21 enables it to take a powerful international brand, credible quality assurance, and multi-jurisdictional certification and add Thomson Learning's expansive content and course development experience.

Thomson believed that the brand names of the institutions involved would be sufficient to attract "brand-conscious" students in the target countries, although it should be noted that that premise had been found wanting in relation to the unknown brands of Cardean and Fathom, virtual universities with contributions from prestige US institutions.

Target courses were to be at postgraduate level, a hotly contested market in which other commercial operators such as the University of Maryland University College already had an established position, although not predominantly in Asia. SK was not considered a competitor to U21Global, since SK's major programmes were in oil-related corporate programmes in the Middle East. The interim U21Global Business Plan included provision for US $700,000 to $1 million per year professors who would combine pedagogical skills for the online environment with discipline skills, to support 24 hour a day teaching/learning activity, assisted by local tutors. The plan has subsequently been adapted to a wholly online environment, without any global star professors.

The success (or otherwise) of U21Global as a business has been affected by a number of factors which point to the difficulty of establishing "the business case" for a global online university, particularly one with no "brand recognition", and one predicated almost entirely on predicted demand for a professional programme.

When U21Global was in establishment phase, the MBA was a high-demand programme across the developed and developing world. Commencing numbers in Australian universities jumped by 53 percent between 2001 and 2003, for example; fee paying students. Oversupply of the course had met the demand for middle and upper management credentials. Total international student enrolments fell 18 percent between 2003 and 2004; total enrolments dropped by nearly a third between 2003 and 2004, and fell further in 2005 (*Financial Review Education*, February 27, 2006, p. 29). Furthermore, many Asian countries have developed their own strong programmes, or are in the process of developing reputations in graduate business programmes. The dramatic fall in IT programme enrolments has been well documented since the dot.com bubble burst in 2001, yet U21 Global persisted in development of its Masters of Science in Information Systems Management (MSISM). Thus, both its flagship programmes (along with their articulating Executive Certificate/Diploma programmes) are in declining demand, indicating that a global programme instituted on predictions for particular professions may itself be subject to the economic forces of globalisation.

However, U21Global's failure to meet its student targets may not be attributable solely to its choice of programmes. The assumed attraction of an online programme with worldwide management/student perspectives was "over-hyped" from the outset, as it was in the EU–UK case. Furthermore, the consortium model has not proved durable: the Global University Alliance led by several Australian universities has quietly disappeared.

The pedagogic model resembles that of UoP Online, with all required resources online, and "a high degree of communication between faculty and students" and student–student, in a problem-based learning approach. The MBA requires eighteen subjects, ten core, and allows credit transfer for only three subjects; yet-to-launch MISM requires twelve subjects, organised around "competency clusters" such as project management, eServices, and organisational change. U21Global has not, however, adopted the short six-week term characteristic of UoP programmes – the semester is twelve weeks, with ten hours per week study expected.

Currently, there are seven full-time academic staff listed on the website (http://www.u21global.edu.sg); each "school" lists many part-time staff, who appear to warrant U21Global claims to a strongly multinational workforce, favouring perhaps the Subcontinent and Sri Lanka.

Adjuncts are required to complete an online induction to teaching in an online environment, and the "global methodology" approach to teaching ("Higher Education", *The Australian*, 2004). By February 2006, U21Global claimed a 1,000-student milestone in the two years since its actual launch of the MBA, with a doubling of enrolments in the last year, well below the server capacity of 100,000. (By comparison Heriot Watts' online MBA boasted 10,000 students worldwide in 2004; Garrett, 2004.) There is no breakdown of the student enrolments into Masters and Executive Certificate/Diploma enrolments, but if US for-profit enrolments are a guide, the majority of students are in short-course programmes. U21Global has employed some innovative marketing to attract these students, notwithstanding physical offices in five countries, in addition to Hong Kong SAR. In January 2004, the newsletter offered US$2,000 off tuition fees (which vary by country) if payment were made via MasterCard. Discounts are available to staff of the University of Melbourne, the Association of Chartered Practicing Accountants, and to a number of Indian companies. Competitions are held for a "free subject enrolment".

Although U21Global continues to promote its wholly online activities, it too, like UoP, has now sought to expand its offerings to "blended learning", offering supplementary classes with two private providers, Loyola Institute of Business Management in South India and the Indian Institute of Management Bangalore. Thomson's enthusiasm for the project may well have waned since its commissioned investigation, *What Happened to E-Learning and Why* (Zemsky and Massy, 2004), found that international e-learning had failed to capture market share.

39.9.4 The African Virtual University

The AVU project was initially conceived in 1997, during the euphoria of the dot.com era, as the World Bank sought to build an agency which would capitalise on the resources of the developed world's universities and deliver education and training into a network of universities which would assist Sub-Saharan Africa to "leapfrog" into the post-industrial world economy. It remains a source of astonishment that anyone believed that the original business plan could work, on technical, administrative, cultural, and, significantly, pedagogic grounds.

Briefly, the Bank, from its Washington, DC, headquarters, gained agreement from a number of European and North American universities and private training companies to use a video satellite network to deliver a limited number of sub-degree programmes to classrooms set aside for participating African universities. For the universities, the inducements were a small number of second-hand computers, a suite of CDROM materials, a satellite dish and technical training for operators, and limited funding during the establishment phase, with the expectation that the operations would be self-funding after the pilot phase (1997–2001), based on charging modest (in US terms) fees. Programmes were to cover Anglophone and Francophone countries.

No training was provided for centre directors or administrators; no administrative or financial systems were established for collection of data or fees from the widespread network of universities; equipment breakdown was frequent. Centres were often poorly supported by the host university, in sub-standard accommodation which affected the performance of computer equipment, as well as the staff. Live broadcasts were often "illegally" taped and simply replayed by the local centres in subsequent course delivery, to eliminate the licence costs of a "new" programme. In many countries, the initial Computer Literacy programmes were highly successful in training aspiring clerical workers gain entry-level employment in computing skills, but there were few employment opportunities for those enticed into programmes such as Java training.

Local centre directors were alert to the pedagogical needs of their students and provided local face-to-face tutors for each programme delivered in classrooms to groups of up to twenty. The most successful centre programmes were not degree level, but non-formal; many centres targeted internal university students and staff rather than adults excluded from on-campus tertiary study, in contravention of the original AVU mission to increase access. A Bank-led strategic review in 2001 proposed a new business plan, predicated on enrolments of 200 equivalent full-time students at each centre, clearly unrealistic in countries where public universities were reluctant to charge fees, where poverty was endemic, and where domestic computer access was limited. Centre directors in a 2002 study were sceptical of attaining this figure, given that "distance" enrolments (excluding the Computer Literacy students) totalled only 325 for *all* Anglophone programmes (Ryan, 2002a).

Since that date, a more realistic plan has been adopted, along with transfer of the project managers from Washington to Nairobi, and an increase in staff numbers and administrative support systems. There has also been an acceptance of the pedagogical need for face-to-face teaching, and training of teaching staff in using "distance" materials and technologies. A hybrid model of distance and class-based delivery is now integral to the "virtual" university approach and underpins Curtin University's relationship with the AVU and its business degree. However, the future of distance education in Africa generally remains fragile: in Zimbabwe, the Open University tripled its fees because of government cuts to its subsidy. Tuition is therefore twice the level of on-campus fees at public residential universities (*Chronicle of Higher Education* (*CHE*), online edition 2002).

39.9.5 IGNOU

Examination of the particular case of IGNOU, the Indira Gandhi National Open University in India, demonstrates the argument, developed further below, that the economics of open and distance education in developing countries suggest that the business case for mass distance education provision in such countries will continue to deter for-profit providers. (Undoubtedly, there are bogus "diploma mills", colleges, and "universities" offering degrees for sale in such countries, as in the developed world, and there are other than accredited institutions also based in these countries. However, the concern here is with bona fide provision by reputable providers.)

IGNOU was established in 1985 with a brief to "democratise higher education" and to meet demand for degree qualifications, particularly for those disadvantaged by gender, caste, or low income (IGNOU, 2006). It was always intended to cater for 18 to 23-year-olds unable to access university, unlike the UKOU, which deliberately targeted adults wanting a "second chance" education. UKOU retention and progression rates benefited from the higher levels of self-discipline and motivation of adults that were subsequently established in the research. It is worth noting that in the West, distance education is strongly the preserve of adult students, not the school-leavers often targeted by open and distance institutions in developing countries. In both the United States (NCES, 2002) and Australia, adults over 24 years constitute the majority of distance students, and young adults are not often encouraged into distance programmes. Panda (2005, p. 209) notes that Indian government policy to increase the proportion of the age cohort 18–23 attending university requires an expansion of distance provision by 30 percent by 2007, to a total of 4 million students, with 50 percent directed to IGNOU. IGNOU's conception of its mission as providing access for the disadvantaged aligns with UNESCO, Commonwealth of Learning (COL), and World Bank goals to promote distance education as a major plank of development aid.

In 2005, IGNOU's enrolment of 1.3 million students constituted 50 percent of all Indian distance enrolments; Panda notes that over 25 percent of all Indian higher education enrolments are via distance provision. This is a staggering proportion: distance enrolment in Australia hovered around 10 percent of total higher education enrolments until the late 1990s and, by 2004, had reached 14 percent, although the real figure in Australia is likely masked by those enrolled in the so-called flexible units that may in effect be non-class based. By contrast, in the United States, NCES (2002) reports that distance students constituted 8 percent of undergraduate and 10 percent of postgraduate enrolments. Examination of the IGNOU programme offerings reveals that many are sub-degree and non-award programmes, and Reddy and Sriastava (2001) flag a strong trend towards professional and vocational programmes by 2000.

Motivation is a key element of persistence in such programmes, and clearly disadvantaged groups are more likely to cease study programmes. As Belawati (1998) points out, the mere receipt of study resources may lead many to believe they can learn independently of the institution. Even in the developed world, distance students are more likely to be among those with what NCES (2002) deem "persistence risk factors", including working full-time while enrolled, having children, no matriculation, and part-time study status.

IGNOU introduced its online-supported programme, the Bachelor of Information Technology (BIT), in 1999. Programme delivery relies on fifty-eight regional centres and 1,409 study centres, which provide equipment and technical and academic support. The centres are a core element of the programme, since modes of delivery include live satellite broadcasts, pre-recorded videos, and CBT-materials, as well as synchronous and asynchronous discussion.

39.10 CONVERGENCE OF ON-CAMPUS AND OFF-CAMPUS MODELS

From the examples above, one must conclude that the increasing use of ICTs in education, and decreasing public funding, is forcing a convergence of distance and classroom-based delivery (see also Tait and Mills, 1999). As students' contribution to their tuition costs has risen, with a concomitant rise in their paid work commitments, as more mature age students demand more convenient timetabling, as online resources have grown, and labour costs have risen along with technology costs, universities have responded by slicing contact time in class-based programmes (OECD, 2005). At the same time, distance providers, even those designing around a "virtual" environment, such as IGNOU's BIT programme, have found that local face-to-face technical and academic support is necessary for students to succeed in the programme. Yet computer- and staff-equipped centres were often inaccessible to those in remote and poor areas of the country (Sharma, 2001). This is at odds with IGNOU's mission and excludes those arguably most in need of the programmes. Reddy and Sriastava (2001) found that 80 percent of the first BIT cohort printed out most of the online or CDROM materials, and many protested about the costs of telephone line and printing involved. Once again, a digital and educational divide seems likely.

Hodge and Hayward (2004) also argue that the commercialisation of distance education has rapidly diminished the equity philosophy of distance educators in most developing nations.

Mingle (as cited in Cunningham et al., 2000) observed sorrowfully that "the market won't support research, arts, science, small institutions, and low income students". And "the market" has no interest in the "difficult" student: Kaplan and the then Sylvan quickly exited remedial teaching programmes based heavily on computerised instruction, in community colleges in the late 1990s.

It seems clear then that the "borders" between distance and on-campus education are diminishing. Convergence of modes of delivery proceeds apace, with increasing numbers of notionally on-campus students in the United States and Australia also enrolling in "flexible" or "distance"/off-campus/online programmes. Students appreciate the convenience of online resources that can be accessed around their working and social lives and are showing a declining preference for traditional face-to-face-only delivery.

Although the OECD (2005, p. 6) confidently asserts that "no clear sustainable business model has yet emerged for commercial provision of e-learning", UoP Online's success suggests there is profit to be made. The OECD report, however, is correct in arguing that there are as yet "very few" transnational online enrolments, and these mostly in the areas of IT and business. UoP Online crosses borders, certainly, but these are mainly *intra*-US borders, notwithstanding their boast of students from 130 countries; mostly these students are US military or US citizens temporarily offshore. Bates (2004) reports the same pattern in the University of British Columbia's online Masters in Educational Technology.

On the evidence of distance programmes which attempt to use digital technologies to support students' learning, we can observe commercialising trends which increasingly exclude those who cannot pay.

In 2004, The Commonwealth of Learning (http://www.col.org/colweb/site) widely promoted distance education as a key element in the achievement of the Millennium Development Goals by 2015. If there is hope in that vision, we must acknowledge the new model of distance education, which combines the use of digital technologies, face-to-face learner support, and independent learning, *and* provide aid to support that model. It *may* mean admitting fewer students, but those admitted will be more likely to complete the qualifications and programmes needed for social and economic progress. Economic rationing through the imposition of student fees may serve the developed world well; it cannot be the basis for education in the developing world.

REFERENCES

Apollo Group. (2005). Retrieved February 1, 2006 from, www.apollogroup.edu/annual-reports /2005.

Australian Education International (AEI). (2006). Retrieved March 7, 2006 from http://aei.dest. gov.au/AEI/PublicationsAndResearch/ResearchDatabase/Default.htm

Bates, A. (2004). Technology and lifelong learning: myths and realities. In *Distance Learning and Technology: Issues and Practices* (D. Murphy, R. Carr, J. Taylor, and W. Tat-meng, Eds.) Hong Kong: OUHK Press, pp. 9–30.

Belawati, T. (1998). Increasing student persistence in Indonesian post-secondary distance education. *Distance Education*, **19**(1), 81–108.

Business Week (2006). Retrieved March 5, 2006 from http://www.businessweek.com/bschools/03/distance_profiles/unext.htm.

Campus Review, June 8, 2005a, p. 5.

Campus Review, October 19, 2005b, p. 1.

Campus Review, January 24, 2006, p. 13.

Castells, M. (2000). *The Rise of the Network Society, The Information Age: Economy, Society and Culture*, Vol. I. Cambridge, MA; Oxford, UK: Blackwell (1996) (Second edition, 2000).

Chronicle of Higher Education, online edition, November 15, 2004.

Chronicle of Higher Education, (online edition; January 31, 2002).

Corporate Universities Xchange (2004). *Sixth Annual Benchmarking*. Report http://www.corpu.com. Retrieved December 12, 2004.

Cunningham, S., Ryan, Y., Stedman, L. et al. (2000). *The Business of Borderless Education, Evaluations and Investigations Program*. Canberra: Department of Employment, Education, Training and Youth Affairs.

Cunningham, S., Tapsall, S., Ryan, Y. et al. (1998). *New Media and Borderless Education: A Review of the Convergence Between Global Media Networks and Higher*

Education Provision, Evaluations and Investigations Program. Canberra: Department of Employment, Education, Training and Youth Affairs.
Crystal, D. (1997). *English as a Global Language*. Cambridge: Cambridge University Press.
Currie, J., De Angelis, R., de Boer, H. et al. (2003). *Global Practices and University Responses*. Westport, CT: Greenwood Press.
Daniel, J. (1996). *Mega-Universities and Knowledge Media: Technology Strategies for Higher Education*. London: Kogan Page.
Darkwa, O. and Mazibuko, F. (2000). *Creating Virtual Learning Communities in Africa: Challenges and Prospects*. Retrieved October 11, 2001 from http:www.firstmonday.dk/issues/issues5_5/darkwa.
Doherty, C. (2004). *Managing Potentials: Cultural Differencing in a Site of Global/Local Education*. Paper presented at Australian Association of Research in Education Annual Conference, 28 November–2 December, University of Melbourne, Victoria.
Duke FUQUA School of Business. (2006a). Retrieved March 5, 2006 from http://www.fuqua.duke.edu/mba/executive/global
Duke FUQUA School of Business. (2006b). Retrieved March 5, 2006 from http://www.economist.com/globalexecutive/education/executive/profile2.cfm?id=duke-fuqua
Dymock, D. and Hobson, P. (1998). Collaborative learning thorough audio conferencing and voicemail – A case study. *Distance Education*, **19**(1), 157–171.
Garrett, R. (2004). The Global Education Index 2004: Part 2: Public companies relationships with non-profit higher education. *The Observatory Report*. Retrieved September 6, 2004 from www.obhe.ac.uk. Subscription required.
Garrett, R. and Verbik, L. (2004). *Transnational Delivery by UK Higher Education, Part 1: Data and Missing Data*. London: The Observatory on Borderless Higher Education. Subscription required.
Gourley, B. (2004). The digital divide as a development issue. In *Distance Learning and Technology: Issues and Practices* (D. Murphy, R. Carr, J. Taylor, and W. Tat-meng eds) Hong Kong: OUHK Press, pp. 31–44.
Harman, G. (2006). Australia as a higher education exporter. *International Higher Education*, **42**, 14–16.
Higher Education Quality Committee. (2003). *Criteria for Quality Distance Education in South Africa*. Johannesburg: Department of Education.
Hodge, N. and Hayward, L. (2004). Redefining roles: University distance education contributing to lifelong learning in a networked world. In *Distance Learning and Technology: Issues and Practices* (D. Murphy, R. Carr, J. Taylor, and W. Tat-meng, Eds) Hong Kong: OUHK Press, pp. 111–128.
IDP Education Australia. (2004). *IDP Survey of International Students in Australian Univerisities*. http://www.idp.com/research/fastfacts/Retrieved 30/3/2004.
IGNOU. (2006). Retrieved March 4, 2006 from http://www.ignou.ac.in
Keegan M. (2000). *E-learning: The Engine of the Knowledge Economy*. NY: Morgan Keegan.
Kelly, P. (2000). Internationalizing the Curriculum: For Profit or Planet. In *The University in Transformation: Global Perspectives on the Futures of the University* (S. Inayatullah, and Gidley, J., Eds.) London: Bergin and Harvey, pp. 161–175.
King, B. (2004). Transnational distance education – the critical role of partnership. In *Distance Learning and Technology: Issues and Practices* (D. Murphy, R. Carr, J. Taylor, and W. Tat-meng, eds.) Hong Kong: OUHK Press, pp. 75–88.
Knight, J. (1994). *Internationalization: Elements and Checkpoints. Ottawa:* CBIE
Knight, J. (2002). *Trade in Higher Education Services: The Implications of GATS*. London: The Observatory on Borderless Higher Education, ACU and CVCP.

Knight, J. (2005). *Borderless, Offshore, Transnational and Cross-border Education: Definition and data Dilemmas*. London: OBHE Report.

Koelman, J. and de Vries, P. (1999). Marketisation, hybrid organizations and accounting in higher education. In *From the Eye of the Storm: Higher Education's Changing Institution* (B. Jongbloed, P.Maassen, and G.Neave, Eds.) Dordrecht: Kluwer Academic Publishers, pp. 165–188.

Marginson, S. and Considine, M. (2000). *The Enterprise University: Power, Governance and Reinvention in Australia*. Cambridge: Cambridge University Press.

Mhehe, E. (2001). Confronting barriers to distance study in Tanzania. In *Using Learning Technologies: International Perspectives and Practices* (L. Burge and M. Haughey, Eds.) London: Routledge, pp. 102–111.

Meister, J. (1998). *Corporate Universities: Lessons for a World-Class Work Force*, New York: McGraw-Hill.

Mooney, P. (2006). The Wild, Wild East. *The Chronicle of Higher Education*, **52**(24), 46.

Moore, M. and Kearsley, G. (1996). *Distance Education: A Systems View*. Belmont. CA: Wadsworth.

Murphy, P., Anzalone, S., Bosch, A., and Moulton, J. (2002). *Enhancing Learning Opportunities in Africa: Distance Education and Information and Communication Technologies for Learning*. Washington DC: The World Bank.

National Center for Education Statistics. (2002). *A Profile of Participation in Distance Education 1999–2000*. Washington DC: NCES.

Neave, G. (2002). Globalization: Threat, Opportunity or Both? *International Association of Universities Newsletter*. Retrieved March 1, 2006 from www.unesco.org/iau/he/globalization.index.html.

Ninnes, P. and Hellsten, M. (eds). (2005). *Internationalizing Higher Education: Critical Explorations of Pedagogy and Policy*. Hong Kong: University of Hong Kong/Springer.

OECD. (2005). *E-learning in Tertiary Education: Where do we stand?* Paris: OECD.

Panda, S. (2005). Higher education at a distance and national development: Reflections on the Indian experience. *Distance Education*, **26**(2), 205–225.

Reddy, V. and Sriastava, M. (2001). Virtual education in a developing nation (India): Experiences of IGNOU. *Turkish Online Journal of Distance Education*, **2**(2), 5–10.

Ryan, Y. (2002a). *AVU Baseline Study*. Unpublished report for AusAID, Canberra.

Ryan, Y. (2002b). *Emerging Indicators of Success and Failure in Borderless Higher Education*. London: The Observatory in Borderless Higher Education, ACU. Retrieved February 20, 2002 from www.obhe.ac.uk Subscription required.

Ryan, Y. and King, R. (2004) Impact of the Internet on Higher Education in Australia and Asia, In *The E-University Compendium: Volume One: Cases, Issues and Themes in Higher Education Distance E-Learning* (P.Bacsich and S, Bristow, eds.) http://www.heacademy.ac.uk/1641.htm

Sharma, R. (2001). Online delivery of programmes: A case study of IGNOU., *International Review of Research in Open and Distance Learning*, **1**(2), 1–15.

Tait, A. and Mills, R. (1999). The Convergence of Distance and Conventional Education: Patterns of Flexibility for the Individual Learner. In *The Convergence of Distance and Conventional Education: Patterns of Flexibility for the Individual Learner* (A. Tait and R. Mills, Eds.) Routledge: London.

The Australian Higher Education, June 1, 2005, p. 28.

The Observatory on Borderless Higher Education. (2006). Retrieved March 7, 2006 from http://www.obhe.ac.uk/aboutus.

The Times of India (2006). Retrieved January 23, 2006 from http://timesofindia.indiatimes.com.

THES, February 17, 2005, p. 12.

THES, December 23, 2005, p. 9.

The University of Phoenix (2006a). Retrieved December 16, 2006 from www.phoenix.edu/about_us/publications.

The University of Phoenix (2006b). Retrieved December 16, 2006 from http://online.phoenix.edu/index.html

UNESCO (2002). *Open and Distance Learning: Trends, Policy and Strategy Considerations.* Paris: UNESCO.

UNESCO-CEPES/Council of Europe. (2001). *The UNESCO-CEPES/Council of Europe Code of Good Practice for the Provision of Transnational Education.* Paris: UNESCO.

Vermeer, R. (2004). Online identity and learning. In *Distance Learning and Technology: Issues and Practices* (D. Murphy, R. Carr, J. Taylor, and W. Tat-meng, Eds.) Hong Kong: OUHK Press, pp. 271–290.

World Bank. (2002). *Constructing Knowledge Societies: New Challenges for Tertiary Education.* Washington DC: The World Bank.

Zemsky, R. and Massy, W. (2004). *What Happened to E-Learning and Why.* University of Pennsylvania: The Learning Alliance for Higher Education and Thomson Corp.

Chapter 40

Economic Models of Distance Education

Greville Rumble

This chapter discusses the development of economic models of distance education, our understanding of the factors that drive costs in distance education, and the way in which such models can be used to investigate the funding of distance education.

40.1 EDUCATIONAL COST MODELS

The economics of education developed in the late 1950s and early 1960s following the publication in the United Kingdom of John Vaizey's *The Costs of Education* (1958) and the delivery in the United States, on 28 December 1960, of Theodore Schultz's lecture on "Investment in Human Capital" to the American Economic Association (Schultz, 1961).

Initially interest focused on attempts to quantify the economic benefits of investment in education, but there were other concerns too – notably the efficiency of public expenditure. Most of the costs in traditional education were driven by class size (ACS), the average number of class contact hours undertaken by students (ASH), and the average number of class hours taught by lecturers (ALH). This in turn determined the number of lecturers (L), the cost of these being determined by the average lecturer pay (ALP) per annum. In addition, there were some fixed costs (F), but these rarely accounted for more than about 20 percent of total costs. These relationships were captured in what came to be known as the fundamental (educational) cost model (Eqn 40.1), in which the total cost (T) equalled:

$$T = (L \times \text{ALP}) + F \qquad (40.1)$$

where

$$L = (S \times \text{ASH}) \div (\text{ACS} \times \text{ALH}) \qquad (40.2)$$

This fundamental cost model was sometimes reduced to what was called the basic cost model in which total costs (T) equalled the number of full-time equivalent students (S) times the direct cost per student (DCS) plus the fixed costs (F):

$$T = (S \times \text{DCS}) + F \tag{40.3}$$

The average cost per student (ACS) was derived by dividing the fixed costs of the system by the number of students, and then adding the DCS:

$$\text{ACS} = (F \div S) + \text{DCS} \tag{40.4}$$

Since the fixed costs were in general a small proportion of the total cost, the potential for economies of scale arising from the spreading of fixed costs across an expanded student body was extremely small. Efficiency studies thus focused on the reduction of the direct cost of per student by, for example,

- reducing student class hours (ASH);
- increasing the average class size (ACS);
- reducing the cost of lecturers (ALP) by hiring adjunct staff on lower salaries and, more commonly, hiring adjunct lecturers by the hour.

As educational budgets exploded, and as interest focused on the need to develop the educational systems of emergent ex-colonies, governments, development agencies such as the World Bank and UNESCO, and aid agencies such as USAID became more interested in whether or not "the new media" (cf. Schramm et al., 1967) could substitute for teachers (thus making up for teacher shortages) and cut educational costs. By the late 1960s, mass media were being used to provide a wide range of educational and training opportunities outside schools and colleges.

Quite separate from all of this, correspondence education had developed in the nineteenth century, initially to provide educational opportunities to those out of school. Later, it came to be used to meet the needs of school- and college-age children, young adults, and adults who were unable to attend an educational institution for classes. Many of the early correspondence education providers operated within the private sector on a for-profit basis, with little public discussion of their commercially sensitive cost data. Publicly funded projects developed towards the end of the nineteenth century. These also showed little interest in the costs of the educational technologies they were using. In part, this reflected a period in which innovation in teaching methods was a largely marginal activity (Coombs, 1968, p. 7). However, the development of large-scale, technology-intensive systems, designed to reach many thousands of learners, and involving very considerable investment in infrastructure and sizeable operating budgets, eventually attracted the attention of economists as governments, development agencies, and managers grappled with the escalating costs of technology-intensive projects. This was particularly true of systems using educational television.

By the early 1970s, a number of agencies such as UNESCO, the World Bank, and USAID had begun to research the costs of technology-based and distance education projects

(Klees et al., 1977; UNESCO, 1977; Eicher et al., 1982). From an economic point of view, the basic cost structure of technology-intensive projects was quickly identified as involving the following elements:

- The cost of developing a curriculum and the learning materials supporting it. Since materials are usually developed with the view that they will last a number of years, these costs are usually annualised over the average life of the materials;
- The cost of copying, storing, and distributing learning materials;
- The annual costs of presenting a course (for example, preparing examination papers);
- The cost of admitting, billing, advising, teaching, examining, and supporting students, and of keeping records on them;
- The annual costs of sustaining the business (leadership, planning, technology, financial, and human resource management).

The basic cost function for educational television systems developed by Jamison et al. (1978, pp. 93–98) indicated that the total costs (TC) of a system were made up of the costs (C) of a number of functions:

$$TC = C_C + C_P + C_T + C_R \tag{40.5}$$

where the subscripts C, P, T, and R refer to central, programming, transmission, and reception, respectively (Eqn 40.5). Each of these constituent components (C_C, C_P, etc.) was further broken down into separate cost functions that reflected the variables driving the costs. Among the main system variables identified (p. 94) were the number of students, the number of hours of programming each year, the area of the region to be served, the number of pages of printed material for each student, the number of students who share a receiver, the fraction of the reception sites located in non-electrified areas, and the number of reception sites. Among the cost variables identified are the cost of project planning and start-up, central administration, the production facility (land and buildings), and the production equipment; the annual cost of programme production; the cost of the transmission facility (land and buildings); the annual cost of power, maintenance, and operating personnel for a transmitter capable of covering the area served; the cost of one receiver; the cost of related reception equipment (e.g. antennae) for reception sites; the cost of building modifications for television reception; the cost per reception site for power generation equipment (required for television only in non-electrified areas); the cost of electric power per reception site per hour (using power lines); the cost of electric power per reception site per hour using local power generation equipment or batteries; the cost per hour for maintenance at each reception site; and the cost of a book per page (pp. 94–95). All capital items were annualised for a given number of years (which varied depending on the nature of the capital item) using the standard annualisation factor, a(r, n) and an appropriate social discount rate (r).

The approach initially used by those modelling the costs of the distance teaching universities was much simpler. Just three-variable, cost-inducing outputs were identified: the number of courses in development/production; the number of courses in presentation; and the number of students. Capital costs were ignored. Wagner's (1977, pp. 370–371) cost function explaining the costs of the British Open University (Eqn 40.6) is a good example of the approach taken:

$$E = \alpha + \beta_n C_n + \chi_p C_p + \delta S \tag{40.6}$$

where

E = the total recurrent expenditure
α = the total fixed costs of the enterprise
β_n = the average variable cost of development/production per standard course equivalent per year
C_n = the number of standard course equivalents in development/production in any year
χ_p = the average variable cost of presentation per standard course equivalent per year
C_p = the number of standard course equivalents in presentation in any year
δ = the average variable cost per full-time equivalent student per year
S = the number of full-time equivalent students.

Both these models assume that the total costs of a "system" are made up of a combination of fixed and variable costs. Fixed costs are those that do not vary with any change in the level of activity; variable costs do change. The total costs of a system (T) will thus be equivalent to the sum of the fixed costs (F) plus the variable cost per unit of activity (V) times the volume of activity (X):

$$T = F + VX \tag{40.7}$$

In this simplified model, the costs of course development and presentation are treated as a "fixed" cost, although obviously this would change were more courses to be added to the profile, and/or development and production levels increased. The average cost per student (A) in this model is equal to the variable cost per student (V) plus a "share" of the overhead costs (F):

$$A = V + F/S \tag{40.8}$$

Run against rising student numbers, Eqn 40.8 will show how average costs fall in a distance education system (Figure 40.1):

Significantly, the cost curve flattens out as student numbers rise and the economies of scale drop off.

Models such as these are usually derived by analysing expenditure in order to identify the money spent in support of each variable. The money spent on each variable is then divided by the volume of each identifiable variable to obtain an average cost per variable unit. So, for example, analysis of the accounts showing a total annual recurrent expenditure of $37,000,000 may show that of this sum $7,200,000 can be attributed to business sustaining activities which may be deemed to be "fixed" within the current level of activities plus or minus, say, 15 percent (the *critical range* in which these costs are said to be fixed). Of the other costs, $16,390,000 is being spent on courses – $14,751,000 on

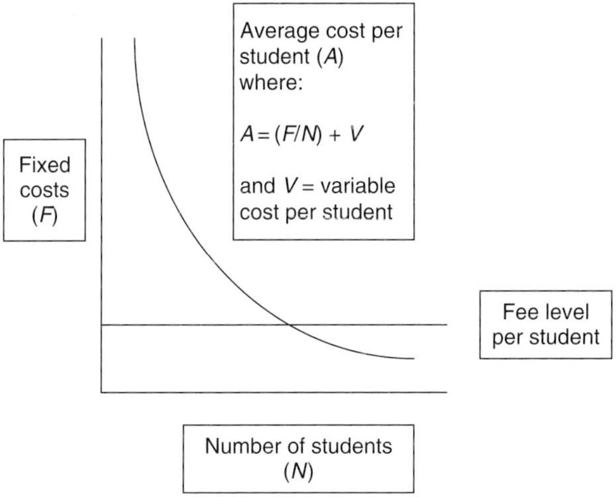

Figure 40.1: Average Cost Per Student Curve in Distance Education

developing each year twenty course modules (an average development cost per module of $737,550), and $1,639,000 on maintaining the 100 courses in the academic profile (an average cost of $16,390 per year per course). The remaining $13,410,000 is spent providing student support to 27,000 students at an average cost of $496.67. These figures can now be fed into Eqn 40.6 to provide values for the model:

$$E = \alpha + \beta_n C_n + \chi_p C_p + \delta S \tag{40.6}$$

(The small difference in total expenditure arises because of the rounding up of the cost per student to two decimal places.) Furthermore, the average cost per student (A) is easy to calculate since this is derived from the following equation:

$$A = \delta + (\alpha + \beta_n C_n + \chi_p C_p / S) \tag{40.9}$$

This model can then be used to assess the implications of changes in the volume of activity: What if student numbers rise to 31,000 and new course development rises to twenty modules per year? How will this affect total expenditure? And how will this affect average costs per student?

The value of models such as that in Eqn 40.6 is seriously weakened by three major flaws. Firstly, the whole model depends on the idea that one can define an average course with an average cost per course, or an average student with an average cost per student. This is at best a convenient fiction. In practice, individual students are likely to be studying full- or part-time, taking subjects that require costly support, and subjects that require relatively little support. Even courses within a subject may have different levels of support designed into them. So at best the models provide us with a crude, aggregated, approximation of costs.

Secondly, a model such as this does not specify "the fundamental variables that affect costs in sufficient detail to be of practical value to people who are trying to prepare an operating budget for an institution" (Rumble et al., 1981, p. 235). For example, the development, production, and delivery cost of a course vary depending on the mix of media, with each technology having a different cost structure. In addition, the way in which technologies are structured, organisationally, varies enormously. Some institutions use in-house facilities; others outsource much of the development and production. Also, organisations vary in the extent to which they use permanent staff on permanent contracts (what is often referred to as core staffing) as opposed to staff on short-term contracts (peripheral staffing). Such differences can affect costs greatly. Similarly, in the case of student costs, while many of the costs of student support are driven by the number of individual students in the system, some are driven by the number of student course enrolments, and others by the number of groups of students.

Thirdly, there is the assumption that fixed costs are indeed fixed. In practice, they are likely to change over time in response to changes in the level of output, and also to changing conditions and expectations.

A further problem with some of the models is that they do not take account of capital costs. Jamison et al. took account of the costs of capital in their models of the costs of educational television systems. However, the models used to cost the distance teaching universities did not do this. Economists generally agree that the costs of capital tied up in projects need to be taken into account (Jamison et al., 1978, p. 32; Wagner, 1982, p. 89; Levin, 1983, pp. 68–69). Not everyone agrees that the cost of capital needs to be taken into account. The use of interest rates to assess the relative cost of public projects involving capital elements does not, in Eicher's view, rest upon a sound theoretical basis for public finance decisions (because such decisions rarely in fact involve a choice between spend and investment for income growth) (Eicher, 1978, p. 13). However, since one of the cost advantages of distance teaching universities is that they do not need to provide lecture halls and seminar rooms, and one of their cost disadvantages is that they may need to provide production, storage, and distribution facilities, this is a serious omission. Indeed, it is difficult to see how a true comparison of costs between a highly capital-intensive and a less-capital-intensive option can be obtained without taking at least the annualised capital cost into account.

The cost of capital is generally done using the annualisation equation that "annualises" capital costs by estimating an average of the combination of depreciation and interest on the un-depreciated portion over the life of the facility (Eqn 40.10):

$$a(r, n) = \frac{r(1+r)^n}{(1+r)^n - 1} \qquad (40.10)$$

where $a(r, n)$ is the annualisation factor, n is the life of the capital equipment, and r is the prevailing rate of interest. It is worth noting, however, that quite small changes in the rate of interest and the lifetime assumptions made will have significant implications for the total cost of the project.

Another problem affects those distance education projects that are embedded in dual-mode institutions (i.e. institutions that teach both by traditional and by distance means). The problem arises because some of the costs of the two approaches may be shared because of the existence of what are called joint products. A *joint product* is one of two or more products in which, initially, a single stream of inputs goes in until a "separation point" is reached, after which the products are acted on separately. For example, academics may develop a course and then teach one version by traditional class-based means and another version by distance means; or a series of lectures delivered in class may be videotaped and subsequently used in a distance programme. Equally, some of the overhead costs of the institution will support the distance programme, and some the off-campus programme, and will therefore need to be apportioned across the products if only for pricing purposes. Rumble (1997, pp. 65–70) identifies no less than six different approaches used to attribute development costs to joint products in mixed-mode institutions, and two approaches to attribute delivery costs. Such variations can radically affect the level of reported costs in systems and can be used both to manipulate data provided to funding bodies and to "justify" different pricing decisions.

In many dual-mode institutions, the initial decision to offer courses by distance means was taken at departmental level, often by a group of enthusiastic academics. Costs were absorbed by enthusiasm as individuals created course materials by videotaping lectures and/or producing lecture notes for a relatively small number of students. Such cottage industries hardly seemed worth costing. Where costs were identified, these seemed to be confined to the costs of copying materials and despatching them to students. As studies by Wagner (1975) and Fwu et al. (1992) showed, the per student costs of videotaping lectures was very small. The additional costs of assessing and supporting the off-campus students were often kept low by using graduate assistants, and in any case, these costs were usually balanced against additional fee income. Such studies that were undertaken tended to focus on the additional costs of producing materials, thus essentially enabling the distance programme to free-ride on the back of the main development effort, which was the cost of developing and supporting the campus-based course.

Occasionally, an attempt was made to acknowledge that the original development costs of the face-to-face course also supported the distance programme. In these cases, the cost of the original development might be calculated and either split 50:50 across the campus and the distance programmes or apportioned on a student number basis. Sometimes the additional costs of the distance course were charged wholly to the distance programme; at other times they were lumped in with the face-to-face development costs and the total development costs shared across the programmes, either 50:50 (a common approach in Australia) or, more unusually, on a student per capita basis. Such differences generally reflected varying attitudes towards funding rather than any wish to get at the different costs of programmes within dual-mode institutions. Overall, most institutions did not bother one way or the other, or took the easy option and shared all costs across all students, without distinction.

On the whole, these different approaches reflected the fact that for many dual-mode institutions, it simply was not worth the bother of tracking costs at course and student levels. Not only were the financial systems in place inadequate for the task, but the level of activity was marginal to the main focus of the institution, which was teaching students face-to-face traditional means. As a result, information vital to rational decision-making about the allocation of resources across programmes of activity was often lacking.

In many ways, the development of online or e-learning has merely replicated the experience of the past. Most projects were initially undertaken by enthusiasts who developed online materials and support systems at the margins of their other work. Materials were generally (and often still are) relatively simple – perhaps a course outline coupled with a bibliography/webliography that provides access both to documents scanned into a (usually) limited e-library for students registered on the course, coupled with pointers to further study online, and to other printed materials. In parallel, there may be a discussion forum within a structured computer conferencing environment. Exercise and assessment material may also be available online. Relatively few online courses offer access to sophisticated materials (video, games, simulations, and virtual reality environments). Academic development costs are kept low, while the impact on staff time is also minimised through restrictions on the number of students. The majority of courses have relatively few students and are supported by a single academic or an academic working with an assistant. Importantly, most courses are run using existing networking facilities and standardised packages that support online teaching and learning. The overall tendency appears to be not to cost provision at the course level.

Yet at both the individual course level and the institutional level, an understanding of the relative costs of provision would help identify the cut-off points at which one model of course development/presentation becomes more or less costly than another. Assuming that one knows the costs of two systems – say a distance learning system and a face-to-face system, it is not too difficult to answer questions concerning the break-even point at which the two systems have a similar unit cost. For example, assume that the fixed costs (F_1) of putting on a traditional face-to-face course with twenty learners is \$4,440, with variable costs (V_1) of \$2,322 per student, while the fixed cost (F_1) of putting on a distance course is \$164,500, with variable costs (V_2) of \$421 per student (the variable cost is equivalent to the DCS in Eqn 40.3 and the variable cost per student in Eqn 40.7). The break-even point (B) at which the two courses have the same unit cost per student is:

$$\begin{aligned} B &= (F1 - F2) \div (V2 - V1) \\ &= (164{,}500 - 4{,}440) \div (2{,}322 - 421) \\ &= 84.2 \text{ students.} \end{aligned} \tag{40.11}$$

Thus, if over a given period of time there are under eighty-four students taking the programme, it will be cheaper, given the relative fixed and variable costs of the option, to teach the course by traditional means; and if there are over eighty-four students, then distance education becomes an economically attractive proposition.

The challenge of accurately developing cost models remains. Each technology has its own cost structure. Cost complexity is then compounded by organisational, staffing, and other factors. The different cost structures mean that a technology that is cheap to use when there are relatively few students enrolled on a course can become relatively expensive in absolute and in unit cost terms if there are lots of students enrolled. Similarly, technologies that are very expensive in unit cost terms when teaching relatively few students may offer economies of scale that make them very attractive for teaching large numbers of students. Since most courses use a combination of technologies, considerable analysis needs to be undertaken if the cheapest option is to be used. (Not, of course, that using the cheapest option is necessarily the only criterion for coming to a judgement on technology mix: other factors, such as access to the technology, ease of use, and robustness, all affect choice.)

The next section looks at some of the factors that affect costs.

40.2 FACTORS DRIVING COSTS IN EDUCATION

Identification of drivers affecting costs in technology-based and face-to-face education has developed over the years. It is now possible to identify in general terms a range of factors that can affect costs. The way in which these factors interact is often complex, however, making it far less easy to specify outside of a specific context exactly what the likely impact of these factors will be on costs.

40.2.1 Media and Technology Choice

Technology choice has a significant affect on both total and average costs. Technology always interacts with human beings; hence a real understanding of the costs of a given technology can only be taken within the context of an understanding of the socio-technical system that surrounds it. A range of socio-technical structures thus support the use of the various media (text, audio, video, face-to-face, and computing) used to support education.

Face-to-face teaching in lectures (any audience size), seminars (small- to medium-sized group teaching), and tutorials or supervisions (one-to-one or one-to-two) involve relatively low fixed costs but, particularly in the case of small- and medium-sized group teaching, incurs a rapid increase in student variable costs because increases in student numbers have to be matched with increases in staff numbers. The average student:staff ratio can vary enormously. In UK higher education, a feature of the past 30 years has been an increase of the average number of students per member of staff. This has had a major effect on the cost structure of campus-based higher education in the United Kingdom. As Scott (1997, p. 38) comments,

> the massification of British higher education is demonstrated [by] the sharp reduction in unit costs. Overall productivity gains of more than 25 percent have been achieved since 1990....This pattern, which exactly matches the expansion of student numbers, closely follows the cost curves in other countries where mass higher education systems developed earlier than in Britain. *It supports the claim that mass systems have a quite different economy from that of élite systems.* [my italics].

Generally speaking, where few students are involved, face-to-face teaching may be the cheapest option. Depending on the technology chosen, for large numbers the labour substitution enabled by distance education can produce a more cost-efficient solution than traditional approaches. Systems that combine technologies' face-to-face contact tend to be the most expensive solutions.

Although distance education systems are generally said to have high fixed costs, but low variable costs per student, each technology has its own cost structure, dependent on the mix of fixed and variable cost elements. In the mid-1990s, Bates (1995, p. 5) indicated that print, audio cassettes, and pre-recorded instructional television were the only media that were relatively low cost for courses with populations of from under 250 students a year to over 1,000 students a year. In addition, radio was also likely to be low cost on courses with populations of 1,000 or more students. Other media, such as good-quality broadcast television, pre-programmed computer-based learning, and multimedia, are much more expensive.

This judgement still holds. However, the problem with such generalisations is that technology costs are in practice susceptible to wide variations. For example, Bates (1995, p. 197) gave a cost range of from Canadian $2,600 to over $21,000 per student hour for the development of online teaching materials, while Arizona Learning Systems (1998, pp. 13–14) suggested costs of from US $6,000 to $1,000,000 for a three-unit Internet course, depending on the approach used. The cheapest approach involved the presentation of simple course outlines and assignments; more expensive options included the provision of text ($12,000), text with reference materials ($18,000), images ($37,500), audio and video ($120,000), simulations ($250,000), and virtual reality ($1,000,000).

One of the interesting features of electronic moderating could be the moderator's experience of the time it takes to support students electronically. In face-to-face tuition, there is a clear cost control mechanism in place – the timetable. The same is not true of online teaching, where the pressure is to respond to students' queries rapidly and individually. Tolley (2000, p. 263) recounts her experience as a tutor on the "correspondence" and "online" versions of an open university course. On the version of the course with scheduled tutorials, she estimated she spent 42 hours (10 hours preparation, 17 hours teaching, 15 hours sent preparing and sending tutorial-related mailings), though this excluded her (unpaid) travel time to the tutorials (12 hours) and the unrelated time she spent marking assignments. On the online version, she spent 120 hours excluding assignment marking. In other words, her workload more than doubled. In addition, working online had a "dramatic effect" on her telephone bill. Crucially she was not paid for the additional time she spent. When tutors begin to demand to be paid for the increased workload, some chickens may come home to roost, either in demands for increased pay or in a reluctance to take the job. Arizona Learning Systems (1998, p. 20) reported that faculty workload costs have pushed the typical direct cost per course enrolment of an Internet course (US$571) above that of traditional classroom instruction ($474), although they suggested that faculty workload could be reduced through improved support and processes such as academic help desks (p. 7). In some cases, colleges have restricted course enrolments in order to bring instructor time down (p. 22). Annand (1999) suggests that it is these costs that may in the end constrain the extent to which large-scale distance teaching universities can adopt online technologies.

The problem of costing such practices arises not just because of inherent differences in complexity in the way in which the technology is used but also because a whole range of organisational and working practices impact on the actual cost of the technology as it is used *in particular circumstances*. There may also be problems because costs in one system may not be directly comparable with those in another. For example, some systems have access to facilities (for example, study centre space or transmission time) at preferential rates; in other cases, costs that in one system fall on the institution's budget may in another be passed on to the students, so that comparisons based on *institutional* budgets are misleading. It is very important, when one comes to compare the costs of one system with another, to be clear about the precise nature of the model being used and to understand how this can affect cost comparisons.

The main message to emerge from these studies is that there are a great many caveats that have to be made to any statement about the costs of technology within education. The problems is that the cost of a given technology is not just driven by the hardware and software costs of that technology, but by other factors – of which the working practices underpinning the use of the technology are perhaps the most important.

40.2.2 Using Existing Materials

The costs of developing courses can be brought down by developing "wrap-around" materials to accompany existing textbooks and other materials and thus "transforming" them into a distance course, by "commodifying" traditional lectures (by, for example, videotaping them) for later use and by buying-in material developed elsewhere by another supplier (Rumble, 1997, pp. 87–91). Certainly, the additional costs of videotaping lectures and reusing them for subsequent generations of students can be very low indeed (Fwu et al., 1992). Studies suggest, however, that the cost advantages of buying-in materials can be overestimated. Although this may be a cheaper option for low student numbers, payments to the providing institution mean that it can be cheaper to develop one's own materials – with Curran (1993, p. 21) suggesting that the break-even point at which this is true can be as low as 123 students on a course.

Because of the high cost of developing materials, there has been increasing interest in reusing materials that have not become dated (see Littlejohn, 2003). The discussion on the reuse of course resources is focused on the concept of a "learning object", defined as a digitalised or non-digitalised entity which can stand on its own and be used, reused, or referenced during technology-supported learning. Learning objects may be media objects, such as a text, video, audio, or graphical elements, interactive objects, such as a simulation, game, or diagram with movable parts, or assessment objects. A learning object contains within itself not just content, which would be a mere "information object," but also the learning context within which the content is used. The rather clumsy word "granularisation" has been coined to refer to the size of learning objects; "levels of granularity" (Duncan 2003, pp. 12, 15) refers to the extent to which courses can be disaggregated into learning objects suitable for reuse elsewhere.

The key, then, is to identify within existing courses, or design into new courses, learning object "chunks" that are self-contained and reusable with the objective to bring down unit production costs. Learning objects support the learning of more students (scalability), increase efficiency with prolonged life (sustainability), and lessen the need to develop new objects in subsequent courses (cannibalisation). Ideally, the cost of identifying suitable learning objects should not be too great. Whether this is so will depend on the extent to which individual learning objects can be adequately described and catalogued in ways that enable would-be users to search for, identify, and access the learning object relatively quickly, and certainly in less time that it takes them to prepare their own materials. It will also depend on the extent of "editing" required to fit a learning object into the recipient's framework – be that a content, linguistic, level, or qualifications framework.

40.2.3 Working Practices and Organisational Structures

Much of the information that we have on the costs of technologies is derived from particular case studies. Although analysts frequently counsel against assuming that the costs in one system will be similar to those in another, the urge to generate guidance for policy-makers often leads to an assumption that the cost experience of one institution will transfer to another. Underlying this assumption is a belief that technology determines the social sphere (that is, the organisational structures, hierarchies, and work roles) within which it is used. Particular levels of costs are then thought to be a natural outcome of the socio-technical conditions engendered by a given technology. While technological determinism has now been discredited (cf. Grint and Woolgar, 1997, pp. 11–14 for a resumé of the arguments), the perspective has a long history and was still being advocated in the 1960s and 1970s (Bell, 1960, 1973; Blauner, 1964; Kerr et al., 1964). Blauner (1964, p. 6), for example, maintained that "the most important single factor that gives an industry a distinctive character is its technology".

A technologically determinist approach to distance education would manifest itself in assumptions that it is the technology itself that determines the structures of distance education systems. There is some evidence of this in recent literature. Thus, Daniel (1996) suggested that what he calls the "mega-universities" (that is, universities that have distance teaching as their primary activity, and in excess of 100,000 active enrolments [p. 29]) "operate differently from other universities in many ways, not least in the way they have redefined the tasks of the academic faculty and introduced a division of labour into the teaching function" (p. 30). He went on to claim that "*changes in technology transform* the *structures* of industries" (p. 80, my italics). Furthermore, he saw this is a continuing process since "it is clear that *new technologies*, such as computer conferencing and the Internet, *will change* the format of university courses taught at a distance" (p. 130, my italics). In point of fact, of course, the relationship of technology to structure, work roles, skill levels, etc. is not simple, not constant across settings and firms, and not determined by the technology itself, but by management. This does not negate the fact that technology can be used by management to reduce costs and that technology change may be accompanied by organisational change.

This kind of technological determinism can blind managers to the very real variations in the way in which technologies are used in practice, and to the wide range of costs that result. In fact, the way in which work is organised around a given technology, and the way in which human resources are engaged in the enterprise (including the use of casual as opposed to core labour), has a profound effect on costs (Rumble, 1997, pp. 83–87).

Many distance teaching systems have industrialised the organisation of materials development, production, and delivery, thus breaking with the traditional craft approaches that characterise traditional education (Peters, 1967, 1973, 1983, 1989). The overall task of teaching can thus be divided into its constituent roles – curriculum design, instructional design, content preparation, materials development, and production – tasks which themselves may require a number of specialisms, tutorial back-up, continuous assessment, and examination script marking. These roles can be given to different people, in part reflecting the need to access specialist knowledge and skills and in part because the very nature of the system would make it difficult for one person to undertake all of the tasks (e.g. to both develop all the materials and teach and assess all the students on a large-scale course). Most large-scale systems have a division of labour between those who develop the materials and those who support and assess the students. However, where student course numbers are low, individual academics may both develop the materials and teach the students (Rumble, 1986, pp. 127–129). Those who believe that the industrialised model reduces academic autonomy and control over the teaching process and thus degrades academic work (e.g. Campion and Renner, 1992; Raggatt, 1993) see this model as particularly attractive. It is one of the reasons why online teaching models are thought to be so attractive – though any in fact any system that involves both the development of online materials and the support of online students is likely to begin to move towards a division of labour if course student numbers increase beyond the support capacity of a small group of academics.

The organisation of the course development process – and the way in which it is planned and controlled – also varies greatly. Course authors can work on their own, with an editor (the author-editor or transformer model), in small groups, or in large course teams (Rumble, 1997, pp. 83–86) – the latter being an expensive way of developing materials (Perry, 1976, p. 91). What is feasible is in part determined by the way in which the curriculum has been divided, and the content organised. Small modules or courses, and those based more heavily around existing texts and materials, allow much greater scope for individual academic control, while large modules and those involving a great deal of specially developed materials are likely to require a big team effort. In general, the use of consultants can bring down costs significantly (Rumble, 1997, p. 87).

The division of academic labour has been accompanied by another feature – the use of short-term and piece-work contracts. The nature of the employment contract is a crucial factor in determining costs. Course developers may be hired on permanent, full-time contracts *of* service to develop course materials. This is the most costly option, with a potential long-term commitment (to holiday, sick, and study leave) up to retirement age. Alternatively, they can be hired on short-term temporary contracts *of* service that limit the long-term liability of the employer, or as consultant authors and materials' developers on contracts *for* service, essentially paid piece-rates for their output. This latter option is relatively cheap. As for the tutors who support the students, many of them are employed on piece-work rates, paid by the hour for their class tutoring, or by the script in respect of assignment and examination scripts marked.

In mixed-mode institutions, course developers may teach on-campus students as well as develop materials. In some systems, staff who have a full teaching load on-campus are bought out to help develop distance teaching materials, to develop either a version of their own existing on-campus courses or a new course (Rumble, 1986, pp. 131–133; 1997, pp. 81–83). However, this does not always happen, with the result that staff may be reluctant to get involved in mixed-mode operations (Ellis, 2000).

Non-academic work – for example, editing, illustration – can also be given to consultants, while whole functions such as printing and the production and transmission of broadcasting may also be outsourced, either to a single supplier or to a number of suppliers. Whether outsourcing actually saves money will depend on circumstances including the relative transaction costs of in-house versus outsourced work, and the extent to which outside providers can offer a price that is competitive.

40.2.4 The Curriculum

The number of courses on offer is also an important variable. The more courses that are offered, the greater the investment in developing, maintaining, and remaking the course materials will be. The number of courses offered depends in part on the number of awards or qualifications on offer, the range of subjects offered within those qualifications, and the extent to which students can choose elective courses as opposed to being restricted to mandatory courses.

The number of years over which courses are presented, and the frequency with which materials have to be remade, will also affect costs. All content dates with the passage of time, but in some subject areas (e.g. computing), knowledge dates extremely quickly, while in other subjects changes of legislation, societal change, and changes in academic interests and the impact of research on the subject, all result in the need to update courses.

40.2.5 The Number of Learners

All commentators recognise that the number of students enrolled in a system is a crucial factor affecting both total system costs and average student costs. Media and technology choice will have a bearing here, given that some technologies lend themselves to economies of scale while others do not. Systems that provide considerable support to students generally deliver significantly less in the way of economies of scale than those providing little or no support.

It is generally assumed that the more students a distance learning system has, the lower the average cost, and this is broadly so. This has led many distance education systems to seek to expand their student numbers year on year. There is, however, a problem with this. What distance educators seem to do in many ways parallels the wasteful practices of the post-Second World War American automobile industry (see Johnson, 1992, pp. 44–46) by assuming that the high overhead costs "inherent" in distance education can be "controlled" by expanding student numbers to position oneself to sell places on courses at a lower rate than more traditional institutions. Thus, the emphasis is placed on driving expansion fast enough to cover overhead costs that are, to a considerable extent, caused by scale and complexity and that are deemed to be "fixed" and hence beyond control. But most, the economies of scale are reaped early on in expansion. The nature of the average cost curve is such that the more students there are in the system, the harder it becomes to achieve significant economies of scale. The pursuit of expansion in itself may cause costs to rise.

Thought must also be given to the number of students at individual course level. For any given student population, the more courses on offer, the lower the average course population. However, students will rarely if ever be distributed equally across the courses. It is much more likely that the 80:20 rule will apply, with 80 percent of the students enrolled on something like 20 percent of the courses, so that one can expect a few courses have very high student populations, and a large number to have relatively few students on them. Planners thus need to consider the likely student population on each course and bear this in mind in selecting the media to be used on each course.

40.3 CONCLUSIONS

These findings suggest that the use of models is fraught with dangers. Rumble et al. (1981), in seeking to develop models that would capture the costs of distance education accurately, argued the need both to analyse costs accurately and to identify quite specifically the drivers that generate cost changes. Such a process lies at the heart of activity-based costing approaches, and it is the only way in which costs can be accurately modelled. Unfortunately, most of the costing systems employed in education still have their foundation in accounting systems that pre-date the development of activity-based costing. Such systems have difficulty in dealing with multi-product systems because (a) they take little or no account of variations in the design of courses and the levels of service offered to different students, but instead assume a "standard" course model and "standard" student incurring "average" direct costs; (b) they often fail to identify the real drivers of costs; and (c) they allocate overheads to products by largely arbitrary means (see Johnson & Kaplan, 1987, for a critique of twentieth-century management accounting systems).

The failure to recognise the wide variation in costs of products and services to students, and the failure to identify the drivers actually pushing costs, means that the models identified above are of limited use in helping decision makers understand and cope with the real behaviour and complexity of costs in distance education systems. This is a major limitation because even within a single institution the range of course "models" and the study patterns of students can vary enormously. This largely invalidates the use of simple cost functions to project forward total system costs in situations where student numbers are increasing or being reduced, or where curriculum, organisational, technological, and process changes are underway. There are also special factors relating to the use of results from analyses undertaken in one jurisdiction (say the United Kingdom) to draw inferences concerning the cost implications of a similar model in, say, a developing country. This is because labour costs are likely to be much lower in the latter, at the same time as the cost of technology inputs are likely to be much higher. Thus, a given technology (say computer-assisted learning) may be a viable and cost-efficient option within a developed country because, when substituted for high-cost labour, it brings the unit costs per learner down; but where the hourly costs of a teacher are pegged to the income expectations of a developing country, the substitution of high-cost imported technology for local labour may actually drive unit costs up (Orivel, 2000, pp. 147–149). These are very real drawbacks, and limit the value of the studies in terms of the practical advice that can be gained from them to guide future decision-making.

On the other hand, the models explored in this chapter can help one to understand the implications of the overall cost structure of a distance education system, and hence come to some broad-brush conclusions. For example, they can identify the interplay between technology choice, curriculum, course life, and student numbers, and provided the data incorporated into them reflects working practices and organisational structures, they can provide decision makers with a "back of the envelope" tool for the analysis and costing of alternative strategies. They can also be extended to identify broad-brush funding requirements.

Funding normally comes from a variety of sources: government, the learners or their families in the form of fees and other payments (for example, for materials), the community (sometimes in kind – for example, the provision of local centre facilities at no cost), the private sector, funding agencies and donors, and the sale of materials and services on the open market.

Equation 40.6 can be modified to take account of these various sources:

$$B = [\alpha + (\beta_n C_n - \beta_g) + (\chi_p C_p - \chi_g) + (\delta - \lambda)S] - (\zeta + \eta) \qquad (40.12)$$

where

B = net profit or loss
α = the total fixed costs of the enterprise
β_n = the average variable cost of development/production per standard course equivalent per year
β_g = the total development grants provided by funders
C_n = the number of standard course equivalents in development/production in any year
χ_p = the average variable cost of presentation per standard course equivalent per year
χ_g = the total funds awarded by finders to support course presentation
C_p = the number of standard course equivalents in presentation in any year
δ = the average variable cost per full-time equivalent student per year
λ = the average fees paid by a student per year
S = the number of full-time equivalent students
ζ = the funders' contributions towards general expenses
η = income from sales of materials.

Provided the limitations of such models are borne in mind, and the values of the various inputs periodically checked against reality, these models can become a valuable adjunct to a more rigorous, activity-based accounting and costing system.

REFERENCES

Annand, D. (1999). The problem of computer conferencing for distance-based universities. *Open Learning*, **14**(3), 47–52.

Arizona Learning Systems. (1998). *Preliminary Cost Methodology for Distance Learning*. Arizona Learning Systems and the State Board of Directors for Community Colleges of Arizona.

Bates, A.W. (1995). *Technology, Open Learning and Distance Education*. London: Routledge.

Bell, D. (1960). *The End of Ideology*. Glencoe, Ill.: The Free Press.

Bell, D. (1973). *The Coming of Post-Industrial Society*. New York: Basic Books.

Blauner, R. (1964). *Alienation and Freedom*. Chicago: Chicago University Press.

Campion, M. and Renner, W. (1992). The supposed demise of Fordism: Implications for distance education and higher education, *Distance Education*, **13**(1), 7–28.

Coombs, P.H. (1968). *The World Educational Crisis: A Systems Analysis*. Oxford: Oxford University Press.

Curran, C. (1993). Scale, cost and quality in small distance teaching universities. In *Organization, Technology and Economics of Education*. Proceedings of the COSTEL Workshop, Copenhagen, 11–12 January 1993 (H. Siggard Jensen and S. Siggard Jensen, eds) Copenhagen: n.p.

Daniel, J.S. (1996). *Mega-Universities and Knowledge Media. Technology Strategies for Higher Education*. London: Kogan Page.

Duncan, C. (2003). Granularization. In *Reusing Online Resources. A Sustainable Approach to e-Learning* (A. Littlejohn, ed.) London: Kogan Page.

Eicher, J.C. (1978). Some thoughts on the economic analysis of new educational media. In UNESCO 1980. *The Economics of New Educational Media. Vol. 2: Cost and Effectiveness*. Paris: The UNESCO Press.

Eicher, J.C., Hawkridge, D., McAnany, E. et al. (1982). *The Economics of New Educational Media. Volume 3: Cost and Effectiveness Overview and Synthesis*. Paris: The UNESCO Press.

Ellis, E.M. (2000). Faculty participation in the Pennsylvania State University World Campus: Identifying barriers to success. *Open Learning*, **15**(3), 233–242.

Fwu, B.J., Jamison, D., Livingston, R. et al. (1992). The National Technological University. In *Vocational Education at a Distance: International Perspectives* G. Rumble and J. Oliveira, eds) London: Kogan Page.

Grint, K. and Woolgar, S. (1997). *The Machine at Work. Technology, Work and Organization*. Cambridge: Polity Press.

Jamison, D.T., Klees, S.J., and Wells, S.J. (1978). *The Costs of Educational Media. Guidelines for Planning and Evaluation*. Beverly Hills: Sage Publications.

Johnson, H.T. (1992). *Relevance Regained: From Top-down Control to Bottom-up Empowerment*. New York: The Free Press.

Johnson, H.T. and Kaplan, R.S. (1987). *Relevance Lost. The Rise and Fall of Management Accounting*. Boston: Harvard Business School Press.

Kerr, C., Dunlop, J.T., Harbinson, F.H., and Myers, C.A. (1964). *Industrialism and Industrial Man.* London: Oxford University Press.

Klees, S.J., Orivel, F., and Wells, S. (1977). *Economic Analysis of Educational Media.* Final Report of the Washington Conference, 2–4 March 1977. Paris/Washington: UNESCO, US AID, ICEM, EDUTEL.

Levin, H.M. (1983). *Cost-effectiveness: A primer.* Beverly Hills: Sage Publications.

Littlejohn, A. (ed.). (2003). *Reusing Online Resources. A Sustainable Approach to E-Learning*, London: Kogan Page.

Orivel, F. (2000). Finance, costs and economics. In *Basic Education at a Distance. World Review of Distance Education and Open Learning, Volume 2* (C. Yates and J. Bradley, eds) London: RoutledgeFalmer.

Perry, W. (1976). *Open University. A Personal Account by the First Vice-Chancellor.* Milton Keynes: Open University Press.

Peters, O. (1967). *Des Fernstudium an Universitätn und Hochschulen.* Weinheim: Beltz.

Peters, O. (1973). *Die didaktische Struktur des Fernunterrichts Untersuchungen zu einer industrialisierten Form des Lehrens und Lernens.* Weinheim: Beltz.

Peters, O. (1983). Distance teaching and industrial production. A comparative interpretation. In *Distance education: international perspectives* (D. Sewart, D. Keegan, and B. Holmberg, eds) London: Croom Helm.

Peters, O. (1989). The iceberg has not melted: further reflections on the concept of industrialisation and distance teaching. *Open Learning*, **4**(2), 3–8.

Raggatt, P. (1993). Post-Fordism and distance education – a flexible strategy for change. *Open Learning*, **8**(1), 21–31.

Rumble, G. (1986). *The Planning and Management of Distance Education.* London: Croom Helm.

Rumble, G. (1997). *The Costs and Economics of Open and Distance Learning.* London: Kogan Page.

Rumble, G., Neil, M., and Tout, A. (1981). Budgetary and resource forecasting. In *Distance Teaching for Higher and Adult Education* (A. Kaye and G. Rumble, eds). London: Croom Helm.

Schramm, W., Coombs, P.H., Kahnert, F., and Lyle, J. (1967). *The new Media: Memo to Educational Planners*, Paris: UNESCO.

Schultz, T. (1961). Investment in human capital. *American Economic Review*, 51, 1–17.

Scott, P. (1997). The postmodern university? In *The Postmodern University? Contested Visions of Higher Education in Society* (A. Smith and F. Webster, eds) Buckingham: Open University Press.

Tolley, S. (2000). How electronic conferencing affects the way we teach. *Open Learning*, **15**(3), 253–265.

UNESCO. (1977). *The Economics of New Educational Media.* Paris: UNESCO.

Vaizey, J. (1958). *The Costs of Education.* London: Faber.

Wagner, L. (1975). Television video-tape systems for off-campus education: A cost analysis of SURGE. *Instructional Science*, **4**(2), 315–332.

Wagner, L. (1977). The economics of the Open University revisited. *Higher Education*, **6**(3), 359–381.

Wagner, L. (1982). *The Economics of Educational Media.* London: The Macmillan Press.

Chapter 41

Business Skills for Managing Flexible Learning

John Mitchell

41.1 INTRODUCTION

This chapter examines the knowledge and skills required of vocational education and training (VET) senior managers in managing flexible learning early in the twenty-first century, when flexible learning is being impacted upon by the availability of the Internet. The argument presented in the chapter is that VET senior managers need an increased understanding of contemporary business knowledge and skills to effectively manage flexible learning, given the availability of the Internet and related new business models for educational organisations. The chapter expands upon the insights into the knowledge and skills required to manage flexible learning that were provided by Peoples et al. (1997), who were writing near the start of the period when the Internet first became available for use within vocational education and training.

The chapter specifically examines the attitudes of senior managers about critical business issues in flexible learning in the VET sector in the state of Victoria, Australia. A consideration of these critical business issues helps clarify the knowledge and skills required of VET senior managers in managing flexible learning.

The chapter is drawn from the author's doctorate of education unpublished thesis (Mitchell, 2004) as well as Mitchell et al. (2001a,b,c).

41.2 DEFINITION OF FLEXIBLE LEARNING

While there is a range of different definitions of the term "flexible learning" available both in the VET sector and in the wider literature, the definition endorsed by the Australian Flexible Learning Framework (AFLF, 2004) is as follows:

> Flexible learning expands choice on what, when, where and how people learn. It supports different styles of learning, including e-learning.

> Flexibility means anticipating, and responding to, the ever-changing needs and expectations of VET clients – enterprises, learners and communities.
>
> (AFLF website, 2004)

This two-part definition suggests that managing flexible learning involves more than supporting different styles of learning: the definition also emphasises the role of flexible learning in expanding choices for learners and meeting the ever-changing needs and expectations of clients. In linking flexible learning to the needs and expectations of VET clients, the definition has ramifications for VET senior managers, and these ramifications are a major focus of discussion in this chapter.

41.3 VET CONTEXT AND TERMS

Before proceeding, explanation is required of key abbreviations and terms used in the chapter, particularly the abbreviations VET and RTO and the term "managers". Providing these explanations will also serve as an introduction to the VET context. The Australian VET sector serviced approximately 1.72 m students in 2003 (NCVER, 2004, p. 1) and consists of over 4,000 Registered Training Organisations (RTOs). Approximately sixty-five of the RTOs in Australia are government-funded Technical and Further Education (TAFE) institutes, and the number is declining due to amalgamations of institutes in Western Australia and South Australia. These TAFE institutes service over 76.8 percent of the national student cohort and 85.8 percent of the national enrolments (NCVER, 2004, p. 8).

While most RTOs in Australian are privately funded, the majority are micro-businesses, often consisting of one to two staff. While this chapter focuses on the managers of RTOs that are beyond the micro-level, and predominantly focuses on the managers in the sixty-five or so TAFE institutes, the discussion in the chapter is relevant to other VET managers, including the senior managers of community-sponsored organisations which service 14.2 percent of the VET student cohort (NCVER, 2004, p. 8) and senior managers of large privately owned RTOs.

41.4 REVIEW OF EARLIER RESEARCH

The chapter includes a review of, and considerable extension to, research undertaken by the author in 2000–2001 and reported upon in Mitchell and others (2001a,b,c). The initial research in 2000–2001 was undertaken for a project commissioned by *TAFE frontiers*, an organisation funded by the Victorian Government to provide staff development and related resources for the Victorian VET sector, to support the implementation of flexible learning and online learning. For *TAFE frontiers*, the VET sector included any organisation involved in the provision of vocational education and training, such as TAFE institutes, private RTOs, Adult and Community Education (ACE) providers or Flexible Learning Networks (*TAFE frontiers*, 2000).

In mid-2000, the Victorian-based *TAFE frontiers* commissioned the author to undertake a research project entitled Flexible Learning Planning and Management Resources. The author engaged three other researchers – Colin Latchem, Tony Bates and Peter Smith – to provide written contributions to specific parts of the project, but not to undertake any original field research.

41.5 ORIGINAL BRIEF

The three purposes of the *TAFE frontiers* project brief were to identify key business issues in flexible learning, to provide high-level briefing papers and to provide professional development sessions, as follows:

1. *Identify key business issues in flexible delivery*
   Identify and prioritise the major management issues and critical business decisions for senior managers involved in developing flexible delivery systems and programmes for vocational education and training.
2. *Provide high-level briefing papers*
   Identify the most significant research, information and management resources relevant to the key issues identified, and prepare fully referenced "monographs" to provide accessible summaries for managers. This will include
   - researching optional formats for monographs and briefing documents, including visual models
   - developing and testing an appropriate format
   - preparing the resources to print-ready stage as a "kit", including quality layout, design and packaging.
3. *Provide professional development*
   Prepare and implement an innovative strategy to disseminate the information resources and engage senior managers in the key issues. The strategy is to include
   - presenting workshops on business planning for flexible delivery, as part of the FlexiNet series, in October
   - preparing the monograph series in web-ready format. (*TAFE frontiers*, 2000, p. 20)

The chapter does not follow the sequence of the three parts of the original project brief, but instead summarises the literature available at the time, provides an analysis of the context for the project, explains and analyses the methodology for the field research, reports on the field research and discusses key findings in the light of contemporary thinking about management. The discussion section of the chapter will then identify implications of the research for VET senior managers. These implications substantially expand on those identified in the original report (Mitchell et al., 2001b,c).

41.6 REVIEW OF NEW BUSINESS MODELS FOR FLEXIBLE LEARNING, 1997–2001

To provide an historical context for the chapter, the following literature review and discussion investigates a number of business issues facing senior managers of adult and higher education, both in Australia and overseas, in relation to flexible learning, earlier this century. The discussion refers to literature in the four to five years leading up to 2001, the year the field research was conducted with Victorian VET senior managers for *TAFE frontiers*. The literature review refers to both Australian and related overseas literature. As there are few similar structures overseas to the Australian VET sector, the review focuses broadly on adult, further and higher education, not just VET. The review is organised around a business theme that emerged in the literature in the period up to and including 2001: the need for senior managers to respond to new and emerging business models.

New business models were promoted as a result of the emergence of the Internet in the late 1990s (Timmers, 1999; Turban et al., 2000). A broad definition of business models is as follows: a description of the relationship between the common components of a business, such as inbound logistics, operations, outbound logistics, marketing, sales and service; and supporting elements, such as human resource management, procurement and technology development. A more exacting definition is provided by Timmers (1999, p. 31), who defines business models as consisting of the following three components: the organisation (or "architecture") of product, service and information flows, a description of the sources of benefits for suppliers and customers, and a description of the sources of revenue.

One business model for the Internet in the late 1990s that contained the three components of the Timmers definition was the "e-mall": a collection of online shops usually grouped around a common brand and an Internet portal, and sometimes sharing the same payment system. The customer benefits from the e-mall model by being able to access a range of shops on the one website and the shop owners benefit from higher "traffic" flows and from sharing the costs of a payment system. Revenue from constructing an e-mall can be derived from membership fees for the e-shop owners, advertising and sometimes a fee on transactions (Timmers, 1999, p. 37). However, for this discussion, the term "business model" is not used in the rigorous sense provided by Timmers: it is used loosely to describe a business strategy, such as the provision of a "virtual" organisation that uses an online platform and does not use traditional "bricks and mortar" campus facilities to deliver education.

New business models for incorporating the Internet with flexible learning were promoted nationally and internationally in the late 1990s (Mitchell, 2000b, p. 10). Driven by the availability of the online medium in the late 1990s, a range of new business models were promoted by private companies providing online courseware and hardware, who suggested that traditional providers could add an e-learning component to their conventional course offerings (Mitchell, 2000a, pp. 23–25). Companies that emerged in the e-learning field at that time included Smartforce, NETg and SkillSoft Corporation (W.R. Hambrecht and Co., 1999, pp. 40–49). With about 4.5 percent share of the US market, over 2,000 corporate customers, and a large global presence, SmartForce was by far the largest e-training company in the US market (p. 51). W.R. Hambrecht & Co. (1999, p. 51) describes the position of SmartForce in the market and its recent change from offering computer-based training (CBT) that involved CD ROMs to a strategy that involved the use of the World Wide Web. In late 1999, SmartForce launched "SmartForce e-Learning", a fully integrated, Internet-based learning solution, representing a fundamental strategy shift that transformed the formerly CBT-focused company into one with an Internet focus (W.R. Hambrecht and Co. 1999, p.51). This change in SmartForce's business model from a focus on CD ROMs to a focus on the World Wide Web demonstrated the impact of the Internet on flexible learning in the late 1990s.

A number of other overseas companies besides SmartForce also began providing online learning or related services in Australia at the turn of the century, including NETg and Monster Learning Asia Pacific (Day, 2000). Day's (2000) survey identified ninety-nine providers of online training in the VET sector in Australia (pp. 9–12). Day (2000, p. 9) used the following criteria to categorise the ninety-nine organisations responding to the survey of online learning providers in Australia: VET online course materials; online assessment tools; online course management systems; online delivery systems; online marketing portals; e-commerce expertise; and venture capitalists. These companies promoted different business models, ranging from those that were using the Internet to deliver learning content to those that primarily used the Internet for marketing purposes.

The Internet created a new dimension for the market place, leading to the development in the late 1990s of the term "marketspace" (Turban et al., 2000, p. 427) and the related need for new business models. Mitchell (2000b, p. 10) found that a variety of business models were being proposed for marketspace, stemming from the nature of the Internet: the Internet is available 24 hours a day, it is global, it is interactive, it enables customisation of services for the individual consumer and it enables both one-to-one and mass marketing. Importantly, marketspace can deliver enhanced benefits to customers, by increasing choice, lowering cost and enabling customisation. Marketspace also enables companies to form new and fluid relationships. Mitchell (2000b, p. 9) found that the international marketspace for online products and services in the VET arena included these key features: many of the online products and services are new, but the potential of the market is considerable; the market is in flux, due to continual changes in the technology available to access the products and services and due to the emergence of new styles of business alliances; and the markets for online products and services vary from country to country, from region to region, and from one industry sector to the next.

The flux in the marketplace is graphically illustrated by the example of a marketing and distribution model for online products in the higher education sector. *Campus Review* (May 31–June 6, 2000, p. 1) reported that the University of Melbourne's Vice Chancellor Professor Alan Gilbert would spend the next 6 months in London "getting the Universitas 21-News Corporation joint venture up and running". The plan was to set up a global education network offering postgraduate courses by News Corp's satellite system as well as over the Internet. Universitas 21 (U21) is an alliance of eighteen universities from around the world. According to *Campus Review* (p. 3), Professor Gilbert convinced News Corporation's Rupert Murdoch that "an incorporated network such as U21 was an attractive partner for a communications and media giant". The report continued,

> Gilbert believes that the income-generating potential of e-education is so vast – he talks of it being worth trillions of dollars within a few years – that this is the only way traditional universities will be able to afford to continue offering on-campus courses.

> He asserts that non-traditional educational providers (an emerging breed of e-education universities) are almost certain to be the prime beneficiaries of an educational boom driven by a strengthening of the global knowledge economy.
>
> (*Campus Review*, May 31–June 6, 2000, p. 1)

If Vice Chancellor Gilbert was right, the question arose as to whether similar international alliances for marketspace could be developed in the VET sector.

One of the few examples of educational providers in the VET sector seeking to develop business models for the global marketspace in this period was the OnFX Consortium of Print and Graphic Arts providers which developed a series of online training modules from 1997–2000 (Mitchell, 2000b, p. 10). The consortium consisted of Southbank Institute of TAFE, Central Western Institute of TAFE, Douglas Mawson Institute of TAFE, Royal Melbourne Institute of Technology, Canberra Institute of Technology and Sydney Institute of Technology. The consortium arranged with Adskill, a training provider in Malaysia, to use the OnFX online training system, and negotiated with parties in New Zealand and Canada. The business model used by the OnFX consortium included a strategic alliance with a private provider of a web-based student management system, Morgan and Banks's TechWorks. The TechWorks online "front-end" to the OnFX online modules enabled students to enrol and pay online at any time, while any of the six TAFE institutes could provide the online tutorial assistance. The OnFX consortium was an early example of VET operating in marketspace, with a business model that included national and international partnerships and an online platform for enrolling, tutoring and accessing learning materials.

While the Universitas 21 and OnFX examples showed that the marketspace potentially offers opportunities, it also presented threats, as competition in marketspace is intense, price pressure is high and customer attention and loyalty are harder to maintain as customers find it easy to switch sites (Mitchell, 2000b, p. 10). Interestingly, Britain's Open University failed in its attempt to launch a US branch: in 2000 it had fewer than 100 students enrolled in the first four courses offered by the inaugural Open University US (*The Australian*, May 31, 2000, p. 40). Cultural reasons explain some of this low enrolment: one of the four courses was on the art of political campaign management, but the Open University found that "professionals were too busy campaigning in an election year" (p. 40). Interestingly, the OnFX Consortium no longer operates and the Universitas 21 initiative was later scaled down, offering a more modest range of programmes.

At the same time as the concept of the marketspace evolved and new business models and providers of online training emerged, a new range of business structures was promoted in the university sector around the world. For example, in 2000 the Association of Commonwealth Universities envisaged four possible scenarios for the future of tertiary education: "the invaders triumph" – tertiary education becomes a global big business dominated by a few players; "the Trojan horse" – institutions seek outside and international partners, offering international award programmes; "community champions" – a wide range of educational services is widely available through community hubs; and "explorers international" – educational service providers are a university/business hybrid (Poole, 2000, p. 48). Hanna (2000, p. 39) suggests that the alternative business structures for the post-secondary sector, with special reference to the United States, included traditional campus-centred institutions; extended institutions; distance education/technology-based institutions; for-profit institutions; competency-based institutions; corporate institutions; strategic alliance institutions; and global institutions. As one example of this development of new business structures, some universities without any previous experience in distance education began to extend their traditional role by providing on-campus courses to a non-traditional student cohort – off-campus, part-time, working adults (Latchem and Hanna, 2001, p. 6).

By the end of the twentieth century, most Australian universities provided programmes through a range of methods in addition to face-to-face instruction, in some cases capturing niche markets, such as large enterprises. For example, Deakin University, a long-standing provider of distance education, through DeakinPrime, secured clients such as Ford Australia, ANZ Bank, the Department of Foreign Affairs and Trade, Australian Society of Certified Practising Accountants and Coles and these corporate enrolments significantly complemented enrolments in Deakin University's mainstream courses (Latchem and Hanna, 2001, p. 6).

One national consortium that increased the options for public access to higher education was Open Learning Australia (OLA). In the late 1990s, the OLA expanded from just one university, Monash, to include eight shareholding universities in a private company: Monash University, RMIT, University of Queensland, Griffith University, Macquarie University, Curtin University of Technology, Swinburne University of Technology and University of South Australia. OLA contracts with its partners and other universities to provide fee-for-service undergraduate, postgraduate, continuing and professional education programmes in Arts, Social Sciences, Business Studies, Science and Technology, Applied Studies and Australian Indigenous Studies and it contracts VET organisations to provide VET courses.

Forming national or international consortia to deliver online learning involved some challenges, as illustrated below. Two international strategic alliances that were formed in the late 1990s that involved Australian educational organisations were Universitas 21, mentioned above, a consortium of eighteen universities led by the University of Melbourne, and the Global University Alliance, which included RMIT University and the University of South Australia, together with the private company NextEd and overseas universities. The following comments from the vice chancellor of the University of South Australia reflect the increasing awareness of some Australian educational leaders that the challenges of forming alliances and competing globally need to be met. In announcing the Global University Alliance involving two Australian and seven overseas universities, vice chancellor of the University of South Australia, Denise Bradley, commented that "learning how to work in alliances and partnerships was a great challenge for universities":

> "The web really does challenge whether you're a local or an international university", she said.
>
> "And you can't just say you're an international university because you take international students in Australia. You have to do more than that".
>
> (*The Australian* 14 June, 2000, p. 38)

The new business model of a "virtual university" was promoted in the mid-1990s, but Farrell (1999) and Cunningham et al. (2000) found that there is more rhetoric than reality in naming some organisations "virtual universities" because there are in fact very few examples of organisations providing entirely online the full range of teaching programmes and services. The United States of America was active in developing virtual universities and its first fully accredited online university was Jones International University, a for-profit organisation owned by Jones Cable, the sixth largest cable operator in the United States. However, Cunningham and others (2000) found that, while many of the factors driving the emergence of alternative education providers in the United States also affect Australia, there are some systemic differences between Australia and the United States that are likely to influence the potential for new providers to operate in Australia. These differences include

> demographic scale, economic size and diversity;
>
> the existence of widespread employer-sponsored tuition subsidies in the US;
>
> Australian higher education is more regulated than in the US in matters such as the use of the "university" label, and the US higher education quality assurance and accreditation systems are diverse and poorly coordinated in comparison to those in Australia;
>
> the industry-orientation and competency basis of the Australian vocational education and training system, which contrasts with the more autonomous and general education oriented community college system in the US;
>
> greater levels of experience in Australia with distance education and part-time higher education students.
>
> (p. xiv)

In summing up this discussion of the new business models for flexible learning, it is clear that the turn of the century was a challenging time for Australian senior managers in all forms of adult, further and university education. Senior managers were presented with the promises of the new business models identified by Poole (2000), Hanna (2000) and other analysts, and promoted by commercial vendors such as SmartForce and exemplified by Universitas 21, the Global University Alliance, OnFX and Jones International University. At the same time, commentators such as Cunningham and others (2000) and Mitchell (2000b) warned about Australian organisations directly imitating overseas business models. Educational senior managers in the late 1990s were required to operate in an historical context where flexible learning and online learning were enmeshed in the excitement and media hype surrounding the Internet, symbolised by the use of the term "marketspace", as discussed above.

41.7 RESEARCH METHODS

The research methods used for the 2000–2001 *TAFE frontiers* project were partly prescribed by the client, although there was scope for the author, in the tender response, to propose both a methodology and the research methods. Defining methods as techniques or procedures (Creswell, 2003, p. 5), the four main research methods used in the TAFE project were a literature review, survey, interviews and workshops. To gauge the views and needs of Victorian VET senior managers in relation to critical issues in flexible learning, two major instruments were used in late 2000 to early 2001: a survey and structured interviews. Additionally, two workshops were conducted in May 2001 to gain feedback on draft sections of the report. The other methods included the circulation of draft reports for validation to two workshop groups and, by mail, to a selected audience. The survey, interview and workshops are discussed below and the literature review was revised and incorporated in earlier sub-sections of the chapter. However, some comments about the composition of the sample of managers will be made before the discussion of techniques.

A total of thirty-eight Victorian VET managers were involved in the interviews and surveys, comprising eighteen interviewees and twenty survey respondents who completed an email survey. Additionally, ninety Victorian VET managers attended one or other of the two half-day workshops, to validate initial draft sections of the final report, and only five of these were from the forty who completed surveys or were interviewed. Six personnel from the ninety participants at the workshops reviewed the full draft of the final report. The client, *TAFE frontiers*, considered the sample of managers at the two workshops, including five of the forty involved in interviews and the survey, to be a sufficient proportion of the Victorian TAFE system to ensure the findings from the field research were accurate, reliable and valid.

41.8 SUMMARY OF FINDINGS

In the interviews for this study the Victorian VET senior managers generally articulated a commitment to embedding a customer-service principle in flexible learning, and identified a range of critical issues in flexible learning that need further attention. Almost all of the interviewees shared a passion for flexible learning, not so much as just another means of providing learning opportunities for students, but as an essential approach to operating in a business-like manner in the VET sector. The managers looked upon flexible delivery as much more than operational issues such as developing a website and using effective instructional design strategies. They saw flexible delivery as integral to contemporary, twenty-first century business practices in VET, which includes being customer-focused and providing the customer with choices. For these managers, flexible learning is about the current generation of VET organisations differentiating themselves from any previous generations who thought that the basis of VET was teacher-dominant classroom instruction. The interviewees articulated their awareness that the world is changing and that customer service is the primary reason for being in business and remaining in business. As one interviewee said,

> We in VET have to keep proving ourselves. The sort of service offered in the past was a "good thing". It was paternalism. That attitude has to change. To stay in business now we have to go and show we are in business.
>
> (Mitchell et al., 2001b, p. 30)

While the interviewees generally agreed that flexible learning will provide customer benefits and keep VET organisations in business, flexible learning provides managers with many challenges, including the need to meet policy directives, to balance educational and business goals, to manage strategic alliances, to identify costs and benefits, to increase staff capability, to manage staff workloads and to cater for a diversity of student needs.

These consistent responses from the interviewees complemented the findings from the survey respondents. The survey provided both quantitative and qualitative data that senior managers rate flexible learning as critical to the future of VET organisations, highlighting the need for managers to develop more skills in aspects of flexible learning such as implementation strategies, cost–benefit analysis and identifying market demand. The survey responses showed that VET managers see flexible learning as multi-faceted and impacting on different aspects of the business. The survey responses also showed that VET senior managers believe that a commitment to flexible learning demonstrates a customer focus. Finally, the survey responses showed that VET senior managers believe that more staff development is required to support flexible learning. The interviews provided rich qualitative data about similar issues.

In brief, both the interviews and survey for the *TAFE frontiers* project suggest that major *strategic* management issues for managers in relation to flexible learning include developing a coherent corporate vision for flexible learning, undertaking strategic planning and developing sustainable competitive advantages; providing leadership in a turbulent environment and providing confidence for staff; bringing about organisational change, increasing organisational capability and addressing issues such as the changing roles of staff; and measuring cost benefits, including addressing the time pressures faced by staff. The interviews and survey for the *TAFE frontiers* study (Mitchell et al., 2001b) suggest that major *operational* management issues in relation to flexible learning include overseeing teaching and learning processes such as the following: staff workload and incentive issues; catering for different learning styles; updating learning resources; segmenting the market, monitoring student demand and marketing effectively; developing learning resources and the infrastructure and addressing related issues, for example intellectual property issues; and providing support services for a variety of learners.

The combined data from the interviews and the survey enable a refinement to be made to the two levels of data noted in the responses to the survey: the operational and the strategic level. The data from both sources support the following, more detailed and diagrammatic representation of critical issues in flexible learning for VET senior managers (Figure 41.1).

The figure is also a reminder that VET senior managers view flexible learning as a core business challenge. The figure shows that flexible learning is seen through the same lenses as senior managers view generic business issues. For these VET senior managers, flexible learning is more than a delivery system or a philosophy about learning. For many senior managers, flexible learning is the way they conduct their business: flexible learning means conducting normal business in response to customers.

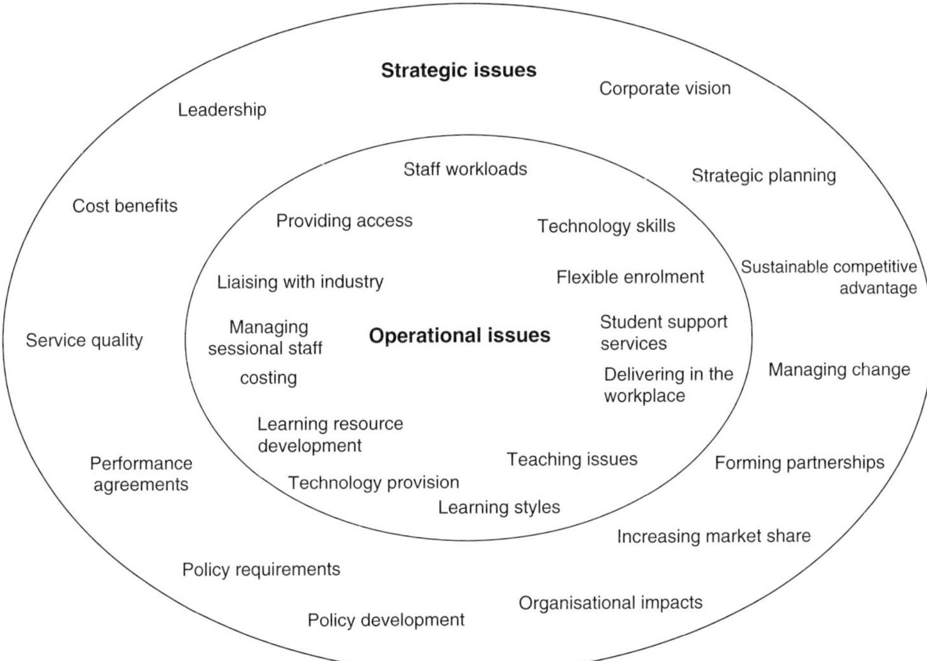

Figure 41.1: Critical Business Issues in Flexible Learning Issues for VET Senior Managers – Identified in the Survey and Interviews for the TAFE Frontiers Study

A discussion follows on one of these critical issues arising from the field research and how it is an indication of the increasing knowledge required by VET managers to manage flexible learning.

41.9 DISCUSSION

The discussion below extends beyond two points that emerged from the field research and that were explored in earlier sections of the chapter: first, that key business decisions need to be taken to effectively manage flexible learning and, second, that the senior managers need both a strategic and a operational understanding of the complexities of flexible learning.

A central theme that emerges from the research reported in the chapter is that VET senior managers need to understand that the scope of flexible learning has expanded since the 1990s and it now includes the business concept of ensuring that their organisation is responsive to customer demand in new ways. The term "scope" is taken to mean the extent or range of application or operation (Delbridge et al., 2001, p. 1692). Interviewees for this study identified as essential features of flexible learning such business concepts as customer service based around customisation to suit the client or the student; the importance of customer satisfaction; and the need to develop flexible ways of delivering and building customer relationships. Flexible learning is, as one senior manager interviewed noted, about "being where the student needs us to be" (Mitchell et al., 2001b, p. 31). Interviewees for this study showed that defining the scope of flexible learning for a VET organisation requires the VET manager to use business knowledge as well as educational knowledge, as it involves determining its potential contribution to the business. Hence, the following discussion employs business concepts such as providing added value to customers and enabling personalised service and self-service, in building on the ideas generated by the interviewees and integrating them into a framework for understanding the new scope of flexible learning in VET.

In discussing the scope of flexible learning, theorists and proponents in the 1990s – for example, Johnson, 1990; ANTA, 1996 – argued that flexible learning is essentially a philosophy rather than a teaching or technology-based methodology. The philosophy included the view that flexible learning can be applied on- and/or off-campus; is based on the needs of the individual rather than the interests of the teacher or organisation; gives the students as much control as possible over the what, when, where and how of their learning; changes the role of the teacher from a source of knowledge to a manager or facilitator of learning. Hence, the philosophy about flexible learning in the 1990s defined elements of a more responsive approach to teaching and learning.

In the 1990s, flexible learning was viewed as operating along a closed–open continuum in terms of boundaries of operation, enrolments, learning routes, delivery methods, time and place of delivery, and accreditation (for example, ANTA, 1996). Mitchell and others (2001c, pp. 8–9) found that in the 1990s, influenced by the prevailing philosophy of flexible learning, some educational organisations were open to all comers, while some restricted their enrolments to specific markets. Some waived entry requirements or recognised prior informal learning; others required the same entry qualifications as conventional organisations. Some placed no limits on their enrolments; others were constrained by government quotas or self-imposed quotas. Some operated multi-entry, multi-exit models with students choosing what they want to learn and accumulating credit as they explore pathways towards their chosen qualifications; others were rigid in their requirements of students. Some were flexible in their timelines, allowing students to take years to complete their studies; others set firm entry and completion dates, requiring re-enrolment whenever students fall behind in their studies. Some programmes were conducted entirely through self-instruction or distance learning; others included face-to-face teaching or practical sessions, on campus or at study centres. The philosophy about flexible learning in the 1990s clearly illuminated organisational arrangements that could be made more responsive to student needs.

While these 1990s tenets are still valuable and relevant to vocational education and training organisations in the current century, additional tenets are necessary to describe the emerging scope of flexible learning in contemporary VET. The field research for *TAFE frontiers* project found widespread agreement with the idea that flexible learning is a philosophy and not simply a methodology; but it is a philosophy describing how the

VET organisation can be positioned as a service business as well as how learning can occur. Interviewees and survey respondents in the study generally confirmed that flexible learning is fundamental to the survival of their organisations. Flexible learning in VET emerges from the *TAFE frontiers* study (Mitchell et al., 2001b,c) as an aid to achieving corporate goals such as improved customer services and enhanced competitive advantage. It is representative of the way business is ideally conducted in VET organisations today.

The *TAFE frontiers* research (Mitchell et al., 2001b,c) shows that flexible learning is ultimately contributing to a customer-centred approach to the provision of VET. In the current decade, "flexibility" in flexible learning is increasingly about providing extra or added value to students and other customers. While the definition of and approach to flexible learning in VET in the early 1990s emphasised two themes – access and equity, on the one hand, and learner-centredness, on the other (Mitchell, 1991) – the definition of flexible learning emerging from the *TAFE frontiers* project takes those two imperatives for granted. The emerging definition places a new emphasis on the value of flexible learning for the individual customer and for the enterprise that requires training. As a result of these findings, it is possible to identify the following additional examples of flexibility that are derived from a customer-centric approach to the provision of VET: some educational organisations offer customers self-service while others provide a mix of self-service and hands-on instruction; some customise educational opportunities for individuals or groups while others modify generic offerings; and some pitch to markets of only one person and others seek mass markets.

This customer-centred approach is the language of contemporary business, used by author such as Cortada (2001, pp. 18–27), who notes that in the contemporary world customers are more in control because they have increased access to information, can negotiate better terms and conditions for goods and services, can return goods faster and can change suppliers quicker, more frequently and easier than in the past. Latchem and Hanna (2001) note that customers have increased expectations of educational organisations:

> Many of today's students are fee-paying. They are more knowledgeable, more discerning, more assertive and more market-oriented. They expect quick outcomes, quality, currency and applicability in their learning, not hype...They expect good "customer relationship management" and some require "customer intimacy", for example, through Web-based customisation.
>
> (p. 17)

Latchem and Hanna (2001) conclude that it is imperative that all educational and training providers see their central mission and purpose as "satisfying the customer's needs" (p. 17).

Case study research by Henry (2001a) on Sunraysia Institute of TAFE in regional and rural Victoria – research that was released simultaneously with the *TAFE frontiers* research discussed here – identified a similar shift in the understanding of flexible delivery within that VET organisation, such that flexible delivery is viewed as the outcome of customer responsiveness:

> The established vision of the Institute as a flexible training provider at this time is associated with its commitment to customer responsiveness. Flexible delivery, as a concept, is intertwined with the prior concept of customer-oriented training delivery. Thus a single model of flexible delivery or a narrow definition of flexible delivery is deemed to be inappropriate. Customer responsiveness is the determining concept with flexible delivery being the term used to describe the strategic and practical outcomes.
>
> (p. 17)

Henry's (2001b) second case study of the Adult Migrant Education Service in Victoria (AMES) showed that flexible delivery is "now not a stand-alone concept at AMES" but is absorbed in the way AMES conducts business:

> Flexible delivery has been absorbed into the way AMES does things in 2001. As AMES has diversified as an education and training provider, the organisation transformed itself to meet its purchaser clients' expectations of flexibility.
>
> (p. 23)

Henry's case study research reinforces the findings from the *TAFE frontiers* project that VET organisations need to be driven by the goal of satisfying customer needs.

Given these research findings by Henry (2001a,b) and in the *TAFE frontiers* project reported in this chapter (Mitchell et al., 2001b,c), a new set of flexible learning tenets can be added to the 1990s tenets for flexible learning listed above, using the language of contemporary business, as follows. Ideally, flexible learning is an essential component of a contemporary VET organisation that is demand-driven not supply-driven; is market-driven not technology-driven; is driven by the value proposition for the customer, i.e. "What is in it for the customer?"; meets customer expectations for attributes such as speed, convenience, personalised service and competitive price; meets customer expectations by enhancing service quality and/or reducing prices and/or improving products; delights the customer, starting with the customer's first contact with the organisation, to enrolling, to receiving services, to after-sales service; seeks repeat business from the customer; retains customers by offering holistic, integrated, personalised service; and values the life-long relationship with the customer. This new scope of flexible learning presents new and ongoing challenges for senior managers in VET.

The discussion above shows that the scope of flexible learning in the 1990s was based on a philosophy of using flexible techniques to suit the convenience of the student, particularly in terms of where and when and how learning took place. The scope of flexible learning in the current century is based more on a philosophy which combines educational and business concepts. The new scope of flexible learning is based on the philosophy that educational organisations exist to provide value to students and other customers and that flexible learning is central to this reason for the organisation's continued existence. A practical consequence of this new scope for flexible learning is that providing customer value through flexible learning requires senior managers to develop new knowledge and skills to identify new market demands, and to develop new services to satisfy these markets.

The above discussion about the changed scope and definition of flexible learning in the VET sector complements and extends other VET research. This new understanding of the scope of flexible learning complements research conducted simultaneously with the 2001 *TAFE frontiers* project by Henry (2001c), who found that the definition of flexible learning was framed by each organisation's strategic positioning and was equated with customer responsiveness:

> The concepts for flexible delivery were framed by each organisation's overall strategic positioning. For example, the Sunraysia Institute's vision was developed in line with its managed response to customer responsiveness. In this way, customer responsiveness became the driver for organisational change within which flexible delivery was given a purpose and a meaning within the Institute's overall strategic planning.
>
> (p. 6)

This discussion of the scope of flexible learning complements the work of McNickle and Cameron (2003), who examined the understanding of middle and senior management of the human resource issues and implications associated with the implementation of flexible delivery within Australian TAFE institutes. McNickle and Cameron provide this summary of how managers see flexible delivery, which covers some but not all of the dimensions captured in the *TAFE frontiers* research project:

> Managers participating in this study understood flexible delivery as including online delivery, distance learning, workplace training and assessment, and a blend of online and face-to-face delivery. They acknowledged the value of flexible delivery in meeting the needs and expectations of learners, industry and the wider community. The capacity to deliver training in a range of modes, at times and in locations suited to the specific requirements of clients, was seen to be a great advantage for TAFE institutes. In addition, flexible delivery had opened up opportunities for institutes to enter new markets, to make training more accessible and to solve some of the problems associated with small class sizes in areas of limited demand.
>
> (2003, p. 8)

This definition is narrower than the scope of flexible learning that emerges from the *TAFE frontiers* research (Mitchell et al., 2001b,c) reported upon in this chapter. Palmieri (2003), who prepared case studies on the same topic as McNickle and Cameron, also took a narrower view of flexible delivery than is taken in this chapter:

> Flexible delivery is a term less used than it once was, because now the emphasis in this field of study is usually on the ramifications of flexibility for the teaching and learning process rather than the processes used to deliver teaching and learning.
>
> (p. 10)

The work of Henry (2001a,b,c) and the research set out in this chapter provides a broader understanding of flexible learning than provided by McNickle and Cameron (2003) and Palmieri (2003), possibly because the latter were not charged with the brief to explore the "ramifications of flexibility", including the ramifications for competitive advantage and customer value.

The above discussion potentially will assist policy-makers in the sector to develop a more thoroughgoing definition than the one used by the major programme in flexible learning in the VET sector, which includes the statement: "Flexibility means anticipating, and responding to, the ever-changing needs and expectations of VET clients – enterprises, learners and communities" (AFLF, 2004). The above discussion suggests that one definition of flexible learning still used by the AFLF is a 1990s position: "Flexible learning expands choice on what, when, where and how people learn. It supports different styles of learning, including e-learning" (AFLF, 2004). In the minds of many VET managers in this current decade, flexible learning is, as Palmieri (2003) notes, much more than flexible teaching and learning processes. This chapter argues that flexible learning is, for many VET managers, fundamental to being in the business of providing vocational education and training.

41.10 CONCLUSION

By focusing the discussion above on the theme of the changed and changing scope of flexible learning, a closer analysis could be made of the business knowledge and skills required to manage flexible learning than was provided by Peoples and others (1997), who reported near the start of the period when the Internet became available for education. While Peoples and others (1997) did not highlight the categories of operational and strategic – preferring instead to identify the knowledge, skills and attitudes of the two categories of VET staff, managers and non-managers – their report did contain a range of operational and strategic skills which can now be extended and refined. For instance, the types of operational skills for managers involved in flexible learning cited by Peoples and others (1997) include selecting appropriate courses for flexible learning, especially online learning, using computer and Internet skills, working in teams and developing flexible enrolling, recording and certifying systems (pp. 34–35). Additional operational issues identified in the field research and set out above included determining staff workloads, developing student support issues and costing flexible learning. Similarly, strategic skills identified by Peoples and others (1997, p. 35) include developing strategic plans for the organisation that include flexible learning and planning for the whole of the organisation to become flexible. Additional strategic skills identified in the field research and reported upon above include identifying sustainable competitive advantage with regard to flexible learning, developing performance agreements for flexible learning and identifying the cost benefits of flexible learning. Table 41.1 summarises these key differences between the report by Peoples and others (1997) and this chapter, drawing particularly on the discussion above and the knowledge and skills summarised in Figure 41.1. This chapter complements the insights of People and others (1997) by using the two categories of operational and strategic.

Table 41.1: The Knowledge and Skills Required of VET Managers to Manage Flexible Learning Identified by Peoples and Others (1997) Compared with the Knowledge and Skills Identified in this Study

Peoples and Others 1997	*Additional Items Identified in this Study*
Knowledge	**Strategic knowledge**
Knowledge of models and underpinning theories of flexible delivery and flexible learning	Developing a corporate vision that includes flexible learning
Knowledge of models of workbased learning	Understanding the organisational impacts of flexible learning
Knowledge of the changes to the training system and the requirements imposed by Training Packages	Understanding the policy requirements of flexible learning
Knowledge and theories underpinning recognition of prior learning	Undertaking policy development around flexible learning
Knowledge of models and theories of online delivery of training	Meeting performance agreements involving flexible learning
	Understanding service quality issues for flexible learning
	An understanding of a range of business models that incorporate flexible learning within the organisation
	Operational knowledge
	Determining staff workloads
	Understanding the teaching issues raised by flexible learning
	Understanding learning styles in relation to flexible learning
Skills	**Strategic skills**
Selecting appropriate courses for flexible learning, especially online delivery	An ability to stimulate innovation to support flexible learning
Delivering strategic plans for the organisation that include flexible delivery and flexible learning	An ability to design and develop organisational capability to support flexible learning
Identifying programs/courses and students best suited for alternate forms of delivery	Providing leadership for flexible learning
Using computer/Internet skills	Undertaking strategic planning that includes flexible learning
Planning for whole of organisation to become flexible	Identifying sustainable competitive advantage with regard to flexible learning
Planning, managing and organising flexible delivery and flexible learning	Managing change related to flexible learning
Working in teams	Forming business partnerships for flexible learning
Liaising and negotiating with internal and external clients	Increasing market share with flexible learning
Applying change management skills	Identifying the cost benefits of flexible learning
Evaluating flexible delivery and flexible learning processes and outcomes	**Operational skills**
Developing flexible enrolling, recording, certifying systems	Developing technology skills
Marketing flexible delivery and flexible learning	Providing flexible enrolment systems
Networking with external clients	Developing student support issues
	Delivering in the workplace
	Marketing flexible learning
	Costing flexible learning
	Providing appropriate technology
	Developing learning resources
	Costing flexible learning options
	Managing sessional staff involved in flexible learning
	Liaising with industry about flexible learning
	Providing increased access through learning

While the knowledge and skills required by VET managers managing flexible learning, as identified by People and others (1997), are still valid early this century, the list in the right-hand column, generated by this chapter, not only sets out an increased amount of knowledge and skills, it also separates them into the categories of operational and strategic, which has the benefit of clarifying the breadth of management knowledge and skills required. Another feature of the items in the right-hand column is the use of contemporary business concepts, such as corporate vision, performance agreements, service quality, sustainable competitive advantage, business partnerships, market share and liaising with industry. This use of business concepts supports the findings of Callan (2001) and Mulcahy (2003) that VET managers are combining business and educational frameworks.

The chapter underlined this tendency for VET managers to approach flexible learning with concepts and attitudes drawn from contemporary business. Table 41.2 lists the attitudes required of VET managers to manage flexible learning, as recorded by People and others (1997), with the attitudes identified in this study.

The right-hand column in Table 41.2 shows that the attitudes towards flexible learning of VET managers, as identified in the chapter, are influenced by the language of contemporary business, especially the emphasis on customer needs and expectations. The right-hand column in Table 41.2 is a sign that VET managers are responding to the call from Latchem and Hanna (2001) that educational institutions "radically overhaul they way they relate to customers" and become more customer focused (p. 16). This list of attitudes is a product of the mixed-mode approach to the research, following Cresswell (2003), which included tapping into the attitudes of respondents through the rating

Table 41.2: The Attitudes Required of VET Managers to Manage Flexible Learning and Identified by Peoples and Others (1997) Compared with the Attitudes Identified by this Study

Attitudes Identified by Peoples and Others 1997	*Additional Attitudes Identified in this Study*
Acceptance of and commitment to flexible delivery/learning	Committed to meeting customer expectations regarding speed, convenience, personalised service, competitive price
Strong customer focus	Demand-driven not supply-driven
Open-mindedness and willingness to change/risk taking	Market-driven not technology driven
Willingness to devolve power	Driven by the value proposition for the customer
Commitment to staff development and learning organisation	Meets customer expectations by enhancing service quality and/or reducing prices and/or improving products
Leading and motivating	Delights the customer, starting with the customer's first contact with the organisation, to enrolling, to receiving services, to after-sales service
	Seeks repeat business from the customer; retains customers by offering holistic, integrated, personalised service
	Values the life-long relationship with the customer

scales in the survey and capturing the richness of the attitudes of the survey respondents and interviewees through the use of open-ended questions in the survey and interview.

The overall finding from the chapter is that VET senior managers need an increased repertoire of knowledge and skills to effectively manage flexible learning than previously summarised by Peoples and others (1997). The knowledge and skills can usefully be categorised as strategic and operational. Much of the knowledge and many of the skills are characteristic of contemporary business, underpinned by business attitudes that are a response to customer expectations. The discussion then noted that this business knowledge and skills include the need to understand that the scope of contemporary flexible learning – in the minds of VET managers – has expanded significantly from its position in the previous decade. In particular, the chapter emphasises the need to develop a new rationale for flexible learning that integrates business thinking with educational ideas to suit the contemporary context for VET.

REFERENCES

Australian Flexible Learning Framework (AFLF). (2004). About the Framework: What is Flexible Learning? Retrieved January 25, 2004 from http://flexiblelearning.net.au/aboutus/whatisfl.htm

Australian National Training Authority (ANTA). (1996). *National Flexible Delivery Taskforce, Final Report*, ANTA, Brisbane.

Callan, V.J. (2001). *What are the Essential Capabilities for those who Manage Training Organisations?*, NCVER, Adelaide.

Campus Review (2000). Article, APN Educational Media Pty Ltd, North Sydney, NSW, pp. 1, 3, 31 May – 6 June.

Cortada, J.W. (2001). *21st Century Business: Managing and Working in the New Digital Economy*. London: Prentice Hall.

Creswell, J.W. (2003) *Research Design. Qualitative, Quantitative and Mixed Methods Approaches* (2nd ed.). Thousand Oaks: Sage Publications.

Cunningham, S., Ryan, Y., Stedman, L. et al. (2000). *The Business of Borderless Education.* Evaluations and Investigations Program, Higher Education Division, Department of Employment, Education, Training and Youth Affairs, Australian Government Publishing Service, Canberra.

Day, G. (2000). *e-VET Australian Survey. Data from Online Survey Forms and Key Findings from Interviews and Workshops.* Richmond Victoria: Education Image.

Delbridge, A., Bernard, J.R.L., Blair, D. et al. (2001). *Macquarie Dictionary*, Revised Third Edition, The Macquarie Library Pty Ltd, Macquarie University, Sydney.

Farrell, G. (ed.). (1999) *The Development of Virtual Education: A Global Perspective.* The Commonwealth of Learning. Retrieved August 25, 2001 from http://www.col.org/virtualed

Hambrecht, W.R., and Co. (1999). *Corporate e-learning: Exploring a New Frontier.* Retrieved April 25, 2004 from http://www.wrhambrecht.com/research/elearning/ir/ir_explore.html.

Hanna, D.E. (2000). Emerging organisational models: The extended traditional university. In *Higher Education in an Era of Digital Competition: Choices and Challenges* (D.E. Hanna, and Associates, eds) Madison: Atwood Publishers, pp. 123–156.

Henry, J. (2001a). *Sunraysia Institute of TAFE: Responding to the Rural Training Market as a Flexible Training Provider. A Case Study in the Strategic Interpretation of Policy.* TAFE frontiers, Melbourne.

Henry, J. (2001b). *Adult Multicultural Education Services: A Diversifying Education and Training Provider. A Case Study in the Maintenance of an Educational Culture in Changing Times.* TAFE frontiers, Melbourne.

Henry, J. (2001c). *Support Services for Flexible Delivery. Model of Organisational Preparedness for Flexible Delivery.* TAFE frontiers, Melbourne.

Johnson, R. (1990). *Open Learning: Policy and Practice*, National Board of Employment Education and Training. Commissioned Report No. 4. Australian Government Publishing Service, Canberra.

Latchem, C. and Hanna, D. (2001). *Leadership for 21st Century Learning: Global Perspectives from Educational Innovators.* London: Kogan Page.

McNickle, C. and Cameron, N. (2003). *The Impact of Flexible Delivery on Human Resource Practices.* NCVER, Adelaide.

Mitchell, J.G. (1991). *An Introduction to Open Learning.* South Australian Department of Employment and Technical and Further Eduction, Adelaide.

Mitchell, J.G. (2000a). *International e-VET Market Research Report, A Report on International Market Research for Australian VET Online Products and Services*, FLAG. Retrived November 11, 2004 from http://flexiblelearning.net.au/evetmarketing/docs/intlmark.rtf

Mitchell, J.G. (2000b). *Business Models for Marketing e-VET, A Report on Business Models for the International Marketing of Australian VET Online Products and Services*, FLAG. Retrieved November 11, 2004 from http://flexiblelearning.net.au/evetmarketing/docs/busmods.PDF

Mitchell, J.G. (2004). *Management of Flexible Learning in Vocational Education and Training* (Doctoral dissertation, Deakin University, 2004).

Mitchell, J.G, Latchem, C., Bates, A., and Smith, P. (2001a). *Critical Issues in Flexible learning for VET Managers: 1. Overview.* TAFE frontiers, Melbourne.

Mitchell, J.G, Latchem, C., Bates, A., and Smith, P. (2001b). *Critical Issues in Flexible learning for VET Managers: 2. Voices from the Field.* TAFE frontiers, Melbourne.

Mitchell, J.G, Latchem, C., Bates, A., and Smith, P. (2001c). *Critical Issues in Flexible Learning for VET Managers: 3. Issues.* TAFE frontiers, Melbourne.

Mulcahy, D. (2003). *Leadership and Management in Vocational Education and Training. Staying Focused on Strategy*, vol.1. NCVER, Adelaide.

National Centre for Vocational Education and Training (NCVER). (2004). *Australian Vocational Education and Training Statistics, Students and Courses 2003.* NCVER, Adelaide.

Palmieri, P. (2003). *The Agile Organisation. Case Studies of the Impact of Flexible Delivery on Human Resource Practices in TAFE.* NCVER, Adelaide.

Peoples, K., Robinson, P., and Calvert, J. (1997). *From Desk to Disk: Staff Development for VET Staff in Flexible Delivery.* ANTA, Brisbane.

Poole, M. (2000). Substance the key factor in new-style university. *The Australian: Higher Education*, May 17, 48.

TAFE frontiers (2000). Major Initiatives, May 2000, *Research and Professional Development, Request for Tenders*, TAFE frontiers, Melbourne.

Timmers, P. (1999). *Electronic Commerce.* Chichester: John Wiley & Sons Ltd.

Turban, E., Lee, J., King, D., and Chung, H. (2000). *Electronic Commerce, A Managerial Perspective.* New Jersey: Prentice Hall.

Chapter 42

Marketing Distance Education: Strategy and Context

James Fong and Norman "Tut" Bailey

A few years ago at an online learning institute attended by members of several esteemed American universities, an opening speaker remarked at the breadth of expectations found by constituents in distance education. According to Harwood (2001):

> Provosts want to see distance-education collaboration become seamless and routine while containing and reducing costs.
>
> Students want personalized learning, active engagement in course content and presentation, and effective feedback on their learning – without an increase in effort on their part.
>
> Faculty want more effective learning without compromising their research and are looking to information technology to eliminate the drudgery aspects of their work.
>
> Faculty also want recognition for their work by internal and external peers, and they want ease of use of distance-education technology.
>
> Information technology staff want scalable, robust and flexible products and services that are easy to train others to use and easy to support. And they want this to come without increased effort or cost.
>
> Learning technology experts want solid assessment data and support for accepted learning standards.
>
> (para. 13–17)

With all of these expectations pulling at online stakeholders, is it any wonder that the marketing and recruitment of students are sometimes afterthoughts in many of these academic discussions about the online learning environment?

42.1 THE GROWING DISTANCE-EDUCATION MARKETPLACE

The significance of this question has become more pronounced in the past 5 years since those remarks. When it comes to participation in distance education at U.S. institutions, nearly 2.33 million students took at least one online course in 2004 (Allen and Seaman, 2005). This figure was an 18.2 percent increase over the previous year, and the growth in online enrollments estimated by institutions was a mean of 19.9 percent and with a median of 10 percent.

Analysis from 2 years prior (Allen and Seaman, 2003) showed that nearly one third (578,000) of online students took courses exclusively online. A recent study by Eduventures, an education research and consulting company, estimated that the "exclusively online" total had more than doubled to 1.2 million as of 2005 (Stokes, 2006, para. 41). Further, Eduventures concluded that more than 30,000 online learners begin taking online courses each month (para. 41).

Finally, from an online-accessibility standpoint, just less than three quarters of all American households have Internet access (Nielsen//NetRatings [sic], 2004). Projections taken as recent as 2 years ago (Sabia and Schoener, 2003) predicted the 75 percent barrier would not be passed until 2006.

Therefore, one could assess that distance-education growth has significant momentum in enrollment and student growth, complemented by the capacity to expand even further.

42.2 THE IMPACT ON HIGHER EDUCATION

From an overarching higher-education perspective, distance-education students are estimated at 7 percent (Aslanian, 2001; Carnevale, 2005c) of students in higher education in the United States. According to the National Center for Education Statistics (NCES) and the U.S. Department of Education's Office of Educational Research and Improvement (as cited in Spanier, 2004), the 628 public 4-year institutions, 1,541 private 4-year institutions, along with the community and junior colleges collectively educate more than fifteen million students at any given time. This does not include the 780 for-profit institutions that also award degrees (para. 7), who make up approximately 4 percent of the student population in higher education (Glazer-Raymo, 2004) and among the broader category of degree-granting institutions, and serve about 2.4 percent of the market (Blumenstyk, 2005a, p. A11).

While a 7 percent sliver of education may seem small in the framework of the student population in higher education, distance education is easily the fastest growing delivery mode for higher education. According to Allen and Seaman (2005), the online enrollment growth rate of 18.2 percent is more than 10 times that projected by the NCES for the entire postsecondary population. With estimates that the overall higher education population will grow to 18.3 million by the year 2013 (NCES, 2005), distance education is positioned to be a significant portion of that growth.

Relative to investment on behalf of higher education, Gold (2004) reports, "Universities are investing substantial monies in the development and deployment of online distance learning environments to meet the needs of adult students and to provide an online modality for education that can compete effectively in the marketplace" (p. 1).

This is one of the main reasons that the distance-education marketplace is increasingly competitive and full of opportunity for existing entities and new entrants. Distance education is a realm where demand exceeds supply (Hanna, 2000), and the medium through which adults are increasingly continuing their education (Askov and Simpson, 2001).

42.3 THE INSTITUTIONAL CONTEXT OF DISTANCE-EDUCATION MARKETING

The present challenges confronting American higher education are changing the climate in which distance education operates, making campuses dramatically more market oriented and competition driven (Turner and Abrahamson, 2003; Couturier and Scurry, 2005; Zemsky et al., 2005). Within this broad perspective of the distance-education marketplace, individual traditional higher education institutions and for-profit providers of education bring different perspectives to the marketing of distance education, and the lines are not necessarily drawn along the for-profit/non-profit line.

As a result, the marketing of distance education is affected, specifically impacting which models, strategies and approaches work best for the specific institution. These factors include program offering, target market, politics within the organization, competition and the stage of progression of each program in the product life cycle among other factors. Unfortunately, a marketing model for one institution may not necessarily work for another (Turner and Abrahamson, 2003). Further, a 2004 study revealed that the second greatest challenge faced by distance-education providers in higher education is marketing and advertising to students. Thirty-two percent of respondents to a survey of university administrators cited this challenge, which trailed only "gaining the support of school and faculty management," and ranked above the issues of technical infrastructure and the "high start-up costs of development and technology" (Acadient, 2004, p. 2).

While traditional marketing philosophy often follows a four P's mentality (Kotler, 2000) of product, place (or distribution), promotion and price, other Ps play a role, such as the people (marketing staff), the people processes (i.e. servicing customers), politics and probably most importantly, positioning.

The remainder of this chapter discusses the factors that influence the marketing of distance education. Critical to this analysis is the interrelated and overlapping field of continuing-education marketing, as 80 percent of continuing-education marketing units also have the responsibility of marketing distance education for their university (Fong and Bailey, 2004; Bailey and Erickson, 2006). This makes the operations and pressures of the distance-education marketplace not clearly distinct for many distance-education providers in higher education, similar to trying to examine an alloy, and the pressures placed on the elements that combine to make it.

42.3.1 Positioning and Strategy

Positioning is consumer perception of an organization that resides in their mind (Trout and Ries, 2000). For higher education institutions, positioning and strategy are critical for their marketing, communication, and product-development decisions. However, within colleges and universities and within the distance-education space, this may not always be the case. It has been observed that many colleges and universities conduct marketing on an ad hoc basis which can ultimately erode the institutions established position. An integrated approach to positioning that reinforces strategy and provides a consistent identity (Hesel, 2004) is more likely to cause a positive marketing effect.

According to Hesel (2004), proper positioning and strategy require defining a number of key elements:

- What should my institution offer?
- Who should my institution offer it to?
- What should the communications say?
- How will it be communicated differently than the competition?
- What do we want to be known for?

Answering these questions among others helps to create a marketing strategy that ultimately makes other decisions such as product and promotion decisions easier, since these actions are not independent of the strategy (Trout and Ries, 1986). An action to develop a distance-education program or degree that is not in alignment with an organization's core competencies is less likely to be sustainable long term. Marketing under conditions where the product strategies are in alignment with the marketing strategy is more likely to be successful (Carnevale and Olsen, 2003), and with a clear strategy in place, distance-education providers – especially colleges and universities – can step out of the trap of "marketing-as-you-go."

Bailey (2005) notes that during the past 20 years, four factors in the field of higher education have tightened the connection between marketing and distance education: the emergence of the for-profit education sector (e.g. Eisenbarth, 2003; Carnevale, 2005b), the growth and diffusion of master's degrees (e.g. Aslanian, 2001; Glazer-Raymo, 2004), the explosion of distance education as a mainstream educational resource for adults (Allen and Seaman, 2003, 2004; Carnevale, 2005c) and the privatization of higher education (e.g. Reich, 2004; Couturier and Scurry, 2005).

42.3.2 Positioning: Choosing the Target Market

In the distance-education marketplace, the target market could be as simple as bachelor or graduate degree seeking individuals or it could be defined as program specific; for example, the Penn State World Campus, the university's distance-education arm, recently announced a degree in turfgrass science aimed at professionals in the field. The target market truly depends on the strategy of the institution and the programing or product.

Experience has shown that even in the broadest definitions for degree seekers, clear differences in market segments do exist. These market segments can be defined in many ways, including stage of technology adoption, geography, demographics, psychographics and usage among others (Weinstein, 1994). Experience has shown that depending on the program or market, distance-education market segments can be as simple as

- young, aspiring white-collar professionals who tend to be males
- teachers in Pennsylvania seeking certification or
- overseas military personnel seeking a degree online in a specific field.

However, as distance education matures, the next cohort of students may be more willing to adopt learning online. In fact, the challenges of almost a decade ago regarding distance education are far different than today.

Recent research (Fong and Miller, 2005) shows that even among a clearly defined segment there are many sub-segment possibilities. Table 42.1 shows that even between a demographic break between a segment with children and one without, there are statistically significant differences.

Table 42.1: Statistical Test Between Households in the United States with or Without Young Children Against Feeling Confident in Abilities to Learn Online

%		***Do you have any children under the age of 10 living at home?***		***Total***
		Yes	***No***	
I feel confident in my abilities to study in web and email-based environment	Strongly agree	48.38	35.57	40.10
	Somewhat agree	25.99	30.63	28.99
	Neither agree nor disagree	15.52	23.12	20.43
	Somewhat disagree	7.22	7.31	7.28
	Strongly disagree	2.89	3.36	3.19
Total		100	100	100
Chi-Square Tests				
	Value	df	Asymp. Sig. (2-sided)	
Pearson Chi-Square	13.83	4	0.00079	
Likelyhood Ratio	13.89	4	0.0077	
Linear-by-Linear Association	7.32	1	0.0068	
N of Valid Cases	783			

The research examined 783 individuals who were between the ages of 21 and 54 who had some college credit, an associates degree or a high school diploma on their interests toward distance education. The research revealed a number of segments and their preferences toward distance education. The research also revealed various potential market positions and customer needs.

42.3.3 Product: Product Life Cycle

It may be inferred that distance education is more evolved for some organizations yet new to others. To understand the differences requires understanding an organization's marketing culture, what stage distance education is within the product life cycle for the institution, competitive and marketplace factors and the constantly changing field of marketing.

As a starting point, a basic product life cycle is provided (Grieves, 2005) in Figure 42.1. The life cycle curve includes four stages: introduction, growth, maturity and decline. Marketing new products at the introduction stage often requires audiences that are earlier adopters, those typically in high demand or need. After the early adopters have been marketed to, other groups must be marketed in a slightly different manner, often times with greater information.

Marketing in the growth stage often has many competitors, and providers enter into the marketplace. It could be argued that marketing distance education over the past five years has been in the growth stage and is still in the growth stage. The industry and ultimately the consumer benefit, as many providers are advertising and educating the consumer base.

It could be argued that distance education is far from the maturity stage, given that some providers have closed their doors or minimized their operations (Boettcher, 2002).

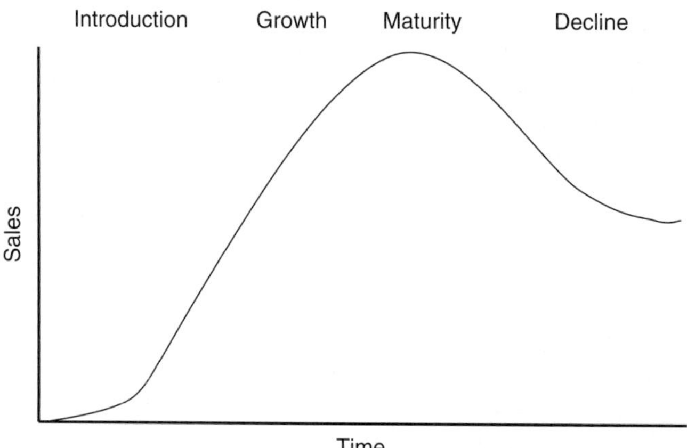

Figure 42.1: The Product Life Cycle

Reports suggest that the field still has significant growth potential (e.g. Allen and Seaman, 2005; Stokes, 2006). The last stage of the product life cycle is decline, a stage which distance education has clearly not entered at this point as previously referenced.

Figure 42.1 shows the product life cycle and one could argue that distance education is around the center of the growth curve, however, it is expected that more competitors will continue to enter the marketplace. In fact, given the ability for colleges and universities to offer online education through the use of external vendor services, as well as gain assistance with support services and marketing, the barriers to entry appear to be few. A review of entry barriers (Porter, 1990) suggests that competitors will expand operations, few will exit the distance-education arena, and development costs will decrease over time. It is expected that technology will impact distance education, and the quality of learning will improve during the growth period, as providers use technology not only to improve quality but also as a competitive advantage (Ebersole, 2004).

42.3.4 Product: New Product Development

In corporate systems, new product development is often driven by a blend of product management or engineering teams working jointly with marketing, whereas marketing's role is to validate or determine need for the product, as well as be in concert with promoting it at a later stage. Companies often rely on a number of new product development processes, such as six sigma based House of Quality/Quality Function Deployment (Hauser and Clausen, 1988) or StageGate (Cooper, 2005), to name a few. However, marketing's role within product development with colleges and universities is often unclear or minimal. In 2004, nearly two-thirds of the institutions surveyed were not using marketing research to drive new programing decisions (Fong and Bailey, 2004). While this rate fell to approximately one-half in 2006 (Bailey and Erickson, 2006), it is still clear that new product development system norms or processes that integrate marketing into the process are lacking.

Often what results is a product portfolio in need of promotion, left to a marketing staff that had little input in shaping and designing. These new product portfolios, especially in a fairly new distribution mode of distance education, often did little to consider cash cows (Boston Consulting Group, 1970) or products that were developed that extended beyond a college's or university's core competencies, strengths or ability to deliver. What was perceived as innovative was a far stretch from what the college or university typically offered. Figure 42.2 shows the product/market strategy grid (Ansoff, 1988), and many of these products were often in the upper right quadrant. As a present day example, one such trend is the response by over 200 colleges and universities to create disaster management or homeland security programs in distance-education, and/or residence-instruction formats. According to the United States Federal Emergency Management Agency (2005), as recently as 1995 only four programs existed in the field. As of 2005, 120 colleges had programs with another forty-eight institutions investigating or developing them. A review of some of these providers shows that while many have expertise, many also do not. Program development efforts are clearly the result of the trend to follow governmental funding, but not validating against supply and demand constraints,

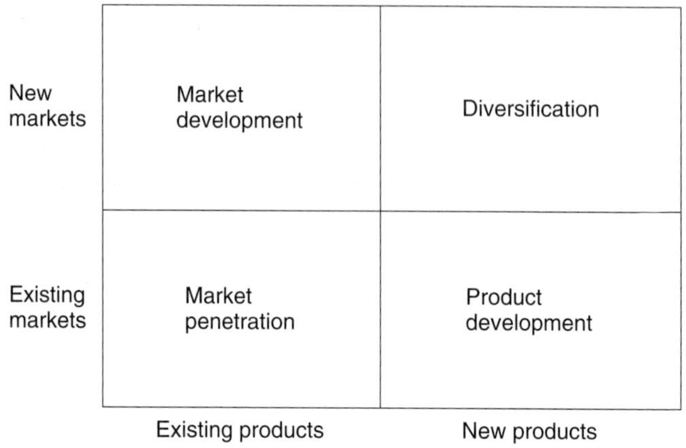

	Existing products	New products
New markets	Market development	Diversification
Existing markets	Market penetration	Product development

Figure 42.2: The Product/Market Strategy Grid

as well as long-term sustainability for each institution offer such a program. A similar occurrence happened in the late 1990s into 2001, when many providers, despite not having a past history in offering technology programs, began to offer Webmaster and other technology programs. What soon resulted was an accelerated downturn due to unstable economies in 2001 and 2002 and excessive supply without sufficient demand. Many providers soon fell out of the market. Without market validation and an established product development system, many providers may drop out of the disaster management or homeland security education market within the next few years.

To help improve the circumstances at higher education institutions, program development processes need to be strategic to leverage existing or critical programs while nurturing innovation at the upper right hand of the grid. Balance between marketing an organization's existing portfolio against a safe number of new ideas, concepts or programs is important in order to not jeopardize its future. A critical tool in the process could be implementing validation or market research efforts.

42.3.5 Politics and Processes: Organizational Readiness

Marketplace implications exist for universities and organizations with the ability to respond internally to critical marketing elements. Personal interviews and surveys suggest that universities spent a good portion of the late 1990s and the first half of the decade of 2000 on revamping or improving their marketing departments (Fong and Bailey, 2004). Compounding this challenge is that universities are adapting to the shifting demographics of a student body that is nearly 50 percent adult students. As of 2000, there were 6.5 million adult learners in higher education who make up 45 percent of the overall higher education population, and this segment of higher education is anticipated to grow to 7.1 million students by 2010 (Aslanian, 2001). According to NCES (cited in Council for Adult and Experiential Learning, 2000), several characteristics are often noted for these adult students: (a) delayed enrollment into postsecondary education;

(b) attend part-time; (c) are financially independent of parents; (d) work full-time while enrolled; (e) have dependents other than a spouse (p. 2).

Prior to this period, colleges and universities typically did not have to have sophisticated marketing personnel. The onset of distance education and shifting demographics, along with the evolution of the Internet and marketing science, facilitated the need for colleges and universities to rethink their staff development needs. Marketers had typically evolved from copywriting, design or public relations jobs. However, with the mainstreaming of distance education and the subsequent increase in competition in higher education, marketers now need to understand: integrated marketing, electronic marketing, database marketing, market research, strategic marketing planning, media selection and planning, and customer relationship management among other skill areas.

Further compounding the issue of marketing staff readiness is that not only do institutions have different markets and programs but they have different goals, revenues and operating cultures (e.g. centralized/decentralized, union/nonunion). College and university administrators often did not comprehend the massive changes happening to the marketing profession. No longer can marketing be driven only by great program designs and ideas. Instead, distance education should be strongly influenced by overarching marketing strategy and executed through well-planned marketing plans and efforts.

42.3.6 The People: Developing a Marketing Staff

As colleges and universities recognize the importance of marketing, the average staff size of marketing departments that conduct distance-education marketing continues to increase (Fong and Bailey, 2004; Bailey and Erickson, 2006). In 2004, the average marketing staff had 5.8 people, which grew to 8.4 in 2006. The contrast of institutional staffing differs greatly by revenue generated by the continuing-education unit. Units with greater than $10 million in revenue on average carry fourteen marketing-staff members, while departments with $3 million or less had only five individuals devoted to marketing (Bailey and Erickson, 2006). Typically, for every seven people working within continuing education, one person is a marketer.

According to three recent studies of continuing- and distance-education marketing professionals (Fong and Bailey, 2004; Bailey and Erickson, 2006), the greatest need among professionals employed in the marketing of continuing or distance education has been a constant – electronic marketing. Over this four-year period, marketing professionals affiliated with the University Continuing Education Association (UCEA) stated that their greatest professional development need was electronic marketing. However, in each of these years, the specific needs of electronic marketing changed. In 2002, marketing professionals needed help getting their Web sites up or organized better to reinforce the needs of their learners. In 2004, the needs evolved to more sophisticated topics, such as Web site optimization, site redesign, pay-per-click campaigns or developing metrics. In 2006, this list of topics grew to include customer relationship management (CRM), and analyzing return on investment (ROI).

Fong and Bailey (2004) and Bailey and Erickson (2006) also determined that marketing staffs are in need of professional development in other marketing areas, such as strategic planning, marketing research and database marketing. In addition, marketing staffs often report to deans, vice presidents or directors of continuing or distance education. The marketing leadership dilemma is that many of these individuals also seek marketing growth and understanding, as many lack significant marketing expertise (Fong et al., 2001). Salary survey comparisons for and among continuing- and distance-education marketers, as well as measuring their experience, may also reveal expertise and readiness of this marketing pool.

42.3.7 Pricing and Budgets

Marketers in any field need to consider pricing as a crucial element of the marketing mix. However, often times with traditional education, credit pricing is fixed and cannot be adapted for competitive market needs. Some universities have adapted their in-residence program credit pricing either up or down for the online market. As a result, differentiated pricing occurs in the marketplace for an institution. Differentiated pricing may be a positive occurrence as price and revenues can be potentially optimized by target market segment. It could, however, be a negative action if consumers are able to identify pricing tiers that do not benefit them.

A critical tool in pricing strategies is having customer and competitor information. Market research and other information tools can assist in defining price sensitivities and opportunities by segment. Simple surveys using methods such as Van Westendoff models (Marketing NPV, 2005) can be applied or even multivariate choice models such as conjoint analysis can be used to measure trade-offs and optimal feature sets.

While pricing strategies remain a largely untapped P in the four P model, often colleges and universities involved in distance education tend to focus on cost and budgets and not necessarily value. Budget models for marketing continuing- and distance-education programs and departments differ dramatically (Fong and Bailey, 2004). Marketing budgets could be program-based, derived from a department budget or institutionally allocated (Eduventures, 2004). Further complicating budgeting are various revenue sharing models and organizational structures (centralized or decentralized) among others. The data available suggest that 7.4 percent of revenues are provided for marketing – 4.7 percent of revenues are for staff and operating costs and 2.7 percent go toward media for continuing education (Bailey and Erickson, 2006). An Eduventures' (2004) report on online education had similar findings, stating that 63 percent of the 69 respondents said their institution spent 5 percent or less and 80 percent of respondents spent 10 percent or less on marketing. However, it appears that these percentages were based exclusively on media expenses, as opposed to operating and media expenses combined.

It can be assumed that marketing budgets for distance-education programs, especially for-profit educational providers, are significantly more. In some cases, institutions are spending two to three times the percentage of revenue. A review of the Apollo Group's (2004) 10-K shows that the organization spends approximately 21 percent.

As the market continues to grow, some marketing organizations try to maintain market share by investing and growing with the market. When an organization cannot invest and maintain market share, but still build revenues, it must acknowledge the fact that a competitor has captured this lost market share, and new entrants may have entered the competitive space.

Over the past few years, continuing-education marketing budgets have increased slightly moving from approximately $737,000 in 2000 to nearly $800,000 in 2006 (Bailey and Erickson, 2006). During this same period of time, 34–43 percent of marketing departments have increased their budget, reflecting a positive connection between increased revenues and marketing budgets for many of these institutions (Fong and Bailey, 2004; Bailey and Erickson, 2006). In fact, between 2004 and 2006, more than two-thirds of continuing-education marketing directors report that their continuing education departments have experienced an increase in revenue predominantly due to marketing expansion and/or an increase in programing (Bailey and Erickson, 2006). However, in 2004 and 2006, 43 percent and 48 percent of these same directors report that their budgets stayed the same, respectively. Further, if coupled with the marketing leaders that reported a decrease, this figure grows to almost 60 percent for both of the studies. Concerns are growing about the increasing expectations to market distance-education programs without devoting or developing the resources to effectively market these programs (Fong and Bailey, 2004; Bailey and Erickson, 2006).

Some of the decrease has been with a reduction of print catalogs and other collateral, while moving much of this content to university Web sites. One would expect that this shift would decrease marketing spending; however, in many circumstances, marketers are spending these savings on marketing campaigns designed to drive prospective students to the Web site. Another factor that may be compounding an increase in marketing expenditures is the continued fracturing or fragmentation of mainstream media such as cable television and radio.

Further increases in expenditures are most likely a result of adding staff and increasing salaries. Colleges and universities are finding that they are lacking key marketing leadership and adding them on their staff. Marketing directors from private industry have been brought into institutions such as Penn State University, the University of Massachusetts Amherst, University of Connecticut, Western Michigan University and Upper Iowa University among others. Marketing staffs are expanding, as well as deepening in terms of their expertise. In terms of expansion, e-marketing, planning, market research and other positions are being added (Fong and Bailey, 2004).

42.3.8 Place or Distribution

Place decisions are often referred to as channel strategies (Hoffman, 2004). The marketing channel is how the product is delivered and experienced so that the transaction can occur. A key factor in the transaction is often the difference between marketing a product versus a service (Zeithaml and Bitner, 2002). In the case of distance education, consumers will typically be exposed through a print advertisement, by receiving a catalog or most likely through the Internet or an organization's Web site.

In the world of online education, an organization's Web site, its reputation and how it communicates with its potential customers are critical in the selection of services. According to the 2005 National Adult Learners Satisfaction-Priorities Report, adult learners indicated that an institution's Web site and its online catalog were the two most important factors that influenced their enrollment (Noel-Levitz, Inc. and Council for Adult and Experiential Learning, 2005). Potential customers do not necessarily get to sample the product or see it through a traditional distribution method like a Wal-Mart superstore or through a car dealership. The service is most often simulated or communicated through the content on the organization's Web site, how the site is organized and whether the promised services can be communicated as deliverable within expected quality limits (Lovelock, 1996).

Place or distribution of online education is expected to take place online, although physical elements can reinforce the experience, i.e. customer service, books, learning materials and regular contact with faculty.

For marketers, the Web site plays a critical role as it is often the storefront or distribution center to the customer. A poorly designed Web site may in fact turn customers away, just as an unclean restaurant impacts the potential dining experience. As part of the marketing mix, place, particularly an organization's Web site, is an integral part of a marketing strategy.

42.3.9 Promotion

What many view as marketing's primary P, promotion is often more successful when driven by a strategy and position. Regardless, promotion can take many forms. For distance education, the most used and fastest growing media is the Internet (Eduventures 2004; Fong and Bailey, 2004). However, many organizations continue to spend resources on offline marketing in forms including print, broadcast such as television and radio, billboards, word of mouth, direct mail, public relations, direct selling and other means. In terms of media selection, continuing education marketers cite that the use of electronic marketing has increased the most, but other areas of increase include the use of public relations, radio and personal selling or tradeshows (Fong and Bailey, 2004).

42.3.10 Promotion: Evolution of the Web

Certainly, the greatest recent marketing and media development has been the Internet. According to Cassar (as cited in Nielsen//NetRatings, 2004) "online access has managed to gain the type of traction that took other media decades to achieve" (p. 1).

Not only has the Internet expanded trade and e-commerce opportunities, but has also served as a marketing medium still in development. While legislation and regulation have not kept pace against SPAM, virus development and identity theft/security threats, the upside has been huge opportunities for legitimate marketing.

Early efforts to use mass e-mails and banners have now evolved into focused efforts around Web site optimization and search engine marketing. The majority of consumers use a search engine to find information, compare products or shop online. Search engine optimization (SEO) campaigns and pay-per-click search engine efforts have been a growing focus among marketers outside of education. Marketers have realized that SEO is probably the single most important marketing tool currently. In the realm of distance education, search engine optimization is no different and in fact is probably more important given the product line of online education. However, it would appear that colleges and universities lag in the area of SEO (Marckini, 2005).

SEO consists of Web site design that focuses on principles that allow for search engines such as Google or Yahoo! to optimally index the site so that when a consumer uses specific keywords, the organization's Web site moves up or down in the rankings. Critical elements to SEO are writing properly for the Web, avoiding or minimizing the use of graphics or animation, creating legitimate links to partners or other related sites and using keywords in title tags, meta-tags and Web site content.

When an organization cannot rise to the top of search-engine rankings by organic (non-paid) means, organizations have been adopting pay-per-click (also known as PPC) campaigns that allow them to purchase advertising space for certain keywords. The advertising space is often on the right-hand side or even the top areas for Google or Yahoo searches. This allows for organizations to promote their programs without being solely dependent on SEO. Colleges and universities are just starting to become aware of the need to re-design their Web sites for SEO. Some of the challenges that colleges and universities face with SEO is that Web design functions can reside within the greater institution's communications department or through an outsourced partner. These individuals may not necessarily have SEO training.

A reflection that colleges and universities may be behind emanates from statistics recently posted by Nielsen, the media ratings provider. The finding suggests that for-profits are spending more and gaining the most impressions in the paid Web advertising medium. In the two most recent Nielsen//NetRatings AdRelevance reports of top online education advertisers, taken in December 2004 and April 2005, more than 83 percent and 88 percent of the online advertising impressions were from for-profits, respectively (The Center for Media Research, 2004; Nielsen//NetRatings, 2005). So while this market segment may represent approximately 3–4 percent of the students, it controls the vast majority of the online media (Bailey, 2005).

Colleges and universities need to assess their marketing budgets, as previously mentioned. However, these budgets need to be assessed on whether marketing expenditures are generating a ROI or have enough marketing weight or impressions in the market. The Nielsen data suggest that the for-profits are marketing to overcome brand awareness issues, but are doing so on a pre-meditated basis to have a consistent or obvious market presence. The question as to why traditional colleges and universities are only spending a fraction needs to be answered. Is it because these institutions have no need as their brand names are stronger than the for-profits, as these institutions are unable to or have not adequately planned for it or as these institutions do not understand the opportunity that is available to them?

Other implications to marketing online are the growing expectation for customization and immediate response. Savvy marketers have created systems such as profiles and tracking systems (using cookies) to personalize greetings, messages and product needs to consumers. While the implications of such may not be of immediate importance to online learners, the ability to customize is becoming more of a necessity as the Internet evolves.

In addition, customer response may also be impacted by 24/7 mentalities for service. Customer service is a critical element of many organizations and should be managed appropriately in the distance-education arena. According to Turner and Abrahamson (2003), concerns are being raised by students in higher-education programs targeting adult learners because "Students are, in short, acting more like consumers than ever before. While universities tend to react slowly to market needs, continuing education units are expected to be more alert and nimble" (para. 8).

Managing expectations about the availability (or lack of it) needs to be adequately communicated to customers and potential customers. The impact on marketing is significant as marketing messages or strategies may leverage or promise a high level of customer service or position the organization as a top-flight provider, which in turn requires customer service to be set at a high level. Other e-marketing strategies that have been observed include creating self-service tools on the institution's Web site, such as frequently asked questions (FAQs), online advising and QandA, virtual open houses where visitors can ask an institution's staff questions and online conferencing with business decision makers regarding distance education.

Given the challenges of marketing a service, as mentioned earlier, some institutions have resorted to overcoming the trial or sampling factor by offering short courses online at no cost. Institutions that have offered this include the University of California at Berkeley and the University of Washington (Chronicle of Higher Education, 2001).

42.3.11 Promotion: Measuring Marketing ROI Through Metrics

Due to the complex structures found in many higher-education institutions, colleges and universities may have difficulty with reporting the return on their marketing investment or isolating which media tends to be working better than others. Institutions do tend to have ratios such as cost per acquisition/student or inquiry/enrollment percentages. However, detail below these critical metrics, such as cost per student via the Web or other media, is often absent for an institution. The basics, such as Web site hits or user sessions, are usually present, but statistics or information that track the Web visitor's origination point, the keywords that were used or at which point on the Web site the customer leaves is often missing in an online marketing effort.

Research shows that few institutions understand database marketing or have dedicated enrollment managers to their distance-education efforts (Fong and Bailey, 2004). As a result, making decisions through data or metrics is typically absent from most institutions. Other results of not having metrics is an inability to eliminate poor media purchases, prioritizing good media choices and being able invest new resources to garner a greater return on investment.

42.4 UNDERSTANDING THE MANY Ps THROUGH MARKET RESEARCH

Market research can help better understand or impact many of the Ps identified earlier. Surprisingly, less than one-half of continuing education marketing departments use market research in their new program and marketing decisions, only 36 percent of continuing-education marketing units see marketing research as a core strength and one-quarter of institutions report spending $0 on marketing research (Bailey and Erickson, 2006). However, it seems that continuing-education departments are beginning to recognize this need, as they are adding capacity through the combination of additional staff and outsourcing of the research function faster than any other area of marketing (Bailey and Erickson, 2006).

Through experiences at a variety of institutions, colleges and universities that integrate or adopt market research into their decision-making processes often shorten timelines for development. For example, University X had spent two years working through whether they should offer a specific degree. At the many gatherings of the institution, various factions would present reasons for progressing while others would present reasons for stopping. As a result, follow-up meetings would occur and other or new members would be brought in to offer their perspectives. Only when market research and new data were presented did a decision result on a "go/no-go" on the program. This phenomenon is not uncommon to colleges and universities, as often the resources do not exist for market research or the belief that the answer was among the stakeholders and it had not been flushed out yet is often common belief.

Market research can help with program development decisions, as well as extend the product life cycle. In the case of the product life cycle, market research can be conducted on struggling online programs to determine or isolate the problem and identify a solution. Experience has shown that problems can arise from many areas including outdated content, the introduction of a competitor, a legislative change that eliminates program need, changes in technology making existing delivery appear obsolete, changes to price sensitivity in the marketplace or the effects of a struggling economy among others. Market research can identify solutions such as introducing new product features; directing the program to other, more needy markets; repositioning the product; selecting new media; or even changing price strategies.

Market research in distance education usually takes one of three forms (Fong, 2004): (a) gathering information that the company has; (b) collecting information that may be available through secondary sources or (c) collecting information through primary sources such as surveys or focus groups.

Implementing market research has never been easier, as what was viewed as expensive and intrusive methods, such as telephone surveys, have migrated to Web surveys and focus groups. Telephone surveys are still used, but often substituted for more cost-efficient and quicker Web surveys for distance-education audiences. The use of Internet panels has also grown to acquire information on narrow market segments, such as those done recently for the University of Massachusetts Amherst (Fong and Miller, 2005).

Organizations that can have a consistent pulse on the market are more likely to be successful in the distance-education field, as it is loaded with uncertainty due to competitive pressures, technology changes and major consumer changes. To implement a process or system would require planning and budgeting for market research. While the publication can no longer be found, the American Marketing Association released a study in the late 1990s that said that many major institutions budgeted one-half of 1 percent to market research. A number of institutions are beginning to adopt this practice of fulfilling market research needs as can be illustrated by three occurrences: (a) the hiring of market research staff (Fong and Bailey, 2004; Bailey and Erickson, 2006); (b) consortiums and collaborations being developed such as the Eduventures Learning Collaborative which has approximately fifty-eight institutions participating (Eduventures, 2005) and (c) actual budgeting and use of market research through outside vendors (Bailey and Erickson, 2006).

42.5 DISCUSSION: MARKETING STRATEGIES FOR THE FUTURE

While this paper identifies many building blocks toward the marketing of distance education, it purposely does not provide a standard or specific model for the implementation of marketing campaigns. The reason for doing so is that the situation differs for each institution and significant analyses and planning must be undertaken to define a strategy, dictate integrated marketing actions and budget and plan accordingly. However, a number of situations may merit one marketing strategy over another.

For example, an established non-profit century-old college or university may have a competitive advantage against a 10-year-old, for-profit provider in the marketplace. On the other hand, experience shows that for-profit providers are often more successful at customer service and marketing and are less likely to be inhibited by bureaucratic processes. It has been observed that some non-profit educational providers are striving to acquire the positive attributes of the for-profits, such as faster, more reliable customer response, quicker program development and more delivery options. At the same time, for-profit providers are positioning themselves as reputable and reliable providers of higher education.

Also, measuring an institution's brand equity is essential in terms of impacting a marketing strategy. Traditional colleges and universities are more likely to have established brands, significant alumni pools to tap, faculty expertise to leverage and greater credibility among corporate hiring executives. It is surmised that for-profits are likely to gain ground on brand equity over time, as the number of graduates increases and influences corporate opinion in the future. Evidence of this can be seen by the fact that major associations or organizations are becoming more open to for-profit providers (Carnevale, 2005a).

In fact, traditional colleges and universities offering online program most likely will see more competitive pressures from for-profit providers of education (Blumenstyk, 2005b).

Presently, the market is favorable due to a still seemingly positive legislative climate, influx of capital and a student base that is more accepting of learning online. However, Blumenstyk also warns of possible hindrances to growth for for-profits, such as issues related to quality and drop-out rates. It can be argued that, while this article identifies friction and competition between traditional and for-profit institutions, the demand for education may not be fulfilled solely from public institutions, and a strong place for for-profits exists in the global education marketplace.

Regarding customer responsiveness, colleges and universities have also been slow in the area of customer relationship management (CRM), as opposed to their for-profit counterparts. It has been observed that many institutions are saddled with legacy student information tracking systems that lack key elements, such as marketing referral tracking information, prospect/inquiry status, non-credit student records and linkages to marketing or financial results. In fact, observation suggests that the larger the institution, the more likely that a prohibitive legacy system is in place. For distance-education providers troubled by CRM, Shaik (2005) has provided some analysis of how to implement a broad-based relationship marketing strategy from a distance-education standpoint, which allows adult educators to apply a marketplace strategy across their organization.

Traditional colleges and universities have a greater ability to address consumers seeking out programs while in the introduction and growth phases of the product life cycle. Quality and reliability are often embedded given an established brand. In marketing models such as Strong's AIDA (attention/interest/desire/action) (as cited in Lascu and Clow, 2005), century-old brands have high brand awareness, desirability and acceptance. Newer brands, such as many for-profits, often do not have widespread awareness and therefore must focus their marketing efforts at developing the market among smaller, more relevant or needy segments, segments that have been largely ignored by traditional colleges and universities.

Some institutions have made dramatic shifts over the past five years to business-to-business markets, as opposed to traditional business-to-consumer advertising. Business-to-business, often referred to as corporate training, has required marketers to shift their strategies and tactics somewhat. Market positioning as a solutions provider or a valued partner has been implemented by some institutions. Corporate universities that leverage colleges and universities have been observed as well. Marketing and advertising of distance-education programs have been directed to human resource professionals, trainers and others that influence the decision-making process in a corporation. Some universities boast that they are contractually serving cohorts of corporate students.

42.6 CONCLUSION

An unprecedented crossroads presently exists for distance-education providers. The acceleration of technology adoption, distance-education participation and academic-degree production are growing at rates never before seen in the history of education in the United States. Moreover, these advances are even exceeding the growth estimates and predictions of professional experts who track the media, delivery systems and higher-education credentials, respectively, for these related entities (Allen and Seaman, 2003, 2004; Glazer-Raymo, 2004; Nielsen//NetRatings, 2004). This growth punctuates the need for distance-education professionals to maintain a high level of respect and vigilance for the marketing of distance education and the need to begin to invest more resources into the marketing of these programs. With the unquestioned growth of distance education, more scholarship needs to be developed to further articulate the impact of professional practice on the field.

Generally, marketing distance education has many challenges as well as rewards. Some of the challenges are a result of a collision between technological, geographical, economical and demographic changes. Colleges and universities, as a result, have to adapt to a constantly changing environment. However, some have taken the time to successfully plan and organize their marketing efforts. They have infused market and competitive data into their decisions, analyzed their situations and opportunities, put in place strategies and realistic plans and have avoided the pitfalls of a slow and bureaucratic process. They abandoned advertising approaches in favor of marketing approaches. They have made distinct choices as to who their customers will or will not be. They have learned what motivates these customers. They have stopped to get their marketing materials and Web sites aligned with their marketing strategy. They have developed programs that customers want and that they can deliver. They have priced them accordingly – to market and to strategy. They have also designed customer response systems that reinforce a strategy and build confidence that distance education can be effectively delivered. They have convinced the consumer that their investment will have a positive return. This is the future of marketing distance education.

REFERENCES

Acādient (2004, April 28). 2004 University Distance Learning Survey. Retrieved July 21, 2004 from: www.acadient.com.

Allen, I.E. and Seaman, J. (2003, September). Sizing the Opportunity: The Quality and Extent of Online Education in the United States, 2002 and 2003. Retrieved May 26, 2005 from: http://www.sloan-c.org/resources/sizing_opportunity.pdf.

Allen, I.E. and Seaman, J. (2004, November). Entering the Mainstream: The Quality and Extent of Online Education in the United States, 2003 and 2004. Retrieved May 26, 2005 from: http://www.sloan-c.org/resources/entering_mainstream.pdf.

Allen, I.E. and Seaman, J. (2005, November). Growing by Degrees: Online Education in the United States, 2005. Retrieved January 3, 2006 from: http://www.sloan-c.org/resources/growing_by_degrees.pdf.

Ansoff, I. (1988). *The New Corporate Strategy*. New York: Wiley.

Apollo Group. (2004). Marketing expenditures excerpted from their 10-K report.

Askov, E. and Simpson, M. (2001). *Researching Distance Education: Penn State's Online Adult Education MEd [sic] Degree on the World Campus* [sic]. Paper presented at the 2001 AVETRA Conference. Retrieved November 10, 2004 from: http://www.avetra.org.au/abstracts_and_papers_2001/Askov-Simpson_full.pdf.

Aslanian, C. (2001). *Adult Students Today*. New York: The College Board.

Bailey, N.T. (2005). *A Critical Review of the Literature for the Marketplace of Online, Graduate-Level Adult Education*. Unpublished master's paper in adult education, The Pennsylvania State University, State College, Pennsylvania, United States.

Bailey, N.T. and Erickson, K.L. (2006, April). 2006 *State of Continuing Education Marketing: How Does Your Organization Size Up?* Paper presented at the 2006 University Continuing Education Association National Conference, San Diego, CA.

Blumenstyk, G. (2005a, January 7). For-profit education: Online courses fuel growth [Electronic version]. *The Chronicle of Higher Education*, **51**(18), A11. Retrieved July 26, 2005 from: http://chronicle.com/weekly/v51/i18/18a01101.htm.

Blumenstyk, G. (2005b, November 25). Higher education 2015: For-profit outlook. *The Chronicle of Higher Education*, **52**(14), A14.

Boettcher, J. (2002). The changing landscape of distance education: What micro-market segment is right for you? [Electronic version]. Syllabus. Retrieved December 18, 2005 from http://www.campus-technology.com/article.asp?id=6474.

Boston Consulting Group. (1970). The Product Portfolio. Retrieved December 18, 2005 from http://www.bostonconsultinggroup.com/.

Carnevale, D. (2005a, September, 23). Employers still prefer traditional degrees over online learning. *The Chronicle of Higher Education*, **52**(5), p. A43.

Carnevale, D. (2005b, February 4). Offering entire degrees online is one key to distance education, survey finds [Electronic version]. *The Chronicle of Higher Education* **51**(22), A31. Retrieved June 28, 2005 from: http://chronicle.com/weekly/v51/i22/22a03101.htm.

Carnevale, D. (2005c, June 28). Online courses continue to grow dramatically, enrolling nearly 1 million, report says. The Chronicle of Higher Education: Today's News. Retrieved June 28, 2005 from: http://chronicle.com/daily/2005/06/20005062802t.htm.

Carnevale, D. and Olsen, F. (2003). How to succeed in distance education. *The Chronicle of Higher Education*, **49**(40), A31.

Chronicle of Higher Education. (2001, July 6). U. of Washington to use short versions of distance courses as marketing tools. *The Chronicle of Higher Education*, **47**(43), 26.

Cooper, R. (2005). *Product Leadership: Creating and Launching Superior New Products*. New York: Basic Books.

Council for Adult and Experiential Learning. (2000). *Serving Adult Learners in Higher Education: Principles of Effectiveness*. New York: Forbes Custom Publishing.

Couturier, L. and Scurry, J. (2005, February). Correcting Course: How We can Restore the Ideals of Public Higher Education in a Market-Driven Era. Retrieved February 17, 2005 from: http://www.futuresproject.org/publications/Correcting_Course.pdf.

Ebersole, J. (2004). Innovation: The new necessity. *Continuing Higher Education Review*, **68**, 57–63.

Eduventures. (2004). Marketing Benchmarking in Online Education 2004.

Eduventures. (2005). Eduventures Learning Collaborative Web site. Retrieved January 8, 2006 from http://www.eduventures.com/

Eisenbarth, G. (2003). The online education market [Electronic version]. *On the Horizon*, **11**(3), 9–15.

Fong, J. (2004, June). *Marketing Workshop*. Presented at University Continuing Education Association Summer Institute for Continuing Education Professionals, Boston, MA.

Fong, J.E. and Bailey, N.T. (2004, February 13). *The State of Continuing Education Marketing: A UCEA Study*. Paper presented at the 2004 University Continuing Education Association Marketing Seminar, Savannah, GA.

Fong, J.E. and Miller, H. (2005). Proprietary survey research conducted on behalf of the University of Massachusetts Amherst.

Fong, J., Mattes, B., and Settle, T. (2001, April 7). *The Changing Role of Continuing Education CEOs*. Paper presented at the 2001 University Continuing Education Association National Conference, Philadelphia, PA.

Glazer-Raymo, J. (2004). Trajectories for professional master's education [Electronic version]. *Communicator*, **37**(2), 1, 2, 5.

Gold, S.S. (2004). An Analysis of the Relationship between Software Facilitated Communication and Student Outcomes in Online Education. (Doctoral dissertation, Northcentral University, 2004). Retrieved November 13, 2004 from: http://wwwlib.umi.com/disserations/preview_page/3118091/10.

Grieves, M. (2005). *Product Lifecycle Management*. New York: McGraw-Hill.

Hanna, D.E. (ed.). (2000). *Higher Education in an era of Digital Competition: Choices and Challenges*. Madison, WI: Atwood Publishing.

Harwood, J. (2001, June). *Welcome Address*. Presented at Learning On-line Institute for the Committee of Institutional Cooperation, University Park, Pennsylvania.

Hauser, J. and Clausen, D. (1988). *The House of Quality*. Boston: The Harvard Business Review.

Hesel, H. (2004, April 30). Know thyself: 5 strategies for marketing a college. *The Chronicle of Higher Education*, **50**(34), B9.

Hoffman, D. (2004). *Marketing Principles and Best Practices*, 3rd ed., Florence, KY: Thomson Southwestern.

Kotler, P. (2000). *Marketing Management (Millennium Edition)*. Upper Saddle River, New Jersey: Prentice Hall.

Lascu D.N. and Clow, K.E. (2005). *Marketing Frontiers: Concepts and Tools*. Cincinnati, OH: Atomic Dog.

Lovelock, C. (1996). *Services Marketing, 3rd ed*. Upper Saddle River, New Jersey: Prentice Hall.

Marckini, F. (2005, February 17). *Search Engine Marketing: From Blueprint to Completion*. Workshop presented at the 2005 University Continuing Education Association Marketing Seminar, New Orleans, Louisiana.

Marketing NPV. (2005). Taking Pricing to the People. Retrieved January 8, 2006 from: http://www.marketingnpv.com/article.asp?ix=1096.

National Center for Educational Statistics. (2005). Projections of Educational Statistics to 2013. Retrieved December 18, 2005 from http://nces.ed.gov/programs/projections/.

Nielsen//NetRatings. (2004, March 18). Three Out of Four Americans have Access to the Internet According to Nielsen//NetRatings. Retrieved June 7, 2005 from: http://www.netratings.com/pr/pr_040318.pdf.

Noel-Levitz, Inc. and Council for Adult and Experiential Learning. (2005). The 2005 National Adult Learners Satisfaction-Priorities Report. Retrieved February 22, 2006 from: www.noellevitz.com.

Porter, M. (1990). *Competitive Strategy: Techniques for Analyzing Industries and Competitors*. New York: The Free Press.

Reich, R. (2004, March 25). *The Destruction of Public Higher Education in America and how the U.K. can Avoid the Same Fate*. Presented at the 2004 Higher Education

Policy Institute Lecture at the Royal Institution, London. Retrieved June 24, 2005 from: http://news.bbc.co.uk/1/hi/education/3564531.stm.

Sabia, A. and Schoener, M. (2003, January). Gartner research: Key Trends. Retrieved December 27, 2005 from: http://140.198.160.116/ie/resources/2003_EMCC_EnvironmentalScan.pdf.

Shaik, N. (2005). *Marketing Distance Learning Programs and Courses: A Relationship Marketing Strategy*. Paper presented at the 2005 Distance Leaning Association proceedings, Jeckyl Island, GA. Retrieved June 24, 2005 from http://www.westga.edu/~distance/ojdla/summer82/shaik82.htm.

Spanier, G.B. (2004, February). *The Privatization of American Public Higher Education*. Presented at Penn State University Faculty Senate, University Park, Pennsylvania.

Stokes, P.J. (2006, January 19). Revamping adult education [Msg 22]. Message posted to The Chronicle of Higher Education Colloquy: http://chronicle.com/colloquy/2006/01/adult/.

The Center for Media Research. (2004, December 5). Education and Careers Sites, Demographics, Advertisers, and ad Types, Sizes and Delivery. Retrieved July 25, 2005 from: http://www.centerformediaresearch.com/cfmr_brief.cfm?fnl=041230.

Trout, J. and Ries, A. (1986). *Marketing Warfare*. New York: McGraw-Hill.

Trout, J. and Ries, A. (2000). *Positioning: The Battle for Your Mind*. New York: McGraw-Hill.

Turner, C. and Abrahamson, T. (2003, March 28). Marketing Continuing Education for the 21st Century: A View from the Top. Lipman-Hearne roundtable discussion retrieved June 25, 2005 from: http://www.lipmanhearne.com/resources/articles/continuingeducation/.

United States Federal Emergency Management Agency. (2005, June 7). *Emergency Management Higher Education Project*. Presented at the Emergency Management Higher Education Conference. Emmitsburg, MD: B. W. Blanchard. Retrieved February 28, 2006 from: http://training.fema.gov.

Weinstein, A. (1994). *Market Segmentation, 2nd ed.*, Chicago: Probus Publishing Company.

Zemsky, R., Wenger, G.R., and Massy, W.F. (2005, July 15). Today's colleges must be market smart and mission centered. *The Chronicle Review*, **51**(45), B6–B7.

Ziethaml, V. and Bitner, M.J. (2002). *Services Marketing: Integrating Customer Focus Across the Firm*. New York: McGraw-Hill.

Chapter 43

The Costs and Effectiveness of Distance Education

Mark Bullen and Adnan Qayyum

43.1 INTRODUCTION

The economics of distance education is a relatively new field of study, emerging in the early 1970s as correspondence-style distance education began to incorporate the use of expensive mass communication technologies such as broadcast television, video and, later, multimedia. In particular, it was the emergence of the mass distance teaching universities like the UK Open University and the other open universities that made the economics of distance education a subject of growing interest to researchers, policy makers and administrators. The economics of distance education has grown in complexity and interest as organizational arrangements and modes of delivery have changed and evolved, and the use of information technology has increased.

With the spread and growth of the Internet, demand for distance education and e-learning has increased significantly and distance education has moved from the margins of education toward the mainstream. Quite rightly, questions about the effectiveness and cost have also increased. However, calculating distance education costs is not a straightforward exercise because of the many variables involved and because it is often difficult to get accurate cost information. The increasing use of digital technologies complicates matters further because the resources used for distance education are more numerous than ever. Additionally, as distance education has moved to the mainstream, it has stimulated a growing interest in comparing the costs and effectiveness of distance education with conventional classroom education and this brings with it a whole set of other challenges.

The economics of distance education and the effectiveness of distance education are two topics that are usually dealt with separately. There is a vast literature that attempts to answer questions about the effectiveness of distance education and technology-based teaching, usually in comparison to face-to-face teaching, using a specific view of effectiveness that tends to conceptualize it mainly in terms of learning outcomes (For a comprehensive meta-analysis of the effectiveness debate, see Bernard et al., 2004). There is also a considerable body of literature that looks at the issues of economics again often in comparison to conventional educational methods (Rumble, 1992). However, costs and effectiveness are rarely looked at together (for some exceptions see Bates, 1995). We take the position that studying these two topics in isolation from each other does not advance our understanding of either topic nor of distance education. It fails to provide practical answers to significant questions about the management and administration of distance education. For example, if we determine that a particular implementation of distance education is cheaper than face-to-face teaching without knowing anything about its effectiveness, this information will do little to help inform decision-making. Similarly, if we discover that particular approaches to distance education are producing spectacular outcomes, measured along a variety of dimensions, we are again left with information that may be interesting, but is of little practical value if we do not have any reliable data on how much it cost to achieve these results. Our premise is that effectiveness is the overarching issue. After all, as educators, our primary concern is how effective our programs are at achieving the various goals we have for them. There will be many different goals for our programs, some of them related to how well the learning outcomes have been achieved by students, but others with social, political, cultural, and economic dimensions. Costs are just one part of the effectiveness equation. No doubt they are a critical part, especially in times of limited funding for education, but they must be examined in relation to the many other dimensions of effectiveness. We treat costs as one dimension of effectiveness. If further research in this area is to produce practical results that can help inform policy and practice, it needs to deal with cost and effectiveness as a form of evaluation. Nonetheless, we will be focusing specifically on the cost dimensions of effectiveness and looking at some of the different costing issues and approaches to thinking about costing.

43.2 OVERVIEW OF THE CHAPTER

We begin this chapter by discussing the concept of effectiveness and arguing that we need to conceive effectiveness more broadly than what is prevalent in the literature that focuses almost exclusively on learning outcomes. We conclude this section with a framework for considering the effectiveness of distance education that includes instructional, social, financial, and organizational issues.

Next we examine the complex array of issues related to the economics of distance education particularly models of costing distance education. We conclude by encouraging cost calculations of distance education courses and programs, in the context of effectiveness and with the understanding that distance education can no longer be thought of as a cheap (in both senses of the word) alternative to conventional teaching.

43.3 THE EFFECTIVENESS QUESTION

Distance educators seem to be consumed by the topic of effectiveness. We seem obsessed with trying to prove the value of what we do, to measure up to some mythical gold standard of "conventional education". Largely this preoccupation with effectiveness has been rooted in the marginal status historically accorded to distance education, to some questionable practices in the early days of correspondence schools and, more recently, of the so-called "digital diploma mills" (Noble, 1999). But if one examines the effectiveness discourse in DE, it is not very deep (Russell, 2001). It is almost always framed in comparative terms. Is distance education "as good as" conventional education? The underlying assumption being that conventional education is some homogeneous practice that has proven its worth and is therefore something to which any new approach must be measured against. The depth and complexity of effectiveness is almost always glossed over in favor of some simplistic, unidimensional notion. Fundamental questions are usually ignored. Questions such as:

- What constitutes effectiveness?
- Why is conventional education assumed to be the measure against which every other approach is compared?
- Can meaningful comparisons really be made between approaches that use fundamentally different methods and media (Clark, 1994; Bates, 2005)?
- Is it defensible to examine the quality and effectiveness of distance education on its own terms?

The purpose of this section of the chapter is to scratch below the surface of the DE effectiveness debate, examine what the literature tells us about effectiveness and propose a framework that will help guide our understanding of what effectiveness is about and how it can inform our understanding of the cost issues. Because, as we will demonstrate, there is little point in developing a sophisticated understanding of the costs of distance education if we do not also deal with effectiveness as this will do little to guide administrative decision-making.

43.4 CONCEPTUALIZING EFFECTIVENESS

Usually when we talk about the effectiveness of distance education there is an assumption that we are talking about one thing, learning. The underlying question that we are attempting to answer is: did the learners learn what they were supposed to? But effectiveness is more multilayered and complex concept than simply a matter of learning. Effectiveness depends upon what the goals are for a course or program, and learning is just one of the important goals for education. Depending on who is asking there are several goals. For distance education managers, trying to understand costs without effectiveness is a fruitless exercise, just as thinking about effectiveness only in terms of learning outcomes is also limiting. It will not give us a full 360-degree view of a distance education course or program that is being scrutinized. The learning may have been effective, but how much instructor time was required to achieve it? How long did it take for the learners to achieve success? How much did it cost to produce the learning materials in the first place? What impact does their learning have on society, their ability to find employment? What did the learners have to sacrifice in order to pay their tuition fees and attend school in the first place? That is to say, what is their opportunity cost? Distance education is a complex educational system that depends on a variety of institutional components for its effectiveness. Student learning in an individual distance education course is just the tip of the iceberg. We cannot ignore the various interrelated factors that contribute to course success and which, like the iceberg, are often not visible but lurking below the surface.

Key instructional, technological, implementation and organizational factors need to be considered when discussing effectiveness. As distance education is a complex system, these factors are not independent of each other and need to be considered together. In order for the distance education system to work effectively, its various components need to work together effectively (Lockee et al., 2002). Distance education effectiveness needs to be viewed holistically, as a concept with many interrelated dimensions in much the same way we would think about education generally. Education is not just about learning; it has social, political, ideological, cultural, and economic dimensions.

So what are the dimensions of effectiveness? To answer that question it is important that we understand what we mean by effectiveness. For the purposes of this chapter, we define effectiveness as being successful in achieving a desired or intended result. Thus, effectiveness will depend on what the desired or intended result is. While learning is clearly one desired or intended result of distance education, it is rarely, if ever, the only result. Indeed, it has been argued that most of the distance teaching universities established from the 1960s through the 1980s had a core mission to broaden access and reach out to underserved populations (Curran, 1999). Certainly, for the developing world, distance education has historically had a strong social mandate of access, capacity building, and economic development that makes the social goals as important as the pedagogical goals (Perraton, 2000). Thus, multiple measures should be used to come to some conclusion about effectiveness. If we think about effectiveness in this way, it can be conceptualized in terms of:

- Student learning
- Participation rates
- Access (who could access the course or program)
- Cost-effectiveness (what are the costs for a given outcome?)
- Cost efficiency (how many resources are required for an effective program)
- Return on investment
- Enrollments and
- Social effectiveness.

Viewed from this multidimensional perspective, it becomes clear that costs are just one of many aspects of effectiveness and that looking at costs in isolation from the other dimensions is akin to asking the question, "how much does a meal cost?", without knowing anything about the meal.

43.5 EFFECTIVENESS AND EVALUATION

Determining the effectiveness of distance education means, by definition, that we are evaluating distance education. Evaluation is the process of making evidence-based judgments about the merit and worth, the value, of a course, program, or initiative.

There is a vast literature on program, course, and student evaluation (Worthen et al., 1997; Guba and Lincoln, 1989; Kirkpatrick, 1998; Stufflebeam, 2000) that can help identify the dimensions of effectiveness and our approaches to determining it. There are parallels between the debate over appropriate evaluation paradigms and the question of how to conceptualize the effectiveness of distance education. Many evaluation researchers (Patton, 1987; Guba and Lincoln, 1989; Earl et al., 2001) have argued for a broader view of evaluation that goes beyond the historically dominant positivist research paradigm on the grounds that this is too limiting and does not allow us to answer the important questions of educational and social program evaluation:

> For example, conventional research methods don't tell us how and why programs work, for whom, and in what circumstances, and don't adequately answer other process and implementation questions. And yet, given the increasingly complex social problems and situations we face today, and the increasingly complex social initiatives and programs developed to solve these problems, these are important questions to address.
>
> (W.K. Kellogg Foundation, 1998, p. 8)

A similar argument can be made about how the effectiveness of distance education is conceptualized and our argument that we need to take a broader view that considers the larger social goals of distance education and the various factors that contribute to its success. If we take this broad view, some of the key questions that should drive our consideration of effectiveness can be drawn from the program evaluation literature, questions such as:

- How does this program work?
- Why has it worked or not worked? For whom and in what circumstances?
- What was the development and implementation process?
- What stumbling blocks were encountered?
- What do the experiences mean to the people involved?
- How do these meanings relate to intended outcomes?
- What lessons have we learned about developing and implementing this program?
- How have contextual factors impacted the development, implementation, success, and stumbling blocks of this program?
- What are the hard-to-measure impacts of this program (ones that cannot be easily quantified)? How can we begin to effectively document these impacts? (W.K. Kellogg Foundation, 1998, p. 12)

Program evaluation literature provides many useful frameworks that help identify factors that contribute to the successful implementation of a distance education program. Stufflebeam (2000) produced one of the most comprehensive evaluation frameworks that covers context, input, process, and product evaluation (CIPP) and attempts to answer four broad questions: What needs to be done? How should it be done? Is it being done? Did it succeed? This last question covers the product evaluation part of the framework and is divided into impact, effectiveness, sustainability, and transportability evaluations. It is this product evaluation component and, more specifically, the impact and effectiveness parts that are most relevant to our conceptualization of distance education effectiveness. Impact and effectiveness evaluation look at how well a program reached its target audience and the quality and significance of the goals or outcomes. Other frameworks are more focused and specific but in general the factors that contribute to effectiveness can be grouped into the following categories (Lockee et al., 2002; Stufflebeam, 2000):

Program inputs
Costs
Human resources
Performance outcomes
Learning outcomes in terms of knowledge skills and attitudes
Programmatic outcomes
Impact on employment, employability
Impact on the organization
Implementation issues
Technology effectiveness
Learner support
Faculty support
Quality assurance, i.e. accreditation.

Other, equally detailed frameworks for evaluation have been proposed but we find it more useful to think about effectiveness at a higher level and suggest the following three broad categories of effectiveness that captures all of the key factors.

Instructional (Learner and Instructor)

- Was the learning effective?
- Knowledge, skills, attitudes
- Faculty preparedness
- Learner support
- Faculty support

Social (Society)

- Was greater access achieved?
- Were the projected participation rates achieved?
- Was economic development affected?
- Employment, employability of graduates

Institutional (Financial and Organizational)

- Were the costs as projected?
- Were the revenues as projected?
- Were enrollments as projected?

- Organizational structure (appropriateness of, change to)
- Institutional change

So we need to think about effectiveness broadly as more than simply the success of students in achieving the stated learning outcomes and we need to think about costs as one of a constellation of factors related to effectiveness. If we do this we are more likely to gain a greater understanding of the quality and value of our distance education programs.

In the next section, we look more closely at some of the key considerations related to costing distance education programs and some of the different ways of approaching costs.

43.6 COSTS OF DISTANCE EDUCATION

Calculating distance education costs without also considering other elements of effectiveness decontextualizes the costing process. Thus, calculating costs should be considered as part of a larger exercise of evaluating effectiveness. Having said that, it is still important to have a good grasp of some of the conceptual issues related to costing and to know the nuts and bolts of cost calculations. In this section, we look at some of the different approaches to costing and try to unravel the complexity of the cost issue.

43.7 CALCULATING THE COSTS OF DISTANCE EDUCATION

Most research on the economics of distance education has focused narrowly on comparisons of unit costs per student between distance and conventional teaching. However, rarely has the research taken full account of all the cost factors and it usually uses full-time education as a basis, not part-time. So, while the results of this research point to lower per unit costs for distance education, Curran (1999) concludes that the results are less favorable to distance education:

> where the basis of comparison is with part-time (rather than wholetime) education; where ancillary activities and outputs, notably research, is taken into account; and where graduates or credits acquired, are taken as the basis of comparison, rather than simple student numbers.
>
> Qualifications of this kind (and the relatively few distance teaching universities which have been the subject of external, methodologically sound, research) would seem to warrant a degree of caution. Perhaps the most one can say is that in appropriate circumstances, distance teaching *can* offer a cost-efficient alternative to more traditional modes of university teaching.
>
> (p. 60)

Clearly then, in calculating and comparing costs, we have to be sure we are comparing apples with apples. This is not straightforward as it is possible to arrive at very different costs for the same distance education course. For instance, a department head will include different variables for calculating the cost of a distance education certificate consisting of four courses, than an instructional designer would to calculate how much one course costs. Simply dividing the certificate cost by four to calculate the cost per course may result in a different cost than calculating each course separately. For the certificate, the department head would have to include joint and indirect costs, costs shared with other departments, such as the cost of buildings, shared equipment, shared administrative services like the finance and human resources department of an institution. Instructional designers usually ignore these variables unless required to include them. Similarly, comparing the cost of a distance education course with classroom courses is not straightforward, as distance education students use different resources than on-campus students. For example, distance students may use more learner support time, but on-campus students may use more expensive infrastructure, like buildings and transportation facilities. Calculating costs appropriately requires describing the cost context and goal clearly and completely.

Of the many models created to calculate costs of distance education and more recently of technology-based teaching in general, the better ones all start with identifying the goals and context of costing (see Bartolic and Bates, 1999; Hislop, 2001; Rumble, 1999, 2001; WCET, 2001). The first step, then, in calculating costs of DE is to write a prose description that addresses two important questions: what problem do you want to address? and what is your context? Answering these questions provides the "decision unit". This will establish the assumptions for any cost calculation and delineate the unit for aggregating costs. Units of aggregation used in distance education cost research include cost per degree, cost per course, cost per student, cost per student contact hour, and cost per student credit. The unit of aggregation will determine what variables to include when calculating costs.

The second step is to write a prose description of the course, degree, or whatever unit will be costed. The prose description will define what data is required to calculate costs. It should include: a detailed description of the activities required to create, deliver and support the course, degree, etc. (e.g. curriculum planning); the resources needed, including staff involved (e.g. subject matter experts), and equipment needed (e.g. printers) to perform the activities.

The third step is to organize activities and resources in a table or spreadsheet (Table 43.1 is a simplified example). The final step is to assign costs to each cell by calculating the monetary value of each resource needed for each activity.

This basic framework is common for most Activity-Based Costing (ABC) efforts. ABC is a method for dividing an organization's practices into discrete activities. Recent versions of ABC (Bacsish et al., 2001) have attempted to identify costs more specifically by having people use timesheets to record time spent on specific activities such as course development, teaching, computer technology support, and marking assignments. For conventional teaching, overall institutional costs are generally divided into different cost categories such as research, teaching, and administration. Calculating costs involves determining how much of a resource is used by allocating expenses in proportion to some estimated aggregate factor. For example, a department might be required to allocate 15 percent of its budget for overheads, such as computer technology support. Using

Table 43.1: Simplified Table of Activities and Expenses

Resources	*Activities*			
	Instruction		*Student Support*	
	curriculum planning	*media design*	*computing support*	*academic counseling*
Subject matter expert				
Instructional designer				
Web designer				

an allocation factor is known as Total Cost Accounting (TCA). TCA only allows for making rough estimates of the costs of activities. ABC is useful for exposing hidden costs that can go unrecorded or are "generally absorbed" into other cost categories. However, ABC tends to account for joint and indirect costs poorly, such as buildings and equipment shared by various departments (e.g. servers). Distance education courses are usually calculated using an ABC approach.

Research indicates important unique features for organizing the tables (i.e. step three above) used to calculate costs of resources needed for DE activities. First, some costs are fixed and other costs vary. There are activities related to creating courses and activities related to delivering the courses to students and supporting students before, during, and after the course. Course-related costs include costs of planning, designing, and creating courses. These are fixed, front-end costs that will not change regardless of student enrollment numbers. Course-related costs include costs for subject-matter experts (e.g. professors), instructional designers, web-programmers, software (unless it is open source), hardware (such as server space), and media production (such as animation or audio clips). Student-related costs include the costs of materials, teaching, marking, administration, and academic and non-academic support for students. These are variable costs that differ according to student enrollments. For example, the cost of printing and distributing course materials depends upon the number of students who need course materials. If there are so many students that one or more instructors must be added, then again, costs will increase.

Research also indicates that indirect resources and unused capacity are rarely included in cost calculations (WCET, 2001). Indirect costs can include costs for buildings, equipment, capital assets (e.g. land), and central administration. Unused capacity is about whether costs of a resource should be based on actual use or full use. For example, a DE institution may have a videoconferencing classroom that is used for 10 hours, though it could be used for 40 hours a week. From an ABC approach, one would only calculate actual use. However, calculating full use gives an institution incentive to use a resource to full capacity and to identify underutilized resources (see WCET, 2001, pp. 13–14 for more). All courses and programs will have indirect costs and costs for unused capacity.[1]

Finally, calculating DE costs must include identifying the lifespan of a course. Course-related (fixed) costs are incurred before a cost is delivered. Student-related (variable) costs are incurred as a course is delivered. DE costs can decrease over years depending on how much revision and maintenance a course requires. Some subject areas require less revision as they have a long lifespan where the course, once created, can be taught with the same content for years (e.g. Introductory Chemistry). Other subjects change rapidly (e.g. Introduction to Computer Programming). If a course has a long shelf life, the high course-related costs can be offset by lower student-related costs in years four and five. The lifespan of a course will affect a course's overall costs.

Given what research indicates, a more appropriate table for organizing costs look like the following.

Table 43.2: Example of a Costs Table that Includes Course Lifespan

	Year One	*Year Two*	*Year Three*	*Year Four*
Course-related Costs				
Curriculum Planning				
Project manager				
Academic approval committee				
Course design				
Subject matter expert				
Instructional designer				
Web designer				
Student-related Costs				
Teaching				
Marking				
Indirect Costs				
Capital assets				
Unused Capacity				

One of the most comprehensive cost-analyses of a distance education program was conducted by Hulsmann (2003). He studied the online Master of Distance Education offered jointly by the University of Oldenburg and the University of Maryland University College. The analysis was able to produce answers to the following questions: How much does it cost? Why does it cost so much or little? Is the model scaleable? What is the ideal class size? What is the teacher time required to teach an online class? Is it cheaper to outsource activities? What are the main avenues of quality investment? While this analysis is one of the few that has been able to accurately document the full costs of developing and delivering a distance education program, you can see from the questions that are covered that no other dimensions of effectiveness, other than costs, are covered. Hence, we are left with results that have questionable practical value as we do not have a full picture of the impact and effectiveness of the program.

What we are advocating is not new. Researchers of educational economics have long advocated that costs should not be examined in isolation. Yet, distance educators have not always heeded this advice. Levin (1983) identified four different types of cost-analyses used in education: cost-effectiveness analysis, cost-benefit analysis, cost-utility analysis, and cost-feasibility analysis. For cost-effectiveness analysis, costs are compared to the effects of the outcome of a project. This requires some measures of a project's effect. Cost-benefit analysis is used to compare costs and benefits of a program with each measured in monetary terms. In cost-utility analysis, alternative options are evaluated by comparing their costs and the estimated qualitative and quantitative value of their outcomes. For a cost-feasibility analysis, a project cost is calculated to decide if it is feasible for a given budget. It is important to note that the first three approaches to cost calculation all require non-cost information to provide context for cost-analysis. This is what we want to highlight. Costs should be calculated in conjunction with analyzing effectiveness, benefit, or utility. Only with cost-feasibility analysis is it honest and meaningful to make decisions based on calculating costs alone.

43.8 CONCLUSION

We have argued in this chapter that the costs of distance education be treated as part of the larger discussion of the effectiveness of distance education. As well, we have urged that effectiveness be conceptualized broadly to include dimensions that go beyond student achievement that tends to be the focus of the effectiveness discourse. The goals of distance education are broad and varied and include social, political, cultural, and economic dimensions in addition to the pedagogical dimensions that tend to be the focus of much of the discussion of effectiveness. Discussing costs without also examining other aspects of effectiveness yields results of limited practical value. So does looking at effectiveness solely in terms of student achievement. We suggest that costs be considered as one factor in a broader framework of effectiveness that includes instructional, social, organizational, and financial factors.

NOTE

1. We do not include the *costs borne by others*. For example, students have to bear technology costs for printing documents provided online. It is now fairly common to not include such costs in the suppliers calculations of costs. For exceptions, see WCET, 2001, p.13 and Hislop, 2001, p. 192.

REFERENCES

Bacsish, P., Ash, C. and Heginbotham, S. (2001). *The Cost of Networked Learning – Phase Two*. Research Report, Sheffield Hallam University.

Bartolic, S. and Bates, A.W. (1999). Investing in online learning: potential benefits and limitations. *Canadian Journal of Communication*, **24**(3), 349–366.

Bates, A.W. (1995). *Technology, Open and Distance Learning*. London: Routledge.

Bates, A.W. (2005). *Technology, E-Learning and Distance Learning*. London: Routledge.

Bernard, R.M., Abrami, P.C., Lou, Y. et al. (2004). How does distance education compare to classroom instruction? A meta-analysis of the empirical literature. *Review of Educational Research*, **74**(3), 379–439.

Clark, R. (1994). Media will never influence learning. *Educational Technology Research and Development*, **42**(2), 21–30.

Curran, C. (1999). Social Costs and Benefits of University Distance Education. In *Socio-Economics of Virtual Universities* (G.E. Ortner and F. Nickolmann, eds) Weinheim: Deutscher Studien Verlag, pp. 53–76.

Earl, S., Carden, F., and Smutylo, T. (2001). *Outcome Mapping: Building Learning and Reflection into Development Programs*. Ottawa: International Development Research Centre.

Guba, E. and Lincoln, Y. (1989). *Fourth Generation Evaluation*. Newbury Park, CA: Sage.

Hislop, G. (2001). "Operating cost of an online degree program", *Proceedings of the 2000 Sloan Summer Workshop on Asynchronous Learning Networks, Vol.2*. Sloan Center for Online Education, pp. 189–202.

Hulsmann, T. (2003). Costs without Camouflage. In *Reflections on Teaching and Learning in an Online Master Program* (U. Bernath and E. Rubin, eds) Oldenburg: BIS, pp. 167–226.

Kirkpatrick, D.L. (1998). *Evaluating Training Programs: The Four Levels*. San Francisco: Berrett-Koehler Publishers.

Levin, H.M. (1983). *Cost-Effectiveness: A Primer*. Newbury Park: Sage.

Lockee, B., Moore, M., and Burton, J. (2002). Measuring success: Evaluation strategies for distance education. *Educause Quarterly*, **1**, 20–26.

Noble, D. (1999). *Digital Diploma Mills, Part IV: Rehearsal for the Revolution*. http://communication.ucsd.edu/DL/ddm4.html. Retrieved January 12, 2006.

Patton, M.Q. (1987). *Creative Evaluation*. Newbury, CA: Sage.

Perraton, H. (ed.). (2000). *Open and Distance Learning in the Developing World*. London and New York: Routledge.

Qayyum, A. (2003). *Comparing apples and Apple computers: Issues in Costing E-Learning and Face-to-Face Teaching*. Unpublished report, MAPLE, UBC.

Rumble, G. (1992). The competitive vulnerability of distance teaching universities. *Open Learning*, **7**(28), 31–45.

Rumble, G. (1999). Cost analysis of distance learning. *Performance Improvement Quarterly*, **12**(2), 122–137.

Rumble, G. (2001): The costs and costing of networked learning, *Journal of Asynchronous Learning Networks*, **5**(2), September.

Russell, T.L. (2001). The No Significant Difference Phenomenon: A Comparative Research Annotated Bibliography on Technology for Distance Education. IDECC, fifth edition.

Stufflebeam, D.L. (2000). Evaluation models. *New Directions for Evaluation no. 89*. San Francisco: Jossey-Bass.

Worthen, B.R., Sanders, J.R., and Fitzpatrick, J.L. (1997). *Program Evaluation: Alternative Approaches and Practical Guidelines* (2nd ed.), White Plains, NY: Longman Inc.

WCET. (2001). *Technology Costing Methodology Handbook – Version 1.0*. Research Report, Western Cooperative for Educational Telecommunications, Boulder, Colorado.

W.K. Kellogg Foundation. (1998). *The W.K.Kellogg Foundation Evaluation Handbook*. http://www.wkkf.org, Retrieved, December 31, 2005.

Chapter 44

International Partnership and Collaboration for Cost-Effective Distance Education

Ellie Chambers and Kevin Wilson

44.1 INTRODUCTION: THE INTERNATIONAL ENVIRONMENT

In the contemporary context, international partnership in the field of higher education must be viewed against a backdrop of rapid technological advance, knowledge-based global economic development and the opening up of the education market to international competition notably via GATS. The GATS agreement (the 1995 General Agreement on Trade in Services) is operated by the World Trade Organisation under the auspices of the UN, the 145 member countries of which account for 97 percent of world trade:

> GATS is the first multi-national agreement [between member countries] to provide legally enforceable rights to trade in all services. It has a built-in commitment to continuous liberalization through periodic negotiations. And it is the world's first multinational agreement on investment, since it covers not just cross-border trade but every possible means of supplying a service, including the right to set up a commercial presence in the export market.
>
> (World Trade Organisation Secretariat, 2002)

While we may be familiar with the notion of liberalisation and globalisation in trade, these ideas are fairly new as applied to services. Education is among the services concerned. And, according to Hawkridge (2005, p. 7), "In the medium- to long-term, GATS has serious organisational, cultural, legal, political and economic implications for ... education".

An internationalisation of higher education, then, seems inevitable and is indeed already underway. It is, of course, predicated on extensive use of information and communications technologies (ICTs), and we may assume that it is likely to have a pronounced effect on distance education. When an institution has these technologies at its disposal and can apply them effectively it is possible to attract and educate students from locations anywhere in the world, provided the necessary technology is available or can be made available there, without the trouble and expense of setting up satellite campuses in those locations. Already institutions such as the UK Open University are offering selected courses to an international student audience which are delivered, supported and assessed entirely online; and this is part of a growing trend. As Hawkridge (2005, p. 2) remarks:

> Proponents [of globalisation] see knowledge as a commodity and education as a service, to be traded globally, and students everywhere as customers whose needs can and must be met through globalisation, which is a creative gale.

They would claim some positive advantages for it: enrichment of curricula, wide provision of high-quality courses and scarce staff expertise made available to students in many countries. Perhaps some of these considerations underlie MIT's decision to make its "courseware" freely available (OpenCourseWare at MIT (US): http://ocw.mit.edu/index.html). But globalisation of higher education has many detractors too, who see it as more of a destructive than a creative force.

While international provision of this kind is predicated on e-learning arrangements, some regard cognition in e-learning as different from that in embodied forms of education, and inferior to it (see Dreyfus, 2001, and also critique of his argument in Blake, 2002). Others fear that global education will tend to impose common curricula, teaching–learning methods and indeed the English language, so ultimately reducing cultural diversity (see Ess, 2001; Chambers, 2002; Mayor and Swann, 2002). Furthermore, global education is seen as incompatible with social objectives in many countries (Stromquist and Monkman, 2000): "nowhere are the poor able to benefit from services they cannot pay for" (Hawkridge, 2005, p. 2). In related vein, the entry into the education market of international corporations such as Microsoft, Pearson and the private "for-profit" Web-based universities, especially those in the United States, is regarded by some (particularly in Europe) as a direct challenge to the integrity of state-supported higher education.

In this world of so-called "borderless education", universities are finding it necessary not only to compete amongst themselves for home and overseas students but also to enter into alliances of various kinds with these private corporations, with media publishing houses, professional associations and other universities, as a means of protecting and/or enhancing their position. Distance education provision cannot be insulated from these trends, and it may certainly be prudent for distance educators to explore the possibilities for wide collaboration. For those in Europe this is given greater urgency by the policy stance of the European Union in promoting trans-European collaboration across the higher education sector, in encouraging the wide-scale application of new technologies to the educational process and in signalling its intention, courtesy of the Lisbon Process, to become by 2010 the world's leading knowledge-driven economy. Meanwhile, it will be to the advantage of distance education institutions to consider some of the issues surrounding the cross-border provision of services within the university sector, to which the GATS agreement lends considerable urgency.

In order to grapple with the underlying issues involved in international partnership, including the cost-effectiveness and quality of its procedures, processes and end-products, this chapter concentrates on a single aspect, that of cooperative arrangements between universities in Europe. It draws, necessarily selectively, on some of the collaborative projects undertaken by member countries of the European Union (EU) from the mid-1990s. While the emphasis is on distance education and open learning, it is clear that the new ICTs are promoting a convergence between on-campus and off-campus provision and this, in turn, is tending to blur the hitherto accepted distinctions between traditional and non-traditional providers in the higher education sector. Such is the fluidity of the situation that, for example, consortia lists emanating from the EU's Socrates Bureau show, as a matter of routine, traditional and non-traditional universities working side by side as partners in international collaborative enterprises.

44.2 COURSE PRODUCTION PARTNERSHIPS

Moving from the *meta* to the *micro* level, it is evident that any single university, distance education provider or otherwise, will have its own set of institutional priorities within which core provision for its own registered, largely home-based, student population is paramount. In the main, such core provision can be provided in-house. There are, however, situations in which collaboration, including cooperation with international partners, can enhance an institutional course offering, though the precise nature of any specific collaboration will vary enormously according to particular circumstance and a host of other internal and external factors.

44.2.1 Advantages of Collaboration for Institutions

Although not an institutional panacea, collaboration has clear-cut attractions and its potential benefits have long been recognised (Moran and Mugridge, 1993). These include the following:

- reducing costs by sharing in the development and production of courses. This is of particular relevance to distance education institutions operating on a business model governed by high fixed, low variable costs. Large development and production costs, allied to the expensive character of multimedia courses, call for high initial financial outlay. Hence any bilateral or multi-lateral pooling arrangement with respect to course development and production costs can potentially work to the advantage of all parties in easing up-front investment on course expenditure;
- widening the curriculum and enhancing the quality of courses by drawing on the expertise of specialist staff from a number of institutions;
- widening the appeal of courses by making them accessible to a range of national student groups, and so attracting larger numbers of students to the participating institutions;
- contributing to staff development through a widening and deepening of professional contacts at academic, teaching and administrative levels; increasing the scope for joint research among academics in the cooperating institutions.

Allied to gains of this kind which can accrue at the organisational level are some positive features of institutional collaboration that, as we shall see, relate expressly to the student experience.

44.2.2 The European Association of Distance Teaching Universities (EADTU)

In the conventional university sector in Europe, the standard form of collaboration has been student exchange. In a number of subject fields such as languages, international business and European studies, a period of study abroad in another European country is deemed a compulsory programme requirement. Over and above specific subject requirements, the process of student exchange has been boosted in the last decade or so by the European Commission's ERASMUS programme. By providing institutional encouragement and financial support for student exchange within Europe, ERASMUS has made it possible for many thousands of European students to spend a study year abroad and, inevitably, such transfer has encouraged cooperation between universities at both academic and administrative levels.

However, in the arena of open and distance learning, ERASMUS has had little appeal. Open and distance education in Europe is largely populated by mature students whose family, work and social obligations compel them to study on a part-time basis. For these students a study year abroad is out of the question. This is why a number of distance education providers have focused their attention on "course" mobility rather than "student" mobility as a possible means of adding an international dimension to their curricula. Putting it crudely, if the students are not able to travel, then the courses can. Thus, high on the agenda of the EADTU – a grouping of national open universities and national associations for distance education formed in the late 1980s – has been the promotion of schemes for joint course development, course transfer and course exchange. Collaborating on courses is a much more complex business than organising student exchange schemes, but the outcomes, for distance education students, can be no less rewarding in providing international enrichment of their studies.

In the case of the EADTU, the perceived merits of course cooperation have led to the formation of programme committees and academic networks in fields such as business studies, humanities, law, science and technology, where detailed collaborative arrangements for joint course activities can be pursued. In exploring the issue of international partnership and collaboration as a cost-effective device for distance education provision, the early experience of the EADTU as an umbrella for cooperative enterprise is instructive in terms of both the intricacies of cross-institutional working and the technicalities of joint cooperation (Wilson, 1994). Three programme committees – European Law, European Business Administration, and Humanities – set to work in the early 1990s to construct a common offering in their respective fields. In the case of both European Law and European Business Administration, masters' programmes were elaborated at the European level, but the tasks of developing and producing the constituent courses were sub-contracted to the individual partner institutions thus avoiding the cumbersome and expensive process of operating with international course teams. While devolution of this kind represented substantial economies of scale with regard to course development and production costs – such a pooling arrangement allowed each of the partners access to a full programme for the "price" of providing a single course – insufficient emphasis on course presentation matters impeded the wider reach of both programmes. There were problems with the translation of courses into a single, common language (i.e. English), difficulties over student registration, over modes of assessment and quality standards and academic recognition within the different national constituencies (Curran, 2004). These are some of the challenges that international collaborative ventures inevitably face.

Although a number of courses were produced and presented within this collaborative framework, few students, if any, enrolled in either of the full programmes. Course enrolment tended to proceed on the basis of home-based student registration, and in these circumstances cost-effectiveness considerations relating to inter-institutional collaboration hardly arise. However, in the third EADTU programme area, the Humanities, the correlation between collaboration and cost-effectiveness can be explored in some detail. Such an exploration involves examination of methods of working as well as the efficacy of the end-product.

44.2.3 "What is Europe?"

In pursuing its objective of promoting a European dimension in the study of the humanities, the EADTU Humanities Programme Committee (HPC) took the view that the traditional curriculum could be enhanced by a select *corps* of courses conceived at a European level and written by authors from different European countries. These courses would draw on different academic traditions and reflect different national perspectives; and their inter-institutional, cross-cultural and trans-national characteristics would provide distance education students, largely unable to study abroad, with a distinctive European strand in their study of the humanities. As a way of proceeding, the HPC focused its early efforts on developing and producing a paradigmatic course that could be offered to students on a pan-European basis. If this outcome could be achieved, it would point to a viable model for future collaboration and joint course building. Out of this thinking emerged the *What is Europe?* course, a scholarly exploration of the many facets of European identity and the first distance education course in European studies to be offered to a wide European student audience.

Like their counterparts in European law and business administration, the partners constituting the HPC rejected the notion of a single international course team and opted for a more flexible and decentralised working arrangement. This covered five stages of inter-related activity:

1. agenda setting and planning at an inter-institutional and trans-national level within the HPC;
2. concurrent development of draft materials in each of the partner institutions along lines agreed by the HPC;
3. pooling of drafts to form a master set of core academic materials;
4. production of the core academic materials in different formats and different languages as required by the different partners;
5. presentation of the course according to the separate teaching, assessment and certification arrangements of each partner institution.

This strategy served to accommodate a major challenge: the very real differences and sets of expectation that exist between international partners. Broad agreement at the outset on the scope, range and content of the course gave the project a European rather than a separate national character. Subdivision of tasks in the course development phase speeded up the process and shortened the lines of communication. Pooling academic materials to form a master-set ready for exploitation reinforced joint ownership of the product. And, finally, the provision for separate institutional styles and procedures in presenting the course to students made for adaptability and flexibility without compromising the European character of the project (Wilson, 2001).

The reception of *What is Europe?* vindicates the chosen course model and attests to the quality of the course. Since its first appearance in 1993, it has been offered to over 4,000 students in different editions and different language formats. There are versions of the course in English, German and Portuguese and there have been adaptations in Dutch, Danish and Swedish. In its English language version it has attracted audiences in Eastern as well as Western Europe and it has reached students as far afield as South-East Asia. In 1994 it was awarded the Daimler-Benz prize for its contribution to an understanding of European educational systems; it served as a focus for an international conference on approaches to the teaching of European studies sponsored by the European Cultural Foundation (Baumeister, 1996); and the four core texts have been published by Routledge as an introductory series in European studies aimed at the undergraduate market (*What is Europe?* series, 1995).

Yet for all its acknowledged success, the *What is Europe?* course has not been followed by others in the same mould – though the subsequent *Paradigms of European Humanities* project deserves honourable mention. In this respect, the expectation of the HPC that the course would serve as the progenitor of a suite of collaboratively developed courses has not been realised. This raises some fundamental questions about the financial underpinning and the cost-effectiveness of distance education courses that are the product of international partnerships. And, in turn, these questions serve to underscore some of the challenges and difficulties faced by institutions attempting to develop collaborative products.

Perhaps the first point to emphasise in this respect is institutional difference – even between institutions that share a common distance education designation. With regard to joint course development and production, problems arise not so much in partners recognising the merits of cooperation as in forging the instruments and procedures through which collaboration can be realised. Goodwill is insufficient. Crucial in this regard is the recognition of, and a respect for, different institutional cultures (Paul, 1990). If a partnership is going to work, the intending partners need to devise modus vivendi that, besides embracing a common goal, take cognisance of the real differences that exist between them. Such differences can be quite extensive, covering aspects as diverse as student entry requirements, methods of course development and production, length of courses, the use of media in courses, quality control procedures, types of student assessment, patterns of student support and the language of course presentation. Failure to accommodate differences of this kind within a partnership arrangement is the principal reason why so many attempts at international co-production of courses come to grief. If some of the potential gains of collaboration are to be realised, it follows that mechanisms for collaboration that are responsive to the varied needs of the different partners are an essential pre-condition of any cooperative arrangement. It was for this reason that the international partnership responsible for the *What is Europe?* course eschewed the notion of a centralised international course team, a fixed course product and a standard method of presentation in favour of a more flexible, adaptable and decentralised approach that went with the grain of the different institutional cultures within the partnership. Such an approach enabled the collaboratively developed course materials to be successfully exploited in different ways according to the different needs of the partners (Wilson, 2004).

While institutional differences were surmounted in the case of the *What is Europe?* project, all this came at a cost. For the lead producer of the first version of the course (the UK Open University), its development and production costs were greater than a comparable in-house product. In order to achieve an English language version of the course, almost half of the core material commissioned by the partners had to be translated and the outcomes negotiated with the respective authors so as to achieve hand-over copy. Apart from the direct costs involved, translation arrangements make additional demands on editorial resources, extend production time-scales and make a project more complex to handle. International commissioning also raises the thorny question of intellectual property rights and makes copyright clearance more complicated than in in-house production. As a UK Open University offering, 400–500 students a year registered for the course over its 6-year lifespan (1993–1998). Such a total enrolment is somewhat below the institutional average for a comparable arts/social sciences course; and so the additional production costs were not covered by increases in student numbers, thus resulting in a high unit-cost ratio for the collaborative course. The experience of the German partner also points in the direction of above average production costs. Although the partner was able to benefit from working with finalised copy as opposed to draft material, in order to achieve a German language version of the course it was faced with a substantial translation bill which more than offset the standard costs of academic commissioning. On the other hand, the Dutch and Danish partners did achieve production savings since they were able to utilise the English language version of the course in their respective programmes. However, their student enrolment remained small and their savings resulted entirely from a generous arrangement which allowed them to offset their input into the development of the course against their access to the published course materials.

Over the years, acquisition by institutions outside the initial partnership of the rights to use some or all of the course materials, together with the royalty income from the commercially published course texts, have made something of a contribution towards offsetting the high production costs. But these sums are not large and cannot disguise the fact that joint course procedures did not lead to across-the-board savings. Judged by the *What is Europe?* case, the justification for this kind of common enterprise lies not so much in the economies to be realised but more on the intrinsic quality of the end-product. The reception of the course, as intimated above, together with the perceptions of tutors and students who have worked with the course materials (see Chambers and Winck, 1996; Clennell and Proctor, 1997) confirm the intellectual calibre and the distinctive character of the collaborative enterprise. Operating as an international partnership tends to generate a richer course product than working within separate national parameters, and it is the course's European character that gives it particular appeal.

Yet, as we saw, the *What is Europe?* project has not paved the way for a suite of collaborative courses emanating from the EADTU stable. Obviously there is a resource issue at work. The high production costs, including translation, editing and copyright clearances, incurred in turning jointly developed materials into a quality distance education course have, in these cash-strapped times, proved to be something of a deterrent. With the exception of the German Fernuniversität, which backed the *Paradigms of European Humanities* project, no EADTU institution has been brave enough to take on the role of lead-producer of a collaboratively developed course with European reach. But it is not simply a question of resource. Within the last 10 years, and particularly over the last five, the application of ICTs to the educational process has begun to open up new possibilities for cooperation between distance educational providers, and this development has altered the trajectory of collaboration. In particular, the impact of computer conferencing has served to shift the emphasis away from joint development and production of published course materials towards joint presentation and teaching of courses, and usually parts of courses. In Europe, ICT developments have been given strong encouragement by the EU's Socrates-Minerva programme which, since its inception in the mid-1990s, has provided financial support for hundreds of collaborative schemes across the higher education sector. Within this strand, a number of projects have sought to utilise computer conferencing and virtual seminars as vehicles for collaborative teaching arrangements.

44.3 VIRTUAL SEMINAR PARTNERSHIPS

Virtual seminars, catering for trans-national student groups, focus on shared teaching and learning rather than joint course production partnerships. They allow for international cooperation without the drawback of requiring large-scale, up-front investment in printed course materials. Web resources can be designated as the core academic material for virtual seminars, thereby eliminating entirely the physical course production process which, as demonstrated, can be very costly. Virtual seminars are delivered on existing learning platforms, either proprietary or open-source, and incur little de novo set-up costs. What is more, because virtual seminars emphasise the value of dialogue, discussion and discourse, they work with the grain of established university teaching, especially in the human and cultural sciences, and thereby facilitate cooperation between traditional and distance education providers. Virtual seminars also have the merit of encouraging collaborative learning through stimulating exchanges between international student working groups. Whereas the *What is Europe?* course promoted a European dimension in the humanities curriculum by allowing for separate national or institutional presentation of jointly prepared academic materials, virtual seminars go one stage further by enabling a jointly planned curriculum to be taught on a common international basis. Nonetheless, in shifting the balance from joint course production to joint course presentation, virtual seminars have their own set of discrete costs. Principal among them are the staff costs of those involved in the shared teaching arrangements and the related training costs of equipping university lecturers with the skills and moderating techniques to operate in a virtual and multi-cultural learning environment.

In order to put flesh on international partnerships predicated on virtual seminar arrangements, and to consider the effectiveness and quality of this kind of collaborative provision, we will examine in some detail a few selected European projects. In the process we will see to what extent the advantages said to accrue from collaborative endeavours are realised in practice. To those institutional advantages adumbrated earlier should be added the gains that relate directly to the student experience: enhancing the effectiveness of study through the involvement of a team of expert teachers and the "added value" of teachers and peers with different perspectives emanating from different national/academic traditions. We will also revisit some of the challenges presented by international partnerships:

- "ownership" of a collaborative project by all the partners, and commitment to its goals;
- different educational traditions, languages and cultures;
- different institutional norms, requirements and programmes of study;
- different assessment and accreditation requirements and regimes;
- "technical" difficulties (such as those which surround metadata and intellectual rights).

The projects selected for discussion include CEFES (Creating a European Forum for European Studies, 1997–2000), DEC.KNOWL (Decentralised Knowledge – Networked Resource-based Learning, 2002–2004) and RESULTS (The Role of Universities in Regional Economic Development, 2003 and ongoing): the main features of these projects are summarised in Table 44.1, later in the chapter.

Table 44.1: Some International Virtual Seminar Projects in Europe: Main Features

Project	*Features*	*Details/Problems*
CEFES (1997–2000)	*Optional computer conferences (three 8-week sequences)	"Bottom up" planning for u-g enrichment; national conferences and "representative speaker" conventions emerged.
	*Curriculum in European Studies (themes, key questions, readings, tasks) *Tutor training	Problems of timing and length of sequences... ...under-determined curriculum for inter-cultural moderation.
DEC.KNOWL (2002–2004)	Virtual seminar (6 weeks, piloted) *plus*	Focus on structural flexibility: decentralised teaching and accreditation programmed in.
	*"Expert groups" for curriculum and technical planning *Shared knowledge base	Preparatory "work package" prepared. Problematic: from tutor- to student-based.
	*Student accreditation	Different institutional norms followed.

(*Continued*)

Table 44.1: (Continued)

Project	*Features*	*Details/Problems*
RESULTS (2003–2006)	Virtual research seminar and accreditation (6 weeks, piloted) *plus*	Masters/research students: collaborative small group work as well as Open Forum
	*Sustainability	Emphasis on sustainability – involving leaders of the research community ("top down"/ mainstreaming).
	*Student research collaboration	Collaboration in student groups leading to discussion of written work, and devolved assessment.
	*Knowledge base	Planned as student-based and dynamic.

44.3.1 CEFES

The CEFES project took as its theme "European Identity" and, over 2 years, enabled some 200 students from different European institutions and countries to engage in discussion of the issues in computer conferences, on a voluntary basis, guided by tutors. These discussions were to be additional, enriching elements in the students' undergraduate education; that is, additional to their home-based courses and, in this case, unassessed. Some of the partners concerned represented dedicated distance education institutions (single mode, such as the Universidade Aberta, Portugal, the Universidad Nacional de Educación a Distancia, Spain, and the UK Open University), two others were dual-mode institutions (the University of Aarhus, Denmark, and Universität Lüneberg, Germany) and one was a fully campus-based institution (the University of Surry, UK): the project was coordinated by the Deutsches Institut für Fernstudienforschung, a German research institute. Three of these six partners had worked together previously, in the *What is Europe?* course team, and so understood each other's institutional context and trusted one other. According to Raybourn et al. (2003, p. 98), these are among the prerequisites for successful intercultural communication:

> Lessons learned from face-to-face communication tell us that the quality of successful collaborations depends largely on sharing cultural and contextual information (Rogers, 1995). Cultural information shared by collaborative organisations or communities of practice (Wenger, 1998) includes the assumptions, values, goals, meanings, and histories shared, negotiated and co-created by its members. Intercultural communication is the exchange of this information and the co-creation of meaning between individuals or among groups (teams, organisations, etc.) that perceive themselves to be different. As our organisations become more diverse, the challenge of intercultural communication is heightened.

Furthermore, these CEFES team members were able to base the new partnership on some of the principles of their earlier collaboration and, along with the new partners, both adapt these principles to the virtual context and develop them further. As we shall see, foremost among them were the principles of flexibility and decentralisation, in recognition of and respect for differences among the partners – the attempt to go with the grain of their institutional and national cultures. Apart from these operational matters, to be successful such partnerships have to be inclusive and they have to be maintained; all the partners must be committed to the project, feel a sense of "ownership" of it and project outcomes must be of real benefit to all concerned. In short, genuine collaboration – resulting in changes to practice in the partner institutions – also depends upon the development of projects from the "bottom up".

Broadly, the CEFES partners set out to do three things:

- together to develop a curriculum for a "course" in European studies that could be integrated into the regular programmes of all the participating universities;
- to run computer conferences on the topics of the course, with occasional invited guest "speakers";
- to train lecturer-tutors in the participating institutions to improve their technical skills and their ability to teach both virtually and cross-culturally (see Baumeister et al., 2000.)

Three modules, or "sequences", comprised the course: The identity of Europe: a historical phenomenon; The Europe of identities: a political phenomenon; Globalisation: implications for European identity. Each sequence was of eight weeks' duration, involving a three-week preparatory period, a four-week international forum (computer conference) and an evaluation period. Each sequence had a syllabus, co-constructed by the partners, consisting of themes, key questions, tasks and readings (in a range of languages, when possible), to be studied during the preparatory period and subsequently discussed in the international forum, in English. English was chosen for the forum because it was the only language all the academics concerned could speak, most regarded it as the lingua franca (although this was itself a topic for debate in the forum), and because for many of their students practising and improving their English was a major attraction of the course. This obviated the need for, and expense of, any translation provision.

The sequences could be studied independently (one or more), as in the first year of the project, or all three sequences could be studied one after the other to form a coherent course, as in the project's second year. First-year practice turned out to be the more successful. European countries have different start dates for academic terms/semesters, different holiday periods, festivals, etc., and finding three blocks of eight weeks during which all the students could participate was well nigh impossible. In the second year of the project student participation tended to fall away as the course progressed, mainly owing to practical difficulties of this kind (Chambers and Winck, 2000). In this form of collaborative endeavour, offering "bite-sized" elements and choice are important aspects of structural flexibility.

Crucially, however, the partnership was maintained successfully and integration of CEFES in the universities' regular programmes was achieved by adoption of a decentralised teaching model. The partners constructed the syllabus for each sequence collaboratively – two institutions, in different countries, took the lead each time, and the outcome was discussed and agreed by all the partners before being implemented. But when it came to the relationship between the CEFES sequence and the institutions' regular courses, each university made its own adaptation. Thus Surrey, as a campus-based university, held CEFES-related face-to-face seminars during the preparatory period and thereafter; just a few of the Surrey students would actually participate in the international forum discussions at any one time, representing the views of their peers. Meanwhile, the Universidade Aberta established a "national conference" on the platform (an idea later taken up by other universities) in which the distance students first discussed the readings set in the syllabus in their own language, thus establishing a surer understanding of the issues before beginning to contribute to the international forum. In fact, as an aid to inclusiveness, what became known as a "representative speaker" convention became established in the project as a whole. This allowed any student group to nominate a few of its number to contribute to the international forum on its behalf, thus sheltering those who felt unsure about their ability to write in English, or just very unconfident to "speak", while enabling them to follow the discussions. The fact that the distance students were usually obliged to operate as individuals made no difference – decentralisation meant that each university was free to make whatever teaching arrangements suited it and its students' best. Thus, everyone could choose to study the CEFES sequence(s) that were of most relevance to their programme of European studies, and do so in ways that best chimed with their circumstances and met their needs.

Inclusiveness and equal ownership of the project were also enhanced by the way in which the international forum was designed to operate. Each virtual seminar was moderated by pairings of tutors from different institutions and countries, so that by the end of the series each national partner institution had taken its turn to lead a conference in cooperation with at least one other. This ensured negotiation and some accommodation between different academic traditions of teaching European studies within Europe, and allowed a range of debating styles to be represented in the discussions (for the different orientations to study across Europe, see Teichler and Maiworm, 1997). Consequently, no single conception of "European studies" would predominate in the discussions and no one culture's perceptions of, for instance, aspects of the past or the implications of globalisation would prevail. But, primarily, the moderators' job was to help students *learn* through and from the process of cross-cultural exchange; the aim of the virtual seminars was a genuine exchange of views across borders – a co-creation of knowledge and understanding. In this connection, teachers whose first language is not English are especially sympathetic to students' attempts to express themselves in a second (or third) language – better able to read between the lines, looking beyond non-standard locutions, grammatical errors and the like, to the core of their meaning – and also sensitive to the students' needs for further explanation and guidance from time to time. A strategy such as this ensures that one such teacher is involved in every conference.

Thorough evaluation of this course supported its overall teaching–learning effectiveness and its quality. The students' aims in participating – "hearing different nationals" views on an "international topic" and "topical events", learning about "attitudes from different national standpoints" – were achieved, and many ended up attesting to "a feeling of solidarity with people I have never seen". A student summed up: "It's a fascinating way of learning, it's active, helps my English, uses modern technology – it's challenging" (Chambers and Winck, 2000, pp. 130–31). The lecturer-tutors had been trained in conference moderation, in face-to-face sessions and online, before the course began. They were new to conference moderation but learned quickly, mainly because computer conferencing goes with the grain of the group-discussion methods conventionally used in the humanities and social sciences. In a tutor forum they frequently discussed such matters as the tension between encouraging students to participate in the conference and their taking a more academic, didactic role in steering the discussion as it progressed. Nevertheless, the evaluators concluded that:

> A major advantage of the CEFES project is that it was naturalistic, involving actual students studying real courses in a range of national and institutional contexts. . . . The evaluation has shown that communication among students and tutors in different European countries via the new electronic technologies is not only feasible but is also a highly appropriate teaching–learning strategy to adopt in the field of European Studies. In enabling students to expose their knowledge and beliefs to those in other national/cultural groups, and to challenge one another, the moderated virtual seminar has the "added value" potential to transform the students' understanding of this subject.
>
> (Chambers and Winck, 2000, p. 132)

44.3.2 DEC.KNOWL

Many of the "bottom up" features of CEFES were reproduced in the DEC.KNOWL project (2002–2004), notably the operations of computer conferencing, the decentralised teaching model and the tutor training programme. In this case, the (single) computer conference was formalised as a "virtual seminar" with a full syllabus "preparatory pack", and "national conferences" and the "representative speaker" convention were introduced from the start. However, there were major differences too. In the first place, this project involved collaboration among colleagues in business studies, all of whom had been known to each other for some time through membership of an international consortium of business schools (the Universities of Reutlingen, Reims, Madrid, Lancaster and Dublin City), including a university in the United States. Second, in addition to constructing a syllabus for the virtual seminar, on aspects of globalisation, the participating institutions set out to construct a knowledge base in international business studies. This would be a wide-ranging resource, including lecture notes, web links to resources and readings, etc., which it was hoped would make the process of curriculum development among the partners more collaborative and exploratory. Third, the students in DEC.KNOWL were offered accreditation for their involvement in the virtual seminar preparatory work and/or the seminar itself.

As regards personnel, we again see at work the principle of building on previous partnerships, of constructing the collaboration on the basis of knowledge and trust. Even so, this partnership was strained by the attempt to construct the shared disciplinary knowledge base (KB) since, among other matters, it raised the question of property rights.

The partners were reluctant simply to "donate" their curriculum designs and lecture notes, or the fruits of their own research in the form of bibliographies and web links, which in higher education are traditionally regarded as institutionally owned or as their personal property (see Johnes, 2004, for the background to these issues). There was also the difficulty of deciding on the right kind of technical platform for the KB, and appropriate metadata for the knowledge objects it contained such that it could be searched (Rae, 2004). The upshot was that the conception of the nature and purposes of the KB changed over the course of the project, from a knowledge repository – a content-oriented academic resource – largely for use by course designers in international studies, to a constantly evolving resource on globalisation for use by students during the virtual seminar, to which they too could contribute. That is, the conception changed from a relatively static structure to a dynamic student-centred process.

In short, the project made the important discovery that there are limits to collaboration, even among colleagues and institutions known to each other. There was little support for the idea of sharing management structures, such as curriculum designs, and resources, and much more enthusiasm for sharing pedagogic ideas and strategies. For a number of reasons, the notion of a "community of experts" freely sharing their expert knowledge did not take root.

As regards accreditation, widely agreed to be important for students' motivation to participate in online discussions (McConnell, 1999; Salmon, 2000), the DEC.KNOWL team made it work for all the partners by adopting a decentralised approach – just as they did for teaching in this and the earlier CEFES project. Rather than trying to reach an agreement about accreditation across the partnership – a particularly sensitive matter for the different institutions – the project left the various partners free to make their own arrangements: "This way each of the partners could harmonise the online seminars within their own standard teaching provision and offer credit according to their own internal procedures" (Wetzel, 2004, p. 59). For example, at Lancaster students were asked to submit an essay based on the discussions experienced in the virtual seminar, which was worth one-third of the marks in a UK 15-credit course (or, around 30 points in the European Credit Transfer Scheme). At Reutlingen, as well as writing an essay on a DEC.KNOWL theme the students' written contributions to the seminar itself were assessed, together worth up to 50 percent of the end-of-course grade. At Reims, students joining the seminar from one programme were assessed (worth one credit towards the final degree), while those from another programme were not. Again, institutional and cultural differences were recognised and respected.

The project also aimed to integrate e-learning into the participating universities' regular programmes of study, and to be sustainable. In this respect the outcome was mixed. Those elements closest to the working lives of the academics concerned were the most successful: constructing the study programme (preparatory work package), tutor training and the conduct of the virtual seminar. Although the partners have run further seminars beyond the life of the project, and new members have joined the partnership, we have seen that the most ambitious element of the programme – constructing the shared knowledge base – was problematic. Making the original KB conception successful would require the input of considerable resource along with changes in institutional culture. In particular, the evaluators concluded, it would require informed leadership – support for collaborative e-learning from influential people at a high level in the universities. "Bottom up" procedures, it emerged, can take partnerships only so far; "top down" characteristics are also necessary if mainstreaming is the aim.

44.3.3 RESULTS

The RESULTS project, which is ongoing, in particular aims to tackle the issue of "buy in" to e-learning by senior staff of the participating universities, as leaders of their research communities. Instead of recruiting undergraduate student participation it enrolled Masters and research students, and their supervisors, in order for innovation to become embedded at higher levels in the institutions. Another major difference between this project and the earlier ones is that the focus of RESULTS is collaborative work among the students, linked to an assessed piece of work. The work package sets up a number of topics, which the students may choose to tackle in international sub-groups of four or five. Each sub-group researches the chosen topic, in ways agreed among them, for a period of 4 weeks. Subsequently, the students individually prepare an assignment in draft form, which is posted in a plenary Open Forum. Following discussions in the Forum, each assignment is re-drafted and submitted for marking to the students' own (home) supervisor – who grades the work in accordance with the rules that normally apply within that institution. In due course, the assignments (plus references and supporting materials) are to be lodged in a knowledge base which will serve as an ongoing teaching and research resource for the partner institutions.

The project has not reported yet, but its aims are clear. We can expect some illuminating findings regarding the workings of literature-led trans-national study groups, as well as the extent to which the strategy to involve more influential partners helps to "mainstream" and sustain e-learning programmes in European universities. Also, the evaluators aim to explore the theoretical notion of the co-creation of knowledge and understanding in the Open Forum, such that a "third culture" emerges:

> A "third culture" is what is created from an intercultural interaction when persons from different cultures communicate equitably and with respect for the other such that the emergent culture reflects appropriate input from each interlocutor. A third culture is the co-creation of meaning in which all interlocutors are participants as well as co-owners. In effect, together users co-create a "third culture" that is neither one nor the other, but a combination of the two, or three, and so on.
>
> (Raybourn et al., 2003, pp. 106).

44.4 CONCLUSION

This chapter has demonstrated that virtual seminar partnership depending on ICTs yields greater advantages to distance education institutions than does the course production partnership model, if only because the costs of the collaboration are greatly reduced. At the same time, virtual seminar partnership can achieve comparable widening of the curriculum, can attract students and enhance their studies through expert team work, and similarly contributes to staff development. It is clear, too, that quality online courses can be produced and delivered successfully when the main challenges of virtual international collaboration are addressed and resolved. Centrally, this involves recognising and respecting differences between the participating nations, cultures and institutions, and attempting to find ways to accommodate those differences. However, some challenges are actually problems that are not at all easy to resolve – the academic sub-culture that values the individual scholar's work above team work and the issues surrounding intellectual property rights, for example – which may indicate outer limits to such collaboration.

As we have seen from the chosen examples of virtual seminar partnership, during approximately a decade of European experimentation the emphasis has shifted from how to forge partnerships between universities that promote meaningful learning opportunities for all their students (for instance, how to mount and run successful virtual seminars, how to integrate assessment of the outcomes in ways that accommodate the different European assessment regimes, how to train teachers effectively) to consideration of the ways in which international e-learning programmes may become embedded in the partner institutions – no longer experiments, but established aspects of university education in Europe for undergraduate and graduate students alike. Such sustainability is among the most pressing and intractable challenges still facing us. And it is clear that it will be achieved only by involving senior staff of the universities in collaborative e-learning projects, and convincing them of their value.

But this is still not enough. Drawing on evaluation of the DEC.KNOWL project, Baumeister and Wilson (2004, pp. 74–5) list all the factors that must be present for successful mainstreaming of e-learning in the university, as follows:

- support for e-learning by influential people at a high level in the university;
- commitment to e-learning by key staff at departmental/faculty level;
- reasonable content area, where e-learning makes sense;
- some resident experts in e-learning (both technical and pedagogic aspects), to advise and provide staff training;
- planned, specific e-learning projects, along with adequate funding to support them and enthusiastic staff members to execute them;
- evaluation of the projects, with the processes and outcomes disseminated widely in the university (and beyond) and fed into e-learning policy development.

Arguably, universities need to experiment among themselves and to understand e-learning processes at every level and in all respects *before* they consider entering into the wider forms of collaboration referred to at the start of the chapter – with global corporations, publishers, etc. For only then will the universities be in a good position to know what they want from such collaborations and to ensure that they work well from their own, and their students', point of view.

ACKNOWLEDGEMENT

The authors would like to thank their colleagues Dr Hans-Peter Baumeister (Reutlingen University) who coordinated the projects discussed in this chapter, and Simon Rae (the UK Open University) for his contributions to evaluation of them. They would also like to thank the tutors and students across Europe who participated in the courses. The courses were funded by the EU in the Socrates/Minerva Programme.

REFERENCES

Baumeister, H-P. (ed.) (1996). *'What is Europe?' Revisited: New Contexts for European Studies*. International conference, Warsaw, September 29–30. Conference Report, Tübingen.

Baumeister, H-P., Williams, J., and Wilson, K.P. (eds). (2000). *Teaching Across Frontiers: A Handbook for International Online Seminars*. Tübingen: Deutsches Institut für Fernstudienforschung an der Universität Tübingen.

Baumeister, H-P. and Wilson, K. (2004). The Dec.Knowl Project: Results and Future Perspectives. In *DEC.KNOWL: Handbook* (K.P. Wilson, ed.) Reutlingen: European School of Business, Reutlingen University, pp. 70–75. (Available at: http://kn.open.ac.uk/public/document.cfm?docid=8281)

Blake, N. (2002). Hubert Dreyfus on Distance Education: Relays of Educational Embodiment. *Educational Philosophy and Theory*, **34**(4), 379–385. (Symposium on Hubert Dreyfus's *On the Internet*.)

Chambers, E.A. (2002). Cultural imperialism or pluralism? Cross-cultural electronic teaching in the Humanities. *Arts and Humanities in Higher Education*, **2**(3), 249–64.

Chambers, E.A. and Winck, M. (1996). *Same Difference? Experience of a European Distance Education Course in Two Cultures*. Tübingen: Deutsches Institut für Fernstudienforschung an der Universität Tübingen.

Chambers, E.A. and Winck, M. (2000). Evaluation of the CEFES project. In *Teaching Across Frontiers: A Handbook for International Online Seminars* (H-P. Baumeister, J. Williams, and K.P. Wilson, eds) Tübingen: Deutsches Institut für Fernstudienforschung an der Universität Tübingen, pp. 123–133.

Clennell, S. and Proctor, P. (eds) (1997). *Studying Europe: Perception and Experience of a Group of Adult Students*. Milton Keynes: The Open University.

Curran, C. (2004). Academic Networking in Europe: The European Association of Distance Teaching Universities. In *Consortia: International Networking Alliances of Universities* (D.C.B. Teather, ed.) Melbourne: Melbourne University Press, pp. 86–102.

Dreyfus, H. (2001). *On the Internet*. New York: Routledge.

Ess, C. (2001). What's culture got to do with it? Cultural collisions in the electronic global village, creative interferences, and the rise of culturally-mediated computing. In *Culture, Technology, Communication: Towards an Intercultural Global Village* (C. Ess and F. Sudweeks, eds) Albany, NY: State University of New York Press, pp. 1–50.

Hawkridge, D. (2005). *Globalisation and Business Education*. Paper presented at The Open University, UK, February 2005.

Johnes, G. (2004). Networking: Synergies and independence. In *DEC.KNOWL: Handbook* (K. Wilson ed.) Reutlingen: European School of Business, Reutlingen University, pp. 11–17. (Available at: http://kn.open.ac.uk/public/document.cfm?docid=8281)

Mayor, B. and Swann, J. (2002). The English language and 'global' teaching. In *Distributed Learning: Social and Cultural Approaches to Practice* (M.R. Lea and K. Nicoll, eds) London: Routledge Falmer, pp. 111–130.

McConnell, D. (1999). Examining a collaborative assessment process in networked lifelong learning. *Journal of Computer Assisted Learning*, **15**, 232–243.

Moran, L. and Mugridge, I. (eds) (1993). *Collaboration in Distance Education: International Case Studies*. London: Routledge.

Paul, R.H. (1990). *Open Learning and Open Management*. London: Kogan Page.

Rae, S. (2004). Constructing the Knowledge Base for the Dec.Knowl Project. In *DEC.KNOWL: Handbook* (K.P. Wilson, ed.) Reutlingen: European School of Business, Reutlingen University, pp. 18–35. (Available at: http://kn.open.ac.uk/public/document.cfm?docid=8281)

Raybourn, E.M., Kings, N., and Davies, J. (2003). Adding cultural signposts in adaptive community-based virtual environments. *Interacting with Computers*, **15**, 91–107.

Rogers, E.M. (1995). *Diffusion of Innovations*. New York: The Free Press.

Salmon, G. (2000). *E-Moderating: The key to Teaching and Learning Online*. London: Kogan Page.

Stromquist, N. and Monkman, K. (2000). *Globalisation and Education: Integration and Contestation Across Cultures*. Lanham, Maryland: Rowman and Littlefield.

Teichler, U. and Maiworm, F. (1997). *The ERASMUS Experience*. Universität Gesamthochschule Kassel.

Wenger, E. (1998). *Communities of Practice: Learning, Meaning, and Identity*. Cambridge: Cambridge University Press.

Wetzel, E. (2004). Assessing Students' Work Online. In *DEC.KNOWL: Handbook* (K.P. Wilson, ed.) Reutlingen: European School of Business, Reutlingen University, pp. 59–64. (Available at: http://kn.open.ac.uk/public/document.cfm?docid=8281)

What is Europe? Series (1995). Volumes 1–4. London: Routledge. Comprising: Rieu, A-M. and Duprat, G. (eds), *European Democratic Culture* (English edition, N. Parker, ed.); Shelley, M. and Winck, M. (eds) *Aspects of European Cultural Diversity*; Waites, B. (ed.), *Europe and the Wider World*; Wilson, K.P. and Van der Dussen, J. (eds), *The History of the Idea of Europe*.

Wilson, K.P. (1994). Joint course and curriculum development. In *Open Learning in the Mainstream* (M. Thorpe and D. Grugeon, eds) London: Longman, pp. 309–317.

Wilson, K.P. (2001). Collaborative approaches to humanities teaching in Europe. In *Contemporary Themes in Humanities Higher Education* (E.A. Chambers, ed.) Kluwer: Dordrecht, pp. 87–106.

Wilson, K. (2004). EADTU initiatives: Collaborative course development and the impact of new technology. In *Consortia: International Networking Alliances of Universities* (D.C.B. Teather, ed.) Melbourne: Melbourne University Press, pp. 103–120.

World Trade Organisation Secretariat (2002). *Trading into the Future*. (Available at: http://www.wto.org)

Chapter 45

The Business of Distance Education: Whose Profit, Whose Loss?

Ted Nunan

45.1 INTRODUCTION

This section of the World handbook is about the business of distance education – both its business in the sense of what are its purposes and achievements within educational systems and whether in pursuing various purposes it acts as a business. Both senses of the business of distance education are taken into account when considering "whose profit, whose loss?" This chapter attempts to identify the groups and individuals to which the terms "profit" and "loss" apply and outline the significance of gains and losses.

There are two major problems faced when considering the "business of distance education" – first, it is assumed that the reader knows what is meant when the term distance education is used and second, who profits and who loses is connected to the diverse uses of distance education as well as its success or otherwise within an educational marketplace.

45.2 DISTANCE EDUCATION: FOR OPPORTUNITY AND ACCESS TO THOSE DISADVANTAGED OR A MOVEMENT TO PROVIDE CONVENIENCE AND FLEXIBILITY OF LEARNING?

Ten years ago, distance education could be identified by its broadly agreed purposes and a set of issues that were pursued by distance educators – as Yoni Ryan (this section) points out a key international journal in the field, Distance Education, was concerned with articles on "traditional concerns" of distance students and teaching and learning from print-based delivery. Recently, Calvert (2005, p. 227) has observed that distance education is now operating in a context of convergence and that it is "becoming synonymous with non-contiguous online learning". Ryan also notes that convergence and the "convenience factor" are changing the core philosophy of "the provision of educational opportunity to those disadvantaged by distance, socio-economic position, or disability". Calvert suggests that distance education has become something that is defined by institutional purposes such as "a means of enrolling more students, broadening their student base, generating fee revenue, offering courses in niche markets and meeting regional commitments cost effectively" rather than being a field of study, practitioner community or area of research.

A converged "distance education" is no longer a distinct area of education. Its existence as a field (for the provision of services for off-campus students or for study and research) or as a process (using media and digital technologies, techniques for e-learning, supporting off-campus students) is now embedded in "blended" forms of education. It operates in diverse contexts for the provision of education and training and is influenced by a range of economic and political forces. Convergence and the forces that are producing "convenience education" are forcing the re-valuing of the traditions of "access and equity". Suellen Tapsall (2001, p. 43) contends that "in the modern Western world, 'distance education' is (also) less about distance and much more about convenience, lifestyle and perception" while Rumble (2001, p. 230) fears that "convenience education" and the temptation for institutions to become increasingly commercial will supplant any progressive access and equity purposes. Distance education is seen as a "leader" in the push to have convenience education conducted like a business as it can be used in flexible, cost-effective ways that provide competitive advantages to institutions. Convenience is a "customer product" of high value, especially where the customer's experiences are part of the product that is purchased!

Within education systems and institutions the values behind "convenience" and "access and equity" co-exist. The provision of educational opportunity through distance education can now be for the disadvantaged or the privileged; distance education can be a system shaped to serve and support off-campus students or a technique that adds convenience for all learners; it can be a distinct education policy area for governments, especially in developing countries, or it can be so difficult to identify that it is not possible to consider it as a policy area; it can be identified by practitioners that have an interest in open access institutions that address educational disadvantagement and provide "second chance" opportunities or it can be seen as the mechanism to provide for-profit training and education for those that can afford to pay for qualifications to enhance their competitive position.

One way of looking at this co-existence is to identify key values or idea systems that have been subject to re-evaluation and change as the purposes of distance education have diversified. For example, the three overlapping concepts of new managerialism, academic capitalism and entrepreneurial universities (Deem, 2001, p. 7) have been used in explaining recent changes in universities in Western countries. These concepts are associated with neo-liberal agendas and they also overlap with "Third Way" thinking where the public service sector has been encouraged to accept the "rhetoric of access and accountability accompanied a drive for efficiency, marketisation and rationalisation of structures and procedures" (Walsh, 2006, p. 98). Consequently, despite the fact that Governments provide between 40–80 percent of university funding in industrialised countries (Marginson and Rhoades, 2002, p. 287), and often use the rhetoric of access and equity for distance education, many of the impacts of Third Way thinking upon the provision of education are the same as those based around neo-liberal ideas.

The literature of educational change points to the currency of the above concepts. Deem and Brehony (2005, p. 225) cite research data for the UK which suggests that "the new managerialism as a general ideology is believed by both manager-academics and other academics and support staff to have permeated (UK) universities". Larry Hanley (2005) has provided an analysis of factors that have changed in American universities and colleges identifying them within the broad framework of academic capitalism, while Marginson and Considine (2000) have written on entrepreneurial universities. The concepts have also been linked to globalisation as has open and distance learning where Edwards and Usher provide post-modern analysis that contends that "open and distance learning is an engine of globalisation because it serves to challenge the foundations of modern education systems" (Monkman and Baird, 2002, p. 501). While there are a range of interpretations of the impacts of the above ideas upon systems and institutions, there is no doubt that these factors have affected practices, practitioners and directions of distance education.

Another way of describing the changes in distance education is to point to the move from a rights-based welfare model of equitable access to quality education to a citizen–consumer model where choices for purchasing education require market knowledge of products and services. Michael Peters (2005, p. 123) notes that "prudentialisation" results when education is addressed to the entrepreneurial self, and such prudentialisation "seeks to 'insure' the citizen-consumer against risk (that is, the risk to each citizen when education is moved from a 'right') in a context where the state has transferred risk to the individual". Under these circumstances, costs and benefits become an important part of the transfer of power to consumers operating their choices in a "market". Choice to consumers, both in terms of which institution and with what products on offer (that is, what convenience) is facilitated by distance education.

The following table gives a brief outline of changes in the ways that key factors associated with managerialism, academic capitalism and entrepreneurialism have been re-valued in distance education. The factors in the table have been chosen because of their usefulness in describing changes within distance education.

	Distance Education as Access and Equity Rights-Based, Welfare Model	*Distance Education as Convenience Citizen–Consumer Model*
Disaggregation of teaching	Industrialised processes within the print-based models of distance education	Further segmentation of processes and products, labour substitution, involvement of delivery managers and technology "carriers", outsourcing
Commodification	Largely print and audio-based learning material	Learning management systems for commodities, modularisation and learning objects, digital capture and distribution
Marketisation	No geographical impediment hindering changing of supplier (technically a postage stamp with a change of address would send assignments to an alternate institution) Directories of institutions and offerings available at national level	Product and service differentiation to influence on and offshore markets, products to address niche markets, possible expansion of markets using distance education processes and products, possible linkages with global expansion/ internationalisation
Managerialism	Distance education centres exist as subsystems within institutions with their own management structures. An area for distinctive institutional policy and procedure	Part of a wider product and delivery strategy for institutions with financial/marketing expertise determining the role and extent of distance education

The above table looks at the two co-existing traditions in distance education (access and equity) and converged distance education (convenience). It identifies the two positions with reference to four factors that have relevance to broader educational strategies used by institutions.

This framework can also provide a useful structure for commenting on the views of the contributors to this section on the business of distance education.

45.3 THE BUSINESS OF DISTANCE EDUCATION

Contributors to this section have looked at costs and cost-effectiveness of "distance education". Rumble looks broadly at factors driving the costs in education and points to ways in which these factors change with diverse uses of distance education techniques; Bullen and Qayyum point to distance moving from margins to mainstream and consider effectiveness as including instructional, social, financial and organisational issues; Fong looks at distance education as a system that operates within a market for its services and as such there are a range of producer and consumer issues that are conditional upon strategy and knowledge of the particular educational market; Chambers and Wilson link cost-effective distance education with international partnership and collaboration and point to the importance of experience with an understanding of e-learning; Ryan talks of a new distance education which blends the use of digital technologies, face-to-face learner support and independent learning. The common factor here is that all of these contributions consider "converged distance education".

Because the focus is on "converged distance education", the notion of attempting to assign costs to a separate thing called distance education is not a particularly useful idea – if it exists, it is converged in one way or another! The converged environment is identified by the activities that are carried out and this brings a focus upon activity-based costing. Likewise, it makes little sense to compare "converged distance education" with some other differently configured educational activity that has different purposes. Cost-effectiveness becomes a more difficult concept with more indicators of effectiveness and debates about which methodology to use in exploring the matter. Consequently, convergence has brought a new set of questions and possible methodologies. Bullen and Qayyum point out "if further research in this area (effectiveness) is to produce practical results that can help inform policy and practice, it needs to deal with cost and effectiveness as a form of evaluation". Their "evaluation approach" is one which attempts to provide evidence about the extent to which indicators of effectiveness point to achievements within a framework of activity-based costing and these indicators will underlie judgements that integrate and interpret the evidence.

Fong, on the other hand, works from an altogether different position by applying a marketing approach. Institutions collect and infuse market and competitive data, strategy, and realistic plans are in place, customers have been identified and motivated, programs are those that customers want and customers have confidence that their investment will have a positive return. In short, the system can be judged effective and the "invisible hand" of the unfettered market has produced the best distribution of goods and services of the best quality and value. Clearly, this view of effectiveness is different from that above!

Rumble's contribution resonates with current developments in education systems in that the models explored "can identify the interplay between technology choice, curriculum, course life, and student numbers and provided the data incorporated into them reflects working practices and organisational structures, they can provide decision makers with a 'back of the envelope' tool for the analysis and costing of alternative strategies". The convenience factor means that it is important to have a tool that can cope with essential drivers of education costs – a tool that accounts for disaggregation of teaching, that has a notion of the price structures of the market and the production and support costs, that responds to technology costs associated with infrastructure and delivery, and that is realistic, practicable, and can be used by management structures to control costs.

The work of the contributors to the section support Calvert's contention that distance education is at the crossroads. It is clear that there is a lack of consensus on how to address change issues – the set of cost drivers used by Rumble would need to be supplemented to be useful for Fong, and, while such drivers might be useful in quantifying magnitudes of effects, they are not judgmental criteria that could be used within the evaluation approach advocated by Bullen and Qayyum. Further, while Bullen and Qayyum see the need to address a series of evaluation questions to look at educational worthwhileness, Fong's system has no place for such questions. With a lack of structure and methodology for consideration of key problems the field will need to return to basics and their associated technical issues.

There is a major need for useful cost models that help managers to form broad-brush conclusions. Traditionally, distance educators have explored costing models – in the West there has been an interest in comparison of costs between face-to-face and distance education – while in Third World countries, governments have been interested in distance education as a development strategy. The need for expertise in this area is evident as

- further supply driven expansion of education systems (and, in particular, post-secondary systems) is not politically possible in Western countries and this means that funding the system or any expansion depends upon user-pays (student fees or loans) or from profits gained from core activities of institutions.
- Neo-liberal and Third Way approaches will continue to frame education from a consumer perspective and consumption issues such as cost, convenience and perceived quality of services and products will shape practice for the citizen–consumer.
- not all institutions will seek to gain income from teaching activity, but the majority will attempt to maintain or gain student numbers using distance education techniques to make studies more convenient for those that attend or to provide study for those who choose not to attend.
- the economics of distance education and market conditions will be a central concern for those institutions that see distance education as a for-profit activity or for those that add to their delivery costs through the use of distance education "convenience" mechanisms such as the provision of hard copy and online learning materials, the use of 24 × 7 help desk facilities, the use of flexible "study periods" and so on.

The fact that institutions need to earn income from core teaching activities means that the cost associated with all teaching needs to be determined so that profit can be calculated and maximised. This issue is central to the existence and continuity of an institution – enterprise is valued and management is directed towards achieving the profits from enterprise.

45.4 GROWTH AND DIVERSITY OF FORMS OF DISTANCE EDUCATION

The question of whose profit, whose loss? can be considered by taking the key factors of disaggregation of teaching, commodification, marketisation and managerialism and predicting winners and losers in circumstances where each factor is changed. It is assumed that various forms of distance education can be described and characterised by the extent to which changes in each of these areas are made in response to the various institutional uses of distance education. Because the four factors that we have identified interconnect when decisions are made about costs and effectiveness for specific institutional uses, their effects upon who profits and who loses will involve considering them together. However, it is useful to provide some further detail about each of the factors before considering their interconnected effects.

45.4.1 Disaggregation of Teaching

Distance education has traditionally made possible some form of unbundling or disaggregation of teaching. Teaching at a distance has often meant using the curriculum and learning materials devised by others; interactions with students through responding to assignments may involve a group of "markers"; and learning support may be provided by specialist staff other than the teacher.

Disaggregation allows cost controls to be established and the implementation of cost efficiencies such as retiring low-volume curricula, restricting options within a curriculum, increasing the shelf life of course materials, substituting cheaper labour for teaching and assessment, purchasing a licence to use curricula and materials rather than developing them and so on. It also reduces teacher controls over the curriculum and teaching processes.

Integrating activities for learning was once the role of the distance teacher – however with disaggregation a new manager is needed to bring together the creation of the curriculum, materials development, technology support, student learning support, teaching, assessment and marking, evaluation of teaching, learning and student satisfaction measures and so on.

There are winners and losers with disaggregation. Clearly teachers lose controls over the teaching and learning environment, and materials production staff and managers have a greater impact upon delivery of teaching and learning. These and other matters will be taken up later.

45.4.2 Commodification

Distance education has always been about commodities as they stand for, and have embedded within them, teaching and learning interactions. Commodification was seen to be a necessary part of providing access to learning for those that chose not to attend an institution as it allowed the distribution of "teaching and learning interactions". A key idea of distance education practice is that commodities contain evidence of excellence in teaching and learning and have the potential to replace face-to-face teaching.

Distance education has traditionally been concerned with quality assurance and quality enhancement of such commodities. Part of the reason for this concern is that the teaching and learning commodities (especially the printed learning materials) are potentially publicly available and are open to scrutiny at any time – classroom teaching, on the other hand, is not generally open for public observation and comment. In addition, there was continuing concern that the "access and equity" version of distance education was "second class" because it lacked face-to-face contact, and quality assurance processes were directed towards ensuring "parity of esteem" for face-to-face and distance education.

However, goods and services are also the "atoms" for developing a market in education. Knowledge products such as learning materials, online tutorials, learning support and help desks and so on can provide a major source of differentiation between institutions. Consequently, the economics of creation, storage, duplication and distribution of digitised commodities is central to convenience or converged distance education.

It is commonly argued that a winner with commodification is the student – quality assurance can result in the availability of high-quality teaching and learning materials and processes and the commodity is usually available for use at times/places convenient for the student. Proponents of choice and free-markets contend that market differentiation results in transparency of customer service standards (commodities and associated services) and that such standards inevitably rise as competition for students increases. So, as this logic goes, the customer always wins! However, as Rumble (2001, p. 230) points out "e-education has the potential to disaggregate the overall product, and charge according to use. In such a system, the poor lose out".

45.4.3 Marketisation

For "converged" or "convenience" distance education, market share of available students is only partly a function of geographic location. Free trade and borderlessness bring the potential for continual competition for "customers" so that institutions cannot afford to ignore the "convenience" factor of distance education in a market where other institutions can offer this service (Nunan, 2005).

While there are questions about whether markets in educational services are global (i.e. that they can reach across cultures) and whether particular models can be developed to service a potentially global market, there is no doubt that some higher education institutions see expansion into "offshore" markets as core business and an essential part of their economic strategy to survive and distance education makes this possible.

45.4.4 Managerialism

Within organisations, managerialism has a focus upon efficiency and effectiveness of the delivery of educational services, work-force shaping to organisational goals and performance monitoring through league tables, indicators and external benchmarking as well as internal mechanisms. Some of the institutional characteristics are financial target-setting and monitoring, the development of internal quasi-markets for services, and formal and regular performance management by line managers. With "converged" distance education managerial controls are put on the planning of educational programs, the monitoring of student input and cohort progression numbers, quality control and the use of student feedback about perceived satisfaction with programs, the costs of changing a program and the frequency of change and so on. Strategic issues about costs are taken up at an institutional executive level.

45.5 INTERCONNECTING THE FACTORS: WHO PROFITS, WHO LOSES?

This section introduces the ways in which the previous four factors work in combination. Many commentators on education have brought together such factors and described their impact with reference to concepts such as globalisation, academic capitalism and borderless education. This section picks up on some of this terminology in considering the interconnected effects.

45.5.1 Stronger Institutional Emphasis upon Academic Capitalism

At a supra-national level, free trade has been seen to include educational goods and services. Agreements such as the General Agreement on Trade in Services (GATS) point to rules that give providers (both public and private) access to global consumers while the Lisbon process provides an exchange rate for parts of a degree (for degrees from differing national jurisdictions). While the Lisbon process can be seen as a response to student mobility (within the European Union) an extension of the idea could see it used for managing course mobility as well as student mobility – that is, courses from another system or jurisdiction being taught and credited in other countries/locations.

At the national level, private providers point to the need for "free competition" as many national governments have conferred a monopoly status for granting degrees upon public universities. While it is the case that private providers can undertake a process of accreditation with regulations defining a system of national higher education awards, such regulation is seen as a cost to business and structured in favour of national systems that have grown from, and are supported by, government funding arrangements. Private providers argue that an unfettered market would produce a better sense of consumer awareness and choice, and that uniform regulatory processes hinder the development and operation of a market in the area.

The spread of "academic capitalism" and non-academic values is a well-recognised characteristic of current university life. Distance education can be an institutional site for activities that are consistent with the values of "academic capitalism". According to Becher (as cited in Calvert, 2005), distance education as a "soft-applied area of study" is "susceptible to dictation by non-academic interests" and managers, delivery technologists, educational designers and marketing staff see a role for themselves within converged distance education. The extent of disaggregation and management input is based on income generating capacities.

Distance education is a loser (as is the whole post-secondary system) from increased academic capitalism as the more that market forces are seen to determine action, the less the need for national policy development in distance education. Some educationists argue that policy development is essential in the area of education as it is not a business. Pusser and Doane (2001, p. 10) for example note that for American education, "public higher education institutions can be seen as political institutions, entities that control significant public resources with the authority to allocate costs and benefits selectively". Craven (2006, p. 6) comments of the Australian system that education is not a true business as "we do not have shareholders, profits and commercial choices in the same way as private enterprise" and "by way of contrast, we have much in common with government" as "we are statutory corporations, with statutory objectives and statutory obligations". While "academic capitalism" brings income and efficiencies through competition to the system there is also the chance that it can bring about a financial crisis and collapse. Consequently, practitioners of distance education need to remind politicians that they have a responsibility for a system which delivers public benefits (that distance education has an important access and equity role) and that ignoring it in policy terms means that their responsibilities to gauge the balance between "public benefit and private good" are not being responsibly handled. Further, politicians have a responsibility to maintain a system that delivers public benefits and that a reliance upon academic capitalism can sow the seeds of the economic collapse of the system as a whole.

Also, academic capitalism brings a further loss to the system in areas of knowledge that have little commercial value – the public and civic functions of such knowledge feed the culture of the nation and its individuals. Generating income through education provides rewards for areas such as management, business and computer science that can be seen to interact with external markets, while studies that bring personal and cultural development are pushed to the margins and fight for their survival.

45.5.2 Disaggregation is an Engine for Casualisation

It is clear that a major loser from casualisation is the academic teacher. Casualisation takes place when part-time and/or staff of lower seniority are substituted for tenured staff to reduce or contain costs. This has the effect of weakening the controls of the faculty over academic and teaching matters. In relation to the way that disaggregation changes the workforce, Hanley (2005, p. 8) reports that the American Association of University professors recently reported that "currently 44.5 percent of all faculty are part time and non-tenure-track positions of all types account for more than 60 percent of all faculty appointments in American higher education".

45.5.3 Managing Costs, Disaggregated Teaching and Managerialism

Cost analysis will become a major concern of distance education. As Rumble notes a smart manager will attempt to go beyond macro-analysis of the type used with activity-based costing and focus upon technology costs, commodity and service costs, work practices and organisational structures, the curriculum and the numbers of learners. The pressure here is to gain control over these costs so that the activities can be marketed, differentiated from others in the market and competitively priced.

Activity-based costing can involve surveying all staff of institutions to measure the proportion of time that they devote to pre-determined "categories of core activities" of the institution. This information can be converted to a cost for an activity and compared with the income gained from the activity. Where activity-based costing links costs to distinctive cohorts of students or delivery mechanisms this can be categorised as "distance teaching costs". New managers or executive positions such as the Head of Marketing have an institutional role in linking activity-based costing with student experience surveys to establish the priorities within institutional strategies for expenditure of resources.

It goes without saying that major winners are those connected with managerial activities. The systems nature of management (exerting controls over the parts to gain increased controls over the whole) means that commodification is likely to be part of the solution to cost containment or competitive differentiation.

45.5.4 Commodification and Marketing

As previously noted commodification refers to providing a commodity that has a role in delivering teaching and learning. While the costs for the design, production and testing of the commodity might be high, these costs are spread over the numbers of students that use the commodity. The use depends upon factors such as the "shelf life" of the commodity, whether it is used in one or many contexts/courses, the number of enrolments of the courses that the product is used within, the mechanism chosen for students to access the product and the existence of competitor products.

Commodities can be combined with particular services to make packages. A package will continue to contain "hard goods" but increasingly these will be mixed with other services and experiences. Packages will give the appearance of choice and the exercise of individual responsibility in the consumer's investment in education. A major issue will be the costs of a package, the quality of the products and services within it and how information about their cost-effectiveness becomes available to those that wish to participate in the market.

Institutions generally market through their graduates, their facilities or their products such as research outcomes, teaching packages, and course and program structures. Packaging commodities can be an aid to marketing a "brand", and winners and losers here can be institutions as such marketing can impact upon student demand for places.

45.5.5 Marketing and the "Consumer Citizen"

Many institutions now have an increasing reliance upon surveys that provide feedback upon all areas of student experience. It is argued that as the overall experience can colour perceptions of specific activities such as teaching it is important to respond to "consumer" needs in areas such as technology, social space, availability and types of food, access to libraries and internet and so on. Such surveys have questions about "the convenience of learning" which provide information about the delivery of distance education. Consumers may recognise convenience through the ways that institutions cite their "flexibility" or characterise studying through "flexible learning" or "e-learning".

While such customer experience surveys are important, there are informal league tables for distance education which are based around particular experiences – the student perception of electronic infrastructure, printed distance teaching materials, learning and other support, interactions with administrators, turn-around times for assessment feedback and the like. For many customers the mainstreaming of distance education within the institution has meant that the league tables for institutions or discipline/professional areas is used for differentiation within a market – they are particularly important as consumers "buy" a product (degree) without any real sense of what experience they are purchasing, and institutional ranking along with the costs is taken as a measure of product differentiation and value for money.

45.6 CONCLUDING STATEMENT

The contributors of this section have demonstrated the range of issues that arise when considering effectiveness and costs of a "converged" distance education. In an attempt to connect with the traditions of distance education (as "access and equity"), four areas that shape current educational debate have been traced for their impact upon newer forms of converged or convenience "distance education". The purpose of tracking changes in these areas has been twofold; to identify characteristics of converged distance education and to point to who profits and who loses in the current educational climate.

This chapter has worked from the position that attempts to reduce the business of distance education to business is to weaken education systems as it advantages those that can pay for education and privileges knowledge areas that connects with the interest of capital. However, if we accept that no political system can afford open and higher education for all, then the balance between paying for the system through the public purse and from charges upon those who benefit from the system remains a contested issue. Regardless of what educators think about the impact of the forces that accompany "converged" distance education the imperative to cost activities and provide convenience and "customer service" will continue. The public funded activities and the for-profit activities of post-secondary institutions are too intertwined to be separated and as a consequence the income-generating activities become the "tail that wags the dog". Consequently, the techniques associated with distance education will continue to be valued for their income-generation capabilities. However, in such circumstances it makes little sense to talk of a separate and identifiable entity called distance education and the convergence of its techniques and knowledge base into the mainstream will continue at a rapid pace.

REFERENCES

Calvert, J. (2005). Distance education at the crossroads. *Distance Education*, **26**(2), 227–238.

Craven, G. (2006). *Universities, Government and Policy: Riding the Whirlwind*, [unpublished paper presented to ATN Universities], Curtin University of Technology, pp. 1–14.

Deem, R. (2001). Globalisation, new managerialism, academic capitalism and entrepreneuralism in universities: Is the local dimension still important? *Comparative Education*, **37**(1), 7–20.

Deem, R. and Brehony, K. (2005). Management as ideology: The case of "new managererialism" in higher education. *Oxford Review of Education*, **31**(2), 217–235.

Hanley, L. (2005). Academic capitalism in the new university. *Radical Teacher*, **73**, 3–7.

Marginson, S. and Considine, M. (2000). *The Enterprise University: Power, Governance and Re-Invention in Australia*, Cambridge: Cambridge University Press.

Marginson, S. and Rhoades, G. (2002). Beyond national states, markets and systems of higher education: A glonacal agency heuristic. *Higher Education*, **42**, 281–309.

Monkman, K. and Baird, M. (2002). Educational change in the context of globalisation. *Comparative Education Review*, **46**(4), 497–508.

Nunan, T. (2005). Markets distance education, and Australian higher education. *International Review of Research in Open and Distance Learning*, **6**(1), 1–11.

Peters, M. (2005). The new prudentialism in education: Actuarial rationality and the entrepreneurial self. *Educational Theory*, **55**(2), 123–136.

Pusser, B., and Doane, D. (2001). Public purpose and private enterprise: The contemporary organisation of postsecondary education. *Change*, **33**(5), 18–22.

Rumble, G. (2001). Just how relevant is e-education to global education needs? *Open Learning*, **16**(3), 223–232.

Tapsall, S. (2001). "All aboard" the borderless education bandwagon. *Open Learning*, **16**(1), 35–46.

Walsh, P. (2006). Narrowed horizons and the impoverishment of educational discourse: Teaching, learning and performing under new educational bureaucracies. *Journal of Education Policy*, **21**(1), 95–117.

Chapter 46

Conclusion: Which Futures for Distance Education?

Terry Evans, Margaret Haughey, and David Murphy

In the opening chapter of this handbook we canvassed the traditions, theoretical approaches and practices that constitute distance education from its early forms of correspondence education through to the virtual worlds of today. We invited our contributors from many different countries with the intention of drawing on a wide range of expertise, interests and backgrounds but in this world of competing commitments and decreasing time some were unable to undertake and others complete their appropriate chapters, hence we do not have quite the representation of nations we had hoped for. Life pressures and the intensification of work took its toll and we are very grateful to all those who were able to complete their commitments and enable us to access such rich and diverse perspectives on distance education today. In each section of the handbook at least one chapter provides a critical perspective on the current position of distance education and its directions for the future. We did this deliberately because, as editors, we did not want the handbook to be seen as a series of contemporary, but static, statements of the world of distance education. In this chapter we wish to close with a few further reflections on the future of distance education.

46.1 DIVERSITY

The themes we chose for the sections reflect trends in distance education. Diversity was a way to give recognition to the increasing acceptance of the range of student concerns and needs, the ever-widening contexts in which distance education is used and the variety of uses of distance education. As a theme, it highlights the need to engage with this increasing complexity in designing for distance education and the importance of recognizing that personal autonomy and choice are factors that increasingly shape what we as distance educators hope to achieve. As is often the case with new developments in the field of human endeavour, it is the wealthiest people and the wealthiest nations that make the running and reap the benefits. Although distance education has a long tradition of providing educational access for those who "miss out", it has often found that the really poor and disadvantaged remain untouched by distance education's facilities and resources. Agencies, such as the Commonwealth of Learning (http://www.col.org/), endeavour to work against this trend, but the task is not easy. The potential of the Web to provide easy access to high-quality distance education is difficult to dispute: from the perspective of the wired and literate. But those who are in no position to dispute – the poor and illiterate – may give a contrary view if they could. Nicholas Negroponte's initiative to provide a means to education through the one laptop per child (OLPC) project, made in 2005, is now coming to fruition with the first dissemination of the US$100 laptops through governments starting in 2008. What then does this mean for the future of distance education?

While definitions of openness differ, the construct generally includes being learner centred; providing for flexibility in learning; removing barriers to learning whether circumstantial, personal, financial or educational; and recognizing prior learning experiences. The roots of distance education have often been concerned with access and equity, whether it has been about providing schooling (see, for example, Gibb, 1986; Haughey and Roberts, 1996) or higher education (see, for example, Harris, 1987; Hay et al., 2002), and this is partly a statement about previous policies for distance education being about "empowering" the poor, persons with disabilities and those who missed a fair share of educational opportunities, especially through reasons of distance from educational institutions. Distance education has served people in these circumstances over previous decades, however, this agenda can be used by others as Harris (1987) showed so clearly in the 1980s, where the UK Open University was used in the earliest days by the educated middle classes (especially teachers) to improve their careers. The Open University goals which were delineated as being open to people, to places, to methods and to ideas, needed its leaders to be vigilant that unanticipated contextual factors such as easier access to financial or technical resources did not distort unduly the original intent. The present emphasis on "customer service" has reinforced the importance of meeting needs and providing individualized student support especially in collaborative and peer learning environments. Inclusiveness and recognition of diversity are not only considerations at the outset but must be ongoing aspects of how we think about distance education.

46.2 TRANSFORMATION OF TEACHING AND LEARNING

What does it mean for those who teach and learn in today's distance education institutions? Our second theme, transformation of teaching and learning, speaks of the changes we see through looking back at earlier eras and examining contemporary transformations in organizational and programme structures, provision of services and in teaching and learning theories.

Over twenty years ago, Evans and Nation posed the question "Which future for distance education?" (Evans and Nation, 1987). In their response they criticized the rise of "instructional industrialism" in distance education (Evans and Nation, 1989a) partly basing their argument on Harris's (1987) work at the UKOU and argued for distance education to involve dialogue (Evans and Nation, 1989b). More recently, they lamented the rise of those "weapons of mass instruction" (PowerPoint lectures, learning management systems, etc.) that have been dominating university education systems and their impact as globalizing forms of distance education (Evans and Nation, 2003). Much has been written about the "technology fix" in distance education but authors in this handbook section point out that the issue is not so much one of fascination with technological toys but the greater issue of its impact on the transformation in society and how this is calling into question previous perspectives in distance education. Historically, visions of the future and the ability to seize on technological innovation and development have long been hallmarks of distance education. Over 150 years ago, Caleb Phillips and Isaac Pitman can be credited with the introduction of correspondence education (Jegede and Naidu, 1999) by grasping the opportunities offered through the emerging technology of a fast and reliable postal service. The well-documented vision and foresight of distance education pioneers during the twentieth century has led us to the current global significance of this mode of education. The role of the UKOU in the remarkable growth of distance education is acknowledged here and elsewhere. What then are the visions for the future which will seize on present technological innovations to transform the next versions of distance education?

The introductory chapter (Chapter 1) reviewed the main theoretical positions and their practical implications for distance education and its mutation into various forms of virtual learning environments. However, as Pauling's chapter (Chapter 20) in this handbook shows, all "traditional" education is under challenge from the new media. Articles in this section point out the renewed emphasis on communications in society and its increasing importance in educational writings from constructivist theories and collaborative learning environments to social software (Anderson, Chapter 9) and connective knowledge (Downes, 2005, 2006) The assumption of course content as already designated, so much a mark of previous forms of distance education, is now being challenged by content creation strategies of today's participants such as e-portfolios and personal learning environments. As we noted in Chapter 1, it is the power relations behind these changes that are important to understand, hence, our question "in whose interests?" posed in various chapters of this handbook.

46.3 LEADERSHIP

In discussing possible scenarios for the future of distance education, King (2003) posits that while one might be the maintenance of the status quo, and another international expansion, other equally likely were the "diminution of the field through disaggregation of function, and (4) loss of identity" (n.p.). The influence of the Internet and the web on societies in general has challenged the utility of previous distance education structures and suggested their absorption into traditional educational structures under blended or hybrid learning options except where the "mega" open universities (Daniel, 1996) can exercise their power. Such discussions led us to focus on leadership as our third theme.

From a clearly positive perspective, some look to the future with a firmly optimistic vision, seemingly preferring to replace the question "What future for distance education?" with the claim that "Distance education is the future!". The most well known of such proponents is Daniel (2007), who has argued that:

> the growth of higher education in the developing world is a tectonic shift that will break up the old order. In a decade or two most university and college students will be in the developing world, which will, by definition, redefine the norms in higher education globally.
>
> How will both the public and the private sector provide higher education to the millions of new students in the developing nations? Much of it will likely follow traditional patterns of classroom teaching on locally owned campuses, but distance learning, offered both locally and across borders... will have an increasingly high profile.
>
> (n.p.)

The prime exemplar Daniel uses to buttress his argument is India, where over two million students (representing 24% of enrolments in higher education) study by distance education. The Indian government is aiming to increase this to 40 percent by 2010. Fundamentally, the argument appears to be that the demand will be such that only by applying distance education systems can it even begin to be met. The note of caution, though, is that distance education proponents must heed "the five A's of affordability, accessibility, appropriateness, accreditation and acceptability" (Daniel, 2007, n.p.) King's suggestion that we are moving to transnational education concurs with Daniel's analysis.

Vision and goals are tightly aligned with leadership. Leadership has been conceptualized as process rather than procedures, focusing on the development of an enabling culture where individual professional development is closely aligned with the desired goals of the group and many of the section's authors have focused on leadership development as key to this process. Equally important are questions of purpose: What leadership goals and in whose interests?

46.4 ACCOUNTABILITY

One of Daniel's key indicators, accountability, was chosen as the focus of the next handbook section because the present orientation in management practices believes that support for education should no longer be based on its value to society and future generations; it must also show how well it has used the society's resources and what its can show as system "outputs". This rationalization of educational spending has greatly influenced how funding is allocated and results reported, so much so that governments have added accountability to their access and equity agendas. One result has been a much greater focus on measurement, whether of practice (and hence "best practices") or of learning "outcomes" through standardized assessments of the total system using key performance indicators. At the same time, the changes in orientation to learning and the results of brain-based research have suggested the value of authentic assessment practices. The use of quality as a marker of high achievement and simultaneously of accountability is a contested terrain.

While many of the accountability practices might seem to be common sense financial practices which provide ways of measuring "the bang for the buck" it is their underlying premises that we must consider. Accountability, efficiency and competitiveness are aspects of a market economy ideology that is reshaping how we think about education. The adoption of a way of thinking about learning and work as performative (Ball, 1998) and productive for society rather as being for individual and societal development is cause for concern. This infusion of neo-liberal thinking has emphasized responding to the needs of the individual, greater competitiveness within the educational sector and an increasing reduction of public-funding sources. All of this has placed greater emphasis on accountability as educational organizations have turned to buying and selling products and marketing services, what Slaughter and Leslie refer to as "academic capitalism" (1997). How then do distance education organizations place them in this landscape of greater managerialism and what does the future hold for them?

46.5 POLICY

While distance education has received greater attention in recent years it has not always resulted in major policy initiatives at national levels. For many countries, including public policies on distance education would mean reformulating their educational landscape and the pressures to do so come from competing ideologies: on one hand is the greater commercialization of education and on the other the reform of the educational system to be more responsive to individual learners as reflected in themes of increased access and equity. Instead, policies that affect distance education have come through legislation on accreditation, access to local markets, quality-assurance systems and funding (Robinson, 2004) and through economic policies that favour flexibility in education and training (Edwards and Tait, 2000). Government legislation has a major impact on the provision of distance education such as when it provides for equivalency of credentials from distance education programmes or when it maintains a separation between the two providers such as requiring that distance education students need to have a percentage of their programme in classroom experiences before graduation. The impact of external providers on the system may result in legislation prohibiting all external providers, the development of a list of approved universities, a requirement to obtain in-country registration or the requirement that all external providers must partner with local providers. Often governance of distance education is achieved through the implementation of standards, where the major work of providing documents showing how the institution is meeting the benchmarks is undertaken by the institution itself. The impact of accreditation seems to be two fold: since few organizations fail to achieve accreditation, it can be seen as ensuring a minimal platform of services, but since the tendency of assurance systems is to measure the tangible, questions have been raised about its focus on measurable outcomes. Government policies of lifelong learning and worker mobility are other instances of indirect impact on the values and choices of distance education institutions.

What seems to be occurring is that educational policy with its emphasis on the vision and values of education for society has been confined to the K-12 sector while in the post-secondary sector, this emphasis has been replaced by one on political possibilities and what governments are willing to fund and support during the term of their mandate. Policies mandate and enable change. They exclude certain topics from the educational debate (for a long time, distance education was in this camp) and they institutionalize how certain topics are to be understood. With the impact of new digital communications technologies, aspects of distance education have become visible on the policy agenda. How they are shaped and supported will help determine the future of distance education.

46.6 BUSINESS

One of the impacts of the new digital technologies has been to globalize the possibilities for the economy of the provision of education for this new knowledge society. At the same time, the introduction of business strategies into education has brought other trends: the reduction of public funding, a consumerist attitude about their education from students and an increase in the number of private-sector providers and entrepreneurial initiatives in transnational education. Increasingly, governments are accepting that private providers have a role in public education provision (Gourley, 2007).

As the "business" of distance education becomes firmly entrenched as an ideological position, and education becomes a "private good" it is to be expected that the benefits will accrue most to those who own the businesses and to the "customers" who pay for the courses. The "customers" may be the "consumers" themselves or their employers or other benefactors who are paying the bills. Control over the curriculum and the pedagogy – or, as Pauling (Chapter 20) suggests, after McLuhan, "the medium" and "the" message" – is an important part of the business strategy. In a "free market" economy, these matters are to be expected and may work to good effect where competition is sound However, the notion of education as a "public good" has underpinned the institutional and governmental development of distance education during the Twentieth Century. In democratic societies with mixed economies, the public benefits of an educated citizenry are seen as necessities for electoral participation and national development. That is, without an informed and educated citizenry democratic societies cannot function, neither can mixed (or solely market) economies operate effectively without informed consumers, nor without competent knowledge workers to develop those economies. In this sense, the business and the (public) service of education are essential elements of contemporary societies, especially in an era of global creative economies (Florida, 2003, 2005). This is arguably the sort of context that most developed nations are accommodating, and with which most developing nations are having to cope.

These effects of globalization have to be placed in the larger context of the General Agreement on Trade in Services (GATS) by the member countries of the World Trade Organization. Many countries are only beginning to recognize the potential impacts of the GATS on their educational provision particularly in relation to foreign provision. In a report for the International Research Foundation for Open Learning and the Commonwealth of Learning, David Hawkridge (2003) noted

> Distance education is simply a particular example of the general case. Universities and colleges offering distance education learning face a bewildering range of competition, public and private, at home and from abroad, all of which is fuelled by rapid technological advances. Crucially, the capacity of both governments and individual institutions to make robust choices is not evenly distributed between the industrialized countries and the low-income countries.
>
> (p. i)

Hawkridge goes on the explain that the trends we have been discussing – the need for worker flexibility, "the demand for education and training in the global economy, the need to reduce the brain drain and the pull of new education markets abroad" – are seen as providing the impetus for this initiative but the drive is coming from the "WTO, multinational companies and corporate universities". He concludes, "Sharing distance education and training functions between institutions offers potential benefits across the full range of functions, as many examples show. Each of the options has serious organizational, cultural, legal, political and economic implications" (p. ii). He goes on to ask a series of questions about who provides redress when transnational agreements malfunction. These are likely to be questions for the near future.

This handbook provides a large volume of material for distance educators, planners and policymakers to use in their work. While the substance and media of our activities may change in the coming years, many of the principles, ideas and theories that support them will remain to be adapted to the prevailing conditions. The contributors to this handbook represent, collectively, centuries of experience and considerable diversity therein. We intend that their work will be a resource to enable many people to construct the next generation of the theory and practice of distance education.

REFERENCES

Ball, S.J. (1998). Performativity and fragmentation in "postmodern schooling," In J. Carter, (Ed.), Postmodernity and the fragmentation of welfare. London: Routledge.

Daniel, J. (1996). *The Mega-Universities and the Knowledge Media*, Kogan Page, London.

Daniel, J. (2007). The Expansion of Higher Education in the Developing World: What can Distance Learning Contribute? *CHEA International Commission Conference 2007*. Retrieved March 21, 2007 from http://www.col.org/colweb/site/pid/4358.

Downes, S. (2005). *An Introduction to Connective Knowledge*. Unpublished paper. (December 22). Available on Stephen's Web, http://www.downes.ca/cgi-bin/page.cgi?post=33034.

Downes, S. (2006). *Learning Networks and Connective Knowledge*. Unpublished paper. (October 16). Available at http://it.coe.uga.edu/itforum/paper92/paper92.html.

Edwards, R. and Tait, A. (2000). Forging policies in flexible learning. In *Flexible Learning, Human Resource and Organizational Development. Putting Theory to Work* (V. Jakupec and J. Garrick, eds) London: Routledge, pp. 130–146.

Evans, T.D. and Nation, D.E. (1987). Which future for distance education? *International Council for Distance Education Bulletin*, **14**, 48–53.

Evans, T.D. and Nation, D.E. (1989a). "Critical reflections in distance education", In *Critical Reflections on Distance Education* (T.D. Evans and D.E. Nation, eds) Falmer Press, London, pp. 237–252.

Evans, T.D. and Nation, D.E. (1989b). Dialogue in practice, research and theory in distance education, *Open Learning*, **4**(2), 37–43.

Evans, T.D. and Nation, D.E. (2003). "Globalisation and the reinvention of distance education." In *The Handbook of Distance Education, Second Edition*, (M.G. Moore, and W. Anderson, eds) Lawrence Erlbaum and associates, Mahwah, NJ, pp. 767–782.

Florida, R. (2003). *The Rise of the Creative Class*. Pluto Press, Melbourne.

Florida, R. (2005). *The Flight of the Creative Class: The New Global Competition for Talent*. Harper Business, New York.

Gibb, P. (1986). *Classrooms a World Apart: The Story of the Broken Hill School of the Air*. Spectrum Publications, Melbourne.

Gourley, B. (2007). How technology is shaping educational agendas. *Address to the 36th Scottish Council Forum, 23 March*. Retrieved from: http://www/open.ac.uk/vice-chancellor/Speeches.

Harris, D. (1987). *Openness and Closure in Distance Education*. Falmer Press, London.

Haughey, M. and Roberts, J. (1996). Canadian policy and practice on open and distance schooling. In *Opening Education: Policies and Practices from Distance Education* (T.D. Evans and D.E. Nation, eds) Routledge, London, pp. 63–76.

Hawkridge, D. (2003). Models for open and distance learning. 2. *Globalisation, Education and Distance Education*. Cambridge, UK: IRFOL & COL.

Hay, R., Lowe, D., Gibb, D.M. et al. (2002). *Breaking the Mould: Deakin University, The First Twenty-Five Years*. Deakin University, Geelong, Victoria.

Jegede, O. and Naidu, S. (1999). Editorial. *E-Journal of Instructional Science and Technology*, 3(1), n.p. Retrieved March 15, 2007 from http://www.usq.edu.au/electpub/e-jist/docs/old/vol3no1/contents.htm.

King, B. (2003). "*Has Distance Education a Future*". Invited keynote at 10th Biennial Cambridge Conference on Open and Distance Education, Maddingley Hall, Cambridge, September 22–26.

Robinson, B. (2004). Governance, accreditation and quality assurance in open and distance education. In *Policy for Open and Distance Learning* (H. Perraton and H. Lentell, eds) London: RoutledgeFalmer & COL, pp. 181–206.

Slaughter, S. and Leslie, L. (1997). Academic capitalism. *Politics, Policies and the Entrepreneurial University*. Baltimore: Johns Hopkins.

Index